Open Country:
Canadian Literature
in English

Open Country:
Canadian Literature
in English

Edited by
Robert Lecker

THOMSON

★

NELSON

Australia   Canada   Mexico   Singapore   Spain   United Kingdom   United States

THOMSON

NELSON

Open Country: Canadian Literature in English

Edited by Robert Lecker

Associate Vice President:
Editorial Director:
Evelyn Veitch

Editor-in-Chief, Higher Education:
Anne Williams

Executive Editor:
Laura Macleod

Marketing Manager:
Shelley Collacutt Miller

Developmental Editor:
Theresa Fitzgerald

Permissions Coordinator:
Wendy Clark

Senior Content Production Manager:
Natalia Denesiuk Harris

Copy Editor:
Erin Moore

Proofreader:
Rodney Rawlings

Indexer:
Newgen

Production Coordinator:
Ferial Suleman

Design Director:
Ken Phipps

Interior Design Modifications:
Katherine Strain

Cover Design:
Dianna Little

Cover Image:
Kyle Stewart, *Summer Field*, oil on canvas. © 2006 Kyle Stewart.

Compositor:
Newgen

Printer:
RR Donnelley

Library and Archives Canada Cataloguing in Publication Data

Lecker, Robert, 1951–
Open country : Canadian literature in English / Robert Lecker.

Includes bibliographical references and index.
ISBN 978-0-17-610398-9

1. Canadian literature (English)
I. Title.

PS8233.L43 2007   C810.8
C2007-903651-1

ISBN-13: 978-0-17-610398-9
ISBN-10: 0-17-610398-8

This book is for Mary, Emily, and Claire

Contents

Preface

Open Country brings together a selection of poetry and fiction by over 100 Canadian authors. In making choices for this anthology, I was guided by a number of editorial aims. I wanted to give the book a contemporary emphasis by including writers who have emerged in the past 10 years. At the same time, I tried to cover writers who have been historically excluded from mainstream anthologies of Canadian literature and to include a greater representation of material from the Maritimes and the West. Although many of the selections include canonical works by some of Canada's best-known writers, I have also chosen some of their lesser-known poetry and fiction in order to challenge traditional assumptions about their output. I hope the extensive explanatory material contained in footnotes throughout the volume will enrich the reading experience.

This anthology is organized chronologically and covers poetry and fiction published between 1825 and 2006. The selections for each author are also organized chronologically to sustain a sense of their personal development. In a few cases, however, I depart from chronology to respect a retrospective unity conferred by the authors themselves. The selections are dated according to the first print publication, when such information is available. If that information is not available, I have used the first book publication, but in some instances, where the date of book publication does not provide an accurate sense of the work's chronological position in an author's oeuvre because of a substantial time lag between composition and book, I have substituted the date of composition when it can be determined. If the work has been revised by the author, I have used the most recent version. In some cases I have silently corrected obvious errors in typography and spelling. In all cases I have sought out the most authoritative version of the work.

Robert Lecker
March 2007

Introduction

National literature anthologies are the product of extensive negotiations. Their editors wrestle with questions about how the nation is represented through its literature and about the extent to which its literary canon should be repudiated or reproduced. They are also forced to make difficult decisions about representing genre, gender, chronology, region, revision, abridgement, and the repertoire of every single author to be included in the chosen group, to name only a few of the contexts that vie with each other for anthological presence. While national literature anthologies may assert various forms of objectivity, in truth such anthologies contribute to a commodification of writing that distorts history and warps our understanding of the relation between a nation and its literature. Any anthology that pretends otherwise is caught in a canonical dream.

Yet that dream remains an inspiring force behind anthologizing national literatures, and the anthologizing of Canadian literature is no exception. In one of the earliest anthologies of Canadian literature — *Selections from Canadian Poets* (1864) — Edward Hartley Dewart argued that "a national literature is an essential element in the formation of national character. It is not merely a record of a country's mental progress: it is the expression of its intellectual life, the bond of national unity, and the guide of national energy." Dewart's view is based on the unquestioned assumption that literature can reflect a national consciousness and that the editor, in turn, can select literature that will perform this act of reflection.

Much has changed since Dewart's time. More than 3,000 anthologies of Canadian literature have been published to date. This statistic suggests that the subject in question — Canadian literature — is unstable and multiple, at best. Anthologies of Canadian literature have always been preoccupied with capturing a moment in the midst of this instability as they navigate the inter-twined concepts of canon and nation. Reading Canadian literature anthologies involves people in the activity of constructing Canada; every anthology pres-ents them with textual versions of the country they know or are getting to know. The idea of Canada presented in anthologies changes in response to shifting concepts of the country and to notions of literary value current in any given period. And different anthologists working in the same era often con-struct Canada in very different ways.

Today, we have come to question the definability of national literatures, just as we have come to interrogate the idea of national literary canons and the systems of authority that traditionally empower them. We also understand that literary history does not exist as a stable object, waiting to be discovered, but is a narrative that changes according to the way it is told and the values of its teller. Despite the best intentions of editors, conditions and limitations lead to selection practices that distort the canon and literary history. What gets published in anthologies (and elsewhere) is never strictly a function of inherent value. Material factors — such as budgets, permissions costs, editorial costs, technological issues, the physical weight of the final product — compromise the editor's choices, making it impossible for any anthology to lay claim to objectivity.

Faced with the conflicts that arise through the process of selection, any editor of a national anthology who attempts to collect "the best" or what is "representative" or "original" is self-deceived. Such terms, being relative, are largely irrelevant. Every anthology is nothing more or less than the narrative record of a series of intense negotiations about literary value at a given historical moment. Every national literary anthology is nothing more or less than the anxious attempt to create a selective narrative of nation, against all odds. I think of these anthologies as multi-faceted jewels on an unfinished necklace, the stories and poems changing with the light. In that kind of flux and compromise, the country itself moves, shifts, responds to tension and flow. It isn't closed, or completed, or stable. It is open country.

II

Open Country. Think of this book as a weather report on a nation, in multiple periods, in dozens of places. Taken together, the stories and poems gathered here create an overall climate, but within that climate there are all kinds of pockets and strange patterns. There are sketches, realistic narratives, colloquial humour, depictions of rural and urban life, psychological dramas, postmodern experiments, confessional and autobiographical tales. The poetry takes us from optimistic perceptions of 18th-century Canada through diverse encounters with the natural world, history, geography, identity, inheritance, and the process of writing itself. There are familiar voices here, and new voices that actively challenge conventional ideas about what it means to be Canadian.

While I understand that my selections are unavoidably compromised, I can also look out at the variegated landscape created through the editorial process. The act of working with all these poems and stories so intimately over such an intense period has collapsed their spatial and temporal identities for me. In some ways, the anthology seems like a palimpsest. I see myself looking down through inscribed layers of voices, geographies, identities. From this vantage point, the most experimental Canadian poets are superimposed on their earliest counterparts. The 19th-century landscape of Charles Sangster appears under or over Robert Kroetsch's postmodern prairie. I see Lorna Crozier's very different prairie through John Steffler's elemental encounter with Newfoundland, while Marlene NourbeSe Philip's intentionally ruptured

English somehow finds itself sharing space with Steve McCaffery's experiments in undermining linguistic convention. Through the same palimpsest, Eden Robinson's stories set in Vancouver's Downtown Eastside mingle with Ivan E. Coyote's self-referential tales about the Yukon and David Bezmozgis's account of the Jewish immigrant experience in Toronto. These writers are all very different, but the collection puts them in intimate proximity.

It will always be possible to argue with the chronological bookends of a national literature anthology. Where does a national literature begin? Through what lens do we see its origins, or its present? I am well aware that those origins could be located in the literature of Canada's Native peoples, or in early travel narratives, or in the long poems of Henry Kelsey and Thomas Cary, or in Canadian slave narratives dating from the late 1700s. There is no definitive point of departure. *Open Country* begins with the celebratory vision of Oliver Goldsmith's *The Rising Village*, which has always struck me as unique in its urgent need to comprehend a Canadian landscape through religious and aesthetic perspectives that try to differentiate (unevenly) between the old world and the new. I have tried to find a more contemporary emphasis by focusing on works by many of Canada's younger poets and fiction writers, and by including a number of voices frequently excluded from anthologies of Canadian literature. Needless to say, many more figures might have been included, and the exclusion of some established writers was often a source of distress.

III

Although I would like to believe that there is an accurate way to describe the process of selection that produced the current volume, such accuracy eludes me. However, I know that several factors were at play. One level of selection reflects the fact that, after studying Canadian literature for close to 30 years, I keep returning to certain works. Call them my personal canon. These are the poems and stories that refuse to stay still, the ones that reward me with different nuances each time I reread them, the ones whose lines or images I carry around and find myself quoting in class to illustrate a point or to isolate a particular moment of pain, or longing, or beauty, or doubt. These are the works that have granted me insight into the creative process and, more often than not, they tend to be poems or stories that explore the problem of their own existence as works of art. This may sound like a postmodern emphasis on self-reflexivity, but in fact I find that kind of implicit aesthetic self-interrogation in a wide range of Canadian writers, from early times to the present. Along with these works, which I selected because they changed me, I chose material that makes me laugh, or that is weird and eccentric, or that plunges us into a world we could never visit without the writer's expert help. I also looked for selections that altered the way I saw Canada, from east to west and north to south. Startling images, unfamiliar landscapes, distinct speech patterns across the land. The more you read Canadian writing, the more you realize what kind of open country Canada is — open to potential, open to different readings, open to multiple voices that won't settle down. I wanted to create an anthology that you could open at random and be instantly drawn into.

It would be both unrealistic and dishonest to say that these selections are strictly personal. Literary taste is a give and take, and it is always affected by others. In this sense, all of my students have contributed to the selection process by teaching me to see the literature through new eyes and by challenging many of my assumptions about how a poem or story works. I owe a lot to the many critics who have commented on these writers over the years and helped me to better understand their work. Every anthologist has to be conscious of other anthologists who have faced similar editorial challenges. This anthology is in conversation with earlier anthologies of Canadian literature; I hope it will converse with others that follow. It is also the product of a healthy negotiation between me and the seven (anonymous) assessors of my initial selections, each of whom made strong arguments in favour of including or excluding various figures, often contradicting each other in the process, so that I was left to make some anxious decisions. Perhaps that anxiety will energize the anthology, give it some uncertain strength. Right down to the last moment, I was adding new material, rethinking the selections I had made, wondering whether I was doing the subject justice. Then I realized that, like all anthologies, this one is just a beginning. The rest is up to you.

ACKNOWLEDGEMENTS

My sincere thanks to the dedicated team of McGill students who helped me with the writing and editing of every aspect of this book: Joel Deshaye, Norah Franklin, Tara Murphy, Julie Peters, and Michelle Thompson. Michelle's assistance in composing the footnotes was extraordinary. I would also like to thank Michael Darling for his expertise, and for the commentary he provided on preliminary versions of the bio-critical essays in *Open Country*. Wendy Wickwire provided crucial scholarly assistance for the commentary on Harry Robinson. All of the bio-critical essays were consistently improved through the editorial skills of Mary Williams.

I want to thank Professor Nathalie Cooke and the Arts Insights Initiative of the Faculty of Arts at McGill University for supporting the research connected with this project. This book would not exist without the wonderful team at Thomson Nelson who helped me bring it to fruition, especially Anne Williams, who got the ball rolling, and the invaluable Natalia Denesiuk Harris, Theresa Fitzgerald, Laura MacLeod, Erin Moore, and Rodney Rawlings. Your efforts are much appreciated.

Finally, I wish to express my appreciation to those who reviewed the anthology: Pamela Banting, University of Calgary; Neil Besner, University of Winnipeg; Albert Braz, University of Alberta; Janice Fiamengo, University of Ottawa; Robert May, Queen's University; Ken McLean, Bishop's University; and Margaret Steffler, Trent University.

Oliver Goldsmith (1794–1861)

Often called the first native-born Canadian poet, Oliver Goldsmith was born in New Brunswick. His father, Henry, a nephew of Anglo-Irish poet and novelist Oliver Goldsmith, was an officer in an Irish regiment during the American Revolutionary War. When the war ended, Henry left for the colony of New Brunswick — then called Acadia — with his wife, Mary, and other British loyalists unwilling to remain in the newly independent states. Acadia was still relatively undeveloped, and the first wave of loyalist émigrés endured great physical hardship.

The Goldsmiths moved to the Annapolis Valley when Oliver was two, and there he attended Halifax Grammar School. He referred to the instruction he received there as "Irish Dog Latin," and he was delighted, at the age of 16 (in 1810), to have the opportunity to leave school and enter the commissariat of the British Army. His father died the following year, and although his mother chose to return to New England, Oliver remained in Canada. While stationed in Nova Scotia, he taught himself French and Spanish, became involved in amateur theatre, and "read many useful and practical Works." In his autobiography, he remarks that during this period he "entered *con spirito* [with spirit] into the Regions of Poetry." Encouraged by friends, and prompted by his lineage — his great-uncle and namesake had authored *The Deserted Village* (1770), an account of the ruination of an Irish town, as well as the enormously popular *Vicar of Wakefield* (1766) — Oliver decided to try his hand at writing.

The result was a narrative poem that Gerald Lynch calls the "indigenous source" of mainstream English Canadian poetry of the 19th century. *The Rising Village* was Goldsmith's only significant work; Lynch calls it "the most ambitious poem of an occasional poet" — a work that, "for numerous literary, historical, and bibliographical reasons [is] a Canadian poem worthy of critical attention and scholarly care."

In content and style, *The Rising Village* recalls *The Deserted Village*. While its themes reflect the natural concerns of a loyal colonist living in a poorly populated territory — conquering nature, battling vice, remaining loyal to the Empire — the poem is never predictable or propagandistic. Some critics have accused Goldsmith of being too idealistic about the role of agrarian colonists in the Empire, and since *The Deserted Village* was critical of the competition between the farming and merchant classes, many assume Goldsmith missed the point of his great-uncle's work. As Lynch points out, however, cooperation between farmers and merchants was a necessary part of colonist mythology, and the fact that the poet incorporated it as an ideal into *The Rising Village* is, if inappropriate, at least understandable.

The Rising Village has four major sections, each written in heroic couplets. The first is an address to the poet's brother Henry and an exhortation to the elder Oliver to inspire this poem in the name of *The Deserted Village*'s unhappy villagers. The poet then compares the solitude, wilderness, and intractable physical environment of Acadia to the gentle British landscape. The first section ends with the establishment of the poem's dominant pattern: a success (a good harvest) followed by a challenge ("savage tribes" drive the settler from his home into the woods). A warning resounds throughout the poem: remain vigilant because for every triumph of order and virtue, disorder and vice will retaliate.

As the second section begins, settler society has tamed the wilderness. The settlers' "scattered huts" have multiplied, the "aggressors" have fled, and the cultivation of the soil and the mind has begun in earnest. The community erects its essential institutions: tavern, church, store, and school. But as soon as the "Rising Village claims a name" and the villagers, released from pioneer toil, begin to settle into their newfound society and security, fresh challenges emerge. The village attracts a charlatan doctor who "cures, by chance," and a schoolmaster whose "skill / Consists in reading, and in writing ill."

In the third section, Goldsmith further explores the populating of the settlement. His conservative nature compels him to caution the reader that even love is a mixed blessing if it encourages rash behaviour, compromises morals, or fosters deceit. He tells the tale of Flora, a maiden whose hopes are betrayed, and offers the meagre consolation that "such tales of real woe" do "not oft … Degrade the land." This underscores the poem's theme of the bond between the character of the land and the moral integrity of its cultivators; it also serves to remind the reader to struggle tirelessly against physical and moral corruption.

The fourth section begins as the poet climbs a hill to survey the settlement's varied achievements, as he has surveyed the mother country's achievements earlier in the poem. The poet offers his thanks to Britannia, again proclaiming her glorious accomplishments in the arts, the sciences, commerce, and war. He sees that having conquered physical and emotional hardship, the Acadians are now prepared to assume their role as Britannia's "Heir," as "the wonder of the Western skies."

The Rising Village was published in London in 1825, making Goldsmith the first Canadian-born poet to publish in England. Although he lamented that his "first effort was criticized with undue severity, abused, and condemned" because he did not "produce a poem like the great Oliver," reviews from the period are either warm or indifferent, and the poem was reprinted in *The Canadian Review & Magazine* in 1826. Still, Goldsmith felt the perceived criticism keenly, and he forswore "the pleasure of any further intercourse" with his muse. He did, however, continue to revise his work, eliminating references that would render it dated, and he published a Canadian edition in 1834.

Goldsmith served in the military in Halifax and Fredericton until 1844, when he was sent to Hong Kong; he was posted to Newfoundland in 1848 and was made deputy commissary general in 1853. In retirement, he toured Ireland. Recalled in 1854, he was sent to the Crimea, but the undertaking proved too arduous for him. He gave up his assignment and went to Liverpool, England, to live with his sister. There he died in 1861.

In 1943, the Reverend Wilfrid E. Myatt edited and published a manuscript that had been in the possession of the Goldsmith family: *The Autobiography of Oliver Goldsmith*. *The Rising Village* was reissued in *Nineteenth-Century Narrative Poems* (1972; edited by David Sinclair); and in 1989, Gerald Lynch edited the 1825 and 1834 versions.

The Rising Village

Thou dear companion of my early years,[1]
Partner of all my boyish hopes and fears,
To whom I oft addressed the youthful strain,
And sought no other praise than thine to gain;
Who oft hast bid me emulate his fame[2]
Whose genius formed the glory of our name:
Say, when thou canst, in manhood's ripened age,
With judgment scan the more aspiring page,
Wilt thou accept this tribute of my lay,
10   By far too small thy fondness to repay?

---

1. The "companion" is Goldsmith's brother, Henry, to whom the poem is dedicated. 2. **emulate his fame** Equal his fame.

Say, dearest Brother, wilt thou now excuse
This bolder flight[3] of my advent'rous muse?
 If, then, adown your cheek a tear should flow,
For Auburn's Village,[4] and its speechless woe;
If, while you weep, you think the "lowly train"[5]
Their early joys can never more regain,
Come, turn with me where happier prospects rise,
Beneath the sternness of our Acadian skies.
And thou, dear spirit![6] whose harmonious lay
Didst lovely Auburn's piercing woes display,   20
Do thou to thy fond relative impart
Some portion of thy sweet poetic art;
Like thine, Oh! let my verse as gently flow,
While truth and virtue in my numbers[7] glow:
And guide my pen with thy bewitching hand,
To paint the Rising Village of the land.
 How chaste and splendid are the scenes that lie
Beneath the circle of Britannia's[8] sky!
What charming prospects there arrest the view,
How bright, how varied, and how boundless too!   30
Cities and plains extending far and wide,
The merchant's glory, and the farmer's pride.
Majestic palaces in pomp display
The wealth and splendour of the regal sway;
While the low hamlet and the shepherd's cot,
In peace and freedom mark the peasant's lot.
There nature's vernal[9] bloom adorns the field,
And Autumn's fruits their rich luxuriance yield.
There men, in busy crowds, with men combine,
That arts may flourish, and fair science shine;   40
And thence, to distant climes their labours send,
As o'er the world their widening views extend.
Compar'd with scenes like these, how lone and drear
Did once Acadia's woods and wilds appear;
Where wandering savages, and beasts of prey,
Displayed, by turns, the fury of their sway.[10]
 What noble courage must their hearts have fired,
How great the ardour which their souls inspired,
Who leaving far behind their native plain,[11]
Have sought a home beyond the Western main;   50

---

3. **This bolder flight** Goldsmith refers to his interest in writing a long poem that was more epic in scope than his shorter
verse. 4. **Auburn's Village** The imaginary town in *The Deserted Village,* a poem written by Oliver Goldsmith's Anglo-Irish
great-uncle. They shared the same name. 5. **"lowly train"** A group of people. 6. **dear spirit!** Goldsmith refers to his great-
uncle. 7. **numbers** Lines of poetry. 8. **Britannia's sky** Britain's sky. 9. **vernal** Spring-time. 10. 45–46: The lines allude to
The Deserted Village: "Where crouching tigers wait their hapless prey, / And savage men more murderous still than they."
11. **their native plain** Their homeland.

And braved the perils of the stormy seas,
In search of wealth, of freedom, and of ease!
Oh! none can tell but they who sadly share
The bosom's anguish, and its wild despair,
What dire distress awaits the hardy bands,
That venture first on bleak and desert lands.[12]
How great the pain, the danger, and the toil,
Which mark the first rude culture of the soil.
When, looking round, the lonely settler sees
His home amid a wilderness of trees:
How sinks his heart in those deep solitudes,
Where not a voice upon his ear intrudes;
Where solemn silence all the waste pervades,
Heightening the horror of its gloomy shades;
Save where the sturdy woodman's strokes resound,
That strew the fallen forest on the ground.
See! from their heights the lofty pines descend,
And crackling, down their pond'rous[13] lengths extend.
Soon from their boughs the curling flames arise,
Mount into the air, and redden all the skies;
And, where the forest once its foliage spread
The golden corn triumphant waves its head.*
  How blest did nature's ruggedness appear
The only source of trouble or of fear;
How happy, did no hardship meet his view,
No other care his anxious steps pursue;
But, while his labour gains a short repose,
And hope presents a solace for his woes,
New ills arise, new fears his peace annoy,
And other dangers all his hopes destroy.
Behold the savage tribes in wildest strain,[14]
Approach with death and terror in their train;
No longer silence o'er the forest reigns,
No longer stillness now her power retains;
But hideous yells announce the murderous band,
Whose bloody footsteps desolate the land;
He hears them oft in sternest mood maintain,
Their right to rule the mountain and the plain;
He hears them doom the *white man's* instant death,
Shrinks from the sentence, while he gasps for breath,

60

70

80

90

---

*The process of clearing land, though simple, is attended with a great deal of labour. The trees are all felled, so as to lie in the same direction; and after the fire has passed over them in that state, whatever may be left is collected into heaps, and reduced to ashes. The grain is then sown between the stumps of the trees, which remain, until the lapse of time, from ten to fifteen years, reduces them to decay.

---

12. desert lands Uninhabited. **13. pond'rous** Massive. **14. wildest strain** Wild-sounding song.

Then, rousing with one effort all his might,
Darts from his hut, and saves himself by flight.
Yet, what a refuge! Here a host of foes,
On every side, his trembling steps oppose;
Here savage beasts around his cottage howl,
As through the gloomy wood they nightly prowl,
Till morning comes, and then is heard no more
The shouts of man, or beast's appalling roar;
The wandering Indian turns another way,
And brutes avoid the first approach of day.   100
  Yet, tho' these threat'ning dangers round him roll,
Perplex his thoughts, and agitate his soul,
By patient firmness and industrious toil,
He still retains possession of the soil;
Around his dwelling scattered huts extend,
Whilst every hut affords another friend.
And now, behold! his bold aggressors fly,
To seek their prey beneath some other sky;
Resign the haunts they can maintain no more,
And safety in far distant wilds explore.   110
His perils vanished, and his fears o'ercome,
Sweet hope portrays a happy peaceful home.
On every side fair prospects charm his eyes,
And future joys in every thought arise.
His humble cot, built from the neighbouring trees,
Affords protection from each chilling breeze;
His rising crops, with rich luxuriance crowned,
In waving softness shed their freshness round;
By nature nourished, by her bounty blest,
He looks to Heaven, and lulls his cares to rest.   120
  The arts of culture now extend their sway,
And many a charm of rural life display.
Where once the pine upreared its lofty head,
The settlers' humble cottages are spread;
Where the broad firs once sheltered from the storm,
By slow degrees a neighbourhood they form;
And, as its bounds, each circling year, increase
In social life, prosperity, and peace,
New prospects rise, new objects too appear,
To add more comfort to its lowly sphere.   130
Where some rude sign or post the spot betrays,
The tavern first its useful[15] front displays.
Here, oft the weary traveller at the close
Of evening, finds a snug and safe repose.
The passing stranger here, a welcome guest,

---

15. **useful** Welcoming.

From all his toil enjoys a peaceful rest;
Unless the host, solicitous to please,
With care officious mar his hope of ease,
With flippant questions to no end confined,
140 Exhaust his patience, and perplex his mind.
    Yet, let no one condemn with thoughtless haste,
The hardy settler of the dreary[16] waste,
Who, far removed from every busy throng,
And social pleasures that to life belong,
Whene'er a stranger comes within his reach,
Will sigh to learn whatever he can teach.
To this, must be ascribed in great degree,
That ceaseless, idle curiosity,
Which over all the Western world prevails,
150 And every breast, or more or less, assails;
Till, by indulgence, so o'erpowering grown,
It seeks to know all business but its own.
Here, oft when winter's dreary terrors reign,
And cold, and snow, and storm, pervade the plain,
Around the birch-wood blaze the settlers draw,
"To tell of all they felt, and all they saw."[17]
When, thus in peace are met a happy few,
Sweet are the social pleasures that ensue.
What lively joy each honest bosom feels,
160 As o'er the past events his memory steals,
And to the listeners paints the dire distress,
That marked his progress in the wilderness;
The danger, trouble, hardship, toil, and strife,
Which chased each effort of his struggling life.
    In some lone spot of consecrated ground,
Whose silence spreads a holy gloom around,
The village church in unadorned array,[18]
Now lifts its turret to the opening day.
How sweet to see the villagers repair
170 In groups to pay their adoration there;
To view, in homespun dress, each sacred morn,
The old and young its hallowed seats adorn,
While, grateful for each blessing God has given,
In pious strains, they waft their thanks to Heaven.
    Oh, heaven-born faith! sure solace of our woes,
How lost is he who ne'er thy influence knows,
How cold the heart thy charity ne'er fires,
How dead the soul thy spirit ne'er inspires!
When troubles vex and agitate the mind,

---

16. **dreary waste** Undeveloped, harsh place. 17. The line recalls *The Deserted Village*: "And tell of all I felt, and all I saw."
18. **unadorned array** Plain-looking.

By gracious Heaven for wisest ends designed,   180
When dangers threaten, or when fears invade,
Man flies to thee for comfort and for aid;
The soul, impelled by thy all-powerful laws,
Seeks safety, only, in a Great First Cause![19]
If, then, amid the busy scene of life,
Its joy and pleasure, care, distrust, and strife;
Man, to his God for help and succour fly,
And on his mighty power to save, rely;
If, then, his thoughts can force him to confess
His errors, wants, and utter helplessness;   190
How strong must be those feelings which impart
A sense of all his weakness to the heart,
Where not a friend in solitude is nigh,
His home the wild, his canopy the sky;
And, far removed from every human arm,
His God alone can shelter him from harm.
   While now the Rising Village claims a name,
Its limits still increase, and still its fame.
The wandering Pedlar, who undaunted traced
His lonely footsteps o'er the silent waste;   200
Who traversed once the cold and snow-clad plain,
Reckless[20] of danger, trouble, or of pain,
To find a market for his little wares,
The source of all his hopes, and all his cares,
Established here, his settled home maintains,
And soon a merchant's higher title gains.
Around his store, on spacious shelves arrayed,
Behold his great and various stock in trade.
Here, nails and blankets, side by side, are seen,
There, horses' collars, and a large tureen;   210
Buttons and tumblers, fish-hooks, spoons and knives,
Shawls for young damsels, flannel for old wives;
Woolcards and stockings, hats for men and boys,
Mill-saws and fenders, silks, and children's toys;
All useful things, and joined with many more,
Compose the well-assorted country store.*
   The half-bred Doctor next then settles down,
And hopes the village soon will prove a town.
No rival here disputes his doubtful skill,
He cures, by chance, or ends each human ill;   220
By turns he physics,[21] or his patient bleeds,

---

*Every shop in America, whether in city or village, in which the most trifling articles are sold, is dignified with the title of a store.

---

19. Great First Cause God. **20. Reckless** Ignoring. **21. physics** Practices medicine, sometimes through bleeding.

Uncertain in what case each best succeeds.
And if, from friends untimely snatched away,
Some beauty fall a victim to decay;
If some fine youth, his parents' fond delight,
Be early hurried to the shades of night,
Death bears the blame, 'tis his envenomed dart
That strikes the suffering mortal to the heart.
  Beneath the shelter of a log-built shed
230   The country school-house next erects its head.
No "man severe,"[22] with learning's bright display,
Here leads the opening blossoms into day;
No master here, in every art refined,
Through fields of science guides the aspiring mind;
But some poor wanderer of the human race,
Unequal to the task, supplies his place,
Whose greatest source of knowledge or of skill
Consists in reading, and in writing ill;[23]
Whose efforts can no higher merit claim,
240   Than spreading Dilworth's[24] great scholastic fame.
No modest youths surround his awful[25] chair,
His frowns to deprecate, or smiles to share,
But all the terrors of his lawful sway[26]
The proud despise, the fearless disobey;
The rugged urchins spurn at all control,
Which cramps the movements of the free-born soul,
Till, in their own conceit so wise they've grown,
They think their knowledge far exceeds his own.
  As thus the village each successive year
250   Presents new prospects, and extends its sphere,
While all around its smiling charms expand,
And rural beauties decorate the land.
The humble tenants, who were taught to know,
By years of suffering, all the weight of woe;
Who felt each hardship nature could endure,
Such pains as time alone could ease or cure,
Relieved from want, in sportive pleasures find
A balm to soften and relax the mind;
And now, forgetful of their former care,
260   Enjoy each sport, and every pastime share.
Beneath some spreading tree's expanded shade
Here many a manly youth and gentle maid,
With festive dances or with sprightly song

---

22. **"man severe"** A reference to *The Deserted Village:* "A man severe he was, and stern to view." 23. **writing ill** A reference to Alexander Pope's *An Essay on Criticism:* "'Tis hard to say, if greater Want of Skill / Appear in *Writing* or in *Judging* ill." 24. **Dilworth's** Thomas Dilworth was an English school teacher and the author of several school books. 25. **awful** Imposing; commanding respect. 26. **lawful sway** Influence.

The summer's evening hours in joy prolong,
And as the young their simple sports renew,
The aged witness, and approve them too.
And when the Summer's bloomy charms are fled,
When Autumn's fallen leaves around are spread,
When Winter rules the sad inverted year,
And ice and snow alternately appear,   270
Sports not less welcome lightly they essay,
To chase the long and tedious hours away.
Here, ranged in joyous groups around the fire,
Gambols and freaks[27] each honest heart inspire;
And if some venturous youth obtain a kiss,
The game's reward, and summit of its bliss,
Applauding shouts the victor's prize proclaim,
And every tongue augments his well-earned fame;
While all the modest fair one's blushes tell
Success had crowned his fondest hopes too well.   280
Dear humble sports, Oh! long may you impart
A guileless pleasure to the youthful heart,
Still may your joys from year to year increase,
And fill each breast with happiness and peace.
   Yet, tho' these simple pleasures crown the year,
Relieve its cares, and every bosom cheer,
As life's gay scenes in quick succession rise,
To lure the heart and captivate the eyes;
Soon vice steals on, in thoughtless pleasure's train,
And spreads her miseries o'er the village plain.   290
Her baneful arts some happy home invade
Some bashful lover, or some tender maid;
Until, at length, repressed by no control,
They sink, debase, and overwhelm the soul.
How many aching breasts now live to know
The shame, the anguish, misery and woe,
That heedless passions, by no laws confined,
Entail forever on the human mind.
Oh, Virtue! that thy powerful charms could bind
Each rising impulse of the erring mind.   300
That every heart might own thy sovereign sway,
And every bosom fear to disobey;
No father's heart would then in anguish trace
The sad remembrance of a son's disgrace;
No mother's tears for some dear child undone
Would then in streams of poignant sorrow run,

---

27. **Gambols and freaks** Games and playfulness.

Nor could my verse the hapless story tell
Of one poor maid who loved — and loved too well.
  Among the youths that graced their native plain,
Albert was foremost of the village train;
310   The hand of nature had profusely shed
Her choicest blessings on his youthful head;
His heart seemed generous, noble, kind, and free,
Just bursting into manhood's energy.
Flora[28] was fair, and blooming as that flower
Which spreads its blossom to the April shower;*
Her gentle manners and unstudied grace
Still added lustre to her beaming face,
While every look, by purity refined,
Displayed the lovelier beauties of her mind.
320   Sweet was the hour, and peaceful was the scene
When Albert first met Flora on the green;
Her modest looks, in youthful bloom displayed,
Then touched his heart, and there a conquest made.
Nor long he sighed, by love and rapture fired,
He soon declared the passion she inspired.
In silence, blushing sweetly, Flora heard
His vows of love and constancy preferred;
And, as his soft and tender suit he pressed,
The maid, at length, a mutual flame confessed.
330   Love now had shed, with visions light as air,
His golden prospects on this happy pair;
Those moments soon rolled rapidly away,
Those hours of joy and bliss that gently play
Around young hearts, ere yet they learn to know
Life's care or trouble, or to feel its woe.
The day was fixed, the bridal dress was made,
And time alone their happiness delayed,
The anxious moment that, in joy begun,
Would join their fond and faithful hearts in one.
340   'Twas now at evening's hour, about the time
When in Acadia's cold and northern clime
The setting sun, with pale and cheerless glow,
Extends his beams o'er trackless[29] fields of snow,
That Flora felt her throbbing heart oppressed
By thoughts, till then, a stranger to her breast.
Albert had promised that his bosom's pride

---

*The May-flower (*Epigaea repens*) is indigenous to the wilds of Acadia, and is in bloom from the middle of April to the end of May. Its leaves are white, faintly tinged with red, and it possesses a delightful fragrance.

---

28. Flora The Greek goddess of flowers and spring. **29. trackless** Barren; windswept.

That very morning should become his bride;
Yet morn had come and passed; and not one vow
Of his had e'er been broken until now.
But, hark! a hurried step advances near, 350
'Tis Albert's breaks upon her listening ear;
Albert's, ah, no! a ruder footstep bore,
With eager haste, a letter to the door;
Flora received it, and could scarce conceal
Her rapture, as she kissed her lover's seal.
Yet, anxious tears were gathered in her eye,
As on the note it rested wistfully;
Her trembling hands unclosed the folded page,
That soon she hoped would every fear assuage,
And while intently o'er the lines she ran, 360
In broken half breathed tones she thus began:
    "Dear Flora, I have left my native plain,
And fate forbids that we shall meet again:
'Twere vain to tell, nor can I now impart
The sudden motive to this change of heart.
The vows so oft repeated to thine ear
As tales of cruel falsehood must appear.
Forgive the hand that deals this treacherous blow,
Forget the heart that can afflict this woe;
Farewell! and think no more of Albert's name, 370
His weakness pity, now involved in shame."
    Ah! who can paint her features as, amazed,
In breathless agony, she stood and gazed!
Oh, Albert, cruel Albert! she exclaimed,
Albert was all her faltering accents named.
A deadly feeling seized upon her frame,
Her pulse throbb'd quick, her colour went and came;
A darting pain shot through her frenzied head,
And from that fatal hour her reason fled!
    The sun had set; his lingering beams of light 380
From western hills had vanished into night.
The northern blast along the valley rolled,
Keen was that blast, and piercing was the cold,
When, urged by frenzy, and by love inspired,
For what but madness could her breast have fired!
Flora, with one slight mantle[30] round her waved,
Forsook her home, and all the tempest braved.
Her lover's falsehood wrung her gentle breast,
His broken vows her tortured mind possessed;
Heedless of danger, on she bent her way 390
Through drifts of snow, where Albert's dwelling lay,

---

30. **mantle** Cloak.

With frantic haste her tottering steps pursued
Amid the long night's darkness unsubdued;
Until, benumbed, her fair and fragile form
Yielded beneath the fury of the storm;
Exhausted nature could no further go,
And, senseless, down she sank amid the snow.
  Now as the morn had streaked the eastern sky
With dawning light, a passing stranger's eye,
400 By chance directed, glanced upon the spot
Where lay the lovely sufferer: To his cot
The peasant bore her, and with anxious care
Tried every art, till hope became despair.
With kind solicitude his tender wife
Long vainly strove to call her back to life;
At length her gentle bosom throbs again,
Her torpid limbs their wonted power obtain;
The loitering current[31] now begins to flow,
And hapless Flora wakes once more to woe:
410 But all their friendly efforts could not find
A balm to heal the anguish of her mind.
  Come hither, wretch, and see what thou hast done,
Behold the heart thou hast so falsely won,
Behold it, wounded, broken, crushed and riven,[32]
By thy unmanly arts to ruin driven;
Hear Flora calling on thy much loved name,
Which, e'en in madness, she forbears to blame.
Not all thy sighs and tears can now restore
One hour of pleasure that she knew before;
420 Not all thy prayers can now remove the pain,
That floats and revels[33] o'er her maddened brain.
Oh, shame of manhood! that could thus betray
A maiden's hopes, and lead her heart away;
Oh, shame of manhood! that could blast her joy,
And one so fair, so lovely, could destroy.
  Yet, think not oft such tales of real woe
Degrade the land, and round the village flow.
Here virtue's charms appear in bright array,
And all their pleasing influence display;
430 Here modest youths, impressed in beauty's train,
Or captive led by love's endearing chain,
And fairest girls whom vows have ne'er betrayed,
Vows that are broken oft as soon as made,
Unite their hopes, and join their lives in one,
In bliss pursue them, as at first begun.
Then, as life's current onward gently flows,

---

31. **loitering current** Circulation of the blood. 32. **riven** Torn apart. 33. **floats and revels** Churns and moves.

With scarce one fault to ruffle its repose,
With minds prepared, they sink in peace to rest,
To meet on high the spirits of the blest.
  While time thus rolls his rapid years away,   440
The Village rises gently into day.
How sweet it is, at first approach of morn,
Before the silvery dew has left the lawn,
When warring winds are sleeping yet on high,
Or breathe as softly as the bosom's sigh,
To gain some easy hill's ascending height,
Where all the landscape brightens with delight,
And boundless prospects stretched on every side,
Proclaim the country's industry and pride.
Here the broad marsh extends its open plain,   450
Until its limits touch the distant main;
There verdant meads along the uplands spring,
And grateful odours to the breezes fling;
Here crops of grain in rich luxuriance rise,
And wave their golden riches to the skies;
There smiling orchards interrupt the scene,
Or gardens bounded by some fence of green;
The farmer's cottage, bosomed 'mong[34] the trees,
Whose spreading branches shelter from the breeze;
The winding stream that turns the busy mill,   460
Whose clacking echos o'er the distant hill;
The neat white church, beside whose walls are spread
The grass-clod hillocks of the sacred dead,
Where rude cut stones or painted tablets tell,
In laboured verse, how youth and beauty fell;
How worth and hope were hurried to the grave,
And torn from those who had no power to save.
  Or, when the Summer's dry and sultry[35] sun
Adown the West his fiery course has run;
When o'er the vale his parting rays of light   470
Just linger, ere they vanish into night,
How sweet to wander round the wood-bound lake,
Whose glassy stillness scarce the zephyrs[36] wake;
How sweet to hear the murmuring of the rill,
As down it gurgles from the distant hill;
The note of Whip-poor-Will how sweet to hear,*

---

*The Whip-poor-Will (*Caprimulgus vociferus*) is a native of America. On a summer's evening the wild and mournful cadence of its note is heard at a great distance; and the traveller listens with delight to the repeated tale of its sorrows.

---

34. bosomed 'mong Encircled by. **35. sultry** Hot. **36. zephyrs** Calm breezes.

When sadly slow it breaks upon the ear,
And tells each night, to all the silent vale,[37]
The hopeless sorrows of its mournful tale.
480 Dear lovely spot! Oh may such charms as these,
Sweet tranquil charms, that cannot fail to please,
Forever reign around thee, and impart
Joy, peace, and comfort to each native heart.
  Happy Acadia! though around thy shore*
Is heard the stormy wind's terrific roar;
Though round thee Winter binds his icy chain,
And his rude tempests sweep along thy plain,
Still Summer comes, and decorates thy land
With fruits and flowers from her luxuriant hand;
490 Still Autumn's gifts repay the labourer's toil
With richest products from thy fertile soil;
With bounteous store his varied wants supply,
And scarce the plants of other suns deny.
How pleasing, and how glowing with delight
Are now thy budding hopes! How sweetly bright
They rise to view! How full of joy appear
The expectations of each future year!
Not fifty Summers yet have blessed thy clime,
How short a period in the page of time!
500 Since savage tribes, with terror in their train,
Rushed o'er thy fields, and ravaged all thy plain.
But some few years have rolled in haste away
Since, through thy vales, the fearless beast of prey,
With dismal yell and loud appalling cry,
Proclaimed his midnight reign of terror nigh.
And now how changed the scene! the first, afar,
Have fled to wilds beneath the northern star;
The last has learned to shun man's dreaded eye,
And, in his turn, to distant regions fly.[38]
510 While the poor peasant, whose laborious care
Scarce from the soil could wring his scanty fare;
Now in the peaceful arts of culture skilled,
Sees his wide barn with ample treasures filled;
Now finds his dwelling, as the year goes round,
Beyond his hopes, with joy and plenty crowned.
  Nor culture's arts, a nation's noblest friend,
Alone o'er Scotia's fields their power extend;

---

*The Provinces of Nova Scotia and New Brunswick now comprehend that part of British North America, which was formerly denominated Acadia, or L'Acadie, by the French, and Nova Scotia by the English.

---

37. silent vale Quiet valley. **38.** 502–510: The lines refer to the dislocation of the native peoples, partially as a result of their efforts to evade the illnesses brought to North America by European settlers, but also because some were co-opted by the British to assist in military operations that forced them to relocate.

From all her shores, with every gentle gale,
Commerce expands her free and swelling sail;
And all the land, luxuriant, rich, and gay,
Exulting owns the splendour of their sway.   520
These are thy blessings, Scotia, and for these,
For wealth, for freedom, happiness, and ease,
Thy grateful thanks to Britain's care are due,
Her power protects, her smiles past hopes renew,
Her valour guards thee, and her councils guide,
Then, may thy parent ever be thy pride!
  Happy Britannia! though thy history's page
In darkest ignorance shrouds thine infant age,
Though long thy childhood's years in error strayed,
And long in superstition's bands delayed;   530
Matur'd and strong, thou shin'st in manhood's prime,
The first and brightest star of Europe's clime.
The nurse of science, and the seat of arts,
The home of fairest forms and gentlest hearts;
The land of heroes, generous, free, and brave,
The noblest conquerors of the field and wave;
Thy flag, on every sea and shore unfurled,
Has spread thy glory, and thy thunder hurled.
When, o'er the earth, a tyrant[39] would have thrown
His iron chain, and called the world his own,   540
Thine arm preserved it, in its darkest hour,
Destroyed his hopes, and crushed his dreaded power,
To sinking nations life and freedom gave,
'Twas thine to conquer, as 'twas thine to save.
  Then blest Acadia! ever may thy name,
Like hers, be graven[40] on the rolls of fame;
May all thy sons, like hers, be brave and free,
Possessors of her laws and liberty;
Heirs of her splendour, science, power, and skill,
And through succeeding years her children still.   550
And as the sun, with gentle dawning ray,
From night's dull bosom wakes, and leads the day,
His course majestic keeps, till in the height
He glows one blaze of pure exhaustless light;
So may thy years increase, thy glories rise,
To be the wonder of the Western skies;
And bliss and peace encircle all thy shore,
Till empires rise and sink, on earth, no more.

                                                                    (1825, rev. 1834)

---

39. **a tyrant** Napolean Bonaparte. 40. **graven** Carved.

Thomas Chandler Haliburton (1796–1865)

Thomas Chandler Haliburton was born on 17 December 1796 in Windsor, Nova Scotia. There he attended the Anglican King's Grammar School and then King's College. After graduating in 1815, he made two voyages to England, and during his second visit, he met and married an English-woman named Louisa Neville. She returned with him to Nova Scotia the following year. In 1821, the couple and their growing family (five daughters and six sons, three of whom died in infancy) moved to Annapolis Royal, where Haliburton established a law practice.

During his visits to England, Haliburton was disappointed in what he considered Britons' inaccurate perceptions of Nova Scotia. In 1823, he wrote *A General Description of Nova Scotia; Illustrated by a New and Correct Map* in an attempt to provide an accurate portrait of his colony to the British, particularly potential emigrants. In his preface to the volume, he observes that "In Great Britain, less is known of Nova Scotia, than of any other Colony she possesses. ... The object of this work is to ... give a true description of its climate and productions, its agriculture and trade, its public institutions and laws." Haliburton's Nova Scotian friends encouraged him to expand *A General Description* into a full-length history of the colony. In 1829, he published the two-volume work *An Historical and Statistical Account of Nova-Scotia.*

In 1826, Haliburton was elected to the House of Assembly as the member for Annapolis Royal. A powerful orator and debater, he pushed for educational reform and battled restrictions on the Roman Catholic population of Nova Scotia. He was frustrated with the apathy of many of his fellow assembly members and with the amount of time it took to accomplish anything in the legislature. In a later sketch, "The Schoolmaster Abroad" (1838), he expresses this dissatisfaction through the character of a drunken English emigrant: "Little ponds never hold big fish, there is nothing but pollywogs, tadpoles, and minims in them. ... Go to every legislature this side of the water from Congress to Halifax, and hear the stuff that is talked ... and then tell me this is a location for anything above mediocrity." In 1829, Haliburton's career in the House of Assembly came to an end when he inherited his late father's judgeship in the Inferior Court of Common Pleas. The Haliburtons moved to Windsor.

In 1835, Haliburton began to publish a series of sketches in the *Novascotian,* which were met with much success. He collected and revised the sketches the following year, publishing them under the title *The Clockmaker; or, The Sayings and Doings of Samuel Slick, of Slickville.* The narrator of these sketches, a British Tory traditionalist called the Squire, rides to Windsor in the company of an American individualist, industrialist, and clock salesman named Sam Slick. As the two men discuss the colony through which they are travelling, Haliburton employs the figure of Slick to satirize the lethargy of Nova Scotians, or "bluenoses," and the colony's social and political scenes. Slick was derived from the Yankee stock character so popular in American humour writing at this time. He speaks in a Yankee dialect, and, with his larger-than-life personality, he recalls Davy Crockett and other figures from the tall-tale genre. "I never seed or heard tell of a country that had so many natural privileges as this," Slick says of Nova Scotia; "[the citizens] have all they can ax, and more than they desarve. ... But they are either asleep, or stone blind to them." British publisher Richard Bentley pirated the first series of *The Clockmaker,* and it was extremely popular with the British public.

In 1841, Haliburton was promoted to the Supreme Court of Nova Scotia. Later that year, his wife, Louisa, died. He continued to write, publishing a new collection of Sam Slick sketches, *The Attaché; or, Sam Slick in England* (1843). He also produced *The Old Judge; or, Life in a Colony*, which was serialized in 1846–47 and published as a collection in 1849. *The Old Judge* is narrated by an Englishman who recounts his experiences as he becomes acquainted with Nova Scotia life in the fictional town of Illinoo. Haliburton's Tory politics and nostalgia for a vanished way of life reach full expression in this work.

After his retirement from the Supreme Court, in 1856, Haliburton moved to England and married his second wife, Sarah Harriet Williams. He became involved in politics once more, this time as the member of the House of Commons for Launceston. In 1858, he was honoured with a Doctor of Civil Law degree from Oxford University. He died on 5 August 1865.

Haliburton's other works include *The Letter-Bag of the Great Western; or, Life in a Steamer* (1840); *The English in America* (1851); *Sam Slick's Wise Saws and Modern Instances; or, What He Said, Did, or Invented* (1853); *Nature and Human Nature* (1855); and *The Season-Ticket* (1860).

Contemporary readers of Haliburton are often uncomfortable with the author's more conservative views, particularly the racist and pro-slavery sentiments he expresses in *The Clock-maker* and *The Old Judge*. Indeed, recent criticism has examined this aspect of his work. George Elliot Clarke, for example, has argued that "To characterize Haliburton as a species of living fossil, a 'provincial' Tory ... is facile and obscuring." Instead, we must look at the ways in which Haliburton's politics are still present in Canadian society — the ways in which his "reactions to slavery, abolitionism, and modernity bare the foundations of English-Canadian conservatism."

Gulling a Blue Nose[1]

I allot, said Mr. Slick, that the Blue Noses are the most gullible folks on the face of the airth — rigular soft horns, that's a fact. Politicks and such stuff set 'em a gapin, like children in a chimbly[2] corner listenen to tales of ghosts, Salem witches, and Nova Scotia snow storms; and while they stand starin and yawpin, all eyes and mouth, they get their pockets picked of every cent that's in 'em. One candidate chap says, "Feller citizens, this country is goin to the dogs hand over hand; look at your rivers, you have no bridges; at your wild lands, you have no roads; at your treasury, you hante got a cent in it; at your markets, things dont fetch nothin; at your fish, the Yankees ketch 'em all. There's nothin behind you but sufferin, around you but poverty, afore you, but slavery and death. What's the cause of this unheerd of awful state of things, ay, what's the cause? Why Judges, and Banks, and Lawyers, and great folks, have swallered all the money. They've got you down, and they'll keep you down to all etarnity, you and your posteriors arter[3] you. Rise up like men, arouse yourselves like freemen, and elect me to the Legislatur, and I'll lead on the small but patriotic band, I'll put the big wigs thro' their facins, I'll make 'em shake in their shoes, I'll knock off your chains and make you free." Well, the goneys[4] fall tu and elect him, and he desarts right away, with balls, rifle, powder horn and all. *He promised too much.*

Then comes a rael good man, and an everlastin fine preacher, a most a special spiritual man, renounces the world, the flesh, and the devil, preaches and prays day and night, so kind to the poor, and so humble, he has no more pride than a babe, and so short-handed he's no butter to his bread — all self denial, mortifyin the flesh. Well, as soon as he can work it, he marries the richest gall in all his flock, and then his bread is buttered on both sides. *He promised too much.*

---

1. **Gulling a Blue Nose** Inhabitants of the Maritimes, especially of Nova Scotia, were called Blue Noses. Gulling means to deceive, or cheat. 2. **chimbly** Chimney corner; hearth. 3. **arter** After. 4. **goneys** Dumb people.

Then comes a Doctor, and a prime article he is too, I've got, says he, a screw augur emetic[5] and hot crop, and if I cant cure all sorts o' things in natur my name aint quack. Well he turns stomach and pocket, both inside out, and leaves poor blue nose — a dead man. *He promised too much.*

Then comes a Lawyer, an honest lawyer too, a rael wonder under the sun, as straight as a shingle in all his dealins. He's so honest he cant bear to hear tell of other lawyers, he writes agin 'em, raves agin 'em, votes agin 'em, they are all rogues but him. He's jist the man to take a case in hand, cause *he* will see justice done. Well, he wins his case, and fobs all for costs, cause he's sworn to see justice done to — himself. *He promised too much.*

Then comes a Yankee Clockmaker, (and here Mr. Slick looked up and smiled,) with his "Soft Sawder," and "Human Natur," and he sells clocks warranted to run from July to Etarnity, stoppages included, and I must say they do run as long as — as long as wooden clocks commonly do, that's a fact. But I'll shew you presently how I put the leak into 'em, for here's a feller a little bit ahead on us, whose flint I've made up my mind to fix this while past. Here we were nearly thrown out of the waggon, by the breaking down of one of those small wooden bridges, which prove so annoying and so dangerous to travellers. Did you hear that are snap? said he, well as sure as fate, I'll break my clocks over them etarnal log bridges, if Old Clay clips over them arter that fashion. Them are poles are plaguy treacherous, they are jist like old Marm Patience Doesgood's teeth, that keeps the great United Independent Democratic Hotel, at Squaw Neck Creek, in Massachusetts, one half gone, and tother half rotten eends. I thought you had disposed of your last Clock, said I, at Colchester, to Deacon Flint. So I did, he replied, the last one I had to sell to *him*, but I got a few left for other folks yet. Now there is a man on this road, one Zeb Allen, a real genu*in*e skinflint, a proper close fisted customer as you'll amost see any where, and one that's not altogether the straight thing in his dealin neither. He dont want no one to live but himself, and he's mighty handsum to me, sayin my Clocks are all a cheat, and that we ruinate the country, a drainin every drop of money out of it, a callin me a Yankee broom and what not. But it tante all jist Gospel that he says. Now I'll put a Clock on him afore he knows it, I'll go right into him as slick as a whistle, and play him to the eend of my line like a trout. I'll have a hook in his gills, while he's a thinkin he's only smellin at the bait. There he is now, I'll be darned if he aint, standin afore his shop door, lookin as strong as high proof Jamaiky;[6] I guess I'll whip it out o' the bung while he's a lookin arter the spicket,[7] and praps he'll be none o' the wiser till he finds it out, neither.

Well Squire, how do you do, said he, how's all to home? Reasonable well, I give you thanks, wont you alight? Cant today, said Mr. Slick, I'm in a considerable of a hurry to katch the Packet, have you any commands for Sow West? I'm going to the Island, and across the Bay to Windsor. Any word that way? No says Mr. Allen, none that I can think on, unless it be to enquire how butter's goin; they tell me cheese is down, and pro*duce* of all kind particular dull this fall. Well, I'm glad I can tell you that question, said Slick, for I don't calculate to return to these parts, butter is risin a cent or two; I put mine off mind at 10 pence. Dont return! possible! why how you talk? have you done with the clock trade? I guess I have, it tante worth follerin now. Most time, said the other, laughing, for by all accounts the clocks warnt worth havin, and most infarnal dear too, folks begin to get their eyes open. It warnt needed in your case, said Mr. Slick, with

---

5. **emetic** A medicine that causes vomiting. 6. **Jamaiky** Rum. 7. **spicket** Spiggot.

that peculiarly composed manner, that indicates suppressed feeling, for you were always wide awake, if all the folks had cut their eye teeth as airly as you did, their'd be plaguy few clocks sold in these parts, I reckon; but you are right, Squire, you may say that, they actilly were *not* worth havin, and that's the truth. The fact is, said he, throwing down his reins, and affecting a most confidential tone, I felt almost ashamed of them myself, I tell you. The long and short of the matter is jist this, they dont make no good ones now-a-days, no more, for they calculate 'em for shippin and not for home use. I was all struck up of a heap when I see'd the last lot I got from the States; I was properly bit by them, you may depend; they didn't pay cost, for I couldn't recommend them with a clear conscience, and I must say I do like a fair deal, for I'm strait up and down, and love to go right ahead, that's a fact. Did you ever see them I fetched when I first came, them I sold over the Bay? No, said Mr. Allen, I cant say I did. Well, continued he, they *were* a prime article, I tell you, no mistake there, fit for any market, its generally allowed there aint the beat of them to be found any where. If you want a clock, and *can* lay your hands on one of them, I advise you not to let go the chance; you'll know 'em by the 'Lowell' mark, for they were all made at Judge Beler's factory. Squire Shepody, down to Five Islands, axed[8] me to get him one, and a special job I had of it, near about more sarch arter it than it was worth, but I did get him one, and particular hansum one it is, copald and gilt superior. I guess its worth ary half dozen in these parts, let tothers be where they may. If I could a got supplied with the like o' them, I could a made a grand spec out of them, for they took at once, and went off quick. Have you got it with you, said Mr. Allen, I should like to see it. Yes, I have it here, all done up in tow, as snug as a bird's egg, to keep it from jarring, for it hurts 'em consumedly to jolt 'em over them are etarnal wooden bridges. But its no use to take it out, it aint for sale, its bespoke, and I would'nt take the same trouble to get another for twenty dollars. The only one that I know of that there's any chance of gettin, is one that Increase Crane has up to Wilmot, they say he's a sellin off.

After a good deal of persuasion, Mr. Slick unpacked the clock, but protested against his asking for it, for it was not for sale. It was then exhibited, every part explained and praised, as new in invention and perfect in workmanship. Now Mr. Allen had a very exalted opinion of Squire Shepody's taste, judgment, and saving knowledge; and, as it was the last and only chance of getting a clock, of such superior quality, he offered to take it at the price the Squire was to have it, at seven pounds ten shillings. But Mr. Slick vowed he could'nt part with it at no rate, he didnt know where he could get the like agin, (for he warnt quite sure about Increase Crane's) and the Squire would be confounded disappointed, he could'nt think of it. In proportion to the difficulties, rose the ardor of Mr. Allen, his offers advanced to £8, to £8 10, to £9. I vow, said Mr. Slick, I wish I had'nt let on that I had it at all. I dont like to refuse you, but where am I to get the like. After much discussion of a similar nature, he consented to part with the clock, though with great apparent reluctance, and pocketed the money with a protest that, cost what it would, he should have to procure another, for he could'nt think of putting the Squire's pipe out arter that fashion, for he was a very clever man, and as fair as a boot jack. Now, said Mr. Slick, as we proceeded on our way, that are feller is properly sarved, he got the most inferior article I had, and I jist doubled the price on him. Its a pity he should be a tellin of lies of the yankees all the time, this will help him now to a little grain of truth. Then mimicking his voice and manner, he repeated Allen's words with a strong nasal

---

8. **axed** Asked.

twang, "Most time for you to give over the clock trade, I guess, for by all accounts they aint worth havin, and most infarnel dear too, folks begin to get their eyes open." Better for you, if you'd a had yourn open, I reckon, a joke is a joke, but I concait you'll find that no joke. The next time you tell stories about Yankee pedlars, put the wooden clock in with the wooden punkin seeds, and Hickory hams, will you? The blue noses, Squire, are all like Zeb Allen, they think they know every thing, but they get gulled from years' eend to years' eend. They expect too much from others, and do too little for themselves. They actilly expect the sun to shine, and the rain to fall, through their little House of Assembly. What have you done for us? they keep axin their members. Who did you spunk up to last Session? jist as if all legislation consisted in attackin some half dozen puss proud folks at Halifax, who are jist as big noodles as they be themselves. You hear nothin but politicks, politicks, politicks, one everlastin sound of give, give, give. If I was Governor I'd give 'em the butt eend of my mind on the subject, I'd crack their pates[9] till I let some light in 'em, if it was me, I know. I'd say to the members, don't come down here to Halifax with your long lockrums about politicks, makin a great touss about nothin; but open the country, foster agricultur, encourage trade, incorporate companies, make bridges, facilitate conveyance, and above all things make a Railroad from Windsor to Halifax; and mind what I tell you now, write it down for fear you should forget it, for it's a fact; and if you don't believe me, I'll lick you till you do, for there aint a word of a lie in it, by Gum: *"One such work as the Windsor Bridge is worth all your laws, votes, speeches and resolutions, for the last ten years, if tied up and put into a meal bag together. If it tante I hope I may be shot."*

(1836)

Catharine Parr Traill (1802–1899)

Throughout Margaret Laurence's novel *The Diviners* (1974), protagonist Morag Gunn holds conversations with an imaginary Catharine Parr Traill. She pictures "C.P.T.," having already cooked breakfast "for the multitude," "cleaning the house, baking two hundred loaves of delicious bread, preserving half a ton of plums, pears, cherries, etcetera. All before lunch." In much of her writing, Traill suggests that a pioneer woman will need a rational outlook and an industrious nature to ensure that her family survives the hardships of life in Canada.

Born Catharine Parr Strickland on 9 January 1802 in Rotherhithe, Kent, in England, Traill moved several times with her family before settling in a large manor house near Southwold, Suffolk, in 1808. After her father, Thomas Strickland, passed away in 1818, she and several of her siblings began to publish their literary efforts to help put bread on the table. Traill wrote a number of didactic narratives during this period, such as *Disobedience; or, Mind What Mama Says* (1819) and *The Keepsake Guineas; or, The Best Use of Money* (1828). Her interest in the natural sciences led her to write *Sketches from Nature; or, Hints to Juvenile Naturalists* (1830) and *Narratives of Nature, and History Book for Young Naturalists* (1831), which encouraged young people to take up botany. Notably, she also wrote *The Young Emigrants; or, Pictures of Life in Canada, Calculated to Amuse and Instruct the Minds of Youth* (1826), a story based on letters from friends who had emigrated to Canada and travel narratives she had read.

---

9. **pates** Heads.

On 13 May 1832, Catharine married a retired lieutenant of the Twenty-First Royal North British Fusiliers. Thomas Traill was a close friend of John Wedderburn Dunbar Moodie, who had recently married Catharine's sister Susanna. In July, both couples immigrated to Upper Canada. The Traills settled north of Peterborough, at Lake Katchawanook (now Lakefield) to be near Catharine's brother, Samuel Strickland, who had emigrated in 1825. The Moodies joined them two years later, after leaving their first settlement.

In 1836, Traill published *The Backwoods of Canada: Being Letters from the Wife of an Emigrant Officer, Illustrative of the Domestic Economy of British America* (1836), an epistolary narrative about her experiences of immigration and domestic life during her first years in Canada. Dissatisfied with the lack of practical and accurate information in much existing emigrant literature, Traill aimed with this work to provide a useful and detailed guide to settler life.

In 1839, financial pressures compelled the Traills to sell their farm. Over the next ten years, they moved from place to place within the Peterborough area as their family grew: the Traills had nine children, two of whom died in infancy. Finally, in 1849, they were able to purchase a property near Rice Lake. Many of Traill's sketches had appeared in British periodicals throughout the 1830s and 1840s. Then, in 1852, she published *The Canadian Crusoes: A Tale of the Rice Lake Plains*, a melodramatic story of three children who get lost in the backwoods of Upper Canada and manage to thrive for two years before they are found. In 1854, she produced *The Female Emigrant's Guide, and Hints on Canadian Housekeeping*, which was republished the following year as *The Canadian Settler's Guide*. Traill intended the work to be an extension of *The Backwoods of Canada*, but this time she divided her advice into accessible sections — such as "Knitting," "Fermentations for Bread," and "Dysentery in Children." "Having myself suffered from the disadvantage of acquiring all my knowledge of Canadian housekeeping by experience," she writes, "and having heard other females similarly situated lament the want of some simple useful book to give them an insight into the customs and occupations incidental to a Canadian settler's life, I have taken upon me to endeavor to supply this want."

In 1857, the Traills' house was destroyed by fire. Two years later, Thomas Traill passed away. With the help of her family and a small British government grant, Catharine built a cottage in Lakefield. There, she continued to write, turning much of her attention to her amateur botany studies. In 1868, her study *Canadian Wild Flowers* appeared, and in 1885, she published a book of much greater scope, entitled *Studies of Plant Life in Canada; or, Gleanings from Forest, Lake and Plain*. These works were the product of years of research and collecting specimens of Canadian flora, a pastime that had brought Traill much joy throughout her life as a settler. In her final decade, Traill published *Pearls and Pebbles; or, Notes of an Old Naturalist* (1894) and *Cot and Cradle Stories* (1895). She died in 1899.

Traill's other works include *The Tell Tale: An Original Collection of Moral and Amusing Stories* (1818); *Little Downy; or, The History of a Field Mouse: A Moral Tale* (1822); *The Juvenile Forget-Me-Not; or, Cabinet of Entertainment and Instruction* (1827); *Lady Mary and Her Nurse; or, A Peep into the Canadian Forest* (1856). The first Canadian edition of *The Backwoods of Canada* appeared in 1929.

The Bereavement

It was one of those soft warm mornings in April, that we not infrequently experience in this country during the melting of the snow, when the thermometer indicates a degree of temperature not less than summer heat. The air was filled with insects which had either revived from their winter torpor or been prematurely awakened to the enjoyment of a bright but brief existence. A few sleepy, dusty looking flies had crept from their hiding places about the window — while some attenuated shadowy spider made vain attempts at commencing a web to entangle them. Without all was gay and cheerful — a thousand spring-like sounds filled the air — flocks of that pleasant warbler, the Canadian song-sparrow, mingled with the neat snow-bird (*fringilla nivalis*) flitted about the low wattled fence of the garden; at the edge of the cedar swamp, might be heard from time to time the rapid strokes of the small spotted wood-pecker, full of energy and animation, the mellow drumming of the Canadian partridge, (or ruffed Grouse,) mingled not unharmoniously with the wild cry of that bold but beautiful depredator, the blue jay. There too was the soft melancholy whispering note of the little chickadee, (*parus palustris*,) as it restlessly pursued its insect prey among the feathery branches of some old gnarled hemlock — the murmuring melody of the breeze stirring the lofty heads of the pines, with the "still sweet sound of waters far away," combining made sweet music to the ear.

Bright and blue as was the sky above, warm and genial as was the air around, and inviting as were the sounds of nature abroad, I yet found myself obliged to be an unwilling prisoner; the newly melted snow had rendered the surface of the ground porous as a sponge; half decomposed ice and pools of water, made the roads and paths impassable. The luxury of India rubbers had scarcely at that time reached our settlement; they were among the rare things heard of but seldom seen. How I envied the more fortunate flocks of wild geese and ducks that were revelling in the azure pools, that lay so invitingly open to them, on the ice-bound lake in front of our log house. Sorely tempted as I was by the bright sunshine, and all spring's pleasant harmonies, to go forth into the newly uncovered fields — yet I dared not risk wetting my feet, having but recently recovered from a severe fit of illness.

I was still lingering at the open door, watching the graceful manoeuvres of the wild fowl on the lake, when my attention was attracted to a bare-footed, bare-headed, uncouth looking girl, who was hurrying towards the wicket, and panting from the speed which she had used. The little damsel, as soon as she could speak, told me she had been sent by her mistress, (a nice young Scotchwoman, wife to the overseer of a neighbouring saw-mill,) to entreat me to go and see her baby, a lovely infant of eight weeks old — which lay dying as she feared. I hesitated. Of what use could I be in a case of such emergency? I asked myself. The road lay through a tangled cedar swamp, the mudholes would be opened by the soft air — and I cast a glance at the wide pools of water, and the honey-combed ice. The bare-legged little messenger seemed to read my thoughts.

"Ye'll no find the path sae vera bad, gif ye'll gang the same gait wi' me. The mistress is greeting, greeting sairly a' the time, about the sick wean — she'll weary till she sees ye coming."

The simple entreaties of the little lassie prevailed over the dread of swamps and mudholes, wet feet and draggled garments. If I could afford no aid to the suffering child, I might yet support and console the afflicted mother — it was worth some little risk. Joy sparkled in the eyes of my little conductress as she watched me adjusting my tartan shawl; and as a reward for my compliance, she declared that I looked "like a bonny Scotch leddy."

My rough but warm-hearted little guide set off at a good round trot before me — heedless of mud or mire, stone or log; plunging most independently through the first, and scrambling fearlessly over the second — more than one high pile of logs she invited me to cross, after having set me the example with the agility, if not with the grace, of a squirrel — I might as well have followed a Will-o-the-Wisp, as little Maggie Freebairn.

Half an hour's quick walking brought me to the dwelling of the young mother and her sick infant. The babe had been ill several days, and many improper remedies had been successively adopted; among the most pernicious of these whisky punch, (the country people, by-the-bye, call all mixtures of spirits and water punch,) and bad port-wine had been forced down the babe's throat. It now lay, convulsed and evidently dying, on the lap of the weeping, sorrowing mother, a pale and wasted shadow of what had been so lovely only a single week before disease had seized it. The hand of Death had set its seal upon it — and "life's young wings were fluttering for their flight!"

By the advice of my sister-in-law, who happened to call in a few minutes after my arrival, we put the babe into a warm bath, and applied gentle friction to its body and extremities; but alas! it was beyond the reach of human skill or human care. It seemed almost cruel to torment it with unavailing remedies. It was sad to see the anguish of the poor mother, as she hung in tearful agony over its pale unconscious face. It was her first-born — her only one, and the bare possibility of parting from it was too bitter a grief to be dwelt upon. With what tender solicitude did her sad eyes wander towards it continually, as it lay upon my knees, while she almost unconsciously performed those household tasks which her situation rendered imperatively necessary, having to cook for some ten or twelve workmen, belonging to the saw-mill. How often would she throw herself upon her knees beside me to take its cold damp hands and place them on her bosom, or bathe them with her scalding tears — and ask with despairing accents, if I thought it could yet recover — and with what eager looks did she listen to the assurances of the compassionate millwrights and lumberers, that the infant would surely live — they had seen many young children brought as low and yet grew up fine stout boys and girls. I felt as if it were cruel to deceive her.

Towards night, the convulsion fits became more frequent, and, yielding to the passionate entreaties of the poor young woman, not to leave her alone with her dying babe, I consented to take share in her painful vigil. The little Scotch lass was again sent forth on a message to my household, and I prepared to act the part of nurse and watcher, while poor Jessy laid down to sleep — that heavy sleep, that the weary in heart and body alone know. Alone, in silence — I watched, by the flickering light cast by the pile of logs that had been carefully built up in the ample chimney (for candle there was none,) the last faint glimmerings of life in the unconscious form that lay upon my lap. No sound but the crackling and settling of the burning logs upon the hearth, the shrill chirp of the crickets, and the deep breathing of the tired slumberers in the loft above, met my ears within the dwelling; the ever moving waters of the river, as they rushed along their rocky bed, was the only sound abroad: and thus I passed the long night.

The first grey dawn found me still watching — I had not the heart to rouse the worn-out mother. I knew she could only waken to renewed anxiety. I felt the chill air of the early frosty morning blow bleak through the wide chinks of the imperfectly framed apartment. The infant appeared to have sunk into a tranquil sleep, and cramped with having maintained one posture for many hours, I now placed it in the cradle, and looked forth upon the face of Nature — and a lovely sight it was! The frosty earth was gemmed with countless diamonds — the mimic picture of those bright orbs above, which were still gleaming down from the clear blue sky; the saffron tint of early dawn was streaking the East. A light curling mist was gathering on the face of the rapid river, which lay before my eyes in all the majesty of its white crested waves, darkly shaded by the then unbroken line of forest on the opposite bank.

The little hamlet with its rude shanties and half erected dwellings and mill, lay scattered before me on the wide area in front — it was a scene of quiet and of freshness, save the rapid restless river rushing over its ledge of limestone rock, and hurrying away beneath the newly erected bridge in its downward course. It recalled to my mind Moore's lines written at the falls of the Mohawk river.[1]

> From rise of morn till set of sun,
> I've seen the mighty Mohawk run —
> *   *   *   *   *
> Rushing alike untired and wild
> Thro' rocks that frowned and flowers that smiled.

From the contemplation of things like these, I turned with a subdued and humbled heart to look upon human suffering and human woe. Without all was beauty and magnificence, for I gazed upon the works of God. Within was sorrow and death — the consequence of man's sin.

On my re-entering the house, I found Jessy sitting beside the cradle — her hopes had risen with the new day.

Her profound sleep had refreshed both body and mind, and she came to her labour of love with renewed spirits. She was anxious to get breakfast for me, but I preferred the reviving influence of the morning air to anything she could offer me, and promising to return in a few hours, I set forth on my solitary walk homeward.

There is no season when gratitude seems more naturally to fill our hearts, than at early dawn — it is the renewal to us of our existence, we feel that we have been cared for and preserved, and we lift our hearts to Him, from whom all blessings flow. How indeed, can we listen to the chorus of thanksgiving poured forth at sunrise, without being assured that an instinctive feeling of gratitude animates all things living — nay, even the very flowers, and trees, and herbs seem to rejoice in their freshness. Do not the Heavens declare the glory of God, and the firmament shew his handy-work!

The day was now risen, and the silent woods seemed suddenly to become eloquent with melodious notes, heard at no other time. The ground was white and crisp with frost, a comfortable change from the soft mud and half melted ice of the preceding day — the breeze blew sharp and cold from the river, but it seemed to revive my exhausted spirits and wearied frame. The wood-peckers were at their ceaseless work, hammering away at the pines and hemlocks — the red squirrels were out crossing my path in every direction, now stopping to regard me with furtive glance, now angrily erecting their beautiful feathery tails and darting up the stem of some rough barked tree, pausing from time to time in their ascent, to chatter forth some indignant remonstrance at my unseasonable intrusion on their privacy at such an hour — seldom, I ween, had lady fair been seen at dawn of day among the deep solitudes of these hemlock and cedar shades, through which I then winded my way. I was lost in a train of reflections to which the novelty of my

---

1. **Moore's lines** Thomas Moore (1779–1852) immortalized the sight of the Mohawk River in his poem entitled "Lines, Written at the Cohoes Falls of the Mohawk River."

situation had given birth, when a heavy tread upon the frozen ground near made me look round, and I perceived my husband advancing among the trees to meet me. He had risen thus early to escort me home.

I had not been home more than two hours, before the little Scotch maid came over to tell me that the babe was dead. The deep sleep, in which I had left it, was its last — it breathed its little life away so peacefully, that it might indeed be said, that it fell asleep and wakened in Heaven. The golden bowl was broken, and the young spirit, wearied with this earthly strife of pain, had returned to God who gave it!

It was evening when I renewed my visit to the house of the afflicted mother. Exhausted with weeping, she lay stretched upon her bed, fevered and ill at ease in body, and bowed down with the grief that belongs to human nature, when deprived of the object of its love. It was her first-born, her only one. It was piteous to hear her sad wailing, as she cast her eyes down upon her arm, and exclaimed:

"It used to lie here — just here, but it will never rest upon my arm again. It is gone — gone — gone!"

I did not then know the pangs of a bereaved mother, mourning for a dear babe, but I have often thought of poor Jessy, since that day — and felt how natural was her sorrow.

It was the third day, after this last sad visit, that I again re-entered the house of mourning. It was a day of sunny brightness. The sounds of business and labour had ceased — the axe no longer made the weeds echo to its heavy strokes, the rush and whirl of the mill-wheels was stopped — it was the Sabbath morning, and silence and repose reigned over that busy spot. The door of the dwelling stood open, and I entered unbidden. A solemn feeling came over me, as I stepped across the threshold, from the broad glare of daylight into the dim religious light of the darkened room. In the centre was a table, decently covered with a snow white damask cloth; beside it sat the father of the child, his hat craped and tied with the simple white riband, symbol of the youth and innocence of the dead; his head was bent down over the big Bible, that rested on his knees; he was habited in decent mourning. As I entered, he raised his head, and bowed with an air of deep reverence, but spoke no word, and I passed on, unwilling to intrude upon his wholesome meditation. The father was gathering strength from the Book of peace and consolation.

At the further end of the apartment stood the mournful mother, her face bowed over the pale shrouded form of the idol of her heart. Her fair hair, gemmed with tears, fell in long soft ringlets over her face, and swept the pallid brow and tiny ice-cold hands of the dead infant; they were wet with the holy weeping of maternal love.

The sound of my steps made her look up, and forgetting all distinctions of rank, and alive only to the sympathy that had been shewn to her in her hour of deep distress, she threw her arms about my neck, and wept — but her grief was softened and subdued. She had schooled her heart to bear the sad reality, and she now sorrowed, as one not without hope.

Silently, she drew from within the folds of her muslin handkerchief, a small packet, carefully fastened with a thread of black silk — it was the fair hair of her lost treasure. She regarded it with a look of inexpressible tenderness, kissed it and replaced it in her bosom — then imprinting a last passionate kiss upon the marble brow and cheek of the dead babe, she suffered me to lead her quietly away, while the men approached to screw down the coffin, and throw the white pall over it.

With tearful earnestness did poor Jessy entreat of me to join in the procession that was to form, but the burial ground was three or four miles off, on the opposite side of the river, and I was unequal to so long a walk.

I watched the funeral train, as it slowly crossed the bridge, and ascended the steep banks of the river, till the last waving of the white pall and scarfs of the mourners was no longer visible among the dark pines. I turned to retrace my steps, and felt that it was better to go into the house of mourning, than the house of mirth.

'Tis a sweet quiet spot, that burial ground in the woods. A few rudely sculptured stones — a heap piled here and there — a simple cross of wood, or a sapling tree planted by some pious hand, are the only memorials, to point out where rest the poor forgotten emigrant or his children. But the pines sigh above them a solemn requiem, the wild birds of the forest sing their lullaby, and the pure white lily of the woods and the blue violet, grow as freely on their green mossy graves, as though they slept within the holy shadow of the sanctuary. Their resting place is indeed hallowed, by the tears and humble prayers of their mournful relatives.

There is one that sleeps there among the children of the soil, unknown and uncared for, save by one who sadly remembers his guileless childhood, his early promise, and the bright example of a talented, but too indulgent father, and of a doting mother —

> "But thoughtless follies led astray
> And stained his name."[2]

Cut off in the reckless levity of youth's mad career, he fills an early grave; and I might say of him in the words of the old Scotch ballad:

> "Ah! little did thy mother think
> The day she cradled thee,
> Through what lands thou should's travel,
> And what death thou should'st die!"

(1846)

Susanna Moodie (1803–1885)

During her first years in Upper Canada, Susanna Moodie longed to return to the land of her birth: "Home!" she exclaims in an early scene in *Roughing It in the Bush* (1852); "the word had ceased to belong to my present — it was doomed to live for ever in the past; for what emigrant ever regarded the country of his exile as his home?"

She was born Susanna Strickland in 1803 in Bungay, Suffolk, in England. In 1808, her parents moved their six daughters and two infant sons to a manor house near Southwold, and there Moodie spent her formative years. The Stricklands believed in educating their daughters, and the young women received lessons in academic subjects in conjunction with more practical studies. Consequently, when their father died, in 1818, leaving their mother in a state of financial instability, five of the Strickland sisters were able to contribute to the financial welfare of the family by publishing their writings.

Moodie published *Spartacus: A Roman Story* in 1822, following it with a number of moral and didactic stories for children. She also became a major contributor to the London magazine *Belle Assemblée* with the help of a family friend, Thomas Harral. During his tenure as editor of the

---

2. The lines are from "A Bard's Epitaph," by Robert Burns (1759–1796).

periodical, Harral published over 50 of Moodie's poems and stories, including several Suffolk sketches. With their personal tone and observational style, these are precursors to her later, more celebrated Canadian sketches.

In the late 1820s, Moodie went through a period of religious exploration. Although her family members were confirmed Anglicans, she began to seek guidance outside of the established church, eventually identifying herself as a Congregationalist. Her collection *Enthusiasm; and Other Poems* (1831) comes out of this time of spiritual searching. Also during these years, Moodie befriended Thomas Pringle, secretary of the Anti-slavery Society in London, and she wrote several pamphlets on behalf of that group. In 1830, Pringle introduced his writer friend to a retired army officer named John Wedderburn Dunbar Moodie. By 1831, Susanna and John were married. Originally from the Orkney Islands, John Moodie had been on a visit to London from his settlement in the Cape colony of South Africa, and he tried to convince his new wife to return there with him. But Susanna was reluctant to live in South Africa, so John devised a new plan: they would immigrate to Canada.

The Moodies embarked from Edinburgh, Scotland, in July of 1832, and they settled near Cobourg in Upper Canada that autumn. They spent almost two years in their first Canadian home before moving north to a bush farm in Douro Township, where the families of Susanna's brother Samuel Strickland and sister Catharine Parr Traill resided. They remained there for six long years. In 1837, the Moodies' fortunes changed when John Moodie left to serve in the militia after the Mackenzie Rebellion. He was first appointed to the position of captain of the Queen's Own of Toronto Regiment, and then he became the militia paymaster. In 1839, he was made sheriff of Hastings County, and he, Susanna, and their five children moved to Belleville. Although John's new position proved to be quite difficult, the Moodies were able to live relatively comfortably for quite some time.

In 1837, Susanna Moodie had written a series of patriotic poems that had been well received by the general public. They had also attracted the attention of a Montreal editor named John Lovell, who asked Moodie to submit her work to his magazine, the *Literary Garland*. Finally enjoying some leisure time in Belleville, Moodie began to write poems, stories, and serials for the *Literary Garland* on a regular basis. In the late 1840s, she and her husband helped to edit a periodical called *Victoria Magazine*, which published work by Catharine Parr Traill, Samuel Strickland, and Agnes Strickland (who had become quite famous in England), among others.

In 1852, Moodie produced an autobiographical narrative interspersed with poetry: *Roughing It in the Bush; or, Forest Life in Canada*. Working from sketches she had written for the *Literary Garland* and *Victoria Magazine*, she composed scenes based on her life in Canada from her arrival at Grosse Isle to her "Adieu to the Woods" in 1840. She included humorous elements and depicted many moments of happiness and instances of bravery. Yet she insisted that the ultimate purpose of the work was to deter families "from sinking their property, and shipwrecking all their hopes, by going to reside in the backwoods of Canada." The book was a huge success.

Attempting to capitalize on the success of *Roughing It*, Moodie expanded one of her short stories to produce the novel *Mark Hurdlestone* (1853). Her publisher requested a second collection of Canadian sketches, and soon Moodie had compiled *Life in the Clearings versus the Bush* (1853). Her objective with this work was to represent Canada in a more positive light. "Since my residence in a settled part of the country," she wrote, "I have enjoyed as much domestic peace and happiness as ever falls to the lot of poor humanity." She declared, "Canada has become almost as dear to me as my native land." Moodie published several more novels in her lifetime, including the autobiographical *Flora Lyndsay; or, Passages in an Eventful Life* (1855), but none was as successful as *Roughing It in the Bush*.

Moodie has achieved an almost mythical status in the Canadian literary imagination, embodying for some the archetypal Canadian struggle between self and wilderness. Margaret

Atwood's celebrated volume of poetry *The Journals of Susanna Moodie* (1970) has perpetuated an image of Moodie as "divided down the middle." In Atwood's reading, the pioneer writer claims "to be an ardent Canadian patriot while all the time she is standing back from the country and criticizing it as though she was a detached observer, a stranger." Atwood's Moodie confesses, "I felt I ought to love / this country. / I said I loved it / and my mind saw double."

A Visit to Grosse Isle

Alas! that man's stern spirit e'er should mar
A scene so pure — so exquisite as this.

The dreadful cholera[1] was depopulating Quebec and Montreal, when our ship cast anchor off Grosse Isle, on the 30th of August, 1832, and we were boarded a few minutes after by the health-officers. One of these gentlemen — a little, shrivelled-up Frenchman — from his solemn aspect and attenuated figure, would have made no bad representative of him who sat upon the pale horse. He was the only grave Frenchman I had ever seen, and I naturally enough regarded him as a phenomenon. His companion — a fine-looking fair-haired Scotchman — though a little consequential in his manners, looked like one who in his own person could combat and vanquish all the evils which flesh is heir to. Such was the contrast between these doctors, that they would have formed very good emblems — one, of vigorous health; the other, of hopeless decay.

Our captain, a rude, blunt north-country sailor, possessing certainly not more polite-ness than might be expected in a bear, received his sprucely dressed visitors on the deck, and, with very little courtesy, abruptly bade them follow him down into the cabin.

The officials were no sooner seated, than glancing hastily round the place, they commenced the following dialogue: —

"From what port, captain?"

Now, the captain had a peculiar language of his own, from which he commonly expunged all the connecting links. Small words, such as "and" and "the," he contrived to dispense with altogether.

"Scotland — sailed from port o' Leith, bound for Quebec, Montreal — general cargo — seventy-two steerage, four cabin passengers — brig *Anne*, one hundred and ninety-two tons burden, crew eight hands." Here he produced his credentials, and handed them to the strangers. The Scotchman just glanced over the documents, and laid them on the table.

"Had you a good passage out?"

"Tedious, baffling winds, heavy fogs, detained three weeks on Banks — foul weather making Gulf — short of water, people out of provisions, steerage passengers starving."

"Any case of sickness or death on board?"

"All sound as crickets."

"Any births?" lisped the little Frenchman.

---

1. Grosse Isle is a small island 48 kilometres (30 miles) east of Quebec City. European immigrants arriving during the great cholera epidemic of 1832 were quarantined there. More than 6,000 Irish immigrants died on the island as a result of the illness.

The captain screwed up his mouth, and after a moment's reflection he replied, "Births? Why, yes; now I think on't, gentlemen, we had one female on board, who produced three at a birth."

"That's uncommon," said the Scotch doctor, with an air of lively curiosity. "Are the children alive and well? I should like much to see them." He started up, and knocked his head, for he was very tall, against the ceiling. "Confound your low cribs! I have nearly dashed out my brains."

"A hard task, that," looked the captain to me. He did not speak, but I knew by his sarcastic grin what was uppermost in his thoughts. "The young ones all males — fine thriving fellows. Step upon deck, Sam Frazer," turning to his steward; "bring them down for doctors to see." Sam vanished, with a knowing wink to his superior, and quickly returned, bearing in his arms three fat, chuckle-headed bull-terriers; the sagacious mother following close at his heels, and looked ready to give and take offence on the slightest provocation.

"Here, gentlemen, are the babies," said Frazer, depositing his burden on the floor. "They do credit to the nursing of the brindled slut."

The old tar laughed, chuckled, and rubbed his hands in an ecstacy of delight at the indignation and disappointment visible in the countenance of the Scotch Esculapius, who, angry as he was, wisely held his tongue. Not so the Frenchman; his rage scarcely knew bounds, — he danced in a state of most ludicrous excitement, — he shook his fist at our rough captain, and screamed at the top of his voice,

"Sacré, you bête! You tink us dog, ven you try to pass your puppies on us for babies?"

"Hout, man, don't be angry," said the Scotchman, stifling a laugh; "you see 'tis only a joke!"

"Joke! me no understand such joke. Bête!" returned the angry Frenchman, bestowing a savage kick on one of the unoffending pups which was frisking about his feet. The pup yelped; the slut barked and leaped furiously at the offender, and was only kept from biting him by Sam, who could scarcely hold her back for laughing; the captain was uproarious; the offended Frenchman alone maintained a severe and dignified aspect. The dogs were at length dismissed, and peace restored.

After some further questioning from the officials, a bible was required for the captain to take an oath. Mine was mislaid, and there was none at hand.

"Confound it!" muttered the old sailor, tossing over the papers in his desk; "that scoundrel, Sam, always stows my traps out of the way." Then taking up from the table a book which I had been reading, which happened to be *Voltaire's History of Charles XII.*, he presented it, with as grave an air as he could assume, to the Frenchman. Taking for granted that it was the volume required, the little doctor was too polite to open the book, the captain was duly sworn, and the party returned to the deck.

Here a new difficulty occurred, which nearly ended in a serious quarrel. The gentlemen requested the old sailor to give them a few feet of old planking, to repair some damage which their boat had sustained the day before. This the captain could not do. They seemed to think his refusal intentional, and took it as a personal affront. In no very gentle tones, they ordered him instantly to prepare his boats, and put his passengers on shore.

"Stiff breeze — short sea," returned the bluff old seaman; "great risk in making land — boats heavily laden with women and children will be swamped. Not a soul goes on shore this night."

"If you refuse to comply with our orders, we will report you to the authorities."

"I know my duty — you stick to yours. When the wind falls off, I'll see to it. Not a life shall be risked to please you or your authorities."

He turned upon his heel, and the medical men left the vessel in great disdain. We had every reason to be thankful for the firmness displayed by our rough commander. That same evening we saw eleven persons drowned, from another vessel close beside us, while attempting to make the shore.

By daybreak all was hurry and confusion on board the *Anne*. I watched boat after boat depart for the island, full of people and goods, and envied them the glorious privilege of once more standing firmly on the earth, after two long months of rocking and rolling at sea. How ardently we anticipate pleasure, which often ends in positive pain! Such was my case when at last indulged in the gratification so eagerly desired. As cabin passengers, we were not included in the general order of purification, but were only obliged to send our servant, with the clothes and bedding we had used during the voyage, on shore, to be washed.

The ship was soon emptied of all her live cargo. My husband went off with the boats, to reconnoitre the island, and I was left alone with my baby, in the otherwise empty vessel. Even Oscar, the Captain's Scotch terrier, who had formed a devoted attachment to me during the voyage, forgot his allegiance, became possessed of the land mania, and was away with the rest. With the most intense desire to go on shore, I was doomed to look and long and envy every boatful of emigrants that glided past. Nor was this all; the ship was out of provisions, and I was condemned to undergo a rigid fast until the return of the boat, when the captain had promised a supply of fresh butter and bread. The vessel had been nine weeks at sea; the poor steerage passengers for the two last weeks had been out of food, and the captain had been obliged to feed them from the ship's stores. The promised bread was to be obtained from a small steam-boat, which plied daily between Quebec and the island, transporting convalescent emigrants and their goods in her upward trip, and provisions for the sick on her return.

How I reckoned on once more tasting bread and butter! The very thought of the treat in store served to sharpen my appetite, and render the long fast more irksome. I could now fully realise all Mrs. Bowdich's longings for English bread and butter, after her three years' travel through the burning African deserts, with her talented husband.

"When we arrived at the hotel at Plymouth," said she, "and were asked what refreshment we chose — 'Tea, and home-made bread and butter,' was my instant reply. 'Brown bread, if you please, and plenty of it.' I never enjoyed any luxury like it. I was positively ashamed of asking the waiter to refill the plate. After the execrable messes, and the hard ship-biscuit, imagine the luxury of a good slice of English bread and butter!"

At home, I laughed heartily at the lively energy with which that charming woman of genius related this little incident in her eventful history, — but, off Grosse Isle, I realised it all.

As the sun rose above the horizon, all these matter-of-fact circumstances were gradually forgotten, and merged in the surpassing grandeur of the scene that rose majestically before me. The previous day had been dark and stormy; and a heavy fog had concealed the mountain chain, which forms the stupendous background to this sublime view, entirely from our sight. As the clouds rolled away from their grey, bald brows, and cast into denser shadow the vast forest belt that girdled them round, they loomed out like mighty giants — Titans of the earth, in all their rugged and awful beauty — a thrill of wonder and delight pervaded my mind. The spectacle floated dimly on my sight — my eyes were blinded with tears — blinded with the excess of beauty. I turned to the right and to the left, I looked up and down the glorious river; never had I beheld so many striking objects blended into one mighty whole! Nature had lavished all her noblest features in producing that enchanting scene.

The rocky isle in front, with its neat farm-houses at the eastern point, and its high bluff at the western extremity, crowned with the telegraph — the middle space occupied by tents and sheds for the cholera patients, and its wooded shores dotted over with motley groups — added greatly to the picturesque effect of the land scene. Then the broad, glittering river, covered with boats darting to and fro, conveying passengers from twenty-five vessels, of various size and tonnage, which rode at anchor, with their flags flying from the mast-head, gave an air of life and interest to the whole. Turning to the south side of the St. Lawrence, I was not less struck with its low fertile shores, white houses, and neat churches, whose slender spires and bright tin roofs shone like silver as they caught the first rays of the sun. As far as the eye could reach, a line of white buildings extended along the bank; their background formed by the purple hue of the dense, interminable forest. It was a scene unlike any I had ever beheld, and to which Britain contains no parallel. Mackenzie, an old Scotch dragoon,[2] who was one of our passengers, when he rose in the morning, and saw the parish of St. Thomas for the first time, exclaimed — "Weel, it beats a'! Can thae white clouts be a' houses? They look like claes[3] hung out to drie!" There was some truth in this odd comparison, and for some minutes, I could scarcely convince myself that the white patches scattered so thickly over the opposite shore could be the dwellings of a busy, lively population.

"What sublime views of the north side of the river those *habitans*[4] of St. Thomas must enjoy," thought I. Perhaps familiarity with the scene has rendered them indifferent to its astonishing beauty.

Eastward, the view down the St. Lawrence towards the Gulf, is the finest of all, scarcely surpassed by anything in the world. Your eye follows the long range of lofty mountains until their blue summits are blended and lost in the blue of the sky. Some of these, partially cleared round the base, are sprinkled over with neat cottages; and the green slopes that spread around them are covered with flocks and herds. The surface of the splendid river is diversified with islands of every size and shape, some in wood, others partially cleared, and adorned with orchards and white farm-houses. As the early sun streamed upon the most prominent of these, leaving the others in deep shade, the effect was strangely novel and imposing. In more remote regions, where the forest has never yet echoed to the woodman's axe, or received the impress of civilisation, the first approach to the shore inspires a melancholy awe, which becomes painful in its intensity.

> Land of vast hills, and mighty streams,
> The lofty sun that o'er thee beams
> On fairer clime sheds not his ray,
> When basking in the noon of day
> Thy waters dance in silver light,
> And o'er them frowning, dark as night,

---

2. **dragoon** Soldier; infantryman. 3. **claes** Clothes. 4. *habitans* Local inhabitants.

Thy shadowy forests, soaring high,
Stretch forth beyond the aching eye,
And blend in distance with the sky.

And silence — awful silence broods
Profoundly o'er these solitudes;
Nought but the lapsing of the floods
Breaks the deep stillness of the woods;
A sense of desolation reigns
O'er these unpeopled forest plains.
Where sounds of life ne'er wake a tone
Of cheerful praise round Nature's throne,
Man finds himself with God — alone.

My day-dreams were dispelled by the return of the boat, which brought my husband and the captain from the island.

"No bread," said the latter, shaking his head; "you must be content to starve a little longer. Provision-ship not in till four o'clock." My husband smiled at the look of blank disappointment with which I received these unwelcome tidings. "Never mind, I have news which will comfort you. The officer who commands the station sent a note to me by an orderly, inviting us to spend the afternoon with him. He promises to show us everything worthy of notice on the island. Captain —— claims acquaintance with me; but I have not the least recollection of him. Would you like to go?"

"Oh, by all means. I long to see the lovely island. It looks a perfect paradise at this distance."

The rough sailor-captain screwed his mouth on one side, and gave me one of his comical looks, but he said nothing until he assisted in placing me and the baby in the boat.

"Don't be too sanguine, Mrs. Moodie; many things look well at a distance which are bad enough when near."

I scarcely regarded the old sailor's warning, so eager was I to go on shore — to put my foot upon the soil of the new world for the first time. I was in no humour to listen to any depreciation of what seemed so beautiful.

It was four o'clock when we landed on the rocks, which the rays of an intensely scorching sun had rendered so hot that I could scarcely place my foot upon them. How the people without shoes bore it, I cannot imagine. Never shall I forget the extraordinary spectacle that met our sight the moment we passed the low range of bushes which formed a screen in front of the river. A crowd of many hundred Irish emigrants had been landed during the present and former day; and all this motley crew — men, women, and children, who were not confined by sickness to the sheds (which greatly resembled cattle-pens) — were employed in washing clothes, or spreading them out on the rocks and bushes to dry.

The men and boys were in the water, while the women, with their scanty garments tucked above their knees, were trampling their bedding in tubs, or in holes in the rocks, which the retiring tide had left half full of water. Those who did not possess washing-tubs, pails, or iron pots, or could not obtain access to a hole in the rocks, were running to and fro, screaming and scolding in no measured terms. The confusion of Babel was among them. All talkers and no hearers — each shouting and yelling in his or her uncouth dialect, and all accompanying their vociferations with violent and extraordinary gestures, quite incomprehensible to the uninitiated. We were literally stunned by the strife of tongues. I shrank, with feelings almost akin to fear, from the hard-featured, sun-burnt harpies, as they elbowed rudely past me.

I had heard and read much of savages, and have since seen, during my long residence in the bush, somewhat of uncivilised life; but the Indian is one of Nature's gentlemen — he never says or does a rude or vulgar thing. The vicious, uneducated barbarians who form the surplus of over-populous European countries, are far behind the wild man in delicacy of feeling or natural courtesy. The people who covered the island appeared perfectly destitute of shame, or even of a sense of common decency. Many were almost naked, still more but partially clothed. We turned in disgust from the revolting scene, but were unable to leave the spot until the captain had satisfied a noisy group of his own people, who were demanding a supply of stores.

And here I must observe that our passengers, who were chiefly honest Scotch labourers and mechanics from the vicinity of Edinburgh, and who while on board ship had conducted themselves with the greatest propriety, and appeared the most quiet, orderly set of people in the world, no sooner set foot upon the island than they became infected by the same spirit of insubordination and misrule, and were just as insolent and noisy as the rest.

While our captain was vainly endeavouring to satisfy the unreasonable demands of his rebellious people, Moodie had discovered a woodland path that led to the back of the island. Sheltered by some hazel-bushes from the intense heat of the sun, we sat down by the cool, gushing river, out of sight, but, alas! not out of hearing of the noisy, riotous crowd. Could we have shut out the profane sounds which came to us on every breeze, how deeply should we have enjoyed an hour amid the tranquil beauties of that retired and lovely spot!

The rocky banks of the island were adorned with beautiful evergreens, which sprang up spontaneously in every nook and crevice. I remarked many of our favourite garden shrubs among these wildings of nature. The fillagree, with its narrow, dark glossy-green leaves; the privet, with its modest white blossoms and purple berries; the lignum-vitae, with its strong resinous odour; the burnet-rose, and a great variety of elegant unknowns.

Here, the shores of the island and mainland, receding from each other, formed a small cove, overhung with lofty trees, clothed from the base to the summit with wild vines, that hung in graceful festoons from the topmost branches to the water's edge. The dark shadows of the mountains, thrown upon the water, as they towered to the height of some thousand feet above us, gave to the surface of the river an ebon hue. The sunbeams, dancing through the thick, quivering foliage, fell in stars of gold, or long lines of dazzling brightness, upon the deep black waters, producing the most novel and beautiful effects. It was a scene over which the spirit of peace might brood in silent adoration; but how spoiled by the discordant yells of the filthy beings who were sullying the purity of the air and water with contaminating sights and sounds!

We were now joined by the sergeant, who very kindly brought us his capful of ripe plums and hazel-nuts, the growth of the island; a joyful present, but marred by a note from Captain ——, who had found that he had been mistaken in his supposed knowledge of us, and politely apologised for not being allowed by the health-officers to receive any emigrant beyond the bounds appointed for the performance of quarantine.

I was deeply disappointed, but my husband laughingly told me that I had seen enough of the island; and turning to the good-natured soldier, remarked, that "it could be no easy task to keep such wild savages in order."

"You may well say that, sir — but our night scenes far exceed those of the day. You would think they were incarnate devils; singing, drinking, dancing, shouting, and cutting antics that would surprise the leader of a circus. They have no shame — are under no restraint — nobody knows them here, and they think they can speak and act as they please; and they are such thieves that they rob one another of the little they possess. The healthy actually run the risk of taking the cholera by robbing the sick. If you have not hired one or two stout, honest fellows from among your fellow-passengers to guard your clothes while they are drying, you will never see half of them again. They are a sad set, sir, a sad set. We could, perhaps, manage the men; but the women, sir! — the women! Oh, sir!"

Anxious as we were to return to the ship, we were obliged to remain until sundown in our retired nook. We were hungry, tired, and out of spirits; the mosquitoes swarmed in myriads around us, tormenting the poor baby, who, not at all pleased with her first visit to the new world, filled the air with cries; when the captain came to tell us, that the boat was ready. It was a welcome sound. Forcing our way once more through the still squabbling crowd, we gained the landing place. Here we encountered a boat, just landing a fresh cargo of lively savages from the Emerald Isle.[5] One fellow, of gigantic proportions, whose long, tattered great-coat just reached below the middle of his bare red legs, and, like charity, hid the defects of his other garments, or perhaps concealed his want of them, leaped upon the rocks, and flourishing aloft his shilelagh,[6] bounded and capered like a wild goat from his native mountains. "Whurrah! my boys!" he cried, "Shure we'll all be jintlemen!"

"Pull away, my lads!" exclaimed our captain. Then turning to me, "Well, Mrs. Moodie, I hope that you have had enough of Grosse Isle. But could you have witnessed the scenes that I did this morning — "

Here he was interrupted by the wife of the old Scotch Dragoon, Mackenzie, running down to the boat, and laying her hand familiarly upon his shoulder, "Captain, dinna forget."

"Forget what?"

She whispered something confidentially in his ear.

"Oh, ho! the brandy!" he responded aloud. "I should have thought, Mrs. Mackenzie, that you had had enough of *that same*, on yon island?"

"Aye, sic a place for *decent* folk," returned the drunken body, shaking her head. "One needs a drap o' comfort, captain, to keep up one's heart avá."

The captain set up one of his boisterous laughs, as he pushed the boat from the shore. "Hollo! Sam Frazer! steer in, we have forgotten the stores."

"I hope not, captain," said I; "I have been starving since daybreak."

"The bread, the butter, the beef, the onions and potatoes are here, sir," said honest Sam, particularising each article.

"All right; pull for the ship. Mrs. Moodie, we will have a glorious supper, and mind you don't dream of Grosse Isle."

---

5. **Emerald Isle** Ireland. 6. **shilelagh** A cudgel made of oak.

In a few moments we were again on board. Thus ended my first day's experience of the land of all our hopes.

(1852)

Our First Settlement, and the Borrowing System

To lend, or not to lend — is that the question?

"Those who go a-borrowing, go a-sorrowing," saith the old adage; and a wiser saw never came out of the mouth of experience. I have tested the truth of this proverb since my settlement in Canada, many, many times, to my cost; and what emigrant has not? So averse have I ever been to this practice, that I would at all times rather quietly submit to a temporary inconvenience than obtain anything I wanted in this manner. I verily believe that a demon of mischief presides over borrowed goods, and takes a wicked pleasure in playing off a thousand malicious pranks upon you the moment he enters your dwelling. Plates and dishes, that had been the pride and ornament of their own cupboard for years, no sooner enter upon foreign service than they are broken; wine-glasses and tumblers, that have been handled by a hundred careless wenches in safety, scarcely pass into the hands of your servants when they are sure to tumble upon the floor, and the accident turns out a compound fracture. If you borrow a garment of any kind, be sure that you will tear it; a watch, that you will break it; a jewel, that you will lose it; a book, that it will be stolen from you. There is no end to the trouble and vexation arising out of this evil habit. If you borrow a horse, and he has the reputation of being the best-behaved animal in the district, you no sooner become responsible for his conduct than he loses his character. The moment that you attempt to drive him, he shows that he has a will of his own, by taking the reins into his own management, and running away in a contrary direction to the road that you wished him to travel. He never gives over his eccentric capers until he has broken his own knees, and the borrowed carriage and harness. So anxious are you about his safety, that you have not a moment to bestow upon your own. And why? — the beast is borrowed, and you are expected to return him in as good condition as he came to you.

But of all evils, to borrow money is perhaps the worst. If of a friend, he ceases to be one the moment you feel that you are bound to him by the heavy clog of obligation. If of a usurer, the interest, in this country, soon doubles the original sum, and you owe an increasing debt, which in time swallows up all you possess.

When we first came to the colony, nothing surprised me more than the extent to which this pernicious custom was carried, both by the native Canadians, the European settlers, and the lower order of Americans. Many of the latter had spied out the goodness of the land, and *borrowed* various portions of it, without so much as asking leave of the absentee owners. Unfortunately, our new home was surrounded by these odious squatters, whom we found as ignorant as savages, without their courtesy and kindness.

The place we first occupied was purchased of Mr. C——, a merchant, who took it in payment of sundry large debts which the owner, a New England loyalist, had been unable to settle. Old Joe H——, the present occupant, had promised to quit it with his family, at the commencement of sleighing; and as the bargain was concluded in the month of September, and we were anxious to plough for fall wheat, it was necessary to be upon the spot. No house was to be found in the immediate neighbourhood, save a small dilapidated log tenement, on an adjoining farm (which was scarcely reclaimed from the bush) that had been some months without an owner. The merchant assured us that this could be made very comfortable until such time as it suited H—— to remove, and the owner was willing to let us have it for the *moderate* sum of four dollars a month.

Trusting to Mr. C——'s word, and being strangers in the land, we never took the precaution to examine this delightful summer residence before entering upon it, but thought ourselves very fortunate in obtaining a temporary home so near our own property, the distance not exceeding half-a-mile. The agreement was drawn up, and we were told that we could take possession whenever it suited us.

The few weeks that I had sojourned in the country had by no means prepossessed me in its favour. The home-sickness was sore upon me, and all my solitary hours were spent in tears. My whole soul yielded itself up to a strong and overpowering grief. One simple word dwelt for ever in my heart, and swelled it to bursting — "Home!" I repeated it waking a thousand times a day, and my last prayer before I sank to sleep was still "Home! Oh, that I could return, if only to die at home!" And nightly I did return; my feet again trod the daisied meadows of England; the song of her birds was in my ears; I wept with delight to find myself once more wandering beneath the fragrant shade of her green hedge-rows; and I awoke to weep in earnest when I found it but a dream. But this is all digression, and has nothing to do with our unseen dwelling. The reader must bear with me in my fits of melancholy, and take me as I am.

It was the 22nd September that we left the Steam-boat Hotel, to take possession of our new abode. During the three weeks we had sojourned at ——, I had not seen a drop of rain, and I began to think that the fine weather would last for ever; but this eventful day arose in clouds. Moodie had hired a covered carriage to convey the baby, the servant-maid, and myself to the farm, as our driver prognosticated[1] a wet day; while he followed with Tom Wilson and the teams that conveyed our luggage.

The scenery through which we were passing was so new to me, so unlike anything that I had ever beheld before, that in spite of its monotonous character, it won me from my melancholy, and I began to look about me with considerable interest. Not so my English servant, who declared that the woods were frightful to look upon; that it was a country only fit for wild beasts; that she hated it with all her heart and soul, and would go back as soon as she was able.

About a mile from the place of our destination the rain began to fall in torrents, and the air, which had been balmy as a spring morning, turned as chilly as that of a November day. Hannah shivered; the baby cried, and I drew my summer shawl as closely round as possible, to protect her from the sudden change in our hitherto delightful temperature. Just then, the carriage turned into a narrow, steep path, overhung with lofty woods, and after labouring up it with considerable difficulty, and at the risk of breaking our necks, it brought us at length to a rocky upland clearing, partially covered with a second growth of timber, and surrounded on all sides by the dark forest.

"I guess," quoth our Yankee driver, "that at the bottom of this 'ere swell, you'll find yourself *to hum*;" and plunging into a short path cut through the wood, he pointed to a miserable hut, at the bottom of a steep descent, and cracking his whip, exclaimed, "'Tis a smart location that. I wish you Britishers may enjoy it."

---

1. **prognosticated** Forecast.

I gazed upon the place in perfect dismay, for I had never seen such a shed called a house before. "You must be mistaken; that is not a house, but a cattle-shed, or pig-sty."

The man turned his knowing, keen eye upon me, and smiled, half-humorously, half-maliciously, as he said,

"You were raised in the old country, I guess; you have much to learn, and more, perhaps, than you'll like to know, before the winter is over."

I was perfectly bewildered — I could only stare at the place, with my eyes swimming in tears; but as the horses plunged down into the broken hollow, my attention was drawn from my new residence to the perils which endangered life and limb at every step. The driver, however, was well used to such roads, and, steering us dexterously between the black stumps, at length drove up, not to the door, for there was none to the house, but to the open space from which that absent but very necessary appendage had been removed. Three young steers and two heifers, which the driver proceeded to drive out, were quietly reposing upon the floor. A few strokes of his whip, and a loud burst of gratuitous curses, soon effected an ejectment; and I dismounted, and took possession of this untenable tenement. Moodie was not yet in sight with the teams. I begged the man to stay until he arrived, as I felt terrified at being left alone in this wild, strange-looking place. He laughed, as well he might, at our fears, and said that he had a long way to go, and must be off; then, cracking his whip, and nodding to the girl, who was crying aloud, he went his way, and Hannah and myself were left standing in the middle of the dirty floor.

The prospect was indeed dreary. Without, pouring rain; within, a fireless hearth; a room with but one window, and that containing only one whole pane of glass; not an article of furniture to be seen, save an old painted pine-wood cradle, which had been left there by some freak of fortune. This, turned upon its side, served us for a seat, and there we impatiently awaited the arrival of Moodie, Wilson, and a man whom the former had hired that morning to assist on the farm. Where they were all to be stowed might have puzzled a more sagacious brain than mine. It is true there was a loft, but I could see no way of reaching it, for ladder there was none, so we amused ourselves, while waiting for the coming of our party, by abusing the place, the country, and our own dear selves for our folly in coming to it.

Now, when not only reconciled to Canada, but loving it, and feeling a deep interest in its present welfare, and the fair prospect of its future greatness, I often look back and laugh at the feelings with which I then regarded this noble country.

When things come to the worst, they generally mend. The males of our party no sooner arrived than they set about making things more comfortable. James, our servant, pulled up some of the decayed stumps, with which the small clearing that surrounded the shanty was thickly covered, and made a fire, and Hannah roused herself from the stupor of despair, and seized the corn-broom from the top of the loaded waggon, and began to sweep the house, raising such an intolerable cloud of dust that I was glad to throw my cloak over my head, and run out of doors, to avoid suffocation. Then commenced the awful bustle of unloading the two heavily-loaded waggons. The small space within the house was soon entirely blocked up with trunks and packages of all descriptions. There was scarcely room to move, without stumbling over some article of household stuff.

The rain poured in at the open door, beat in at the shattered window, and dropped upon our heads from the holes in the roof. The wind blew keenly through a thousand apertures in the log walls; and nothing could exceed the uncomfortableness of our situation. For a long time the box which contained a hammer and nails was not to be found. At length Hannah discovered it, tied up with some bedding which she was opening out in order to dry. I fortunately spied the door lying among some old boards at the back of the house, and Moodie immediately commenced fitting it to its place. This, once accomplished, was a great addition to our comfort. We then nailed a piece of white cloth entirely over the broken window, which, without diminishing the light, kept out the rain. James constructed a ladder out of the old bits of boards, and Tom Wilson assisted him in stowing the luggage away in the loft.

But what has this picture of misery and discomfort to do with borrowing? Patience, my dear, good friends; I will tell you all about it by-and-bye.

While we were all busily employed — even the poor baby, who was lying upon a pillow in the old cradle, trying the strength of her lungs, and not a little irritated that no one was at leisure to regard her laudable endeavours to make herself heard — the door was suddenly pushed open, and the apparition of a woman squeezed itself into the crowded room. I left off arranging the furniture of a bed, that had been just put up in a corner, to meet my unexpected, and at that moment, not very welcome guest. Her whole appearance was so extraordinary that I felt quite at a loss how to address her.

Imagine a girl of seventeen or eighteen years of age, with sharp, knowing-looking features, a forward, impudent carriage, and a pert, flippant voice, standing upon one of the trunks, and surveying all our proceedings in the most impertinent manner. The creature was dressed in a ragged, dirty purple stuff gown, cut very low in the neck, with an old red cotton handkerchief tied over her head; her uncombed, tangled locks falling over her thin, inquisitive face, in a state of perfect nature. Her legs and feet were bare, and, in her coarse, dirty red hands, she swung to and fro an empty glass decanter.

"What can she want?" I asked myself. "What a strange creature!"

And there she stood, staring at me in the most unceremonious manner, her keen black eyes glancing obliquely to every corner of the room, which she examined with critical exactness.

Before I could speak to her, she commenced the conversation by drawling through her nose,

"Well, I guess you are fixing here."

I thought she had come to offer her services; and I told her that I did not want a girl, for I had brought one out with me.

"How!" responded the creature, "I hope you don't take me for a help. I'd have you to know that I'm as good a lady as yourself. No; I just stepped over to see what was going on. I seed the teams pass our'n about noon, and I says to father, 'Them strangers are cum; I'll go and look arter them.' 'Yes,' says he, 'do — and take the decanter along. May be they'll want one to put their whiskey in.' 'I'm goin' to,' says I; so I cum across with it, an' here it is. But, mind — don't break it — 'tis the only one we have to hum; and father says 'tis so mean to drink out of green glass."

My surprise increased every minute. It seemed such an act of disinterested generosity thus to anticipate wants we had never thought of. I was regularly taken in.

"My good girl," I began, "this is really very kind — but — "

"Now, don't go to call me 'gall' — and pass off your English airs on us. We are *genuine* Yankees, and think ourselves as good — yes, a great deal better than you. I am a young lady."

"Indeed!" said I, striving to repress my astonishment. "I am a stranger in the country, and my acquaintance with Canadian ladies and gentlemen is very small. I did not mean to offend you by using the term girl; I was going to assure you that we had no need of the decanter. We have bottles of our own — and we don't drink whiskey."

"How! Not drink whiskey? Why, you don't say! How ignorant you must be! may be they have no whiskey in the old country?"

"Yes, we have; but it is not like the Canadian whiskey. But, pray take the decanter home again — I am afraid that it will get broken in this confusion."

"No, no; father told me to leave it — and there it is;" and she planted it resolutely down on the trunk. "You will find a use for it till you have unpacked your own."

Seeing that she was determined to leave the bottle, I said no more about it, but asked her to tell me where the well was to be found.

"The well!" she repeated after me, with a sneer. "Who thinks of digging wells when they can get plenty of water from the creek? There is a fine water privilege not a stone's-throw from the door," and, jumping off the box, she disappeared as abruptly as she had entered. We all looked at each other; Tom Wilson was highly amused, and laughed until he held his sides.

"What tempted her to bring this empty bottle here?" said Moodie. "It is all an excuse; the visit, Tom, was meant for you."

"You'll know more about it in a few days," said James, looking up from his work. "That bottle is not brought here for nought."

I could not unravel the mystery, and thought no more about it, until it was again brought to my recollection by the damsel herself.

Our united efforts had effected a complete transformation in our uncouth dwelling. Sleeping-berths had been partitioned off for the men; shelves had been put up for the accommodation of books and crockery, a carpet covered the floor, and the chairs and tables we had brought from —— gave an air of comfort to the place, which, on the first view of it, I deemed impossible. My husband, Mr. Wilson, and James, had walked over to inspect the farm, and I was sitting at the table at work, the baby creeping upon the floor, and Hannah preparing dinner. The sun shone warm and bright, and the open door admitted a current of fresh air, which tempered the heat of the fire.

"Well, I guess you look smart," said the Yankee damsel, presenting herself once more before me. "You old country folks are so stiff, you must have every thing nice, or you fret. But, then, you can easily do it; you have *stacks* of money; and you can fix everything right off with money."

"Pray take a seat," and I offered her a chair, "and be kind enough to tell me your name. I suppose you must live in the neighbourhood, although I cannot perceive any dwelling near us."

"My name! So you want to know my name. I arn't ashamed of my name; 'tis Emily S——. I am eldest daughter to the *gentleman* who owns this house."

"What must the father be," thought I, "if he resembles the young *lady*, his daughter?"

Imagine a young lady, dressed in ragged petticoats, through whose yawning rents peeped forth, from time to time, her bare red knees, with uncombed elf-locks, and a face and hands that looked as if they had been unwashed for a month — who did not know A from B, and despised those who did. While these reflections, combined with a thousand ludicrous images, were flitting through my mind, my strange visitor suddenly exclaimed,

"Have you done with that 'ere decanter I brought across yesterday?"

"Oh, yes! I have no occasion for it." I rose, took it from the shelf, and placed it in her hand.

"I guess you won't return it empty; that would be mean, father says. He wants it filled with whiskey."

The mystery was solved, the riddle made clear. I could contain my gravity no longer, but burst into a hearty fit of laughter, in which I was joined by Hannah. Our young lady was mortally offended; she tossed the decanter from hand to hand, and glared at us with her tiger-like eyes.

"You think yourselves smart! Why do you laugh in that way?"

"Excuse me — but you have such an odd way of borrowing that I cannot help it. This bottle, it seems, was brought over for your own convenience, not for mine. I am sorry to disappoint you, but I have no whiskey."

"I guess spirits will do as well; I know there is some in that keg, for I smells it."

"It contains rum for the workmen."

"Better still. I calculate when you've been here a few months, you'll be too knowing to give rum to your helps. But old country folks are all fools, and that's the reason they get so easily sucked in, and be so soon wound-up. Cum, fill the bottle, and don't be stingy. In this country we all live by borrowing. If you want anything, why just send and borrow from us."

Thinking that this might be the custom of the country, I hastened to fill the decanter, hoping that I might get a little new milk for the poor weanling child in return; but when I asked my liberal visitor if she kept cows, and would lend me a little new milk for the baby, she burst out into high disdain. "Milk! Lend milk? I guess milk in the fall is worth a York shilling a quart. I cannot sell you a drop under."

This was a wicked piece of extortion, as the same article in the town, where, of course, it was in greater request, only brought three-pence the quart.

"If you'll pay me for it, I'll bring you some to-morrow. But mind — cash down."

"And when do you mean to return the rum?" I said, with some asperity.

"When father goes to the creek." This was the name given by my neighbours to the village of P———, distant about four miles.

Day after day I was tormented by this importunate creature; she borrowed of me tea, sugar, candles, starch, blueing, irons, pots, bowls — in short, every article in common domestic use — while it was with the utmost difficulty we could get them returned. Articles of food, such as tea and sugar, or of convenience, like candles, starch, and soap, she never dreamed of being required at her hands. This method of living upon their neighbours is a most convenient one to unprincipled people, as it does not involve the penalty of stealing; and they can keep the goods without the unpleasant necessity of returning them, or feeling the moral obligation of being grateful for their use. Living eight miles from ———, I found these constant encroachments a heavy burden on our poor purse; and being ignorant of the country, and residing in such a lonely, out-of-the-way place, surrounded by these savages, I was really afraid of denying their requests.

The very day our new plough came home, the father of this bright damsel, who went by the familiar and unenviable title of *Old Satan*, came over to borrow it (though we afterwards found out that he had a good one of his own). The land had never been broken up, and was full of rocks and stumps, and he was anxious to save his own from injury; the consequence was that the borrowed implement came home unfit for use, just at the very time that we wanted to plough for fall wheat. The same happened to a spade and trowel, bought in order to plaster the house. Satan asked the loan of them for *one* hour for the same purpose, and we never saw them again.

The daughter came one morning, as usual, on one of these swindling expeditions, and demanded of me the loan of some *fine slack*. Not knowing what she meant by *fine slack*, and weary of her importunities, I said I had none. She went away in a rage. Shortly after she came again for some pepper. I was at work, and my work-box was open upon the table, well stored with threads and spools of all descriptions. Miss Satan cast her hawk's eye into it, and burst out in her usual rude manner,

"I guess you told me a tarnation big lie the other day."

Unaccustomed to such language, I rose from my seat, and pointing to the door, told her to walk out, as I did not choose to be insulted in my own house.

"Your house! I'm sure it's father's," returned the incorrigible wretch. "You told me that you had no *fine slack*, and you have *stacks* of it."

"What is fine slack?" said I, very pettishly.

"The stuff that's wound upon these 'ere pieces of wood," pouncing as she spoke upon one of my most serviceable spools.

"I cannot give you that; I want it myself."

"I didn't ask you to give it. I only wants to borrow it till father goes to the creek."

"I wish he would make haste, then, as I want a number of things which you have borrowed of me, and which I cannot longer do without."

She gave me a knowing look, and carried off my spool in triumph.

I happened to mention the manner in which I was constantly annoyed by these people, to a worthy English farmer who resided near us; and he fell a-laughing, and told me that I did not know the Canadian Yankees as well as he did, or I should not be troubled with them long.

"The best way," says he, "to get rid of them, is to ask them sharply what they want; and if they give you no satisfactory answer, order them to leave the house; but I believe I can put you in a better way still. Buy some small article of them, and pay them a trifle over the price, and tell them to bring the change. I will lay my life upon it that it will be long before they trouble you again."

I was impatient to test the efficacy of his scheme. That very afternoon Miss Satan brought me a plate of butter for sale. The price was three and nine-pence; twice the sum, by-the-bye, that it was worth.

"I have no change," giving her a dollar; "but you can bring it me to-morrow."

Oh, blessed experiment! for the value of one quarter dollar I got rid of this dishonest girl for ever; rather than pay me, she never entered the house again.

About a month after this, I was busy making an apple-pie in the kitchen. A cadaverous-looking woman, very long-faced and witch-like, popped her ill-looking visage into the door, and drawled through her nose,

"Do you want to buy a *rooster*?"

Now, the sucking-pigs with which we had been regaled every day for three weeks at the tavern, were called *roasters;* and not understanding the familiar phrases of the country, I thought she had a sucking-pig to sell.

"Is it a good one?"

"I guess 'tis."

"What do you ask for it?"

"Two Yorkers."

"That is very cheap, if it is any weight. I don't like them under ten or twelve pounds."

"Ten or twelve pounds! Why, woman, what do you mean? Would you expect a rooster to be bigger nor a turkey?"

We stared at each other. There was evidently some misconception on my part.

"Bring the roaster up; and if I like it, I will buy it, though I must confess that I am not very fond of roast pig."

"Do you call this a pig?" said my she-merchant, drawing a fine game-cock from under her cloak.

I laughed heartily at my mistake, as I paid her down the money for the bonny bird. This little matter settled, I thought she would take her departure; but that roaster proved the dearest fowl to me that ever was bought.

"Do you keep backy and snuff here?" says she, sideling close up to me.

"We make no use of those articles."

"How! Not use backy and snuff? That's oncommon."

She paused, then added in a mysterious, confidential tone,

"I want to ask you how your tea-caddy stands?"

"It stands in the cupboard," said I, wondering what all this might mean.

"I know that; but have you any tea to spare?"

I now began to suspect what sort of a customer the stranger was.

"Oh, you want to borrow some? I have none to spare."

"You don't say so. Well now, that's stingy. I never asked anything of you before. I am poor, and you are rich; besides, I'm troubled so with the headache, and nothing does me any good but a cup of strong tea."

"The money I have just given you will buy a quarter of a pound of the best."

"I guess that isn't mine. The fowl belonged to my neighbour. She's sick; and I promised to sell it for her to buy some physic. Money!" she added, in a coaxing tone, "Where should I get money? Lord bless you! people in this country have no money; and those who come out with piles of it, soon lose it. But Emily S—— told me that you are nation rich, and draw your money from the old country. So I guess you can well afford to lend a neighbour a spoonful of tea."

"Neighbour! Where do you live, and what is your name?"

"My name is Betty Fye — old Betty Fye; I live in the log shanty over the creek, at the back of your'n. The farm belongs to my eldest son. I'm a widow with twelve sons; and 'tis —— hard to scratch along."

"Do you swear?"

"Swear! What harm? It eases one's mind when one's vexed. Everybody swears in this country. My boys all swear like Sam Hill; and I used to swear mighty big oaths till about a month ago, when the Methody[2] parson told me that if I did not leave it off I should go to a tarnation bad place; so I dropped some of the worst of them."

"You would do wisely to drop the rest; women never swear in my country."

"Well, you don't say! I always heer'd they were very ignorant. Will you lend me the tea?"

The woman was such an original that I gave her what she wanted. As she was going off, she took up one of the apples I was peeling.

---

2. **Methody** Methodist.

"I guess you have a fine orchard?"

"They say the best in the district."

"We have no orchard to hum, and I guess you'll want *sarce*."

"Sarce! What is sarce?"

"Not know what sarce is? You are clever! Sarce is apples cut up and dried, to make into pies in the winter. Now do you comprehend?"

I nodded.

"Well, I was going to say that I have no apples, and that you have a tarnation big few of them; and if you'll give me twenty bushels of your best apples, and find me with half a pound of coarse thread to string them upon, I will make you a barrel of sarce on shares — that is, give you one, and keep one for myself."

I had plenty of apples, and I gladly accepted her offer, and Mrs. Betty Fye departed, elated with the success of her expedition.

I found to my cost, that, once admitted into the house, there was no keeping her away. She borrowed everything that she could think of, without once dreaming of restitution. I tried all ways of affronting her, but without success. Winter came, and she was still at her old pranks. Whenever I saw her coming down the lane, I used involuntarily to exclaim, "Betty Fye! Betty Fye! Fye upon Betty Fye! The Lord deliver me from Betty Fye!" The last time I was honoured with a visit from this worthy, she meant to favour me with a very large order upon my goods and chattels.

"Well, Mrs. Fye, what do you want *to-day*?"

"So many things that I scarce know where to begin. Ah, what a thing 'tis to be poor! First, I want you to lend me ten pounds of flour to make some Johnnie cakes."

"I thought they were made of Indian meal?"

"Yes, yes, when you've got the meal. I'm out of it, and this is a new fixing of my own invention. Lend me the flour, woman, and I'll bring you one of the cakes to taste."

This was said very coaxingly.

"Oh, pray don't trouble yourself. What next?" I was anxious to see how far her impudence would go, and determined to affront her if possible.

"I want you to lend me a gown, and a pair of stockings. I have to go to Oswego to see my husband's sister, and I'd like to look decent."

"Mrs. Fye, I never lend my clothes to any one. If I lent them to you, I should never wear them again."

"So much the better for me," (with a knowing grin). "I guess if you won't lend me the gown, you will let me have some black slack to quilt a stuff petticoat, a quarter of a pound of tea and some sugar; and I will bring them back as soon as I can."

"I wonder when that will be. You owe me so many things that it will cost you more than you imagine to repay me."

"Sure you're not going to mention what's past, I can't owe you much. But I will let you off the tea and the sugar, if you will lend me a five-dollar bill." This was too much for my patience longer to endure, and I answered sharply,

"Mrs. Fye, it surprises me that such proud people as you Americans should condescend to the meanness of borrowing from those whom you affect to despise. Besides, as you never repay us for what you pretend to borrow, I look upon it as a system of robbery. If strangers unfortunately settle among you, their good-nature is taxed to supply your domestic wants, at a ruinous expense, besides the mortification of finding that they have been deceived and tricked out of their property. If you would come honestly to me and say, 'I want these things, I am too poor to buy them myself, and would be obliged to you to give them to me,' I should then acknowledge you as a common beggar, and treat you accordingly; give or not give, as it suited my convenience. But in the way in which you obtain these articles from me, you are spared even a debt of gratitude; for you well know that the many things which you have borrowed from me will be a debt owing to the day of judgment."

"S'pose they are," quoth Betty, not in the least abashed at my lecture on honesty, "you know what the Scripture saith, 'It is more blessed to give than to receive.'"

"Ay, there is an answer to that in the same book, which doubtless you may have heard," said I, disgusted with her hypocrisy, "'The wicked borroweth, and payeth not again.'"

Never shall I forget the furious passion into which this too apt quotation threw my unprincipled applicant. She lifted up her voice and cursed me, using some of the big oaths temporarily discarded for *conscience* sake. And so she left me, and I never looked upon her face again.

When I removed to our own house, the history of which, and its former owner, I will give by-and-by, we had a bony, red-headed, ruffianly American squatter, who had "left his country for his country's good," for an opposite neighbour. I had scarcely time to put my house in order before his family commenced borrowing, or stealing from me. It is even worse than stealing, the things procured from you being obtained on false pretences — adding lying to theft. Not having either an oven or a cooking stove, which at that period were not so cheap or so common as they are now, I had provided myself with a large bake-kettle as a substitute. In this kettle we always cooked hot cakes for breakfast, preferring that to the trouble of thawing the frozen bread. This man's wife was in the habit of sending over for my kettle whenever she wanted to bake, which, as she had a large family, happened nearly every day, and I found her importunity a great nuisance.

I told the impudent lad so, who was generally sent for it; and asked him what they did to bake their bread before I came.

"I guess we had to eat cakes in the pan; but now we can borrow this kettle of your'n, mother can fix bread."

I told him that he could have the kettle this time; but I must decline letting his mother have it in future, for I wanted it for the same purpose.

The next day passed over. The night was intensely cold, and I did not rise so early as usual in the morning. My servant was away at a quilting bee, and we were still in bed, when I heard the latch of the kitchen-door lifted up, and a step crossed the floor. I jumped out of bed, and began to dress as fast as I could, when Philander called out, in his well-known nasal twang,

"Missus! I'm come for the kettle."

I (*through the partition*): "You can't have it this morning. We cannot get our breakfast without it."

Philander: "Nor more can the old woman to hum," and, snatching up the kettle, which had been left to warm on the hearth, he rushed out of the house, singing, at the top of his voice,

"Hurrah for the Yankee Boys!"

When James came home for his breakfast, I sent him across to demand the kettle, and the dame very coolly told him that when she had done with it I *might* have it, but she defied him to take it out of her house with her bread in it.

One word more about this lad, Philander, before we part with him. Without the least intimation that his company would be agreeable, or even tolerated, he favoured us with it at all hours of the day, opening the door and walking in and out whenever he felt inclined. I had given him many broad hints that his presence was not required, but he paid not the slightest attention to what I said. One morning he marched in with his hat on, and threw himself down in the rocking-chair, just as I was going to dress my baby.

"Philander, I want to attend to the child; I cannot do it with you here. Will you oblige me by going into the kitchen?"

No answer. He seldom spoke during these visits, but wandered about the room, turning over our books and papers, looking at and handling everything. Nay, I have even known him to take a lid off from the pot on the fire, to examine its contents.

I repeated my request.

Philander: "Well, I guess I sha'n't hurt the young 'un. You can dress her."

I: "But not with you here."

Philander: "Why not? We never do anything that we are ashamed of."

I: "So it seems. But I want to sweep the room — you had better get out of the dust."

I took the broom from the corner, and began to sweep; still my visitor did not stir. The dust rose in clouds; he rubbed his eyes, and moved a little nearer to the door. Another sweep, and, to escape its inflictions, he mounted the threshold. I had him now at a fair advantage, and fairly swept him out, and shut the door in his face.

Philander (*looking through the window*): "Well, I guess you did me then; but 'tis deuced hard to outwit a Yankee."

This freed me from his company, and he, too, never repeated his visit; so I found by experience, that once smartly rebuked, they did not like to try their strength with you a second time.

When a sufficient time had elapsed for the drying of my twenty bushels of apples, I sent a Cornish lad, in our employ, to Betty Fye's, to inquire if they were ready, and when I should send the cart for them.

Dan returned with a yellow, smoke-dried string of pieces, dangling from his arm. Thinking that these were a specimen of the whole, I inquired when we were to send the barrel for the rest.

"Lord, ma'am, this is all there be."

"Impossible! All out of twenty bushels of apples!"

"Yes," said the boy, with a grin. "The old witch told me that this was all that was left of your share; that when they were fixed enough, she put them under her bed for safety, and the mice and the children had eaten them all up but this string."

This ended my dealings with Betty Fye.

I had another incorrigible borrower in the person of old Betty B——. This Betty was unlike the rest of my Yankee borrowers; she was handsome in her person, and remarkably civil, and she asked for the loan of everything in such a frank, pleasant manner, that for some time I hardly knew how to refuse her. After I had been a loser to a considerable extent, and declined lending her any more, she refrained from coming to the house herself, but sent in her name the most beautiful boy in the world; a perfect cherub, with regular features, blue, smiling eyes, rosy cheeks, and lovely curling auburn hair, who said, in the softest tones imaginable, that mammy had sent him, with her *compliments*, to the English lady to ask the loan of a little sugar or tea. I could easily have refused the mother, but I could not find it in my heart to say nay to her sweet boy.

There was something original about Betty B———, and I must give a slight sketch of her.

She lived in a lone shanty in the woods, which had been erected by lumberers some years before, and which was destitute of a single acre of clearing; yet Betty had plenty of potatoes, without the trouble of planting, or the expense of buying; she never kept a cow, yet she sold butter and milk; but she had a fashion, and it proved a convenient one to her, of making pets of the cattle of her neighbours. If our cows strayed from their pastures, they were always found near Betty's shanty, for she regularly supplied them with salt, which formed a sort of bond of union between them; and, in return for these little attentions, they suffered themselves to be milked before they returned to their respective owners. Her mode of obtaining eggs and fowls was on the same economical plan, and we all looked upon Betty as a sort of freebooter, living upon the property of others. She had had three husbands, and he with whom she now lived was not her husband, although the father of the splendid child whose beauty so won upon my woman's heart. Her first husband was still living (a thing by no means uncommon among persons of her class in Canada), and though they had quarrelled and parted years ago, he occasionally visited his wife to see her eldest daughter, Betty the younger, who was his child. She was now a fine girl of sixteen, as beautiful as her little brother. Betty's second husband had been killed in one of our fields by a tree falling upon him while ploughing under it. He was buried upon the spot, part of the blackened stump forming his monument. In truth, Betty's character was none of the best, and many of the respectable farmers' wives regarded her with a jealous eye.

"I am so jealous of that nasty Betty B———," said the wife of an Irish captain in the army, and our near neighbour, to me, one day as we were sitting at work together. She was a West Indian, and a negro by the mother's side, but an uncommonly fine-looking mulatto, very passionate, and very watchful over the conduct of her husband. "Are you not afraid of letting Captain Moodie go near her shanty?"

"No, indeed; and if I were so foolish as to be jealous, it would not be of old Betty, but of the beautiful young Betty, her daughter." Perhaps this was rather mischievous on my part, for the poor dark lady went off in a frantic fit of jealousy, but this time it was not of old Betty.

Another American squatter was always sending over to borrow a small-tooth comb, which she called a *vermin destroyer*; and once the same person asked the loan of a towel, as a friend had come from the States to visit her, and the only one she had, had been made into a best "pinny" for the child; she likewise begged a sight in the looking-glass, as she wanted to try on a new cap, to see if it were fixed to her mind. This woman must have been a mirror of neatness when compared with her dirty neighbours.

One night I was roused up from my bed for the loan of a pair of "steelyards."[3] For what purpose, think you, gentle reader? To weigh a new-born infant. The process was performed by tying the poor squalling thing up in a small shawl, and suspending it to one of the hooks. The child was a fine boy, and weighed ten pounds, greatly to the delight of the Yankee father.

One of the drollest[4] instances of borrowing I have ever heard of was told me by a friend. A maid-servant asked her mistress to go out on a particular afternoon, as she was going to have a party of her friends, and wanted the loan of the drawing-room.

---

3. **steelyards**   Scale. 4. **drollest**   Most amusing.

It would be endless to enumerate our losses in this way; but, fortunately for us, the arrival of an English family in our immediate vicinity drew off the attention of our neighbours in that direction, and left us time to recover a little from their persecutions.

This system of borrowing is not wholly confined to the poor and ignorant; it pervades every class of society. If a party is given in any of the small villages, a boy is sent round from house to house, to collect all the plates and dishes, knives and forks, teaspoons and candlesticks, that are presentable, for the use of the company.

During my stay at the hotel, I took a dress out of my trunk, and hung it up upon a peg in my chamber, in order to remove the creases it had received from close packing. Returning from a walk in the afternoon, I found a note upon my dressing table, inviting us to spend the evening with a clergyman's family in the village; and as it was nearly time to dress, I went to the peg to take down my gown. Was it a dream? — the gown was gone. I re-opened the trunk, to see if I had replaced it; I searched every corner of the room, but all in vain; nowhere could I discover the thing I sought. What had become of it? The question was a delicate one, which I did not like to put to the young ladies of the truly respectable establishment; still, the loss was great, and at that moment very inconvenient. While I was deliberating on what course to pursue, Miss S—— entered the room.

"I guess you missed your dress," she said, with a smile.

"Do you know where it is?"

"Oh, sure. Miss L——, the dressmaker, came in just after you left. She is a very particular friend of mine, and I showed her your dress. She admired it above all things, and borrowed it, to get the pattern for Miss R——'s wedding dress. She promised to return it to-morrow."

"Provoking! I wanted it to-night. Who ever heard of borrowing a person's dress without the leave of the owner? Truly, this is a free-and-easy country!"

One very severe winter night, a neighbour borrowed of me a blanket — it was one of my best — for the use of a stranger who was passing the night at her house. I could not well refuse; but at that time, the world pressed me sore, and I could ill spare it. Two years elapsed, and I saw no more of my blanket; at length I sent a note to the lady, requesting it to be returned. I got a very short answer back, and the blanket, alas! worn threadbare; the borrower stating that she had sent the article, but really she did not know what to do without it, as she wanted it to cover the children's bed. She certainly forgot that I, too, had children, who wanted covering as well as her own. But I have said so much of the ill results of others' borrowing, that I will close this sketch by relating my own experience in this way.

After removing to the bush, many misfortunes befel us, which deprived us of our income, and reduced us to great poverty. In fact we were strangers, and the knowing ones took us in; and for many years we struggled with hardships which would have broken stouter hearts than ours, had not our trust been placed in the Almighty, who among all our troubles never wholly deserted us.

While my husband was absent on the frontier during the rebellion, my youngest boy fell very sick, and required my utmost care, both by night and day. To attend to him properly, a candle burning during the night was necessary. The last candle was burnt out; I had no money to buy another, and no fat from which I could make one. I hated borrowing; but, for the dear child's sake, I overcame my scruples, and succeeded in procuring a candle from a good neighbour, but with strict injunctions (for it was *her last*), that I must return it if I did not require it during the night.

I went home quite grateful with my prize. It was a clear moonlight night — the dear boy was better, so I told old Jenny, my Irish servant, to go to bed, as I would lie down in my clothes by the child, and if he were worse I would get up and light the candle. It happened that a pane of glass was broken out of the window-frame, and I had supplied its place by fitting in a shingle; my friend Emilia S—— had a large Tom-cat, who, when his mistress was absent, often paid me a predatory or borrowing visit; and Tom had a practice of pushing in this wooden pane, in order to pursue his lawless depredations. I had forgotten all this, and never dreaming that Tom would appropriate such light food, I left the candle lying in the middle of the table, just under the window.

Between sleeping and waking, I heard the pane gently pushed in. The thought instantly struck me that it was Tom, and that, for lack of something better, he might steal my precious candle.

I sprang up from the bed, just in time to see him dart through the broken window, dragging the long white candle after him. I flew to the door, and pursued him *half* over the field, but all to no purpose. I can see him now, as I saw him then, scampering away for dear life, with his prize trailing behind him, gleaming like a silver tail in the bright light of the moon.

Ah! never did I feel more acutely the truth of the proverb, "Those that go a-borrowing go a-sorrowing," than I did that night. My poor boy awoke ill and feverish, and I had no light to assist him, or even to look into his sweet face, to see how far I dared hope that the light of day would find him better.

(1852)

Brian, the Still-Hunter

"O'er memory's glass I see his shadow flit,
Though he was gathered to the silent dust
Long years ago. A strange and wayward man,
That shunn'd companionship, and lived apart;
The leafy covert of the dark brown woods,
The gleamy lakes, hid in their gloomy depths,
Whose still, deep waters never knew the stroke
Of cleaving oar, or echoed to the sound
Of social life, contained for him the sum
Of human happiness. With dog and gun,
Day after day he track'd the nimble deer
Through all the tangled mazes of the forest."

It was early day. I was alone in the old shanty, preparing breakfast, and now and then stirring the cradle with my foot, when a tall, thin, middle-aged man walked into the house, followed by two large, strong dogs.

Placing the rifle he had carried on his shoulder, in a corner of the room, he advanced to the hearth, and without speaking, or seemingly looking at me, lighted his pipe, and commenced smoking. The dogs, after growling and snapping at the cat, who had not given the strangers a very courteous reception, sat down on the hearth-stone on either side of their taciturn master, eyeing him from time to time, as if long habit had made them understand all his motions. There was a great contrast between the dogs. The one was a brindled bulldog of the largest size, a most formidable and powerful brute; the other a staghound, tawny, deep-chested, and strong-limbed. I regarded the man and his hairy companions with silent curiosity.

He was between forty and fifty years of age; his head, nearly bald, was studded at the sides with strong, coarse, black curling hair. His features were high, his complexion brightly dark, and his eyes, in size, shape, and colour, greatly resembled the eyes of a hawk. The face itself was sorrowful and taciturn; and his thin, compressed lips looked as if they were not much accustomed to smile, or often to unclose to hold social communion with any one. He stood at the side of the huge hearth, silently smoking, his eyes bent on the fire, and now and then he patted the heads of his dogs, reproving their exuberant expression of attachment, with — "Down, Music; down, Chance!"

"A cold, clear morning," said I, in order to attract his attention and draw him into conversation.

A nod, without raising his head, or withdrawing his eyes from the fire, was his only answer; and, turning from my unsociable guest, I took up the baby, who just then awoke, sat down on a low stool by the table, and began feeding her. During this operation, I once or twice caught the stranger's hawk-eye fixed upon me and the child, but word spoke he none; and presently, after whistling to his dogs, he resumed his gun, and strode out.

When Moodie and Monaghan came in to breakfast, I told them what a strange visitor I had had; and Moodie laughed at my vain attempt to induce him to talk.

"He is a strange being," I said; "I must find out who and what he is."

In the afternoon an old soldier, called Layton, who had served during the American war, and got a grant of land about a mile in the rear of our location, came in to trade for a cow. Now, this Layton was a perfect ruffian; a man whom no one liked, and whom all feared. He was a deep drinker, a great swearer, in short, a perfect reprobate; who never cultivated his land, but went jobbing about from farm to farm, trading horses and cattle, and cheating in a pettifogging way. Uncle Joe had employed him to sell Moodie a young heifer, and he had brought her over for him to look at. When he came in to be paid, I described the stranger of the morning; and as I knew that he was familiar with every one in the neighbourhood, I asked if he knew him.

"No one should know him better than myself," he said; "'tis old Brian B——, the still-hunter,[1] and a near neighbour of your'n. A sour, morose, queer chap he is, and as mad as a March hare! He's from Lancashire, in England, and came to this country some twenty years ago, with his wife, who was a pretty young lass in those days, and slim enough then, though she's so awful fleshy now. He had lots of money, too, and he bought four hundred acres of land, just at the corner of the concession line, where it meets the main road. And excellent land it is; and a better farmer, while he stuck to his business, never went into the bush, for it was all bush here then. He was a dashing, handsome fellow, too, and did not hoard the money, either; he loved his pipe and his pot too well; and at last he left off farming, and gave himself to them altogether. Many a jolly booze he and I have had, I can tell you. Brian was an awful passionate man, and, when the liquor was in, and the wit was out, as savage and as quarrelsome as a bear. At such times there was no one but Ned Layton dared go near him. We once had a pitched battle, in which I was conqueror; and ever arter he yielded a sort of sulky obedience to all I said to him. Arter being on the spree for a week or two, he would take fits of remorse, and return home to his wife; would fall down at her knees, and ask her forgiveness, and

---

1. **still-hunter** A hunter who ambushes his prey by stealth.

cry like a child. At other times he would hide himself up in the woods, and steal home at night, and get what he wanted out of the pantry, without speaking a word to any one. He went on with these pranks for some years, till he took a fit of the blue devils.

"'Come away, Ned, to the —— lake, with me,' said he; 'I am weary of my life, and I want a change.'

"'Shall we take the fishing-tackle?' says I. 'The black bass are in prime season, and F—— will lend us the old canoe. He's got some capital rum up from Kingston. We'll fish all day, and have a spree at night.'

"'It's not to fish I'm going,' says he.

"'To shoot, then? I've bought Rockwood's new rifle.'

"'It's neither to fish nor to shoot, Ned: it's a new game I'm going to try; so come along.'

"Well, to the —— lake we went. The day was very hot, and our path lay through the woods, and over those scorching plains, for eight long miles. I thought I should have dropped by the way; but during our long walk my companion never opened his lips. He strode on before me, at a half-run, never once turning his head.

"'The man must be the devil!' says I, 'and accustomed to a warmer place, or he must feel this. Hollo, Brian! Stop there! Do you mean to kill me?'

"'Take it easy,' says he; 'you'll see another day arter this — I've business on hand, and cannot wait.'

"Well, on we went, at the same awful rate, and it was mid-day when we got to the little tavern on the lake shore, kept by one F——, who had a boat for the convenience of strangers who came to visit the place. Here we got our dinner, and a glass of rum to wash it down. But Brian was moody, and to all my jokes he only returned a sort of grunt; and while I was talking with F——, he steps out, and a few minutes arter we saw him crossing the lake in the old canoe.

"'What's the matter with Brian?' says F——; 'all does not seem right with him, Ned. You had better take the boat, and look arter him.'

"'Pooh!' says I; 'he's often so, and grows so glum now-a-days that I will cut his acquaintance altogether if he does not improve.'

"'He drinks awful hard,' says F——; 'may be he's got a fit of the delirium-tremulous. There is no telling what he may be up to at this minute.'

"My mind misgave me, too, so I e'en takes the oars, and pushes out, right upon Brian's track; and, by the Lord Harry! if I did not find him, upon my landing on the opposite shore, lying wallowing in his blood, with his throat cut. 'Is that you, Brian?' says I, giving him a kick with my foot, to see if he was alive or dead. 'What upon earth tempted you to play me and F—— such a dirty, mean trick, as to go and stick yourself like a pig, bringing such a discredit upon the house? — and you so far from home and those who should nurse you.'

"I was so mad with him, that (saving your presence, ma'am) I swore awfully, and called him names that would be ondacent to repeat here; but he only answered with groans and a horrid gurgling in his throat. 'It's choking you are,' said I, 'but you shan't have your own way, and die so easily, either, if I can punish you by keeping you alive.' So I just turned him upon his stomach, with his head down the steep bank; but he still kept choking and growing black in the face."

Layton then detailed some particulars of his surgical practice which it is not necessary to repeat. He continued,

"I bound up his throat with my handkerchief, and took him neck and heels, and threw him into the bottom of the boat. Presently he came to himself a little, and sat up in the boat; and — would you believe it? — made several attempts to throw himself in the water. 'This will not do,' says I; 'you've done mischief enough already by cutting your weasand![2] If you dare to try that again, I will kill you with the oar.' I held it up to threaten him; he was scared, and lay down as quiet as a lamb. I put my foot upon his breast. 'Lie still, now! or you'll catch it.' He looked piteously at me; he could not speak, but his eyes seemed to say, 'Have pity upon me, Ned; don't kill me.'

"Yes, ma'am; this man, who had just cut his throat, and twice arter that tried to drown himself, was afraid that I should knock him on the head and kill him. Ha! ha! I shall never forget the work that F—— and I had with him arter I got him up to the house.

"The doctor came, and sewed up his throat; and his wife — poor crittur! — came to nurse him. Bad as he was, she was mortal fond of him! He lay there, sick and unable to leave his bed, for three months, and did nothing but pray to God to forgive him, for he thought the devil would surely have him for cutting his own throat; and when he got about again, which is now twelve years ago, he left off drinking entirely, and wanders about the woods with his dogs, hunting. He seldom speaks to any one, and his wife's brother carries on the farm for the family. He is so shy of strangers that 'tis a wonder he came in here. The old wives are afraid of him; but you need not heed him — his troubles are to himself, he harms no one."

Layton departed, and left me brooding over the sad tale which he had told in such an absurd and jesting manner. It was evident from the account he had given of Brian's attempt at suicide, that the hapless hunter was not wholly answerable for his conduct — that he was a harmless maniac.

The next morning, at the very same hour, Brian again made his appearance; but instead of the rifle across his shoulder, a large stone jar occupied the place, suspended by a stout leather thong. Without saying a word, but with a truly benevolent smile, that flitted slowly over his stern features, and lighted them up, like a sunbeam breaking from beneath a stormy cloud, he advanced to the table, and unslinging the jar, set it down before me, and in a low and gruff, but by no means an unfriendly voice, said, "Milk, for the child," and vanished.

"How good it was of him! How kind!" I exclaimed, as I poured the precious gift of four quarts of pure new milk out into a deep pan. I had not asked him — had never said that the poor weanling wanted milk. It was the courtesy of a gentleman — of a man of benevolence and refinement.

For weeks did my strange, silent friend steal in, take up the empty jar, and supply its place with another replenished with milk. The baby knew his step, and would hold out her hands to him and cry, "Milk!" and Brian would stoop down and kiss her, and his two great dogs lick her face.

"Have you any children, Mr. B——?"

"Yes, five; but none like this."

"My little girl is greatly indebted to you for your kindness."

"She's welcome, or she would not get it. You are strangers; but I like you all. You look kind, and I would like to know more about you."

---

2. **weasand** Windpipe.

Moodie shook hands with the old hunter, and assured him that we should always be glad to see him. After this invitation, Brian became a frequent guest. He would sit and listen with delight to Moodie while he described to him elephant-hunting at the Cape; grasping his rifle in a determined manner, and whistling an encouraging air to his dogs. I asked him one evening what made him so fond of hunting.

"'Tis the excitement," he said; "it drowns thought, and I love to be alone. I am sorry for the creatures, too, for they are free and happy; yet I am led by an instinct I cannot restrain to kill them. Sometimes the sight of their dying agonies recalls painful feelings; and then I lay aside the gun, and do not hunt for days. But 'tis fine to be alone with God in the great woods — to watch the sunbeams stealing through the thick branches, the blue sky breaking in upon you in patches, and to know that all is bright and shiny above you, in spite of the gloom that surrounds you."

After a long pause, he continued, with much solemn feeling in his look and tone,

"I lived a life of folly for years, for I was respectably born and educated, and had seen something of the world, perhaps more than was good, before I left home for the woods; and from the teaching I had received from kind relatives and parents I should have known how to have conducted myself better. But, madam, if we associate long with the depraved and ignorant, we learn to become even worse than they are. I felt deeply my degradation — felt that I had become the slave to low vice; and in order to emancipate myself from the hateful tyranny of evil passions, I did a very rash and foolish thing. I need not mention the manner in which I transgressed God's holy laws; all the neighbours know it, and must have told you long ago. I could have borne reproof, but they turned my sorrow into indecent jests, and, unable to bear their coarse ridicule, I made companions of my dogs and gun, and went forth into the wilderness. Hunting became a habit. I could no longer live without it, and it supplies the stimulant which I lost when I renounced the cursed whiskey bottle.

"I remember the first hunting excursion I took alone in the forest. How sad and gloomy I felt! I thought that there was no creature in the world so miserable as myself. I was tired and hungry, and I sat down upon a fallen tree to rest. All was still as death around me, and I was fast sinking to sleep, when my attention was aroused by a long, wild cry. My dog, for I had not Chance then, and he's no hunter, pricked up his ears, but instead of answering with a bark of defiance, he crouched down, trembling, at my feet. 'What does this mean?' I cried, and I cocked my rifle and sprang upon the log. The sound came nearer upon the wind. It was like the deep baying of a pack of hounds in full cry. Presently a noble deer rushed past me, and fast upon his trail — I see them now, like so many black devils — swept by a pack of ten or fifteen large, fierce wolves, with fiery eyes and bristling hair, and paws that seemed hardly to touch the ground in their eager haste. I thought not of danger, for, with their prey in view, I was safe; but I felt every nerve within me tremble for the fate of the poor deer. The wolves gained upon him at every bound. A close thicket intercepted his path, and, rendered desperate, he turned at bay. His nostrils were dilated, and his eyes seemed to send forth long streams of light. It was wonderful to witness the courage of the beast. How bravely he repelled the attacks of his deadly enemies, how gallantly he tossed them to the right and left, and spurned them from beneath his hoofs; yet all his struggles were useless, and he was quickly overcome and torn to pieces by his ravenous foes. At that moment he seemed more unfortunate than even myself, for I could not see in what manner he had deserved his fate. All his speed and energy, his courage and fortitude, had been exerted in vain. I had tried to destroy myself; but he, with every effort vigorously made for self-preservation, was doomed to meet the fate he dreaded! Is God just to his creatures?"

With this sentence on his lips, he started abruptly from his seat and left the house.

One day he found me painting some wild flowers, and was greatly interested in watching the progress I made in the group. Late in the afternoon of the following day he brought me a large bunch of splendid spring flowers.

"Draw these," said he; "I have been all the way to the —— lake plains to find them for you."

Little Katie, grasping them one by one, with infantile joy, kissed every lovely blossom.

"These are God's pictures," said the hunter, "and the child, who is all nature, understands them in a minute. Is it not strange that these beautiful things are hid away in the wilderness, where no eyes but the birds of the air, and the wild beasts of the wood, and the insects that live upon them, ever see them? Does God provide, for the pleasure of such creatures, these flowers? Is His benevolence gratified by the admiration of animals whom we have been taught to consider as having neither thought nor reflection? When I am alone in the forest, these thoughts puzzle me."

Knowing that to argue with Brian was only to call into action the slumbering fires of his fatal malady, I turned the conversation by asking him why he called his favourite dog Chance?

"I found him," he said, "forty miles back in the bush. He was a mere skeleton. At first I took him for a wolf, but the shape of his head undeceived me. I opened my wallet,[3] and called him to me. He came slowly, stopping and wagging his tail at every step, and looking me wistfully in the face. I offered him a bit of dried venison, and he soon became friendly, and followed me home, and has never left me since. I called him Chance, after the manner I happened with him; and I would not part with him for twenty dollars."

Alas, for poor Chance! he had, unknown to his master, contracted a private liking for fresh mutton, and one night he killed no less than eight sheep that belonged to Mr. D——, on the front road; the culprit, who had been long suspected, was caught in the very act, and this *mischance* cost him his life. Brian was sad and gloomy for many weeks after his favourite's death.

"I would have restored the sheep fourfold," he said, "if he would but have spared the life of my dog."

My recollections of Brian seem more particularly to concentrate in the adventures of one night, when I happened to be left alone, for the first time since my arrival in Canada. I cannot now imagine how I could have been such a fool as to give way for four-and-twenty hours to such childish fears; but so it was, and I will not disguise my weakness from my indulgent reader.

Moodie had bought a very fine cow of a black man, named Mollineux, for which he was to give twenty-seven dollars. The man lived twelve miles back in the woods; and one fine, frosty spring day — (don't smile at the term frosty, thus connected with the genial season of the year; the term is perfectly correct when applied to the Canadian spring, which, until the middle of May, is the most dismal season of the year) — he and John Monaghan took a rope, and the dog, and sallied forth to fetch the cow home. Moodie said that they should be back by six o'clock in the evening, and charged me to have something cooked for supper when they returned, as he doubted not their long

3. **wallet** Pack.

walk in the sharp air would give them a good appetite. This was during the time that I was without a servant, and living in old Mrs. ——'s shanty.

The day was so bright and clear, and Katie was so full of frolic and play, rolling upon the floor, or toddling from chair to chair, that the day passed on without my feeling remarkably lonely. At length the evening drew nigh, and I began to expect my husband's return, and to think of the supper that I was to prepare for his reception. The red heifer that we had bought of Layton, came lowing to the door to be milked; but I did not know how to milk in those days, and, besides this, I was terribly afraid of cattle. Yet, as I knew that milk would be required for the tea, I ran across the meadow to Mrs. Joe, and begged that one of her girls would be so kind as to milk for me. My request was greeted with a rude burst of laughter from the whole set.

"If you can't milk," said Mrs. Joe, "it's high time you should learn. My girls are above being helps."

"I would not ask you but as a great favour; I am afraid of cows."

"*Afraid of cows!* Lord bless the woman! A farmer's wife, and afraid of cows!"

Here followed another laugh at my expense; and, indignant at the refusal of my first and last request, when they had all borrowed so much from me, I shut the inhospitable door, and returned home.

After many ineffectual attempts, I succeeded at last, and bore my half-pail of milk in triumph to the house. Yes! I felt prouder of that milk than many an author of the best thing he ever wrote, whether in verse or prose; and it was doubly sweet when I considered that I had procured it without being under any obligation to my ill-natured neighbours. I had learned a useful lesson of independence, to which in after-years I had often again to refer.

I fed little Katie and put her to bed, made the hot cakes for tea, boiled the potatoes, and laid the ham, cut in nice slices, in the pan, ready to cook the moment I saw the men enter the meadow, and arranged the little room with scrupulous care and neatness. A glorious fire was blazing on the hearth, and everything was ready for their supper; and I began to look out anxiously for their arrival.

The night had closed in cold and foggy, and I could no longer distinguish any object at more than a few yards from the door. Bringing in as much wood as I thought would last me for several hours, I closed the door; and for the first time in my life I found myself at night in a house entirely alone. Then I began to ask myself a thousand torturing questions as to the reason of their unusual absence. Had they lost their way in the woods? Could they have fallen in with wolves (one of my early bugbears)? Could any fatal accident have befallen them? I started up, opened the door, held my breath, and listened. The little brook lifted up its voice in loud, hoarse wailing, or mocked, in its babbling to the stones, the sound of human voices. As it became later, my fears increased in proportion. I grew too superstitious and nervous to keep the door open. I not only closed it, but dragged a heavy box in front, for bolt there was none. Several ill-looking men had, during the day, asked their way to Toronto. I felt alarmed, lest such rude wayfarers should come to-night and demand a lodging, and find me alone and unprotected. Once I thought of running across to Mrs. Joe, and asking her to let one of the girls stay with me until Moodie returned; but the way in which I had been repulsed in the evening prevented me from making a second appeal to their charity.

Hour after hour wore away, and the crowing of the cocks proclaimed midnight, and yet they came not. I had burnt out all my wood, and I dared not open the door to fetch in more. The candle was expiring in the socket, and I had not courage to go up into the loft and procure another before it went finally out. Cold, heart-weary, and faint, I sat and cried. Every now and then the furious barking of the dogs at the neighbouring farms, and the loud cackling of the geese upon our own, made me hope that they were coming; and then I listened till the beating of my own heart excluded all other sounds. Oh, that unwearied brook! how it sobbed and moaned like a fretful child; — what unreal terrors and fanciful illusions my too active mind conjured up, whilst listening to its mysterious tones!

Just as the moon rose, the howling of a pack of wolves, from the great swamp in our rear, filled the whole air. Their yells were answered by the barking of all the dogs in the vicinity, and the geese, unwilling to be behind-hand in the general confusion, set up the most discordant screams. I had often heard, and even been amused, during the winter, particularly on thaw nights, with hearing the howls of these formidable wild beasts; but I had never before heard them alone, and when one dear to me was abroad amid their haunts. They were directly in the track that Moodie and Monaghan must have taken; and I now made no doubt that they had been attacked and killed on their return through the woods with the cow, and I wept and sobbed until the cold grey dawn peered in upon me through the small dim windows. I have passed many a long cheerless night, when my dear husband was away from me during the rebellion, and I was left in my forest home with five little children, and only an old Irish woman to draw and cut wood for my fire, and attend to the wants of the family, but that was the saddest and longest night I ever remember.

Just as the day broke, my friends the wolves set up a parting benediction, so loud, and wild, and near to the house, that I was afraid lest they should break through the frail window, or come down the low wide chimney, and rob me of my child. But their detestable howls died away in the distance, and the bright sun rose up and dispersed the wild horrors of the night, and I looked once more timidly around me. The sight of the table spread, and the uneaten supper, renewed my grief, for I could not divest myself of the idea that Moodie was dead. I opened the door, and stepped forth into the pure air of the early day. A solemn and beautiful repose still hung like a veil over the face of Nature. The mists of night still rested upon the majestic woods, and not a sound but the flowing of the waters went up in the vast stillness. The earth had not yet raised her matin hymn to the throne of the Creator. Sad at heart, and weary and worn in spirit, I went down to the spring and washed my face and head, and drank a deep draught of its icy waters. On returning to the house, I met, near the door, old Brian the hunter, with a large fox dangling across his shoulder, and the dogs following at his heels.

"Good God! Mrs. Moodie, what is the matter? You are early abroad this morning, and look dreadful ill. Is anything wrong at home? Is the baby or your husband sick?"

"Oh!" I cried, bursting into tears, "I fear he is killed by the wolves."

The man stared at me, as if he doubted the evidence of his senses, and well he might; but this one idea had taken such strong possession of my mind that I could admit no other. I then told him, as well as I could find words, the cause of my alarm, to which he listened very kindly and patiently.

"Set your heart at rest; your husband is safe. It is a long journey on foot to Mollineux, to one unacquainted with a blazed path in a bush road. They have staid all night at the black man's shanty, and you will see them back at noon."

I shook my head and continued to weep.

"Well, now, in order to satisfy you, I will saddle my mare, and ride over to the nigger's, and bring you word as fast as I can."

I thanked him sincerely for his kindness, and returned, in somewhat better spirits, to the house. At ten o'clock my good messenger returned with the glad tidings that all was well.

The day before, when half the journey had been accomplished, John Monaghan let go the rope by which he led the cow, and she had broken away through the woods, and returned to her old master; and when they again reached his place, night had set in, and they were obliged to wait until the return of day. Moodie laughed heartily at all my fears; but indeed I found them no joke.

Brian's eldest son, a lad of fourteen, was not exactly an idiot, but what, in the old country, is very expressively termed by the poor people a "natural." He could feed and assist himself, had been taught imperfectly to read and write, and could go to and from the town on errands, and carry a message from one farm-house to another; but he was a strange, wayward creature, and evidently inherited, in no small degree, his father's malady.

During the summer months he lived entirely in the woods, near his father's dwelling, only returning to obtain food, which was generally left for him in an outhouse. In the winter, driven home by the severity of the weather, he would sit for days together moping in the chimney-corner, without taking the least notice of what was passing around him. Brian never mentioned this boy — who had a strong, active figure; a handsome, but very inexpressive face — without a deep sigh; and I feel certain that half his own dejection was occasioned by the mental aberration of his child.

One day he sent the lad with a note to our house, to know if Moodie would purchase the half of an ox that he was going to kill. There happened to stand in the corner of the room an open wood box, into which several bushels of fine apples had been thrown; and, while Moodie was writing an answer to the note, the eyes of the idiot were fastened, as if by some magnetic influence, upon the apples. Knowing that Brian had a very fine orchard, I did not offer the boy any of the fruit. When the note was finished, I handed it to him. The lad grasped it mechanically, without removing his fixed gaze from the apples.

"Give that to your father, Tom."

The boy answered not — his ears, his eyes, his whole soul, were concentrated in the apples. Ten minutes elapsed, but he stood motionless, like a pointer at dead set.

"My good boy, you can go."

He did not stir.

"Is there anything you want?"

"I want," said the lad, without moving his eyes from the objects of his intense desire, and speaking in a slow, pointed manner, which ought to have been heard to be fully appreciated, "I want ap-ples!"

"Oh, if that's all, take what you like."

The permission once obtained, the boy flung himself upon the box with the rapacity of a hawk upon its prey, after being long poised in the air, to fix its certain aim; thrusting his hands to the right and left, in order to secure the finest specimens of the coveted fruit, scarcely allowing himself time to breathe until he had filled his old straw hat, and all his pockets, with apples. To help laughing was impossible; while this new Tom o' Bedlam darted from the house, and scampered across the field for dear life, as if afraid that we should pursue him, to rob him of his prize.

It was during this winter that our friend Brian was left a fortune of three hundred pounds per annum; but it was necessary for him to return to his native country, in order to take possession of the property. This he positively refused to do; and when we remonstrated with him on the apparent imbecility of this resolution, he declared that he would not risk his life, in crossing the Atlantic twice, for twenty times that sum. What strange inconsistency was this, in a being who had three times attempted to take away that which he dreaded so much to lose accidentally!

I was much amused with an account which he gave me, in his quaint way, of an excursion he went upon with a botanist, to collect specimens of the plants and flowers of Upper Canada.

"It was a fine spring day, some ten years ago, and I was yoking my oxen to drag in some oats I had just sown, when a little, fat, punchy man, with a broad, red, good-natured face, and carrying a small black leathern wallet across his shoulder, called to me over the fence, and asked me if my name was Brian B——? I said, 'Yes; what of that?'

"'Only you are the man I want to see. They tell me that you are better acquainted with the woods than any person in these parts; and I will pay you anything in reason if you will be my guide for a few days.'

"'Where do you want to go?' said I.

"'Nowhere in particular,' says he. 'I want to go here and there, in all directions, to collect plants and flowers.'

"That is still-hunting with a vengeance, thought I. 'To-day I must drag in my oats. If to-morrow will suit, we will be off.'

"'And your charge?' said he. 'I like to be certain of that.'

"'A dollar a-day. My time and labour upon my farm, at this busy season, is worth more than that.'

"'True,' said he. 'Well, I'll give you what you ask. At what time will you be ready to start?'

"'By daybreak, if you wish it.'

"Away he went; and by daylight next morning he was at my door, mounted upon a stout French pony. 'What are you going to do with that beast?' said I. 'Horses are of no use on the road that you and I are to travel. You had better leave him in my stable.'

"'I want him to carry my traps,' said he; 'it may be some days that we shall be absent.'

"I assured him that he must be his own beast of burthen, and carry his axe, and blanket, and wallet of food upon his own back. The little body did not much relish this arrangement; but as there was no help for it, he very good-naturedly complied. Off we set, and soon climbed the steep ridge at the back of your farm, and got upon —— lake plains. The woods were flush with flowers; and the little man grew into such an ecstacy, that at every fresh specimen he uttered a yell of joy, cut a caper in the air, and flung himself down upon them, as if he was drunk with delight. 'Oh, what treasures! what treasures!' he cried. 'I shall make my fortune!'

"It is seldom I laugh," quoth Brian, "but I could not help laughing at this odd little man; for it was not the beautiful blossoms, such as you delight to paint, that drew forth these exclamations, but the queer little plants, which he had rummaged for at the roots of old trees, among the moss and long grass. He sat upon a decayed trunk, which lay in our path, I do believe for a long hour, making an oration over some greyish things, spotted with red, that grew upon it, which looked more like mould than plants, declaring himself repaid for all the trouble and expense he had been at, if it were only to obtain a sight of them. I gathered him a beautiful blossom of the lady's slipper; but he pushed it back when I presented it to him, saying, 'Yes, yes; 'tis very fine. I have seen that often before; but these lichens are splendid.'

"The man had so little taste that I thought him a fool, and so I left him to talk to his dear plants, while I shot partridges for our supper. We spent six days in the woods, and the little man filled his black wallet with all sorts of rubbish, as if he wilfully shut his eyes to the beautiful flowers, and chose only to admire ugly, insignificant plants that everybody else passes by without noticing, and which, often as I had been in the woods, I never had observed before. I never pursued a deer with such earnestness as he continued his hunt for what he called 'specimens.'

"When we came to the Cold Creek, which is pretty deep in places, he was in such a hurry to get at some plants that grew under the water, that in reaching after them he lost his balance and fell head over heels into the stream. He got a thorough ducking, and was in a terrible fright; but he held on to the flowers which had caused the trouble, and thanked his stars that he had saved them as well as his life. Well, he was an innocent man," continued Brian; "a very little made him happy, and at night he would sing and amuse himself like a child. He gave me ten dollars for my trouble, and I never saw him again; but I often think of him, when hunting in the woods that we wandered through together, and I pluck the wee plants that he used to admire, and wonder why he preferred them to the fine flowers."

When our resolution was formed to sell our farm, and take up our grant of land in the backwoods, no one was so earnest in trying to persuade us to give up this ruinous scheme as our friend Brian B——, who became quite eloquent in his description of the trials and sorrows that awaited us. During the last week of our stay in the township of H——, he visited us every evening, and never bade us good-night without a tear moistening his cheek. We parted with the hunter as with an old friend; and we never met again. His fate was a sad one. After we left that part of the country, he fell into a moping melancholy, which ended in self-destruction. But a kinder, warmer-hearted man, while he enjoyed the light of reason, has seldom crossed our path.

(1852)

Adieu to the Woods

Adieu! — adieu! — when quivering lips refuse
    The bitter pangs of parting to declare;
And the full bosom feels that it must lose
    Friends who were wont its inmost thoughts to share;
When hands are tightly clasp'd, 'mid struggling sighs
And streaming tears, those whisper'd accents rise,
    Leaving to God the objects of our care
In that short, simple, comprehensive prayer —
                    ADIEU!

Never did eager British children look for the first violets and primroses of spring with more impatience than my baby boys and girls watched, day after day, for the first snowflakes that were to form the road to convey them to their absent father.

"Winter never means to come this year. It will never snow again?" exclaimed my eldest boy, turning from the window on Christmas-day, with the most rueful aspect that ever greeted the broad, gay beams of the glorious sun. It was like a spring day. The little lake in front of the window glittered like a mirror of silver, set in its dark frame of pine woods.

I, too, was wearying for the snow, and was tempted to think that it did not come as early as usual, in order to disappoint us. But I kept this to myself, and comforted the expecting child with the oft-repeated assertion that it would certainly snow upon the morrow.

But the morrow came and passed away, and many other morrows, and the same mild, open weather prevailed. The last night of the old year was ushered in with furious storms of wind and snow; the rafters of our log cabin shook beneath the violence of the gale, which swept up from the lake like a lion roaring for its prey, driving the snow-flakes through every open crevice, of which there were not a few, and powdering the floor until it rivalled in whiteness the ground without.

"Oh, what a dreadful night!" we cried, as we huddled, shivering, around the old broken stove. "A person abroad in the woods to-night would be frozen. Flesh and blood could not long stand this cutting wind."

"It reminds me of the commencement of a laughable extempore ditty," said I to my young friend, A. C——, who was staying with me, "composed by my husband, during the first very cold night we spent in Canada":

Oh, the cold of Canada nobody knows,
The fire burns our shoes without warming our toes;
Oh, dear, what shall we do?
Our blankets are thin, and our noses are blue —
Our noses are blue, and our blankets are thin,
It's at zero without, and we're freezing within!
(*Chorus*). Oh, dear, what shall we do?

"But, joking apart, my dear A——, we ought to be very thankful that we are not travelling this night to B——."

"But to-morrow," said my eldest boy, lifting up his curly head from my lap. "It will be fine to-morrow, and we shall see dear papa again."

In this hope he lay down on his little bed upon the floor, and was soon fast asleep; perhaps dreaming of that eagerly-anticipated journey, and of meeting his beloved father.

Sleep was a stranger to my eyes. The tempest raged so furiously without that I was fearful the roof would be carried off the house, or that the chimney would take fire. The night was far advanced when old Jenny and myself retired to bed.

My boy's words were prophetic; that was the last night I ever spent in the bush — in the dear forest home which I had loved in spite of all the hardships which we had endured since we pitched our tent in the backwoods. It was the birthplace of my three boys, the school of high resolve and energetic action in which we had learned to meet calmly, and successfully to battle with the ills of life. Nor did I leave it without many regretful tears, to mingle once more with a world to whose usages, during my long solitude, I had become almost a stranger, and to whose praise or blame I felt alike indifferent.

When the day dawned, the whole forest scenery lay glittering in a mantle of dazzling white; the sun shone brightly, the heavens were intensely blue, but the cold was so severe that every article of food had to be thawed before we could get our breakfast. The very blankets that covered us during the night were stiff with our frozen breath. "I hope the sleighs won't come to-day," I cried; "we should be frozen on the long journey."

About noon two sleighs turned into our clearing. Old Jenny ran screaming into the room, "The masther has sent for us at last! The sleighs are come! Fine large sleighs, and illigant teams of horses! Och, and it's a cowld day for the wee things to lave the bush."

The snow had been a week in advance of us at B——, and my husband had sent up the teams to remove us. The children jumped about, and laughed aloud for joy. Old Jenny did not know whether to laugh or cry, but she set about helping me to pack up trunks and bedding as fast as our cold hands would permit.

In the midst of the confusion, my brother arrived, like a good genius, to our assistance, declaring his determination to take us down to B—— himself in his large lumber-sleigh. This was indeed joyful news. In less than three hours he despatched the hired sleighs with their loads, and we all stood together in the empty house, striving to warm our hands over the embers of the expiring fire.

How cold and desolate every object appeared! The small windows, half blocked up with snow, scarcely allowed a glimpse of the declining sun to cheer us with his serene aspect. In spite of the cold, several kind friends had waded through the deep snow to say, "God bless you! — Good-bye;" while a group of silent Indians stood together, gazing upon our proceedings with an earnestness which showed that they were not uninterested in the scene. As we passed out to the sleigh, they pressed forward, and silently held out their hands, while the squaws kissed me and the little ones with tearful eyes. They had been true friends to us in our dire necessity, and I returned their mute farewell from my very heart.

Mr. S—— sprang into the sleigh. One of our party was missing. "Jenny!" shouted my brother, at the top of his voice, "it is too cold to keep your mistress and the little children waiting."

"Och, shure thin, it is I that am comin'!" returned the old body, as she issued from the house.

Shouts of laughter greeted her appearance. The figure she cut upon that memorable day I shall never forget. My brother dropped the reins upon the horses' necks, and fairly roared. Jenny was about to commence her journey to the front in three hats. Was it to protect her from the cold? Oh, no; Jenny was not afraid of the cold! She could have eaten her breakfast on the north side of an iceberg, and always dispensed with shoes, during the most severe of our Canadian winters. It was to protect these precious articles from injury.

Our good neighbour, Mrs. W——, had presented her with an old sky-blue drawn-silk bonnet, as a parting benediction. This, by way of distinction, for she never had possessed such an article of luxury as a silk bonnet in her life, Jenny had placed over the coarse calico cap, with its full furbelow[1] of the same yellow, ill-washed, homely material, next to her head; over this, as second in degree, a sun-burnt straw hat, with faded pink ribbons, just showed its broken rim and tawdry trimmings; and, to crown all, and serve as a guard to the rest, a really serviceable grey-beaver bonnet, once mine, towered up as high as the celebrated crown in which brother Peter figures in Swift's "Tale of a Tub."

"Mercy, Jenny! Why, old woman, you don't mean to go with us that figure?"

---

1. furbelow Trim made of fabric.

"Och, my dear heart! I've no band-box to kape the cowld from desthroying my illigant bonnets," returned Jenny, laying her hand upon the side of the sleigh.

"Go back, Jenny; go back," cried my brother. "For God's sake take all that tom-foolery from off your head. We shall be the laughing-stock of every village we pass through."

"Och, shure now, Mr. S——, who'd think of looking at an owld crathur[2] like me! It's only yersel' that would notice the like."

"All the world, everybody would look at you, Jenny. I believe that you put on those hats to draw the attention of all the young fellows that we shall happen to meet on the road. Ha, Jenny!"

With an air of offended dignity, the old woman returned to the house to re-arrange her toilet, and provide for the safety of her "illigant bonnets," one of which she suspended to the strings of her cloak, while she carried the third dangling in her hand; and no persuasion of mine would induce her to put them out of sight.

Many painful and conflicting emotions agitated my mind, but found no utterance in words, as we entered the forest path, and I looked my last upon that humble home consecrated by the memory of a thousand sorrows. Every object had become endeared to me during my long exile from civilised life. I loved the lonely lake, with its magnificent belt of dark pines sighing in the breeze; the cedar-swamp, the summer home of my dark Indian friends; my own dear little garden, with its rugged snake-fence which I had helped Jenny to place with my own hands, and which I had assisted the faithful woman in cultivating for the last three years, where I had so often braved the tormenting musquitoes, black-flies, and intense heat, to provide vegetables for the use of the family. Even the cows, that had given a breakfast for the last time to my children, were now regarded with mournful affection. A poor labourer stood in the doorway of the deserted house, holding my noble water-dog, Rover, in a string. The poor fellow gave a joyous bark as my eyes fell upon him.

"James J——, take care of my dog."

"Never fear, ma'am, he shall bide with me as long as he lives."

"He and the Indians at least feel grieved for our departure," I thought. Love is so scarce in this world that we ought to prize it, however lowly the source from whence it flows.

We accomplished only twelve miles of our journey that night. The road lay through the bush, and along the banks of the grand, rushing, foaming Otonabee river, the wildest and most beautiful of forest streams. We slept at the house of kind friends, and early in the morning resumed our long journey, but minus one of our party. Our old favourite cat, Peppermint, had made her escape from the basket in which she had been confined, and had scampered off, to the great grief of the children.

As we passed Mrs. H——'s house, we called for dear Addie. Mr. H—— brought her in his arms to the gate, well wrapped up in a large fur cape and a warm woollen shawl.

"You are robbing me of my dear little girl," he said. "Mrs. H—— is absent; she told me not to part with her if you should call; but I could not detain her without your consent. Now that you have seen her, allow me to keep her for a few months longer?"

Addie was in the sleigh. I put my arm about her. I felt I had my child again, and I secretly rejoiced in the possession of my own. I sincerely thanked him for his kindness, and Mr. S—— drove on.

---

2. **crathur** Creature.

At Mr. R——'s, we found a parcel from dear Emilia, containing a plum-cake and other good things for the children. Her kindness never flagged.

We crossed the bridge over the Otonabee, in the rising town of Peterborough, at eight o'clock in the morning. Winter had now set in fairly. The children were glad to huddle together in the bottom of the sleigh, under the buffalo skins and blankets; all but my eldest boy, who, just turned of five years old, was enchanted with all he heard and saw, and continued to stand up and gaze around him. Born in the forest, which he had never quitted before, the sight of a town was such a novelty that he could find no words wherewith to express his astonishment.

"Are the houses come to see one another?" he asked. "How did they all meet here?"

The question greatly amused his uncle, who took some pains to explain to him the difference between town and country. During the day, we got rid of old Jenny and her bonnets, whom we found a very refractory travelling companion; as wilful, and far more difficult to manage than a young child. Fortunately, we overtook the sleighs with the furniture, and Mr. S—— transferred Jenny to the care of one of the drivers; an arrangement that proved satisfactory to all parties.

We had been most fortunate in obtaining comfortable lodgings for the night. The evening had closed in so intensely cold that although we were only two miles from C——, Addie was so much affected by it that the child lay sick and pale in my arms, and, when spoken to, seemed scarcely conscious of our presence.

My brother jumped from the front seat, and came round to look at her. "That child is ill with the cold; we must stop somewhere to warm her, or she will hardly hold out till we get to the inn at C——."

We were just entering the little village of A——, in the vicinity of the courthouse, and we stopped at a pretty green cottage, and asked permission to warm the children. A stout, middle-aged woman came to the sleigh, and in the kindest manner requested us to alight.

"I think I know that voice," I said. "Surely it cannot be Mrs. S——, who once kept the —— hotel at C——?"

"Mrs. Moodie, you are welcome," said the excellent woman, bestowing upon me a most friendly embrace; "you and your children. I am heartily glad to see you again after so many years. God bless you all!"

Nothing could exceed the kindness and hospitality of this generous woman; she would not hear of our leaving her that night, and, directing my brother to put up his horses in her stable, she made up an excellent fire in a large bed-room, and helped me to undress the little ones who were already asleep, and to warm and feed the rest before we put them to bed.

This meeting gave me real pleasure. In their station of life, I seldom have found a more worthy couple than this American and his wife; and, having witnessed so many of their acts of kindness, both to ourselves and others, I entertained for them a sincere respect and affection, and truly rejoiced that Providence had once more led me to the shelter of their roof.

Mr. S—— was absent, but I found little Mary — the sweet child who used to listen with such delight to Moodie's flute — grown up into a beautiful girl; and the baby that was, a fine child of eight years old. The next morning was so intensely cold that my brother would not resume the journey until past ten o'clock, and even then it was a hazardous experiment.

We had not proceeded four miles before the horses were covered with icicles. Our hair was frozen as white as old Time's solitary forelock, our eyelids stiff, and every limb aching with cold.

"This will never do," said my brother, turning to me; "the children will freeze. I never felt the cold more severe than this."

"Where can we stop?" said I; "we are miles from C——, and I see no prospect of the weather becoming milder."

"Yes, yes; I know, by the very intensity of the cold, that a change is at hand. We seldom have more than three very severe days running, and this is the third. At all events, it is much warmer at night in this country than during the day; the wind drops, and the frost is more bearable. I know a worthy farmer who lives about a mile a-head; he will give us house-room for a few hours; and we will resume our journey in the evening. The moon is at full; and it will be easier to wrap the children up, and keep them warm when they are asleep. Shall we stop at Old Woodruff's?"

"With all my heart." My teeth were chattering with the cold, and the children were crying over their aching fingers at the bottom of the sleigh.

A few minutes' ride brought us to a large farm-house, surrounded by commodious sheds and barns. A fine orchard opposite, and a yard well-stocked with fat cattle and sheep, sleek geese, and plethoric-looking[3] swine, gave promise of a land of abundance and comfort. My brother ran into the house to see if the owner was at home, and presently returned, accompanied by the staunch Canadian yeoman and his daughter, who gave us a truly hearty welcome, and assisted in removing the children from the sleigh to the cheerful fire, that made all bright and cozy within.

Our host was a shrewd, humorous-looking Yorkshireman. His red, weather-beaten face, and tall, athletic figure, bent as it was with hard labour, gave indications of great personal strength; and a certain knowing twinkle in his small, clear grey eyes, which had been acquired by long dealing with the world, with a quiet, sarcastic smile that lurked round the corners of his large mouth, gave you the idea of a man who could not easily be deceived by his fellows; one who, though no rogue himself, was quick in detecting the roguery of others. His manners were frank and easy, and he was such a hospitable entertainer that you felt at home with him in a minute.

"Well, how are you, Mr. S——?" cried the farmer, shaking my brother heartily by the hand. "Toiling in the bush still, eh?"

"Just in the same place."

"And the wife and children?"

"Hearty. Some half-dozen have been added to the flock since you were our way."

"So much the better — so much the better. The more the merrier, Mr. S——; children are riches in this country."

"I know not how that may be; I find it hard to clothe and feed mine."

"Wait till they grow up; they will be brave helps to you then. The price of labour — the price of labour, Mr. S——, is the destruction of the farmer."

"It does not seem to trouble you much, Woodruff," said my brother, glancing round the well-furnished apartment.

---

3. **plethoric-looking** Well fed.

"My son and S—— do it all," cried the old man. "Of course the girls help in busy times, and take care of the dairy, and we hire occasionally; but small as the sum is which is expended in wages during seed-time and harvest, I feel it, I can tell you."

"You are married again, Woodruff?"

"No, sir," said the farmer, with a peculiar smile; "not yet:" which seemed to imply the probability of such an event. "That tall gal is my eldest daughter; she manages the house, and an excellent housekeeper she is. But I cannot keep her for ever." With a knowing wink, "Gals will think of getting married, and seldom consult the wishes of their parents upon the subject when once they have taken the notion into their heads. But 'tis natural, Mr. S——, it is natural; we did just the same when we were young."

My brother looked laughingly towards the fine, handsome young woman, as she placed upon the table hot water, whiskey, and a huge plate of plum-cake, which did not lack a companion, stored with the finest apples which the orchard could produce.

The young girl looked down, and blushed.

"Oh, I see how it is, Woodruff! You will soon lose your daughter. I wonder that you have kept her so long. But who are these young ladies?" he continued, as three girls very demurely entered the room.

"The two youngest are my darters, by my last wife, who, I fear, mean soon to follow the bad example of their sister. The other *lady*," said the old man, with a reverential air, "is a *particular* friend of my eldest darter's."

My brother laughed slily, and the old man's cheek took a deeper glow as he stooped forward to mix the punch.

"You said that these two young ladies, Woodruff, were by your last wife. Pray how many wives have you had?"

"Only three. It is impossible, they say in my country, to have too much of a good thing."

"So I suppose you think," said my brother, glancing first at the old man and then towards Miss Smith. "Three wives! You have been a fortunate man, Woodruff, to survive them all."

"Ay, have I not, Mr. S——? But to tell you the truth, I have been both lucky and unlucky in the wife way," and then he told us the history of his several ventures in matrimony, with which I shall not trouble my readers.

When he had concluded, the weather was somewhat milder, the sleigh was ordered to the door, and we proceeded on our journey, resting for the night at a small village about twenty miles from B——, rejoicing that the long distance which separated us from the husband and father was diminished to a few miles, and that, with the blessing of Providence, we should meet on the morrow.

About noon we reached the distant town, and were met at the inn by him whom one and all so ardently longed to see. He conducted us to a pretty, neat cottage, which he had prepared for our reception, and where we found old Jenny already arrived. With great pride the old woman conducted me over the premises, and showed me the furniture "the masther" had bought; especially recommending to my notice a china tea-service, which she considered the most wonderful acquisition of the whole.

"Och! who would have thought, a year ago, misthress dear, that we should be living in a mansion like this, and ating off raal chaney? It is but yesterday that we were hoeing praties in the field."

"Yes, Jenny, God has been very good to us, and I hope that we shall never learn to regard with indifference the many benefits which we have received at His hands."

Reader! it is not my intention to trouble you with the sequel of our history. I have given you a faithful picture of a life in the backwoods of Canada, and I leave you to draw from it your own conclusions. To the poor, industrious working man it presents many advantages; to the poor gentleman, *none!* The former works hard, puts up with coarse, scanty fare, and submits, with a good grace, to hardships that would kill a domesticated animal at home. Thus he becomes independent, inasmuch as the land that he has cleared finds him in the common necessaries of life; but it seldom, if ever, in remote situations, accomplishes more than this. The gentleman can neither work so hard, live so coarsely, nor endure so many privations as his poorer but more fortunate neighbour. Unaccustomed to manual labour, his services in the field are not of a nature to secure for him a profitable return. The task is new to him, he knows not how to perform it well; and, conscious of his deficiency, he expends his little means in hiring labour, which his bush-farm can never repay. Difficulties increase, debts grow upon him, he struggles in vain to extricate himself, and finally sees his family sink into hopeless ruin.

If these sketches should prove the means of deterring one family from sinking their property, and shipwrecking all their hopes, by going to reside in the backwoods of Canada, I shall consider myself amply repaid for revealing the secrets of the prison-house, and feel that I have not toiled and suffered in the wilderness in vain.

(1852)

Charles Sangster (1822–1893)

When Charles Sangster's *The St. Lawrence and the Saguenay* first appeared, in 1856, the response was overwhelmingly positive. With his first published work, Sangster had established himself as "the Wordsworth of Canada," "the Father of Canadian Poetry," "a credit to Canadian literature," and "the first important national poet." Contemporary critics, however, tend to criticize Sangster for viewing Canada through a British lens. Sangster was influenced by British Romantics like Byron, whose *Childe Harold's Pilgrimage* serves as the model for the travel narrative *The St. Lawrence and the Saguenay*. He also employed the Spenserian sonnet form in this poem and evoked a Wordsworthian awe of the sublime in nature. Furthermore, many critics have identified echoes of Tennyson, Milton, Coleridge, Shelley, and Shakespeare in Sangster's work.

Kingston, Upper Canada, where Sangster was born in 1822, was one of the larger Canadian cities in the 19th century. It was an orderly place set in natural surroundings that would inspire Sangster to write. When he was two, his father died of a sudden illness, leaving his mother to care for five children alone. She "honorably brought up and provided for [us] by the labor of her hands," Sangster wrote. At age 15, Sangster left home to earn money for his family by filling cartridges for William Lyon Mackenzie's rebels. By his own admission, his literary education was "defective" — "I would have read more in my younger days," but "books were not to be had."

Sangster travelled extensively throughout his life — especially to Montreal and New York — often in his capacity as subeditor for the *British Whig,* a position he held from 1849 to1864. In 1853, he journeyed along the St. Lawrence River writing a travelogue for the *Whig* entitled "Etchings by the Way." In it, he muses, "what do your readers want to be told about the Rapids? — nothing. Not a man Jack of them but has probably seen them a score of times, and appreciated their wild beauty."

Later, in writing *The St. Lawrence and the Saguenay,* Sangster drew a new map of Canadian space and asked his readers to put down their works of British literature — thus "rous[ing] the lounging student from his book" — and take a close look at their own country. He names and describes Quebec sites such as Lachine, "The Royal Mount," Richelieu, Les Éboulements, and Quebec City. He also makes references to important figures in Canadian history, such as Major General James Wolfe and the Marquis de Montcalm. The volume contains many references to the epic 1759 battle of the Plains of Abraham, in which antagonists Wolfe and Montcalm both died and British control over Canada was secured.

Sangster again takes up a military theme in "Brock," a poem from his second publication, *Hesperus and Other Poems and Lyrics* (1860). The work was commissioned for a memorial to British Major-General Sir Isaac Brock, who died defending Canada in the Battle of Queenston Heights.

There were few Canadian influences for Sangster to draw from. His work belongs to the vital tradition of Canadian travel writing — a tradition he shared with the likes of Oliver Goldsmith, Joseph Howe, Isabella Valancy Crawford, and Major John Richardson. He was particularly impressed by Charles Heavysege, who contributed greatly to what Sangster called "our yet scanty stock of poetic literature." Though Sangster was known to be a solitary figure, he was acquainted with several Canadian writers, including Susanna Moodie, William Kirby, George Stewart, and the Reverend E.H. Dewart.

Love is a recurring theme in Sangster's melancholy and Romantic poetry. The poet's travelling companion in *The St. Lawrence and the Saguenay* is a mysterious and wild "Maiden," whose "intellectual eyes" reflect spiritual love. Sangster often uses biblical imagery and allusions to Milton's *Paradise Lost* to express his desire to reconcile pure Christian spiritual love and human passion.

Sangster's life was marked by suffering. His first wife, Mary, died of pneumonia less than two years after their wedding. His subsequent marriage to Henrietta Meagher, while enduring, was unhappy. In 1868, he gave up his job as a reporter for the *Daily News,* which he had taken on in 1864, to become a clerk at the federal post office in Ottawa. The work was stressful, and his health was already precarious. He had not written a word since the publication of *Hesperus* in 1860. In 1875, he had a complete nervous breakdown; when he was ready to resume work, he transferred to another post office position, which he held for 10 years. He suffered another nervous collapse in 1885 and retired the following year.

In 1888, Sangster wrote to W.D. Lighthall, "I have written comparatively nothing for the past 20 years — I might say positively nothing … so steady were my duties, and so much did they unfit me for any, even the slightest, literary endeavour." In 1891, he sent his unpublished manuscripts to Lighthall, explaining, "my idea was to save them, not to the world, but to 'this Canada of ours,' which, as you know, has occupied much of my thoughts in the rhyming way for many years." Sangster never aspired to fame and fortune. Instead, his goal was to contribute to a national literary tradition that he believed would one day be great: "Fame is dross to me. I write because I believe it to be a duty; and, succeed or fail, what little light I have shall not be hidden under a bushel. I have but one hope — one great hope — and it is great — you know it." Charles Sangster died in 1893. The manuscripts he had sent to Lighthall were published as *Norland Echoes and Other Strains and Lyrics* in 1975 and *The Angel Guest and Other Poems and Lyrics* in 1976.

From *The St. Lawrence and the Saguenay*

I.

There is but one to whom my hopes are clinging
As clings the bee unto the morning flower,

There is but one to whom my thoughts are winging
Their dove-like passage through each silent hour:
One who has made my heart her summer bower.
Feeling and passion there forever bloom
For her, who, by her love's mysterious power,
Dispels the languor of my spirit's gloom,
And lifts my dead heart up, like Lazarus from the tomb.

II.

Maiden! from whose large, intellectual[1] eyes,   10
My soul first drank love's immortality,
Plume my weak spirit for its chosen skies,
'T would falter in its mission without thee.
Conduct its flight; and if its musings be
Oft'ner of earth than heaven, bear awhile
With what is native to mortality:
It dare not err exulting in thy smile:
Look on it with thine eyes, and keep it free from guile.[2]

III.

The bark[3] leaps love-fraught from the land; the sea
Lies calm before us. Many an isle is there,   20
Clad with soft verdure;[4] many a stately tree
Uplifts its leafy branches through the air;
The amorous current bathes the islets fair,
As we skip, youth-like, o'er the limpid[5] waves;
White cloudlets speck the golden atmosphere,
Through which the passionate sun looks down, and graves
His image on the pearls that boil from the deep caves,

IV.

And bathe the vessel's prow. Isle after isle
Is passed, as we glide tortuously through
The opening vistas, that uprise and smile   30
Upon us from the ever-changing view.
Here nature, lavish of her wealth, did strew
Her flocks of panting islets on the breast
Of the admiring River, where they grew,
Like shapes of Beauty, formed to give a zest
To the charmed mind, like waking Visions of the Blest.

V.

The silver-sinewed arms of the proud Lake,
Love-wild, embrace each islet tenderly,
The zephyrs kiss the flowers when they wake

---

1. **intellectual** Intelligent. 2. **guile** Deception. 3. **bark** Ship. 4. **verdure** Vegetation. 5. **limpid** Clear.

40   At morn, flushed with a rare simplicity;
      See how they bloom around yon birchen[6] tree,
      And smile along the bank, by the sandy shore,
      In lovely groups — a fair community!
      The embossed rocks glitter like golden ore,
      And here, the o'erarching trees form a fantastic bower.

VI.

      Red walls of granite rise on either hand,
      Rugged and smooth; a proud young eagle soars
      Above the stately evergreens, that stand
      Like watchful sentinels on these God-built towers;
50   And near yon beds of many-colored flowers
      Browse two majestic deer, and at their side
      A spotted fawn all innocently cowers;
      In the rank[7] brushwood it attempts to hide,
      While the strong-antlered stag steps forth with lordly stride,

VII.

      And slakes his thirst, undaunted, at the stream.
      Isles of o'erwhelming beauty! surely here
      The wild enthusiast might live, and dream
      His life away. No Nymphic trains appear,
      To charm the pale Ideal Worshipper
60   Of Beauty; nor Nereids[8] from the deeps below;
      Nor hideous Gnomes, to fill the breast with fear;
      But crystal streams through endless landscapes flow,
      And o'er the clustering Isles the softest breezes blow.

LYRIC TO THE ISLES.

      Here the Spirit of Beauty keepeth
          Jubilee for evermore;
      Here the Voice of Gladness leapeth,
          Echoing from shore to shore.
      O'er the hidden watery valley,
          O'er each buried wood and glade,
70   Dances our delighted galley,[9]
          Through the sunlight and the shade —
      Dances o'er the granite cells,
      Where the Soul of Beauty dwells:

      Here the flowers are ever springing,
          While the summer breezes blow;

---

6. **birchen** Birch. 7. **rank** Luxurious and abundant. 8. **Nereids** Sea nymphs in Greek mythology. 9. **galley** Boat.

Here the hours[10] are ever clinging,
  Loitering before they go;
Playing round each beauteous islet,
  Loath to leave the sunny shore,
Where, upon her couch of violet,   80
  Beauty sits for evermore —
Sits and smiles by day and night,
Hand in hand with pure Delight.

Here the Spirit of Beauty dwelleth
  In each palpitating tree,
In each amber wave that welleth
  From its home, beneath the sea;
In the moss upon the granite,
  In each calm, secluded bay,
With the zephyr trains that fan it   90
  With their sweet breaths all the day —
On the waters, on the shore,
Beauty dwelleth evermore!

VIII.

  Yes, here the Genius of Beauty truly dwells.
  I worship Truth and Beauty in my soul.
  The pure and prismatic globule that upwells
  From the blue deep; the psalmy waves that roll
  Before the hurricane; the outspread scroll
  Of heaven, with its written tomes of stars;
  The dew-drop on the leaf: These I extol,   100
  And all alike — each one a Spirit-Mars,[11]
Guarding my Victor-Soul above Earth's prison bars.

IX.

  There was a stately Maiden once, who made
  These Isles her home. Oft has her lightsome skiff
  Toyed with the waters; and the velvet glade,
  The shadowy woodland, and the granite cliff,
  Joyed at her footsteps. Here the Brigand Chief,[12]
  Her father, lived, an outlaw. Her soul's pride
  Was ministering to his wants. In brief,
  The wildest midnight she would cross the tide,   110
Full of a daughter's love, to hasten to his side.

---

10. hours Goddesses of the seasons; the *Horae* of classical mythology. **11. Spirit-Mars** A heavenly or spiritual guardian, named after the Greek god of war. **12. Brigand Chief** A reference to Bill Johnston, a famous pirate.

X.

Queen of the Isles![13] she well deserved the name:
In look, in action, in repose a Queen!
Some Poet-Muse may yet hand down to fame
Her woman's courage, and her classic mien;
Some Painter's skill immortalize the scene,
And blend with it that Maiden's history;
Some Sculptor's hand from the rough marble glean
An eloquent Thought, whose truthfulness shall be
120　The expounder of her worth and moral dignity.

XI.

On, through the lovely Archipelago,
Glides the swift bark. Soft summer matins ring
From every isle. The wind fowl come and go,
Regardless of our presence. On the wing,
And perched upon the boughs, the gay birds sing
Their loves: This is their summer paradise;
From morn till night their joyous caroling
Delights the ear, and through the lucent skies
Ascends the choral hymn in softest symphonies.

XII.

130　The Spring is gone — light, genial-hearted Spring!
Whose breath gives odor to the violet,
Crimsons the wild rose, tints the blackbird's wing,
Unfolds the buttercup. Spring that has set
To music the laughter of the rivulet,
Sent warm pulsations through the hearts of hills,
Reclothed the forests, made the valleys wet
With pearly dew, and waked the grave old mills
From their calm sleep, by the loud rippling of the rills.[14]

XIII.

Long years ago the early Voyageurs
140　Gladdened these wilds with some romantic air;
The moonlight, dancing on their dripping oars,
Showed the slow batteaux[15] passing by with care,
Impelled by rustic crews, as debonnair[16]
As ever struck pale Sorrow dumb with Song:
Many a dropping spirit longed to share
Their pleasant melodies, that swept among
The echo-haunted woods, in accents clear and strong.

---

13. **Queen of the Isles**　Bill Johnston's daughter, Kate. 14. **rills**　Small streams. 15. **batteaux**　Flat-bottomed boats.
16. **debonnair**　Handsome; gracious.

XIV.

See, we have left the Islands far behind,
And pass into a calm, pellucid Lake.
Merrily dance the billows! for the wind   150
Rises all fresh and healthful in our wake,
Up start large flocks of waterfowl, that shake
The spray from their glossed plumage, as they fly
To seek the shelter of some island brake;[17]
Now like dark clouds they seem against the sky,
So vast the numbers are that pass us swiftly by.

XV.

Merrily dance the billows! Cheerily leaps
Our fearless bark! — it loves to skim the sea,
The River and the Lake, when o'er them sweeps
The swift unwearied billow fearlessly.   160
Stretches its spotless sail! — it tightens — see!
How the wind curves the waters all around,
Ploughing into their bosoms fitfully.
Hark to the tempest's dismal shriek! its bound,
Like to an earthquake, makes the river's depths resound.

XVI.

Through the dense air the terror-stricken clouds
Fly, tortured by the pursuing hurricane.
Fast bound the milky billows — the white shrouds
That wind around the mariner on the main.[18]
Nay, shrink not, dark-eyed one! they weave no chain   170
For us — we're free! Ha! ha! our gallant bark
Spurns the white wave with eloquent disdain.
She laughs to scorn the waters wild and dark,
She revels in the Storm, the Tempest loves to mark.

XVII.

Hoarsely reverberates the thunder loud
Through the charged air. The fiery lightnings leap
Forth, from their mystic dwelling in the cloud;
Electric shafts through all the heavens sweep,
And penetrate the surface of the deep,
Like flaming arrows from the bow of wrath,   180
Shot down some dark and cloud-pavilioned steep;
Each red-hot bolt the fearful power hath
To scatter blight and death along its burning path.

---

17. brake A place overgrown with bushes or brambles. **18. main** Ocean.

XVIII.

A wild joy fills my overburdened brain.
My ears drink from each thunder peal.
I glory in the lightings and the rain.
There is no joy like this! With thee to feel
And share each impulse, makes my spirit kneel.
Sing to me, love! my heart is painted with bliss!
190   Thy voice alone can quicken and unseal
The inner depths of feeling. Grant me this:
Flood me with Song, and loose the founts[19] of Happiness.

(1856)

Isabella Valancy Crawford (1850–1887)

Born in Dublin in 1850, Isabella Valancy Crawford is today remembered as an independent-minded writer who was well versed in her craft. She was among the first to explore post-colonial themes in Canadian literature. Her poems were ambivalent about the consequences of colonialism in North America, and they were also provocative in terms of their sexual content.

Crawford was personally affected by colonial expansion. Her family came to North America in 1858, settling in Canada West (now part of Southern Ontario). Her father was the first doctor in the town of Paisley and the township treasurer, but his alcoholism undermined his medical practice, and his misappropriation of public funds led to his disgrace as a civil servant. He tried to re-establish his practice in the Kingston area, and then at Lakefield, where the Crawfords befriended Catharine Parr Traill and her family. The Crawfords settled for a while in Peterborough, and Dr. Crawford died there in 1875.

Even before her father's death, Isabella had begun to take responsibility for her impoverished family. In 1873, she had started to publish her poetry in Toronto periodicals, including the *Mail*, the *National,* and the *Evening Telegram;* her fiction appeared in American tabloids. That year, one of her stories won a $600 prize, but the company that had awarded it defaulted after paying her only $100. This incident foreshadowed a lifetime of financial disappointment — through no fault of her own, she would never manage to earn a comfortable living as a writer. Nevertheless, she was able to support herself and her mother through her diligent literary efforts. She published two serialized novels, one in the *Evening Globe* and the other in *Fireside Weekly*.

In about 1876, Crawford moved with her mother to the bigger market of Toronto, where she eventually learned that of all her talents, poetry would be the least likely to bring her wealth. In 1884, after engaging in a long and fruitless search for a publisher, she selected 43 of her poems and published them independently as *Old Spookses' Pass, Malcolm's Katie and Other Poems*.

Although her significance went unrecognized during her lifetime, Crawford has since been identified as the first poet to explore Canada's distinctive vernacular in literary form. In a further innovation, she sexualized the Canadian landscape. This erotic tendency is most obvious in "The Lily Bed." A longer poem, "Malcolm's Katie," makes similar use of the lily as a symbol for the female body; it also explores the imperial and expansionist rhetoric of English literature in colonial times. For Crawford, colonization was akin to sexual exploitation and violence.

In her long poem *Hugh and Ion* (posthumously published in 1977), the poet sympathizes with a figure who resembles Métis leader Louis Riel, whose rebellion was defeated by Prime Minister

---

19. founts Fountains.

John A. Macdonald's North West Mounted Police at Batoche (in what is now Saskatchewan) in 1885. Yet in her poem "The Rose of a Nation's Thanks" she commends the police. Such conflicts form a subtext in her career as a poet and writer: she admired the Ojibwa people who inhabited the area where she was raised for their spiritual and practical respect for the earth, but she also realized that her livelihood as a poet would be affected if she did not portray the experience of European colonists in a positive manner. She may have felt guilty about colonialism, but her response to such feelings was complex.

Although she was frequently depressed by her situation, Crawford did not entirely lose hope. She continued to pursue her writing and other interests, including playing the piano. Maintaining a habit she had established years before, she read widely in the area of English Romantic and Victorian classic literature, favouring Blake, Burns, Tennyson, Whitman, and Longfellow, as well as earlier figures such as Herrick, Jonson, and Shakespeare. She also remained interested in French poetry and music and works of world religion as diverse as the Bhagavad Gita, the Rig Veda, the Koran, the Talmud, and the Zend-Avesta. Stricken by a winter cold in January 1887, Crawford refused to confine herself to her bed and died some weeks later of congenital heart failure, the same disease that had killed her father and most of her siblings. She was only 36 years old.

In the first half of the 20th century, critics and other poets became interested in her work, especially her poetry. A.J.M. Smith wrote that "'Malcolm's Katie' is the first, and not one of the least, of the few poems that can really be called Canadian, because its language and its imagery, the sensibility it reveals and the vision it embodies is indigenously northern and western, a product not of England or the States but of Canada." For her subtlety in crafting a mythic narrative, Northrop Frye hailed Crawford, asserting that her work displayed a mythopoeic imagination. Later, however, she was scorned for her clumsiness and jingoism. Louis Dudek was especially harsh. In 1979, he denounced her work as "hollow convention" and "counterfeit"; he insisted that Crawford was a "failed poet." But even as he levelled these criticisms — at a symposium on Crawford's life and oeuvre — other scholars were publishing evaluations of her work that made claims for her learnedness, depth, and range of style and maintained that although her poetry was at times formal and dense (even confusing), it could also be energetic, humorous, and erotic. *The Collected Poems of Isabella Valancy Crawford* was published in 1905 and reissued in 1972 with an introduction by James Reaney.

Malcolm's Katie: A Love Story

Part I.

Max plac'd a ring on little Katie's hand,
A silver ring that he had beaten out
From that same sacred coin — first well-priz'd wage
For boyish labour, kept thro' many years.
"See, Kate," he said, "I had no skill to shape
"Two hearts fast bound together, so I grav'd
"Just K. and M., for Katie and for Max."
"But, look; you've run the lines in such a way,
"That M. is part of K., and K. of M.,"
Said Katie, smiling. "Did you mean it thus?   10
"I like it better than the double hearts."
"Well, well," he said, "but womankind is wise!

"Yet tell me, dear, will such a prophecy
"Not hurt you sometimes, when I am away?
"Will you not seek, keen ey'd, for some small break
"In those deep lines, to part the K. and M.
"For you? Nay, Kate, look down amid the globes
"Of those large lilies that our light canoe
"Divides, and see within the polish'd pool

20   "That small, rose face of yours, — so dear, so fair, —
"A seed of love to cleave into a rock,
"And bourgeon[1] thence until the granite splits
"Before its subtle strength. I being gone —
"Poor soldier of the axe — to bloodless fields
"(Inglorious battles, whether lost or won)
"That sixteen-summer'd heart of yours may say:
"'I but was budding, and I did not know
"'My core was crimson and my perfume sweet;
"'I did not know how choice a thing I am;

30   "'I had not seen the sun, and blind I sway'd
"'To a strong wind, and thought because I sway'd,
"''Twas to the wooer of the perfect rose —
"'That strong, wild wind has swept beyond my ken —
"'The breeze I love sighs thro' my ruddy leaves.'"
"O, words!" said Katie, blushing, "only words!
"You build them up that I may push them down;
"If hearts are flow'rs, I know that flow'rs can root —
"Bud, blossom, die — all in the same lov'd soil;
"They do so in my garden. I have made

40   "Your heart my garden. If I am a bud
"And only feel unfoldment feebly stir
"Within my leaves, wait patiently; some June,
"I'll blush a full-blown rose, and queen it, dear,
"In your lov'd garden. Tho' I be a bud,
"My roots strike deep, and torn from that dear soil
"Would shriek like mandrakes — those witch things I read
"Of in your quaint old books. Are you content?"
"Yes — crescent-wise — but not to round, full moon.
"Look at yon hill that rounds so gently up

50   "From the wide lake; a lover king it looks,
"In cloth of gold, gone from his bride and queen:
"And yet delay'd, because her silver locks
"Catch in his gilded fringes; his shoulders sweep
"Into blue distance, and his gracious crest,
"Not held too high, is plum'd with maple groves; —
"One of your father's farms. A mighty man,
"Self-hewn from rock, remaining rock through all."

---

1. **bourgeon** To bud; sprout.

"He loves me, Max," said Katie. "Yes, I know —
"A rock is cup to many a crystal spring.
"Well, he is rich; those misty, peak-roof'd barns —   60
"Leviathans rising from red seas of grain —
"Are full of ingots, shaped like grains of wheat.
"His flocks have golden fleeces, and his herds
"Have monarchs worshipful, as was the calf
"Aaron call'd from the furnace; and his ploughs,
"Like Genii chained, snort o'er his mighty fields.
"He has a voice in Council and in Church — "
"He work'd for all," said Katie, somewhat pain'd.
"Aye, so, dear love, he did; I heard him tell
"How the first field upon his farm was ploughed.   70
"He and his brother Reuben, stalwart lads,
"Yok'd themselves, side by side, to the new plough;
"Their weaker father, in the grey of life
"(But rather the wan age of poverty
"Than many winters), in large, gnarl'd hands
"The plunging handles held: with mighty strains
"They drew the ripping beak through knotted sod,
"Thro' tortuous lanes of blacken'd, smoking stumps;
"And past great flaming brush heaps, sending out
"Fierce summers, beating on their swollen brows.   80
"O, such a battle! had we heard of serfs
"Driven to like hot conflict with the soil,
"Armies had march'd and navies swiftly sail'd
"To burst their gyves.[2] But here's the little point —
"The polish'd di'mond pivot on which spins
"The wheel of Difference — they OWN'D the rugged soil,
"And fought for love — dear love of wealth and pow'r,
"And honest ease and fair esteem of men;
"One's blood heats at it!" "Yet you said such fields
"Were all inglorious," Katie, wondering, said.   90
"Inglorious? Yes; they make no promises
"Of Star or Garter,[3] or the thundering guns
"That tell the earth her warriors are dead.
"Inglorious! Aye, the battle done and won
"Means not — a throne propp'd up with bleaching bones;
"A country sav'd with smoking seas of blood;
"A flag torn from the foe with wounds and death;
"Or Commerce, with her housewife foot upon
"Colossal bridge of slaughter'd savages,
"The Cross laid on her brawny shoulder, and   100
"In one sly, mighty hand her reeking sword,
"And in the other all the woven cheats

---

2. gyves Shackles. **3. Star or Garter** An order of knighthood in Britain.

"From her dishonest looms. Nay, none of these.
"It means — four walls, perhaps a lowly roof;
"Kine in a peaceful posture; modest fields;
"A man and woman standing hand in hand
"In hale old age, who, looking o'er the land,
"Say: 'Thank the Lord, it all is mine and thine!'
"It means, to such thew'd warriors of the Axe
110   "As your own father; — well, it means, sweet Kate,
"Outspreading circles of increasing gold,
"A name of weight; one little daughter heir,
"Who must not wed the owner of an axe,
"Who owns naught else but some dim, dusky woods
"In a far land; two arms indifferent strong — "
"And Katie's heart," said Katie, with a smile;
For yet she stood on that smooth, violet plain,
Where nothing shades the sun; nor quite believed
Those blue peaks closing in were aught but mist
120   Which the gay sun could scatter with a glance.
For Max, he late had touch'd their stones, but yet
He saw them seam'd with gold and precious ores,
Rich with hill flow'rs and musical with rills.
"Or that same bud that will be Katie's heart,
"Against the time your deep, dim woods are clear'd,
"And I have wrought my father to relent."
"How will you move him, sweet? Why, he will rage
"And fume and anger, striding o'er his fields,
"Until the last-bought king of herds lets down
130   "His lordly front, and rumbling thunder from
"His polish'd chest, returns his chiding tones.
"How will you move him, Katie, tell me how?"
"I'll kiss him and keep still — that way is sure,"
Said Katie, smiling. "I have often tried."
"God speed the kiss," said Max, and Katie sigh'd,
With pray'rful palms close seal'd, "God speed the axe!"

———————

O, light canoe, where dost thou glide?
Below thee gleams no silver'd tide,
But concave Heaven's chiefest pride.

———————

140   *Above thee burns Eve's rosy bar;*
Below thee throbs her darling star;
Deep 'neath thy keel her round worlds are!

———————

Above, below, O sweet surprise.
To gladden happy lover's eyes;
No earth, no wave — all jewell'd skies!

Part II.

The South Wind laid his moccasins aside,
Broke his gay calumet of flow'rs, and cast
His useless wampum,[4] beaded with cool dews,
Far from him, northward; his long, ruddy spear
Flung sunward, whence it came, and his soft locks   150
Of warm, fine haze grew silver as the birch,
His wigwam of green leaves began to shake;
The crackling rice-beds scolded harsh like squaws;
The small ponds pouted up their silver lips;
The great lakes ey'd the mountains, whisper'd "Ugh!
"Are ye so tall, O chiefs? Not taller than
"Our plumes can reach," and rose a little way,
As panthers stretch to try their velvet limbs,
And then retreat to purr and bide their time.
At morn the sharp breath of the night arose   160
From the wide prairies, in deep-struggling seas,
In rolling breakers, bursting to the sky;
In tumbling surfs, all yellow'd faintly thro'
With the low sun — in mad, conflicting crests,
Voic'd with low thunder from the hairy throats
Of the mist-buried herds; and for a man
To stand amid the cloudy roll and moil,
The phantom waters breaking overhead,
Shades of vex'd billows bursting on his breast,
Torn caves of mist wall'd with a sudden gold,   170
Reseal'd as swift as seen — broad, shaggy fronts,
Fire-ey'd and tossing on impatient horns
The wave impalpable — was but to think
A dream of phantoms held him as he stood.
The late, last thunders of the summer crash'd,
Where shrieked great eagles, lords of naked clifts.
The pulseless forest, lock'd and interlock'd
So closely, bough with bough, and leaf with leaf,
So serf'd[5] by its own wealth, that while from high
The Moons of Summer kiss'd its green-gloss'd locks,   180
And round its knees the merry West Wind danc'd,
And round its ring, compacted emerald,
The South Wind crept on moccasins of flame,
And the red fingers of th' impatient Sun
Pluck'd at its outmost fringes — its dim veins

---

4. **wampum** Beads made by North American natives, used as currency. 5. **serf'd** Satisfied.

Beat with no life — its deep and dusky heart,
In a deep trance of shadow, felt no throb
To such soft wooing answer: thro' its dream
Brown rivers of deep waters sunless stole;
190   Small creeks sprang from its mosses, and amaz'd,
Like children in a wigwam curtain'd close
Above the great, dead heart of some red chief,
Slipp'd on soft feet, swift stealing through the gloom,
Eager for light and for the frolic winds.
In this shrill Moon the scouts of Winter ran
From the ice-belted north, and whistling shafts
Struck maple and struck sumach — and a blaze
Ran swift from leaf to leaf, from bough to bough;
Till round the forest flash'd a belt of flame
200   And inward lick'd its tongues of red and gold
To the deep, tranced inmost heart of all.
Rous'd the still heart — but all too late, too late.
Too late, the branches welded fast with leaves,
Toss'd, loosen'd, to the winds — too late the Sun
Pour'd his last vigor to the deep, dark cells
Of the dim wood. The keen, two-bladed Moon
Of Falling Leaves roll'd up on crested mists;
And where the lush, rank[6] boughs had foiled the Sun
In his red prime, her pale, sharp fingers crept
210   After the wind and felt about the moss,
And seem'd to pluck from shrinking twig and stem
The burning leaves — while groan'd the shudd'ring wood.
Who journey'd where the prairies made a pause,
Saw burnish'd ramparts flaming in the sun,
With beacon fires, tall on their rustling walls.
And when the vast, horn'd herds at sunset drew
Their sullen masses into one black cloud,
Rolling thund'rous o'er the quick pulsating plain,
They seem'd to sweep between two fierce red suns
220   Which, hunter-wise, shot at their glaring balls[7]
Keen shafts, with scarlet feathers and gold barbs.
By round, small lakes with thinner forests fring'd,
More jocund[8] woods that sung about the feet
And crept along the shoulders of great cliffs,
The warrior stags, with does and tripping[9] fawns,
Like shadows black upon the throbbing mist
Of evening's rose, flash'd thro' the singing woods —
Nor tim'rous, sniff'd the spicy, cone-breath'd air;
For never had the patriarch of the herd
230   Seen, limn'd against the farthest rim of light

---

6. **rank** Luxurious and abundant. 7. **glaring balls** Eyes. 8. **jocund** Cheerful; merry. 9. **tripping** Sprightly.

Of the low-dipping sky, the plume or bow
Of the red hunter; nor, when stoop'd to drink,
Had from the rustling rice-beds heard the shaft
Of the still hunter hidden in its spears;
His bark canoe close-knotted in its bronze,
His form as stirless as the brooding air,
His dusky eyes, too, fix'd, unwinking, fires;
His bow-string tighten'd till it subtly sang
To the long throbs, and leaping pulse that roll'd
And beat within his knotted, naked breast.   240
There came a morn. The Moon of Falling Leaves,
With her twin silver blades, had only hung
Above the low-set cedars of the swamp
For one brief quarter, when the Sun arose
Lusty with light and full of summer heat,
And, pointing with his arrows at the blue,
Clos'd, wigwam curtains of the sleeping Moon,
Laugh'd with the noise of arching cataracts,
And with the dove-like cooing of the woods,
And with the shrill cry of the diving loon,   250
And with the wash of saltless, rounded seas,
And mock'd the white Moon of the Falling Leaves.
"Esa! esa! shame upon you, Pale Face!
"Shame upon you, Moon of Evil Witches!
"Have you kill'd the happy, laughing Summer?
"Have you slain the mother of the flowers
"With your icy spells of might and magic?
"Have you laid her dead within my arms?
"Wrapp'd her, mocking, in a rainbow blanket?
"Drown'd her in the frost-mist of your anger?   260
"She is gone a little way before me;
"Gone an arrow's flight beyond my vision;
"She will turn again and come to meet me,
"With the ghosts of all the slain flowers.
"In a blue mist round her shining tresses,
"In a blue smoke in her naked forests —
"She will linger, kissing all the branches;
"She will linger, touching all the places,
"Bare and naked, with her golden fingers,
"Saying, 'Sleep, and dream of me, my children;   270
"'Dream of me, the mystic Indian Summer;
"'I, who, slain by the cold Moon of Terror,
"'Can return across the Path of Spirits,
"'Bearing still my heart of love and fire,
"'Looking with my eyes of warmth and splendour,
"'Whisp'ring lowly thro' your sleep of sunshine,
"'I, the laughing Summer, am not turn'd

"'Into dry dust, whirling on the prairies, —
"'Into red clay, crush'd beneath the snowdrifts.
280   "'I am still the mother of sweet flowers
"'Growing but an arrow's flight beyond you —
"'In the Happy Hunting Ground — the quiver
"'Of great Manitou, where all the arrows
"'He has shot from his great bow of Pow'r,
"'With its clear, bright, singing cord of Wisdom,
"'Are re-gather'd, plum'd again and brighten'd,
"'And shot out, re-barb'd with Love and Wisdom;
"'Always shot, and evermore returning.
"'Sleep, my children, smiling in your heart-seeds
290   "'At the spirit words of Indian Summer!'
"Thus, O Moon of Falling Leaves, I mock you!
"Have you slain my gold-ey'd squaw, the Summer?"
The mighty morn strode laughing up the land,
And Max, the labourer and the lover, stood
Within the forest's edge, beside a tree;
The mossy king of all the woody tribes,
Whose clatt'ring branches rattl'd, shuddering,
As the bright axe cleav'd moon-like thro' the air,
Waking strange thunders, rousing echoes link'd
300   From the full, lion-throated roar, to sighs
Stealing on dove-wings thro' the distant aisles.
Swift fell the axe, swift follow'd roar on roar,
Till the bare woodland bellow'd in its rage,
As the first-slain slow toppl'd to his fall.
"O King of Desolation, art thou dead?"
Thought Max, and laughing, heart and lips, leap'd on
The vast, prone trunk. "And have I slain a King?
"Above his ashes will I build my house —
"No slave beneath its pillars, but — a King!"
310   Max wrought alone, but for a half-breed lad,
With tough, lithe sinews and deep Indian eyes,
Lit with a Gallic sparkle. Max, the lover, found
The labourer's arms grow mightier day by day —
More iron-welded as he slew the trees;
And with the constant yearning of his heart
Towards little Kate, part of a world away,
His young soul grew and shew'd a virile front,
Full muscl'd and large statur'd, like his flesh,
Soon the great heaps of brush were builded high,
320   And, like a victor, Max made pause to clear
His battle-field, high strewn with tangl'd dead.
Then roar'd the crackling mountains, and their fires
Met in high heaven, clasping flame with flame.
The thin winds swept a cosmos of red sparks

Across the bleak, midnight sky: and the sun
Walk'd pale behind the resinous, black smoke.
And Max car'd little for the blotted sun,
And nothing for the startl'd, outshone stars;
For Love, once set within a lover's breast,
Has its own Sun — its own peculiar sky,   330
All one great daffodil — on which do lie
The sun, the moon, the stars — all seen at once,
And never setting; but all shining straight
Into the faces of the trinity, —
The one belov'd, the lover, and sweet Love!
It was not all his own, the axe-stirr'd waste.
In these new days men spread about the earth
With wings at heel[10] — and now the settler hears,
While yet his axe rings on the primal woods,
The shrieks of engines rushing o'er the wastes;   340
Nor parts his kind to hew his fortunes out.
And as one drop glides down the unknown rock
And the bright-threaded stream leaps after it
With welded billions, so the settler finds out
His solitary footsteps beaten out,
With the quick rush of panting, human waves
Upheav'd by throbs of angry poverty,
And driven by keen blasts of hunger, from
Their native strands — so stern, so dark, so dear!
O, then, to see the troubl'd, groaning waves,   350
Throb down to peace in kindly, valley beds,
Their turbid bosoms clearing in the calm
Of sun-ey'd Plenty — till the stars and moon,
The blessed sun himself, has leave to shine
And laugh in their dark hearts! So shanties grew
Other than his amid the blacken'd stumps;
And children ran with little twigs and leaves
And flung them, shouting, on the forest pyres
Where burn'd the forest kings — and in the glow
Paus'd men and women when the day was done.   360
There the lean weaver ground anew his axe,
Nor backward look'd upon the vanish'd loom,
But forward to the ploughing of his fields,
And to the rose of Plenty in the cheeks
Of wife and children — nor heeded much the pangs
Of the rous'd muscles tuning to new work.
The pallid clerk look'd on his blister'd palms
And sigh'd and smil'd, but girded up his loins
And found new vigour as he felt new hope.

---

10. **With wings at heel** Rapidly.

370 The lab'rer with train'd muscles, grim and grave,
   Look'd at the ground and wonder'd in his soul,
   What joyous anguish stirr'd his darken'd heart,
   At the mere look of the familiar soil,
   And found his answer in the words — "*Mine own!*"
   Then came smooth-coated men, with eager eyes,
   And talk'd of steamers on the cliff-bound lakes;
   And iron tracks across the prairie lands;
   And mills to crush the quartz of wealthy hills;
   And mills to saw the great, wide-arm'd trees;
380 And mills to grind the singing stream of grain;
   And with such busy clamour mingled still
   The throbbing music of the bold, bright Axe —
   The steel tongue of the Present, and the wail
   Of falling forests — voices of the Past.
   Max, social-soul'd, and with his practised thews,
   Was happy, boy-like, thinking much of Kate,
   And speaking of her to the women-folk,
   Who, mostly, happy in new honeymoons
   Of hope themselves, were ready still to hear
390 The thrice-told tale of Katie's sunny eyes
   And Katie's yellow hair, and household ways;
   And heard so often, "There shall stand our home —
   "On yonder slope, with vines about the door!"
   That the good wives were almost made to see
   The snowy walls, deep porches, and the gleam
   Of Katie's garments flitting through the rooms;
   And the black slope all bristling with burn'd stumps
   Was known amongst them all as "Max's House."

   O, *Love builds on the azure sea,*
400 *And Love builds on the golden sand;*
   And Love builds on the rose-wing'd cloud.
   And sometimes Love builds on the land.

   O, *if Love build on sparkling sea —*
   And if Love build on golden strand[11] *—*
   And if Love build on rosy cloud —
   To Love these are the solid land.

---

11. **strand** Shore.

O, Love will build his lily walls,
And Love his pearly roof will rear, —
On cloud or land, or mist or sea —
Love's solid land is everywhere!   410

Part III.

The great farm house of Malcolm Graem stood
Square shoulder'd and peak roof'd upon a hill,
With many windows looking everywhere;
So that no distant meadow might lie hid,
Nor corn-field hide its gold — nor lowing herd
Browse in far pastures, out of Malcolm's ken.
He lov'd to sit, grim, grey, and somewhat stern,
And thro' the smoke-clouds from his short clay pipe
Look out upon his riches; while his thoughts
Swung back and forth between the bleak, stern past,   420
And the near future, for his life had come
To that close balance, when, a pendulum,
The memory swings between the "Then" and "Now";
His seldom speech ran thus two diff'rent ways:
"When I was but a laddie, thus I did";
Or, "Katie, in the fall I'll see to build
"Such fences or such sheds about the place;
"And next year, please the Lord, another barn."
Katie's gay garden foam'd about the walls,
'Leagur'd[12] the prim-cut modern sills, and rush'd   430
Up the stone walls — and broke on the peak'd roof.
And Katie's lawn was like a poet's sward,[13]
Velvet and sheer and di'monded with dew;
For such as win their wealth most aptly take
Smooth, urban ways and blend them with their own;
And Katie's dainty raiment[14] was as fine
As the smooth, silken petals of the rose;
And her light feet, her nimble mind and voice,
In city schools had learn'd the city's ways,
And grafts upon the healthy, lovely vine   440
They shone, eternal blossoms 'mid the fruit.
For Katie had her sceptre in her hand
And wielded it right queenly there and here,
In dairy, store-room, kitchen — ev'ry spot
Where women's ways were needed on the place.
And Malcolm took her through his mighty fields,
And taught her lore about the change of crops;
And how to see a handsome furrow plough'd;

---

12. **Leagur'd** Surrounded. 13. **sward** Lawn or meadow. 14. **raiment** Clothing; attire.

And how to choose the cattle for the mart;
450   And how to know a fair day's work when done;
And where to plant young orchards; for he said,
"God sent a lassie, but I need a son —
"Bethankit for His mercies all the same."
And Katie, when he said it, thought of Max —
Who had been gone two winters and two springs,
And sigh'd, and thought, "Would he not be your son?"
But all in silence, for she had too much
Of the firm will of Malcolm in her soul
To think of shaking that deep-rooted rock;
460   But hop'd the crystal current of his love
For his one child, increasing day by day,
Might fret with silver lip until it wore
Such channels thro' the rock that some slight stroke
Of circumstance might crumble down the stone.
The wooer, too, had come, Max prophesied;
Reputed wealthy; with the azure eyes
And Saxon-gilded locks — the fair, clear face,
And stalwart form that most women love,
And with the jewels of some virtues set
470   On his broad brow. With fires within his soul
He had the wizard skill to fetter down[15]
To that mere pink, poetic, nameless glow,
That need not fright a flake of snow away —
But, if unloos'd, could melt an adverse rock
Marrow'd with iron, frowning in his way.
And Malcolm balanc'd him by day and night;
And with his grey-ey'd shrewdness partly saw
He was not one for Kate; but let him come,
And in chance moments thought: "Well, let it be —
480   "They make a bonnie pair — he knows the ways
"Of men and things: can hold the gear I give,
"And, if the lassie wills it, let it be."
And then, upstarting from his midnight sleep,
With hair erect and sweat upon his brow
Such as no labor e'er had beaded there;
Would cry aloud, wide-staring thro' the dark —
"Nay, nay; she shall not wed him — rest in peace."
Then fully waking, grimly laugh and say:
"Why did I speak and answer when none spake?"
490   But still lie staring, wakeful, through the shades;
List'ning to the silence, and beating still
The ball of Alfred's merits to and fro —
Saying, between the silent arguments:

---

15. **fetter down** Control.

"But would the mother like it, could she know?
"I would there was a way to ring a lad
"Like a silver coin, and so find out the true;
"But Kate shall say him 'Nay' or say him 'Yea'
"At her own will." And Katie said him "Nay,"
In all the maiden, speechless, gentle ways
A woman has. But Alfred only laugh'd   500
To his own soul, and said in his wall'd mind:
"O, Kate, were I a lover, I might feel
"Despair flap o'er my hopes with raven wings;
"Because thy love is giv'n to other love.
"And did I love — unless I gain'd thy love,
"I would disdain the golden hair, sweet lips,
"Air-blown form and true violet eyes;
"Nor crave the beauteous lamp without the flame;
"Which in itself would light a charnel house.
"Unlov'd and loving, I would find the cure   510
"Of Love's despair in nursing Love's disdain —
"Disdain of lesser treasure than the whole.
"One cares not much to place against the wheel
"A di'mond lacking flame — nor loves to pluck
"A rose with all its perfume cast abroad
"To the bosom of the gale. Not I, in truth!
"If all man's days are three-score years and ten,
"He needs must waste them not, but nimbly seize
"The bright, consummate blossom that his will
"Calls for most loudly. Gone, long gone the days   520
"When Love within my soul for ever stretch'd
"Fierce hands of flame, and here and there I found
"A blossom fitted for him — all up-fill'd
"With love as with clear dew — they had their hour
"And burn'd to ashes with him, as he droop'd
"In his own ruby fires. No Phœnix he,
"To rise again because of Katie's eyes,
"On dewy wings, from ashes such as his!
"But now, another Passion bids me forth,
"To crown him with the fairest I can find,   530
"And makes me lover — not of Katie's face,
"But of her father's riches! O, high fool,
"Who feels the faintest pulsing of a wish
"And fails to feed it into lordly life!
"So that, when stumbling back to Mother Earth,
"His freezing lip may curl in cold disdain
"Of those poor, blighted fools who starward stare
"For that fruition, nipp'd and scanted here.
"And, while the clay o'ermasters all his blood —
"And he can feel the dust knit with his flesh —   540

"He yet can say to them, 'Be ye content;
"'I tasted perfect fruitage thro' my life,
"'Lighted all lamps of passion, till the oil
"'Fail'd from their wicks; and now, O now, I know
"'There is no Immortality could give
"'Such boon as this — to simply cease to be!
"'*There* lies your Heaven, O ye dreaming slaves,
"'If ye would only live to make it so;
"'Nor paint upon the blue skies lying shades
550   "'Of — what *is not*. Wise, wise and strong the man
"'Who poisons that fond haunter of the mind,
"'Craving for a hereafter with deep draughts
"'Of wild delights — so fiery, fierce, and strong,
"'That when their dregs are deeply, deeply drain'd,
"'What once was blindly crav'd of purblind[16] Chance,
"'Life, life eternal — throbbing thro' all space,
"'Is strongly loath'd — and with his face in dust,
"'Man loves his only Heav'n — six feet of Earth!'
"So, Katie, tho' your blue eyes say me 'Nay,'
560   "My pangs of love for gold must needs be fed,
"And shall be, Katie, if I know my mind."
Events were winds close nestling in the sails
Of Alfred's bark,[17] all blowing him direct
To his wish'd harbour. On a certain day,
All set about with roses and with fire;
One of three days of heat which frequent slip,
Like triple rubies, in between the sweet,
Mild, emerald days of summer, Katie went,
Drawn by a yearning for the ice-pale blooms,
570   Natant[18] and shining — firing all the bay
With angel fires built up of snow and gold.
She found the bay close pack'd with groaning logs,
Prison'd between great arms of close-hing'd wood,
All cut from Malcolm's forests in the west,
And floated hither to his noisy mills;
And all stamp'd with the potent "G." and "M.,"
Which much he lov'd to see upon his goods,
The silent courtiers owning him their king.
Out clear beyond, the rustling ricebeds sang,
580   And the cool lilies starr'd the shadow'd wave.
"This is a day for lily-love," said Kate,
While she made bare the lilies of her feet,
And sang a lily-song that Max had made,
That spoke of lilies — always meaning Kate.

———

16. **purblind** Slow in understanding; dull. 17. **bark** Ship. 18. **Natant** Floating.

"White Lady of the silver'd lakes,
Chaste Goddess of the sweet, still shrines,
    The jocund river fitful makes,
By sudden, deep gloom'd brakes,[19]
Close shelter'd by close weft and woof of vine,
Spilling a shadow gloomy-rich as wine,   590
Into the silver throne where thou dost sit,
Thy silken leaves all dusky round thee knit!

————

"Mild soul of the unsalted wave!
  White bosom holding golden fire!
Deep as some ocean-hidden cave
  Are fix'd the roots of thy desire,
Thro' limpid currents stealing up,
And rounding to the pearly cup.
    Thou dost desire,
With all thy trembling heart of sinless fire,   600
    But to be fill'd
    With dew distill'd
From clear, fond skies that in their gloom
Hold, floating high, thy sister moon.
Pale chalice of a sweet perfume,
Whiter-breasted than a dove —
To thee the dew is — love!"

————

Kate bared her little feet, and pois'd herself
On the first log close grating on the shore;
And with bright eyes of laughter, and wild hair —   610
A flying wind of gold — from log to log
Sped, laughing as they wallow'd in her track,
Like brown-scal'd monsters rolling, as her foot
Spurn'd each in turn with its rose-white sole.
A little island, out in middle wave,
With its green shoulder held the great drive[20] brac'd
Between it and the mainland; here it was
The silver lilies drew her with white smiles;
And as she touch'd the last great log of all,
It reel'd, upstarting, like a column brac'd   620
A second on the wave — and when it plung'd
Rolling upon the froth and sudden foam,

---

19. **brakes** Places overgrown with bushes or brambles. 20. **drive** A group of logs floating down a river.

Katie had vanish'd, and with angry grind
The vast logs roll'd together, — nor a lock
Of drifting, yellow hair — an upflung hand,
Told where the rich man's chiefest treasure sank
Under his wooden wealth. But Alfred, laid
With pipe and book upon the shady marge
Of the cool isle, saw all, and seeing hurl'd
630   Himself, and hardly knew it, on the logs.
By happy chance a shallow lapp'd the isle
On this green bank; and when his iron arms
Dash'd the bark'd monsters, as frail stems of rice,
A little space apart, the soft, slow tide
But reach'd his chest, and in a flash he saw
Kate's yellow hair, and by it drew her up,
And lifting her aloft, cried out, "O, Kate!"
And once again said, "Katie! is she dead?"
For like the lilies broken by the rough
640   And sudden riot of the armor'd logs,
Kate lay upon his hands; and now the logs
Clos'd in upon him, nipping his great chest,
Nor could he move to push them off again
For Katie in his arms. "And now," he said,
"If none should come, and any wind arise
"To weld these woody monsters 'gainst the isle,
"I shall be crack'd like any broken twig;
"And as it is, I know not if I die,
"For I am hurt — aye, sorely, sorely hurt!"
650   Then look'd on Katie's lily face, and said,
"Dead, dead or living? Why, an even chance.
"O lovely bubble on a troubl'd sea,
"I would not thou shouldst lose thyself again
"In the black ocean whence thy life emerg'd,
"But skyward steal on gales as soft as love,
"And hang in some bright rainbow overhead,
"If only such bright rainbow spann'd the earth."
Then shouted loudly, till the silent air
Rous'd like a frighten'd bird, and on its wings
660   Caught up his cry and bore it to the farm.
There Malcolm, leaping from his noontide sleep,
Upstarted as at midnight, crying out,
"She shall not wed him — rest you, wife, in peace!"
They found him, Alfred, haggard-ey'd and faint,
But holding Katie ever towards the sun,
Unhurt, and waking in the fervent heat.
And now it came that Alfred, being sick
Of his sharp hurts and tended by them both,
With what was like to love, being born of thanks,

Had choice of hours most politic[21] to woo,   670
And used his deed as one might use the sun,
To ripen unmellow'd fruit; and from the core
Of Katie's gratitude hop'd yet to nurse
A flow'r all to his liking — Katie's love.
But Katie's mind was like the plain, broad shield
Of a table di'mond, nor had a score of sides;
And in its shield, so precious and so plain,
Was cut, thro' all its clear depths — Max's name.
And so she said him "Nay" at last, in words
Of such true-sounding silver that he knew   680
He might not win her at the present hour,
But smil'd and thought — "I go, and come again!
"Then shall we see. Our three-score years and ten
"Are mines of treasure, if we hew them deep,
"Nor stop too long in choosing out our tools!"

Part IV.

From his far wigwam sprang the strong North Wind
And rush'd with war-cry down the steep ravines,
And wrestl'd with the giants of the woods;
And with his ice-club beat the swelling crests
Of the deep watercourses into death;   690
And with his chill foot froze the whirling leaves
Of dun and gold and fire in icy banks;
And smote the tall reeds to the harden'd earth;
And sent his whistling arrows o'er the plains,
Scatt'ring the ling'ring herds — and sudden paus'd
When he had frozen all the running streams,
And hunted with his war-cry all the things
That breath'd about the woods, or roam'd the bleak
Bare prairies swelling to the mournful sky.
"White squaw," he shouted, troubl'd in his soul,   700
"I slew the dead, wrestl'd with naked chiefs
"Unplum'd before, scalped of their leafy plumes;
"I bound sick rivers in cold thongs of death,
"And shot my arrows over swooning plains,
"Bright with the paint of death — and lean and bare.
"And all the braves of my loud tribe will mock
"And point at me — when our great chief, the Sun,
"Relights his Council fire in the Moon
"Of Budding Leaves: 'Ugh, ugh! he is a brave!
"'He fights with squaws and takes the scalps of babes!'   710
"And the least wind will blow his calumet —

---

21. **politic** Advantageous.

"Fill'd with the breath of smallest flow'rs — across
"The war-paint on my face, and pointing with
"His small, bright pipe, that never moved a spear
"Of bearded rice, cry, 'Ugh! he slays the dead!'
"O, my white squaw, come from thy wigwam grey,
"Spread thy white blanket on the twice-slain dead,
"And hide them, ere the waking of the Sun!"

———————

High grew the snow beneath the low-hung sky,
720   *And all was silent in the Wilderness;*
In trance of stillness Nature heard her God
Rebuilding her spent fires, and veil'd her face
While the Great Worker brooded o'er His work.

———————

"Bite deep and wide, O Axe, the tree,
What doth thy bold voice promise me?"

———————

"I promise thee all joyous things,
That furnish forth the lives of kings!

———————

"For ev'ry silver ringing blow,
Cities and palaces shall grow!"

———————

730   "Bite deep and wide, O Axe, the tree,
Tell wider prophecies to me."

———————

"When rust hath gnaw'd me deep and red,
A nation strong shall lift his head!

———————

"His crown the very Heav'ns shall smite,
Æons shall build him in his might!"

———————

"Bite deep and wide, O Axe, the tree;
Bright Seer, help on thy prophecy!"

———————

Max smote the snow-weigh'd tree and lightly laugh'd.
"See, friend," he cried to one that look'd and smil'd,
"My axe and I — we do immortal tasks —   740
"We build up nations — this my axe and I!"
"O," said the other with a cold, short smile,
"Nations are not immortal! Is there now
"One nation thron'd upon the sphere of earth,
"That walk'd with the first Gods, and saw
"The budding world unfold its slow-leav'd flow'r?
"Nay; it is hardly theirs to leave behind
"Ruins so eloquent that the hoary sage
"Can lay his hand upon their stones, and say:
"'These once were thrones!' The lean, lank lion peals   750
"His midnight thunders over lone, red plains.
"Long-ridg'd and crested on their dusty waves
"With fires from moons red-hearted as the sun;
"And deep re-thunders all the earth to him.
"For, far beneath the flame-fleck'd, shifting sands,
"Below the roots of palms, and under stones
"Of younger ruins, thrones, tow'rs and cities
"Honeycomb the earth. The high, solemn walls
"Of hoary ruins — their foundings all unknown
"(But to the round-ey'd worlds that walk   760
"In the blank paths of Space and blanker Chance) —
"At whose stones young mountains wonder, and the seas'
"New-silv'ring, deep-set valleys pause and gaze,
"Are rear'd upon old shrines, whose very Gods
"Were dreams to the shrine-builders of a time
"They caught in far-off flashes — as the child
"Half thinks he can remember how one came
"And took him in her hand and shew'd him that,
"He thinks, she call'd the sun. Proud ships rear high
"On ancient billows that have torn the roots   770
"Of cliffs, and bitten at the golden lips
"Of firm, sleek beaches, till they conquer'd all,
"And sow'd the reeling earth with salted waves.
"Wrecks plunge, prow foremost, down still, solemn slopes,
"And bring their dead crews to as dead a quay;
"Some city built before that ocean grew,
"By silver drops from many a floating cloud,
"By icebergs bellowing in their thoes of death,
"By lesser seas toss'd from their rocking cups,
"And leaping each to each; by dew-drops flung   780

"From painted sprays, whose weird leaves and flow'rs
"Are moulded for new dwellers on the earth,
"Printed in hearts of mountains and of mines.
"Nations immortal? Where the well-trimm'd lamps
"Of long-past ages, when Time seem'd to pause
"On smooth, dust-blotted graves that, like the tombs
"Of monarchs, held dead bones and sparkling gems?
"She saw no glimmer on the hideous ring
"Of the black clouds; no stream of sharp, clear light
790 "From those great torches, pass'd into the black
"Of deep oblivion. She seem'd to watch, but she
"Forgot her long-dead nations. When she stirr'd
"Her vast limbs in the dawn that forc'd its fire
"Up the black East, and saw the imperious red
"Burst over virgin dews and budding flow'rs,
"She still forgot her molder'd thrones and kings,
"Her sages and their torches, and their Gods,
"And said, 'This is my birth — my primal day!'
"She dream'd new Gods, and rear'd them other shrines,
800 "Planted young nations, smote a feeble flame
"From sunless flint, re-lit the torch of mind;
"Again she hung her cities on the hills,
"Built her rich tow'rs, crown'd her kings again,
"And with the sunlight on her awful wings
"Swept round the flow'ry cestus[22] of the earth,
"And said, 'I build for Immortality!'
"Her vast hand rear'd her tow'rs, her shrines, her thrones;
"The ceaseless sweep of her tremendous wings
"Still beat them down and swept their dust abroad;
810 "Her iron finger wrote on mountain sides
"Her deeds and prowess — and her own soft plume
"Wore down the hills! Again drew darkly on
"A night of deep forgetfulness; once more
"Time seem'd to pause upon forgotten graves —
"Once more a young dawn stole into her eyes —
"Again her broad wings stirr'd, and fresh, clear airs,
"Blew the great clouds apart; — again Time said,
"'This is my birth — my deeds and handiwork
"'Shall be immortal.' Thus and so dream on
820 "Fool'd nations, and thus dream their dullard sons.
"Naught is immortal save immortal — Death!"
Max paus'd and smil'd: "O, preach such gospel, friend,
"To all but lovers who most truly love;
"For *them*, their gold-wrought scripture glibly reads,
"All else is mortal but immortal — Love!"

---

22. **cestus** Girdle; belt.

"Fools! fools!" his friend said, "most immortal fools! —
"But pardon, pardon, for, perchance, you love?"
"Yes," said Max, proudly smiling, "thus do I
"Possess the world and feel eternity!"
Dark laughter blacken'd in the other's eyes: 830
"Eternity! why, did such Iris-arch
"Enring our worm-bored planet, never liv'd
"One woman true enough such tryst[23] to keep!"
"I'd swear by Kate," said Max; and then, "I had
"A mother, and my father swore by her."
"By Kate? Ah, that were lusty oath, indeed!
"Some other man will look into her eyes,
"And swear me roundly, 'By true Catherine!'
"As Troilus swore by Cressèd — so they say."
"You never knew my Kate," said Max, and pois'd   840
His axe again on high. "But let it pass —
"You are too subtle for me; argument
"Have I none to oppose yours with — but this,
"Get you a Kate, and let her sunny eyes
"Dispel the doubting darkness in your soul."
"And have not I a Kate? Pause, friend, and see.
"She gave me this faint shadow of herself
"The day I slipp'd the watch-star of our loves —
"A ring — upon her hand — she loves me, too;
"Yet tho' her eyes be suns, no Gods are they   850
"To give me worlds, or make me feel a tide
"Of strong Eternity set towards my soul;
"And tho' she loves me, yet am I content
"To know she loves me by the hour — the year —
"Perchance the second — as all women love."
The bright axe falter'd in the air, and ripp'd
Down the rough bark, and bit the drifted snow,
For Max's arm fell, wither'd in its strength,
'Long by his side. "Your Kate," he said; "your Kate!"
"Yes, mine, while holds her mind that way, my Kate;   860
"I sav'd her life, and had her love for thanks;
"Her father is Malcolm Graem — Max, my friend,
"You pale! What sickness seizes on your soul?"
Max laugh'd, and swung his bright axe high again:
"Stand back a pace — a too far-reaching blow
"Might level your false head with yon prone trunk —
"Stand back and listen while I say, 'You lie!'
"That is my Katie's face upon your breast,
"But 'tis my Katie's love lives in my breast —

---

23. **tryst** Appointment; meeting.

870   "Stand back, I say! my axe is heavy, and
        "Might chance to cleave a liar's brittle skull.
        "Your Kate! your Kate! your Kate! — hark, how the woods
        "Mock at your lie with all their woody tongues.
        "O, silence, ye false echoes! Not his Kate
        "But mine — I'm certain I will have your life!"
        All the blue heav'n was dead in Max's eyes;
        Doubt-wounded lay Kate's image in his heart,
        And could not rise to pluck the sharp spear out.
        "Well, strike, mad fool," said Alfred, somewhat pale;
880   "I have no weapon but these naked hands."
        "Aye, but," said Max, "you smote my naked heart!
        "O shall I slay him? — Satan, answer me —
        "I cannot call on God for answer here.
        "O Kate — !"
        A voice from God came thro' the silent woods
        And answer'd him — for suddenly a wind
        Caught the great tree-tops, con'd with high-pil'd snow,
        And smote them to and fro, while all the air
        Was sudden fill'd with busy drifts, and high
890   White pillars whirl'd amid the naked trunks,
        And harsh, loud groans, and smiting, sapless boughs
        Made hellish clamour in the quiet place.
        With a shrill shriek of tearing fibres, rock'd
        The half-hewn tree above his fated head;
        And, tott'ring, asked the sudden blast, "Which way?"
        And, answ'ring its windy arms, crash'd and broke
        Thro' other lacing boughs, with one loud roar
        Of woody thunder; all its pointed boughs
        Pierc'd the deep snow — its round and mighty corpse,
900   Bark-flay'd and shudd'ring, quiver'd into death.
        And Max — as some frail, wither'd reed, the sharp
        And piercing branches caught at him, as hands
        In a death-throe, and beat him to the earth —
        And the dead tree upon its slayer lay.
        "Yet hear we much of Gods; — if such there be,
        "They play at games of chance with thunderbolts,"
        Said Alfred, "else on me this doom had come.
        "This seals my faith in deep and dark unfaith!
        "Now, Katie, are you mine, for Max is dead —
910   "Or will be soon, imprison'd by those boughs,
        "Wounded and torn, sooth'd by the deadly palms
        "Of the white, trait'rous frost; and buried then
        "Under the snows that fill those vast, grey clouds,
        "Low-sweeping on the fretted[24] forest roof.

---

24. **fretted** Ornamental design work.

"And Katie shall believe you false — not dead;
"False, false! — and I? O, she shall find me true —
"True as a fabl'd devil to the soul
"He longs for with the heat of all Hell's fires.
"These myths serve well for simile, I see.
"And yet — down, Pity! Knock not at my breast,   920
"Nor grope about for that dull stone my heart;
"I'll stone thee with it, Pity! Get thee hence,
"Pity, I'll strangle thee with naked hands;
"For thou dost bear upon thy downy breast
"Remorse, shap'd like a serpent, and her fangs
"Might dart at me and pierce my marrow thro'.
"Hence, beggar, hence — and keep with fools, I say!
"He bleeds and groans! Well, Max, thy God or mine,
"Blind Chance, here play'd the butcher — 'twas not I.
"Down hands! Ye shall not lift his fall'n head.   930
"What cords tug at ye? What? Ye'd pluck him up
"And staunch his wounds? There rises in my breast
"A strange, strong giant, throwing wide his arms
"And bursting all the granite of my heart!
"How like to quiv'ring flesh a stone may feel!
"Why, it has pangs! I'll none of them. I know
"Life is too short for anguish and for hearts —
"So I wrestle with thee, giant! and my will
"Turns the thumb, and thou shalt take the knife.
"Well done! I'll turn thee on the arena dust,   940
"And look on thee. What? thou wert Pity's self,
"Stol'n in my breast; and I have slaughter'd thee —
"But hist — where hast thou hidden thy fell snake,
"Fire-fang'd Remorse? Not in my breast, I know,
"For all again is chill and empty there,
"And hard and cold — the granite knitted up.
"So lie there, Max — poor fond and simple Max,
"'Tis well thou diest; earth's children should not call
"Such as thee father — let them ever be
"Father'd by rogues and villains, fit to cope   950
"With the foul dragon Chance, and the black knaves
"Who swarm in loathsome masses in the dust.
"True Max, lie there, and slumber into death."

Part V.

Said the high hill, in the morning: "Look on me —
"Behold, sweet earth, sweet sister sky, behold
"The red flames on my peaks, and how my pines
"Are cressets[25] of pure gold; my quarried scars

---

25. **cressets** Torches mounted on or suspended from a pole.

"Of black crevasse and shadow-fill'd canon,[26]
"Are trac'd in silver mist. Now on my breast
960   "Hang the soft purple fringes of the night;
"Close to my shoulder droops the weary moon,
"Dove-pale, into the crimson surf the sun
"Drives up before his prow; and blackly stands
"On my slim, loftiest peak, an eagle with
"His angry eyes set sunward, while his cry
"Falls fiercely back from all my ruddy heights;
"And his bald eaglets, in their bare, broad nest,
"Shrill pipe their angry echoes: 'Sun, arise,
"'And show me that pale dove, beside her nest,
970   "'Which I shall strike with piercing beak and tear
"'With iron talons for my hungry young.'"
And that mild dove, secure for yet a space,
Half waken'd, turns her ring'd and glossy neck
To watch dawn's ruby pulsing on her breast,
And see the first bright golden motes slip down
The gnarl'd trunks about her leaf-deep nest,
Nor sees nor fears the eagle on the peak.

———————

"Aye, lassie, sing — I'll smoke my pipe the while,
"And let it be a simple, bonnie song,
980   "Such as an old, plain man can gather in
"His dulling ear, and feel it slipping thro'
"The cold, dark, stony places of his heart."
"Yes, sing, sweet Kate," said Alfred in her ear;
"I often heard you singing in my dreams
"When I was far away the winter past."
So Katie on the moonlit window lean'd,
And in the airy silver of her voice
Sang of the tender, blue "Forget-me-not."

———————

"Could every blossom find a voice,
        And sing a strain to me,
990   I know where I would place my choice,
        Which my delight should be.
    I would not choose the lily tall,
        The rose from musky grot;

---

26. canon Canyon.

But I would still my minstrel call
The blue 'Forget-me-not!'

————

"And I on mossy bank would lie
Of brooklet, ripp'ling clear;
And she of the sweet azure eye,
    Close at my list'ning ear,   1000
Should sing into my soul a strain
    Might never be forgot —
So rich with joy, so rich with pain,
The blue 'Forget-me-not!'

————

"Ah, ev'ry blossom hath a tale
    With silent grace to tell,
From rose that reddens to the gale
    To modest heather bell;
But O, the flow'r in ev'ry heart
    That finds a sacred spot   1010
To bloom, with azure leaves apart,
    Is the 'Forget-me-not!'

————

"Love plucks it from the mosses green
    When parting hours are nigh,
And places it Love's palms between,
    With many an ardent sigh;
And bluely up from grassy graves
    In some lov'd churchyard spot,
It glances tenderly and waves,
    The dear 'Forget-me-not!'"   1020

————

And with the faint, last cadence, stole a glance
At Malcolm's soften'd face — a bird-soft touch
Let flutter on the rugged, silver snarls
Of his thick locks, and laid her tender lips
A second on the iron of his hand.
"And did you ever meet," he sudden ask'd
Of Alfred, sitting pallid in the shade,
"Out by yon unco²⁷ place, a lad — a lad

———————————————

27. **unco** Unusual; extraordinary.

"Nam'd Maxwell Gordon; tall, and straight, and strong;
1030   "About my size, I take it, when a lad?"
And Katie at the sound of Max's name,
First spoken for such a space by Malcolm's lips,
Trembl'd and started, and let down her brow,
Hiding its sudden rose on Malcolm's arm.
"Max Gordon? Yes. Was he a friend of yours?"
"No friend of mine, but of the lassie's here —
"How comes he on? I wager he's a drone,
"And never will put honey in the hive."
"No drone," said Alfred, laughing; "when I left,
1040   "He and his axe were quarr'ling with the woods
"And making forests reel — love steels a lover's arm."
O, blush that stole from Katie's swelling heart,
And with its hot rose brought the happy dew
Into her hidden eyes. "Aye, aye! is that the way?"
Said Malcolm, smiling. "Who may be his love?"
"In that he is a somewhat simple soul,
"Why, I suppose he loves — " he paused, and Kate
Look'd up with two "Forget-me-nots" for eyes,
With eager jewels in their centres set
1050   Of happy, happy tears, and Alfred's heart
Became a closer marble than before.
" — Why I suppose he loves — his lawful wife."
"His wife! his wife!" said Malcolm, in amaze,
And laid his heavy hand on Katie's head;
"Did you two play me false, my little lass?
"Speak and I'll pardon! Katie, lassie, what?"
"He has a wife," said Alfred, "lithe and bronz'd,
"An Indian woman, comelier than her kind;
"And on her knee a child with yellow locks,
1060   "And lake-like eyes of mystic Indian brown.
"And so you knew him? He is doing well."
"False, false!" said Katie, lifting up her head.
"O, you know not the Max my father means!"
"He came from yonder farm-house on the slope."
"Some other Max — we speak not of the same."
"He has a red mark on his temple set."
"It matters not — 'tis not the Max we know."
"He wears a turquoise ring slung round his neck."
"And many wear them — they are common stones."
1070   "His mother's ring — her name was Helen Wynde."
"And there be many Helens who have sons."
"O Katie, credit me — it is the man."
"O not the man! Why, you have never told
"Us of the true soul that the true Max has;
"The Max we know has such a soul, I know."

"How know you that, my foolish little lass?"
Said Malcolm, a storm of anger bound
Within his heart, like Samson with green withs —
"Belike it is the false young cur we know!"
"No, no," said Katie, simply, and low-voic'd;   1080
"If he were traitor I must needs be false,
"For long ago love melted our two hearts,
"And time has moulded those two hearts in one,
"And he is true since I am faithful still."
She rose and parted, trembling as she went,
Feeling the following steel of Alfred's eyes,
And with the icy hand of scorn'd mistrust
Searching about the pulses of her heart —
Feeling for Max's image in her breast.
"To-night she conquers Doubt; to-morrow's noon   1090
"His following soldiers sap the golden wall,
"And I shall enter and possess the fort,"
Said Alfred, in his mind. "O Katie, child,
"Wilt thou be Nemesis,[28] with yellow hair,
"To rend my breast? for I do feel a pulse
"Stir when I look into thy pure-barb'd eyes —
"O, am I breeding that false thing, a heart,
"Making my breast all tender for the fangs
"Of sharp Remorse to plunge their hot fire in?
"I am a certain dullard! Let me feel   1100
"But one faint goad, fine as a needle's point,
"And it shall be the spur in my soul's side
"To urge the madd'ning thing across the jags
"And cliffs of life, into the soft embrace
"Of that cold mistress, who is constant too,
"And never flings her lovers from her arms —
"Not-Death, for she is still a fruitful wife,
"Her spouse the Dead, and their cold marriage yields
"A million children, born of mould'ring flesh —
"So Death and Flesh live on — immortal they!   1110
"I mean the blank-ey'd queen whose wassail bowl[29]
"Is brimm'd from Lethe,[30] and whose porch is red
"With poppies, as it waits the panting soul —
"She, she alone is great! No scepter'd slave
"Bowing to blind, creative giants, she;
"No forces seize her in their strong, mad hands,
"Nor say, 'Do this — be that!' Were there a God,
"His only mocker, she, great Nothingness!

---

28. Nemesis The Greek goddess of divine retribution. **29. wassail bowl** Liquor or punch bowl. **30. Lethe** River in Hades, whose water caused forgetfulness in those who drank from it.

"And to her, close of kin, yet lover too,
1120   "Flies this large nothing that we call the soul."

———

Doth true Love lonely grow?
             Ah, no! ah, no!
Ah, were it only so —

That it alone might show
Its ruddy rose upon its sapful tree,
  Then, then in dewy morn,
  Joy might his brow adorn
With Love's young rose as fair and glad as he.

———

But with Love's rose doth blow,
1130   *Ah, woe! ah, woe!*
Truth with its leaves of snow,
And Pain and Pity grow
With Love's sweet roses on its sapful tree!
  Love's rose buds not alone,
  But still, but still doth own
A thousand blossoms cypress-hued to see!

Part VI.

Who curseth Sorrow knows her not at all.
Dark matrix she, from which the human soul
Has its last birth; whence, with its misty thews,
1140 *Close-knitted in her blackness, issues out.*
Strong for immortal toil up such great heights.
As crown o'er crown rise through Eternity.
Without the loud, deep clamour of her wail,
The iron of her hands, the biting brine
Of her black tears, the Soul but lightly built
Of indeterminate spirit, like a mist
Would lapse to Chaos in soft, gilded dreams,
As mists fade in the gazing of the sun.
Sorrow, dark mother of the soul, arise!
1150 *Be crown'd with spheres where thy bless'd children dwell.*
Who, but for thee, were not. No lesser seat
Be thine, thou Helper of the Universe,
Than planet on planet pil'd! — thou instrument
Close-clasp'd within the great Creative Hand!

———

The Land had put his ruddy gauntlet on,
Of harvest gold, to dash in Famine's face.
And like a vintage wain,[31] deep dy'd with juice,
The great moon falter'd up the ripe, blue sky,
Drawn by silver stars — like oxen white
And horn'd with rays of light. Down the rich land   1160
Malcolm's small valleys, fill'd with grain, lip-high,
Lay round a lonely hill that fac'd the moon,
And caught the wine-kiss of its ruddy light.
A cusp'd, dark wood caught in its black embrace
The valleys and the hill, and from its wilds,
Spic'd with dark cedars, cried the Whip-poor-will.
A crane, belated, sail'd across the moon.
On the bright, small, close-link'd lakes green islets lay,
Dusk knots of tangl'd vines, or maple boughs,
Or tuft'd cedars, boss'd upon the waves.   1170
The gay, enamell'd children of the swamp
Roll'd a low bass to treble, tinkling notes
Of little streamlets leaping from the woods.
Close to old Malcolm's mills, two wooden jaws
Bit up the water on a sloping floor;
And here, in season, rush'd the great logs down,
To seek the river winding on its way.
In a green sheen, smooth as a Naiad's locks,
The water roll'd between the shudd'ring jaws —
Then on the river-level roar'd and reel'd —   1180
In ivory-arm'd conflict with itself.
"Look down," said Alfred, "Katie, look and see
"How that but pictures my mad heart to you.
"It tears itself in fighting that mad love
"You swear is hopeless — hopeless — is it so?"
"Ah, yes!" said Katie, "ask me not again."
"But Katie, Max is false; no word has come,
"Nor any sign from him for many months,
"And — he is happy with his Indian wife."
She lifted eyes fair as the fresh, grey dawn   1190
With all its dews and promises of sun.
"O, Alfred! — saver of my little life —
"Look in my eyes and read them honestly."
He laugh'd till all the isles and forests laugh'd.
"O simple child! what may the forest flames
"See in the woodland ponds but their own fires?
"And have you, Katie, neither fears nor doubts?"

---

31. wain Farm wagon; cart.

She, with the flow'r-soft pinkness of her palm
Cover'd her sudden tears, then quickly said:
1200   "Fears — never doubts, for true love never doubts."
Then Alfred paus'd a space, as one who holds
A white doe by the throat and searches for
The blade to slay her. "This your answer still —
"You doubt not — doubt not this far love of yours,
"Tho' sworn a false young recreant, Kate, by me?"
"He is as true as I am," Katie said;
"And did I seek for stronger simile,
"I could not find such in the universe!"
"And were he dead? What, Katie, were he dead —
1210   "A handful of brown dust, a flame blown out —
"What then would love be strongly true to — Naught?"
"Still true to Love my love would be," she said,
And, faintly smiling, pointed to the stars.
"O fool!" said Alfred, stirr'd — as craters rock
To their own throes — and over his pale lips
Roll'd flaming stone, his molten heart. "Then, fool —
"Be true to what thou wilt — for he is dead.
"And there have grown this gilded summer past
"Grasses and buds from his unburied flesh.
1220   "I saw him dead. I heard his last, loud cry,
"'O Kate!' ring thro' the woods; in truth I did."
She half raised up a piteous, pleading hand,
Then fell along the mosses at his feet.
"Now will I show I love you, Kate," he said,
"And give you gift of love; you shall not wake
"To feel the arrow, feather-deep, within
"Your constant heart. For me, I never meant
"To crawl an hour beyond what time I felt
"The strange, fang'd monster that they call Remorse
1230   "Fold round my waken'd heart. The hour has come;
"And as Love grew, the welded folds of steel
"Slipp'd round in horrid zones. In Love's flaming eyes
"Stared its fell eyeballs, and with Hydra[32] head
"It sank hot fangs in breast, and brow and thigh.
"Come, Kate! O Anguish is a simple knave
"Whom hucksters[33] could outwit with small trade lies,
"When thus so easily his smarting thralls
"May flee his knout! Come, come, my little Kate;
"The black porch with its fringe of poppies waits —
1240   "A propylaeum[34] hospitably wide, —

---

32. Hydra Multi-headed serpent slain by Hercules. **33. hucksters** Peddlers; hawkers. **34. propylaeum** Entrance or vestibule to a temple area.

"No lictors with their fasces[35] at its jaws,
"Its floor as kindly to my fire-vein'd feet
"As to thy silver, lilied, sinless ones.
"O you shall slumber soundly, tho' the white,
"Wild waters pluck the crocus of your hair,
"And scaly spies stare with round, lightless eyes
"At your small face laid on my stony breast.
"Come, Kate! I must not have you wake, dear heart,
"To hear you cry, perchance, on your dead Max."
He turn'd her still face close upon his breast,   1250
And with his lips upon her soft, ring'd hair,
Leap'd from the bank, low shelving o'er the knot
Of frantic waters at the long slide's foot.
And as the sever'd waters crash'd and smote
Together once again, — within the wave
Stunn'd chamber of his ear there peal'd a cry:
"O Kate! stay, madman; traitor, stay! O Kate!"

_____

Max, gaunt as prairie wolves in famine time,
With long-drawn sickness, reel'd upon the bank —
Katie, new-rescu'd, waking in his arms.   1260
On the white riot of the waters gleam'd,
The face of Alfred, calm, with close-seal'd eyes,
And blood red on his temple where it smote
The mossy timbers of the groaning slide.
"O God!" said Max, as Katie's opening eyes
Looked up to his, slow budding to a smile
Of wonder and of bliss, "My Kate, my Kate!"
She saw within his eyes a larger soul
Than that light spirit that before she knew,
And read the meaning of his glance and words.   1270
"Do as you will, my Max. I would not keep
"You back with one light-falling finger-tip!"
And cast herself from his large arms upon
The mosses at his feet, and hid her face
That she might not behold what he would do;
Or lest the terror in her shining eyes
Might bind him to her, and prevent his soul
Work out its greatness; and her long, wet hair
Drew, mass'd, about her ears, to shut the sound
Of the vex'd waters from her anguish'd brain.   1280
Max look'd upon her, turning as he look'd.
A moment came a voice in Katie's soul:

---

35. **fasces** A bundle of roots bound around an axe to symbolize magisterial power.

"Arise, be not dismay'd, arise and look;
"If he should perish, 'twill be as a God,
"For he would die to save his enemy."
But answer'd her torn heart: "I cannot look —
"I cannot look and see him sob and die
"In those pale, angry arms. O, let me rest
"Blind, blind and deaf until the swift-pac'd end.
1290   "My Max! O God — was that his Katie's name?"
Like a pale dove, hawk-hunted, Katie ran,
Her fear's beak in her shoulder; and below,
Where the coil'd waters straighten'd to a stream,
Found Max all bruis'd and bleeding on the bank,
But smiling with man's triumph in his eyes,
When he has on fierce Danger's lion neck
Plac'd his right hand and pluck'd the prey away.
And at his feet lay Alfred, still and white,
A willow's shadow tremb'ling on his face.
1300   "There lies the false, fair devil, O my Kate,
"Who would have parted us, but could not, Kate!"
"But could not, Max," said Katie. "Is he dead?"
But, swift perusing Max's strange, dear face,
Close clasp'd against his breast — forgot him straight
And ev'ry other evil thing upon
The broad green earth.

Part VII.

Again rang out the music of the axe,
And on the slope, as in his happy dreams,
The home of Max with wealth of drooping vines
1310   On the rude walls; and in the trellis'd porch
Sat Katie, smiling o'er the rich, fresh fields;
And by her side sat Malcolm, hale and strong;
Upon his knee a little, smiling child,
Nam'd — Alfred, as the seal of pardon set
Upon the heart of one who sinn'd and woke
To sorrow for his sins — and whom they lov'd
With gracious joyousness — nor kept the dusk
Of his past deeds between their hearts and his.
Malcolm had follow'd with his flocks and herds
1320   When Max and Katie, hand in hand, went out
From his old home; and now, with slow, grave smile,
He said to Max, who twisted Katie's hair
About his naked arm, bare from his toil:
"It minds me of old times, this house of yours;

"It stirs my heart to hearken to the axe,
"And hear the windy crash of falling trees;
"Aye, these fresh forests make an old man young."
"Oh, yes!" said Max, with laughter in his eyes;
"And I do truly think that Eden bloom'd
"Deep in the heart of tall, green maple groves,   1330
"With sudden scents of pine from mountain sides,
"And prairies with their breasts against the skies.
"And Eve was only little Katie's height."
"Hoot, lad! you speak as ev'ry Adam speaks
"About his bonnie Eve; but what says Kate?"
"O Adam had not Max's soul," she said;
"And these wild woods and plains are fairer far
"Than Eden's self. O bounteous mothers they!
"Beck'ning pale starvelings with their fresh, green hands,
"And with their ashes mellowing the earth,   1340
"That she may yield her increase willingly.
"I would not change these wild and rocking³⁶ woods,
"Dotted by little homes of unbark'd trees,
"Where dwell the fleers from the waves of want, —
"For the smooth sward of selfish Eden bowers,
"Nor — Max for Adam, if I knew my mind!"

                                                                   (1884)

The Rose

The Rose was given to man for this:
    He, sudden seeing it in later years,
Should swift remember Love's first lingering kiss
    And Grief's last lingering tears;

Or, being blind, should feel its yearning soul
    Knit all its piercing perfume round his own,
Till he should see on memory's ample scroll
    All roses he had known;

Or, being hard, perchance his finger-tips
    Careless might touch the satin of its cup,   10
And he should feel a dead babe's budding lips
    To his lips lifted up;

Or, being deaf and smitten with its star,
    Should, on a sudden, almost hear a lark
Rush singing up — the nightingale afar
    Sing thro' the dew-bright dark;

---

36. **rocking** Swaying.

Or, sorrow-lost in paths that round and round
    Circle old graves, its keen and vital breath
Should call to him within the yew's bleak bound
20   Of Life, and not of Death.

(1883)

The Dark Stag

A startled stag, the blue-grey Night,
    Leaps down beyond black pines.
Behind — a length of yellow light —
    The hunter's arrow shines:
His moccasins are stained with red,
    He bends upon his knee,
From covering peaks his shafts are sped,
The blue mists plume his mighty head, —
    Well may the swift Night flee!
10   The pale, pale Moon, a snow-white doe,
    Bounds by his dappled flank:
They beat the stars down as they go,
    Like wood-bells growing rank.
The winds lift dewlaps from the ground,
    Leap from the quaking reeds;
Their hoarse bays shake the forests round,
With keen cries on the track they bound, —
    Swift, swift the dark stag speeds!

Away! his white doe, far behind,
20   Lies wounded on the plain;
Yells at his flank the nimblest wind,
    His large tears fall in rain;
Like lily-pads, small clouds grow white
    About his darkling way;
From his bald nest upon the height
The red-eyed eagle sees his flight;
He falters, turns, the antlered Night, —
    The dark stag stands at bay!

His feet are in the waves of space;
30   His antlers broad and dun
He lowers; he turns his velvet face
    To front the hunter, Sun;
He stamps the lilied clouds, and high
    His branches fill the west.
The lean stork sails across the sky,
The shy loon shrieks to see him die,
    The winds leap at his breast.

Roar the rent lakes as thro' the wave
　　Their silver warriors plunge,
As vaults from core of crystal cave　　　　　　　　　40
　　The strong, fierce muskallunge;
Red torches of the sumach glare,
　　Fall's council-fires are lit;
The bittern, squaw-like, scolds the air;
The wild duck splashes loudly where
　　The rustling rice-spears knit.

Shaft after shaft the red Sun speeds:
　　Rent the stag's dappled side,
His breast, fanged by the shrill winds, bleeds,
　　He staggers on the tide;　　　　　　　　　　　50
He feels the hungry waves of space
　　Rush at him high and blue;
Their white spray smites his dusky face,
Swifter the Sun's fierce arrows race
　　And pierce his stout heart thro'.

His antlers fall; once more he spurns
　　The hoarse hounds of the day;
His blood upon the crisp blue burns,
　　Reddens the mounting spray;
His branches smite the wave — with cries　　　　60
　　The loud winds pause and flag —
He sinks in space — red glow the skies,
The brown earth crimsons as he dies,
　　The strong and dusky stag.

　　　　　　　　　　　　　　　　　　　　　(1883)

The Canoe

My masters twain made me a bed
Of pine-boughs resinous, and cedar;
Of moss, a soft and gentle breeder
Of dreams of rest; and me they spread
With furry skins, and laughing said,
"Now she shall lay her polish'd sides,
As queens do rest, or dainty brides,
Our slender lady of the tides!"

My masters twain their camp-soul lit,
Streamed incense from the hissing cones,　　　　10
Large, crimson flashes grew and whirl'd
Thin, golden nerves of sly light curl'd
Round the dun camp, and rose faint zones,

Half way about each grim bole knit,
Like a shy child that would bedeck
With its soft clasp a Brave's red neck;
Yet sees the rough shield on his breast,
The awful plumes shake on his crest,
And fearful drops his timid face,
20   Nor dares complete the sweet embrace.

Into the hollow hearts of brakes,
Yet warm from sides of does and stags,
Pass'd to the crisp dark river flags;
Sinuous, red as copper snakes,
Sharp-headed serpents, made of light,
Glided and hid themselves in night.

My masters twain, the slaughter'd deer
Hung on fork'd boughs — with thongs of leather.
Bound were his stiff, slim feet together —
30   His eyes like dead stars cold and drear;
The wand'ring firelight drew near
And laid its wide palm, red and anxious,
On the sharp splendor of his branches;
On the white foam grown hard and sere
    On flank and shoulder.
Death — hard as breast of granite boulder,
    And under his lashes
Peer'd thro' his eyes at his life's gray ashes.

My masters twain sang songs that wove
40   (As they burnish'd hunting blade and rifle)
A golden thread with a cobweb trifle —
Loud of the chase, and low of love.

"O Love, art thou a silver fish?
Shy of the line and shy of gaffing,
Which we do follow, fierce, yet laughing,
Casting at thee the light-wing'd wish,
And at the last shall we bring thee up
From the crystal darkness under the cup
    Of lily folden,
50   On broad leaves golden?

"O Love! art thou a silver deer,
Swift thy starr'd feet as wing of swallow,
While we with rushing arrows follow;
And at the last shall we draw near,
And over thy velvet neck cast thongs —

Woven of roses, of stars, of songs?
  New chains all molden
  Of rare gems olden!"

They hung the slaughter'd fish like swords
On saplings slender — like scimitars
Bright, and ruddied from new-dead wars,
Blaz'd in the light — the scaly hordes.
                                        60

They pil'd up boughs beneath the trees,
Of cedar-web and green fir tassel;
Low did the pointed pine tops rustle,
The camp fire blush'd to the tender breeze.

The hounds laid dew-laps on the ground,
With needles of pine sweet, soft, and rusty —
Dream'd of the dead stag stout and lusty;
A bat by the red flames wove its round.
                                        70

The darkness built its wigwam walls
Close round the camp, and at its curtain
Press'd shapes, thin woven and uncertain,
As white locks of tall waterfalls.

                                      (1884)

The Lily Bed

His cedar paddle, scented, red,
He thrust down through the lily bed;

Cloaked in a golden pause he lay,
Locked in the arms of the placid bay.

Trembled alone his bark canoe
As shocks of bursting lilies flew

Thro' the still crystal of the tide,
And smote the frail boat's birchen side;

Or, when beside the sedges thin
Rose the sharp silver of a fin;
                                      10

Or when, a wizard swift and cold,
A dragon-fly beat out in gold

And jewels all the widening rings
Of waters singing to his wings;

Or, like a winged and burning soul,
Dropped from the gloom an oriole

On the cool wave, as to the balm
Of the Great Spirit's open palm

The freed soul flies. And silence clung
20 To the still hours, as tendrils hung,

In darkness carven, from the trees,
Sedge-buried to their burly knees.

Stillness sat in his lodge of leaves;
Clung golden shadows to its eaves,

And on its cone-spiced floor, like maize,
Red-ripe, fell sheaves of knotted rays.

The wood, a proud and crested brave;
Bead-bright, a maiden, stood the wave.

And he had spoke his soul of love
30 With voice of eagle and of dove.

Of loud, strong pines his tongue was made;
His lips, soft blossoms in the shade,

That kissed her silver lips — her's cool
As lilies on his inmost pool —

Till now he stood, in triumph's rest,
His image painted in her breast.

One isle 'tween blue and blue did melt, —
A bead of wampum from the belt

Of Manitou — a purple rise
40 On the far shore heaved to the skies.

His cedar paddle, scented, red,
He drew up from the lily bed;

All lily-locked, all lily-locked,
His light bark in the blossoms rocked.

Their cool lips round the sharp prow sang,
Their soft clasp to the frail sides sprang,

With breast and lip they wove a bar.
Stole from her lodge the Evening Star;

With golden hand she grasped the mane
Of a red cloud on her azure plain.

50

It by the peaked, red sunset flew;
Cool winds from its bright nostrils blew.

They swayed the high, dark trees, and low
Swept the locked lilies to and fro.

With cedar paddle, scented, red,
He pushed out from the lily bed.

(1884)

Charles G.D. Roberts (1860–1943)

Charles George Douglas Roberts was born on 10 January 1860, in Douglas, New Brunswick. When he was only a few months old, his father, George Goodridge Roberts, was made Anglican rector of Westcock, New Brunswick, and the family relocated there. Roberts spent his youth in Tantramar county near the now renowned marshes. These rural surroundings shaped his childhood experience and informed his later writing. Because the area lacked a proper educational institution, George Goodridge Roberts acted as a tutor for his son. The child was assigned farm duties on the plot of land that bordered the parish, and his father also taught him woodcraft and hunting.

In 1874, Roberts's father became the rector of Christ Church Parish Church in Fredericton, and the family moved once more. Roberts adjusted well to city life and to institutionalized learning. He received a classical education at the Fredericton Collegiate School — his cousin and close friend Bliss Carman was a fellow student — and in 1879, he graduated from the University of New Brunswick with training in the British literary tradition, honours in mental and moral philosophy and political economy, a scholarship in Latin and Greek, and recognition for Latin prose composition.

Roberts's academic achievements landed him a position as headmaster of the grammar school in Chatham, New Brunswick. In the autumn of 1880, he published *Orion and Other Poems*, and it met with great acclaim. That winter, he married Mary Isabel Fenety, and the next few years were active ones for the Roberts family. Charles struggled to find employment that better suited his needs and interests. In 1881, he was awarded a master's degree from the University of New Brunswick; and in 1882, he became principal of the York Street School in Fredericton. Still feeling that his job was consuming time and energy that would be better spent writing, Roberts moved his young family to Toronto, where he became the editor of Goldwin Smith's new periodical *The Week*. Unfortunately, Smith's political views — namely, his support for the annexation of Canada by the United States — clashed with Roberts's growing Canadian nationalism. The poet left *The Week* in February of 1884.

After a period of upheaval and uncertainty, Roberts found stable employment as a professor at King's College in Windsor, Nova Scotia, in 1885. He stayed there for the next 10 years. This decade was to be the most productive of Roberts's life. He published two volumes of poetry — *In Divers Tones* (1886) and *Songs of the Common Day and Ave* (1893) — and he began to publish fiction, including a collection of animal stories, *Earth's Enigmas* (1895), and several novels. But Roberts's restlessness persisted. In the spring of 1897, he left his family in Fredericton (he and

Mary would remain separated, and she died in 1930) to work in New York; in 1907, he left North America for Europe.

While overseas, Roberts fought in World War I, first for the British, and then for Canada. When he returned to Canada in 1925 on a lecture tour, he discovered that he had become famous in his home country. He spent the rest of his years writing, lecturing, and working on the editorial boards of various Canadian literary projects.

In his early writing, Roberts was clearly influenced by the British Romantic tradition, especially by the poetry of John Keats. Like his British predecessors, Roberts revelled in both pastoral and sublime images of nature. Yet he departed from these conventions in describing the changeable and sometimes violent Canadian wilderness. Critics hold that Roberts's poetry underwent a transformation during his New York years. His later works betray the influence of the Pre-Raphaelites — or, as critic James Cappon notes, "the sentimental and erotic poetry of the Rossetti school." Of the vast amount of fictional and non-fictional prose Roberts produced in the course of his career, his animal stories are the most celebrated examples. In these works, the author blends the conventions of the animal adventure story and the animal biography with impeccable attention to detail. He is considered to be a master of the genre.

Roberts holds a curious position in Canadian literary history. As Glenn Clever points out, "on the one hand called the Father of Canadian Literature, and on the other one of the recipients of F.R. Scott's opprobrium in 'The Canadian Authors Meet,' Roberts has no reserved seat in the Canadian literary pantheon." Indeed, literary critics see Roberts at the head of the group of writers known as the Confederation Poets; the enthusiasm and energy with which he promoted these and other Canadian writers during his lifetime are truly remarkable. However, the generation of poets that succeeded Roberts viewed the Confederation School as representative of a Romantic poetic tradition that had to be jettisoned to make room for new, more modern Canadian voices. Consequently, although Roberts is regularly acknowledged in anthologies and histories of Canadian literature, there is a lack of critical attention to his oeuvre.

The Tantramar[1] Revisited

Summers and summers have come, and gone with the flight of the swallow;
Sunshine and thunder have been, storm, and winter, and frost;
Many and many a sorrow has all but died from remembrance,
Many a dream of joy fall'n in the shadow of pain.
Hands of chance and change have marred, or moulded, or broken,
Busy with spirit or flesh, all I most have adored;
Even the bosom of Earth is strewn with heavier shadows, —
Only in these green hills, aslant to the sea, no change!
Here where the road that has climbed from the inland valleys and woodlands,
10   Dips from the hill-tops down, straight to the base of the hills, —
Here, from my vantage-ground, I can see the scattering houses,
Stained with time, set warm in orchards, meadows, and wheat,
Dotting the broad bright slopes outspread to southward and eastward,
Wind-swept all day long, blown by the south-east wind.

---

1. **Tantramar** Saltwater tidal marsh on the isthumus between New Brunswick and Nova Scotia.

Skirting the sunbright uplands stretches a riband[2] of meadow,
Shorn of the labouring grass, bulwarked[3] well from the sea,
Fenced on its seaward border with long clay dikes[4] from the turbid[5]
Surge and flow of the tides vexing the Westmoreland shores.
Yonder, toward the left, lie broad the Westmoreland marshes, —

Miles on miles they extend, level, and grassy, and dim,   20
Clear from the long red sweep of flats to the sky in the distance,
Save for the outlying heights, green-rampired[6] Cumberland Point;
Miles on miles outrolled, and the river-channels divide them, —
Miles on miles of green, barred by the hurtling gusts.
Miles on miles beyond the tawny bay is Minudie.
There are the low blue hills; villages gleam at their feet.
Nearer a white sail shines across the water, and nearer
Still are the slim, gray masts of fishing boats dry on the flats.
Ah, how well I remember those wide red flats, above tide-mark
Pale with scurf of the salt, seamed and baked in the sun!   30
Well I remember the piles of blocks and ropes, and the net-reels
Wound with the beaded nets, dripping and dark from the sea!
Now at this season the nets are unwound; they hang from the rafters
Over the fresh-stowed hay in upland barns, and the wind
Blows all day through the chinks,[7] with the streaks of sunlight, and sways them
Softly at will; or they lie heaped in the gloom of a loft.

Now at this season the reels are empty and idle; I see them
Over the lines of the dykes, over the gossiping grass.
Now at this season they swing in the long strong wind, thro' the lonesome
Golden afternoon, shunned by the foraging gulls.   40
Near about sunset the crane will journey homeward above them;
Round them, under the moon, all the calm night long,
Winnowing soft gray wings of marsh-owls wander and wander,
Now to the broad, lit marsh, now to the dusk of the dike.
Soon, thro' their dew-wet frames, in the live keen freshness of morning,
Out of the teeth of the dawn blows back the awakening wind.
Then, as the blue day mounts, and the low-shot shafts of the sunlight
Glance from the tide to the shore, gossamers[8] jewelled with dew
Sparkle and wave, where late sea-spoiling fathoms of drift-net
Myriad-meshed, uploomed sombrely over the land.   50

Well I remember it all. The salt raw scent of the margin;
While, with men at the windlass, groaned each reel, and the net,
Surging in ponderous lengths, uprose and coiled in its station;
Then each man to his home, — well I remember it all!

---

2. **riband** Ribbon. 3. **bulwarked** Protected by a breakwater. 4. **dikes** Short walls of earth to prevent flooding.
5. **turbid** Clouded. 6. **green-rampired** Protected by green embankments. 7. **chinks** Cracks. 8. **gossamers** Something delicate or light.

Yet, as I sit and watch, this present peace of the landscape, —
Stranded boats, these reels empty and idle, the hush,
One grey hawk slow-wheeling above yon cluster of haystacks, —
More than the old-time stir this stillness welcomes me home.
Ah, the old-time stir, how once it stung me with rapture, —
60   Old-time sweetness, the winds freighted with honey and salt!
Yet will I stay my steps and not go down to the marsh-land, —
Muse and recall far off, rather remember than see, —
Lest on too close sight I miss the darling illusion,
Spy at their task even here the hands of chance and change.

(1883)

The Furrow

How sombre slope these acres to the sea
    And to the breaking sun! The sun-rise deeps
    Of rose and crocus, whence the far dawn leaps,
Gild[1] but with scorn their grey monotony.

The glebe[2] rests patient for its joy to be.
    Past the salt field-foot many a dim wing sweeps;
    And down the field a first slow furrow creeps,
Pledge of near harvests to the unverdured[3] lea.

With clank of harness tramps the serious team.[4]
10   With sea air thrills their nostrils. Some wise crows
    Feed confidently behind the ploughman's feet.
In the early chill the clods fresh cloven steam,
    And down its griding[5] path the keen share[6] goes.
    So, from a scar, best flowers the future's sweet.

(1890)

The Sower

A brown, sad-coloured hillside, where the soil
    Fresh from the frequent harrow,[1] deep and fine,
    Lies bare; no break in the remote sky-line,
Save where a flock of pigeons streams aloft,
Startled from feed in some low-lying croft,
    Or far-off spires[2] with yellow of sunset shine;
    And here the Sower, unwittingly divine,
Exerts the silent forethought of his toil.

---

1. **Gild** Coated, made bright. 2. **glebe** A church's farmable land; the term is primarily British. 3. **unverdured** Not greened by vegetation. 4. **team** Working cattle. 5. **griding** Cutting with a harsh sound. 6. **share** Plowshare.

---

1. **harrow** Farming tool dragged over land to level and groom it. 2. **spires** Point which tapers and points upwards.

Alone he treads the glebe,[3] his measured stride
   Dumb[4] in the yielding soil; and though small joy   10
   Dwell in his heavy face, as spreads the blind
Pale grain from his dispensing palm aside,
   This plodding churl[5] grows great in his employ; —
God-like, he makes provision for mankind.

(1884)

The Potato Harvest

A high bare field, brown from the plough, and borne
   Aslant from sunset; amber wastes of sky
   Washing the ridge; a clamour of crows that fly
In from the wide flats where the spent tides mourn
To yon their rocking roosts in pines wind-torn;
   A line of grey snake-fence, that zigzags by
   A pond, and cattle; from the homestead nigh
The long deep summonings of the supper horn.

Black on the ridge, against that lonely flush,
   A cart, and stoop-necked oxen; ranged beside   10
     Some barrels; and the day-worn harvest-folk,
Here emptying their baskets, jar the hush
   With hollow thunders. Down the dusk hillside
     Lumbers the wain;[1] and day fades out like smoke.

(1886)

The Waking Earth

With shy bright clamour the live brooks sparkle and run.
   Freed flocks confer about the farmstead ways.
   The air's a wine of dreams and shining haze,
Beaded with bird-notes thin, — for Spring's begun!
The sap flies upward. Death is over and done.
   The glad earth wakes; the glad light breaks; the days
   Grow round, grow radiant. Praise for the new life! Praise
For bliss of breath and blood beneath the sun!

What potent wizardry the wise earth wields,
To conjure with a perfume! From bare fields   10
   The sense drinks in a breath of furrow and sod.
And lo, the bound of days and distance yields;

---

3. **glebe** A church's farmable land; the term is primarily British. 4. **Dumb** Silent. 5. **churl** Rustic person.

1. **Lumbers the wain** The farm cart moves slowly and clumsily.

And fetterless[1] the soul is flown abroad,
Lord of desire and beauty, like a god!

(1889)

The Cow Pasture

I see the harsh, wind-ridden, eastward hill,
   By the red cattle pastured, blanched with dew;
   The small, mossed hillocks where the clay gets through;
The grey webs woven on milkweed tops at will.
The sparse, pale grasses flicker, and are still.
   The empty flats yearn seaward. All the view
   Is naked to the horizon's utmost blue;
And the bleak spaces stir me with strange thrill.

Not in perfection dwells the subtler power
10   To pierce our mean content, but rather works
        Through incompletion, and the need that irks, —
Not in the flower, but effort toward the flower.
        When the want stirs, when the soul's cravings urge,
        The strong earth strengthens, and the clean heavens purge.

(1893)

When Milking-Time Is Done

When milking-time is done, and over all
   This quiet Canadian inland forest home
   And wide rough pasture-lots the shadows come,
And dews, with peace and twilight voices, fall,
From moss-cooled watering-trough to foddered[1] stall
   The tired plough-horses turn, — the barnyard loam[2]
   Soft to their feet, — and in the sky's pale dome
Like resonant chords the swooping night-hawks call.

The frogs, cool-fluting ministers of dream,
10   Make shrill the slow brook's borders; pasture bars
        Down clatter, and the cattle wander through, —
Vague shapes amid the thickets; gleam by gleam
        Above the wet grey wilds emerge the stars,
        And through the dusk the farmstead fades from view.

(1889)

---

1. fetterless Unbound.

---

1. foddered Containing food for farm animals. **2. loam** Heavy soil.

Frogs

Here in the red heart of the sunset lying,
   My rest an islet of brown weeds blown dry,
   I watch the wide bright heavens, hovering nigh,
My plain and pools in lucent[1] splendour dyeing.
My view dreams over the rosy wastes, descrying
   The reed-tops fret the solitary sky;
   And all the air is tremulous to the cry
Of myriad frogs on mellow pipes replying.

For the unrest of passion here is peace,
   And eve's cool drench for midday soil and taint.   10
To tired ears how sweetly brings release
   This limpid[2] babble from life's unstilled complaint;
   While under tired eyelids lapse and faint
The noon's derisive visions — fade and cease.

                     (1888)

The Pea-Fields

These are the fields of light, and laughing air,
   And yellow butterflies, and foraging bees,
   And whitish, wayward blossoms winged as these,
And pale green tangles like a seamaid's hair.
Pale, pale the blue, but pure beyond compare,
   And pale the sparkle of the far-off seas,
   A-shimmer like these fluttering slopes of peas,
And pale the open landscape everywhere.

From fence to fence a perfumed breath exhales
   O'er the bright pallor of the well-loved fields, —   10
My fields of Tantramar in summer-time;
   And, scorning the poor feed their pasture yields,
Up from the bushy lots the cattle climb,
   To gaze with longing through the grey, mossed rails.

                     (1891)

The Mowing

This is the voice of high midsummer's heat.
   The rasping vibrant clamour soars and shrills
   O'er all the meadowy range of shadeless hills,
As if a host of giant cicadae[1] beat

---

1. lucent Clear or shining. **2. limpid** Clear.

---

1. cicadae Type of bug similar to locusts or crickets, which make cricket-like sounds.

The cymbals of their wings with tireless feet,
   Or brazen grasshoppers with triumphing note
   From the long swath proclaimed the fate that smote
The clover and timothy-tops and meadowsweet.

The crying knives glide on; the green swath lies.
10   And all noon long the sun, with chemic[2] ray,
   Seals up each cordial essence in its cell,
That in the dusky stalls, some winter's day,
   The spirit of June, here prisoned by his spell,
May cheer the herds with pasture memories.

(1890)

The Winter Fields

Winds here, and sleet, and frost that bites like steel.
   The low bleak hill rounds under the low sky.
   Naked of flock and fold the fallows[1] lie,
Thin streaked with meagre drift. The gusts reveal
By fits the dim grey snakes of fence, that steal
   Through the white dusk. The hill-foot poplars sigh,
   While storm and death with winter trample by,
And the iron fields ring sharp, and blind lights reel.

Yet in the lonely ridges, wrenched with pain,
10   Harsh solitary hillocks,[2] bound and dumb,
Grave glebes[3] close-lipped beneath the scourge and chain,
   Lurks hid the germ of ecstasy — the sum
Of life that waits on summer, till the rain
   Whisper in April and the crocus come.

(1890)

The Flight of the Geese

I hear the low wind wash the softening snow,
   The low tide loiter down the shore. The night,
   Full filled with April forecast, hath no light.
The salt wave on the sedge-flat pulses slow.
Through the hid furrows lisp in murmurous flow
   The thaw's shy ministers; and hark! The height
   Of heaven grows weird and loud with unseen flight
Of strong hosts prophesying as they go!

High through the drenched and hollow night their wings
10   Beat northward hard on Winter's trail. The sound

---

2. **chemic** Chemical.

---

1. **fallows** Unseeded farmland. 2. **hillocks** Small hills. 3. **glebes** Farmable church lands.

Of their confused and solemn noises, borne
Athwart[1] the dark to their long Arctic morn,
   Comes with a sanction and an awe profound,
A boding of unknown, foreshadowed things.

(1890)

O Solitary of the Austere Sky

O Solitary of the austere sky,
   Pale presence of the unextinguished star,
That from thy station where the spheres wheel by,
   And quietudes of infinite patience are,
Watchest this wet, grey-visaged world emerge, —
   Cold pinnacle on pinnacle, and deep
On deep of ancient wood and wandering surge, —
   Out of the silence and the mists of sleep;
How small am I in thine august[1] regard!
   Invisible, — and yet I know my worth!   10
When comes the hour to break this prisoning shard,
   And reunite with Him that breathed me forth,
Then shall this atom of the Eternal Soul
Encompass thee in its benign control!

(1892)

The Iron Edge of Winter

The glory of the leaves was gone; the glory of the snow was not yet come; and the world, smitten with bitter frost, was grey like steel. The ice was black and clear and vitreous[1] on the forest pools. The clods on the ploughed field, the broken hillocks in the pasture, the ruts of the winding backwoods road, were hard as iron and rang under the travelling hoof. The silent, naked woods, moved only by the bleak wind drawing through them from the north, seemed as if life had forgotten them.

Suddenly there came a light thud, thud, thud, with a pattering of brittle leaves; and a leisurely rabbit hopped by, apparently on no special errand. At the first of the sounds, a small, ruddy head with bulging, big, bright eyes had appeared at the mouth of a hole under the roots of an ancient maple. The bright eyes noted the rabbit at once, and peered about anxiously to see if any enemy were following. There was no danger in sight.

Within two or three feet of the hole under the maple the rabbit stopped, sat up as if begging, waved its great ears to and fro, and glanced around inquiringly with its protruding, foolish eyes. As it sat up, it felt beneath its whitey fluff of a tail something hard which was not a stone, and promptly dropped down again on all fours to investigate. Poking its nose among the leaves and scratching with its fore-paws, it uncovered a

---

1. **Athwart** Across.

---

1. **august** Awe-inspiring or majestic.

---

1. **vitreous** Glass-like.

pile of beech-nuts, at which it began to sniff. The next instant, with a shrill, chattering torrent of invective,[2] a red squirrel whisked out from the hole under the maple, and made as if to fly in the face of the big, good-natured trespasser. Startled and abashed by this noisy assault, the rabbit went bounding away over the dead leaves and disappeared among the desolate grey arches.

The silence was effectually dispelled. Shrieking and scolding hysterically, flicking his long tail in spasmodic jerks, and calling the dead solitudes to witness that the imbecile intruder had uncovered one of his treasure-heaps, the angry squirrel ran up and down the trunk for at least two minutes. Then, his feelings somewhat relieved by this violent outburst, he set himself to gathering the scattered nuts and bestowing them in new and safer hiding-places.

In this task he had little regard for convenience, and time appeared to be no object whatever. Some of the nuts he took over to a big elm fifty paces distant, and jammed them one by one, solidly and conscientiously, into the crevices of the bark. Others he carried in the opposite direction, to the edge of the open where the road ran by. These he hid under a stone, where the passing wayfarer might step over them, indeed, but would never think of looking for them. While he was thus occupied, an old countryman slouched by, his heavy boots making a noise on the frozen ruts, his nose red with the harsh, unmitigated cold. The squirrel, mounted on a fence stake, greeted him with a flood of whistling and shrieking abuse; and he, not versed in the squirrel tongue, muttered to himself half enviously: "Queer how them squur'ls can keep so cheerful in this weather." The tireless little animal followed him along the fence rails for perhaps a hundred yards, seeing him off the premises and advising him not to return, then went back in high feather to his task. When all the nuts were once more safely hidden but two or three, these latter he carried to the top of a stump close beside the hole in the maple, and proceeded to make a meal. The stump commanded a view on all sides; and as he sat up with a nut between his little, handlike, clever fore-paws, his shining eyes kept watch on every path by which an enemy might approach.

Having finished the nuts, and scratched his ears, and jumped twice around the stump as if he were full of erratically acting springs, he uttered his satisfaction in a long, vibrant chir-r-r-r, and started to re-enter his hole in the maple-roots. Just at the door, however, he changed his mind. For no apparent reason he whisked about, scurried across the ground to the big elm, ran straight up the tall trunk, and disappeared within what looked like a mass of sticks perched among the topmost branches.

The mass of sticks was a deserted crow's nest, which the squirrel, not content with one dwelling, had made over to suit his own personal needs. He greatly improved upon the architecture of the crows, giving the nest a tight roof of twigs and moss, and lining the snug interior with fine dry grass and soft fibres of cedar-bark. In this secure and softly swaying refuge, far above the reach of prowling foxes, he curled himself up for a nap after his toil.

He slept well, but not long; for the red squirrel has always something on his mind to see to. In less than half an hour he whisked out again in great excitement, jumped from branch to branch till he was many yards from his own tree, and then burst forth into vehement chatter. He must have dreamed that some one was rifling his hoards, for he ran eagerly from one hiding-place to another and examined them all suspiciously. As he had at least two-score[3] to inspect, it took him some time; but not till

---

2. **invective** Aggressive verbal abuse. 3. **two-score** Forty.

he had looked at every one did he seem satisfied. Then he grew very angry, and scolded and chirruped, as if he thought some one had made a fool of him. That he had made a fool of himself probably never entered his confident and self-sufficient little head.

While indulging this noisy volubility[4] he was seated on the top of his dining-stump. Suddenly he caught sight of something that smote him into silence and for the space of a second turned him to stone. A few paces away was a weasel, gliding toward him like a streak of baleful[5] light. For one second only he crouched. Then his faculties returned, and launching himself through the air he landed on the trunk of the maple and darted up among the branches.

No less swiftly the weasel followed, hungry, bloodthirsty, relentless on the trail. Terrified into folly by the suddenness and deadliness of the peril, the squirrel ran too far up the tree and was almost cornered. Where the branches were small there was no chance to swing to another tree. Perceiving this mistake, he gave a squeak of terror, then bounded madly right over his enemy's head, and was lucky enough to catch foothold far out on a lower branch. Recovering himself in an instant, he shot into the next tree, and thence to the next and the next. Then, breathless from panic rather than from exhaustion, he crouched trembling behind a branch and waited.

The weasel pursued more slowly, but inexorably as doom itself. He was not so clever at branch-jumping as his intended prey, but he was not to be shaken off. In less than a minute he was following the scent up the tree wherein the squirrel was hiding; and again the squirrel dashed off in his desperate flight. Twice more was this repeated, the squirrel each time more panic-stricken and with less power in nerve or muscle. Then wisdom forsook his brain utterly. He fled straight to his elm and darted into his nest in the swaying top. The weasel, running lithely up the ragged trunk, knew that the chase was at an end. From this *cul de sac* the squirrel had no escape.

But Fate is whimsical in dealing with the wild kindreds. She seems to delight in unlooked-for interventions. While the squirrel trembled in his dark nest, and the weasel, intent upon the first taste of warm blood in his throat, ran heedlessly up a bare stretch of trunk, there came the chance which a foraging hawk had been waiting for. The hawk, too, had been following this breathless chase, but ever baffled by intervening branches. Now he swooped and struck. His talons had the grip of steel. The weasel, plucked irresistibly from his foothold, was carried off writhing to make the great bird's feast. And the squirrel, realizing at last that the expected doom had been somehow turned aside, came out and chattered feebly of his triumph.

(1908)

Ernest Thompson Seton (1860–1946)

In his own time, Ernest Thompson Seton was internationally recognized as a naturalist, a painter, an illustrator, a prolific author of articles, and a woodsman. Over the course of his life, he received numerous commendations for his work in the natural and biological sciences. In the world of literature, however, he is better known for co-inventing, with Charles G.D. Roberts, the realistic animal story. For these stories, Seton drew on his extensive observations of animals in wilderness environments. The close attention Seton pays to the behaviour of individual animals stands, in a

---

4. **volubility** Chattiness. 5. **baleful** Villainous.

sense, as a critique of the more generic portrayals of animals offered by fiction writers and natural historians during the late 19th century.

Seton was born in South Shields, England, and he immigrated to Canada with his family in 1866. He was one of 10 sons. The Setons lived in Lindsay, Ontario, for four years, moving to Toronto in 1870. Seton excelled at his studies. He attended the Toronto Grammar School, the Ontario College of Art, and the Royal Academy of Art in England. By 1881, he had returned to Canada and was living in Carberry, Manitoba, where he undertook his first serious work as a nature artist. In 1892, Seton spent several months studying and trapping wolves in New Mexico, and he recounted this experience in "Lobo, the King of Currumpaw." He married a wealthy socialite and suffragette named Grace Gallatin in 1896; they had a daughter, Ann, in 1904, who (under the name Anya Seton) would go on to write popular historical novels. Seton retired to New Mexico in 1930. In 1934, he and Grace divorced, and the following year he married Julia Buttree, with whom he lived for the rest of his days at Seton Village, the naturalist centre they established near Santa Fe.

Seton wrote about 10,000 scientific and popular articles between 1884 and 1940. His literary career, however, began in 1894, with the publication of "Lobo," which was republished to great acclaim in his 1898 collection *Wild Animals I Have Known*. "Lobo," along with Charles G.D. Roberts's "Do Seek Their Meat from God" (1892), marked the introduction of a new fiction genre: the realistic animal story.

This type of tale departs from the traditional animal story in some important ways. Typical British animal fiction of the 19th century depicts animals as people in furry suits. They speak English, belong to various social classes, and often wear human clothing. Seton, however, was determined to present animals as animals, not as humans in disguise. In his "Note to the Reader" in *Wild Animals*, he calls his tales "biographies," and he claims to have taken "every incident … from life," as he witnessed it, or from reports by credible sources. His animals have unique personalities, display emotions, and occasionally seem capable of rational thought; they also communicate with one another, but, unlike the animals of Seton's literary predecessors, they are not overtly anthropomorphized.

Seton did not want to impose human values on the natural world or make animals symbolize human ideas. He was very careful to distinguish between what humans attribute to animals for symbolic purposes and what animals actually do. Like the authors who preceded him, he acknowledged that the human imagination can use the animal kingdom to better understand itself, but, with his stories, he was the first to argue that our conception of animals and the animals themselves are two very different things.

If either Seton's storytelling or his scientific method can be said to have a moral, it is "We and the beasts are kin." Each animal deserves, as does each human being, unbiased individual consideration. Seton was, ironically, both Romantic and Darwinian in his perspective, and he often chose as his animal subjects the most heroic, lonely, singular, or sublime. His preference for heroic narratives — in which one noble animal bests, for a time, either a human or another animal, and, after engaging in spectacular feats of cunning or strength, dies — makes his claim to realism somewhat problematic.

After *Wild Animals I Have Known*, Seton went on to publish over 20 collections of animal biographies. He also wrote "The Wild Animal Play for Children" (1900), and he published short stories for children and a novel, *The Preacher of Cedar Mountain* (1917). His interest in woodcraft inspired him to write guides and manuals based on his experiences as a naturalist and his knowledge of Native practices and folklore. One of them, *The Birch-Bark Roll* (1906), formed the basis for his boys' program, called the Woodcraft Indians. Seton sent a copy of the book to Lord

Baden-Powell, a British army general with a great interest in scouting. In 1908, when he founded the Boy Scouts, Baden-Powell adapted many of the Woodcraft Indians' practices and included them in his own manual, *Scouting for Boys*. In 1910, the Woodcraft Indians merged with the newly incorporated Boy Scouts of America. Seton, who had authored the *Boy Scouts of America Official Manual*, became the organization's first chief scout; however, in 1915, after he had protested the growing militarization of the group, Seton was dismissed — ostensibly because new rules required all scouts to be American citizens.

Seton's Woodcraft Indians program emphasized spiritual and emotional well-being as well as wilderness training. Much of his Woodcraft philosophy he owed to Native North American spiritualism, and he actively sympathized with and advocated Native causes throughout his life. Prior to the outbreak of World War II, Seton travelled across Canada, the U.S., and abroad, lecturing and writing articles. He died in Santa Fe at the age of 86.

Lobo, the King of Currumpaw

I

Currumpaw is a vast cattle range in northern New Mexico. It is a land of rich pastures and teeming flocks and herds, a land of rolling mesas[1] and precious running waters that at length unite in the Currumpaw River, from which the whole region is named. And the king whose despotic power was felt over its entire extent was an old gray wolf.

Old Lobo, or the king, as the Mexicans called him, was the gigantic leader of a remarkable pack of gray wolves, that had ravaged the Currumpaw Valley for a number of years. All the shepherds and ranchmen knew him well, and, wherever he appeared with his trusty band, terror reigned supreme among the cattle, and wrath and despair among their owners. Old Lobo was a giant among wolves, and was cunning and strong in proportion to his size. His voice at night was well-known and easily distinguished from that of any of his fellows. An ordinary wolf might howl half the night about the herdsman's bivouac[2] without attracting more than a passing notice, but when the deep roar of the old king came booming down the cañon, the watcher bestirred himself and prepared to learn in the morning that fresh and serious inroads had been made among the herds.

Old Lobo's band was but a small one. This I never quite understood, for usually, when a wolf rises to the position and power that he had, he attracts a numerous following. It may be that he had as many as he desired, or perhaps his ferocious temper prevented the increase of his pack. Certain is it that Lobo had only five followers during the latter part of his reign. Each of these, however, was a wolf of renown, most of them were above the ordinary size, one in particular, the second in command, was a veritable giant, but even he was far below the leader in size and prowess. Several of the band, besides the two leaders, were especially noted. One of those was a beautiful white wolf, that the Mexicans called Blanca; this was supposed to be a female, possibly Lobo's mate. Another was a yellow wolf of remarkable swiftness, which, according to current stories had, on several occasions, captured an antelope for the pack.

---

1. **mesas** Flat, elevated pieces of land surrounded by steep downward cliffs; common in the Southwestern U.S.
2. **bivouac** Temporary camp.

It will be seen, then, that these wolves were thoroughly well-known to the cow-boys and shepherds. They were frequently seen and oftener heard, and their lives were intimately associated with those of the cattlemen, who would so gladly have destroyed them. There was not a stockman on the Currumpaw who would not readily have given the value of many steers for the scalp of any one of Lobo's band, but they seemed to possess charmed lives, and defied all manner of devices to kill them. They scorned all hunters, derided all poisons, and continued, for at least five years, to exact their tribute from the Currumpaw ranchers to the extent, many said, of a cow each day. According to this estimate, therefore, the band had killed more than two thousand of the finest stock, for, as was only too well-known, they selected the best in every instance.

The old idea that a wolf was constantly in a starving state, and therefore ready to eat anything, was as far as possible from the truth in this case, for these freebooters were always sleek and well-conditioned, and were in fact most fastidious about what they ate. Any animal that had died from natural causes, or that was diseased or tainted, they would not touch, and they even rejected anything that had been killed by the stockmen. Their choice and daily food was the tenderer part of a freshly killed yearling heifer.[3] An old bull or cow they disdained, and though they occasionally took a young calf or colt, it was quite clear that veal or horseflesh was not their favorite diet. It was also known that they were not fond of mutton, although they often amused themselves by killing sheep. One night in November, 1893, Blanca and the yellow wolf killed two hundred and fifty sheep, apparently for the fun of it, and did not eat an ounce of their flesh.

These are examples of many stories which I might repeat, to show the ravages of this destructive band. Many new devices for their extinction were tried each year, but still they lived and throve in spite of all the efforts of their foes. A great price was set on Lobo's head, and in consequence poison in a score of subtle forms was put out for him, but he never failed to detect and avoid it. One thing only he feared — that was firearms, and knowing full well that all men in this region carried them, he never was known to attack or face a human being. Indeed, the set policy of his band was to take refuge in flight whenever, in the daytime, a man was descried, no matter at what distance. Lobo's habit of permitting the pack to eat only that which they themselves had killed, was in numerous cases their salvation, and the keenness of his scent to detect the taint of human hands or the poison itself, completed their immunity.

On one occasion, one of the cowboys heard the too familiar rallying-cry of Old Lobo, and stealthily approaching, he found the Currumpaw pack in a hollow, where they had "rounded up" a small herd of cattle. Lobo sat apart on a knoll, while Blanca with the rest was endeavoring to "cut out" a young cow, which they had selected; but the cattle were standing in a compact mass with their heads outward, and presented to the foe a line of horns, unbroken save when some cow, frightened by a fresh onset of the wolves, tried to retreat into the middle of the herd. It was only by taking advantage of these breaks that the wolves had succeeded at all in wounding the selected cow, but she was far from being disabled, and it seemed that Lobo at length lost patience with his followers, for he left his position on the hill, and, uttering a deep roar, dashed toward the herd. The terrified rank broke at his charge, and he sprang in among them. Then the cattle scattered like the pieces of a bursting bomb. Away went the chosen victim, but ere she had gone twenty-five yards Lobo was upon her. Seizing her by the neck he

---

3. **heifer** Female cow that has not yet borne a calf.

suddenly held back with all his force and so threw her heavily to the ground. The shock must have been tremendous, for the heifer was thrown heels over head. Lobo also turned a somersault, but immediately recovered himself, and his followers falling on the poor cow, killed her in a few seconds. Lobo took no part in the killing — after having thrown the victim, he seemed to say, "Now, why could not some of you have done that at once without wasting so much time?"

The man now rode up shouting, the wolves as usual retired, and he, having a bottle of strychnine, quickly poisoned the carcass in three places, then went away, knowing they would return to feed, as they had killed the animal themselves. But next morning, on going to look for his expected victims, he found that, although the wolves had eaten the heifer, they had carefully cut out and thrown aside all those parts that had been poisoned.

The dread of this great wolf spread yearly among the ranchmen, and each year a larger price was set on his head, until at last it reached $1,000, an unparalleled wolf-bounty, surely; many a good man has been hunted down for less. Tempted by the promised reward, a Texan ranger named Tannerey came one day galloping up the cañon of the Currumpaw. He had a superb outfit for wolf-hunting — the best of guns and horses, and a pack of enormous wolf-hounds. Far out on the plains of the Pan-handle,[4] he and his dogs had killed many a wolf, and now he never doubted that, within a few days, old Lobo's scalp would dangle at his saddle-bow.[5]

Away they went bravely on their hunt in the gray dawn of a summer morning, and soon the great dogs gave joyous tongue to say that they were already on the track of their quarry. Within two miles, the grizzly band of Currumpaw leaped into view, and the chase grew fast and furious. The part of the wolf-hounds was merely to hold the wolves at bay till the hunter could ride up and shoot them, and this usually was easy on the open plains of Texas; but here a new feature of the country came into play, and showed how well Lobo had chosen his range; for the rocky cañons of the Currumpaw and its tributaries intersect the prairies in every direction. The old wolf at once made for the nearest of these and by crossing it got rid of the horsemen. His band then scattered and thereby scattered the dogs, and when they reunited at a distant point of course all of the dogs did not turn up, and the wolves no longer outnumbered, turned on their pursuers and killed or desperately wounded them all. That night when Tannerey mustered his dogs, only six of them returned, and of these, two were terribly lacerated. This hunter made two other attempts to capture the royal scalp, but neither of them was more successful than the first, and on the last occasion his best horse met its death by a fall; so he gave up the chase in disgust and went back to Texas, leaving Lobo more than ever the despot of the region.

Next year, two other hunters appeared, determined to win the promised bounty. Each believed he could destroy this noted wolf, the first by means of a newly devised poison, which was to be laid out in an entirely new manner; the other a French Canadian, by poison assisted with certain spells and charms, for he firmly believed that Lobo was a veritable "loup-garou,"[6] and could not be killed by ordinary means. But cunningly compounded poisons, charms, and incantations were all of no avail against this grizzly devastator. He made his weekly rounds and daily banquets as aforetime, and

---

4. **Pan-handle** Long, thin, protruding section of land. 5. **saddle-bow** The raised front piece of a saddle. 6. **loup-garou** Werewolf.

before many weeks had passed, Calone and Laloche gave up in despair and went elsewhere to hunt.

In the spring of 1893, after his unsuccessful attempt to capture Lobo, Joe Calone had a humiliating experience, which seems to show that the big wolf simply scorned his enemies, and had absolute confidence in himself. Calone's farm was on a small tributary of the Currumpaw, in a picturesque cañon, and among the rocks of this cañon, within a thousand yards of the house, old Lobo and his mate selected their den and raised their family that season. There they lived all summer, and killed Joe's cattle, sheep, and dogs, but laughed at all his poisons and traps, and rested securely among the recesses of the cavernous cliffs, while Joe vainly racked his brain for some method of smoking them out, or of reaching them with dynamite. But they escaped entirely unscathed, and continued their ravages as before. "There's where he lived all last summer," said Joe, pointing to the face of the cliff, "and I couldn't do a thing with him. I was like a fool to him."

II

This history, gathered so far from the cowboys, I found hard to believe until in the fall of 1893, I made the acquaintance of the wily marauder,[7] and at length came to know him more thoroughly than anyone else. Some years before, in the Bingo days, I had been a wolf-hunter, but my occupations since then had been of another sort, chaining me to stool and desk. I was much in need of a change, and when a friend, who was also a ranch-owner on the Currumpaw, asked me to come to New Mexico and try if I could do anything with this predatory pack, I accepted the invitation and, eager to make the acquaintance of its king, was as soon as possible among the mesas of that region. I spent some time riding about to learn the country, and at intervals, my guide would point to the skeleton of a cow to which the hide still adhered, and remark, "That's some of his work."

It became quite clear to me that, in this rough country, it was useless to think of pursuing Lobo with hounds and horses, so that poison or traps were the only available expedients. At present we had no traps large enough, so I set to work with poison.

I need not enter into the details of a hundred devices that I employed to circumvent this "loup-garou"; there was no combination of strychnine, arsenic, cyanide, or prussic acid, that I did not essay; there was no manner of flesh that I did not try as bait; but morning after morning, as I rode forth to learn the result, I found that all my efforts had been useless. The old king was too cunning for me. A single instance will show his wonderful sagacity. Acting on the hint of an old trapper, I melted some cheese together with the kidney fat of a freshly killed heifer, stewing it in a china dish, and cutting it with a bone knife to avoid the taint of metal. When the mixture was cool, I cut it into lumps, and making a hole in one side of each lump, I inserted a large dose of strychnine and cyanide, contained in a capsule that was impermeable by any odor; finally I sealed the holes up with pieces of the cheese itself. During the whole process, I wore a pair of gloves steeped in the hot blood of the heifer, and even avoided breathing on the baits. When all was ready, I put them in a raw-hide bag rubbed all over with blood, and rode forth dragging the liver and kidneys of the beef at the end of a rope. With this I made a ten-mile circuit, dropping a bait at each quarter of a mile, taking the utmost care, always, not to touch any with my hands.

---

7. **marauder** One who roams and raids; in this case, Lobo.

Lobo, generally, came into this part of the range in the early part of each week, and passed the latter part, it was supposed, around the base of Sierra Grande. This was Monday, and that same evening, as we were about to retire, I heard the deep bass howl of his majesty. On hearing it one of the boys briefly remarked, "There he is, we'll see."

The next morning I went forth, eager to know the result. I soon came on the fresh trail of the robbers, with Lobo in the lead — his track was always easily distinguished. An ordinary wolf's forefoot is 4 1/2 inches long, that of a large wolf 4 3/4 inches, but Lobo's, as measured a number of times, was 5 1/2 inches from claw to heel; I afterward found that his other proportions were commensurate, for he stood three feet high at the shoulder, and weighed 150 pounds. His trail, therefore, though obscured by those of his followers, was never difficult to trace. The pack had soon found the track of my drag, and as usual followed it. I could see that Lobo had come to the first bait, sniffed about it, and finally had picked it up.

Then I could not conceal my delight. "I've got him at last," I exclaimed; "I shall find him stark within a mile," and I galloped on with eager eyes fixed on the great broad track in the dust. It led me to the second bait and that also was gone. How I exulted — I surely have him now and perhaps several of his band. But there was the broad paw-mark still on the drag; and though I stood in the stirrup and scanned the plain I saw nothing that looked like a dead wolf. Again I followed — to find now that the third bait was gone — and the king-wolf's track led on to the fourth, there to learn that he had not really taken a bait at all, but had merely carried them in his mouth. Then having piled the three on the fourth, he scattered filth over them to express his utter contempt for my devices. After this he left my drag and went about his business with the pack he guarded so effectively.

This is only one of many similar experiences which convinced me that poison would never avail to destroy this robber, and though I continued to use it while awaiting the arrival of the traps, it was only because it was meanwhile a sure means of killing many prairie wolves and other destructive vermin.

About this time there came under my observation an incident that will illustrate Lobo's diabolic cunning. These wolves had at least one pursuit which was merely an amusement, it was stampeding and killing sheep, though they rarely ate them. The sheep are usually kept in flocks of from one thousand to three thousand under one or more shepherds. At night they are gathered in the most sheltered place available, and a herdsman sleeps on each side of the flock to give additional protection. Sheep are such senseless creatures that they are liable to be stampeded by the veriest trifle, but they have deeply ingrained in their nature one, and perhaps only one, strong weakness, namely, to follow their leader. And this the shepherds turn to good account by putting half a dozen goats in the flock of sheep. The latter recognize the superior intelligence of their bearded cousins, and when a night alarm occurs they crowd around them, and usually are thus saved from a stampede and are easily protected. But it was not always so. One night late in last November, two Perico shepherds were aroused by an onset of wolves. Their flocks huddled around the goats, which being neither fools nor cowards, stood their ground and were bravely defiant; but alas for them, no common wolf was heading this attack. Old Lobo, the weir-wolf, knew as well as the shepherds that the goats were the moral force of the flock, so hastily running over the backs of the densely packed sheep, he fell on these leaders, slew them all in a few minutes, and soon had the luckless sheep stampeding in a thousand different directions. For weeks afterward I was almost daily accosted by some anxious shepherd, who asked, "Have you seen any stray OTO sheep lately?" and usually I was obliged to say I had; one day it was, "Yes, I came on some five or six carcasses by Diamond Springs;" or another, it was to the effect that I had seen a small "bunch" running on the Malpai Mesa; or again, "No, but Juan Meira saw about twenty, freshly killed, on the Cedra Monte two days ago."

At length the wolf traps arrived, and with two men I worked a whole week to get them properly set out. We spared no labor or pains, I adopted every device I could think of that might help to insure success. The second day after the traps arrived, I rode around to inspect, and soon came upon Lobo's trail running from trap to trap. In the dust I could read the whole story of his doings that night. He had trotted along in the darkness, and although the traps were so carefully concealed, he had instantly detected the first one. Stopping the onward march of the pack, he had cautiously scratched around it until he had disclosed the trap, the chain, and the log, then left them wholly exposed to view with the trap still unsprung, and passing on he treated over a dozen traps in the same fashion. Very soon I noticed that he stopped and turned aside as soon as he detected suspicious signs on the trail and a new plan to outwit him at once suggested itself. I set the traps in the form of an H; that is, with a row of traps on each side of the trail, and one on the trail for the cross-bar of the H. Before long, I had an opportunity to count another failure. Lobo came trotting along the trail, and was fairly between the parallel lines before he detected the single trap in the trail, but he stopped in time, and why or how he knew enough I cannot tell, the Angel of the wild things must have been with him, but without turning an inch to the right or left, he slowly and cautiously backed on his own tracks, putting each paw exactly in its old track until he was off the dangerous ground. Then returning at one side he scratched clods and stones with his hind feet till he had sprung every trap. This he did on many other occasions, and although I varied my methods and redoubled my precautions, he was never deceived, his sagacity seemed never at fault, and he might have been pursuing his career of rapine[8] to-day, but for an unfortunate alliance that proved his ruin and added his name to the long list of heroes who, unassailable when alone, have fallen through the indiscretion of a trusted ally.

III

Once or twice, I had found indications that everything was not quite right in the Currumpaw pack. There were signs of irregularity, I thought; for instance there was clearly the trail of a smaller wolf running ahead of the leader, at times, and this I could not understand until a cowboy made a remark which explained the matter.

"I saw them to-day," he said, "and the wild one that breaks away is Blanca." Then the truth dawned upon me, and I added, "Now, I know that Blanca is a she-wolf, because were a he-wolf to act thus, Lobo would kill him at once."

This suggested a new plan. I killed a heifer, and set one or two rather obvious traps about the carcass. Then cutting off the head, which is considered useless offal,[9] and quite beneath the notice of a wolf, I set it a little apart and around it placed six powerful steel traps properly deodorized and concealed with the utmost care. During my operations I kept my hands, boots, and implements smeared with fresh blood, and afterward sprinkled the ground with the same, as though it had flowed from the head; and when the traps were buried in the dust I brushed the place over with the skin of a coyote, and

---

8. **rapine** Plunder, destruction. 9. **offal** Unusable parts of a dead animal.

with a foot of the same animal made a number of tracks over the traps. The head was so placed that there was a narrow passage between it and some tussocks, and in this passage I buried two of my best traps, fastening them to the head itself.

Wolves have a habit of approaching every carcass they get the wind of, in order to examine it, even when they have no intention of eating of it, and I hoped that this habit would bring the Currumpaw pack within reach of my latest stratagem. I did not doubt that Lobo would detect my handiwork about the meat, and prevent the pack approaching it, but I did build some hopes on the head, for it looked as though it had been thrown aside as useless.

Next morning, I sallied forth to inspect the traps, and there, oh, joy! were the tracks of the pack, and the place where the beef-head and its traps had been was empty. A hasty study of the trail showed that Lobo had kept the pack from approaching the meat, but one, a small wolf, had evidently gone on to examine the head as it lay apart and had walked right into one of the traps.

We set out on the trail, and within a mile discovered that the hapless wolf was Blanca. Away she went, however, at a gallop, and although encumbered by the beef-head, which weighed over fifty pounds, she speedily distanced my companion who was on foot. But we overtook her when she reached the rocks, for the horns of the cow's head became caught and held her fast. She was the handsomest wolf I had ever seen. Her coat was in perfect condition and nearly white.

She turned to fight, and raising her voice in the rallying cry of her race, sent a long howl rolling over the cañon. From far away upon the mesa came a deep response, the cry of Old Lobo. That was her last call, for now we had closed in on her, and all her energy and breath were devoted to combat.

Then followed the inevitable tragedy, the idea of which I shrank from afterward more than at the time. We each threw a lasso over the neck of the doomed wolf, and strained our horses in opposite directions until the blood burst from her mouth, her eyes glazed, her limbs stiffened and then fell limp. Homeward then we rode, carrying the dead wolf, and exulting over this, the first death-blow we had been able to inflict on the Currumpaw pack.

At intervals during the tragedy, and afterward as we rode homeward, we heard the roar of Lobo as he wandered about on the distant mesas, where he seemed to be searching for Blanca. He had never really deserted her, but knowing that he could not save her, his deep-rooted dread of firearms had been too much for him when he saw us approaching. All that day we heard him wailing as he roamed in his quest, and I remarked at length to one of the boys, "Now, indeed, I truly know that Blanca was his mate."

As evening fell he seemed to be coming toward the home cañon for his voice sounded continually nearer. There was an unmistakable note of sorrow in it now. It was no longer the loud, defiant howl, but a long, plaintive wail; "Blanca! Blanca!" he seemed to call. And as night came down, I noticed that he was not far from the place where we had overtaken her. At length he seemed to find the trail, and when he came to the spot where we had killed her, his heart-broken wailing was piteous to hear. It was sadder than I could possibly have believed. Even the stolid cowboys noticed it, and said they had "never heard a wolf carry on like that before." He seemed to know exactly what had taken place, for her blood had stained the place of her death.

Then he took up the trail of the horses and followed it to the ranch-house. Whether in hopes of finding her there, or in quest of revenge, I know not, but the latter was what he found, for he surprised our unfortunate watchdog outside and tore him to little bits within fifty yards of the door. He evidently came alone this time, for I found but one trail next morning, and he had galloped about in a reckless manner that was very unusual with him. I had half expected this, and had set a number of additional traps about the pasture. Afterward I found that he had indeed fallen into one of these, but such was his strength, he had torn himself loose and cast it aside.

I believed that he would continue in the neighborhood until he found her body at least, so I concentrated all my energies on this one enterprise of catching him before he left the region, and while yet in this reckless mood. Then I realized what a mistake I had made in killing Blanca, for by using her as a decoy I might have secured him the next night.

I gathered in all the traps I could command, one hundred and thirty strong steel wolf-traps, and set them in fours in every trail that led into the cañon; each trap was separately fastened to a log, and each log was separately buried. In burying them, I carefully removed the sod and every particle of earth that was lifted we put in blankets, so that after the sod was replaced and all was finished the eye could detect no trace of human handiwork. When the traps were concealed I trailed the body of poor Blanca over each place, and made of it a drag that circled all about the ranch, and finally I took off one of her paws and made with it a line of tracks over each trap. Every precaution and device known to me I used, and retired at a late hour to await the result.

Once during the night I thought I heard Old Lobo, but was not sure of it. Next day I rode around, but darkness came on before I completed the circuit of the north cañon, and I had nothing to report. At supper one of the cowboys said, "There was a great row among the cattle in the north cañon this morning, maybe there is something in the traps there." It was afternoon of the next day before I got to the place referred to, and as I drew near a great grizzly form arose from the ground, vainly endeavoring to escape, and there revealed before me stood Lobo, King of the Currumpaw, firmly held in the traps. Poor old hero, he had never ceased to search for his darling, and when he found the trail her body had made he followed it recklessly, and so fell into the snare prepared for him. There he lay in the iron grasp of all four traps, perfectly helpless, and all around him were numerous tracks showing how the cattle had gathered about him to insult the fallen despot, without daring to approach within his reach. For two days and two nights he had lain there, and now was worn out with struggling. Yet, when I went near him, he rose up with bristling mane and raised his voice, and for the last time made the cañon reverberate with his deep bass roar, a call for help, the muster call of his band. But there was none to answer him, and, left alone in his extremity, he whirled about with all his strength and made a desperate effort to get at me. All in vain, each trap was a dead drag of over three hundred pounds, and in their relentless fourfold grasp, with great steel jaws on every foot, and the heavy logs and chains all entangled together, he was absolutely powerless. How his huge ivory tusks did grind on those cruel chains, and when I ventured to touch him with my rifle-barrel he left grooves on it which are there to this day. His eyes glared green with hate and fury, and his jaws snapped with a hollow "chop," as he vainly endeavored to reach me and my trembling horse. But he was worn out with hunger and struggling and loss of blood, and he soon sank exhausted to the ground.

Something like compunction came over me, as I prepared to deal out to him that which so many had suffered at his hands.

"Grand old outlaw, hero of a thousand lawless raids, in a few minutes you will be but a great load of carrion.[10] It cannot be otherwise." Then I swung my lasso and sent it whistling over his head. But not so fast; he was yet far from being subdued, and, before the supple coils had fallen on his neck he seized the noose and, with one fierce chop, cut through its hard thick strands, and dropped it in two pieces at his feet.

Of course I had my rifle as a last resource, but I did not wish to spoil his royal hide, so I galloped back to the camp and returned with a cowboy and a fresh lasso. We threw to our victim a stick of wood which he seized in his teeth, and before he could relinquish it our lassoes whistled through the air and tightened on his neck.

Yet before the light had died from his fierce eyes, I cried, "Stay, we will not kill him; let us take him alive to the camp." He was so completely powerless now that it was easy to put a stout stick through his mouth, behind his tusks, and then lash his jaws with a heavy cord which was also fastened to the stick. The stick kept the cord in, and the cord kept the stick in so he was harmless. As soon as he felt his jaws were tied he made no further resistance, and uttered no sound, but looked calmly at us and seemed to say, "Well, you have got me at last, do as you please with me." And from that time he took no more notice of us.

We tied his feet securely, but he never groaned, nor growled, nor turned his head. Then with our united strength were just able to put him on my horse. His breath came evenly as though sleeping, and his eyes were bright and clear again, but did not rest on us. Afar on the great rolling mesas they were fixed, his passing kingdom, where his famous band was now scattered. And he gazed till the pony descended the pathway into the cañon, and the rocks cut off the view.

By travelling slowly we reached the ranch in safety, and after securing him with a collar and a strong chain, we staked him out in the pasture and removed the cords. Then for the first time I could examine him closely, and proved how unreliable is vulgar report when a living hero or tyrant is concerned. He had *not* a collar of gold about his neck, nor was there on his shoulders an inverted cross to denote that he had leagued himself with Satan. But I did find on one haunch a great broad scar, that tradition says was the fang-mark of Juno, the leader of Tannerey's wolf-hounds — a mark which she gave him the moment before he stretched her lifeless on the sand of the cañon.

I set meat and water beside him, but he paid no heed. He lay calmly on his breast, and gazed with those steadfast yellow eyes away past me down through the gateway of the cañon, over the open plains — his plains — nor moved a muscle when I touched him. When the sun went down he was still gazing fixedly across the prairie. I expected he would call up his band when night came, and prepared for them, but he had called once in his extremity, and none had come; he would never call again.

A lion shorn of his strength, an eagle robbed of his freedom, or a dove bereft of his mate, all die, it is said, of a broken heart; and who will aver that this grim bandit could bear the three-fold brunt, heart-whole? This only I know, that when the morning dawned, he was lying there still in his position of calm repose, but his spirit was gone — the old king-wolf was dead.

I took the chain from his neck, a cowboy helped me to carry him to the shed where lay the remains of Blanca, and as we laid him beside her, the cattle-man exclaimed: "There, you *would* come to her, now you are together again."

(1898)

---

10. **carrion** Decaying flesh.

Bliss Carman (1861–1929)

William Bliss Carman was born on 15 April 1861 in Fredericton, New Brunswick. Along with his cousin, Charles G.D. Roberts, he received a classical education at the Fredericton Collegiate School and the University of New Brunswick. After graduating, in 1881, he enrolled in Oxford University but left after only a few days of classes for Edinburgh, Scotland. He entered Edinburgh University, where he studied physics, mathematics, and philosophy, but he felt dissatisfied and alienated in these new surroundings. He returned to Canada in 1883. From 1886 to 1888, he studied English literature and philosophy at Harvard and, although he did not earn a degree, the experience was an enriching one. He was influenced by his Harvard professors, particularly Dr. Josiah Royce, under whom he studied the work of Ralph Waldo Emerson (a distant relative of Carman's) and American transcendentalism. Settling into Cambridge life, Carman became acquainted with several like-minded young artists who called themselves the Twentieth Century Group. Through this affiliation, he met Richard Hovey, who would become his close friend and collaborator.

After publishing a handful of poems in various Canadian and American periodicals, Carman decided that he wanted to become a professional poet. In order to support himself as he pursued this ambition, he took a series of temporary editorial jobs at the *Boston Transcript,* the *Independent,* the *Atlantic Monthly,* and *Cosmopolitan.* In 1894, he became founding editor of a periodical called the *Chap Book* for Stone and Kimball Press in Cambridge.

Carman's first collection of poetry, *Low Tide on Grand Pré: A Book of Lyrics,* appeared in 1893 to enthusiastic reviews at home and abroad. With these early poems, he created a mysterious and mystical aesthetic, evoking atmosphere and emotion through natural imagery. Explaining his methods in a personal letter, he remarked, "I try to arrest and put in permanent form the emotional life of situations. I imagine an incident and then attempt to wring from it whatever lyric rapture it contains and embody *this* for the soul of my work, giving the fewest possible explanatory side hints that shall still be sufficient to reveal the situation or circumstance." Carman employs a metaphorical language that creates an impression of coherence but becomes more difficult to decipher under scrutiny. In "A Sea-Drift," for example, he combines imagery of harmony and discord in nature to evoke the ambivalent emotions of unfulfilled desire: "As the seaweed swims the sea / In the ruin after storm, / Sunburnt memories of thee / Through the twilight float and form. / And desire, when thou art gone, / Roves his desolate domain, / As the meadow-birds at dawn / Haunt the spaces of the rain."

Carman's real breakthrough occurred when he and Hovey published their collaborative efforts *Songs from Vagabondia* (1894) and *More Songs from Vagabondia* (1896). *Last Songs from Vagabondia* was published in 1900, the year that Hovey died. With the *Vagabondia* series, Carman and Hovey attempted to distance themselves from British models and, drawing inspiration from American transcendentalism, adopt what they saw as a North American style. "Off with the fetters / That chafe and restrain / Off with the chain!" Hovey announces in the first volume. In some of the more serious *Vagabondia* poems, Carman and Hovey explore the spiritual state one attains when one casts off the social world and retreats into nature. The mystical language of these works echoes that of Carman's earlier verse.

Having established a wide audience, Carman wrote prolifically, producing approximately 30 volumes in under 35 years. His five-volume *Pipes of Pan* was published over three years, beginning in 1902. In 1904, he composed *Sappho: One Hundred Lyrics*, in which he falls back on his classical education to imagine that he is translating the lost works of the early 7th century BC Greek poet.

In the early 1900s, Carman came under the powerful influence of François Delsarte, a French singer who had developed a style of orating and acting based on the theory that all human movement expresses rationality, spirituality, and physicality. After Delsarte died, in 1871, his proponents used his method to design a set of physical exercises for people seeking psychological, spiritual, and bodily health. Hovey's wife, Henrietta Knapp Russell, became an instructor of the Delsartean method. Russell introduced Carman to one of her students, Mary Perry King, in 1896, and Carman joined with King and her husband to establish a school for Delsartean exercise — the Unitrinian School of Personal Harmonizing.

Beginning in 1904, Carman published a series of prose works defending his view of art and its relationship to nature and human life. *The Kinship of Nature* (1904), *The Friendship of Art* (1904), and *The Poetry of Life* (1905) appeared in quick succession. In 1908, he produced *The Making of Personality,* in which he presented his theories of Delsartean-inspired "Unitrinianism." He wrote, "we have … to take into consideration the essential threefold unity of personality in any attempt at education, — the indivisible relation between body-building and character-building." This notion led him, in collaboration with King, to combine poetry and movement to create several lyric masques. In 1913, the pair composed *Daughters of Dawn: A Lyrical Pageant or Series of Historic Scenes for Presentation with Music and Dancing* for a recital at their Unitrinian school. In 1914, they created *Earth Deities, and Other Rhythmic Masques*.

From 1919 to 1920, Carman suffered from tuberculosis. When he had recovered, he travelled across Canada and the United States giving readings and lectures. This tour sealed his reputation in his homeland: at the inaugural dinner of the Canadian Authors Association in 1922, he was feted as Canada's unofficial poet laureate. In 1928, he was honoured with the Lorne Pierce Medal for his contribution to Canadian letters. He died in 1929 in New Canaan, Connecticut.

Low Tide on Grand Pré[1]

The sun goes down, and over all
These barren reaches by the tide
Such unelusive glories fall,
I almost dream they yet will bide
Until the coming of the tide.

And yet I know that not for us,
By any ecstasy of dream,
He lingers to keep luminous
A little while the grievous stream,
Which frets, uncomforted of dream —

A grievous stream, that to and fro
Athrough the fields of Acadie[2]
Goes wandering, as if to know
Why one beloved face should be
So long from home and Acadie.

Was it a year or lives ago
We took the grasses in our hands,

10

---

1. **Grand Pré** Settlement on the shores of the Minas Basin, Nova Scotia. 2. **Acadie** French colony in Eastern Canada which contained Grand Pré.

And caught the summer flying low
Over the waving meadow lands,
20   And held it there between our hands?

The while the river at our feet —
A drowsy inland meadow stream —
At set of sun the after-heat
Made running gold, and in the gleam
We freed our birch upon the stream.

There down along the elms at dusk
We lifted dripping blade to drift,
Through twilight scented fine like musk,
Where night and gloom awhile uplift,
30   Nor sunder[3] soul and soul adrift.

And that we took into our hands
Spirit of life or subtler thing —
Breathed on us there, and loosed the bands
Of death, and taught us, whispering,
The secret of some wonder-thing.

Then all your face grew light, and seemed
To hold the shadow of the sun;
The evening faltered, and I deemed
That time was ripe, and years had done
40   Their wheeling underneath the sun.

So all desire and all regret,
And fear and memory, were naught;
One to remember or forget
The keen delight our hands had caught;
Morrow and yesterday were naught.

The night has fallen, and the tide. ...
Now and again comes drifting home,
Across these aching barrens wide,
A sigh like driven wind or foam:
50   In grief the flood is bursting home.

(1887)

A Northern Vigil

Here by the gray north sea,
   In the wintry heart of the wild,

---

3. **sunder** Divide.

Comes the old dream of thee,
   Guendolen,[1] mistress and child.

The heart of the forest grieves
   In the drift against my door;
A voice is under the eaves,
   A footfall on the floor.

Threshold, mirror and hall,
   Vacant and strangely aware,   10
Wait for their soul's recall
   With the dumb expectant air.

Here when the smouldering west
   Burns down into the sea,
I take no heed of rest
   And keep the watch for thee.

I sit by the fire and hear
   The restless wind go by,
On the long dirge and drear,
   Under the low bleak sky.   20

When day puts out to sea
   And night makes in for land,
There is no lock for thee,
   Each door awaits thy hand!

When night goes over the hill
   And dawn comes down the dale,
It's O for the wild sweet will
   That shall no more prevail!

When the zenith[2] moon is round,
   And snow-wraiths gather and run,   30
And there is set no bound
   To love beneath the sun,

O wayward will, come near
   The old mad wilful way,
The soft mouth at my ear
   With words too sweet to say!

Come, for the night is cold,
   The ghostly moonlight fills

---

1. **Guendolen** King Arthur's half-fairy lover; they had a child together. 2. **zenith** Full.

Hollow and rift and fold
40   Of the eerie Ardise hills!

The windows of my room
   Are dark with bitter frost,
The stillness aches with doom
   Of something loved and lost.

Outside, the great blue star
   Burns in the ghostland pale,
Where giant Algebar[3]
   Holds on the endless trail.

Come, for the years are long,
50   And silence keeps the door,
Where shapes with the shadows throng
   The firelit chamber floor.

Come, for thy kiss was warm,
   With the red embers' glare
Across thy folding arm
   And dark tumultuous hair!

And though thy coming rouse
   The sleep-cry of no bird,
The keepers of the house
60   Shall tremble at thy word.

Come, for the soul is free!
   In all the vast dreamland
There is no lock for thee,
   Each door awaits thy hand.

Ah, not in dreams at all,
   Fleering, perishing, dim,
But thy old self, supple and tall,
   Mistress and child of whim!

The proud imperious[4] guise,
70   Impetuous and serene,
The sad mysterious eyes,
   And dignity of mien!

Yea, wilt thou not return,
   When the late hill-winds veer,

---

3. **Algebar** Brightest star in the Orion constellation. 4. **imperious** Haughty.

And the bright hill-flowers burn
  With the reviving year?

When April comes, and the sea
  Sparkles as if it smiled,
Will they restore to me
  My dark Love, empress and child?   80

The curtains seem to part;
  A sound is on the stair,
As if at the last … I start;
  Only the wind is there.

Lo, now far on the hills
  The crimson fumes uncurled,
Where the caldron mantles and spills
  Another dawn on the world!

(1893)

By the Aurelian Wall

In Memory of John Keats[1]

By the Aurelian Wall,[2]
Where the long shadows of the centuries fall
From Caius Cestius'[3] tomb,
A weary mortal seeking rest found room
For quiet burial,

Leaving among his friends
A book of lyrics.
Such untold amends
A traveller might make
In a strange country, bidden to partake   10
Before he farther wends;

Who slyly should bestow
The foreign reed-flute they had seen him blow
And finger cunningly,
On one of the dark children standing by,
Then lift his cloak and go.

The years pass. And the child
Thoughtful beyond his fellows, grave and mild,
Treasures the rough-made toy,

---

1. Keats British poet John Keats (1795–1821). **2. Aurelian Wall** City walls built around Rome under Emperor Aurelian between 270 and 273 BC. **3. Caius Cestius** Ancient Roman consul.

20   Until one day he blows it for clear joy,
       And wakes the music wild.

       His fondness makes it seem
       A thing first fashioned in delirious dream,
       Some god had cut and tried,
       And filled with yearning passion, and cast aside
       On some far woodland stream, —

       After long years to be
       Found by the stranger and brought over sea,
       A marvel and delight
30   To ease the noon and pierce the dark blue night,
       For children such as he.

       He learns the silver strain
       Wherewith the ghostly houses of gray rain
       And lonely valleys ring,
       When the untroubled whitethroats[4] make the spring
       A world without a stain;

       Then on his river reed,
       With strange and unsuspected notes that plead
       Of their own wild accord
40   For utterances no bird's throat could afford,
       Lifts it to human need.

       His comrades leave their play,
       When calling and compelling far away
       By river-slope and hill,
       He pipes their wayward footsteps where he will,
       All the long lovely day.

       Even his elders come.
       "Surely the child is elvish," murmur some,
       And shake the knowing head;
50   "Give us the good old simple things instead,
       Our fathers used to hum."

       Others at open door
       Smile when they hear what they have hearkened for
       These many summers now,
       Believing they should live to learn somehow
       Things never known before.

---

4. **whitethroats** European songbird.

But he can only tell
How the flute's whisper lures him with a spell,
Yet always just eludes
The lost perfection over which he broods;   60
And how he loves it well.
Till all the country-side,
Familiar with his piping far and wide,
Has taken for its own
That weird enchantment down the evening blown, —
Its glory and its pride.

And so his splendid name,
Who left the book of lyrics and small fame
Among his fellows then,
Spreads through the world like autumn — who knows when? —   70
Till all the hillsides flame.

Grand Pré[5] and Margaree[5]
Hear it upbruited from the unresting sea;
And the small Gaspereau,[5]
Whose yellow leaves repeat it, seems to know
A new felicity.

Even the shadows tall,
Walking at sundown through the plain, recall
A mound the grasses keep,
Where once a mortal came and found long sleep   80
By the Aurelian Wall.

                                                                   (1893)

I Loved Thee, Atthis, in the Long Ago

I loved thee, Atthis, in the long ago,
When the great oleanders were in flower
In the broad herded meadows full of sun.
And we would often at the fall of dusk
Wander together by the silver stream,
When the soft grass-heads were all wet with dew
And purple-misted in the fading light.
And joy I knew and sorrow at thy voice,
And the superb magnificence of love, —
The loneliness that saddens solitude,   10
And the sweet speech that makes it durable, —
The bitter longing and the keen desire,
The sweet companionship through quiet days
In the slow ample beauty of the world,

---

5. **Grand Pré, Margaree, Gaspereau** Towns in Nova Scotia.

And the unutterable glad release
Within the temple of the holy night.
O Atthis, how I loved thee long ago
In that fair perished summer by the sea!

(1903)

Vestigia

I took a day to search for God,
And found Him not. But as I trod
By rocky ledge, through woods untamed,
Just where one scarlet lily flamed,
I saw His footprint in the sod.

Then suddenly, all unaware,
Far off in the deep shadows, where
A solitary hermit thrush
Sang through the holy twilight hush —
10   I heard His voice upon the air.

And even as I marvelled how
God gives us Heaven here and now,
In a stir of wind that hardly shook
The poplar leaves beside the brook —
His hand was light upon my brow.

At last with evening as I turned
Homeward, and thought what I had learned
And all that there was still to probe —
I caught the glory of His robe
20   Where the last fires of sunset burned.

Back to the world with quickening start
I looked and longed for any part
In making saving Beauty be ...
And from that kindling ecstasy
I knew God dwelt within my heart.

(1921)

The Winter Scene

I

The rutted roads are all like iron; skies
Are keen and brilliant; only the oak-leaves cling
In the bare woods, or the hardy bitter-sweet;
Drivers have put their sheepskin jackets on;
And all the ponds are sealed with sheeted ice
That rings with stroke of skate and hockey-stick,

Or in the twilight cracks with running whoop.
Bring in the logs of oak and hickory,
And make an ample blaze on the wide hearth.
Now is the time, with winter o'er the world,   10
For books and friends and yellow candle-light,
And timeless lingering by the setting fire.
While all the shuddering stars are keen with cold.

II

Out from the silent portal of the hours,
When frosts are come and all the hosts put on.
Their burnished gear to march across the night
And o'er a darkened earth in splendor shine,
Slowly above the world Orion[1] wheels
His glittering square, while on the shadowy hill
And throbbing like a sea-light through the dusk,   20
Great Sirius[2] rises in his flashing blue.
Lord of the winter night, august[3] and pure,
Returning year on year untouched by time,
To hearten faith with thine unfaltering fire,
There are no hurts that beauty cannot ease,
No ills that love cannot at last repair,
In the victorious progress of the soul.

III

Russet and white and gray is the oak wood
In the great snow. Still from the North it comes,
Whispering, settling, sifting through the trees,   30
O'erloading branch and twig. The road is lost.
Clearing and meadow, stream and ice-bound pond
Are made once more a trackless wilderness
In the white hush where not a creature stirs;
And the pale sun is blotted from the sky.
In that strange twilight the lone traveller halts
To listen to the stealthy snowflakes fall.
And then far off toward the Stamford[4] shore,
Where through the storm the coastwise liners go,
Faint and recurrent on the muffled air,   40
A foghorn booming through the Smother[5] — hark!

IV

When the day changed and the mad wind died down,
The powdery drifts that all day long had blown

---

1. Orion In classical myth, a giant hunter of the Pleiades; in astronomy, a major constellation. **2. Sirius** Orion's dog; also the brightest star in the constellation Canis Major. **3. august** Awe-inspiring or majestic. **4. Stamford** Coastal town in Connecticut on a common eastern ship route. **5. Smother** Oppressively thick smoke.

Across the meadows and the open fields,
Or whirled like diamond dust in the bright sun,
Settled to rest, and for a tranquil hour
The lengthening bluish shadows on the snow
Stole down the orchard slope, and a rose light
Flooded the earth with beauty and with peace.
50 Then in the west behind the cedars black
The sinking sun stained red the winter dusk
With sullen flare upon the snowy ridge, —
As in a masterpiece by Hokusai,[6]
Where on a background gray, with flaming breath
A scarlet dragon dies in dusky gold.

(1929)

E. Pauline Johnson (1861–1913)

Emily Pauline Johnson was one of the most popular Canadian poets of her day. When she died, a massive crowd marched in her funeral procession. Her ashes were interred in Vancouver's Stanley Park, and a monument was erected there in her honour. A likeness of Johnson was printed on a stamp in 1961. Margaret Atwood once wanted to write a libretto for an opera based on her life, and *Maclean's* magazine included her on its list of the 26 Canadians "who inspired the world."

Johnson led an uncommon life. She was born and grew up on the Six Nations Reserve near Brantford, Ontario. Her father was a Mohawk, and her mother was an Englishwoman. They placed great value on interracial cooperation in the political sphere as well as in the home, and from them Pauline inherited a lifelong admiration for both Native and imperial traditions. As a young adult, Pauline read Byron, Scott, Longfellow, Tennyson, and Keats, but she also absorbed the stories of her grandfather, the influential Mohawk chief Sakayengwaraton (John Smoke Johnson).

After her father's death, in 1884, Johnson began supplementing the family income by writing. Her first two poems appeared that year in the British periodical *The Week* and a New York publication called *Gems of Poetry*. In 1886, she assumed the name Tekahionwake, which had belonged to her great-grandfather, Jacob Johnson. By 1889, after her inclusion in W.D. Lighthall's anthology *Songs of the Great Dominion*, she was established as an authentic "Indian" voice.

From 1892 to 1909, Johnson toured Canada, the United States, and England, appearing in Native dress for the first half of each performance and in an evening gown for the second half. In 1895, she published *The White Wampum*, a tremendously successful volume, and she followed it with the equally successful *Canadian Born* in 1903. Her muse, however, was not stimulated by success, and her output became infrequent. After she retired from performing, she released one more volume, *Flint and Feather* (1911). Although it was subtitled *The Complete Poems,* it did not include some pieces that had been published earlier in magazines.

Johnson's poetry reflects what she called, in an 1890 letter to a friend, the "double motive" of her work. She was determined to "stand by" her "blood" by challenging the racial stereotypes about Natives — particularly Native women — fostered by the literature of the day. As she noted in "A Strong Race Opinion: On the Indian Girl in Modern Fiction" (which appeared in the *Toronto Sunday Globe* in May 1892), Canadian authors rarely wrote about Native women who possessed

6. **Hokusai** Katsushika Hokusai (1760–1849), Japanese artist most famous for his "Thirty-Six Views of Mount Fuji."

"originality" or "singularity." Instead, she argued, they perpetuated a type learned from literature and not from life: the Native heroine "grubs in the mud like a turtle, climbs trees like a raccoon, and tears and soils her gown like a madwoman." Johnson's poems — even those that speak on behalf of nations, like "A Cry from an Indian Wife" — always ensure that Native women are not "hampered with being obliged to continually be national first and natural afterwards." By focusing on unique lives rather than stereotypes, Johnson was better able to assert the validity of her own divided heritage and to challenge the arrogant assumptions made by Whites who "write up Indian stuff" without ever having "met a 'real live' Redman."

Johnson's second motive, as she joked to her friend, was to become a "millionairess." The comment reminds us that her poems were performance pieces — she wanted them to have popular appeal. Many of her verses are ballad-like, with enticing rhymes and lilting metres. Moreover, her conscious decision to write accessibly, and to use the first person when addressing either the audience or an unseen "you," reflected her admiration for oral storytelling. By drawing on oral modes, she indicated her faith in the power of direct communication to counter assumptions about race and gender. (She explored this power in "The Pilot of the Plains," in which a Native girl's band is only convinced of her "Pale-face" lover's fidelity after they sit, "all silent," and listen to his death-cry on the winds.)

Many of Johnson's poems do not deal explicitly with Native themes, instead focusing on love or nature; however, she evokes nature with a physical passion that is unusual for that period. In "The Idlers," for example, the natural world facilitates a sexual longing that is not fearful or uncertain, but experienced, anticipatory, and, eventually, burdened by regret. Johnson — as her biographers Carole Gerson and Veronica Strong-Boag note — was radical in her descriptions of female sexuality.

Johnson's work was enthusiastically received by her peers the Confederation poets, but her themes and her forms were too popular and political to appeal to the next generation of modernist poets, who valued intellectually difficult verse and believed that commercial success was the antithesis of aesthetic achievement. However, Johnson has lately been identified as someone who challenged the limitations placed on femininity and racial identity in an imperial and patriarchal society, and there is renewed interest in her poems. Her influence on Native writers has been profound and consistent.

Johnson's reputation as a poet and performer tends to obscure her vigorous and more extensive career as a prose writer: from 1890 to 1911, she produced stories and articles on topics ranging from race relations to outdoor sports. Her *Legends of Vancouver*, a series of short pieces inspired by the stories of Squamish chief Su-à-pu-luck (Joe Capilano), was immensely popular. In 1913, Johnson died of breast cancer, and two collections of her prose (*The Moccasin Maker* and *The Shagganappi*) were published posthumously. The profits from these two volumes were sufficient to clear her medical debts.

A Cry from an Indian Wife

My Forest Brave, my Red-skin love, farewell;
We may not meet to-morrow; who can tell
What mighty ills befall our little band,
Or what you'll suffer from the white man's hand?
Here is your knife! I thought 'twas sheathed for aye.
No roaming bison calls for it to-day;
No hide of prairie cattle will it maim;
The plains are bare, it seeks a nobler game:

'Twill drink the life-blood of a soldier host.
10   Go; rise and strike, no matter what the cost.
      Yet stay. Revolt not at the Union Jack,
      Nor raise thy hand against this stripling pack
      Of white-faced warriors, marching West to quell
      Our fallen tribe that rises to rebel.
      They all are young and beautiful and good;
      Curse to the war that drinks their harmless blood.
      Curse to the fate that brought them from the East
      To be our chiefs — to make our nation least
      That breathes the air of this vast continent.
20   Still their new rule and council is well meant.
      They but forget we Indians owned the land
      From ocean unto ocean; that they stand
      Upon a soil that centuries agone
      Was our sole kingdom and our right alone.
      They never think how they would feel to-day,
      If some great nation came from far away,
      Wresting their country from their hapless braves,
      Giving what they gave us — but wars and graves.
      Then go and strike for liberty and life,
30   And bring back honour to your Indian wife.
      Your wife? Ah, what of that, who cares for me?
      Who pities my poor love and agony?
      What white-robed priest prays for your safety here,
      As prayer is said for every volunteer
      That swells the ranks that Canada sends out?
      Who prays for vict'ry for the Indian scout?
      Who prays for our poor nation lying low?
      None — therefore take your tomahawk and go.
      My heart may break and burn into its core,
40   But I am strong to bid you go to war.
      Yet stay, my heart is not the only one
      That grieves the loss of husband and of son;
      Think of the mothers o'er the inland seas;
      Think of the pale-faced maiden on her knees;
      One pleads her God to guard some sweet-faced child
      That marches on toward the North-West wild.
      The other prays to shield her love from harm,
      To strengthen his young, proud uplifted arm.
      Ah, how her white face quivers thus to think,
50   Your tomahawk his life's best blood will drink.
      She never thinks of my wild aching breast,
      Nor prays for your dark face and eagle crest
      Endangered by a thousand rifle balls,
      My heart the target if my warrior falls.
      O! coward self I hesitate no more;

Go forth, and win the glories of the war.
Go forth, nor bend to greed of white men's hands,
By right, by birth we Indians own these lands,
Though starved, crushed, plundered, lies our nation low ...
Perhaps the white man's God has willed it so.   60

(1885)

The Idlers

The sun's red pulses beat,
Full prodigal of heat,
Full lavish of its lustre unrepressed;
But we have drifted far
From where his kisses are,
And in this landward-lying shade we let our paddles rest.

The river, deep and still,
The maple-mantled hill,
The little yellow beach whereon we lie,
The puffs of heated breeze,   10
All sweetly whisper — These
Are days that only come in a Canadian July.

So, silently we two
Lounge in our still canoe,
Nor fate, nor fortune matters to us now:
So long as we alone
May call this dream our own,
The breeze may die, the sail may droop, we care not when or how.

Against the thwart, near by,
Inactively you lie,   20
And all too near my arm your temple bends.
Your indolently crude,
Abandoned attitude,
Is one of ease and art, in which a perfect languor blends.

Your costume, loose and light,
Leaves unconcealed your might
Of muscle, half-suspected, half defined;
And falling well aside,
Your vesture opens wide,
Above your splendid sunburnt throat that pulses unconfined.   30

With easy unreserve,
Across the gunwale's[1] curve,

---

1. **gunwale** The upper rim of a boat's walls.

Your arm superb is lying, brown and bare;
Your hand just touches mine
With import firm and fine,
(I kiss the very wind that blows about your tumbled hair).

Ah! Dear, I am unwise
In echoing your eyes
Whene'er they leave their far-off gaze, and turn
40   To melt and blur my sight,
For every other light
Is servile to your cloud-grey eyes, wherein cloud shadows burn.

But once, the silence breaks,
But once, your ardour wakes
To words that humanize this lotus-land;
So perfect and complete
Those burning words and sweet,
So perfect is the single kiss your lips lay on my hand.

The paddles lie disused,
50   The fitful breeze abused,
Has dropped to slumber, with no after-blow;
And hearts will pay the cost,
For you and I have lost
More than the homeward blowing wind that died an hour ago.

(1890)

The Pilot of the Plains

"False," they said, "thy Pale-face lover, from the land of waking morn;
Rise and wed thy Redskin wooer, nobler warrior ne'er was born;
Cease thy watching, cease thy dreaming,
    Show the white thine Indian scorn."

Thus they taunted her, declaring, "He remembers naught of thee:
Likely some white maid he wooeth, far beyond the inland sea."
But she answered ever kindly,
    "He will come again to me,"

Till the dusk of Indian summer crept athwart the western skies;
10   But a deeper dusk was burning in her dark and dreaming eyes,
As she scanned the rolling prairie,
    Where the foothills fall, and rise.

Till the autumn came and vanished, till the season of the rains,
Till the western world lay fettered in midwinter's crystal chains,
Still she listened for his coming,
    Still she watched the distant plains.

Then a night with nor'land tempest, nor'land snows a-swirling fast,
Out upon the pathless prairie came the Pale-face through the blast,
Calling, calling, "Yakonwita,
    I am coming, love, at last."   20

Hovered night above, about him, dark its wings and cold and dread;
Never unto trail or tepee were his straying footsteps led;
Till benumbed, he sank, and pillowed
    On the drifting snows his head,

Saying, "O! my Yakonwita call me, call me, be my guide
To the lodge beyond the prairie — for I vowed ere winter died
I would come again, belovèd;
    I would claim my Indian bride."

"Yakonwita, Yakonwita!" Oh, the dreariness that strains
Through the voice that calling, quivers, till a whisper but remains,   30
"Yakonwita, Yakonwita,
    I am lost upon the plains."

But the Silent Spirit hushed him, lulled him as he cried anew,
"Save me, save me! O! belovèd, I am Pale but I am true.
Yakonwita, Yakonwita
    I am dying, love, for you."

Leagues afar, across the prairie, she had risen from her bed,
Roused her kinsmen from their slumber: "He has come tonight," she said.
    "I can hear him calling, calling;
    But his voice is as the dead.   40

"Listen!" and they sate[1] all silent, while the tempest louder grew,
And a spirit-voice called faintly, "I am dying, love, for you."
Then they wailed, "O! Yakonwita.
    He was Pale, but he was true."

Wrapped she then her ermine round her, stepped without the tepee door,
Saying, "I must follow, follow, though he call for evermore,
Yakonwita, Yakonwita";
    And they never saw her more.

Late at night, say Indian hunters, when the starlight clouds or wanes,
Far away they see a maiden, misty as the autumn rains,   50
Guiding with her lamp of moonlight
    Hunters lost upon the plains.

                             (1891)

---

1. **sate** Archaic form of "sat."

The Cattle Thief

They were coming across the prairie, they were galloping hard and fast;
For the eyes of those desperate riders had sighted their man at last —
Sighted him off to Eastward, where the Cree encampment lay,
Where the cotton woods fringed the river, miles and miles away.
Mistake him? Never! Mistake him? the famous Eagle Chief!
That terror to all the settlers, that desperate Cattle Thief —
That monstrous, fearless Indian, who lorded it over the plain,
Who thieved and raided, and scouted, who rode like a hurricane!
But they've tracked him across the prairie; they've followed him hard and fast;
10   For those desperate English settlers have sighted their man at last.

Up they wheeled to the tepees, all their British blood aflame,
Bent on bullets and bloodshed, bent on bringing down their game;
But they searched in vain for the Cattle Thief: that lion had left his lair,
And they cursed like a troop of demons — for the women alone were there.
"The sneaking Indian coward," they hissed; "he hides while yet he can;
He'll come in the night for cattle, but he's scared to face a *man*."
"Never!" and up from the cotton woods rang the voice of Eagle Chief;
And right out into the open stepped, unarmed, the Cattle Thief.
Was that the game they had coveted? Scarce fifty years had rolled
20   Over that fleshless, hungry frame, starved to the bone and old;
Over that wrinkled, tawny skin, unfed by the warmth of blood.
Over those hungry, hollow eyes that glared for the sight of food.

He turned, like a hunted lion: "I know not fear," said he;
And the word outleapt from his shrunken lips in the language of the Cree.
"I'll fight you, white-skins, one by one, till I kill you *all*," he said;
But the threat was scarcely uttered, ere a dozen balls of lead
Whizzed through the air about him like a shower of metal rain,
And the gaunt old Indian Cattle Thief dropped dead on the open plain.
And that band of cursing settlers gave one triumphant yell,
30   And rushed like a pack of demons on the body that writhed and fell.
"Cut the fiend up into inches, throw his carcass on the plain;
Let the wolves eat the cursed Indian, he'd have treated us the same."
A dozen hands responded, a dozen knives gleamed high,
But the first stroke was arrested by a woman's strange, wild cry.
And out into the open, with a courage past belief,
She dashed, and spread her blanket o'er the corpse of the Cattle Thief;
And the words outleapt from her shrunken lips in the language of the Cree,
"If you mean to touch that body, you must cut your way through *me*."
And that band of cursing settlers dropped backward one by one,
40   For they knew that an Indian woman roused, was a woman to let alone.
And then she raved in a frenzy that they scarcely understood,
Raved of the wrongs she had suffered since her earliest babyhood:
"Stand back, stand back, you white-skins, touch that dead man to your shame;

You have stolen my father's spirit, but his body I only claim.
You have killed him, but you shall not dare to touch him now he's dead.
You have cursed, and called him a Cattle Thief, though you robbed him first of bread —
Robbed him and robbed my people — look there, at that shrunken face,
Starved with a hollow hunger, we owe to you and your race.
What have you left to us of land, what have you left of game,
What have you brought but evil, and curses since you came?   50
How have you paid us for our game? how paid us for our land?
By a *book*, to save our souls from the sins *you* brought in your other hand.
Go back with your new religion, we never have understood
Your robbing an Indian's *body*, and mocking his *soul* with food.
Go back with your new religion, and find — if find you can —
The *honest* man you have ever made from out a *starving* man.
You say your cattle are not ours, your meat is not our meat;
When *you* pay for the land you live in, *we'll* pay for the meat we eat.
Give back our land and our country, give back our herds of game;
Give back the furs and the forests that were ours before you came;   60
Give back the peace and the plenty. Then come with your new belief,
And blame, if you dare, the hunger that *drove* him to be a thief."

(1895)

Ojistoh

I am Ojistoh, I am she, the wife
Of him whose name breathes bravery and life
And courage to the tribe that calls him chief.
I am Ojistoh, his white star, and he
Is land, and lake, and sky — and soul to me.

Ah! But they hated him, those Huron braves,
Him who had flung their warriors into graves,
Him who had crushed them underneath his heel,
Whose arm was iron, and whose heart was steel
To all — save me, Ojistoh, chosen wife   10
Of my great Mohawk, white star of his life.

Ah! but they hated him, and councilled long
With subtle witchcraft how to work him wrong;
How to avenge their dead, and strike him where
His pride was highest, and his fame most fair.
Their hearts grew weak as women at his name:
They dared no war-path since my Mohawk came
With ashen bow, and flinten arrow-head
To pierce their craven bodies; but their dead
Must be avenged. Avenged? They dared not walk   20
In day and meet his deadly tomahawk;

They dared not face his fearless scalping knife;
So — Niyoh![1] — then they thought of me, his wife.

O! evil, evil face of them they sent
With evil Huron speech: "Would I consent
To take of wealth? be queen of all their tribe?
Have wampum ermine?" Back I flung the bribe
Into their teeth, and said, "While I have life
Know this — Ojistoh is the Mohawk's wife."

30   Wah! how we struggled! But their arms were strong.
They flung me on their pony's back, with thong
Round ankle, wrist, and shoulder. Then upleapt
The one I hated most: his eye he swept
Over my misery, and sneering said,
"Thus, fair Ojistoh, we avenge our dead."

And we rode, rode as a sea wind-chased,
I, bound with buckskin to his hated waist,
He, sneering, laughing, jeering, while he lashed
The horse to foam, as on and on we dashed.
40   Plunging through creek and river, bush and trail,
On, on we galloped like a northern gale.
At last, his distant Huron fires aflame
We saw, and nearer, nearer still we came.

I, bound behind him in the captive's place,
Scarcely could see the outline of his face.
I smiled, and laid my cheek against his back:
"Loose thou my hands," I said. "This pace let slack.
Forget we now that thou and I are foes.
I like thee well, and wish to clasp thee close;
50   I like the courage of thine eye and brow;
I like thee better than my Mohawk now."

He cut the cords; we ceased our maddened haste
I wound my arms about his tawny waist;
My hand crept up the buckskin of his belt;
His knife hilt in my burning palm I felt;
One hand caressed his cheek, the other drew
The weapon softly — "I love you, love you,"
I whispered, "love you as my life."
And — buried in his back his scalping knife.

60   Ha! how I rode, rode as a sea wind-chased,
Mad with sudden freedom, mad with haste,

---

1. **Niyoh** According to Johnson, the Mohawk word for "God."

Back to my Mohawk and my home. I lashed
That horse to foam, as on and on I dashed.
Plunging through creek and river, bush and trail,
On, on I galloped like a northern gale.
And then my distant Mohawk's fires aflame
I saw, as nearer, nearer still I came,
My hands all wet, stained with a life's red dye,
But pure my soul, pure as those stars on high —
"My Mohawk's pure white star, Ojistoh, still am I."   70

(1895)

The Corn Husker

Hard by the Indian lodges, where the bush
  Breaks in a clearing, through ill-fashioned fields,
She comes to labour, when the first still hush
  Of autumn follows large and recent yields.

Age in her fingers, hunger in her face,
  Her shoulders stooped with weight of work and years,
But rich in tawny colouring of her race,
  She comes a-field to strip the purple ears.

And all her thoughts are with the days gone by,
  Ere might's injustice banished from their lands   10
Her people, that today unheeded lie,
  Like the dead husks that rustle through her hands.

(1896)

Archibald Lampman (1861–1899)

In an 1884 letter to his friend J.A. Ritchie, Archibald Lampman remarked, "I have been endeavouring to think up some plan for a strictly Canadian poem, local in its incident and spirit, but cosmopolitan in form and manner. It is a hard thing to get at." Lampman did achieve his goal in poems such as "Morning on the Lièvres" (1888), but he was still deeply indebted to classical and British Romantic themes and subjects in many of his works. In his 1891 lecture "Two Canadian Poets," he locates his literary circle at the initial stages of a developing tradition. "A good deal is being said about Canadian Literature," he notes, and much of it has to do with "whether a Canadian Literature exists. Of course it does not." He adds that in time, Canada's "social and climatic conditions" will "evolve a race of people, having a peculiar national temperament and bent of mind, and when that is done we shall have a *Canadian* literature."

Lampman was born on 17 November 1861 in Morpeth, Canada West (now Ontario). In 1866, his father was appointed rector of the Perrytown Anglican church and, within a year, the family had relocated yet again — this time to Gore's Landing, on Rice Lake. Although he had been seriously weakened by rheumatic fever, Lampman spent his childhood years outdoors, rambling along the lakeshore. The famous Strickland sisters — Susanna Moodie and Catharine Parr Traill — were members of the Rice Lake community, and the Lampmans became acquainted with them. The family left Gore's Landing for Cobourg in 1874.

When he was 15, Lampman became a student at Trinity College School in Port Hope, and in 1879 he entered Trinity College in Toronto. There, he joined the college's literary institute; he published his first writing, mainly critical prose, in the campus periodical, *Rouge et Noir*. Graduating in 1882, he was hired as a teacher at Orangeville High School. He quickly developed an aversion to teaching, however, and the following year he moved to Ottawa, where he settled into a permanent position at the Post Office Department.

In an 1883 letter, Lampman wrote of the city he now called home, "this is a place not of 'wind and flowers, full of sweet trees and colour of glad grass' [quoting Swinburne], but a place of chill fierce colds, full of rheumatism and damned snowstorms"; he described his post office job as "easy monotonous work." In his ample spare time, he read and wrote. "I have grown wonderfully prolific of verse since I came here," he declared. "I am belching forth like a volcano." His poetic technique improved, and he began to establish associations with other intellectuals in the city. His closest friend was fellow poet Duncan Campbell Scott, a clerk in the Department of Indian Affairs. The two men belonged to the Ottawa Literary and Scientific Society, and they attended society meetings together. Sharing an appreciation for nature, they went on many canoe trips in regions north of the city.

Throughout the 1880s, Lampman's interest in politics grew. He joined the Ottawa Progressive Club, and he and his friends met informally to discuss current events and social problems. He also appears to have been a member of the Fabian Society (a socialist organization), and this has caused scholars to speculate about his socialist leanings. His "Essay on Socialism" (circa 1895) reveals a committed yet moderate view. Lampman's socialist orientation also emerges in his city poems. In "The City of the End of Things," for example, he describes "multitudes of men" who "built [a] city in their pride, / Until its might was made"; but now, "of that prodigious race, / Three only in an iron tower, / Set like carved idols face to face, / Remain the masters of its power."

In 1887, Lampman married Maud Playter. He had been publishing his poetry in various Canadian and American periodicals, such as Goldwin Smith's *The Week* (Toronto), of which Charles G.D. Roberts was the editor, but Maud helped him to fund the publication of his first collection: *Among the Millet, and Other Poems* (1888). The poems in this volume derive from the British Romantic tradition, reflecting themes of reverence and humility in the face of the beauty of the natural world. In "Winter Hues Recalled," the speaker stumbles upon a "sunset's rapid hand of fire, / Sudden, mysterious, every moment deepening / To some new majesty of rose or flame." He stands "Like one spell-bound / Caught in the presence of some god." For Lampman, the poetic imagination, often depicted as a dreamlike state, is the way to a higher truth.

Among the Millet was a success, and Lampman began to enjoy a reputation as one of Canada's most promising poets. From 1892 to 1893, he collaborated with Scott and William Wilfred Campbell on a weekly column for the Toronto *Globe* called "At the Mermaid Inn." Lampman contributed over 85 reviews, essays, poems, literary news stories, and position pieces to the column; these have been collected and published in *At the Mermaid Inn: Wilfred Campbell, Archibald Lampman, Duncan Campbell Scott in The Globe 1892–93* (1979, edited by Barrie Davies).

At around this time, Lampman formed a close relationship with a young woman named Katherine Thompson Waddell, a fellow Post Office Department employee whom he considered his "spiritual mate." He was still a married man, and his feelings for Waddell troubled him. Ultimately, Waddell put an end to their relationship. Lampman wrote many poems for her, which were never published in his lifetime, and these have been collected in *Lampman's Kate: Late Love Poems of Archibald Lampman 1887–1897* (1975, edited by Margaret Whitridge).

In 1895, Lampman was made a fellow of the Royal Society of Canada. The following year, a Boston publisher produced *Lyrics of Earth* (although the edition was dated 1895). Lampman began to prepare a third volume of poetry, *Alcyone* (1899), but he did not live to see it published. He died, weakened by pneumonia, on 10 February 1899, in Ottawa. In 1900, Scott compiled a memorial edition of his friend's poetry, *The Poems of Archibald Lampman*. He went on to compile *Lyrics of Earth: Sonnets and Ballads* (1925); *At the Long Sault and Other New Poems* (1943, with E.K. Brown); and the *Selected Poems of Archibald Lampman* (1947).

The Railway Station

The darkness brings no quiet here, the light
   No waking: ever on my blinded brain
   The flare of lights, the rush, and cry, and strain,
The engines' scream, the hiss and thunder smite:
I see the hurrying crowds, the clasp, the flight,
   Faces that touch, eyes that are dim with pain:
   I see the hoarse wheels turn, and the great train
Move labouring out into the bourneless night.
So many souls within its dim recesses,
   So many bright, so many mournful eyes: 10
Mine eyes that watch grow fixed with dreams and guesses;
   What threads of life, what hidden histories,
What sweet or passionate dreams and dark distresses,
   What unknown thoughts, what various agonies!

                              (1887)

In October

Along the waste, a great way off, the pines
   Like tall slim priests of storm, stand up and bar
The low long strip of dolorous[1] red that lines
   The under west, where wet winds moan afar.
The cornfields all are brown, and brown the meadows
   With the brown leaves' wind-heapèd traceries,[2]
And the brown thistle stems that cast no shadows,
   And bear no bloom for bees.

As slowly earthward leaf by red leaf slips,
   The sad trees rustle in chill misery,   10
A soft strange inner sound of pain-crazed lips,
   That move and murmur incoherently;
As if all leaves, that yet have breath, were sighing,
   With pale hushed throats, for death is at the door,
So many low soft masses for the dying
   Sweet leaves that live no more.

---

1. dolorous Sorrowful. **2. traceries** Delicate patterns of lines.

Here I will sit upon this naked stone,
   Draw my coat closer with my numbèd hands,
And hear the ferns sigh, and the wet woods moan,
20   And send my heart out to the ashen lands;
And I will ask myself what golden madness,
   What balmèd breaths of dreamland spicery,
What visions of soft laughter and light sadness
   Were sweet last month to me.

The dry dead leaves flit by with thin weird tunes,
   Like failing murmurs of some conquered creed,
Graven in mystic markings with strange runes,
   That none but stars and biting winds may read;
Here I will wait a little; I am weary,
30   Not torn with pain of any lurid hue,
But only still and very gray and dreary,
   Sweet sombre lands, like you.

(1888)

Heat

From plains that reel to southward, dim,
   The road runs by me white and bare;
Up the steep hill it seems to swim
   Beyond, and melt into the glare.
Upward half-way, or it may be
   Nearer the summit, slowly steals
A hay-cart, moving dustily
   With idly clacking wheels.

By his cart's side the wagoner
10   Is slouching slowly at his ease,
Half-hidden in the windless blur
   Of white dust puffing to his knees.
This wagon on the height above,
   From sky to sky on either hand,
Is the sole thing that seems to move
   In all the heat-held land.

Beyond me in the fields the sun
   Soaks in the grass and hath his will;
I count the marguerites one by one;
20   Even the buttercups are still.
On the brook yonder not a breath
   Disturbs the spider or the midge.
The water-bugs draw close beneath
   The cool gloom of the bridge.

Where the far elm-tree shadows flood
  Dark patches in the burning grass,
The cows, each with her peaceful cud,
  Lie waiting for the heat to pass.
From somewhere on the slope near by
  Into the pale depth of the noon   30
A wandering thrush slides leisurely
  His thin revolving tune.

In intervals of dreams I hear
  The cricket from the droughty ground;
The grasshoppers spin into mine ear
  A small innumerable sound.
I lift mine eyes sometimes to gaze:
  The burning sky-line blinds my sight:
The woods far off are blue with haze:
  The hills are drenched in light.   40

And yet to me not this or that
  Is always sharp or always sweet;
In the sloped shadow of my hat
  I lean at rest, and drain the heat;
Nay more, I think some blessèd power
  Hath brought me wandering idly here:
In the full furnace of this hour
  My thoughts grow keen and clear.

                                                    (1888)

Winter Evening

To-night the very horses springing by
Toss gold from whitened nostrils. In a dream
The streets that narrow to the westward gleam
Like rows of golden palaces; and high
From all the crowded chimneys tower and die
A thousand aureoles.[1] Down in the west
The brimming plains beneath the sunset rest,
One burning sea of gold. Soon, soon shall fly
The glorious vision, and the hours shall feel
A mightier master; soon from height to height,   10
With silence and the sharp unpitying stars,
Stern creeping frosts, and winds that touch like steel,
Out of the depth beyond the eastern bars,
Glittering and still shall come the awful night.

                                                    (1888)

---

1. aureoles Rings of light.

Among the Timothy

Long hours ago, while yet the morn was blithe,[1]
  Nor sharp athirst had drunk the beaded dew,
A mower came, and swung his gleaming scythe
  Around this stump, and, shearing slowly, drew
    Far round among the clover, ripe for hay,
      A circle clean and gray;
And here among the scented swathes that gleam,
  Mixed with dead daisies, it is sweet to lie
  And watch the grass and the few-clouded sky,
10   Nor think but only dream.

For when the noon was turning, and the heat
  Fell down most heavily on field and wood,
I too came hither, borne on restless feet,
  Seeking some comfort for an aching mood.
    Ah! I was weary of the drifting hours,
      The echoing city towers,
The blind gray streets, the jingle of the throng,
  Weary of hope that like a shape of stone
  Sat near at hand without a smile or moan,
20   And weary most of song.

And those high moods of mine that sometime made
  My heart a heaven, opening like a flower
A sweeter world where I in wonder strayed,
  Begirt[2] with shapes of beauty and the power
    Of dreams that moved through that enchanted clime
      With changing breaths of rhyme,
Were all gone lifeless now, like those white leaves
  That hang all winter, shivering dead and blind
  Among the sinewy beeches in the wind,
30   That vainly calls and grieves.

Ah! I will set no more mine overtaskèd brain
  To barren search and toil that beareth nought,
For ever following with sore-footed pain
  The crossing pathways of unbournèd thought;
    But let it go, as one that hath no skill,
      To take what shape it will,
An ant slow-burrowing in the earthy gloom,
  A spider bathing in the dew at morn,
  Or a brown bee in wayward fancy borne
40   From hidden bloom to bloom.

---

1. **blithe** Pleasant. 2. **Begirt** Encircled by.

Hither and thither o'er the rocking grass
   The little breezes, blithe as they are blind,
Teasing little slender blossoms pass and pass,
   Soft-footed children of the gipsy wind,
     To taste of every purple-fringèd head
       Before the bloom is dead;
And scarcely heed the daisies that, endowed
   With stems so short they cannot see, up-bear
   Their innocent sweet eyes distressed, and stare
     Like children in a crowd.   50

Not far to fieldward in the central heat,
   Shadowing the clover, a pale poplar stands
With glimmering leaves that, when the wind comes, beat
   Together like innumerable small hands,
     And with the calm, as in vague dreams astray,
       Hang wan and silver-gray;
Like sleepy maenads,[3] who in pale surprise,
   Half-wakened by a prowling beast, have crept
   Out of the hidden covert, where they slept,
     At noon with languid[4] eyes.   60

The crickets creak, and through the noonday glow,
   That crazy fiddler of the hot mid-year,
The dry cicada plies his wiry bow
   In long-spun cadence, thin and dusty sere;
     From the green grass the small grasshoppers' din
       Spreads soft and silvery thin;
And ever and anon a murmur steals
   Into mine ears of toil that moves alway,
   The crackling rustle of the pitch-forked hay
     And lazy jerk of wheels.   70

As so I lie and feel the soft hours wane,
   To wind and sun and peaceful sound laid bare,
That aching dim discomfort of the brain
   Fades off unseen, and shadowy-footed care
     Into some hidden corner creeps at last
       To slumber deep and fast;
And gliding on, quite fashioned to forget,
   From dream to dream I bid my spirit pass
   Out into the pale green ever-swaying grass
     To brood, but no more fret.   80

And hour by hour among all shapes that grow
   Of purple mints and daisies gemmed with gold

---

3. maenads Female worshipper of Dionysus in Greek mythology. **4. languid** Listless.

In sweet unrest my visions come and go;
   I feel and hear and with quiet eyes behold;
   And hour by hour, the ever-journeying sun,
     In gold and shadow spun,
Into mine eyes and blood, and through the dim
   Green glimmering forest of the grass shines down,
   Till flower and blade, and every cranny brown,
90   And I are soaked with him.

(1888)

The Frogs

I

Breathers of wisdom won without a quest,
   Quaint uncouth[1] dreamers, voices high and strange;
   Flutists of lands where beauty hath no change,
And wintry grief is a forgotten guest,
Sweet murmurers of everlasting rest,
   For whom glad days have ever yet to run,
   And moments are as aeons, and the sun
But ever sunken half-way toward the west.

Often to me who heard you in your day,
10   With close rapt ears, it could not choose but seem
That earth, our mother, searching in what way
   Men's hearts might know her spirit's inmost dream;
     Ever at rest beneath life's change and stir,
     Made you her soul, and bade you pipe for her.

II

In those mute days when spring was in her glee,
   And hope was strong, we knew not why or how,
And earth, the mother, dreamed with brooding brow,
Musing on life, and what the hours might be,
When love should ripen to maternity,
20   Then like high flutes in silvery interchange
   Ye piped with voices still and sweet and strange,
And ever as ye piped, on every tree

The great buds swelled; among the pensive woods
   The spirits of first flowers awoke and flung
From buried faces the close-fitting hoods,
   And listened to your piping till they fell,
   The frail spring-beauty with her perfumed bell,
The wind-flower, and the spotted adder-tongue.

---

1. **uncouth** Ungraceful.

III

All the day long, wherever pools might be
  Among the golden meadows, where the air   30
  Stood in a dream, as it were moorèd there
For ever in a noon-tide reverie,
Or where the birds made riot of their glee
  In the still woods, and the hot sun shone down,
  Crossed with warm lucent shadows on the brown
Leaf-paven pools, that bubbled dreamily,

Or far away in whispering river meads
  And watery marshes where the brooding noon,
  Full with the wonder of its own sweet boon,
Nestled and slept among the noiseless reeds,   40
  Ye sat and murmured, motionless as they,
  With eyes that dreamed beyond the night and day.

IV

And when day passed and over heaven's height,
  Thin with the many stars and cool with dew,
  The fingers of the deep hours slowly drew
The wonder of the ever-healing night,
No grief or loneliness or rapt delight
  Or weight of silence ever brought to you
  Slumber or rest; only your voices grew
More high and solemn; slowly with hushed flight   50

Ye saw the echoing hours go by, long-drawn,
  Nor ever stirred, watching with fathomless eyes,
  And with your countless clear antiphonies[2]
Filling the earth and heaven, even till dawn,
  Last-risen, found you with its first pale gleam,
  Still with soft throats unaltered in your dream.

V

And slowly as we heard you, day by day,
  The stillness of enchanted reveries
  Bound brain and spirit and half-closèd eyes,
In some divine sweet wonder-dream astray;   60
To us no sorrow or upreared dismay
  Nor any discord came, but evermore
  The voices of mankind, the outer roar,
Grew strange and murmurous, faint and far away.

Morning and noon and midnight exquisitely,
  Rapt with your voices, this alone we knew,

---

2. **antiphonies** Exchanges between two musical voices.

Cities might change and fall, and men might die,
   Secure were we, content to dream with you
      That change and pain are shadows faint and fleet,
70   And dreams are real, and life is only sweet.

(1888)

Morning on the Lièvres[1]

Far above us where a jay
Screams his matins[2] to the day,
Capped with gold and amethyst,
Like a vapour from the forge
Of a giant somewhere hid,
Out of hearing of the clang
Of his hammer, skirts of mist
Slowly up the woody gorge
Lift and hang.

10   Softly as a cloud we go,
Sky above and sky below,
Down the river; and the dip
Of the paddles scarcely breaks,
With the little silvery drip
Of the water as it shakes
From the blades, the crystal deep
Of the silence of the morn,
Of the forest yet asleep;
And the river reaches borne
20   In a mirror, purple gray,
Sheer away
To the misty line of light,
Where the forest and the stream
In the shadow meet and plight,
Like a dream.

From amid a stretch of reeds,
Where the lazy river sucks
All the water as it bleeds
From a little curling creek,
30   And the muskrats peer and sneak
In around the sunken wrecks
Of a tree that swept the skies
Long ago,
On a sudden seven ducks
With a splashy rustle rise,

---

1. **Lièvres** River in Southern Quebec. 2. **matins** Morning prayer.

Stretching out their seven necks,
One before, and two behind,
And the others all arow,
And as steady as the wind
With a swivelling whistle go, 40
Through the purple shadow led,
Till we only hear their whir
In behind a rocky spur,
Just ahead.

(1888)

In November

With loitering step and quiet eye,
Beneath the low November sky,
I wandered in the woods, and found
A clearing, where the broken ground
Was scattered with black stumps and briers,
And the old wreck of forest fires.
It was a bleak and sandy spot,
And, all about, the vacant plot,
Was peopled and inhabited
By scores of mulleins[1] long since dead. 10
A silent and forsaken brood
In that mute opening of the wood,
So shrivelled and so thin they were,
So gray, so haggard, and austere,
Not plants at all they seemed to me,
But rather some spare company
Of hermit folk, who long ago,
Wandering in bodies to and fro,
Had chanced upon this lonely way,
And rested thus, till death one day 20
Surprised them at their compline[2] prayer,
And left them standing lifeless there.

There was no sound about the wood
Save the wind's secret stir. I stood
Among the mullein-stalks as still
As if myself had grown to be
One of their sombre company,
A body without wish or will.
And as I stood, quite suddenly,
Down from a furrow in the sky 30
The sun shone out a little space

---

1. **mulleins** Woolly-leafed plant. 2. **compline** Final canonical hour (of seven) sung before bedtime.

Across that silent sober place,
Over the sand heaps and brown sod,
The mulleins and dead goldenrod,
And passed beyond the thickets gray,
And lit the fallen leaves that lay,
Level and deep within the wood,
A rustling yellow multitude.

And all around me the thin light,
40   So sere, so melancholy bright,
Fell like the half-reflected gleam
Or shadow of some former dream;
A moment's golden reverie
Poured out on every plant and tree
A semblance of weird joy, or less,
A sort of spectral happiness;
And I, too, standing idly there,
With muffled hands in the chill air,
Felt the warm glow about my feet,
50   And shuddering betwixt cold and heat,
Drew my thoughts closer, like a cloak,
While something in my blood awoke,
A nameless and unnatural cheer,
A pleasure secret and austere.

(1890)

The City of the End of Things

Beside the pounding cataracts[1]
Of midnight streams unknown to us
'Tis builded in the leafless tracts
And valleys huge of Tartarus.[2]
Lurid and lofty and vast it seems;
It hath no rounded name that rings,
But I have heard it called in dreams
The City of the End of Things.

Its roofs and iron towers have grown
10   None knoweth how high within the night,
But in its murky streets far down
A flaming terrible and bright
Shakes all the stalking shadows there,
Across the walls, across the floors,
And shifts upon the upper air

---

1. **cataracts** Heavy falls of water. 2. **Tartarus** Depth of Hades reserved for guilty mortals in Greek mythology; famously sunless.

From out a thousand furnace doors;
And all the while an awful sound
Keeps roaring on continually,
And crashes in the ceaseless round
Of a gigantic harmony. 20
Through its grim depths re-echoing
And all its weary height of walls,
With measured roar and iron ring,
The inhuman music lifts and falls.
Where no thing rests and no man is,
And only fire and night hold sway;
The beat, the thunder and the hiss
Cease not, and change not, night nor day.
And moving at unheard commands,
The abysses and vast fires between, 30
Flit figures that with clanking hands
Obey a hideous routine;
They are not flesh, they are not bone,
They see not with the human eye,
And from their iron lips is blown
A dreadful and monotonous cry;
And whoso of our mortal race
Should find that city unaware,
Lean Death would smite him face to face,
And blanch him with its venomed air: 40
Or caught by the terrific spell,
Each thread or memory snapt and cut,
His soul would shrivel and its shell
Go rattling like an empty nut.

It was not always so, but once,
In days that no man thinks upon,
Fair voices echoed from its stones,
The light above it leaped and shone:
Once there were multitudes of men,
That built that city in their pride, 50
Until its might was made, and then
They withered age by age and died.
But now of that prodigious race,
Three only in an iron tower,
Set like carved idols face to face,
Remain the masters of its power;
And at the city gate a fourth,
Gigantic and with dreadful eyes,
Sits looking toward the lightless north,
Beyond the reach of memories; 60
Fast rooted to the lurid floor,

A bulk that never moves a jot,
In his pale body dwells no more,
Or mind or soul, — an idiot!
But sometime in the end those three
Shall perish and their hands be still,
And with the master's touch shall flee
Their incommunicable skill.
A stillness absolute as death
70   Along the slacking wheels shall lie,
And, flagging at a single breath,
The fires that moulder out and die.
The roar shall vanish at its height,
And over that tremendous town
The silence of eternal night
Shall gather close and settle down.
All its grim grandeur, tower and hall,
Shall be abandoned utterly,
And into rust and dust shall fall
80   From century to century;
Nor ever living thing shall grow,
Nor trunk of tree, nor blade of grass;
No drop shall fall, no wind shall blow,
Nor sound of any foot shall pass:
Alone of its accursèd state,
One thing the hand of Time shall spare,
For the grim Idiot at the gate
Is deathless and eternal there.

                                                      (1894)

Winter Uplands

The frost that stings like fire upon my cheek,
The loneliness of this forsaken ground,
The long white drift upon whose powdered peak
I sit in the great silence as one bound;
The rippled sheet of snow where the wind blew
Across the open fields for miles ahead;
The far-off city towered and roofed in blue
A tender line upon the western red;
The stars that singly, then in flocks appear,
10   Like jets of silver from the violet dome,
So wonderful, so many and so near,
And then the golden moon to light me home —
The crunching snowshoes and the stinging air,
And silence, frost and beauty everywhere.

                                                      (1899)

At the Long Sault: May, 1660[1]

Under the day-long sun there is life and mirth
   In the working earth,
And the wonderful moon shines bright
   Through the soft spring night,
The innocent flowers in the limitless woods are springing
   Far and away
   With the sound and the perfume of May,
And ever up from the south the happy birds are winging,
   The waters glitter and leap and play
   While the grey hawk soars.   10

But far in an open glade of the forest set
   Where the rapid plunges and roars,
Is a ruined fort with a name that men forget, —
   A shelterless pen
   With its broken palisade,
   Behind it, musket in hand,
   Beyond message or aid
   In this savage heart of the wild,
Mere youngsters, grown in a moment to men,
   Grim and alert and arrayed,   20
   The comrades of Daulac[2] stand.
Ever before them, night and day,
   The rush and skulk and cry
Of foes, not men but devils, panting for prey;
   Behind them the sleepless dream
Of the little frail-walled town, far away by the plunging stream,
   Of maiden and matron and child,
With ruin and murder impending, and none but they
   To beat back the gathering horror
   Deal death while they may,   30
   And then die.

Day and night they have watched while the little plain
Grew dark with the rush of the foe, but their host
Broke ever and melted away, with no boast
But to number their slain;
   And now as the days renew
   Hunger and thirst and care
Were they never so stout, so true,
   Press at their hearts; but none
Falters or shrinks or utters a coward word,   40
   Though each setting sun

---

1. **At the Long Sault: May, 1660** About 700 Iroquois fighters attacked a 16-person camp of French settlers here, beside the St. Lawrence River. 2. **Daulac** Commander of the French garrison at Montreal, who defended the fort at Long Sault.

Brings from the pitiless wild new hands to the Iroquois horde,
And only to them despair.

Silent, white-faced, again and again
Charged and hemmed round by furious hands,
Each for a moment faces them all and stands
In his little desperate ring; like a tired bull moose
Whom scores of sleepless wolves, a ravening pack,
Have chased all night, all day
50   Through the snow-laden woods, like famine let loose;
And he turns at last in his track
Against a wall of rock and stands at bay;
Round him with terrible sinews and teeth of steel
They charge and recharge; but with many a furious plunge and wheel,
Hither and thither over the trampled snow,
He tosses them bleeding and torn;
Till, driven, and ever to and fro
Harried, wounded and weary grown,
His mighty strength gives way
60   And all together they fasten upon him and drag him down.

So Daulac turned him anew
With a ringing cry to his men
In the little raging forest glen,
And his terrible sword in the twilight whistled and slew.
And all his comrades stood
With their backs to the pales, and fought
Till their strength was done;
The thews that were only mortal flagged and broke
Each struck his last wild stroke,
70   And they fell one by one,
And the world that had seemed so good
Passed like a dream and was naught.

And then the great night came
With the triumph-songs of the foe and the flame
Of the camp-fires.
Out of the dark the soft wind woke,
The song of the rapid rose alway
And came to the spot where the comrades lay,
Beyond help or care,
80   With none but the red men round them
To gnash their teeth and stare.

All night by the foot of the mountain
    The little town lieth at rest,
The sentries are peacefully pacing;
    And neither from East nor from West

Is there rumour of death or of danger;
   None dreameth tonight in his bed
That ruin was near and the heroes
   That met it and stemmed it are dead.

But afar in the ring of the forest,   90
   Where the air is so tender with May
And the waters are wild in the moonlight,
   They lie in their silence of clay.

The numberless stars out of heaven
   Look down with a pitiful glance;
And the lilies asleep in the forest
   Are closed like the lilies of France.

                                                  (1943)

Duncan Campbell Scott (1862–1947)

In his 1922 presidential address to the Royal Society of Canada, entitled "Poetry and Progress," Duncan Campbell Scott reflected upon the Modern movement in poetry and in the arts in general. "A virus has infected all the arts," he declared. "The desire for rebellious, violent and discordant expression has invaded even the serene province of Music." Scott's assertion is remarkable, as he is often remembered as the Confederation poet who came closest to creating a modern aesthetic in his work.

Scott was born on 2 August 1862 in Ottawa. His father was a Methodist minister, and the Scott family moved often to accommodate his various appointments. Scott spent his childhood in Ottawa; Smith's Falls, Ontario; and Stanstead, Quebec. In 1879, he had to abandon his formal education due to financial constraints, and he went to work as a clerk in the Department of Indian Affairs in Ottawa. He remained with the department throughout his entire working life, becoming superintendent of Indian education in 1909, and deputy superintendent general of Indian affairs in 1913.

Scott had an interest in visual art and a passion for music (he was a talented pianist), but he did not consider writing poetry or fiction until he met Archibald Lampman, in the mid-1880s. Lampman was working at the Post Office Department, and the two became great friends. During the 1890s, they indulged their shared passion for the outdoors, taking a number of canoe trips.

Scott's reputation grew as his work started to appear in various Canadian and American periodicals. He collaborated with Lampman and Wilfred Campbell on a weekly literary column for the Toronto *Globe* called "At the Mermaid Inn," and in 1893, he published his first book: *The Magic House and Other Poems*. With some exceptions ("At the Cedars," for example), the collection reveals the poet's indebtedness to the British Romantics and Victorians. In "The Fifteenth of April," he describes a natural world transformed by a pastoral imagination: "Under Venus sings the vesper sparrow, / Down a path of rosy gold / Floats the slender moon; / Ringing from the rounded barrow / Rolls the robin's tune." In "To Winter," Scott uses elevated diction and tropes of the sublime in nature to portray the season: "Come, O thou conqueror of the flying year; / Come from thy fastness of the Arctic suns; / Mass on the purple waste and wide frontier / Thy wanish hosts and silver clarions."

In 1894, Scott married a concert violinist named Belle Warner Botsford, and the following year, their first and only child, Elizabeth Duncan, was born. Tragically, she died when she was just 12 years old. Scott's poem "The Closed Door" is an elegy for his daughter.

In 1896, Scott published *In the Village of Viger*, a collection of sketches about life in small-town French Canada inspired by his experiences as a youth in rural Quebec; in 1898, he produced a second collection of poetry, entitled *Labour and the Angel*. In 1899, Lampman passed away, and Scott quickly applied himself to memorializing his friend's life and work, preparing *The Poems of Archibald Lampman* for publication in 1900. He subsequently compiled three more collections of Lampman's poetry. Lampman had been a fellow of the Royal Society of Canada, and Scott was elected to replace him in 1899.

In 1905, Scott was appointed commissioner for Treaty 9 (the James Bay Treaty), and he spent the next two summers negotiating land claims with Cree and Ojibway tribes in Northern Ontario. He drew on his travels in the Canadian wilderness to write *New World Lyrics* (1905) and *Via Borealis* (1906). It is in these two works that Scott really began to transform his experiences with Native peoples into poetic material. This has troubled many contemporary critics, who point to the disparity between Scott's seemingly sympathetic portraits of Native communities and individuals and the fact that Scott deployed the government projects that displaced them. It is difficult to reconcile a poem like "On the Way to the Mission" (1905), which explores the destructive effects of the fur trade on the Native population, with Scott's accounts of his work with Indian affairs — in which he makes assertions such as the Native people of Canada need "to develop and mature under protection until they, one and all, reach their destined goal, full British citizenship."

In 1929, Scott's wife passed away. Several years later, he married a poet named Elise Aylen. When Scott retired from the civil service, in 1932, he and Elise travelled through Europe, the United States, and western Canada. Many of the poems in his collection *The Green Cloister: Later Poems* (1935) were inspired by these travels. Scott's final publication was *The Circle of Affection, and Other Pieces in Prose and Verse* (1947), a collection of old and new stories, essays, and poems. He died on 19 December 1947.

The Onondaga[1] Madonna

She stands full-throated and with careless pose,
This woman of a weird and waning race,
The tragic savage lurking in her face,
Where all her pagan passion burns and glows;
Her blood is mingled with her ancient foes,
And thrills with war and wilderness in her veins;
Her rebel lips are dabbled with the stains
Of feuds and forays and her father's woes.

And closer in the shawl about her breast,
The latest promise of her nation's doom,
Paler than she her baby clings and lies,

10

---

1. **Onondaga** A tribe of the Iroquois.

The primal warrior gleaming from his eyes;
He sulks, and burdened with his infant gloom,
He draws his heavy brows and will not rest.

(1898)

The Piper of Arll

There was in Arll a little cove
  Where the salt wind came cool and free:
A foamy beach that one would love,
  If he were longing for the sea.

A brook hung sparkling on the hill,
  The hill swept far to ring the bay;
The bay was faithful, wild or still,
  To the heart of the ocean far away.

There were three pines above the comb
  That, when sun flared and went down,   10
Grew like three warriors reaving home
  The plunder of a burning town.

A piper lived within the grove,
  Tending the pasture of his sheep;
His heart was swayed with faithful love,
  From the springs of God's ocean clear and deep.

And there a ship one evening stood,
  Where ship had never stood before;
A pennon[1] bickered red as blood,
  An angel glimmered at the prore.[2]   20

About the coming on of dew,
  The sails burned rosy, and the spars
Were gold, and all the tackle grew
  Alive with ruby-hearted stars.

The piper heard an outlanded[3] tongue,
  With music in the cadenced fall;
And when the fairy lights were hung,
  The sailors gathered one and all,

And leaning on the gunwales[4] dark,
  Crusted with shells and dashed with foam,   30
With all the dreaming hills to hark,
  They sang their longing songs of home.

---

1. pennon Banner. **2. prore** A ship's prow. **3. outlanded** Foreign. **4. gunwales** Upper edge of a ship.

When the sweet airs had fled away,
   The piper, with a gentle breath,
Moulded a tranquil melody
   Of lonely love and longed-for death.

When the fair sound began to lull,
   From out the fireflies and the dew,
A silence held the shadowy hull,
40   Until the eerie tune was through.

Then from the dark and dreamy deck
   An alien song began to thrill;
It mingled with the drumming beck,
   And stirred the braird[5] upon the hill.

Beneath the stars each sent to each
   A message tender, till at last
The piper slept upon the beach,
   The sailors slumbered round the mast.

Still as a dream till nearly dawn,
50   The ship was bosomed on the tide;
The streamlet murmuring on and on,
   Bore the sweet water to her side.

Then shaking out her lawny[6] sails,
   Forth on the misty sea she crept;
She left the dawning of the dales,
   Yet in his clock the piper slept.

And when he woke he saw the ship,
   Limned[7] black against the crimson sun;
Then from the disc he saw her slip,
60   A wraith of shadow — she was gone.

He threw his mantle[8] on the beach,
   He went apart like one distraught,
His lips were moved — his desperate speech
   Stormed his inviolable thought.

He broke his human-throated reed,
   And threw it in the idle rill;
But when his passion had its mead,[9]
   He found it in the eddy[10] still.

---

5. braird New plants sprouting. **6. lawny** Like very thin cotton. **7. limned** Outlined. **8. mantle** Cloak. **9. mead** Heavy, honey-based liquor. **10. eddy** Swirl of water.

He mended well the patient flue,[11]
  Again he tried its varied stops;
The closures answered right and true,
  And starting out in piercing drops,   70

A melody began to drip
  That mingled with a ghostly thrill
The vision-spirit of the ship,
  The secret of his broken will.

Beneath the pines he piped and swayed,
  Master of passion and of power;
He was his soul and what he played,
  Immortal for a happy hour.   80

He, singing into nature's heart,
  Guiding his will by the world's will,
With deep, unconscious, child-like art
  Had sung his soul out and was still.

And then at evening came the bark
  That stirred his dreaming heart's desire;
It burned slow lights along the dark
  That died in glooms of crimson fire.

The sailors launched a sombre boat,
  And bent with music at the oars;   90
The rhythm throbbing every throat,
  And lapsing round the liquid shores,

Was that true tune the piper sent,
  Unto the wave-worn mariners,
When with the beck and ripple blent
  He heard that outland song of theirs.

Silent they rowed him, dip and drip,
  The oars beat out an exequy,[12]
They laid him down within the ship,
  They loosed a rocket to the sky.   100

It broke in many a crimson sphere
  That grew to gold and floated far,
And left the sudden shore-line clear,
  With one slow-changing, drifting star.

---

11. **flue** Windway in a pipe. 12. **exequy** Funeral ritual.

Then out they shook the magic sails,
    That charmed the wind in other seas,
From where the west line pearls and pales,
    They waited for a ruffling breeze.

But in the world there was no stir,
110   The cordage[13] slacked with never a creak,
They heard the flame begin to purr
    Within the lantern at the peak.

They could not cry, they could not move,
    They felt the lure from the charmed sea;
They could not think of home or love
    Or any pleasant land to be.

They felt the vessel dip and trim,[14]
    And settle down from list to list;
They saw the sea-plane heave and swim
120   As gently as a rising mist.

And down so slowly, down and down,
    Rivet by rivet, plank by plank;
A little flood of ocean flown
    Across the deck, she sank and sank.

From knee to breast the water wore,
    It crept and crept; ere they were ware
Gone was the angel at the prore,
    They felt the water float their hair.

They saw the salt plain spark and shine,
130   They threw their faces to the sky;
Beneath a deepening film of brine
    They saw the star-flash blur and die.

She sank and sank by yard and mast,
    Sank down the shimmering gradual dark;
A little drooping pennon last
    Showed like the black fin of a shark.

And down she sank till, keeled in sand,
    She rested safely balanced true,
With all her upward gazing band,
140   The piper and the dreaming crew.

---

13. **cordage** Bulk of cords. 14. **trim** Adjust in response to the movement of wind and sea.

And there, unmarked of any chart,
   In unrecorded deeps they lie,
Empearled within the purple heart
   Of the great sea for aye and aye.

Their eye are ruby in the green
   Long shaft of sun that spreads and rays,
And upward with a wizard sheen
   A fan of sea-light leaps and plays.

Tendrils of or and azure creep,
   And globes of amber light are rolled,   150
And in the gloaming of the deep
   Their eyes are starry pits of gold.

And sometimes in the liquid night
   The hull is changed, a solid gem,
That glows with a soft stony light,
   The lost prince of a diadem.[15]

And at the keel a vine is quick,
   That spreads its bines[16] and works and weaves
O'er all the timbers veining thick
   A plenitude of silver leaves.   160

                                                 (1895)

Night Hymns on Lake Nipigon[1]

Here in the midnight, where the dark mainland and island
Shadows mingle in shadow deeper, profounder,
Sing we the hymns of the churches, while the dead water
Whispers before us.

Thunder is travelling slow on the path of the lightning;
One after one the stars and the beaming planets
Look serene in the lake from the edge of the storm-cloud,
Then have they vanished.

While our canoe, that floats dumb in the bursting thunder,
Gathers her voice in the quiet and thrills and whispers,   10
Presses her prow in the star-gleam, and all her ripple
Lapses in blackness.

Sing we the sacred ancient hymns of the churches,
Chanted first in old-world nooks of the desert,

---

15. **diadem** Crown. 16. **bines** Clasping tendrils, for climbing.

1. **Lake Nipigon** Body of water north of Lake Superior in Ontario; once Ojibwan land.

While in the wild, pellucid[2] Nipigon reaches
Hunted the savage.

Now have the ages met in the Northern midnight,
And on the lonely, loon-haunted Nipigon reaches
Rises the hymn of triumph and courage and comfort,
20   Adeste Fideles.[3]

Tones that were fashioned when the faith brooded in darkness,
Joined with sonorous vowels in the noble Latin,
Now are married with the long-drawn Ojibwa,
Uncouth and mournful.

Soft with the silver drip of the regular paddles
Falling in rhythm, timed with the liquid, plangent[4]
Sounds from the blades where the whirlpools break and are carried
Down into darkness;

Each long cadence,[5] flying like a dove from her shelter
30   Deep in the shadow, wheels for a throbbing moment,
Poises in utterance, returning in circles of silver
To nest in the silence.

All wild nature stirs with the infinite, tender
Plaint[6] of a bygone age whose soul is eternal,
Bound in the lonely phrases that thrill and falter
Back into quiet.

Back they falter as the deep storm overtakes them,
Whelms them in splendid hollows of booming thunder,
Wraps them in rain, that, sweeping, breaks and onrushes
40   Ringing like cymbals.

(1900)

The Forsaken

I

Once in the winter
Out on a lake
In the heart of the north-land,
Far from the Fort
And far from the hunters,
A Chippewa woman
With her sick baby,

---

2. **pellucid** Clear. 3. **Adeste Fideles** The "O Come All Ye Faithful" hymn. 4. **plangent** Loud but sorrowful.
5. **cadence** Patterns of rhythm and pitch, especially at the end of a phrase (musical or spoken). 6. **Plaint** Expression
of suffering.

Crouched in the last hours
Of a great storm.
Frozen and hungry,   10
She fished through the ice
With a line of the twisted
Bark of the cedar,
And a rabbit-bone hook
Polished and barbed;
Fished with the bare hook
All through the wild day,
Fished and caught nothing;
While the young chieftain
Tugged at her breasts,
Or slept in the lacings   20
Of the warm *tikanagan*.[1]
All the lake-surface
Streamed with the hissing
Of millions of iceflakes
Hurled by the wind;
Behind her the round
Of a lonely island
Roared like a fire
With the voice of the storm
In the deeps of the cedars.   30
Valiant, unshaken,
She took of her own flesh,
Baited the fish-hook,
Drew in a gray-trout,
Drew in his fellows,
Heaped them beside her,
Dead in the snow.
Valiant, unshaken,
She faced the long distance,   40
Wolf-haunted and lonely,
Sure of her goal
And the life of her dear one:
Tramped[2] for two days,
On the third in the morning,
Saw the strong bulk
Of the Fort by the river,
Saw the wood-smoke
Hand soft in the spruces,
Heard the keen yelp   50
Of the ravenous huskies
Fighting for whitefish:
Then she had rest.

---

1. **tikanagan** A board and carrying bag used by the Cree to carry young children safely. 2. **Tramped** Trudged.

II

Years and years after,
When she was old and withered,
When her son was an old man
And his children filled with vigour,
They came in their northern tour on the verge of winter,
To an island in a lonely lake.
60   There one night they camped, and on the morrow
Gathered their kettles and birch-bark
Their rabbit-skin robes and their mink-traps,
Launched their canoes and slunk away through the islands,
Left her alone forever,
Without a word of farewell,
Because she was old and useless,
Like a paddle broken and warped,
Or a pole that was splintered.
Then, without a sigh,
70   Valiant, unshaken,
She smoothed her dark locks under her kerchief,
Composed her shawl in state,
Then folded her hands ridged with sinews and corded with veins,
Folded them across her breasts spent with the nourishment of children,
Gazed at the sky past the tops of the cedars,
Saw two spangled[3] nights arise out of the twilight,
Saw two days go by filled with the tranquil sunshine,
Saw, without pain, or dread, or even a moment of longing:
Then on the third great night there came thronging and thronging
80   Millions of snowflakes out of a windless cloud;
They covered her close with a beautiful crystal shroud,
Covered her deep and silent.
But in the frost of the dawn,
Up from the life below,
Rose a column of breath
Through a tiny cleft in the snow,
Fragile, delicately drawn,
Wavering with its own weakness,
In the wilderness a sign of the spirit,
90   Persisting still in the sight of the sun
Till day was done.
Then all light was gathered up by the hand of God and hid in His breast,
Then there was born a silence deeper than silence,
Then she had rest.

(1903)

---

3. spangled Starry.

On the Way to the Mission

They dogged him all one afternoon,
Through the bright snow,
Two whitemen servants of greed;
He knew that they were there,
But he turned not his head;
He was an Indian trapper;
He planted his snow-shoes firmly,
He dragged the long toboggan
Without rest.

The three figures drifted   10
Like shadows in the mind of a seer;
The snow-shoes were whisperers
On the threshold of awe;
The toboggan made the sound of wings,
A wood-pigeon sloping to her nest.

The Indian's face was calm.
He strode with the sorrow of fore-knowledge,
But his eyes were jewels of content
Set in circles of peace.

They would have shot him;   20
But momently in the deep forest,
They saw something flit by his side:
Their hearts stopped with fear.
Then the moon rose.
They would have left him to the spirit,

But they saw the long toboggan
Rounded well with furs,
With many a silver fox-skin,
With the pelts of mink and of otter.
They were the servants of greed;   30
When the moon grew brighter
And the spruces were dark with sleep,
They shot him.
When he fell on a shield of moonlight
One of his arms clung to his burden;
The snow was not melted:
The spirit passed away.

Then the servants of greed
Tore off the cover to count their gains;
They shuddered away into the shadows,   40
Hearing each the loud heart of the other.
Silence was born.

There in the tender moonlight,
    As sweet as they were in life,
Glimmered the ivory features,
    Of the Indian's wife.

In the manner of Montagnais[1] women
    Her hair was rolled with braid;
Under her waxen fingers
50   A crucifix was laid.

He was drawing her down to the Mission,
    To bury her there in spring,
When the bloodroot comes and the windflower
    To silver everything.

But as a gift of plunder
    Side by side were they laid,
The moon went on to her setting
    And covered them with shade.

                         (1905)

The Height of Land

Here is the height of land:
The watershed on either hand
Goes down to Hudson Bay
Or Lake Superior;
The stars are up, and far away
The wind sounds in the wood, wearier
Than the long Ojibwa cadence
In which Potàn the Wise
Declares the ills of life
10   And Chees-que-ne-ne makes a mournful sound
Of acquiescence.[1] The fires burn low
With just sufficient glow
To light the flakes of ash that play
At being moths, and flutter away
To fall in the dark and die as ashes:
Here there is peace in the lofty air,
And Something comes by flashes
Deeper than peace; —
The spruces have retired a little space
20   And left a field of sky in violet shadow
With stars like marigolds in a water-meadow.

---

1. Montagnais An Algonquin tribe.

---

1. acquiescence Reluctant consent.

Now the Indian guides are dead asleep;
There is no sound unless the soul can hear
The gathering of the waters in their sources.

We have come up through the spreading lakes
From level to level, —
Pitching our tents sometimes over a revel
Of roses that nodded all night,
Dreaming within our dreams,
To wake at dawn and find that they were captured   30
With no dew on their leaves;
Sometimes mid sheaves
Of bracken² and dwarf-cornel,³ and again
On a wide blue-berry plain
Brushed with the shimmer of a bluebird's wing;
A rocky islet followed
With one lone poplar and a single nest
Of white-throat-sparrows that took no rest
But sang in dreams or woke to sing, —
To the last portage and the height of land — :   40
Upon one hand
The lonely north enlaced with lakes and streams,
And the enormous targe of Hudson Bay,
Glimmering all night
In the cold arctic light;
On the other hand
The crowded southern land
With all the welter⁴ of the lives of men.
But here is peace, and again
That Something comes by flashes   50
Deeper than peace, — a spell
Golden and inappellable⁵
That gives the inarticulate part
Of our strange being one moment of release
That seems more native than the touch of time,
And we must answer in chime;
Though yet no man may tell
The secret of that spell
Golden and inappellable.

Now are there sounds walking in the wood,   60
And all the spruces shiver and tremble,
And the stars move a little in their courses.

---

2. **bracken** A type of fern. 3. **dwarf-cornel** Low, berried plant. 4. **welter** Disorienting muddle.
5. **inappellable** Unnameable or uncallable.

The ancient disturber of solitude
Breathes a pervasive sigh,
And the soul seems to hear
The gathering of the waters at their sources;
Then quiet ensues and pure starlight and dark;
The region-spirit murmurs in meditation,
The heart replies in exaltation
70 And echoes faintly like a inland shell
Ghost tremors of the spell;
Thought reawakens and is linked again
With all the welter of the lives of men.

Here on the uplands where the air is clear
We think of life as of a stormy scene, —
Of tempest, of revolt and desperate shock;
And here, where we can think, on the bright uplands
Where the air is clear, we deeply brood on life
Until the tempest parts, and it appears
80 As simple as to the shepherd seems his flock:
A Something to be guided by ideals —
That in themselves are simple and serene —
Of noble deed to foster noble thought,
And noble thought to image noble deed,
Till deed and thought shall interpenetrate,
Making life lovelier, till we come to doubt
Whether the perfect beauty that escapes
Is beauty of deed or thought or some high thing
Mingled of both, a greater boon than either:
90 Thus we have seen in the retreating tempest
The victor-sunlight merge with the ruined rain,
And from the rain and sunlight spring the rainbow.

The ancient disturber of solitude
Stirs his ancestral potion in the gloom,
And the dark wood
Is stifled with the pungent fume
Of charred earth burnt to the bone
That takes the place of air.
Then sudden I remember when and where, —
100 The last weird lakelet[6] foul with weedy growths
And slimy viscid[7] things the spirit loathes,
Skin of vile water over viler mud
Where the paddle stirred unutterable stenches,
And the canoes seemed heavy with fear,

---

6. **lakelet** Small lake. 7. **viscid** Sticky.

Not to be urged toward the fatal shore
Where a bush fire, smouldering, with sudden roar
Leaped on a cedar and smothered it with light
And terror. It had left the portage-height
A tangle of slanted spruces burned to the roots,
Covered still with patches of bright fire   110
Smoking with incense of the fragrant resin
That even then began to thin and lessen
Into the gloom and glimmer of ruin.

'Tis overpast. How strange the stars have grown;
The presage of extinction glows on their crests
And they are beautied with impermanence;
They shall be after the race of men
And mourn for them who snared their fiery pinions,[8]
Entangled in the meshes of bright words.

A lemming stirs the fern and in the mosses   120
Eft-minded things feel the air change, and dawn
Tolls out from the dark belfries of the spruces.
How often in the autumn of the world
Shall the crystal shrine of dawning be rebuilt
With deeper meaning! Shall the poet then,
Wrapped in his mantle on the height of land,
Brood on the welter of the lives of men
And dream of his ideal hope and promise
In the blush sunrise? Shall he base his flight
Upon a more compelling law than Love   130
As Life's atonement; shall the vision
Of noble deed and noble thought immingled
Seem as uncouth to him as the pictograph
Scratched on the cave side by the cave-dweller
To us of the Christ-time? Shall he stand
With deeper joy, with more complex emotion,
In closer commune with divinity,
With the deep fathomed, with the firmament charted,
With life as simple as a sheep-boy's song,
What lies beyond a romaunt[9] that was read   140
Once on a morn of storm and laid aside
Memorious with strange immortal memories?
Or shall he see the sunrise as I see it
In shoals of misty fire the deluge-light
Dashes upon and whelms[10] with purer radiance,

---

8. pinions Wings. **9. romaunt** Conventional verse romance. **10. whelms** Engulfs.

And feel the lulled earth, older in pulse and motion,
Turn the rich lands and inundant[11] oceans
To the flushed color, and hear as now I hear
The thrill of life beat up the planet's margin
150 And break in the clear susurrus[12] of deep joy
That echoes and reëchoes in my being?
O Life is intuition the measure of knowledge
And do I stand with heart entranced and burning
At the zenith[13] of our wisdom when I feel
The long light flow, the long wind pause, the deep
Influx of spirit, of which no man may tell
The Secret, golden and inappellable?

           (1916)

At Gull Lake: August, 1810

Gull Lake set in the rolling prairie —
Still there are reeds on the shore,
As of old the poplars shimmer
As summer passes;
Winter freezes the shallow lake to the core;
Storm passes,
Heat parches the sedges and grasses,
Night comes with moon-glimmer,
Dawn with the morning-star;
10 All proceeds in the flow of Time
As a hundred years ago.

Then two camps were pitched on the shore,
The clustered teepees
Of Tabashaw Chief of the Saulteaux.[1]
And on a knoll tufted with poplars
Two gray tents of a trader —
Nairne of the Orkneys.[2]
Before his tents under the shade of the poplars
Sat Keejigo, third of the wives
20 Of Tabashaw Chief of the Saulteaux;
Clad in the skins of antelopes
Broidered with porcupine quills
Coloured with vivid dyes,
Vermilion here and there
In the roots of her hair,
A half-moon of powder-blue

---

11. **inundant** Uncontainable. 12. **susurrus** Whisper. 13. **zenith** Pinnacle.

---

1. **Tabashaw Chief of the Saulteux** The Saulteaux decended from the Ojibwa and migrated to the Prairies. 2. **Nairne of the Orkneys** Scottish trader (from the Orkney Islands).

On her brow, her cheeks
Scored with light ochre streaks.
Keejigo daughter of Launay
The Normandy hunter[3]   30
And Oshawan of the Saulteaux,
Troubled by fugitive visions
In the smoke of the camp-fires,
In the close dark of the teepee,
Flutterings of colour
Along the flow of the prairies,
Spangles of flower tints
Caught in the wonder of dawn,
Dreams of sounds unheard —
The echoes of echo,   40
Star she was named for
Keejigo, star of the morning,
Voices of storm —
Wind-rush and lightning, —
The beauty of terror;
The twilight moon
Coloured like a prairie lily,
The round moon of pure snow,
The beauty of peace;
Premonitions of love and of beauty   50
Vague as shadows cast by a shadow.
Now she had found her hero,
And offered her body and spirit
With abject unreasoning passion,
As Earth abandons herself
To the sun and the thrust of the lightning.
Quiet were all the leaves of the poplars,
Breathless the air under their shadow,
As Keejigo spoke of these things to her heart
In the beautiful speech of the Saulteaux.   60

    The flower lives on the prairie,
    The wind in the sky,
    I am here my beloved;
    The wind and the flower.

    The crane hides in the sand-hills,
    Where does the wolverine hide?
    I am here my beloved,
    Heart's-blood on the feathers
    The foot caught in the trap.

---

3. **Launay the Normandy hunter** A French man; Keejigo is half-white.

70   *Take the flower in your hand,*
       The wind in your nostrils;
       I am here my beloved;
       Release the captive
       Heal the wound under the feathers.

       A storm-cloud was marching
       Vast on the prairie,
       Scored with livid[4] ropes of hail,
       Quick with nervous vines of lightning —
       Twice had Nairne turned her away
80   Afraid of the venom of Tabashaw,
       Twice had the Chief fired at his tents
       And now when two bullets
       Whistled above the encampment
       He yelled "Drive this bitch to her master."

       Keejigo went down a path by the lake;
       Thick at the tangled edges,
       The reeds and the sedges
       Were gray as ashes
       Against the death-black water;
90   The lightning scored with double flashes
       The dark lake-mirror and loud
       Came the instant thunder.
       Her lips still moved to the words of her music,
       "Release the captive,
       Heal the wound under the feathers."

       At the top of the bank
       The old wives caught her and cast her down
       Where Tabashaw crouched by his camp-fire.
       He snatched a live brand from the embers,
100   Seared her cheeks,
       Blinded her eyes,
       Destroyed her beauty with fire,
       Screaming, "Take that face to your lover."
       Keejigo held her face to the fury
       And made no sound.
       The old wives dragged her away
       And threw her over the bank
       Like a dead dog.

       Then burst the storm —
110   The Indians' screams and the howls of the dogs
       Lost in the crash of hail

---

4. **livid** Gloomy or angry.

That smashed the sedges and reeds,
Stripped the poplars of leaves,
Tore and blazed onwards,
Wasting itself with riot and tumult —
Supreme in the beauty of terror.

The setting sun struck the retreating cloud
With a rainbow, not an arc but a column
Built with the glory of seven metals;
Beyond in the purple deeps of the vortex   120
Fell the quivering vines of the lightning.
The wind withdrew the veil from the shrine of the moon,
She rose changing her dusky shade for the glow
Of the prairie lily, till free of all blemish of colour
She came to her zenith[5] without a cloud or a star,
A lovely perfection, snow-pure in the heaven of midnight.
After the beauty of terror the beauty of peace.

But Keejigo came no more to the camps of her people;
Only the midnight moon knew where she felt her way,
Only the leaves of autumn, the snows of winter   130
Knew where she lay.

                                                                    (1935)

Stephen Leacock (1869–1944)

In his posthumously published memoir, Stephen Leacock wrote that his mother had been forced to cope with 11 children and an alcoholic husband; the family had lived in debt while enduring the father's violent behaviour and extended absences. When Leacock graduated from Upper Canada College, at the age of 18, his father came home to the family he had practically abandoned. Enraged at his impertinence, the young Leacock marched him to the train station and threatened him with a buggy whip. "If you come back," he said, "I'll kill you!" Such behaviour is highly uncharacteristic of the Stephen Leacock we know through his other writings. In the course of his literary career, he consistently expressed his morality through humour, not indignation. He was a kind-hearted humorist and a life-long teacher — a humanist who helped define Canadian culture.

Leacock was born in England in1869. In 1876, he and his family settled on a farm in Ontario, near the shores of Lake Simcoe. His mother hired a tutor to help preserve the children's Victorian sensibilities, and her plan succeeded — Leacock never stopped believing in the Empire and imperialism. But he tempered this with an abiding faith in cooperation, not domination. He earned a B.A. in modern languages from the University of Toronto in 1891 and then taught for eight years at his old college, but he did not find the work challenging. Of his university years, he wrote: "I spent my entire time in the acquisition of languages, living, dead, and half-dead, and knew nothing of the outside world. In this diligent pursuit of words I spent about sixteen hours of each day."

Before completing his Ph.D., he moved to Montreal to take up a position at McGill University as a special lecturer in political science and history. In 1900, he married Beatrix Hamilton, and six

---

5. **zenith** Pinnacle.

years later, he published the textbook *Elements of Political Science*, which was adopted by more than 30 universities and translated into several languages. In 1910, he inaugurated a tradition of publishing a book of humour per year. The first was *Literary Lapses*, an enlarged edition of a volume he had already self-published. It was a comic tour de force, a showcase for the wide variety of comic techniques that Leacock would employ in future books, including illogical thinking: "Just think of it. A hundred years ago there were no bacilli, no ptomaine poisoning, no diphtheria, and no appendicitis. Rabies was but little known, and only imperfectly developed." This book, and *Nonsense Novels* (1911), betrayed the stylistic influence on Leacock of English nonsense humour.

Then, in 1912, Leacock published *Sunshine Sketches of a Little Town*. It would become his most famous work. It describes the small lakeside town of Mariposa (modelled on Orillia, Ontario), its hapless inhabitants, and the pressures of modernity and urban culture on their rural lifestyle. Because Leacock's depiction of the townspeople is affectionate, indulgent of their foibles and follies, the author is generally viewed as an ironist, not a satirist. In *Arcadian Adventures with the Idle Rich*, which appeared in 1914, Leacock offered a contrast to Mariposa — a big city, based on Montreal. In this book, he criticizes class and materialism, suggesting that urban society is less compassionate than small-town society. Despite the themes he raised here, Leacock distrusted socialism, as evidenced by some of his books from the 1920s and 1930s, and he was fond of Montreal, publishing *Montreal, Seaport and City* in 1942.

Leacock produced three history books the same year *Arcadian Adventures* appeared. He also wrote biographies. His first was *Mark Twain* (1932), a study of the writer who had influenced him more than any other. In fact, when Leacock's work first appeared, his publisher called him "the Canadian Mark Twain."

McGill forced Leacock to retire at the age of 66. He had enjoyed a long and distinguished career at the university (becoming a full professor in 1908), and he felt disappointed and angry at this turn of events. Writing now claimed most of his attention. *Humor: Its Theory and Technique* — in which Leacock defines humour as "what we laugh at" — appeared in 1935, and it is still a standard reference on the subject. He then published a series of books with a political orientation, among them *My Discovery of the West* (1937), which dealt with the economic prospects of the Western Canadian provinces with the rise of the Social Credit movement.

In 1941, *Canada: The Foundations of Its Future* (a book commissioned by Seagram's distillery) appeared. In it, Leacock remarks: "There is not as yet a Canadian literature. ... Nor is there similarly a Canadian humour, nor any particularly Canadian way of being funny." He was being typically modest. For many years, he had been widely considered the funniest writer in English, setting the standard for ironic, self-deprecating humour. He died of cancer in 1944 in a Toronto hospital, predeceased by his wife (who had died in 1925), and survived by their son, Stephen Junior.

My Financial Career

When I go into a bank I get rattled. The clerks rattle me; the wickets rattle me; the sight of the money rattles me; everything rattles me.

The moment I cross the threshold of a bank and attempt to transact business there, I become an irresponsible idiot.

I knew this beforehand, but my salary had been raised to fifty dollars a month and I felt that the bank was the only place for it.

So I shambled in and looked timidly round at the clerks. I had an idea that a person about to open an account must needs consult the manager.

I went up to a wicket marked "Accountant." The accountant was a tall, cool devil. The very sight of him rattled me. My voice was sepulchral.

"Can I see the manager?" I said, and added solemnly, "alone." I don't know why I said "alone."

"Certainly," said the accountant, and fetched him.

The manager was a grave, calm man. I held my fifty-six dollars clutched in a crumpled ball in my pocket.

"Are you the manager?" I said. God knows I didn't doubt it.

"Yes," he said.

"Can I see you," I asked, "alone?" I didn't want to say "alone" again, but without it the thing seemed self-evident.

The manager looked at me in some alarm. He felt that I had an awful secret to reveal.

"Come in here," he said, and led the way to a private room. He turned the key in the lock.

"We are safe from interruption here," he said. "Sit down."

We both sat down and looked at each other. I found no voice to speak.

"You are one of Pinkerton's men, I presume," he said.

He had gathered from my mysterious manner that I was a detective. I knew what he was thinking, and it made me worse.

"No, not from Pinkerton's," I said, seeming to imply that I came from a rival agency.

"To tell the truth," I went on, as if I had been prompted to lie about it, "I am not a detective at all. I have come to open an account. I intend to keep all my money in this bank."

The manager looked relieved but still serious; he concluded now that I was a son of Baron Rothschild or a young Gould.

"A large account, I suppose," he said.

"Fairly large," I whispered, "I propose to deposit fifty-six dollars now and fifty dollars a month regularly."

The manager got up and opened the door. He called to the accountant.

"Mr. Montgomery," he said unkindly loud, "this gentleman is opening an account, he will deposit fifty-six dollars. Good morning."

I rose.

A big iron door stood open at the side of the room.

"Good morning," I said, and stepped into the safe.

"Come out," said the manager coldly, and showed me the other way.

I went up to the accountant's wicket and poked the ball of money at him with a quick convulsive movement as if I were doing a conjuring trick.

My face was ghastly pale.

"Here," I said, "deposit it." The tone of the words seemed to mean, "Let us do this painful thing while the fit is on us."

He took the money and gave it to another clerk.

He made me write the sum on a slip and sign my name in a book. I no longer knew what I was doing. The bank swam before my eyes.

"Is it deposited?" I asked in a hollow, vibrating voice.

"It is," said the accountant.

"Then I want to draw a cheque."

My idea was to draw out six dollars of it for present use. Someone gave me a cheque-book through a wicket and someone else began telling me how to write it out. The people in the bank had the impression that I was an invalid millionaire. I wrote something on the cheque and thrust it in at the clerk. He looked at it.

"What! are you drawing it all out again?" he asked in surprise. Then I realised that I had written fifty-six instead of six. I was too far gone to reason now. I had a feeling that it was impossible to explain the thing. All the clerks had stopped writing to look at me.

Reckless with misery, I made a plunge.

"Yes, the whole thing."

"You withdraw your money from the bank?"

"Every cent of it."

"Are you not going to deposit any more?" said the clerk, astonished.

"Never."

An idiot hope struck me that they might think something had insulted me while I was writing the cheque and that I had changed my mind. I made a wretched attempt to look like a man with a fearfully quick temper.

The clerk prepared to pay the money.

"How will you have it?" he said.

"What?"

"How will you have it?"

"Oh" — I caught his meaning and answered without even trying to think — "in fifties."

He gave me a fifty-dollar bill.

"And the six?" he asked dryly.

"In sixes," I said.

He gave it me and I rushed out.

As the big door swung behind me I caught the echo of a roar of laughter that went up to the ceiling of the bank. Since then I bank no more. I keep my money in cash in my trousers pocket and my savings in silver dollars in a sock.

(1910)

The Whirlwind Campaign in Mariposa

It was Mullins, the banker, who told Mariposa all about the plan of a Whirlwind Campaign and explained how it was to be done. He'd happened to be in one of the big cities when they were raising money by a Whirlwind Campaign for one of the universities, and he saw it all.

He said he would never forget the scene on the last day of it, when the announcement was made that the total of the money raised was even more than what was needed. It was a splendid sight — the business men of the town all cheering and laughing and shaking hands, and the professors with the tears streaming down their faces, and the Deans of the Faculties, who had given money themselves, sobbing aloud.

He said it was the most moving thing he ever saw.

So, as I said, Henry Mullins, who had seen it, explained to the others how it was done. He said that first of all a few of the business men got together quietly — very quietly, indeed the more quietly the better — and talked things over. Perhaps one of them would dine — just quietly — with another one and discuss the situation. Then these two would invite a third man — possibly even a fourth — to have lunch with them and talk in a general way — even talk of other things part of the time. And so on in this way things would be discussed and looked at in different lights and viewed from different angles and then when everything was ready they would go at things with a rush. A central committee would be formed and sub-committees, with captains of each group and recorders and secretaries, and on a stated day the Whirlwind Campaign would begin.

Each day the crowd would all agree to meet at some stated place and eat lunch together — say at a restaurant or at a club or at some eating place. This would go on every day with the interest getting keener and keener, and everybody getting more and more excited, till presently the chairman would announce that the campaign had succeeded and there would be the kind of scene that Mullins had described.

So that was the plan that they set in motion in Mariposa.

* * * * *

I don't wish to say too much about the Whirlwind Campaign itself. I don't mean to say that it was a failure. On the contrary, in many ways it couldn't have been a greater success, and yet somehow it didn't seem to work out just as Henry Mullins had said it would. It may be that there are differences between Mariposa and the larger cities that one doesn't appreciate at first sight. Perhaps it would have been better to try some other plan.

Yet they followed along the usual line of things closely enough. They began with the regular system of some of the business men getting together in a quiet way.

First of all, for example, Henry Mullins came over quietly to Duff's rooms, over the Commercial Bank, with a bottle of rye whiskey, and they talked things over. And the night after that George Duff came over quietly to Mullins's rooms over the Exchange Bank, with a bottle of Scotch whiskey. A few evenings after that Mullins and Duff went together, in a very unostentatious way, with perhaps a couple of bottles of rye, to Pete Glover's room over the hardware store. And then all three of them went up one night with Ed Moore, the photographer, to Judge Pepperleigh's house under pretence of having a game of poker. The very day after that, Mullins and Duff and Ed Moore, and Pete Glover and the judge got Will Harrison, the harness maker, to go out without any formality on the lake on the pretext of fishing. And the next night after that Duff and Mullins and Ed Moore and Pete Glover and Pepperleigh and Will Harrison got Alf Trelawney, the postmaster, to come over, just in a casual way, to the Mariposa House, after the night mail, and the next day Mullins and Duff and —

But, pshaw! you see at once how the thing is worked. There's no need to follow that part of the Whirlwind Campaign further. But it just shows the power of organization.

And all this time, mind you, they were talking things over, and looking at things first in one light and then in another light — in fact, just doing as the big city men do when there's an important thing like this under way.

So after things had been got pretty well into shape in this way, Duff asked Mullins one night, straight out, if he would be chairman of the Central Committee. He sprung it on him and Mullins had no time to refuse, but he put it to Duff straight whether he would be treasurer. And Duff had no time to refuse.

* * * * *

That gave things a start, and within a week they had the whole organization on foot. There was the Grand Central Committee and six groups or sub-committees of twenty men each, and a captain for every group. They had it all arranged on the lines most likely to be effective.

In one group there were all the bankers, Mullins and Duff and Pupkin (with the cameo pin), and about four others. They had their photographs taken at Ed Moore's studio, taken in a line with a background of icebergs — a winter scene — and a pretty penetrating crowd they looked, I can tell you. After all, you know, if you get a crowd of representative bank men together in any financial deal, you've got a pretty considerable leverage right away.

In the second group were the lawyers, Nivens and Macartney and the rest — about as level-headed a lot as you'd see anywhere. Get the lawyers of a town with you on a thing like this and you'll find you've got a sort of brain power with you that you'd never get without them.

Then there were the business men — there was a solid crowd for you — Harrison, the harness maker, and Glover, the hardware man, and all that gang, not talkers, perhaps, but solid men who can tell you to a nicety how many cents there are in a dollar. It's all right to talk about education and that sort of thing, but if you want driving power and efficiency, get business men. They're seeing it every day in the city, and it's just the same in Mariposa. Why, in the big concerns in the city, if they found out a man was educated, they wouldn't have him — wouldn't keep him there a minute. That's why the business men have to conceal it so much.

Then in the other teams there were the doctors and the newspaper men and the professional men like Judge Pepperleigh and Yodel the auctioneer.

* * * * *

It was all organized so that every team had its headquarters, two of them in each of the three hotels — one upstairs and one down. And it was arranged that there would be a big lunch every day, to be held in Smith's caff, round the corner of Smith's Northern Health Resort and Home of the Wissanotti Angler — you know the place. The lunch was divided up into tables, with a captain for each table to see about things to drink, and of course all the tables were in competition with one another. In fact the competition was the very life of the whole thing.

It's just wonderful how these things run when they're organized. Take the first luncheon, for example. There they all were, every man in his place, every captain at his post at the top of the table. It was hard, perhaps, for some of them to get there. They had very likely to be in their stores and banks and offices till the last minute and then make a dash for it. It was the cleanest piece of team work you ever saw.

You have noticed already, I am sure, that a good many of the captains and committee men didn't belong to the Church of England Church. Glover, for instance, was a Presbyterian, till they ran the picket fence of the manse[1] two feet on to his property, and after that he became a free-thinker. But in Mariposa, as I have said, everybody likes to be in everything and naturally a Whirlwind Campaign was a novelty. Anyway it would have been a poor business to keep a man out of the lunches merely on account of his religion. I trust that the day for that kind of religious bigotry is past.

---

1. **manse** Church minister's residence.

Of course the excitement was when Henry Mullins at the head of the table began reading out the telegrams and letters and messages. First of all there was a telegram of good wishes from the Anglican Lord Bishop of the Diocese to Henry Mullins and calling him Dear Brother in Grace — the Mariposa telegraph office is a little unreliable and it read: "Dear Brother in grease," but that was good enough. The Bishop said that his most earnest wishes were with them.

Then Mullins read a letter from the Mayor of Mariposa — Pete Glover was mayor that year — stating that his keenest desires were with them; and then one from the Carriage Company saying that its heartiest good will was all theirs; and then one from the Meat Works saying that its nearest thoughts were next to them. Then he read one from himself, as head of the Exchange Bank, you understand, informing him that he had heard of his project and assuring him of his liveliest interest in what he proposed.

At each of these telegrams and messages there was round after round of applause, so that you could hardly hear yourself speak or give an order. But that was nothing to when Mullins got up again, and beat on the table for silence and made one of those crackling, concise speeches — just the way business men speak — the kind of speech that a college man simply can't make. I wish I could repeat it all. I remember that it began: "Now boys, you know what we're here for, gentlemen," and it went on just as good as that all through.

When Mullins had done he took out a fountain pen and wrote out a cheque for a hundred dollars, conditional on the fund reaching fifty thousand. And there was a burst of cheers all over the room.

Just the moment he had done it, up sprang George Duff — you know the keen competition there is, as a straight matter of business, between the banks in Mariposa — up sprang George Duff, I say, and wrote out a cheque for another hundred conditional on the fund reaching seventy thousand. You never heard such cheering in your life.

And then when Netley walked up to the head of the table and laid down a cheque for a hundred dollars conditional on the fund reaching one hundred thousand the room was in an uproar. A hundred thousand dollars! Just think of it! The figures fairly stagger one. To think of a hundred thousand dollars raised in five minutes in a little place like Mariposa!

And even that was nothing! In less than no time there was such a crowd round Mullins trying to borrow his pen all at once that his waistcoat was all stained with ink. Finally when they got order at last, and Mullins stood up and announced that the conditional fund had reached a quarter of a million, the whole place was a perfect babel of cheering. Oh, these Whirlwind Campaigns are wonderful things!

* * * * *

I can tell you the Committee felt pretty proud that first day. There was Henry Mullins looking a little bit flushed and excited, with his white waistcoat and an American Beauty rose, and with ink marks all over him from the cheque signing; and he kept telling them that he'd known all along that all that was needed was to get the thing started and telling again about what he'd seen at the University Campaign and about the professors crying, and wondering if the high-school teachers would come down for the last day of the meetings.

Looking back on the Mariposa Whirlwind, I can never feel that it was a failure. After all, there is a sympathy and a brotherhood in these things when men work shoulder to shoulder. If you had seen the canvassers of the Committee going round the town that evening shoulder to shoulder from the Mariposa House to the Continental and up to Mullins's rooms and over to Duff's shoulder to shoulder, you'd have understood it.

I don't say that every lunch was quite such a success as the first. It's not always easy to get out of the store if you're a busy man, and a good many of the Whirlwind Committee found that they had just time to hurry down and snatch their lunch and get back again. Still, they came, and snatched it. As long as the lunches lasted, they came. Even if they had simply to rush it and grab something to eat and drink without time to talk to anybody, they came.

No, no, it was not lack of enthusiasm that killed the Whirlwind Campaign in Mariposa. It must have been something else. I don't just know what it was but I think it had something to do with the financial, the bookkeeping side of the thing.

It may have been, too, that the organization was not quite correctly planned. You see, if practically everybody is on the committees, it is awfully hard to try to find men to canvass, and it is not allowable for the captains and the committee men to canvass one another, because their gifts are spontaneous. So the only thing that the different groups could do was to wait round in some likely place — say the bar parlour of Smith's Hotel — in the hope that somebody might come in who could be canvassed.

You might ask why they didn't canvass Mr. Smith himself, but of course they had done that at the very start, as I should have said. Mr. Smith had given them two hundred dollars in cash conditional on the lunches being held in the caff of his hotel; and it's awfully hard to get a proper lunch — I mean the kind to which a Bishop can express regret at not being there — under a dollar twenty-five. So Mr. Smith got back his own money, and the crowd began eating into the benefactions, and it got more and more complicated whether to hold another lunch in the hope of breaking even, or to stop the campaign.

It was disappointing, yes. In spite of all the success and the sympathy, it was disappointing. I don't say it didn't do good. No doubt a lot of the men got to know one another better than ever they had before. I have myself heard Judge Pepperleigh say that after the campaign he knew all of Pete Glover that he wanted to. There was a lot of that kind of complete satiety. The real trouble about the Whirlwind Campaign was that they never clearly understood which of them were the whirlwind and who were to be campaign.

Some of them, I believe, took it pretty much to heart. I know that Henry Mullins did. You could see it. The first day he came down to the lunch, all dressed up with the American Beauty and the white waistcoat. The second day he only wore a pink carnation and a grey waistcoat. The third day he had on a dead daffodil and a cardigan undervest, and on the last day, when the high-school teachers should have been there, he only wore his office suit and he hadn't even shaved. He looked beaten.

It was that night that he went up to the rectory to tell the news to Dean Drone. It had been arranged, you know, that the rector should not attend the lunches, so as to let the whole thing come as a surprise; so that all he knew about it was just scraps of information about the crowds at the lunch and how they cheered and all that. Once, I believe, he caught sight of the Newspacket with the two-inch headline: A QUARTER OF A MILLION, but he wouldn't let himself read further because it would have spoilt the surprise.

I saw Mullins, as I say, go up the street on his way to Dean Drone's. It was middle April and there was ragged snow on the streets, and the nights were dark still, and cold. I saw Mullins grit his teeth as he walked, and I know that he held in his coat pocket his own cheque for the hundred, with the condition taken off it, and he said that there were so many skunks in Mariposa that a man might as well be in the Head Office in the city.

The Dean came out to the little gate in the dark — you could see the lamplight behind him from the open door of the rectory — and he shook hands with Mullins and they went in together.

(1912)

Frederick Philip Grove (1879–1948)

Frederick Philip Grove was born Felix Paul Berthold Friedrich Greve on 14 February 1879 in Radomno, Prussia. In 1881, his family moved to Hamburg, Germany, where he attended grammar school. He was an exceptional student. Grove enrolled in Friedrich-Wilhelms University, Bonn, in 1898, but he left without completing his program of study in philology and spent the summer of 1901 travelling through Italy. Settling in Munich, Germany, with the intention of resuming his university studies, he decided instead to devote himself to writing. In 1902, he privately published two books: a collection of poems, *Wanderungen* ("The Wanderings"); and a drama, *Helena und Damon*. He also began to earn money by translating English works into German.

Around this time, Grove appears to have become involved with a married woman named Elsa Endell (née Ploetz), and they eloped to Italy. Grove funded the trip with money he had misappropriated from a former colleague at Bonn, Herman F.C. Kilian, and in 1903, he was charged with fraud. After serving a one-year prison sentence, Grove attempted to work his way out of debt, producing German translations of works by writers such as Oscar Wilde, Walter Pater, Jonathan Swift, Gustave Flaubert, and André Gide, whom he had met in 1904. His financial difficulties persisted, however, and in 1909, he faked his suicide and fled with Elsa to the United States. The couple spent two years farming in Kentucky. In 1911, Grove abandoned Elsa, worked for a period as a labourer, and finally made his way to Canada. In January of 1913, he took up a teaching position in Manitoba under the name Frederick Philip Grove. The following year, he married a Canadian woman named Catherine Wiens, and he became a citizen of Canada in 1921.

Grove's first work written in English was *Over Prairie Trails* (1922). It is composed of seven sketches based on Grove's weekend commutes from Gladstone, Manitoba, where he was employed as a teacher in 1917, to Falmouth, where Catherine and their daughter were residing. In his descriptions of the Canadian prairies, Grove often reflects on the beauty and serenity of the natural world. In his introductory notes, for example, he maintains that these trips "made [his] life worth living," and that he loves "Nature more than Man." In "Dawn and Diamonds," he senses "the whole creation breathing in its sleep — as if it was soundlessly stirring in dreams."

More frequently, though, Grove imagines himself in opposition to natural forces. In "Snow" (a chapter in *Over Prairie Trails*) nature is aggressive and terrifying in its sublimity. The narrator observes a cliff of snow that looks "so harsh, so millennial-old, so antediluvian and pre-adamic!" He notes, "I still remember with particular distinctness the slight dizziness that overcame me, the sinking feeling in my heart, the awe, and the foreboding that I had challenged a force in Nature which might defy all tireless effort and the most fearless heart." *Over Prairie Trails* was a success, and upon publishing its sequel, *The Turn of the Year* (1923), Grove retired from teaching to make more time for his writing.

In 1925, he published *Settlers of the Marsh*. Influenced by the naturalist movement in late-19th-century European writing, the novel is often lauded as one of the first works of Canadian prairie realism. It tells the story of a Swedish-born Canadian settler, Niels Lindstedt, who falls in love with a woman named Ellen Amundsen. Ellen returns his affections, but she has resolved never to marry, so Niels weds a widow, Clara Vogel, only to discover after three years of marriage that she is the "town whore." Niels murders his wife, finds redemption and peace of mind in prison, and finally enters into a union with Ellen. The plotline is rather theatrical, and the novel did not sell well when it first appeared. What is remarkable, though, is Grove's naturalistic treatment of female sexuality in his portrayal of the dynamic and passionate Clara. Later in his life, he would (somewhat overconfidently) compare this work to Flaubert's *Madame Bovary*: "a serious work of art was classed as pornography; but with this difference that the error, in Flaubert's case, increased the sales; he lived in France. In my case, and in Canada, it killed them."

After the publication of his semi-autobiographical account of the North American immigrant experience, *A Search for America* (1927), and a second Canadian novel, *Our Daily Bread* (1928), Grove went on several cross-country reading tours. In 1929, he moved with his family to Ottawa to become president of Ariston Press, but when the company failed, Grove purchased a farm near Simcoe, Ontario, and they moved again; a son was born to the Groves in 1930. In the early years of the Depression, Grove had to sell most of his land; nearly destitute, he neglected his writing for almost 10 years. In 1939, he published *Two Generations: A Story of Present-Day Ontario*, a novel inspired by his experiences as a dairy farmer. Unlike the Groves, however, the couple in this story are successful in their venture.

During the last years of his life, Grove wrote two novels: *The Master of the Mill* (1944) and *Consider Her Ways* (1947). He also published a work of fictionalized autobiography entitled *In Search of Myself* (1946), which was honoured with a Governor General's Award in 1947. Grove died the following year.

In Search of Myself is a fascinating read because, although the details Grove provides about the latter half of his life are accurate, the first sections of the book, which concern his years in Europe, are largely fabricated. Grove writes that he was born in Russia to an Anglo-Swedish father and a Scottish mother; yet both his parents were German. And missing from his account is any mention of Elsa Endell and Herman Kilian. The book was considered a reliable source of information on Grove's life until 1971, when D.O. Spettigue discovered the author's identity as Greve. In his 1974 edition of the book, Spettigue attributes Grove's fabrications not only to the fact that he had to conceal his identity upon arriving in North America, but also to the author's impulse to adhere to a pattern in Canadian autobiographical immigrant literature. Like Susanna Moodie, for example, Grove idealizes his European past and depicts Canada as a country in which an immigrant must endure poverty and hardship in order to emerge with some sense of belonging.

Among Grove's other works are *Fanny Essler* (1905), *Maurermeister Ihles Haus* (1906), *It Needs to Be Said* (1929), *The Yoke of Life* (1930), and *Fruits of the Earth* (1933). Throughout his career, he published about 30 short stories in various Canadian literary magazines. In 1971, Desmond Pacey collected many of these in *Tales from the Margin: The Selected Short Stories of Frederick Philip Grove*.

The House of Many Eyes

It was a January thaw, such as is common in the western provinces. There were two and a half feet of snow on the ground where it was level and sheltered. On the fields and roads, the water which formed was merely absorbed by the underlying loose, almost powdery masses, compacting them into spongy ice; but in town the eaves kept dripping for two whole days, ceasing to do so only with the chill of the night.

At the very east end of Fisher Landing, beyond the mill, stood a single house of peculiar, almost orientally fantastic roof-forms. It had once been the property of some great "booster"[1] who had aimed at giving expression to his contempt for mere practicality by building into it many reentrant angles, a *porte-cochère*,[2] and broken lines bewildering in their chaotic tangle. It was a very large house, for a small town. But, as rapidly almost as it had been run up, regardless of expense, it had decayed; for, though, in summer, it commanded a pretty view of the rapids of Fisher Creek, below the mill-race,[3] it was, in winter, too far from the centre of the town to be a desirable residence for doctor, lawyer, or business man. What, to its original owner, must have appealed as its very beauty, had, in its decay, become its flagrant and ostentatious ugliness: down to its cracked and scaling paint in two contrasting shades of green with arabesque orange ornaments. Besides, it enjoyed the reputation, justly no doubt, of being the coldest house in town; for there was hardly a room within its compass which did not have a triple exposure to the weather.

Nearly every western town has some such, if not several, relics of a past prosperity which proclaim both the purse-proud lack of taste and the improvident lavishness of a generation of newly-rich promoters, parasitic upon the pioneer.

Thus, this particular house gave his first impression of the town to him who approached Fisher Landing from the west. At a distance, it greeted the new-comer many-eyed, snowy, garish like a decayed woman of the street[4] who flaunts her paint and her cheap jewelry, her once ostentatious but now frayed wraps, in a mistaken estimate of her irresistible charms. As the traveller approached, he saw the broken panes, the chipped-off paint, the cracking and warping boards, the bulging walls, and the once perpendicular corner-posts sadly out of plumb; just as he would see the poor, foolish pretence on passing, in the street, the once gay but now aging cocotte[5] overflowing with fat.

Such houses, abounding in towns like Fisher Landing, stand mostly vacant. Since the original builder or a later purchaser has long since wearied of paying the annual charges, they are owned by the town, which has acquired them for the accumulated tax-bill. The town, anxious at all times to secure revenue, rents them for whatever periods and at whatever rentals it can, to transients; or, failing such, it houses in them its poor who have become a public charge; for of them too, there are plenty in such places which exist with no other justification but the promoters' ingenuity and greed.

At the present time the particular house in question had been assigned to a married but childless couple by name of Creighton.

The Creightons had, a few years ago, come from England under the provisions of the Empire Settlement Act.[6] A farm had been bought for them out of government funds; they to pay for it in annual instalments distributed over thirty years. From the

---

1. **booster** During the development of the Canadian West, a resident of a fledgling town who sought to promote it by making extravagant claims and predictions for its future. 2. *porte-cochère* Covered stopping-place for carriages dropping off visitors to a house; common in 19th-century mansions. 3. **mill-race** A stream of water that is channelled to turn a mill wheel. 4. **woman of the street** Prostitute. 5. **cocotte** Female prostitute. 6. **Empire Settlement Act** A British act of 1922 that subsidized the emigration of British settlers to colonial countries. The unsuccessful "Three Thousand Families" initiative of 1925 was meant to help British emigrants start farms on the Canadian prairies.

beginning, since they had been townspeople[7] — Mr. Creighton had run a "pub" in a suburb of London — they had not made a success of the farming business. In fact, they would never have gone to the farm had it not been that they had engaged to do so in order to secure free transportation from overseas. Though they had lived in the country, Tom Creighton had, almost from the beginning, daily walked the three miles into Fisher Landing and worked at odd jobs — raking and mowing lawns, spading up flower beds, digging wells in summer; and shovelling snow or helping Pete Harrington saw wood in winter. They had prospered in a modest way though they had defaulted on the payments for the farm; so much so that, after three years of his pretence at farming, Tom Creighton had bought a circular saw and an engine of his own, on credit. With this outfit he had set up in competition with Pete Harrington, his former employer who farmed north of the town, underbidding him by ten cents the cord of wood. At this new business, too, he had been reasonably successful though "the better class of citizens" remained loyal to Pete who, for many years, had supplied the town with its fuel.

Then a terrible accident had happened to Tom.

One day in spring when, as the consequence of a sudden and unlooked-for recrudescence[8] of winter, the demand for the saw had been urgent and universal, Tom Creighton, in order to keep pace with Pete Harrington — Pete was a giant in stature and strength — had hired a half-grown boy of fifteen to help him. This boy, reckless and irresponsible — his task being to hand the cord-lengths up on the tilting table[9] — had, at a moment when Tom's back was turned, thrown a heavy stick on to that table with such force that the table swung forward, against the rapidly, because idly, revolving saw, before the sidewise motion of the stick of wood had been arrested. The highly tempered and therefore brittle blade had, under the impact, and with a sound of "ping," burst into a score of fragments which were hurled into space with the full and unretarded force of a nine-horse-power engine. One of the fragments had entered the skull and brain of the lead-horse, killing it as a big-game bullet would fell a moose; another had entered Tom Creighton's back, near the spine, where it had lodged.

Henceforth, Tom Creighton had been a cripple. In spite of all Dr. Stanhope could do, he never walked upright again but remained bent double. Besides, he was periodically visited by next to unbearable pains.

The Creightons had promptly moved into town. Mrs. Creighton was a tall, strong, and competent woman, who, though she had never done any actual work, outside of her household, was well able to look after herself. People took pity on their plight; and Mrs. Creighton soon had all the washing to do which she could take care of, both at home and at various houses where she went by the day or the half day.

At first, when this arrangement was being entered into, the Creightons, under the shadow of the disaster which had befallen them, had felt grateful that at least they could still make an honest living. But, as month after month had gone by, a change had crept into their mutual relations.

They had rented the many-eyed house. Mrs. Creighton rose at five or six in the morning and prepared breakfast; she came home again at five or six in the evening and prepared supper. The noon-day lunch Tom contrived to prepare for himself, his wife having put things handy for him in the morning. Tom Creighton felt grateful to his wife for what she did; she might have sent him to some public institution. Mrs. Creighton

---

7. **townspeople** Not accustomed to rural life. 8. **recrudescence** Reappearance. 9. **tilting table** Flat, adjustable table used for cutting lumber.

pitied him in his helplessness; for even when there were no pains, it took him ten minutes to climb down the stairway from his room to the kitchen.

But, as time went by and the memory of past sufferings and anxieties faded, the situation came to be accepted as an irremediable fact; and it defined itself by contrast to other households where the man was the bread-winner. More and more Tom Creighton — partly from a desire on his part to do the share of the work which in regular households is done by the woman, partly under the passive pressure exerted by his wife who simply ceased doing certain things — began to be the household drudge. Again, as formerly, before the accident which had disabled him, he rose, as winter came, first in the morning and lighted the fires. Since this took three or four times as long as it used to do, he had to rise in the small hours of the night in order to have a room warm by the time his wife came down. Next, he began to set the tables and even to cook the meals.

Concurrently with this development, their attitude to each other changed. Tom Creighton forgot that he had at least half voluntarily assumed his duties; and he saw as the only motive of his performing them the passive pressure exerted by his wife. She, too, forgot that she had at first been glad to be able to go to work; it was true that she sometimes did more than she could without feeling over-burdened; but she assumed the speech and manners of the "boss" in the house, speaking sometimes as if she blamed her husband for his disability. Rarely, henceforth, did she consider his wishes; she acted and spoke as if she considered him an encumbrance. As a matter of fact, she sometimes thought of how much of her earning she might lay by if she were single, thus insuring herself against want in old age.

It showed in such trifles as this.

Tom Creighton smoked a pipe. He liked a certain kind of tobacco of which he consumed a pound a month, at a cost of a dollar and eighty cents. In the beginning, his wife had invariably brought home, on the first of every month, a pound tin of it; and Tom, having more leisure to smoke in than formerly, was sorely tempted to ask for a pound and a half, but refrained from doing so in order not to put an unnecessary burden on his wife; he timed himself, sucking an empty pipe rather than refilling it before he could do so without danger of exceeding his monthly allowance.

But when, on the first of October, his wife had brought him a pound of a different brand, cheaper by thirty cents, he had silently revolted. She, noticing it, had felt angered and resolved then and there to bring only a half-pound tin the next time. What an idea of his to smoke away month after month the earnings of a whole day's work, and her work at that!

Other trifles furnished the subject for silent comment and criticism: hundreds of trifles; yes, finally every single trifle of which their daily intercourse consisted.

On the particular afternoon of the day in the January thaw of which we were speaking, Tom Creighton lay on his bed in the front room upstairs which faced north. Outside, the sun shone brightly; and the moisture with which the air was saturated imparted to the day a springlike quality full of hope. Other people thought of the fact that such a thaw, three months hence, would mean the end of winter; or they rejoiced at least in the general sparkle and glitter, in the very whiteness of the world. But Tom Creighton lay there, his dull look fastened to the wall where a little trickle of water seeped down from the ceiling; for in this crazy-built house with the many angles in the roof the joints were pulling apart. Snow had accumulated above as it does in holes in the ground; whereas it slipped down from other houses.

"Yes," thus his thought ran, "Not even a decent house to live in! Not even a tiny little box of a house with two or three rooms at most, as we should have! We've got to rent this big maze of a thing, with ten rooms all piled topsy-turvy as out of a toy box! A ten-year old child could have built more sensibly! And why? Because we could not rent a hen-roost for less money!"

He groaned.

Then he thought of his wife; and his thought of her was tinged with hatred. Did she smile when she came home? God forbid! A serious, weary, superior, dissatisfied expression lay on her still handsome features, as if she hated the very thought of entering the house which held him.

Again he groaned.

"As if it were my fault! As if I had made myself a cripple on purpose! What did she come home for anyway, at noon? To spy on me! She might have stayed at the Bailies'; she had an all-day job to do there, confound it! A head-ache! As if Mrs. Bailie wouldn't have given her a head-ache wafer! ... And how she said that! 'I wish you would not smoke in here; I have a head-ache!' Where the devil am I to smoke if not in the only room that is heated? Am I to sit outside?"

The kitchen was a large room; and there were two stoves: a cookstove and a small, so-called "air-tight" heater of tin. He lay and re-visualized his wife's entrance, knitting his pale, sickly-looking forehead into a frown. First of all, she had gone to that heater and raised the lid. Seeing a fresh piece of wood in it, she had said querulously, "It seems to me you might let one fire go out over noon on a day like this. I've got to work for that wood. Besides, you always lie down upstairs after dinner. What's the use of putting a fresh stick in just before?"

He thought and thought of that.

"I could have answered her, to be sure. But the dickens of it is, she is right. She works for the money! It's her money we are spending! It's best to keep quiet ... Only she might think of the fact that I suffer most from the situation. It's coarse of her to throw it in my face that way! Yes, coarse and indelicate! Does she think I like her to go and make the living? A man's got his pride! Doggone it! This life is a burden!"

And again he fastened his eye on the wall and that slow, slow trickle of water from the leaky roof.

"Eh!" he said aloud with the accent of utter disgust.

But his thought returned to his wife. She was the dominant fact in his life. He hated her very strength and efficiency: the very means which kept them from starving or becoming a public charge. He almost wished she, too, were crippled so that they'd at least be on a level.

But suddenly his thoughts took a turn. Sit outside? Let the fires go out? Save fuel? Ostentatiously and out of spite?

She inflicted suffering on him, mental suffering worse than physical pain.

He would punish her! Surely, he would punish her!

He painted the situation to himself in elaborate detail; from his intimate knowledge of her he guessed at the very words which she would use; and he prepared his answers, carefully, testingly, trying his very intonations so as to give them the proper sting.

Thus the afternoon wore on. He pulled his nickel watch and looked at the time. It was four o'clock. His wife had said she would be home shortly after five.

Painfully indeed, but much more painfully in appearance than in fact — as if there had been a witness — he lifted himself into a sitting position on his bed, throwing off the blanket; and slowly, bent double, leaning on his cane, he made his way to the stairway and down, descending step for step.

In the kitchen, he looked into the tin heater which was tightly closed off. The single stick which he had put in at noon and on which his wife had remarked was still smouldering. Carefully, with poker and ash-shovel, he picked it out and placed it in the fire-box of the cook-stove. Then he opened the outside door to let the room cool off. On the cook-stove, over the smouldering piece of wood, he placed a kettle half full of water.

Outside, it being midwinter, it had already begun to freeze again; it had done so now for the last two or three nights. He shivered even in the kitchen.

At last he closed the door, took a chair and dragged it over the floor, through the unfurnished and darkened front room which had once been the parlour of the house and out, through the front door, to the porch.

Then he returned for his old sheep-skin coat and his cane which he had left behind.

From the porch, he moved his chair down into the still slushy front yard and across it to the tumble-down fence along the roadside. And lastly he fetched coat and cane which he had left behind again and sat down in the chair, throwing the coat over his bent and crippled back; for he could not do it without help.

It was a quarter to five when he had thus installed himself. The sun was sinking to the crest of the hills to the west.

He looked at the house and laughed contemptuously. "There's the snow on the roof that's melting into the house! And what a colour! That green! Like poison! And that silly, orange ornament running under the eaves! Disgusting! And all the points of the roof! No wonder the doggone thing is cold! And windows! Let's see. How many windows are there in that old parlour? There's the bay window in front, as large as five ordinary windows thrown together! And two on each side! Nine windows in one room! I'll be jiggered! I will! And open to the nice, cosy north wind on three sides! Some way of building that is! A blasted house!"

For twenty minutes he sat, bent over, his elbows resting on his knees, shivering in the evening chill, for the slushy snow was congealing now into a hard, rigid crust.

Then, slowly and carefully, so it would not hurt — but also in order to impress a possible spectator with his infirmities — he turned his head and peered along the street, towards town, or rather towards the mill which blocked the road.

Yes, his wife was coming; and her approach made him feel almost gay, for the tragi-comedy which he was enacting would come to a head now; but he also felt nervous; he was not entirely without dread of the coming encounter.

"Well," Mrs. Creighton exclaimed ironically when she reached the yard gate. "What's the latest? Do you want to catch your death of cold? Sitting out here in the yard?"

Hurriedly he gathered up his cane. "I'm going in," he said with feigned and exaggerated meekness. "I didn't expect you so soon."

"What's the idea?" Reading his mind fully, she could not suppress an impulse of anger.

"Well," he said apologetically, "it was warmer out here than inside."

"What? Haven't you got a fire?"

"No," he replied innocently. "That is, I've just lit one in the cook-stove. I understood you to say ..." He paused at the recollection; a feeling of impotent rebellion overpowered him; and he spat his words out venomously. "I understood you to say that a cripple like me has no right to a fire in the heater ... Don't deny it now! That's what you said! Even if those weren't the exact words!"

Mrs. Creighton stood and stared at him. Strangely, she understood the full psychology of the situation; she even understood that there was only one remedy, that of "having it out" on the spot, of letting it come to a quarrel which would clear the atmosphere. But she also felt that it was just such a quarrel he was "driving for"; and, perversely, though she wished for it herself, she would not, at this moment, give him the satisfaction of letting him have his way.

She shrugged her shoulders, walked away with quick steps which made her broad hips quiver under her coat, entered the house, and slammed the door in his face.

(1929)

E.J. Pratt (1882–1964)

E.J. Pratt, born in 1882, was the child of a Methodist minister who agreed to finance his son's college education on the condition that he, too, would become a minister. After his ordination, in 1913, Pratt experienced a crisis of faith — not an uncommon occurrence among Christians in the late Victorian period. This crisis evolved into a long-term questioning, which was exacerbated by his exposure (while at Methodist College in 1900) to the Darwinian works of T.H. Huxley and Herbert Spencer. In "From Stone to Steel," Pratt applied the concept of evolution to Jesus, the pinnacle of moral development; but he also suggested that despite Christ's highly evolved compassion, people fluctuate between savagery and civility — the line between the two is "tissue thin."

Pratt's faith in Christian compassion endured, but throughout his life, his uneasiness with dogmatic religion would be intensified by a series of traumatic experiences connected to Newfoundland, the province in which he grew up. At 16, he witnessed a mass funeral of local sealers who had frozen to death at sea; at 22, he lost his father to cancer; when he was 30, the *Titanic* sank, the woman he wanted to marry died of tuberculosis, and one of his professors (who was also a friend) drowned; in 1916, when he was 34, the Newfoundland regiment of the Canadian army was decimated at the Battle of Somme. And in 1924, when Pratt was 42, his oldest brother killed himself. These events worked their way into his poems — for example, "The Ice-Floes," "The Toll of the Bells," and *The Titanic*.

After moving to Toronto in 1907, Pratt earned four degrees, including a Ph.D. in Pauline eschatology completed in 1917. The following year he married Viola Whitney (they would have one child, Claire, born in 1921). He continued his studies, and by 1919, he held four academic degrees (the last he attained was a Ph.D.). Determined to avoid the ministry, he accepted a professorship in English literature at Victoria College, part of the University of Toronto. While he was hired mainly for his promise as a poet, he found that he was well suited to the scholarly life. Aspects of literary research appear in his poems, which illustrate Pratt's fascination with history and theories of evolution and psychoanalysis — ideas that were reshaping the cultural and literary landscapes. His work was not always innovative: his early poems bear the imprint of the Romantic poets Byron, Shelley, and Wordsworth; their influence is apparent in the privately printed *Rachel* (1917). In his World War I poems, however, he began to eschew Romanticism and embrace the realist sensibility of John Masefield and Carl Sandburg.

Pratt's interest in the relationship of people to nature did not wane — witness the infamous collision between ship and iceberg in the long poem *The Titanic* (1935) — but post-war disillusionment crushed his Romantic fervour for rebellion. By the time his first commercially printed book, *Newfoundland Verse* (1923), appeared, Pratt had absorbed the Imagism of other modernist poets, but he retained his interest in the long narrative poem. The blend of the contemporary and the historical proved popular and, in the context of surging nationalism prompted by the 1917 Canadian victory at Vimy Ridge, so would his book's descriptions of a distinctly Canadian wilderness. His next book, *Titans* (1926), was hailed as one of the first works of Canadian literature that could not have been written by an Englishman.

Although many of Pratt's poems were serious, he balanced them with a lighthearted and eccentric sense of humour. Such levity characterized *The Witches' Brew* (1925), a book that marked the introduction of the Pratt persona for public consumption — the poet as entertainer. However, he usually returned to tragic themes. With *The Titanic*, an epic poem that recounts the sinking of the ill-fated vessel in the icy waters off Newfoundland, Pratt combines moment-by-moment reportage and dramatic dialogue to thrilling effect. Dorothy Livesay applauded the work, identifying it as the embodiment of a new form: the documentary poem. Pratt would explore this form further in *Dunkirk* (1941) and *Behind the Log* (1947). *The Titanic* begins fatalistically, but its moral is humanistic: people can avert disaster if they resist the hubris that arises from an unquestioning belief in technological progress (the *Titanic* was supposedly "unsinkable").

While he had already won a Governor General's Award for *The Fable of the Goats and Other Poems* (1937), which seemed to predict the next war, it was *Brébeuf and His Brethren* (1940) that became his greatest wartime success. This work, in which Pratt accurately and vividly renders the martyrdom of the Jesuit missionaries in New France, won him his second Governor General's Award. In an age of bitter cynicism, of polarized opinions on war and peace, Pratt offered a balanced but firm view that was predictably too cynical for some critics and not cynical enough for others. In his long poem *The Truant* (1943), he evokes the struggle between the volatile human spirit, as embodied by the "bucking truant," and the deterministic universe, as personified by the absurd "great Panjandrum." The work inspired Pratt's friend Northrop Frye to remark that he "had felt not simply that I had heard the greatest of all Canadian poems, but that the voice of humanity had spoken once more."

He would win the Governor General's Award again, for *Towards the Last Spike* (1954), which appeared the year after he retired from Victoria College. Another national epic, *Towards the Last Spike* depicts the construction of the Canadian Pacific Railway, an undertaking that involved staggering engineering feats and explosive political scandals. This poem differs from *The Titanic* in that it expresses a general approval of technological progress; the railway had, after all, geographically united the country, and Canadian nationalism was a subtext of much of Pratt's oeuvre. As one of six poets included in the influential *New Provinces* anthology (1936), Pratt had helped to galvanize the country's poetry scene and, by co-founding and editing *Canadian Poetry Magazine* (from 1936 to 1943), he solidified his reputation as a major Canadian poet.

Pratt died on 26 April 1964, in Toronto. Among his other poetic works are *The Iron Door* (1927), *The Roosevelt and the Antinoë* (1930), *Still Life and Other Verse* (1943), *Collected Poems* (1944, 1958), and the posthumous *Complete Poems* (1989).

Newfoundland

Here the tides flow,
And here they ebb;
Not with that dull, unsinewed tread of waters
Held under bonds to move

Around unpeopled shores —
Moon-driven through a timeless circuit
Of invasion and retreat;
But with a lusty stroke of life
Pounding at stubborn gates,
10   That they might run
Within the sluices of men's hearts,
Leap under throb of pulse and nerve,
And teach the sea's strong voice
To learn the harmonies of new floods,
The peal of cataract,
And the soft wash of currents
Against resilient banks,
Or the broken rhythms from old chords
Along dark passages
20   That once were pathways of authentic fires.

Red is the sea-kelp on the beach,
Red as the heart's blood,
Nor is there power in tide or sun
To bleach its stain.
It lies there piled thick
Above the gulch-line.[1]
It is rooted in the joints of rocks,
It is tangled around a spar,
It covers a broken rudder,
30   *It is red as the heart's blood,*
And salt as tears.

Here the winds blow,
And here they die,
Not with that wild, exotic rage
That vainly sweeps untrodden shores,
But with familiar breath
Holding a partnership with life,
Resonant with the hopes of spring,
Pungent with the airs of harvest.
40   They call with the silver fifes of the sea,
They breathe with the lungs of men,
They are one with the tides of the sea,
They are one with the tides of the heart,
They blow with the rising octaves of dawn,
They die with the largo[2] of dusk,
Their hands are full to the overflow,
In their right is the bread of life,
In their left are the waters of death.

---

1. **gulch-line** Long and narrow cove (Newfoundland slang). 2. **largo** Slow musical tempo; "widely" or "broadly."

Scattered on boom
And rudder and weed
Are tangles of shells;
Some with backs of crusted bronze,
And faces of porcelain blue,
Some crushed by the beach stones
To chips of jade;
And some are spiral-cleft
Spreading their tracery[3] on the sand
In the rich veining of an agate's[4] heart;
And others remain unscarred,
To babble of the passing of the winds.

Here the crags
Meet with winds and tides —
Not with that blind interchange
Of blow for blow
That spills the thunder of insentient seas;
But with the mind that reads assault
In crouch and leap and the quick stealth,
Stiffening the muscles of the waves.
Here they flank the harbours,
Keeping watch
On thresholds, altars and the fires of home,
Or, like mastiffs,[5]
Over-zealous,
Guard too well.

Tide and wind and crag,
Sea-weed and sea-shell
And broken rudder —
And the story is told
Of human veins and pulses,
Of eternal pathways of fire,
Of dreams that survive the night,
Of doors held ajar in storms.

(1923)

50

60

70

80

The Highway

What aeons passed without a count or name,
Before the cosmic seneschal,[1]
Succeeding with a plan

---

3. **tracery** Delicate pattern of lines. **4. agate** Type of quartz with layered, swirling colours. **5. mastiffs** Large, sturdy breed of dog.

---

1. **seneschal** In a royal, medieval house, an officer in charge of household affairs.

Of weaving stellar patterns from a flame,
Announced at his high carnival
An orbit — with Aldebaran![2]

And when the drifting years had sighted land,
And hills and plains declared their birth
Amid volcanic throes,
10   What was the lapse before the marshal's hand
Had found a garden on the earth,
And led forth June with her first rose?

And what the gulf between that and the hour,
Late in the simian-human day,
When Nature kept her tryst
With the unfoldment of the star and flower —
When in her sacrificial way
Judea blossomed with her Christ!

But what made *our* feet miss the road that brought
20   The world to such a golden trove,
In our so brief a span?
How may we grasp again the hand that wrought
Such light, such fragrance, and such love,
O star! O rose! O Son of Man?

(1931)

From Stone to Steel

From stone to bronze, from bronze to steel[1]
Along the road-dust of the sun,
Two revolutions of the wheel
From Java[2] to Geneva[3] run.

The snarl Neanderthal is worn
Close to the smiling Aryan[4] lips,
The civil polish of the horn
Gleams from our praying finger tips.

The evolution of desire
10   Has but matured a toxic wine,

---

2. **Aldebaran** Very bright star in the Taurus constellation; from "dabaran," meaning "follower of the Pleiades." The Pleiades are both a star cluster themselves and a set of seven sister nymphs in classical mythology.

---

1. **stone, bronze, steel** Ages of human history. 2. **Java** Indonesian island made famous in the late 19th century by the discovery of fossils of *homo erectus* ("Java man"), which lived between two–one million years ago and provided a potential evolutionary link between apes and humans. 3. **Geneva** City in Switzerland, famous for its humanitarian treaties (Geneva conventions, the first of which was adopted in 1864) and, in Pratt's time, home of the League of Nations. 4. **Aryan** In 20th-century usage, a non-Jewish caucasian.

Drunk long before its heady fire
Reddened Euphrates[5] or the Rhine.[6]

Between the temple and the cave
The boundary lies tissue-thin:
The yearlings still the altars crave
As satisfaction for a sin.

The road goes up, the road goes down —
Let Java or Geneva be —
But whether to the cross or crown,
The path lies through Gethsemane.[7]   20

(1932)

The Man and the Machine

By right of fires that smelted ore
Which he had tended years before,
The man whose hands were on the wheel
Could trace his kinship through her steel,
Between his body warped and bent
In every bone and ligament,
And this "eight-cylinder" stream-lined,
The finest model yet designed.
He felt his lesioned pulses strum
Against the rhythm of her hum,   10
And found his nerves and sinews knot
With sharper spasm as she climbed
The steeper grades, so neatly timed
From storage tank to piston shot —
This creature with the cougar grace,
This man with slag[1] upon his face.

(1932)

The Submarine[1]

The young lieutenant in command
Of the famous submarine, the K-
148,[2] had scanned
The sea circumference all day:
A thousand times or so his hand
Revolved the prism in the hope

---

5. **Euphrates** River in South-West Asia; cited in the Bible as one of the rivers in Paradise. 6. **Rhine** A river through Switzerland, Germany, and the Netherlands. 7. **Gethsemane** The garden near Jerusalem where Christ was betrayed by Judas Iscariot. Also where he prayed, the night before his crucifixion, for the sins of the world.

---

1. **slag** Scum residue left by smelting processes used to purify metals.

---

1. **The Submarine** Pratt wrote this poem in response to the 1937 Lloyd Bacon film *Submarine D-1*, which was praised for its realism. 2. **the K-148** A large and new naval ship.

That the image of the ship expected,
But overdue, might be reflected
Through the lenses of his periscope.
10   'Twas getting late, and not a mark
Had troubled the monotony
Of every slow expanding arc

Of the horizon. Suddenly
His grip froze to the handle! What
Was that amorphous yellow spot
To the north-east? Was it the lift
Of a wave, a curl of foam, a drift
Of cloud? Too slow for foam, too fast
For cloud. A minute more. At last
20   The drift was taking shape; his stroke
Of luck had fallen — it was SMOKE!

An hour of light in the western sky,
And thirty seconds for descent;
The quarry ten miles off. Stand by!
The valves were opened — flood and vent —
And the water like a rumble of thunder
Entered the tanks. Two generators
Sparked her fins and drove her under
Down the ocean escalators.

30   No forebear of the whale or shark,
No saurian of the Pleiocene,[3]
Piercing the sub-aquatic dark
Could rival this new submarine.
The evolution of the sea
Had brought forth many specimens
Conceived in horror — denizens[4]
Whose vast inside economy
Not only reproduced their broods,
But having shot them from their wombs,
40   Devoured them in their family feuds
And passed them through their catacombs.
But was there one in all their race
Combined such terror with such grace,
As this disturber of the glooms,
This rapid sinuous oval form
Which knew unerringly the way
To sound and circumvent a storm
Or steal a march upon her prey?

---

3. saurian of the Pleiocene "Saurian" means lizardlike, while the "Pleiocene" was a geological era that lasted between 5.3 million and 1.8 million years ago; a dinosaur. **4. denizens** Citizens.

No product she of Nature's dower,
No casual selection wrought her   50
Or gave her such mechanic power
To breathe above or under water.

In her thoracic[5] cavities
One hundred tons of batteries
Were ready, on the dive, to start
The musculation of the heart.
And where outside a Ming museum
Could any antiquarian find
An assemblage such as here was shrined
Within the vault of her peritoneum?   60
Electric switches, indicators,
Diving alarm-horns, oscillators,
Rudder controls, and tubes and dials,
Yellow, white, magenta vials,
Pipes to force out battery gases,
Pressure gauges, polished brasses,
Surrounded human figures caught
At their positions, silent, taut,
Like statues in the tungsten light,
While just outside the cell was night   70
And a distant engine's monotone
Tapping at a telephone.
And now two hundred feet below
She held her bearings towards her foe,
While silence and the darkness flowed
Along an unnavigated road.

In half an hour she stopped and blew
The water ballast with her air,
Rose stealthily to surface where
Upon the mirror in full view,   80
Cutting an Atlantic swarth
The trail of smoke turned out to be
A fat mammalian of the sea,
Set on a course north-east by north,
And heavy with maternity.
Within her framework iron-walled
A thousand bodies were installed,
A snug and pre-lacteal brood
Drawing from her warmth and food,
Awaiting in two days or three   90
A European delivery.
Blood of tiger, blood of shark,

---

5. **thoracic** Of the thorax.

What a prey to stalk and strike
From an ambush in the dark
Thicket of the sea!

   Now like
The tiger-shark viviparous[6]
Who with her young grown mutinous
Before the birth-hour with the smell
Of blood inside the mother, will expel
100 Them from her body to begin
At once the steerage of the fin,
The seizure of the jaw, the click
Of serried teeth fashioned so well
Pre-natally to turn the trick
Upon a shoal of mackerel —
So like the shark, the submarine
Ejected from her magazine
The first one of her foetal young.
It ran along the trolley, swung
110 Into a flooded tube and there
Under a jet of compressed air
It found the sea. A trip-latch in
The tube a second later sprung
A trigger, and the turbine power
Acting on the driving fin
Paced it at fifty miles per hour.

So huge and luscious was this feast,
The 148 released
Three others to offset the chance
120 Of some erratic circumstance
Of aim or speed or tide or weather.
And during this time nothing was seen
Except to an eye in the submarine
Of that bevy of sharks on the sea together,
So accurately spaced one after the other,
And driven by thirst derived from the mother.
Each seemed on the glass a tenuous feather
Of gold such as a curlew in flight
Would make with its nether wing skimming the swell;
130 Not a hint of a swerve to the left or right,
The gyros were holding the balance so well.

The rich-ripe mammal was swimming straight
On the course of her chart with unconcerned leisure,

---

6. **viviparous** Giving birth to live young (e.g., rather than eggs).

Her steady keel and uniform rate
Combining so perfectly with the deep black
Of the hull — silhouette against the back-
Drop of the sunset to etch and measure
The target — when three of those shafts of foam
At the end of their amber stretch struck home.
The first one barely missed — to plough   140
A harmless path across her bow:
The next tore like a scimitar
Through flesh to rip the jugular;
Boilers and bulkheads broke apart
When the third torpedo struck the heart;
And with what logic did the fourth
Cancel the course north-east by north,
Hitting abaft the beam to rut
The exploding nitrates through her gut.

The young commander's time was short   150
To log the items for report.
Upon the mirror he descried
Three cavernous wounds in the mammal's side —
Three crumbled dykes[7] through which the tide
Of a gluttonous Atlantic poured;
A heavy starboard list with banks
Of smoke fluted with steam which soared
From a scramble of pipes within her flanks;
Twin funnel-nostrils belching red,
A tilting stern, a plunging head,   160
The foundering angle in position,
And the sea's reach for a thousand souls
In the last throe of the parturition.[8]

Now with her hyper-sensitive feel
Of her master's hands on the controls —
A pull of a switch, a turn of a wheel,
The submarine, like the deep-sea shark,
Went under cover, away from the light
And limn of the sunset, from the sight
Of the stars, to a native lair as dark   170
As a kraken's[9] grave. She took her course
South-west by south — for what was the source
Of that hum to the port picked up by the oscillator?
A rhythm too rapid, too hectic for freighter
Or liner! This was her foe, not her prey:

---

7. **dykes** Embankments meant to prevent floods. 8. **parturition** Childbirth. 9. **kraken** Massive octopus-like monster in Norwegian legend; allegedly causes whirlpools.

Faster and louder, and heading her way!
Beyond the depth where the tanks could flood 'er,
She drove her nose down with the diving rudder,
Far from the storm of shells or thrust
180   Of the ram, away from the gear-wrenching zone
Of the depth-bomb, away from the scent and lust
Of a killer whose might was as great as her own.

(1938)

The Truant

"What have you there?" the great Panjandrum[1] said
To the Master of the Revels who had led
A bucking truant with a stiff backbone
Close to the foot of the Almighty's throne.

"Right Reverend, most adored,
And forcibly acknowledged Lord
By the keen logic of your two-edged sword!
This creature has presumed to classify
Himself — a biped, rational, six feet high
10   And two feet wide; weighs fourteen stone;[2]
Is guilty of a multitude of sins.
He has abjured his choric[3] origins,
And like an undomesticated slattern,[4]
Walks with tangential step unknown
Within the weave of the atomic pattern.
He has developed concepts, grins
Obscenely at your Royal bulletins,
Possesses what he calls a will
Which challenges your power to kill."

20   "What is his pedigree?"

"The base is guaranteed, your Majesty —
Calcium, carbon, phosphorus, vapour
And other fundamentals spun
From the umbilicus of the sun,
And yet he says he will not caper
Around your throne, nor toe the rules
For the ballet of the fiery molecules."

"His concepts and denials — scrap them, burn them —
To the chemists with them promptly."

---

1. Panjandrum Self-important official. **2. stone** Imperial unit of weight, equal to 14 pounds. **3. choric** Related to a chorus. **4. slattern** Untidy woman or prostitute.

"Sire,
The stuff is not amenable to fire. 30
Nothing but their own kind can overturn them.
The chemists have sent back the same old story —
'With our extreme gelatinous apology,
We beg to inform your Imperial Majesty,
Unto whom be dominion and power and glory,
There still remains that strange precipitate
Which has the quality to resist
Our oldest and most trusted catalyst.
It is a substance we cannot cremate
By temperatures known to our Laboratory.'" 40

And the great Panjandrum's face grew dark —
"I'll put those chemists to their annual purge,
And I myself shall be the thaumaturge[5]
To find the nature of this fellow's spark.
Come, bring him nearer by yon halter rope:
I'll analyse him with the cosmoscope."[6]

Pulled forward with his neck awry,
The little fellow six feet short,
Aware he was about to die,
Committed grave contempt of court 50
By answering with a flinchless stare
The Awful Presence seated there.

The ALL HIGH swore until his face was black.
He called him a coprophagite,[7]
A genus *homo*, egomaniac,
Third cousin to the family of worms,
A sporozoan[8] from the ooze of night,
Spawn of a spavined troglodyte:[9]
He swore by all the catalogue of terms
Known since the slang of carboniferous Time. 60
He said that he could trace him back
To pollywogs and earwigs in the slime.
And in his shrillest tenor he began
Reciting his indictment of the man,
Until he closed upon this capital crime —
"You are accused of singing out of key,
(A foul unmitigated dissonance)
Of shuffling in the measures of the dance,
Then walking out with that defiant, free

---

5. **thaumaturge** One who performs miracles or magic. 6. **cosmoscope** Pratt invented this term. 7. **coprophagite** One who eats feces. Pratt's term. 8. **sporozoan** Spore-producing parasites transmitted by blood-sucking insects.
9. **troglodyte** Prehistoric race of cave-dwelling humans.

70 Toss of your head, banging the doors,
    Leaving a stench upon the jacinth[10] floors.
    You have fallen like a curse
    On the mechanics of my Universe.

    "Herewith I measure out your penalty —
    Hearken while you hear, look while you see:
    I send you now upon your homeward route
    Where you shall find
    Humiliation for your pride of mind.
    I shall make deaf the ear, and dim the eye,
80 Put palsy[11] in your touch, make mute
    Your speech, intoxicate your cells and dry
    Your blood and marrow, shoot
    Arthritic needles through your cartilage,
    And having parched you with old age,
    I'll pass you wormwise through the mire;
    And when your rebel will
    Is mouldered, all desire
    Shrivelled, all your concepts broken,
    Backward in dust I'll blow you till
90 You join my spiral festival of fire.[12]
    Go, Master of the Revels — I have spoken."

    And the little genus *homo*, six feet high,
    Standing erect, countered with this reply —
    "You dumb insouciant invertebrate,
    You rule a lower than a feudal state —
    A realm of flunkey decimals that run,
    Return; return and run; again return,
    Each group around its little sun,
    And every sun a satellite.
100 There they go by day and night,
    Nothing to do but run and burn,
    Taking turn and turn about,
    Light-year in and light-year out,
    Dancing, dancing in quadrillions,
    Never leaving their pavilions.

    "Your astronomical conceit
    Of bulk and power is anserine.[13]
    Your ignorance so thick,
    You did not know your own arithmetic.
110 We flung the graphs about your flying feet;
    We measured your diameter —

---

10. jacinth Fiery-toned precious stone. **11. palsy** Muscular condition causing tremors. **12. spiral festival of fire** Reference to Dante's spiralling plunge into Hell in *The Divine Comedy*. There may also be a reference to Dante's eventual ascent into Heaven at line 138. **13. anserine** Foolish.

Merely a line
Of zeros prefaced by an integer.
Before we came
You had no name.
You did not know direction or your pace;
We taught you all you ever knew
Of motion, time and space.
We healed you of your vertigo
And put you in our kindergarten show,   120
Perambulated[14] you through prisms, drew
Your mileage through the Milky Way,
Lassoed your comets when they ran astray,
Yoked[15] Leo, Taurus, and your team of Bears[16]
To pull our kiddy cars of inverse squares.[17]

"Boast not about your harmony,
Your perfect curves, your rings
Of pure and endless light[18] — 'Twas we
Who pinned upon your seraphim their wings,
And when your brassy heavens rang   130
With joy that morning while the planets sang
Their choruses of archangelic lore,
'Twas we who ordered the notes upon their score
Out of our winds and strings.
Yes! all your shapely forms
Are ours — parabolas of silver light,
Those blueprints of your spiral stairs
From nadir[19] depth to zenith[20] height,
Coronas,[21] rainbows after storms,
Auroras on your eastern tapestries   140
And constellations over western seas.

"And when, one day, grown conscious of your age,
While pondering an eolith,[22]
We turned a human page
And blotted out a cosmic myth
With all its baby symbols to explain
The sunlight in Apollo's eyes,
Our rising pulses and the birth of pain,
Fear, and that fern-and-fungus breath
Stalking our nostrils to our caves of death —   150

---

14. Perambulated Guided. **15. Yoked** Latched together (usually refers to animals bound together to pull something).
16. Leo, Taurus, Bears Constellations of stars. **17. inverse squares** Measurement of gravity's force to its distance from
an object; one decreases proportionally to the other's increase. **18. pure and endless light** From the opening lines of Henry
Vaughan's "The World" (17th c.). **19. nadir** In astronomy, the point directly below the observer; a low point. **20. zenith** In
astronomy, the point directly above the observer; a high point. **21. Coronas** Sets of concentric circles of light around a
luminous body. **22. eolith** Crude, ancient stone artifact originally thought to be a primitive tool made by humans in the
Pleiocene era; proven, after Pratt's time, to be naturally occurring rather than manmade.

That day we learned how to anatomize
Your body, calibrate your size
And set a mirror up before your face
To show you what you really were — a rain
Of dull Lucretian atoms[23] crowding space,
A series of concentric waves which any fool
Might make by dropping stones within a pool,
Or an exploding bomb forever in flight
Bursting like hell through Chaos and Old Night.[24]

160   "You oldest of the hierarchs
Composed of electronic sparks,
We grant you speed,
We grant you power, and fire
That ends in ash, but we concede
To you no pain nor joy nor love nor hate,
No final tableau of desire,
No causes won or lost, no free
Adventure at the outposts — only
The degradation of your energy
170   When at some late
Slow number of your dance your sergeant-major Fate
Will catch you blind and groping and will send
You reeling on that long and lonely
Lockstep of your wave-lengths towards your end.

    "We who have met
With stubborn calm the dawn's hot fusillades;
Who have seen the forehead sweat
Under the tug of pulleys on the joints,
Under the liquidating tally
180   Of the cat-and-truncheon bastinades;[25]
Who have taught our souls to rally
To mountain horns and the sea's rockets
When the needle ran demented through the points;
We who have learned to clench
Our fists and raise our lightless sockets
To morning skies after the midnight raids,
Yet cocked our ears to bugles on the barricades,
And in cathedral rubble found a way to quench
A dying thirst within a Galilean valley
190   No! by the Rood,[26] we will not join your ballet."

(1942)

---

23. Lucretian atoms Lucretius (94–49 BC) recommended casting off the gods on the grounds that the world was composed of tiny atoms whose movements were without purpose. **24. Chaos and Old Night** From *Paradise Lost*, 1.543; describes existence before God created the universe. **25. cat-and-truncheon bastinades** Beating with a cat-o'-nine-tails or club. **26. by the Rood** "by the Cross," a mild (archaic) religious oath.

Still Life

To the poets who have fled
To pools where little breezes dusk and shiver,
Who need still life to deliver
Their souls of their songs,
We offer roses blanched of red
In the Orient gardens,
With April lilies to limn
On the Japanese urns —
And time, be it said,
For a casual hymn   10
To be sung for the hundred thousand dead
In the mud of the Yellow River.[1]

And if your metric paragraphs
Incline to Western epitaphs,
Be pleased to return to a plain
Where a million lie
Under a proletarian sky,
Waiting to trouble
Your lines on the scorched Ukrainian[2] stubble.
On the veined marble of their snows   20
Indite a score to tether
The flight of your strain;
Or should you need a rougher grain
That will never corrode with weather,
Let us propose
A stone west of the bend where the Volga[3] flows
To lick her cubs on the Stalingrad[4] rubble.

Hasten, for time may pass you by,
Mildew the reed and rust the lyre;
Look — that Tunisian glow will die   30
As died the Carthaginian fire![5]
Today the autumn tints are on
The trampled grass at Marathon.[6]
Here are the tales to be retold,
Here are the songs to be resung.
Go, find a cadence for that field-grey mould

---

1. **Yellow River** A river in China prone to flooding; its levees were broken in 1938 by nationalist troops to push back the Japanese force. As a result, at least 300,000 Chinese people drowned; this poem was written in 1939. 2. **Ukrainian** Under communist rule, Ukraine had struggled with economic (and agricultural) devastation, racial purges, and famine throughout the 1930s. 3. **Volga** River in Western Russia. 4. **Stalingrad** Now Volgograd, Russia. Named after Joseph Stalin in 1925, Stalingrad was a site of political struggle during the early days of the Soviet Union. 5. **Carthaginian fire** During the fall of Carthage, Romans set the Phoenician fleet of ships on fire; Carthage was also infamous for sacrificing children to the gods by fire. 6. **Marathon** Grecian site of the Battle of Marathon, 490 BC, which required a Phidippides, a messenger, to run from Marathon to Athens (42 km).

Outcropping on the Parthenon.
Invoke, in other than the Latin tongue,
A Mediterranean Muse
40   To leave her pastoral loves —
The murmurs of her soft Theocritean[7] fold,
Mimosa, oleander,
Dovecotes and olive groves,
And court the shadows where the night bedews
A Roman mausoleum hung
Upon the tides from Candia to Syracuse.[8]

(1943)

Marjorie Pickthall (1883–1922)

Few poets, living or dead, have faced the extremes of praise and contempt that Marjorie Pickthall has. By the time she was 16 many readers had seized on her as the new voice of Canadian writing and assigned her the impossible task of preserving romanticism from the early stirrings of modernism. As a result, in her lifetime she enjoyed literary fame and easy access to print, publishing more than 200 stories over the course of her short career. Yet posthumously she has suffered some of the harshest judgements in Canadian literary history. Skeptics like W.E. Collin and former sympathizer E.J. Pratt criticized her lack of real-world experience and accused her of mimicry and emotional vagueness; her poetry was dismissed as flat, over-stylized, and blandly feminine. For the bulk of the 20th century, her work (if cited at all) was used primarily to demonstrate the backwardness of Canada's literary culture before the advent of modernism. Only recently, through the efforts of feminist critics, has Pickthall's work been granted a place of respect within the Canadian canon.

Although many critics have viewed Pickthall as a dreamy visionary desperate to flee the world around her, the poet's life was shaped by her intense relationships with people and places. Born in 1883, in Middlesex, England, she grew up in Toronto. Her parents encouraged her to learn to play the violin, paint, and write poetry. The fusion of these skills — an ear for rhythm, tone, and cadence, an eye for colour and balance, and an understanding of the sensual potential of language — would become fundamental to her work. As a child, she read Kipling, Stevenson, and Conrad, and she later became an admirer of Duncan Campbell Scott. She was still enrolled at the Bishop Strachan School for Girls when her first short story was published, in 1898. "Two Ears" appeared in the *Globe,* and although Pickthall was only 15 when she wrote it, Lorne Pierce, one of her most vocal advocates, later called it "Kipling all over again." Pickthall has described John Maclean's *The Indians, Their Manners and Customs* as an invaluable resource, and its influence can be seen in her first novel, *A Tale of the Early Settlement of Ontario,* which launched her career as a serious writer in 1905. Her early prose is heavily focused on battles for survival, often against epic historical, legendary, or natural backdrops.

In 1910, her mother died, a calamity that put Pickthall's physical and emotional health under serious strain. She would not recover for years, and for a time she stopped writing entirely. During

---

7. **Theocritean** Of Theocritus, the creator of Greek idyllic poetry. 8. **Candia to Syracuse** From an ancient city on the island of Crete to Sicily.

this period, she worked at the library of Victoria College at the University of Toronto, and the friends she made there eventually encouraged her to resume writing. She moved back to England in 1912 to live with relatives, and there she embraced her creative work with new vigour.

The thousand-copy first run of her 1913 poetry collection *The Drift of Pinions* sold out within 10 days. The poems focused on the affinity of temporal beauty and holiness, pitting worship of beauty against worldly decay. In her idealization of art and spiritualized approach to earthly decline, she had more in common with the decadent and Pre-Raphaelite poets of the late 19th century than with most of her Canadian contemporaries. In "The Pool," she articulates her relationship with poetry, nature, and divine beauty: on the one hand, she takes refuge from the world by submersing herself in the pool; on the other, she uses her reflection in the pool to describe the experience of being both female subject and object (in contrast to the way British male aestheticists used the female form as a projection of their own virtues). The *The Drift of Pinions* poems were published in magazines and journals across North America. With the onset of World War I, Pickthall found herself inhabiting a dual life. As an artist, she published another novel, *Little Hearts* (1915) (set in 18th-century Devonshire), and another collection of poetry, *The Lamp of Poor Souls* (1916); in the latter, she experimented with free verse in poems like "Improvisation on the Flute," in which she uses the transformative power of night to express female eroticism through male desire. As a civilian, she aided the war effort by driving an ambulance and working as a farm labourer. For a sheltered girl who hated crowds, this was a time of remarkable activity and engagement with the world.

Following the war, Pickthall moved to Bowershalke in Salisbury, England, where she visited Stonehenge and became fascinated with the Druids and English chivalric mythology. By 1920, however, she was yearning for Canada and returned home. She stayed briefly with her father in Toronto before moving west to Vancouver. Her last years were immensely productive — the year of her death, 1922, saw the release of *The Woodcarver's Wife and Other Poems*, a verse drama and poetry collection in which she addresses the destructive, even murderous, power of art, particularly at its intersection with religion.

Pickthall died at the age of 28 of an embolus following surgery. In the year and a half after her death, no less than 10 articles of ardent praise for Pickthall were published in literary journals across North America. Soon after, with her father's publication of her *Angels' Shoes and Other Stories* (1923), a collection of prose melodramas, and *The Complete Poems of Marjorie Pickthall* (1925), her twofold reputation was secured. To some, her work would never be more than romanticism's last gasp, but others would remember the colour, musicality, and refined quality of her voice. At her best, Pickthall presented a subtle, spiritual view of nature, history, and the human spirit with a lyrical beauty that even her harshest critics acknowledge. Her detailed symbolism, drawn often from myth, archetype, or texts like John Henry Ingram's *Flora Symbolica*, ultimately served her own high romantic ideals of truth and beauty. Although hers was perhaps the last literary generation that could indulge in such ideals, Pickthall remained optimistic about the new century and her homeland. In response to Rupert Brooke's claim that Canadian history lacked legendary figures, she expressed absolute faith that they would be found: "The material is there, wherever there is longing, sacrifice, or the sense of fate."

Dream River

Wind-silvered willows hedge the stream,
And all within is hushed and cool.
The water, in an endless dream,

Goes sliding down from pool to pool.
And every pool a sapphire is,
From shadowy deep to sunlit edge,
Ribboned around with irises
And cleft with emerald spears of sedge.

O, every morn the winds are stilled,
10   The sunlight falls in amber bars.
O, every night the pools are filled
With silver brede[1] of shaken stars.
O, every morn the sparrow flings
His elfin trills athwart the hush,
And here unseen at eve there sings
One crystal-throated hermit-thrush.

(1905)

The Pool

Come with me, follow me, swift as a moth,
Ere the wood-doves waken.
Lift the long leaves and look down, look down
Where the light is shaken,
Amber and brown,
On the woven ivory roots of the reed,
On a floating flower and a weft[1] of weed
And a feather of froth.

Here in the night all wonders are,
10   Lapped in the lift of the ripple's swing, —
A silver shell and a shaken star,
And a white moth's wing.
Here the young moon when the mists unclose
Swims like the bud of a golden rose.

I would live like an elf where the wild grapes cling,
I would chase the thrush
From the red rose-berries.
All the day long I would laugh and swing
With the black choke-cherries.

20   I would shake the bees from the milkweed blooms,
And cool, O cool,
Night after night I would leap in the pool,
And sleep with the fish in the roots of the rush.

---

1. **brede** Braid.

---

1. **weft** Strips of material used crosswise in weaving.

Clear, O clear my dreams should be made
Of emerald light and amber shade,
Of silver shallows and golden glooms.
Sweet, O sweet my dreams should be
As the dark, sweet water enfolding me
Safe as a blind shell under the sea.

(1913)

Improvisation on the Flute

My lost delight, my guest,
Fled from me when I stirred,
Silently as the bird
That has no nest.

She has gathered darkness to build her a nest
And the little leaves of cloud.
She crouches with her breast against darkness,
And hides as a hare in the meadows of night.
It covers her like long grass
Whose blossom is all of stars;   10
Crocus-stars, stars of anemone
Where cling the moths that are the longings of men.
She is born of the evening,
When the moon breathes the scent of young thyme,
And the dead shepherds hear the sheep cropping in the dew.

She is slain of the morning,
When the thin willow-leaves tremble like fire
Burning the branches,
As if each were a sorrow that burned and shone
Forever.   20
My shadow, my desire,
Come to me, listen, and stay,
Ah, never?
With the day
She is gone, she is gone
Away
Forever —
My guest, my lost delight,
Come nearer, star by star.
Sweet as the lips of night   30
Your kisses are.

(1916)

Miranda's Tomb

Miranda?[1] She died soon, and sick for home.
And dark Ilario the Milanese
Carved her in garments 'scutcheoned[2] to the knees,
Holding one orchard-spray as fresh as foam.
One heart broke, many grieved. Ilario said:
"The summer is gone after her. Who knows
If any season shall renew his rose?
But this rose lives till Beauty's self be dead."
So wrought he, days and years, and half aware
10 Of a small, striving, sorrowing quick thing,
Wrapped in a furred sea-cloak, and deft to bring
Tools to his hand or light to the dull air.
Ghost, spirit, flame, he knew not, — could but tell
It had loved her, and its name was Ariel.[3]

(1922)

The Spell

Rainy moors and a green hollow of rushes,
A pool like glass that gives on an empty room,
An orchard full of the happy fluting of thrushes,
And a lilac hedge in bloom, —

The towered beech-wood barren of blade or flower,
Leaf on leaf in a depth like the depth of the sea,
Dewy at noon, — these things from of old have power
To set my spirit free.

But only the gray downs gold in the cowslip weather,
10 Curve on curve as clean as the breast of the foam,
And the cloud-white thorn and the white cloud blowing together
Can call my spirit home.

(1925)

The Princess in the Tower

I was happier up in the room
At the head of the long blue stair
Than here in the garden's gloom
With roses to wear.

When stars my window were riming
I would lean out over the snow
And hear him climbing, climbing
A long way below.

---

1. **Miranda** The daughter of Prospero in *The Tempest*. 2. **'scutcheoned** Decorated. 3. **Ariel** Sprite in *The Tempest*.

But I was happy and lonely
As the heart of a mountain pool,   10
With stars and shadows only
Made beautiful.

Then he came. He said "How chill is
This height I have won!
I will love you among the lilies,
And ride ere the sun."

So I followed him into the night
A long way down.
I would I were back on the height,
With dawn for a crown.   20

(1927)

Ethel Wilson (1888–1980)

Ethel Wilson published her first book, *Hetty Dorval*, in 1947, when she was nearly 60 years old. A retiring woman and the wife of a respected doctor, she worried about the reviews the book might receive and shied away from the public exposure it would bring. Her professional confidence did not improve substantially until she was well established in her relatively short career. Born in 1888 to missionary parents in South Africa, Wilson lost her mother when she was very young; her father passed away a few years later, after they had gone to live in England. The resulting lack of confidence and persistent sense of vulnerability that dogged Wilson in life manifested itself in her fiction as a preoccupation with accidents, precariously forestalled disaster, and the slips and mistakes that shape lives.

In 1898, she went to live in Vancouver, British Columbia, with her maternal grandmother, who tried to help her rebuild what she had lost, which, Wilson noted, "was really everything." Wilson proved to be such an excellent student that her grandmother decided she should receive a first-rate traditional education and sent her to Trinity Hall School in Staffordshire, England. Desperately homesick, Wilson made no friends until her second year, when she attained popularity based on her sports and debating skills. Returning to Vancouver in 1906, she earned a teaching certificate but found that she disliked teaching (although she would continue in the profession); she took painting lessons from Emily Carr but quit when she concluded that she had little talent. Wilson would live with her grandmother until she was 31 years old, never finding her ideal calling. In 1921, two years after her grandmother died, she married Wallace Wilson, and he would become the centre of her life.

Then, during the Great Depression of the 1930s, Wilson began to write. She contributed short stories to magazines like the *New Statesman* and penned the travel sketches and tales of family life that she would later weave into the novel *The Innocent Traveller*. She also wrote her first novel, *Hetty Dorval*. This story of an irresponsible adventuress who must eventually pay for the damage she does to others was an ambitious experiment in narrative perspective: the sophisticated Hetty is revealed to the reader through the eyes of the neophyte Frankie. In it, Wilson explores an essential conundrum of our condition: we are simultaneously solitary beings and part of human society.

In 1949, after years of writing and revision, Wilson finally produced *The Innocent Traveller*. This novel, comprising a series of sketches featuring a clan of middle-class Englishwomen living in Vancouver, has been described by critic Beverley Mitchell as "a study of the factors which make for satisfactory living and peaceful dying." Wilson would later remark that she was pleased with this work because in it she was able to encapsulate her own upbringing while presenting a kind of social history of her adopted city. In 1952, Wilson published *The Equations of Love*, which was made up of two novellas: *Tuesday and Wednesday* and *Lilly's Story*. Each features characters who are buffeted by fate and never manage to penetrate the surface of experience, thus allowing their creator to explore, as Wilson herself puts it, "the irrelevance of cause and effect amongst us … and the instability and suggestibility of emotion and behaviour." *Tuesday and Wednesday* depicts two days in the life of a very ordinary married couple, at the end of which the husband dies; *Lilly's Story* concerns a woman who, to protect her daughter, manufactures a new identity for herself, in the process undermining her own chance for happiness. The circumstances of each tale highlight Wilson's keen sense of irony.

Two years later, in 1954, Wilson published *Swamp Angel*, which would come to be seen as her most successful work. In it, Maggie Vardoe abandons the ruins of her second marriage and goes to work at a fishing lodge in northern B.C.; the peace she is seeking in these tranquil surroundings remains elusive, however, and her flight is revealed to be a quest for a more profound spiritual healing — a recurring motif in Wilson's oeuvre. Maggie meets up with her eccentric friend Nell Severance, a retired circus performer who reminds her of a past she is struggling to forget, and she is called upon to help others in need of compassionate attention. Finally, however, Maggie does move towards wholeness and independence, but she balances this with the realization of another pervasive Wilson theme, which she articulates towards the novel's conclusion: "We are all in it together. 'No Man is an Island, I am involved in Mankinde,' and we have no immunity and we may as well realize it."

Wilson's next novel, *Love and Salt Water* (1956), would be her last. It failed to match the success of *Swamp Angel*. Mitchell observes that Wilson clearly struggled with its creation: its "inconsistencies and discrepancies … are evidence that this novel has been reworked." It follows heroine Ellen Cuppy as she emerges from a traumatic childhood and moves towards adult consciousness; her journey is built on an array of familiar Wilson preoccupations: human interdependence, the ineffable workings of chance, the healing power of love. As is most of Wilson's fiction, *Love and Salt Water* is recounted from the perspective of an omniscient narrator who observes characters from a great distance through the lens of mature experience.

Most of the short stories Wilson submitted to magazines were collected in *Mrs. Golightly and Other Stories*, which appeared in 1961. The collection is a testament to the author's remarkable range — from complex experiments in narrative voice ("A Drink with Adolphus"), to absurdist reportage ("Mr. Sleepwalker"), to moral parable ("The Window"), to gentle comedy (the title story).

Wilson gradually overcame her inherent shyness to the extent that she gave several talks on Canadian literature at the University of British Columbia and became involved in West Coast writing circles, hosting a creative writers' group in her home. She became friends with poet Earle Birney, but they clashed when Birney's fervent nationalism became too much for Wilson, who strongly believed that the writer must protect a private, non-political space for her art. She also befriended Margaret Laurence, recognizing the younger writer's prodigious talent.

In 1966, Wallace died, and Wilson was devastated; she suffered a stroke shortly afterwards and gave up writing. Desmond Pacey published an important study of her work in 1967. She had been awarded the Royal Society of Canada's Lorne Pierce Medal in 1964, and six years later she received the Order of Canada Medal of Service. Academic interest in Wilson increased after her death, in 1980: the University of Ottawa published the proceedings of its 1981 Ethel Wilson

Symposium; in 1985, the Ethel Wilson Prize, B.C.'s top fiction award, was established; and in 2003, David Stouck produced *Ethel Wilson: A Critical Biography.*

Mr. Sleepwalker

During the time that Mary Manly's husband was in Australia, Mrs. Manly had an experience that was peculiar. I should like to say that up to the time that her husband went to the war, Mrs. Manly had never shown any tendency to undue imagination, nervousness, hysteria, nor to any of those weaknesses which are supposed to be the prerogative of her sex, but are not — any of which might have been considered responsible for the mounting episodes which culminated in her nearly killing Mr. Sleepwalker. Let us begin with Mary Manly, because we do not know very much about the past of Mr. Sleepwalker. It would be provocative, but not fair, to speculate about Mr. Sleepwalker's past, but unless we knew something about his origin and his history, the speculations would be useless, and disturbing.

Mary Davidson married Hugh Manly who was a forester in the government service of British Columbia, and so able a man was Hugh Manly in the matter of conservation of forests, marketing of lumber — especially as these things applied to the Province of British Columbia whose forests are among her noblest treasures — that his government began to send him on long journeys to foreign countries where export trade might be developed, and it became no great surprise — but a source of something like grief — to Mary when Hugh walked in for dinner, and said later on in the evening as he often did, "Well, it looks as though I'm off again," and Mary would learn that Hugh was being sent by his government to South Africa, or to the United Kingdom, or to Sweden, and so it was that Mary had to gear herself — as they say — to these absences which became to her a mounting sorrow, because she loved her husband beyond expression, and he loved only her. Each time that Hugh left he said something like this, "Next time, darling, we'll see if you can't come too," and Mary would say, "Yes, next time, Hugh." But next time Hugh might go to Hyderabad, and how can a young wife whimsically accompany her husband to Hyderabad, when there is a future to look to. I mention all this because it is possible that the unhappiness of repeated separation in a world whose essential limit is bounded by the life and love of two people closely united, may have done something to Mary's otherwise calm and extroverted nature, and may have made her susceptible to outside influence of an esoteric, supra-human, or even sub-human kind.

Just at the time when it seemed that Hugh had approached the point in his chosen profession at which he could say, "Come with me and be damned to everything and hang the expense," there came the war. Hugh went to the war, and Mary's sense of separation became exacerbated to the point where it was anguish. Are we who love each other so dearly, she said to herself, always to be deprived of our greatest joy, and have I to accustom myself to the theory that we belong to each other *in absentia* only, for it is an actual fact that the woman in the next apartment and I have lived for seven years with only one wall dividing us, and we do not belong to each other; while Hugh and I, who belong to each other, have lived for seven years with half the world between us most of the time. And now this war!

She busied herself at once, but in spite of being daily involved in responsibility and detail, her other life — that is to say her absent life with Hugh — gradually became more real to her than the life of meetings, administration, billeting, in which her body was engaged, especially after Hugh left for overseas. ("Onlie the body's busy, and pretends.") Again I say that this other-worldness, which developed in Mary, and in many other young women like her during those years, but more in Mary Manly, because absence and frustration had already made some mark on her before the war began, may have been responsible for many queer things, one way and another. Directly the war was over, Hugh came home (fortunately) and was placed at once at the head of his department; and before the two had spent a month together, Hugh was sent to Australia. "You're coming this time, Mary, and no nonsense about it," said Hugh, and Mary with rapture prepared to go, broke her left elbow, and Hugh went without her.

To go now to Mr. Sleepwalker.

Before Hugh went overseas he was stationed for a while in Winnipeg. Mary camp-followed him to Winnipeg, and it was in Winnipeg that she first saw Mr. Sleepwalker. It was in a street car. The street car swinging along Portage Avenue was full, and Mary stood, holding onto a strap. She looked idly about her, and the swaying of the street car so determined that her eyes fell upon this person and that sitting in the row of seats immediately beside the entrance to the street car. She saw a small slim man sitting in this seat, with people on either side of him. Mary's whole attention was taken by this man, although no one else seemed to observe him, and as the body of someone swaying beside her interposed between her and the small man seated, she did not see him, and then she saw him again.

She became violently curious about the small man, and began to speculate about him. He appeared unaware of people around him, and certainly unaware of Mary's occasional scrutiny. If I were accustomed to menservants, thought Mary, or if we lived in a different age, I should think that this little man is, or has been, a "gentleman's gentleman." He is drilled in some precision of thought and action, and he hides behind that soft and deferential pose and immobility some definite and different entity. The small man sat erect, looking straight ahead of him, servile yet proud, his hands — in worn black gloves — folded on the head of his walking stick which rested between his knees. His hat was a kind of square obsolete bowler. He wore a wing collar, and a small black tie of the kind known as a string tie. His black suit was old, worn and very neat. Below the anachronistic hat was the face that so attracted and repelled Mary Manly. The features were neat and of a prissy femininity. The eyes were a warm stealthy reddish brown. His hair descended in reddish brown sideburns; otherwise he was clean-shaven. The hair was soft and unlike the hair of a man; in fact it resembled a soft fur. His mouth was set — so, with gentility. He is a mixture, thought Mary, as she watched the little man, now and again obscured from her, of gentility — a fake product of civilization — and of something feral,[1] I do not know what. I seem to have seen those russet eyes, she continued to herself, in some animal. Is it a fox? No, I know no more about foxes than about gentlemen's gentlemen, and yet it seems like a fox. Or a watching hawk. Or some red-eyed rodent. And why is he in the middle of Canada, in Winnipeg, new city of grain, utility and railroads, looking like this, dressed like this? He is as much a phenomenon in his dreadful respectability, riding on an unlikely street car in the city of Winnipeg as if he wore a crown, or a gray topper, or a sarong. What life does he lead, and why is he here? The small man sat alone, it appeared, in his personal and genteel world, politely apart from those who rubbed shoulders with him or crowded his neatly-brushed worn buttoned boots, and he looked straight ahead of him. Mary

---

1. **feral** Wild.

now avoided looking at the small man, because, so lively had been her interest in his peculiarities, she was afraid that he might become aware of her, and she did not want this to happen; so she turned her back, and faced in the other direction. Then she got off the street car and, for the moment, forgot him.

On the next evening, Hugh came in from barracks, and they had dinner together. Mary tried to tell Hugh about the small man on the street car, but found that she was unable to describe him in such a way as would interest Hugh; and when Hugh told her, as he did, that he was ordered east and that he thought that embarkation would be the next step, this drove other thoughts from Mary's mind and she determined at once to move east also, because, as she said, "We may as well continue living together, Hugh, in our own peculiar haphazard fashion. I have really loved it in Winnipeg, and who knows but that they may keep you in the east longer than you think. So I shall not go back to Vancouver. I shall go east, too." Mary then prepared to go east, following Hugh, who left at a day's notice.

She had by this time attained (she thought) a fairly philosophic regard for things as they have to be, realizing of course that she was only one of the millions of persons — friend and enemies — whose lives were dislocated by war; that she could expect no special privilege because she was Mary Manly, wife of Hugh Manly (usually *in absentia*); and that she could and must assume the matter-of-factness which is necessary in the successful conduct of life, which other people achieve so admirably, and which passes very well for courage. So she took life as it came, allowing herself to hope, as was natural, that her husband would be kept in Canada, although a part of each of them wished that he would be sent away and would see action, but safely, with everybody else, and no favours sought or granted. Mary said good-bye to her friends in Winnipeg, many of whom, like herself, were also in motion one way or another, and then, late one night, she boarded the eastbound train.

Because Mary was what is called a good train traveller, she soon bestowed her things neatly away and settled down for the remainder of the night in her lower berth. She slept at once, and only in a half-conscious and comfortable way was she aware of the stopping, starting, moaning, creaking of the great train. Suddenly she was awakened by a quiet. The train was standing still, perhaps in a siding, because there seemed to be no noise, or it may have been in the night-time stillness of the railway station of a town. Mary was half awake, and did not care. She was sleepily aware of stillness, of time and place suspended — and then of persons passing quietly, almost stealthily, in the aisle outside her curtain … the porter … perhaps … passenger … porter … a murmur … a smell … earth … rotted wood … an animal … in the sleeping-car … impossible … a smell … earth … rotted wood … an animal … it passed. She fell asleep.

When day broke, the train had left Manitoba and was speeding into the vast western wooded lake-strewn regions of Ontario. The train stopped at Chapleau for twenty minutes. Mary got out, and wandered, as she always did at Chapleau station, to the small stone memorial that bears the name of Louis Hémon.[2] Why, she wondered, did Louis Hémon come to Canada, write his book which, although unknown to most young Canadians, had already dimmed to a reputation faintly classic, and die. And why did Louis Hémon die, still young, at Chapleau, straggling rawly beside its railway station and its forests. A young man stood beside her and studied the carved words. Mary

---

2. **Louis Hémon** 19th-century French writer, hit by a train in Ontario. The novel is *Maria Chapdelaine*, which he wrote in Quebec.

looked up at him and spoke tentatively. "Do you know why Louis Hémon came here?" she asked.

"Sawry," said the young man awkwardly, "I never heard of him. I was kinda wondering myself who he was," and he strolled away.

Mary turned and walked briskly up and down the platform, with the breeze and against the breeze that blew refreshingly through Chapleau. She heard the cry "All aboard." She turned towards her own porter at her own car. As she waited to mount the steps, she saw walking down the platform the small man in black whom she had seen in the Winnipeg street car. She was startled to see the small figure in motion. He walked, one might say, with as much stillness as he sat, regarding no one. He walked with his arms at his sides, guarded, genteel, like a black-suited doll. She climbed on the train, entered her car, and found her seat. She did not see him again.

When she rejoined Hugh in Halifax, there were many urgent things to think about without recalling to mind the small man whose hair was like fur, and so it seemed that he had never been. Hugh's convoy sailed, and Mary Manly went back to Vancouver and put herself at once to work.

It was months later that Mary Manly and Thérèse Leduc went to a movie together. At the end of the first picture, the two people who were sitting beside Mary went out, and, in the dark, another occupant took the seat beside her. Suddenly Mary's attention was taken from the screen by the scent, slight at first, then stronger, of, perhaps, an animal, or, perhaps, rotted wood, thick and dank (but how could it be rotted wood?). This smell was not at first heavy, but pervasive, and was very unpleasant to her. It became at last heavy in the air, and made her uneasy. It recalled to her a journey ... a what? ... some smell ... not train smell ... something that passed by. She tried to look at the person next to her without appearing to do so. This was difficult. She murmured to Thérèse Leduc, "Do you smell anything queer?"

"No," whispered Thérèse. "What kind of thing?"

"I don't know," answered Mary.

"I smell nothing," said Thérèse.

The smell persisted. Suddenly the skin on the back of Mary's neck seemed to prickle. The man (it was a man) who sat beside her, was small, and sat very still. Mary sat still too, and thought, "I want to get up and leave. I can't. That is unreasonable." But at last she whispered to Thérèse, "I'm sorry, Terry, but the man beside me *does* smell. Let's get out ... perhaps we can move. Let's go your way."

The two women got up and shuffled out of the long end of the row.

"How disgusting!" expostulated Thérèse.

"Yes, wasn't it? It really *was*," said Mary, but she did not explain that the smell was not what Terry thought it was. Not dirt. Nothing like dirt. Something animal. Something wild. They found other seats, but Mary could not give her attention to the play. After the movie, she discovered also that she could not tell Thérèse about the small man, and about this animal smell which she had begun to associate with him. The thing was fanciful, and Mary did not like to be thought fanciful. Most of all, she did not like to admit to herself that she was fanciful. But there it was. She put her mind to other things, and that was not very difficult.

Some time later, as Mary rose from her knees in church, she did not need to look in order to see who it was that had come into the pew and had now dropped on his knees beside her. The feral scent wafted and then hung heavy. The small man in black drew himself up to his seat, and sat, doll-like, prim, just as (Mary knew) she had seen him sit in the street car on Portage Avenue. She saw him as plainly now as though her physical eyes observed the genteel shape, the russet fur of the sideburns, the prissy set of the mouth. He sat beside her, she knew, correct, genteel, yet vulpine, if it was vulpine. Mary's head began to spin. My imagination plays tricks, or does it? she asked herself ... Soon, of course, I shall see the two people in front of me move, turn slightly, disturbed by the smell that disturbs me. It cannot be to me, me alone, that it comes. He carries it round with him. Others *must* smell it — always. He is horrible, horrible. But now I can't leave ... I must stay ... he can never have observed me (for we never think, do we, that we are the observed ones; always we are the observers), I shall sit here. I shall stay for the service, and out-stay him. But he is horrible. And a revulsion at the proximity of this small being almost overcame her, and she felt faint.

The little man sat still; his worn-gloved hands were on his knees, she could see. He took his Prayer Book and found his place, following the service respectfully, and in an accustomed manner. Mary's mind worked obliquely, directed, in spite of herself, towards the small man.

But the two people in front of her did not turn round, disturbed by the alien smell of rotted wood, of something animal, unknown.

Mary out-sat the service. Then, with elaborate negligence, while the small man was leaving and after he had left, she put on her gloves, leaned back in her pew and awaited the end of the slowly-drifting columns of church goers moving with slightly rocking inhibited motion down the aisles. Then she joined the departing stream at its end, went out into the open air, felt refreshed and, by a foolishly roundabout way, returned home.

I shall tell Hugh, she thought. It's very silly. I take this too seriously, and if I tell Hugh, I'll get rid of it. The thing bothers me out of all proportion. What concerns me is the war, and Hugh, and my jobs of work to do, and my life that I have always had; and a small being that smells like — perhaps — a weasel or a musk-rat has no part and does not matter. So she wrote, but when she read the letter that she had written to Hugh, her story seemed idiotic. She tore the letter up, and wrote again and did not mention the small man. Hugh, she thought, would not in any case be amused. She could not make the story amusing. She could just make it sound silly. Hugh might be interested in a man that smelled like an animal (she had seldom smelled an animal), but she would not be able to conceal from him the fact that something was being established that affected her unreasonably and unpleasantly; it seemed to her that the small man, in spite of his apparent immobility and unawareness, was in some peculiar way, aware of her also. This, of course, was possible, yet unlikely and very unpleasant. She neither saw the small man, nor did the strange scent reach her, for a long time.

One night it rained. Mary drove carefully in her little car. She picked up her cousin, Cora Wilmot, and drove through the lashing rain, and through the lights and reflections of lights, cross-hatched in the early dark in splashing pools and pavements, lighted by and left behind by the beams of her own headlights, onto Granville Street Bridge. She drove carefully in the late dinner-time traffic, peering through the rainstorm. She drove rather slowly. Cora, beside her, peered too. Then the thing nearly happened.

Just before Mary reached the narrow span of the bridge, Cora cried out, and stifled her cry. Off the slightly raised platform-like sidewalk of the bridge, into the light of the headlights of Mary's slowly-moving car, stepped a small man. He faced the lights of the car, and seemed to look through the windshield of the car and at, or into, the occupants. The lights showed all in one flash the white face (and Mary could see the lighted russet eyes), the intolerable propriety of mouth and chin, dark lines of hair framing the almost rectangular face. The man threw up his arms with the stiff gesture of a marionette. Mary swerved sharply to the left into whatever cars there might be, into the span, if need be, rather than touch, or become involved in any way with the man who had stepped in front of her car. She did not touch him. She touched neither cars nor span. She did not speak. She drove to the end of the bridge, up Granville Street hill, through lights, darkness and rain, and then she pulled up at the side of the road. She was trembling violently. Cora was voluble.

"That horrible little man!" she said, "*What* was he doing? *Why* did he do it? He did it on purpose! No one crosses the bridge there! There's nothing to cross for! Oh Mary, what a narrow shave! Let's sit here a while. What a face! He looked as if he could see us, as if he was looking at us! I'll never forget him, will you? Do you feel like driving now? Let's get there, and then they'll give us a drink before dinner, and that will help us both."

"Yes," said Mary, and she drove on. He saw me, she thought, as I drove so slowly in the lights, and then he stepped out.

Before the end of the year, Hugh came home, the war being incredibly over. And then, as I said, Hugh went to Australia, and Mary, with the complicated fracture of her left arm in a sling, stayed at home.

Many and many a time, towards the end of the war, and now, when alone, when sleeping, and at waking, she seemed to see the doll-like figure of the small man with her motor lights full on his white face. She saw a marionette's gesture — two dark arms flung stiffly upwards, she swerved, she drove on in her dream. And then, the obsession became less frequent. Nevertheless, within herself, she knew that she had begun to be afraid of something.

Hugh wrote from Melbourne, "I'm going to be here longer than we thought. Just as soon as that elbow is better enough cable me. I'll advise you, and you get a passage by air. And at last … " The load of aggravation lifted from Mary, and she began to lie about her elbow in order to get away and to join Hugh in Australia. However, their friend the doctor, Johnny Weston, put her off for a week.

One afternoon she returned from John's surgery with the permission that she might now make arrangements for her flight to Australia, and so she cabled to Hugh. Such a thing as this had never happened to Mary Manly before. She went home, and in her ecstasy, her rapture, she telephoned Thérèse Leduc and Cora, and anybody else that came to mind, to tell them that she was flying to Australia to join Hugh.

There came a ring at the door of the flat. Still careful of her clumsy left arm, Mary went lightly to the door and opened it. A feral smell entered the apartment, followed by the small respectable man who had stood outside Mary's door and had rung her doorbell. The man was dressed as usual in black. As he stepped humbly but without question into the hall, he took off his obsolete square-shaped bowler hat, laid it upon a table, turned and shut the door in a serviceable manner, and then advanced obsequiously on Mary. In his hand he carried a small black valise.[3] Scent hung heavy and it was the smell of fear.

Mary was aghast. Her right hand flew to her mouth. She pressed the back of her hand to her mouth and gazed at the small man over her hand. She did not think, I am

---

3. **valise** Suitcase.

alone in this apartment with this unpleasant little creature. She did not think at all. The air was full of the dank wild earthy smell of something old and unknown. She backed, and obsequiously the small man advanced upon her. She saw the russet animal eyes, the reddish animal fur. She saw the prissy gentility of the lips. She smelled the smell.

"Sleepwalker," said the man softly, looking at her.

Mary snatched up a small bronze vase, and hit the man hard upon the side of the head. He looked at her with infinite surprise and reproach, swayed, and sank to the floor. He lay there like a large black-garbed doll, and blood began to flow from the wound on his head. His eyes were closed and he was very pale.

Mary stood looking down upon him, and tried to measure what she had done. "Three minutes ago," she thought, "I was mad with joy because I was going to Hugh, and now perhaps I have killed a man who is a stranger." She now felt curiously hard and not at all frightened. She went to the telephone and called John Weston at his surgery.

"John," she said, "this is Mary Manly. I am at home. I think I have killed a man. Please come." And she hung up the telephone and went back to the small man who lay as she had left him.

I am very stupid, thought Mary, because I do not know whether he is unconscious or whether he is dead, and I don't know how to find out such things. At least I will bathe his head, and perhaps if he is unconscious he will rally a bit. She got water and a cloth, and although it was repugnant to her, she knelt down and bathed the wound which she had inflicted on the small respectable man. He stirred. He opened his eyes and looked steadily at her. She rose to her feet and looked down at him.

"Dear lady," whispered the man, still prostrate on the floor, "whatever made you do that to me?" and his eyes were indeed the eyes of an animal.

Well, thought Mary, I can see that this is going to be a very odd conversation. She could not answer his question, and so she said, "I am very, very sorry that I have done this to you, but why are you here? And why did you walk into my flat like that? And what was that you said to me when you came in?" It gave her satisfaction that John Weston would soon come, and would act as some kind of a solvent to this situation.

The man sat up slowly, and felt his head. He looked at his red hand with surprise, and again looked up at Mrs. Manly.

"Name of Sleepwalker," he said, "carrying a line of ladies' underwear samples of special buys in rayon, silk, crêpe, also ladies' hosiery put out by the Silki-Silk Company with agents in all major cities of Canada," and he looked at the black valise which lay where it had fallen.

"Oh," said Mary, feeling very silly indeed. "And do you really mean that your name is Sleepwalker?"

"Name of Handel Sleepwalker," said Mr. Sleepwalker, and subsided again into a faint on the floor.

The doorbell rang, and Mary opened the door to Dr. Weston. Because Dr. Weston was ruffled, and had — unwillingly — left his patients when Mary summoned him so imperatively and strangely, he had, since leaving his consulting-room, built up a genuine and justified annoyance mixed with real uneasiness, and because he could find no other object for his annoyance, he had hung it upon Mary Manly. Therefore by the time Dr. Weston arrived at Mary's apartment he was very angry indeed with her for having killed a man at a quarter-past five in the afternoon, for having taken him forcibly from his consultations and for having chosen to do this at a time when Hugh was not at home and therefore was unable to take the matter in hand. Although a very good friend of Hugh and Mary, Dr. Weston was not at that moment in the frame of mind to shoulder the results of murder. This is why, when Mary opened the door with a sense of relief, John Weston dismayed her by a complete absence of sympathy; he turned on her an angry face, and roared at her in an injured manner, "What on Earth *have* you been doing?" as if she were guilty. Well, so she was.

Mary, aware of all that had gone before that was so ridiculously unexplainable at that very instant, realized that she had to cope with her own emotions to attend — in the first place — to Mr. Sleepwalker who lay inert on the living-room floor, and to manage Dr. Weston either by returning anger for anger, innocence for anger, or by disregarding anger. This latter she decided to do.

"Come," she said. She turned and indicated Mr. Sleepwalker with an air quite sublime. "You see!"

When Dr. Weston saw the actual body of Mr. Sleepwalker lying on the floor of the room in which Dr. Weston and his wife had so often enjoyed a cocktail, and saw Mr. Sleepwalker's blood upon the carpet, and saw Mary standing there pale, helpless, bandaged and gentle, other feelings began to take possession of him. He kneeled down and examined the prostrate one. Then he looked up and said to Mary in a fretful tone, "He's not dead at all!"

Well, really, thought Mary, this is too much! Does John expect that one should make sure of *killing* someone before disturbing him! John is going to be aggravating, I can see. But she said simply, "Oh, John, I am so thankful. This has been very alarming."

"Did *you* hit him?" asked Dr. Weston, scrambling to his feet.

"Oh yes, I hit him."

"Why … ?"

"He *terrified* me," said Mary. "He stole into the room when I opened the door, and followed me up, and did not explain his business, and then he said something that frightened me very much. And here I was with my bad arm and alone, and before I realized what I was doing, John, I hit him with that little vase."

"What did he say to you?" asked Dr. Weston.

Mr. Sleepwalker spoke from the floor. His eyes were closed. He said softly, "I did not indeed desire to frighten the dear lady; I merely told the dear lady my name."

Dr. Weston shot a very baleful look at Mary; he became suspicious of her again (and there were all those patients in the waiting-room).

"And what *is* your name?" asked Dr. Weston.

"Sleepwalker," said Mr. Sleepwalker, opening his eyes.

"And where do you live?" asked Dr. Weston.

Mr. Sleepwalker closed his eyes again. "I am afraid," he said, "that for the moment I am unable to remember."

"Well, where would you like us to take you?" asked the doctor.

"Yes, where would you like us to take you?" asked Mary, eagerly.

Mr. Sleepwalker paused for a moment. Then, "I would like to stay ere," he said.

"That is impossible, quite impossible," said Dr. Weston crossly. "You can take him to the hospital, Mary. He's all right to move, and a day or two will be all that's needed."

"John," said Mary, taking the doctor aside, "do you notice a very queer smell in this room?"

"No, I don't," said the doctor. "Do you?"

She did not answer. "I will get an ambulance if you will arrange with the hospital," she said.

"I would much prefer," said a silky voice from the floor, "if the dear lady would take me to the ospital erself. Far be it indeed to go in an ambulance."

Mary scowled at the doctor, who said at once, "No, we'll get an ambulance. See if you can sit up now."

Mr. Sleepwalker obediently sat up, a little black figure with legs outstretched on the floor. The doctor supported him.

"Now into this chair."

"I am a poor man," said Mr. Sleepwalker, sitting up straight and stiff in the chair, with his disfigured head.

"I will pay for your ambulance, Mr. Sleepwalker, and I will pay for your days in the hospital as long as Dr. Weston says that you must stay," said Mary.

"Oh, ow kind, dear lady," said Mr. Sleepwalker humbly, and Mary thought, What a brute I am, I've never abased myself and really apologized for hitting him! "I shall get you some tea," she said. Meanwhile, the doctor was busy at the telephone. He looked at his watch. "Don't leave me!" murmured Mary as she brushed past him in the hall, and Dr. Weston gave her an un-affectionate look. She took a tray in to Mr. Sleepwalker, who gazed round the room as though he were memorizing it.

"I shall burn this tray, break the cup and saucer, give away the chair, and send the carpet to the cleaners, or we can sell it — in fact, we might leave the flat. I can't bear to have had this little horror in the room," Mary said to herself unfairly, forgetting that she was very lucky.

Mr. Sleepwalker coughed. "One thing may I hask," he said.

"What," said Mary.

"I should like to hask," he said, "that the dear lady will visit me in the ospital."

Mary considered. That was the very least she could do.

"Yes, of course I will," she said, trying to sound hearty.

"Oh, thank you, *thank* you," said Mr. Sleepwalker. The doctor came out of the hall.

"I have arranged for the bed and the ambulance," he said, looking again at his watch. "Some time I will hear more about this." He had one leg out of the door.

"You will stay!" besought Mary with agitation, seizing his arm.

The doctor put down his overcoat again. "Very well, I will stay," he said irritably, and thought of his waiting-room. He did not like Mary Manly at all just now, whether because she had or had not killed Mr. Sleepwalker (although on the whole he was relieved that she had not); but chiefly he disliked Mary because she had behaved in an irrational manner — he disapproved of people being irrational — and had called him away from his surgery in the middle of the afternoon. He whirled to the telephone, and Mary heard him say brusquely, "I'll be back. Keep Mrs. Jenkins, and tell Mr. Howe I'll see him tomorrow, and explain to the two others that I'll see them tomorrow, and give them a time, and tell Mrs. Boniface that I'll drop in on the way home, and don't let the Jackson boy go home till I've seen him and … "

"Oh Lord," thought Mary, contrite, "what have I done to all these people! Poor Johnny!" and she tried to look pathetic, but it was no good.

The ambulance arrived, and Dr. Weston sped away. Two burly ambulance men helped Mr. Sleepwalker; he walked between them in his still fashion. One big man carried his absurdly small valise. The other one took charge of the obsolete hat. Mary stood.

At the door Mr. Sleepwalker made as if to turn.

"I do hask, dear lady, that you will recollect your promise?" he said, with a question.

"I will indeed," said Mary heartily and with the greatest repugnance.

She heard the door close. She turned and opened all the windows, and did what she could to the room. Then she telephoned Cora. "Cora," she said, "a very peculiar thing has happened. I won't tell you over the telephone, but here, but for the grace of God, sits your cousin, the famous murderess ..." a thought checked her, "or," and she laughed. "the famous huntress."

"What *do* you mean!" asked Cora.

"Well," said Mary slowly, "you remember the night we nearly ran that man down on the bridge?"

"Yes, yes," said Cora.

"Well," continued Mary slowly, "it's the same man. Coincidence, of course, of the most extraordinary kind" (was it coincidence?) "and it's left me rather shaken."

"Too much happens to you. Come at once and have dinner," said Cora.

"I will," said Mary gratefully.

As Mary Manly went to her cousin's house, she asked herself some questions. If I wished to go to the bottom of the queerness of this, if I had any scientific curiosity and not just a detestation of the whole affair, I would take up a notebook and pencil, and question that ... that ... person (she avoided even his name). I would say to him, Was your aunt a fox, or was your grandmother a weasel, and of course, he would say no, and where should I find myself then? I could ask him if he seeks me in particular, and how, and why. But I am such a coward that I don't want to know. Then I would say, My good sir, do you know that you smell? And if he said yes, I should have to ask him, Do some people (such as I) and not other people, recognize this animal (yes, I should have to say "animal") scent? I can see how totally impossible such a conversation is, and so I shall leave it alone, and shall admit, to myself, and not to others, only the fact that this man frightens me....

When Mary left Cora the next morning (for Cora easily persuaded her to stay the night), she knew that the talk of her attack upon Mr. Sleepwalker would spread among her friends and acquaintances, and that it would be well and properly launched by Cora. She realized that she would be the object of universal pity ("Poor Mrs. Manly, wasn't it dreadful for her! The man, my dear, walked straight into the flat, and there was Mary all alone, with a broken arm ... I think she's very good not to prosecute! And so brave. The most extraordinary coincidence, my dear! Cora Wilmot says ...") and that this was not quite fair to Mr. Sleepwalker who, after all, was the one who had been hit on the temple with a bronze vase and was now in hospital. She knew that she would be decried as soft, foolish, and too kind because she had provided the ambulance and was about to pay the hospital bill. However, she had to choose between all or nothing, and the section of the story which was in Cora's possession and which Cora would launch on all their acquaintances with her well-known energy, approximated to nothing, and that was best.

The following afternoon Mary said to herself as she alighted clumsily with parcels at the hospital, This (calling on this man, I mean) is the most unpleasant thing that I have deliberately done in my whole life. I don't call hitting ... Mr. Sleepwalker ... deliberate. It was instinctive. If only Hugh were with me it would be easier. However, as she had that afternoon received a cable from Hugh which read: "Cheers and cheers take first passage and cable me," she felt more carefree than she would have thought possible. I can tell this ... individual ... she thought, that I am going to Australia (that seems far enough away) — which is true — that I'm going tomorrow, which is not true, but it is true enough. And she entered the hospital.

She found Mr. Sleepwalker propped up a little on his pillows, looking very pale. His head was bandaged, and when she saw the bandage, she felt much more guilty than when, in the storm of terror, she had struck down Mr. Sleepwalker and had seen him lying on the floor, with blood flowing upon the carpet.

Patients in the adjacent beds regarded her apathetically. Mr. Sleepwalker looked earnestly, too earnestly, at her. I should, of course, give him my hand, she said to herself, this hand which has struck him down. But she did not wish to do so. She found that her feelings were strangely involved. In order to avoid touching Mr. Sleepwalker's hand, and for no more altruistic reason, Mary had filled her good hand with flowers, and carried magazines and a box of chocolates under her arm. As she disposed these articles awkwardly about Mr. Sleepwalker's bed, the handshaking moment passed, as she had intended it should. A nurse, seeing her arm in a sling, brought forward a chair. Mary smiled at her, thanked her, and sat down.

"I hope you are not too uncomfortable," she said.

"Oh, no, thank you, dear lady," said Mr. Sleepwalker. "This is a very nice ospital, nicer than what I was in in England that time the dogs bit me."

"Dogs … !" said Mary.

"Ounds," said Mr. Sleepwalker.

Mr. Sleepwalker's bandages really afflicted Mary. They made her feel more guilty even than her own conscience. However, she could not afford to get soft about Mr. Sleepwalker, even though she had hit him with a vase.

"I am sorry that I cannot have a nice long chat," she said untruthfully, "but the fact is that I am flying to Australia tomorrow to join my husband."

"Come a little closer, dear lady," said Mr. Sleepwalker. His reddish eyes were fixed upon her. Mary made hitching noises with her chair, but she was near enough. She began to feel faint. "I should like to go to Australia," he said. "Oh, ow I should like!"

"Australia is, I am sure, a very nice country," replied Mary with considerable idiocy. I must keep this impersonal, she thought, and proceeded to talk about Australia, of which she knew very little. "So you see I cannot stay any longer; in fact, I must go. Everything will be arranged, the bill, you know. I am so very sorry for what I did to you. It was really some terrible misunderstanding."

The little man in the bed continued to look earnestly at her.

"It as been a pleasure indeed to meet you, dear lady," he said in his soft voice. (What an extraordinary statement! thought Mary.) "May I thank you indeed for your kindness, and may I tell you, dear lady, ow grateful I ave always been to you, and ow I ave frequently and in oh ever so many places enjoyed your delicious smell … fragrance, I *should* say."

"My … ! my … !" stammered Mary, and sprang to her feet. She stood for one moment looking down at Mr. Sleepwalker. Then she turned and the patients saw her running like a hare out of the ward.

(1961)

W.W.E. Ross (1894–1966)

In his public life, William Wrightson Eustace Ross was a distinguished geophysicist. In private, he quietly pursued an interest in the literary classics and in writing poetry. He published just three books in his lifetime, and the first two he financed himself, using only the initials E.R. to indicate his authorship. He was reclusive and often depressed, and it took strong encouragement from other writers to convince him to publish his writings. Although Raymond Souster read Ross's imagist poems and would later tout him as Canada's first modern poet, Ross never achieved renown.

Born in Peterborough, Ontario, Ross was raised in Pembroke. After graduating from high school, he enrolled at the University of Toronto. In the summers of his university years, he worked in northern Ontario as a chainman on a surveying crew. Obliged to canoe and hike to survey sites, Ross was exposed to the Canadian wilderness made famous by the Group of Seven painters. He later incorporated imagery of the natural world into his poetry, but he rejected the traditional European Romantic motifs.

In 1914, Ross graduated with a degree in chemistry, and soon after that he enlisted in the signal corps of the Canadian Army. He served overseas during World War I, but he was never forthcoming about the experience. According to Barry Callaghan, "No one knew that [Ross] had fought in the First World War, that he had been gassed in the trenches, that he'd suffered shell-shock." Returning from Europe, he embarked on two careers: scientist and poet. In 1924, he married Mary Lowry and joined the Dominion Astrophysical Observatory in Agincourt (north of Toronto); he eventually became the director of the Magnetic Observatory.

The year before, he had begun writing poems, and in 1928, he published some of them in the United States; Marianne Moore's journal the *Dial*, and then the Chicago journal *Poetry* welcomed his poems. Many of these reappeared in his self-published *Laconics* (1930). The term "laconic" — which means terse, succinct — well describes the quality of these poems, and their author's personality. In a 1956 letter to Ralph Gustafson, Ross explained that "Practically all the first section of that book *Laconics* was written one night in April, 1928, after an evening's discussion of Canadian nationalism with friends of ours. The laconics form was developed in 1925 in an attempt to find one that would be 'native' and yet not 'free verse,' one that would be unrhymed and yet definitely a 'form.'" Developing a native form was important to Ross. He disagreed with A.J.M. Smith's view that modern poetry should be cosmopolitan and believed instead that a poet is always associated with a place. In his most innovative works — most of which are written in narrow stanzas, sometimes even in two columns that can be read left-to-right *or* top-to-bottom — he incorporated elements of a landscape recognizable to Canadians. *Laconics* was Ross's first, and arguably best, book: "It never 'clicked' so well before or since as that night in 1928."

Certainly, something clicked: to a 1931 issue of *Poetry*, Marianne Moore contributed an admiring review of Ross's work (perhaps not surprisingly, since she was one of his influences, along with Max Jacob, Ezra Pound, and E.E. Cummings). After Ross published *Sonnets* in 1932 (still identifying himself only by his initials), Moore applauded his work for its "freshness, responsibility, and authenticity of locality." *Sonnets*, however, was not as formally interesting or as innovative as *Laconics*; Ross himself admitted that he was uncertain about some of the phrasings he had used in it.

In the 1920s and 1930s, the transition to modernism was far from complete in Canada — few readers favoured the new styles. Ross became less interested in publishing his poems. He was overcome by shyness and uncertainty. In the 1940s, his introversion burgeoned into a serious depression, which, Callaghan suggests, was linked to the shell shock he had suffered during the war. It seemed that the world wars allowed Ross an opportunity to vent the anger and contempt he otherwise kept well under control. Callaghan maintains that Ross "wrote preposterous letters to the newspapers, curmudgeonly letters, bigoted, always supporting the British or Ulster Orange cause, ripe with diatribe.... No one knew that [Ross] was a mesmerist who believed that during the Second World War he had received messages from spirits, messages that he took so seriously he wrote to the U.S. War Department warning them that there was going to be an invasion of western Ireland."

In the 1950s and 1960s, Ross attracted the attention of some younger, more established poets, who helped enrich his literary reputation. Raymond Souster edited a retrospective selection of Ross's poems, *Experiment 1923–29* (1956), which led to Ross being recognized as Canada's first imagist poet. Ross remained unwilling to publish a book of his poems with a commercial press, but anthologizers managed to convince him to participate in their projects. His work was included in his friend Ralph Gustafson's *The Penguin Book of Canadian Verse* (1958); and A.J.M. Smith won Ross's permission to publish some of his poems in *The Oxford Book of Canadian Verse* (1960).

In 1966, when he was 72, Ross died of cancer. Souster and J.R. Colombo published Ross's first collection, *Shapes and Sounds*, in 1968. The volume charts Ross's poetry chronologically, from 1923 to 1958, in the process revealing that Ross's poetic method was considerably ahead of his time.

Lovers

We shall be
lovers of
all that is
lovely and
gentle and
bold

Fearing no
death but the
lapse of our
souls and the   10
sluggardly
peevish

Death that curves
mouldering
out of the
mouths of our
idleness

We shall be
lovers of
stars and the   20
light of the
full round moon

When in her
splendour she
rises at
set of the
sun.

(1926)

Wild Rose

Delicate
is the light
petal of
wild rose that
stands by the
pathway

Fragile and
delicate,
lightest of
10   pressure will
unbalance
fatally

Faintest of
touches will
start from its
base this light
petal of
wild rose

Delicate
20   fragile and
apt to be
swept away
suddenly.

(1926)

Curving, the Moon

Curving, the moon
over the mirror lake;
the new moon
thinly curving
over the lake.

Below, the pine
standing dark and tall,
through its black
topmost branches
10   the curved limb
of the new moon.

Rising, it leaps from the ground,
immobile —
the dark pine

moon-illuminated
on the shore
of mirror-lake.

Is it a breeze?
No sound from the pine,
but on the water   20
a long shadow
ripples.

                                                                    (1926)

The Diver

I would like to dive
Down
Into this still pool
Where the rocks at the bottom are safely deep,

Into the green
Of the water seen from within,
A strange light
Streaming past my eyes —

Things hostile;
You cannot stay here, they seem to say;   10
The rocks, slime-covered, the undulating
Fronds of weeds —

And drift slowly
Among the cooler zones;
Then, upward turning,
Break from the green glimmer

Into the light,
White and ordinary of the day,
And the mild air,
With the breeze and the comfortable shore.   20

                                                                    (1927)

Good Angels

Good   angels
angels   pausing
pause   a moment
they remain   do not fly
still a   away
moment   away now
If they shall   perhaps
remain   more than

	a moment	more than
10	If angels	momentarily —
	If they should	remain
	more than	a moment —
	But no	no
	they do not	do not remain
	more than	momentarily
	Good angels	pause
	touch	a moment
	then pass	pass
	are gone	are gone

(1928)

First Snow

Let the first
snow fall
white upon
fields and the
roofs of the
houses

freshly.
Let it remain a
time on them,
10   covering

all of the
dust, and the
dried-up
leaves of the
field-weeds,

hiding old
traces;
making all
new, for a time.

(1958)

Raymond Knister (1899–1932)

John Raymond Knister was born in 1899 in the farming community of Ruscom, Ontario. As a youth, he read voraciously and widely; he preferred studying to doing farm work and was glad to spend a year at the University of Toronto, in 1919. Poor health, however, forced him to return to his father's farm, where he would work until 1923. In "Canadian Literati," Knister observes that those years changed his view of farm life and the course of his literary career: his resentment of hard labour vanished and was replaced by the desire to express "something about the life that [he] lived, and all the other farm people round [him]."

In his precious spare time, he wrote short stories and poems about farming, as well as book reviews for a Windsor paper, the *Border Cities Star*. But Knister laboured 14 to 16 hours a day on the farm, and the work was repetitive and exhausting. Trying to write left him with a strong sense that subsistence-level work inhibits the development of art on individual and national levels. Indeed, several of Knister's protagonists are sensitive boys whose potential is quashed by agrarian life, and in his introduction to *Canadian Short Stories* (1928), he says that the initial "material" work of nation-building must have barred all but "more than usually vigorous talent" from achieving "any sort of adequate expression" in Canada. So when Knister was offered an internship as an assistant editor for the *Midland*, an Iowa-based magazine that had published two of his stories, he accepted. He left the farm permanently in 1924.

The position was part-time, and Knister could fill his free hours with writing and study. He composed two novels (*Group Portrait* and *Turning Loam*, both unpublished) and attended classes at Iowa State University. When his internship terminated, he moved to Chicago, where he drove a taxi and continued to write.

That Knister set his early stories on farms or in Chicago demonstrates his growing commitment to write about, as he called it, "experienced reality." He believed that good writing should be as "real" as possible, but that realism itself is only "means to an end … the end being a personal projection of the world." He admired the stories of Anton Chekhov and 19th-century American writers like Henry James because, as he says in "Democracy and the Short Story," they never allowed their realism to compromise the "emotional authenticity" of their work. In "Canadian Literature: A General Impression," Knister declares that pure realism does not, alone, qualify as art: it must possess "a depth of knowledge and conviction and authenticity of feeling together with a more revealing portrayal of our inner life."

Knister's realistic detail and his emphasis on the "inner life" of his characters aligned him more closely with modern experimental prose writers abroad than it did with popular writers in Canada. While the editor of the *Toronto Star Weekly* criticized Knister's contributions for being "too real," the prestigious *This Quarter*— a Parisian review that published Ernest Hemingway and James Joyce — accepted a poem and two stories, including "The Fate of Mrs Lucier" (1925). Knister's themes of isolation, initiation, and psychological development, as well as his powerful imagery, poetic prose style, and extensive vocabulary, appealed to the European avant-garde but repelled the editors of Canadian magazines (whose offerings were intended as light, pleasant reading). Nonetheless, Knister moved to Toronto in 1926 and freelanced for the *Toronto Star Weekly* and *Saturday Night*. When the *Star Weekly* rejected a number of stories by Knister's peer Morley Callaghan, Knister concluded that the editor "was instinctively on his guard against anything approaching artistic integrity," and "it was only because he wanted a quantity of 'farm stuff' that he tolerated my stories."

In 1927, Knister married Myrtle Gamble and moved to Hanlan's Point, Ontario, where he wrote his first published novel, *White Narcissus* (1929). The plot is fairly straightforward: Richard Milne proposes to his childhood sweetheart, Ada, who feels obliged to remain at home with her unhappy parents. *White Narcissus* features a number of characters who focus to the point of blindness on a single object; but the character of Milne, a writer, comes to appreciate that a narrow material obsession can limit the broad vision an artist requires in order to apprehend the internal and external components of reality.

How to, in his words, "come to grips with reality" is the question Knister believed Canadian writers needed to address. He had been asked to edit a volume of Canadian short fiction for Macmillan; in 1928, he released *Canadian Short Stories*, which included works by Callaghan, Stephen Leacock, Charles G.D. Roberts, and Duncan Campbell Scott. In the introduction, he cautiously assessed the state of Canadian letters. He maintained that the country's stories, for material and economic reasons, had emerged from "foreign models" in a state of "spirited emulation at best, or a shallow imitativeness at worst." While he had acknowledged elsewhere that imitation is a vital part of learning the technique of writing, Knister urged Canadians to apply "the variety and potency" of English and American influences to their own unique experiences — to be "rooted in the soil."

After editing *Canadian Short Stories*, Knister moved his family to Port Dover, Ontario, where he wrote his second novel. *My Star Predominant* (1934) is a fictionalized biography of John Keats in his final years (the book had won first prize, guaranteed publication, in the Graphic Publishers' Canadian Novel Contest). Both *My Star Predominant* and *White Narcissus* are written in a highly poetic style, have writers as protagonists, and to some degree reflect their author's development as an artist.

From 1931 to 1932, Knister lived in and around Montreal, where he made the acquaintance of Leo Kennedy. Though his name does not appear in the book, Knister helped Kennedy plan *New Provinces* (1936), a volume of contemporary Canadian verse containing the work of Kennedy, Robert Finch, A.M. Klein, F.R. Scott, and A.J.M. Smith. His own poetry is marked by experimentation with imagist techniques, although he employed several forms, including the long poem and the prose-poem.

Knister drowned in 1932 while swimming in Lake St. Clair. Dorothy Livesay speculated upon the circumstances surrounding his death in her memoir of him, which was commissioned to accompany a 1940 volume of his poetry. In 1979, Knister's daughter, Imogen Knister Givens, released a statement refuting Livesay's account, citing factual errors. Much of Knister's work remained unpublished during his short lifetime. The first substantial edition of his selected prose was released in 1976, but Knister wrote a great deal, and many of his stories, critical articles, reviews, and journalistic pieces remain uncollected.

The Fate of Mrs Lucier

She rocked in her living-room, an arm uplifted, holding a curling iron to her hair. She talked with great calmness to Mrs Slagwin, the only neighbour to whom she could tell her story. With careful fingers she separated each string of hair, and wound it about the iron which she withdrew from the gas heater beside her. Her even plaintive drawl moved on, on, her features were as pastelike as ever throughout, her wide milky eyes as slow. Yet there was something dogged[1] about her attitude; she actually burned her clay-coloured hair by her deliberation with the tongs.... Her face was grey, as twisted leaves beside a frosty road are grey.

"I felt," she said lingeringly, "that I might lose control of myself any minute." And such an event as the visit of her middle-aged cousin from the West with a son and nephew she did not know, was scarcely more than mentioned.

She had been back to Huntville to see Ruby on the farm. Since she and Lyniol had rented it to the son-in-law and retired, she had felt out of place. The ways of even the church people and women's societies in the city misgave her.[2] But at Ruby's she was at home; she went about noting changes in the house and farm yard, more absorbed, almost, than when she stayed there month after month. The worst thing was leaving Lyniol, who was not likely to take care of himself in her absence; his neck looked thinner than ever, each time she returned home. And when he was working at the mill that way, he would eat one meal at least in restaurants; and that was so expensive.

---

1. **dogged** Persistent. 2. **misgave her** Caused her to doubt.

On these visits to Ruby Mrs Lucier was apt to forget that she was the visitor, and not a rabbit-like woman never leaving the farm save for church; strange to any other countryside, and never conceiving the city. Before she knew December had turned, and it would look odd to be back again at Christmas, if she stayed longer. Ruby, driving her to the station in the buggy, insisted again that the parents should come to "her" home, this first Christmas. Perhaps that would be nicer, Mrs Lucier reflected in the train. Ruby had not left her horse, and Fred Langton, the agent, had seen that she got on safely. "Thank you. I'll — I'll be all right now," she told his back as he hurried to the baggage end of the train.

Though it did not stop more than a minute, she had a chance from the plush seat to see the village, dirty and amorphous as though behind a grimed pane, — its murky lights starting in the mist from hunchback dwellings, its cinder-veneered mud fleetly changed through a bell's clanging to fields with narrow bright pools, reeling jagged forests — to see these with something of a stranger's objectiveness. They stayed with her.

Limply uninterested, but not aware of dejection, she did not see the other passengers, humanly. She scarcely dared to look about her. This was a situation, and the vague potentialities of travel made her uncomfortable. She smoothed her black skirt, looking directly ahead; regularly she looked at individuals and to the pane, her mind marking time thirty-five miles to Blenden, where she was to take the inter-urban car to the city.

Here it was foggier still, shouts and the slow blasts of the engine echoed lonely, and the fence wires were wet before all that space of bare country about the two-roomed station squatted in the light of stretched wires and rails. Night was coming too soon. She hurried inside.

The waiting-room, with its dusty floor, blue-gray wainscotting and plaster, long brown bench, was spacious and echoing after her habitude of tiny cluttered farmhouse rooms. She pushed her suitcase half under the middle of the bench, and sat looking into the red-seamed bed of coal in the open tall portly coal stove on its sheet iron platform, and the huge iron spittoon[3] containing sawdust. The single lamp, above the wicket,[4] cast shadows, and by a dusty reflector, a ray that seemed made of motes.

Just when she had got herself settled men entered one after another: three — and then the stout, dull-eyed station agent, wearing an unofficial cap with the earflaps down, dispatches and lantern in his hands. "Looks like pretty raw night out," he said generally, in a tenor, and crowding into his office closed the door. The train hooted back lonely.

Two of the three men stared after him. The oldest made some reply, disposing a miscellany of luggage. He was a short, jagged-whiskered, hard-bitten man, respectable enough, Mrs Lucier thought, in dress; he did not have much to say to the others. They were younger: one of stocky-slender build, determined-looking, wide-shouldered; perhaps thirty-seven years old, yellow-faced with high cheek bones and heavy, straight-hanging lips and sloping flat forehead. He too sat down, and then rose as though conscious of a long wait, to walk about with the other, perhaps younger, very tall with a short blue overcoat beneath which light trousers showed and long shoes. Jauntily[5] rode his cylindrical head a cloth hat, over his long seamed dark countenance with its curly lips and slanting chin.

The words tossed among the three were random, abrupt, and casual, as though they were impatient, or tired of each other's company. Mrs Lucier couldn't tell what they

---

3. **spittoon** Receptacle for spit. 4. **wicket** Ticket-window. 5. **Jauntily** Stylishly.

said. She was given up to the sensation of being thus alone. Truly, since their retirement, she had seen more than in all the years before! What would Lyniol say to see her
now? The young men, first one, then the other, sat down moodily.

How long before the street car would come? She had forgotten whether it were due
at seventeen minutes after seven or seventeen minutes to eight. At least the wait was
always endless, each time she had to remind herself that it really would come to an end.
What if the car should be late reaching the city — a night like this? Lyniol would be
worried.... Perhaps he would go away and leave her to get home alone. The streets were
so misleading at night, and where could she inquire the way? If he could, if he could!
She shivered and held her body erect leaning forward with mourner's mien.

Less than a week ago she had read of a wreck, and there were plenty of others of which
she wouldn't hear. She began to prefigure details. Just what would she do in a wreck?
One would be thrown headlong, of course, backward or forward, depending upon the
direction of the oncoming train. The windows in pieces would fly to slash faces.
Probably the whole train would be thrown into the ditch, but the car in which she
rode would not get the greatest shock. Unless it were full she always was careful to
choose a car as near the middle of the train as possible.... Hadn't she made some mistake
and got into the last one? Which car — ? She came back with a start to the waiting
room.... But even in the middle of the train you wouldn't be safe, if it were "telescoped."

The men were looking at her. If only someone would say something. The two
younger ones crossed in their walks as they stopped at a red-veined map of Canada, and
muttered something to each other. Instantly all her senses were alert, she was watching.
... Yes, when one of them, the tall sinister one, came to the older man on the bench he
half-whispered, "Like her ..." wasn't it? And both of them looked at her, a cold
calculation. If something didn't happen she would scream — and if it did.

... No, it was not a train she was to take, of course. But even street cars might have
accidents. There was the great ditch, or the electricity might run amuck and kill people,
somehow. She always thought of how a car looked from outside, clanging briskly along
in the night, while at a burst of light, a flash from overhead, her heart leaped to her
mouth. Bowling recklessly along, the people exasperatingly oblivious and — it seemed,
since the windows were so bright — gay. Like Lyniol. She recalled her annoyance with
his sitting blandly unconscious in front of the telephone, not six feet from it, in a
thunderstorm, really paying no attention to her warnings. In a buggy, when the wheels
slipped into a rut, she might scream, she couldn't help it.... And that time she had gone
with Lyniol to London Fair, when Ruby was small. She had no purse, and Lyniol had
gone away "for a minute." He came back with some neighbours he had found, and
joked, really joked at her agony: "I thought you'd gone and left me." With the only
asperity she knew she recalled almost the chief misunderstanding with Lyniol. He had
refused to shoot a cat which had scratched her. The cat might very well go mad, and
then.... She lay awake nights thinking about it.

Yet sitting there it seemed to her that only in the last three months had she come to know
the plenary terror of the world. In the city you could not forget, ever, all the desperate
things, men and machines ready always to maim or rob, kill, and disfigure. How was any
one to know when she was beside a thug, a hold-up man? (Would the car never come?)
Only afterward, robbed, or never, if the revolver or chisel were brought out ...

When she looked again the older man glanced again at her. It was feigned recognition, that was what it was! She did not know where to turn. They began to speak very casually about something … trying to allay her suspicions, but they only made them more painful. She was not so easily fooled.

Looking about the room like a caged bird, it appeared vast, and her death-screams would be lost in a corner…. Perhaps the agent had gone home, out a back way. There was silence…. What was more deceptive than time, going on, and on, even when it seemed to stand still? Fast or slow. She might have been there only a few minutes. Perhaps the car wasn't coming at all that night. There was no traffic now at the Lake, since the exodus from the summer resort; and perhaps the company had become so careless that they wouldn't mind missing a train now and then. Or a strike. What was the last she had read in the paper of the municipal dissention? After all she had been at the farm for two weeks, and she couldn't tell what was going on. Perhaps Lyniol would arrive at the door any minute with a hired car, jitney. If it were not he, but someone else, who pretended … that Lyniol was sick, wanted her at once. Then these three men would appear, would demand passage. The driver couldn't refuse … or perhaps it was all made up, the driver hired, bribed.

By refusing to look at the men she had recreated them hideously in her mind's eye, and she was surprised that they were not so gruesome after all, but like three ordinary travellers of a not too successful class. The tall youth lounged to a seat near the door. Why *must* he sit near the door? The yellow-faced one began a discussion of motor tires with the old man, which he joined. Perhaps they were thinking of that, of a car they had waiting outside. They thought that she was wealthy, had smuggled goods over the river at Detroit…. Anyway, imagine three men travelling together! A long man and a short looked sinister enough, too chummy ("thick as thieves"). But when there were three, and they looked as travel-worn as these, as tired of each other and as familiar…. The youth laughed suddenly at some saying, and the yellow-faced man smiled, showing strong dark teeth. The man with the jagged beard hid his merriment grimly beneath it, and became the most terrible of all.

For moments at a time she could not hear or know what went on. Her mind raced like an unloaded engine. With an effort of the neck she stared all about. There was no place. In the ceiling was a trapdoor the colour of the plaster. Could she be sure the shadow did not swerve? If it opened suddenly and a rope descended. All kinds of ways, all kinds of places for putting victims' bodies. The stove door yawning before her hot eyes!

The talk had stopped for a long time now, but again one of the men was walking about, yawning loudly, hands clasped behind him. "And this is the East!" he muttered passing her. The East, the East; wasn't that some sort of password? She searched her memory for shreds of an old newspaper serial. She looked up timidly as a rabbit from brush watches a passing hunter. The smell of coal had gone, the blue gas no longer twined upward from the middle of the stove; the hollow vast of the room was desperately cold…. The windows deep with blackness gathered from the immense night, the dreary hum of telegraph wires to immeasurably distant bright cities, like paradises.

The telegraph clacked and twittered, prickling along her nerves like red-hot pins in memory. A vast insufferable quiet held the little station between forefinger and thumb, in gingerly patience. No breath. The stout agent appeared, drawing a bunch of keys from the door. Was he going to lock the office for the night? He put them in his pocket.

"Car's kind of late tonight," he said cheerfully. Perhaps he was in the plot. "Makes it kind of bad for you people. Oh, well, she'll be here any time now."

Swinging the coal scuttle up, he threw its contents into the stove. He slammed the door to, opened the bottom damper, shook the gate. He was going home, he was leaving her —

The bearded man was answering him, benevolently. "Quite a little wait for you too? Do you have to stay until it gets here?" He was going to offer to wait instead, and then, then — !

"Oh, no, I go home, as soon as the express pulls out." The clear full tones drew the woman back to reality.

Mrs Lucier rose after a futile movement abruptly, and walked shaking half across the room. The motion roused her to another self, but she was watching if They made a suspicious move. The wicket was closed, the door closed — Perhaps all —

"Did you want something, lady?" the agent asked her wild look.

"A — a return ticket to Huntville. The train, there is a train goes, isn't there, soon now?" her voice did reach him.

"Why, yes, due in about six minutes. On time too." He would think she had forgotten something at home. Warmer air came through the wicket. They would think she had — remembered something — that she was being pursued — and follow her. And in the village, all dark, they could — They weren't buying tickets, to be sure. But even that meant nothing.

But the great light of the train shone into the station windows as the ticket was stamped and shoved through to her hand. The lamp was dimmed. Her heart leaped. With trepidation and quivering foretaste of triumph Mrs Lucier marched to her suitcase.

The tremor of the platform, emerging from blackness like a raft out of depths thrilled her as always on taking a journey. But she climbed into the train with such a feeling of refuge as home could never give. (She saw a living-room at home — Ruby's home — in all its dear monotony.) The world was shut out and she saw the victims of its innumerable crimes, their torturings, last writhings.... Warm, light, the gliding, soporifically swinging train was like heaven, in which sprawled tired bored gods. They didn't even notice her. Everything glided forward with a non-deceptive illusion of soundlessness, past that same bushland, glittering water, sodden fields blotted now. Only the blackness of void, effectively held at bay, lay behind those windows. She needn't look. The trip was less than an hour, but it was passing.... The night would face her again.

A uniformed boy entered with a tray slung from his neck, and announced with perfunctory but clearly audible monotone, "Apples, oranges, chocolates, peanuts ..." Just loudly enough to waken the men dozing under newspapers, or an occasional woman, head nodding on a hand propped to the windowsill. Mrs Lucier had an impulse to buy. Unheard-of action, it would express in a way her triumph, her thanksgiving at escape. The boy clairvoyantly half-paused, but went on, "Apples, chewing-gum, oranges, chocolates, peanuts!" The door opened and slammed against a sound of rushing wheels and rushing wind.

The brakeman called "Huntville, Huntville!" at each end of the aisle, and before she knew it she was walking with accelerated steps to the door, receiving the final jolt outside at the platform railing. She glimpsed the station in large squares of light emanating from the train windows.

Mrs Lucier shied from the cars, glancing beneath, and hurried down the cinder path to the road. Fred Langton coming from the head of train, greeted her, surprised. She hesitated. "Yes," she answered, turning half around, her suitcase swinging. "Yes," she added nervously. Then she went on again in the fog toward the street remembering that his way home led in a different direction, and she could scarcely ask him …

She went forward past the little houses. Their lights in back rooms were dimmed by fog. Dark moisture stood on the narrow cement sidewalk under a light, and heavy beads hung on an intricate front lawn wire fence. Heavy drops spattered her hat and the pavement as she hurried forward, a dark half-bent figure, long-skirted, dragging the suitcase.

The sidewalk went past the last house, on to the muffled brick church at the corner. Then there was the cinder path to the graveyard, and after that she walked more hurriedly, stumbling, along the road by the deep mist-filled ditch. She swerved and held to the middle way, because of the ditch. But there might be buggies, or an unlighted car. Along the edge again, her shoes squelched neatly in the seeping limp grass. She gripped the handle of her suitcase for a leap either way. It was just after long struggle and seeming escape that things happened. It was just, after half a mile in wet clay she came to a wide frame house set back from the road.

She crossed the ditch over a shaky plank bridge and stood, savouring triumph and dread, panting, her hands on the iron damp gate. All about was the fog covering the fields. The branches of a large maple curved down and let fall irregular drops in a pattern of sound upon the grass and the rustling water of the ditch. Yet it was almost bright. There should have been a moon, she realized. Buildings and trees stood out clouded, in a lifting haze. Her gloves had become wet through on the iron. The light remained in this house, and she opened the gate and gathering herself together went boldly to the front door.

"Well, Agatha Lucier! You *did* come in to see me before you left! I was wondering — Come right in." The large woman seized and kissed her, still talking, her head held at the kissing angle. "Here's Mrs Lucier, Andy, Alice." Children were entering from the kitchen where they had been hindering homework. "But have you had supper?"

"No. I mean, I — My, isn't Alice growing!" Mrs Lucier exclaimed with mild fervour. "And Andy! Why he's as big as his father, nearly." She felt bold, and backed by the gods of circumstance.

"And walking were you, alone? Isn't it raining?"

"Oh, you know I'm never afraid of the dark."

An hour later, after a substantial meal, Mrs Lucier peered from the window, fancying a light through the fog-waves. Ruby's light? But she would not call up and have Ruby's man come for her. It was too terrible a night. Besides, it was more than half-past nine o'clock.

She wouldn't tell Ruby, not right away. Yet … "I made up my mind I'd just have to come back. One minute, and I'd lost control of myself." Sometime she would have to tell.

(1925)

F.R. Scott (1899–1985)

Attempting to define his poetics in 1958, F.R. Scott spoke of writing as "an exploring of the frontiers of the world inside and the world outside man." Many of his poems traverse these boundaries, moving from microcosm to macrocosm, from "verse" to "universe." There are two strains in his work: a private, sometimes spiritual lyric mode; and a public, social, and often satirical voice. For Scott, life was a "flow of events and experiences" that "constantly meets us and passes behind." He wrote, "we are faced with infinite choices and possibilities. What we call creative living is the ability to pick out of the total flow those special elements which are significant."

Francis Reginald Scott was born on 1 August 1899 in Quebec City. His father, Frederick George Scott, was an Anglican clergyman and a writer known in his day as "the poet of the Laurentians." In 1916, F.R. Scott left home to study at Bishop's College in Lennoxville. There he developed an interest in European history and in poetry, favouring the British Romantics and the early verse of Alfred Lord Tennyson. Upon his graduation, in 1919, Scott received a Rhodes Scholarship to further his education at Oxford. Continuing his study of history at Oxford's Magdalen College, he earned a B.A. in 1922 and a B.Litt. the following year.

When Scott returned to Canada, in 1923, he began teaching at Lower Canada College in Montreal; then, in 1924, he enrolled in the Faculty of Law at McGill University. During his first year at McGill, he began to meet regularly with a circle of friends to discuss Canadian politics and culture. They called themselves "the group," and their sessions aroused a sense of nationalism in Scott that would influence many of the artistic and political choices he made throughout his life. In 1925, Scott joined A.J.M. Smith and Allan Latham on the editorial board of the literary supplement to the *McGill Daily*. When the supplement's funds were cut off by the student union, the editorial board members and colleagues Leon Edel and A.P.R. Coulborn founded a new periodical: the *McGill Fortnightly Review*.

The *Fortnightly Review* became an outlet for modern poetry in Canada at a time when Romanticism and Victorianism still dominated the Canadian literary scene. Its editors, frustrated with the conservatism of the newly formed Canadian Authors Association, advocated change. Scott expressed these sentiments in his 1927 poem "The Canadian Authors Meet": "The air is heavy with Canadian topics, / And Carman, Lampman, Roberts, Campbell, Scott, / Are measured for their faith and philanthropics, / Their zeal for God and King, their earnest thought." Scott lamented, "O Canada, O can / a day go by without new authors springing / To paint the native maple," but he still struggled to find an aesthetic that would allow him to depict Canadian imagery in a modernist context. At times, he risked lapsing into the Romantic mode, but his efforts influenced a later generation of writers — among them Margaret Atwood and Al Purdy — who would also turn to the Canadian landscape for poetic material.

In 1928, Scott, with Louis Schwartz and Leo Kennedy, founded the *Canadian Mercury*. The same year, he accepted a position teaching law at McGill and married Montreal artist Marian Dale. In the 1930s, Scott shifted his primary focus from literature to politics. The effects of the Depression on the country compelled him to help find a way to create a more socially responsible and independent Canada. In 1932, he became a founding member of the League for Social Reconstruction. The following year, he contributed to the Regina Manifesto, which would become the platform of the Cooperative Commonwealth Federation (CCF), the forerunner of the New Democratic Party. In 1935, he became a member of the Canadian Institute of International Affairs, remaining with the organization until 1957; he also served as the CCF's national chairman from 1942 to 1950.

Through all of this, Scott maintained his involvement with the Canadian literary scene. In 1936, he co-edited, with Smith, *New Provinces* — the first anthology of Canadian modern verse.

In 1942, he helped to establish the little magazine *Preview*, and he was still on board in 1945, when the periodical merged with its rival *First Statement* to become the *Northern Review*. He composed poetry, but his style was changing in ways that corresponded with his awakened political consciousness. In "Social Notes I, 1932" and "Social Notes II, 1935," for example, he attempted to reveal the limitations of the capitalist system through unadorned speech and juxtaposition: "Come and see the vast natural wealth of this mine. / In the short space of ten years / It has produced six American millionaires / And two thousand pauperized Canadian families." In 1945, Scott published his first collection of poetry, *Overture*, which included political writing and more personal lyric verse.

In 1952, Scott worked as a United Nations technical assistant in Burma, and in 1955 he served as chairman of the Canadian Writers Conference. Throughout the 1950s, he put his knowledge of constitutional law into practice in two Supreme Court cases against Quebec's conservative Duplessis regime. In the 1960s, he appeared once more before the Supreme Court of Canada, this time to defend D.H. Lawrence's 1928 novel *Lady Chatterley's Lover* from censorship.

As a native of Quebec, Scott had always been attracted to French Canadian culture. In the late 1940s, he began translating the work of various Québécois poets, and in 1962, he produced *St-Denys Garneau and Anne Hébert: Translations/Traductions*. He later published his correspondence with Hébert concerning his translation of her work: *Dialogue sur la traduction à propos du "Tombeau des rois"* appeared in 1970. In 1977, he compiled an anthology of his translations; entitled *Poems of French Canada*, it won the 1978 Canada Council translation prize. In the introduction, Scott expressed his desire to help "build a Canada that would allow the two principal cultures to flourish freely." The same ambition had led him to become a member of the Royal Commission on Bilingualism and Biculturalism from 1963 to 1971.

The rise of Quebec separatism in the late 1960s and the 1970s, followed by the 1980 Quebec referendum, had a profound effect on Scott. He became disillusioned with politics, and the stress of active involvement was taking its toll on his health. He slowly began to withdraw from public life. In 1981, he published *The Collected Poems of F.R. Scott*, and it garnered a 1982 Governor General's Award. Scott died in Montreal in 1985.

North Stream

Ice mothers me
My bed is rock
Over sand I move silently.

I am crystal clear
To a sunbeam.
No grasses grow in me
My banks are clean.

Foam runs from the rapid
To rest on my dark pools.

(1945)

Laurentian Shield

Hidden in wonder and snow, or sudden with summer,
This land stares at the sun in a huge silence

Endlessly repeating something we cannot hear.
Inarticulate, arctic,
Not written on by history, empty as paper,
It leans away from the world with songs in its lakes
Older than love, and lost in the miles.

This waiting is wanting.
It will choose its language
10   When it has chosen its technic,
A tongue to shape the vowels of its productivity.

A *language of flesh and roses.*[1]

Now there are pre-words,
Cabin syllables,
Nouns of settlement
Slowly forming, with steel syntax,
The long sentence of its exploitation.

The first cry was the hunter, hungry for fur,
And the digger for gold, nomad, no-man, a particle;
20   Then the bold commands of monopolies, big with machines,
Carving their kingdoms out of the public wealth;
And now the drone of the plane, scouting the ice,
Fills all the emptiness with neighbourhood
And links our future over the vanished pole.

But a deeper note is sounding, heard in the mines,
The scattered camps and the mills, a language of life,
And what will be written in the full culture of occupation
Will come, presently, tomorrow,
From millions whose hands can turn this rock into children.

(1946)

Lakeshore

The lake is sharp along the shore
Trimming the bevelled[1] edge of land
To level curves; the fretted sands
Go slanting down through liquid air
Till stones below shift here and there
Floating upon their broken sky

---

1. *A language of flesh and roses* Poet Stephen Spender's description of a modern industrial landscape and the human values it manifests; from *The Making of a Poem* (1955).

1. **bevelled** Slanted.

All netted by the prism wave
And rippled where the currents are.

I stare through windows at this cave
Where fish, like planes, slow-motioned, fly.   10
Poised in a still of gravity
The narrow minnow, flicking fin,
Hangs in a paler, ochre sun,
His doorways open everywhere.

And I am a tall frond that waves
Its head below its rooted feet
Seeking the light that draws it down
To forest floors beyond its reach
Vivid with gloom and eerie dreams.

The water's deepest colonnades   20
Contract the blood, and to this home
That stirs the dark amphibian
With me the naked swimmers come
Drawn to their prehistoric womb.

They too are liquid as they fall
Like tumbled water loosed above
Until they lie, diagonal,
Within the cool and sheltered grove
Stroked by the fingertips of love.

Silent, our sport is drowned in fact   30
Too virginal for speech or sound
And each is personal and laned
Along his private aqueduct.[2]

Too soon the tether of the lungs
Is taut and straining, and we rise
Upon our undeveloped wings
Toward the prison of our ground
A secret anguish in our thighs
And mermaids in our memories.

This is our talent, to have grown   40
Upright in posture, false-erect,
A landed gentry, circumspect,[3]
Tied to a horizontal soil
The floor and ceiling of the soul;

---

2. **aqueduct** Channel or canal. 3. **circumspect** Cautious.

Striving, with cold and fishy care
To make an ocean of the air.

Sometimes, upon a crowded street,
I feel the sudden rain come down
And in the old, magnetic sound
50   I hear the opening of a gate
That loosens all the seven seas.
Watching the whole creation drown
I muse, alone, on Ararat.[4]

(1950)

A Grain of Rice

Such majestic rhythms, such tiny disturbances.
The rain of the monsoon falls, an inescapable treasure,
Hundreds of millions live
Only because of the certainty of this season,
    The turn of the wind.

The frame of our human house rests on the motion
Of earth and of moon, the rise of continents,
Invasion of deserts, erosion of hills,
    The capping of ice.

10   Today, while Europe tilted, drying the Baltic,
I read of a battle between brothers in anguish,
    A flag moved a mile.

And today, from a curled leaf cocoon, in the course of its rhythm,
I saw the break of a shell, the creation
Of a great Asian moth, radiant, fragile,
Incapable of not being born, and trembling
    To live its brief moment.

Religions build walls round our love, and science
Is equal of truth and of error. Yet always we find
20   Such ordered purpose in cell and in galaxy,
So great a glory in life-thrust and mind-range,
Such widening frontiers to draw out our longings,
    We grow to one world
    Through enlargement of wonder.

(1954)

---

4. **Ararat** In the Biblical story, the landing place of Noah's ark after the great flood.

National Identity

The Canadian Centenary Council[1]
Meeting in le Reine Elizabeth[2] hotel
To seek those symbols
Which will explain ourselves to ourselves
Evoke bi-cultural responses
And prove that something called Canada
Really exists in the hearts of all
Handed out to every delegate
At the start of proceedings
A portfolio of documents   10
On the cover of which appeared
In gold letters
     not
A Mari Usque Ad Mare[3]
     not
Dieu Et Mon Droit[4]
     not
E Pluribus Unum[5]
     but
COURTESY OF COCA-COLA LIMITED   20

                                   (1963)

A Lass in Wonderland

I went to bat for the Lady Chatte[1]
  Dressed in my bib and gown.[2]
The judges three glared down at me
  The priests patrolled the town.

My right hand shook as I reached for that book
  And rose to play my part.
For out on the street were the marching feet
  Of the League of the Sacred Heart.[3]

The word "obscene" was supposed to mean
  "Undue exploitation of sex."   10
This wording's fine for your needs and mine
  But it's far too free for Quebec's.

---

1. **Canadian Centenary Council** Convened in 1962 to seek ideas and financial support for Canada's 100th Anniversary from private citizens (especially businessmen). 2. **le Reine Elizabeth** A hotel in Montreal. 3. *A Mari Usque Ad Mare* Canada's motto, Latin for "from sea to sea." 4. *Dieu Et Mon Droit* Britain's motto, French for "God and my right." 5. *E Pluribus Unum* Motto of the United States, Latin for "from many, one."

1. **Lady Chatte** *Lady Chatterley's Lover*, the novel by D.H. Lawrence that featured taboo language and sex scenes. In 1962, the book was brought before the Supreme Court on obscenity charges in *Brodie v. the Queen*, but Scott (as a lawyer) successfully defended it. 2. **bib and gown** A lawyer's attire. 3. **League of the Sacred Heart** A Montreal-based men's Christian group who thought the novel obscene (La Ligue du Sacré-Coeur).

I tried my best, with unusual zest,
  To drive my argument through.
But I soon got stuck on what rhymes with "muck"
  And that dubious word "undue."

So I raised their sights to the Bill of Rights[4]
  And cried: "Let freedom ring!"
Showed straight from the text that freedom of sex
20   Was as clear as anything.

Then I plunged into love, the spell that it wove,
  And its attributes big and bold
Till the legal elect all stood erect
  As my rapturous tale was told.

The judges' sighs and rolling of eyes
  Gave hope that my case was won,
Yet Mellors and Connie[5] still looked pretty funny
  Dancing about in the sun.

What hurt me was not that they did it a lot
30   And even ran out in the rain,
'Twas those curious poses with harebells[6] and roses
  And that dangling daisy-chain.

Then too the sales made in the paperback trade
  Served to aggravate judicial spleen,[7]
For it seems a high price will make any book nice
  While its mass distribution's obscene.

Oh Letters and Law are found in the raw
  And found on the heights sublime,
But D.H. Lawrence would view with abhorrence
40   This Jansenist[8] pantomime.

                                                    (1964)

Harry Robinson (1900–1990)

By the early 1970s the aboriginal languages of British Columbia were disappearing, pushed towards extinction by English. Only the oldest generations of speakers continued to speak their first languages on a regular basis. In the south central region, one such elder was Harry Robinson.

---

4. **Bill of Rights** Passed in Canada in 1960, secured the right to freedom of expression. Scott thought it thoroughly inadequate. 5. **Mellors and Connie** Oliver Mellors and Constance Chatterley, the novel's main characters. 6. **harebells** Bell-shaped flower (campanula). 7. **spleen** Anger. 8. **Jansenist** Christian theological theory that humans are essentially depraved and predestined to be saved or damned.

A member of the Lower Similkameen Band near Keremos, Robinson was steeped in his language and culture. He had learned much of this as a child from his maternal grandmother and other community elders. As he explained: "I got enough people to tell me. That's why I know." Concerned that many of his listeners could not understand his Okanagan tales, he began adapting his stories to English. It became his way of preserving what he held as important about his people, their stories, and their past.

Robinson received his only formal education during a five-month period when he was a teenager; he was ultimately forced to quit school because it was 12 miles away and the journey back and forth over such a distance was too demanding. In 1912, he took his first paying job, threshing wheat and oats, and five years after that he became a ranch hand. In 1922, with the help of a friend, he learned to read and·write. He married Matilda Johnny, a widow, in 1924, and through her he acquired four large pieces of ranch land. Robinson would remain a successful rancher until he retired, in 1972, two years after Matilda's death. In retirement, he found that he at last had time to share the stories he had absorbed during his youth.

Robinson was saddened to see that radio and television were replacing traditional storytelling, and he was also concerned that fewer and fewer people could speak Okanagan. He resolved to do what he could to preserve his oral heritage by translating and adapting his stories into English. It was a difficult process.

In 1977, Robinson encountered Wendy Wickwire, who would compile his stories in three volumes. Wickwire's compilations are the only available published sources of Robinson's work in English. Although Wickwire cautions readers to consider the sorts of adaptations that Robinson made for her benefit, she believes that *Write It on Your Heart: The Epic World of an Okanagan Storyteller* (1989), *Nature Power: In the Spirit of an Okanagan Storyteller* (1992), and *Living by Stories: A Journey of Landscape and Memory* (2005) stand as a fair representation of his repertory. Robinson's concern with ecological and social matters is evident in all of them.

Robinson explained that his stories represented two types: *chap-TEEK-whl,* or creation stories from a mythological age when people lived as "animal-people" — part human, part animal; and *shmee-MA-ee,* stories from the more recent times, when people lived as "human-people," or as people as we know them today. Many of Robinson's stories relate the misadventures of Coyote. Others, like "You Think It's a Stump, but That's My Grandfather," describe the experiences of *shoo-MISH,* or guardian spirits who bestow special powers on certain people.

Some of Robinson's stories focus on conflicts that took place in postcontact times. White people, or *SHA-ma's,* assume a negative presence in Robinson's story, "Twins: White and Indian" (in *Write It on Your Heart*), which combines elements of both myth and historical narrative. Here, Coyote is one of the first beings created by God, or the Big Chief. Robinson, who regarded Coyote as his own first ancestor, presented him as sometimes good and sometimes bad but never inherently evil like his twin brother — the first ancestor of Whites.

In "Coyote Makes a Deal with the King of England," Coyote travels to England to bargain with the king over troubles incurred by the arrival of *SHA-ma's* in North America. By using his special powers, Coyote secures a promise of a law that would keep the peace in Canada and prevent further colonial exploitation. The king orders that the law be written down in a book, "The Black and White," and that it be taken to various places in Canada. Robinson recalled meeting a man in 1917 who claimed to have accompanied the person delegated to deliver the book to the legislature in Victoria, B.C. Robinson's concern, and his reason for telling the story, was to convey that this important book was intentionally hidden from view.

Nevertheless, Robinson's story is a powerful allegory about the actual treaties signed by colonizers and Native peoples, many of which were forgotten or wilfully neglected by successive

Canadian governments. It vividly illustrates Robinson's belief that the power given to *SHA-ma's* is the power of the written word, while the power given to the Okanagan peoples is the *shoo-MISH* — the power of the heart and mind. Robinson deploys Coyote to appropriate the written word in order to improve the transitional world in which we live. Robinson himself did much the same thing with his efforts to project the oral tradition of his people to the broader community; couching the tales of his Okanagan elders in written English and imbuing them with a contemporary political consciousness, he ensured their survival. The impact and influence of Robinson's undertaking is evident in Cherokee writer Thomas King's account of reading Robinson's work for the first time. King was struck by how well Robinson "understood the power of the oral voice in a written piece … it was *inspirational* … I remember sitting in my office, just sort of sweating, reading this stuff: it was so *good.*" Harry Robinson died on 25 January 1990; he was 90 years old.

You Think It's a Stump, but That's My Grandfather

Left alone by his father, his uncles and the other hunters, a boy finds himself singing with another young boy and his grandfather beside a smooth stump.

Shash-AP-kin.
That's his Indian name.
White people call it Shash-AP-kin.
Indians call it Shash-ap-KANE.
That means "Smooth Stump."
Supposing if — now here's this —
    that's the stump right there.
And underneath the stump was washed out
    and washed out,
        and then there's kind of hole underneath.
The roots look like that.
And it's kind of — the chipmunk or anything can get under
    that.
And this stump was a-standing in the place
    where this snow slide at every year.
But, they must've grow there a long, long time.
But maybe not sliding place at that time.
But somehow, when the earthquake and the rocks was sliding,
    and they open up like —
        and when the snow comes
            and after that slide every year.
But this tree was growing there right where the slide goes.
But hit by a big stone and broke.
But only stump — so high.

The stump is still there.
It turn into a hard wood, more like a pitch.

Then every time when they had a snow slide,
  it was always mixed with rocks and things, you know.
Then the rocks, the small rocks, they hit them
  and — just like they resting or something.
And they smooth.
Just smooth, but stump.
And underneath, they kind of washed.
And there was kind of hole underneath.

But right in the steep hill
  and the place was like that.
That's where the snow slide every year.
And Shash-AP-kin, he was just a young,
  about ten years old, eleven years old,
    something like that.
And he was left there by the hunter.
His dad, and the other hunters, they tell 'em,

  "You stay here.
    You wait here.
    It's too far for you to walk.
    You stay 'round here.
    We can hunt that way, make a turn
      and a circle,
        and then we come back.
    Towards evening we come by
      and then you can go back with us to the camp."

You know, they tell 'em lies to leave 'em there.
Just like George Jim.
Yeah.
So the older people, his dad and his uncle and the others,
  they thought they going to leave him there by himself.
Maybe some animal, maybe bird or something,
  they might met them.
And talk to 'em.
So he can be power man.
They think — but they didn't tell 'em.
They just tell 'em,

  "You, you might get tired if you go along.
    You too young.
    You going to get tired.
    You stay here and we hunt.
    We come back and then you can go back with us
      to the camp."

So he thinks,

> "Well, that's good enough,
> > because that's too far.
> > I get tired if I go along."

So he satisfied to be there alone.
So these other people went.
But he's left there all by himself.
So finally, he looked around and he go down that way
> where he could see that the nice and smooth.
Quite a ways.
Where the snow slide.
But this was in the summer — no snow.
So he looked that place
> and then he could see that stump,
> > quite a ways down.
So he thought,

> "Maybe I go and see that.
> > Looks like a rock or looks like a stump or something.
> > Maybe I go down there and take a look."

So he went down and he come to this stump.
Before he get too close,
> and he looked.
By God, that stump was just as smooth,
> just like somebody rub it nice and smooth.
And they go little ways.
Looked around.
Then they see the chipmunk.
Running from little ways.
And they run to get under that stump.
Because it's high from the ground
> and they get under that.

He pick up a stick,
> and he thought he go over there
> > and is going to make a fun with that chipmunk.
He put the stick underneath, you know.
He going to scare 'em out of there
> and then he's going to make 'em run away.
Or else, he's going to make fun.

When he get there,
> and he get the stick,
> > and they puts the stick under the stump, you know,
> > > to try to get the chipmunk out of that.
But, the first thing they do,
> the chipmunk, it get out of that stump on the other side.

But he get up.
And there was another boy, like him.
Just a boy, just like him.
Get out of the stump and he stand up.
Was another boy.
And told 'em,

    "Well, boy, you're here."

    "Yeah."

    "You think you're going to make a fun out of me."

    "Well," he says.
    "That's what I think."

    "You do not think of that.
       You my friend.
       You boy, and I'm a boy.
       We both boy.
       So, it's better to be friends
          instead of making fun out of me.
       Now, I'm going to tell you something.
       This stump — you think it's a stump —
          but that's my grandfather.
       He's very, very old man.
       Old, old man.
       He can talk to you.
       He can tell you what you going to be.
       When you get to be middle-aged, or more.
       But you're not going to be like that now,
          right away.
       Later on.
       When you get to be middle-aged.
       My grandfather that will tell you …"

Then, just in a second, then he could see,
   supposed to be the son
   but he was an old, old man.
He setting there.
And he talked.
And told 'em,

    "You see me.
       You see my body.
       It was hit by the bullet for many, many years.
       Hit by the bullet.

That's why you could see, all smooth.
That's bullet marks.
And the bullet, when they hit me — the bullet —
    they never go through my skin.
They never go through my body.
For a long, long time.
You look how old I was.
I been hit with a bullet for many years.
I never get killed.
The bullet never go in through my body.
So now, that's the way you going to be.
When you get to be a man.
If somebody shoots you,
    with the bow and arrow, or gun."

At those days, they had the gun,
    like the first gun like they have.

    "Then, if anybody shoot you,
        you going to be just like me.
    The bullet never will go into your skin.
    And that's going to be your power."

And he started to sing.
He sing the song.
That old man.
And the chipmunk was a boy,
    turn to be a boy.
He sing the song.
The both of 'em talked to him.
And he's got two power.
And he sing the song.
The three of 'em sing the song,
    for a while.
Then told 'em that, that would be enough.
Then, in the same way, he don't know what happened
    and he went to sleep.

First thing he know, he was WAY down.
He must've rolled, or sliding, or somehow,
    but WAY down.
When he wake up.
And he wake up and then his people were around,
    way up there, looking for him.
They couldn't find 'em.
But he get up and he could see his people WAY up.
And then he got up and they holler.

Then, these other people,
　My God!, they holler way down.
They must've go down that way.

But the last he knew, right by that stump.
No more.
But he might've walked down or might've rolled.
Nobody know.
But he was WAY down when they come to him.

But he knows already what he's going to be
　when he get to be a man.
So, that's the way he get his power.
Then, when he get to be a man,
　'bout middle age or more,
　　and told him again,

　　"Now is his time. For you
　　　You're not going to use your power for anybody.
　　　Just for you."

So that's Shash-AP-kin is a power man
　but his power, never use for anybody,
　　you know, just for himself.

Then, one time, just so they could show, I think,
　somehow that they had trouble with the white people.
And finally these white people,
　those days, all the white people that comes,
　　they all bad, you know.
They mean.
They tough.
So they — they shoot him.
He shoot him with a rifle.
But they never get him.
They never kill him.
Those days, there's different rifles they use.
They got the powder they put right in the rifle.
Then put the lead in there
　and put the rag in there
　　and put powder to the rag.
Then put some more rags.
Then they put the lead in.
And then they put some more rags on top of the lead,
　to keep the lead in place.
Then — they got the hammer just like the other gun.
Then they pull the trigger.

Then this is expired or exploded.
Then the bullet went, "Bang!"
Then they smoke.
They fired two shots.
They got two bar,[1] you know, more like a shotgun.
Fire the both of 'em.
Quite the smoke.

When they shoots him with that.
When the smoke was all over,
   he still there.
He never gots hurt.
The bullet never go in.
But they know, they shoot him not far.
They hit it all right.
But the bullet never go through on his body.
And that's just to show to the white,
   or to the other Indians.
So that's how they know he's a power man.
Just for himself.
So he live till he get old.
Very old — can be about seventy or more.

(1992)

A.J.M. Smith (1902–1980)

Arthur James Marshall Smith was born on 8 November 1902 in Westmount, Quebec. He developed a passion for literature at a young age. In his brief autobiographical essay "The Confessions of a Compulsive Anthologist" (1976), he remembers discovering *The New Poetry: An Anthology* (1917), edited by Harriet Monroe and Alice Corbin Henderson, and reading "with delight and fascination the 'new' poetry of Ezra Pound, Wallace Stevens, T.S. Eliot, [W.B.] Yeats in his middle period, Conrad Aiken, and H.D." Travelling with his parents to England in 1918, he expanded his exploration of modern poetry by browsing in Harold Monro's Poetry Bookshop in Bloomsbury, London.

In 1921, Smith enrolled in the B.Sc. program at McGill University. He had begun composing his own poetry, self-consciously imitating the modern forms and themes with which he was so enamoured. He submitted his work to the *McGill Daily*, and he soon became editor of its literary supplement. Dissatisfied with the poetry being published in his home country, he bemoaned the lack of Canadian verse that was "new, intelligent and contemporary."

Canadian writers such as Arthur Stringer and Dorothy Livesay were already experimenting with imagist techniques and free-verse form, but Smith and fellow poet F.R. Scott were frustrated with what they saw as the Victorian conservatism of the Canadian literary scene and the tendency of the Canadian Authors Association to embrace a nationalistic and romantic poetry of the Canadian landscape. The two founded the *McGill Fortnightly Review*, in which they advocated

---

1. **bar** Barrels.

the modernization of Canadian verse. They and two other writers they published in the review — Leon Edel and Leo Kennedy — are often referred to as the McGill Movement, and the review is credited with being one of the first outlets for modern poetry in Canada.

In 1925, Smith completed his undergraduate program; he then continued his studies at McGill, writing a thesis on Yeats and earning a master's degree. After graduation, he began working as a high school teacher in Montreal, and a year later he married Jeannie Dougall Robins. In 1927, the couple moved to Scotland, where Smith began his doctoral studies at the University of Edinburgh. During his years abroad, Smith published poetry in English, American, and Canadian journals. He also remained engaged in the modernist cause at home. In 1928, he published a controversial essay in the *Canadian Forum* entitled "Wanted — Canadian Criticism," in which he claimed that Canadian writers had to compose uplifting and patriotic poetry if they wanted critical attention and commercial success. He insisted that creative energy would be more valuably spent on intellectual poetry rooted in "modernity and tradition."

Smith returned to Canada in 1929. He took another high school teaching job in Montreal because the Great Depression had taken its toll on academia, and he was unable to find work at a university. He would eventually secure a long-term post at Michigan State College (later Michigan State University) in East Lansing. In the early 1930s, he collaborated with F.R. Scott and Leo Kennedy on an anthology that would announce the arrival of modern poetry in Canada. In 1936, the book was published as *New Provinces: Poems of Several Authors*, and it featured work by Smith, Scott, Kennedy, A.M. Klein, Robert Finch, and E.J. Pratt. The volume has since been recognized as a key document in Canadian literary history; a new edition appeared in 1976.

In 1941, Smith was awarded a Guggenheim Fellowship to research and compile *The Book of Canadian Poetry: A Critical and Historical Anthology*. It was published in 1943. In it, he aimed to present a "more balanced view of the development of Canadian poetry." Smith did, of course, import his own biases into the work. He divided Canadian poetry into two strains — the "native" and the "cosmopolitan" — and he clearly championed the latter. In his introduction, he stated that native poetry "has attempted to describe and interpret whatever is essentially and distinctively Canadian and thus come to terms with an environment that is only now ceasing to be colonial." Cosmopolitan poetry, "from the very beginning, has made a heroic effort to transcend colonialism by entering into the universal, civilizing culture of ideas." Many readers objected to this distinction. John Sutherland responded by producing *Other Canadians: Anthology of the New Poetry in Canada; 1940–1946* (1947). In his introduction, he argued that Smith's so-called cosmopolitan poetry does not, in fact, "transcend colonialism," as "it is the product of a cultured English group who are out of touch with a people who long ago began adjusting themselves to life on this continent." Later editions of *The Book of Canadian Poetry* did not include the native/cosmopolitan division.

Smith's first collection of poetry, *News of the Phoenix and Other Poems*, appeared in 1943, and it won a Governor General's Award. In 1945, Smith was given a Rockefeller grant to compile an anthology of Canadian prose. The project was enormous: the first volume, *The Book of Canadian Prose* (later renamed *The Colonial Century*), was published in 1965; the second volume, *The Canadian Century*, did not appear until 1973. In the meantime, Smith worked on non-Canadian anthologies — *Seven Centuries of Verse — English and American* (1947) and *The Worldly Muse* (1951) — and collaborated with F.R. Scott on *The Blasted Pine: An Anthology of Satire, Invective, and Disrespectful Verse Chiefly by Canadian Writers* (1957).

Smith's career as a critic and anthologist has tended to overshadow his poetic achievements. He was a deliberate poet who valued technique, a polished product, and an intellectual tone. In a paper entitled "The Poetic Process: On the Making of Poems," he reflected, "I suppose I am what is called an academic poet ... It implies (or should imply) an awareness of tradition and an understanding of the forces that bring about change, development, progress, and growth." Smith was not entirely free of the romantic tendencies he so disparaged, and he worked hard to edit these impulses out of his work and to "sing" what he felt was a more "difficult, lonely music."

The list of Smith's poetry collections includes *A Sort of Ecstasy* (1954), *Collected Poems* (1962), *Poems: New and Collected* (1967), and *The Classic Shade: Selected Poems* (1978). Smith died in East Lansing, Michigan, in 1980.

The Lonely Land[1]

Cedar and jagged fir
uplift sharp barbs
against the gray
and cloud-piled sky;
and in the bay
blown spume and windrift
and thin, bitter spray
snap
at the whirling sky;
10 and the pine trees
lean one way.

A wild duck calls
to her mate,
and the ragged
and passionate tones
stagger and fall,
and recover,
and stagger and fall,
on these stones —
20 are lost
in the lapping of water
on smooth, flat stones.

This is a beauty
of dissonance,
this resonance
of stony strand,
this smoky cry
curled over a black pine
like a broken
30 and wind-battered branch
when the wind
bends the tops of the pines
and curdles the sky
from the north.

---

1. **The Lonely Land**   Originally titled "The Lonely Land: Group of Seven."

This is the beauty
of strength
broken by strength
and still strong.

(1926)

A Hyacinth[1] for Edith[2]

Now that the ashen rain of gummy April
Clacks like a weedy and stain'd mill,

So that all the tall purple trees
Are pied[3] porpoises in swishing seas,

And the yellow horses and milch[4] cows
Come out of their long frosty house

To gape at the straining flags
The brown pompous hill wags,[5]

I'll seek within the wood's black plinth[6]
A candy-sweet sleek wooden hyacinth —   10

And in its creaking naked glaze,
And in the varnish of its blaze,

The bird of ecstasy shall sing again,
The bearded sun shall spring again —

A new ripe fruit upon the sky's high tree,
A flowery island in the sky's wide sea —

And childish cold ballades, long dead, long mute,
Shall mingle with the gayety of bird and fruit,

And fall like cool and soothing rain
On all the ardour, all the pain   20

Lurking within this tinsel paradise
Of trams and cinemas and manufactured ice,

Till I am grown again my own lost ghost
Of joy, long lost, long given up for lost,

---

1. Hyacinth Smith alludes to the hyacinth myth in Eliot's *The Waste Land.* **2. Edith** Edith Sitwell (1882–1964), imaginative British poet. She uses couplets in her collection, "Bucolic Comedies." The poem contains several references to Sitwell's poem. **3. pied** Multi-coloured. **4. milch** Milk. **5. wags** Shakes. **6. plinth** In architecture, a base for a statue or column.

And walk again the wild and sweet wildwood
Of our lost innocence, our ghostly childhood.

(1927)

Prothalamium[1]

Here in this narrow room there is no light;
The dead tree sings against the window pane;
Sand shifts a little, easily; the wall
Responds a little, inchmeal, slowly, down.

My sister, whom my dust shall marry, sleeps
Alone, yet knows what bitter root it is
That stirs within her; see, it splits the heart —
Warm hands grown cold, grown nerveless as a fin,
And lips enamelled to a hardness —
10   Consummation ushered in
By wind in sundry corners.

This holy sacrament was solemnized
In harsh poetics a good while ago —
At Malfy[2] and the Danish battlements,[3]
And by that preacher from a cloud in Paul's.[4]

No matter: each must read the truth himself,
Or, reading it, reads nothing to the point.
Now these are me, whose thought is mine, and hers,
Who are alone here in this narrow room —
20   Tree fumbling pane, bell tolling,[5]
Ceiling dripping and the plaster falling,
And Death, the voluptuous, calling.

(1928)

Like an Old Proud King in a Parable

A bitter king[1] in anger to be gone
From fawning courtier and doting queen
Flung hollow sceptre and gilt[2] crown away,
And breaking bound of all his counties green
He made a meadow in the northern stone
And breathed a palace of inviolable air
To cage a heart that carolled like a swan,

---

1. **Prothalamium** A wedding song or poem sung before the bridal chamber. 2. **Malfy** *The Duchess of Malfi* was a tragic play by John Webster (1580–1634). 3. **Danish battlements** Refers to Shakespeare's *Hamlet*. 4. **Paul's** Reference to a passage in Izaak Walton's *Life of Dr. Donne*. 5. **bell tolling** From Donne's "Meditation XVII."

1. **king** The biblical King Solomon. Anne Compton argues that "the King is gestural. ... The tale is fabulous, not realistic. ... The parable presents not a single, exemplary life but a generic 'hero,' an amalgamation." 2. **gilt** Coated with gold leaf.

And slept alone, immaculate and gay,
With only his pride for a paramour.

O who is that bitter king? It is not I.   10

Let me, I beseech thee, Father, die
From this fat royal life, and lie
As naked as a bridegroom by his bride,
And let that girl be the cold goddess Pride:

And I will sing to the barren rock
Your difficult, lonely music, heart,
Like an old proud king in a parable.

                                                                               (1928)

Noctambule[1]

Under the flag of this pneumatic[2] moon,
— Blown up to bursting, whitewashed white,
And painted like the moon — the piracies of day
Scuttle the crank hulk of witless night.
The great black innocent Othello of a thing
Is undone by the nice clean pockethandkerchief
Of 6 a.m., and though the moon is only an old
Wetwash snotrag — horsemeat for good rosbif[3] —
Perhaps to utilize substitutes is what
The age has to teach us,   10
                            wherefore let the loud
Unmeaning warcry of treacherous daytime
Issue like whispers of love in the moonlight,
— Poxy[4] old cheat!
        So mewed the lion,
Until mouse roared once and after lashed
His tail: Shellshock[5] came on again, his skin
Twitched in the rancid margarine,[6] his eye
Like a lake isle in a florist's window:
Reality at two removes,[7] and mouse and moon   20
Successful.

                                                                               (1935)

---

1. Noctambule From the Latin *nocta*, meaning "night," and *ambulare*, meaning "to walk." The speaker is a noctambulist, sleepwalking at night. **2. pneumatic** Filled with air. **3. rosbif** Roastbeef. **4. Poxy** Contemptible. **5. Shellshock** A reaction to the stress of combat, especially prevalent in soldiers from the World Wars, and similar to Post-Traumatic Stress Disorder. A few common symptoms include nightmares, flashbacks, anxiety, and insomnia. **6. margarine** Developed for soldiers as a cheap substitute for butter. **7. at two removes** A reference to George Herbert's poem "Jordan (I)."

The Archer

Bend back thy bow, O Archer, till the string
Is level with thine ear, thy body taut,
Its nature art, thyself thy statue wrought
Of marble blood, thy weapon the poised wing
Of coiled and aquiline[1] Fate. Then, loosening, fling
The hissing arrow like a burning thought
Into the empty sky that smokes as the hot
Shaft plunges to the bullseye's quenching ring.

So for a moment, motionless, serene,
10   Fixed between time and time, I aim and wait;
Nothing remains for breath now but to waive
His prior claim and let the barb fly clean
Into the heart of what I know and hate —
That central black, the ringed and targeted grave.

(1937)

Metamorphosis

This flesh repudiates[1] the bone
    With such dissolving force,
In such a tumult to be gone,
    Such longing for divorce,
As leaves the livid[2] mind no choice
    But to conclude at last
That all this energy and poise
    Were but designed to cast
A richer flower from the earth
10   Surrounding its decay,
And like a child whose fretful mirth
    Can find no constant play,
Bring one more transient form to birth
    And fling the old away.

(1957)

The Wisdom of Old Jelly Roll[1]

How all men wrongly death to dignify
Conspire, I tell. Parson, poetaster,[2] pimp,

---

1. **aquiline** Like an eagle (especially the beak).

1. **repudiates** Rejects. 2. **livid** Caught by strong emotion.

1. **Jelly Roll** Ferdinand Joseph La Menthe (Jelly Roll Morton), an early jazz musician from Louisiana (1885–1941).
2. **poetaster** Bad poet.

Each acts or acquiesces.[3] They prettify,
Dress up, deodorize, embellish, primp,
And make a show of Nothing. Ah, but met-
aphysics laughs: she touches, tastes, and smells
— Hence knows — the diamond holes that make a net.
Silence resettled testifies to bells.
"Nothing" depends on "Thing," which is or was:
So death makes life or makes life's worth, a worth   10
Beyond all highfalutin'[4] woes or shows
To publish and confess. "Cry at the birth,
Rejoice at the death," old Jelly Roll said,
Being on whisky, ragtime, chicken, and the scriptures fed.

(1962)

Morley Callaghan (1903–1990)

Morley Callaghan was born in Toronto in 1903 and lived in that city all of his life. He was a prolific novelist and short story writer whose credo was exemplified by his statement "Tell the truth cleanly." His career in journalism and training in law inspired a practical outlook — he once declared, "I'd be damned if the glory of literature was in the metaphor." Callaghan's parents loved poetry and read it aloud to the family; they were also drawn to liberal politics and raised their children in the Roman Catholic faith.

Callaghan was a student at the University of Toronto from 1921 to 1925, and during that period he worked part time as a reporter for the *Daily Star*. He regularly clashed with his editor and was fired and rehired several times over. In 1924, he also became acquainted with fellow *Star* reporter Ernest Hemingway, who was similarly frustrated with the boss and left after a few months. In Hemingway, Callaghan found affirmation of the terse, imagistic writing style he favoured, and they formed a friendship. When Hemingway returned to Paris, he took with him some of the short stories Callaghan had written and showed them to other writers and a few publishers. Meanwhile, Callaghan continued to write fiction and began articling for law school (he was called to the bar in 1928, but he would never practise law).

After publishing some stories, he travelled to New York where he met well-known writers of the time — figures such as William Carlos Williams, Katherine Ann Porter, and Sinclair Lewis. In New York, Callaghan met Maxwell Perkins of the publishing company Scribner's, and in 1928 Scribner's published Callaghan's first novel, *Strange Fugitive*. The novel introduced readers to Callaghan's fascination with criminals, whom he depicted as alienated anti-heroes on a violent trajectory. The novel owes much to the Hollywood gangster classics so popular with filmgoers at the time, as it chronicles the rise and fatal fall of Harry Trotter, a working-class bully who loses his job, steals a truckload of illegal liquor, and becomes a bootlegger. Callaghan etched Trotter's dark world in a realist style with moralistic overtones — one reviewer of the time remarked that Callaghan "tells his plot like a crack reporter" — and the tale, however formulaic, was a popular success. Starting in 1928, Callaghan made the first of 14 contributions to Edward J. O'Brien's *The Best Short Stories*.

---

3. **acquiesces** Concedes. 4. **highfalutin'** Pretentious.

In 1929, Scribner's issued a collection of Callaghan's short fiction entitled *A Native Argosy;* the same year, Callaghan wed Loretto Dee, and they went to Paris for several months. In Paris, Callaghan spent a lot of time with Hemingway. They were both skilled amateur boxers and often sparred. One day, F. Scott Fitzgerald was timing a match between them and let a round go into overtime, at which point Callaghan knocked Hemingway down (but not out). Tempers flared, but the three men reconciled. Later, a rumour circulated that Callaghan had flattened Hemingway to put an end to his incessant bragging. Though false, the rumour was so persistent that it eventually soured their friendship, and it did not help that Callaghan was often accused of being Hemingway's imitator. Callaghan would later write a memoir of these experiences — *That Summer in Paris* (1963).

The decade of the 1930s was a highly productive time for Callaghan. He and his wife had two sons, and he published several novels in quick succession: *It's Never Over* (1930), *No Man's Meat* (1931), *A Broken Journey* (1932), *Such Is My Beloved* (1934), *They Shall Inherit the Earth* (1935), and *More Joy in Heaven* (1937). His second short fiction collection, *Now That April's Here and Other Stories*, appeared in 1936. The novels reflect the author's experience of the Depression and his gradual shift away from naturalism towards Christian theology. Callaghan had met Jacques Maritain in Toronto in 1933, and the French Catholic philosopher inspired him to find a way to embody a heightened Christian humanism and sense of personal virtue in his work. Maritain's formidable effect is apparent in, for example, the characterization of *Such Is My Beloved*'s Father Dowling, the idealistic hero who tries to save two prostitutes in his parish. The bishop intervenes to avoid a scandal, the women are arrested, and Father Dowling sinks into a depression so deep that he is committed to an asylum. The irony of this dynamic — as one's involvement with others increases, so does one's personal isolation — would become a motif in Callaghan's writing.

In 1939, with the rise of fascism in Europe, the outbreak of war, and the establishment of a wartime economy that could support only mainstream arts, Callaghan entered what he called "the dark period" of his life. His stories were now frequently rejected by publishers. He mustered the determination to write two plays, but he could not get them produced right away, so he began to work for the Canadian Broadcasting Corporation, becoming a popular host and panel member on a number of radio series; he also contributed sports columns and editorials to *New World Illustrated*.

In 1948, Callaghan published *Luke Baldwin's Vow*, a novel for young people based on an earlier short story of the same name, and *The Varsity Story*, a novel about a fundraising scheme set at the University of Toronto. Then, in 1951, he produced *The Loved and the Lost*, the now very dated story of a White woman who, in defiance of the social conventions of her day, has affairs with Black men in Montreal's jazz community. It would win him a Governor General's Award. He followed this success with *The Many Colored Coat* (1960) and *A Passion in Rome* (1961), two more realist novels that expanded on his stated conviction that "all great writers are really moralists."

Through the 1960s and 1970s, Callaghan's work became more self-reflexive. In the novel *A Fine and Private Place* (1975), for example, he drew on his own life to create a portrait of an under-appreciated novelist and his critics. Nearing the end of his career, Callaghan published *Season of the Witch* (1976); *Close to the Sun Again* (1977); *The Enchanted Pimp* (1978), which he expanded into *Our Lady of the Snows* (1985); and *A Wild Old Man on the Road* (1988), a thinly veiled autobiography set in the 1920s. In 1983, he produced *A Time for Judas*, a revisionist interpretation of the crucifixion of Christ.

Despite his sense of having never received the recognition he deserved, by the time Callaghan died, in 1990, at the age of 87, he had won several prestigious awards, including over $70,000 in literary prizes, and he was made a Companion of the Order of Canada in 1982.

The Blue Kimono

It was hardly more than dawn when George woke up suddenly. He lay wide awake listening to a heavy truck moving on the street below; he heard one truck driver shout angrily to another; he heard the noises of doors slamming, of women taking in the milk, of cars starting, and sometime later on in the morning, he wondered where all these people went when they hurried out briskly with so much assurance.

Each morning he wakened a little earlier and was wide awake. But this time he was more restless than ever and he thought with despair. "We're unlucky, that's it. We've never had any luck since we've come here. There's something you can't put your hands on working to destroy us. Everything goes steadily against us from bad to worse. We'll never have any luck. I can feel it. We'll starve before I get a job."

Then he realized that his wife, Marthe, was no longer in the bed beside him. He looked around the room that seemed so much larger and so much emptier in that light and he thought, "What's the matter with Marthe? Is it getting that she can't sleep?" Sitting up, he peered uneasily into the room's dark corners. There was a light coming from the kitchenette. As he got out of bed slowly, with his thick hair standing up straight all over his head, and reached for his slippers and dressing gown, the notion that something mysterious and inexorable[1] was working to destroy them was so strong in him that he suddenly wanted to stand in front of his wife and shout in anger, "What can I do? You tell me something to do. What's the use of me going out to the streets today? I'm going to sit down here and wait, day after day." That time when they had first got married and were secure now seemed such a little faraway forgotten time.

In his eagerness to make his wife feel the bad luck he felt within him, he went striding across the room, his old, shapeless slippers flapping on the floor, his dressing gown only half pulled on, looking in that dim light like someone huge, reckless, and full of sudden savage impulse, who wanted to pound a table and shout. "Marthe, Marthe," he called, "what's the matter with you? Why are you up at this time?"

She came into the room carrying their two-year-old boy. "There's nothing the matter with me," she said. "I got up when I heard Walter crying." She was a small, slim, dark woman with black hair hanging on her shoulders, a thin eager face, and large soft eyes, and as she walked over to the window with the boy she swayed her body as though she were humming to him. The light from the window was now a little stronger. She sat there in her old blue kimono holding the boy tight and feeling his head with her hand.

"What's the matter with him?" George said.

"I don't know. I heard him whimpering, so I got up. His head felt so hot."

"Is there anything I can do?" he said.

"I don't think so."

She seemed so puzzled, so worried and aloof from even the deepest bitterness within him, that George felt impatient, as if it were her fault that the child was sick. For a while he watched her rocking back and forth, always making the same faint humming sound, with the stronger light showing the deep frown on her face, and he couldn't seem to think of the child at all. He wanted to speak with sympathy, but he burst out, "I had to get up because I couldn't go on with my own thoughts. We're unlucky, Marthe. We haven't had a day's luck since we've come to this city. How much longer can this go on before they throw us out on the street? I tell you we never should have come here."

---

1. **inexorable** Inevitable.

She looked up at him indignantly. He couldn't see the fierceness in her face because her head was against the window light. Twice he walked the length of the room, then he stood beside her, looking down at the street. There was now traffic and an increasing steady hum of motion. He felt chilled and his fingers grasped at the collar of his dressing gown, pulling it across his chest. "It's cold here, and you can imagine what it'll be like in winter," he said. And when Marthe again did not answer, he said sullenly, "You wanted us to come here. You wanted us to give up what we had and come to a bigger city where there were bigger things ahead. Where we might amount to something because of my fine education and your charming manner. You thought we didn't have enough ambition, didn't you?"

"Why talk about it now, George?"

"I want you to see what's happened to us."

"Say I'm responsible. Say anything you wish."

"All right. I'll tell you what I feel in my bones. Luck is against us. Something far stronger than our two lives is working against us. I was thinking about it when I woke up. I must have been thinking about it all through my sleep."

"We've been unlucky, but we've often had a good time, haven't we?" she said.

"Tell me honestly, have we had a day's luck since we got married?" he said brutally.

"I don't know," she said with her head down. Then she looked up suddenly, almost pleading, but afraid to speak.

The little boy started to whimper and then sat up straight, pushing away the blanket his mother tried to keep around him. When she insisted on covering him, he began to fight and she had a hard time holding him till suddenly he was limp in her arms, looking around the darkened room with the bright wonder that comes in a child's fevered eyes.

George watched Marthe trying to soothe the child. The morning light began to fall on her face, making it seem a little leaner, a little narrower and so dreadfully worried. A few years ago everybody used to speak about her extraordinary smile, about the way the lines around her mouth were shaped for laughter, and they used to say, too, that she had a mysterious, tapering, Florentine[2] face. Once a man had said to George, "I remember clearly the first time I met your wife. I said to myself, 'Who is the lady with that marvelous smile?'"

George was now looking at this face as though it belonged to a stranger. He could think of nothing but the shape of it. There were so many angles in that light; it seemed so narrow. "I used to think it was beautiful. It doesn't look beautiful. Would anybody say it was beautiful?" he thought, and yet these thoughts had nothing to do with his love for her.

In some intuitive way she knew that he was no longer thinking of his bad luck, but was thinking of her, so she said patiently, "Walter seems to have quite a fever, George." Then he stopped walking and touched Walter's head, which was very hot.

"Here, let me hold him a while and you get something," he said. "Get him some aspirin."

"I'll put it in orange juice, if he'll take it," she said.

"For God's sake, turn on the light, Marthe," he called. "This ghastly light is getting on my nerves."

---

2. **Florentine** Of Florence, the Italian city.

He tried talking to his son while Marthe was away. "Hello, Walter, old boy, what's the matter with you? Look at me, big boy, say something bright to your old man." But the little boy shook his head violently, stared vacantly at the wall a moment, and then tried to bury his face in his father's shoulder. So George, looking disconsolately[3] around the cold room, felt that it was more barren than ever.

Marthe returned with the orange juice and the aspirin. They both began to coax Walter to take it. They pretended to be drinking it themselves, made ecstatic noises with their tongues as though it were delicious and kept it up till the boy cried, "Orange, orange, me too," with an unnatural animation. His eyes were brilliant. Then he swayed as if his spine were made of putty and fell back in his mother's arms.

"We'd better get a doctor in a hurry, George," Marthe said.

"Do you think it's that bad?"

"Look at him," she said, laying him on the bed. "I'm sure he's very sick. You don't want to lose him, do you?" and she stared at Walter, who had closed his eyes and was sleeping.

As Marthe in her fear kept looking up at George, she was fingering her old blue kimono, drawing it tighter around her to keep her warm. The kimono had been of a Japanese pattern adorned with clusters of brilliant flowers sewn in silk. George had given it to her at the time of their marriage; now he stared at it, torn as it was at the arms, with pieces of old padding hanging out at the hem, with the light colored lining showing through in many places, and he remembered how, when the kimono was new, Marthe use to make the dark hair across her forehead into bangs, fold her arms across her breasts, with her wrists and hands concealed in the sleeve folds, and go around the room in the bright kimono, taking short, prancing steps, pretending she was a Japanese girl.

The kimono now was ragged and gone; it was gone, he thought, like so many bright dreams and aspirations they had once had in the beginning, like so many fine resolutions he had sworn to accomplish, like so many plans they had made and hopes they had cherished.

"Marthe, in God's name," he said suddenly, "the very first money we get, even if we just have enough to put a little down, you'll have to get a decent dressing gown. Do you hear?"

She was startled. Looking up at him in bewilderment, she swallowed hard, then turned her eyes down again.

"It's terrible to have to look at you in that thing," he muttered.

After he had spoken in this way he was ashamed, and he was able to see for the first time the wild terrified look on her face as she bent over Walter.

"Why do you look like that?" he asked. "Hasn't he just got a little fever?"

"Did you see the way he held the glass when he took the orange juice?"

"No. I didn't notice."

"His hand trembled. Earlier, when I first went to him, and gave him a drink I noticed the strange trembling in his hand."

"What does it mean?" he said, awed by the fearful way she was whispering.

"His body seemed limp and he could not sit up either. Last night I was reading about such symptoms in the medical column in the paper. Symptoms like that with a fever are symptoms of infantile paralysis."

---

3. **disconsolately** Inconsolably.

"Where's the paper?"

"Over there on the table."

George sat down and began to read the bit of newspaper medical advice; over and over he read it, very calmly. Marthe had described the symptoms accurately; but in a stupid way he could not get used to the notion that his son might have such a dreadful disease. So he remained there calmly for a long time.

And then he suddenly realized how they had been dogged by bad luck; he realized how surely everything they loved was being destroyed day by day and he jumped up and cried out, "We'll have to get a doctor." And as if he realized to the full what was inevitably impending, he cried out, "You're right, Marthe, he'll die. That child will die. It's the luck that's following us. Then it's over. Everything's over. I tell you I'll curse the day I ever saw the light of the world. I'll curse the day we ever met and ever married. I'll smash everything I can put my hands on in this world."

"George, don't go on like that. You'll bring something dreadful down on us," she whispered in terror.

"What else can happen? What else can happen to us worse than this?"

"Nothing, nothing, but please don't go on saying it, George."

Then they both bent down over Walter and they took turns putting their hands on his head. "What doctor will come to us at this house when we have no money?" he kept muttering. "We'll have to take him to a hospital." They remained kneeling together, silent for a long time, almost afraid to speak.

Marthe said suddenly, "Feel, feel his head. Isn't it a little cooler?"

"What could that be?"

"It might be the aspirin working on him."

So they watched, breathing steadily together while the child's head gradually got cooler. Their breathing and their silence seemed to waken the child, for he opened his eyes and stared at them vaguely. "He must be feeling better," George said. "See the way he's looking at us."

"His head does feel a lot cooler."

"What could have been the matter with him, Marthe?"

"It must have been a chill. Oh, I hope it was only a chill."

"Look at him, if you please. Watch me make the rascal laugh."

With desperate eagerness George rushed over to the table, tore off a sheet of newspaper, folded it into a thin strip about eight inches long and twisted it like a cord. Then he knelt down in front of Walter and cried, "See, see," and thrust the twisted paper under his own nose and held it with his upper lip while he wiggled it up and down. He screwed up his eyes diabolically. He pressed his face close against the boy's.

Laughing, Walter put out his hand. "Let me," he said. So George tried to hold the paper moustache against Walter's lip. But that was no good. Walter pushed the paper away and said, "You, you."

"I think his head is cool now," Marthe said. "Maybe he'll be all right."

She got up and walked away from the bed, over to the window with her head down. Standing up, George went to follow her, but his son shouted tyrannically so he had to kneel down and hold the paper moustache under his nose and say, "Look here, look, Walter."

Marthe was trying to smile as she watched them. She took one deep breath after another, as though she would never succeed in filling her lungs with air. But even while she stood there, she grew troubled. She hesitated, she lowered her head and wanted to say, "One of us will find work of some kind, George," but she was afraid.

"I'll get dressed now," she said quietly, and she started to take off her kimono.

As she held it on her arm, her face grew full of deep concern. She held the kimono up so the light shone on the gay silken flowers. Sitting down in the chair, she spread the faded silk on her knee and looked across the room at her sewing basket, which was on the dresser by the mirror. She fumbled patiently with the lining, patting the places that were torn; and suddenly she was sure she could draw the torn parts together and make it look bright and new.

"I think I can fix it up so it'll look fine, George," she said.

"Eh?" he said. "What are you bothering with that for?" Then he ducked down to the floor again and wiggled his paper moustache fiercely at the child.

(1936)

Earle Birney (1904–1995)

Earle Birney once declared that "living art, like anything else, stays alive only by changing. The young artist must constantly examine the forms and the aesthetic theories he has inherited; he must reject most of them, and he must search for new ones." Birney held to this credo. His restless mind led him from the traditional forms and themes of the Canadian Romantics to the revisionist aesthetics of the Canadian modernists; he would eventually experiment with concrete, computer, and found poetry. Birney also travelled extensively, believing that through relentless exploration, both physical and mental, he could acquire a greater self-knowledge and understanding of humankind.

Birney was born on 14 May 1904 in Calgary, Alberta. As a young adult, he toiled as a labourer for several years to earn enough money for university. In 1922, he enrolled at the University of British Columbia and began to work towards a degree in English literature. In his third year, he became editor-in-chief of the university periodical the *Ubyssey*, in which he published his first poetry. After completing his degree, in 1927, he began graduate work and accepted a teaching position in the English department of the University of Utah. He then moved on to the University of Toronto to finish his doctoral thesis on irony in Chaucer. In the early 1930s, he became involved in Marxist-Leninist politics, and when he was granted a fellowship to complete his doctorate in London, England, he became active in the Independent Labour Party; in 1935, he travelled to Norway to interview Leon Trotsky in exile.

He received his doctorate from the University of Toronto in 1936 and became literary editor of the *Canadian Forum*, a left-leaning journal committed to literary and political issues. He was, however, becoming increasingly disillusioned with all forms of communism, and when Trotsky announced his support for Russia's invasion of Finland in 1939 he was dismayed. He began to turn his attention to poetry, informing his mentor Garnett Sedgewick, "I will luxuriate once more in scepticism and political idleness, and try, if it is not too late, to do some real writing instead of the weekly political hack work I've devoted my spare time to for the last eight long bitter years."

Reworking some older material and composing new verses, Birney produced his first collection of poetry: *David and Other Poems* (1942). It earned him a Governor General's Award. World War II had been raging since 1939, and the title poem, with its themes of paralysis, choice, consequence, and lost innocence, touched a chord with readers. The climax of the poem occurs when David, paralyzed by a fall while mountain climbing, begs his friend Bob (the poem's speaker) to push him over a ledge. Suddenly in control of David's fate, Bob chooses to accede to his friend's request, asserting that "none but the sun and incurious clouds have lingered / Around the marks of … That day, the last of my youth, on the last of our mountains."

In 1940, Birney had married Esther Bull and enlisted in the Canadian Officers Training Corps. He joined the Canadian Active Army in 1942. The following year, he left Esther and their young son to go to England and serve as a personnel selection officer. The job involved conducting psychological and psychiatric assessments of Canadian soldiers and assigning them to the positions for which they seemed best suited. Later, in his first novel, *Turvey* (1949), he wrote about his experiences abroad. When he returned to Canada, Birney published a volume of poetry entitled *Now Is Time* (1945), and it won him a second Governor General's Award. He found employment at the CBC as a supervisor of foreign-language radio broadcasts to Europe, but he soon returned to teaching, this time at the University of British Columbia. Although he continued to publish poetry, he remained attracted to the medium of radio, and he began to write verse dramas for the CBC drama department. Many of these plays were collected in *Words on Waves: The Selected Radio Plays of Earle Birney* (1985).

Having been granted tenure at UBC, Birney found more time for travelling and writing. He undertook several major reading tours and recounted many of his travel experiences in the poetry he published during this period. *Near False Creek Mouth* (1964), for example, is an exploration of the poet's responses to a journey he made to the Caribbean, South America, and then Spain. In "For George Lamming," the poet is jolted by the realization that he is very different from the people who surround him in Kingston, Jamaica: "on a wall mirror / my face assaulted me / stunned to see itself / like a white snail / in the supple dark flowers." However, Birney ultimately regarded cultural differences as superficial and posited the connectedness of all human beings.

In 1965, he resigned from UBC and served as writer-in-residence at various institutions in Canada and the United States. Towards the end of the decade, he started to experiment with concrete and computer poetry, producing *pnomes jukollages & other stunzas* (1969). Leaving the academic life behind, Birney immersed himself in writing, revising, and travelling. He and Esther ended their marriage in 1977. Birney would spend the rest of his life with Wailan Low, and he included warm poetic tributes to her in his final collection, *Last Makings* (1991); these pieces are exceptional for Birney, who had never before written personal love poetry.

Birney wrote in order to interpret the state of the world. Because he was often discouraged with society, many of his verses are bitter and pessimistic, but beneath his frustration there was always faith in the possibility of hope and change, and a profound sense of humour. He insisted that "there's more to writing than howling. There's singing. And isn't there lots still to sing about too?"

David

I

David and I that summer cut trails on the Survey,
All week in the valley for wages, in air that was steeped
In the wail of mosquitoes, but over the sunalive week-ends
We climbed, to get from the ruck[1] of the camp, the surly

---

1. **ruck** Mess.

Poker, the wrangling, the snoring under the fetid
Tents, and because we had joy in our lengthening coltish
Muscles, and mountains for David were made to see over,
Stairs from the valleys and steps to the sun's retreats.

II

Our first was Mount Gleam. We hiked in the long afternoon
To a curling lake and lost the lure of the faceted   10
Cone in the swell of its sprawling shoulders. Past
The inlet we grilled our bacon, the strips festooned[2]

On a poplar prong, in the hurrying slant of the sunset.
Then the two of us rolled in the blanket while round us the cold
Pines thrust at the stars. The dawn was a floating
Of mists till we reached to the slopes above timber, and won

To snow like fire in the sunlight. The peak was upthrust
Like a fist in a frozen ocean of rock that swirled
Into valleys the moon could be rolled in. Remotely unfurling
Eastward the alien prairie glittered. Down through the dusty   20

Skree[3] on the west we descended, and David showed me
How to use the give of shale[4] for giant incredible
Strides. I remember, before the larches'[5] edge,
That I jumped on a long green surf of juniper flowing

Away from the wind, and landed in gentian and saxifrage[6]
Spilled on the moss. Then the darkening firs
And the sudden whirring of water that knifed down a fern-hidden
Cliff and splashed unseen into mist in the shadows.

III

One Sunday on Rampart's arête a rainsquall caught us,
And passed, and we clung by our blueing fingers and bootnails   30
An endless hour in the sun, not daring to move
Till the ice had steamed from the slate. And David taught me

How time on a knife-edge can pass with the guessing of fragments
Remembered from poets, the naming of strata beside one,
And matching of stories from schooldays…. We crawled astride
The peak to feast on the marching ranges flagged

By the fading shreds of the shattered stormcloud. Lingering
There it was David who spied to the south, remote,

---

2. **festooned** Hung. 3. **skree** Loose debris on a steep rock face. 4. **shale** Layered, unstable sedimentary rock.
5. **larches** Coniferous trees. 6. **gentian, saxifrage** Wild, flowering plants.

And unmapped, a sunlit spire on Sawback, an overhang
40   Crooked like a talon. David named it the Finger.

That day we chanced on the skull and the splayed white ribs
Of a mountain goat underneath a cliff-face, caught
On a rock. Around were the silken feathers of hawks.
And that was the first I knew that a goat could slip.

IV

And then Inglismaldie.[7] Now I remember only
The long ascent of the lonely valley, the live
Pine spirally scarred by lightning, the slicing pipe
Of invisible pika,[8] and great prints, by the lowest

Snow, of a grizzly. There it was too that David
50   Taught me to read the scroll of coral in limestone
And the beetle-seal[9] in the shale of ghostly trilobites,[10]
Letters delivered to man from the Cambrian[11] waves.

V

On Sundance we tried from the col and the going was hard.
The air howled from our feet to the smudged rocks
And the papery lake below. At an outthrust we baulked
Till David clung with his left to a dint in the scarp,

Lobbed the iceaxe over the rocky lip,
Slipped from his holds and hung by the quivering pick,
Twisted his long legs up into space and kicked
60   To the crest. Then, grinning, he reached with his freckled wrist

And drew me up after. We set a new time for that climb.
That day returning we found a robin gyrating
In grass, wing-broken. I caught it to tame but David
Took and killed it, and said, "Could you teach it to fly?"

VI

In August, the second attempt, we ascended The Fortress,[12]
By the forks of the Spray we caught five trout and fried them
Over a balsam fire. The woods were alive
With the vaulting of mule-deer and drenched with clouds all the morning,

Till we burst at noon to the flashing and floating round
70   Of the peaks. Coming down we picked in our hats the bright

---

7. **Inglismaldie** Large mountain in Banff National Park's Fairholme Range, Alberta. Part of the Rockies. **8. pika** Rock rabbits. **9. beetle-seal** Egyptians commonly used carved beetle seals. **10. trilobites** Primitive, Precambrian dwellers of the ocean floor; many fossils have been found in the Rockies. **11. Cambrian** Geological era, 542–488 million years ago. **12. The Fortress** Mountain near Inglismaldie.

And sunhot raspberries, eating them under a mighty
Spruce, while marten moving like quicksilver scouted us.

VII

But always we talked of the Finger on Sawback, unknown
And hooked, till the first afternoon in September we slogged
Through the musky woods, past a swamp that quivered with frog-song,
And camped by a bottle-green lake. But under the cold

Breath of the glacier sleep would not come, the moon-light
Etching the Finger. We rose and trod past the feathery
Larch, while the stars went out, and the quiet heather
Flushed, and the skyline pulsed with the surging bloom   80

Of incredible dawn in the Rockies. David spotted
Bighorns[13] across the moraine[14] and sent them leaping
With yodels the ramparts redoubled and rolled to the peaks,
And the peaks to the sun. The ice in the morning thaw

Was a gurgling world of crystal and cold blue chasms,
And seracs[15] that shone like frozen saltgreen waves.
At the base of the Finger we tried once and failed. Then David
Edged to the west and discovered the chimney;[16] the last

Hundred feet we fought the rock and shouldered and kneed
Our way for an hour and made it. Unroping we formed   90
A cairn[17] on the rotting tip. Then I turned to look north
At the glistening wedge of giant Assiniboine,[18] heedless

Of handhold. And one foot gave. I swayed and shouted.
David turned sharp and reached out his arm and steadied me,
Turning again with a grin and his lips ready
To jest. But the strain crumbled his foothold. Without

A gasp he was gone. I froze to the sound of grating
Edge-nails and fingers, the slither of stones, the lone
Second of silence, the nightmare thud. Then only
The wind and the muted beat of unknowing cascades.   100

VIII

Somehow I worked down the fifty impossible feet
To the ledge, calling and getting no answer but echoes

---

13. Bighorns Wild mountain sheep. **14. moraine** Heap of debris left behind by a glacier. **15. seracs** Pointed peaks of ice
in a glacial crevasse. **16. chimney** A slim, vertical passage through a body of rock. **17. cairn** Pile of stones amassed as a
monument. **18. Assiniboine** This mountain's peak is at least 457 metres (1,500 feet) taller than the neighbouring ones.

Released in the cirque,[19] and trying not to reflect
What an answer would mean. He lay still, with his lean

Young face upturned and strangely unmarred, but his legs
Splayed beneath him, beside the final drop,
Six hundred feet sheer to the ice. My throat stopped
When I reached him, for he was alive. He opened his gray

Straight eyes and brokenly murmured "over ... over."
110   And I, feeling beneath him a cruel fang
Of the ledge thrust in his back, but not understanding,
Mumbled stupidly, "Best not to move," and spoke

Of his pain. But he said, "I can't move.... If only I felt
Some pain." Then my shame stung the tears to my eyes
As I crouched, and I cursed myself, but he cried
Louder, "No, Bobbie! Don't ever blame yourself.

I didn't test my foothold." He shut the lids
Of his eyes to the stare of the sky, while I moistened his lips
From our water flask and tearing my shirt into strips
120   I swabbed the shredded hands. But the blood slid

From his side and stained the stone and the thirsting lichens,[20]
And yet I dared not lift him up from the gore
Of the rock. Then he whispered, "Bob, I want to go over!"
This time I knew what he meant and I grasped for a lie

And said, "I'll be back here by midnight with ropes
And men from the camp and we'll cradle you out." But I knew
That the day and the night must pass and the cold dews
Of another morning before such men unknowing

The ways of mountains could win to the chimney's top.
130   And then, how long? And he knew ... and the hell of hours
After that, if he lived till we came, roping him out.
But I curled beside him and whispered, "The bleeding will stop.

You can last." He said only, "Perhaps.... For what? A wheelchair,
Bob?" His eyes brightening with fever upbraided[21] me.
I could not look at him more and said, "Then I'll stay
With you." But he did not speak, for the clouding fever.

I lay dazed and stared at the long valley,
The glistening hair of a creek on the rug stretched

---

19. cirque Bowl structure in a mountain range, usually containing a lake. **20. lichens** Fungus and algae growing together in a crust. **21. upbraided** Reproached.

By the firs, while the sun leaned round and flooded the ledge,
The moss, and David still as a broken doll.   140

I hunched to my knees to leave, but he called and his voice
Now was sharpened with fear. "For Christ's sake push me over!
If I could move.... Or die...." The sweat ran from his forehead,
But only his eyes moved. A hawk was buoying

Blackly its wings over the wrinkled ice.
The purr of a waterfall rose and sank with the wind.
Above us climbed the last joint of the Finger
Beckoning bleakly the wide indifferent sky.

Even then in the sun it grew cold lying there.... And I knew
He had tested his holds. It was I who had not.... I looked   150
At the blood on the ledge, and the far valley. I looked
At last in his eyes. He breathed, "I'd do it for you, Bob."

IX
I will not remember how nor why I could twist
Up the wind-devilled peak, and down through the chimney's empty
Horror, and over the traverse alone. I remember
Only the pounding fear I would stumble on It

When I came to the grave-cold maw of the bergschrund[22] ... reeling
Over the sun-cankered snowbridge, shying the caves
In the névé[23] ... the fear, and the need to make sure It was there
On the ice, the running and falling and running, leaping   160

Of gaping greenthroated crevasses, alone and pursued
By the Finger's lengthening shadow. At last through the fanged
And blinding seracs I slid to the milky wrangling
Falls at the glacier's snout, through the rocks piled huge

On the humped moraine, and into the spectral larches,
Alone. By the glooming lake I sank and chilled
My mouth but I could not rest and stumbled still
To the valley, losing my way in the ragged marsh.

I was glad of the mire that covered the stains, on my ripped
Boots, of his blood, but panic was on me, the reek   170
Of the bog, the purple glimmer of toadstools obscene
In the twilight. I staggered clear to a firewaste,[24] tripped

---

22. **bergschrund** Deep crevasses where a glacier has separated from rock. 23. **névé** A field of tightly packed, granular snow. 24. **firewaste** Area desolated by fire.

And fell with a shriek on my shoulder. It somehow eased
My heart to know I was hurt, but I did not faint
And I could not stop while over me hung the range
Of the Sawback. In blackness I searched for the trail by the creek

And found it.... My feet squelched a slug and horror
Rose again in my nostrils. I hurled myself
Down the path. In the woods behind some animal yelped.
180   Then I saw the glimmer of tents and babbled my story.

I said that he fell straight to the ice where they found him,
And none but the sun and incurious clouds have lingered
Around the marks of that day on the ledge of the Finger,
That day, the last of my youth, on the last of our mountains.

(1941)

Anglosaxon Street

Dawndrizzle ended   dampness steams from
Blotching brick and   blank plasterwaste
Faded housepatterns   hoary and finicky
unfold stuttering   stick like a phonograph

Here is a ghetto   gotten for goyim[1]
O with care denuded   of nigger and kike[2]
No coonsmell[3] rankles   reeks only cellarrot
attar of carexhaust   catcorpse and cookinggrease
Imperial hearts   heave in this haven
10   Cracks across windows   are welded with slogans
There'll Always Be An England[4]   enhances geraniums
and V's for Victory[5]   vanquish the housefly

Ho! with climbing sun   march the bleached beldames[6]
festooned with shopping bags   farded[7] flatarched
bigthewed[8] Saxonwives   stepping over buttrivers
waddling back wienerladen   to suckle smallfry

Hoy! with sunslope   shrieking over hydrants
flood from learninghall   the lean fingerlings
Nordic nobblecheeked   not all clean of nose
20   leaping Commandowise   into leprous lanes

---

1. **goyim** Generally negative term for a non-Jewish person. 2. **nigger, kike** Derogatory terms for blacks and Jews, respectively. 3. **coonsmell** "Coon" was a common racial slur in the early 20th century for a black person. 4. **There'll Always Be An England** English patriotic song from World War II. 5. **V's for Victory** Allies' slogan from World War II. 6. **beldames** Old, ugly woman. 7. **farded** With a painted face. 8. **bigthewed** Large-muscled.

What! after whistleblow!   spewed from wheelboat
after daylong doughtiness[9]   dire handplay
in sewertrench or sandpit   come Saxonthegns[10]
Junebrown Jutekings[11]   jawslack for meat

Sit after supper   on smeared doorsteps
not humbly swearing   hatedeeds on Huns[12]
profiteers politicians   pacifists Jews

Then by twobit magic   to muse in movie
unlock picturehoard   or lope to alehall
soaking bleakly   in beer skittleless[13]   30

Home again to hotbox   and humid husbandhood
in slumbertrough adding   sleepily to Anglekin[14]
Alongside in lanenooks   carling[15] and leman[16]
caterwaul[17] and clip   careless of Saxonry
with moonglow and haste   and a higher heartbeat

Slumbers now slumtrack   unstinks cooling
waiting brief for milkmaid   mornstar and worldrise

(1942)

Vancouver Lights

About me the night   moonless   wimples[1] the mountains
wraps ocean   land   air   and mounting
sucks at the stars   The city   throbbing below
webs the sable peninsula   The golden
strands overleap the seajet   by bridge and buoy
vault the shears of the inlet   climb the woods
toward me   falter   and halt   Across to the firefly
haze of a ship on the gulf's erased horizon
roll the lambent[2] spokes of a lighthouse

Through the feckless[3] years we have come to the time   10
when to look on this quilt of lamps is a troubling delight
Welling from Europe's bog   through Africa flowing
and Asia   drowning the lonely lumes[4] on the oceans
tiding up over Halifax   now to this winking
outpost comes flooding the primal ink

---

9. **doughtiness** Bravery. 10. **Saxonthegns** Thanes, an aristocratic class of early England. 11. **Jutekings** Kings of Germanic tribes of Jutland, which attacked England in the 5th century. 12. **Huns** Nomadic Western-Asian peoples who conquered Europe in the 4th–5th centuries. 13. **skittleless** "Skittles" are pins in the British game of ninepin (similar to bowling). 14. **Anglekin** The early Germanic inhabitants of Britain. 15. **carling** A crossbeam in a ship. 16. **leman** Sweetheart (medieval). 17. **caterwaul** A long wail.

1. **wimples** Surrounds. 2. **lambent** Graceful, radiant. 3. **feckless** Futile. 4. **lumes** Lights.

On this mountain's brutish forehead with terror of space
I stir   of the changeless night and the stark ranges
of nothing   pulsing down from beyond and between
the fragile planets   We are a spark beleaguered
20   by darkness   this twinkle we make in a corner of emptiness
how shall we utter our fear that the black Experimentress
will never in the range of her microscope find it?   Our Phoebus[5]
himself is a bubble that dries on Her slide   while the Nubian[6]
wears for an evening's whim a necklace of nebulae

Yet we must speak   we the unique glowworms
Out of the waters and rocks of our little world
we conjured these flames   hooped these sparks
by our will   From blankness and cold we fashioned stars
to our size   and signalled Aldebaran[7]
30   This must we say   whoever may be to hear us
if murk devour   and none weave again in gossamer:

                                        These rays were ours
we made and unmade them   Not the shudder of continents
doused us   the moon's passion   nor crash of comets
In the fathomless heat of our dwarfdom   our dream's combustion
we contrived the power   the blast that snuffed us
No one bound Prometheus[8]   Himself he chained
and consumed his own bright liver   O stranger
Plutonian[9]   descendant   or beast in the stretching night —
40   there was light

(1942)

Bushed

He invented a rainbow but lightning struck it
shattered it into the lake-lap of a mountain
so big his mind slowed when he looked at it

Yet he built a shack on the shore
learned to roast porcupine belly and
wore the quills on his hatband

At first he was out with the dawn
whether it yellowed bright as wood-columbine
or was only a fuzzed moth in a flannel of storm
10   But he found the mountain was clearly alive

---

5. **Phoebus** Classical god of the sun. 6. **Nubian** Native of Nubia, an ancient region of southern Egypt and northern Sudan; Birney uses the term to allude to the night sky. 7. **Aldebaran** Bright star in the Taurus constellation; from *dabaran*, meaning "follower of the Pleiades." The Pleiades are both a star cluster themselves and a set of seven sister nymphs in classical mythology. 8. **Prometheus** Titan who stole fire from the gods and gave it to the mortals. 9. **Plutonian** Reference to Pluto, god of the underworld.

sent messages whizzing down every hot morning
boomed proclamations at noon and spread out
a white guard of goat
before falling asleep on its feet at sundown

When he tried his eyes on the lake   ospreys
would fall like valkyries[1]
choosing the cut-throat
He took then to waiting
till the night smoke rose from the boil of the sunset

But the moon carved unknown totems   20
out of the lakeshore
owls in the beardusky woods derided him
moosehorned cedars circled his swamps and tossed
their antlers up to the stars
then he knew   though the mountain slept   the winds
were shaping its peak to an arrowhead
poised

And now he could only
bar himself in and wait
for the great flint to come singing into his heart   30

(1951)

The Bear on the Delhi Road

Unreal   tall as a myth
by the road the Himalayan bear
is beating the brilliant air
with his crooked arms
About him two men   bare
spindly as locusts   leap

One pulls on a ring
in the great soft nose   His mate
flicks   flicks with a stick
up at the rolling eyes   10

They have not led him here
down from the fabulous hills
to this bald alien plain
and the clamorous world   to kill
but simply to teach him to dance

---

1. **valkyries** Female figures in Norse mythology who gathered the best of the fallen soldiers for use by Odin, the chief god.

They are peaceful both   these spare
men of Kashmir[1]   and the bear
alive is their living   too
If   far on the Delhi way
20   around him galvanic[2] they dance
it is merely to wear   wear
from his shaggy body the tranced
wish forever to stay
only an ambling bear
four-footed in berries

It is no more joyous for them
in this hot dust to prance
out of reach of the praying claws
sharpened to paw for ants
30   in the shadows of deodars[3]
It is not easy to free
myth from reality
or rear this fellow up
to lurch   lurch with them
in the tranced dancing of men

(1960)

Can. Lit.

(or *them able to leave her ever*)

since we'd always sky about
when we had eagles they flew out
leaving no shadow bigger than wren's
to trouble even our broodiest hens

too busy bridging loneliness
to be alone
we hacked in railway ties
what Emily[1] etched in bone

we French&English never lost
10   our civil war
endure it still
a bloody civil bore

---

1. Kashmir Region straddling India, Pakistan, and China; north of Delhi. **2. galvanic** Energetically. **3. deodars** A Himalayan cedar.

---

1. Emily American poet Emily Dickinson (1830–1886), especially active during the American Civil War.

the wounded sirened off
no Whitman[2] wanted
it's only by our lack of ghosts
we're haunted

(1962)

El Greco: *Espolio*

The carpenter is intent on the pressure of his hand

on the awl[1]   and the trick of pinpointing his strength
through the awl to the wood   which is tough
He has no effort to spare for despoilings[2]
or to worry if he'll be cut in on the dice
His skill is vital to the scene   and the safety of the state
Anyone can perform the indignities   It's his hard arms
and craft that hold the eyes of the convict's women
There is the problem of getting the holes exact
(in the middle of this elbowing crowd)   10
and deep enough to hold the spikes
after they've sunk through those bared feet
and inadequate wrists he knows are waiting behind him

He doesnt sense perhaps that one of the hands
is held in a curious gesture over him —
giving   or asking   forgiveness? —
but he'd scarcely take time to be puzzled by poses
Criminals come in all sorts
as anyone knows who makes crosses
are as mad or sane as those who decide on their killings   20
Our one at least has been quiet so far
though they say he talked himself into this trouble
a carpenter's son who got notions of preaching

Well here's a carpenter's son[3] who'll have carpenter sons
God willing   and build what's wanted
temples or tables   mangers or crosses
and shape them decently
working alone in that firm and profound abstraction
which blots out the bawling of rag-snatchers
To construct with hands   knee-weight   braced thigh   30
keeps the back turned from death

---

2. Whitman American poet Walt Whitman (1819–1892), also engaged with the Civil War.

---

1. awl Steel spike used to scratch lines for woodworking. **2. despoilings** Loss by force. **3. carpenter's son** Jesus of
Nazareth was the son of a carpenter, but the speaker is referring to himself.

But it's too late now for the other carpenter's boy
to return to this peace before the nails are hammered

(1961)

November Walk Near False Creek Mouth

I

The time is the last of warmth
and the fading of brightness
     before the final flash and the night

I walk as the earth turns
from its burning father
here on this lowest edge of mortal city
where windows flare on faded flats
and the barren end of the ancient English
     who tippled mead in Alfred's hall[1]
10   and took tiffin in lost Lahore[2]
drink now their fouroclock chainstore tea
sighing like old pines as the wind turns

The beat is the small   slap   slapping
of the tide sloping   slipping
its long soft fingers into the tense
joints of the trapped seawall

More ones than twos on the beaches today
strolling   or stranded as nations
woolly mermaids   dazed on beachlogs
20   a kept dog   sniffing   leading his woman
Seldom the lovers   seldom as reason
They will twine indoors from now to May
or ever to never   except the lovers
of what is not city   the refugees
     from the slow volcano
     the cratered rumbling   sirening vents
     the ashen air   the barren spilling
     compulsive rearing of glassy cliff
     from city
30   they come to the last innocent warmth
and the fading
before the unimaginable brightness

---

1. **mead in Alfred's hall** Alfred the Great ruled England from 849–899; mead is a honey-based liquor, popular at the time.
2. **Lahore** Northeastern major city in Pakistan; reached its peak in the 16th century.

II

The theme lies in the layers
made and unmade by the nudging   lurching
spiralling down from nothing

down through the common explosion of time
through the chaos of suns
to the high seas of the spinning air
where the shelves form   and re-form down
through cirrus[3] to clouds on cracking peaks   40
to the terraced woods and the shapeless town
and its dying shapers

The act is the sliding out
to the shifting rotting
folds of the sands that lip
slipping to reefs and sinking cliffs
that ladder down to the ocean's abyss
and farther down through a thousand seas
of the mantling rock
to the dense unbeating black unapproachable   50
heart of this world

Lanknosed[4] lady sits on a seawall
not alone   she sits with an older book
Who is it?   Shakespeare   Sophocles   Simenon?[5]
They are tranced as sinners unafraid
in the common gaze to pursue
under hard covers their private quaint barren
affair   though today there is no unbusy body
but me to throw them a public look

    not this wrinkled triad of tourists   60
    strayed off the trail from the rank zoo
    peering away from irrelevant sea
    seeking a starred sign for the bus-stop
    They dangle plastic totems   a kewpie[6]
    a Hong Kong puzzle for somebody's child
    who waits to be worshipped
    back on the prairie farm

    No nor the two manlings
    all muscles and snorkels and need to shout
    with Canadian voices   Nipponese[7] bodies   70

---

3. **cirrus** Thin, fleecy cloud. 4. **Lanknosed** Long-nosed. 5. **Shakespeare, Sophocles, Simenon** William Shakespeare
(1564–1616), Greek poet Sophocles (495–506 BC), and Belgian-American novelist Georges Simenon (1903–1989).
6. **kewpie** A brand of small, fat doll. 7. **Nipponese** Japanese.

racing each other into the chilling waters
last maybe of whatever summer's swimmers

Nor for certain the gamey old gaffer
asleep on the bench like a local Buddha
above them   buttonedup mackinaw[8]
Sally Ann trousers   writing in stillness
his own last book   under the squashed
cock of his hat   with a bawdy plot
she never will follow

80   A tremor only of all his dream
runs like fear from under the hat
through the burned face to twitch
one broken boot   at the other end
of the bench as I pass

dreaming my own unraveled plots
between eating water and eaten shore
    in this hour of the tired and homing
retired   dissolving
    in the days of the separate wait
90   for the mass dying
and I   having clambered down to the last
shelf of the gasping world of lungs
do not know why I too wait   and stare
before descending the final step
into the clouds of the sea

III

The beat beating   is the soft cheek
nudging of the sly   shoving   almost
immortal ocean at work
on the earth's liquidation

100   Outward the sun   explodes light
like a mild rehearsal of light to come
over the vitreous[9] waters
At this edge of the blast
a young girl sits on a granite bench
so still as if already only
silhouette burned in the stone

Two women pass in a cloud of words
    ... so I said   You're *not*!?

---

8. mackinaw Short, often plaid, wool coat. **9. vitreous** Glasslike.

and she said   I *am*!
I'm one of the Lockeys!
Not the Lockeys of *Out*garden surely
I said   *Yes* she said   but I live
in Winnipeg now   Why for heaven's *sake*
I said   then you *must* know Carl *Thorson*?
Carl? she said   he's my cousin by marriage
He *is* I said   why he's *mine* too! So....   110

Born from the glare come the freakish forms
of tugs   all bows and swollen funnels
straining to harbour in False Creek
and blindly followed by mute scows[10]   120
   with islets of gravel to thicken the city
   and square bowls of saffron sawdust
   the ground meal of the manstruck forest
or towing shining grids of the trees stricken

At the edge of knowledge the *Prince Apollo*
   (or is it the *Princess Helen*[11]?)
floats in a paperblue fusion of air
gulf   Mykenean islands[12]
and crawls with its freight of flesh
toward the glare and the night waiting   130
behind the hidden Gate of the Lions[13]

IV

The beat is the slap slip   nudging
as the ledges are made   unmade
by the lurching swaying of all the world
that lies under the spinning air

from the dead centre and the fiery circles
up through the ooze to black liquidities
up to the vast moats
where the doomed whales are swimming
by the weedy walls of sunless Carcassonnes[14]   140
rising   rising   to the great eels waiting
in salt embrasures[15]   and swirling up
to the twilit roofs that floor the Gulf
up to the crab-scratched sands
of the dappled Banks

---

10. **scows** Flat-bottomed boats. 11. **Apollo, Helen** Apollo was the Greek god of archery, medicine, and truth. Helen's abduction by Paris of Troy initiated the Trojan War. 12. **Mykenean islands** Greek islands in the Aegean Sea, named after the Trojan War hero Mycenae. 13. **Gate of the Lions** A gate in Jerusalem's old city walls. 14. **Carcassonnes** Medieval walled city in southern France. 15. **embrasures** Small openings in fort walls through which cannons were fired.

into the sunblazed living mud
and the radiant mussels
that armour the rocks

150   and I on the path at the high-tide edge
           wandering under the leafless maples
           between the lost salt home
           and the asphalt ledge where carhorns call
           call in the clotting air by a shore
           where shamans never again will sound
           with moon-snail conch the ritual plea
           to brother salmon or vanished seal
           and none ever heard
           the horn of Triton[16] or merman

V

160   *The beat is the bob   dip   dipping*
           in the small waves   of the ducks shoring
           and the shored rocks that seem to move
           from turning earth or breathing ocean
           in the dazzling slant of the cooling sun

           Through piled backyards of the sculptor sea
           I climb   over discarded hemlock saurians[17]
                Medusae cedar-stumps   muscled horsemen
                Tartars or Crees[18]   sandsunk forever
           and past the raw sawed butt
                telltale with brands
170   of a buccaneered boom-log
                whisked away to a no-question mill

           all the swashing topmost reach of the sea
                that is also the deepest
                reach of wrens   the vanishing squirrel
                and the spilling city
           the stinking ledge disputed by barnacles
           waiting for tiderise to kick in their food
           contested by jittery sandfleas
           and hovering gulls that are half-sounds only
180   traced overhead   lone as my half-thoughts
                wheeling too with persistence of hunger
                or floating on scraps of flotsam

---

16. **Triton** Greek merman god, son of Poseidon, god of the sea; controlled the waves by blowing a conch-shell horn.
17. **saurians** Dinosaurs. 18. **Tartars, Crees** Tartars were a Central Asian ethnic group who invaded westward in the middle ages; the Cree are an indigenous group from Western Canada (now dispersed throughout).

VI

Slowly   scarcely sensed   the beat
has been quickening now as the air
from the whitened peaks is falling
faraway sliding   pouring down
through the higher canyons and over
knolls and roofs to a oneway urgent
procession of rhythms

blowing the haze from False Creek's girders   190
where now I walk as the waves stream
from my feet to the bay to the far shore
where they lap like dreams that never reach

The tree-barbed tip of Point Grey's lance
has failed again to impale the gone sun
Clouds and islands float together
out from the darkening bandsaw of suburbs
and burn like sodium over the sunset waters

Something   is it only the wind?
above a jungle of harbour masts   200
is playing paperchase with the persons
of starlings   They sift and fall
stall and soar   turning
  as I too turn   with the need to feel
  once more the yielding of moist sand
  and thread the rocks back to the seawall

shadowed and empty now
of booklost ladies or flickering wrens
and beyond to the Boats for Hire
where a thin old Swede clings in his chair   210
like hope to the last light

eyeing bluely the girls with rackets
padding back from belated tennis
while herring gulls make civic statues
of three posts on the pier
and all his child-bright boats
heave unwanted to winter sleep

  Further the shore dips   and the sea   sullen
  with sludge from floors of barges   spits
  arrogantly over the Harbour Board's wall   220
  and only the brutish prow of something
  a troller perhaps   lies longdrowned

on an Ararat[19] of broken clamshells
and the flakings of dead crabs

The shore snouts up again
spilling beachlogs glossy and dry
as sloughed snakeskins
but with sodden immovable hearts
heigh ho the logs that no one wants
230   and the men that sit on the logs
that no one wants
while the sea repeats what it said
to the first unthinking frogs
and the green wounds of the granite stones

By cold depths and by cliffs
whose shine will pass any moment now
the shore puts an end to my ledge
and I climb past the dried shell
of the children's pool   waiting like faith
240   for summer   to where the last leaves
of the shore's alders[20]   glistening with salt
have turned the ragged lawns
to a battlefield bright with their bodies

VII

For the time is after the scarring of maples
torn by the fall's first fury of air
on the nearest shelf above brine and sand
where the world of the dry troubling begins

the first days of the vitreous fusing
of deserts   the proud irradiations of air
250   in the years when men rise
and fall   from the moon's ledge

while the moon sends   as before
the waters swirling up and back
from the bay's world
to this darkening bitten shore
I turn to the terraced road
the cold steps to the bland new block
the human-encrusted reefs
that rise here higher than firs or singing
260   up to aseptic[21] penthouse hillforts

---

19. Ararat In the Biblical story, the landing place of Noah's ark after the great flood; a mountain in Turkey.
20. alders Woody flowering shrubs. **21. aseptic** Sterile.

to antennae above the crosses
pylons marching over the peaks
of mountains without Olympus[22]

Higher than clouds and strata of jetstreams
the air-roads wait the two-way traffic
And beyond?   The desert planets
What else?   a galaxy-full perhaps
of suns and penthouses waiting

But still on the highest shelf of ever
washed by the curve of timeless returnings
lies the unreached unreachable nothing
whose winds wash down to the human shores
and slip   shoving

into each thought nudging my footsteps now
as I turn to my brief night's ledge

in the last of warmth
and the fading of brightness
on the sliding edge of the beating sea

270

(1964)

Sinclair Ross (1908–1996)

Sinclair Ross was born on a farm near Shellbrook, Saskatchewan, in 1908. When he was seven years old, his parents separated, and his mother left the farm, taking young "Jimmy" (as he was known to his friends) with her and leaving the two older Ross children behind. She managed to support herself and her son by working as a housekeeper for a series of employers, but she was never able to come to terms with her slide in social status — Ross recalls that she told "great whoppers" about her past in order to save face, and this would become one bone of contention between them as Ross matured. But Ross did learn from his mother the joys and pitfalls of imaginative escape.

His early education was sporadic and his access to literature limited, but he loved to read, so he visited and revisited all the classic texts he could lay his hands on, among them works by Shakespeare and George Eliot. Encouraged by his mother, he became a voracious reader, and as he grew, his taste in literature became broad and eclectic. In a 1976 letter to critic Lorraine McMullen, he included a list of books he had enjoyed, but he also observed, "I have never been a 'disciple' of anyone. I have often been impressed by a book or author, but it has been my way to wish I could do it and pass on."

In 1924, after completing grade 11, Ross went to work for the Royal Bank in Abbey, Saskatchewan. He would work for that institution continuously — except for a four-year stint

---

22. **Olympus** Mount Olympus was the home of the Greek gods.

in the army — until he retired. Still sharing living quarters with his domineering mother, he taught Sunday school and played piano in church in his spare time. During the nine years the two lived in Saskatchewan, Ross wrote several stories and submitted them to magazines, meeting with little success. In 1933, the bank transferred him to Winnipeg, Manitoba, and the next year his "No Other Way" won third prize in the *Nash's Pall Mall Magazine* short story competition. The story was published in that British periodical accompanied by a biographical note, in which Ross said he was exploiting the short story form "to build up a better technique without the cramping grind that writing a novel after office hours demands."

The contest win heralded a change in Ross's publishing fortunes. Between 1935 and 1950, *Queen's Quarterly* would publish all but three of his short stories, including "A Field of Wheat" (1935), "The Lamp at Noon" (1938), "The Painted Door" (1939), and "Cornet at Night" (1939). The stylistic development between "No Other Way" and "A Field of Wheat" was notable. Ross had found his voice, expressing himself in a mix of simple sentences, elliptical dashes, and sentence fragments; his preoccupation with the phrasing and rhythm of prose is evident and clearly enhanced by his musical abilities.

Ross's stories were collected in *The Lamp at Noon and Other Stories* (1968) and *The Race and Other Stories* (1982). Most are set in rural Saskatchewan during the Great Depression and they are concerned with the individual imagination simultaneously oppressed by wilderness and aroused by the beauty of the natural world; they feature artist figures who feel smothered by the tedium of rural existence and married couples whose relations are strained by the rigours of farm life. Small children are engulfed by their parents' oppressive relationships, and boys (like Tom in "A Cornet at Night") are attracted to young male artists who do not conform to masculine norms. The stories Ross wrote after 1938 also explore illicit sex, marital infidelity, and the prospect of living with guilt and suffering. The author's own unresolved sexuality — he was drawn to both men and women — feeds a thematic tension in much of his fiction.

In 1941, Ross published the novel *As for Me and My House*. It was well, if sparsely, reviewed, but it sold poorly. Years later, in 1957, it was reissued as part of McClelland and Stewart's popular and influential New Canadian Library series, at which point it received a new wave of critical attention and became a standard on university syllabi. It chronicles, in diary form, the thoughts of a pastor's wife during a conflict-ridden year spent in Horizon, a small prairie town hit hard by the Depression. Mr. Bentley has lost his faith and struggles to find salvation through art; Mrs. Bentley, while accusing her husband of infidelity, pursues a close friendship with their neighbour, Paul. As the year progresses, the battle of wills between the childless Bentleys rages quietly.

By employing Mrs. Bentley as first-person narrator of his tale, Ross creates a spiral of complications. As critic Morton L. Ross notes, the reader is treated to the "spectacle of a remarkably active, complex, and dynamic consciousness, a shaping intelligence fully engaged, not to say embattled, with her world." But Mrs. Bentley (whose first name we never learn) is a highly unreliable narrator who withholds information and manipulates her audience's perceptions. The reader is forced to question every aspect of the dramatic reality as it unfolds. *As for Me and My House* is a conflicted and difficult text, and this may account for the lukewarm reception it initially received and the fascination it holds for critics of a more recent era, who thrive on textual ambiguity.

In 1942, Ross joined the army and was sent to London, England, to work at Canadian Army Headquarters. He remained at the post until 1946. When he was demobilized, he resumed his employment at the Royal Bank; he was transferred to the bank's main branch in Montreal, where he would stay until he retired.

After an extended interval, Ross produced a second novel: *The Well* (1958). Like *As for Me and My House*, it focuses on revealing the psychological reality of a single character, but here Ross returns to the technique of third-person narration he used in his short fiction. The central character, Chris Rowe, is a petty criminal who takes refuge on a prairie farm, offering his services as a hired man. Soon, however, he is drawn into an illicit liaison with the farmer's young wife, who tries to draw him into a plot to murder her wealthy husband. *Whir of Gold* (1970), Ross's third novel, is set in Montreal; it also incorporates a love triangle and features a restless young man — Sonny McAlpine, who dreams of being a clarinetist. Both novels portray divided loyalties and claustrophobic heterosexual relations.

Ross's most experimental novel is *Sawbones Memorial* (1974). It marks the first time that Ross abandoned a single narrative voice, opting instead for a series of voices, and it is modelled on *Diner en ville* by avant-garde French novelist Claude Mauriac. Set in the fictional town of Upward, Saskatchewan, it is cobbled together from snippets of conversation, bits of interior monologue, and speech — all depicting a gathering in celebration of the town doctor, who is retiring. Through the interwoven narrative, revelations are made and characters develop as celebrants talk, think, give speeches, and sing. We discover that Doc Hunter, who has risen in social standing by outwardly adhering to the town's moral conventions, has made some questionable professional decisions and has been unfaithful to his wife. Upward, which initially appears orderly and benign, gradually emerges as community tainted by corruption and repression.

Retiring in 1968, Ross went to live for a time in Greece and Spain. In 1980, he returned to Canada, eventually settling in Vancouver. Recognition of his literary contribution was long in coming, but a symposium on his work was held at the University of Ottawa in 1990; two years later, he was made a Member of the Order of Canada, and in 1993, the Saskatchewan Arts Board honoured him with a lifetime achievement award. Ross died in 1996, after a 20-year battle with Parkinson's disease.

The Lamp at Noon

A little before noon she lit the lamp. Demented wind fled keening past the house: a wail through the eaves that died every minute or two. Three days now without respite it had held. The dust was thickening to an impenetrable fog.

She lit the lamp, then for a long time stood at the window motionless. In dim, fitful outline the stable and oat granary still were visible; beyond, obscuring fields and landmarks, the lower of dust clouds made the farmyard seem an isolated acre, poised aloft above a sombre void. At each blast of wind it shook, as if to topple and spin hurtling with the dust-reel into space.

From the window she went to the door, opening it a little, and peering toward the stable again. He was not coming yet. As she watched there was a sudden rift overhead, and for a moment through the tattered clouds the sun raced like a wizened orange. It shed a soft, diffused light, dim and yellow as if it were the light from the lamp reaching out through the open door.

She closed the door, and going to the stove tried the potatoes with a fork. Her eyes all the while were fixed and wide with a curious immobility. It was the window. Standing at it, she had let her forehead press against the pane until the eyes were strained apart and rigid. Wide like that they had looked out of the deepening ruin of the storm. Now she could not close them.

The baby started to cry. He was lying in a homemade crib over which she had arranged a tent of muslin.[1] Careful not to disturb the folds of it, she knelt and tried to still him, whispering huskily in a singsong voice that he must hush and go to sleep again. She would have liked to rock him, to feel the comfort of his little body in her arms, but a fear obsessed her that in the dust-filled air he might contract pneumonia. There was dust sifting everywhere. Her own throat was parched with it. The table had been set less than ten minutes, and already a film was gathering on the dishes. The little cry continued, and with wincing, frightened lips she glanced around as if to find a corner where the air was less oppressive. But while the lips winced the eyes maintained their wide, immobile stare. "Sleep," she whispered again. "It's too soon for you to be hungry. Daddy's coming for his dinner."

He seemed a long time. Even the clock, still a few minutes off noon, could not dispel a foreboding sense that he was longer than he should be. She went to the door again — and then recoiled slowly to stand white and breathless in the middle of the room. She mustn't. He would only despise her if she ran to the stable looking for him. There was too much grim endurance in his nature ever to let him understand the fear and weakness of a woman. She must stay quiet and wait. Nothing was wrong. At noon he would come — and perhaps after dinner stay with her awhile.

Yesterday, and again at breakfast this morning, they had quarrelled bitterly. She wanted him now, the assurance of his strength and nearness, but he would stand aloof, wary, remembering the words she had flung at him in her anger, unable to understand it was only the dust and wind that had driven her.

Tense, she fixed her eyes upon the clock, listening. There were two winds: the wind in flight, and the wind that pursued. The one sought refuge in the eaves, whimpering, in fear; the other assailed it there, and shook the eaves apart to make it flee again. Once as she listened this first wind sprang inside the room, distraught like a bird that has felt the graze of talons on its wing; while furious the other wind shook the walls, and thudded tumbleweeds against the window till its quarry glanced away again in fright. But only to return — to return and quake among the feeble eaves, as if in all this dust-mad wilderness it knew no other sanctuary.

Then Paul came. At his step she hurried to the stove, intent upon the pots and frying-pan. "The worst wind yet," he ventured, hanging up his cap and smock. "I had to light the lantern in the tool shed, too."

They looked at each other, then away. She wanted to go to him, to feel his arms supporting her, to cry a little just that he might soothe her, but because his presence made the menace of the wind seem less, she gripped herself and thought, "I'm in the right. I won't give in. For his sake, too, I won't."

He washed, hurriedly, so that a few dark welts of dust remained to indent upon his face a haggard strength. It was all she could see as she wiped the dishes and set the food before him: the strength, the grimness, the young Paul growing old and hard, buckled against a desert even grimmer than his will. "Hungry?" she asked, touched to a twinge of pity she had not intended. "There's dust in everything. It keeps coming faster than I can clean it up."

He nodded. "Tonight, though, you'll see it go down. This is the third day."

---

1. **muslin** A cotton fabric, usually used for sheets.

She looked at him in silence a moment, and then as if to herself muttered broodingly, "Until the next time. Until it starts again."

There was a dark resentment in her voice now that boded another quarrel. He waited, his eyes on her dubiously as she mashed a potato with her fork. The lamp between them threw strong lights and shadows on their faces. Dust and drought, earth that betrayed alike his labour and his faith, to him the struggle had given sternness, an impassive courage. Beneath the whip of sand his youth had been effaced. Youth, zest, exuberance — there remained only a harsh and clenched virility that yet became him, that seemed at the cost of more engaging qualities to be fulfilment of his inmost and essential nature. Whereas to her the same debts and poverty had brought a plaintive indignation, a nervous dread of what was still to come. The eyes were hollowed, the lips pinched dry and colourless. It was the face of a woman that had aged without maturing, that had loved the little vanities of life, and lost them wistfully.

"I'm afraid, Paul," she said suddenly. "I can't stand it any longer. He cries all the time. You will go, Paul — say you will. We aren't living here — not really living — "

The pleading in her voice now, after its shrill bitterness yesterday, made him think that this was only another way to persuade him. He answered evenly, "I told you this morning, Ellen; we keep on right where we are. At least I do. It's yourself you're thinking about, not the baby."

This morning such an accusation would have stung her to rage; now, her voice swift and panting, she pressed on, "Listen, Paul — I'm thinking of all of us — you, too. Look at the sky — what's happening. Are you blind? Thistles and tumbleweeds — it's a desert. You won't have a straw this fall. You won't be able to feed a cow or a chicken. Please, Paul, say we'll go away — "

"Go where?" His voice as he answered was still remote and even, inflexibly in unison with the narrowed eyes and the great hunch of muscle-knotted shoulder. "Even as a desert it's better than sweeping out your father's store and running his errands. That's all I've got ahead of me if I do what you want."

"And here — " she faltered. "What's ahead of you here? At least we'll get enough to eat and wear when you're sweeping out his store. Look at it — look at it, you fool. Desert — the lamp lit at noon — "

"You'll see it come back. There's good wheat in it yet."

"But in the meantime — year after year — can't you understand, Paul? We'll never get them back — "

He put down his knife and fork and leaned toward her across the table. "I can't go, Ellen. Living off your people — charity — stop and think of it. This is where I belong. I can't do anything else."

"Charity!" she repeated him, letting her voice rise in derision. "And this — you call this independence! Borrowed money you can't even pay the interest on, seed from the government — grocery bills — doctor bills — "

"We'll have crops again," he persisted. "Good crops — the land will come back. It's worth waiting for."

"And while we're waiting, Paul!" It was not anger now, but a kind of sob. "Think of me — and him. It's not fair. We have our lives, too, to live."

"And you think that going home to your family — taking your husband with you — "

"I don't care — anything would be better than this. Look at the air he's breathing. He cries all the time. For his sake, Paul. What's ahead of him here, even if you do get crops?"

He clenched his lips a minute, then, with his eyes hard and contemptuous, struck back, "As much as in town, growing up a pauper. You're the one who wants to go, it's not for his sake. You think that in town you'd have a better time — not so much work — more clothes — "

"Maybe — " She dropped her head defencelessly. "I'm young still. I like pretty things."

There was silence now — a deep fastness of it enclosed by rushing wind and creaking walls. It seemed the yellow lamplight cast a hush upon them. Through the haze of dusty air the walls receded, dimmed, and came again. At last she raised her head and said listlessly, "Go on — your dinner's getting cold. Don't sit and stare at me. I've said it all."

The spent quietness in her voice was even harder to endure than her anger. It reproached him, against his will insisted that he see and understand her lot. To justify himself he tried, "I was a poor man when you married me. You said you didn't mind. Farming's never been easy, and never will be."

"I wouldn't mind the work or the skimping if there was something to look forward to. It's the hopelessness — going on — watching the land blow away."

"The land's all right," he repeated. "The dry years won't last forever."

"But it's not just dry years, Paul!" The little sob in her voice gave way suddenly to a ring of exasperation. "Will you never see? It's the land itself — the soil. You've plowed and harrowed until there's not a root or fibre left to hold it down. That's why the soil drifts — that's why in a year or two there'll be nothing left but the bare clay. If in the first place you farmers had taken care of your land — if you hadn't been so greedy for wheat every year — "

She had taught school before she married him, and of late in her anger there had been a kind of disdain, an attitude almost of condescension, as if she no longer looked upon the farmers as her equals. He sat still, his eyes fixed on the yellow lamp flame, and seeming to know her words had hurt him, she went on softly, "I want to help you, Paul. That's why I won't sit quiet while you go on wasting your life. You're only thirty — you owe it to yourself as well as me."

He sat staring at the lamp without answering, his mouth sullen. It seemed indifference now, as if he were ignoring her, and stung to anger again she cried, "Do you ever think what my life is? Two rooms to live in — once a month to town, and nothing to spend when I get there. I'm still young — I wasn't brought up this way."

"You're a farmer's wife now. It doesn't matter what you used to be, or how you were brought up. You get enough to eat and wear. Just now that's all I can do. I'm not to blame that we've been dried out five years."

"Enough to eat!" she laughed back shrilly. "Enough salt pork — enough potatoes and eggs. And look — " Springing to the middle of the room she thrust out a foot for him to see the scuffed old slipper. "When they're completely gone I suppose you'll tell me I can go barefoot — that I'm a farmer's wife — that it's not your fault we're dried out — "

"And what about these?" He pushed his chair away from the table now to let her see what he was wearing. "Cowhide — hard as boards — but my feet are so calloused I don't feel them any more."

Then he stood up, ashamed of having tried to match her hardships with his own. But frightened now as he reached for his smock she pressed close to him. "Don't go yet. I brood and worry when I'm left alone. Please, Paul — you can't work on the land anyway."

"And keep on like this? You start before I'm through the door. Week in and week out — I've troubles enough of my own."

"Paul — please stay — " The eyes were glazed now, distended a little as if with the intensity of her dread and pleading. "We won't quarrel any more. Hear it! I can't work — I just stand still and listen — "

The eyes frightened him, but responding to a kind of instinct that he must withstand her, that it was his self-respect and manhood against the fretful weakness of a woman, he answered unfeelingly, "In here safe and quiet — you don't know how well off you are. If you were out in it — fighting it — swallowing it — "

"Sometimes, Paul, I wish I was. I'm so caged — if I could only break away and run. See — I stand like this all day. I can't relax. My throat's so tight it aches — "

With a jerk he freed his smock from her clutch. "If I stay we'll only keep on all afternoon. Wait till tomorrow — we'll talk things over when the wind goes down."

Then without meeting her eyes again he swung outside, and doubled low against the buffets of the wind, fought his way slowly toward the stable. There was a deep hollow calm within, a vast darkness engulfed beneath the tides of moaning wind. He stood breathless a moment, hushed almost to a stupor by the sudden extinction of the storm and the stillness that enfolded him. It was a long, far-reaching stillness. The first dim stalls and rafters led the way into cavern-like obscurity, into vaults and recesses that extended far beyond the stable walls. Nor in these first quiet moments did he forbid the illusion, the sense of release from a harsh, familiar world into one of peace and darkness. The contentious mood that his stand against Ellen had roused him to, his tenacity and clenched despair before the ravages of wind, it was ebbing now, losing itself in the cover of darkness. Ellen and the wheat seemed remote, unimportant. At a whinny from the bay mare, Bess, he went forward and into her stall. She seemed grateful for his presence, and thrust her nose deep between his arm and body. They stood a long time motionless, comforting and assuring each other.

For soon again the first deep sense of quiet and peace was shrunken to the battered shelter of the stable. Instead of release or escape from the assaulting wind, the walls were but a feeble stand against it. They creaked and sawed as if the fingers of a giant were tightening to collapse them; the empty loft sustained a pipelike cry that rose and fell but never ended. He saw the dust-black sky again, and his fields blown smooth with drifted soil.

But always, even while listening to the storm outside, he could feel the tense and apprehensive stillness of the stable. There was not a hoof that clumped or shifted, not a rub of halter against manger. And yet, though it had been a strange stable, he would have known, despite the darkness, that every stall was filled. They, too, were all listening.

From Bess he went to the big grey gelding, Prince. Prince was twenty years old, with rib-grooved sides and high, protruding hipbones. Paul ran his hand over the ribs, and felt a sudden shame, a sting of fear that Ellen might be right in what she said. For wasn't it true — nine years a farmer now on his own land, and still he couldn't even feed his horses? What, then could he hope to do for his wife and son?

There was much he planned. And so vivid was the future of his planning, so real and constant, that often the actual present was but half felt, but half endured. Its difficulties were lessened by a confidence in what lay beyond them. A new house — land for the boy — land and still more land — or education, whatever he might want.

But all the time was he only a blind and stubborn fool? Was Ellen right? Was he trampling on her life, and throwing away his own? The five years since he married her, were they to go on repeating themselves, five, ten, twenty, until all the brave future he looked forward to was but a stark and futile past?

She looked forward to no future. She had no faith or dream with which to make the dust and the poverty less real. He understood suddenly. He saw her face again as only a few minutes ago it had begged him not to leave her. The darkness round him now was as a slate on which her lonely terror limned itself. He went from Prince to the other horses, combing their manes and forelocks with his fingers, but always it was her face before him, its staring eyes and twisted suffering. "See Paul — I stand like this all day. I just stand still — My throat's so tight it aches — "

And always the wind, the creak of walls, the wild lipless wailing through the loft. Until at last as he stood there, staring into the livid face before him it seemed that this scream of wind was a cry from her parched and frantic lips. He knew it couldn't be, he knew that she was safe within the house, but still the wind persisted in a woman's cry. The cry of a woman with eyes like those that watched him through the dark. Eyes that were mad now — lips that even as they cried still pleaded, "See Paul — I stand like this all day. I just stand still — so caged! If I could only run!"

He saw her running, pulled and driven headlong by the wind, but when at last he returned to the house, compelled by his anxiety, she was walking quietly back and forth with the baby in her arms. Careful, despite his concern, not to reveal a fear or weakness that she might think capitulation to her wishes, he watched a moment through the window, and then went off to the tool shed to mend harness. All afternoon he stitched and riveted. It was easier with the lantern lit and his hands occupied. There was a wind whining high past the tool shed too, but it was only wind. He remembered the arguments with which Ellen had tried to persuade him away from the farm, and one by one he defeated them. There would be rain again — next year or the next. Maybe in his ignorance he had farmed his land the wrong way, seeding wheat every year, working the soil till it was lifeless dust — but he would do better now. He would plant clover and alfalfa, breed cattle, acre by acre and year by year restore to his land its fibre and fertility. That was something to work for, a way to prove himself. It was ruthless wind, blackening the sky with his earth, but it was not his master. Out of his land it had made a wilderness. He now, out of the wilderness, would make a farm and home again.

Tonight he must talk with Ellen. Patiently, when the wind was down, and they were both quiet again. It was she who had told him to grow fibrous crops, who had called him an ignorant fool because he kept on with summer fallow and wheat. Now she might be gratified to find him acknowledging her wisdom. Perhaps she would begin to feel the power and steadfastness of the land, to take a pride in it, to understand that he was not a fool, but working for her future and their son's.

And already the wind was slackening. At four o'clock he could sense a lull. At five, straining his eyes from the tool shed doorway, he could make out a neighbour's buildings half a mile away. It was over — three days of blight and havoc like a scourge — three days so bitter and so long that for a moment he stood still, unseeing, his senses idle with a numbness of relief.

But only for a moment. Suddenly he emerged from the numbness; suddenly the fields before him struck his eyes to comprehension. They lay black, naked. Beaten and mounded smooth with dust as if a sea in gentle swell had turned to stone. And though he had tried to prepare himself for such a scene, though he had known since yesterday that not a blade would last the storm, still now, before the utter waste confronting him, he sickened and stood cold. Suddenly like the fields he was naked. Everything that had sheathed him a little from the realities of existence: vision and purpose, faith in the land, in the future, in himself — it was all rent now, stripped away. "Desert," he heard her voice begin to sob. "Desert, you fool — the lamp lit at noon!"

In the stable again, measuring out their feed to the horses, he wondered what he would say to her tonight. For so deep were his instincts of loyalty to the land that still, even with the images of his betrayal stark upon his mind, his concern was how to withstand her, how to go on again and justify himself. It had not occurred to him yet that he might or should abandon the land. He had lived with it too long. Rather was his impulse still to defend it — as a man defends against the scorn of strangers even his most worthless kin.

He fed his horses, then waited. She too would be waiting, ready to cry at him, "Look now — that crop that was to feed and clothe us! And you'll still keep on! You'll still say 'Next year — there'll be rain next year'!"

But she was gone when he reached the house. The door was open, the lamp blown out, the crib empty. The dishes from their meal at noon were still on the table. She had perhaps begun to sweep, for the broom was lying in the middle of the floor. He tried to call, but a terror clamped upon his throat. In the wan, returning light it seemed that even the deserted kitchen was straining to whisper what it had seen. The tatters of the storm still whimpered through the eaves, and in their moaning told the desolation of the miles they had traversed. On tiptoe at last he crossed to the adjoining room; then at the threshold, without even a glance inside to satisfy himself that she was really gone, he wheeled again and plunged outside.

He ran a long time — distraught and headlong as a few hours ago he had seemed to watch her run — around the farmyard, a little distance into the pasture, back again blindly to the house to see whether she had returned — and then at a stumble down the road for help.

They joined him in the search, rode away for others, spread calling across the fields in the direction she might have been carried by the wind — but nearly two hours later it was himself who came upon her. Crouched down against a drift of sand as if for shelter, her hair in matted strands around her neck and face, the child clasped tightly in her arms.

The child was quite cold. It had been her arms, perhaps, too frantic to protect him, or the smother of dust upon his throat and lungs. "Hold him," she said as he knelt beside her. "So — with his face away from the wind. Hold him until I tidy my hair."

Her eyes were still wide in an immobile stare, but with her lips she smiled at him. For a long time he knelt transfixed, trying to speak to her, touching fearfully with his fingertips the dust-grimed cheeks and eyelids of the child. At last she said, "I'll take him again. Such clumsy hands — you don't know how to hold a baby yet. See how his head falls forward on your arm."

Yet it all seemed familiar — a confirmation of what he had known since noon. He gave her the child, then, gathering them up in his arms, struggled to his feet, and turned toward home.

It was evening now. Across the fields a few spent clouds of dust still shook and fled. Beyond, as if through smoke, the sunset smouldered like a distant fire.

He walked with a long dull stride, his eyes before him, heedless of her weight. Once he glanced down and with her eyes she still was smiling. "Such strong arms, Paul — and I was so tired just carrying him...."

He tried to answer, but it seemed that now the dusk was drawn apart in breathless waiting, a finger on its lips until they passed. "You were right, Paul...." Her voice came whispering, as if she too could feel the hush. "You said tonight we'd see the storm go down. So still now, and a red sky — it means tomorrow will be fine."

(1938)

A.M. Klein (1909–1972)

In January of 1943, A.M. Klein wrote a letter to his friend A.J.M. Smith, who was putting the finishing touches on *The Book of Canadian Poetry* (1943), an anthology that would include Klein's work. Responding to Smith's request for a brief statement of his artistic values, Klein declared: "I am surprised that you ask it. You know that such questions elicit only the sheerest of arrogant balderdash.... Simply expressed, I write poetry only to reveal my civilization, my sensitivities, my craftsmanship."

Throughout his literary career, the poet wrote on behalf of his civilization. Not only did he continually delve into his Jewish heritage and historical and contemporary Jewish themes, but he also wrote perceptively and compassionately of the culture of his French Canadian neighbours. He wrote to reveal his sensitivities; his poetry, fiction, criticism, and journalism, though often addressed to a large reading public, were rooted in a very personal vision. His oeuvre displays his craftsmanship, as he experimented with countless traditional verse forms and skilfully employed numerous genres. And his work demonstrates his love of language — a love evident in his poem "Portrait of the Poet as Landscape."

However, in his observations to Smith, Klein failed to acknowledge the element of social consciousness in his work. Although he may not have believed that his writing could affect the world, the desire for social change infused his writing. In his verse and prose, he confronted anti-Semitism and condemned Nazism; and through his use of Zionist themes, he expressed his commitment to the establishment of a Jewish nation.

Abraham Moses Klein was born in 1909, in Ratno, Ukraine. In 1910, his family immigrated to Montreal and took up residence in the Jewish ghetto, whose nucleus was St. Lawrence Boulevard. Klein had an Orthodox upbringing in this community, and he contemplated entering a yeshiva, but he finally chose to pursue a secular education. Graduating from McGill University with a B.A. in 1930, he went on to study law at the University of Montreal. In 1939, he established his own law firm.

During his university years, Klein was increasingly drawn to Zionism. He became involved with Canadian Young Judaea, a Zionist youth movement, and he edited its magazine, the *Judaean*. Klein had been writing poetry since the age of 16, and at McGill he became acquainted with a group of writers — A.J.M. Smith, F.R. Scott, Leo Kennedy, and Leon Edel — who were promoting Canadian modernism in the *McGill Fortnightly Review*. As a result, Klein began to work more intently on his poetry, and soon he was publishing work in the *Menorah Journal* (New York) and *Poetry* (Chicago).

After graduation, Klein worked for the *Canadian Zionist* and the *Canadian Jewish Chronicle*, writing prolifically during a period that encompassed the rise of Nazism, World War II, and the establishment of the state of Israel. He also became a speechwriter for Samuel Bronfman (the president of the Canadian Jewish Congress) and was involved with the CCF (the forerunner of the NDP). During these years, Klein continued to work on his poetry and fiction. His first published collection of poetry, *Hath Not a Jew…* appeared in 1940; his second, *Poems*, appeared in 1944. These volumes contain pieces that range in form from satire to psalm, and the poet's tone fluctuates from playful and witty to prophetic and severe. He repeatedly returns to the theme of anti-Semitism, and many of the poems convey a great sense of gravity. Also in 1944, Klein published *The Hitleriad*, a satiric attack on Nazism written in a style that recalls that of Alexander Pope's mock-epic poem *The Dunciad*. *The Hitleriad* was not well received — Klein's choice of genre was deemed inappropriate for the work's subject.

In the early 1940s, Klein's exchanges with some of the poets working on the journals *Preview* and *First Statement* — such as Patrick Anderson, P.K. Page, and Irving Layton — prompted him to explore a more unadorned, less romantic style. During this time, he produced *The Rocking Chair and Other Poems,* which won the Governor General's Award in 1949. The poems in this volume centre on the province of Quebec and its citizens. French Canadian society, with its determination to preserve its traditions and cultural identity, reminded Klein of his own culture; he has been credited with creating an accurate and empathetic portrait of a group that was routinely over-looked by Canada's English-speaking majority.

In 1949, the Canadian Jewish Congress sent Klein to Israel to report on the newly established state. His only published novel, *The Second Scroll* (1951), is a product of this experi-ence. Klein had been studying and publishing on James Joyce's *Ulysses*, and there are many similarities between Joyce's novel and his own. Like Joyce, Klein employs unconventional methods of storytelling, uses poetic language interwoven with allusion, and creates layers of meaning through symbolism and mythology.

In 1954, Klein had a nervous breakdown. He was ultimately forced to withdraw from public life; he suspended contact with friends and associates and gave up writing. Depression dogged him until he died, in 1972. Klein's long silence has been the subject of much conjecture. It led poets such as Irving Layton and Leonard Cohen to carefully consider what it means to engage in "the destructive element" of our time.

Design for Mediaeval Tapestry

Somewhere a hungry muzzle rooted.
The frogs among the sedges croaked.
Into the night a screech-owl hooted.

A clawed mouse squeaked and struggled, choked.
The wind pushed antlers through the bushes.
Terror stalked through the forest, cloaked.

Was it a robber broke the hushes?
Was it a knight in armoured thews,[1]
Walking in mud, and bending rushes?

Was it a provost[2] seeking Jews?
The Hebrews shivered; their teeth rattled;
Their beards glittered with gelid[3] dews.

10

---

1. **thews** Muscles. 2. **provost** Administrative official, or the head of a cathedral. 3. **gelid** Icy.

Gulped they their groans, for silence tattled;
They crushed their sighs, for quiet heard;
They had their thoughts on Israel battled

By pagan and by Christian horde.
They moved their lips in pious anguish.
They made no sound. They never stirred.

* * *

Reb[4] Zadoc Has Memories.

Reb Zadoc's brain is a German town:
20   Hermits come from lonely grottos
Preaching the right for Jews to drown;

Soldiers who vaunt their holy mottos
Stroking the cross that is a sword;
Barons plotting in cabal sottos,[5]

A lady spitting on the abhorred.
The market-place and faggot-fire[6] —
A hangman burning God's true word;

A clean-shaved traitor-Jew; a friar
Dropping his beads upon his paunch;
30   The heavens speared by a Gothic spire;[7]

The Judengasse[8] and its stench
Rising from dark and guarded alleys
Where Jew is neighboured to harlot-wench

Perforce ecclesiastic malice;
The exile-booths of Jacob where
Fat burghers[9] come to pawn a chalice

While whistling a Jew-hating air;
Peasants regarding Jews and seeking
The hooves, the tail, the horn-crowned hair;

40   And target for a muddy streaking,
The yellow badge[10] upon the breast,
The vengeance of a papal wreaking;

---

4. Reb Title similar to Mr. **5. cabal sottos** Sottos are low places; Jews have been anti-semitically accused of forming cabals, small and sinister religious groups. **6. faggot-fire** "Faggot" once meant "burning stick." **7. spire** Point of a steeple or roof. **8. Judengasse** German term for a Jewish ghetto. **9. burghers** Middle-class citizens. **10. yellow badge** Jews were forced to wear identifying badges.

The imposts paid for this fine crest;
Gay bailiffs serving writs of seizure;
Even the town fool and his jest —

Stroking his beard with slowly leisure,
A beard that was but merely down,
Rubbing his palms with gloating pleasure,

Counting fictitious crown after crown.
Reb Zadoc's brain is a torture-dungeon; 50
Reb Zadoc's brain is a German town.

Reb Daniel Shochet[11] *Reflects.*

The toad seeks out its mud; the mouse discovers
The nibbled hole; the sparrow owns its nest;
About the blind mole earthy shelter hovers.

The louse avows the head where it is guest;
Even the roach calls some dark fent his dwelling.
But Israel owns a sepulchre, at best.

Nahum-this-also-is-for-the-good[12] *Ponders.*

The wrath of God is just. His punishment
Is most desirable. The flesh of Jacob
Implores the scourge. For this was Israel meant. 60

Below we have no life. But we will wake up
Beyond, where popes will lave our feet, where princes
Will heed our insignificantest hiccup.

The sins of Israel only blood-shed rinses.
We teach endurance. Lo, we are not spent.
We die, we live; at once we are three tenses.

Our skeletons are bibles; flesh is rent
Only to prove a thesis, stamp a moral.
The rack prepared: for this was Israel meant.

---

11. Shochet Butcher of kosher meat. **12. Nahum-this-also-is-for-the-good** Nahum of Gizmo was a Talmudic rabbi who often said, "This also is for the good." His name means "comforter."

Isaiah Epicure[13] *Avers.*

70   Seek reasons; rifle your theology;
      Philosophize; expend your dialectic;
      Decipher and translate God's diary;

      Discover causes, primal and eclectic;
      I cannot; all I know is this:
      That pain doth render flesh most sore and hectic;

      That lance-points prick; that scorched bones hiss;
      That thumbscrews agonize, and that a martyr
      Is mad if he considers these things bliss.

Job Reviles.

      God is grown ancient. He no longer hears.
80   He has been deafened by his perfect thunders.
      With clouds for cotton he has stopped his ears.

      The Lord is purblind;[14] and his heaven sunders
      Him from the peccadillos[15] of this earth.
      He meditates his youth; he dreams; he wonders.

      His cherubs have acquired beards and girth.
      They cannot move to do his bidding. Even
      The angels yawn. Satan preserves his mirth.

      How long, O Lord, will Israel's heart be riven?
      How long will we cry to a dotard[16] God
90   To let us keep the breath that He has given?

      How long will you sit on your throne, and nod?

Judith[17] *Makes Comparisons.*

      Judith had heard a troubadour
      Singing beneath a castle-turret
      Of truth, chivàlry, and honòur,
      Of virtue, and of gallant merit, —
      Judith had heard a troubadour

---

13. Isaiah Epicure Isaiah is a major Jewish prophet; "Epicure" carries connotations of religious doubt (from the Hebrew), and of pleasure-seeking (Latin). **14. purblind** Nearly blind, or generally unperceptive. **15. peccadillos** Minor sins. **16. dotard** One who has lost his intellect to age. **17. Judith** Seduced and killed the captain of an army that had her city under siege in the biblical Book of Judith; translated in the middle ages. While she succeeded in the biblical telling, her city was, historically speaking, destroyed by the siege.

Lauding the parfait[18] knightly spirit,
Singing beneath the ivied wall.
The cross-marked varlet[19] Judith wrestled
Was not like these at all, at all …   100

Ezekiel the Simple Opines.

If we will fast for forty days; if we
Will read the psalms thrice over; if we offer
To God some blossom-bursting litany,

And to the poor a portion of the coffer;
If we don sack-cloth, and let ashes rain
Upon our heads, despite the boor and scoffer,[20]

Certes,[21] these things will never be again.

Solomon Talmudi Considers His Life.

Rather that these blood-thirsty pious vandals,
Bearing sable[22] in heart, and gules[23] on arm,
Had made me ready for the cerement-candles,   110

Than that they should have taken my one charm
Against mortality, my exegesis:[24]
The script that gave the maggot the alarm.

Jews would have crumpled Rashi's[25] simple thesis
On reading this, and Ibn Ezra's[26] version;
Maimonides[27] they would have torn to pieces.

For here, in black and white, by God's conversion,
I had plucked secrets from the pentateuch,[28]
And gathered strange arcana[29] from dispersion,

The essence and quintessence of the book!   120
Green immortality smiled out its promise —
I hung my gaberdine[30] on heaven's hook.

---

18. parfait Medieval term for "perfect" or "chivalrous." **19. varlet** Rascal or servant. **20. boor and scoffer** Rude fellow
and mocker. **21. Certes** Medieval term for "certainly." **22. sable** Black. **23. gules** Red, in heraldry. **24. exegesis** The
interpretation of Judeo-Christian texts. **25. Rashi** Rabbi Solomon bar Isaac (1040–1105), wrote accessible but thorough
commentaries on the Talmud and Tanakh. **26. Ibn Ezra** Exegetic scholar (1089–1164). **27. Maimonides** Exegetic and
Jewish legal scholar (1135–1204). **28. pentateuch** The first five books of Hebrew scripture. **29. arcana** Specialized
knowledge. **30. gaberdine** Smock.

Refuting Duns, and aquinatic Thomas,[31]
Confounding Moslems, proving the one creed
A simple sentence broken by no commas,

I thought to win myself eternal meed,[32]
I thought to move the soul with sacred lever
And lift the heart to God in very deed.

Ah, woe is me, and to my own endeavour,
130   That on that day they burned my manuscript,
And lost my name, for certain, and for ever!

Simeon Takes Hints from His Environs.

Heaven is God's grimace at us on high.
This land is a cathedral; speech, its sermon.
The moon is a rude gargoyle in the sky.

The leaves rustle. Come, who will now determine
Whether this be the wind, or priestly robes.
The frogs croak out ecclesiastic German,

Whereby our slavish ears have punctured lobes.
The stars are mass-lamps on a lofty altar;
140   Even the angels are Judaeophobes.

There is one path; in it I shall not falter.
Let me rush to the bosom of the state
And church, grasp lawyer-code and monkish psalter,

And being Christianus Simeon, late
Of Jewry, have much comfort and salvation —
Salvation in this life, at any rate.

Esther[33] Hears Echoes of His Voice.

How sweetly did he sing grace after meals!
He now is silent. He has fed on sorrow.
He lies where he is spurned by faithless heels.

150   His voice was honey. Lovers well might borrow
Warmth from his words. His words were musical.
Making the night so sweet, so sweet the morrow!

---

31. Duns, aquinatic Thomas Duns Scotus, Christian theologian (1266–1308) and St. Thomas Aquinas (1225–1274) disagreed over the nature of matter and other issues. **32. meed** Deserved reward. **33. Esther** In the Hebrew Bible, saved the Jews from genocide by pleading with her husband, King Ahasuerus, who granted the Jews new legal rights.

Can I forget the tremors of his call?
Can kiddush benediction[34] be forgotten?
His blood is spilled like wine. The earth is sharp with gall.

As soothing as the promises begotten
Of penitence and love; as lovely as
The turtle-dove; as soft as snow in cotton,

Whether he lulled a child or crooned the laws,
And sacred as the eighteen prayers, so even   160
His voice. His voice was so. His voice that was ...

* * *

The burgher sleeps beside his wife, and dreams
Of human venery,[35] and Hebrew quarry.
His sleep contrives him many little schemes.

There will be Jews, dead, moribund and gory;
There will be booty; there will be dark maids,
And there will be a right good spicy story ...

* * *

The moon has left her vigil. Lucifer[36] fades.
Whither shall we betake ourselves, O Father?
Whither to flee? And where to find our aids?   170

The wrath of people is like foam and lather,
Risen against us. Wherefore, Lord, and why?
The winds assemble; the cold and hot winds gather

To scatter us. They do not heed our cry.
The sun rises and leaps the red horizon,
And like a bloodhound swoops across the sky.

(1931)

Heirloom

My father bequeathed me no wide estates;
No keys and ledgers were my heritage;
Only some holy books with *yahrzeit* dates[1]
Writ mournfully upon a blank front page —

---

34. **kiddush benediction** Celebratory prayer, usually over wine, during a festival. 35. **venery** Sexual pursuits.
36. **Lucifer** The morning star.

---

1. *yahrzeit* **dates** The dates of the deaths of ancestors.

Books of the Baal Shem Tov,[2] and of his wonders;
Pamphlets upon the devil and his crew;
Prayers against road demons, witches, thunders;
And sundry other tomes[3] for a good Jew.

Beautiful: though no pictures on them, save
10   The scorpion crawling on a printed track;
The Virgin floating on a scriptural wave,
Square letters twinkling in the Zodiac.

The snuff left on this page, now brown and old,
The tallow stains of midnight liturgy —
These are my coat of arms, and these unfold
My noble lineage, my proud ancestry!

And my tears, too, have stained this heirloomed ground,
When reading in these treatises some weird
Miracle, I turned a leaf and found
20   A white hair fallen from my father's beard.

(1934)

Autobiographical

1

Out of the ghetto[1] streets where a Jewboy
Dreamed pavement into pleasant bible-land,
Out of the Yiddish slums where childhood met
The friendly beard, the loutish Sabbath-goy,[2]
Or followed, proud, the Torah-escorting band,
Out of the jargoning[3] city I regret,
Rise memories, like sparrows rising from
The gutter-scattered oats,
Like sadness sweet of synagogal hum,
10   Like Hebrew violins
Sobbing delight upon their eastern notes.

2

Again they ring their little bells, those doors
Deemed by the tender-year'd, magnificent:
Old Ashkenazi's cellar, sharp with spice;
The widows' double-parloured candy-stores
And nuggets sweet bought for one sweaty cent;

---

2. Baal Shem Tov Rabbi Yisroel ben Eliezer (1698–1760), generally thought the founder of Hasidic Judaism; he valued moral action above asceticism. **3. sundry other tomes** Various other books.

---

1. ghetto Area populated by Jews. **2. Sabbath-goy** Non-Jewish person employed by a Jewish community to do tasks on the Sabbath. **3. jargoning** Cacophonous.

The warm fresh-smelling bakery, its pies,
Its cakes, its navel'd bellies of black bread;
The lintels candy-poled
Of barber-shop, bright-bottled, green, blue, red;   20
And fruit-stall piled, exotic,
And the big synagogue. door, with letters of gold.

3

Again my kindergarten home is full —
Saturday night — with kin and compatriot:
My brothers playing Russian card-games; my
Mirroring sisters looking beautiful,
Humming the evening's imminent fox-trot;
My uncle Mayer, of blessed memory,
Still murmuring Maariv,[4] counting holy words;
And the two strangers, come   30
Fiery from Volhynia's murderous hordes[5] —
The cards and humming stop.
And I too swear revenge for that pogrom.[6]

4

Occasions dear: the four-legged aleph[7] named
And angel pennies dropping on my book;
The rabbi patting a coming scholar-head;
My mother, blessing candles, Sabbath-flamed,
Queenly in her Warsovian perruque;[8]
My father pickabacking me to bed
To tell tall tales about the Baal Shem Tov,[9] —   40
Letting me curl his beard.
O memory of unsurpassing love,
Love leading a brave child
Through childhood's ogred corridors, unfear'd!

5

The week in the country at my brother's — (May
He own fat cattle in the fields of heaven!)
Its picking of strawberries from grassy ditch,
Its odour of dogrose and of yellowing hay, —
Dusty, adventurous, sunny days, all seven! —
Still follow me, still warm me, still are rich   50
With the cow-tinkling peace of pastureland.
The meadow'd memory

---

4. **Maariv** A religious service in the evening. 5. **Volhynia's murderous hoards** Volhynia is a Ukrainian province that was the site of various pogroms against the Jews. 6. **pogrom** A planned massacre of Jews. 7. **four-legged aleph** The first letter in the Hebrew alphabet. 8. **Warsovian perruque** Wig worn by orthodox Jewish women. 9. **Baal Shem Tov** Rabbi Yisroel ben Eliezer (1698–1760), generally thought the founder of Hasidic Judaism; he valued moral action above scholarship.

Is sodded with its clover, and is spanned
By that same pillow'd sky
A boy on his back one day watched enviously.

6

And paved again the street: the shouting boys
Oblivious of mothers on the stoops
Playing the robust robbers and police,
The corn-cob battle, — all high-spirited noise
60   Competitive among the lot-drawn groups.
Another day, of shaken apple-trees
In the rich suburbs, and a furious dog,
And guilty boys in flight;
Hazelnut games, and games in the synagogue, —
The burrs, the Haman rattle,[10]
The Torah-dance on Simchas-Torah night.

7

Immortal days of the picture-calendar
Dear to me always with the virgin joy
Of the first flowering of senses five,
70   Discovering birds, or textures, or a star,
Or tastes sweet, sour, acid, those that cloy;
And perfumes. Never was I more alive.
All days thereafter are a dying-off,
A wandering away
From home and the familiar. The years doff
Their innocence.
No other day is ever like that day.

8

I am no old man fatuously[11] intent
On memoirs, but in memory I seek
80   The strength and vividness of nonage days,
Not tranquil recollection of event.
It is a fabled city that I seek;
It stands in Space's vapours and Time's haze;
Thence comes my sadness in remembered joy
Constrictive of the throat;
Thence do I hear, as heard by a Jewboy
The Hebrew violins,
Delighting in the sobbed oriental note.

(1942)

---

10. Haman rattle When the Book of Esther is read aloud, children shake rattles to drown out the name of Haman, the villain. **11. fatuously** Foolishly.

Portrait of the Poet as Landscape

I

Not an editorial-writer, bereaved with bartlett,[1]
mourns him, the shelved Lycidas.[2]
No actress squeezes a glycerine tear for him.
The radio broadcast lets his passing pass.
And with the police, no record. Nobody, it appears,
either under his real name or his alias,
missed him enough to report.

It is possible that he is dead, and not discovered.
It is possible that he can be found some place
in a narrow closet, like the corpse in a detective story,   10
standing, his eyes staring, and ready to fall on his face.
It is also possible that he is alive
and amnesiac, or mad, or in retired disgrace,
or beyond recognition lost in love.

We are sure only that from our real society
he has disappeared; he simply does not count,
except in the pullulation[3] of vital statistics —
somebody's vote, perhaps, an anonymous taunt
of the Gallup poll,[4] a dot in a government table —
but not felt, and certainly far from eminent —   20
in a shouting mob, somebody's sigh.

O, he who unrolled our culture from his scroll —
the prince's quote, the rostrum-rounding[5] roar —
who under one name made articulate
heaven, and under another the seven-circled air,[6]
is, if he is at all, a number, an x,
a Mr. Smith in a hotel register, —
incognito, lost, lacunal.[7]

II

The truth is he's not dead, but only ignored —
like the mirroring lenses forgotten on a brow   30
that shine with the guilt of their unnoticed world.
The truth is he lives among neighbours, who, though they will allow
him a passable fellow, think him eccentric, not solid,
a type that one can forgive, and for that matter, forego.

---

1. **bartlett** *Bartlett's Familiar Quotations,* a reference book of famous quotes. 2. **Lycidas** John Milton's pastoral elegy for the drowned poet Edward King (1612–1637). 3. **pullulation** Creation. 4. **Gallup poll** Large-scale poll of public opinion. 5. **rostrum-rounding** Rostrums are podiums for public oration. 6. **seven-circled air** A reference to Dante's *Inferno.* Various actions were punished in different circles. 7. **lacunal** Occupying an empty space.

Himself he has his moods, just like a poet.
Sometimes, depressed to nadir,[8] he will think all lost,
will see himself as throwback, relict, freak,
his mother's miscarriage, his great-grandfather's ghost,
and he will curse his quintuplet senses, and their tutors
40   in whom he put, as he should not have put, his trust.

Then he will remember his travels over that body —
the torso verb, the beautiful face of the noun,
and all those shaped and warm auxiliaries!
A first love it was, the recognition of his own.
Dear limbs adverbial, complexion of adjective,
dimple and dip of conjugation!

And then remember how this made a change in him
affecting for always the glow and growth of his being;
how suddenly was aware of the air, like shaken tinfoil,
50   of the patents of nature, the shock of belated seeing,
the lonelinesses peering from the eyes of crowds;
the integers of thought; the cube-roots of feeling.

Thus, zoomed to zenith,[9] sometimes he hopes again,
and sees himself as a character, with a rehearsed role:
the Count of Monte Cristo, come for his revenges;
the unsuspected heir, with papers; the risen soul;
or the chloroformed prince awakening from his flowers;
or — deflated again — the convict on parole.

III

He is alone; yet not completely alone.
60   Pins on a map of a colour similar to his,
each city has one, sometimes more than one:
here, caretakers of art, in colleges;
in offices, there, with arm-bands, and green-shaded;
and there, pounding their catalogued beats in libraries, —

everywhere menial, a shadow's shadow.
And always for their egos — their outmoded art.
Thus, having lost the bevel[10] in the ear,
they know neither up nor down, mistake the part
for the whole, curl themselves in a comma,
70   talk technics, make a colon their eyes. They distort —

such is the pain of their frustration — truth
to something convolute and cerebral.
How they do fear the slap of the flat of the platitude!

---

8. nadir Lowest point. **9. zenith** Pinnacle. **10. bevel** Tool for drawing proper angles.

Now Pavlov's victims,[11] their mouths water at bell,
the platter empty.
     See they set twenty-one jewels
into their watches; the time they do not tell!

Some, patagonian[12] in their own esteem,
and longing for the multiplying word,
join party and wear pins, now have a message,
an ear, and the convention-hall's regard.   80
Upon the knees of ventriloquists, they own,
of their dandled brightness, only the paint and board.

And some go mystical, and some go mad.
One stares at a mirror all day long, as if
to recognize himself; another courts
angels, — for here he does not fear rebuff;
and a third, alone, and sick with sex, and rapt,
doodles him symbols convex and concave.

O schizoid solitudes! O purities
curdling upon themselves! Who live for themselves,   90
or for each other, but for nobody else;
desire affection, private and public loves;
and friendly, and then quarrel and surmise
the secret perversions of each other's lives.[13]

IV

He suspects that something has happened, a law
been passed, a nightmare ordered. Set apart,
he finds himself, with special haircut and dress,
as on a reservation. Introvert.
He does not understand this; sad conjecture
muscles and palls thrombotic[14] on his heart.   100

He thinks an impostor, having studied his personal biography,
his gestures, his moods, now has come forward to pose
in the shivering vacuums his absence leaves.
Wigged with his laurel, that other, and faked with his face,
he pats the heads of his children, pecks his wife,
and is at home, and slippered, in his house.

---

11. Pavlov's victims Ivan Pavlov (1849–1936), Nobel-prize-winning psychologist, was famous for his experiments in conditioned reactions. **12. patagonian** According to accounts of Ferdinand Magellan's co-explorers, the Indian inhabitants of Patagonia (an area of Argentina) were giants. **13. secret perversions of each other's lives** May refer to the attacks of John Sutherland, founder of the influential magazine *First Statement*, on Patrick Anderson, founder of rival magazine *Preview*; in 1943 Sutherland accused Anderson of practising "abnormal sex," or homosexuality. **14. palls thrombotic** Covering of clotted blood.

So he guesses at the impertinent silhouette
that talks to his phone-piece and slits open his mail.
Is it the local tycoon who for a hobby
110   plays poet, he so epical in steel?
The orator, making a pause? Or is that man
he who blows his flash of brass in the jittering hall?

Or is he cuckolded by the troubadour
rich and successful out of celluloid?
Or by the don who unrhymes atoms? Or
the chemist death built up? Pride, lost impostor'd pride,
it is another, another, whoever he is,
who rides where he should ride.

V

Fame, the adrenalin: to be talked about;
120   to be a verb; to be introduced as *The*;
to smile with endorsement from slick paper; make
caprices[15] anecdotal; to nod to the world; to see
one's name like a song upon the marquees played;
to be forgotten with embarrassment; to be —
to be.

It has its attractions, but is not the thing;
nor is it the ape mimesis[16] who speaks from the tree
ancestral; nor the merkin joy[17] ...
Rather it is stark infelicity
130   which stirs him from his sleep, undressed, asleep
to walk upon roofs and window-sills and defy
the gape of gravity.

VI

Therefore he seeds illusions. Look, he is
the nth Adam taking a green inventory
in world but scarcely uttered, naming, praising,
the flowering fiats[18] in the meadow, the
syllabled fur, stars aspirate, the pollen
whose sweet collision sounds eternally.
For to praise

140   the world — he, solitary man — is breath
to him. Until it has been praised, that part
has not been. Item by exciting item —
air to his lungs, and pressured blood to his heart. —

---

15. caprices Impulsive changes of mind. **16. mimesis** "The mimicry or imitation practiced by the ape" (Klein). **17. merkin joy** Merkins are pubic wigs for women; the phrase refers to masturbation. **18. fiats** Proclamations.

they are pulsated, and breathed, until they map,
not the world's, but his own body's chart!

And now in imagination he has climbed
another planet, the better to look
with single camera view upon this earth —
its total scope, and each afflated tick,
its talk, its trick its tracklessness — and this,   150
this he would like to write down in a book!

To find a new function for the déclassé[19] craft
archaic like the fletcher's;[20] to make a new thing;
to say the word that will become sixth sense;
perhaps by necessity and indirection bring
new forms to life, anonymously, new creeds —
O, somehow pay back the daily larcenies of the lung!

These are not mean ambitions. It is already something
merely to entertain them. Meanwhile, he
makes of his status as zero a rich garland,   160
a halo of his anonymity,
and lives alone, and in his secret shines
like phosphorus. At the bottom of the sea.

(1945)

The Rocking Chair

It seconds the crickets of the province. Heard
in the clean lamplit farmhouses of Quebec, —
wooden, — it is no less a national bird;
and rivals, in its cage, the mere stuttering clock.
To its time, the evenings are rolled away;
and in its peace the pensive mother knits
contentment to be worn by her family,
grown-up, but still cradled by the chair in which she sits.

It is also the old man's pet, pair to his pipe,
the two aids of his arithmetic and plans;   10
plans rocking and puffing into market-shape;
and it is the toddler's game and dangerous dance.
Moved to the verandah, on summer Sundays, it is,
among the hanging plants, the girls, the boy-friends,
sabbatical and clumsy, like the white haloes
dangling above the blue serge[1] suits of the young men.

---

19. **déclassé** Outmoded. 20. **fletcher's** A fletcher is a maker of arrows.

---

1. **serge** Wool material.

It has a personality of its own;
is a character (like that old drunk Lacoste,
exhaling amber, and toppling on his pins);
20   it is alive; individual; and no less
an identity than those about it. And
it is tradition. Centuries have been flicked
from its arcs, alternately flicked and pinned.
It rolls with the gait of St. Malo.[2] It is act

and symbol, symbol of this static folk
which moves in segments, and returns to base, —
a sunken pendulum: *invoke, revoke*;
loosed yon, leashed hither, motion on no space.
O, like some Anjou[3] ballad, all refrain,
30   which turns about its longing, and seems to move
to make a pleasure out of repeated pain,
its music moves, as if always back to a first love.

(1945)

Dorothy Livesay (1909–1996)

For most of her career, Dorothy Livesay was critical of poetry that "came from literature rather than life." Hoping to influence the world beyond the academic and literary domains, she attempted to develop a poetic language that would capture more authentic rhythms and speech patterns. In her poem "Without the Benefit of Tape," she announces: "The real poems are being written in outports" and "on backwoods farms … The living speech is shouted out / by men and women leaving railway lines / to trundle home, pack-sacked."

Even when she first started to write poetry, at age 12, Livesay favoured the natural rhythms of free verse over the more constrictive, traditional forms. Born in Winnipeg in 1909, she grew up in a literary household. Her parents were journalists who had met while working on the Winnipeg *Telegram*. Her father, John F.B. Livesay, went on to found and manage the Canadian Press. Her mother, Florence Randal Livesay, wrote poetry and fiction and translated works of Ukrainian literature. In 1920, the family moved to Toronto, where Dorothy attended Glen Mawr, a private girls' school. In her *Journey with My Selves: A Memoir 1909–1963* (1991), she recalls how she and her friend Eugenia Watts were consumed by "literary exploration" during these years. In 1927, Livesay began to study modern languages at Trinity College, University of Toronto. A year later, she produced her first volume of poetry, *Green Pitcher*, and she won the Jardine Memorial Prize for her poem "City Wife." She spent her junior year abroad at the Université d'Aix-Marseille, and upon graduating from Trinity in 1931, she returned to France to write a *thèse d'études supérieures* at the Sorbonne. A second volume of poetry, *Signpost* (1932), appeared several months after she returned to Toronto.

Livesay's early literary efforts demonstrate the influence of the imagist movement on her thinking. Her mother subscribed to *Poetry* (a Chicago journal), and Livesay was drawn to contributors like H.D., Ezra Pound, and Amy Lowell. On the Canadian literary scene, she admired

---

2. **gait of St. Malo** with a sailor's gait; St. Malo is the port town in northern France from which Jacques Cartier sailed on his first voyage to Canada. 3. **Anjou** A province of France. Klein refers to the repetitive nature of French-Canadian songs rooted in the French tradition.

imagists Arthur Stringer and Louise Morey Bowman. Raymond Knister, with whom she was acquainted, also played a major role in her development as a poet. Many of the poems in *Green Pitcher* and *Signpost* are written in free verse and employ simple forms and unadorned imagery. Nevertheless, Livesay also drew on traditional forms, and some of her depictions of nature reveal a Romantic influence.

Yet even before her second collection was published, Livesay's poetics were changing. In Paris, she became involved in the French political scene. She read Karl Marx and Friedrich Engels, and she attended rallies at which she witnessed police brutalizing the unemployed. Returning to Canada, she was confronted with the effects of the Great Depression on her country, and she began to reconsider her role as a poet — "a poem must speak more about the times." In Toronto, she joined several socialist and proletarian artist groups and wrote agitprop poetry for the magazine *Masses*. Enrolling in a social work program at the University of Toronto, she spent a year as an apprentice to the Montreal Family Service Bureau and travelled to New Jersey to work with families on relief. By this time, she was a member of the Communist Party, and she expended much energy composing leaflets and chants for picket lines. Literary critics have often suggested that this stage in Livesay's poetic career was a regrettable one. Desmond Pacey was glad that "the sensitive reverberator" eventually "prevailed over the agitator." But later in her life, Livesay would make no apologies for this; in 1977, she collected her literary creations and other artefacts from the 1930s in *Right Hand Left Hand*.

In 1936, Livesay became a member of the editorial board of the left-wing periodical *New Frontier*. She moved to Vancouver, and in 1937, she married Duncan Macnair, with whom she would have two children. Although she had become skeptical of communism, she did not abandon her activist pursuits. In 1944, she published a collection of poems, *Day and Night*, for which she received the Governor General's Award. The volume included a selection of poems she had written over the previous decade, and many contained social commentary. "Day and Night," for example, deals with the racial prejudice she witnessed as a social worker in New Jersey and concludes with a call to revolution: "Day and night / Night and day / Till life is turned / The other way!" The collection also incorporates poetry that originated in a more private vision, including personal expressions to her loved ones.

Following the publication of *Day and Night*, Livesay worked in Europe as a journalist for the *Toronto Daily Star* and produced a second Governor General's Award–winning volume, *Poems for People* (1947). She also wrote several lengthy "documentaries," including "Call My People Home" (1950), a poem for radio that focused on the treatment of Japanese Canadians in British Columbia during World War II. Livesay insisted on describing these works as "documentary poems." In a 1969 paper called "The Documentary Poem: A Canadian Genre," she traces the tradition from Isabella Valancy Crawford to E.J. Pratt, Earle Birney, and Anne Marriott. She published many of these long poems in the collection *The Documentaries* (1969).

In 1956, Livesay received a teaching degree from the University of British Columbia, and in 1958, she went to the University of London to study British teaching methods. Returning briefly to Canada after the death of Macnair, she began to work for UNESCO — first in Paris, and then in northern Rhodesia (now Zambia) as a field worker. She again took up residence in Vancouver, in 1963, teaching creative writing courses at UBC and earning an M.Ed. with her thesis "Rhythm and Sound in Contemporary Canadian Poetry." The *Tish* group — Canadian poets Frank Davey, Fred Wah, George Bowering, David Dawson, and James Reid, who were influenced by the Black Mountain poets in the U.S. — attracted Livesay at this point. Inspired by her association with them, she published *The Unquiet Bed* (1967) and *Plainsongs* (1969). Many of the poems in these collections examine prescribed cultural roles for women, and critics were impressed by Livesay's frank treatment of love and sexuality.

She was an important voice in Canadian literature and criticism throughout her long life. She served as writer-in-residence at universities in five provinces; she organized two anthologies of writing by Canadian women; and, in 1975, she founded and then edited the journal *CV/II*. Livesay died in 1996.

Green Rain

I remember long veils of green rain
Feathered like the shawl of my grandmother —
Green from the half-green of the spring trees
Waving in the valley.

I remember the road
Like the one which leads to my grandmother's house,
A warm house, with green carpets,
Geraniums, a trilling canary
And shining horse-hair chairs;
10 And the silence, full of the rain's falling
Was like my grandmother's parlour
Alive with herself and her voice, rising and falling —
Rain and wind intermingled.

I remember on that day
I was thinking only of my love
And of my love's house.
But now I remember the day
As I remember my grandmother.
I remember the rain as the feathery fringe of her shawl.

(1930)

Day and Night

1

Dawn, red and angry, whistles loud and sends
A geysered shaft of steam searching the air.
Scream after scream announces that the churn
Of life must move, the giant arm command.
Men in a stream, a moving human belt
Move into sockets, every one a bolt.
The fun begins, a humming, whirring drum —
Men do a dance in time to the machines.

2

One step forward
10 Two steps back
Shove the lever,
Push it back

While Arnot whirls
A roundabout
And Geoghan shuffles
Bolts about.

One step forward
Hear it crack
Smashing rhythm —
Two steps back   20

Your heart-beat pounds
Against your throat
The roaring voices
Drown your shout

Across the way
A writhing whack
Sets you spinning
Two steps back —

One step forward
Two steps back.   30

3
Day and night are rising and falling
Night and day shift gears and slip rattling
Down the runway, shot into storerooms
Where only arms and a note-book remember
The record of evil, the sum of commitments.
We move as through sleep's revolving memories
Piling up hatred, stealing the remnants,
Doors forever folding before us —
And where is the recompense, on what agenda
Will you set love down? Who knows of peace?   40

Day and night
Night and day
Light rips into ribbons
What we say.

I called to love
Deep in dream:
Be with me in the daylight
As in gloom.

Be with me in the pounding
In the knives against my back   50
Set your voice resounding
Above the steel's whip crack.

High and sweet
Sweet and high
Hold, hold up the sunlight
In the sky!

Day and night
Night and day
Tear up all the silence
60   Find the words I could not say ...

4

We were stoking coal in the furnaces; red hot
They gleamed, burning our skins away, his and mine.
We were working together, night and day, and knew
Each other's stroke; and without words, exchanged
An understanding about kids at home,
The landlord's jaw, wage-cuts and overtime.
We were like buddies, see? Until they said
That nigger is too smart the way he smiles
And sauces back the foreman; he might say
70   Too much one day, to others changing shifts.
Therefore they cut him down, who flowered at night
And raised me up, day hanging over night —
So furnaces could still consume our withered skin.

Shadrach, Meshach and Abednego[1]
Turn in the furnace, whirling slow.
        Lord, I'm burnin' in the fire
        Lord, I'm steppin' on the coals
        Lord, I'm blacker than my brother
        Blow your breath down here.

80   Boss, I'm smothered in the darkness
        Boss, I'm shrivellin' in the flames
        Boss, I'm blacker than my brother
        Blow your breath down here.
Shadrach, Meshach and Abednego
Burn in the furnace, whirling slow.

5

Up in the roller room, men swing steel
Swing it, zoom; and cut it, crash.
Up in the dark the welder's torch
Makes sparks fly like lightning reel.

---

1. Shadrach, Meshach, and Abednego   In the story of the fiery furnace from the Book of Daniel, these three youths defy King Nebuchadnezzar's order to worship a golden idol. The king has them thrown into a furnace, but they survive, and the king orders everyone to worship their god.

Now I remember storm on a field   90
The trees bow tense before the blow
Even the jittering sparrows' talk
Ripples into the still tree shield.

We are in storm that has no cease
No lull before, no after time
When green with rain the grasses grow
And air is sweet with fresh increase.

We bear the burden home to bed
The furnace glows within our hearts:
Our bodies hammered through the night   100
Are welded into bitter bread.

Bitter, yes:
But listen, friend:
We are mightier
In the end.

We have ears
Alert to seize
A weakness
In the foreman's ease

We have eyes   110
To look across
The bosses' profit
At our loss.

Are you waiting?
Wait with us
After evening
There's a hush —

Use it not
For love's slow count:
Add up hate   120
And let it mount

Until the lifeline
Of your hand
Is calloused with
A fiery brand!

Add up hunger,
Labour's ache
These are figures
That will make

130 The page grow crazy
     Wheels go still,
     Silence sprawling
     On the till —

     Add your hunger,
     Brawn and bones,
     Take your earnings:
     Bread, not stones!

     6

     Into thy maw I commend my body
     But the soul shines without
140 A child's hands as a leaf are tender
     And draw the poison out.

     Green of new leaf shall deck my spirit
     Laughter's roots will spread:
     Though I am overalled and silent
     Boss, I'm far from dead!

     One step forward
     Two steps back
     Will soon be over:
     Hear it crack!

150 The wheels may whirr
     A roundabout
     And neighbour's shuffle
     Drown your shout

     The wheel must limp
     Till it hangs still
     And crumpled men
     Pour down the hill.

     Day and night
     Night and day
160 Till life is turned
     The other way!

                                        (1936)

London Revisited: 1946

     1

     In the cavern of cold
     Chill of the world
     Turn of the old

Year's leaf to the soil
September to sere
In the cave of the year
The long fingered wall
Of the house disembowelled
Stares in a prayer
Voiceless, unvowelled: 10
Inerasably stained
The stone is unveiled.
(But down in the pit
Where the cellar was hit
It is green, it is gold:
From the grass and leaf mould
Willow herb's knit
With goldenrod's hold.)
In the cave of the year
The underground ride   20
Heart knocks in fear
Map is no guide —
Whose is this hand
Chained to your side?

2

Once it was death's. We saw
The bone of the beast
Stretcher bearer's torch
Flashed on his dark feast
Once in the tense sky
Riveted with blood   30
We visioned blank defeat
The iron flood
Had not our prophets cried
Ruin! No release!
And politicians lied
Predicting peace?
Now in the surging street
Sway and sweep of song
It is not death whose arm
Hurries us along   40
It is not death, for that
We met with a proud smile
Tossing a hand grenade
At the rocket's snarl
It is not death, but he
We feared, we fled:
Our brother, searching us —
Love's lightning tread.

3

Coming upon this face as to a map
50   Learning the contours not from street to street
But from the coloured ink, the gay red arteries
The yellow wrinkles and the shaded brow:
Coming to London with an eager now
The printed Golders dancing on the Green[1]
The happy Shepherds hunting in the Bush[2]
Coming to Chelsea[3] and the brush
Of autumn tarnishing a square
(Whether a sheltered court, demure, austere
Or narrow alley where the children flare
60   Their whittled voices on the nipping air) —
Coming with guide and gift, I fell
Blundering through dark, around
No builded wall
I fell and heard my fall
Echoing through the tall
Rubble of rift and wreck
Down to the low unreaching wretched wall
Through the last door hung
On naked nail
70   And the stairs flung
Up to the gap of hell:
And above, no ceiling
And below, no wall.

4

O feet that found the way to bed,
The narrow place where prayers were said;
That danced a circle on the floor
And kicked a hollow on the door
O feet that morning noon and night
Suffered the hour to be delight
80   Or stood upon the edge of mist
And felt the earth, and met, and kissed —
Into the parapet[4] of time
Memorial tower of the mind
You have ascended in a climb
Sudden as a flying bomb
You have left the city's face
Scarred and grimed by human hand

---

1. **Golders … Green** An area of London. 2. **Shepherds … Bush** Another district in London. 3. **Chelsea** London district, in which Sloane Square is found. 4. **parapet** Defensive wall.

And all the magic of her map
Crumbling in brick and sand.

* * * *

And though the Michaelmas[5] is here   90
A mauve repose on mildewed stain
And children swing on girders grown
Rusty with the wrack of rain
And though the mushroom houses grow
In prim, prefabricated row;
Where debris was, a park will be
And here a chaste community —
Still lies the skeleton behind,
The bony manufactured grin
The voice we heard time out of mind   100
That rustles when the leaves are thin;
And still the footprints trace the map
Scuttle across the veins and flaws
Reverberating on the heart
To warn the way that winter was.

(1947)

Bartok[1] and the Geranium

She lifts her green umbrellas
Towards the pane
Seeking her fill of sunlight
Or of rain;
Whatever falls
She has no commentary
Accepts, extends,
Blows out her furbelows,
Her bustling boughs;

And all the while he whirls   10
Explodes in space,
Never content with this small room:
Not even can he be
Confined to sky
But must speed high and higher still
From galaxy to galaxy,
Wrench from the stars their momentary notes
Steal music from the moon.

---

5. **Michaelmas** A celebration on 29 September for the archangel Michael.

1. **Bartok** Béla Bartok (1881–1945), modernist Hungarian composer.

20

She's daylight
He is dark
She's heaven-held breath
He storms and crackles
Spits with hell's own spark.

Yet in this room, this moment now
These together breathe and be:
She, essence of serenity,
He in a mad intensity
Soars beyond sight
Then hurls, lost Lucifer,

30

From heaven's height.

And when he's done, he's out:
She leans a lip against the glass
And preens herself in light.

(1952)

Lament

for J.F.B.L.[1]

What moved me, was the way your hand
Lay in my hand, not withering,
But warm, like a hand cooled in a stream
And purling still; or a bird caught in a snare
Wings folded stiff, eyes in a stare,
But still alive with the fear,
Heart hoarse with hope —
So your hand, your dead hand, my dear.

And the veins, still mounting as blue rivers,

10

Mounting towards the tentative finger-tips,
The delta where four seas come in —
Your fingers promontories[2] into colourless air
Were rosy still — not chalk (like cliffs
You knew in boyhood, Isle of Wight[3]):
But blushed with colour from the sun you sought
And muscular from garden toil;
Stained with the purple of an iris bloom,
Violas grown for a certain room;
Hands seeking faïence,[4] filagree,

20

Chinese lacquer and ivory —

---

1. **J.F.B.L.** Livesay's father, John Frederick Bligh Livesay. 2. **promontories** Protrusions, especially of rock. 3. **Isle of Wight** A British island-district where John Frederick Bligh Livesay grew up. 4. **faïence** Colourful glazed pottery.

Brussels lace; and a walnut piece
Carved by a hand now phosphorus.

What moved me, was the way your hand
Held life, although the pulse was gone.
The hand that carpentered a children's chair,
Carved out a stair
Held leash upon a dog in strain
Gripped wheel, swung sail,
Flicked horse's rein
And then again   30
Moved kings and queens meticulous on a board,
Slashed out the cards, cut bread, and poured
A purring cup of tea;

The hand so neat and nimble
Could make a tennis partner tremble,
Write a resounding round
Of sonorous verbs and nouns —
Hand that would not strike a child, and yet
Could ring a bell and send a man to doom.

And now unmoving in this Spartan room   40
The hand still speaks:
After the brain was fogged
And the tight lips tighter shut,
After the shy appraising eyes
Relinquished fire for the sea's green gaze —
The hand still breathes, fastens its hold on life;
Demands the whole, establishes the strife.

What moved me, was the way your hand
Lay cool in mine, not withering;
As bird still breathes, and stream runs clear —   50
So your hand; your dead hand, my dear.

                                                              (1953)

The Three Emilys[1]

These women crying in my head
Walk alone, uncomforted:
The Emily's, these three
Cry to be set free —
And others whom I will not name

---

1. **Three Emilys** Bronte (1818–1848), British poet; Dickinson (1830–1886), American poet; and Carr (1871–1945), Canadian artist and writer.

Each different, each the same.
Yet they had liberty!
Their kingdom was the sky:
They batted clouds with easy hand,
10 Found a mountain for their stand;
From wandering lonely they could catch
The inner magic of a heath —
A lake their palette, any tree
Their brush could be.
And still they cry to me
As in reproach —
I, born to hear their inner storm
Of separate man in woman's form,
I yet possess another kingdom, barred
20 To them, these three, this Emily.
I move as mother in a frame,
My arteries
Flow the immemorial way
Towards the child, the man;
And only for brief span
Am I an Emily on mountain snows
And one of these.
And so the whole that I possess
Is still much less —
30 They move triumphant through my head:
I am the one
Uncomforted.

(1953)

The Notations of Love

i

You left me nothing, when
you bared me to the light
gently took off all my skin
undressed me to the bone

you left me nothing, yet
softly I melted down
into the earthy green
grass grew between my thighs

and when a flower shot
10 out of my unclenched teeth
you left me nothing but
a tongue to say it with.

ii
in my mouth
no love?
only cruelty   you say

take love   take love
is my reply
the hard way

twisted and sparse
to find   facing the rock
the fountain's force.   20

iii
Crow's feet your finger follows
circling my eyes
and on the forehead's field
a skeleton of leaves

Only the lips stay fresh
only the tongue
unsheathes its secret skin
and bolts
the lightning in.   30

iv
I used to think
that Siamese twins
occurred only
in Siam[1]
once disabused
I find their trace
no matter where
I am

especially around
these absences   40
our minds are twins
they circle and unite
my left arm is your right arm
bound   even in flight

---

1. **Siam** Now Thailand.

v

My legs stretched two ways   disparate
until you came
and joined them
(lying down between)
now, even when we separate
50   my legs coil close
and feet unite:
they form a pedestal
whereon I turn, in sleep
circling, serene —
no longer desperate.

vi

I was naked
and you clothed
me[2]

so, in the dead
60   of night
you whisper-
ed
no other word
        of praise
you found, in day
bright light
to say

but day or night, I
am undressed

70   dance
differently.

(1967)

Sheila Watson (1909–1998)

When Sheila Watson died, in 1998, her family and friends discovered that she had left three posthumous requests concerning her remains. She was to be cremated, and she wanted her ashes scattered at the mouth of the Fraser River, more at Dog Creek, while the third portion was to be buried in Toronto in the back yard of F. T. Flahiff, her friend and biographer. Multiple interment instructions seem appropriate to Watson, a writer whose oeuvre testifies to her attraction to multiple voices.

This attraction is nowhere more evident than in *The Double Hook* (1959), an experimental novel that had a dramatic impact on Canadian literature. Sometimes considered the first modern — even postmodern — Canadian novel, it heralded a shift away from traditional writing

---

2. **I was naked and you clothed me** From Matthew 25:36.

in this country. In 1985, Stephen Scobie wrote of Watson: "There is no point in listing names of those who have been influenced by her; such a list would have to include every serious writer in Canada for the last twenty years." Had Scobie drawn up such a list, some names more familiar to most readers than Watson's would have appeared on it — among them, Robert Kroetsch, Daphne Marlatt, Michael Ondaatje, Margaret Atwood, and bpNichol.

Watson would rarely comment on *The Double Hook*, but she did say that "somehow or other I had to get the authorial voice out of the novel for it to say what I wanted it to say. I didn't want a voice talking about something … I was thinking rather of a cry of voices … crying out in the wilderness. Something like the voices one hears in early litanies — voices reaching beyond themselves." She achieved this effect by writing a discontinuous prose-poetic narrative whose characters are rooted in the valleys of British Columbia but who are still archetypal, religious, or mythological figures. Drawing from the Bible, Greek mythology, and First Nations narratives, she universalized her story. The novel's genesis in the Great Depression of the 1930s in part accounts for its inherent bleakness: it begins with a murder and explores abandonment, violence, and suicide, with a brief turnaround at the end. The birth of a child — a surprising finale, which Atwood called "Baby *ex machina*" — is considered by some critics to be a sign of Christian redemption, but others have noted that God is not evident in the novel; there is, however, Coyote, an Aboriginal trickster figure who symbolizes balance, not good or evil.

Although Toronto, Edmonton, and Calgary appear briefly in *The Double Hook,* small B.C. towns are the novel's matrix. Watson (née Doherty) was born in New Westminster, B.C., at a psychiatric hospital where her father was superintendent. Schooled at convents, she moved on to university, earning a B.A. in honours English from the University of British Columbia in 1931; she was awarded an academic teaching certificate in 1932 and an M.A. from UBC in 1933, with a focus on the works of Addison and Swift. Struggling to find employment in the Depression era, she finally secured a teaching post in the remote community of Dog Creek. The government closed the school, and she went on to teach high school in Langley, but when she and a number of colleagues expressed interest in organizing a union, they were fired. In Langley, in 1938, Watson started to write. Her first novel was *Deep Hollow Creek,* which was not published until much later (1992), and which has generally been considered a testing ground for the concepts that would give rise to *The Double Hook.*

Leaving Langley, she took a teaching job in Duncan, and there she met poet Wilfred Watson, the man she would marry. Together they lived in a succession of Canadian cities — including Calgary, where Watson wrote *The Double Hook.* In 1954, they moved to France, and Watson published "Brother Oedipus" in *Queen's Quarterly.* It was her first publication; although she had written the pieces for *Four Stories* between 1948 and 1950, she did not publish the volume until 1979. In 1957, Watson embarked on a Ph.D. at the University of Toronto, writing her dissertation on Wyndham Lewis under the direction of Marshall McLuhan. In 1961, she and her husband took faculty jobs at the University of Alberta, in Edmonton; and in 1965, she received her doctorate. Watson retired from teaching in 1975. In the course of her tenure at Alberta, she enjoyed a reputation as an excellent teacher and co-founded with her husband *White Pelican,* an avant-garde journal of the literary and visual arts.

After her retirement, when *Four Stories* appeared, Watson's fascination with myth became even more evident. In "Antigone," for example, all the characters have the names of mythic figures. Watson places them in a contemporary setting — the psychiatric hospital where she was born — and charts their journey towards redemption. In the course of this journey, Antigone defies the hierarchical order of the hospital, threatening to upset the balance between sanity and insanity that preserves order in the hospital. Watson was essentially a modernist writer, but by questioning the master narratives of myth and dissolving the centrality of the author, she introduced some key elements of postmodernism. In 1984, she published *Five Stories,* adding "And the Four Animals" to the original quartet of short fiction. This story differs from the others in that it is set in Dog Creek and picks up the themes of *The Double Hook.*

In expressing admiration for the author's unflagging curiosity and independence, George Bowering relates that "In her old age Sheila Watson developed the habit of falling off things she had clambered onto to look for something.... It was after one such fall that she broke her hip in January of her 89th year, and she died in a Nanaimo hospital where Wilfred was already an inpatient. He died shortly thereafter."

Antigone[1]

My father[2] ruled a kingdom on the right bank of the river. He ruled it with a firm hand and a stout heart though he was often more troubled than Moses,[3] who was simply trying to bring a stubborn and moody people under God's yoke. My father ruled men who thought they were gods or the instruments of gods, or, at very least, god-afflicted and god-pursued. He ruled Atlas[4] who held up the sky, and Hermes[5] who went on endless messages, and Helen[6] who'd been hatched from an egg, and Pan[7] the gardener, and Kallisto[8] the bear, and too many others to mention by name. Yet my father had no thunderbolt, no trident, no helmet of darkness. His subjects were delivered bound into his hands. He merely watched over them as the hundred-handed ones watched over the dethroned Titans[9] so that they wouldn't bother Hellas[10] again.

Despite the care which my father took to maintain an atmosphere of sober common sense in his whole establishment, there were occasional outbursts of self-indulgence which he could not control. For instance, I have seen Helen walking naked down the narrow cement path under the chestnut trees for no better reason, I suppose, than that the day was hot and the white flowers themselves lay naked and expectant in the sunlight. And I have seen Atlas forget the sky while he sat eating the dirt which held him up. These were things which I was not supposed to see.

If my father had been as sensible through and through as he was thought to be, he would have packed me off to boarding school when I was old enough to be disciplined by men. Instead he kept me at home with my two cousins who, except for the accident of birth, might as well have been my sisters. Today I imagine people concerned with our welfare would take such an environment into account. At the time I speak of most people thought us fortunate — especially the girls whose fathers' affairs had come to an unhappy issue. I don't like to revive old scandal and I wouldn't except to deny it; but it takes only a few impertinent newcomers in any community to force open cupboards which had been decently sealed by time. However, my father was so busy setting his kingdom to rights that he let weeds grow up in his own garden.

---

1. **Antigone** In classical mythology, buries her deceased and disgraced brother (Polynices) in defiance of a royal decree and is sentenced to starve in a cave. 2. **My father** Oedipus, though they share a mother (Iocaste). Most famously, Oedipus unknowingly kills his father and impregnates his mother; he spends his later life in exile. Antigone, Ismene, Polynices, and Eteocles are his children. His kingdom is Thebes. 3. **Moses** Brought the Ten Commandments down from the mountain and led the Jews out of Egypt. 4. **Atlas** In classical mythology, Atlas was forced to stand at the edge of the world and hold up the sky as punishment for waging war on the Olympian gods. 5. **Hermes** Classical god of travel, literature, science, and commerce. 6. **Helen** In classical mythology, Helen's abduction by Paris of Troy initiated the Trojan War. 7. **Pan** Classical guardian of shepherds and flocks, who had the hindquarters of a goat; famously lusty. 8. **Kallisto** A chaste nymph of Artemis (goddess of the hunt) whom Zeus tricked into accepting his advances; Artemis changed her into a bear for not upholding her vow of virginity. 9. **Titans** A classical race of deities who unsuccessfully waged war on the Olympian gods. 10. **Hellas** Greek name for Greece.

As I said, if my father had had all his wits about him he would have sent me to boarding school — and Antigone and Ismene[11] too. I might have fallen in love with the headmaster's daughter and Antigone might have learned that no human being can be right always. She might have found out besides that from the seeds of eternal justice grow madder flowers than any which Pan grew in the gardens of my father's kingdom.

Between the kingdom which my father ruled and the wilderness flows a river. It is this river which I am crossing now. Antigone is with me.

How often can we cross the same river, Antigone asks.

Her persistence annoys me. Besides, Heraklitos[12] made nonsense of her question years ago. He saw a river too — the Inachos, the Kephissos, the Lethaios.[13] The name doesn't matter. He said: See how quickly the water flows. However agile a man is, however nimbly he swims, or runs, or flies, the water slips away before him. See, even as he sets down his foot the water is displaced by the stream which crowds along in the shadow of its flight.

But after all, Antigone says, one must admit that it is the same kind of water. The oolichan[14] runs in it as they ran last year and the year before. The gulls cry above the same banks. Boats drift towards the Delta and circle back against the current to gather up the catch.

At any rate, I tell her, we're standing on a new bridge. We are standing so high that the smell of mud and river weeds passes under us out to the straits. The unbroken curve of the bridge protects the eye from details of river life. The bridge is foolproof as a clinic's passport to happiness.

The old bridge still spans the river, but the cat-walk with its cracks and knot-holes, with its gap between planking and hand-rail has been torn down. The centre arch still grinds open to let boats up and down the river, but a child can no longer be walked on it or swung out on it beyond the water-gauge at the very centre of the flood.

I've known men who scorned any kind of bridge, Antigone says. Men have walked into the water, she says, or, impatient, have jumped from the bridge into the river below.

But these, I say, didn't really want to cross the river. They went Persephone's[15] way, cradled in the current's arms, down the long halls under the pink feet of the gulls, under the booms and tow-lines, under the soft bellies of the fish.

Antigone looks at me.

There's no coming back, she says, if one goes far enough.

I know she's going to speak of her own misery and I won't listen. Only a god has the right to say: Look what I suffer. Only a god should say: What more ought I to have done for you that I have not done?

Once in winter, she says, a man walked over the river.

Taking advantage of nature, I remind her, since the river had never frozen before.

---

11. Ismene After her sister, Antigone, is sentenced to death for burying Polynices against the orders of King Creon, Ismene claims she helped Antigone and thus should die as well. Antigone insists that Ismene is innocent. **12. Heraklitos** Heracles (Hercules), the classical hero who was forced to do 12 labours as punishment for the murder of his wife and children. **13. Inachos, Kephissos, Lethaios** Rivers in Greece. Lethe was a river in Hades, the classical underworld; exposure to its waters caused forgetfulness. **14. oolichan** A small fish common to the Western coast of North America. **15. Persephone** Goddess of spring who was captured by Hades, god of the underworld, and forced to live there as his queen.

Yet he escaped from the penitentiary, she says. He escaped from the guards walking round the walls or standing with their guns in the sentry-boxes at the four corners of the enclosure. He escaped.

Not without risk, I say. He had to test the strength of the ice himself. Yet safer perhaps than if he had crossed by the old bridge where he might have slipped through a knot-hole or tumbled out through the railing.

He did escape, she persists, and lived forever on the far side of the river in the Alaska tea and bulrushes. For where, she asks, can a man go farther than to the outermost edge of the world?

The habitable world, as I've said, is on the right bank of the river. Here is the market with its market stalls — the coops of hens, the long-tongued geese, the haltered calf, the bearded goat, the shoving pigs, and the empty bodies of cows and sheep and rabbits hanging on iron hooks. My father's kingdom provided asylum in the suburbs. Near it are the convent, the churches, and the penitentiary. Above these on the hill the cemetery looks down and on the river itself.

It is a world spread flat, tipped up into the sky so that men and women bend forward, walking as men walk when they board a ship at high tide. This is the world I feel with my feet. It is the world I see with my eyes.

I remember standing once with Antigone and Ismene in the square just outside the gates of my father's kingdom. Here from a bust set high on a cairn[16] the stone eyes of Simon Fraser[17] look from his stone face over the river that he found.

It is the head that counts, Ismene said.

It's no better than an urn, Antigone said, one of the urns we see when we climb to the cemetery above.

And all I could think was that I didn't want an urn, only a flat green grave with a chain about it.

A chain won't keep out the dogs, Antigone said.

But his soul could swing on it, Ismene said, like a bird blown on a branch in the wind.

And I remember Antigone's saying: The cat drags its belly on the ground and the rat sharpens its tooth in the ivy.

I should have loved Ismene, but I didn't. It was Antigone I loved. I should have loved Ismene because, although she walked the flat world with us, she managed somehow to see it round.

The earth is an oblate spheroid, she'd say. And I knew that she saw it there before her comprehensible and whole like a tangerine spiked through and held in place while it rotated on the axis of one of Nurse's steel sock needles. The earth was a tangerine and she saw the skin peeled off and the world parcelled out into neat segments, each segment sweet and fragrant in its own skin.

It's the head that counts, she said.

In her own head she made diagrams to live by, cut and fashioned after the eternal patterns spied out by Plato as he rummaged about in the sewing basket of the gods.

I should have loved Ismene. She would live now in some prefabricated and perfect chrysolite[18] by some paradigm which made love round and whole. She would simply live and leave destruction in the purgatorial ditches outside her own walled paradise.

---

16. **cairn** Pile of stones forming a monument. 17. **Simon Fraser** Explorer who charted most of British Columbia (1776–1862). He also charted the Fraser River, which has since been named after him. 18. **chrysolite** A mineral silicate. Watson may be suggesting a "chrysalis"— a cocooned moth or butterfly in its transformative stage.

Antigone is different. She sees the world flat as I do and feels it tip beneath her feet. She has walked in the market and seen the living animals penned and the dead hanging stiff on their hooks. Yet she defies what she sees with a defiance which is almost denial. Like Atlas she tries to keep the vaulted sky from crushing the flat earth. Like Hermes she brings a message that there is life if one can escape to it in the brush and bulrushes in some dim Hades[19] beyond the river. It is defiance not belief and I tell her that this time we walk the bridge to a walled cave where we can deny death no longer.

Yet she asks her questions still. And standing there I tell her that Heraklitos has made nonsense of her question. I should have loved Ismene for she would have taught me what Plato meant when he said in all earnest that the union of the soul with the body is in no way better than dissolution. I expect that she understood things which Antigone is too proud to see.

I turn away from her and flatten my elbows on the high wall of the bridge. I look back at my father's kingdom. I see the terraces rolling down from the red-brick buildings with their barred windows. I remember hands shaking the bars and hear fingers tearing up paper and stuffing it through the meshes. Diktynna,[20] mother of nets and high leaping fear. O Artemis,[21] mistress of wild beasts and wild men.

The inmates are beginning to come out on the screened verandahs. They pace up and down in straight lines or stand silent like figures which appear at the same time each day from some depths inside a clock.

On the upper terrace Pan the gardener is shifting sprinklers with a hooked stick. His face is shadowed by the brim of his hat. He moves as economically as an animal between the beds of lobelia and geranium. It is high noon.

Antigone has cut out a piece of sod and has scooped out a grave. The body lies in a coffin in the shade of the magnolia tree. Antigone and I are standing. Ismene is sitting between two low angled branches of the monkey puzzle tree. Her lap is filled with daisies. She slits the stem of one daisy and pulls the stem of another through it. She is making a chain for her neck and a crown for her hair.

Antigone reaches for a branch of the magnolia. It is almost beyond her grip. The buds flame above her. She stands on a small fire of daisies which smoulder in the roots of grass.

I see the magnolia buds. They brood above me, whiteness feathered on whiteness. I see Antigone's face turned to the light. I hear the living birds call to the sun. I speak private poetry to myself: Between four trumpeting angels at the four corners of the earth a bride stands before the altar in a gown as white as snow.

Yet I must have been speaking aloud because Antigone challenges me: You're mistaken. It's the winds the angels hold, the four winds of the earth. After the just are taken to paradise the winds will destroy the earth. It's a funeral, she says, not a wedding.

She looks towards the building.

Someone is coming down the path from the matron's house, she says.

I notice that she has pulled one of the magnolia blossoms from the branch. I take it from her. It is streaked with brown where her hands have bruised it. The sparrow which she has decided to bury lies on its back. Its feet are clenched tight against the feathers of its breast. I put the flower in the box with it.

---

19. **Hades** The classical underworld; also refers to its god of the same name. 20. **Diktynna** Goddess of Mount Dikte, birthplace of Zeus. Her name is from the Greek for "hunting nets." 21. **Artemis** In classical mythology, the chaste goddess of the hunt.

Someone is coming down the path. She is wearing a blue cotton dress. Her cropped head is bent. She walks slowing carrying something in a napkin.

It's Kallisto the bear, I say. Let's hurry. What will my father say if he sees us talking to one of his patients?

If we live here with him, Antigone says, what can he expect? If he spends his life trying to tame people he can't complain if you behave as if they were tame. What would your father think, she says, if he saw us digging in the Institution lawn?

Pat comes closer. I glower at him. There's no use speaking to him. He's deaf and dumb.

Listen, I say to Antigone, my father's not unreasonable. Kallisto thinks she's a bear and he thinks he's a bear tamer, that's all. As for the lawn, I say quoting my father without conviction, a man must have order among his own if he is to keep order in the state.

Kallisto has come up to us. She is smiling and laughing to herself. She gives me her bundle.

Fish, she says.

I open the napkin.

Pink fish sandwiches, I say.

For the party, she says.

But it isn't a party, Antigone says. It's a funeral.

For the funeral breakfast, I say.

Ismene is twisting two chains of daisies into a rope. Pan has stopped pulling the sprinkler about. He is standing beside Ismene resting himself on his hooked stick. Kallisto squats down beside her. Ismene turns away, preoccupied, but she can't turn far because of Pan's legs.

> Father said we never should
> Play with madmen in the wood.

I look at Antigone.

It's my funeral, she says.

I go over to Ismene and gather up a handful of loose daisies from her lap. The sun reaches through the shadow of the magnolia tree.

It's my funeral, Antigone says. She moves possessively towards the body.

An ant is crawling into the bundle of sandwiches which I've put on the ground. A file of ants is marching on the sparrow's box.

I go over and drop daisies on the bird's stiff body. My voice speaks ritual words: Deliver me, O Lord, from everlasting death on this dreadful day. I tremble and am afraid.

The voice of a people comforts me. I look at Antigone. I look her in the eye.

It had better be a proper funeral then, I say.

Kallisto is crouched forward on her hands. Tears are running down her cheeks and she is licking them away with her tongue.

My voice rises again: I said in the midst of my days, I shall not see —

Antigone just stands there. She looks frightened, but her eyes defy me with their assertion.

It's my funeral, she says. It's my bird. I was the one who wanted to bury it.

She is looking for a reason. She will say something which sounds eternally right.

Things have to be buried, she says. They can't be left lying around anyhow for people to see.

Birds shouldn't die, I tell her. They have wings. Cats and rats haven't wings.

Stop crying, she says to Kallisto. It's only a bird.

It has a bride's flower in its hand, Kallisto says.

We shall rise again, I mutter, but we shall not all be changed.

Antigone does not seem to hear me.

Behold, I say in a voice she must hear, in a moment, in the twinkling of an eye, the trumpet shall sound.

Ismene turns to Kallisto and throws the daisy chain about her neck.

Shall a virgin forget her adorning or a bride the ornament of her breast?

Kallisto is lifting her arms towards the tree.

The bridegroom has come, she says, white as a fall of snow. He stands above me in a great ring of fire.

Antigone looks at me now.

Let's cover the bird up, she says. Your father will punish us all for making a disturbance.

He has on his garment, Kallisto says, and on his thigh is written King of Kings.

I look at the tree. If I could see with Kallisto's eyes I wouldn't be afraid of death, or punishment, or the penitentiary guards. I wouldn't be afraid of my father's belt or his honing strap or his bedroom slipper. I wouldn't be afraid of falling into the river through a knot-hole in the bridge.

But, as I look, I see the buds falling like burning lamps and I hear the sparrow twittering in its box: Woe, woe, woe because of the three trumpets which are yet to sound.

Kallisto is on her knees. She is growling like a bear. She lumbers over the sandwiches and mauls them with her paw.

Ismene stands alone for Pan the gardener has gone.

Antigone is fitting a turf in place above the coffin. I go over and press the edge of the turf with my feet. Ismene has caught me by the hand.

Go away, Antigone says.

I see my father coming down the path. He has an attendant with him. In front of them walks Pan holding the sprinkler hook like a spear.

What are you doing here? my father asks.

Burying a bird, Antigone says.

Here? my father asks again.

Where else could I bury it? Antigone says.

My father looks at her.

This ground is public property, he says. No single person has any right to an inch of it.

I've taken six inches, Antigone says. Will you dig the bird up again?

Some of his subjects my father restrained since they were moved to throw themselves from high places or to tear one another to bits from jealousy or rage. Others who disturbed the public peace he taught to walk in the airing courts or to work in the kitchen or in the garden.

If men live at all, my father said, it is because discipline saves their life for them.

From Antigone he simply turned away.

(1984)

Anne Wilkinson (1910–1961)

In her autobiographical writing, Anne Wilkinson often reflects upon the way in which her identity is tied to her memories of childhood. She cherishes her connection to her past, at times feeling closer to these reminiscences than to her own children. The bond becomes complicated, however, when the places and people of her youth begin to disappear. Recalling a visit to the property where her late grandfather's house once stood, she writes that she "tried to build it up again in my imagination, brick by brick. Nothing happened. It was as if I had gone to a looking-glass expecting to meet my own image and had found no self reflected back to me."

Throughout her poetry and prose, Wilkinson envisions these instances of physical loss as moments of awakening from eternity into "Time." For this reason, she imagines "legacy" as something that is simultaneously eternal and ephemeral. In the poem "Summer Acres," for example, she recognizes the enduring legacy of her family and their summer home as it shapes her own body and those of her children, but she feels stifled by the knowledge that "the family are temples / Whose columns will tumble." Images of life and death intermingle as she imagines herself shaking the "half mast … scarlet flags" of her forebears from the "green virility of trees."

Wilkinson (née Gibbons) was born in 1910 in Toronto, Ontario. Her mother belonged to the prominent Osler family, who settled Ontario's Tecumseh Township in the early 1800s and boasted three generations of lawyers, doctors, and politicians. Wilkinson spent her childhood in London, Ontario, returning to Toronto after the death of her father, in 1919. She was educated by governesses and tutors, and at a private school in Toronto, progressive boarding schools in California and Connecticut, and a finishing school in Paris. In 1932, she married Frederick Wilkinson, and they moved first to London, England, and then to New York so that Frederick could complete his postgraduate medical training. They finally settled in Toronto, where they would raise three children.

Wilkinson had been writing poetry since she was a teenager, but she had destroyed all of her early efforts. In the mid-1940s, she began to preserve her writing, publishing pieces in various Canadian periodicals. In 1949, she became involved in the Toronto art scene, finding work as a reader for an arts magazine called *here and now;* later that year, she was promoted to the position of literary editor.

Wilkinson's first collection of poetry, *Counterpoint to Sleep*, appeared in 1951. Critics immediately recognized her facility with language, but some felt that the poet had been too deliberately obscure in her composition. Her imagery can be arresting. In "Winter Sketch, Rockcliffe, Ottawa," she describes the coming change of season in corporeal terms: "Till April babble swells the shroud to breast / So milky full the whole north swills, licking / A world of sugar from encrusted nipples." Furthermore, she often adjusts her metaphors within a single poem, challenging the reader to pinpoint her meaning. This technique is integral to her style, however, and it is effective when she is attempting to create a sense of instability or movement. In "Lake Song," for example, the constant shifts in imagery create a feeling of ebb and flow that replicates the undulation of the water she describes in the poem.

A second collection, *The Hangman Ties the Holly*, appeared in 1955 to more consistently positive reviews. Often seen as Wilkinson's most polished and coherent work, many of these poems develop and refine the themes that underlie *Counterpoint to Sleep*. In "Lens," for example, Wilkinson explores the "poet's eye" of her earlier poem "A Poet's-Eye View," only here it is imagined as a "good lens" used to supplement her "woman's eye." She writes, "My woman's iris circles / A blind pupil; / The poet's eye is crystal, / Polished to accept the negative, / The contradictions in a proof / And the accidental / Candour of the shadows."

The years following the publication of *The Hangman Ties the Holly* were troubled ones for Wilkinson. She and her husband divorced in 1954, and the stress of their separation was heightened for her by the declining health of her mother. Wilkinson was writing a history of her maternal family that would eventually be published as *Lions in the Way: A Discursive History of the Oslers* (1956), but her mother died before it was finished. Wilkinson was devastated, and she abandoned her writing for over a year. Finally, she began to compile a third collection, *Heresies and Other Poems*.

There has been some debate as to whether Wilkinson's later poems reflect the turmoil of her personal life during this period. The tone of "Nature Be Damned" is dark and despairing. In it, she acknowledges that a love for the natural world does not ultimately protect one from its forces, and there does not seem to be a solution to this problem. She writes, "I hide my skin within the barren city / Where artificial moons pull no man's tide, / And so escape my green love till the day / Vine breaks through brick and strangles me." The same sentiments underlie "Nursery Rhyme," as the earth that hides "the small white bones of a child" is referred to as "mother earth indeed." But the poem "Unicorn" offers a slightly different vision. The speaker searches for a unicorn. Unable to find it, she returns "home, empty, quite in despair"; yet, once she shakes "the rain / From [her] good eye," she sees the unicorn running down her "tumbling stair." Here, Wilkinson suggests that pain and despair are subjective, and we can escape them if we allow ourselves to re-envision the world.

Wilkinson did not publish these poems during her lifetime; she died in 1961 of lung cancer. She had also been writing an autobiography when her health declined, and an abridged version of the work appeared in the *Tamarack Review* later that year as "Four Corners of My World." In 1968, A.J.M. Smith published this piece and much of Wilkinson's previously unpublished poetry in *The Collected Poems of Anne Wilkinson and a Prose Memoir*. In 1992, Joan Coldwell published Wilkinson's journals and the unabridged version of her autobiography as *The Tightrope Walker: Autobiographical Writings of Anne Wilkinson*. Most recently, Dean Irvine has collected Wilkinson's entire poetic oeuvre in *Heresies: The Complete Poems of Anne Wilkinson (1924–1961)* (2004).

Summer Acres

I

These acres breathe my family,
Holiday with seventy summers' history.
My blood lives here,
Sunned and veined three generations red
Before my bones were formed.

My eyes are wired to the willow
That wept for my father,
My heart is boughed by the cedar
That covers with green limbs the bones of my children,
My hands are white with a daisy, sired   10
By the self same flower my grandfather loved;

My ears are tied to the tattle of water
That echoes the vows of ancestral lovers,
My skin is washed by a lather of waves
That bathed the blond bodies of uncles and aunts
And curled on the long flaxen hair of my mother;

My feet step soft on descendants of grass
That was barely brushed
By the wary boots of a hummingbird woman,
20   The Great Great Grandmother
Of my mid-century children.

II

September born, reared in the sunset hour,
I was the child of old men heavy with honour;
I mourned the half mast time of their death and sorrowed
A season for leaves, shaking their scarlet flags
From green virility of trees.

As ears spring cartilaged from skulls
So my ears spring from the sound of water
And the whine of autumn in the family tree.
30   How tired, how tall grow the trees
Where the trees and the family are temples
Whose columns will tumble, leaf over root to their ruin.

Here, in my body's home my heart dyes red
The last hard maple in their acres.
Where birch and elm and willow turn,
Gently bred, to gold against the conifers.
I hail my fathers, sing their blood to the leaf.

(1951)

Lake Song

Willow weep, let the lake lap up your green trickled tears.
Water, love, lip the hot roots, cradle the leaf;
Turn a new moon on your tongue, water, lick the deaf rocks,
With silk of your pebble-pitched song, water, wimple the beach;
Water, wash over the feet of the summer-bowed trees,
Wash age from the face of the stone.

I am a hearer of water;
My ears hold the sound and the feel of the sound of it mortally.
My skin is in love with lake water,
10   My skin is in love and it sings in the arms of its lover,

My skin is the leaf of the willow,
My nerves are the roots of the weeping willow tree.

My blood is a clot in the stone,
The blood of my heart is fused to a pit in the rock;
The lips of my lover can wear away stone,
My lover can free the blocked heart;
The leaf and the root and the red sap will run with lake water,
The arms of my lover will carry me home to the sea.

(1951)

Lens

I

The poet's daily chore
Is my long duty;
To keep and cherish my good lens
For love and war
And wasps about the lilies
And mutiny within.

My woman's eye is weak
And veiled with milk;
My working eye is muscled
With a curious tension,   10
Stretched and open
As the eyes of children;
Trusting in its vision
Even should it see
The holy holy spirit gambol[1]
Counterheadwise,
Lithe[2] and warm as any animal.

My woman's iris circles
A blind pupil;
The poet's eye is crystal,   20
Polished to accept the negative,
The contradictions in a proof
And the accidental
Candour of the shadows;

The shutter, oiled and smooth
Clicks on the grace of heroes

---

1. gambol Skip playfully. **2. Lithe** Flexible.

Or on some bestial act
When lit with radiance
The afterwords the actors speak
30   Give depths to violence,

Or if the bull is great
And the matador
And the sword
Itself the metaphor.

II

In my dark room the years
Lie in solution,
Develop film by film.
Slow at first and dim
Their shadows bite
40   On the fine white pulp of paper.

An early snap of fire
Licking the arms of air
I hold against the light, compare
The details with a prehistoric view
Of land and sea
And cradles of mud that rocked
The wet and sloth[3] of infancy.

A stripe of tiger, curled
And sleeping on the ribs of reason
50   Prints as clear
As Eve and Adam, pearled
With sweat, staring at an apple core;

And death, in black and white
Or politic in green and Easter film,
Lands on steely points, a dancer
Disciplined to the foolscap stage,
The property of poets
Who command his robes, expose
His moving likeness on the page.

(1955)

---

3. sloth Indolence.

In June and Gentle Oven

In June and gentle oven
Summer kingdoms simmer
As they come
And flower and leaf and love
Release
Their sweetest juice.

No wind at all
On the wide green world
Where fields go stroll-
Ing by   10
And in and out
An adder of a stream
Parts the daisies
On a small Ontario farm.

And where, in curve of meadow,
Lovers, touching, lie,
A church of grass stands up
And walls them, holy, in.

Fabulous the insects
Stud the air   20
Or walk on running water,
Klee-drawn saints
And bright as angels are.

Honeysuckle here
Is more than bees can bear
And time turns pale
And stops to catch its breath
And lovers slip their flesh

And light as pollen
Play on treble water   30
Till bodies reappear
And a shower of sun
To dry their languor.

Then two in one the lovers lie
And peel the skin of summer
With their teeth
And suck its marrow from a kiss
So charged with grace
The tongue, all knowing

40   Holds the sap of June
      Aloof from seasons, flowing.

      (1955)

Letter to My Children

      I guided you by rote —
      Nipple to spoon, from spoon
      To knife and fork,
      And many a weak maternal morning
      Bored the breakfast hour
      With "manners make the man,"
      And cleanliness I kissed
      But shunned its neighbour,
      Puzzled all my days
10   By the "I" in godliness.

      Before you turn
      And bare your faultless teeth at me
      Accept a useless gift, apology,
      Admit I churched you in the rites
      Of trivia
      And burned the family incense
      At a false god's altar.

      If we could start again,
      You, newbegotten, I
20   A clean stick peeled
      Of twenty paper layers of years
      I'd tell you only what you know
      But barely know you know,
      Teach one commandment,
      "Mind the senses and the soul
      Will take care of itself,
      Being five times blessed."

      (1955)

Variations on a Theme

"A man needs only to be turned round once with his eyes shut in this world to be lost."

— THOREAU

I
      There is always a first flinging
      Of the blood about in circles,
      A falling down, a sickness ringing

In the ear, a swivelling eye
Uprooting tree whose tendrils flower
On sagging skin of sky.

Green blades cut, they spin so fast.
Round and round, a child on grass
Whose name in anagram is lost.

II

I turned round once; I shut my eyes;   10
I opened them on truth or lies.
And this is what I saw though
Cannot say: or false or true.

From arteries in graves, columns
Rose to soil the sky, and down
Their fluted sides the overflow
Slid to earth, unrolled and spread
On stalk and stone its plushy red.

Trees had shed their limbs, become
Mobile marble guards. Secret   20
Their manoeuvres in this land;
And while they marched a mad dog's tooth,
Rabid violet, tore half my hand.

The wind blew from the south
Before I turned, but here a north
Wind blew, and I was lost. It blew
A milch cow[1] dry, a new moon down;
Then higher roared until it blew
Seven fuses of the sun.

III

We shut our eyes and turned once round   30
And were up borne by our down fall.
Such life was in us on the ground
That while we moved, earth ceased to roll,
And oceans lagged, and all the flames
Except our fire, and we were lost
In province that no settler names.

IV

I shut my eyes and turned once round;
I opened them on alien air;

---

1. **milch cow** Milk cow.

Sea had shrunk to farmer's pond
40   And sky was pink and distance near.
A forest and its nights were now
Woodpile for an old man's fire;
And where above me one black crow
Had cawed my spring, two dirty doves
Sang daintily. I stoned the birds
But no stone hit, for of white gloves
My hands were made; I stole a stick
To break the sky; it did not crack;
I could not curse — though I was lost,
50   Had trespassed on some stranger's dream
Where swan forswears his lust,
The gull his scream.

               (1957)

Irving Layton (1912–2006)

In 1952, Irving Layton played a long, fierce game of handball with his friend Louis Dudek, having agreed that whoever won was destined to become the greater poet. Layton triumphed, and in his memoir he insists that Dudek was resigned to his fate as a minor poet. The anecdote illustrates Layton's propensity for exaggeration and self-aggrandizement — he also once asserted that he had been born circumcised, and this qualified him as the new messiah.

His personal life, his poems, and his reviews all bear the mark of his powerful personality. No other Canadian poet has sustained such an energetic, sometimes vituperative, critique of post–World War II culture and of "philistine" Canadians, in particular. Although he published his first volume of poetry with First Statement Press in 1945, Layton did not achieve renown as a poet until the mid-1950s. Some of his poems were unabashedly erotic, reflecting the influence of D.H. Lawrence, and with them, Layton fed into the brewing sexual revolution that would erupt in the 1960s. Appearing regularly on the CBC TV debating program *Fighting Words,* he promoted himself relentlessly, finally attracting the attention of a commercial publisher. In *A Red Carpet for the Sun* (1959), Layton collected the best of his work, winning critical admiration and gaining a national audience. The volume won him a Governor General's Award.

The award confirmed for Layton that his early struggles had not been in vain. Born Israel Pincu Lazarovitch in Romania in 1912, he moved to Montreal with his family in 1913. They settled in a poor neighbourhood around rue St. Urbain, the multi-ethnic thoroughfare made famous by the novels of Mordecai Richler. At an early age, Layton acquired street smarts, and as a high school student he developed a passion for ideas and literature, which helped him to become a formidable debater and orator. In the 1940s, he enlisted in the Canadian Army, obtaining an honourable discharge a year later after endangering other soldiers during a training exercise (or so he says in his memoir); he earned a master's degree in political science from McGill University; he became a high school teacher, tutor, and college lecturer; he involved himself in *First Statement* magazine with Dudek and John Sutherland; and he published his first books at his own expense, despite the fact that he was struggling to support his second wife and his children.

Tenacity became the hallmark of Layton's life and his writing, which for him were insepa-rable. His poems of the 1950s were strongly influenced by Nietzsche's *Thus Spake Zarathustra* (which he called "a great and amazing book") and *The Will to Power* ("a colourful description of life's exuberance"), even though Nietzsche's reputation had been tainted by the appropriation of his ideas by the Nazi regime. Later, Layton's appreciation of Marx and his socialist politics would prompt the anti-communist American government to refuse him entry into the United States. Frustrated by this barrier erected between him and a large potential audience, the author of "Whatever Else Poetry Is Freedom" was forced to travel instead to countries such as Italy and Greece, where he was well received. He also undertook a reading tour of Canada in 1964 with Leonard Cohen, Phyllis Gotlieb, and Earle Birney. The National Film Board of Canada filmed the tour and released parts of the footage in 1965 as *Ladies and Gentlemen ... Mr. Leonard Cohen* — an indication that Cohen was supplanting Layton as the nation's most popular poet.

But Cohen was Layton's chosen one: he was the only contemporary Canadian poet Layton considered to be truly vital and original (aside from himself, of course). Despite this firm choice, and despite the fact that his frequent denunciations of others were often extremely caustic, Layton was a generous mentor to many other younger poets, including Al Purdy and Eli Mandel. But the midst of the fray was his natural habitat. In poems, reviews, and letters, he insulted the critics of his work and rebuked friends who disagreed with him (including Dudek, with whom Layton was especially harsh).

He also attacked all kinds of institutions for their hypocrisy, including Christianity. Critique of religion is central to his work, especially his later output. An atheist rebelling against his strict Jewish upbringing, Layton became convinced that it was his duty to reclaim Jesus as a Jew (as in "Song of a Frightened Jewish Boy") and denounce Christianity as a perversion of Christ's teachings. His general fascination with the human potential for violence is vividly illustrated in "Butterfly on Rock" and "Still Life" from *Balls for a One-Armed Juggler* (1963), poems in which animals are the victims. Later, this preoccupation metamorphosed into rage over the genocide of Jews during the Holocaust, and he wrote many poems condemning Nazi atrocities and supporting Jewish nationalism. Rejoicing in the success of Israel during the Six-Day War in "The New Sensibility" from *The Shattered Plinths* (1968), he claims that "The up-to-date poet / besides labouring at his craft / should be a dead shot." Similarly, in "For My Two Sons, Max and David," he directs his children to "Be gunners in the Israeli Air Force."

With time, Layton's controversiality lost its novelty and edge. In a 1979 review, his friend Purdy wrote that "Layton has been imitating himself for years, in a perfect parody of his own style, and has written nearly all of his poems before, some many times." Nevertheless, Layton's notorious ego would not be quelled. He said of Yahweh in "Credo" from *Europe and Other Bad News* (1981), "I laughed him out of the heavens / long ago." He failed, however, to realize one of his greatest ambitions: winning the Nobel Prize. He was nominated for a 1982 Nobel, but the laurels were claimed by Gabriel García Márquez.

In the course of his life, Irving Layton wrote more than 40 books of prose and poetry and married five times. In 1994, he was diagnosed with Alzheimer's disease, and he died in 2006 at the age of 93.

The Swimmer

The afternoon foreclosing, see
The swimmer plunges from his raft,
Opening the spray corollas[1] by his act of war —

---

1. **corollas** Inner petals of a flower.

The snake heads strike
Quickly and are silent.

Emerging see how for a moment
A brown weed with marvellous bulbs,
He lies imminent upon the water
While light and sound come with a sharp passion
10   From the gonad[2] sea around the Poles
And break in bright cockle-shells about his ears.

He dives, floats, goes under like a thief
Where his blood sings to the tiger shadows
In the scentless greenery that leads him home,
A male salmon down fretted stairways
Through underwater slums …

Stunned by the memory of lost gills
He frames gestures of self-absorption
Upon the skull-like beach;
20   Observes with instigated eyes
The sun that empties itself upon the water,
And the last wave romping in
To throw its boyhood on the marble sand.

(1945)

Composition in Late Spring

When Love ensnares my mind unbidden
       I am lost in the usual way
On a crowded street or avenue
Where I am lord of all the marquees,
And the traffic cop moving his lips
       Like a poet composing
Whistles a discovery of sparrows
About my head.

My mind, full of goats and pirates
10   And simpler than a boy's,
I walk through a forest of white arms
That embrace me like window-shoppers;
Friends praise me like a Turkish delight[1]
       Or a new kind of suspender
And children love me
Like a story.

---

2. **gonad** Organ (in men or women) that produces reproductive sex cells.

---

1. **Turkish delight** Sweet, sticky candy.

Conscience more flat than cardboard
      Over the gap in a sole,
I avoid the fanatic whose subway
Collapsed in his brain;
There's a sinking, but the madonna   20
      Who clings to my hairlock
Is saved: on shore the damned ones
Applaud with the vigour of bees.

The sparrows' golden plummeting
      From fearful rooftop
Shows the flesh dying into sunshine.
Fled to the green suburbs, Death
Lies scared to death under a heap of bones.
      Beauty buds from mire   30
And I, a singer in season, observe
Death is a name for beauty not in use.

No one is more happy, none can do more tricks.
      The sun melts like butter
Over my sweetcorn thoughts;
And, at last, both famous and good
I'm a Doge,[2] a dog
      At the end of a terrace
Where poems like angels like flakes of powder
Quaver above my prickling skin.   40

(1954)

The Birth of Tragedy

And me happiest when I compose poems.
      Love, power, the huzza of battle
      are something, are much;
yet a poem includes them like a pool
      water and reflection.
In me, nature's divided things —
      tree, mould on tree —
      have their fruition;
I am their core. Let them swap,
bandy,[1] like a flame swerve
I am their mouth; as a mouth I serve.   10

And I observe how the sensual moths
      big with odour and sunshine

---

2. **Doge** Until the 18th century, an elected leader of some Italian republics, like Venice.

---

1. **bandy** To pass back and forth.

dart into the perilous shrubbery;
or drop their visiting shadows
   upon the garden I one year made
of flowering stone to be a footstool
   for the perfect gods:
   who, friends to the ascending orders,
20 sustain all passionate meditations
and call down pardons
for the insurgent blood.

A quiet madman, never far from tears,
   I lie like a slain thing
   under the green air the trees
inhabit, or rest upon a chair
   towards which the inflammable air
tumbles on many robins' wings;
   noting how seasonably
30   leaf and blossom uncurl
and living things arrange their death,
while someone from afar off
blows birthday candles for the world.

               (1954)

The Fertile Muck

There are brightest apples on those trees
  but until I, fabulist, have spoken
they do not know their significance
or what other legends are hung like garlands
  on their black boughs twisting
like a rumour. The wind's noise is empty.

Nor are the winged insects better off
  though they wear my crafty eyes
wherever they alight. Stay here, my love;
10 you will see how delicately they deposit
  me on the leaves of elms
or fold me in the orient dust of summer.

And if in August joiners and bricklayers
  are thick as flies around us
building expensive bungalows for those
who do not need them, unless they release
  me roaring from their moth-proofed cupboards
their buyers will have no joy, no ease.

I could extend their rooms for them without cost
20 and give them crazy sundials

to tell the time with, but I have noticed
how my irregular footprint horrifies them
 evenings and Sunday afternoons:
they spray for hours to erase its shadow.

How to dominate reality? Love is one way;
 imagination another. Sit here
beside me, sweet; take my hard hand in yours.
We'll mark the butterflies disappearing over the hedge
 with tiny wristwatches on their wings:
our fingers touching the earth, like two Buddhas.   30

                    (1956)

Whatever Else Poetry Is Freedom

Whatever else poetry is freedom.
Forget the rhetoric, the trick of lying
All poets pick up sooner or later. From the river,
Rising like the thin voice of grey castratos[1] — the mist;
Poplars and pines grow straight but oaks are gnarled;
Old codgers[2] must speak of death, boys break windows;
Women lie honestly by their men at last.

And I who gave my Kate a blackened eye
Did to its vivid changing colours
Make up an incredible musical scale;   10
And now I balance on wooden stilts and dance
And thereby sing to the loftiest casements.
See how with polish I bow from the waist.
Space for these stilts! More space or I fail!

And a crown I say for my buffoon's head.
Yet no more fool am I than King Canute,[3]
Lord of our tribe, who scanned and scorned;
Who half-deceived, believed; and, poet, missed
The first white waves come nuzzling at his feet;
Then damned the courtiers and the foolish trial   20
With a most bewildering and unkingly jest.

It was the mist. It lies inside one like a destiny.
A real Jonah[4] it lies rotting like a lung.
And I know myself undone who am a clown
And wear a wreath of mist for a crown;

---

1. **castratos** Castrated male singers whose voices consequently remain soprano after puberty. 2. **codgers** Old men.
3. **King Canute** Danish king who ruled England from 1016 to 1035. Prompted by the flattery of courtiers, he commanded the sea to recede; after failing, he refused to wear his crown again. 4. **Jonah** Hebrew prophet who was disobedient to God, and consequently swallowed by a large fish.

Mist with the scent of dead apples,
Mist swirling from black oily waters at evening,
Mist from the fraternal graves of cemeteries.

It shall drive me to beg my food and at last
30   Hurl me broken I know and prostrate on the road;
Like a huge toad I saw, entire but dead,
That Time mordantly⁵ had blacked; O pressed
To the moist earth it pled for entry.
I shall be I say that stiff toad for sick with mist
And crazed I smell the odour of mortality.

And Time flames like a paraffin⁶ stove
And what it burns are the minutes I live.
At certain middays I have watched the cars
Bring me from afar their windshield suns;
40   What lay to my hand were blue fenders,
The suns extinguished, the drivers wearing sunglasses.
And it made me think I had touched a hearse.

So whatever else poetry is freedom. Let
Far off the impatient cadences reveal
A padding for my breathless stilts. Swivel,
O hero, in the fleshy groves, skin and glycerine,
And sing of lust, the sun's accompanying shadow
Like a vampire's wing, the stillness in dead feet —
Your stave⁷ brings resurrection, O aggrievèd⁸ king.

(1958)

For Mao Tse-Tung:¹
A Meditation on Flies and Kings

So, circling about my head, a fly.
Haloes of frantic monotone.
Then a smudge of blood smoking
On my fingers, let Jesus and Buddha cry.

Is theirs the way? Forgiveness of hurt?
Leprosariums?² Perhaps. But I
Am burning flesh and bone,
An indifferent creature between
Cloud and a stone;

---

5. **mordantly** Corrosively. 6. **paraffin** In its oil form, kerosene. 7. **stave** Staff. 8. **aggrievèd** Wronged.

1. **Mao Tse-Tung** Chairman of the Communist Party of China, leader of China from 1949 until his death in 1976.
2. **Leprosariums** Treatment hospitals for those suffering from leprosy.

Smash insects with my boot,
Feast on torn flowers, deride[3]
the nonillion[4] bushes by the road
(Their patience is very great.)
Jivatma,[5] they endure,
Endure and proliferate.

And the meek-browed and poor
In their solid tenements
(Etiolated,[6] they do not dance.)
Worry of priest and of commissar:
None may re-create them who are
Lowly and universal as the moss
Or like vegetation the winds toss
Sweeping to the open lake and sky.
I put down these words in blood
And would not be misunderstood:
They have their Christs and their legends
And out of their pocks[7] and ailments
Weave dear enchantments —
Poet and dictator, you are as alien as I.

On this remote and classic lake
Only the lapsing of the water can I hear
And the cold wind through the sumac.
The moneyed and their sunburnt children
Swarm other shores. Here is ecstasy,
The sun's outline made lucid
By each lacustral[8] cloud
And man naked with mystery.
They dance best who dance with desire,
Who lifting feet of fire from fire
Weave before they lie down
A red carpet for the sun.

I pity the meek in their religious cages
And flee them; and flee
The universal sodality[9]
Of joy-haters, joy-destroyers
(O Schiller,[10] wine-drunk and silly!)
The sufferers and their thick rages;
Enter this tragic forest where the trees

10

20

30

40

---

3. **deride** To laugh at with contempt. 4. **nonillion** Amount of 10^{30}. 5. **Jivatma** Sanskrit term for the individual soul, as well as the unified body of life. 6. **Etiolated** Drained of colour, weakened. 7. **pocks** Pus-blisters or their resultant scars. 8. **lacustral** Of lakes or ponds. 9. **sodality** Fellowship. 10. **Schiller** Friedrich Schiller (1759–1805), poet and philosopher who suggested that true freedom entailed being free from one's animal desires; he also believed that beauty could coax people to goodness.

Uprear as if for the graves of men,
50   All function and desire to offend
With themselves finally done;
And mark the dark pines farther on,
The sun's fires touching them at will,
Motionless like silent khans[11]
Mourning serene and terrible
Their Lord entombed in the blazing hill.

(1958)

A Tall Man Executes a Jig

I

So the man spread his blanket on the field
And watched the shafts of light between the tufts
And felt the sun push the grass towards him;
The noise he heard was that of whizzing flies,
The whistlings of some small imprudent birds,
And the ambiguous rumbles of cars
That made him look up at the sky, aware
Of the gnats that tilted against the wind
And in the sunlight turned to jigging motes.
10   Fruitflies he'd call them except there was no fruit
About, spoiling to hatch these glitterings,
These nervous dots for which the mind supplied
The closing sentences from Thucydides,[1]
Or from Euclid[2] having a savage nightmare.

II

Jig jig, jig jig. Like minuscule black links
Of a chain played with by some playful
Unapparent hand or the palpitant[3]
Summer haze bored with the hour's stillness.
He felt the sting and tingle afterwards
20   Of those leaving their orthodox unrest,
Leaving their undulant[4] excitation
To drop upon his sleeveless arm. The grass,
Even the wildflowers became black hairs
And himself a maddened speck among them.
Still the assaults of the small flies made him

---

11. khans Rulers of certain Asiatic communities.

1. closing sentences from Thucydides From Greek writer-historian Thucydides's *History of the Peloponnesian War*, in which a soldier seeks a way back to his army to apologize for his failings, and offers a sacrifice to Artemis, goddess of the hunt and the wild. The closing sentences of the *History* are missing. Layton equates the gnats with the ellipses typically used to note the incompletion. **2. Euclid** Greek mathematician (330–275 BC); especially interested in geometry. **3. palpitant** Trembling. **4. undulant** Wave-like.

Glad at last, until he saw purest joy
In their frantic jiggings under a hair,
So changed from those in the unrestraining air.

III

He stood up and felt himself enormous.
Felt as might Donatello[5] over stone,   30
Or Plato, or as a man who has held
A loved and lovely woman in his arms
And feels his forehead touch the emptied sky
Where all antinomies[6] flood into light.
Yet jig jig jig, the haloing black jots
Meshed with the wheeling fire of the sun:
Motion without meaning, disquietude
Without sense or purpose, ephemerides[7]
That mottled the resting summer air till
Gusts swept them from his sight like wisps of smoke.   40
Yet they returned, bringing a bee who, seeing
But a tall man, left him for a marigold.

IV

He doffed his aureole[8] of gnats and moved
Out of the field as the sun sank down,
A dying god upon the blood-red hills.
Ambition, pride, the ecstasy of sex,
And all circumstance of delight and grief,
That blood upon the mountain's side, that flood
Washed into a clear incredible pool
Below the ruddied peaks that pierced the sun.   50
He stood still and waited. If ever
The hour of revelation was come
It was now, here on the transfigured steep.
The sky darkened. Some birds chirped. Nothing else.
He thought the dying god had gone to sleep:
An Indian fakir[9] on his mat of nails.

V

And on the summit of the asphalt road
Which stretched towards the fiery town, the man
Saw one hill raised like a hairy arm, dark
With pines and cedars against the stricken sun   60
— The arm of Moses or of Joshua.[10]

---

5. **Donatello** Italian Renaissance artist and sculptor (1386–1466). 6. **antinomies** Paradoxes or contradictions.
7. **ephemerides** An ephemerid is a mayfly. Layton may also be referring to the ephemeral presence of the flies.
8. **aureole** A halo of light. 9. **fakir** A Muslim or Hindu ascetic, often performing miraculous feats of endurance.
10. **Moses, Joshua** Hebrew prophets. Layton alludes to Exodus 10:22, in which Moses raises his arm to bring darkness to
Egypt, and to Joshua 10:12, in which Joshua commands the sun to stand still.

He dropped his head and let fall the halo
Of mountains, purpling and silent as time,
To see temptation coiled before his feet:
A violated grass snake that lugged
Its intestine like a small red valise.[11]
A cold-eyed skinflint[12] it now was, and not
The manifest of that joyful wisdom,
The mirth and arrogant green flame of life;

70   Or earth's vivid tongue that flicked in praise of earth.

VI

And the man wept because pity was useless.
"Your jig's up; the flies come like kites,"[13] he said
And watched the grass snake crawl towards the hedge,
Convulsing and dragging into the dark
The satchel filled with curses for the earth,
For the odours of warm sedge, and the sun,
A blood-red organ in the dying sky.
Backwards it fell into a grassy ditch
Exposing its underside, white as milk,

80   And mocked by wisps of hay between its jaws;
And then it stiffened to its final length.
But though it opened its thin mouth to scream
A last silent scream that shook the black sky,
Adamant and fierce, the tall man did not curse.

VII

Beside the rigid snake the man stretched out
In fellowship of death; he lay silent
And stiff in the heavy grass with eyes shut,
Inhaling the moist odours of the night
Through which his mind tunnelled with flicking tongue

90   Backwards to caves, mounds, and sunken ledges
And desolate cliffs where come only kites,
And where of perished badgers and racoons
The claws alone remain, gripping the earth.
Meanwhile the green snake crept upon the sky,
Huge, his mailed[14] coat glittering with stars that made
The night bright, and blowing thin wreaths of cloud
Athwart the moon; and as the weary man
Stood up, coiled above his head, transforming all.

(1963)

---

11. valise Suitcase. **12. skinflint** A person who is reluctant to spend money. **13. kites** Hawks. **14. mailed** Armoured.

To the Victims of the Holocaust

Your terrible deaths are forgotten;
no one speaks of them any more.

The novelty of tattooed forearms
wore off quickly; people now say
your deaths are pure invention, a spoof.

More corrosive of human pride
than Copernicus or Darwin,[1] your martyrdoms
must lie entombed in silence.

The devil himself is absolved, polyhistors[2]
naming him the only fascist in Europe   10
ignorant you were changed into soap and smoke.

That's how the wind blows. Tomorrow
some *goy*[3] will observe you never existed
and the Holocaust your just deserts[4]
for starting wars and revolutions.

I live among the blind, the deaf, and the dumb.
I live among amnesiacs.

My murdered kin
let me be your parched and swollen tongue
uttering the maledictions[5]   20
bullets and gas silenced on your lips.

Fill, fill my ears with your direst curses.
I shall tongue them, unappeasable shades,
till the sun turns black in the sky.

(1978)

P.K. Page (1916–)

In 1977, P.K. Page taught a creative writing course at the University of Victoria and then vowed never to teach again. She was disheartened by the closed-mindedness of students who thought they had nothing to learn and who wanted to be free from influence. Page was frustrated, too, that they were unwilling to experiment, to exchange the subjective "I" for the objective eye. For Page — as both a poet and a painter who began her career in the 1930s, when modern visual media was poised to transform 20th-century culture — the eye is a vital motif.

---

1. **Copernicus, Darwin** Copernicus (1473–1543) speculated that the earth was not the centre of the universe; Darwin (1809–1882) explained that humans evolved from apes. 2. **polyhistors** Historians. 3. *goy* Disparaging term for a non-Jewish person. 4. **just deserts** Appropriate punishment. 5. **maledictions** Slander or cursing.

Page's interest in objectivity links her to the tradition of modernist poetry, which was influenced by French symbolist poets such as Baudelaire. His technique of *correspondances horizontales* entailed taking material objects and relating them to other objects, leading eventually to a vertical or abstract understanding of the poet's emotions. T.S. Eliot developed an analogous idea — the concept of the objective correlative. He further insisted that poetry should avoid focusing on personality and instead concentrate on images and their symbolic values. Page brought these tenets to her early work, along with the imagism and surrealism she gleaned from writers such as Federico García Lorca and painters such as Salvador Dali.

These values were also associated with the group of poets who published *Preview* magazine in Montreal in the 1940s. Although she was born in England in 1916 and raised in Alberta, Page spent her formative years after high-school in Montreal. There she joined the *Preview* group (Patrick Anderson, F.R. Scott, Neufville Shaw, and later A.M. Klein). These poets wanted their work to promote objectivity, compression, formalism, and an urbane, intellectual, and moderately socialist political conscience. In the responses to her work prior to the publication of *Cry Ararat! Poems Selected and New* (1967), she was often associated with the poetics and politics of *Preview,* even after its amalgamation with competitor *First Statement.*

Her affinities with *Preview* appear especially in *As Ten, As Twenty* (1946). This book, her first, contained her most anthologized works, including "The Stenographers" and "The Landlady," which epitomize her compassion for working people in an oppressive and alienating modern world. The collection also includes "Stories of Snow," which predicts the poetic comparisons she would make between snowy Canada and the much warmer countries she visited during her travels in the 1950s and 1960s. Her work of the 1940s embraces the metaphysical perspective of Eliot and W.H. Auden, and earlier poets such as W.B. Yeats.

The year *As Ten, As Twenty* was published, Page moved to Ottawa to be a scriptwriter for the National Film Board. Over the next four years, she wrote the poems that would form *The Metal and the Flower* (1954), the elegant and spare collection that won a Governor General's Award and that emphasized her interest in perception and vision — an interest particularly evident in such poems as "Photos of a Salt Mine," "Portrait of Marina," and "The Permanent Tourists." In Ottawa, she also met and married the NFB commissioner, Arthur Irwin (a past editor of *Maclean's* magazine). Irwin later became a diplomat, and they spent many years abroad, beginning with Australia (1953–56), then Brazil (1957–59), and Mexico and Guatemala (1960–64); they also lived in New York for parts of 1959 and 1960, when Irwin worked for the United Nations. These sojourns strengthened the elements of social protest and ecological concern in Page's later poems. They also led to a dramatic change in artistic direction — around 1956, she appeared to have abandoned poetry in favour of painting.

Her 10-year poetic silence began when, unable to speak Portuguese or relate to Brazilians except as an outsider, she resorted to describing her situation in images. She produced drawings and then paintings in a variety of media and eventually exhibited her work in Ontario, British Columbia, and Mexico under the name P.K. Irwin. Some of her visual art is reproduced in *Cry Ararat!*, *The Glass Air* (1985), and *Brazilian Journal* (1987); some is held by the National Gallery in Ottawa.

With her poem "After Rain" (written in 1954, published in 1956), Page anticipates her poetic silence and foreshadows the more personal work that she would produce after returning to poetry in 1967 with *Cry Ararat!* That year was Canada's centennial, and Page had only recently returned to the country and its literary community, having settled with her husband in Victoria in 1964. This more personal work coincides with the wave of nationalist sentiment in Canada in the late 1960s and Page's re-immersion in Canadian poetry, including the work of those who influenced her later books — among them, Patrick Lane, Margaret Avison, Gwendolyn MacEwen, and Margaret

Atwood. Due to their new degree of warmth, her post-silence poems were well received; by comparison, the 1940s reviews of Page's work written by *First Statement*'s John Sutherland were qualified in their praise. In her later work, she expands her concept of vision to the highly personal yet transcendental realm, perhaps because of a growing interest in Sufi philosophy (an Islamic mystical tradition) and the role of the poet as visionary prophet.

In her mid-70s, Page reflected on her long career as an artist in *Hologram: A Book of Glosas* (1994). This book contains 14 *glosas,* an early Renaissance form of Spanish origin. Each *glosa* begins with a stanza from a poem by someone else, and each line of the stanza becomes the closing line in a stanza of Page's own new poem. Page chose this intertextual form as an homage to poets who had influenced her over the years, including George Woodcock, Leonard Cohen, and Mark Strand. Through the startling juxtaposition of one poet's lines with another's, Page returned to one of the imagist principles that informed her early poetry, as if she had elegantly rounded a circle.

More recently, her book *Cosmologies: Poems Selected and New* (2003) experiments with circular forms such as the *pantoum* and the villanelle, whose repetitions heighten the effect of her subject: parallel universes. The *pantoum* unfolds through a series of staggered repetitions and ends by repeating the first line. The villanelle, too, returns to its beginning, using two parallel refrains that meet at the end. In using these forms (and the *glosa*), Page demonstrated her technical facility and her interest in the dimensional transparency of both vision and language.

Page followed *Cry Ararat!* with *The Sun and the Moon and Other Fictions* (1973), edited by Margaret Atwood and including the short novel that she had originally published under the pseudonym Judith Cape. Page went on to publish many more books over the years; most recently, she produced a verse memoir entitled *Hand Luggage* (2006).

The Stenographers [1]

After the brief bivouac[2] of Sunday,
their eyes, in the forced march of Monday to Saturday,
hoist the white flag, flutter in the snow-storm of paper,
haul it down and crack in the mid-sun of temper.

In the pause between the first draft and the carbon
they glimpse the smooth hours when they were children —
the ride in the ice-cart, the ice-man's name,
the end of the route and the long walk home;

remember the sea where floats at high tide
were sea marrows growing on the scatter-green vine
or spools of grey toffee, or wasps' nests on water;
remember the sand and the leaves of the country.

Bell rings and they go and the voice draws their pencil
like a sled across snow; when its runners are frozen
rope snaps and the voice then is pulling no burden
but runs like a dog on the winter of paper.

10

---

1. **Stenographers** Professionals employed to take dictation. 2. **bivouac** A temporary military encampment.

Their climates are winter and summer — no wind
for the kites of their hearts — no wind for a flight;
a breeze at the most, to tumble them over
20 and leave them like rubbish — the boy-friends of blood.

In the inch of the noon as they move they are stagnant.
The terrible calm of the noon is their anguish;
the lip of the counter, the shapes of the straws
like icicles breaking their tongues, are invaders.

Their beds are their oceans — salt water of weeping
the waves that they know — the tide before sleep;
and fighting to drown they assemble their sheep
in columns and watch them leap desks for their fences
and stare at them with their own mirror-worn faces.

30 In the felt of the morning the calico-minded,[3]
sufficiently starched, insert papers, hit keys,
efficient and sure as their adding machines;
yet they weep in the vault, they are taut as net curtains
stretched upon frames. In their eyes I have seen
the pin men of madness in marathon trim
race round the track of the stadium pupil.

(1942)

Stories of Snow

Those in the vegetable rain retain
an area behind their sprouting eyes
held soft and rounded with the dream of snow
precious and reminiscent as those globes —
souvenir of some never-nether land —
which hold their snow-storms circular, complete,
high in a tall and teakwood cabinet.

In countries where the leaves are large as hands
where flowers protrude their fleshy chins
10 and call their colours,
an imaginary snow-storm sometimes falls
among the lilies.
And in the early morning one will waken
to think the glowing linen of his pillow
a northern drift, will find himself mistaken
and lie back weeping.
And there the story shifts from head to head,

---

3. **calico-minded** Calico is a type of cotton fabric.

of how in Holland, from their feather beds
hunters arise and part the flakes and go
forth to the frozen lakes in search of swans —   20
the snow-light falling white along their guns,
their breath in plumes.
While tethered in the wind like sleeping gulls
ice-boats wait the raising of their wings
to skim the electric ice at such a speed
they leap jet strips of naked water,
and how these flying, sailing hunters feel
air in their mouths as terrible as ether.
And on the story runs that even drinks
in that white landscape dare to be no colour;   30
how flasked and water clear, the liquor slips
silver against the hunters' moving hips.
And of the swan in death these dreamers tell
of its last flight and how it falls, a plummet,
pierced by the freezing bullet
and how three feathers, loosened by the shot,
descend like snow upon it.
While hunters plunge their fingers in its down
deep as a drift, and dive their hands
up to the neck of the wrist   40
in that warm metamorphosis of snow
as gentle as the sort that woodsmen know
who, lost in the white circle, fall at last
and dream their way to death.

And stories of this kind are often told
in countries where great flowers bar the roads
with reds and blues which seal the route to snow —
as if, in telling, raconteurs unlock
the colour with its complement and go
through to the area behind the eyes   50
where silent, unrefractive whiteness lies.

(1945)

The Permanent Tourists

Somnolent[1] through landscapes and by trees
nondescript, almost anonymous,
they alter as they enter foreign cities —
the terrible tourists with their empty eyes
longing to be filled with monuments.

---

1. **Somnolent** Sleepy.

Verge upon statues in the public squares
remembering the promise of memorials
yet never enter the entire event
as dogs, abroad in any kind of weather,
10   move perfectly within their rainy climate.

Lock themselves into snapshots on the steps
of monolithic bronze as if suspecting
the subtle mourning of the photograph
might later conjure in the memory
all they are now incapable of feeling.

And search all heroes out: the boy who gave
his life to save a town; the stolid queen;
forgotten politicians minus names
and the plunging war dead, permanently brave,
20   forever and ever going down to death.

Look, you can see them nude in any café
reading their histories from the bill of fare,
creating futures from a foreign teacup.
Philosophies like ferns bloom from the fable
that travel is broadening at the café table.

Yet somehow beautiful, they stamp the plaza.
Classic in their anxiety they call
all sculptured immemorial stone
into their passive eyes, as rivers
30   draw ruined columns to their placid glass.

(1948)

Arras[1]

Consider a new habit — classical,
and trees espaliered[2] on the wall like candelabra.
How still upon that lawn our sandalled feet.

But a peacock rattling his rattan tail and screaming
has found a point of entry. Through whose eye
did it insinuate in furled disguise
to shake its jewels and silk upon that grass?

The peaches hang like lanterns. No one joins
those figures on the arras.

---

1. **Arras** A tapestry with a complex weave. 2. **espaliered** Trained to grow flat against a wall.

Who am I   10
or who am I become that walking here
I am observer, other, Gemini,[3]
starred for a green garden of cinema?

I ask, what did they deal me in this pack?
The cards, all suits, are royal when I look.
My fingers slipping on a monarch's face
twitch and grow slack.
I want a hand to clutch, a heart to crack.

No one is moving now, the stillness is
infinite. If I should make a break …   20
take to my springy heels …? But nothing moves.
The spinning world is stuck upon its poles,
the stillness points a bone at me. I fear
the future on this arras.
                         I confess:

It was my eye.

Voluptuous it came.
Its head the ferrule[4] and its lovely tail
folded so sweetly; it was strangely slim
to fit the retina. And then it shook   30
and was a peacock — living patina,[5]
eye-bright, maculate![6]
Does no one care?

I thought their hands might hold me if I spoke.
I dreamed the bite of fingers in my flesh,
their poke smashed by an image, but they stand
as if within a treacle,[7] motionless,
folding slow eyes on nothing.
                         While they stare
another line has trolled the encircling air,   40
another bird assumes its furled disguise.

                                             (1954)

Photos of a Salt Mine

How innocent their lives look,
how like a child's
dream of caves and winter, both combined;

---

3. Gemini Zodiac sign of the twins. **4. ferrule** Metal reinforcement at the end of a tube. **5. patina** A film left behind by oxidizing metal; a sheen produced over time. **6. maculate** Spotted or tarnished. **7. treacle** Molasses.

the steep descent to whiteness
and the stope[1]
with its striated[2] walls
their folds all leaning as if pointing to
the greater whiteness still,
that great white bank
10 with its decisive front,
that seam upon a slope,
salt's lovely ice.
And wonderful underfoot the snow of salt
the fine
particles a broom could sweep,
one thinks
muckers[3] might make angels in its drifts
as children do in snow,
lovers in sheets,
20 lie down and leave imprinted where they lay
a feathered creature holier than they.
And in the outworked stopes
with lamps and ropes
up miniature matterhorns[4]
the miners climb
probe with their lights
the ancient folds of rock —
syncline and anticline[5] —
and scoop from darkness an Aladdin's cave:[6]
30 rubies and opals glitter from its walls.
But hoses douse the brilliance of these jewels,
melt fire to brine.
Salt's bitter water trickles thin and forms,
slow fathoms down,
a lake within a cave,
lacquered with jet —
white's opposite.
There grey on black the boating miners float
to mend the stays and struts of that old stope
40 and deeply underground
their words resound,
are multiplied by echo, swell and grow
and make a climate of a miner's voice.
So all the photographs like children's wishes
are filled with caves or winter,

---

1. **stope** Excavation or mining in vertical shafts. 2. **striated** Full of parallel grooves. 3. **muckers** Idlers.
4. **matterhorns** Peaks; from Matterhorn, a mountain on the border of Switzerland and Italy. 5. **syncline, anticline**
Downward-curving fold and arch-shaped fold, respectively. 6. **Aladdin's cave** From a story in the *One Thousand and One
Nights,* a cave filled with booby-trapped treasures.

innocence
has acted as a filter,
selected only beauty from the mine.
Except in the last picture,
it is shot 50
from an acute high angle. In a pit
figures the size of pins are strangely lit
and might be dancing but you know they're not.
Like Dante's vision of the nether hell[7]
men struggle with the bright cold fires of salt,
locked in the black inferno of the rock:
the filter here, not innocence but guilt.

(1954)

T-Bar

Relentless, black on white, the cable runs
through metal arches up the mountain side.
At intervals giant pickaxes are hung
on long hydraulic springs. The skiers ride
propped by the axehead, twin automatons
supported by its handle, one each side.

In twos they move slow motion up the steep
incision in the mountain. Climb. Climb.
Somnambulists,[1] bolt upright in their sleep
their phantom poles swung lazily behind, 10
while to the right, the empty T-bars keep
in mute descent, slow monstrous jigging time.

Captive the skiers now and innocent,
wards of eternity, each pair alone.
They mount the easy vertical ascent,
pass through successive arches, bride and groom,
as through successive naves,[2] are newly wed
participants in some recurring dream.

So do they move forever. Clocks are broken.
In zones of silence they grow tall and slow,
inanimate dreamers, mild and gentle-spoken 20
blood-brothers of the haemophilic[3] snow

---

7. Dante's vision of the nether hell Both fire and ice play prominent roles in the circles of Hell described in Dante's
Divine Comedy.

1. Somnambulists Sleepwalkers. **2. naves** Areas in a church. **3. haemophilic** One who has haemophilia, a condition in
which blood does not clot easily.

until the summit breaks and they awaken
imagos[4] from the stricture[5] of the tow.

Jerked from her chrysalis the sleeping bride
suffers too sudden freedom like a pain.
The dreaming bridegroom severed from her side
singles her out, the old wound aches again.
Uncertain, lost, upon a wintry height
30   these two, not separate, but no longer one.

Now clocks begin to peck and sing. The slow
extended minute like a rubber band
contracts to catapult them through the snow
in tandem trajectory while behind
etching the sky-line, obdurate[6] and slow
the spastic T-bars pivot and descend.

(1954)

After Rain

The snails have made a garden of green lace:
broderie anglaise from the cabbages,
chantilly from the choux-fleurs, tiny veils —
I see already that I lift the blind
upon a woman's wardrobe of the mind.

Such female whimsy floats about me like
a kind of tulle, a flimsy mesh,
while feet in gum boots[1] pace the rectangles —
garden abstracted, geometry awash —
10   an unknown theorem argued in green ink,
dropped in the bath.
Euclid[2] in glorious chlorophyll, half drunk.

I none too sober slipping in the mud
where rigged with guys[3] of rain
the clothes-reel gauche[4]
as the rangey skeleton of some
gaunt delicate spidery mute
is pitched as if
listening;
20   while hung from one thin rib
a silver web —

---

4. **imagos** The last stage in the metamorphosis of insects. 5. **stricture** Contraction. 6. **obdurate** Inflexible.

---

1. **gum boots** Boots for wet weather. 2. **Euclid** Greek mathematician (330–275 BC) who was especially interested in geometry. 3. **guys** Ropes or cables used to secure an object. 4. **gauche** Clumsy; unsophisticated.

its infant, skeletal, diminutive,
now sagged with sequins, pulled ellipsoid,[5]
glistening.

I suffer shame in all these images.
The garden is primeval, Giovanni
in soggy denim squelches by my hub
over his ruin,
shakes a doleful head.
But he so beautiful and diademmed,[6]   30
his long Italian hands so wrung with rain
I find his ache exists beyond my rim
and almost weep to see a broken man
made subject to my whim.

O choir him, birds, and let him come to rest
within this beauty as one rests in love,
till pears upon the bough
encrusted with
small snails as pale as pearls
hang golden in   40
a heart that knows tears are a part of love.

And choir me too to keep my heart a size
larger than seeing, unseduced by each
bright glimpse of beauty striking like a bell,
so that the whole may toll,
its meaning shine
clear of the myriad images that still —
do what I will — encumber its pure line.

(1956)

Cook's Mountains[1]

By naming them he made them.
They were there
before he came
but they were not the same.
It was his gaze
that glazed each one.
He saw
the Glass House Mountains in his glass.
They shone.

---

5. **ellipsoid** Rounded. 6. **diademmed** Crowned.

1. **Cook's Mountains** The Glass House Mountains of Queensland, Australia, named by explorer James Cook in 1770; he likened their shape to British greenhouses.

10   And still they shine.
        We saw them as we drove —
        sudden, surrealist, conical
        they rose
        out of the rain forest.
        The driver said,
        "Those are the Glass House Mountains up ahead."

        And instantly they altered to become
        the sum of shape and name.
        Two strangenesses united into one
20   more strange than either.
        Neither of us now
        remembers how they looked before they broke
        the light to fragments as the driver spoke.

        Like mounds of mica,[2]
        hive-shaped hothouses,[3]
        mountains of mirror glimmering
        they form
        in diamond panes behind the tree ferns of
        the dark imagination,
30   burn and shake
        the lovely light of Queensland like a bell
        reflecting Cook upon a deck
        his tongue
        silvered with paradox and metaphor.

                                                          (1967)

After Reading *Albino Pheasants*[1]

    For Pat Lane

    Pale beak … *pale eye* … the dark imagination
    flares like magnesium. Add but *pale flesh*
    and I am lifted to a weightless world:
    watered cerulean,[2] chrome-yellow (light)
    and green, veronese[3] — if I remember — a soft wash
    recalls a summer evening sky.

    At Barro de Navidad[4] we watched the sky
    fade softly like a bruise. Was it imagination
    that showed us Venus phosphorescent[5] in a wash

---

2. mica Minerals forming thin, brittle, translucent layers. **3. hothouses** Greenhouses.

1. *Albino Pheasants* Poem by Patrick Lane, published in 1977. "Pale beak," "pale eye," and "pale flesh" are from the poem. See Lane's "Albino Pheasants" in this volume. **2. cerulean** A sky-blue. **3. veronese** A bright greem popularized in Italian art of Verona. **4. Barro de Navidad** A coastal town in Mexico. **5. phosphorescent** Emitting light.

of air and ozone? — a phosphorescence flesh   10
wears like a mantle in bright moonlight,
a natural skin-tone in that other world.

Why should I wish to escape this world?
Why should three phrases alter the colour of the sky
the clarity, texture even, of the light?
What is there about the irrepressible imagination
that the adjective *pale* modifying *beak*, *eye* and *flesh*
can set my sensibilities awash?

If with my thickest brush I were to lay a wash
of thinnest watercolour I could make a world   20
as unlike my own dense flesh
as the high-noon midsummer sky;
but it would not catch at my imagination
or change the waves or particles of light

yet *pale* can tip the scales, make light
this heavy planet. If I were to wash
everything I own in mercury, would imagination
run rampant in that suddenly silver world —
free me from gravity, set me floating sky-
ward — thistledown — permanently disburdened of my flesh?   30

Like cygnets[6] hatched by ducks, our minds and flesh
are imprinted early — what to me is light
may be dark to one born under a sunny sky.
And however cool the water my truth won't wash
without shrinking except in its own world
which is one part matter, nine parts imagination.

I fear flesh which blocks imagination,
the light of reason which constricts the world.
Pale beak ... pale eye ... pale flesh ... My sky's awash.

                                                                               (1978)

Margaret Avison (1918–)

Although Margaret Avison stated in a 1948 review that to write poetry is "to discipline speech into clarity," her own work has featured wordplay, unusual syntax, and intertextual references, all of which force the reader to search for meaning. Furthermore, many of her allusions — like those to early astronomers Tycho Brahe and Johannes Kepler in "Dispersed Titles" — might be unfamiliar to students of literature.

---

6. **cygnets** Young swans.

Avison was born in 1918 in Galt, Ontario (now Cambridge), to a strongly Methodist family. From Ontario, the family moved to Saskatchewan and then to Calgary, Alberta. In her early teen years, Avison was horrified by the plight of starving people during the Great Depression, and she stopped eating in protest. Her fast became what we would now call anorexia nervosa, and it took her three years to recover her health. She would need 30 more years to recover her faith, and she was still searching when she published her first book, *Winter Sun* (1960), in which she displays her interest in history and scientific reality rather than religion.

She had been reluctant to publish a collection, but she had already built an enthusiastic readership through her contributions to prestigious journals such as *Poetry* and *Contemporary Verse*. She was included in *The Book of Canadian Poetry* (1943) when she was only 25 (though she had published her first poem at 14). But, bolstered by the encouragement of friends, she produced *Winter Sun,* which received accolades for its "superb poetic dexterity." It won the Governor General's Award.

It was a bleak but urbane book — abstract and detached in its treatment of death (as in "The Apex Animal," "On the Death of France Darte Scott," or "Jael's Part"), but cosmopolitan in its modernist approach to traditional forms such as the sonnet. In the sequence that ends with "Butterfly Bones: Sonnet against Sonnets," the poet wonders whether the sonnet's rigid form could "strike men blind / like Adam's lexicon locked in the mind." A rejection of dogmatic obeisance to both religion and poetic tradition is hinted at in the previous sonnet, as well — the inscrutable "Snow," which also employs metaphors of vision: "Nobody stuffs the world in at your eyes. / The optic heart must venture: a jail-break / And re-creation." In other words, the heart must learn to see, because the eye and the mind will be blind without it.

In 1963, Avison began graduate work at the University of Toronto, where she had earned a B.A. in 1940 from Victoria College. Her M.A. thesis was on Byron's *Don Juan,* which attests to the influence of the Romantic poets on her work and on her interest in the sublime. Also in 1963, Avison returned to the church, partly inspired by William James's *The Varieties of Religious Experience* (1902) and the Gospel of Saint John. She spent two intense months writing the poems for her next book, *The Dumbfounding* (1966), and she also attended the famous summer poetry workshop at the University of British Columbia. Some critics maintain that the new styles introduced by the American poets conducting the workshop were powerfully attractive to the young Canadian poets who attended it, and that Canadian poetry was thus altered forever. But Avison cannot be included in this generalization. She was too independent to associate herself closely with the groups that formed at the workshop; instead, she resisted trends, especially with *The Dumbfounding* and the unfashionably religious books that she produced after it. In short, Avison became a religious writer in an increasingly secular age.

Perhaps because of her renewed sense of having a message to convey, her poems became more accessible and sensuous, stressing daily, physical experience over intellectual, metaphysical conceits. Shortly after publishing *The Dumbfounding,* she began lecturing at the University of Toronto's Scarborough College while working on a Ph.D., which she would never finish. In 1968, she started to work full time at the Presbyterian Church Mission in downtown Toronto, and from 1972 to 1973, she served as writer-in-residence at the University of Western Ontario. In 1978, she published *Sunblue,* which one critic identified as a devotional book in the English tradition; the titles of many of the poems clearly signal their religious orientation — for example, "He Couldn't Be Safe (Isaiah 53:5)." Still, *Sunblue* begins with a series of sketches of Toronto and the surrounding area, and urban space is a motif throughout the collection.

Avison's Toronto teaching experiences inspired *Sunblue*'s "Strong Yellow, for Reading Aloud," which contains a dialogue between "Miss Avison" and some students who wonder why she wrote "The Apex Animal." In "Strong Yellow," she distinguishes between nature in the form of the horse in "The Apex Animal" and God. Nevertheless, she remains ambiguous about the relationship between nature and God until, in "Potentiality" from *Not Yet but Still* (1997), she suggests that nature and God share "a bond that makes them one."

Avison did not stop contemplating the mysteries of Christianity, nor did she abandon her Christian projects. From 1978 to 1986, she worked at Toronto's Mustard Seed Mission, and she was appointed an Officer of the Order of Canada in 1985. In 1989, she published *No Time,* which won her a second Governor General's Award. It was only the fourth book in a career that had started in the 1930s. One commentator described *No Time* as a "gritty religious vision"; the extended meditations on death in "The Jo Poems" and "My Mother's Death" are balanced with "Radical Hope," which "gives life worth … hid in a seed for growth" and "Enduring," which evokes trees that "wait their lifetimes … for the sounding / the long wind moves them to." Again, nature and religion are merged in metaphor.

According to one critic, there are 111 question marks in only 63 poems in *Not Yet but Still*, but in her next book, *Concrete and Wild Carrot* (2002), Avison was not so tentative. In "Dividing Goods," the poet notes that "They say it's wrong to / push a parable." She acknowledges that "Words have their life too, won't / compact into a theorem," but she pushes her parables with confidence in this book. The collection won the 2003 Griffin Prize. Avison's next book, *Momentary Dark* (2006), extended some of the spatial and environmental themes from earlier books into a meditation on urban green spaces.

Snow

Nobody stuffs the world in at your eyes.
The optic heart must venture: a jail-break
And re-creation. Sedges and wild rice
Chase rivery pewter. The astonished cinders quake
With rhizomes.¹ All ways through the electric air
Trundle² candy-bright discs; they are desolate
Toys if the soul's gates seal, and cannot bear,
Must shudder under, creation's unseen freight.
But soft, there is snow's legend: colour of mourning
Along the yellow Yangtze³ where the wheel   10
Spins an indifferent stasis that's death's warning.
Asters of tumbled quietness reveal
Their petals. Suffering this starry blur
The rest may ring your change, sad listener.

(1960)

---

1. **rhizomes** A root which grows underground and sends up new shoots. 2. **Trundle** Roll unevenly. 3. **Yangtze** The longest river in China, which runs from the Tibetan Plateau into the East China Sea at Shanghai.

The Apex[1] Animal

A Horse, thin-coloured as oranges ripened in freight-cars
which have shaken casements through the miles of night
across three nights of field and waterfront warehouses —
rather, the narrow Head of the Horse[2]
with the teeth shining and white ear-tufts:
It, I fancy, and from experience
commend the fancy to your inner eye,
It is the One, in a patch of altitude
troubled only by clarity of weather,
10 Who sees, the ultimate Recipient
of what happens, the One Who is aware
when, in the administrative wing
a clerk returns from noon-day, though
the ointment of mortality
for one strange hour, in all his lustreless life,
has touched his face.

(For that Head of a Horse there is no question
whether he spent the noon-hour with a friend,
below street-level, or on the parapet[3] —
20 a matter which may safely rest
in mortal memory.)

(1960)

Strong Yellow, for Reading Aloud

written for and read to English 389's class when asked to comment on my poem
"The Apex Animal," etc.

A painted horse,
a horse-sized clay horse, really,
like blue riverclay, painted,
with real mural eyes — or a
Clydesdale[1] with his cuff-tufts
barbered[2] — the mane
marcelled[3] like a conch and cropped and plastered down like a
merry-go-round pony's
without the varnish —
10 all kinds confounding,
yet a powerful presence

---

1. **Apex** Climax or peak. 2. **Head of the Horse** It has been suggested that this refers to the Horsehead Nebula, a cloud of gases and energy which is shaped like a horse's head. 3. **parapet** Defensive wall.

1. **Clydesdale** Scottish farm-horses, with long hair covering the lower legs and hooves (cuff-tufts). 2. **barbered** The tails and manes of Clydesdale horses are often kept short; an additional pun may come from the Barb, or Barbary, horse, which was first found in Northern Africa. 3. **marcelled** Curled.

on the rainy Sunday diningroom wall,
framed by a shallow niche ...

Q: "Miss Avison could you
    relate that to the 'head of a horse'?"

No. No. That one
was strong yellow — almost tangerine, with
white hairs, the eyes
whited too as if
pulled back by the hair   20
so the eyeballs would water with wind in them,
one you'd call Whitey, maybe,
though he was not, I say,
white ...

Q: "Auburn?"

It was not a horse-shaped horse,
or sized.   It loomed.   Only the
narrow forehead part, the
eyes starting   loose and appled,
and shoulder-streaming part ...   30
Colour? a stain on the
soiled snow-mattress-colour of
the office-day noon-hour mezzanine[4]
            that is the sky downtown.

Q: "The Head of the Horse
    'sees' you say in that poem.
    Was that your vision of
    God, at that period
    in your development?"

Who I was then we   40
both approach timorously[5] —
or I do, believe me!
But I think, reading the lines,
the person looking *up* like that
was squeezed solid, only a crowd-pressed
mass of herself at shoulder
level, as it were, or at least
nine to noon, and the p.m. still to come
day *in* day *out*   as the saying goes
which pretty well covers everything   50
or seems to, in *and* out then,
        when it's like that: no heart, no surprises, no

---

4. **mezzanine** Low balcony or landing. 5. **timorously** Apprehensively.

people-scope, no utterances,
no strangeness, no nougat of delight
     to touch, and worse,
no secret cherished in the
midriff then.

Whom you look up from that to
is Possibility not
60 God.
   I'd think …

Q: "Strong yellow."

Yes! Not the clay-blue
with rump and hoof and all and almost
eyelashes, the pupil
fixed on you, on that wall of
fake hunt, fake aristocracy
in this fake Sunday
diningroom I was telling
70 about. …

              (1978)

Meeting Together of Poles and Latitudes (in Prospect)

Those who fling off, toss head,
 taste the bitter morning, and have at it —
 thresh, knead, dam, weld,
 wave baton, force
 marches through squirming bogs,
 not from contempt, but
 from thrust, unslakable[1] thirsty,
 amorous of every tower and twig, and
 yet like railroad engines with
10 longings for their landscapes (pistons pounding)
 rock fulminating[2] through
 wrecked love, unslakably loving —

Seldom encounter at the Judgment Seat
those who are flung off, sit
 dazed awhile, gather concentration,
 follow vapor-trails with shriveling wonder,
 pilfer,[3] mow, play jongleur[4]
 with mathematic signs, or

---

1. unslakable Insatiably. **2. fulminating** Exploding. **3. pilfer** Steal. **4. jongleur** Medieval minstrel and entertainer.

tracing the forced marches make
peculiar cats-cradles of telephone wire,   20
lap absently at sundown, love
as the stray dog on foreign hills
a bone-myth, atavistically,[5]
needing more faith, and fewer miles, but
slumber-troubled by it,
wanting for death that
myth-clay, though
scratch-happy in these (foreign) brambly wilds;

But when they approach each other
The place is an astonishment: 30
Runways shudder with little planes
practicing folk-dance steps or
playing hornet,
sky makes its ample ruling
clear as a primary child's exercise-book
in somebody else's language,
and the rivers under the earth
foam without whiteness, domed down,
as they foam indifferently every
day and night (if you'd call that day and night)   40
not knowing how they wait, at the node, the
curious encounter.

                                                                   (1966)

Searching and Sounding

In July this early sky is
a slope-field, a tangled
shining — blue-green, moist, in
heaped up pea-vines, in milk-hidden
tendrils, in light so strong
it seems a shadow of
further light, were the heart
large enough to find its succulence[1]
and feed and not be glutted there.

I look for you   10
who only know the
melding and the forming of such heart,

and find you here
in the sour air

---

5. **atavistically** Relapsing to previously held traits after a period of difference; an evolutionary throwback.

---

1. **succulence** Juicy richness; succulent plants retain water and thus need little to survive.

of a morning-after rooming-house[2] hall-bedroom;
not in Gethsemane's[3] grass, perfumed with prayer,
but here,
seeking to cool the grey-stubbled cheek
    and the filth-choked throat
20   and the scalding self-loathing heart, and
failing, for he is
sick,
for I …

I run from you to
the blinding blue of the
loveliness of this wasting
morning, and know
it is only with you
I can find the fields of brilliance
30 to burn out the sockets of the eyes that want no
weeping
though I am he
      or I am
a babbling boy
aged twenty, mentally distracted, blunted
by sedatives and too-long innocence
without your hand, teaching his the axe-heft or
    throttle-bar or
      grease-monkey's gun or
40   any craft or art.

And as I run I cry
"But I need something human,
somebody now, here, with me."
Running from you.
The sunlight is sundered by cloud-mass.

My heart is sore, as its
bricked-in ovens smoulder,
for I know whose hand at my elbow
I fling from me as I run.

50 But you have come and sounded
a music around me, newly,

as though you can clear
all tears from our eyes only
if we sound the wells of weeping with

---

2. **rooming-house** A boarding house, where the house-owner may also provide meals. 3. **Gethsemane's** The garden near Jerusalem where Christ was betrayed by Judas Iscariot. Also where he prayed, the night before his crucifixion, for the sins of the world.

another's heart, and hear
another's music only.

Lord, the light deepens as the
summer day goes down
in lakes of stillness.
Dwarf that I am, and spent,   60
touch my wet face with
the little light I can bear now, to mirror,
and keep me
close, into sleeping.

——————

From the pearl and grey of daybreak
you have brought me to
sandstone, baldness, the place
of jackals, the sparrow's skull,
tumbled skeletons of what were
hills clothed in forest   70
and spongy meadows, the place of
baked stone, dryness, famine,
of howling among the tombs.

   From the first dews, the
      grasses at their budding,
         fragrance of mountain snow
            and sunfat cedars
to the farthest reaches
where your Descent began, on the beach gravel
ground by sea-slimed teeth ...   80
those bloodless horses ...

To what strange fruits in
the ocean's orchards?

Reaching
with Light that is perfect, needed no
   kernels to swell nor juices to syrup nor
   any more making — *all* newness —
   all being
that the remotest fishrib,
the hairiest pink-thing there   90
might as one fragment
make towards the fullness you
put off, there, on the
ravening shore I view, from
my gull-blanched cliffs,
and shiver.

GATHER my fragments towards
the radium,[4] the
all-swallowing moment
100   once more.

(1966)

Just Left *or* The Night Margaret Laurence[1] Died

Bare branches studded once with jewelled birds
Someone inexorably[2] plunders
One by one till an
Impoverished wintry sky from hill to
Darkening hill reveals
Untreasured tree-spikes, almost only
(One bunched bird left
His eye aglimmer there).

Waiting, dim
10   Loneliness, place of
That withdrawing vision —
More than the well of light from
The first far planet —
Fills, fills, fills, fills.

Mutable mortal night
Blinds mortal day
Still to changelessness.

The perched, askew,
Will ruffle still as the day-ocean
20   Lips in and foams towards flood of
All emptiness exposed.

(1989)

Al Purdy (1918–2000)

"This is my last book," declared Al Purdy in the preface to *Beyond Remembering* (2000), the collection of poems published the year he died of lung cancer. Such bluntness was typical of Purdy, whose post-1960 work was plain-spoken, informal, comic but also contemplative. In the 20 years prior to what he called his "watershed" *Poems for All the Annettes* (1962) and *The Cariboo Horses* (1965), he laboured to overcome the influence of poets such as Bliss Carman and Charles G.D. Roberts. Their mark on his work remained strong from his self-published *The Enchanted*

---

4. radium A luminous, bright white metallic element.

1. Margaret Laurence Canadian writer (1926–1987); Laurence was diagnosed with lung cancer in 1986 and, following a grave prognosis, committed suicide on 5 January 1987. **2. inexorably** Persistently.

Echo (1944) to his 1950s offerings. Eventually, however, following the example of poets Milton Acorn and Irving Layton, he crafted the distinctive style that won him readers, two Governor General's Awards, and inclusion in the Order of Canada.

Purdy's late maturation might be attributed to the tenacious influence of the Confederation poets and also to the transient lifestyle of his youth. He was born in Wooler, Ontario, in 1918; he was raised there and in Trenton, where a munitions factory had exploded not long before his birth. His one novel, the semi-autobiographical *A Splinter in the Heart* (1990), describes growing up in the aftermath of this event. He learned to read at about age seven, and he often read a book a day. He even feigned a serious illness for "a month or so," he wrote, so that he could stay home from school and read. His unsatisfied interest in books and nascent nonconformist attitude prompted him to quit school at the age of 16.

Temporarily free from institutional constraints, he hitchhiked and hid on trains travelling across the country, and in the process he gained an understanding of hardship, of self-reliance, and of Canadian geography — all of which would later inform his poetry. His working-class ethic solidified when he served in the Royal Canadian Air Force in Canada through World War II, and later, when he worked at various jobs, including taxi driver and machine operator in a mattress factory.

In 1941, Purdy met Eurithe Parkhurst, who would become a central, recurring figure in his poems, one seemingly unfazed by the poet's excesses and unimpressed by his calling. He married her shortly thereafter. The relationship between this female figure and the speaker in Purdy's poems is charged with mixed feelings: lust, contempt, frustration, jealousy, wonder, love, admiration. He tends to invite outrage by teasing the women who appear in his poems, such as "For Norma in Lieu of an Orgasm," which implies that a poem is like sexual pleasure. Notably, however, women rarely agree with him in his poems. He portrays them as independent beings who can only be clumsily assimilated into a poetic vision, as in "The Horseman of Agawa."

Although Purdy might have learned some of his masculine posturing from Layton, he also learned to satirize it, as in "At the Quinte Hotel," in which he argues that men may fight each other, but they can also talk intimately by "quietly making love / in the brief prelude to infinity." When Purdy and Eurithe moved to Montreal, in 1956, he renewed a friendship with Layton that had begun via correspondence. Layton's warmth and generosity towards younger poets attracted Purdy to him, as did his energy and ambition, which were hallmarks of the Montreal poetry scene in the late 1950s. Soon after, however, Purdy and Eurithe settled in rural Ontario, where property was affordable.

In Ameliasburg, he built the A-frame house that would later be a humble mecca for young Canadian writers and the site of a vast personal library. Purdy's collection of thousands of books included many signed first editions by his favourite authors, especially Canadian ones. Acorn helped Purdy to build the house and also convinced Purdy that a poet's voice could be vernacular and written in open verse. Under this influence — along with that of Layton and a host of other modernist poets — Purdy began to let go of traditional forms and nurture his own anti-academic (even anti-intellectual) stance, one that viewed brawling and beer drinking as part of an acceptable poetic culture. When Vancouver bookseller Steve McIntyre told him that serious writers needed to know the classics, Purdy diligently read Thomas Mann, Marcel Proust, and Virginia Woolf, among others, but he much preferred contemporary works, even pulp fiction. Nevertheless, evidence of his wide reading appears in all his writing, especially his poems. His allusions show that he was familiar with D.H. Lawrence, Charles Bukowski, Louis Dudek, E.J. Pratt, Malcolm Lowry, Earle Birney, Pablo Neruda, Rainer Maria Rilke, T.S. Eliot, Marianne Moore, Dylan Thomas, Philip Larkin, W.B. Yeats, and P.K. Page, among many others.

Purdy travelled as widely as he read. His most productive trip was to Baffin Island, in the summer of 1965, which resulted in *North of Summer* (1967), one of the many books that reveal his interest in Canada's indigenous peoples. He also wrote about his voyages to the Cariboo region of British Columbia, Hiroshima, Greece, Italy, England, and Cuba. These trips refined his sense of the Canadian identity and how it differed from that of other countries.

Purdy's national poetic and his distinctive voice developed with the rising tide of Canadian nationalism that followed the onset of 20th-century modernism. Canadian nationalism permeates his work to such an extent that he rarely questions it. In the preface to *The New Romans* (1968), a book of Canadian opinions on America, he writes that "there are few things I find more irritating about my own country than this so-called 'search for an identity,' an identity which I've never doubted having in the first place." Many of Purdy's most important poems — such as "The Country North of Belleville," "Wilderness Gothic," "At the Quinte Hotel," and "The Horseman of Agawa" — invoke this identity through description of specific places that have historical or autobiographical importance. The general reading public and critics alike responded favourably to these poems, and the more elegiac ones of the 1980s and 1990s, and Purdy was frequently invited to give readings from his work across the country.

Through his many friendships and his huge body of work, Purdy influenced many Canadian poets, including Margaret Atwood, George Bowering, and Michael Ondaatje, to name but a few. He wrote over 30 books of poetry, one novel, two memoirs, many reviews, and he also edited several books, including the influential anthology of Canadian poetry called *Storm Warning: The New Canadian Poets* (1971) and its sequel (1976).

The Country North of Belleville[1]

Bush land scrub land —
     Cashel Township and Wollaston
Elzevir McClure and Dungannon
green lands of Weslemkoon Lake[2]
where a man might have some
     opinion of what beauty
is and none deny him
          for miles —

10   Yet this is the country of defeat
where Sisyphus[3] rolls a big stone
year after year up the ancient hills
picnicking glaciers have left strewn
with centuries' rubble
          backbreaking days
          in the sun and rain
when realization seeps slow in the mind
without grandeur or self-deception in
          noble struggle
of being a fool —

---

1. **Belleville** City in Hastings County, Southeastern Ontario, near the Bay of Quinte and Lake Ontario. The County sits on the Canadian Shield, an extensive rock formation covered with only a thin layer of soil. 2. **Cashel Township, Wollaston, Elzevir, McClure, Dungannon, Weslemkoon Lake** Locations in or around Hastings County. 3. **Sisyphus** Cruel King of Corinth who was condemned forever to roll a huge stone up a hill in Hades, only to have it roll down again on nearing the top.

A country of quiescence[4] and still distance   20
a lean land
       not like the fat south
with inches of black soil on
       earth's round belly —
And where the farms are
       it's as if a man stuck
both thumbs in the stony earth and pulled

           it apart
           to make room
enough between the trees   30
for a wife
       and maybe some cows and
       room for some
of the more easily kept illusions —

And where the farms have gone back
to forest
       are only soft outlines
       shadowy differences —
Old fences drift vaguely among the trees
       a pile of moss-covered stones   40
gathered for some ghost purpose
has lost meaning under the meaningless sky
       — they are like cities under water
and the undulating green waves of time
       are laid on them —

This is the country of our defeat
       and yet
during the fall plowing a man
might stop and stand in a brown valley of the furrows
       and shade his eyes to watch for the same   50
       red patch mixed with gold
       that appears on the same
       spot in the hills
       year after year
       and grow old
plowing and plowing a ten-acre field until
the convolutions[5] run parallel with his own brain —

And this is a country where the young
           leave quickly
unwilling to know what their fathers know   60
or think the words their mothers do not say —

---

4. **quiescence** Inactivity. 5. **convolutions** Rows.

Herschel Monteagle and Faraday
lakeland rockland and hill country
a little adjacent to where the world is
a little north of where the cities are and
sometime
we may go back there
                              to the country of our defeat
Wollaston Elzevir and Dungannon
70   and Weslemkoon lake land
where the high townships of Cashel
                              McClure and Marmora[6] once were —
But it's been a long time since
and we must enquire the way
          of strangers —

                                                                        (1965)

The Cariboo Horses

At 100 Mile House[1] the cowboys ride in rolling
stagey cigarettes with one hand reining
half-tame bronco rebels on a morning grey as stone
— so much like riding dangerous women
          with whiskey coloured eyes —
such women as once fell dead with their lovers
with fire in their heads and slippery froth on thighs
— Beaver or Carrier[2] women maybe or
          Blackfoot squaws[3] far past the edge of this valley
10   on the other side of those two toy mountain ranges
          from the sunfierce plains beyond

But only horses
                    waiting in stables
hitched at taverns
                    standing at dawn
pastured outside the town with
jeeps and fords and chevys and
busy muttering stake trucks rushing
importantly over roads of man's devising
20   over the safe known roads of the ranchers
families and merchants of the town
                    On the high prairie
are only horse and rider
                    wind in dry grass

---

6. **Herschel, Monteagle, Faraday, Marmora** More townships in the area.

1. **100 Mile House** Municipality of the Cariboo District of central British Columbia. 2. **Beaver or Carrier** Anglicized names for two western First Nations communities, the Dunneza people of Alberta and the Dakelh of British Columbia. 3. **Blackfoot squaws** The Blackfoot are an Albertan First Nations community.

clopping in silence under the toy mountains
dropping sometimes and
        lost in the dry grass
        golden oranges of dung

Only horses
      no stopwatch memories or palace ancestors   30
not Kiangs[4] hauling undressed stone in the Nile Valley
and having stubborn Egyptian tantrums or
Onagers[5] racing thru Hither Asia and
the last Quagga[6] screaming in African highlands
      lost relatives of these
      whose hooves were thunder
the ghosts of horses battering thru the wind
whose names were the wind's common usage
whose life was the sun's
      arriving here at chilly noon   40
      in the gasoline smell of the
      dust and waiting 15 minutes
      at the grocer's

(1965)

Home-Made Beer

I was justly annoyed 10 years ago
in Vancouver: making beer in a crock
under the kitchen table when this
next-door youngster playing with my own
kid managed to sit down in it and
emerged with one end malted —
With excessive moderation I yodelled
at him
      "Keep your ass out of my beer!"
      and the little monster fled —   10
Whereupon my wife appeared from the bathroom
where she had been brooding for days
over the injustice of being a woman and
attacked me with a broom —
With commendable savoir faire I broke
the broom across my knee (it hurt too) and
then she grabbed the breadknife and made
for me with fairly obvious intentions —
I tore open my shirt and told her calmly
with bared breast and a minimum of boredom   20
      "Go ahead! Strike! Go ahead!"

---

4. Kiangs Wild donkeys from Southern Asia, sometimes used as work-animals. **5. Onagers** Similar to Kiangs in species type and origin, but have been used to pull chariots. **6. Quagga** Now-extinct African relative of the zebra.

Icicles dropped from her fiery eyes as she
snarled
      "I wouldn't want to go to jail
      for killing a thing like you!"
I could see at once that she loved me
tho it was cleverly concealed —
For the next few weeks I had to distribute
the meals she prepared among neighbouring
30   dogs because of the rat poison and
addressed her as Missus Borgia —
That was a long time ago and while
at the time I deplored her lack of
self-control I find myself sentimental
about it now for it can never happen again —

Sept. 22, 1964: PS, I was wrong —

                                                    (1965)

When I Sat Down to Play the Piano

He cometh forth hurriedly from his tent
and looketh for a quiet sequestered vale[1]
he carrieth a roll of violet toilet tissue
and a forerunner goeth ahead to do him honour
yclept[2] a snotty-nosed Eskimo kid
He findeth a quiet glade among great stones
squatteth forthwith and undoeth trousers
Irrational Man by Wm. Barrett[3] in hand
while the other dismisseth mosquitoes
10   and beginneth the most natural of natural functions
buttocks balanced above the boulders
Then
        dogs[1]
          Dogs[3]
            DOGS[12]
                  all shapes and sizes
all colours and religious persuasion
a plague of dogs rushing in
having been attracted by the philosophic climate
20   and being wishful to learn about existential dogs
and denial of the self with regard to bitches
But let's call a spade a shovel
therefore there I am I am I think that is
surrounded by a dozen dozen fierce Eskimo dogs
with an inexplicable (to me) appetite

---

1. vale Valley or sheltered place. **2. yclept** Called (medieval term). **3.** *Irrational Man* **by Wm. Barrett** A work of
existential philosophy by William Barrett, 1962.

for human excrement
        Dear Ann Landers
what would you do?
        Dear Galloping Gourmet[4]
what would *you* do   30
        in a case like this?
Well I'll tell you
NOT A DAMN THING
You just squat there cursing hopelessly
while the kid throws stones
and tries to keep them off and out from under
as a big black husky dashes in
swift as an enemy submarine
white teeth snapping at the anus
I shriek   40
        and shriek
        (the kid laughs)
        and hold onto my pants
        sans dignity
        sans intellect
        sans Wm. Barrett
        and damn near sans anus
Stand firm little Eskimo kid
it giveth candy if I had any
it giveth a dime in lieu of same   50
STAND FIRM
Oh avatar of Olympian excellence[5]
noble Eskimo youth do your stuff
Zeus[6] in the Arctic dog pound
Montcalm at Quebec[7]
Horatius at the bridge[8]
Leonidas at Thermopylae[9]
Custer's last stand at Little Big Horn[10]
"KEEP THEM DAMN DOGS OFF
YOU MISERABLE LITTLE BRAT!"   60

Afterwards
Achilles[11] retreateth without honour
unzippered and sullen

---

4. **Galloping Gourmet** A television cooking show hosted by Graham Kerr. 5. **avatar of Olympian excellence** A manifestation of a godlike figure. 6. **Zeus** Leader of the classical gods. 7. **Montcalm at Quebec** Louis-Joseph de Montcalm (1712–1759), leader of French troops in what is now Quebec, who lost the territory to the British on the Plains of Abraham. 8. **Horatius at the bridge** Roman hero who stood alone on a bridge into Rome and tried unsuccessfully to defend it from attacking Etruscan troops. 9. **Leonides at Thermopylae** Greek king of Sparta (crowned about 488 BC) who led a small army into the hopeless Battle of Thermopylae against the Persians. 10. **Custer's last ... Big Horn** George Armstrong Custer (1839–1876), American commander in the Civil War who died at the Battle of the Little Bighorn, which he fought against a coalition of Native Americans. 11. **Achilles** Greek mythical hero of the Trojan War; withdrew from battle when angered by Agamemnon, his commander who took Chryseis, a woman Achilles prized, for a slave.

and sulketh in his tent till next time appointed
his anus shrinketh
he escheweth[12] all forms of laxative and physick[13] meanwhile
and prayeth for constipation
addresseth himself to the Eskimo brat miscalled
       "Lo tho I walk thru the valley of[14]
70   the shadowy kennels
          in the land of permanent ice cream
             I will fear no huskies
              for thou art with me
    and slingeth thy stones forever and ever
           thou veritable David[15]
                          Amen"

PS Next time I'm gonna take a gun

(1967)

Trees at the Arctic Circle

(*Salix Cordifolia* — *Ground Willow*)

They are 18 inches long
or even less
crawling under rocks
grovelling among the lichens[1]
bending and curling to escape
making themselves small
finding new ways to hide
Coward trees
I am angry to see them
10 like this
not proud of what they are
bowing to weather instead
careful of themselves
worried about the sky
afraid of exposing their limbs
like a Victorian married couple

I call to mind great Douglas firs
I see tall maples waving green
and oaks like gods in autumn gold

---

12. **escheweth** Shuns. 13. **physick** Medicine. 14. **Lo tho I walk thru …** Cf. Psalms 23: "though I walk through the valley of the shadow of death, I will fear no evil." 15. **David** Hebrew prophet who slew the monster Goliath and became king of Israel.

---

1. **lichens** Fungus that grows with algae on trees.

the whole horizon jungle dark
and I crouched under that continual night
But these
even the dwarf shrubs of Ontario
mock them
Coward trees

And yet — and yet —
their seed pods glow
like delicate grey earrings
their leaves are veined and intricate
like tiny parkas
They have about three months
to make sure the species does not die
and that's how they spend their time
unbothered by any human opinion
just digging in here and now
sending their roots down down down
And you know it occurs to me
                about 2 feet under
those roots must touch permafrost
ice that remains ice forever
and they use it for their nourishment
they use death to remain alive

I see that I've been carried away
in my scorn of the dwarf trees
most foolish in my judgements
To take away the dignity
                of any living thing
even tho it cannot understand
                the scornful words
is to make life itself trivial
and yourself the Pontifex Maximus[2]
                of nullity[3]
I have been stupid in a poem
I will not alter the poem
but let the stupidity remain permanent
as the trees are
in a poem
the dwarf trees of Baffin Island

20

30

40

50

Pangnirtung
(1967)

---

2. Pontifex Maximus A pope. **3. nullity** Nothingness.

Wilderness Gothic

Across Roblin Lake,[1] two shores away,
they are sheathing the church spire[2]
with new metal. Someone hangs in the sky
over there from a piece of rope,
hammering and fitting God's belly-scratcher,
working his way up along the spire
until there's nothing left to nail on —

Perhaps the workman's faith reaches beyond:
touches intangibles, wrestles with Jacob,[3]
10   replacing rotten timber with pine thews,
pounds hard in the blue cave of the sky,
contends heroically with difficult problems of
gravity, sky navigation and mythopoeia,[4]
his volunteer time and labour donated to God,
minus sick benefits of course on a non-union job —

Fields around are yellowing into harvest,
nestling and fingerling are sky and water borne,
death is yodelling quiet in green woodlots,
and bodies of three young birds have disappeared
20   in the sub-surface of the new county highway —

That picture is incomplete, part left out
that might alter the whole Dürer[5] landscape:
gothic ancestors peer from medieval sky,
dour faces trapped in photograph albums escaping
to clop down iron roads with matched greys:
work-sodden wives groping inside their flesh
for what keeps moving and changing and flashing
beyond and past the long frozen Victorian day.
A sign of fire and brimstone? A two-headed calf
30   born in the barn last night? A sharp female agony?
An age and a faith moving into transition,
the dinner cold and new-baked bread a failure,
deep woods shiver and water drops hang pendant,
double-yolked eggs and the house creaks a little —
Something is about to happen. Leaves are still.
Two shores away, a man hammering in the sky.
Perhaps he will fall.

(1968)

---

1. **Roblin Lake** Lake near Kingston, Ontario. 2. **spire** Roof-point. 3. **Jacob** Early Hebrew prophet who struggled with his impious brother Esau throughout his life. The night before Jacob faced his brother for the final time, a stranger appeared and wrestled with Jacob all night, afterwards blessing him with the name of Israel. 4. **mythopoeia** Myth-making or myth-finding. 5. **Dürer** Albrecht Dürer (1471–1528), German painter, printer, and mathematician.

Lament for the Dorsets
(Eskimos extinct in the 14th century AD)

Animal bones and some mossy tent rings
scrapers and spearheads   carved ivory swans
all that remains of the Dorset giants
who drove the Vikings back to their long ships[1]
talked to spirits of earth and water
— a picture of terrifying old men,
so large they broke the backs of bears
so small they lurk behind bone rafters
in the brain of modern hunters
among good thoughts and warm things   10
and come out at night
to spit on the stars

The big men with clever fingers
who had no dogs and hauled their sleds
over the frozen northern oceans
awkward giants
                   killers of seal
they couldn't compete with little men
who came from the west with dogs
Or else in a warm climatic cycle   20
the seals went back to cold waters
and the puzzled Dorsets scratched their heads
with hairy thumbs around 1350 AD
— couldn't figure it out
went around saying to each other
plaintively[2]
            "What's wrong? What happened?
            Where are the seals gone?"
And died

Twentieth-century people   30
apartment dwellers
executives of neon death
warmakers with things that explode
— they have never imagined us in their future
how could we imagine them in the past
squatting among the moving glaciers
six hundred years ago

---

1. **drove the Vikings … long ships** The Dorsets are known for their size but not for their aggression. In fact, the Dorsets disappeared at roughly the same time the Vikings retreated from North America. 2. **plaintively** Sorrowfully.

with glowing lamps?
As remote or nearly
40   as the trilobites³ and swamps
when coal became
or the last great reptile hissed
at a mammal the size of a mouse
that squeaked and fled

Did they ever realize at all
what was happening to them?
Some old hunter with one lame leg
a bear had chewed
sitting in a caribou-skin tent
50   — the last Dorset?
Let's say his name was Kudluk
and watch him sitting there
carving 2-inch ivory swans
for a dead grand-daughter
taking them out of his mind
the places in his mind
where pictures are
He selects a sharp stone tool
to gouge a parallel pattern of lines
60   on both sides of the swan
holding it with his left hand
bearing down and transmitting
his body's weight
from brain to arm and right hand
and one of his thoughts
turns to ivory
The carving is laid aside
in beginning darkness
at the end of hunger
70   and after a while wind
blows down the tent and snow
begins to cover him

After 600 years
the ivory thought
is still warm

(1968)

---

3. trilobites Primitive, Precambrian dwellers of the ocean floor; found commonly in fossils.

At the Quinte Hotel[1]

I am drinking
I am drinking beer with yellow flowers
in underground sunlight
and you can see that I am a sensitive man
And I notice that the bartender is a sensitive man too
so I tell him about his beer
I tell him the beer he draws
is half fart and half horse piss
and all wonderful yellow flowers
But the bartender is not quite   10
so sensitive as I supposed he was
the way he looks at me now
and does not appreciate my exquisite analogy
Over in one corner two guys
are quietly making love
in the brief prelude to infinity
Opposite them a peculiar fight
enables the drinkers to lay aside
their comic books and watch with interest
as I watch with interest   20
A wiry little man slugs another guy
then tracks him bleeding into the toilet
and slugs him to the floor again
with ugly red flowers on the tile
three minutes later he roosters over
to the table where his drunk friend sits
with another friend and slugs both
of em ass-over-electric-kettle
so I have to walk around
on my way for a piss   30
Now I am a sensitive man
so I say to him mildly as hell
"You shouldn'ta knocked over that good beer
with them beautiful flowers in it"
So he says to me "Come on"
So I Come On
like a rabbit with weak kidneys I guess
like a yellow streak charging
on flower power I suppose
& knock the shit outa him & sit on him   40
(he is just a little guy)
and say reprovingly
"Violence will get you nowhere this time chum
Now you take me

---

1. **Quinte Hotel** In Belleville, Ontario.

I am a sensitive man
and would you believe I write poems?"
But I could see the doubt in his upside down face
in fact in all the faces
"What kinda poems?"
50   "Flower poems"
"So tell us a poem"
I got off the little guy but reluctantly
for he was comfortable
and told them this poem
They crowded around me with tears
in their eyes and wrung my hands feelingly
for my pockets for
it was a heart-warming moment for Literature
and moved by the demonstrable effect
60   of great Art and the brotherhood of people I remarked
" — the poem oughta be worth some beer"
It was a mistake of terminology
for silence came
and it was brought home to me in the tavern
that poems will not really buy beer or flowers
or a goddam thing
and I was sad
for I am a sensitive man

(1968)

The Horseman of Agawa
(Indian rock-painting under the cliffs of Lake Superior)

It's spring and the steel platforms tourists usually stand on
are not installed yet so we take our chances
but I have to abandon my beer and use both hands for safety
We clamber down rocks unsteady as children
reach slanting stone ledges under the hundred-foot walls
my wife skipping ahead so nimbly I'm jealous of her
and say "Wait for me, dammit" but she won't
then take my shoes off and go barefoot

She sees the painting first and calls "Here!"
10   her face flattens and dissolves into no expression
I balance myself beside her on the tilted ledge
that slides off into deep water and the rock hurts my feet
but I feel the same way she does as the rock horseman canters
by two feet from my nose forever or nearly
The painted horseman rides over four moons (or suns) on his trail
whose meaning must be a four-day journey somewhere

the red iron oxide faded from Lake Superior storms
and maybe two hundred years since the Ojibway artist
     stood there
balance above water like us   20
and drew with his fingers on the stone canvas
with fish eggs or bear grease to make the painting permanent
pitting fish eggs and bear grease against eternity
which is kind of ludicrous or kind of beautiful I guess

I have too many thoughts about the horseman
I might select one and say this is a signpost this painting
(in fact I've just done that)
a human-as-having-babies signpost
but also dammit part of the spirit
a thought taken out from inside the head and carefully left here   30
like saying I love you to stone
I think that after the Ojibway are all dead
and all the bombs in the white world have fizzed into harmlessness
the ghost of one inept hunter who always got lost
and separated from his friends because he had a lousy sense
     of direction
that man can come here to get his bearings calling out
to his horse his dog or himself because he's alone
in the fog in the night in the rain in his mind and say
"My friends where are you?"   40
and the rock walls will seize his voice
and break it into a million amplified pieces of echoes
that will find the ghosts of his friends in the tombs of their dust

But I mistrust the mind-quality that tempts me
to embroider and exaggerate things
          I just watch my wife's face
she is quiet as she generally is because I do most of the talking
it is forty years old and has felt the pain of children
the pettiness of day-to-day living and getting thousands of meals
but standing on the rock face of Lake Superior   50
it is not lessened in any way
with a stillness of depth that reaches where I can't follow
all other thoughts laid aside in her brain
on her face I see the Ojibway horseman painting the rock with
     red fingers
and he speaks to her as I could not
in pictures without handles of words
into feeling into being here by direct transmission
from the stranded Ojibway horseman
And I change it all back into words again for that's the best I can do   60
but they only point the way we came from for who knows where
     we are

under the tall stone cliffs with water dripping down on us
or returned from a long journey and calling out to our friends

But the rock blazes into light when we leave the place
or else the sun shines somewhere else and I didn't notice it
and my secret knowing is knowing what she knows
and can't say and I can only indicate
reclaim my half-empty beer and drink it and tie my shoes
70 follow her up the tangled rocks past the warning sign for strangers
and wait till she turns around

(1973)

Piling Blood

It was powdered blood
in heavy brown paper bags
supposed to be strong enough
to prevent the stuff from escaping
but didn't

We piled it ten feet high
right to the shed roof
working at Arrow Transfer
on Granville Island[1]
10 The bags weighed 75 pounds
and you had to stand on two
of the bags to pile the top rows
I was six feet three inches
and needed all of it

I forgot to say
the blood was cattle blood
horses sheep and cows
to be used for fertilizer
the foreman said
20 It was a matter of some delicacy
to plop the bags down softly
as if you were piling dynamite
if you weren't gentle
the stuff would belly out
from bags in brown clouds
settle on your sweating face
cover hands and arms
enter ears and nose
seep inside pants and shirt
30 reverting back to liquid blood

---

1. **Arrow Transfer, Granville Island** A Vancouver neighbourhood; Arrow Transfer was a transportation and shipping company.

and you looked like
you'd been scalped
by a tribe of
particularly unfriendly
Indians and forgot to die

We piled glass as well
it came in wooden crates
two of us hoicking[2] them
off trucks into warehouses
every crate   40
weighing 200 pounds
By late afternoon
my muscles would twitch and throb
in a death-like rhythm
from hundreds of bags of blood
and hundreds of crates of glass

Then at Burns' slaughterhouse
on East Hastings Street
I got a job part time
shouldering sides of frozen beef   50
hoisting it from steel hooks
staggering to and from
the refrigerated trucks
and eerie freezing rooms
with breath a white vapour
among the dangling corpses
and the sound of bawling animals
screeched down from an upper floor
with their throats cut
and blood gurgling into special drains   60
for later retrieval

And the blood smell clung to me
clung to clothes and body
sickly and sweet
and I heard the screams
of dying cattle
and I wrote no poems
there were no poems
to exclude the screams
which boarded the streetcar   70
and travelled with me
till I reached home
turned on the record player
and faintly

---

2. **hoicking** Hoisting.

in the last century
heard Beethoven weeping

(1984)

Say the Names

— say the names say the names
and listen to yourself
an echo in the mountains
Tulameen   Tulameen[1]
say them like your soul
was listening and overhearing
and you dreamed you dreamed
you were a river
and you were a river
10   Tulameen   Tulameen
— not the flat borrowed imitations
of foreign names
not Brighton Windsor Trenton[2]
but names that ride the wind
Spillimacheen and Nahanni
Kleena Kleene and Horsefly
Illecillewaet and Whachamacallit
Lillooet and Kluane[3]
Head-Smashed-In Buffalo Jump
20   and the whole sky falling
when the buffalo went down
Similkameen and   Nahanni
say them say them remember
if ever you wander elsewhere
"the North as a deed and forever"
Kleena Kleene   Nahanni
Osoyoos and Similkameen[4]
say the names
as if they were your soul
30   lost among the mountains
a soul you mislaid
and found again rejoicing
Tulameen   Tulameen
till the heart stops beating

say the names

(1999)

---

1. **Tulameen** Small community East of Vancouver in British Columbia; the name is from a Nlaka'pamux (Thompson River Indian) word for "red earth." 2. **Brighton, Windsor, Trenton** Ontario cities named after British ones. 3. **Spillimacheen … Kluane** British Columbian locations named for First Nations words or communities (except Whachamacallit, a Purdy original). 4. **Osoyoos, Similkameen** Osoyoos is the Anglicization of an Okanaga word for "the narrows of the lake"; Similkameen is a river named after a First Nations tribe.

Raymond Souster (1921–)

In a career spanning more than 60 years, Raymond Souster has established himself as one of the most consistent poets in Canadian literature. Frank Davey characterized his work as a "peculiar combination of pastoralism and romantic realism" containing "disarming lyrics in which the craft is concealed so that incidents and scenes have all possible prominence." The narrative element of his early and late work focused especially on scenes of Toronto life. Souster was born in that city in 1921, and he has never lived elsewhere, except during World War II. Reflecting on his preoccupation with the neighbourhoods and landmarks of his home, Souster said, "I suppose I am truly an unrepentant regionalist."

After graduating from high school, in 1939, he went to work for the Imperial Bank (now the Canadian Imperial Bank of Commerce). He would remain a banker for more than four decades. In 1940, Souster published his first mature poem, "Nocturnal," in *Canadian Forum,* which was edited by Earle Birney. The war had broken out in Europe, and he enlisted in the Royal Canadian Air Force (RCAF). Souster was prevented from being a pilot by his bad eyesight, so he was put in charge of equipment stores. He was stationed for most of the war in the Maritimes, but in 1943, he went to see Louis Dudek in Montreal. There he met John Sutherland, who was running *First Statement* magazine. Souster published some of his early poems in its pages, but they were dismissed as juvenile. This reaction foreshadowed one to which Souster would be subjected throughout his career — some critics would complain that his consistent oeuvre was dull, clichéd, and poorly crafted.

Sutherland inspired Souster to start his own magazine. While stationed at Sydney, Nova Scotia, Souster started *Direction,* using RCAF equipment and supplies to mimeograph it. He sent copies to newspapers, other writers, editors, and critics. Like many small literary magazines, *Direction* was mainly a vehicle for the work of its editor; Souster and most of his generation were simply unable to find other outlets for their work in the tiny, exclusive publishing industry.

Souster's first book publication was *Unit of Five* (1944), a volume he shared with P.K. Page, Dudek, Ronald Hambleton, and James Wreford. It was a strong enough debut to allow him to place *Go to Sleep, World* (1947) with Ryerson Press. His next publishing venture was the little magazine *Enterprise,* which he produced entirely on his typewriter, 20 carbon copies per issue. He was isolated, he knew few potential contributors, and the magazine failed. In 1951, however, Souster and Dudek started *Contact* as an alternative to *Northern Review,* which they thought was too Canadian and not cosmopolitan enough. They wanted international credibility. From *Contact* emerged Contact Press, which published *Cerberus* (1952), a collection of prefaces and poems by Souster, Dudek, and Irving Layton, all of whom were owners of the press. Despite contributions from these up-and-comers and from some influential American poets, the magazine ceased publishing in 1954. Contact Press would last through Layton's withdrawal into 1967, when Peter Miller, their other partner, quit for family reasons and took his financial support with him. Contact Press had an impressive list, including books by Davey, Phyllis Webb, Eli Mandel, D.G. Jones, Alden Nowlan, Al Purdy, Milton Acorn, Gwendolyn MacEwen, George Bowering, and Margaret Atwood.

During the early days of his involvement in the little magazine and press community, Souster published several of his own books, including his *Selected Poems* (1956). Despite his stature on the literary scene, fewer than 500 copies of that volume were printed, and his readership remained small. In the 1950s, Souster learned about the short lines and concrete vocabulary of imagism through the work of William Carlos Williams. By the mid-1950s, his style had crystallized. He continued to produce and publish, and he soon had enough material to compose *The Colour of the Times* (1964), his collected poems. It won a Governor General's Award, and at last he had a broader readership. For the next two decades, he would be known primarily for the style he'd found through Williams.

In 1965, Souster responded to a comment his friend Cid Corman had made about *Ten Elephants on Yonge Street* (1965), saying, "I know I get sloppy very often, too sentimental, but I *hope* I never get Ezra Pound *cold*, Robert Creeley *controlled*." Perhaps because he was pondering his weaknesses as a poet, Souster began to spend less time writing. In 1966, he edited the influential anthology of new Canadian poetry, *New Wave Canada*. After *As Is* (1967), he initiated an extended process of publishing collections of his past work. *Lost & Found: Uncollected Poems 1945–1965* (1968) appeared, and then *So Far, So Good* (1969); eventually, Oberon Press would launch a long series of Souster's collected poems that would extend from 1980 to the present.

Souster rarely wrote essays, reviews, or prefaces that would provide insight into his work, so "Get the Poem Outdoors" (1969) serves as a retrospective manifesto of his poetics and its central dichotomy. "Get the poem outdoors under any pretext," he writes. "[R]each through the open window if you have to, kidnap it right / off the poet's desk, / then walk the poem in the garden, hold it up among the soft / yellow garlands of the willow." The inside/outside dichotomy ironically suggests that the poet's desk is a bureaucratic object, something easily associated with Souster's profession as a banker. He defended that career choice by claiming that "people are my top interest," and people did provide him with material for many of his poems; however, in his poetry Souster argues that beyond the confines of office and factory there is a more creative life, more real and vital than poetry. For this reason, he avoids artifice and tries to convey a simple image or story — he wants to direct the reader outside the poem.

Shifting direction somewhat, Souster began writing prose poems in the early 1970s. He also returned to the documentary style of his first three books with the continuing "Pictures from a Long Lost World" sequence. A critic once wrote that, faced with Souster's narrative poems, "one sometimes feels that the story is a little too staged for the poem's benefit." This could be due to Souster's thematic insistence on nostalgia and memory — every incident, no matter how mundane, has for him a timeless quality, and he wants to commemorate it in a poem.

In the next three decades, Souster published many new volumes. Some of them explore baseball, some jazz, some World War II, others death and loss. These unadorned topics are the substance of a career of considerable importance in Canadian modernism.

Young Girls

With night full of spring and stars we stand
here in this dark doorway and watch the young
girls pass, two, three together, hand in hand.
They are like flowers whose fragrance hasn't sprung
or awakened, whose bodies now dimly feel
the flooding, upward welling of the trees;
whose senses, caressed by the wind's soft fingers, reel
with a mild delirium that makes them ill at ease.

They lie awake at night, unable to sleep,
10   then walk the streets, kindled by strange desires;
they steal lightning glances at us, unable to keep

control upon those subterranean fires.
We whistle after them, then laugh, for they
stiffen, not knowing what to do or say.

(1946)

Study: The Bath

In the dim light
of the bathroom
a woman steps from white tub,
towel around her shoulders.

Drops of water glisten
on her body
from slight buttocks,
neck, tight belly,
fall at intervals
from the slightly plumed   10
oval of crotch.

The neck bent forward,
eyes collected,
her attention gathered
at the end of fingers,

lovingly removing
dead, flaked skin
from the twin nipples.

(1954)

Two Dead Robins

In the driveway, their bodies so small
I almost stepped on them, two baby robins,
enormous mouths, bulging eyes, bodies thin wire
stretched over taut skin frames, bones showing
like aroused veins.
                    It looked as though they'd either
tried to fly from the nest above
or the wind had swept them down. For some reason
I couldn't bear to pick them up in my hands,
so got a spade and buried them quickly   10
at the back of the garden, thinking as I did it

how many will die today, have much worse burial
than these two my shovel mixes under?

(1955)

The Six-Quart Basket

The six-quart basket,
one side gone,
half the handle torn off,

sits in the centre of the lawn
and slowly fills up
with the white fruits of the snow.

(1958)

Get the Poem Outdoors

Get the poem outdoors under any pretext,
reach through the open window if you have to, kidnap it right
    off the poet's desk,
then walk the poem in the garden, hold it up among the soft
    yellow garlands of the willow,

command of it no further blackness, no silent cursing at
    midnight, no puny whimpering in the endless small hours,
no more shivering in the cold-storage room of the winter heart,

tell it to sing again, loud and then louder so it brings the whole
10   neighbourhood out, but who cares,
ask of it a more human face, a new tenderness, with even the
    sentimental allowed between the hours of nine and five,

then let it go, stranger in a fresh green world, to wander down
    the flowerbeds,
let it go to welcome each bird that lights on the still-barren
    mulberry tree.

(1969)

Mavis Gallant (1922–)

Mavis Gallant (née de Trafford Young) was born in Montreal to an English father and a Canadian mother of mixed descent. She spent her childhood in unfamiliar cultural environments: an English Protestant, she entered a Jansenist convent boarding school at the age of four, and later, after the death of her father in 1932, she was shunted between 17 other schools and foster homes in Canada and the United States. Because her father died when she was young and because she always felt alienated from her mother who would abandon her repeatedly and without notice, Gallant had little in the way of a stable family life. In a 1978 interview Gallant said that all of this upheaval in her childhood ultimately benefited her fiction, since there was "no milieu" that she couldn't "immediately understand." Throughout her career Gallant has published stories that explore the often strained relationship between adults and children — many of them figurative exiles — who come from broken or dysfunctional families. In her fiction, she follows these children into their later lives, presenting us with complex narratives about the broken lines of communication that often characterize families, or marriages, or even countries at different points in time.

In 1941, at the age of 18, she returned to Montreal from New York where she had been living for several years under foster care. She eventually found work as a journalist for the Montreal *Standard* (1944–1950). At 20, she married John Gallant, a Winnipeg musician, but they divorced three years later. She was a zealous worker at the *Standard,* contributing over 60 feature articles; however, she was unhappy with the growing number of content restrictions imposed on her by the paper's editors, and she wanted to write fiction full time. She had been publishing short stories in magazines and in the *Standard* since 1944; not surprisingly, many of these early stories focused on the themes of loneliness and alienation that would mark her most accomplished later work. She resigned her position at the *Standard* in 1950 and moved to Europe, where she established herself as a regular contributor to the *New Yorker,* beginning in 1951. After travelling through Europe for much of the decade, Gallant decided to make Paris her home; she settled there in 1961. Her wide-ranging journalism and essays have been collected in *Paris Notebooks* (1986), which provides a fascinating example of Gallant's ability to blend political commentary and critique with astute observations about architecture, art, and culture.

Since moving to Paris, Gallant has published over 120 stories, a number of which are set in Canada, particularly those collected in *Home Truths,* which won the Governor General's Award for fiction in 1981. In the introduction to *Home Truths,* Gallant refutes the critics who claim she has turned her back on Canada, describing her connection to her country as implicit in all of her writing. For Gallant, "deeper culture is contained in memory. Memory is something that cannot be subsidized or ordained … and it is inseparable from language."

While she has written two successful novels and one well-received play, she excels at the short story form. *The Other Paris* (1956) provides insight into Gallant's narrative technique, which has been described as "spiralling," or "circling." The collection features characters who revise their memories in order to make the past more acceptable or to isolate themselves from the world. In exploring the effects of the past upon the present Gallant allows her story lines to move through characters' shifting emotions and perspectives. One of Gallant's great strengths as a writer is her ability to let silences and unfinished sentences speak for a character's state of mind: what remains unspoken becomes a powerful means of expressing desire, knowledge, longing, uncertainty, fear, unhappiness, or pain.

Three of the four chapters in Gallant's first novel, *Green Water, Green Sky* (1959), were initially published as linked stories. In both this novel and her second one — *A Fairly Good Time* (1970) — she continues to explore the consequences of preserving, re-creating, or destroying one's memories; however, *A Fairly Good Time* employs devices such as journals, letters, and interior monologues to link episodes and chapters together more closely. In her second collection of stories, *My Heart Is Broken* (1964), Gallant's thoughts on memory become darker. Characters like Jean in "Its Image on the Mirror" are too self-aware to find fulfillment in an imaginary past. They only learn more about themselves when they change the way they view their memories; whether they have the power to change anything else about themselves is uncertain. In this and subsequent works, characters have intense reactions to reflections — either their physical reflections in glass or mirrors, or abstract reflections, things they recognize about themselves in others. On another level, the characters in *My Heart Is Broken* reflect the values and concerns of their historical periods. Their personal dramas come to symbolize the larger historical dramas that colour public awareness.

Gallant is interested in the ways that memory distorts history, and she is always drawing our attention to the discrepancies between imagination and actuality, often as it emerges in the friction between diverse cultures or national points of view. Many of her stories present us with contrasting visions of post-war Europe, seen through the eyes of Europeans and their North American contemporaries, who often pursue fantasies of an exotic foreign landscape that has ceased to exist. One of the best examples of Gallant's focus on the post-war consciousness can be found in her collection entitled *The Pegnitz Junction* (1973), which demonstrates Gallant's ability to control narrative perspective. In an interview with Geoff Hancock, she said that she wrote the book in an effort to explain the "small possibilities [of Fascism] in people." The stories depict personal breakdowns, like Ernst's in "Ernst in Civilian Clothes," but they also explore Germany's cultural disintegration following World War II. The challenge of entering foreign cultures or new eras is a frequent theme in Gallant's work. Her authorial viewpoint is detached and sharp, but ultimately compassionate towards her characters in their vulnerability. In the title story from *The Pegnitz Junction*, however, the narrative point of view varies. Competing perspectives sometimes interact without conversation or dialogue, and the effect is to make the characters seem mentally attuned to one another, although each one is involved in an attempt to understand his or her past during a train voyage between France and Germany. In this way Gallant explores the intertwining of personal and public history.

In *From the Fifteenth District* (1979), Gallant's fifth collection, the paradoxes of memory contribute to the nuances that define character. All of the stories focus on exiles and immigrants. One of the strongest pieces in the collection is "The Moslem Wife," a novella which tells the story of a compromised marriage in an expatriate British community at the beginning of the World War II. When her husband Jack leaves for America during the war, Netta is left in charge of the family hotel in France. Its eventual occupation, first by Italians and then by Germans, forces Netta to confront her own sense of history and memory. Eventually, Jack returns, and Netta must again evaluate her own position as a woman, and as a wife. Netta Asher acquires self-awareness through her "dark ... deadly memory" but she must resign herself to living with her husband's selective memory.

Prior to being published in book form, most of Gallant's stories appeared in the *New Yorker*. Her *Overhead in a Balloon: Stories of Paris* (1985) included satires of the Paris literary scene. In 1988, she released a collection called *In Transit*. In 1993, she published *Across the Bridge*, which focused on domestic scenes and contained some memorable Canadian stories, including "1933," "The Chosen Husband," and "The Fenton Child." The year 1996 saw the publication of her substantial *Selected Stories*. Her early Paris stories were collected by Michael Ondaatje in 2002, and Russell Banks collected the Linnet Muir series and other selected Montreal tales in *Varieties of Exile* (2003).

In 1981, Gallant was made an Officer of the Order of Canada; she became a Companion of the Order in 1993. She won the Canada-Australia Literary Prize in 1983 and spent that year as writer-in-residence at the University of Toronto. Gallant has received three honorary doctorates, and she won the Canada Council Molson Prize for the Arts in 1996. The documentary film *Paris Stories: The Writing of Mavis Gallant* aired in 2006. Gallant continues to reside in Paris.

The Moslem Wife

In the south of France, in the business room of a hotel quite near to the house where Katherine Mansfield[1] (whom no one in this hotel had ever heard of) was writing "The Daughters of the Late Colonel," Netta Asher's father announced that there would never

---

1. **Katherine Mansfield** Modernist writer (1888–1923) from New Zealand. "The Daughters of the Late Colonel" was written in Paris and published in 1921.

be a man-made catastrophe in Europe again. The dead of that recent war, the doomed nonsense of the Russian Bolsheviks had finally knocked sense into European heads. What people wanted now was to get on with life. When he said "life," he meant its commercial business.

Who would have contradicted Mr. Asher? Certainly not Netta. She did not understand what he meant quite so well as his French solicitor seemed to, but she did listen with interest and respect, and then watched him signing papers that, she knew, concerned her for life. He was renewing the long lease her family held on the Hotel Prince Albert and Albion. Netta was then eleven. One hundred years should at least see her through the prime of life, said Mr. Asher, only half jokingly, for of course he thought his seed was immortal.

Netta supposed she might easily live to be more than a hundred — at any rate, for years and years. She knew that her father did not want her to marry until she was twenty-six and that she was then supposed to have a pair of children, the elder a boy. Netta and her father and the French lawyer shook hands on the lease, and she was given her first glass of champagne. The date on the bottle was 1909, for the year of her birth. Netta bravely pronounced the wine delicious, but her father said she would know much better vintages before she was through.

Netta remembered the handshake but perhaps not the terms. When the lease had eighty-eight years to run, she married her first cousin, Jack Ross, which was not at all what her father had had in mind. Nor would there be the useful pair of children — Jack couldn't abide them. Like Netta he came from a hotelkeeping family where the young were like blight. Netta had up to now never shown a scrap of maternal feeling over anything, but Mr. Asher thought Jack might have made an amiable parent — a kind one, at least. She consoled Mr. Asher on one count, by taking the hotel over in his lifetime. The hotel was, to Netta, a natural life; and so when Mr. Asher, dying, said, "She behaves as I wanted her to," he was right as far as the drift of Netta's behaviour was concerned but wrong about its course.

The Ashers' hotel was not down on the seafront, though boats and sea could be had from the south-facing rooms.

Across a road nearly empty of traffic were handsome villas, and behind and to either side stood healthy olive trees and a large lemon grove. The hotel was painted a deep ochre with white trim. It had white awnings and green shutters and black iron balconies as lacquered and shiny as Chinese boxes. It possessed two tennis courts, a lily pond, a sheltered winter garden, a formal rose garden, and trees full of nightingales. In the summer dark, *belles-de-nuit*[2] glowed pink, lemon, white, and after their evening watering they gave off a perfume that varied from plant to plant and seemed to match the petals' coloration. In May the nights were dense with stars and fireflies. From the rose garden one might have seen the twin pulse of cigarettes on a balcony, where Jack and Netta sat drinking a last brandy-and-soda before turning in. Most of the rooms were shuttered by then, for no traveller would have dreamed of being south except in winter. Jack and Netta and a few servants had the whole place to themselves. Netta would hire workmen and have the rooms that needed it repainted — the blue cardroom, and the red-walled bar, and the white dining room, where Victorian mirrors gave back glossy walls and blown curtains and nineteenth-century views of the Ligurian coast,[3] the work

---

2. *belles-de-nuit* Bell-shaped flowers. 3. **Ligurian coast** The part of the Italian coast on the Mediterranean Sea that borders France.

of an Asher great-uncle. Everything upstairs and down was soaked and wiped and polished, and even the pictures were relentlessly washed with soft cloths and ordinary laundry soap. Netta also had the boiler overhauled and the linen mended and new monograms embroidered and the looking glasses resilvered and the shutters taken off their hinges and scraped and made spruce green again for next year's sun to fade, while Jack talked about decorators and expert gardeners and even wrote to some, and banged tennis balls against the large new garage. He also read books and translated poetry for its own sake and practiced playing the clarinet. He had studied music once, and still thought that an important life, a musical life, was there in the middle distance. One summer, just to see if he could, he translated pages of St. John Perse,[4] which were as blank as the garage wall to Netta, in any tongue.

Netta adored every minute of her life, and she thought Jack had a good life too, with nearly half the year for the pleasures that suited him. As soon as the grounds and rooms and cellar and roof had been put to rights, she and Jack packed and went travelling somewhere. Jack made the plans. He was never so cheerful as when buying Baedekers and dragging out their stickered trunks. But Netta was nothing of a traveller. She would have been glad to see the same sun rising out of the same sea from the window every day until she died. She loved Jack, and what she liked best after him was the hotel. It was a place where, once, people had come to die of tuberculosis, yet it held no trace or feeling of danger. When Netta walked with her workmen through sheeted summer rooms, hearing the cicadas and hearing Jack start, stop, start some deeply alien music (alien even when her memory automatically gave her a composer's name), she was reminded that here the dead had never been allowed to corrupt the living; the dead had been dressed for an outing and removed as soon as their first muscular stiffness relaxed. Some were wheeled out in chairs, sitting, and some reclined on portable cots, as if merely resting.

That is why there is no bad atmosphere here, she would say to herself. Death has been swept away, discarded. When the shutters are closed on a room, it is for sleep or for love. Netta could think this easily because neither she nor Jack was ever sick. They knew nothing about insomnia, and they made love every day of their lives — they had married in order to be able to.

Spring had been the season for dying in the old days. Invalids who had struggled through the dark comfort of winter took fright as the night receded. They felt without protection. Netta knew about this, and about the difference between darkness and brightness, but neither affected her. She was not afraid of death or of the dead — they were nothing but cold, heavy furniture. She could have tied jaws shut and weighted eyelids with native instinctiveness, as other women were born knowing the temperature for an infant's milk.

"There are no ghosts," she could say, entering the room where her mother, then her father had died. "If there were, I would know."

Netta took it for granted, now she was married, that Jack felt as she did about light, dark, death, and love. They were as alike in some ways (none of them physical) as a couple of twins, spoke much the same language in the same accents, had the same jokes — mostly about other people — and had been together as much as their families would let them for most of their lives. Other men seemed dull to Netta — slower, perhaps, lacking the

---

4. **St. John Perse** Alexis Léger (1887–1975), French poet, diplomat, and Nobel Prize winner.

spoken shorthand she had with Jack. She never mentioned this. For one thing, both of them had the idea that, being English, one must not say too much. Born abroad, they worked hard at an Englishness that was innocently inaccurate, rooted mostly in attitudes. Their families had been innkeepers along this coast for a century, even before Dr. James Henry Bennet[5] had discovered "the Genoese Rivieras." In one of his guides to the region, a "Mr. Ross" is mentioned as a hotel owner who will accept English bank checks, and there is a "Mr. Asher," reliable purveyor of English groceries. The most trustworthy shipping agents in 1860 are the Montale brothers, converts to the Anglican Church, possessors of a British *laissez-passer*[6] to Malta and Egypt. These families, by now plaited like hair, were connections of Netta's and Jack's and still in business from beyond Marseilles to Genoa.[7] No wonder that other men bored her, and that each thought the other both familiar and unique. But of course they were unalike too. When once someone asked them, "Are you related to Montale,[8] the poet?" Netta answered, "What poet?" and Jack said, "I wish we were."

There were no poets in the family. Apart from the great-uncle who had painted landscapes, the only person to try anything peculiar had been Jack, with his music. He had been allowed to study, up to a point; his father had been no good with hotels — had been a failure, in fact, bailed out four times by his cousins, and it had been thought, for a time, that Jack Ross might be a dunderhead too. Music might do him; he might not be fit for anything else.

Information of this kind about the meaning of failure had been gleaned by Netta years before, when she first became aware of her little cousin. Jack's father and mother — the commercial blunderers — had come to the Prince Albert and Albion to ride out a crisis. They were somewhere between undischarged bankruptcy and annihilation, but one was polite: Netta curtsied to her aunt and uncle. Her eyes were on Jack. She could not read yet, though she could sift and classify attitudes. She drew near him, sucking her lower lip, her hands behind her back. For the first time she was conscious of the beauty of another child. He was younger than Netta, imprisoned in a portable-fence arrangement in which he moved tirelessly, crabwise, hanging on a barrier he could easily have climbed. He was as fair as his Irish mother and sunburned a deep brown. His blue gaze was not a baby's — it was too challenging. He was naked except for shorts that were large and seemed about to fall down. The sunburn, the undress were because his mother was reckless and rather odd. Netta — whose mother was perfect — wore boots, stockings, a longsleeved frock, and a white sun hat. She heard the adults laugh and say that Jack looked like a prizefighter. She walked around his prison, staring, and the blue-eyed fighter stared back.

The Rosses stayed for a long time, while the family sent telegrams and tried to rise money for them. No one looked after Jack much. He would lie on a marble step of the staircase watching the hotel guests going into the cardroom or the dining room. One night, for a reason that remorse was to wipe out in a minute, Netta gave him such a savage kick (though he was not really in her way) that one of his legs remained paralyzed for a long time.

---

5. **Dr. James Henry Bennet** Victorian, British doctor and early visitor of the Genoese Riviera when it first became accessible by train; wrote home about his travels. 6. *laissez-passer* Government-administered travel document similar to a passport. 7. **Marseilles to Genoa** Marseilles, coastal city in Southeastern France; Genoa, Italian coastal city about 150 km from the French border. 8. **Montale** Eugenio Montale (1896–1981), Italian poet and Nobel Prize winner.

"*Why* did you do it?" her father asked her — this in the room where she was shut up on bread and water. Netta didn't know. She loved Jack, but who would believe it now? Jack learned to walk, then to run, and in time to ski and play tennis; but her lifelong gift to him was a loss of balance, a sudden lopsided bend of a knee. Jack's parents had meantime been given a small hotel to run at Bandol. Mr. Asher, responsible for a bank loan, kept an eye on the place. He went often, in a hotel car with a chauffeur, Netta perched beside him. When, years later, the families found out that the devoted young cousins had become lovers, they separated them without saying much. Netta was too independent to be dealt with. Besides, her father did not want a rift; his wife had died, and he needed Netta. Jack, whose claim on music had been the subject of teasing until now, was suddenly sent to study in England. Netta saw that he was secretly dismayed. He wanted to be almost anything as long as it was impossible, and then only as an act of grace. Netta's father did think it was his duty to tell her that marriage was, at its best, a parched arrangement, intolerable without a flow of golden guineas and fresh blood. As cousins, Jack and Netta could not bring each other anything except stale money. Nothing stopped them: they were married four months after Jack became twenty-one. Netta heard someone remark at her wedding, "She doesn't need a husband," meaning perhaps the practical, matter-of-fact person she now seemed to be. She did have the dry, burned-out look of someone turned inward. Her dark eyes glowed out of a thin face. She had the shape of a girl of fourteen. Jack, who was large, and fair, and who might be stout at forty if he wasn't careful, looked exactly his age, and seemed quite ready to be married.

Netta could not understand why, loving Jack as she did, she did not look more like him. It had troubled her in the past when they did not think exactly the same thing at almost the same time. During the secret meetings of their long engagement she had noticed how even before a parting they were nearly apart — they had begun to "unmesh," as she called it. Drinking a last drink, usually in the buffet of a railway station, she would see that Jack was somewhere else, thinking about the next-best thing to Netta. The next-best thing might only be a book he wanted to finish reading, but it was enough to make her feel exiled. He often told Netta, "I'm not holding on to you. You're free," because he thought it needed saying, and of course he wanted freedom for himself. But to Netta "freedom" had a cold sound. Is that what I do want, she would wonder. Is that what I think he should offer? Their partings were often on the edge of parting forever, not just because Jack had said or done or thought the wrong thing but because between them they generated the high sexual tension that leads to quarrels. Barely ten minutes after agreeing that no one in the world could possibly know what they knew, one of them, either one, could curse the other out over something trivial. Yet they were, and remained, much in love, and when they were apart Netta sent him letters that were almost despairing with enchantment.

Jack answered, of course, but his letters were cautious. Her exploration of feeling was part of an unlimited capacity she seemed to have for passionate behavior, so at odds with her appearance, which had been dry and sardonic even in childhood. Save for an erotic sentence or two near the end (which Netta read first) Jack's messages might have been meant for any girl cousin he particularly liked. Love was memory, and he was no good at the memory game; he needed Netta there. The instant he saw her he knew all he had missed. But Netta, by then, felt forgotten, and she came to each new meeting aggressive and hurt, afflicted with the physical signs of her doubts and injuries — cold sores, rashes, erratic periods, mysterious temperatures. If she tried to discuss it he would say, "We aren't going over all that again, are we?" Where Netta was concerned he had settled for the established faith, but Netta, who had a wilder, more secret God, wanted a prayer a minute, not to speak of unending miracles and revelations.

When they finally married, both were relieved that the strain of partings and of tense disputes in railway stations would come to a stop. Each privately blamed the other for past violence, and both believed that once they could live openly, without interference, they would never have a disagreement again. Netta did not want Jack to regret the cold freedom he had vainly tried to offer her. He must have his liberty, and his music, and other people, and, oh, anything he wanted — whatever would stop him from saying he was ready to let her go free. The first thing Netta did was to make certain they had the best room in the hotel. She had never actually owned a room until now. The private apartments of her family had always been surrendered in a crisis: everyone had packed up and moved as beds were required. She and Jack were hopelessly untidy, because both had spent their early years moving down hotel corridors, trailing belts and raincoats, with tennis shoes hanging from knotted strings over their shoulders, their arms around books and sweaters and gray flannel bundles. Both had done lessons in the corners of lounges, with cups and glasses rattling, and other children running, and English voices louder than anything. Jack, who had been vaguely educated, remembered his boarding schools as places where one had a permanent bed. Netta chose for her marriage a south-facing room with a large balcony and an awning of dazzling white. It was furnished with lemonwood that had been brought to the Riviera by Russians for their own villas long before. To the lemonwood Netta's mother had added English chintzes;[9] the result, in Netta's eyes, was not bizarre but charming. The room was deeply mirrored; when the shutters were closed on hot afternoons a play of light became as green as a forest on the walls, and as blue as seawater in the glass. A quality of suspension, of disbelief in gravity, now belonged to Netta. She became tidy, silent, less introspective, as watchful and as reflective as her bedroom mirrors. Jack stayed as he was, luckily; any alteration would have worried her, just as a change in an often-read story will trouble a small child. She was intensely, almost unnaturally happy.

One day she overheard an English doctor, whose wife played bridge every afternoon at the hotel, refer to her, to Netta, as "the little Moslem wife." It was said affectionately, for the doctor liked her. She wondered if he had seen through walls and had watched her picking up the clothing and the wet towels Jack left strewn like clues to his presence. The phrase was collected and passed from mouth to mouth in the idle English colony. Netta, the last person in the world deliberately to eavesdrop (she lacked that sort of interest in other people), was sharp of hearing where her marriage was concerned. She had a special antenna for Jack, for his shades of meaning, secret intentions, for his innocent contradictions. Perhaps "Moslem wife" meant several things, and possibly it was plain to anyone with eyes that Jack, without meaning a bit of harm by it, had a way with women. Those he attracted were a puzzling lot, to Netta. She had already catalogued them — elegant elderly parties with tongues like carving knives; gentle, clever girls who flourished on the unattainable; untouchable-daughter types, canny about their virginity, wondering if Jack would be father enough to justify the sacrifice. There was still another kind — tough, sunburned, clad in dark colors — who made Netta think in the vocabulary of horoscopes: Her gem — diamonds. Her color — black. Her language — worse than Netta's. She noticed that even when Jack had no real use for a woman he never made it apparent; he adopted anyone who took a liking to him.

---

9. **chintzes** Bright cotton fabrics with a print.

He assumed — Netta thought — a tribal, paternal air that was curious in so young a man. The plot of attraction interested him, no matter how it turned out. He was like someone reading several novels at once, or like someone playing simultaneous chess.

Netta did not want her marriage to become a world of stone. She said nothing except, "Listen, Jack, I've been at this hotel business longer than you have. It's wiser not to be too pally with the guests." At Christmas the older women gave him boxes of expensive soap. "They must think someone around here wants a good wash," Netta remarked. Outside their fenced area of private jokes and private love was a landscape too open, too light-drenched, for serious talk. And then, when? Jack woke up quickly and early in the morning and smiled as naturally as children do. He knew where he was and the day of the week and the hour. The best moment of the day was the first cigarette. When something bloody happened, it was never before six in the evening. At night he had a dark look that went with a dark mood, sometimes. Netta would tell him that she could see a cruise ship floating on the black horizon like a piece of the Milky Way, and she would get that look for an answer. But it never lasted. His memory was too short to let him sulk, no matter what fragment of night had crossed his mind. She knew, having heard other couples all her life, that at least she and Jack never made the conjugal sounds that passed for conversation and that might as well have been bow-wow and quack quack.

If, by chance, Jack found himself drawn to another woman, if the tide of attraction suddenly ran the other way, then he would discover in himself a great need to talk to his wife. They sat out on their balcony for much of one long night and he told her about his Irish mother. His mother's eccentricity — "Vera's dottiness," where the family was concerned — had kept Jack from taking anything seriously. He had been afraid of pulling her mad attention in his direction. Countless times she had faked tuberculosis and cancer and announced her own imminent death. A telephone call from a hospital had once declared her lost in a car crash. "It's a new life, a new life," her husband had babbled, coming away from the phone. Jack saw his father then as beautiful. Women are beautiful when they fall in love, said Jack; sometimes the glow will last a few hours, sometimes even a day or two.

"You know," said Jack, as if Netta knew, "the look of amazement on a girl's face ..."

Well, that same incandescence had suffused Jack's father when he thought his wife had died, and it continued to shine until a taxi deposited dotty Vera with her cheerful announcement that she had certainly brought off a successful April Fool. After Jack's father died she became violent. "Getting away from her was a form of violence in me," Jack said. "But I did it." That was why he was secretive; that was why he was independent. He had never wanted any woman to get her hands on his life.

Netta heard this out calmly. Where his own feelings were concerned she thought he was making them up as he went along. The garden smelled coolly of jasmine and mimosa. She wondered who his new girl was, and if he was likely to blurt out a name. But all he had been working up to was that his mother — mad, spoiled, devilish, whatever she was — would need to live with Jack and Netta, unless Netta agreed to giving her an income. An income would let her remain where she was — at the moment, in a Rudolf Steiner community[10] in Switzerland, devoted to medieval gardening and to

---

10. Rudolf Steiner community Rudolf Steiner (1861–1925) was an Austrian philosopher, writer, and educator who advocated ethical individualism combined with spiritualism. Many communities were founded on the basis of his ideas, including the Waldorf schools, which provided a means of applying his philosophy to childhood education.

getting the best out of Goethe. Netta's father's training prevented even the thought of spending the money in such a manner.

"You won't regret all you've told me, will you?" she asked. She saw that the new situation would be her burden, her chain, her mean little joke sometimes. Jack scarcely hesitated before saying that where Netta mattered he could never regret anything. But what really interested him now was his mother.

"Lifts give her claustrophobia," he said. "She mustn't be higher than the second floor." He sounded like a man bringing a legal concubine[11] into his household, scrupulously anxious to give all his women equal rights. "And I hope she will make friends," he said. "It won't be easy, at her age. One can't live without them." He probably meant that he had none. Netta had been raised not to expect to have friends: you could not run a hotel and have scores of personal ties. She expected people to be polite and punctual and to mean what they said, and that was the end of it. Jack gave his friendship easily, but he expected considerable diversion in return.

Netta said dryly, "If she plays bridge, she can play with Mrs. Blackley." This was the wife of the doctor who had first said "Moslem wife." He had come down here to the Riviera for his wife's health; the two belonged to a subcolony of flat-dwelling expatriates. His medical practice was limited to hypochondriacs and rheumatic patients. He had time on his hands: Netta often saw him in the hotel reading room, standing, leafing — he took pleasure in handling books. Netta, no reader, did not like touching a book unless it was new. The doctor had a trick of speech Jack loved to imitate: he would break up his words with an extra syllable, some words only, and at that not every time. "It is all a matter of stu-hyle," he said, for "style," or, Jack's favorite, "Oh, well, in the end it all comes down to su-hex." "Uh-hebb and flo-ho of hormones" was the way he once described the behavior of saints — Netta had looked twice at him over that. He was a firm agnostic and the first person from whom Netta heard there existed a magical Dr. Freud. When Netta's father had died of pneumonia, the doctor's "I'm su-horry, Netta" had been so heartfelt she could not have wished it said another way.

His wife, Georgina, could lower her blood pressure or stop her heartbeat nearly at will. Netta sometimes wondered why Dr. Blackley had brought her to a soft climate rather than to the man at Vienna he so admired. Georgina was well enough to play fierce bridge, with Jack and anyone good enough. Her husband usually came to fetch her at the end of the afternoon when the players stopped for tea. Once, because he was obliged to return at once to a patient who needed him, she said, "Can't you be competent about anything?" Netta thought she understood, then, his resigned repetition of "It's all su-hex." "Oh, don't explain. You bore me," said his wife, turning her back.

Netta followed him out to his car. She wore an India shawl that had been her mother's. The wind blew her hair; she had to hold it back. She said, "Why don't you kill her?"

"I am not a desperate person," he said. He looked at Netta, she looking up at him because she had to look up to nearly everyone except children, and he said, "I've wondered why we haven't been to bed."

"Who?" said Netta. "You and your wife? Oh. You mean me." She was not offended, she just gave the shawl a brusque tug and said, "Not a hope. Never with a guest," though of course that was not the reason.

---

11. **concubine** Kept mistress.

"You might have to, if the guest were a maharaja,"[12] he said, to make it all harmless. "I am told it is pu-hart of the courtesy they expect."

"We don't get their trade," said Netta. This had not stopped her liking the doctor. She pitied him, rather, because of his wife, and because he wasn't Jack and could not have Netta.

"I do love you," said the doctor, deciding finally to sit down in his car. "Ee-nee-ormously." She watched him drive away as if she loved him too, and might never see him again. It never crossed her mind to mention any of this conversation to Jack.

That very spring, perhaps because of the doctor's words, the hotel did get some maharaja trade — three little sisters with ebony curls, men's eyebrows, large heads, and delicate hands and feet. They had four rooms, one for their governess. A chauffeur on permanent call lodged elsewhere. The governess, who was Dutch, had a perfect triangle of a nose and said "whom" for "who," pronouncing it "whum." The girls were to learn French, tennis, and swimming. The chauffeur arrived with a hairdresser, who cut their long hair; it lay on the governess's carpet, enough to fill a large pillow. Their toe- and fingernails were filed to points and looked like a kitten's teeth. They came smiling down the marble staircase, carrying new tennis racquets, wearing blue linen skirts and navy blazers. Mrs. Blackley glanced up from the bridge game as they went by the cardroom. She had been one of those opposed to their having lessons at the English Lawn Tennis Club, for reasons that were, to her, perfectly evident.

She said, loudly, "They'll have to be in white."

"End whay, pray?" cried the governess, pointing her triangle nose.

"They can't go on the courts except in white. It is a private club. Entirely white."

"Whum do they all think they are?" the governess asked, prepared to stalk on. But the girls, with their newly cropped heads, and their vulnerable necks showing, caught the drift and refused to go.

"Whom indeed," said Georgina Blackley, fiddling with her bridge hand and looking happy.

"My wife's seamstress could run up white frocks for them in a minute," said Jack. Perhaps he did not dislike children all that much.

"Whom could," muttered Georgina.

But it turned out that the governess was not allowed to choose their clothes, and so Jack gave the children lessons at the hotel. For six weeks they trotted around the courts looking angelic in blue, or hopelessly foreign, depending upon who saw them. Of course they fell in love with Jack, offering him a passionate loyalty they had nowhere else to place. Netta watched the transfer of this gentle, anxious gift. After they departed, Jack was bad-tempered for several evenings and then never spoke of them again; they, needless to say, had been dragged from him weeping.

When this happened the Rosses had been married nearly five years. Being childless but still very loving, they had trouble deciding which of the two would be the child. Netta overheard "He's a darling, but she's a sergeant major and no mistake. And so *mean*." She also heard "He's a lazy bastard. He bullies her. She's a fool." She searched her heart again about children. Was it Jack or had it been Netta who had first said no? The only child she had ever admired was Jack, and not as a child but as a fighter, defying

---

12. **maharaja** An Indian prince.

her. She and Jack were not the sort to have animal children, and Jack's dotty mother would probably soon be child enough for any couple to handle. Jack still seemed to adopt, in a tribal sense of his, half the women who fell in love with him. The only woman who resisted adoption was Netta — still burned-out, still ardent, in a manner of speaking still fourteen. His mother had turned up meanwhile, getting down from a train wearing a sly air of enjoying her own jokes, just as she must have looked on the day of the April Fool. At first she was no great trouble, though she did complain about an ulcerated leg. After years of pretending, she at last had something real. Netta's policy of silence made Jack's mother confident. She began to make a mockery of his music: "All that money gone for nothing!" Or else, "The amount we wasted on schools! The hours he's thrown away with his nose in a book. All that reading — if at least it had got him somewhere." Netta noticed that he spent more time playing bridge and chatting to cronies in the bar now. She thought hard, and decided not to make it her business. His mother had once been pretty; perhaps he still saw her that way. She came of a ramshackle family with a usable past; she spoke of the Ashers and the Rosses as if she had known them when they were tinkers. English residents who had a low but solid barrier with Jack and Netta were fences-down with his mad mother: they seemed to take her at her own word when it was about herself. She began then to behave like a superior sort of guest, inviting large parties to her table for meals, ordering special wines and dishes at inconvenient hours, standing endless rounds of drinks in the bar.

Netta told herself, Jack wants it this way. It is his home too. She began to live a life apart, leaving Jack to his mother. She sat wearing her own mother's shawl, hunched over a new, modern adding machine, punching out accounts. "Funny couple," she heard now. She frowned, smiling in her mind; none of these people knew what bound them, or how tied they were. She had the habit of dodging out of her mother-in-law's parties by saying, "I've got such an awful lot to do." It made them laugh, because they thought this was Netta's term for slave-driving the servants. They thought the staff did the work, and that Netta counted the profits and was too busy with bookkeeping to keep an eye on Jack — who now, at twenty-six, was as attractive as he ever would be.

A woman named Iris Cordier was one of Jack's mother's new friends. Tall, loud, in winter dully pale, she reminded Netta of a blond penguin. Her voice moved between a squeak and a moo, and was a mark of the distinguished literary family to which her father belonged. Her mother, a Frenchwoman, had been in and out of nursing homes for years. The Cordiers haunted the Riviera, with Iris looking after her parents and watching their diets. Now she lived in a flat somewhere in Roquebrune[13] with the survivor of the pair — the mother, Netta believed. Iris paused and glanced in the business room where Mr. Asher had signed the hundred-year lease. She was on her way to lunch — Jack's mother's guest, of course.

"I say, aren't you Miss Asher?"

"I was." Iris, like Dr. Blackley, was probably younger than she looked. Out of her own childhood Netta recalled a desperate adolescent Iris with middle-aged parents clamped like handcuffs on her life. "How is your mother?" Netta had been about to say "How is Mrs. Cordier?" but it sounded servile.

"I didn't know you knew her."

"I remember her well. Your father too. He was a nice person."

---

13. **Roquebrune** Southern French tourist town near the Italian border.

"And still is," said Iris, sharply. "He lives with me, and he always will. French daughters don't abandon their parents." No one had ever sounded more English to Netta. "And your father and mother?"

"Both dead now. I'm married to Jack Ross."

"Nobody told me," said Iris, in a way that made Netta think, Good Lord, Iris too? Jack could not possibly seem like a patriarchal figure where she was concerned; perhaps this time the game was reversed and Iris played at being tribal and maternal. The idea of Jack, or of any man, flinging himself on that iron bosom made Netta smile. As if startled, Iris covered her mouth. She seemed to be frightened of smiling back.

Oh, well, and what of it, Iris too, said Netta to herself, suddenly turning back to her accounts. As it happened, Netta was mistaken (as she never would have been with a bill). That day Jack was meeting Iris for the first time.

The upshot of these errors and encounters was an invitation to Roquebrune to visit Iris's father. Jack's mother was ruthlessly excluded, even though Iris probably owed her a return engagement because of the lunch. Netta supposed that Iris had decided one had to get past Netta to reach Jack — an inexactness if ever there was one. Or perhaps it was Netta Iris wanted. In that case the error became a farce. Netta had almost no knowledge of private houses. She looked around at something that did not much interest her, for she hated to leave her own home, and saw Iris's father, apparently too old and shaky to get out of his armchair. He smiled and he nodded, meanwhile stroking an aged cat. He said to Netta, "You resemble your mother. A sweet woman. Obliging and quiet. I used to tell her that I longed to live in her hotel and be looked after."

Not by me, thought Netta.

Iris's amber bracelets rattled as she pushed and pulled everyone through introductions. Jack and Netta had been asked to meet a young American Netta had often seen in her own bar, and a couple named Sandy and Sandra Braunsweg, who turned out to be Anglo-Swiss and twins. Iris's long arms were around them as she cried to Netta, "Don't you know these babies?" They were, like the Rosses, somewhere in their twenties. Jack looked on, blue-eyed, interested, smiling at everything new. Netta supposed that she was now seeing some of the rather hard-up snobbish — snobbish what? "Intelligumhen-sia," she imagined Dr. Blackley supplying. Having arrived at a word, Netta was ready to go home; but they had only just arrived. The American turned to Netta. He looked bored, and astonished by it. He needs the word for "bored," she decided. Then he can go home, too. The Riviera was no place for Americans. They could not sit all day waiting for mail and the daily papers and for the clock to show a respectable drinking time. They made the best of things when they were caught with a house they'd been rash enough to rent unseen. Netta often had them then *en pension*[14] for meals: a hotel dining room was one way of meeting people. They paid a fee to use the tennis courts, and they liked the bar. Netta would notice then how Jack picked up any accent within hearing.

Jack was now being attentive to the old man, Iris's father. Though this was none of Mr. Cordier's business, Jack said, "My wife and I are first cousins, as well as second cousins twice over."

"You don't look it."

---

14. *en pension* Accommodation with meals included.

Everyone began to speak at once, and it was a minute or two before Netta heard Jack again. This time he said, "We are from a family of great ..." It was lost. What now? Great innkeepers? Worriers? Skinflints?[15] Whatever it was, old Mr. Cordier kept nodding to show he approved.

"We don't see nearly enough of young men like you," he said.

"True!" said Iris loudly. "We live in a dreary world of ill women down here." Netta thought this hard on the American, on Mr. Cordier, and on the male Braunsweg twin, but none of them looked offended. "I've got no time for women," said Iris. She slapped down a glass of whiskey so that it splashed, and rapped on a table with her knuckles. "Shall I tell you why? Because women don't tick over. They just simply don't tick over." No one disputed this. Iris went on: Women were underinformed. One could have virile conversations only with men. Women were attached to the past through fear, whereas men had a fearless sense of history. "Men tick," she said, glaring at Jack.

"I am not attached to a past," said Netta, slowly. "The past holds no attractions." She was not used to general conversation. She thought that every word called for consideration and for an answer. "Nothing could be worse than the way we children were dressed. And our mothers — the hard waves of their hair, the white lips. I think of those pale profiles and I wonder if those women were ever young."

Poor Netta, who saw herself as profoundly English, spread consternation by being suddenly foreign and gassy. She talked the English of expatriate children, as if reading aloud. The twins looked shocked. But she had appealed to the American. He sat beside her on a scuffed velvet sofa. He was so large that she slid an inch or so in his direction when he sat down. He was Sandra Braunsweg's special friend: they had been in London together. He was trying to write.

"What do you mean?" said Netta. "Write what?"

"Well — a novel, to start," he said. His father had staked him to one year, then another. He mentioned all that Sandra had borne with, how she had actually kicked and punched him to keep him from being too American. He had embarrassed her to death in London by asking a waitress, "Miss, where's the toilet?"

Netta said, "Didn't you mind being corrected?"

"Oh, no. It was just friendly."

Jack meanwhile was listening to Sandra telling about her English forebears and her English education. "I had many years of undeniably excellent schooling," she said. "Mitten Todd."

"What's that?" said Jack.

"It's near Bristol. I met excellent girls from Italy, Spain. I took *him* there to visit," she said, generously including the American. "I said, 'Get a yellow necktie.' He went straight out and bought one. I wore a little Schiaparelli.[16] Bought in Geneva but still a real ... A yellow jacket over a gray ... Well, we arrived at my excellent old school, and even though the day was drizzly I said, 'Put the top of the car back.' He did so at once, and then he understood. The interior of the car harmonized perfectly with the yellow and gray." The twins were orphaned. Iris was like a mother.

"When Mummy died we didn't know where to put all the Chippendale,"[17] said Sandra, "Iris took a lot of it."

---

15. **Skinflints** Frugal spenders. 16. **Schiaparelli** Elsa Schiaparelli (1890–1973), pre-eminent Parisian fashion designer of the 1920s and 1930s. 17. **Chippendale** Very high-quality furniture made by Thomas Chippendale (1718–1779).

Netta thought, She is so silly. How can he respond? The girl's dimples and freckles and soft little hands were nothing Netta could have ever described: she had never in her life thought a word like "pretty." People were beautiful or they were not. Her happiness had always been great enough to allow for despair. She knew that some people thought Jack was happy and she was not.

"And what made you marry your young cousin?" the old man boomed at Netta. Perhaps his background allowed him to ask impertinent questions; he must have been doing so nearly forever. He stroked his cat; he was confident. He was spokesman for a roomful of wondering people.

"Jack was a moody child and I promised his mother I would look after him," said Netta. In her hopelessly un-English way she believed she had said something funny.

At eleven o'clock the hotel car expected to fetch the Rosses was nowhere. They trudged home by moonlight. For the last hour of the evening Jack had been skewered on virile conversations, first with Iris, then with Sandra, to whom Netta had already given "Chippendale" as a private name. It proved that Iris was right about concentrating on men and their ticking — Jack even thought Sandra rather pretty.

"Prettier than me?" said Netta, without the faintest idea what she meant, but aware she had said something stupid.

"Not so attractive," said Jack. His slight limp returned straight out of childhood. *She* had caused his accident.

"But she's not always clear," said Netta. "Mitten Todd, for example."

"Who're you talking about?"

"Who are *you*?"

"Iris, of course."

As if they had suddenly quarrelled they fell silent. In silence they entered their room and prepared for bed. Jack poured a whiskey, walked on the clothes he had dropped, carried his drink to the bathroom. Through the half-shut door he called suddenly, "Why did you say that asinine[18] thing about promising to look after me?"

"It seemed so unlikely, I thought they'd laugh." She had a glimpse of herself in the mirrors picking up his shed clothes.

He said, "Well, is it true?"

She was quiet for such a long time that he came to see if she was still in the room. She said, "No, your mother never said that or anything like it."

"We shouldn't have gone to Roquebrune," said Jack. "I think those bloody people are going to be a nuisance. Iris wants her father to stay here, with the cat, while she goes to England for a month. How do we get out of that?"

"By saying no."

"I'm rotten at no."

"I told you not to be too pally with women," she said, as a joke again, but jokes were her way of having floods of tears.

Before this had a chance to heal, Iris's father moved in, bringing his cat in a basket. He looked at his room and said, "Medium large." He looked at his bed and said, "Reasonably long." He was, in short, daft about measurements. When he took books

---

18. **asinine** Foolish.

out of the reading room, he was apt to return them with "This volume contains about 70,000 words" written inside the back cover.

Netta had not wanted Iris's father, but Jack had said yes to it. She had not wanted the sick cat, but Jack had said yes to that too. The old man, who was lost without Iris, lived for his meals. He would appear at the shut doors of the dining room an hour too early, waiting for the menu to be typed and posted. In a voice that matched Iris's for carrying power, he read aloud, alone: "Consommé. Good Lord, again? Is there a choice between the fish and the cutlet? I can't possibly eat all of that. A bit of salad and a boiled egg. That's all I could possibly want." That was rubbish, because Mr. Cordier ate the menu and more, and if there were two puddings, or a pudding and ice cream, he ate both and asked for pastry, fruit, and cheese to follow. One day, after Dr. Blackley had attended him for faintness, Netta passed a message on to Iris, who had been back from England for a fortnight now but seemed in no hurry to take her father away.

"Keith Blackley thinks your father should go on a diet."

"He can't," said Iris. "Our other doctor says dieting causes cancer."

"You can't have heard that properly," Netta said.

"It is like those silly people who smoke to keep their figures," said Iris. "Dieting."

"Blackley hasn't said he should smoke, just that he should eat less of everything."

"My father has never smoked in his life," Iris cried. "As for his diet, I weighed his food out for years. He's not here forever. I'll take him back as soon as he's had enough of hotels."

He stayed for a long time, and the cat did too, and a nuisance they both were to the servants. When the cat was too ailing to walk, the old man carried it to a path behind the tennis courts and put it down on the gravel to die. Netta came out with the old man's tea on a tray (not done for everyone, but having him out of the way was a relief) and she saw the cat lying on its side, eyes wide, as if profoundly thinking. She saw unlicked dirt on its coat and ants exploring its paws. The old man sat in a garden chair, wearing a panama hat, his hands clasped on a stick. He called, "Oh, Netta, take her away. I am too old to watch anything die. I know what she'll do," he said, indifferently, his voice falling as she came near. "Oh, I know that. Turn on her back and give a shriek. I've heard it often."

Netta disburdened her tray onto a garden table and pulled the tray cloth under the cat. She was angered at the haste and indecency of the ants. "It would be polite to leave her," she said. "She doesn't want to be watched."

"I always sit here," said the old man.

Jack, making for the courts with Chippendale, looked as if the sight of the two conversing amused him. Then he understood and scooped up the cat and tray cloth and went away with the cat over his shoulder. He laid it in the shade of a Judas tree, and within an hour it was dead. Iris's father said, "I've got no one to talk to here. That's my trouble. That shroud was too small for my poor Polly. Ask my daughter to fetch me."

Jack's mother said that night, "I'm sure you wish that I had a devoted daughter to take me away too." Because of the attention given the cat she seemed to feel she had not been nuisance enough. She had taken to saying, "My leg is dying before I am," and imploring Jack to preserve her leg, should it be amputated, and make certain it was buried with her. She wanted Jack to be close by at nearly any hour now, so that she could lean on him. After sitting for hours at bridge she had trouble climbing two flights of stairs; nothing would induce her to use the lift.

"Nothing ever came of your music," she would say, leaning on him. "Of course, you have a wife to distract you now. I needed a daughter. Every woman does." Netta managed to trap her alone, and forced her to sit while she stood over her. Netta said, "Look, Aunt Vera, I forbid you, I absolutely forbid you, do you hear, to make a nurse of Jack, and I shall strangle you with my own hands if you go on saying nothing came of his music. You are not to say it in my hearing or out of it. Is that plain?"

Jack's mother got up to her room without assistance. About an hour later the gardener found her on a soft bed of wallflowers. "An inch to the left and she'd have landed on a rake," he said to Netta. She was still alive when Netta knelt down. In her fall she had crushed the plants, the yellow minted *giroflées de Nice*. Netta thought that she was now, at last, for the first time, inhaling one of the smells of death. Her aunt's arms and legs were turned and twisted; her skirt was pulled so that her swollen leg showed. It seemed that she had jumped carrying her walking stick — it lay across the path. She often slept in an armchair, afternoons, with one eye slightly open. She opened that eye now and, seeing she had Netta, said, "My son." Netta was thinking, I have never known her. And if I knew her, then it was Jack or myself I could not understand. Netta was afraid of giving orders, and of telling people not to touch her aunt before Dr. Blackley could be summoned, because she knew that she had always been mistaken. Now Jack was there, propping his mother up, brushing leaves and earth out of her hair. Her head dropped on his shoulder. Netta thought from the sudden heaviness that her aunt had died, but she sighed and opened that one eye again, saying this time, "Doctor?" Netta left everyone doing the wrong things to her dying — no, her murdered — aunt. She said quite calmly into a telephone, "I am afraid that my aunt must have jumped or fallen from the second floor."

Jack found a letter on his mother's night table that began, "Why blame Netta? I forgive." At dawn he and Netta sat at a card table with yesterday's cigarettes still not cleaned out of the ashtray, and he did not ask what Netta had said or done that called for forgiveness. They kept pushing the letter back and forth. He would read it and then Netta would. It seemed natural for them to be silent. Jack had sat beside his mother for much of the night. Each of them then went to sleep for an hour, apart, in one of the empty rooms, just as they had done in the old days when their parents were juggling beds and guests and double and single quarters. By the time the doctor returned for his second visit Jack was neatly dressed and seemed wide awake. He sat in the bar drinking black coffee and reading a travel book of Evelyn Waugh's[19] called *Labels*. Netta, who looked far more untidy and underslept, wondered if Jack wished he might leave now, and sail from Monte Carlo on the Stella Polaris.[20]

Dr. Blackley said, "Well, you are a dim pair. She is not in pu-hain, you know." Netta supposed this was the roundabout way doctors have of announcing death, very like "Her sufferings have ended." But Jack, looking hard at the doctor, had heard another meaning. "Jumped or fell," said Dr. Blackley. "She neither fell nor jumped. She is up there enjoying a damned good thu-hing."

Netta went out and through the lounge and up the marble steps. She sat down in the shaded room on the chair where Jack had spent most of the night. Her aunt did not look like anyone Netta knew, not even like Jack. She stared at the alien face and said, "Aunt Vera, Keith Blackley says there is nothing really the matter. You must have made

---

19. **Evelyn Waugh** British writer and satirist (1903–1966). 20. **Stella Polaris** Early 20th-century ocean liner.

a mistake. Perhaps you fainted on the path, overcome by the scent of wallflowers. What would you like me to tell Jack?"

Jack's mother turned on her side and slowly, tenderly, raised herself on an elbow. "Well, Netta," she said, "I daresay the fool is right. But as I've been given quite a lot of sleeping stuff, I'd as soon stay here for now."

Netta said, "Are you hungry?"

"I should very much like a ham sandwich on English bread, and about that much gin with a lump of ice."

She began coming down for meals a few days later. They knew she had crept down the stairs and flung her walking stick over the path and let herself fall hard on a bed of wallflowers — had even plucked her skirt up for a bit of accuracy; but she was also someone returned from beyond the limits, from the other side of the wall. Once she said, "It was like diving and suddenly realizing there was no water in the sea." Again, "It is not true that your life rushes before your eyes. You can see the flowers floating up to you. Even a short fall takes a long time."

Everyone was deeply changed by this incident. The effect on the victim herself was that she got religion hard.

"We are all hopeless nonbelievers!" shouted Iris, drinking in the bar one afternoon. "At least, I hope we are. But when I see you, Vera, I feel there might be something in religion. You look positively temperate."

"I am allowed to love God, I hope," said Jack's mother.

Jack never saw or heard his mother anymore. He leaned against the bar, reading. It was his favorite place. Even on the sunniest of afternoons he read by the red-shaded light. Netta was present only because she had supplies to check. Knowing she ought to keep out of this, she still said, "Religion is more than love. It is supposed to tell you why you exist and what you are expected to do about it."

"You have no religious feelings at all?" This was the only serious and almost the only friendly question Iris was ever to ask Netta.

"None," said Netta. "I'm running a business."

"I love God as Jack used to love music," said his mother. "At least he said he did when we were paying for lessons."

"Adam and Eve had God," said Netta. "They had nobody but God. A fat lot of good that did them." This was as far as their dialectic went. Jack had not moved once except to turn pages. He read steadily but cautiously now, as if every author had a design on him. That was one effect of his mother's incident. The other was that he gave up bridge and went back to playing the clarinet. Iris hammered out an accompaniment on the upright piano in the old music room, mostly used for listening to radio broadcasts. She was the only person Netta had ever heard who could make Mozart sound like an Irish jig. Presently Iris began to say that it was time Jack gave a concert. Before this could turn into a crisis Iris changed her mind and said what he wanted was a holiday. Netta thought he needed something: he seemed to be exhausted by love, friendship, by being a husband, someone's son, by trying to make a world out of reading and sense out of life. A visit to England to meet some stimulating people, said Iris. To help Iris with her tiresome father during the journey. To visit art galleries and bookshops and go to concerts. To meet people. To talk.

This was a hot, troubled season, and many persons were planning journeys — not to meet other people but for fear of a war. The hotel had emptied out by the end of

March. Netta, whose father had known there would never be another catastrophe, had her workmen come in, as usual. She could hear the radiators being drained and got ready for painting as she packed Jack's clothes. They had never been separated before. They kept telling each other that it was only for a short holiday — for three or four weeks. She was surprised at how neat marriage was, at how many years and feelings could be folded and put under a lid. Once, she went to the window so that he would not see her tears and think she was trying to blackmail him. Looking out, she noticed the American, Chippendale's lover, idly knocking a tennis ball against the garage, as Jack had done in the early summers of their life; he had come round to the hotel looking for a partner, but that season there were none. She suddenly knew to a certainty that if Jack were to die she would search the crowd of mourners for a man she could live with. She would not return from the funeral alone.

Grief and memory, yes, she said to herself, but what about three o'clock in the morning?

By June nearly everyone Netta knew had vanished, or, like the Blackleys, had started to pack. Netta had new tablecloths made, and ordered new white awnings, and two dozen rosebushes from the nursery at Cap Ferrat.[21] The American came over every day and followed her from room to room, talking. He had nothing better to do. The Swiss twins were in England. His father, who had been backing his writing career until now, had suddenly changed his mind about it — now, when he needed money to get out of Europe. He had projects for living on his own, but they required a dose of funds. He wanted to open a restaurant on the Riviera where nothing but chicken pie would be served. Or else a vast and expensive café where people would pay to make their own sandwiches. He said that he was seeing the food of the future, but all that Netta could see was customers asking for their money back. He trapped her behind the bar and said he loved her; Netta made other women look like stuffed dolls. He could still remember the shock of meeting her, the attraction, the brilliant answer she had made to Iris about attachments to the past.

Netta let him rave until he asked for a loan. She laughed and wondered if it was for the chicken-pie restaurant. No — he wanted to get on a boat sailing from Cannes. She said, quite cheerfully, "I can't be Venus[22] and Barclays Bank.[23] You have to choose."

He said, "Can't Venus ever turn up with a letter of credit?"

She shook her head. "Not a hope."

But when it was July and Jack hadn't come back, he cornered her again. Money wasn't in it now: his father had not only relented but had virtually ordered him home. He was about twenty-two, she guessed. He could still plead successfully for parental help and for indulgence from women. She said, no more than affectionately, "I'm going to show you a very pretty room."

A few days later Dr. Blackley came alone to say goodbye.

"Are you really staying?" he asked.

"I am responsible for the last eighty-one years of this lease," said Netta. "I'm going to be thirty. It's a long tenure. Besides, I've got Jack's mother and she won't leave. Jack has a chance now to visit America. It doesn't sound sensible to me, but she writes encouraging him. She imagines him suddenly very rich and sending for her. I've

---

21. **Cap Ferrat** French seaside town. 22. **Venus** Classical goddess of love. 23. **Barclays Bank** A British bank.

discovered the limit of what you can feel about people. I've discovered something else," she said abruptly. "It is that sex and love have nothing in common. Only a coincidence, sometimes. You think the coincidence will go on and so you get married. I suppose that is what men are born knowing and women learn by accident."

"I'm su-horry."

"For God's sake, don't be. It's a relief."

She had no feeling of guilt, only of amazement. Jack, as a memory, was in a restricted area — the tennis courts, the cardroom, the bar. She saw him at bridge with Mrs. Blackley and pouring drinks for temporary friends. He crossed the lounge jauntily with a cluster of little dark-haired girls wearing blue. In the mirrored bedroom there was only Netta. Her dreams were cleansed of him. The looking glasses still held their blue-and-silver-water shadows, but they lost the habit of giving back the moods and gestures of a Moslem wife.

About five years after this, Netta wrote to Jack. The war had caught him in America, during the voyage his mother had so wanted him to have. His limp had kept him out of the Army. As his mother (now dead) might have put it, all that reading had finally got him somewhere: he had spent the last years putting out a two-pager on aspects of European culture — part of a scrupulous effort Britain was making for the West. That was nearly all Netta knew. A Belgian Red Cross official had arrived, apparently in Jack's name, to see if she was still alive. She sat in her father's business room, wearing a coat and a shawl because there was no way of heating any part of the hotel now, and she tried to get on with the letter she had been writing in her head, on and off, for many years.

"In June, 1940, we were evacuated," she started, for the tenth or eleventh time. "I was back by October. Italians had taken over the hotel. They used the mirror behind the bar for target practice. Oddly enough it was not smashed. It is covered with spiderwebs, and the bullet hole is the spider. I had great trouble over Aunt Vera, who disappeared and was found finally in one of the attic rooms.

"The Italians made a pet of her. Took her picture. She enjoyed that. Everyone who became thin had a desire to be photographed, as if knowing they would use this intimidating evidence against those loved ones who had missed being starved. Guilt for life. After an initial period of hardship, during which she often had her picture taken at her request, the Italians brought food and looked after her, more than anyone. She was their mama. We were annexed territory and in time we had the same food as the Italians. The thin pictures of your mother are here on my desk.

"She buried her British passport and would never say where. Perhaps under the Judas tree with Mr. Cordier's cat, Polly. She remained just as mad and just as spoiled, and that became dangerous when life stopped being ordinary. She complained about me to the Italians. At that time a complaint was a matter of prison and of death if it was made to the wrong person. Luckily for me, there was also the right person to take the message.

"A couple of years after that, the Germans and certain French took over and the Italians were shut up in another hotel without food or water, and some people risked their well-being to take water to them (for not everyone preferred the new situation, you can believe me). When she was dying I asked her if she had a message for one Italian officer who had made such a pet of her and she said, 'No, why?' She died without a word for anybody. She was buried as 'Rossini,' because the Italians had changed people's names. She had said she was French, a Frenchwoman named Ross, and so some peculiar civil status was created for us — the two Mrs. Rossinis.

"The records were topsy-turvy; it would have meant going to the Germans and explaining my dead aunt was British, and of course I thought I would not. The death certificate and permission to bury are for a Vera Rossini. I have them here on my desk for you with her pictures.

"You are probably wondering where I have found all this writing paper. The Germans left it behind. When we were being shelled I took what few books were left in the reading room down to what used to be the wine cellar and read by candlelight. You are probably wondering where the candles came from. A long story. I even have paint for the radiators, large buckets that have never been opened.

"I live in one room, my mother's old sitting room. The business room can be used but the files have gone. When the Italians were here your mother was their mother, but I was not their Moslem wife, although I still had respect for men. One yelled '*Luce*, *luce*,'[24] because your mother was showing a light. She said, 'Bugger you, you little toad.' He said, 'Granny, I said "*luce*," not "*Duce*."'[25]

"Not long ago we crept out of our shelled homes, looking like cave dwellers. When you see the hotel again, it will be functioning. I shall have painted the radiators. Long shoots of bramble come in through the cardroom windows. There are drifts of leaves in the old music room and I saw scorpions and heard their rustling like the rustle of death. Everything that could have been looted has gone. Sheets, bedding, mattresses. The neighbors did quite a lot of that. At the risk of their lives. When the Italians were here we had rice and oil. Your mother, who was crazy, used to put out grains to feed the mice.

"When the Germans came we had to live under Vichy law,[26] which meant each region lived on what it could produce. As ours produces nothing, we got quite thin again. Aunt Vera died plump. Do you know what it means when I say she used to complain about me?

"Send me some books. As long as they are in English. I am quite sick of the three other languages in which I've heard so many threats, such boasting, such a lot of lying.

"For a time I thought people would like to know how the Italians left and the Germans came in. It was like this: They came in with the first car moving slowly, flying the French flag. The highest-ranking French official in the region. Not a German. No, just a chap getting his job back. The Belgian Red Cross people were completely uninterested and warned me that no one would ever want to hear.

"I suppose that you already have the fiction of all this. The fiction must be different, oh very different, from Italians sobbing with homesickness in the night. The Germans were not real, they were specially got up for the events of the time. Sat in the white dining room, eating with whatever plates and spoons were not broken or looted, ate soups that were mostly water, were forbidden to complain. Only in retreat did they develop faces and I noticed then that some were terrified and many were old. A radio broadcast from some untouched area advised the local population not to attack them as they retreated, it would make wild animals of them. But they were attacked by some young boys shooting out of a window and eight hostages were taken, including the son of the man who cut the maharaja's daughters' black hair, and they were shot and left along the wall of a café on the more or less Italian side of the border. And the man who owned the café was killed too, but later, by civilians — he had given names to the

---

24. *Luce* "Light," in Italian. 25. *Duce* "Leader"; strongly associated with Mussolini, fascist leader of Italy during World War II. 26. **Vichy law** French laws adopted by leader Philippe Pétain during the Nazi occupation of France in World War II; Jews were displaced into camps and otherwise persecuted, and economic zones were isolated.

Gestapo once, or perhaps it was something else. He got on the wrong side of the right side at the wrong time, and he was thrown down the deep gorge between the two frontiers.

"Up in one of the hill villages Germans stayed till no one was alive. I was at that time in the former wine cellar, reading books by candlelight.

"The Belgian Red Cross team found the skeleton of a German deserter in a cave and took back the helmet and skull to Knokke-le-Zoute[27] as souvenirs.

"My war has ended. Our family held together almost from the Napoleonic adventures. It is shattered now. Sentiment does not keep families whole — only mutual pride and mutual money."

This true story sounded so implausible that she decided never to send it. She wrote a sensible letter asking for sugar and rice and for new books; nothing must be older than 1940.

Jack answered at once: there were no new authors (he had been asking people). Sugar was unobtainable, and there were queues for rice. Shoes had been rationed. There were no women's stockings but lisle,[28] and the famous American legs looked terrible. You could not find butter or meat or tinned pineapple. In restaurants, instead of butter you were given miniature golf balls of cream cheese. He supposed that all this must sound like small beer to Netta.

A notice arrived that a CARE package awaited her at the post office. It meant that Jack had added his name and his money to a mailing list. She refused to sign for it; then she changed her mind and discovered it was not from Jack but from the American she had once taken to such a pretty room. Jack did send rice and sugar and delicious coffee but he forgot about books. His letters followed; sometimes three arrived in a morning. She left them sealed for days. When she sat down to answer, all she could remember were implausible things.

Iris came back. She was the first. She had grown puffy in England — the result of drinking whatever alcohol she could get her hands on and grimly eating her sweets allowance: there would be that much less gin and chocolate for the Germans if ever they landed. She put her now wide bottom on a comfortable armchair — one of the few chairs the first wave of Italians had not burned with cigarettes or idly hacked at with daggers — and said Jack had been living with a woman in America and to spare the gossip had let her be known as his wife. Another Mrs. Ross? When Netta discovered it was dimpled Chippendale, she laughed aloud.

"I've seen them," said Iris. "I mean I saw them together. King Charles and a spaniel. Jack wiped his feet on her."

Netta's feelings were of lightness, relief. She would not have to tell Jack about the partisans hanging by the neck in the arches of the Place Masséna at Nice. When Iris had finished talking, Netta said, "What about his music?"

"I don't know."

"How can you not know something so important?"

"Jack had a good chance at things, but he made a mess of everything," said Iris. "My father is still living. Life really is too incredible for some of us."

---

27. **Knokke-le-Zoute** Resort town on the Belgian North Sea. 28. **lisle** Cotton-thread weave.

A dark girl of about twenty turned up soon after. Her costume, a gray dress buttoned to the neck, gave her the appearance of being in uniform. She unzipped a military-looking bag and cried, in an unplaceable accent, "Hallo, hallo, Mrs. Ross? A few small gifts for you," and unpacked a bottle of Haig, four tins of corned beef, a jar of honey, and six pairs of American nylon stockings, which Netta had never seen before, and were as good to have under a mattress as gold. Netta looked up at the tall girl.

"Remember? I was the middle sister. With," she said gravely, "the typical middle-sister problems." She scarcely recalled Jack, her beloved. The memory of Netta had grown up with her. "I remember you laughing," she said, without loving that memory. She was a severe, tragic girl. "You were the first adult I ever heard laughing. At night in bed I could hear it from your balcony. You sat smoking with, I suppose, your handsome husband. I used to laugh just to hear you."

She had married an Iranian journalist. He had discovered that political prisoners in the United States were working under lamentable conditions in tin mines. President Truman had sent them there. People from all over the world planned to unite to get them out. The girl said she had been to Germany and to Austria, she had visited camps, they were all alike, and that was already the past, and the future was the prisoners in the tin mines.

Netta said, "In what part of the country are these mines?"

The middle sister looked at her sadly and said, "Is there more than one part?"

For the first time in years, Netta could see Jack clearly. They were silently sharing a joke; he had caught it too. She and the girl lunched in a corner of the battered dining room. The tables were scarred with initials. There were no tablecloths. One of the great-uncle's paintings still hung on a wall. It showed the Quai Laurenti, a country road alongside the sea. Netta, who had no use for the past, was discovering a past she could regret. Out of a dark, gentle silence — silence imposed by the impossibility of telling anything real — she counted the cracks in the walls. When silence failed she heard power saws ripping into olive trees and a lemon grove. With a sense of deliverance she understood that soon there would be nothing left to spoil. Her great-uncle's picture, which ought to have changed out of sympathetic magic, remained faithful. She regretted everything now, even the three anxious little girls in blue linen. Every calamitous season between then and now seemed to descend directly from Georgina Blackley's having said "white" just to keep three children in their place. Clad in buttoned-up gray, the middle sister now picked at corned beef and said she had hated her father, her mother, her sisters, and most of all the Dutch governess.

"Where is she now?" said Netta.

"Dead, I hope." This was from someone who had visited camps. Netta sat listening, her cheek on her hand. Death made death casual: she had always known. Neither the vanquished in their flight nor the victors returning to pick over rubble seemed half so vindictive as a tragic girl who had disliked her governess.

Dr. Blackley came back looking positively cheerful. In those days men still liked soldiering. It made them feel young, if they needed to feel it, and it got them away from home. War made the break few men could make on their own. The doctor looked years younger, too, and very fit. His wife was not with him. She had survived everything, and the hardships she had undergone had completely restored her to health — which had made it easy for her husband to leave her. Actually, he had never gone back, except to wind up the matter.

"There are things about Georgina I respect and admire," he said, as husbands will say from a distance. His war had been in Malta. He had come here, as soon as he could, to the shelled, gnawed, tarnished coast (as if he had not seen enough at Malta) to ask Netta to divorce Jack and to marry him, or live with him — anything she wanted, on any terms.

But she wanted nothing — at least, not from him.

"Well, one can't defeat a memory," he said. "I always thought it was mostly su-hex between the two of you."

"So it was," said Netta. "So far as I remember."

"Everyone noticed. You would vanish at odd hours. Dis-huppear."

"Yes, we did."

"You can't live on memories," he objected. "Though I respect you for being faithful, of course."

"What you are talking about is something of which one has no specific memory," said Netta. "Only of seasons. Places. Rooms. It is as abstract to remember as to read about. That is why it is boring in talk except as a joke, and boring in books except for poetry."

"You never read poetry."

"I do now."

"I guessed that," he said.

"That lack of memory is why people are unfaithful, as it is so curiously called. When I see closed shutters I know there are lovers behind them. That is how the memory works. The rest is just convention and small talk."

"Why lovers? Why not someone sleeping off the wine he had for lunch?"

"No. Lovers."

"A middle-aged man cutting his toenails in the bathtub," he said with unexpected feeling. "Wearing bifocal lenses so that he can see his own feet."

"No, lovers. Always."

He said, "Have you missed him?"

"Missed who?"

"Who the bloody hell are we talking about?"

"The Italian commander billeted here. He was not a guest. He was here by force. I was not breaking a rule. Without him I'd have perished in every way. He may be home with his wife now. Or in that fortress near Turin where he sent other men. Or dead." She looked at the doctor and said, "Well, what would you like me to do? Sit here and cry?"

"I can't imagine you with a brute."

"I never said that."

"Do you miss him still?"

"The absence of Jack was like a cancer which I am sure has taken root, and of which I am bound to die," said Netta.

"You'll bu-hury us all," he said, as doctors tell the condemned.

"I haven't said I won't." She rose suddenly and straightened her skirt, as she used to do when hotel guests became pally. "Conversation over," it meant.

"Don't be too hard on Jack," he said.

"I am hard on myself," she replied.

After he had gone he sent her a parcel of books, printed on grayish paper, in warped wartime covers. All of the titles were, to Netta, unknown. There was *Fireman Flower* and

The Horse's Mouth and *Four Quartets* and *The Stuff to Give the Troops* and *Better Than a Kick in the Pants* and *Put Out More Flags.*[29] A note added that the next package would contain Henry Green and Dylan Thomas.[30] She guessed he would not want to be thanked, but she did so anyway. At the end of her letter was "Please remember, if you mind too much, that I said no to you once before." Leaning on the bar, exactly as Jack used to, with a glass of the middle sister's drink at hand, she opened *Better Than a Kick in the Pants* and read, " … two Fascists came in, one of them tall and thin and tough looking; the other smaller, with only one arm and an empty sleeve pinned up to his shoulder. Both of them were quite young and wore black shirts."

Oh, thought Netta, I am the only one who knows all this. No one will ever realize how much I know of the truth, the truth, the truth, and she put her head on her hands, her elbows on the scarred bar, and let the first tears of her after-war run down her wrists.

The last to return was the one who should have been first. Jack wrote that he was coming down from the north as far as Nice by bus. It was a common way of travelling and much cheaper than by train. Netta guessed that he was mildly hard up and that he had saved nothing from his war job. The bus came in at six, at the foot of the Place Masséna. There was a deep-blue late-afternoon sky and pale sunlight. She could hear birds from the public gardens nearby. The Place was as she had always seen it, like an elegant drawing room with a blue ceiling. It was nearly empty. Jack looked out on this sunlighted, handsome space and said, "Well, I'll just leave my stuff at the bus office, for the moment" — perhaps noticing that Netta had not invited him anywhere. He placed his ticket on the counter, and she saw that he had not come from far away: he must have been moving south by stages. He carried an aura of London pub life; he had been in London for weeks.

A frowning man hurrying to wind things up so he could have his first drink of the evening said, "The office is closing and we don't keep baggage here."

"People used to be nice," Jack said.

"Bus people?"

"Just people."

She was hit by the sharp change in his accent. As for the way of speaking, which is something else again, he was like the heir to great estates back home after a Grand Tour. Perhaps the estates had run down in his absence. She slipped the frowning man a thousand francs, a new pastel-tinted bill, on which the face of a calm girl glowed like an opal. She said, "We shan't be long."

She set off over the Place, walking diagonally — Jack beside her, of course. He did not ask where they were headed, though he did make her smile by saying, "Did you bring a car?," expecting one of the hotel cars to be parked nearby, perhaps with a driver to open the door; perhaps with cold chicken and wine in a hamper, too. He said, "I'd forgotten about having to tip for every little thing." He did not question his destination, which was no farther than a café at the far end of the square. What she felt at that instant was intense revulsion. She thought, I don't want him, and pushed away some invisible flying thing — a bat or blown paper. He looked at her with surprise. He must have been wondering if hardship had taught Netta to talk in her mind.

---

29. *Fireman Flower … Put Out More Flags* Novels by American, British, and Irish writers. **30. Henry Green, Dylan Thomas** Green was a British satirical novelist (1905–1973); Thomas was a Welsh writer and poet (1914–1953).

This is it, the freedom he was always offering me, she said to herself, smiling up at the beautiful sky.

They moved slowly along the nearly empty square, pausing only when some worn-out Peugeot[31] or an old bicycle, finding no other target, made a swing in their direction. Safely on the pavement, they walked under the arches where partisans[32] had been hanged. It seemed to Netta the bodies had been taken down only a day or so before. Jack, who knew about this way of dying from hearsay, chose a café table nearly under a poor lad's bound, dangling feet.

"I had a woman next to me on the bus who kept a hedgehog all winter in a basketful of shavings," he said. "He can drink milk out of a wineglass." He hesitated. "I'm sorry about the books you asked for. I was sick of books by then. I was sick of rhetoric and culture and patriotic crap."

"I suppose it is all very different over there," said Netta.

"God, yes."

He seemed to expect her to ask questions, so she said, "What kind of clothes do they wear?"

"They wear quite a lot of plaids and tartans. They eat at peculiar hours. You'll see them eating strawberries and cream just when you're thinking of having a drink."

She said, "Did you visit the tin mines, where Truman sends his political prisoners?"

"*Tin* mines?" said Jack. "No."

"Remember the three little girls from the maharaja trade?"

Neither could quite hear what the other had to say. They were partially deaf to each other.

Netta continued softly, "Now, as I understand it, she first brought an American to London, and then she took an Englishman to America."

He had too much the habit of women, he was playing too close a game, to waste points saying, "Who? What?"

"It was over as fast as it started," he said. "But then the war came and we were stuck. She became a friend," he said. "I'm quite fond of her" — which Netta translated as, "It is a subterranean river that may yet come to light." "You wouldn't know her," he said. "She's very different now. I talked so much about the south, down here, she finally found some land going dirt cheap at Bandol.[33] The mayor arranged for her to have an orchard next to her property, so she won't have neighbors. It hardly cost her anything. He said to her, 'You're very pretty.'"

"No one ever had a bargain in property because of a pretty face," said Netta.

"Wasn't it lucky," said Jack. He could no longer hear himself, let alone Netta. "The war was unsettling, being in America. She minded not being active. Actually she was using the Swiss passport, which made it worse. Her brother was killed over Bremen.[34] She needs security now. In a way it was sorcerer and apprentice between us, and she suddenly grew up. She'll be better off with a roof over her head. She writes a little now. Her poetry isn't bad," he said, as if Netta had challenged its quality.

"Is she at Bandol now, writing poetry?"

"Well, no." He laughed suddenly. "There isn't a roof yet. And, you know, people don't sit writing that way. They just think they're going to."

"Who has replaced you?" said Netta. "Another sorcerer?"

---

31. Peugeot A brand of French car. **32. partisans** Members of the French resistance. **33. Bandol** French wine region. **34. Bremen** German city.

"Oh, *he* ... he looks like George II in a strong light. Or like Queen Anne. Queen Anne and Lady Mary, somebody called them." Iris, that must have been. Queen Anne and Lady Mary wasn't bad — better than King Charles and his spaniel. She was beginning to enjoy his story. He saw it, and said lightly, "I was too preoccupied with you to manage another life. I couldn't see myself going on and on away from you. I didn't want to grow middle-aged at odds with myself."

But he had lost her; she was enjoying a reverie about Jack now, wearing one of those purple sunburns people acquire at golf. She saw him driving an open car, with large soft freckles on his purple skull. She saw his mistress's dog on the front seat and the dog's ears flying like pennants. The revulsion she felt did not lend distance but brought a dreamy reality closer still. He must be thirty-four now, she said to herself. A terrible age for a man who has never imagined thirty-four.

"Well, perhaps you have made a mess of it," she said, quoting Iris.

"What mess? I'm here. *He* — "

"Queen Anne?"

"Yes, well, actually Gerald is his name; he wears nothing but brown. Brown suit, brown tie, brown shoes. I said, '*He* can't go to Mitten Todd. He won't match.'"

"Harmonize," she said.

"That's it. Harmonize with the — "

"What about Gerald's wife? I'm sure he has one."

"Lucretia."

"No, really?"

"On my honor. When I last saw them they were all together, talking."

Netta was remembering what the middle sister had said about laughter on the balcony. She couldn't look at him. The merest crossing of glances made her start laughing rather wildly into her hands. The hysterical quality of her own laughter caught her in midair. What were they talking about? He hitched his chair nearer and dared to take her wrist.

"Tell me, now," he said, as if they were to be two old confidence men getting their stories straight. "What about you? Was there ever ... " The glaze of laughter had not left his face and voice. She saw that he would make her his business, if she let him. Pulling back, she felt another clasp, through a wall of fog. She groped for this other, invisible hand, but it dissolved. It was a lost, indifferent hand; it no longer recognized her warmth. She understood: He is dead ... Jack, closed to ghosts, deaf to their voices, was spared this. He would be spared everything, she saw. She envied him his imperviousness, his true unhysterical laughter.

Perhaps that's why I kicked him, she said. I was always jealous. Not of women. Of his short memory, his comfortable imagination. And I am going to be thirty-seven and I have a dark, an accurate, a deadly memory.

He still held her wrist and turned it another way, saying, "Look, there's paint on it."

"Oh, God, where is the waiter?" she cried, as if that were the one important thing. Jack looked his age, exactly. She looked like a burned-out child who had been told a ghost story. Desperately seeking the waiter, she turned to the café behind them and saw the last light of the long afternoon strike the mirror above the bar — a flash in a tunnel; hands juggling with fire. That unexpected play, at a remove, borne indoors, displayed to anyone who could stare without blinking, was a complete story. It was the brightness on the looking glass, the only part of a life, or a love, or a promise, that could never be concealed, changed, or corrupted.

Not a hope, she was trying to tell him. He could read her face now. She reminded herself, If I say it, I am free. I can finish painting the radiators in peace. I can read every book in the world. If I had relied on my memory for guidance, I would never have crept out of the wine cellar. Memory is what ought to prevent you from buying a dog after the first dog dies, but it never does. It should at least keep you from saying yes twice to the same person.

"I've always loved you," he chose to announce — it really was an announcement, in a new voice that stated nothing except facts.

The dark, the ghosts, the candlelight, her tears on the scarred bar — *they* were real. And still, whether she wanted to see it or not, the light of imagination danced all over the square. She did not dare to turn again to the mirror, lest she confuse the two and forget which light was real. A pure white awning on a cross street seemed to her to be of indestructible beauty. The window it sheltered was hollowed with sadness and shadow. She said with the same deep sadness, "I believe you." The wave of revulsion receded, sucked back under another wave — a powerful adolescent craving for something simple, such as true love.

Her face did not show this. It was set in adolescent stubbornness, and this was one of their old, secret meetings when, sullen and hurt, she had to be coaxed into life as Jack wanted it lived. It was the same voyage, at the same rate of speed. The Place seemed to her to be full of invisible traffic — first a whisper of tires, then a faint, high screeching, then a steady roar. If Jack heard anything, it could be only the blood in the veins and his loud, happy thought. To a practical romantic like Jack, dying to get Netta to bed right away, what she was hearing was only the uh-hebb and flo-ho of hormones, as Dr. Blackley said. She caught a look of amazement on his face: *Now* he knew what he had been deprived of. *Now* he remembered. It had been Netta, all along.

Their evening shadows accompanied them over the long square. "I still have a car," she remarked. "But no petrol. There's a train." She did keep on hearing a noise, as of heavy traffic rushing near and tearing away. Her own quiet voice carried across it, saying, "Not a hope." He must have heard that. Why, it was as loud as a shout. He held her arm lightly. He was as buoyant as morning. This *was* his morning — the first light on the mirror, the first cigarette. He pulled her into an archway where no one could see. What could I do, she asked her ghosts, but let my arm be held, my steps be guided?

Later, Jack said that the walk with Netta back across the Place Masséna was the happiest event of his life. Having no reliable counter-event to put in its place, she let the memory stand.

(1979)

Robin Blaser (1925–)

In his 1967 essay "The Fire," Robin Blaser argues that the lyric voice and imagist technique employed by many of his contemporaries is narrow and limited: "the psychological accuracy" of a "perception is not enough; the sculptural imagistic quality is not enough; and the very aesthetic quality of taking the one image, or even three images as a whole, the beauty of the idea that you can write a single poem, is a lie." For Blaser, "the processional aspect of the world has to be caught in the language also." This constant negotiation between the image and the world is, in his view, a form of resistance. By engaging with the plural, infinite, and ever-changing world outside him, he is endeavouring to combat not only rigid and inward-looking poetry, but also the fixed and self-important language of public discourse in general.

Blaser was born on 18 May 1925 in Denver, Colorado. His father and maternal grandmother worked for the railroad, and he spent most of his youth in various small communities across Idaho. Remembering his childhood, Blaser writes, "we lived in houses that were always by the railroad tracks, sometimes between two railbeds — the houses were remodeled railway cars. ... Towns I lived in had populations of 8 persons, 14, seldom 20." The family eventually settled in Twin Falls.

In the early 1940s, Blaser briefly attended both Northwestern University and the College of Idaho at Caldwell before embarking upon a long period of study at the University of California at Berkeley in 1944. At Berkeley, Blaser took courses in medieval, Renaissance, and Romantic literatures and became involved in the lively artistic community that had sprung up around the university. This off-campus experience was crucial to Blaser's development as a poet. In a 2002 interview, he explains that "in the English Department you couldn't really study twentieth-century stuff. You had the New Criticism that could read T.S. Eliot perhaps, but it could not read anything else." His introduction to "what would be called modern poetry" occurred when he met Robert Duncan, a fellow poet who hosted a reading group in his home. With Duncan, Blaser read James Joyce, García Lorca, W.B. Yeats, Ezra Pound, and Stéphane Mallarmé, among others. Along with their friend Jack Spicer, the two began to work on poetic projects as part of what they called "the Berkeley Renaissance."

At Berkeley, Blaser often felt overshadowed by his two colleagues. In 1955, he graduated with master's degrees in arts and library science and moved to Boston to work at Harvard's Widener Library; he soon became acquainted with the members of the Cambridge Poets' Theatre, among them John Ashbery and Frank O'Hara. With this new distance from Spicer and Duncan, Blaser began to develop his own distinct writing style, attempting to "find a line" that would not only hold his personal perceptions of the world but also "tie a reader to the poems" rather than to their author. His Boston poem "Herons" (circa 1956–1958) speaks of this poetic awakening: "For years I've heard / others speak like birds. / ... One day I spoke / articulate / the words *tic-ed* / in my throat. / It was / as if love woke / after anger. / The words / sure — / Listen."

In 1959, Blaser moved back to Berkeley, and in 1960, several of his poems were published in Donald Allen's major anthology *The New American Poetry 1945–1960*. Around this time, Spicer began to develop a poetic practice that he called "dictation," maintaining that instead of manip-ulating language to their own purposes, poets should serve as mediums for messages coming from outside themselves. This technique worked well for Blaser's purposes, and he began to explore dictation in his *Cups* series (circa 1959–1960). Unlike Spicer, however, Blaser envisioned writing as a constant exchange between the inside and outside, or self and world. Speaking alongside a host of other voices, whose works he often quoted at length, he would imagine that he was creating a shared space, or community. In *Cups,* he speaks of this difference: "Jack talked. His determined privacy against / my public face. The poem / by dictation."

The atmosphere of the Berkeley poetic community in the 1960s was tense, however, as Spicer and Duncan had begun to grow apart and Blaser was often caught in the middle of their disagreements. In 1964, Blaser published a translation of Gérard de Nerval's *Les Chimères,* which he had produced in accordance with his own experimental theories of translation: "not the word for word crib, but the actual heat of the process which gave form to the poems." Duncan publicly attacked his methods and did his own, more traditional translation. When, in 1965, Spicer died as a result of alcoholism, Blaser decided it was time to leave Berkeley a second time.

Blaser had become increasingly involved in the literary scene in Vancouver, British Columbia, and in 1966, he accepted a position in the English department at Simon Fraser University. He remained there until his retirement, in 1986, becoming a Canadian citizen in 1972. In Vancouver, Blaser formed friendships and connections with Canadian poets such as George Bowering, Angela Bowering, Phyllis Webb, bpNichol, Michael Ondaatje, and Daphne Marlatt. Several of these writers were in attendance when he recorded his series of autobiographical tapes, *Astonishments* (1974).

Until the 1990s, Blaser had only published his work in anthologies and in a few small-press chapbooks. In fact, he considers all of his poetic efforts to be a part of one long poem entitled *The Holy Forest*. In 1993, he published an edition of the poem, and in 2003, he produced a revised and expanded version. The title *The Holy Forest* is an allusion to Dante's *The Divine Comedy*, which begins with the poet lost in a "dark wood" of spiritual uncertainty. Blaser imagines the "events" that comprise his long poem as "noises in the forest," asserting that "forests are where one is lost, and sometimes found." This is an apt description of his poem, and many critics have used the metaphor to describe the experience of reading this, at times, rather difficult work.

In the late 1990s, Blaser put poetry aside to write the libretto for British composer Sir Harrison Birtwistle's opera *The Last Supper* (2000). In the libretto, Blaser imagines that Jesus Christ and his disciples are "invited back into Space/Time" to look "through the three zeros of the year 2000" at the history of Christianity. He suggests that spirituality should play a role in all of our lives, but he also conveys his frustration with organized religion, particularly with the institution of Christianity. In one powerful scene, the actor playing Christ washes "the dust of centuries" from the feet of the disciples. In doing so, he wipes away "pre-emptions of God's judgement"; "the State confused with God"; "hatred of the body"; and "the dust of unmournable wars and killing fields." Blaser now lives in Vancouver with his partner, David Farwell.

The Medium

it is essentially reluctance   the language
a darkness, a friendship, tying to the real
but it is unreal

the clarity desired, a wish for true sight,
all tangling

"you" tried me, the everyday which
caught me, turning the house

in the wind, a lovecraft   the political
was not my business   I could not look

without seeing the decay, the shit poured   10
on most things, by indifference, the personal

power which is simply that,   demanding a friend
take dullness out of the world   (he doesn't know
his lousy emptiness)   I slept

in a fire   on my book bag, one dried wing
of a white moth   the story is of a man
who lost his way in the holy wood

because the way had never been taken without
at least two friends,   one on each side,

20   and I believe my dream said one of the others
always led   now left to acknowledge,

he can't breathe, the darkness bled
the white wing,   one   of the body

of the moth that moved him, of the other
wing,   the language is bereft

(1964)

Image-Nation 12 (Actus[1]

so the ground flows   and the heavens are propositional
gifts   of birth   an accomplishment of thought   where
one sits in silence   a word-boundary

so the companions move
who belong to their work   strange unfamiliarity
of the familiar

I make out a boat   the soul's image   a voice   a residence
and the disappearance from a work   over the last
blind note   "Oh, a boat of friends"   the music of,
10   logos[2] of   a blinding instrument   our words, mine
among them   wash at the perilous   social, political,
hellish and heavenly parts
                    the world is in accordance with my
                    perspective in order to be independent
                    of me   is   for me in order to be without me
I make a boat out of an apple tree,
both ends are golden   (Veda[3]
the labyrinthine differences

or I'm a horseman with prowess
20   in the rodeo,
but what will is the shape of the horse

---

1. Actus Latin; may be translated as "action," "moving through," or "perfection." **2. logos** Logic, reason **3. Veda** "Vedas" are the primary scriptures of Hinduism.

the uncertain Wavering   swift to harry[4]

gods and goddesses at the ends of our words,
dead or alive

discoursing   that is to say, running around arranging
things, ourselves among them   *centrifugal, after our brief*
hangup   among things   working again and again with that
operational language   always, an incorporeal matter, sharp
as sticks and stones

visible   visible   visible   heart-heartless   30

a wreckage, if he goes there   and I love these instabilities
of unstable institutions   we speak
                                                     a washboard

the **Sudden**   radiates   the work of it
drinks us up

                                                     washing
a shirt of silk
                    a mallet of gold
                                a washboard of silver
in the sea   (Veda   40
invisible   invisible   invisible   heart
less

•

I water my dragon steeds   at a constellation
and tie the reins to the sunrise-tree

to enter on wheels

I break a sprig of the sunset-tree   holding
its red flowers
                            this, Ch'u Yuan,[5] is
a journey
                    of the bird-throat   50
                                        indeterminate
musical   shore   of
                            the invisible

---

4. **harry** To attack, harass, or ravage. 5. **Ch'u Yuan** Chinese poet and statesman (340–278 BC) who committed suicide; his
death is now commemorated with the Duan Yu (Dragon Boat) Festival.

behind the face,
   the masked procession
through "you" I conceal my loneliness from myself
and make a way into the multitude and into love
by lies, for my heart cannot bear the terror, and
compels me to talk as if I were two

60 you are invited into an elevator
it has no windows
you are invited into a glass house,
a reversible abode
       not in time
but not out of it either
        the horizon
momentary shaped and formal
by a Suddenness like a hillside

dragons chimeras of the past the future
70 or elsewhere present a gift of
wildness of the behaviour of violet
and pepper-flower
      wild-logos, Ch'u Yuan, *knots*
the lithe light-trails of ivy
       around the
  wheels

 •

in the Cold Mountain pool black water
swept by the wind
      upside-down trees
80 and sky, shadowy, at the bottom
        other step-stone
holes in the world
      the work folding
a dragon at the edge of the sea my enlargement
of the pond
     where the story went
wild fiery under the leaves

I am glad you cherish the sea, Emily Dickinson[6] wrote, *we*
correspond though I never met him

---

6. **Emily Dickinson** American poet (1830–1886).

moiling   the sunlight washing   90
        and original stratum of men and women's thought

•

Unarm, Eros,[7]

                shaping
                                and unshaped, Eros,
there-then

                                                    (1974)

The Truth Is Laughter 6

moving from one room to another   a shocked,
resilient heart, owning nothing, as Yeats[1] says,
perhaps in the depths of the eyes, the latest
image held of a shimmering city,   of breathless
trees grown out of holes in the sidewalk,   of
the cold, bent body of startled thought fallen
solitary, ass over teakettle, or lost in the
whirl of this destiny or that one   do they spin
inside themselves?   like so many gods we are
told are projections of our own violence? the   10
hunched beauty covering that possibility   the
bells of the day ring from room to room the
restless mind twists around corners, angles,
over lighted floors, the moment beyond itself
like the single day, April, 1767, Jefferson[2]
planted Carnations, Indian pink, Marygold, Globe
violet, Sensitive plant, Cockscomb, a flower like
Broom, Umbrella, Laurel, Almonds, Muscle plums,
Cayenne pepper, and 12 cuttings of Gooseberries
and the country was Argo,[3] he said,   a solitude   20
conscious of itself   a green bottle behind the
fan   *the giant confined in the body's prison*
roams at will among the stars   far, in the
projection of infinite love in a finite room
today, the winter shines   winter-shine
Blake said, "When Thought is closed in Caves. Then
love shall shew its root in deepest Hell."   out
of perspective   out of the picture   not in the frame
"I cannot," he wrote, "consider death as anything
but a removing from one room to another."   30

                                                    (1983)

---

7. *Eros* Greek term for erotic drive.

---

1. **Yeats** Irish poet and Nobel prize winner (1865–1939). 2. **April, 1767, Jefferson** Thomas Jefferson, third president of
the United States (1743–1826). 3. **Argo** The ship on which Jason sailed in his search for the Golden Fleece.

Image-Nation 21 (territory

wandering to the other, wandering
the spiritual realities, skilled in all
ways of contending, he did not search
out death or courage, did not
found something, a country,
or end it, but made it endless,
that is his claim to fame, to
seek out what is beyond any single
man or woman, or the multiples
10   of them   the magic country that
is homeland

the bridges   I strained for, strings
of my vastness in language, and
the cars rushed by in both
directions flashing at one another

the mechanic of splendour, sought
after, chanted in the windy
cables   and the river sailed,
haphazard, under the solitude

20   he had only the stories to tell, naked
and plotless, the spiritual territories,
earth-images and sky-maps, dark
at the edges

the mechanic of the marvellous dreamed
of Stalin and Hitler and the ordinary,
endlessly knew where he had gone
and, then, came back, whatever happens
if, I said — I was talking to religionists —
you gain social justice,
30   solve the whole terror, then where
is god?   certainly not in happiness
and since god is not in unhappiness,
there you have it   the skilled
adventure in hostilities with no name

(1988)

Margaret Laurence (1926–1987)

"I didn't pick [the subject] because it would have a wide appeal ... I wrote because it was there to be written." Although Margaret Laurence made this statement in reference to her novel *The Fire-Dwellers* (1969), she could have been speaking about any of her literary endeavours. From *A Tree for Poverty* (1954), her translations of Somali oral tales and lyrics she feared would "otherwise be lost in another fifty years," to *A Bird in the House* (1970), the collection of semi-autobiographical short stories she produced in order to write herself "out of [her] past," Laurence always poured her energy into projects she believed were in need of her attention.

Of course, she did achieve "wide appeal" as a result of these pursuits. In Canada, Laurence is celebrated for her ability to articulate a distinctly Canadian experience and tradition, specifically in her Manawaka novels. Poet and author Kristjana Gunnars writes: "Margaret Laurence has been a founding mother of Canadian literature. She has given voice to the Manitoba prairie. She has raised the value of all sectors of society by showing the full humanity of the most neglected and forgotten among us. From her example we have learned the value of Canadian literature and culture." Laurence has also made her mark outside of Canada. In writing her African stories, she contributed to a budding literary movement in Nigeria that focused on the oral tradition of its people. Her works have been translated into many languages, and her fiction is read internationally.

Born Jean Margaret Wemyss on 18 July 1926, Laurence spent her early years in Neepawa, Manitoba. This prairie community consisting primarily of families of British, Anglo-Irish, and Scottish backgrounds would become the writer's model for the fictional town of Manawaka. Laurence's parents died when she was a child, and her maternal grandfather and her aunt (who had married her widowed father) became her guardians. Laurence's grandfather, the inspiration for Timothy Connor in *A Bird in the House*, was strict and controlling; but her aunt was compassionate, and it was she who encouraged the child to read and write.

In 1944, Laurence left Neepawa to attend Winnipeg's United College, where she studied English literature and began to publish poetry and prose fiction in the college periodicals *The Manitoban* and *Vox*. In 1947, she graduated with the highest marks in her class for English and was awarded a prize for poetry. The same year, she married Jack Laurence. She began work as a reporter for both *The Westerner* and the Winnipeg *Citizen,* but soon after that she and Jack moved to England. In 1950, Jack was hired as the civil engineer in charge of building a series of dams in the British Protectorate of Somaliland (now Somalia), and the couple went to live in Africa — first in Somaliland, and then in Gold Coast (now Ghana).

When Laurence left England, she was working on a novel set in the Canadian prairies. As she became increasingly fascinated with Somali culture, however, she abandoned the project and began to concentrate on her immediate surroundings. This new focus proved to be fruitful. Over the next 20 years, she produced *A Tree for Poverty; The Tomorrow-Tamer* (1963), a series of short stories first published individually in various periodicals; *This Side Jordan* (1960), a novel about the Ghanaian struggle for independence; *The Prophet's Camel Bell* (1963), an adaptation of the detailed journal she kept during her time in Africa; and *Long Drums and Cannons* (1968), a study of English-language writing in Nigeria. Much of Laurence's African fiction explores the situation of the indigenous peoples under the British colonial establishment and the interaction between the two cultures. Post-colonial theorists have begun to reconsider these projects and to dismantle the critical narrative that regards these works as juvenilia — or, in the words of one critic, Laurence's "training ground" for her later fiction.

In 1957, Laurence returned to Canada, accompanied by her husband and their two children, who had been born in Africa. The family settled in Vancouver. Laurence discontinued work on a second African novel and began to write *The Stone Angel* (1964), a novel set in the fictional Manawaka. Having written so prolifically about a culture that was not her own, she was finally ready to turn her attention to Canada. In a letter to friend and fellow writer Adele Wiseman, she remarked, "I feel the urge to write about the only people I can possibly know about from the inside … I feel I might at last be able to look at people here without blinking."

In 1962, she separated from Jack and moved back to England with the children. There she completed *The Stone Angel*. She also wrote *A Jest of God* (1966), which won a Governor General's Award; *The Fire-Dwellers* (1969); and *A Bird in the House* (1970). She returned to Canada for good in 1974 and completed what is now known as the five-part "Manawaka cycle" with *The Diviners* (1974); once again, she was honoured with a Governor General's Award. In Laurence's Manawaka fiction, the protagonists are women struggling to come to terms with their pasts or searching for independence and identity. Feminist scholars have shown a particular interest in the novels and in Laurence's exploration of the situation of Canadian women in the 20th century.

When Laurence had finished the Manawaka series, she wrote several books for children: *The Olden Days Coat* (1979), *Six Darn Cows* (1979), and *The Christmas Birthday Story* (1980). She also wrote short non-fictional works; in 1976, she published *Heart of a Stranger*, a collection of short essays and articles. In the early 1980s, she started to write her memoirs, *Dance on the Earth*. Laurence died in 1987, after a battle with cancer, leaving her daughter Jocelyn to complete the editorial process. The memoirs were published in 1989.

To Set Our House in Order

When the baby was almost ready to be born, something went wrong and my mother had to go into hospital two weeks before the expected time. I was wakened by her crying in the night, and then I heard my father's footsteps as he went downstairs to phone. I stood in the doorway of my room, shivering and listening, wanting to go to my mother but afraid to go lest there be some sight there more terrifying than I could bear.

"Hello — Paul?" my father said, and I knew he was talking to Dr. Cates. "It's Beth. The waters have broken, and the fetal position doesn't seem quite — well, I'm only thinking of what happened the last time, and another like that would be — I wish she were a little huskier, damn it — she's so — no, don't worry, I'm quite all right. Yes, I think that would be the best thing. Okay, make it as soon as you can, will you?"

He came back upstairs, looking bony and dishevelled in his pyjamas, and running his fingers through his sand-coloured hair. At the top of the stairs, he came face to face with Grandmother MacLeod, who was standing there in her quilted black satin dressing gown, her slight figure held straight and poised, as though she were unaware that her hair was bound grotesquely like white-feathered wings in the snare of her coarse night-time hairnet.

"What is it, Ewen?"

"It's all right, Mother. Beth's having — a little trouble. I'm going to take her into the hospital. You go back to bed."

"I told you," Grandmother MacLeod said in her clear voice, never loud, but distinct and ringing like the tap of a sterling teaspoon on a crystal goblet, "I did tell you, Ewen, did I not, that you should have got a girl in to help her with the housework? She would have rested more."

"I couldn't afford to get anyone in," my father said. "If you thought she should've rested more, why didn't you ever — oh God, I'm out of my mind tonight — just go back to bed, Mother, please. I must get back to Beth."

When my father went down to the front door to let Dr. Cates in, my need overcame my fear and I slipped into my parents' room. My mother's black hair, so neatly pinned up during the day, was startlingly spread across the white pillowcase. I stared at her, not speaking, and then she smiled and I rushed from the doorway and buried my head upon her.

"It's all right, honey," she said. "Listen, Vanessa, the baby's just going to come a little early, that's all. You'll be all right. Grandmother MacLeod will be here."

"How can she get the meals?" I wailed, fixing on the first thing that came to mind. "She never cooks. She doesn't know how."

"Yes, she does," my mother said. "She can cook as well as anyone when she has to. She's just never had to very much, that's all. Don't worry — she'll keep everything in order, and then some."

My father and Dr. Cates came in, and I had to go, without ever saying anything I had wanted to say. I went back to my own room and lay with the shadows all around me. I listened to the night murmurings that always went on in that house, sounds which never had a source, rafters and beams contracting in the dry air, perhaps, or mice in the walls, or a sparrow that had flown into the attic through the broken skylight there. After a while, although I would not have believed it possible, I slept.

The next morning I questioned my father. I believed him to be not only the best doctor in Manawaka, but also the best doctor in the whole of Manitoba, if not in the entire world, and the fact that he was not the one who was looking after my mother seemed to have something sinister about it.

"But it's always done that way, Vanessa," he explained. "Doctors never attend members of their own family. It's because they care so much about them, you see, and — "

"And what?" I insisted, alarmed at the way he had broken off. But my father did not reply. He stood there, and then he put on that difficult smile with which adults seek to conceal pain from children. I felt terrified, and ran to him, and he held me tightly.

"She's going to be fine," he said. "Honestly she is. Nessa, don't cry — "

Grandmother MacLeod appeared beside us, steel-spined despite her apparent fragility. She was wearing a purple silk dress and her ivory pendant. She looked as though she were all ready to go out for afternoon tea.

"Ewen, you're only encouraging the child to give way," she said. "Vanessa, big girls of ten don't make such a fuss about things. Come and get your breakfast. Now, Ewen, you're not to worry. I'll see to everything."

Summer holidays were not quite over, but I did not feel like going out to play with any of the kids. I was very superstitious, and I had the feeling that if I left the house, even for a few hours, some disaster would overtake my mother. I did not, of course, mention this feeling to Grandmother MacLeod, for she did not believe in the existence of fear, or if she did, she never let on. I spent the morning morbidly, in seeking hidden places in the house. There were many of these — odd-shaped nooks under the stairs, small and loosely nailed-up doors at the back of clothes closets, leading to dusty tunnels and forgotten recesses in the heart of the house where the only things actually to be seen were drab oil paintings stacked upon the rafters, and trunks full of outmoded clothing and old photograph albums. But the unseen presences in these secret places I knew to be those of every person, young or old, who had ever belonged to the house and had died, including Uncle Roderick who got killed on the Somme, and the baby who would have been my sister if only she had managed to come to life. Grandfather MacLeod, who had died a year after I was born, was present in the house in more tangible form. At the top of the main stairs hung the mammoth picture of a darkly uniformed man riding upon a horse whose prancing stance and dilated nostrils suggested that the battle was not yet over, that it might indeed continue until Judgment Day. The stern man was actually the Duke of Wellington, but at the time I believed him to be my grandfather MacLeod, still keeping an eye on things.

We had moved in with Grandmother MacLeod when the Depression got bad and she could no longer afford a housekeeper, but the MacLeod house never seemed like home to me. Its dark red brick was grown over at the front with Virginia creeper that turned crimson in the fall, until you could hardly tell brick from leaves. It boasted a small tower in which Grandmother MacLeod kept a weedy collection of anaemic ferns. The verandah was embellished with a profusion of wrought-iron scrolls, and the circular rose-window upstairs contained glass of many colours which permitted an outlooking eye to see the world as a place of absolute sapphire or emerald, or if one wished to look with a jaundiced eye, a hateful yellow. In Grandmother MacLeod's opinion, their features gave the house style.

Inside, a multitude of doors led to rooms where my presence, if not actually forbidden, was not encouraged. One was Grandmother MacLeod's bedroom, with its stale and old-smelling air, the dim reek of medicines and lavender sachets. Here resided her monogrammed dresser silver, brush and mirror, nail-buffer and button hook and scissors, none of which must even be fingered by me now, for she meant to leave them to me in her will and intended to hand them over in the same flawless and unused condition in which they had always been kept. Here, too, were the silver-framed photographs of Uncle Roderick — as a child, as a boy, as a man in his Army uniform. The massive walnut spool bed had obviously been designed for queens or giants, and my tiny grandmother used to lie within it all day when she had migraine, contriving somehow to look like a giant queen.

The living room was another alien territory where I had to tread warily, for many valuable objects sat just-so on tables and mantelpiece, and dirt must not be tracked in upon the blue Chinese carpet with its birds in eternal motionless flight and its water-lily buds caught forever just before the point of opening. My mother was always nervous when I was in this room.

"Vanessa, honey," she would say, half apologetically, "why don't you go and play in the den, or upstairs?"

"Can't you leave her, Beth?" my father would say. "She's not doing any harm."

"I'm only thinking of the rug," my mother would say, glancing at Grandmother MacLeod, "and yesterday she nearly knocked the Dresden shepherdess off the mantel. I mean, she can't help it, Ewen, she has to run around — "

"Goddamn it, I know she can't help it," my father would growl, glaring at the smirking face of the Dresden shepherdess.

"I see no need to blaspheme, Ewen," Grandmother MacLeod would say quietly, and then my father would say he was sorry, and I would leave.

The day my mother went to the hospital, Grandmother MacLeod called me at lunch-time, and when I appeared, smudged with dust from the attic, she looked at me distastefully as though I had been a cockroach that had just crawled impertinently out of the woodwork.

"For mercy's sake, Vanessa, what have you been doing with yourself? Run and get washed this minute. Here, not that way — you use the back stairs, young lady. Get along now. Oh — your father phoned."

I swung around. "What did he say? How is she? Is the baby born?"

"Curiosity killed a cat," Grandmother MacLeod said, frowning. "I cannot understand Beth and Ewen telling you all these things, at your age. What sort of vulgar person you'll grow up to be, I dare not think. No, it's not born yet. Your mother's just the same. No change."

I looked at my grandmother, not wanting to appeal to her, but unable to stop myself. "Will she — will she be all right?"

Grandmother MacLeod straightened her already-straight back. "If I said definitely yes, Vanessa, that would be a lie, and the MacLeods do not tell lies, as I have tried to impress upon you before. What happens is God's will. The Lord giveth, and the Lord taketh away."

Appalled, I turned away so she would not see my face and my eyes. Surprisingly, I heard her sigh and felt her papery white and perfectly manicured hand upon my shoulder.

"When your Uncle Roderick got killed," she said, "I thought I would die. But I didn't die, Vanessa."

At lunch, she chatted animatedly, and I realised she was trying to cheer me in the only way she knew.

"When I married your Grandfather MacLeod," she related, "he said to me, 'Eleanor, don't think because we're going to the prairies that I expect you to live roughly. You're used to a proper house, and you shall have one.' He was as good as his word. Before we'd been in Manawaka three years, he'd had this place built. He earned a good deal of money in his time, your grandfather. He soon had more patients than either of the other doctors. We ordered our dinner service and all our silver from Birks' in Toronto. We had resident help in those days, of course, and never had less than twelve guests for dinner parties. When I had a tea, it would always be twenty or thirty. Never any less than half a dozen different kinds of cake were ever served in this house. Well, no one seems to bother much these days. Too lazy, I suppose."

"Too broke," I suggested. "That's what Dad says."

"I can't bear slang," Grandmother MacLeod said. "If you mean hard up, why don't you say so? It's mainly a question of management, anyway. My accounts were always in good order, and so was my house. No unexpected expenses that couldn't be met, no fruit cellar running out of preserves before the winter was over. Do you know what my father used to say to me when I was a girl?"

"No," I said. "What?"

"God loves Order," Grandmother MacLeod replied with emphasis. "You remember that, Vanessa. God loves Order — he wants each one of us to set our house in order. I've never forgotten those words of my father's. I was a MacInnes before I got married. The MacInnes is a very ancient clan, the lairds of Morven and the constables of the Castle of Kinlochaline.[1] Did you finish that book I gave you?"

"Yes," I said. Then, feeling some additional comment to be called for, "It was a swell book, Grandmother."

This was somewhat short of the truth. I had been hoping for her cairngorm brooch[2] on my tenth birthday, and had received instead the plain-bound volume entitled *The Clans and Tartans of Scotland*. Most of it was too boring to read, but I had looked up the motto of my own family and those of some of my friends' families. *Be then a wall of brass*.

---

1. **lairds … Kinlochaline** Landowners in Morven, Scotland, and owners of the Castle of Kinlochaline, which was burned by a rival clan in the 1645 Civil War. 2. **cairngorm brooch** A lapel pin of smoky quartz.

Learn to suffer. Consider the end. Go carefully. I had not found any of these slogans reassuring. What with Mavis Duncan learning to suffer, and Laura Kennedy considering the end, and Patsy Drummond going carefully, and I spending my time in being a wall of brass, it did not seem to me that any of us were going to lead very interesting lives. I did not say this to Grandmother MacLeod.

"The MacInnes motto is *Pleasure Arises from Work*," I said.

"Yes," she agreed proudly. "And an excellent motto it is, too. One to bear in mind."

She rose from the table, rearranging on her bosom the looped ivory beads that held the pendant on which a fullblown ivory rose was stiffly carved.

"I hope Ewen will be pleased," she said.

"What at?"

"Didn't I tell you?" Grandmother MacLeod said. "I hired a girl this morning, for the housework. She's to start tomorrow."

When my father got home that evening, Grandmother MacLeod told him her good news. He ran one hand distractedly across his forehead.

"I'm sorry, Mother, but you'll just have to unhire her. I can't possibly pay anyone."

"It seems distinctly odd," Grandmother MacLeod snapped, "that you can afford to eat chicken four times a week."

"Those chickens," my father said in an exasperated voice, "are how people are paying their bills. The same with the eggs and the milk. That scrawny turkey that arrived yesterday was for Logan MacCardney's appendix, if you must know. We probably eat better than any family in Manawaka, except Niall Cameron's. People can't entirely dispense with doctors or undertakers. That doesn't mean to say I've got any cash. Look, Mother, I don't know what's happening with Beth. Paul thinks he may have to do a Caesarean. Can't we leave all this? Just leave the house alone. Don't touch it. What does it matter?"

"I have never lived in a messy house, Ewen," Grandmother MacLeod said, "and I don't intend to begin now."

"Oh Lord," my father said. "Well, I'll phone Edna, I guess, and see if she can give us a hand, although God knows she's got enough, with the Connor house and her parents to look after."

"I don't fancy having Edna Connor in to help," Grandmother MacLeod objected.

"Why not?" my father shouted. "She's Beth's sister, isn't she?"

"She speaks in such a slangy way," Grandmother MacLeod said. "I have never believed she was a good influence on Vanessa. And there is no need for you to raise your voice to me, Ewen, if you please."

I could barely control my rage. I thought my father would surely rise to Aunt Edna's defence. But he did not.

"It'll be all right," he soothed her. "She'd only be here for part of the day, Mother. You could stay in her room."

Aunt Edna strode in the next morning. The sight of her bobbed black hair and her grin made me feel better at once. She hauled out the carpet sweeper and the weighted polisher and got to work. I dusted while she polished and swept, and we got through the living room and front hall in next to no time.

"Where's her royal highness, kiddo?" she enquired.

"In her room," I said. "She's reading the catalogue from Robinson & Cleaver."

"Good Glory, not again?" Aunt Edna cried. "The last time she ordered three linen tea-clothes and two dozen serviettes. It came to fourteen dollars. Your mother was absolutely frantic. I guess I shouldn't be saying this."

"I knew anyway," I assured her. "She was at the lace handkerchiefs section when I took up her coffee."

"Let's hope she stays there. Heaven forbid she should get onto the banqueting cloths. Well, at least she believes the Irish are good for two things — manual labour and linen-making. She's never forgotten Father used to be a blacksmith, before he got the hardware store. Can you beat it? I wish it didn't bother Beth."

"Does it?" I asked, and immediately realised this was a wrong move, for Aunt Edna was suddenly scrutinising me.

"We're making you grow up before your time," she said. "Don't pay attention to me, Nessa. I must've got up on the wrong side of the bed this morning."

But I was unwilling to leave the subject.

"All the same," I said thoughtfully, "Grandmother MacLeod's family were the lairds of Morven and the constables of the Castle of Kinlochaline. I bet you didn't know that."

Aunt Edna snorted. "Castle, my foot. She was born in Ontario, just like your Grandfather Connor, and her father was a horse doctor. Come on, kiddo, we'd better shut up and get down to business here."

We worked in silence for a while.

"Aunt Edna — " I said at last, "what about Mother? Why won't they let me go and see her?"

"Kids aren't allowed to visit maternity patients. It's tough for you, I know that. Look, Nessa, don't worry. If it doesn't start tonight, they're going to do the operation. She's getting the best of care."

I stood there, holding the feather duster like a dead bird in my hands. I was not aware that I was going to speak until the words came out.

"I'm scared," I said.

Aunt Edna put her arms around me, and her face looked all at once stricken and empty of defences.

"Oh, honey, I'm scared, too," she said.

It was this way that Grandmother MacLeod found us when she came stepping lightly down into the front hall with the order in her hand for two dozen lace-bordered handkerchiefs of pure Irish linen.

I could not sleep that night, and when I went downstairs, I found my father in the den. I sat down on the hassock beside his chair, and he told me about the operation my mother was to have the next morning. He kept on saying it was not serious nowadays.

"But you're worried," I put in, as though seeking to explain why I was.

"I should at least have been able to keep from burdening you with it," he said in a distant voice, as though to himself. "If only the baby hadn't got itself twisted around — "

"Will it be born dead, like the little girl?"

"I don't know," my father said. "I hope not."

"She'd be disappointed, wouldn't she, if it was?" I said bleakly, wondering why I was not enough for her.

"Yes, she would," my father replied. "She won't be able to have any more, after this. It's partly on your account that she wants this one, Nessa. She doesn't want you to grow up without a brother or sister."

"As far as I'm concerned, she didn't need to bother," I retorted angrily.

My father laughed. "Well, let's talk about something else, and then maybe you'll be able to sleep. How did you and Grandmother make out today?"

"Oh, fine, I guess. What was Grandfather MacLeod like, Dad?"

"What did she tell you about him?"

"She said he made a lot of money in his time."

"Well, he wasn't any millionaire," my father said, "but I suppose he did quite well. That's not what I associate with him, though."

He reached across to the bookshelf, took out a small leather-bound volume and opened it. On the pages were mysterious marks, like doodling, only much neater and more patterned.

"What is it?" I asked.

"Greek," my father explained. "This is a play called *Antigone*.[3] See, here's the title in English. There's a whole stack of them on the shelves there. *Oedipus Rex. Electra. Medea*.[4] They belonged to your Grandfather MacLeod. He used to read them often."

"Why?" I enquired, unable to understand why anyone would pore over those undecipherable signs.

"He was interested in them," my father said. "He must have been a lonely man, although it never struck me that way at the time. Sometimes a thing only hits you a long time afterwards."

"Why would he be lonely?" I wanted to know.

"He was the only person in Manawaka who could read these plays in the original Greek," my father said. "I don't suppose many people, if anyone, had even read them in English translations. Maybe he would have liked to be a classical scholar — I don't know. But his father was a doctor, so that's what he was. Maybe he would have liked to talk to somebody about these plays. They must have meant a lot to him."

It seemed to me that my father was talking oddly. There was a sadness in his voice that I had never heard before, and I longed to say something that would make him feel better, but I could not, because I did not know what was the matter.

"Can you read this kind of writing?" I asked hesitantly.

My father shook his head. "Nope. I was never very intellectual, I guess. Rod was always brighter than I, in school, but even he wasn't interested in learning Greek. Perhaps he would've been later, if he'd lived. As a kid, all I ever wanted to do was go into the merchant marine."

"Why didn't you, then?"

"Oh well," my father said offhandedly, "a kid who'd never seen the sea wouldn't have made much of a sailor. I might have turned out to be the seasick type."

I had lost interest now that he was speaking once more like himself.

"Grandmother MacLeod was pretty cross today about the girl," I remarked.

"I know," my father nodded. "Well, we must be as nice as we can to her, Nessa, and after a while she'll be all right."

Suddenly I did not care what I said.

"Why can't she be nice to us for a change?" I burst out. "We're always the ones who have to be nice to her."

---

3. *Antigone* A play by Sophocles. 4. *Oedipus Rex, Electra, Medea* Greek plays.

My father put his hand down and slowly tilted my head until I was forced to look at him.

"Vanessa," he said, "she's had troubles in her life which you really don't know much about. That's why she gets migraine sometimes and has to go to bed. It's not easy for her these days, either — the house is still the same, so she thinks other things should be, too. It hurts her when she finds they aren't."

"I don't see — " I began.

"Listen," my father said, "you know we were talking about what people are interested in, like Grandfather MacLeod being interested in Greek plays? Well, your grandmother was interested in being a lady, Nessa, and for a long time it seemed to her that she was one."

I thought of the Castle of Kinlochaline, and of horse doctors in Ontario.

"I didn't know — " I stammered.

"That's usually the trouble with most of us," my father said. "You go on to bed now. I'll phone tomorrow from the hospital as soon as the operation's over."

I did sleep at last, and in my dreams I could hear the caught sparrow fluttering in the attic, and the sound of my mother crying, and the voices of the dead children.

My father did not phone until afternoon. Grandmother MacLeod said I was being silly, for you could hear the phone ringing all over the house, but nevertheless I refused to move out of the den. I had never before examined my father's books, but now, at a loss for something to do, I took them out one by one and read snatches here and there. After I had been doing this for several hours, it dawned on me that most of the books were of the same kind. I looked again at the titles.

Seven-League Boots. Arabia Deserta. The Seven Pillars of Wisdom. Travels in Tibet. Count Lucknor the Sea Devil.[5] And a hundred more. On a shelf by themselves were copies of the *National Geographic* magazine, which I looked at often enough, but never before with the puzzling compulsion which I felt now, as though I were on the verge of some discovery, something which I had to find out and yet did not want to know. I riffled through the picture-filled pages. Hibiscus and wild orchids grew in a soft-petalled confusion. The Himalayas stood lofty as gods, with the morning sun on their peaks of snow. Leopards snarled from the vined depths of a thousand jungles. Schooners buffetted their white sails like the wings of giant angels against the great sea winds.

"What on earth are you doing?" Grandmother MacLeod enquired waspishly, from the doorway. "You've got everything scattered all over the place. Pick it all up this minute, Vanessa, do you hear?"

So I picked up the books and magazines, and put them all neatly away, as I had been told to do.

When the telephone finally rang, I was afraid to answer it. At last I picked it up. My father sounded faraway, and the relief in his voice made it unsteady.

"It's okay, honey. Everything's fine. The boy was born alive and kicking after all. Your mother's pretty weak, but she's going to be all right."

I could hardly believe it. I did not want to talk to anyone. I wanted to be by myself, to assimilate the presence of my brother, towards whom, without ever having seen him yet, I felt such tenderness and such resentment.

---

5. *Seven-League ... Sea Devil* A mix of European myths, travelogues, the autobiography of Lawrence of Arabia, and the American poetic retelling of a German naval officer's life (Count Lucknor).

That evening, Grandmother MacLeod approached my father, who, still dazed with the unexpected gift of neither life now being threatened, at first did not take her seriously when she asked what they planned to call the child.

"Oh, I don't know. Hank, maybe, or Joe. Fauntleroy, perhaps."

She ignored his levity.

"Ewen," she said, "I wish you would call him Roderick."

My father's face changed. "I'd rather not."

"I think you should," Grandmother MacLeod insisted, very quietly, but in a voice as pointed and precise as her silver nail-scissors.

"Don't you think Beth ought to decide?" my father asked.

"Beth will agree if you do."

My father did not bother to deny something that even I knew to be true. He did not say anything. Then Grandmother MacLeod's voice, astonishingly, faltered a little.

"It would mean a great deal to me," she said.

I remembered what she had told me — *When your Uncle Roderick got killed, I thought I would die. But I didn't die.* All at once, her feeling for that unknown dead man became a reality for me. And yet I held it against her, as well, for I could see that it had enabled her to win now.

"All right," my father said tiredly. "We'll call him Roderick."

Then, alarmingly, he threw back his head and laughed.

"Roderick Dhu!" he cried. "That's what you'll call him, isn't it? Black Roderick. Like before. Don't you remember? As though he were a character out of Sir Walter Scott,[6] instead of an ordinary kid who — "

He broke off, and looked at her with a kind of desolation in his face.

"God, I'm sorry, Mother," he said. "I had no right to say that."

Grandmother MacLeod did not flinch, or tremble, or indicate that she felt anything at all.

"I accept your apology, Ewen," she said.

My mother had to stay in bed for several weeks after she arrived home. The baby's cot was kept in my parents' room, and I could go in and look at the small creature who lay there with his tightly closed fists and his feathery black hair. Aunt Edna came in to help each morning, and when she had finished the housework, she would have coffee with my mother. They kept the door closed, but this did not prevent me from eavesdropping, for there was an air register in the floor of the spare room, which was linked somehow with the register in my parents' room. If you put your ear to the iron grille, it was almost like a radio.

"Did you mind very much, Beth?" Aunt Edna was saying.

"Oh, it's not the name I mind," my mother replied. "It's just the fact that Ewen felt he had to. You know that Rod had only had the sight of one eye, didn't you?"

"Sure, I knew. So what?"

"There was only a year and a half between Ewen and Rod," my mother said, "so they often went around together when they were youngsters. It was Ewen's air-rifle that did it."

---

6. **Roderick Dhu, Black Roderick, Sir Walter Scott** Sir Walter Scott (1771–1832), Scottish historical novelist, wrote about the Jacobite uprising in Scotland (1668–1746) in which Black Roderick (Dhu) was a major clan leader.

"Oh Lord," Aunt Edna said heavily. "I suppose she always blamed him?"

"No, I don't think it was so much that, really. It was how he felt himself. I think he even used to wonder sometimes if — but people shouldn't let themselves think like that, or they'd go crazy. Accidents do happen, after all. When the war came, Ewen joined up first. Rod should never have been in the Army at all, but he couldn't wait to get in. He must have lied about his eyesight. It wasn't so very noticeable unless you looked at him closely, and I don't suppose the medicals were very thorough in those days. He got in as a gunner, and Ewen applied to have him in the same company. He thought he might be able to watch out for him, I guess, Rod being — at a disadvantage. They were both only kids. Ewen was nineteen and Rod was eighteen when they went to France. And then the Somme.[7] I don't know, Edna, I think Ewen felt that if Rod had had proper sight, or if he hadn't been in the same outfit and had been sent somewhere else — you know how people always think these things afterwards, not that it's ever a bit of use. Ewen wasn't there when Rod got hit. They'd lost each other somehow, and Ewen was looking for him, not bothering about anything else, you know, just frantically looking. Then he stumbled across him quite by chance. Rod was still alive, but — "

"Stop it, Beth," Aunt Edna said, "You're only upsetting yourself."

"Ewen never spoke of it to me." my mother went on, "until once his mother showed me the letter he'd written to her at the time. It was a peculiar letter, almost formal, saying how gallantly Rod had died, and all that. I guess I shouldn't have, but I told him she'd shown it to me. He was very angry that she had. And then, as though for some reason he were terribly ashamed, he said — *I had to write something to her, but men don't really die like that, Beth. It wasn't that way at all.* It was only after the war that he decided to come back and study medicine and go into practice with his father."

"Had Rod meant to?" Aunt Edna asked.

"I don't know," my mother said slowly. "I never felt I should ask Ewen that."

Aunt Edna was gathering up the coffee things, for I could hear the clash of cups and saucers being stacked on the tray.

"You know what I heard her say to Vanessa once, Beth? *The MacLeods never tell lies.* Those were her exact words. Even then, I didn't know whether to laugh or cry."

"Please, Edna — " my mother sounded worn out now. "Don't."

"Oh Glory," Aunt Edna said remorsefully, "I've got all the delicacy of a two-ton truck. I didn't mean Ewen, for heaven's sake. That wasn't what I meant at all. Here, let me plump up your pillows for you."

Then the baby began to cry, so I could not hear anything more of interest. I took my bike and went out beyond Manawaka, riding aimlessly along the gravel highway. It was late summer, and the wheat had changed colour, but instead of being high and bronzed in the fields, it was stunted and desiccated, for there had been no rain again this year. But in the bluff where I stopped and crawled under the barbed wire fence and lay stretched out on the grass, the plentiful poplar leaves were turning to a luminous yellow and shone like church windows in the sun. I put my head down very close to the earth and looked at what was going on there. Grasshoppers with enormous eyes ticked and twitched around me, as though the dry air were perfect for their purposes. A ladybird laboured mightily to climb a blade of grass, fell off, and started all over again, seeming to be unaware that she possessed wings and could have flown up.

---

7. **the Somme** The Battle of the Somme, one of the most calamitous of World War I, occurred in 1916 at this French river.

I thought of the accidents that might easily happen to a person — or, of course, might not happen, might happen to somebody else. I thought of the dead baby, my sister, who might as easily have been I. Would she, then, have been lying here in my place, the sharp grass making its small toothmarks on her brown arms, the sun warming her to the heart? I thought of the leather-bound volumes of Greek, and the six different kinds of iced cakes that used to be offered always in the MacLeod house, and the pictures of leopards and green seas. I thought of my brother, who had been born alive after all, and now had been given his life's name.

I could not really comprehend these things, but I sensed their strangeness, their disarray. I felt that whatever God might love in this world, it was certainly not order.

(1970)

Robert Kroetsch (1927–)

Robert Kroetsch was born in 1927 in Heisler, Alberta, to parents of German descent who were wheat and cattle farmers. Throughout his career he has used his prairie origins as a backdrop and as a central metaphor in his writing, which often explores and transforms ideas about how "the home place" provides a source of inspiration and identity. For Kroetsch, this search for origins involves him in developing a prairie-oriented sense of "local pride" that articulates a "dream of origins," one that will "tell *our* story" by speaking in "the grammar of our days."

This grammar embodies the dialectical tensions central to Kroetsch's work. As a boy, he developed an allergy to grain dust and could not work in the fields with the men, so he grew up in the company of the women of the household. Performing neither men's nor women's farm chores, he had time to read and tend the garden. He would channel these early experiences into a body of writing characterized by playful reversals of gender binaries; the Governor General's Award–winning *The Studhorse Man* (1969), a novel that is considered a landmark in postmodern Canadian literature, is rife with such play.

In 1948, Kroetsch earned a B.A. in English and philosophy from the University of Alberta and then headed north. He was employed as a labourer on the Slave River and in the Northwest Territories, seeking experiences (and productive silences) that would help him write his first novel, the relatively traditional *But We Are Exiles* (1965). Kroetsch spent six summers in the north. He was a boat purser (a financial accountant) on the Mackenzie River, and then found employment on the United States Air Force base (now closed) at Goose Bay, Labrador. Deciding against a life in the military, he enrolled in graduate school, first at McGill University in Montreal and then at Middlebury College in Vermont. He received his M.A. in 1956 and moved to Iowa, where he earned his Ph.D. in 1961. His thesis was an unpublished novel, *Coulee Hill*, which contained his first attempt at writing about a studhorse man (a person who travels from farm to farm with a stallion that can be hired for mating purposes).

Hazard Lepage, the titular character in Kroetsch's third novel, *The Studhorse Man*, is an ironic hero whose erratic voyage parodies and ironically deconstructs conventional ideas about masculinity, identity, and the nature of literary truth. The story parodies *The Odyssey*, but it also incorporates Plains Indians mythology. For instance, in one scene, rancher Marie Eshpeter hunts Lepage as if he were a coyote — the trickster figure in many Native cultures. Kroetsch himself often adopts the trickster persona, a role that allows him to play — sometimes devilishly — with traditional stories and conventional ideas about Canadian history and culture.

Kroetsch wrote *The Studhorse Man* while teaching at the State University of New York at Binghamton, where he spent 14 years. Meanwhile, Kroetsch was collecting the lyric pieces that comprise *The Stone Hammer Poems* (1975), which explore Kroetsch's persistent attempt to under-stand the spatial, temporal, and linguistic impulses shaping his double career as writer and teacher. Kroetsch's attraction to the double-sided nature of experience emerges in his early use of a three-line stanza with split, binary lines. The poems also demonstrate his increasing attraction to the ideas of several postmodern theorists, among them the French critic Roland Barthes, whose thinking about the relation between writers and readers allowed Kroetsch to experiment with the ways in which this relation came to influence the evolution of Canadian writing.

One of his most interesting critical essays is devoted to the Canadian long poem, which he reads as an erotic form that enables play, doubt, plurality, and constantly shifting notions of place and time. Kroetsch observes that the long poem is central to his aesthetic: "by its very length, " he says, it "allows the exploration of the failure of system and grid." As a poet, novelist, and critic Kroetsch is always resisting closure: he pursues process, rather than product; he values the dynamic possibilities offered by the storytelling act. At once colloquial, anecdotal, and formally complex, Kroetsch's work articulates a radical theory of writing that subverts the conventional and celebrates the force of things unfinished, tentative, just-formed. As Kroetsch's many essays demonstrate, and as his book-length interview with Shirley Neuman reveals, Kroetsch's theoretical interests are wide ranging and touch on crucial ideas about influence, myth, game theory, western Canadian writing, and the rethinking of personal and national concepts of identity. This may explain why Kroetsch is often referred to as "Mr. Canadian Postmodern."

Kroetsch's preoccupation with the border and borderland consciousness were of increasing critical interest in 1972, when Kroetsch and his colleague William V. Spanos founded *Boundary 2: A Journal of Post-Modern Literature*. The journal embraced anti-traditional and experimental models of literature and philosophy. Its contributors brought ideas from contemporary European philosophy to North America, applying them to the work of writers such as Samuel Beckett and Thomas Pynchon. Through *Boundary 2,* and through teaching a course on American poetry that became a course on the long poem, Kroetsch reinforced the connections between literary theory and his own work. After publishing the novel *Gone Indian* (1973), he produced *The Ledger* (1975), his first long poem experiment. The book (which is based on a metaphor derived from accounting) invokes a postmodern binary between debit and credit, past and future, self and community. Although the poet insists that his debts to the past are "PAID IN FULL" he admits that "Tombstones are hard / to kill."

After returning to Canada to serve as writer-in-residence at the University of Manitoba, Kroetsch published the novel *Badlands* (1975) and the long poem *Seed Catalogue* (1977). With *The Ledger, Seed Catalogue* became part of a larger work eventually presented as *Field Notes* (1981) and *Completed Field Notes* (1989). Kroetsch grounded these poems in the western Canadian tradition of the tall tale. Deliberately evasive, Kroetsch's poems showed their creator's interest in what was absent rather than present and exhibited his trickster-like conviction that the poet should not be defined.

Kroetsch accepted a permanent professorship at Manitoba in 1978 and published *What the Crow Said,* an episodic novel steeped in oral tradition. The poetry he wrote over the next ten years became the basis for *Field Notes*. With *The Sad Phoenician* (1979), he continued to experiment with language and poetic grammar, stating, "believe you me I have a few tricks up my sleeve myself." *Advice to My Friends* (1985) was "a continuing poem" to his influences Eli Mandel, Fred Wah, Smaro Kamboureli (his second wife), and bpNichol, as well as other writers, among them Michael Ondaatje.

In the mid-1990s, Kroetsch retired from teaching and then published *A Likely Story: The Writing Life* (1995), a memoir. Shortly thereafter, he completed *The Man from the Creeks* (1998), a novel that elaborates on Robert Service's *The Shooting of Dan McGrew*. Since then, he has published two volumes of poetic sketches — *The New World and Finding It* (1999) and *The Hornbooks of Rita K.* (2001). The latter is the work of a fictional archivist who writes about Rita Kleinhart (who appears as Kroetsch's lover at the end of *A Likely Story*), a reclusive western poet who publishes very brief poems; sharing the poet's initials, Kleinhart is Kroetsch's alter ego.

Kroetsch, who often makes himself a character in his own work, appears in *The Snowbird Poems* (2004) as a retired northerner who flees cold winters for tropical climes. After the book's publication, Kroetsch moved from Winnipeg to warmer, if not sunnier, Victoria, British Columbia.

Meditation on Tom Thomson[1]

Tom Thomson I love you   therefore I apologize
for what I must say   but I must say
damn your jack pines   they are beautiful

I love your bent trees   and I love your ice
in spring   candled into its green rot
and I love the way you drowned   all alone

with your canoe   and our not even knowing
the time of day   and the grave mystery
of your genius   interrupted   is *our* story

10   and art, man, art   is the essential
luxury   the imperative QUESTION(?)
the re-sounding say   of the night's loon

and holy shit mother   the muskeg[2] snatch
of the old north   the bait that caught
the fishing father   into his own feast

the swimming art-man   who did not drown
in the lake   in his pictures
who drowned   for murder or grief or

the weave of the water   would not hold
20   the shoulders of the sky   were deep
the maelstrom[3] would not spin   to spit him

free, daddy, FREE FREE FREE   (but I must say
DAMN your jack pines)   for the whorl
of the whirlpool breaks us   one by one

we stretch and tear   the joints
opening like curtains   on a cool
Algonquin morning   onto a red sun

---

1. Tom Thomson Canadian artist (1877–1917) who frequently painted natural scenes in Northern Ontario, and drowned while on a canoe trip. **2. muskeg** A type of North American bog. **3. maelstrom** Whirlpool, or similar swirling chaos.

or down onto the black bottom   or far
(the grammar of our days   is ill defined)
or rapt in the root and fire   of that wind   30

bent forest   (about your pine trees
this evening   one of them moved
across my wall)   daring the light

daring the bright and lover's leap   across
the impassible gap   the uncertain
principle of time and space   straight down

he dove   and he would seize unearthly
shades   and he would seize the drowned land
the picture from the pool   the pool's picture

and the gods cried   Tom, Tom, you asshole   40
let go   and you had found their secret
and would not ever   let go   they cry

                                                        (1973)

Pumpkin: A Love Poem

Inside the pumpkin   I feel much better
I feel   loyalty to my pioneering
ancestors   I have entered

new territory   I feel a bit
sticky, yes, cramped   but I feel
much better   trying to smile

I take out my knife   I cut
one triangular   hole
into the pale flesh   of my new

head   and then, gently   10
the tip of the knife   to my left
eyeball,   gently I twist

lift the old eye   to its new vision
of pea vines   snared in wire
and lettuce   gone to towering seed

and then   oh, what the hell
the second eye   no, not
quite yet   as blind as

20   love, I cut the new nose   flared
    to demonstrate my   innate
    ferocity   I slice off

    my nose   and let it
    sniff its way   into the scent of
    staked tomatoes   and drying dill

    I cut the new mouth   the place that
    must be   toothed and jagged
    the slit   that will

    sneer   and then, about to
    slice out   the old
30   I feel   on my pressing groin

    the new mouth   on my cradled
    like the seeds that   cradle
    the new mouth   pressing

    and then   squirming uneasily
    inside the pumpkin   I am able
    just barely   able to unzip

    and she, outside   walking
    in her garden   sees
    my magnificent   unfallen

40   nature   my recovered ancestry
    of borders   bravely crossed
    and husbandry[1]   triumphant

    What are you doing   in my
    pumpkin   she says, and I
    muffled   sticky   humped

    (I feel much better)   go
    away, I shout   can't you see
    at last   can't you see

    leave me alone   (thrusting
50   with all my innate   ferocity)
    at last, at last   can't you see
    I'm fucking the whole world.

(1975)

---

1. **husbandry** Cultivation of crops.

Stone Hammer Poem

1.

This stone
become a hammer
of stone, this maul

is the colour
of bone (no,
bone is the colour
of this stone maul).

The rawhide loops
are gone, the
hand is gone, the   10
buffalo's skull
is gone;

the stone is
shaped like the skull
of a child.

2.

This paperweight on my desk

where I begin
this poem   was

found in a wheatfield
lost (this hammer,   20
this poem).

Cut to a function,
this stone was
(the hand is   gone —

3.

Grey, two-headed,
the pemmican maul[1]

fell from the travois[2] or
a boy playing   lost it in
the prairie wool or
a squaw   left it in   30
the brain of a buffalo or

---

1. pemmican maul A stone work hammer. **2. travois** Early transportation device used by First Nations communities; a
hide secured between two poles, which is dragged by an animal.

it is a million
years older than
the hand that
chipped stone or
raised slough[3]
water (or blood) or

4.

This stone maul
was found.

40   In the field
my grandfather
thought
was his

my father
thought was his

5.

It is a stone
old as the last
Ice Age, the
retreating/ the
50   recreating ice,
the retreating
buffalo, the
retreating Indians

(the saskatoons bloom
white (infrequently
the chokecherries the
highbush cranberries the
pincherries bloom
white along the barbed
60   wire fence (the
pemmican   winter

6.

This stone maul
stopped a plough
long enough for one
Gott im Himmel.[4]

The Blackfoot (the
Cree?) not

---

3. slough Swamp. **4. *Gott im Himmel*** German for "God in Heaven."

finding the maul
cursed.

?did he curse   70
?did he try to
go back
?what happened
I have to/ I want
to know (not know)
?WHAT HAPPENED

7.

The poem
is the stone
chipped and hammered
until it is shaped   80
like the stone
hammer, the maul.

8.

Now the field is
mine because
I gave it
(for a price)

to a young man
(with a growing son)
who did not

notice that the land   90
did not belong

to the Indian who
gave it to the Queen
(for a price) who
gave it to the CPR⁵
(for a price) which
gave it to my grandfather
(for a price) who
gave it to my father
(50 bucks an acre   100
Gott im Himmel I cut
down all the trees I
picked up all the stones) who

gave it to his son
(who sold it)

---

5. **CPR** Canadian Pacific Railway.

9.
This won't
surprise you.

My grandfather
lost the stone maul.

10.

110   My father (retired)
grew raspberries.
He dug in his potato patch.
He drank one glass of wine
each morning.
He was lonesome
for death.

He was lonesome for the
hot wind on his face, the smell
of horses, the distant
120   hum of a threshing machine,
the oilcan he carried, the weight
of a crescent wrench in his hind pocket.

He was lonesome for his absent
son and his daughters,
for his wife, for his own
brothers and sisters and
his own mother and father.

He found the stone maul
on a rockpile in the
130   north-west corner of what
he thought of
as his wheatfield.

He kept it (the
stone maul) on the railing
of the back porch in
a raspberry basket.

11.

I keep it
on my desk
(the stone).

140   Sometimes I use it
in the (hot) wind
(to hold down paper)

smelling a little of cut
grass or maybe even of
ripening wheat or of
buffalo blood hot
in the dying sun.

Sometimes I write
my poems for that

stone hammer.   150

                                                                    (1975)

Seed Catalogue

1.

No. 176 — *Copenhagen Market Cabbage*: "This *new introduction*,
strictly speaking, is in every respect a *thoroughbred*, a *cabbage* of *highest
pedigree*, and is *creating considerable flurry* among *professional gardeners*
all *over the world*."

We took the storm windows/off
the south side of the house
and put them on the hotbed.
Then it was spring. Or, no:
then winter was ending.

> "I wish to say we had lovely success   10
> this summer with the seed purchased
> of you. We had the finest Sweet
> Corn in the county, and Cabbage
> were dandy."
> — W.W. Lyon, South Junction, Man.

> My mother said:
> Did you wash your ears?
> You could grow cabbages
> in those ears.

Winter was ending.   20
This is what happened:
we were harrowing the garden.
You've got to understand this.
I was sitting on the horse.
The horse was standing still.
I fell off.

The hired man laughed: how
in hell did you manage to
fall off a horse that was
30   *standing still?*

Bring me the radish seeds,
my mother whispered.

Into the dark of January
the seed catalogue bloomed

a winter proposition, if
spring should come, then,

with illustrations:

No. 25 — McKenzie's *Improved Golden Wax Bean:* "THE MOST
PRIZED OF ALL BEANS. *Virtue* is its own reward. We have had
40   *many expressions* from *keen discriminating gardeners extolling our seed*
and *this variety."*

Beans, beans,
the musical fruit;
the more you eat,
the more you virtue.

My mother was marking the first row
with a piece of binder twine, stretched
between two pegs.

The hired man laughed: just
50   about planted the little bugger.
Cover him up and see what grows.

My father didn't laugh. He was puzzled
by any garden that was smaller than a
quarter-section of wheat and summerfallow.

the home place: N.E. 17-42-16-W4th Meridian.

the home place: one and a half miles west of Heisler, Alberta,
on the correction line road
and three miles south.

No trees
60   around the house.
Only the wind.

Only the January snow.
Only the summer sun.
The home place:
a terrible symmetry.

How do you grow a gardener?

      Telephone Peas
      Garden Gem Carrots
      Early Snowcap Cauliflower
      Perfection Globe Onions   70
      Hubbard Squash
      Early Ohio Potatoes

This is what happened — at my mother's wake. This
is a fact — the World Series was in progress. The
Cincinnati Reds were playing the Detroit Tigers.[1]
It was raining. The road to the graveyard was barely
passable. The horse was standing still. Bring me
the radish seeds, my mother whispered.

2.

My father was mad at the badger: the badger was digging holes in
the potato patch, threatening man and beast with broken limbs (I   80
quote). My father took the double-barrelled shotgun out into the
potato patch and waited.

Every time the badger stood up, it looked like a little man, come out
of the ground. Why, my father asked himself — Why would so fine a
fellow live under the ground? Just for the cool of roots? The solace
of dark tunnels? The blood of gophers?

My father couldn't shoot the badger. He uncocked the shotgun,
came back to the house in time for breakfast. The badger dug another hole. My father got made again. They carried on like that all
summer.   90

    Love is an amplification
    by doing/over and over.

    Love is a standing up   METONYMY
    to the loaded gun.

    Love is a burrowing.

---

1. **World Series … Detroit Tigers** The year is 1940.

One morning my father actually shot at the badger. He killed a
magpie that was pecking away at a horse turd about fifty feet
beyond and to the right of the spot where the badger had been
standing.

100   A week later my father told the story again. In that version he intended to hit the magpie. Magpies, he explained, are a nuisance.
They eat robins' eggs. They're harder to kill than snakes, jumping
around the way they do, nothing but feathers.

Just call me sure-shot,
my father added.

3.

No. 1248 — *Hubbard Squash*: "As *mankind* seems to have a *particular
fondness* for squash, *Nature* appears to have *especially* provided this
matchless variety of *superlative flavour.*"

> *Love is a leaping up*
110   > *and down.*
>
> *Love*
> *is a beak in the warm flesh.*

"As a cooker, it heads the list for warted squash. The
vines are of strong running growth; the fruits are large,
olive shaped, of a deep rich green colour, the rind is
smooth …"

But how do you grow a lover?

This is the God's own truth:
playing dirty is a mortal sin
120   the priest told us, you'll go to hell
and burn forever (with illustrations) —

it was our second day of catechism[2]
— Germaine and I went home that
afternoon   if it's that bad, we
said to each other   we realized
we better quit   we realized

let's do it just one last time
and quit.

---

2. **catechism** A series of questions and answers summarizing the principles of Christianity.

This is the God's own truth:
catechism, they called it,   130
the boys had to sit in the pews
on the right, the girls on the left.
Souls were like underwear that you

wore inside. If boys and girls sat
together —

Adam and Eve got caught
playing dirty.

This is the truth.
We climbed up into a granary
full of wheat   to the gunny³ sacks   140
the binder twine was shipped in —

we spread the paper from the sacks
smooth sheets   on the soft wheat
Germaine and I   we were like/one

we had discovered, don't ask me
how, where — but when the priest said
playing dirty we knew — well —

he had named it   he had named
our world   out of existence
(the horse   was standing still)   150

— This is my first confession. Bless me father I played
    dirty so long, just the other day, up in the granary
    there by the car shed — up there on the Brantford Binder
    Twine gunny sacks and the sheets of paper — Germaine
    with her dress up and her bloomers⁴ down —

— Son. For penance, keep your peter in your pants
    for the next thirteen years.

But how —

        Adam and Eve and Pinch-Me
        went down to the river to swim —   160
        Adam and Eve got drownded.

But how do you grow a lover?

        We decided we could do it
        just one last time.

---

3. **gunny** Burlap. 4. **bloomers** Loose, old-fashioned women's underwear.

4.

It arrived in winter, the seed catalogue, on a January
day. It came into town on the afternoon train.

Mary Hauck, when she came west from Bruce County, Ontario,
arrived in town on a January day. She brought along
her hope chest.

170   She was cooking in the Heisler Hotel. The Heisler Hotel
            burned down on the night of June 21, 1919. Everything
            in between: lost. Everything: an absence

            of satin sheets
            of embroidered pillowcases
            of tea-towels and English china
            of silver serving spoons.

            How do you grow a prairie town?

                                        The gopher was the model.
                                        Stand up straight:
180   telephone poles
                                        grain elevators
                                        church steeples.
                                        Vanish, suddenly: the
                                        gopher was the model.

            How do you grow a past/
            to live in

            the absence of silkworms
            the absence of clay and wattles[5] (whatever the hell
                        they are)
190   the absence of Lord Nelson[6]
            the absence of kings and queens
            the absence of a bottle opener, and me with a vicious
                        attack of the 26-ounce flu
            the absence of both Sartre and Heidegger[7]
            the absence of pyramids
            the absence of lions
            the absence of lutes, violas and xylophones
            the absence of a condom dispenser in the Lethbridge Hotel and
                        me about to screw an old Blood whore. I was
200   in love.

---

5. wattles Rods or sticks bound together to make fences, roofs, etc. **6. Lord Nelson** British admiral in the Napoleonic
Wars. **7. Sartre, Heidegger** Existential philosophers.

the absence of the Parthenon, not to mention the Cathédrale de
        Chartres[8]
the absence of psychiatrists
the absence of sailing ships
the absence of books, journals, daily newspapers and everything
        else but the *Free Press Prairie Farmer* and *The*
        Western Producer
the absence of gallows (with apologies to Louis Riel)[9]
the absence of goldsmiths
the absence of the girl who said that if the Edmonton Eskimos   210
        won the Grey Cup she'd let me kiss her
        nipples in the foyer of the Palliser Hotel. I
        don't know where she got to.
the absence of Heraclitus[10]
the absence of the Seine, the Rhine, the Danube, the Tiber and
        the Thames. Shit, the Battle River[11] ran dry
        one fall. The Strauss boy could piss across it.
        He could piss higher on a barn wall than any
        of us. He could piss right clean over the
        principal's new car.   220
the absence of ballet and opera
the absence of Aeneas[12]

How do you grow a prairie town?

Rebuild the hotel when it burns down. Bigger. Fill it
full of a lot of A-1 Hard Northern Bullshitters.

— You ever hear the one about the woman who buried
  her husband with his ass sticking out of the ground
  so that every time she happened to walk by she could
  give it a swift kick?

— Yeh, I heard it.   230

5.

I planted some melons, just to see what would
happen. Gophers ate everything.

              I applied to the Government.
              I wanted to become a postman,
              to deliver real words
              to real people.

---

8. Parthenon, Cathédrale de Chartres Ancient Greek Temple of Athena (goddess of wisdom) and a famous cathedral in France. **9. Louis Riel** Métis leader (1844–1885) who was hanged for treason. **10. Heraclitus** Ancient Greek philosopher. **11. Seine … Thames, Battle River** Rivers in Europe; Battle River, the exception, runs between Alberta and Saskatchewan. **12. Aeneas** The epic hero of Virgil's *Aenead*.

                                         There was no one to receive
                                         my application

I don't give a damn if I do die do die do die do die do die
240   do die do die do die do die do die do die do die do die do
      die do die do die do die do die do die do die do die do die
      do

6.

No. 339 — *McKenzie's Pedigreed Early Snowcap Cauliflower*: "Of the
many *varieties of vegetables* in *existence*, *Cauliflower* is *unquestionably*
one of the *greatest inheritances* of the *present generation*, *particularly*
Western Canadians. There is *no place* in the *world* where *better*
cauliflowers can be *grown* than right here in the *West*. The *finest*
specimens we have *ever seen*, larger and of *better quality*, are *annually*
grown here on our *prairies*. Being *particularly a high altitude plant* it
250   *thrives* to a *point of perfection* here, *seldom seen* in *warmer climes*."

But how do you grow a poet?

Start: with an invocation
invoke —

His muse is
his muse/if
memory is

and you have
no memory then
no meditation
260   no song (shit
      we're up against it)

                                         how about that girl
                                         you felt up in the
                                         school barn or that
                                         girl you necked with
                                         out by Hastings' slough
                                         and ran out of gas with
                                         and nearly froze to
                                         death with/or that
270   girl in the skating
                                         rink shack who had on
                                         so much underwear you
                                         didn't have enough
                                         prick to get past her/
                                         CCM skates

Once upon a time in the village of Heisler —

— Hey, wait a minute.
That's a story.

How do you grow a poet?

For appetite: cod-liver   280
oil.
For bronchitis: mustard
plasters.
For pallor and failure to fill
the woodbox: sulphur
& molasses.
For self-abuse: ten Our
Fathers & ten Hail Marys.
For regular bowels: Sunny Boy
Cereal.   290

How do you grow a poet?

"It's a pleasure to advise that I
won the First Prize at the Calgary
Horticultural Show … This is my
first attempt. I used your seeds."

Son, this is a crowbar.
This is a willow fencepost.
This is a sledge.
This is a roll of barbed wire.
This is a bag of staples.   300
This is a claw hammer.

We give form to this land by running
a series of posts and three strands
of barbed wire around a quarter-section.

First off I want you to take that
crowbar and driver 1,156 holes
in that gumbo.
And the next time you want to
write a poem
we'll start the haying.   310

How do you grow a poet?

This is a prairie road.
This road is the shortest distance
Between nowhere and nowhere.
This road is a poem.

Just two miles up the road
you'll find a porcupine
dead in the ditch. It was
trying to cross the road.

320   As for the poet himself
we can find no record
of his having traversed
the land/in either direction

no trace of his coming
or going/only a scarred
page, a spoor of wording
a reduction to mere black

and white/a pile of rabbit
turds that tells us
330   all spring long
where the track was

poet ... say uncle.

How?

Rudy Wiebe:[13] "You must lay great black steel lines of
fiction, break up that space with huge design and, like
the fiction of the Russian steppes, build a giant
artifact. No song can do that ..."

February 14, 1976. Rudy, you
took us there: to the Oldman River
340   Lorna & Byrna, Ralph & Steve and me
you showed us where
the Bloods surprised the Crees
in the next coulee[14]/surprised
them to death. And after
you showed us Rilke's word
Lebensgliedes.[15]

Rudy: Nature thou art.

7.

Brome Grass (Bromus Inermis): "No amount of cold will kill it. It
withstands the summer suns. Water may stand on it for several

---

13. **Rudy Wiebe** Canadian author (b. 1934); the quote is from his essay "On the Trail of Big Bear," in which he argued that
an epic might redeem the Canadian landscape by inflecting it with legend. 14. **coulee** Deep ravine. 15. **Rilke's word**
Lebensgliedes Rainer Maria Rilke (1875–1926) was a German poet; the phrase translates as something like "life-limb."
It suggests both the penis and a botanical limb.

weeks without apparent injury. The roots push through the soil,   350
throwing up new plants continually. It *starts quicker* than other
grasses in the spring. *Remains green* longer in the fall. *Flourishes un-*
der absolute neglect."

The end of winter:
seeding/time.

How do you grow
a poet?

(a)
I was drinking with Al Purdy. We went round and round
in the restaurant on top of the Chateau Lacombe. We
were the turning centre in the still world, the winter   360
of Edmonton was hardly enough to cool our out-sights.

The waitress asked us to leave. She was rather insistent;
we were bad for business, shouting poems at the paying
customers. Twice, Purdy galloped a Cariboo horse[16]
right straight through the dining area.

Now that's what I call
a piss-up.
                              "No song can do that."

(b)
No. 2362 — *Imperialis Morning*
Glory: "This is the wonderful *Jap-*   370
anese Morning Glory, celebrated the
world over for its *wondrous beauty*
of both flowers and foliage."

Sunday, January 12, 1975. This evening after
rereading *The Double Hook*:[17] looking at Japanese prints.
Not at actors. Not at courtesans. Rather: Hiroshige's
series, *Fifty-Three Stations on the Tokaido*.[18]

From the *Tokaido* series: "Shono-Haku-u." The
bare-assed travellers, caught in a sudden shower.
Men and trees, bending. How it is in a rain shower/   380

---

16. **Purdy, Cariboo horse** "The Cariboo Horses" is one of Al Purdy's best-known poems. 17. *The Double Hook* The 1966
experimental novel by Canadian writer Sheila Watson (1909–1998). 18. **Hiroshige's series,** *Fifty-Three Stations on the*
Tokaido Hiroshige was a Japanese artist of ukiyo-e, woodblock prints of Japanese landscapes. The Fifty-Three Stations
print series was inspired by his trip down the Tokaido River.

that you didn't see coming. And couldn't have avoided/
even if you had.

> The double hook:
> The home place.
>
> The stations of the way:
> The other garden
>
> *Flourishes.*
> *Under absolute neglect.*

(c)
Jim Bacque[19] said (I was waiting for a plane,

390   after a reading; Terminal 2, Toronto) — he said,
You've got to deliver the pain to some woman,
don't you?

— Hey, Lady.
You at the end of the bar.
I wanna tell you something.

— Yuh?

— Pete Knight — of Crossfield,
Alberta. Bronc-Busting Champion
of the World. You ever hear of

400   Pete Knight, the King of All
Cowboys, Bronc-Busting Champion
of the world?

— Huh-uh.

— You know what I mean? King
of *All* Cowboys … Got
killed — by a horse.
He fell off.

— You some kind of nut
or something?

8.

410   We silence words
by writing them down.

---

19. **Jim Bacque** Canadian novelist and editor.

THIS IS THE LAST WILL AND TESTAMENT
OF ME, HENRY L. KROETSCH:

(a) [yes, his first bequest]

To my son Frederick my carpenter tools.

It was his first bequest. First,
a man must build.

Those horse-barns around Heisler —
those perfectly designed barns
with the rounded roofs — only Freddie   420
knew how to build them. He mapped
the parklands with perfect horse-barns.

       I remember my Uncle Freddie.
       (The farmers no longer
       use horses.)

       Back in the 30s, I remember
       he didn't have enough money
       to buy a pound of coffee.

       Every morning at breakfast
       he drank a cup of hot water   430
       with cream and sugar in it.

       Why, I asked him one morning —
       I wasn't all that old — why
       do you do that? I asked him.

       Jesus Christ, he said. He was
       a gentle man, really. Don't you
       understand *anything*?

9.

The danger of merely living.

a shell/exploding
in the black sky: a   440
strange planting

a bomb/exploding
in the earth: a
strange

man/falling
on the city.
Killed him dead.

It was a strange
planting.

450   the absence of my cousin who was shot down while bombing
the city that was his maternal great-grandmother's
birthplace. He was the navigator. He guided himself
to that fatal occasion:

> — a city he had
>   forgotten
> — a woman he had
>   forgotten

He intended merely to release a cargo of bombs on a
target and depart. The exploding shell was:

460   a) an intrusion on a design that was not his, or

b) an occurrence which he had in fact, unintentionally,
   himself designed, or

c) it is essential that we understand this matter
   because:

He was the first descendant of that family to return
to the Old Country. He took with him: a cargo of bombs.

Anna Weller: *Geboren* Köln, 1849.
Kenneth MacDonald: Died Cologne, 1943.[20]

A terrible symmetry.

470   A strange muse: forgetfulness. Feeding her far children
to ancestral guns, blasting them out of the sky, smack/
into the earth. Oh, she was the mothering sort. Blood/
on her green thumb.

10.

After the bomb/blossoms   *Poet, teach us*
After the city/falls   *to love our dying*
After the rider/falls

---

20. *Geboren* "Born" in German. The German name for the city of Cologne is Köln.

(the horse
standing still)

West is a winter place.
The palimpsest[21] of prairie

under the quick erasure
of snow, invites a flight.   480

How/do you grow a garden?

(a)

> No. 3060 — *Spencer Sweet Pea*:
> Pkt $.10; oz $.25;
> quarter lb $.75; half lb $1.25.

Your sweet peas
climbing the staked
chicken wire,
climbing the stretched
binder twine by
the front porch   490

taught me the smell
of morning, the grace
of your tired
hands, the strength
of a noon sun, the
colour of prairie grass

taught me the smell
of my sweating armpits.

(b)

How do you a garden grow?
How do you grow a garden?   500

"Dear Sir,
  The longest brome grass I remember seeing was one night in Brooks. We
were on our way up to the Calgary Stampede, and reached Brooks about
11 P.M., perhaps earlier because there was still a movie on the drive-in
screen. We unloaded Cindy, and I remember tying her up to the truck box
and the brome grass was up to her hips. We laid down in the back of the
truck — on some grass I pulled by hand — and slept for about three hours,
then drove into Calgary.

Amie"

---

21. palimpsest A manuscript on which more than one text has been written, with the earlier writing incompletely erased
and still visible.

(c)

No trees
around the house,
only the wind.
Only the January snow.
Only the summer sun.

Adam and Eve got drownded —
510   *Who was left?*

(1977)

Phyllis Webb (1927–)

In her 1962 book *The Sea Is Also a Garden,* Phyllis Webb states: "to consider the numerous methods of killing oneself, / that is surely the finest exercise of the imagination." Rejecting the taboo of speaking about suicide, Webb established herself as a poet who was brave enough to confront the worst despair. In 1977, when her friend Lilo Berliner killed herself following the suicide of anthropologist Wilson Duff, Webb coped by using her imagination to consider the act of suicide and its alternatives. *Wilson's Bowl* (1980) was the result — a book of existential gravity and an extension of the political activism manifest in her early poetry. She also ran in a 1949 provincial election.

As a young graduate of a literature and philosophy program at the University of British Columbia, Webb did not win a seat in the Victoria riding where she campaigned for the Cooperative Commonwealth Federation (CCF, the predecessor of the NDP). She did, however, meet poet F.R. Scott, who was chairman of the CCF from 1942 to 1952. Scott convinced Webb to move to Montreal, and there she met the people involved in *Preview* and *First Statement* magazines and many of their friends. Between 1950 and 1957, she encountered Irving Layton, Louis Dudek, Eli Mandel, Gael Turnbull, Leonard Cohen, Al Purdy, and others while working as a secretary at McGill University. Her importance to this new community was proven when her work was included in the poetry book *Trio*, a 1954 collaboration with Turnbull and Mandel. That year, she travelled to England and Ireland to see the land of Yeats and Joyce, and in 1957 she won a Canadian Government Overseas Award that took her to Paris for two years. French existentialism and the absurdist theatre of Jean-Paul Sartre influenced her work after her first book, *Even Your Right Eye* (1956), especially *The Sea Is Also a Garden.*

"Poetics Against the Angel of Death," from the latter volume, combines her existentialism with the preoccupations of her next book. She writes, "I am sorry to speak of death again / (some say I'll have a long life)." Her apology is a decoy; the poem is actually a critique of a masculine poetry exemplified by Wordsworth, her angel of death. To resist the traditional power and rhythmic bluntness of iambic pentameter, she began to employ Eastern models, stating, "I want to die / writing Haiku / or, better, / long lines, clean and syllabic as knotted bamboo. Yes!"

Such clean and usually brief lines became the basis for *Naked Poems* (1965), the text that secured her reputation as a poet. In 1960, she moved to Vancouver to begin graduate studies at the University of British Columbia, but she did not pursue the degree. She did, however, join a group of writers that included Earle Birney, George Woodcock, and Jane Rule. Through these three, she was also influenced by the American Black Mountain School — whose proponents

included Charles Olsen, Denise Levertov, Robert Creeley, Robert Duncan, and Allen Ginsberg —
several of whom conducted a writing workshop in Vancouver in the summer of 1963. The Black
Mountain tendency towards experimentation, rebellion against tradition, and promotion of
alternative voices inspired Webb to be more daring in dealing with sexuality and feminism in
her work.

"Suite 1," from *Naked Poems*, merges these interests with a minimalism reminiscent of
Japanese haiku. Hinting at a lesbian relationship, the poem describes how "Your mouth blesses me /
all over," "here / and here and / here / and over and / over." In *Naked Poems*, female vulnerability
gives way to a new goddess: "We disappear in the musk of her coming." Affirming women's
sexuality, looking inward and valuing subjectivity, and continuing to examine morbid preoccupations, Webb established herself as a writer who shared a lineage with Virginia Woolf and Emily
Dickinson.

Although she had periods of exhaustion, of despair, and of relative solitude in the late 1960s
and early 1970s, Webb was neither psychologically ill nor reclusive. In fact, she was highly visible.
In 1964, for instance, she worked full time for the Canadian Broadcasting Corporation (CBC)
conducting television interviews with a who's who of Canadian authors. She then co-founded the
long-running radio program *Ideas,* serving as executive producer from 1967 to 1969. She retired
from the CBC after winning a major grant from the Canada Council. In 1972, she settled on Salt
Spring Island, taking on freelance journalism work and teaching creative writing classes. Except
for *Selected Poems* (1971), she did not publish another book of poetry until *Wilson's Bowl*,
15 years after *Naked Poems.*

Of the Black Mountain poets, Robert Duncan most influenced Webb's manipulation of poetic
forms. In *Water and Light: Ghazals and Anti Ghazals* (1984), she takes the 8th-century Persian
form and alters it with a modernist dialectic of opposition. While in *Wilson's Bowl* Webb was
exploring the politics of anarchy after being introduced to the works of Russian Pyotr Kropotkin and
American Paul Goodman, in *Water and Light* she was inspired, by the work of Adrienne Rich, to
return to a feminist approach.

This approach appears subtly in "The Way of All Flesh" from her next book of poetry,
Hanging Fire (1990). The poem criticizes the reader who fails to see the implications of old age.
The poet compares the elderly body to a car that "has crashed at the bottom of the hill; / its motor
purrs like a sick cat, / and you read this as contentment." The cat is not content — it is frustrated.
A recurring symbol for women in Webb's poems, the cat in this case is the bitter spirit of a woman
who campaigned for a better world that has never fully materialized.

Nevertheless, the title poem of *Hanging Fire* casts any bitterness into question. Although it
is technically a two-line poem, it can be read as a concrete poem, a single line drawn as a wave:

> hanging f   hanging f
>   ire   ire …

The wave might be a gesture of goodbye, but it also suggests that the *ire* has dropped out of the
fire — the poet's creative "fire" is not fuelled by anger. Alternately, the poem can be read as a
repeated cutting-off of breath, a stoppage of poetry signalled by the repeated truncations after the
"f" sound, with the resulting "ire / ire / ire."

Although Webb has not published another book of poetry, she did assemble the essay collection *Nothing but Brush Strokes* (1995), which offers reflections on the critical and creative processes in addition to autobiographical information, photographs, and works drawn from *Talking*
(1982), her earlier essay collection. She also published *The Vision Tree: Selected Poems* (1982),
which won a Governor General's Award.

Lament

Knowing that everything is wrong,
how can we go on giving birth
either to poems or the troublesome lie,
to children, most of all, who sense
the stress in our distracted wonder
the instant of their entry with their cry?

For every building in this world
receives our benediction of disease.
Knowing that everything is wrong
10   means only that we all know where we're going.

But I, how can I, I,
craving the resolution of my earth
take up my little gang of sweet pretence
and saunter day-dreary down the alleys, or pursue
the half-disastrous night? Where is that virtue
I would claim with tense impersonal unworth,
where does it dwell, that virtuous land
where one can die without a second birth?

It is not here, neither in the petulance
20   of my cries, nor in the tracers of my active fear,
not in my suicide of love, my dear.
That place of perfect animals and men
is simply the circle we would charm our children in
and why we frame our lonely poems in
the shape of a frugal sadness.

(1956)

Breaking

Give us wholeness, for we are broken.
But who are we asking, and why do we ask?
Destructive element heaves close to home,
our years of work broken against a breakwater.[1]

Shattered gods, self-iconoclasts,[2]
it is with Lazarus[3] unattended we belong
(the fall of the sparrow is unbroken song).
The crucifix has clattered to the ground,
the living Christ has spent a year in Paris,

---

1. **breakwater** An offshore structure designed to slow down waves coming in from the ocean. 2. **self-iconoclasts** One who destroys their own positive public image. 3. **Lazarus** Biblical figure whom Jesus revived from the dead.

travelled on the Metro, fallen in the Seine.[4]
We would not raise our silly gods again.
Stigmata[5] sting, they suddenly appear
on every blessed person everywhere.
If there is agitation there is cause.

Ophelia, Hamlet, Othello, Lear,[6]
Kit Smart, William Blake, John Clare,[7]
Van Gogh, Henry IV of Pirandello,
Gerard de Nerval, Antonin Artaud[8]
bear a crown of darkness.
It is better so.

Responsible now each to his own attack,
we are bequeathed their ethos and our death.
Greek marble white and whiter grows
breaking into history of a west.
If we could stand so virtuously white
crumbling in the terrible Grecian light.

There is a justice in destruction.
It isn't "isn't fair."
A madhouse is designed for the insane,
a hospital for wounds that will re-open;
a war is architecture for aggression,
and Christ's stigmata body-minted token.
What are we whole or beautiful or good for
but to be absolutely broken?

10

20

30

(1962)

Making

Quilted
patches, unlike the smooth silk loveliness
of the bought,
this made-ness out of self-madness
thrown across their bones to keep them warm.
It does.

Making
under the patches a smooth silk loveliness
of parts:

---

4. **Seine** French river that runs through Paris. 5. **Stigmata** Religious phenomenon in which people inexplicably develop the injuries received by Christ in his crucifixion. 6. **Ophelia ... Lear** Central characters of Shakespearean tragedies. 7. **Kit Smart ... Clare** Christopher Smart (1722–1771), Blake (1757–1827), and Clare (1793–1864), British writers and poets. 8. **Van Gogh ... Artaud** Vincent Van Gogh (1853–1890); *Henry IV* is a play by Luigi Pirandello (1867–1936); de Nerval, French romantic poet (1808–1855); Artaud, French playwright of the Theatre of Cruelty (1896–1948).

10   two bodies are better than one for this quilting,
        throwing into the dark a this-ness that was not.
        It does.

        Fragments
        of the splintered irrelevance of doubt, sharp
        hopes, spear and splice into a nice consistency as once
        under the pen, the brush, the sculptor's hand
        music was made, arises now, blossom on fruit-tree bough.
        It does.

        Exercise,
20   exegesis[1] of the will captures and lays
        haloes around bright ankles of a saint.
        Exemplary under the tree,
        Buddha glows out now
        making the intolerable, accidental sky
        patch up its fugitive ecstasies.
        It does.

        It does,
        and, all doing done, a child on the street runs
        dirty from sun
30   to the warm infant born to soiled sheets
        and stares at the patched external face.
        It does.

        From the making made and, made, now making
        certain order — thus excellent despair
        is laid, and in the room the patches of the quilt
        seize light and throw it back upon the air.
        A grace is made, a loveliness is caught
        quilting a quiet blossom as a work.
        It does.

40   And do you,
        doubting, fractured, and untaught, St. John of the Cross,[2]
        come down and patch the particles and throw
        across the mild unblessedness of day
        lectures to the untranscended soul.
        Then lotus-like you'll move upon the pond,
        the one-in-many, the many-in-the-one,
        making a numbered floral-essenced sun
        resting upon the greening padded frond,
        a patched, matched protection for Because.

---

1. exegesis Critical analysis of the Bible (or any text, more generally). **2. St. John of the Cross** (1542–1591) Spanish mystic and poet who was an important figure in the Catholic Reformation.

And for our dubious value it will do.   50
It always does.

(1962)

Poetics Against the Angel of Death

I am sorry to speak of death again
(some say I'll have a long life)
but last night Wordsworth's "Prelude"[1]
suddenly made sense — I mean the measure,
the elevated tone, the attitude
of private Man speaking to public men.
Last night I thought I would not wake again
but now with this June morning I run ragged to elude
the Great Iambic Pentameter
who is the Hound of Heaven[2] in our stress   10
because I want to die
writing Haiku
or, better,
long lines, clean and syllabic as knotted bamboo. Yes!

(1962)

---

1. Wordsworth's "Prelude" William Wordsworth (1770–1850) was the pre-eminent Romantic writer in Britain. His *Prelude* is a long, autobiographical poem written in a lofty tone and blank verse (unrhymed iambic pentameter). **2. Hound of Heaven** Religious poem by British poet Francis Thompson (1859–1907); the poem describes a God who pursues nonbelievers rather than abandoning them.

Suite 1

MOVING
to establish distance
between our houses.

It seems
I welcome you in.

Your mouth blesses me
all over.

There is room.

AND
here
and here and
here
and over   and
over   your mouth

TONIGHT
quietness.   In me
and the room.

I am enclosed
by a thought

and some walls.

THE BRUISE

Again you have left
your mark.

Or we
have.

Skin shuddered
secretly

FLIES

tonight
in this room
two flies
on the ceiling
are making
love
quietly.   Or
so it seems
down here

YOUR BLOUSE

I people
this room
with things, a
chair,   a lamp,   a
fly   two books by
Marianne Moore.[1]

I have thrown my
blouse on the floor.

Was it only
last night?

---

1. Marianne Moore American modernist poet (1887–1972).

YOU
took

with so much
gentleness

my dark

Suite 2

While you were away

I held you like this
in my mind.

It is a good mind
that can embody
perfection   with exactitude.

The sun comes through
plum curtains.

I said
the sun is gold

in your eyes.

It isn't the sun
you said.

On the floor your blouse.
The plum light
falls more golden

going down.

Tonight
quietness
in the room.

We knew.

Then you must go.
I sat cross-legged
on the bed.
There is no room
for self-pity
I said.

I lied.

In the gold darkening
light

you dressed.

I hid my face
in my hair.

The room that held you

is still here.

You brought me clarity.

Gift after gift
I wear.

Poems   naked
in the sunlight

on the floor.

(1965)

Rilke[1]

Rilke, I speak your name I throw it away
with your angels, your angels, your statues
and virgins, and a horse in a field held
at the hoof by wood. I cannot take so much
tenderness, tenderness, snow falling like lace
over your eyes year after year as the poems
receded, roses, the roses, sinking in snow
in the distant mountains.

Go away with your women to Russia or take them
10   to France, and take them or don't the poet is
in you, the spirit, they love that.
(I met one in Paris, her death leaning outward,
death in all forms. The letters you'd sent her,
she said, stolen from a taxi.)

Rilke.
Clowns and angels held your compassion.
You could sit in a room saying nothing,
nothing. Your admirers thought you were there,
a presence, a wisdom. But you had to leave
20   everyone once, once at least. That was your
hardness.

This page is a shadowed hall in Duino Castle.[2]
Echoes. The echoes.
I don't know why I'm here.

(1971)

Treblinka[1] Gas Chamber

Klostermayer ordered another count of the children.
Then their stars[2] were snipped off and thrown into
the center of the courtyard. It looked like a field of
buttercups. — Joseph Hyams, *A Field of Buttercups*

fallingstars
      "a field of
             buttercups"
        yellow stars
            of David
10   falling

---

1. Rilke Rainer Maria Rilke (1875–1926), German poet and prose lyricist. **2. Duino Castle** Duino, Italy, is the site of Rilke's *Duino Elegies*.

---

1. Treblinka A Nazi internment camp in Poland during World War II, where over 780,000 Jews were killed. **2. stars** Stars of David, which Jews were forced to wear on armbands to mark themselves as Jews.

the prisoners
       the children
             falling
     in heaps
         on one another
              they go down

Thanatos[3]
    showers
       his dirty breath
             they must breathe   20
                 him in
      they see stars
          behind their
             eyes

David's
    "a field of
         buttercups"
    a metaphor
        where all that's
           left lies down   30

(1980)

Heidegger,[1] notes of music

Heidegger, notes of music
in his name.

The rose blooms because it blooms in the trellis.
A scale of black death because a scale of black death.

Around me, little creakings
of the house. Day's end.

The universe opens. I close.
And open, just to surprise you.

Come loves, little sheep, into
the barricades of the Fall Fair.   10

(1984)

---

3. **Thanatos** In classical Greek mythology, the personification of death.

1. **Heidegger** Martin Heidegger (1889–1976) was a German existentialist philosopher who argued that confronting the question of the meaning of being, including one's own death, was a crucial aspect of authentic human experience.

"Attend"

Between "attached" and "aloft"
getting the poem on the page
a voice tells her on this day
attend.
Harrowed[1] she is, anguished
by this day's dailiness
teenaged son in danger
following forwardness
as the poem records Bach
10   in invisible margins, neighbour
pruning his shrubs, her babysitter sorting out her own love-
life at Bino's Pancake House.

This is the way the world —
this is the way I pick up on
the voice in my head today
offering "valium," substance
long gone, used up in my last
big job and love affair,
20   its breakdown. *Velvet*, it leads
me on, vole, variorum,[2] text to —
— *stumbling block*, unblocked
and falling over myself in files,
folios,[3] fricatives,[4] freesias — ah
freesias, the scent, spring, sickness,
planting now in Fall my hyacinths —
you brought me hyacinths — and Edith
Sitwellian rain,[5] bombs falling
on London, that old poverty.

30   So I go, so she
sits at her desk, attending.
To wedding plans, Matisse[6] in the
offing,[7] possible poems
feared and held off for a moment
in her new life, or old one
revised, rough-drafted in the
coil of my cigarette smoke, my next

---

1. Harrowed Tormented. **2. vole, variorum** "Vole" can alternately refer to a mouse-like rodent or a series of attempts at something important; a "variorum" is a collection of editions of the same work, as edited by different editors. **3. folios** A high-quality printed collection of works. **4. fricatives** Speech sounds wherein the breath creates friction in the vocal tract (e.g. *S, f, v* sounds). **5. hyacinths, Edith Sitwellian rain** Refers to A.J.M. Smith's poem "A Hyacinth for Edith," which was in tribute to the experimental British poet Edith Sitwell. **6. Matisse** French artist known, like Edith Sitwell, for his use of vibrant colour (1869–1954). **7. in the offing** Likely to occur soon; not far off.

word being "lavender," Lavender
Allen, childhood friend, far back,
Victorian Lavender's innocence
gone surely by now, my own
purple's vengeance, as Bach
counterpoints his clear-eyed
fingering of her poems and mine,
the freeplay, the scandal
murmuring in shrubs this strange
infinitive (listen, I can't believe
it) — *to frolic.*

40

for Sharon Thesen[8]

(1990)

Hugh Hood (1928–2000)

Hugh Hood was born in Toronto to a staunchly Catholic family in 1928. He attended Catholic schools and was exposed to Catholic theology through much of his childhood reading. In his essay "Before the Flood," he fondly recalls learning to read using Benziger's *Bible History,* memorizing catechism at school, and hearing the New Testament read in church. His upbringing led him to see within the mundane world — which he recorded in minute detail in his fiction — evidence of a higher spiritual order.

"After Holy Scripture," Hood quips, he was brought up on "Englishness," since secular children's literature in 1930s Toronto was mostly British. He quickly recognized, however, that the social order presented in British literature was distinct from his own, and while still a child he perceived a need to "articulate what we're doing here" in Canada.

Hood attended the University of Toronto from 1947 to 1955, completing a Ph.D. dissertation on the British Romantic poets. By 1957, he had married painter Noreen Mallory and was writing in earnest. Four years later, he accepted a permanent teaching position in the English department at l'Université de Montréal. Over the next 38 years, Hood would produce ten collections of short fiction, five novels, a 12-volume novel sequence called The New Age/Le nouveau siècle, and five works of non-fiction.

Hood's first collection of short stories, *Flying a Red Kite* (1962), concentrates on spiritual transformations. As a graduate student, Hood had become a proponent of Samuel Taylor Coleridge's Trinitarian philosophy — the notion that the material world (represented by Christ) is constantly uniting with the spiritual dimension (God), and that their union creates a synthesizing third element (the Holy Spirit). According to Hood, who had always been opposed to dualist philosophies, "bringing together the spiritual intelligence and the world of the senses and the world of the incarnate is the fundamental task of any thinker whether he's a poet or a theologian." The sensory objects in Hood's stories — like the red kite, the gorilla mask in "Going Out as a Ghost," or the sailboat in "An Allegory of Man's Fate" — can therefore trigger spiritual revelations. This narrative device has been likened to the Renaissance practice of drawing emblems (pictures that convey an allegory or moral fable), and Hood used it to illuminate further structures of meaning within a story. In "Flying

---

8. **Sharon Thesen** Canadian poet.

a Red Kite," for example, the harried protagonist is transformed as he contemplates his daughter's cross-like kite in the sky, and the day's events reveal themselves to be part of a carefully constructed allegory of lapsed faith. In Hood's short fiction, the contemplation of images and objects brings the reader closer to the story's moral centre.

Hood's precise diction, historically accurate settings, and journalistic prose style obscure the allegorical mode of his stories for many readers, who assume that they are dealing with straightforward realism (Hood himself prefers the term "super-realism," which he defines in "Sober Colouring" as "art which exhibits the transcendental element dwelling in living things"). *White Figure, White Ground* (1964), Hood's first published novel, may seem to be a tale about a painter's quest to find his dead father's house and discover a new art form; but Alex's experiments with light and colour lead him to an artistic revelation that is also spiritual: "All art is religious if it's any good at all."

Hood was concerned with the civic as well as the spiritual dimension of fiction writing. In the winter of 1970–1971, he joined forces with John Metcalf, Ray Smith, Clark Blaise, and Ray Fraser to form the Montreal Storytellers group. Devoted to broadening interest in Canadian prose and fiction, the group gave dynamic performances to high school, college, and university classes for several years and demonstrated to all that prose readings merited public attention and financial support.

Hood had demonstrated his abiding interest in Montreal — its urban culture, its art scene, its corporate life, its politics — several years earlier with *Around the Mountain: Scenes from Montreal Life* (1967). Like Edmund Spenser's *Shepheardes Calendar,* it is a series of 12 sketches in the pastoral tradition: each corresponds to a month of the year and marks a stage in either the ascent or descent of Mount Royal. As the seasons change and the reader ascends or descends this mountain in the heart of Montreal, the city's virtues and faults are weighed in relation to larger historical cycles.

Around the Mountain was the first of Hood's many literary explorations of Montreal. In his second novel, however, he focused on a very different city: Hollywood. *The Camera Always Lies* (1967) employs the conventions of medieval romance to tell the story of aspiring actress Rose Leclair, who, like Eurydice in Greek mythology, is rescued from the underworld — of the American film industry. Hood's explorations of popular culture, industry, and political institutions take a less whimsical turn in the novel *You Can't Get There from Here* (1972). Set in fictional Leofrica, it is a Menippean satire (defined by Northrop Frye as a work concerned "less with people ... than with mental attitudes," which "presents people as mouthpieces of the ideas they represent") in which Anthony Jedeb — prime minister designate of the newly independent nation — becomes a Christ figure when he is murdered at the behest of international corporate powers.

In 1975, Hood published *The Swing in the Garden,* the first volume in his 12-part New Age series. In this series, he sought to create, in his own words, "an enormous social mythology, an enormous prism to rotate, to see yourself and your neighbours and friends and your grandparents." Using a "documentary fantasy" style that combined the real and the imagined, Hood hoped to articulate the past "in terms of the institutions that we're so intensely aware of that we don't even think we're thinking about them." He tried to instill in his readers a sense of "what our society's worth, what it teaches us."

The New Age novels span a hundred years of Canadian history, from 1900 to 2000. Encyclopedic in scope, they catalogue an enormous array of Canadian things, people, places, ideas, and events (including the Canadian Pacific Railway, Eaton's catalogues, and socialism). They loosely follow the life of Matt Goderich, who is close in age and perspective to Hood; however, some books focus extensively on secondary characters, like Matt's father (*Black and White Keys* [1982]) and Matt's brother (*Tony's Book* [1988]). All the novels feature what Hood calls an "expanding and contracting narrative consciousness," which means that the voice of 35-year-old Matt might express what nine-year-old Matt sees (or vice versa).

When developing his theory of narrative consciousness for The New Age, Hood drew upon William Wordsworth's notion of "spots of time" — formative events that upon reflection allow one to comprehend one's own spiritual or artistic development. The series also displays the influence of Marcel Proust, whom Hood admired for his intellectual analysis of historical time, and British writer Anthony Powell, from whom Hood learned that "an infinite series of social relations," particularly between generations, is available to an author who can "move around in [his] time span."

The novels are not chronological, nor are they consistent in setting. *Reservoir Ravine* (1979) is about the courtship of Matt's parents and is set entirely in the 1920s, while *Great Realizations* (1997) is set in 2004. Events occur in Toronto, Montreal, Saskatchewan, England, Italy, and the fictional town of Stoverville, Ontario. In *Black and White Keys,* Matt's father, Andrew, is challenged to uncover the Christian response to Nazism and war crimes; in *Dead Men's Watches* (1995), Matt confronts his homophobia as his friend Sinclair dies of AIDS. The final volume, *Near Water,* sees Matt's erudition crumble after a stroke. Hood himself died of Parkinson's disease before he could finish the novel; his colleague William Keith completed it, and it was published in 2000.

Hood hoped his opus would be as important to Canadian letters as Proust's *À la recherche du temps perdu* was to French literature; however, his Christian content and his somewhat conservative narrative forms continue to separate him from the mainstream of Canadian writing. His short story collections include *The Fruit Man, the Meat Man, and the Manager* (1971), a highly allegorical work with Trinitarian themes; *Dark Glasses* (1976); *August Nights* (1985); and *Light Shining out of Darkness* (2001). *After All!*, the fifth and final volume of Hood's *Collected Stories*, was released in 2003. Other long works include the novel *A Game of Touch* (1970) and the novella *Five New Facts About Giorgione* (1987). His essays have been gathered in *The Governor's Bridge Is Closed* (1973), *Trusting the Tale* (1983), and *Unsupported Assertions* (1991). Hood twice received the University of Western Ontario President's Medal. He was made an Officer of the Order of Canada in 1988.

Going Out as a Ghost

The children were preparing for Halloween, a festival they preferred to Christmas. The sombre mysterious end of October, when it grows colder and nobody yet knows how cold it may become, had always seemed more inviting to them than the steady weather of the solstice. They set great store by their costumes — had in different years presented themselves as Laurel and Hardy, four Marx brothers, knights in armour and hairy serfs, the two ends of a horse. They were a quartet agreeably near in age inclined to form pairs, liking to complement one another: master and slave, fat man and thin.

Their father, a confused man, joked with them about the reach and complication of these conceptions. "Going to go out this year?" he would inquire as they grew older. "What are you going out as?" The boys would argue between themselves, the girls exchange secret smiles, giving nothing away.

"I'll throw a sheet over my head and cut holes in it," their father would say at the very last minute. "I'm going out as a ghost." And the entire family would laugh uproariously, for this struck them as the lowest deep of impoverished fantasy. "Going out as a ghost," they all sang together, laughing, but inwardly troubled by the concept of dressing up as a clown or a cowboy. Such children could — probably did — miss altogether the intense, absorbed September and October during which the dress-up box was emptied, filled, emptied: old organdy and silk from costumes of years past held to the light. They had also a property box filled with daggers, stilettos, swords, false noses, wigs, grotesque false ears. Theatrical make-up was available, nose putty, crêpe hair. A family half sunk in show-business. All this began in late summer with vacation still in progress.

"If you're going into town, bring back my gorilla mask," said the older of the boys to his father on a Wednesday in late August. "I want to compare the fur."

"Where is it in the house? In your closet?"

"It's hanging on the light fixture in our room," said the younger boy. "I hung it there to make it look like a head sticking out of the wall."

"There should be a gorilla's hind-end sticking out of the wall in the next bedroom," said the father. He chatted amusingly with the children, but the image of the gorilla mask stayed with him disagreeably as he drove into the city. One of those rubber, over-the-head, monster disguises which can be found at theatrical costumers, it had been a birthday gift to his son, who had a collection of them: Dracula, Frankenstein's monster, the Wolf-Man, the Gorilla. In a poor light the thing was genuinely horrific and might prove shocking to householders on that dreary night nine weeks in the future. He was troubled by the human cast of the bestial shape. The coarse red of the cheeks, upturned snout, matted dangling hair, the powdery texture of the pliant[1] rubbery skin. The boys played up certain simian[2] characteristics in their movements; they liked to lower their hands around their knees by flexing the knee-joints. They would gibber in simulated ape-language. The younger boy often hung head downward in trees. With the gorilla mask over either head, full disguise was at once effected, a whole transformation of behaviour threatened. "Now I'm going to tear you limb from limb," they would say.

He had further worries, minor repairs impending on his automobile, which gave trouble as he drove along; the radiator leaked, spreading the odour of coolant through the passenger compartment, the smell of ethylene glycol,[3] and some sweetish, doubtless wholly poisonous, additive — radiator cleanser or sealer; there might be holes in the hoses. Late in the day he arrived in his city neighbourhood and left the auto with a local service man who at once, before his eyes, dismantled it, rendering it inoperative. "Tomorrow, one o'clock," said the mechanic, a highly trustworthy man.

"Going back to the country in the afternoon."

"You can have it by one. Not before."

He was glad to leave his car sitting on the lot, always felt better about it at such times, as one does about the seriously-ill member of the family who is at last "in good hands." As he walked the short distance to his empty house, it began to rain, then in the next hour settled into a steady downpour. He let himself in, stepped over the pile of mail lying on the floor below the letter slot, into the quiet hall. He had always liked the look of this house in the late afternoon with no electric light on; what light there was entered freely through large windows front and rear, then diffused itself into the corners of dark halls. He mounted to the second floor and standing in the doorway of his sons' bedroom he saw the gorilla mask hanging over the light socket, from which the bulb had been removed. Outside the rain continued to fall; it was now very dark for this time of year. The house was shut tight and stuffy, yet the mask moved and lifted slightly in some faint air current. He stared. He decided to have his evening meal delivered, Chinese, or barbecued chicken, no need to go out again. He might call a friend, see if he wanted to watch a late movie. What else had the kids asked for, was it masking tape?

---

1. **pliant** Flexible. 2. **simian** Ape-like. 3. **ethylene glycol** Chemical found in antifreeze.

Later he shuffled through the mail, discarded almost all, phoned for chicken, phoned David, who agreed to drive round at 9:30. Unmarried, self-employed, chronically at loose ends at night, David seemed pleased to be asked. "There are two good films on tonight," he said. "I hope my car starts." He came a little early, barely past nine, surprising his host, who was ensconced before the TV in the basement, picking chicken from the spaces between his teeth, listening to the rain, not making much sense of the program he watched, which was loud. The doorbell rang several times before he grasped that it was not part of the soundtrack, which might well have had bells in it.

He switched on the porch light and peered out at the rain. Might as well be Halloween, he thought, and opened the door for David. "You're early."

"You said any time. You're alone, right? How much do you charge to haunt a house anyway?"

"What makes you say that?"

"I just thought of it. Your house is always a little haunted, you know." This seemed a disobliging[4] comment which he could only ignore; they descended to the TV which they watched with pleasure for over an hour, until the telephone rang. This bell, different in tone from the doorbell, could not be assimilated to the sound of TV, had to be answered at once or attention would stray. He climbed unwillingly to the ground floor and went to the telephone in the studio at the very back of the house, where he fondled the clamorous instrument, gazing through the huge window at shining wetness. He put the receiver to his ear.

"Bet you don't know who this is," said a melodious voice. The line clicked and crackled strangely; the voice echoed, seemed familiar, then wholly unrecognizable. He had heard it, he knew, but how very long ago. "Bet you don't know who this is … this is … is … who?"

"We were in school together," he said firmly, shutting off the unsteady echoes.

The voice cooed, "You're getting close."

He listened harder; he had heard the voice somewhere in the past. There was a *castrato*[5] music to it, high, sexually elastic though certainly male. "It's Philly White."

"Who?"

"Philly White. We went to parish school together, don't you remember the Whites, my brother Bob, my sister Pauline? We made our First Holy Communion together."

"So we did. So we did. Of course I remember. You had smallpox when we were in, the third grade?"

He could remember the effects of the disease vividly, the spoiled face, the depth of indentation of the small round scars, about the size of a flake of confetti. His complexion had been like his name, white, the holes in his face changing colour as embarrassment or exposure moved the boy. He had often been in trouble with the teachers, hadn't been heard from in forty years. The voice was irrefutable testimony, when linked to a past and a name.

"I'm here at the Prevention Centre on Parthenais Street." The voice in the receiver pronounced the name wrong, as an Ontarian would, and translated the name of the institution too literally. *Centre de Prevention* doesn't mean "prevention centre," it means "detention centre," a quasi-jail where persons are held to await trial or, in certain cases, sentencing after conviction. Until now he had never heard of the place or seen it,

---

4. disobliging Impolite. **5.** *castrato* Male singer castrated before puberty in order to preserve his soprano or alto voice.

knew nothing about it, couldn't have identified it from glimpses at a distance. It is a deceptive building. It is the embodiment of a lie. It doesn't look like what it is; suicide is routine inside. Men have spent fifteen months there awaiting trial, the presumed innocent often treated far worse than the proven guilty — because the innocence is purely formal and presumptive. Most inmates are habitual offenders. None of this was familiar to him. "What are they holding you for?" he asked.

"Some trouble about a cheque. Well, actually two cheques. Three. You knew my family, you knew Bob was ordained, you knew ... I was married there for a while; then I moved out west. I had a car business in Vancouver and then came back east. Two little girls. We're separated now of course ... you're the only one here in the city ... I don't want my wife to know yet. I was hoping for a reconciliation. I want to get straightened out and start again."

"What's the charge?" He felt proud of the way he phrased the question; he had no contact with police, courts, criminals, or even people who were being held, detained, prevented. "Have they got anything to go on?"

"Actually ... " indecision floated into the quivering voice. "I can't talk any more; they're taking me back. They might let you see me. Could you try to see me?"

"The charge?"

"Matter of two years ... I've been sentenced ... " He never found out whether the term of the sentence was two years, or whether a longer term might be reduced to two for good conduct. "They're deciding whether to send me to a dry-out clinic. There's a problem of alcoholism. And they're waiting for information from Vancouver."

"What sort of information?" He felt damp; the studio was damp.

" ... conviction for fraud ... not serious."

"What else?"

"Hotel bills in Dorval. They brought me in from Dorval. I was there a month. I have to go now." It sounded as if the call had been cut off at the main switchboard. He put the receiver into its cradle and took several deep breaths, then called downstairs. In a few moments, David appeared from the depths. "You're missing some good take-offs," he said.

"Will you do me a favour?"

"Yes."

"My car's in for repair and I have to go out unexpectedly. Would you do me a great kindness and drive me across town? I'm not sure exactly where to go. Do you know where Parthenais is?"

They had to unearth David's street-guide in the glove compartment, then consult its small print as they drove along Sherbrooke in the persistent rain; the windows kept fogging over; it was difficult to see. Parthenais was well out toward the east end, past De Lorimier almost at D'Iberville. They turned south when they came to it, down the steep hill toward De Maisonneuve. In a few minutes a massive dark shape stood up indistinctly before them, an ultra-modern office building fourteen stories high, in glassy black plastic siding, standing on a small plot of land surrounded by chain-link fence topped with multiple strands of shining barbed wire. It reminded him of a shiny polished dark mono-lith seen in some science-fiction film. Some sort of object of perverse worship. Close up, the building looked like most others built around 1969. They parked across the narrow street and approached the main entrance which opened into a spacious glassed-in hall two stories high, with an elevator bank to the right and a reception desk nearby. One or two guards idled in the corners, paying no attention to them. He asked at the desk if he would be able to see Philly White, and the receptionist — perfectly agreeable and forthcoming — laughed jovially.

"Tomorrow, 1:30. Come back then."

"He seemed in pain or frightened. Could he be afraid of something?"

"Tomorrow, 1:30. Come back then."

One of the guards moved indecisively.

Time to get out of here while we still can, he thought. He felt great waves of imaginary fugitive guilt washing over him. Hundreds of movies lodged in his memory now rose up to frighten, to accuse. He thought of the fearful ending of *I Am a Fugitive from a Chain Gang*[6] and hastened away. "What do you do, how do you live?" "I steal."

Driving homeward, David said, "I didn't care much for the atmosphere ... "

He had to force himself to return the next afternoon. Just before he left the house, he got a call from a police sergeant in Dorval. "... heard from Philly White this morning — he's not a bad fellow, Philly, he wouldn't hurt anybody. He has no violence on his record."

"Record? What record?"

"Oh a long, long record. Four convictions in BC. Fraudulent auto sales with forgery. Fraudulent roofing contracts. But no violence, I was glad when he told me he found a friend to help him out. If I come by your house, can I give you his radio? He left it in the cells here and I know he'll miss it. That Parthenais ... it isn't like the Dorval Jail. It's no picnic, you bet." He recited a series of calamitous occurrences which had taken place at the detention centre. Group suicides, self-mutilations. "So you see if old Philly has a friend to help, I'll be glad. His family won't do nothing."

"His family aren't here. His mother is dead and they all live in Toronto."

"Did he tell you that? His mother lives in Montréal with one of his sisters and one brother. They don't go to see him. His wife and kids are here too."

"Does his wife know he's awaiting sentence?"

"No, she doesn't know a thing ... nobody knows anything about Philly White for sure. Can I drop off his radio?"

"I'm not sure I'm going to be here. I have to go to the country. I have to go pick up my car. I don't believe I can make it; the family's expecting me back. I have to go and ..."

"He'll be disappointed. He said you were coming down."

"He seems to say whatever he likes."

"That's right."

"Mail him the radio. I'll be away."

"No. No. I think I'll deliver it by hand."

The car was ready when he went over to get it. "It's ready; it's ready. You said it would be," he said happily; the garageman looked at him in surprise.

"It always is."

"A pleasure ... a pleasure."

The building on Parthenais looked more horrible in bright sunshine than in rainy darkness. Huge, slab-sided, far too glassy. Your gaze went right through it and out the other side. He went in, explained his errand to the man on the desk — the same man as

---

6. *I Am a Fugitive from a Chain Gang* The 1932 film based on the life of Robert Elliott Burns, who escaped from a Georgia prison and wrote about the injustice of forced prison labour.

the night before; didn't he ever sleep? And ascended to the tenth floor in an ordinary elevator. At the third, fifth and eighth floors it stopped automatically; he peered out without ostentation.[7] Each floor seemed perfectly normal; you could see across the hall and out the windows. Ordinary office space. The view grew progressively more distant and spread-out as the car rose in the shaft. He was prepared for a handsome prospect as he stepped out on ten, and was chilled and repelled by the barred, electrically-locked gate, the approaches beyond it to heavy steel doors. The four top floors of the building form a maximum security jail. There is no exercise yard. There is no sports program. Prisoners may use one of three small recreation areas for periods of up to one hour, every second day, if they aren't receiving special discipline.

" … you are not permitted to see him. What gave you the idea you could see him? Are you a relative?"

"No, he told me on the phone that …"

"I'm sorry, sir. His case is awaiting disposition. Only relatives."

"He told me he had no relatives nearer than Toronto."

"He told you a lie."

"Does his wife come to see him? How long has he been in here? I want to try to help."

"You aren't an officer of the John Howard Society?"

"No, nothing like that."

"Not a lawyer conferring with a judge about the sentence?"

"No, no."

The walls of this dreadful bullpen — a long counter or booth like that in a government liquor store or customs house — were painted a very pale grey-blue which did nothing to conceal their metallic chill. He began to look around wildly.

"What is your name, sir? Why did you come here?"

"This man called me on the telephone last night and told me he was in trouble; he didn't say how serious it was, but I gathered that he felt pretty desperate … "

" … they'll all tell you that."

"Yes, I'm sure they will. I would myself, I think, if I had to stay here. Can't you tell me anything at all?"

"I've never seen the man."

"How do you know so much about him?"

"I'm simply following general regulations, sir."

"And he has no right to a visitor, like he claimed?"

"Certain relatives, his lawyer of record, officially authorized prison visitors."

"All right, then, a sergeant from Dorval is bringing in his radio. He left it there. Would you see that he gets it?"

"I don't know anything about that at all."

He left the bullpen and walked quickly through the massive doors. He felt very glad that they opened for him, that the elevator came, some time after he pressed the DOWN button. All the way out to the street and into the driver's seat of his car, he felt as if a hand might descend on his shoulder. There was a parking ticket under the left windshield wiper. The rubberized gorilla mask smiled up at him from where he had dropped it

7. **ostentation** Pretension.

on the front seat. He felt intensely happy to see it there. Happy that he'd remembered it, that his children enjoyed having it. He made the best of his way out of town.

The mask alone was not enough, naturally. Four imaginative new costumes were required. The boys decided to go out as soldiers of the American Civil War, one in blue uniform, one in grey;[8] design and fitting of these intricate costumes occupied much of September and early October.

"What are you going out as?"

"Soldiers of the War Between the States, as they would have been dressed at Gettysburg." The younger son was a student of Civil War history and a bitter partisan of the North, an admirer of Lincoln and Grant.

"But don't you think Lee was the greatest general of that war?"

"He lost, didn't he?"

Not much to be said to that.

And of course, he reflected, on the essential issue of slavery the North had been in the right. He was certain of that; what could possibly be urged in favour of slavery, of imprisonment, detention, referral to clinic? He felt mixed up, his head crowded with civilized misgiving. He started to get letters addressed to Philly White, in his care. He wouldn't open them and couldn't decide what to do with them. Some were post-marked Vancouver. One looked like an Income Tax refund cheque. A month after the first phone call, there came another. "Yes, it's me. I want to thank you for everything you've done for me. Sergeant Bastien told me how you helped him."

"The man from Dorval with your radio."

"He said how kind you were."

"Were you actually talking to Sergeant Bastien?" It had become important to extract some unambiguous, verifiable statement.

"Not actually talking to him in so many words … exactly."

"How then?"

"Well, he got through to me all right. These veteran police officers have ways of dealing with things that you and I wouldn't think of."

"I didn't do anything for you, White. I have no intention of doing anything for you." He at least could be unambiguous, or hoped he could.

"But you came down to the Prevention Centre to see me, didn't you?"

"I did. Anybody would have done that."

"But you came twice, didn't you?"

"How do you know?"

"I know." There was a noxious[9] appeal to this way of talking. He felt himself being drawn into the position of co-conspirator and even accomplice. He had enough free-floating fear of having done something criminal in his imagination without this.

"Just handle my mail for me," begged White.

"Why can't it go directly to jail?" he felt dreadfully like laughing. He thought, "Go directly to Jail; do not pass GO; do not collect $200"; he remembered the cards in the pile marked "Get out of Jail free."

"Would you like your wife to have to send her letters to such a place?"

"No."

"Do this for me then, for the sake of the old days."

---

8. soldiers of the American Civil War … blue uniform … grey Soldiers from the North wore blue uniforms, while soldiers from the South wore grey uniforms. **9. noxious** Harmful.

"What old days? Do you know, I can barely remember you. That's 40 years ago. I don't have any responsibility for you."

"We are all responsible for one another," said White.

"Then why did you … never mind."

"I can use your address?"

"I'll forward anything that arrives."

The call was abruptly ended by that strange echoing click suggestive of constant switchboard surveillance. He wondered who was listening, and thought of making misleading and ambiguous remarks the next time White telephoned, just to give the listeners something to think about, realizing at the same moment that such an action would cause them to set up a dossier on him, which would then have the assured and interminable existence of an official file.

A flood of correspondence ensued, much of it from distant provinces, all addressed to his quiet Montréal street, all for Philly White. He would wait for three or four days till he had a dozen or so items, then bundle them together in a single large envelope and forward it to Parthenais Street. Certain letters obviously got through to White, who discussed them in later phone calls. Some were perhaps suppressed by the authorities or censored by them, but on the whole White seemed well abreast of his outside affairs; he had now been at the Centre de Prevention for August, September, most of October — almost thirteen weeks; this was nothing compared to the detention of other unfortunates. The top floors were designed to hold 250 inmates, all in one way or another of special status. Either they could not be brought to trial because the prosecutor's case was incomplete, or the dockets[10] were overburdened, or their lawyers were evading the event for tactical reasons: those in this last category might wait forever without their process coming on. Many died on Parthenais Street without receiving either condemnation or justification. And there were always more than 300 crowded into the cells.

There were many like White whose guilt had been legally established. Convicted, criminals in the eyes of the law, sentenced, as yet undisposed of, they could not be conveniently put away and forgotten in this or that prison because a humane penology[11] wished to "cure" them — in White's case apparently to dry the liquor out of him and begin treatment for alcoholism. A cured alcoholic, he might no longer be a fraud-artist and con-man, but this was doubtful. The alcoholism and the pathological addiction to lying might be elements of deeper ruin, probably were.

Nobody knows what is truly criminal, who are culpable. There are legal definitions, always abstract, inexact. There is observably bad — at least socially unacceptable — behaviour: what is called the "psychopathic personality" where social responsibility is rejected together with the possibility of truthfulness. What oppressed the listener to Philly White's phone calls was that he never, even by accident, said the plain truth.

Disguise abounded; cold came on. Toward the end of the month the boys completed their Civil War costumes and began to parade around the house in them, looking from a short distance wonderfully authentic. The younger lad had constructed one of those flat, forward-slanting Confederate caps with a badge of crossed rifles over the peak, and the letters C.S.A. sewn into it irregularly. The effect was truly persuasive. He had a cardboard musket and a water bottle. He kept saying, "Pickett's charge[12] represented the

---

10. dockets Schedules for cases waiting to be reviewed by the court. **11. penology** The study of prison management and criminal rehabilitation. **12. Pickett's charge** A failed assault by the Confederate Army against the Union Army during the Battle of Gettysburg in the American Civil War.

high-water mark of the Confederacy," and his father never managed to establish what that meant. The other boy had decided to approach the northern infantryman's dress with less historical correctness and more freedom of interpretation. He carried a powder-horn[13] — more appropriate for the Revolutionary War — and wore a shaggy false beard made of stuff chopped from an old Borghana coat of their mother's, which gave him an unexpectedly Russian air.

The girls hovered over alternatives. Then in a late fury of artistic creation they evolved two superb and original designs. For the younger girl, the baby of the family, they made a horse's body from a painted and draped cardboard carton fitted around her waist like an Eskimo's kayak. This was completed by floppy artificial legs hanging from a painted saddle — a caricature of a circus equestrienne. Her sister had then simply to dress herself as a ringmaster: red coat, tall hat, white breeches, riding whip, and the illusion was perfect and striking.

Mixed images of strangely-caparisoned, smallish persons capering around him wound their way into their father's worried judgment. All day on the 31st of the month he lazed around the house among orange and black festoons,[14] expecting some sort of resolution of the affair of White the bunco steerer.[15] The weekend before, all clocks had been put back. It was full dark by six pm. The children departed for their exciting annual night walk, gangs of neighbourhood kids beginning to press the doorbell. The phone rang in the midst of other urgent pealings, as he raised his coffee cup to his lips. Of course it was his old friend on Parthenais Street, with his first concrete demand for money. "If you'll just make the one payment for me, $184.80, we can retain ownership, they won't repossess. It's in the wife's name. I'll tell you where to send your cheque, and thanks for what you're trying to do. I really mean it."

He felt great anger squeezing his throat. "You don't mean it at all," he said, "You're just trying it on. I knew it would get to this point. A hundred and eighty from the poor sucker for openers, eh? It's finished, White, you get me? That's it. Don't call again and don't have any more mail sent here. I thought you needed me. I thought you meant it. All just a big con. You're still at it even though they've locked you up. You've been sentenced. How come they don't put you where you belong?"

"*They're* trying to help me."

"Let them! Whoever *they* are."

"I'm only trying to make contact."

"Good-bye White. Don't call again."

He hoped the listeners got it all; there wouldn't be any more calls. The doorbell rang and he walked through the house, opened the door and confronted a small visitant dressed as a ghost. He handed this person many sugary treats, then shut the door. I did right, he told himself, I did right (wrong), I did right, right (wrong), I did right …

(1976)

---

13. **powder-horn** Hollow object used for carrying gunpowder. 14. **festoons** Ribbons. 15. **bunco steerer** A person who organizes a swindle or scam.

Timothy Findley (1930–2002)

Timothy Findley was born in the wealthy Toronto district of Rosedale in 1930. Suffering from recurring illnesses throughout his childhood, he finally left school at 16 to study with a tutor, insisting that he be taught only literature and history. When a spinal injury ruined his chance to become a ballet dancer, he tried acting. He would remain a professional actor for 15 years, performing with Alec Guinness at the Stratford Festival in 1953 and then touring with a production of Thornton Wilder's *The Matchmaker*. He settled briefly in California, but job opportunities were scarce, so in 1958 he returned to Toronto. Four years later, he met his lifetime partner, William Whitehead, and they went to live in a farmhouse in Cannington, Ontario. Encouraged by other actors and playwrights, Findley began writing short stories as well as television and radio plays for the Canadian Broadcasting Corporation.

His experience as an actor influenced the development of his fictional characters. It taught him how to imagine a character's psychology and motivation, and he came to believe that writers should explore their characters, not determine them. In his first novel, *The Last of the Crazy People* (1967), he surprised himself by concluding that the only suitable ending would be to have his main character kill his entire family. Young Hooker Winslow inhabits a perplexing and conflict-ridden world. As his family members withdraw into silence, secrecy, and self-destructive behaviour, his feelings of confusion over his nascent sexuality and his place in the world intensify, with murderous results. As a homosexual, Findley himself felt ostracized by his family and by conservative Toronto society at large, and he was compelled to explore the pernicious effects of sexual discrimination in his writing. The odious patriarch in his next novel, *The Butterfly Plague* (1969), assumes that homosexuality is a disease, like hemophilia. This novel, set in 1938 Hollywood as war looms in Europe, also deals with themes of decay, despair, and fascism, which Findley perceives in the ideals of physical perfection and heterosexuality.

Findley's first two novels had been rejected by Canadian publishers and were published in Great Britain. His first book to be published in Canada was *The Wars* (1977), and it won a Governor General's Award. Using the wartime correspondence of an uncle as well as some family photos, and employing the techniques of flashback and repetition, Findley fabricates the story of Robert Ross, a World War I soldier who is being investigated by a researcher. A rich concoction of themes, the novel dramatizes the way in which we manipulate memory to alleviate trauma and exposes the horrific inhumanity of our political systems, which create victims of those who are vulnerable or unconventional. Findley insisted that a controversial scene in which Ross is raped not be cut from the book because he wanted to stress that the young men who fought in the war were metaphorically raped by their parents' generation.

In *Famous Last Words* (1981), Findley again uses the novel form to interrogate the ways we record history by experimenting with such devices as having the narrator interrupt the story to cast doubt upon the truthfulness of a given character. This time, the backdrop is World War II. Like *The Wars*, this novel was an early exemplar of Canadian historiographic metafiction. Concerned with writing about writing (metafiction) and writing about the writing of history (historiography), it encompassed both forms in a story within a story. The first tells of Hugh Selwyn Mauberley (a character borrowed from Ezra Pound's *Cantos*). Discovered dead with his writing instrument in hand and his tale scrawled on the walls, Mauberley has composed his own epitaph: "All I have written here is true, except the lies." The second story is of the soldiers who find the body — the men who must interpret and judge the accuracy of what Mauberley has written. In his novels, Findley is less interested in telling neglected stories than in recasting familiar historical and literary characters. In *Famous Last Words,* he also retells the real-life story of King Edward VIII, who provoked scandal by abdicating the throne in 1936 to marry an American divorcee. The juxtaposition of historical (Edward) and literary (Mauberley) characters demonstrates that their value in fictional narrative is equal and that to approach the truth, we must engage in multiple interpretations.

Not Wanted on the Voyage (1984) is a similar exercise in reinterpretation. Basing his novel on the biblical tale of Noah, Findley undertakes major revisions: he chooses a contemporary setting, shows that Noah's patriarchal authority in the God-appointed mission to save beasts and humankind from the Flood is illegitimate, and even has a blind cat narrate part of the story. Appearing at a time when gender studies were attaining increased importance, the novel was understood as a feminist text, and it outraged readers who believed that biblical mythology was sacrosanct.

The year 1984 saw the publication of *Dinner Along the Amazon,* a collection containing three decades of Findley's short fiction plus one new story. Then came *The Telling of Lies* (1986), a mystery novel, and *Stones* (1988), a collection of new short stories. In the latter two books, Findley established a theme that would pervade his later work: the politics of psychiatry and madness. *Headhunter* (1993) focuses on an ambitious psychiatrist named Kurtz who inflicts drug-therapy and sleep-deprivation experiments on his patients — experiments related to his own involvement in pornography, incest, child abuse, and murder. In 1993, Findley's play *The Stillborn Lover* was produced and published, and he followed this with a rapid (even for such a prolific writer) series of publications: the novel *The Piano Man's Daughter* (1995), which also deals with madness, fascistic ideologies, and the search for personal identity; the novella *You Went Away* (1996); and a third collection of short stories, *Dust to Dust* (1997), which is especially concerned with varieties of death (massacre, drowning, disease).

The last major novel of Findley's career was *Pilgrim* (1999), which contains a sampling of the elements of his oeuvre: historical figures, subversive gender politics, a psychiatric focus, some fantasy, and violence in many forms, especially suicide. The titular character, a patient in a psychiatric hospital under the supervision of Carl Jung, tries repeatedly to kill himself, but he is unable to remain dead, so he travels through time to converse with some great artists (Oscar Wilde, Leonardo da Vinci, and Henry James). Because the novel expands to include other characters who read Pilgrim's journals, the familiar element of metafiction is also present.

Findley's final novel was *Spadework* (2001), which was set in Stratford, Ontario, in the theatre community he knew so well. In the course of his productive career, he also published several more plays and three memoirs; the last, *Journeyman* (2003), was published posthumously. Findley was made an Officer of the Order of Canada in 1986, and a Chevalier de l'Ordre des Arts et des Lettres (France) ten years later. He died in Provence, France, on 20 June 2002.

Dreams

For R.E. Turner

Doctor Menlo was having a problem: he could not sleep and his wife — the other Doctor Menlo — was secretly staying awake in order to keep an eye on him. The trouble was that, in spite of her concern and in spite of all her efforts, Doctor Menlo — whose name was Mimi — was always nodding off because of her exhaustion.

She had tried drinking coffee, but this had no effect. She detested coffee and her system had a built-in rejection mechanism. She also prescribed herself a week's worth of Dexedrine[1] to see if that would do the trick. *Five mg at bedtime* — all to no avail. And

---

1. **Dexedrine** A stimulant.

even though she put the plastic bottle of small orange hearts beneath her pillow and kept augmenting her intake, she would wake half an hour later with a dreadful start to discover the night was moving on to morning.

Everett Menlo had not yet declared the source of his problem. His restless condition had begun about ten days ago and had barely raised his interest. Soon, however, the time spent lying awake had increased from one to several hours and then, on Monday last, to all-night sessions. Now he lay in a state of rigid apprehension — eyes wide open, arms above his head, his hands in fists — like a man in pain unable to shut it out. His neck, his back and his shoulders constantly harried him with cramps and spasms. Everett Menlo had become a full-blown insomniac.

Clearly, Mimi Menlo concluded, her husband was refusing to sleep because he believed something dreadful was going to happen the moment he closed his eyes. She had encountered this sort of fear in one or two of her patients. Everett, on the other hand, would not discuss the subject. If the problem had been hers, he would have said *such things cannot occur if you have gained control of yourself.*

Mimi began to watch for the dawn. She would calculate its approach by listening for the increase of traffic down below the bedroom window. The Menlos' home was across the road from The Manulife Centre — corner of Bloor and Bay streets. Mimi's first sight of daylight always revealed the high, white shape of its terraced storeys. Their own apartment building was of a modest height and colour — twenty floors of smoky glass and polished brick. The shadow of the Manulife would crawl across the bedroom floor and climb the wall behind her, grey with fatigue and cold.

The Menlo beds were an arm's length apart, and lying like a rug between them was the shape of a large, black dog of unknown breed. All night long, in the dark of his well, the dog would dream and he would tell the content of his dreams the way that victims in a trance will tell of being pursued by posses of their nameless fears. He whimpered, he cried and sometimes he howled. His legs and his paws would jerk and flail and his claws would scrabble desperately against the parquet floor. Mimi — who loved this dog — would lay her hand against his side and let her fingers dabble in his coat in vain attempts to soothe him. Sometimes, she had to call his name in order to rouse him from his dreams because his heart would be racing. Other times, she smiled and thought: *at least there's one of us getting some sleep.* The dog's name was Thurber and he dreamed in beige and white.

Everett and Mimi Menlo were both psychiatrists. His field was schizophrenia; hers was autistic children. Mimi's venue was the Parkin Institute at the University of Toronto; Everett's was the Queen Street Mental Health Centre. Early in their marriage they had decided never to work as a team and not — unless it was a matter of financial life and death — to accept employment in the same institution. Both had always worked with the kind of physical intensity that kills, and yet they gave the impression this was the only tolerable way in which to function. It meant there was always a sense of peril in what they did, but the peril — according to Everett — made their lives worth living. This, at least, had been his theory twenty years ago when they were young.

Now, for whatever unnamed reason, peril had become his enemy and Everett Menlo had begun to look and behave and lose his sleep like a haunted man. But he refused to comment when Mimi asked him what was wrong. Instead, he gave the worst of all possible answers a psychiatrist can hear who seeks an explanation of a patient's silence: he said there was *absolutely nothing wrong.*

"You're sure you're not coming down with something?"

"Yes."

"And you wouldn't like a massage?"

"I've already told you: no."

"Can I get you anything?"

"No."

"And you don't want to talk?"

"That's right."

"Okay, Everett …"

"Okay, what?"

"Okay, nothing. I only hope you get some sleep tonight."

Everett stood up. "Have you been spying on me, Mimi?"

"What do you mean by *spying?*"

"Watching me all night long."

"Well, Everett, I don't see how I can fail to be aware you aren't asleep when we share this bedroom. I mean — I can hear you grinding your teeth. I can see you lying there wide awake."

"When?"

"All the time. You're staring at the ceiling."

"I've never stared at the ceiling in my whole life. I sleep on my stomach."

"You sleep on your stomach *if* you sleep. But you have not been sleeping. Period. No argument."

Everett Menlo went to his dresser and got out a pair of clean pyjamas. Turning his back on Mimi, he put them on.

Somewhat amused at the coyness of this gesture, Mimi asked what he was hiding.

"Nothing!" he shouted at her.

Mimi's mouth fell open. Everett never yelled. His anger wasn't like that; it manifested itself in other ways, in silence and withdrawal, never shouts.

Everett was staring at her defiantly. He had slammed the bottom drawer of his dresser. Now he was fumbling with the wrapper of a pack of cigarettes.

Mimi's stomach tied a knot.

Everett hadn't touched a cigarette for weeks.

"Please don't smoke those," she said. "You'll only be sorry if you do."

"And you," he said, "will be sorry if I don't."

"But, dear …" said Mimi.

"Leave me for Christ's sake alone!" Everett yelled.

Mimi gave up and sighed and then she said: "all right. Thurber and I will go and sleep in the living-room. Goodnight."

Everett sat on the edge of his bed. His hands were shaking.

"Please," he said — apparently addressing the floor. "Don't leave me here alone. I couldn't bear that."

This was perhaps the most chilling thing he could have said to her. Mimi was alarmed; her husband was genuinely terrified of something and he would not say what it was. If she had not been who she was — if she had not known what she knew — if her years of training had not prepared her to watch for signs like this, she might have been better off. As it was, she had to face the possibility the strongest, most sensible man on earth was having a nervous breakdown of major proportions. Lots of people have breakdowns, of course; but not, she had thought, the gods of reason.

"All right," she said — her voice maintaining the kind of calm she knew a child afraid of the dark would appreciate. "In a minute I'll get us something to drink. But first, I'll go and change …."

Mimi went into the sanctum of the bathroom, where her nightgown waited for her — a portable hiding-place hanging on the back of the door. "You stay there," she said to Thurber, who had padded after her. "Mama will be out in just a moment."

Even in the dark, she could gauge Everett's tension. His shadow — all she could see of him — twitched from time to time and the twitching took on a kind of lurching rhythm, something like the broken clock in their living-room.

Mimi lay on her side and tried to close her eyes. But her eyes were tied to a will of their own and would not obey her. Now she, too, was caught in the same irreversible tide of sleeplessness that bore her husband backward through the night. Four or five times she watched him lighting cigarettes — blowing out the matches, courting disaster in the bedclothes — conjuring the worst of deaths for the three of them: a flaming pyre on the twentieth floor.

All this behaviour was utterly unlike him; foreign to his code of disciplines and ethics; alien to everything he said and believed. *Openness, directness, sharing of ideas, encouraging imaginative response to every problem. Never hide troubles. Never allow despair …* These were his directives in everything he did. Now, he had thrown them over.

One thing was certain. She was not the cause of his sleeplessness. She didn't have affairs and neither did he. He might be ill — but whenever he'd been ill before, there had been no trauma; never a trauma like this one, at any rate. Perhaps it was something about a patient — one of his tougher cases; a wall in the patient's condition they could not break through; some circumstance of someone's lack of progress — a sudden veering towards a catatonic state,[2] for instance — something that Everett had not foreseen that had stymied[3] him and was slowly … what? Destroying his sense of professional control? His self-esteem? His scientific certainty? If only he would speak.

Mimi thought about her own worst case: a child whose obstinate refusal to communicate was currently breaking her heart and, thus, her ability to help. If ever she had needed Everett to talk to, it was now. All her fellow doctors were locked in a battle over this child; they wanted to take him away from her. Mimi refused to give him up; he might as well have been her own flesh and blood. Everything had been done — from gentle holding sessions to violent bouts of manufactured anger — in her attempt to make the child react. She was staying with him every day from the moment he was roused to the moment he was induced to sleep with drugs.

His name was Brian Bassett and he was eight years old. He sat on the floor in the furthest corner he could achieve in one of the observation-isolation rooms where all the autistic children were placed when nothing else in their treatment — nothing of love or expertise — had managed to break their silence. Mostly, this was a signal they were coming to the end of life.

There in his four-square, glass-box room, surrounded by all that can tempt a child if a child can be tempted — toys and food and story-book companions — Brian Bassett was in the process, now, of fading away. His eyes were never closed and his arms were restrained. He was attached to three machines that nurtured him with all that science

---

2. **catatonic state** A condition characterized by muscle rigidity and mental stupor. 3. **stymied** Frustrated.

can offer. But of course, the spirit and the will to live cannot be fed by force to those who do not want to feed.

Now, in the light of Brian Bassett's utter lack of willing contact with the world around him — his utter refusal to communicate — Mimi watched her husband through the night. Everett stared at the ceiling, lit by the Manulife building's distant lamps, borne on his back further and further out to sea. She had lost him, she was certain.

When, at last, he saw that Mimi had drifted into her own and welcome sleep, Everett rose from his bed and went out into the hall, past the simulated jungle of the solarium, until he reached the dining-room. There, all the way till dawn, he amused himself with two decks of cards and endless games of Dead Man's Solitaire.

Thurber rose and shuffled after him. The dining-room was one of Thurber's favourite places in all his confined but privileged world, for it was here — as in the kitchen — that from time to time a hand descended filled with the miracle of food. But whatever it was that his master was doing up there above him on the table-top, it wasn't anything to do with feeding or with being fed. The playing cards had an old and dusty dryness to their scent and they held no appeal for the dog. So he once again lay down and he took up his dreams, which at least gave his paws some exercise. This way, he failed to hear the advent of a new dimension to his master's problem. This occurred precisely at 5:45 A.M. when the telephone rang and Everett Menlo, having rushed to answer it, waited breathless for a minute while he listened and then said: "yes" in a curious, strangulated fashion. Thurber — had he been awake — would have recognized in his master's voice the signal for disaster.

For weeks now, Everett had been working with a patient who was severely and uniquely schizophrenic. This patient's name was Kenneth Albright, and while he was deeply suspicious, he was also oddly caring. Kenneth Albright loved the detritus[4] of life, such as bits of woolly dust and wads of discarded paper. He loved all dried-up leaves that had drifted from their parent trees and he loved the dead bees that had curled up to die along the window-sills of his ward. He also loved the spiderwebs seen high up in the corners of the rooms where he sat on plastic chairs and ate with plastic spoons.

Kenneth Albright talked a lot about his dreams. But his dreams had become, of late, a major stumbling block in the process of his recovery. Back in the days when Kenneth had first become Doctor Menlo's patient, the dreams had been overburdened with detail: "over-cast," as he would say, "with characters" and over-produced, again in Kenneth's phrase, "as if I were dreaming the dreams of Cecil B. DeMille."[5]

Then he had said: "but a person can't really dream someone else's dreams. Or can they, Doctor Menlo?"

"No" had been Everett's answer — definite and certain.

Everett Menlo had been delighted, at first, with Kenneth Albright's dreams. They had been immensely entertaining — complex and filled with intriguing detail. Kenneth himself was at a loss to explain the meaning of these dreams, but as Everett had said, it wasn't Kenneth's job to explain. That was Everett's job. His job and his pleasure. For quite a long while, during these early sessions, Everett had written out the dreams, taken them home and recounted them to Mimi.

---

4. **detritus** Debris. 5. **Cecil B. DeMille** An American filmmaker (1881–1959) who was known for his elaborate sets.

Kenneth Albright was a paranoid schizophrenic. Four times now, he had attempted suicide. He was a fiercely angry man at times — and at other times as gentle and as pleasant as a docile child. He had suffered so greatly, in the very worst moments of his disease, that he could no longer work. His job — it was almost an incidental detail in his life and had no importance for him, so it seemed — was returning reference books, in the Metro Library, to their places in the stacks. Sometimes — mostly late of an afternoon — he might begin a psychotic episode of such profound dimensions that he would attempt his suicide right behind the counter and even once, in the full view of everyone, while riding in the glass-walled elevator. It was after this last occasion that he was brought, in restraints, to be a resident patient at the Queen Street Mental Health Centre. He had slashed his wrists with a razor — but not before he had also slashed and destroyed an antique copy of *Don Quixote*,[6] the pages of which he pasted to the walls with blood.

For a week thereafter, Kenneth Albright — just like Brian Bassett — had refused to speak or to move. Everett had him kept in an isolation cell, force-fed and drugged. Slowly, by dint of patience, encouragement and caring even Kenneth could recognize as genuine, Everett Menlo had broken through the barrier. Kenneth was removed from isolation, pampered with food and cigarettes, and he began relating his dreams.

At first there seemed to be only the dreams and nothing else in Kenneth's memory. Broken pencils, discarded toys and the telephone directory all had roles to play in these dreams but there were never any people. All the weather was bleak and all the landscapes were empty. Houses, motor cars and office buildings never made an appearance. Sounds and smells had some importance; the wind would blow, the scent of unseen fires was often described. Stairwells were plentiful, leading nowhere, all of them rising from a subterranean world that Kenneth either did not dare to visit or would not describe.

The dreams had little variation, one from another. The themes had mostly to do with loss and with being lost. The broken pencils were all given names and the discarded toys were given to one another as companions. The telephone books were the sources of recitations — hours and hours of repeated names and numbers, some of which — Everett had noted with surprise — were absolutely accurate.

All of this held fast until an incident occurred one morning that changed the face of Kenneth Albright's schizophrenia forever; an incident that stemmed — so it seemed — from something he had dreamed the night before.

Bearing in mind his previous attempts at suicide, it will be obvious that Kenneth Albright was never far from sight at the Queen Street Mental Health Centre. He was, in fact, under constant observation; constant, that is, as human beings and modern technology can manage. In the ward to which he was ultimately consigned, for instance, the toilet cabinets had no doors and the shower-rooms had no locks. Therefore, a person could not ever be alone with water, glass or shaving utensils. (All the razors were cordless automatics.) Scissors and knives were banned, as were pieces of string and rubber bands. A person could not even kill his feet and hands by binding up his wrists or ankles. Nothing poisonous was anywhere available. All the windows were barred. All the double doors between this ward and the corridors beyond were doors with triple locks and a guard was always near at hand.

---

6. *Don Quixote* The 1604 Spanish novel of romantic idealism and comic satire by Miguel de Cervantes.

Still, if people want to die, they will find a way. Mimi Menlo would discover this to her everlasting sorrow with Brian Bassett. Everett Menlo would discover this to his everlasting horror with Kenneth Albright.

On the morning of April 19th, a Tuesday, Everett Menlo, in the best of health, had welcomed a brand-new patient into his office. This was Anne Marie Wilson, a young and brilliant pianist whose promising career had been halted mid-flight by a schizophrenic incident involving her ambition. She was, it seemed, no longer able to play and all her dreams were shattered. The cause was simple, to all appearances: Anne Marie had a sense of how, precisely, the music should be and she had not been able to master it accordingly. "Everything I attempt is terrible," she had said — in spite of all her critical accolades and all her professional success. Other doctors had tried and failed to break the barriers in Anne Marie, whose hands had taken on a life of their own, refusing altogether to work for her. Now it was Menlo's turn and hope was high.

Everett had been looking forward to his session with this prodigy. He loved all music and had thought to find some means within its discipline to reach her. She seemed so fragile, sitting there in the sunlight, and he had just begun to take his first notes when the door flew open and Louise, his secretary, had said: "I'm sorry, Doctor Menlo. There's a problem. Can you come with me at once?"

Everett excused himself.

Anne Marie was left in the sunlight to bide her time. Her fingers were moving around in her lap and she put them in her mouth to make them quiet.

Even as he'd heard his secretary speak, Everett had known the problem would be Kenneth Albright. Something in Kenneth's eyes had warned him there was trouble on the way: a certain wariness that indicated all was not as placid as it should have been, given his regimen of drugs. He had stayed long hours in one position, moving his fingers over his thighs as if to dry them on his trousers; watching his fellow patients come and go with abnormal interest — never, however, rising from his chair. An incident was on the horizon and Everett had been waiting for it, hoping it would not come.

Louise had said that Doctor Menlo was to go at once to Kenneth Albright's ward. Everett had run the whole way. Only after the attendant had let him in past the double doors, did he slow his pace to a hurried walk and wipe his brow. He didn't want Kenneth to know how alarmed he had been.

Coming to the appointed place, he paused before he entered, closing his eyes, preparing himself for whatever he might have to see. *Other people have killed themselves: I've seen it often enough*, he was thinking. *I simply won't let it affect me.* Then he went in.

The room was small and white — a dining room — and Kenneth was sitting down in a corner, his back pressed out against the walls on either side of him. His head was bowed and his legs drawn up and he was obviously trying to hide without much success. An intern was standing above him and a nurse was kneeling down beside him. Several pieces of bandaging with blood on them were scattered near Kenneth's feet and there was a white enamel basin filled with pinkish water on the floor beside the nurse.

"Morowetz," Everett said to the intern. "Tell me what has happened here." He said this just the way he posed such questions when he took the interns through the wards at examination time, quizzing them on symptoms and prognoses.

But Morowetz the intern had no answer. He was puzzled. What had happened had no sane explanation.

Everett turned to Charterhouse, the nurse.

"On the morning of April 19th, at roughly ten-fifteen, I found Kenneth Albright covered with blood," Ms Charterhouse was to write in her report. "His hands, his arms, his face and his neck were stained. I would say the blood was fresh and the patient's clothing — most notably his shirt — was wet with it. Some — a very small amount of it — had dried on his forehead. The rest was uniformly the kind of blood you expect to find free-flowing from a wound. I called for assistance and meanwhile attempted to ascertain where Mister Albright might have been injured. I performed this examination without success. I could find no source of bleeding anywhere on Mister Albright's body."

Morowetz concurred.

The blood was someone else's.

"Was there a weapon of any kind?" Doctor Menlo had wanted to know.

"No, sir. Nothing," said Charterhouse.

"And was he alone when you found him?"

"Yes, sir. Just like this in the corner."

"And the others?"

"All the patients in the ward were examined," Morowetz told him.

"And?"

"Not one of them was bleeding."

Everett said: "I see."

He looked down at Kenneth.

"This is Doctor Menlo, Kenneth. Have you anything to tell me?"

Kenneth did not reply.

Everett said: "When you've got him back in his room and tranquillized, will you call me, please?"

Morowetz nodded.

The call never came. Kenneth had fallen asleep. Either the drugs he was given had knocked him out cold, or he had opted for silence. Either way, he was incommunicado.

No one was discovered bleeding. Nothing was found to indicate an accident, a violent attack, an epileptic seizure. A weapon was not located. Kenneth Albright had not a single scratch on his flesh from stem, as Everett put it, to gudgeon.[7] The blood, it seemed, had fallen like the rain from heaven: unexplained and inexplicable.

Later, as the day was ending, Everett Menlo left the Queen Street Mental Health Centre. He made his way home on the Queen streetcar and the Bay bus. When he reached the apartment, Thurber was waiting for him. Mimi was at a goddamned meeting.

That was the night Everett Menlo suffered the first of his failures to sleep. It was occasioned by the fact that, when he wakened sometime after three, he had just been dreaming. This, of course, was not unusual — but the dream itself was perturbing. There was someone lying there, in the bright white landscape of a hospital dining-room. Whether it was a man or a woman could not be told, it was just a human body, lying down in a pool of blood.

Kenneth Albright was kneeling beside this body, pulling it open the way a child will pull a Christmas present open — yanking at its strings and ribbons, wanting only to see the contents. Everett saw this scene from several angles, never speaking, never being spoken to. In all the time he watched — the usual dream eternity — the silence was

---

7. **stem ... to gudgeon** A nautical expression meaning from the front of a ship to the back.

broken only by the sound of water dripping from an unseen tap. Then, Kenneth Albright rose and was covered with blood, the way he had been that morning. He stared at Doctor Menlo, looked right through him and departed. Nothing remained in the dining-room but plastic tables and plastic chairs and the bright red thing on the floor that once had been a person. Everett Menlo did not know and could not guess who this person might have been. He only knew that Kenneth Albright had left this person's body in Everett Menlo's dream.

Three nights running, the corpse remained in its place and every time that Everett entered the dining-room in the nightmare he was certain he would find out who it was. On the fourth night, fully expecting to discover he himself was the victim, he beheld the face and saw it was a stranger.

But there are no strangers in dreams; he knew that now after twenty years of practice. *There are no strangers; there are only people in disguise.*

Mimi made one final attempt in Brian Bassett's behalf to turn away the fate to which his other doctors — both medical and psychiatric — had consigned him. Not that, as a group, they had failed to expend the full weight of all they knew and all they could do to save him. One of his medical doctors — a woman whose name was Juliet Bateman — had moved a cot into his isolation room and stayed with him twenty-four hours a day for over a week. But her health had been undermined by this and when she succumbed to the Shanghai flu she removed herself for fear of infecting Brian Bassett.

The parents had come and gone on a daily basis for months in a killing routine of visits. But parents, their presence and their loving, are not the answer when a child has fallen into an autistic state. They might as well have been strangers. And so they had been advised to stay away.

Brian Bassett was eight years old — *unlucky eight,* as one of his therapists had said — and in every other way, in terms of physical development and mental capability, he had always been a perfectly normal child. Now, in the final moments of his life, he weighed a scant thirty pounds, when he should have weighed twice that much.

Brian had not been heard to speak a single word in over a year of constant observation. Earlier — long ago as seven months — a few expressions would visit his face from time to time. Never a smile — but often a kind of sneer, a passing of judgment, terrifying in its intensity. Other times, a pinched expression would appear — a signal of the shyness peculiar to autistic children, who think of light as being unfriendly.

Mimi's militant efforts in behalf of Brian had been exemplary. Her fellow doctors thought of her as *Bassett's crazy guardian angel.* They begged her to remove herself in order to preserve her health. Being wise, being practical, they saw that all her efforts would not save him. But Mimi's version of being a guardian angel was more like being a surrogate warrior: a hired gun or a samurai. Her cool determination to thwart the enemies of silence, stillness and starvation gave her strengths that even she had been unaware were hers to command.

Brian Bassett, seated in his corner on the floor, maintained a solemn composure that lent his features a kind of unearthly beauty. His back was straight, his hands were poised, his hair was so fine he looked the very picture of a spirit waiting to enter a newborn creature. Sometimes Mimi wondered if this creature Brian Bassett waited to inhabit could be human. She thought of all the animals she had ever seen in all her travels and she fell upon the image of a newborn fawn as being the most tranquil and the most in need of stillness in order to survive. If only all the natural energy and curiosity of a newborn beast could have entered into Brian Bassett, surely, they would have transformed the boy in the corner into a vibrant, joyous human being. But it was not to be.

On the 29th of April — one week and three days after Everett had entered into his crisis of insomnia — Mimi sat on the floor in Brian Bassett's isolation room, gently massaging his arms and legs as she held him in her lap.

His weight, by now, was shocking — and his skin had become translucent. His eyes had not been closed for days — for weeks — and their expression might have been carved in stone.

"Speak to me. Speak," she whispered to him as she cradled his head beneath her chin. "Please at least speak before you die."

Nothing happened. Only silence.

Juliet Bateman — wrapped in a blanket — was watching through the observation glass as Mimi lifted up Brian Bassett and placed him in his cot. The cot had metal sides — and the sides were raised. Juliet Bateman could see Brian Bassett's eyes and his hands as Mimi stepped away.

Mimi looked at Juliet and shook her head. Juliet closed her eyes and pulled her blanket tighter like a skin that might protect her from the next five minutes.

Mimi went around the cot to the other side and dragged the IV stand in closer to the head. She fumbled for a moment with the long plastic lifelines — anti-dehydrants, nutrients — and she adjusted the needles and brought them down inside the nest of the cot where Brian Bassett lay and she lifted up his arm in order to insert the tubes and bind them into place with tape.

This was when it happened — just as Mimi Menlo was preparing to insert the second tube.

Brian Bassett looked at her and spoke.

"No," he said. "Don't."

Don't meant death.

Mimi paused — considered — and set the tube aside. Then she withdrew the tube already in place and she hung them both on the IV stand.

All right, she said to Brian Bassett in her mind, *you win.*

She looked down then with her arm along the side of the cot — and one hand trailing down so Brian Bassett could touch it if he wanted to. She smiled at him and said to him: "Not to worry. Not to worry. None of us is ever going to trouble you again." He watched her carefully. "Goodbye, Brian," she said. "I love you."

Juliet Bateman saw Mimi Menlo say all this and was fairly sure she had read the words on Mimi's lips just as they had been spoken.

Mimi started out of the room. She was determined now there was no turning back and that Brian Bassett was free to go his way. But just as she was turning the handle and pressing her weight against the door — she heard Brian Bassett speak again.

"Goodbye," he said.

And died.

Mimi went back to Juliet Bateman, too, and they stayed with him another hour before they turned out his lights. "Someone else can cover his face," said Mimi. "I'm not going to do it." Juliet agreed and they came back out to tell the nurse on duty that their ward had died and their work with him was over.

On the 30th of April — a Saturday — Mimi stayed home and made her notes and she wondered if and when she would weep for Brian Bassett. Her hand, as she wrote, was steady and her throat was not constricted and her eyes had no sensation beyond the burning itch of fatigue. She wondered what she looked like in the mirror, but resisted that discovery. Some things could wait. Outside it rained. Thurber dreamed in the corner. Bay Street rumbled in the basement.

Everett, in the meantime, had reached his own crisis and because of his desperate straits a part of Mimi Menlo's mind was on her husband. Now he had not slept for almost ten days. *We really ought to consign ourselves to hospital beds*, she thought. Somehow, the idea held no persuasion. It occurred to her that laughter might do a better job, if only they could find it. The brain, when over-extended, gives us the most surprisingly simple propositions, she concluded. *Stop*, it says to us. *Lie down and sleep*.

Five minutes later, Mimi found herself still sitting at the desk, with her fountain pen capped and her fingers raised to her lips in an attitude of gentle prayer. It required some effort to re-adjust her gaze and re-establish her focus on the surface of the window glass beyond which her mind had wandered. Sitting up, she had been asleep.

Thurber muttered something and stretched his legs and yawned, still asleep. Mimi glanced in his direction. *We've both been dreaming*, she thought, *but his dream continues*.

Somewhere behind her, the broken clock was attempting to strike the hour of three. Its voice was dull and rusty, needing oil.

Looking down, she saw the words BRIAN BASSETT written on the page before her and it occurred to her that, without his person, the words were nothing more than extrapolations from the alphabet — something fanciful we call a "name" in the hope that, one day, it will take on meaning.

She thought of Brian Bassett with his building blocks — pushing the letters around on the floor and coming up with more acceptable arrangements: *TINA STERABBS ... IAN BRETT BASS ... BEST STAB the RAIN*: a sentence. He had known all along, of course, that *BRIAN BASSETT* wasn't what he wanted because it wasn't what he was. He had come here against his will, was held here against his better judgment, fought against his captors and finally escaped.

But where was here to Ian Brett Bass? Where was here to Tina Sterabbs? Like Brian Bassett, they had all been here in someone else's dreams, and had to wait for someone else to wake before they could make their getaway.

Slowly, Mimi uncapped her fountain pen and drew a firm, black line through Brian Bassett's name. *We dreamed him*, she wrote, *that's all. And then we let him go*.

Seeing Everett standing in the doorway, knowing he had just returned from another Kenneth Albright crisis, she had no sense of apprehension. All this was only as it should be. Given the way that everything was going, it stood to reason Kenneth Albright's crisis had to come in this moment. If he managed, at last, to kill himself then at least her husband might begin to sleep again.

Far in the back of her mind a carping, critical voice remarked that any such thoughts were *deeply unfeeling and verging on the barbaric*. But Mimi dismissed this voice and another part of her brain stepped forward in her defence. *I will weep for Kenneth Albright*, she thought, *when I can weep for Brian Bassett. Now, all that matters is that Everett and I survive*.

Then she strode forward and put out her hand for Everett's briefcase, set the briefcase down and helped him out of his topcoat. She was playing wife. It seemed to be the thing to do.

For the next twenty minutes Everett had nothing to say, and after he had poured himself a drink and after Mimi had done the same, they sat in their chairs and waited for Everett to catch his breath.

The first thing he said when he finally spoke was: "finish your notes?"

"Just about," Mimi told him. "I've written everything I can for now." She did not elaborate. "You're home early," she said, hoping to goad him into saying something new about Kenneth Albright.

"Yes," he said. "I am." But that was all.

Then he stood up — threw back the last of his drink and poured another. He lighted a cigarette and Mimi didn't even wince. He had been smoking now three days. The atmosphere between them had been, since then, enlivened with a magnetic kind of tension. But it was a moribund[8] tension, slowly beginning to dissipate.

Mimi watched her husband's silent torment now with a kind of clinical detachment. This was the result, she liked to tell herself, of her training and her discipline. The lover in her could regard Everett warmly and with concern, but the psychiatrist in her could also watch him as someone suffering a nervous breakdown, someone who could not be helped until the symptoms had multiplied and declared themselves more openly.

Everett went into the darkest corner of the room and sat down hard in one of Mimi's straight-backed chairs: the ones inherited from her mother. He sat, prim, like a patient in a doctor's office, totally unrelaxed and nervy; expressionless. Either he had come to receive a deadly diagnosis, or he would get a clean bill of health.

Mimi glided over to the sofa in the window, plush and red and deeply comfortable; a place to recuperate. The view — if she chose to turn only slightly sideways — was one of the gentle rain that was falling onto Bay Street. Sopping-wet pigeons huddled on the window-sill; people across the street in the Manulife building were turning on their lights.

A renegade robin, nesting in their eaves, began to sing.

Everett Menlo began to talk.

"Please don't interrupt," he said at first.

"You know I won't," said Mimi. It was a rule that neither one should interrupt the telling of a case until they had been invited to do so.

Mimi put her fingers into her glass so the ice-cubes wouldn't click. She waited.

Everett spoke — but he spoke as if in someone else's voice, perhaps the voice of Kenneth Albright. This was not entirely unusual. Often, both Mimi and Everett Menlo spoke in the voices of their patients. What was unusual, this time, was that, speaking in Kenneth's voice, Everett began to sweat profusely — so profusely that Mimi was able to watch his shirt front darkening with perspiration.

"As you know," he said, "I have not been sleeping."

This was the understatement of the year. Mimi was silent.

"I have not been sleeping because — to put it in a nutshell — I have been afraid to dream."

---

8. moribund Dying.

Mimi was somewhat startled by this. Not by the fact that Everett was afraid to dream, but only because she had just been thinking of dreams herself.

"I have been afraid to dream, because in all my dreams there have been bodies. Corpses. Murder victims."

Mimi — not really listening — idly wondered if she had been one of them.

"In all my dreams, there have been corpses," Everett repeated. "But I am not the murderer. Kenneth Albright is the murderer, and, up to this moment, he has left behind him fifteen bodies: none of them people I recognize."

Mimi nodded. The ice-cubes in her drink were beginning to freeze her fingers. Any minute now, she prayed, they would surely melt.

"I gave up dreaming almost a week ago," said Everett, "thinking that if I did, the killing pattern might be altered; broken." Then he said tersely: "it was not. The killings have continued...."

"How do you know the killings have continued, Everett, if you've given up your dreaming? Wouldn't this mean he had no place to hide the bodies?"

In spite of the fact she had disobeyed their rule about not speaking, Everett answered her.

"I know they are being continued because I have seen the blood."

"Ah, yes. I see."

"No, Mimi. No. You do not see. The blood is not a figment of my imagination. The blood, in fact, is the only thing not dreamed." He explained the stains on Kenneth Albright's hands and arms and clothes and he said: "It happens every day. We have searched his person for signs of cuts and gashes — even for internal and rectal bleeding. Nothing. We have searched his quarters and all the other quarters in his ward. His ward is locked. His ward is isolated in the extreme. None of his fellow patients was ever found bleeding — never had cause to bleed. There were no injuries — no self-inflicted wounds. We thought of animals. Perhaps a mouse — a rat. But nothing. Nothing. Nothing ... We also went so far as to strip-search all the members of the staff who entered that ward and I, too, offered myself for this experiment. Still nothing. Nothing. No one had bled."

Everett was now beginning to perspire so heavily he removed his jacket and threw it on the floor. Thurber woke and stared at it, startled. At first, it appeared to be the beast that had just pursued him through the woods and down the road. But, then, it sighed and settled and was just a coat; a rumpled jacket lying down on the rug.

Everett said: "we had taken samples of the blood on the patient's hands — on Kenneth Albright's hands and on his clothing and we had these samples analysed. No. It was not his own blood. No, it was not the blood of an animal. No, it was not the blood of a fellow patient. No, it was not the blood of any members of the staff...."

Everett's voice had risen.

"Whose blood was it?" he almost cried. "Whose the hell was it?"

Mimi waited.

Everett Menlo lighted another cigarette. He took a great gulp of his drink.

"Well ..." He was calmer now; calmer of necessity. He had to marshall the evidence. He had to put it all in order — bring it into line with reason. "Did this mean that — somehow — the patient had managed to leave the premises — do some bloody deed and return without our knowledge of it? That is, after all, the only possible explanation. Isn't it?"

Mimi waited.

"Isn't it?" he repeated.

"Yes," she said. "it's the only possible explanation."

"Except there is no way out of that place. There is absolutely no way out."

Now, there was a pause.

"But one," he added — his voice, again, a whisper.

Mimi was silent. Fearful — watching his twisted face.

"Tell me," Everett Menlo said — the perfect innocent, almost the perfect child in quest of forbidden knowledge. "Answer me this — be honest: is there blood in dreams?"

Mimi could not respond. She felt herself go pale. Her husband — after all, the sanest man alive — had just suggested something so completely mad he might as well have handed over his reason in a paper bag and said to her, *burn this*.

"The only place that Kenneth Albright goes, I tell you, is into dreams," Everett said. "That is the only place beyond the ward into which the patient can or does escape."

Another — briefer — pause.

"It is real blood, Mimi. Real. And he gets it all from dreams. My *dreams*."

They waited for this to settle.

Everett said: "I'm tired. I'm tired. I cannot bear this any more. I'm tired...."

Mimi thought, *good. No matter what else happens, he will sleep tonight.*

He did. And so, at last, did she.

Mimi's dreams were rarely of the kind that engender fear. She dreamt more gentle scenes with open spaces that did not intimidate. She would dream quite often of water and of animals. Always, she was nothing more than an observer; roles were not assigned her; often, this was sad. Somehow, she seemed at times locked out, unable to participate. These were the dreams she endured when Brian Bassett died: field trips to see him in some desert setting; underwater excursions to watch him floating amongst the seaweed. He never spoke, and, indeed, he never appeared to be aware of her presence.

That night, when Everett fell into his bed exhausted and she did likewise, Mimi's dream of Brian Bassett was the last she would ever have of him and somehow, in the dream, she knew this. What she saw was what, in magical terms, would be called a disappearing act. Brian Bassett vanished. Gone.

Sometime after midnight on May Day[9] morning, Mimi Menlo awoke from her dream of Brian to the sound of Thurber thumping the floor in a dream of his own.

Everett was not in his bed and Mimi cursed. She put on her wrapper and her slippers and went beyond the bedroom into the hall.

No lights were shining but the street lamps far below and the windows gave no sign of stars.

Mimi made her way past the jungle, searching for Everett in the living-room. He was not there. She would dream of this one day; it was a certainty.

"Everett?"

He did not reply.

Mimi turned and went back through the bedroom.

"Everett?"

She heard him. He was in the bathroom and she went in through the door.

---

9. **May Day** Holiday marking the arrival of spring on May 1.

"Oh," she said, when she saw him. "Oh, my God."

Everett Menlo was standing in the bathtub, removing his pyjamas. They were soaking wet, but not with perspiration. They were soaking wet with blood.

For a moment, holding his jacket, letting its arms hang down across his belly and his groin, Everett stared at Mimi, blank-eyed from his nightmare.

Mimi raised her hands to her mouth. She felt as one must feel, if helpless, watching someone burn alive.

Everett threw the jacket down and started to remove his trousers. His pyjamas, made of cotton, had been green. His eyes were blinded now with blood and his hands reached out to find the shower taps.

"Please don't look at me," he said. "I … Please go away."

Mimi said: "no." She sat on the toilet seat. "I'm waiting here," she told him, "until we both wake up."

(1988)

Alice Munro (1931–)

Dance of the Happy Shades, Alice Munro's first book, was published in 1968. With this collection of stories that delve beneath the placid exterior of small-town southwestern Ontario life, Munro won critical recognition and started building a loyal readership. She has since been widely recognized as one of the world's finest writers of short fiction in English. Louis MacKendrick explains the broad appeal of Munro's work — which is characterized by its wealth of telling detail, its emotional nuance, and its precise rendering of everyday experience — by pointing out that the stories "retain probability and authenticity while they also delight the attentive reader with their fictionality: their realities are constructs of rare skill and masterful invention."

Alice Laidlaw was raised on a farm near Wingham, Ontario. Her father ran a fox farm and her mother was a school teacher until she developed Parkinson's disease. Although her mother required a great deal of care, Alice earned top marks in high school, for which she was rewarded with a scholarship and bursary, and in 1949, she enrolled in the journalism program at the University of Western Ontario. She transferred to the English literature program in 1950, and that year she published her first story: "The Dimensions of a Shadow" appeared in the university magazine *Folio*.

In 1951, before finishing her degree, Alice married James Munro and the couple moved to Vancouver. She later remarked that she would not have decided to marry young and start a family if she had been able to afford to continue her university studies. She had three daughters, and she worried constantly that her commitment to her children and to her ailing mother would keep her from writing. She managed to carve out quiet time to pursue her art by getting up very early in the morning, and she eventually established a pattern of publishing one or two stories a year in journals and magazines.

Domestic demands eased as her children grew, and she was able to produce her first collection, *Dance of the Happy Shades*, in 1968. The book won the Governor General's Award for fiction. In this collection, Munro established an approach to character that would become increasingly sophisticated in coming years. She focused on the eccentricities and biases that made each of her characters distinct, and she placed those sharply realized characters in settings that came alive through Munro's attention to the details, rituals, and idiosyncrasies that mark small-town life. In some ways, these early stories are reminiscent, in Canadian terms, of the preoccupation with odd characters and back road experiences that can be found in the fiction of female writers of the American south, including Carson McCullers, Flannery O'Connor, and Eudora Welty. Munro paid particular attention to the trials and victories of her female protagonists, whose frank encounters with sex, or social delinquency, or financial circumstances made them unique.

Although Munro's stories are as rich as any novel, she is in fact the author of only one book that bears that description. *Lives of Girls and Women*, which appeared in 1971, is the story of Del Jordan, an adolescent whose artistic coming of age in the small town of Jubilee is portrayed with equal attention to the surface details that make Jubilee seem so real and to Del's developing consciousness, which is always trying to make sense of daily life in terms of art. The novel is a *kunstlerroman* — the story of an artist's initiation, or coming of age. As she says towards the end of the novel, which Del narrates retrospectively, life is a mixture of what is hidden and what is revealed, of "deep caves and kitchen linoleum." We see Del overcome a series of daunting obstacles in order to achieve physical and emotional independence. In the process, she moves from childhood to womanhood and becomes an artist — a writer of fiction. Asked to comment on the many parallels between *Lives* and her own experience, Munro described the book as "autobiographical in form but not in fact."

Munro divorced her husband in 1973, taught briefly at Notre Dame University in Nelson, British Columbia, and then moved to London, Ontario. She commuted to York University in Toronto, where she had been hired to teach creative writing. In 1974, she published *Something I've Been Meaning to Tell You* and established a friendship with Gerald Fremlin, whom she had first met as a student at Western. They married in 1976. Munro also engaged an agent and began to place her work with the *New Yorker* magazine, which would become a regular outlet for her fiction.

Who Do You Think You Are?, published in 1978, earned Munro another Governor General's Award and a spot on the Booker Prize short list. This work, another series of linked stories, explores a terrain similar to that of *Lives of Girls and Women:* a small-town girl — named Rose — matures to womanhood and escapes a milieu of conventional values to pursue her ambitions in the wider world. Although it is hard to credit today, the author's implicit insistence that women should not be confined to narrow domestic roles outraged many at the time. Munro was compelled to speak out publicly against censorship in 1978 when an initiative was mounted to ban *Lives of Girls and Women* and Margaret Laurence's *The Diviners* (1974) from schools.

In the 1980s, Munro entered a period of travel, journeying to Australia, China, and Scandinavia; she also served as writer-in-residence at various universities. *The Moons of Jupiter* appeared in 1982, followed, in 1986, by *The Progress of Love*. It earned Munro a third Governor General's Award. The book demonstrated that she had embarked on a new phase in her writing. Although her realist technique and characterization were not much altered, and her concern with relationships between the sexes and family members persisted, she was now engaged in an exploration of such themes as mortality and self-delusion, and the tone of the fiction had darkened. She began to focus more closely on memory and perception and the ways in which they distort reality.

These stories also experimented with meta-textuality — they were stories about the act of storytelling — and in that sense they had an uncharacteristic complexity, but Munro would later abandon such formal manipulation, claiming it was "too fancy."

In her next work, *Friend of My Youth* (1990), Munro's thematic concerns remained essentially unchanged, but the stories in this collection are marked by a density of narrative layering, as are the stories in *Open Secrets* (1994). The latter's ironic title implies an ease of access, but most of the secrets contained within are never fully revealed. In these stories, which broach such dark topics as child molestation, rape, and murder, Munro suggests that there are no secrets that can explain the mysteries and depravities of human existence. As one reviewer has observed, in *Open Secrets,* Munro highlights lessons that are "partial and ambiguous but likely also to be momentous. Gradually, time and experience obscure the easy lessons.... What we once thought true may be lost under the ongoing and always surprising accumulation of event and perception."

The American writer Jonathan Franzen provides a succinct description of the originality of Munro's stories. He says:

> More than any writer since Chekhov, Munro strives for and achieves, in each of her stories, a gestaltlike completeness in the representation of a life. She always had a genius for developing and unpacking moments of epiphany. But it's in the three collections since *Selected Stories* (1996) that she's taken the really big, world-class leap and become a master of suspense. The moments she's pursuing now aren't moments of realization; they're moments of fateful, irrevocable, dramatic action. And what this means for the reader is you can't even begin to guess at a story's meaning until you've followed every twist; it's always the last page or two that switches all lights on.

With *The Love of a Good Woman* (1998), which won the Giller Prize, and *Hateship, Friendship, Courtship, Loveship, Marriage* (2001), Munro returned to a more straightforward form of storytelling, but the critical and public response to her offerings remained consistently laudatory. Reaching her seventies, Munro told interviewers that she might not produce another book, but she continues to write: *Runaway* was published in 2005, and *The View from Castle Rock* (Munro's most overtly autobiographical collection) appeared in 2006.

The Bear Came over the Mountain

Fiona lived in her parents' house, in the town where she and Grant went to university. It was a big, bay-windowed house that seemed to Grant both luxurious and disorderly, with rugs crooked on the floors and cup rings bitten into the table varnish. Her mother was Icelandic — a powerful woman with a froth of white hair and indignant far-left politics. The father was an important cardiologist, revered around the hospital but happily subservient at home, where he would listen to strange tirades with an absent-minded smile. All kinds of people, rich or shabby-looking, delivered these tirades, and kept coming and going and arguing and conferring, sometimes in foreign accents. Fiona had her own little car and a pile of cashmere sweaters, but she wasn't in a sorority, and this activity in her house was probably the reason.

Not that she cared. Sororities were a joke to her, and so was politics, though she liked to play "The Four Insurgent Generals"[1] on the phonograph, and sometimes also she played the "Internationale,"[2] very loud, if there was a guest she thought she could make nervous. A curly-haired, gloomy-looking foreigner was courting her — she said he was a Visigoth[3] — and so were two or three quite respectable and uneasy young interns. She made fun of them all and of Grant as well. She would drolly repeat some of his small-town phrases. He thought maybe she was joking when she proposed to him, on a cold bright day on the beach at Port Stanley.[4] Sand was stinging their faces and the waves delivered crashing loads of gravel at their feet.

---

1. **The Four Insurgent Generals** A Spanish song of political resistance. 2. **Internationale** The anthem of international socialism. 3. **Visigoth** A Germanic tribe that threatened the Roman Empire during its decline. 4. **Port Stanley** Town in Ontario, on Lake Erie.

"Do you think it would be fun — " Fiona shouted. "Do you think it would be fun if we got married?"

He took her up on it, he shouted yes. He wanted never to be away from her. She had the spark of life.

Just before they left their house Fiona noticed a mark on the kitchen floor. It came from the cheap black house shoes she had been wearing earlier in the day.

"I thought they'd quit doing that," she said in a tone of ordinary annoyance and perplexity, rubbing at the gray smear that looked as if it had been made by a greasy crayon.

She remarked that she would never have to do this again, since she wasn't taking those shoes with her.

"I guess I'll be dressed up all the time," she said. "Or semi dressed up. It'll be sort of like in a hotel."

She rinsed out the rag she'd been using and hung it on the rack inside the door under the sink. Then she put on her golden-brown fur-collared ski jacket over a white turtle-necked sweater and tailored fawn slacks. She was a tall, narrow-shouldered woman, seventy years old but still upright and trim, with long legs and long feet, delicate wrists and ankles and tiny, almost comical-looking ears. Her hair, which was light as milkweed fluff, had gone from pale blond to white somehow without Grant's noticing exactly when, and she still wore it down to her shoulders, as her mother had done. (That was the thing that had alarmed Grant's own mother, a small-town widow who worked as a doctor's receptionist. The long white hair on Fiona's mother, even more than the state of the house, had told her all she needed to know about attitudes and politics.)

Otherwise Fiona with her fine bones and small sapphire eyes was nothing like her mother. She had a slightly crooked mouth which she emphasized now with red lipstick — usually the last thing she did before she left the house. She looked just like herself on this day — direct and vague as in fact she was, sweet and ironic.

Over a year ago Grant had started noticing so many little yellow notes stuck up all over the house. That was not entirely new. She'd always written things down — the title of a book she'd heard mentioned on the radio or the jobs she wanted to make sure she did that day. Even her morning schedule was written down — he found it mystifying and touching in its precision.

7 a.m. Yoga. 7:30–7:45 teeth face hair. 7:45–8:15 walk. 8:15 Grant and Breakfast.

The new notes were different. Taped onto the kitchen drawers — Cutlery, Dishtowels, Knives. Couldn't she have just opened the drawers and seen what was inside? He remembered a story about the German soldiers on border patrol in Czechoslovakia during the war. Some Czech had told him that each of the patrol dogs wore a sign that said *Hund*. Why? said the Czechs, and the Germans said, Because that is a *hund*.

He was going to tell Fiona that, then thought he'd better not. They always laughed at the same things, but suppose this time she didn't laugh?

Worse things were coming. She went to town and phoned him from a booth to ask him how to drive home. She went for her walk across the field into the woods and came home by the fence line — a very long way round. She said that she'd counted on fences always taking you somewhere.

It was hard to figure out. She said that about fences as if it was a joke, and she had remembered the phone number without any trouble.

"I don't think it's anything to worry about," she said. "I expect I'm just losing my mind."

He asked if she had been taking sleeping pills.

"If I have I don't remember," she said. Then she said she was sorry to sound so flippant.

"I'm sure I haven't been taking anything. Maybe I should be. Maybe vitamins."

Vitamins didn't help. She would stand in doorways trying to figure out where she was going. She forgot to turn on the burner under the vegetables or put water in the coffeemaker. She asked Grant when they'd moved to this house.

"Was it last year or the year before?"

He said that it was twelve years ago.

She said, "That's shocking."

"She's always been a bit like this," Grant said to the doctor. "Once she left her fur coat in storage and just forgot about it. That was when we were always going somewhere warm in the winters. Then she said it was unintentionally on purpose, she said it was like a sin she was leaving behind. The way some people made her feel about fur coats."

He tried without success to explain something more — to explain how Fiona's surprise and apologies about all this seemed somehow like routine courtesy, not quite concealing a private amusement. As if she'd stumbled on some adventure that she had not been expecting. Or was playing a game that she hoped he would catch on to. They had always had their games — nonsense dialects, characters they invented. Some of Fiona's made-up voices, chirping or wheedling (he couldn't tell the doctor this), had mimicked uncannily the voices of women of his that she had never met or known about.

"Yes, well," the doctor said. "It might be selective at first. We don't know, do we? Till we see the pattern of the deterioration, we really can't say."

In a while it hardly mattered what label was put on it. Fiona, who no longer went shopping alone, disappeared from the supermarket while Grant had his back turned. A policeman picked her up as she walked down the middle of the road, blocks away. He asked her name and she answered readily. Then he asked her the name of the prime minister of the country.

"If you don't know that, young man, you really shouldn't be in such a responsible job."

He laughed. But then she made the mistake of asking if he'd seen Boris and Natasha.

These were the Russian wolfhounds she had adopted some years ago as a favor to a friend, then devoted herself to for the rest of their lives. Her taking them over might have coincided with the discovery that she was not likely to have children. Something about her tubes being blocked, or twisted — Grant could not remember now. He had always avoided thinking about all that female apparatus. Or it might have been after her mother died. The dogs' long legs and silky hair, their narrow, gentle, intransigent faces made a fine match for her when she took them out for walks. And Grant himself, in those days, landing his first job at the university (his father-in-law's money welcome in spite of the political taint), might have seemed to some people to have been picked up on another of Fiona's eccentric whims, and groomed and tended and favored. Though he never understood this, fortunately, until much later.

She said to him, at suppertime on the day of the wandering-off at the supermarket, "You know what you're going to have to do with me, don't you? You're going to have to put me in that place. Shallowlake?"

Grant said, "Meadowlake. We're not at that stage yet."

"Shallowlake, Shillylake," she said, as if they were engaged in a playful competition. "Sillylake. Sillylake it is."

He held his head in his hands, his elbows on the table. He said that if they did think of it, it must be as something that need not be permanent. A kind of experimental treatment.

A rest cure. There was a rule that nobody could be admitted during the month of December. The holiday season had so many emotional pitfalls. So they made the twenty-minute drive in January. Before they reached the highway the country road dipped through a swampy hollow now completely frozen over. The swamp-oaks and maples threw their shadows like bars across the bright snow.

Fiona said, "Oh, remember."

Grant said, "I was thinking about that too."

"Only it was in the moonlight," she said.

She was talking about the time that they had gone out skiing at night under the full moon and over the black-striped snow, in this place that you could get into only in the depths of winter. They had heard the branches cracking in the cold.

So if she could remember that so vividly and correctly, could there really be so much the matter with her?

It was all he could do not to turn around and drive home.

There was another rule which the supervisor explained to him. New residents were not to be visited during the first thirty days. Most people needed that time to get settled in. Before the rule had been put in place, there had been pleas and tears and tantrums, even from those who had come in willingly. Around the third or fourth day they would start lamenting and begging to be taken home. And some relatives could be susceptible to that, so you would have people being carted home who would not get on there any better than they had before. Six months later or sometimes only a few weeks later, the whole upsetting hassle would have to be gone through again.

"Whereas we find," the supervisor said, "we find that if they're left on their own they usually end up happy as clams. You have to practically lure them into a bus to take a trip to town. The same with a visit home. It's perfectly okay to take them home then, visit for an hour or two — they're the ones that'll worry about getting back in time for supper. Meadowlake's their home then. Of course, that doesn't apply to the ones on the second floor, we can't let them go. It's too difficult, and they don't know where they are anyway."

"My wife isn't going to be on the second floor," Grant said.

"No," said the supervisor thoughtfully. "I just like to make everything clear at the outset."

They had gone over to Meadowlake a few times several years ago, to visit Mr. Farquar, the old bachelor farmer who had been their neighbor. He had lived by himself in a drafty brick house unaltered since the early years of the century, except for the addition of a refrigerator and a television set. He had paid Grant and Fiona unannounced but well-spaced visits and, as well as local matters, he liked to discuss books he had been reading — about the Crimean War or Polar explorations or the history of firearms. But after he went to Meadowlake he would talk only about the routines of the place, and they got the idea that their visits, though gratifying, were a social burden for him. And Fiona in particular hated the smell of urine and bleach that hung about, hated the perfunctory bouquets of plastic flowers in niches in the dim, low-ceilinged corridors.

Now that building was gone, though it had dated only from the fifties. Just as Mr. Farquar's house was gone, replaced by a gimcrack[5] sort of castle that was the weekend home of some people from Toronto. The new Meadowlake was an airy, vaulted building whose air was faintly pleasantly pine-scented. Profuse and genuine greenery sprouted out of giant crocks.

Nevertheless, it was the old building that Grant would find himself picturing Fiona in during the long month he had to get through without seeing her. It was the longest month of his life, he thought — longer than the month he had spent with his mother visiting relatives in Lanark County, when he was thirteen, and longer than the month that Jacqui Adams spent on holiday with her family, near the beginning of their affair. He phoned Meadowlake every day and hoped that he would get the nurse whose name was Kristy. She seemed a little amused at his constancy, but she would give him a fuller report than any other nurse he got stuck with.

Fiona had caught a cold, but that was not unusual for newcomers.

"Like when your kids start school," Kristy said. "There's a whole bunch of new germs they're exposed to, and for a while they just catch everything."

Then the cold got better. She was off the antibiotics, and she didn't seem as confused as she had been when she came in. (This was the first time Grant had heard about either the antibiotics or the confusion.) Her appetite was pretty good, and she seemed to enjoy sitting in the sunroom. She seemed to enjoy watching television.

One of the things that had been so intolerable about the old Meadowlake had been the way the television was on everywhere, overwhelming your thoughts or conversation wherever you chose to sit down. Some of the inmates (that was what he and Fiona called them then, not residents) would raise their eyes to it, some talked back to it, but most just sat and meekly endured its assault. In the new building, as far as he could recall, the television was in a separate sitting room, or in the bedrooms. You could make a choice to watch it.

So Fiona must have made a choice. To watch what?

During the years that they had lived in this house, he and Fiona had watched quite a bit of television together. They had spied on the lives of every beast or reptile or insect or sea creature that a camera was able to reach, and they had followed the plots of what seemed like dozens of rather similar fine nineteenth-century novels. They had slid into an infatuation with an English comedy about life in a department store and had watched so many reruns that they knew the dialogue by heart. They mourned the disappearance of actors who died in real life or went off to other jobs, then welcomed those same actors back as the characters were born again. They watched the floorwalker's hair going from black to gray and finally back to black, the cheap sets never changing. But these, too, faded; eventually the sets and the blackest hair faded as if dust from the London streets

---

5. **gimcrack** Flashy but impractical.

was getting in under the elevator doors, and there was a sadness about this that seemed to affect Grant and Fiona more than any of the tragedies on *Masterpiece Theatre*, so they gave up watching before the final end.

Fiona was making some friends, Kristy said. She was definitely coming out of her shell.

What shell was that? Grant wanted to ask, but checked himself, to remain in Kristy's good graces.

If anybody phoned, he let the message go onto the machine. The people they saw socially, occasionally, were not close neighbors but people who lived around the countryside, who were retired, as they were, and who often went away without notice. The first years that they had lived here Grant and Fiona had stayed through the winter. A country winter was a new experience, and they had plenty to do, fixing up the house. Then they had gotten the idea that they too should travel while they could, and they had gone to Greece, to Australia, to Costa Rica. People would think that they were away on some such trip at present.

He skied for exercise but never went as far as the swamp. He skied around and around in the field behind the house as the sun went down and left the sky pink over a countryside that seemed to be bound by waves of blue-edged ice. He counted off the times he went round the field, and then he came back to the darkening house, turning the television news on while he got his supper. They had usually prepared supper together. One of them made the drinks and the other the fire, and they talked about his work (he was writing a study of legendary Norse wolves and particularly of the great Fenris wolf who swallows up Odin[6] at the end of the world) and about whatever Fiona was reading and what they had been thinking during their close but separate day. This was their time of liveliest intimacy, though there was also, of course, the five or ten minutes of physical sweetness just after they got into bed — something that did not often end up in sex but reassured them that sex was not over yet.

In a dream Grant showed a letter to one of his colleagues whom he had thought of as a friend. The letter was from the roommate of a girl he had not thought of for a while. Its style was sanctimonious and hostile, threatening in a whining way — he put the writer down as a latent lesbian. The girl herself was someone he had parted from decently, and it seemed unlikely that she would want to make a fuss, let alone try to kill herself, which was what the letter was apparently, elaborately, trying to tell him.

The colleague was one of those husbands and fathers who had been among the first to throw away their neckties and leave home to spend every night on a floor mattress with a bewitching young mistress, coming to their offices, their classes, bedraggled and smelling of dope and incense. But now he took a dim view of such shenanigans, and Grant recollected that he had in fact married one of those girls, and that she had taken to giving dinner parties and having babies, just as wives used to do.

"I wouldn't laugh," he said to Grant, who did not think he had been laughing. "And if I were you I'd try to prepare Fiona."

So Grant went off to find Fiona in Meadowlake — the old Meadowlake — and got into a lecture theater instead. Everybody was waiting there for him to teach his class.

---

6. **Fenris, Odin** Fenris is a wolf in Norse mythology that grows too large for the gods to control, and consequently eats Odin, the chief god, during Ragnarok, the battle at the end of the world.

And sitting in the last, highest row was a flock of cold-eyed young women all in black robes, all in mourning, who never took their bitter stares off him and conspicuously did not write down, or care about, anything he was saying.

Fiona was in the first row, untroubled. She had transformed the lecture room into the sort of corner she was always finding at a party — some high-and-dry spot where she drank wine with mineral water, and smoked ordinary cigarettes and told funny stories about her dogs. Holding out there against the tide, with some people who were like herself, as if the dramas that were being played out in other corners, in bedrooms and on the dark verandah, were nothing but childish comedy. As if chastity was chic, and reticence a blessing.

"Oh, phooey," Fiona said. "Girls that age are always going around talking about how they'll kill themselves."

But it wasn't enough for her to say that — in fact, it rather chilled him. He was afraid that she was wrong, that something terrible had happened, and he saw what she could not — that the black ring was thickening, drawing in, all around his windpipe, all around the top of the room.

He hauled himself out of the dream and set about separating what was real from what was not.

There had been a letter, and the word "RAT" had appeared in black paint on his office door, and Fiona, on being told that a girl had suffered from a bad crush on him, had said pretty much what she said in the dream. The colleague hadn't come into it, the black-robed women had never appeared in his classroom, and nobody had committed suicide. Grant hadn't been disgraced, in fact he had got off easily when you thought of what might have happened just a couple of years later. But word got around. Cold shoulders became conspicuous. They had few Christmas invitations and spent New Year's Eve alone. Grant got drunk, and without its being required of him — also, thank God, without making the error of confession — he promised Fiona a new life.

The shame he felt then was the shame of being duped, of not having noticed the change that was going on. And not one woman had made him aware of it. There had been the change in the past when so many women so suddenly became available — or it seemed that way to him — and now this new change, when they were saying that what had happened was not what they had had in mind at all. They had collaborated because they were helpless and bewildered, and they had been injured by the whole thing, rather than delighted. Even when they had taken the initiative they had done so only because the cards were stacked against them.

Nowhere was there any acknowledgment that the life of a philanderer (if that was what Grant had to call himself — he who had not had half as many conquests or complications as the man who had reproached him in his dream) involved acts of kindness and generosity and even sacrifice. Not in the beginning, perhaps, but at least as things went on. Many times he had catered to a woman's pride, to her fragility, by offering more affection — or a rougher passion — than anything he really felt. All so that he could now find himself accused of wounding and exploiting and destroying self-esteem. And of deceiving Fiona — as of course he had deceived her — but would it have been better if he had done as others had done with their wives and left her?

He had never thought of such a thing. He had never stopped making love to Fiona in spite of disturbing demands elsewhere. He had not stayed away from her for a single night. No making up elaborate stories in order to spend a weekend in San Francisco or in a tent on Manitoulin Island. He had gone easy on the dope and the drink and he had continued to publish papers, serve on committees, make progress in his career. He had never had any intention of throwing up work and marriage and taking to the country to practice carpentry or keep bees.

But something like that had happened after all. He took an early retirement with a reduced pension. The cardiologist had died, after some bewildered and stoical time alone in the big house, and Fiona had inherited both that property and the farmhouse where her father had grown up, in the country near Georgian Bay. She gave up her job, as a hospital coordinator of volunteer services (in that everyday world, as she said, where people actually had troubles that were not related to drugs or sex or intellectual squabbles). A new life was a new life.

Boris and Natasha had died by this time. One of them got sick and died first — Grant forgot which one — and then the other died, more or less out of sympathy.

He and Fiona worked on the house. They got cross-country skis. They were not very sociable, but they gradually made some friends. There were no more hectic flirtations. No bare female toes creeping up under a man's pants leg at a dinner party. No more loose wives.

Just in time, Grant was able to think, when the sense of injustice wore down. The feminists and perhaps the sad silly girl herself and his cowardly so-called friends had pushed him out just in time. Out of a life that was in fact getting to be more trouble than it was worth. And that might eventually have cost him Fiona.

On the morning of the day when he was to go back to Meadowlake for the first visit, Grant woke early. He was full of a solemn tingling, as in the old days on the morning of his first planned meeting with a new woman. The feeling was not precisely sexual. (Later, when the meetings had become routine, that was all it was.) There was an expectation of discovery, almost a spiritual expansion. Also timidity, humility, alarm.

He left home too early. Visitors were not allowed before two o'clock. He did not want to sit out in the parking lot, waiting, so he made himself turn the car in a wrong direction.

There had been a thaw. Plenty of snow was left, but the dazzling hard landscape of earlier winter had crumbled. These pocked heaps under a gray sky looked like refuse in the fields.

In the town near Meadowlake he found a florist's shop and bought a large bouquet. He had never presented flowers to Fiona before. Or to anyone else. He entered the building feeling like a hopeless lover or a guilty husband in a cartoon.

"Wow. Narcissus this early," Kristy said. "You must've spent a fortune." She went along the hall ahead of him and snapped on the light in a closet, or sort of kitchen, where she searched for a vase. She was a heavy young woman who looked as if she had given up in every department except her hair. That was blond and voluminous. All the puffed-up luxury of a cocktail waitress's style, or a stripper's, on top of such a workaday face and body.

"There, now," she said, and nodded him down the hall. "Name's right on the door."

So it was, on a nameplate decorated with bluebirds. He wondered whether to knock, and did, then opened the door and called her name.

She wasn't there. The closet door was closed, the bed smoothed. Nothing on the bedside table, except a box of Kleenex and a glass of water. Not a single photograph or picture of any kind, not a book or a magazine. Perhaps you had to keep those in a cupboard.

He went back to the nurses' station, or reception desk, or whatever it was. Kristy said "No?" with a surprise that he thought perfunctory.

He hesitated, holding the flowers. She said, "Okay, okay — let's set the bouquet down here." Sighing, as if he was a backward child on his first day at school, she led him along a hall, into the light of the huge sky windows in the large central space, with its cathedral ceiling. Some people were sitting along the walls, in easy chairs, others at tables in the middle of the carpeted floor. None of them looked too bad. Old — some of them incapacitated enough to need wheelchairs — but decent. There used to be some unnerving sights when he and Fiona went to visit Mr. Farquar. Whiskers on old women's chins, somebody with a bulged-out eye like a rotted plum. Dribblers, head wagglers, mad chatterers. Now it looked as if there'd been some weeding out of the worst cases. Or perhaps drugs, surgery had come into use, perhaps there were ways of treating disfigurement, as well as verbal and other kinds of incontinence — ways that hadn't existed even those few years ago.

There was, however, a very disconsolate woman sitting at the piano, picking away with one finger and never achieving a tune. Another woman, staring out from behind a coffee urn and a stack of plastic cups, looked bored to stone. But she had to be an employee — she wore a pale-green pants outfit like Kristy's.

"See?" said Kristy in a softer voice. "You just go up and say hello and try not to startle her. Remember she may not — Well. Just go ahead."

He saw Fiona in profile, sitting close up to one of the card tables, but not playing. She looked a little puffy in the face, the flab on one cheek hiding the corner of her mouth, in a way it hadn't done before. She was watching the play of the man she sat closest to. He held his cards tilted so that she could see them. When Grant got near the table she looked up. They all looked up — all the players at the table looked up, with displeasure. Then they immediately looked down at their cards, as if to ward off any intrusion.

But Fiona smiled her lopsided, abashed, sly, and charming smile and pushed back her chair and came round to him, putting her fingers to her mouth.

"Bridge," she whispered. "Deadly serious. They're quite rabid about it." She drew him towards the coffee table, chatting. "I can remember being like that for a while at college. My friends and I would cut class and sit in the common room and smoke and play like cutthroats. One's name was Phoebe, I don't remember the others."

"Phoebe Hart," Grant said. He pictured the little hollow-chested, black-eyed girl, who was probably dead by now. Wreathed in smoke, Fiona and Phoebe and those others, rapt as witches.

"You knew her too?" said Fiona, directing her smile now towards the stone-faced woman. "Can I get you anything? A cup of tea? I'm afraid the coffee isn't up to much here."

Grant never drank tea.

He could not throw his arms around her. Something about her voice and smile, familiar as they were, something about the way she seemed to be guarding the players and even the coffee woman from him — as well as him from their displeasure — made that not possible.

"I brought you some flowers," he said. "I thought they'd do to brighten up your room. I went to your room, but you weren't there."

"Well, no," she said. "I'm here."

Grant said, "You've made a new friend." He nodded towards the man she'd been sitting next to. At this moment that man looked up at Fiona and she turned, either because of what Grant had said or because she felt the look at her back.

"It's just Aubrey," she said. "The funny thing is I knew him years and years ago. He worked in the store. The hardware store where my grandpa used to shop. He and I were always kidding around and he could not get up the nerve to ask me out. Till the very last weekend and he took me to a ball game. But when it was over my grandpa showed up to drive me home. I was up visiting for the summer. Visiting my grandparents — they lived on a farm."

"Fiona. I know where your grandparents lived. It's where we live. Lived."

"Really?" she said, not paying full attention because the card-player was sending her his look, which was not one of supplication but command. He was a man of about Grant's age, or a little older. Thick coarse white hair fell over his forehead, and his skin was leathery but pale, yellowish-white like an old wrinkled-up kid glove. His long face was dignified and melancholy, and he had something of the beauty of a powerful, discouraged, elderly horse. But where Fiona was concerned he was not discouraged.

"I better go back," Fiona said, a blush spotting her newly fattened face. "He thinks he can't play without me sitting there. It's silly, I hardly know the game anymore. I'm afraid you'll have to excuse me."

"Will you be through soon?"

"Oh, we should be. It depends. If you go and ask that grim-looking lady nicely she'll get you some tea."

"I'm fine," Grant said.

"So I'll leave you then, you can entertain yourself? It must all seem strange to you, but you'll be surprised how soon you get used to it. You'll get to know who everybody is. Except that some of them are pretty well off in the clouds, you know — you can't expect them all to get to know who *you* are."

She slipped back into her chair and said something into Aubrey's ear. She tapped her fingers across the back of his hand.

Grant went in search of Kristy and met her in the hall. She was pushing a cart on which there were pitchers of apple juice and grape juice.

"Just one sec," she said to him, as she stuck her head through a doorway. "Apple juice in here? Grape juice? Cookies?"

He waited while she filled two plastic glasses and took them into the room. Then she came back and put two arrowroot cookies on paper plates.

"Well?" she said. "Aren't you glad to see her participating and everything?"

Grant said, "Does she even know who I am?"

He could not decide. She could have been playing a joke. It would not be unlike her. She had given herself away by that little pretense at the end, talking to him as if she thought perhaps he was a new resident. If that was what she was pretending. If it was a pretense.

But would she not have run after him and laughed at him then, once the joke was over? She would not have just gone back to the game, surely, and pretended to forget about him. That would have been too cruel.

Kristy said, "You just caught her at sort of a bad moment. Involved in the game."

"She's not even playing," he said.

"Well, but her friend's playing. Aubrey."

"So who is Aubrey?"

"That's who he is. Aubrey. Her friend. Would you like a juice?"

Grant shook his head.

"Oh, look," said Kristy. "They get these attachments. That takes over for a while. Best buddy sort of thing. It's kind of a phase."

"You mean she really might not know who I am?"

"She might not. Not today. Then tomorrow — you never know, do you? Things change back and forth all the time and there's nothing you can do about it. You'll see the way it is once you've been coming here for a while. You'll learn not to take it all so serious. Learn to take it day by day."

Day by day. But things really didn't change back and forth, and he didn't get used to the way they were. Fiona was the one who seemed to get used to him, but only as some persistent visitor who took a special interest in her. Or perhaps even as a nuisance who must be prevented, according to her old rules of courtesy, from realizing that he was one. She treated him with a distracted, social sort of kindness that was successful in holding him back from the most obvious, the most necessary question. He could not demand of her whether she did or did not remember him as her husband of nearly fifty years. He got the impression that she would be embarrassed by such a question — embarrassed not for herself but for him. She would have laughed in a fluttery way and mortified him with her politeness and bewilderment, and somehow she would have ended up not saying either yes or no. Or she would have said either one in a way that gave not the least satisfaction.

Kristy was the only nurse he could talk to. Some of the others treated the whole thing as a joke. One tough old stick laughed in his face. "That Aubrey and that Fiona? They've really got it bad, haven't they?"

Kristy told him that Aubrey had been the local representative of a company that sold weed killer — "and all that kind of stuff" — to farmers.

"He was a fine person," she said, and Grant did not know whether this meant that Aubrey was honest and openhanded and kind to people, or that he was well spoken and well dressed and drove a good car. Probably both.

And then when he was not very old or even retired — she said — he had suffered some unusual kind of damage.

"His wife is the one takes care of him usually. She takes care of him at home. She just put him in here on temporary care so she could get a break. Her sister wanted her to go to Florida. See, she's had a hard time, you wouldn't ever have expected a man like him — They just went on a holiday somewhere and he got something, like some bug, that gave him a terrible high fever? And it put him in a coma and left him like he is now."

He asked her about these affections between residents. Did they ever go too far? He was able now to take a tone of indulgence that he hoped would save him from any lectures.

"Depends what you mean," she said. She kept writing in her record book while deciding how to answer him. When she finished what she was writing she looked up at him with a frank smile.

"The trouble we have in here, it's funny, it's often with some of the ones that haven't been friendly with each other at all. They maybe won't even know each other, beyond knowing, like, is it a man or a woman? You'd thing it'd be the old guys trying to crawl in bed with the old women, but you know half the time it's the other way round. Old women going after the old men. Could be they're not so wore out, I guess."

Then she stopped smiling, as if she was afraid she had said too much, or spoken callously.

"Don't take me wrong," she said. "I don't mean Fiona. Fiona is a lady."

Well, what about Aubrey? Grant felt like saying. But he remembered that Aubrey was in a wheelchair.

"She's a real lady," Kristy said, in a tone so decisive and reassuring that Grant was not reassured. He had in his mind a picture of Fiona, in one of her long eyelet-trimmed blue-ribboned nightgowns, teasingly lifting the covers of an old man's bed.

"Well, I sometimes wonder — " he said.

Kristy said sharply, "You wonder what?"

"I wonder whether she isn't putting on some kind of a charade."

"A what?" said Kristy.

Most afternoons the pair could be found at the card table. Aubrey had large, thick-fingered hands. It was difficult for him to manage his cards. Fiona shuffled and dealt for him and sometimes moved quickly to straighten a card that seemed to be slipping from his grasp. Grant would watch from across the room her darting move and quick, laughing apology. He could see Aubrey's husbandly frown as a wisp of her hair touched his cheek. Aubrey preferred to ignore her as long as she stayed close.

But let her smile her greeting at Grant, let her push back her chair and get up to offer him tea — showing that she had accepted his right to be there and possibly felt a slight responsibility for him — and Aubrey's face took on its look of sombre consternation. He would let the cards slide from his fingers and fall on the floor, to spoil the game.

So that Fiona had to get busy and put things right.

If they weren't at the bridge table they might be walking along the halls, Aubrey hanging on to the railing with one hand and clutching Fiona's arm or shoulder with other. The nurses thought that it was a marvel, the way she had got him out of his wheelchair. Though for longer trips — to the conservatory at one end of the building or the television room at the other — the wheelchair was called for.

The television seemed to be always turned to the sports channel and Aubrey would watch any sport, but his favorite appeared to be golf. Grant didn't mind watching that with them. He sat down a few chairs away. On the large screen a small group of spectators and commentators followed the players around the peaceful green, and at appropriate moments broke into a formal sort of applause. But there was silence everywhere as the player made his swing and the ball took its lonely, appointed journey across the sky. Aubrey and Fiona and Grant and possibly others sat and held their breaths, and then Aubrey's breath broke out first, expressing satisfaction or disappointment. Fiona's chimed in on the same note a moment later.

In the conservatory there was no such silence. The pair found themselves a seat among the most lush and thick and tropical-looking plants — a bower, if you like — which Grant had just enough self-control to keep from penetrating. Mixed in with the rustle of the leaves and the sound of splashing water was Fiona's soft talk and her laughter.

Then some sort of chortle. Which of them could it be?

Perhaps neither — perhaps it came from one of the impudent flashy-looking birds who inhabited the corner cages.

Aubrey could talk, though his voice probably didn't sound the way it used to. He seemed to say something now — a couple of thick syllables. *Take care. He's here. My love.*

On the blue bottom of the fountain's pool lay some wishing coins. Grant had never seen anybody actually throwing money in. He stared at these nickels and dimes and quarters, wondering if they had been glued to the tiles — another feature of the building's encouraging decoration.

Teenagers at the baseball game, sitting at the top of the bleachers out of the way of the boy's friends. A couple of inches of bare wood between them, darkness falling, quick chill of the evening late in the summer. The skittering of their hands, the shift of haunches, eyes never lifted from the field. He'll take off his jacket, if he's wearing one, to lay it around her narrow shoulders. Underneath it he can pull her closer to him, press his spread fingers into her soft arm.

Not like today when any kid would probably be into her pants on the first date.

Fiona's skinny soft arm. Teenage lust astonishing her and flashing along all the nerves of her tender new body, as the night thickens beyond the lighted dust of the game.

Meadowlake was short on mirrors, so he did not have to catch sight of himself stalking and prowling. But every once in a while it came to him how foolish and pathetic and perhaps unhinged he must look, trailing around after Fiona and Aubrey. And having no luck in confronting her, or him. Less and less sure of what right he had to be on the scene but unable to withdraw. Even at home, while he worked at his desk or cleaned up the house or shovelled snow when necessary, some ticking metronome in his mind was fixed on Meadowlake, on his next visit. Sometimes he seemed to himself like a mulish[7] boy conducting a hopeless courtship, sometimes like one of those wretches who follow celebrated women through the streets, convinced that one day these women will turn around and recognize their love.

He made a great effort, and cut his visits down to Wednesdays and Saturdays. Also he set himself to observing other things about the place, as if he was a sort of visitor at large, a person doing an inspection or a social study.

Saturdays had a holiday bustle and tension. Families arrived in clusters. Mothers were usually in charge, they were like cheerful but insistent sheepdogs herding the men and children. Only the smallest children were without apprehension. They noticed right away the green and white squares on the hall floors and picked one color to walk on, the other to jump over. The bolder ones might try to hitch rides on the back of wheelchairs. Some persisted in these tricks in spite of scolding, and had to be removed to the car. And how happily, then, how readily, some older child or father volunteered to do the removing, and thus opt out of the visit.

It was the women who kept the conversation afloat. Men seemed cowed[8] by the situation, teenagers affronted. Those being visited rode in a wheelchair or stumped along with a cane, or walked stiffly, unaided, at the procession's head, proud of the turnout but somewhat blank-eyed, or desperately babbling, under the stress of it. And now surrounded by a variety of outsiders these insiders did not look like such regular people after

---

7. **mulish** Stubborn. 8. **cowed** Intimidated.

all. Female chins might have had their bristles shaved to the roots and bad eyes might be hidden by patches or dark lenses, inappropriate utterances might be controlled by medication, but some glaze remained, a haunted rigidity — as if people were content to become memories of themselves, final photographs.

Grant understood better now how Mr. Farquar must have felt. People here — even the ones who did not participate in any activities but sat around watching the doors or looking out the windows — were living a busy life in their heads (not to mention the life of their bodies, the portentous shifts in their bowels, the stabs and twinges every-where along the line), and that was a life that in most cases could not very well be described or alluded to in front of visitors. All they could do was wheel or somehow propel themselves about and hope to come up with something that could be displayed or talked about.

There was the conservatory to be shown off, and the big television screen. Fathers thought that was really something. Mothers said the ferns were gorgeous. Soon every-body sat down around the little tables and ate ice cream — refused only by the teenagers, who were dying of disgust. Women wiped away the dribble from shivery old chins and men looked the other way.

There must be some satisfaction in this ritual, and perhaps even the teenagers would be glad, one day, that they had come. Grant was no expert on families.

No children or grandchildren appeared to visit Aubrey, and since they could not play cards — the tables being taken over for the ice cream parties — he and Fiona stayed clear of the Saturday parade. The conservatory was far too popular then for any of their intimate conversations.

Those might be going on, of course, behind Fiona's closed door. Grant could not manage to knock, though he stood there for some time staring at the Disney birds with an intense, a truly malignant dislike.

Or they might be in Aubrey's room. But he did not know where that was. The more he explored this place, the more corridors and seating spaces and ramps he discovered, and in his wanderings he was still apt to get lost. He would take a certain picture or chair as a landmark, and the next week whatever he had chosen seemed to have been placed somewhere else. He didn't like to mention this to Kristy, lest she think he was suffering some mental dislocations of his own. He supposed this constant change and rearranging might be for the sake of the residents — to make their daily exercise more interesting.

He did not mention either that he sometimes saw a woman at a distance that he thought was Fiona, but then thought it couldn't be, because of the clothes the woman was wearing. When had Fiona ever gone in for bright flowered blouses and electric blue slacks? One Saturday he looked out a window and saw Fiona — it must be her — wheeling Aubrey along one of the paved paths now cleared of snow and ice, and she was wearing a silly woolly hat and a jacket with swirls of blue and purple, the sort of thing he had seen on local women at the supermarket.

The fact must be that they didn't bother to sort out the wardrobes of the women who were roughly the same size. And counted on the women not recognizing their own clothes anyway.

They had cut her hair, too. They had cut away her angelic halo. On a Wednesday, when everything was more normal and card games were going on again, and the women in the Crafts Room were making silk flowers or costumed dolls without anybody hanging around to pester or admire them, and when Aubrey and Fiona were again in evidence so that it was possible for Grant to have one of his brief and friendly and maddening conversations with his wife, he said to her, "Why did they chop off your hair?"

Fiona put her hands up to her head, to check.

"Why — I never missed it," she said.

He thought he should find out what went on on the second floor, where they kept the people who, as Kristy said, had really lost it. Those who walked around down here holding conversations with themselves or throwing out odd questions at a passerby ("Did I leave my sweater in the church?") had apparently lost only some of it.

Not enough to qualify.

There were stairs, but the doors at the top were locked and only the staff had the keys. You could not get into the elevator unless somebody buzzed for it to open, from behind the desk.

What did they do, after they lost it?

"Some just sit," said Kristy. "Some sit and cry. Some try to holler the house down. You don't really want to know."

Sometimes they got it back.

"You go in their rooms for a year and they don't know you from Adam. Then one day, it's oh, hi, when are we going home. All of a sudden they're absolutely back to normal again."

But not for long.

"You think, wow, back to normal. And then they're gone again." She snapped her fingers. "Like so."

In the town where he used to work there was a bookstore that he and Fiona had visited once or twice a year. He went back there by himself. He didn't feel like buying anything, but he had made a list and picked out a couple of the books on it, and then bought another book that he noticed by chance. It was about Iceland. A book of nineteenth-century watercolors made by a lady traveller to Iceland.

Fiona had never learned her mother's language and she had never shown much respect for the stories that it preserved — the stories that Grant had taught and written about, and still did write about, in his working life. She referred to their heroes as "old Njal" or "old Snorri."[9] But in the last few years she had developed an interest in the country itself and looked at travel guides. She read about William Morris's trip, and Auden's. She didn't really plan to travel there. She said the weather was too dreadful. Also — she said — there ought to be one place you thought about and knew about and maybe longed for — but never did get to see.

When Grant first started teaching Anglo-Saxon and Nordic Literature he got the regular sort of students in his classes. But after a few years he noticed a change. Married women started going back to school. Not with the idea of qualifying for a better job or for any job but simply to give themselves something more interesting to think about than their usual housework and hobbies. To enrich their lives. And perhaps it followed naturally that the men who taught them these things would become part of the enrichment, that

---

9. **Njal, Snorri** Njal is the hero of an Icelandic epic; Snorri Sturlusun (1178–1241) was a Norse mythologist and historian.

these men would seem to these women more mysterious and desirable than the men they still cooked for and slept with.

The studies chosen were usually Psychology or Cultural History or English Literature. Archaeology or Linguistics was picked sometimes but dropped when it turned out to be heavy going. Those who signed up for Grant's courses might have a Scandinavian background, like Fiona, or they might have learned something about Norse mythology from Wagner or historical novels. There were also a few who thought he was teaching a Celtic language and for whom everything Celtic had a mystic allure.

He spoke to such aspirants fairly roughly from his side of the desk.

"If you want to learn a pretty language, go and learn Spanish. Then you can use it if you go to Mexico."

Some took his warning and drifted away. Others seemed to be moved in a personal way by his demanding tone. They worked with a will and brought into his office, into his regulated, satisfactory life, the great surprising bloom of their mature female compliance, their tremulous hope of approval.

He chose the woman named Jacqui Adams. She was the opposite of Fiona — short, cushiony, dark-eyed, effusive. A stranger to irony. The affair lasted for a year, until her husband was transferred. When they were saying good-bye, in her car, she began to shake uncontrollably. It was as if she had hypothermia. She wrote to him a few times, but he found the tone of her letters overwrought and could not decide how to answer. He let the time for answering slip away while he became magically and unexpectedly involved with a girl who was young enough to be her daughter.

For another and more dizzying development had taken place while he was busy with Jacqui. Young girls with long hair and sandalled feet were coming into his office and all but declaring themselves ready for sex. The cautious approaches, the tender intimations of feeling required with Jacqui were out the window. A whirlwind hit him, as it did many others, wish becoming action in a way that made him wonder if there wasn't something missed. But who had time for regrets? He heard of simultaneous liaisons, savage and risky encounters. Scandals burst wide open, with high and painful drama all round but a feeling that somehow it was better so. There were reprisals — there were firings. But those fired went off to teach at smaller, more tolerant colleges or Open Learning Centers, and many wives left behind got over the shock and took up the costumes, the sexual nonchalance of the girls who had tempted their men. Academic parties, which used to be so predictable, became a minefield. An epidemic had broken out, it was spreading like the Spanish flu. Only this time people ran after contagion, and few between sixteen and sixty seemed willing to be left out.

Fiona appeared to be quite willing, however. Her mother was dying, and her experience in the hospital led her from her routine work in the registrar's office into her new job. Grant himself did not go overboard, at least in comparison with some people around him. He never let another woman get as close to him as Jacqui had been. What he felt was mainly a gigantic increase in well-being. A tendency to pudginess that he had had since he was twelve years old disappeared. He ran up steps two at a time. He appreciated as never before a pageant of torn clouds and winter sunset seen from his office window, the charm of antique lamps glowing between his neighbors' living-room curtains, the cries of children in the park at dusk, unwilling to leave the hill where they'd been tobogganing. Come summer, he learned the names of flowers. In his classroom, after coaching by his nearly voiceless mother-in-law (her affliction was cancer of the throat), he risked reciting and then translating the majestic and gory ode, the head-ransom, the Hofuolausn,[10] composed to honor King Eric Blood-axe by the skald[11] whom that king had condemned to death. (And who was then, by the same king — and by the power of poetry — set free.) All applauded — even the peaceniks in the class whom he'd cheerfully taunted earlier, asking if they would like to wait in the hall. Driving home that day or maybe another he found an absurd and blasphemous quotation running around in his head.

And so he increased in wisdom and stature —

And in favor with God and man.[12]

That embarrassed him at the time and gave him a superstitious chill. As it did yet. But so long as nobody knew, it seemed not unnatural.

He took the book with him, the next time he went to Meadowlake. It was a Wednesday. He went looking for Fiona at the card tables and did not see her.

A woman called out to him, "She's not here. She's sick." Her voice sounded self-important and excited — pleased with herself for having recognized him when he knew nothing about her. Perhaps also pleased with all she knew about Fiona, about Fiona's life here, thinking it was maybe more than he knew.

"He's not here either," she said.

Grant went to find Kristy.

"Nothing, really," she said, when he asked what was the matter with Fiona. "She's just having a day in bed today, just a bit of an upset."

Fiona was sitting straight up in the bed. He hadn't noticed, the few times that he had been in this room, that this was a hospital bed and could be cranked up in such a way. She was wearing one of her high-necked maidenly gowns, and her face had a pallor that was not like cherry blossoms but like flour paste.

Aubrey was beside her in his wheelchair, pushed as close to the bed as it could get. Instead of the nondescript open-necked shirts he usually wore, he was wearing a jacket and a tie. His natty-looking tweed hat was resting on the bed. He looked as if he had been out on important business.

To see his lawyer? His banker? To make arrangements with the funeral director?

Whatever he'd been doing, he looked worn out by it. He too was gray in the face.

They both looked up at Grant with a stony, grief-ridden apprehension that turned to relief, if not to welcome, when they saw who he was.

Not who they thought he'd be.

They were hanging on to each other's hands and they did not let go.

The hat on the bed. The jacket and tie.

It wasn't that Aubrey had been out. It wasn't a question of where he'd been or whom he'd been to see. It was where he was going.

Grant set the book down on the bed beside Fiona's free hand.

"It's about Iceland," he said. "I thought maybe you'd like to look at it."

"Why, thank you," said Fiona. She didn't look at the book. He put her hand on it.

"Iceland," he said.

---

10. **Hofuolausn** "Head's Ransom," a poem created and recited for King Eirik Bloodaxe by Egill Skalla-Grimsson, a prisoner, to save his life. 11. **skald** Viking court poet (in this case, Egill). 12. **And ... man** Luke 2:52.

She said, "Ice-land." The first syllable managed to hold a tinkle of interest, but the second fell flat. Anyway, it was necessary for her to turn her attention back to Aubrey, who was pulling his great thick hand out of hers.

"What is it?" she said. "What is it, dear heart?"

Grant had never heard her use this flowery expression before.

"Oh, all right," she said. "Oh, here." And she pulled a handful of tissues from the box beside her bed.

Aubrey's problem was that he had begun to weep. His nose had started to run, and he was anxious not to turn into a sorry spectacle, especially in front of Grant.

"Here. Here," said Fiona. She would have tended to his nose herself and wiped his tears — and perhaps if they had been alone he would have let her do it. But with Grant there Aubrey would not permit it. He got hold of the Kleenex as well as he could and made a few awkward but lucky swipes at his face.

While he was occupied, Fiona turned to Grant.

"Do you by any chance have any influence around here?" she said in a whisper. "I've seen you talking to them — "

Aubrey made a noise of protest or weariness or disgust. Then his upper body pitched forward as if he wanted to throw himself against her. She scrambled half out of bed and caught him and held on to him. It seemed improper for Grant to help her, though of course he would have done so if he'd thought Aubrey was about to tumble to the floor.

"Hush," Fiona was saying. "Oh, honey. Hush. We'll get to see each other. We'll have to. I'll go and see you. You'll come and see me."

Aubrey made the same sound again with his face in her chest, and there was nothing Grant could decently do but get out of the room.

"I just wish his wife would hurry up and get here," Kristy said. "I wish she'd get him out of here and cut the agony short. We've got to start serving supper before long and how are we supposed to get her to swallow anything with him still hanging around?"

Grant said, "Should I stay?"

"What for? She's not sick, you know."

"To keep her company," he said.

Kristy shook her head.

"They have to get over these things on their own. They've got short memories usually. That's not always so bad."

Kristy was not hard-hearted. During the time he had known her Grant had found out some things about her life. She had four children. She did not know where her husband was but thought he might be in Alberta. Her younger boy's asthma was so bad that he would have died one night in January if she had not got him to the emergency ward in time. He was not on any illegal drugs, but she was not so sure about his brother.

To her, Grant and Fiona and Aubrey too must seem lucky. They had got through life without too much going wrong. What they had to suffer now that they were old hardly counted.

Grant left without going back to Fiona's room. He noticed that the wind was actually warm that day and the crows were making an uproar. In the parking lot a woman wearing a tartan pants suit was getting a folded-up wheelchair out of the trunk of her car.

The street he was driving down was called Black Hawks Lane. All the streets around were named for teams in the old National Hockey League. This was in an outlying section of the town near Meadowlake. He and Fiona had shopped in the town regularly but had not become familiar with any part of it except the main street.

The houses looked to have been built all around the same time, perhaps thirty or forty years ago. The streets were wide and curving and there were no sidewalks — recalling the time when it was thought unlikely that anybody would do much walking ever again. Friends of Grant's and Fiona's had moved to places something like this when they began to have their children. They were apologetic about the move at first. They called it "going out to Barbecue Acres."

Young families still lived here. There were basketball hoops over garage doors and tricycles in the driveways. But some of the houses had gone downhill from the sort of family homes they were surely meant to be. The yards were marked by car tracks, the windows were plastered with tinfoil or hung with faded flags.

Rental housing. Young male tenants — single still, or single again.

A few properties seemed to have been kept up as well as possible by the people who had moved into them when they were new — people who hadn't had the money or perhaps hadn't felt the need to move on to someplace better. Shrubs had grown to maturity, pastel vinyl siding had done away with the problem of repainting. Neat fences or hedges gave the sign that the children in the houses had all grown up and gone away, and that their parents no longer saw the point of letting the yard be a common run-through for whatever new children were loose in the neighborhood.

The house that was listed in the phone book as belonging to Aubrey and his wife was one of these. The front walk was paved with flagstones and bordered by hyacinths that stood as stiff as china flowers, alternately pink and blue.

Fiona had not got over her sorrow. She did not eat at mealtimes, though she pretended to, hiding food in her napkin. She was being given a supplementary drink twice a day — someone stayed and watched while she swallowed it down. She got out of bed and dressed herself, but all she wanted to do then was sit in her room. She wouldn't have taken any exercise at all if Kristy or one of the other nurses, and Grant during visiting hours, had not walked her up and down in the corridors or taken her outside.

In the spring sunshine she sat, weeping weakly, on a bench by the wall. She was still polite — she apologized for her tears, and never argued with a suggestion or refused to answer a question. But she wept. Weeping had left her eyes raw-edged and dim. Her cardigan — if it was hers — would be buttoned crookedly. She had not got to the stage of leaving her hair unbrushed or her nails uncleaned, but that might come soon.

Kristy said that her muscles were deteriorating, and that if she didn't improve soon they would put her on a walker.

"But you know once they get a walker they start to depend on it and they never walk much anymore, just get wherever it is they have to go."

"You'll have to work at her harder," she said to Grant. "Try to encourage her."

But Grant had no luck at that. Fiona seemed to have taken a dislike to him, though she tried to cover it up. Perhaps she was reminded, every time she saw him, of her last minutes with Aubrey, when she had asked him for help and he hadn't helped her.

He didn't see much point in mentioning their marriage, now.

She wouldn't go down the hall to where most of the same people were still playing cards. And she wouldn't go into the television room or visit the conservatory.

She said that she didn't like the big screen, it hurt her eyes. And the birds' noise was irritating and she wished they would turn the fountain off once in a while.

So far as Grant knew, she never looked at the book about Iceland, or at any of the other — surprisingly few — books that she had brought from home. There was a reading room where she would sit down to rest, choosing it probably because there was seldom anybody there, and if he took a book off the shelves she would allow him to read to her. He suspected that she did that because it made his company easier for her — she was able to shut her eyes and sink back into her own grief. Because if she let go of her grief even for a minute it would only hit her harder when she bumped into it again. And sometimes he thought she closed her eyes to hide a look of informed despair that it would not be good for him to see.

So he sat and read to her out one of these old novels about chaste love, and lost-and-regained fortunes, that could have been the discards of some long-ago village or Sunday school library. There had been no attempt, apparently, to keep the contents of the reading room as up-to-date as most things in the rest of the building.

The covers of the books were soft, almost velvety, with designs of leaves and flowers pressed into them, so that they resembled jewelry boxes or chocolate boxes. That women — he supposed it would be women — could carry home like treasure.

The supervisor called him into her office. She said that Fiona was not thriving as they had hoped.

"Her weight is going down even with the supplement. We're doing all we can for her."

Grant said that he realized they were.

"The thing is, I'm sure you know, we don't do any prolonged bed care on the first floor. We do it temporarily if someone isn't feeling well, but if they get too weak to move around and be responsible we have to consider upstairs."

He said he didn't think that Fiona had been in bed that often.

"No. But if she can't keep up her strength, she will be. Right now she's borderline."

He said that he had thought the second floor was for people whose minds were disturbed.

"That too," she said.

He hadn't remembered anything about Aubrey's wife except the tartan suit he had seen her wearing in the parking lot. The tails of the jacket had flared open as she bent into the trunk of the car. He had got the impression of a trim waist and wide buttocks.

She was not wearing the tartan suit today. Brown belted slacks and a pink sweater. He was right about the waist — the tight belt showed she made a point of it. It might have been better if she hadn't, since she bulged out considerably above and below.

She could be ten or twelve years younger than her husband. Her hair was short, curly, artificially reddened. She had blue eyes — a lighter blue than Fiona's, a flat robin's-egg or turquoise blue — slanted by a slight puffiness. And a good many wrinkles made more noticeable by a walnut-stain makeup. Or perhaps that was her Florida tan.

He said that he didn't quite know how to introduce himself.

"I used to see your husband at Meadowlake. I'm a regular visitor there myself."

"Yes," said Aubrey's wife, with an aggressive movement of her chin.

"How is your husband doing?"

The "doing" was added on at the last moment. Normally he would have said, "How is your husband?"

"He's okay," she said.

"My wife and he struck up quite a close friendship."

"I heard about that."

"So. I wanted to talk to you about something if you had a minute."

"My husband did not try to start anything with your wife, if that's what you're getting at," she said. "He did not molest her in any way. He isn't capable of it and he wouldn't anyway. From what I heard it was the other way round."

Grant said, "No. That isn't it at all. I didn't come here with any complaints about anything."

"Oh," she said. "Well, I'm sorry. I thought you did."

That was all she was going to give by way of apology. And she didn't sound sorry. She sounded disappointed and confused.

"You better come in, then," she said. "It's blowing cold in through the door. It's not as warm out today as it looks."

So it was something of a victory for him even to get inside. He hadn't realized it would be as hard as this. He had expected a different sort of wife. A flustered homebody, pleased by an unexpected visit and flattered by a confidential tone.

She took him past the entrance to the living room, saying, "We'll have to sit in the kitchen where I can hear Aubrey." Grant caught sight of two layers of front-window curtains, both blue, one sheer and one silky, a matching blue sofa and a daunting pale carpet, various bright mirrors and ornaments.

Fiona had a word for those sort of swooping curtains — she said it like a joke, though the women she'd picked it up from used it seriously. Any room that Fiona fixed up was bare and bright — she would have been astonished to see so much fancy stuff crowded into such a small space. He could not think what that word was.

From a room off the kitchen — a sort of sunroom, though the blinds were drawn against the afternoon brightness — he could hear the sounds of television.

Aubrey. The answer to Fiona's prayers sat a few feet away, watching what sounded like a ball game. His wife looked in at him. She said, "You okay?" and partly closed the door.

"You might as well have a cup of coffee," she said to Grant.

He said, "Thanks."

"My son got him on the sports channel a year ago Christmas, I don't know what we'd do without it."

On the kitchen counters there were all sorts of contrivances and appliances — coffeemaker, food processor, knife sharpener, and some things Grant didn't know the names or uses of. All looked new and expensive, as if they had just been taken out of their wrappings, or were polished daily.

He thought it might be a good idea to admire things. He admired the coffeemaker she was using and said that he and Fiona had always meant to get one. This was absolutely untrue — Fiona had been devoted to a European contraption that made only two cups at a time.

"They gave us that," she said. "Our son and his wife. They live in Kamloops. B.C. They send us more stuff than we can handle. It wouldn't hurt if they would spend the money to come and see us instead."

Grant said philosophically, "I suppose they're busy with their own lives."

"They weren't too busy to go to Hawaii last winter. You could understand it if we had somebody else in the family, closer at hand. But he's the only one."

The coffee being ready, she poured it into two brown-and-green ceramic mugs that she took from the amputated branches of a ceramic tree trunk that sat on the table.

"People do get lonely," Grant said. He thought he saw his chance now. "If they're deprived of seeing somebody they care about, they do feel sad. Fiona, for instance. My wife."

"I thought you said you went and visited her."

"I do," he said. "That's not it."

Then he took the plunge, going on to make the request he'd come to make. Could she consider taking Aubrey back to Meadowlake maybe just one day a week, for a visit? It was only a drive of a few miles, surely it wouldn't prove too difficult. Or if she'd like to take the time off — Grant hadn't thought of this before and was rather dismayed to hear himself suggest it — then he himself could take Aubrey out there, he wouldn't mind at all. He was sure he could manage it. And she could use a break.

While he talked she moved her closed lips and her hidden tongue as if she was trying to identify some dubious flavor. She brought milk for his coffee, and a plate of ginger cookies.

"Homemade," she said as she set the plate down. There was challenge rather than hospitality in her tone. She said nothing more until she had sat down, poured milk into her coffee and stirred it.

Then she said no.

"No. I can't do that. And the reason is, I'm not going to upset him."

"Would it upset him?" Grant said earnestly.

"Yes, it would. It would. That's no way to do. Bringing him home and taking him back. Bringing him home and taking him back, that's just confusing him."

"But wouldn't he understand that it was just a visit? Wouldn't he get into the pattern of it?"

"He understands everything all right." She said this as if he had offered an insult to Aubrey. "But it's still an interruption. And then I've got to get him all ready and get him into the car, and he's a big man, he's not so easy to manage as you might think. I've got to maneuver him into the car and pack his chair along and all that and what for? If I go to all that trouble I'd prefer to take him someplace that was more fun."

"But even if I agreed to do it?" Grant said, keeping his tone hopeful and reasonable. "It's true, you shouldn't have the trouble."

"You couldn't," she said flatly. "You don't know him. You couldn't handle him. He wouldn't stand for you doing for him. All that bother and what would he get out of it?"

Grant didn't think he should mention Fiona again.

"It'd make more sense to take him to the mall," she said. "Where he could see kids and whatnot. If it didn't make him sore about his own two grandsons he never gets to see. Or now the lake boats are starting to run again, he might get a charge out of going and watching that."

She got up and fetched her cigarettes and lighter from the window above the sink. "You smoke?" she said.

He said no thanks, though he didn't know if a cigarette was being offered.

"Did you never? Or did you quit?"

"Quit," he said.

"How long ago was that?"

He thought about it.

"Thirty years. No — more."

He had decided to quit around the time he started up with Jacqui. But he couldn't remember whether he quit first, and thought a big reward was coming to him for quitting, or thought that the time had come to quit, now that he had such a powerful diversion.

"I've quit quitting," she said, lighting up. "Just made a resolution to quit quitting, that's all."

Maybe that was the reason for the wrinkles. Somebody — a woman — had told him that women who smoked developed a special set of fine facial wrinkles. But it could have been from the sun, or just the nature of her skin — her neck was noticeably wrinkled as well. Wrinkled neck, youthfully full and up-tilted breasts. Women of her age usually had these contradictions. The bad and good points, the genetic luck or lack of it, all mixed up together. Very few kept their beauty whole, though shadowy, as Fiona had done.

And perhaps that wasn't even true. Perhaps he only thought that because he'd known Fiona when she was young. Perhaps to get that impression you had to have known a woman when she was young.

So when Aubrey looked at his wife did he see a high-school girl full of scorn and sass, with an intriguing tilt to her robin's-egg blue eyes, pursing her fruity lips around a forbidden cigarette?

"So your wife's depressed?" Aubrey's wife said. "What's your wife's name? I forget."

"It's Fiona."

"Fiona. And what's yours? I don't think I ever was told that."

Grant said, "It's Grant."

She stuck her hand out unexpectedly across the table.

"Hello, Grant. I'm Marian."

"So now we know each other's name," she said, "there's no point in not telling you straight out what I think. I don't know if he's still so stuck on seeing your — on seeing Fiona. Or not. I don't ask him and he's not telling me. Maybe just a passing fancy. But I don't feel like taking him back there in case it turns out to be more than that. I can't afford to risk it. I don't want him getting hard to handle. I don't want him upset and carrying on. I've got my hands full with him as it is. I don't have any help. It's just me here. I'm it."

"Did you ever consider — it *is* very hard for you — " Grant said — "did you ever consider his going in there for good?"

He had lowered his voice almost to a whisper, but she did not seem to feel a need to lower hers.

"No," she said. "I'm keeping him right here."

Grant said, "Well. That's very good and noble of you."

He hoped the word "noble" had not sounded sarcastic. He had not meant it to be.

"You think so?" she said. "Noble is not what I'm thinking about."

"Still. It's not easy."

"No, it isn't. But the way I am, I don't have much choice. If I put him in there I don't have the money to pay for him unless I sell the house. The house is what we own outright. Otherwise I don't have anything in the way of resources. I get the pension next year, and I'll have his pension and my pension, but even so I could not afford to keep him there and hang on to the house. And it means a lot to me, my house does."

"It's very nice," said Grant.

"Well, it's all right. I put a lot into it. Fixing it up and keeping it up."

"I'm sure you did. You do."

"I don't want to lose it."

"No."

"I'm not *going* to lose it."

"I see your point."

"The company left us high and dry," she said. "I don't know all the ins and outs of it, but basically he got shoved out. It ended up with them saying he owed them money and when I tried to find out what was what he just went on saying it's none of my business. What I think is he did something pretty stupid. But I'm not supposed to ask, so I shut up. You've been married. You are married. You know how it is. And in the middle of me finding out about this we're supposed to go on this trip with these people and can't get out of it. And on the trip he takes sick from this virus you never heard of and goes into a coma. So that pretty well gets *him* off the hook."

Grant said, "Bad luck."

"I don't mean exactly that he got sick on purpose. It just happened. He's not mad at me anymore and I'm not mad at him. It's just life."

"That's true."

"You can't beat life."

She flicked her tongue in a cat's businesslike way across her top lip, getting the cookie crumbs. "I sound like I'm quite the philosopher, don't I? They told me out there you used to be a university professor."

"Quite a while ago," Grant said.

"I'm not much of an intellectual," she said.

"I don't know how much I am, either."

"But I know when my mind's made up. And it's made up. I'm not going to let go of the house. Which means I'm keeping him here and I don't want him getting it in his head he wants to move anyplace else. It was probably a mistake putting him in there so I could get away, but I wasn't going to get another chance, so I took it. So. Now I know better."

She shook out another cigarette.

"I bet I know what you're thinking," she said. "You're thinking there's a mercenary type of a person."

"I'm not making judgments of that sort. It's your life."

"You bet it is."

He thought they should end on a more neutral note. So he asked her if her husband had worked in a hardware store in the summers, when he was going to school.

"I never heard about it," she said. "I wasn't raised here."

Driving home, he noticed that the swamp hollow that had been filled with snow and the formal shadows of tree trunks was now lighted up with skunk lilies. Their fresh, edible-looking leaves were the size of platters. The flowers sprang straight up like candle flames, and there were so many of them, so pure a yellow, that they set a light shooting up from the earth on this cloudy day. Fiona had told him that they generated a heat of their own as well. Rummaging around in one of her concealed pockets of information, she said that you were supposed to be able to put your hand inside the curled petal and feel the heat. She said that she had tried it, but she couldn't be sure if what she felt was heat or her imagination. The heat attracted bugs.

"Nature doesn't fool around just being decorative."

He had failed with Aubrey's wife. Marian. He had foreseen that he might fail, but he had not in the least foreseen why. He had thought that all he'd have to contend with would be a woman's natural sexual jealousy — or her resentment, the stubborn remains of sexual jealousy.

He had not had any idea of the way she might be looking at things. And yet in some depressing way the conversation had not been unfamiliar to him. That was because it reminded him of conversations he'd had with people in his own family. His uncles, his relatives, probably even his mother, had thought the way Marian thought. They had believed that when other people did not think that way it was because they were kidding themselves — they had got too airy-fairy, or stupid, on account of their easy and protected lives or their education. They had lost touch with reality. Educated people, literary people, some rich people like Grant's socialist in-laws had lost touch with reality. Due to an unmerited good fortune or an innate silliness. In Grant's case, he suspected, they pretty well believed it was both.

That was how Marian would see him certainly. A silly person, full of boring knowledge and protected by some fluke from the truth about life. A person who didn't have to worry about holding on to his house and could go around thinking his complicated thoughts. Free to dream up the fine, generous schemes that he believed would make another person happy.

What a jerk, she would be thinking now.

Being up against a person like that made him feel hopeless, exasperated, finally almost desolate. Why? Because he couldn't be sure of holding on to himself against that person? Because he was afraid that in the end they'd be right? Fiona wouldn't feel any of that misgiving. Nobody had beat her down, narrowed her in, when she was young. She'd been amused by his upbringing, able to think its harsh notions quaint.

Just the same, they have their points, those people. (He could hear himself now arguing with somebody. Fiona?) There's some advantage to the narrow focus. Marian would probably be good in a crisis. Good at survival, able to scrounge for food and able to take the shoes off a dead body in the street.

Trying to figure out Fiona had always been frustrating. It could be like following a mirage. No — like living in a mirage. Getting close to Marian would present a different problem. It would be like biting into a litchi nut.[13] The flesh with its oddly artificial allure, its chemical taste and perfume, shallow over the extensive seed, the stone.

He might have married her. Think of it. He might have married some girl like that. If he'd stayed back where he belonged. She'd have been appetizing enough, with her choice breasts. Probably a flirt. The fussy way she had of shifting her buttocks on the kitchen chair, her pursed mouth, a slightly contrived air of menace — that was what was left of the more or less innocent vulgarity of a small-town flirt.

She must have had some hopes, when she picked Aubrey. His good looks, his salesman's job, his white-collar expectations. She must have believed that she would end up better off than she was now. And so it often happened with those practical people. In spite of their calculations, their survival instincts, they might not get as far as they had quite reasonably expected. No doubt it seemed unfair.

---

13. litchi nut Fleshy, sweet fruit with a hard, slightly poisonous pit.

In the kitchen the first thing he saw was the light blinking on his answering machine. He thought the same thing he always thought now. Fiona.

He pressed the button before he got his coat off.

"Hello, Grant. I hope I got the right person. I just thought of something. There is a dance here in town at the Legion supposed to be for singles on Saturday night, and I am on the supper committee, which means I can bring a free guest. So I wondered whether you would happen to be interested in that? Call me back when you get a chance."

A woman's voice gave a local number. Then there was a beep, and the same voice started talking again.

"I just realized I'd forgot to say who it was. Well you probably recognized the voice. It's Marian. I'm still not so used to these machines. And I wanted to say I realize you're not single and I don't mean it that way. I'm not either, but it doesn't hurt to get out once in a while. Anyway, now I've said all this I really hope it's you I'm talking to. It did sound like your voice. If you are interested you can call me and if you are not you don't need to bother. I just thought you might like the chance to get out. It's Marian speaking. I guess I already said that. Okay, then. Good-bye."

Her voice on the machine was different from the voice he'd heard a short time ago in her house. Just a little different in the first message, more so in the second. A tremor of nerves there, an affected nonchalance, a hurry to get through and a reluctance to let go.

Something had happened to her. But when had it happened? If it had been immediate, she had concealed it very successfully all the time he was with her. More likely it came on her gradually, maybe after he'd gone away. Not necessarily as a blow of attraction. Just the realization that he was a possibility, a man on his own. More or less on his own. A possibility that she might as well try to follow up.

But she'd had the jitters when she made the first move. She had put herself at risk. How much of herself, he could not yet tell. Generally a woman's vulnerability increased as time went on, as things progressed. All you could tell at the start was that if there was an edge of it now, there'd be more later.

It gave him a satisfaction — why deny it? — to have brought that out in her. To have roused something like a shimmer, a blurring, on the surface of her personality. To have heard in her testy, broad vowels this faint plea.

He set out the eggs and mushrooms to make himself an omelette. Then he thought he might as well pour a drink.

Anything was possible. Was that true — was anything possible? For instance, if he wanted to, would he be able to break her down, get her to the point where she might listen to him about taking Aubrey back to Fiona? And not just for visits, but for the rest of Aubrey's life. Where could that tremor lead them? To an upset, to the end of her self-preservation? To Fiona's happiness?

It would be a challenge. A challenge and a creditable feat. Also a joke that could never be confided to anybody — to think that by his bad behavior he'd be doing good for Fiona.

But he was not really capable of thinking about it. If he did think about it, he'd have to figure out what would become of him and Marian, after he'd delivered Aubrey to Fiona. It would not work — unless he could get more satisfaction than he foresaw, finding the stone of blameless self-interest inside her robust pulp.

You never quite knew how such things would turn out. You almost knew, but you could never be sure.

She would be sitting in her house now, waiting for him to call. Or probably not sitting. Doing things to keep herself busy. She seemed to be a woman who would keep busy. Her house had certainly shown the benefits of nonstop attention. And there was Aubrey — care of him had to continue as usual. She might have given him an early supper — fitting his meals to a Meadowlake timetable in order to get him settled for the night earlier and free herself of his routine for the day. (What would she do about him when she went to the dance? Could he be left alone or would she get a sitter? Would she tell him where she was going, introduce her escort? Would her escort pay the sitter?)

She might have fed Aubrey while Grant was buying the mushrooms and driving home. She might now be preparing him for bed. But all the time she would be conscious of the phone, of the silence of the phone. Maybe she would have calculated how long it would take Grant to drive home. His address in the phone book would have given her a rough idea of where he lived. She would calculate how long, then add to that time for possible shopping for supper (figuring that a man alone would shop every day). Then a certain amount of time for him to get around to listening to his messages. And as the silence persisted she would think of other things. Other errands he might have had to do before he got home. Or perhaps a dinner out, a meeting that meant he would not get home at suppertime at all.

She would stay up late, cleaning her kitchen cupboards, watching television, arguing with herself about whether there was still a chance.

What conceit on his part. She was above all things a sensible woman. She would go to bed at her regular time thinking that he didn't look as if he'd be a decent dancer anyway. Too stiff, too professorial.

He stayed near the phone, looking at magazines, but he didn't pick it up when it rang again.

"Grant. This is Marian. I was down in the basement putting the wash in the dryer and I heard the phone and when I got upstairs whoever it was had hung up. So I just thought I ought to say I was here. If it was you and if you are even home. Because I don't have a machine obviously, so you couldn't leave a message. So I just wanted. To let you know.

"'Bye."

The time was now twenty-five after ten.

'Bye.

He would say that he'd just got home. There was no point in bringing to her mind the picture of his sitting here, weighing the pros and cons.

Drapes. That would be her word for the blue curtains — drapes. And why not? He thought of the ginger cookies so perfectly round that she'd had to announce they were homemade, the ceramic coffee mugs on their ceramic tree. A plastic runner, he was sure, protecting the hall carpet. A high-gloss exactness and practicality that his mother had never achieved but would have admired — was that why he could feel this twinge of bizarre and unreliable affection? Or was it because he'd had two more drinks after the first?

The walnut-stain tan — he believed now that it was a tan — of her face and neck would most likely continue into her cleavage, which would be deep, crepey-skinned, odorous and hot. He had that to think of, as he dialled the number that he had already written down. That and the practical sensuality of her cat's tongue. Her gem-stone eyes.

Fiona was in her room but not in bed. She was sitting by the open window, wearing a seasonable but oddly short and bright dress. Through the window came a heady, warm blast of lilacs in bloom and the spring manure spread over the fields.

She had a book open in her lap.

She said, "Look at this beautiful book I found, it's about Iceland. You wouldn't think they'd leave valuable books lying around in the rooms. The people staying here are not necessarily honest. And I think they've got the clothes mixed up. I never wear yellow."

"Fiona ... ," he said.

"You've been gone a long time. Are we all checked out now?"

"Fiona, I've brought a surprise for you. Do you remember Aubrey?"

She stared at him for a moment, as if waves of wind had come beating into her face. Into her face, into her head, pulling everything to rags.

"Names elude me," she said harshly.

Then the look passed away as she retrieved, with an effort, some bantering grace. She set the book down carefully and stood up and lifted her arms to put them around him. Her skin or her breath gave off a faint new smell, a smell that seemed to him like that of the stems of cut flowers left too long in their water.

"I'm happy to see you," she said, and pulled his earlobes.

"You could have just driven away," she said. "Just driven away without a care in the world and forsook me. Forsooken me. Forsaken."

He kept his face against her white hair, her pink scalp, her sweetly shaped skull. He said, Not a chance.

(2001)

Alden Nowlan (1933–1983)

In a 1975 interview, Alden Nowlan said that he found it frustrating when readers, misled by his simple and direct style, formed uncomplicated assumptions about his work. He asserted, "the biggest risk a person runs who tries to write as I do is the casual superficial glance. 'Oh, that's all there is to it,' you know. I'm always quoting Mailer who quoted Gide, who probably quoted somebody else — 'Please do not understand me too quickly.'"

Nowlan's tone is generally so honest and vulnerable that one believes he is being absolutely candid. Yet "truth" is not a static entity in his writing. In "The Seasick Sailor, and Others," for example, the reality of the imagination is different from the reality of experience, as "the woman / who has scarcely spoken to a man except her / brother / and who works in a room no larger than a / closet ... will write as well as anyone who ever lived / about vast, open spaces and the desires of / the flesh." In "Beginning," contradictory truths exist simultaneously for two lovers whose urges are "most lovely, most abhorred." Indeed, in Nowlan's writing, "truth" is various and constantly changing.

Easy conclusions should likewise not be formed about Nowlan's childhood. Born in Stanley, in Nova Scotia's Annapolis Valley, on 25 January 1933, at the height of the Depression, he was shaped by the poverty of his early years. He did not experience the conveniences of modern life until he left home, in 1952. Nowlan's mother was only 15 at the time of his birth, and when he was just a few years old, she left the family. His father was a labourer who worked for over 50 years without ever finding permanent employment. Nowlan dropped out of school in grade five, but he was a voracious reader, and he educated himself with the books he borrowed from the regional library. However, his lively intellect isolated him from his community, and the lack of companionship made him feel as though he were "living alone on an island."

Critics have made much of all this, yet Nowlan insists that his childhood "wasn't as harrowing as it sounds." He writes, "I didn't *feel* particularly poor, ignorant and isolated until I was about fifteen and the outside world, that until then had seemed half-mythical, began to be wholly real to me." Nowlan dramatizes this difference between being poor and feeling poor in "And He Wept Aloud, So That the Egyptians Heard It." The speaker lashes out at the flies in his grandfather's house because he sees "their symbolism: / Baal-Zebub, / god of the poor and out-cast." Yet he soon realizes that his grandfather has not even noticed the flies. The speaker feels immensely guilty for having shaken the older man into this awareness. He has encroached upon his grandfather's world just as he has invaded the world of the flies, and he leaves them to rebuild.

As an adolescent, Nowlan worked with his father as a mill hand and a pulpwood cutter. He also began to write. When he was 17, his first poem was published by a periodical based in Eagle Creek, Oregon, called the *Bridge*. In 1952, he left the Annapolis Valley for Hartland, New Brunswick, to work as a news editor at the *Hartland Observer*. In his free time, he wrote poetry, which he submitted to little magazines. In 1958, he published a pamphlet called *The Rose and the Puritan;* this he followed with a longer collection, *A Darkness in the Earth* (1959). By 1962, he had published *Wind in a Rocky Country* (1960), *Under the Ice* (1961), and *The Things Which Are* (1962); he had also been awarded a Canada Council Junior Arts Fellowship.

In 1963, Nowlan moved to St. John, New Brunswick, where he worked as an editor for the *Saint John Telegraph Journal*. A year later, he married Claudine Orser and became a stepfather to her son, Johnnie. Soon after that, Nowlan was diagnosed with throat cancer. He recovered, but only after undergoing three major operations, during which his thyroid and parts of his larynx were removed. He continued to write while he was sick, and in 1967, he published *Bread, Wine and Salt*, which included several poems about his hospital experiences. The same year, he was honoured with a Canada Council Arts Grant and a Guggenheim Fellowship; in 1968, *Bread, Wine and Salt* received a Governor General's Award.

There is a noticeable difference between Nowlan's early and later verse, in tone and in theme. In his mature poetry, his form is more relaxed and open, and he deals with more intimate subject matter. The forging of emotional connections between himself and his community had become a priority for him, especially after his battle with cancer. Some critics perceived immense growth in Nowlan, praising his ability to capture human feeling. But others claimed that he had lapsed into a kind of prosaic sentimentality. Responding to this criticism, the poet insisted, "to be a writer you have to run the risk of making a fool of yourself. When I run the risk of sounding prosaic I run the risk deliberately — just as I run the risk of sounding sentimental … sentimentality is very close to the things that *genuinely* move people."

In 1969, Nowlan became writer-in-residence at the University of New Brunswick. Over the following years, he published several more collections of poetry, a fictional memoir entitled *Various Persons Named Kevin O'Brien* (1973), a collection of essays called *Double Exposure* (1978), four plays, and a work of local history entitled *Campobello: The Outer Island* (1975). He also wrote columns for the *Telegraph-Journal* and the *Atlantic Advocate,* and he would remain active as a freelance journalist for the rest of his career.

Having spent the majority of his life in the Maritimes, Nowlan often focused on this region of Canada in his writing. His interest in human nature led him to write about what he saw as the specific character of the Maritime people. In "They Go Off to Seek Their Fortunes," for example, he imagines Maritimers travelling in other parts of Canada. He writes, "They tell strangers / where they're from and where they're going and how much / their second cousins make in Sudbury. They

say, / 'I'm from the island,' or 'I'm from the bay,' / as if there were only one of each in the world."
He describes their behaviour in minute detail: "They greet one another / with a meaningful
movement that is part / bow, part shrug, part nod, accompanied / by a slight pursing of the lips, /
the barest suggestion of a wink."

Indeed, because of poems like this there has been much debate as to whether Nowlan was
a regionalist poet or a universalist one. Attempting to negotiate this issue, W.J. Keith notes that
"Nowlan clearly is a regionalist, since the vast majority of his poems (even those that may sound
philosophical or even abstract) arise out a specific and intensely local matrix; on the other hand, he
is just as clearly one of those authors who … transcend the limits of their regionalism to become
writers of national and even international significance." Nowlan died on 27 June 1983.

Warren Pryor

When every pencil meant a sacrifice
his parents boarded him at school in town,
slaving to free him from the stony fields,
the meagre acreage that bore them down.

They blushed with pride when, at his graduation,
they watched him picking up the slender scroll,
his passport from the years of brutal toil
and lonely patience in a barren hole.

When he went in the Bank their cups ran over.
10   They marvelled how he wore a milk-white shirt
work days and jeans on Sundays. He was saved
from their thistle-strewn farm and its red dirt.

And he said nothing. Hard and serious
like a young bear inside his teller's cage,
his axe-hewn hands upon the paper bills
aching with empty strength and throttled rage.

(1961)

The Bull Moose

Down from the purple mist of trees on the mountain,
lurching through forests of white spruce and cedar,
stumbling through tamarack swamps,
came the bull moose
to be stopped at last by a pole-fenced pasture.

Too tired to turn or, perhaps, aware
there was no place left to go, he stood with the cattle.
They, scenting the musk of death, seeing his great head
like the ritual mask of a blood god, moved to the other end
10   of the field, and waited.

The neighbours heard of it, and by afternoon
cars lined the road. The children teased him
with alder switches[1] and he gazed at them
like an old, tolerant collie. The women asked
if he could have escaped from a Fair.

The oldest man in the parish remembered seeing
a gelded[2] moose yoked with an ox for plowing.
The young men snickered and tried to pour beer
down his throat, while their girl friends took their pictures.

And the bull moose let them stroke his tick-ravaged flanks,   20
let them pry open his jaws with bottles, let a giggling girl
plant a little purple cap
of thistles on his head.

When the wardens came, everyone agreed it was a shame
to shoot anything so shaggy and cuddlesome.
He looked like the kind of pet
women put to bed with their sons.

So they held their fire. But just as the sun dropped in the river
the bull moose gathered his strength
like a scaffolded king, straightened and lifted his horns   30
so that even the wardens backed away as they raised their rifles.
When he roared, people ran to their cars. All the young men
leaned on their automobile horns as he toppled.

(1962)

And He Wept Aloud, So That the Egyptians Heard It

In my grandfather's house
for the first time in years,
houseflies big as bumblebees
playing crazy football
in the skim-milk-coloured windows,

leap-frogging from
the cracked butter saucer
to our tin plates of
rainbow trout and potatoes, catching the bread
on its way to our mouths,   10
    mounting one another
      on the rough deal table.

---

1. **alder switches** Alder branches used as whips. 2. **gelded** Castrated.

It was not so much their filth
as their numbers and persistence and —
oh, admit this, man, there's no point in poetry
if you withhold the truth
once you've come by it —
　　　their symbolism:
　　　Baal-Zebub,[1]
20　　god of the poor and outcast,

that enraged me, made me snatch the old man's
Family Herald, attack them like a maniac,
lay to left and right until the window sills
over-flowed with their smashed corpses,
until bits of their wings
stuck to my fingers,
until the room buzzed with their terror …

And my grandfather, bewildered and afraid,
came to help me:
30　　　"never seen a year
　　　when the flies were so thick"
as though he'd seen them at all before I came!

His voice so old and baffled and pitiful
that I threw my club into the wood box and sat down
　　　and wanted to beg his forgiveness
as we ate on in silence broken only
by the almost inaudible humming
of the flies rebuilding their world.

(1967)

The Mysterious Naked Man

A mysterious naked man has been reported
on Cranston Avenue. The police are performing
the usual ceremonies with coloured lights and sirens.
Almost everyone is outdoors and strangers are conversing
　　　excitedly
as they do during disasters when their involvement is
　　　peripheral.
"What did he look like?" the lieutenant is asking.
"I don't know," says the witness. "He was naked."
10　　There is talk of dogs — this is no ordinary case

---

1. **Baal-Zebub**　Judeo-Christian demon; name means "lord of the flies."

of indecent exposure, the man has been seen
a dozen times since the milkman spotted him and now
the sky is turning purple and voices
carry a long way and the children
have gone a little crazy as they often do at dusk
and cars are arriving
from other sections of the city.
And the mysterious naked man
is kneeling behind a garbage can or lying on his belly
in somebody's garden   20
or maybe even hiding in the branches of a tree,
where the wind from the harbour
whips at his naked body,
and by now he's probably done
whatever it was he wanted to do
and wishes he could go to sleep
or die
or take
or take to the air like Superman.

(1969)

On the Barrens

"Once when we were hunting cattle
        on the barrens,"
so began many of the stories they told,
gathered in the kitchen, a fire still
        the focus of life then,
the teapot on the stove as long as
        anyone was awake,
mittens and socks left to thaw on
        the open oven door,
chunks of pine and birch piled   10
        halfway to the ceiling,
and always a faint smell of smoke
        like spice in the air,
the lamps making their peace with
        the darkness,
the world not entirely answerable
        to man.

They took turns talking, the listeners
        puffed their pipes,
he whose turn it was to speak used his   20
        as an instrument,
took his leather pouch from a pocket
        of his overalls,
gracefully, rubbed tobacco between
        his rough palms

as he set the mood, tamped it into
    the bowl
at a moment carefully chosen, scratched
    a match when it was necessary
30 to prolong the suspense. If his pipe
    went out it was no accident,
if he spat in the stove it was done
    for a purpose.
When he finished he might lean back
    in his chair so that it stood
on two legs; there'd be a short silence.

The barrens were flat clay fields,
    twenty miles from the sea
and separated from it by dense woods
40   and farmlands.
They smelled of salt and the wind
    blew there
constantly as it does on the shore
    of the North Atlantic.

There had been a time, the older men
    said, when someone had owned
the barrens but something had happened
long ago and now anyone who wanted to
    could pasture there.
50 The cattle ran wild all summer,
sinewy little beasts, ginger-coloured
    with off-white patches,
grazed there on the windswept barrens
    and never saw a human
until fall when the men came to round
    them up,
sinewy men in rubber boots and tweed caps
    with their dogs beside them.

Some of the cattle would by now have
60   forgotten
there'd been a time before they'd
    lived on the barrens.
They'd be truly wild, dangerous, the
    men would loose the dogs on them,
mongrel collies, barn dogs with the
    dispositions of convicts
who are set over their fellows,
    the dogs would go for the nose,
sink their teeth in the tender flesh,
70   toss the cow on its side,

bleating, hooves flying, but shortly
    tractable.[1]
There were a few escaped,
    it was said, and in a little while
they were like no other cattle —
    the dogs feared them,
they roared at night and the men
    lying by their camp-fires
heard them and moaned in their sleep,
    the next day tracking them   80
found where they'd pawed the moss,
    where their horns had scraped
bark from the trees — all the stories
    agreed
in this: now there was nothing to do
    but kill them.

(1977)

Austin Clarke (1934–)

Austin Chesterfield Clarke was born in Barbados in 1934 to a 16-year-old mother. Daily survival was a struggle, but Clarke's young mother recognized a precocious intelligence in her son and resolved that he would receive a good education. She enrolled him in the best schools she could afford and insisted that he channel all of his energies into his studies — this would be his one chance to escape an existence of grinding and demoralizing poverty. In the 1950s, he spent two years at Harrison College studying English literature, Latin, and Roman history, and there he was made to feel an outsider among the offspring of the island's White elite, a disillusioning experience that filled him with, he recalls, "aggression and ambition" for something better.

After graduation, Clarke taught secondary school, became involved in the Barbados Labour Party, and wrote poetry. In 1955, he moved to Toronto to study economics and political science at Trinity College, but he was aggrieved to discover that his carefully acquired fluency with the British tradition did not guarantee his acceptance in Canadian society, and his attitude towards his colonial past darkened further. His program at Trinity proved unfulfilling, and he dropped out. In 1957, he married Betty Reynolds and launched a search for a good job. Two years later, he was hired as a reporter for the *Daily Press* in Timmins, Ontario.

At this time, Clarke began to explore his Barbadian identity in writing. He also started to read the works of other West Indian writers, and they taught him the power of using dialect in fiction. Encouraged by the publication of a short story in Toronto's *Evidence* magazine, Clarke began writing fiction full time in 1962. From 1963 to 1967, at the behest of the CBC, he interviewed prominent Black political figures and artists, including Malcolm X and Imamu Amiri Baraka (LeRoi Jones). In this charged period, Clarke also helped to establish the Toronto Caribana Festival and participated in demonstrations against racial discrimination.

Beginning in the late 1960s, Clarke accepted a number of visiting lecturer appointments at several prestigious American universities (including Yale, Brandeis, and Duke), and at these

---

1. **tractable** Manageable.

institutions he met many Black intellectuals and activists. At this point, he had two published novels under his belt — *Survivors of the Crossing* (1964) and *Amongst Thistles and Thorns* (1965) — both set in Barbados. *Survivors* is a straightforward narrative about a cane-cutter's failed attempt to organize a strike. Employing vivid imagery and rhythmic Barbadian speech patterns, it dramatizes the way colonialism has crippled Barbadian society. *Amongst Thistles and Thorns,* the coming-of-age story of a Barbadian boy, is a first-person narrative constructed of flashbacks, dream sequences, and internal monologues. It also introduces character types who reappear in Clarke's later works: courageous women forced into demeaning labour and socially powerless men emasculated by their failure as providers. Most prominently, however, *Amongst Thistles and Thorns* is a condemnation of the destructive effect of colonial education on Black identity, a topic Clarke would return to in his memoir of his school years, *Growing Up Stupid Under the Union Jack* (1980) and in a fictionalized autobiography, *Proud Empires* (1986).

In 1967, Clarke published *The Meeting Point,* the first novel of his Toronto trilogy. Along with *Storm of Fortune* (1971) and *The Bigger Light* (1975), it shows how the identity problems faced by postcolonial peoples are not solved by immigrating to Canada — in fact, they are exacerbated. The stories focus on a group of West Indian domestics and their community of spouses, lovers, friends, acquaintances, and employers, and it traces the immigrants' search for elusive stability in an environment fraught with bigotry, casual cruelties, and dead ends — a place where material success often demands the sacrifice of one's heritage. Although the trio of novels are realist in style, Clarke has stated that fiction is "a concentrated assault upon realism, changing the realism to suit the idiosyncrasies of the person created." Throughout the series, however, the author projects a narrative impartiality that suggests his analysis of race relations is objective — or, as he puts it, "nonvindictive."

From 1974 to 1975, Clarke was a cultural attaché to the Barbadian embassy in Washington. He then became general manager of the Caribbean Broadcasting Corporation and an advisor to the prime minister of Barbados. He based his satirical novel *The Prime Minister* (1977) on his experiences as a civil servant. Despite the frustrations and disappointments he endured in this capacity, he would run in an Ontario provincial election and work for the Canadian Immigration and Refugee Board (1988–1993).

After publishing the autobiographical *Growing Up Stupid* and *Proud Empires,* Clarke produced the novel *The Origin of Waves* (1997). In it, two Barbadians rediscover one another and exchange memories in a Toronto bar. The complex narrative structure reaches into their separate pasts, intertwining them. Clarke followed this with the novel *The Question* (1999). *The Polished Hoe,* published in 2002, is Clarke's most acclaimed novel to date, winning the Giller Prize and the Commonwealth Writers Prize. Set on the West Indian island of Bimshire in 1952, the story unfolds over the course of 24 hours. Mary Mathilda confesses to the murder of Mr. Bellfeels, to whom she has been mistress and employee for over 30 years. Clarke intersperses her statement to the local policeman, whom she has known all of her life, with recollections of her crime and her past, in the process evoking a history tainted by slavery as well as the post-colonial Black diaspora. Told in Mary's voice, blending Bahamian dialect with standard English, the novel reflects the sensuality and richness of Caribbean culture.

Though best known for his novels, Clarke has produced seven collections of short fiction. In the introduction to the most political of these, *Nine Men Who Laughed* (1986), he says that he wants his stories to "destroy the definitions that *others* have used to portray so-called immigrants, black people." Clarke has also published several works of non-fiction, including the pamphlet *Public Enemies: Police Violence and Black Youth* (1992), a memoir of Sam Selvon called *A Passage Back Home* (1994), and *Pigtails 'n' Breadfruit: The Rituals of Slave Food, A Barbadian Memoir* (1999).

In 1998, Clarke was made a member of the Order of Canada, and the following year, he was awarded the W.O. Mitchell Literary Prize. He continues to live in Toronto.

A Short Drive

This Saturday afternoon at three, with the first real light, and the first cleansed skies washed so blue after the rains, there was a constant breeze and upon the breeze came the coolness and the strong smell of patchouli and summer flowers. It was tantalizing as the smell of saltiness and of fresh fish brought out of the sea on a beach in Barbados. Gwen was a woman with a touch of this saltiness on her breath. And the woman back in Toronto, on Lascelles Boulevard, she too carried a trace of the smell; but her real smell was of lavender.

Calvin sat nobly and like an emperor, stiff, with the pride of new ownership, behind the steering wheel, reduced to the size of a toy wheel against his imposing size, of the Volkswagen which he had just bought, "hot," he said, for seventy-five dollars. He called it his "Nazzi bug." And he too looked clean, as the skies. His skin, on his arms up to his elbow; his neck, right into the V of the black dashiki[1]; his legs from below the knee and down to his toes, all this flesh was "oiled, Jack," he said. He had "shampooled" his round-shaped Afro, and it was glistening although he had used Duke Greaseless Hairdressing for Men. He had given me some, but my hair did not accept the same shine as his. He looked clean. And he looked like a choice piece of pork seasoned and ready for the greased pan and the oven. He would not like this comparison. But I have to say he looked clean.

His legs were thin and had no calf. This was the first time I had seen Calvin dressed in anything but grey-green plaid trousers and blue blazer. Today, he was in cut-down jeans, which gave me the first glimpse of his legs. I could not believe his long stories over beer in frosted mugs and Polish sausages, about playing running back for the college football team. The black dashiki with its V-neck and sleeves trimmed in black, red, and green, tempered somewhat the informality of his casual dress.

"Pass the paper bag. Glove compartment. Take a sip, brother," he said, holding the steering wheel with his left hand, and a Salem in the other. "And keep your motherfucking head *down*. In case the *man*."

The puttering VW rollicked over the gravel road at a slow pace. Its dashboard was cluttered with additional things which Calvin had installed. Cassette tape deck *and* eight-track tape deck, AM-FM radio and a shortwave radio, a contraption which looked like a walkie-talkie, and two clocks. One he said gave the time in the Northeast, and the other the time of the South, of the city of Birmingham, Alabama, where we were, and had been together since the beginning of the summer semester. Looking at this dashboard, I was reminded of the glimpse of the cockpit of the plane in which I had travelled two months earlier from Toronto to teach the summer course, in which Calvin was an auditor. I had never heard that term before. But Calvin was my student. And as the heavy Southern nights spun themselves out into greater monotony, he became my guide to where the action was, and almost my friend. The noisy VW moved slowly over the rutted road, and I could see in the distance the sights and substance and large properties, the grace and the Southern architecture in the residential exclusive district

---

1. **dashiki** A West African shirt for men, loosely fitting, with embroidery on the collar and sleeves.

we were passing on our right hand. We were driving so slow that I thought it was a mistake, that Calvin lived in this district, and that we would turn into one of the magnificent gates, any minute now. One of these mansions I had passed, in the dark last night, searching in vain for Gwen's apartment. I now could see the structure I had mistaken for the house. It is a white-painted gazebo with Grecian pillars. And in the gazebo is a child's swing and a white-painted iron chair and iron table. There is no child in the swing, now.

"Ripple?" Calvin said, after a large gulp, wiping away the evidence with the hand that held the Salem, just in case. "This is the real shit." Last night, at the bar with the frosted beer mugs and huge Polish sausages, Calvin ordered two gigantic T-bone steaks and two bottles of Mommessin red wine, both of which I paid for. This Ripple wine, which cut into my throat like a razor blade dipped in molasses, must have been a ritualistic thing to go with his cut-down jeans and the dashiki. Or it might have been cultural. I took a second swig from the bottle hardly concealed in the brown paper bag, and squeezed my eyes shut, and shook my head. "This be the real shit," he said, disagreeing with my reaction.

On our left hand, we were passing men, slow as in a shutter speed to capture even the whiz of movement, men bent almost in the shape of hairpins, doubled-up, close to the grass which was so green it looked blue; they resembled gigantic mushrooms painted onto the sprawling lawns, in their broad-brimmed hats necessary to protect themselves against the brutality of the sun, and the exhaustion that the humidity seemed to sap from their bodies. I could see them move their hands as if they were playing with the grass, but at the completion of each piston-like action, the effort in their movements appearing slowed down by the encompassing grandeur of the afternoon. When this act of slashing the blades of grass was completed, a shower of grass lifted itself on impact, a blade of steel flashed like lightning, and the grass was scattered harmlessly over the lawn.

"Mexicans," Calvin said, as if he didn't like Mexicans, and with some bitterness; and as if he was pronouncing a sentence not only on them, but also upon their labour.

They were soaked to their backs and their shapeless clothes made them look Indian to me. But the formlessness of their shirts and pants was the designer's label of hard labour. They could have been Chinese standing up to their ankles in water and growing rice.

"Amerrikah! Home of the motherfucking *free*, Jack!" Calvin said. "This South's shaped my personality, and this university's fucked it up, with the result that I don't know *who* I am. I was happier in Atlanta on 'Fayette Street in the black area." I did not know what he was talking about. I was admiring the Mexicans. They looked now like figures in a tableau, painted against the bluegrass lawns; and the manner in which they had thrown out the proficiency and precision of the power mower by the bare strength of their hands made me deaf to Calvin's protestations. And it seemed that they were showing the superiority of their knowledge of nature and things and their own past, in this temporary but scorching menialness of labour, and expressing their own protest, as Calvin was with words, with the violence of their muscular arms.

Calvin was now slouched behind the steering wheel, as if the Ripple had suddenly changed the composition of the blood in his veins. His right arm was extended so that his fingers just touched the steering wheel, as if we wanted no closer association with it. As if he was despising the wheel, the VW, along with the statement he had just made about rejection. "What the fuck am I getting a college education for? And writing academic papers on reductionism for?" I still did not understand what he was talking about. But he brought the VW to an uncertain stop. We were under a tree. Calvin had told me the name of this tree. They were all over the South; and they cluttered the path through the woods to a building on campus where convocations were held. The first time Calvin told me the name of this tree, he told me about a woman named Billie Holiday. I did not know whom he was talking about; but he started to sing the words of a song, "Strange Fruit," and we were inhaling the sweet smell of the magnolia trees and the wind was unforgiving in bringing the strong Southern smell to our nostrils. I would have trouble remembering the name of the woman who sang this song, and more often the title of the song slipped my memory. But I remembered one line, only one line of the song about Southern trees. *Blood on the leaves, and blood at the root.* Calvin had sung the entire song from memory. He sang it off-key. And now, this afternoon, the VW stopped uncertainly because he had never accumulated the thirty dollars to fix the brakes, we were stopped under a tree. I looked up into the thick branches of the tree under which we had walked to the place which served beer in frosted glasses and huge Polish sausages, and only the raindrops accumulated on the leaves dropped into my face.

"What kind of tree is that? I don't think we have these trees in Toronto."

"The size, or the name?" Calvin asked.

The mouth of the Ripple bottle was in his mouth. A little of the wine escaped his lips, and it ran slowly down into his beard, but I could still see the rich colour of red, like blood.

"The name."

"Poplar. This be a poplar tree."

We were shaded by the tree. And I was beginning to feel great relief from the humidity which embraced me like a tight-fitting shirt.

Southern trees bear strange fruit.

Calvin's singing had not improved in the month since I had first heard it. I smiled at his rendition.

Black bodies hanging in the Southern breeze.

We remained in the shade, and I could feel the breeze, making my body cool, as if I was being dipped slowly into seawater. I was comfortable. But Calvin was not: sadness appeared in his eyes. His lips formed themselves into a sneer. He moved his body, and the bottle of Ripple became heavy and caused the seat and the leather to cry out. The leather on the seats of the VW was the most valuable feature of the old rumbling automobile. He moved his body in the small space we shared, and I could smell his perspiration, and his breath laden with the menthol from the Salems, and the sickening sweetness of the Ripple.

"Dualism, my brother," he said. He leaned over, took the bottle from me, and drained it dry. "What the fuck? I've seen the ass-whuppings in Selma, Bamma, Little Rock."[2]

The breeze stopped. In the languor of the afternoon we were once more lumbering over the road, which turned to hard, dried, uncared-for-dirt. It was sad. The sadness was like the sudden fall of dust under the low-hanging trees, when the scent of magnolia rises like shimmering zzz's you see, if you kneel down, rising from a hot tarred road.

"What do you want to be, then? What do you want to make of your life, if not be a scholar?"

"Miles!"

---

2. **Selma, Bamma, Little Rock** Selma, Alabama, and Little Rock, Arkansas; both cities were sites of significant protest marches during the early days of the American Civil Rights Movement.

"Away from Birmingham?"

"Miles Davis!"[3]

I did not know what to say to this: Calvin's feelings and fantasies seemed to inflate his thin body, making him large and grand and strong as the running back he always boasted he was when he played for his college football team.

"As Barry White says, bro', *let the music play*. Let the music play on. Let the motherfucking music *play*, Jack! I be Miles. I am Miles. Or, I am Coltrane. Trane. I am Otis. I'm Nina Simone. And I am 'Retha![4] And I am on stage at the biggest theatre in the South, but not the Opry,[5] and *thousands* are out there in the dark screaming my name. My toon. My voice. My riffs. My trumpet. My tenor horn. It's the same fucking thing, Jack. Let the music *play*."

The smell of Calvin's Salems, the old odour that had settled inside the VW, filled my nostrils; and with these smells was the smell of clothes that are wet, and drying in the back seat. I could also smell the oiliness of Southern-fried chicken from Chicken Box Number Two. We had eaten chicken many times in the VW, deliberately not eating in restaurants, as if we were still suffering from the segregation of accommodation. Eating in the VW allowed us greater ease of checking out the beautiful women coming out of the women's residence in their pink shorts, and white shorts, and blue shorts. Perhaps we had left some uneaten boxes in the back seat.

We were by ourselves on this road of dried mud now, running by a field in which grew something I could not recognize. Corn came to mind, as this place shared the geography of that island where I came from. Corn came naturally to mind, but there was not the lusciousness in the endless spread of green that made me feel we were adrift on the sea; we were alone, although far to the right I could see the smudged whiteness of the pillars and other parts of the architecture from colonial times; and closer on our right, some small houses, and from them sentinels[6] of rising white smoke that turned blue as it reached high above our heads. And still the sun was shining.

And then in the distance, like the call of my mother's voice, miles away, but only a few yards from the makeshift cricket pitch we had gouged out of our own mud to play the game, my mother's voice calling me home for dinner: rice cooked with few split peas because there was a war on, and served with salt fish from the Grand Banks of New-foundland, thin and flat and full of bones, but transformed by the improvised wisdom in these things of my mother, and soaked in lard oil, tangy from the cheap butter it was said we imported from Australia, to us in a commonwealth of nations, friends; and tomatoes picked from our backyard; that welcoming call, that wrenched me from my friends and playmates, disappointed that I had not hit the ball for six, or four, or even a single in the hot, hot-competing afternoon. So did this sound come to me, unanchored in this vastness of living, thriving green, in the rickety VW with a stranger, drinking Ripple concealed in a brown paper bag from the eyes of the sheriff.

In the blue-white distance I heard the heavy rumbling of a train. A freight train. I followed the train as it wriggled its way like a worm through the greenness on the land, as it moved like a large worm, and in my mind, through the history its approach was unravelling and through the myths of trains, men on the run travelled on them; men

---

3. Miles Davis Jazz musician, trumpeter, composer (1926–1991). **4. Coltrane, Otis, Nina Simone, 'Retha** John Coltrane (jazz musician, 1926–1967), Otis Redding (soul singer, 1941–1967), Nina Simone (jazz and soul musician and activist, 1933–2003), and Aretha Franklin (soul singer, born 1942). **5. Opry** *The Grand Ole Opry* was a radio and television program broadcast live from Nashville, Tennessee, the cradle of American country music. **6. sentinels** Guards or watchmen.

fleeing women and wives and child payments hid on them; and men in chains and those who escaped from chain gangs were placed on them. The best blues were written about them. The rumbling of this train, like the rumbling of that train in the cowboy movies of the Old West, seemed interminable as a toothache that comes at sunset and that lasts throughout the groaning night, like a string pulled by a magician from the palm of one hand, like the worm you pull from the soft late grass-covered ground that does not end, and that makes you late to go fishing. I heard a siren. Or a whistle? There were so many sirens I was hearing this summer in Birmingham because of civil rights and fights with sheriffs, that I sometimes mistook the sound. I heard a siren. The siren killed the sound of the train.

"Police cruiser?" I asked Calvin. "Or ambulance?"

"In this neighbourhood, could be either. Both. Chitlins and hog maws.[7] One goes with the other."

"Cops coming through the grass?" I still did not know what was planted in the growing vastness surrounding me.

Calvin lit another Salem. The VW was immediately filled with smoke. This lasted for one moment. Then, it was filled with a tingling, sweet, and bitter smell. It was not the Salem that Calvin had lighted. It was not a Salem. But he filled his lungs with the smoke, and then shot two unbroken thin and fierce jets of white from his nostrils, making him look, in that moment, like a walrus; speaking through smoke and coughing at the same time as if his thinness meant tuberculosis, and with his breath held, he said, "What can we in the South do, with this dualism thing? Before it fucks us up?"

"Education could never be so destructive."

"Spoken like a true West Indian who knows nothing about the South, and Amerrikah."

"Education is freedom."

"Spoken like a man who's never lived in Birmingham, or in any city in the South!"

"You need education."

"We need a black thang. We don't need no education, brother. A black thang. And a black conclusion."

"And what about your seminar on reductionism?"

"Shit! Can you see me discussing that at my mother's Sunday dinner table? She be calling the cops thinking this nigger's crazy!"

The VW became quiet, still filled with the strange smoke. The words Calvin was using were larger than the capacity of the small "Bug," too bulging with the possibility of explosion and violence. I went back to the Mexicans on the lawns. I began to have the sensation of being rocked from side to side. But it could have been the vibration of the freight train, which had not yet come to its end from within the tunnel created by the endless fields of growing things. Looking outside through the steam of smoke from Calvin's fag,[8] I saw pieces of cement and concrete and paper blowing along the narrow sidewalks and into the street. The light here was harsh. There were no flowers. There were no poplar trees. The trees here were stubby, but they did not shade the blinding, shimmering waves that came off the surface of the sidewalk. I wished, at that moment, that I was back in Toronto among the red brick, the dirty red brick and cobblestones, passing shops that sold the *New York Times* and the *Times Literary Supplement*, and that

---

7. **Chitlins and hog maws** "Chitlins" are pig's intestines, prepared as food in the South; "hog maws" are pig's stomach stuffed with potatoes and sausage. 8. **fag** Cigarette.

sold Condor and Erinmore pipe tobacco and French cigarettes and French leathers or letters — I never knew which was the proper term — things I was accustomed to, and knew how to handle, among the buildings that were not so imposing and the short streets. Space there was more manageable. I wished for the softness of streets shaded by small trees, and lined with cars, many of which belonged to students and were broken into; with garbage pails of green and other wrecks; and I wanted the softness of the northern seductive and betraying nights, and to be among the unthreateningness of broken-down homes with cloth at their windows and with unpainted boards nailed across the windows and the doors, derelicts[9] from the nights of rioting in the cities in the North — Detroit, New York, Washington, D.C.; and missed by Toronto.

Calvin must have been buried in similar thoughts of wanting to be elsewhere, must have come to a conclusion of similar importance, or to some agreeable compromise with his thoughts about education, for he straightened his back, and the vigour and youth of his years came back into his body. His eyes were bright again; and the whiteness in them shone. The dashiki he was wearing made him look noble like an emperor, stiff and proud with knowing where he was.

"This is the very last time I be laying this paranoid shit on you, brother. You are my guest here in this city. I am a Southerner, and we Southerners 're hospitable people. I'm gonna show y'all some real Southern shit now, y'all!"

He had lit a Salem before he spoke. He was the kind of man who could not make a serious statement before he had first lit a cigarette. Smoke streamed through his nostrils, and he looked like a walrus again.

"I'm an Amerrikan. This is my motherfucking country."

"You were born here, man."

"I'm a Southerner. So, let's have some Ripple. Let's drink this shit."

It was a long road. There were no street lights. Dust swirled round the tires of the VW, as it pierced its single weak headlamp through the oncoming darkness. "If the man don't get me for this Ripple, he sure's shit gonna get me for this light!" The moon was a dark sliver of lead, far off to the right. Calvin was still in his cut-down jeans and dashiki. But I had changed. I was in white. White Levi's and a white dashiki, bought from the Soul Brother Store. When I went into the store, dark and musty and smelling of old cigars, the owner greeted me, "Brother, come in, brother!" He charged me twenty dollars more than the price I had seen on the same clothes in two other, white stores on the same integrated street. But I did not divulge this to Calvin.

"Lay it on me, brother!" Calvin had said in admiration and in approval, when he picked me up.

"Be cool, man," I had told him, trying hard to be cool.

"Gwen's opened your nose!" he said, meaning that Gwen was educating me in the ways of the South.

"Shee-it!" I said, hoping it came out right, and heavy, and properly Southern.

"Shit!" Calvin said. His speech was like a crisp bullet in my chest.

Now, driving along this road, in the middle, there was no dividing line, and if there was, we could not see it; in the swirling flour of this thin road, cramped in the VW, with the smell of smoke, a trace of leather, and the acrid[10] and sweet languor[11] from the fumes

---

9. **derelicts** Abandoned residences. 10. **acrid** Bitter or sharp. 11. **languor** Dreaminess or laziness.

of Ripple, making less speed than the rattle of the muffler suggested, and hitting stones in the middle of the road, the two of us, rebellious and drunk in our joy, were like escaped prisoners; but I, like a man redeemed, Gwen had said, when I was at the door like a gentleman, "Shee-it, you ain't leaving here to walk those dark streets, at this hour, man. This is the South," saying it with a pronounced West Indian accent; we were now, Calvin and I, screaming and hollering as if we were both born in the ecstasy of mad Southern Saturday nights in Birmingham.

Calvin slapped an eight-track tape into the player. "My Favorite Things" came out. The hymn-like introduction, like a chant, coiled around the jazz solo, reminded me of matins at St. Matthias Anglican Church in Barbados, and especially evensong and service.[12] I could picture myself walking in that peaceful sacred light, one hour after the sun had gone down behind the tall casuarinas, trees that reached the sky, in my imagination, when there was slice of a moon, like this one here in Birmingham, and walking between thick green sugar canes in my black John Whites that kicked up almost as much dust as the tires of this old VW. And each time Coltrane repeated the main statement of the tune, I could hear and recall the monotony of the tolling bells. There, my mother walked beside me, in contented sloth of age, of sickness, and of Christianity. Here, I bent my neck to the charmed pull of the music.

Calvin is silent beside me. This music is his. I have heard this music before, probably, all the places and things and colours that the music is showing me I have faced in Toronto. The tape is scratched badly.

In the distance, pointed out to us by the weak left headlamp, is a barn, or a factory, perhaps something that was once used as a portable camp for soldiers. Soldiers are always on my mind in Birmingham, this summer. The Civil War, a magazine swears in its cover story, is about to be fought again: white people versus black people. Soldiers with muskets, vertical straps of leather aslant their shoulders, fighting for the *other* cause. And the flag of their confederation with its own two vertical blue slashes across its broad bloodied shoulder, signifying something different. This building in the shortening distance sits in a square stubbornness in the middle of the single headlamp, with no grace of architecture like the white-painted gazebo. From this distance it is black. It soon looks brown. Light from inside the building is being forced through small windows that are covered by blinds made of sacks for sugar, not for Bohemian style, but from economy. And as we get nearer still, the truth of its dimension, size, and colour, is exposed to us.

Coltrane's tenor saxophone reminds me of the singing of old women, repeating the verse of the hymn as if their age has crippled their recollection of succeeding verses. So, I begin to think again of my mother, leading the song at the Mothers' Union service, going over it again. "Rock of Ages." This saxophone is not speaking of such desperation, though.

We are approaching Gwen's wooden house.

Calvin stops the VW, for no reason; and I realize he's always doing this, but this time he parks it, and it rocks forward and backward, just before the engine dies. We are now bathed in the light from the naked fluorescent bulb on Gwen's porch. I did not see this light the night of the party. The rain was too heavy that night.

"You're really into Trane playing 'Love Supreme'!" he said.

"Not 'My Favorite Things'?"

---

12. **matins, evensong, service** Anglican Church rituals.

"'Love Supreme,' brother."

How many other things in this city of Birmingham, this South, in this culture, in this short time here had I got wrong? I had heard a train, but was there a train rolling through the green fields like a lawnmower? I had seen a moon, but now that we were stopped, there was no moon.

"A *love supreme, a love supreme, a love supreme,*" Calvin said. "Nineteen times Trane chants it." I can see movement in Gwen's house, at the side, for the bedrooms are at the side.

Calvin got out, leaving me in the car, slammed the door shut, and stood beside the car. A splattering of water hit the gravel. I imagined steam rising. I could smell the sting of the water. And then I too got out, and shook my legs, each one, to straighten the seams of my tight-fitting jeans. Calvin was still peeing and shaking. Some men can pee as long as horses. But it looked more as if he was being shaken by the peeing, in short spasms of delight and relief. Each time I thought that Calvin was finished, he shook again. I was wrong about the name of the tune on the eight-track. I was wrong about my mother. It was not "Rock of Ages." It was not even the walk through the country lane going to St. Matthias Anglican Church for evensong and service that had pulled those memories from me. It was I myself. As a chorister in the St. Michael's Cathedral, singing a song of praise. Was it Easter I was thinking about? Easter? Or Christmas? Rogations Day? Quinquagesima Sunday?[13] Could it have been Lent? *O, all ye beasts of the sea, praise ye the Lord. O, all you fish of the sea, praise ye the Lord?* Could it have been that? Yes. That was the comparison of the repetition which the beauty of the saxophone ought to have brought back.

"Every time I hear Trane playing 'Love Supreme,' I gotta have me at least *one* smoke, and … " He seemed short of breath, all of a sudden. His words were cut short. Nevertheless, there was a lingering, a drawing out of the enunciation of his words. His words would be cut off. In mid-sentence. As if he were struggling. For breath. And trying to talk at the same time. The middle door on the porch opened and light flowed weakly out, and I could see Calvin's eyes, now red and fierce and, at the same time, peaceful, and filled with water. But he was not in tears. He was happy. "Want a joint? Can you handle this shit, brother?"

"I'm cool, man."

"Shit'll kill you. It's a motherfucker. It kills the black artist, and the black musician."

"I'm cool, man."

"Know something? Let's not waste time with these chicks. Forget Gwen." I was wondering what kind of a man Calvin was. "Let's talk, brother. You're going back up to Toronto, next week, and when you're gone, ain't nobody I can talk to, nobody on this campus, in this city, in this fucking country. Let's talk. And I gonna cut out all these 'motherfuckers' and 'shits' in my speech, and just talk." I was sure he was reading my mind. But I was getting accustomed to his speech, peppered with his Southern or American violence. "I've been checking you out back there, while you were talking to yourself, as Trane was grooving. Bet you didn't realize you were talking to yourself? 'Love Supreme' is a motherfuc — is a fantastic piece, freaks me out too, every time I listen to it. At least five times a day. And if I have a joint, shee — well, it's fantastic." He

---

13. **Rogations Day, Quinquagesima Sunday** Holy Sundays in the Anglican faith.

took the last, deep, noisy pull on the cigarette, now no longer than his fingernail. "'Love Supreme' brings back memories of something my grandmother used to hum, just after she lit the kerosene lamps every evening. Some white folks calls this shit a canticle.[14] Took me years to stop confusing canticle with cuticle. Heh-heh! But, anyhow. This canticle thing has a Latin name. Man! I kicked more ass, I was superior to everybody in my class in Latin in high school. Hate the thing now, though. But I know it all, by heart. Had to learn it by heart. Been learning it by heart from hearing my grandmother, singing it for years. Listen. *O, all ye works of the Lord, bless ye the Lord: praise him, and magnify him forever.* Want to hear more?"

"Didn't know you were Anglican."

"Baptist! To the bone. But I read that shit in a book that had words like *works, nights, days, whales, water,* etcetera, etcetera, and all were spelled with a capital letter. Isn't that something? The English be strange motherfuckers. Strange people. In the South, right here in this city of Birmingham, we worship the English, culturally I mean. The English use colons like Coltrane uses the E-flat! Baptist to the bone! Baptist to the bone. And anti-English, except culturally." He threw the marijuana cigarette, now smaller than his fingernail, through the window. The VW's engine started as if the whole car was about to explode. It stuttered, and finally, it turned over. "Life is better without chicks around. Sometimes. We're going to the Stallion Club, where there's the best rib sandwiches and fried chicken in the whole city of Birmingham! If not in the whole South!"

Pandemonium,[15] sweet as pecan pie and ice cream, struck me full in the face, the moment the door of the Stallion Club was opened, when Calvin pushed me inside, first. The room was dark. Bodies were moving. The laughter was loud and sweet and black and jocular and exaggerated. Smoke was rising and swirling. And above the lighter darkness of the bodies in the room, the smoke remained there like halos. The music was climbing the walls. Music such as this I had never heard. It was like a baptism, a final submergence in the hidden, secret beauty of the South. Loud and full, enunciating each vowel, each nuance possible of behaviour, each instrument, each riff. I heard a voice pleading, *"Didn't I do it, baby? Didn't I? Didn't I do it, baby?"* and I looked towards the stage, in the deeper darkness there, through the large, slow-moving dancers, expecting to see Aretha Franklin in the flesh. What a victory it would be, to know her, in this thick-fleshed Southern, warm night! I was overcome by the music. I could feel my entire body relax. I could smell the odours around me. I could feel my blood. I could feel the difference, and the meaning of my presence in the South. The fried chicken. The bar-becued ribs. The tingling, sweet nausea of burnt hair. The cosmetics and lotions in the glassy, bushy "pompadoos," as Calvin called them, on the fat, healthy jowls of the men and women dancing. I could feel my own body give off a stifled exhaust of smell. I could feel the sweat and the excitement under my armpits. A housefly was in the room. It came and rested on my top lip, and I did not brush it away. I was, for the first time, at home in the noise, the smells, the fragrance, the sounds and the voice of this city of Birmingham. And they all made me nervous, as they made me good. *"Didn't I do it, baby? Didn't I ... "* I was like a man drowning in this foam of a wave that one moment ago had been wafting me in its freshness; I was moving towards the front of the swaying crowd that was coupled in its own sweetness. I looked into their faces. And those faces

---

14. **canticle** Song with a Biblical text. 15. **Pandemonium** Chaos.

that were not buried into the necks and shoulders of men and women wore flat expressions. Masks. No one was smiling. No one was grinning. No one was laughing as he danced. No teeth showed in this relaxed, coagulating, heavy, and soft coupling of the music with the voice. It was as if the voice was giving them a message they all knew and desired. I could feel and taste the powerfulness in the large room. It was like a country. A country of men and women, all of the same colour, the same breathing. And this became my baptism: I had never imagined it was possible to be in a room so large with only black people. Never in Toronto. Never even in Barbados. I looked around to see, just in case. And there was none, not one white person. It was a beautiful sensation, and it frightened me. This is why I thought of powerfulness. And now I knew what it meant. I could feel it in my blood. Two large women, heavy in their thighs, heavy in their bosoms, heavy in their arms, heavy in their waists, each one about fifty-five years old, were tied together in the slow almost unmoving dance; their breasts pressed against each other, thighs glued together beneath their miniskirts, looking like logs of mahogany polished to a high magnificent sheen, arms lassoed to arms like tentacles, or in a Boston crab, and with the weight of their waists pressed together, begrudging space and denying any man's hand from forcing itself between their impenetrable love, close as if they were Siamese; love for the music and for the voice that pumped this love from one into the other, blood through veins, these two women moved in their heaviness like oil on shining glass, oblivious to the fact that there were hundreds dancing along with them. They moved as if they were on ice. They moved, only because I had seen them leave one spot small as a dime, and occupy another dime's area, not that they themselves could ever know that they had moved. They were close to me now, and I stood for a moment and watched them. I watched them grinding out their satisfaction and their ageless joy in this heavy, segregated world, in this black section of this city, safe amongst numbers, and amongst blackness created through the dance. *Didn't I do it, baby?*; a black world and a black poem which the dance itself had formed and had drawn a circle around. "This is a black world," Calvin said, having to shout to be heard.

I was now only three paces from the stage. I stood. I had to stand, for the bodies were not moving now. They were grinding. I was the only one who moved. I was the only one out of the rhythm. Inching to the stage, I was the only one out of place.

"*Didn't I do it, baby?*"

The face of the singer was bathed in black perspiration. It was like the water of baptism and revival. And it was growing out of the body, like strength. Not dripping like an exertion. The thin, tight body looked as if it was being tormented. I could see this through the slits of space in the crowd as the dancers moved. I could see it as a slice of fish, a slice of a human being, slithering in the shimmering sequins on the long dress that was like an extra skin. She was bathed in the white material of the dress, like a dolphin. "*Didn't I do it, baby?*"

"This sister can whup Aretha's ass any … " And Calvin's voice was blocked out, for a moment, by the passing of the two women between us. " … any mother — any day!" Here in this room, I needed space even to hear. The song came to a perspiring end. It was a soft end. And it was followed by an explosion of applause. Handkerchiefs, fingers, and Kleenexes came out to repair the cheeks, and wipe away the beads that had damaged the neckline and the collar and the forehead for the duration of that lovemaking rendition. And before the women and men had completed the renovation of their cosmetics, the mermaid of a woman on the stage began another song. "A *midnight train to Georgia* … " Without warning, without even a desire to join in this dance and in this circle, for I was out of place, inarticulate, foreign, without speech and gesticulation, one of the fat ladies took me into her arms. It was like a mother knowing before the expression of pain is moaned, how to take her child into the safety of her breast and bosom. I sank deep and comfortable in the billows of her love, as her arms wrapped my smaller body in embrace so much like my mother's that I felt I could fall off into a sweet slumber and surrender myself to her; except that the song was raging through the magnolia and pine and poplar woods of a land that held such frightening memories. And Calvin was there to witness my surrender, and perhaps, in a seminar on black behaviour, live to tell the story. But she held me close. She held me tight. She held her left arm round my waist, and her right hand on the softness of my bottom. I began to travel all those miles between the never-ending rails of steel, going from one place I did not know, to a place which was even farther removed from my present; but to a place which was identifiable, as I was able to *know* where I am now. And so, I buried myself in her flesh, her perfume acting as a mild chloroform, and I found that Gwen and the woman in Toronto climbed into the sweet delirium along with the woman holding me, and I paid no regard to those two encumbrances, and allowed myself to be moved so very slowly by her, by her body that was guiding me, and by her blood which I thought I could taste. But that would have been, in addition to the unseemly, unnatural acts, incest. I was dancing with my mother. The smell of her body, and the strength in her legs, which were tightened round my left leg, was like the tightness of a thick towel after a bath deep in winter. I could hardly breathe. But I could just as easily have died in her arms.

The housefly I had seen earlier returned and lighted on the woman's mouth. She pursed her lips, unwilling to release one hand and let go of my body; and the fly fled. It probably had learned, through its ugly leaden antennae, what thunderous violence her anger would give rise to, in the slap the woman would have used.

Her lips were rouged in deep red. Like the blood inside her body which I felt I could feel and taste. But I was not entirely passive in my enjoyment. My eight fingers were pressed deeply into her soft flesh. With difficulty I tried to move to the music, in my own slow, sweet time. It was like poetry; and I thought of poetry. *And green and golden I was huntsman and herdsman …*

"Are you screwing me, nigger?" she asked. And then laughed. A breath of Jack Daniels came to my nostrils when she spoke. I could feel her weight. I had made a wrong step, and her weight fell upon me. And I wondered what it would be like, if by accident, I were to make another wrong step, and she were to fall on top of me. "You want me?" She whispered this into my ear. I smelled her lipstick. I smelled her Jack Daniels again. "You're screwing me, ain't you?" Her mouth was at my ear. I smelled her perfume, and the cosmetics and the treatment in her processed hair. She tightened her grip on me. She tightened her grip more. My breathing became more difficult. And then she groaned, in a short spasm. *My wishes raced through the house-high hay, and nothing I cared … that time allows.* "You like me, don't you, small-island man?"

Whatever Georgia was, whatever was the ruggedness of its landscape, whether of rocks or of stones, green fields of sugar cane or of cotton and corn, the concluding journey was before me. The singer was washed in perspiration, pouring out of her body with a sensual righteousness; the sequins in her dress moved as she breathed, from her ankles to her covered arms, like pistons on the very train that was pulling into Georgia, long after midnight. *Oh as I was young and easy in the mercy of her means, time held me green and dying though I sang in my chains like the sea.*

"I want you, nigger. I have to have you."

I could feel it. I could feel the soft inside of her thighs. I was hard. The singer was coming home. Two sequined arms dropped at her side, in victory like that which concludes exhaustion of the flesh. And sudden so, the strong feeling thundered down. The rain had arrived.

"You want me, don't ya? I want *you*."

"No, I don't want you," I said.

"Well, fuck it! Nigger, you's *mine!*"

"*Clovis!*" It was Calvin, like a referee forcing himself between two locked boxers. "Clovis! Take your motherfucking hands off the brother! The brother's with me, motherfucker!" And Calvin ripped at Clovis's head, as if he was delivering a jab to the face. And when Calvin's hand returned from the face, in it was the wig which had contained such allure and fragrance of Duke Greaseless Hairdressing for Women. His head was shaven bald, and was shining and he was shaking with anger; and he said in a huskier voice, "Shit, Cal! I thought the nigger was mine!"

"Motherfucker!" Calvin pushed him off.

A few men and women danced close to us, looked at me and danced away. I stood looking at Clovis's shining head.

"Motherfucker, this is a Yale professor!"

"I could've *swear*, Cal, honey, the nigger was mine. I am very sorry, sir, I am very sorry," Clovis said, offering me his hands. I remembered his hands were very soft. But by this time, I was feeling the eruption in my bowels; and Calvin, sensing this, and intent upon freeing me from this assault, this offence, and knowing that I had lusted after the wrong person, was easing me with some force through the thick of the crowd, to the entrance. On the way out, I barely recognized Clovis's voice, as he stood where he was, saying, "I knew the nigger looked strange, as if he didn't belong here, weren't one of us, weren't from the South, so what the fuck was I supposed to think?"

I could not wait until I was on the gravel patch in front of the entrance of the Stallion Club, before the vomit spewed down on my white dashiki, onto my white cotton Levi's, into my shoes, with the noise and the slime and the bad taste, and Calvin talking and talking.

"Shit, brother, couldn't you *tell?*"

"How?"

"Didn't you see the motherfucker didn't have no breasts? Couldn't you see?"

"How? I was mesmerized by the woman singing 'Midnight Train to Georgia.'"

"That motherfucker was a man too, brother!" The vomit punctuated whatever else he was about to say. It was coming out with pain and with violence, as if I was trying to rip something awful, something vile, some sin, some hurt clean from my insides.

"I was in love with the woman singing 'Midnight Train.'"

"The woman singing is also a man," Calvin said. Pity and disappointment in me registered in his explanation. "The woman is a motherfucking man, brother! This be the South. Birmingham. In the South, it be so fucked up, you can't tell one motherfucker from the next."

"I thought the man was a woman."

"It's a motherfucking *man*, Jack! A *man!*"

He lit a Salem. "Sure's hell ain't Toronto, Jack!"

(1992)

Leonard Cohen (1934–)

Leonard Cohen was born in 1934, in the affluent Montreal neighbourhood of Westmount. He started to write poetry and play the guitar at 16, and in 1951 he formed a country and western band — the Buckskin Boys. He studied at McGill University, winning the MacNaghten Prize for poetry, and he graduated with a B.A. in 1955. While at McGill, Cohen took classes with F.R. Scott and Louis Dudek, and these well-established poets encouraged Cohen to write. Dudek was involved with the preparation and editing of the McGill Poetry Series, and in 1956, Cohen's first collection of poetry, *Let Us Compare Mythologies,* was published as volume one of the project.

The collection dwells on tradition and romance, but it also introduces some later Cohen themes, like violence and self-sabotage. In "Poem," he writes that he "heard of a man / who says words so beautifully / that if he only speaks their name / women give themselves to him." Implying that this man will steal his lover, Cohen establishes the recurring subject of his own cuckolding. In "Lovers," the tone is grimmer because the lovers are separated not by a seductive poet but by soldiers during the Holocaust: "He tried to kiss her burning breasts / As she burned in the fire."

After leaving McGill, Cohen enrolled in a literature program at Columbia University, but in New York he wrote more than he studied. He won a Canada Council grant in 1959 and another two years later; in 1961, he travelled to Cuba and was there during the Bay of Pigs invasion, a sign of his willingness to explore foreign cultures and forms of political and cultural resistance. Cohen also bought a house on the Greek island of Hydra and lived there intermittently over the next seven years. This island refuge also provided the source of inspiration for many of Cohen's celebratory and frequently self-interrogating love poems.

With *The Spice-Box of Earth* (1961), Cohen's style transformed from lush neo-Romantic to terse modernist. He was motivated by his mentor Irving Layton, who argued that poets should never anchor themselves in one style. The influence of Cohen's other notable precursor, A.M. Klein, appears in several poems that focus on the Jewish tradition (such as "Out of the Land of Heaven"). Layton's anger and Klein's despair over the Holocaust filtered into the younger poet's work, darkening it. In "A Kite Is a Victim," for example, a child's toy becomes a symbol of the tethered spirit — "you can always haul it down / to tame it in your drawer." The collection recorded Cohen's transition to a bleak adult world. *Flowers for Hitler* (1964) reveals an unflinching, even cynical imagination. The poet admits, "I have lied … I have conspired against love … I have tortured." He implies that an even worse apocalypse than the Holocaust is imminent; North Americans feared that the 1962 Cuban missile crisis would propel the world into nuclear war. In "Style," the atoms in a nuclear bomb have a foreboding "silence like the space / between insects in a swarm / … and [the bomb] is aimed at us." Later, in "How to Speak Poetry" (1978), Cohen mocks his own assumptions about the transcendent powers of the poet, anchoring his cynicism in relation to a post-Holocaust world in which ideas about truth, morality, and artistic value have all been called into question.

In 1965, the National Film Board of Canada released the documentary *Ladies and Gentleman … Mr. Leonard Cohen,* and Cohen's reputation as the country's leading poet was set. Despite this rise to poetic prominence, however, Cohen's attention was focused elsewhere. In 1963, he had published a novel entitled *The Favourite Game,* which traced the development of Lawrence Breavman, a poet in search of the "highest beauty." Breavman's interest in modernist poetry is reflected in the novel's economical style, and Cohen's interest in formal experimentation is evident in the combination of prose sections, lists, diary entries, letters, and the narrative's episodic structure. Its originality notwithstanding, *The Favourite Game* was eclipsed by Cohen's second novel, an extravaganza of styles and forms.

Published in 1966, *Beautiful Losers* had been written in 1964 during a writing binge fuelled by hashish and amphetamines. Two of the main characters question the validity of history: one is a historian frustrated by the way documents prevent him from accessing the past, and the other is an anarchist who insists on inventing the past. The other two main characters, the historian's wife and Catherine Tekakwitha, a 17th-century female Iroquois saint, raise questions about the value of self-sacrifice; they show that martyrdom is ultimately inspired by social and sexual oppression. A hyperactive, politically controversial, and sporadically pornographic novel, it mercilessly criticized Jesuit missionaries and the Canadian government for their implicit and explicit promotion of conservative moral codes. In tone, it was highly spiritual but deeply irreverent. In form, it ranged from stream-of-consciousness prose, through devotional poetry, to comic-book advertisements. Because of these qualities — and the depiction of graphic sex among its bisexual characters — *Beautiful Losers* was both a risky publishing venture and a startlingly fresh postmodern experiment.

Regardless of all of his successes, Cohen was dissatisfied with his career. Announcing to his friends that he would become the Canadian Bob Dylan, he moved to New York City and joined its artistic subculture. His first album, *Songs of Leonard Cohen* (1967), sold well and put him in contact with performers such as Judy Collins, Janis Joplin (the subject of "Chelsea Hotel #2"), and Dylan. His next books of poetry, the slim *Parasites of Heaven* (1966) and *Selected Poems: 1956– 1968* (1968) were spinoff successes: *Selected Poems* sold 200,000 copies in its first three months. When it was chosen to receive a Governor General's Award, Cohen declined, saying "the poems themselves forbid it absolutely." Later, in 1993, he would accept a Governor General's Award for the performing arts, not for poetry.

Cohen moved to Nashville to record *Songs from a Room* — another hit — in 1968. From 1971 to 1984 he released seven albums, but they were not as successful as his first two. Between tours — and between relationships with famous women such as Joplin, Joni Mitchell, and Rebecca De Mornay — Cohen began to visit a Zen Buddhist monastery in Mount Baldy, California, and it would become his frequent retreat. Years later, in 1996, he was ordained a monk with the name *Jikan,* meaning "Silent One."

Fame, however, weighed heavily on Cohen. He was frequently depressed. In 1972, he released another poetry collection, *The Energy of Slaves*. In one of its many untitled poems, he writes: "This is a threat / Do you know what a threat is / I have no private life / You will commit suicide / or become like me." These poems are mostly stripped of poetic niceties such as rhyme, traditional form, and punctuation. Instead, they focus on tone and convey resentfulness, disaffection, and anger. With each book, Cohen has changed his style and form, and *Death of a Ladies' Man* (1978) is the most radical example. Most of the pieces are prose poems. Many of them are followed by vicious critiques by a fictional reviewer. Cohen was interested in undermining himself as an artist — even the reviewer's praise has caveats or is tainted by cliché. Layton once said that Cohen was "a narcissist who hates himself."

With the release of *I'm Your Man* (1988) and *The Future* (1992), Cohen re-emerged as an influential musician. Then, in 1993, he published a major collection of his poems and songs, *Stranger Music*. He altered or rearranged some of the poems, especially from *Death of a Lady's Man,* and claimed to be happier with them. By including songs alongside poems, he demonstrated that he sees them as connected genres.

Cohen turned 50 in 1984 and published *Book of Mercy*, which has one psalm for each of his years. An unassuming, meditative collection, it reacquainted Cohen's readers with his Jewish heritage. Its companion, *Book of Longing* (2006), did not appear for another 22 years. He was prompted to publish it after a former manager allegedly defrauded him of several million dollars.

Dedicated to Layton, this bestseller includes Cohen's line drawings of nude women and of himself as a dour-looking old man. In *Book of Longing*, preoccupied, as usual, with sex and love, Cohen yearns for youth in the face of age.

Poem

I heard of a man
who says words so beautifully
that if he only speaks their name
women give themselves to him.

If I am dumb beside your body
while silence blossoms like tumours on our lips
it is because I hear a man climb the stairs
and clear his throat outside our door.

(1956)

I Have Not Lingered in European Monasteries

I have not lingered in European monasteries
and discovered among the tall grasses tombs of knights
who fell as beautifully as their ballads tell;
I have not parted the grasses
or purposefully left them thatched.

I have not released my mind to wander and wait
in those great distances
between the snowy mountains and the fishermen,
like a moon,
or a shell beneath the moving water.   10

I have not held my breath
so that I might hear the breathing of G-d,
or tamed my heartbeat with an exercise,
or starved for visions.
Although I have watched him often
I have not become the heron,
leaving my body on the shore,
and I have not become the luminous trout,
leaving my body in the air.

I have not worshipped wounds and relics,   20
or combs of iron,
or bodies wrapped and burnt in scrolls.

I have not been unhappy for ten thousand years.
During the day I laugh and during the night I sleep.
My favourite cooks prepare my meals,

my body cleans and repairs itself,
and all my work goes well.

(1961)

Style

I don't believe the radio stations
of Russia and America
but I like the music and I like
the solemn European voices announcing jazz
I don't believe opium or money
though they're hard to get
and punished with long sentences
I don't believe love
in the midst of my slavery I
10   do not believe
I am man sitting in a house
on a treeless Argolic island[1]
I will forget the grass of my mother's lawn
I know I will
I will forget the old telephone number
Fitzroy seven eight two oh
I will forget my style
I will have no style
I hear a thousand miles of hungry static
20   and the old clear water eating rocks
I hear the bells of mules eating
I hear the flowers eating the night
under their folds
Now a rooster with a razor
plants the haemophilia gash across
the soft black sky
and now I know for certain
I will forget my style
Perhaps a mind will open in this world
30   perhaps a heart will catch rain
Nothing will heal and nothing will freeze
but perhaps a heart will catch rain
America will have no style
Russia will have no style
It is happening in the twenty-eighth year
of my attention
I don't know what will become
of the mules with their lady eyes
or the old clear water
40   or the giant rooster

---

1. **Argolic island** Classical islands in the Mediterranean Sea that were visited by Jason on the ship *Argo*.

The early morning greedy radio eats
the governments one by one the languages
the poppy fields one by one
Beyond the numbered band
a silence develops for every style
for the style I laboured on
an external silence like the space
between insects in a swarm
electric unremembering
and it is aimed at us   50
(I am sleepy and frightened)
it makes toward me brothers

(1964)

What I'm Doing Here

I do not know if the world has lied
I have lied
I do not know if the world has conspired against love
I have conspired against love
The atmosphere of torture is no comfort
I have tortured
Even without the mushroom cloud
still I would have hated
Listen
I would have done the same things   10
even if there were no death
I will not be held like a drunkard
under the cold tap of facts
I refuse the universal alibi

Life an empty telephone booth passed at night
and remembered
like mirrors in a movie palace lobby consulted
only on the way out
like a nymphomaniac who binds a thousand
into strange brotherhood   20
I wait
for each one of you to confess

(1964)

Suzanne[1]

Suzanne takes you down
to her place near the river
you can hear the boats go by

---

1. **Suzanne** Suzanne Verdal, Montreal dancer and wife of sculptor Armand Vaillancourt; "Suzanne" was first published as a poem, though Cohen later turned it into a song.

you can spend the night beside her
And you know that she's half crazy
but that's why you want to be there
and she feeds you tea and oranges
that come all the way from China
And just when you mean to tell her
10   that you have no love to give her
she gets you on her wavelength
and she lets the river answer
that you've always been her lover
> *And you want to travel with her*
> *you want to travel blind*
> *and you know that she can trust you*
> *for you've touched her perfect body*
> *with your mind*

And Jesus was a sailor
20   when he walked upon the water
and he spent a long time watching
from his lonely wooden tower
and when he knew for certain
only drowning men could see him
he said All men will be sailors then
until the sea shall free them
but he himself was broken
long before the sky would open
forsaken, almost human
30   he sank beneath your wisdom like a stone

(1967)

Famous Blue Raincoat

It's four in the morning, the end of December. I'm writing you now just to see if you're better. New York is cold but I like where I'm living. There's music on Clinton Street all through the evening. I hear that you're building your little house deep in the desert. You're living for nothing now. I hope you're keeping some kind of record. *Yes, and Jane came by with a lock of your hair. She said that you gave it to her the night that you planned to go clear. Did you ever go clear?*

The last time we saw you you looked so much older. Your famous blue raincoat was torn at the shoulder. You'd been to the station to meet every train but then you came home without Lili Marlene. And you treated my woman to a flake of your life. And when she came back she was nobody's wife. *I see you there with a rose in your teeth, one more thin gypsy thief. Well, I see Jane's awake. She sends her regards.*

And what can I tell you my brother my killer? What can I possibly say? I guess that I miss you. I guess I forgive you. I'm glad that you stood in my way. If you ever come by here for Jane or for me, I want you to know that your enemy is sleeping. I want you to know that his woman is free. *Yes, and thanks for the trouble you took from her eyes. I thought it was there for good, so I never tried.*

And Jane came by with a lock of your hair. She said that you gave it to her that night that you planned to go clear.

Sincerely, L. Cohen.

(1971)

The Poems Don't Love Us Any More

The poems don't love us any more
they don't want to love us
they don't want to be poems
Do not summon us, they say
We can't help you any longer

There's no more fishing
in the Big Hearted River
Leave us alone
We are becoming something new

They have gone back into the world   10
to be with the ones
who labour with their total bodies
who have no plans for the world
They never were entertainers

I live on a river in Miami
under conditions I cannot describe
I see them sometimes
half-rotted half-born
surrounding a muscle
like a rolled-up sleeve   20
lying down in their jelly
to make love with the tooth of a saw

(1972)

How to Speak Poetry

Take the word butterfly. To use this word it is not necessary to make the voice weigh less than an ounce or equip it with small dusty wings. It is not necessary to invent a sunny day or a field of daffodils. It is not necessary to be in love, or to be in love with butterflies. The word butterfly is not a real butterfly. There is the word and there is the butterfly. If you confuse these two items people have the right to laugh at you. Do not make so much of the word. Are you trying to suggest that you love butterflies more perfectly than anyone else, or really understand their nature? The word butterfly is merely data. It is not an opportunity for you to hover, soar, befriend flowers, symbolize beauty and frailty, or in any way impersonate a butterfly. Do not act out words. Never act out words. Never try to leave the floor when you talk about flying. Never close your eyes and jerk your head to one side when you talk about death. Do not fix your burning eyes on me when you speak about love. If you want to impress me when you speak about love put your hand in your pocket or under your dress and play with yourself. If ambition and the hunger for applause have driven you to speak about love you should learn how to do it without disgracing yourself or the material.

What is the expression which the age demands? The age demands no expression whatever. We have seen photographs of bereaved Asian mothers. We are not interested in the agony of your fumbled organs. There is nothing you can show on your face that can match the horror of this time. Do not even try. You will only hold yourself up to the scorn of those who have felt things deeply. We have seen newsreels of humans in the extremities of pain and dislocation. Everyone knows you are eating well and are even being paid to stand up there. You are playing to people who have experienced a catastrophe. This should make you very quiet. Speak the words, convey the data, step aside. Everyone knows you are in pain. You cannot tell the audience everything you know about love in every line of love you speak. Step aside and they will know what you know because they know it already. You have nothing to teach them. You are not more beautiful than they are. You are not wiser. Do not shout at them. Do not force a dry entry. That is bad sex. If you show the lines of your genitals, then deliver what you promise. And remember that people do not really want an acrobat in bed. What is our need? To be close to the natural man, to be close to the natural woman. Do not pretend that you are a beloved singer with a vast loyal audience which has followed the ups and downs of your life to this very moment. The bombs, flame-throwers, and all the shit have destroyed more than just the trees and villages. They have also destroyed the stage. Did you think that your profession would escape the general destruction? There is no more stage. There are no more footlights. You are among the people. Then be modest. Speak the words, convey the data, step aside. Be by yourself. Be in your own room. Do not put yourself on.

This is an interior landscape. It is inside. It is private. Respect the privacy of the material. These pieces were written in silence. The courage of the play is to speak them. The discipline of the play is not to violate them. Let the audience feel your love of privacy even though there is no privacy. Be good whores. The poem is not a slogan. It cannot advertise you. It cannot promote your reputation for sensitivity. You are not a stud. You are not a killer lady. All this junk about the gangsters of love. You are students of discipline. Do not act out the words. The words die when you act them out, they wither, and we are left with nothing but your ambition.

Speak the words with the exact precision with which you would check out a laundry list. Do not become emotional about the lace blouse. Do not get a hard-on when you say panties. Do not get all shivery just because of the towel. The sheets should not provoke a dreamy expression about the eyes. There is no need to weep into the handkerchief. The socks are not there to remind you of strange and distant voyages. It is just your laundry. It is just your clothes. Don't peep through them. Just wear them.

The poem is nothing but information. It is the Constitution of the inner country. If you declaim it and blow it up with noble intentions then you are no better than the politicians whom you despise. You are just someone waving a flag and making the cheapest appeal to a kind of emotional patriotism. Think of the words as science, not as art. They are a report. You are speaking before a meeting of the Explorers' Club of the National Geographic Society. These people know all the risks of mountain climbing. They honour you by taking this for granted. If you rub their faces in it that is an insult to their hospitality. Tell them about the height of the mountain, the equipment you used, be specific about the surfaces and the time it took to scale it. Do not work the audience for gasps and sighs. If you are worthy of gasps and sighs it will not be from your appreciation of the event but from theirs. It will be in the statistics and not the trembling of the voice or the cutting of the air with your hands. It will be in the data and the quiet organization of your presence.

Avoid the flourish. Do not be afraid to be weak. Do not be ashamed to be tired. You look good when you're tired. You look like you could go on forever. Now come into my arms. You are the image of my beauty.

(1978)

Closing Time

So we're drinking and we're dancing
and the band is really happening
and the Johnny Walker wisdom running high
And my very sweet companion
she's the Angel of Compassion
and she's rubbing half the world against her thigh
Every drinker, every dancer
lifts a happy face to thank her
and the fiddler fiddles something so sublime
All the women tear their blouses off   10
and the men they dance on the polka-dots
and it's partner found and it's partner lost
and it's hell to pay when the fiddler stops
It's closing time

We're lonely, we're romantic
and the cider's laced with acid
and the Holy Spirit's crying, "Where's the beef?"[1]
And the moon is swimming naked
and the summer night is fragrant
with a mighty expectation of relief   20
So we struggle and we stagger
down the snakes and up the ladder
to the tower where the blessed hours chime
And I swear it happened just like this:
a sigh, a cry, a hungry kiss
the Gates of Love they budged an inch
I can't say much has happened since
but closing time

I loved you for your beauty
but that doesn't make a fool of me —   30
you were in it for your beauty too

1. **"Where's the beef?"** This slogan from a 1980s hamburger commercial is used to imply a lack of substance.

I loved you for your body
there's a voice that sounds like G-d to me
declaring that your body's really you
I loved you when our love was blessed
and I love you now there's nothing left
but sorrow and a sense of overtime
And I miss you since our place got wrecked
I just don't care what happens next
40   looks like freedom but it feels like death
it's something in between, I guess
it's closing time
And I miss you since the place got wrecked
by the winds of change and the weeds of sex
looks like freedom but it feels like death
it's something in between, I guess
it's closing time

We're drinking and we're dancing
but there's nothing really happening
50   the place is dead as Heaven on a Saturday night
And my very close companion
gets me fumbling, gets me laughing
she's a hundred but she's wearing something tight
And I lift my glass to the Awful Truth
which you can't reveal to the Ears of Youth
except to say it isn't worth a dime
And the whole damn place goes crazy twice
and it's once for the Devil and it's once for Christ
but the Boss don't like these dizzy heights —
60   we're busted in the blinding lights
of closing time

(1992)

Leon Rooke (1934–)

Leon Rooke was born in North Carolina in 1934. He and his siblings were separated from their parents in 1940 and sent to live on their grandparents' farm. Rooke grew up poor, but he managed to raise enough money to attend Mars Hill College, where he wrote and directed his first play. After two years, in 1955, he transferred to the University of North Carolina at Chapel Hill, where he majored in journalism before switching to dramatic arts. Rooke has said that hearing his plays read back to him repeatedly by actors tuned his ear to the sounds of words committed to the printed page. At UNC, he began writing short stories, publishing them in literary magazines, and he won several college awards.

Drafted from university into the armed forces in 1957, Rooke returned to UNC in 1960 and entered graduate school on a fellowship to study screenwriting. He soon dropped out of the program, however, and began to work as a writer for the University News Bureau, creating stage and radio plays in his free time. Later, he co-edited the *Anvil,* a progressive newspaper devoted to politics and the arts. Rooke married Constance Raymond in 1969, and they moved to British Columbia, where Constance became a professor of English at the University of Victoria and an editor of the *Malahat Review*. Rooke was glad to leave the United States. From 1963 to 1965, he had worked on social initiatives to assist African American youths, and he was increasingly disgusted by the resistance he saw to the civil rights movement.

Rooke has said that he learned a great deal about style and storytelling from the South's literary giants (like Edgar Allan Poe, William Faulkner, Flannery O'Connor), but his southern heritage also instilled in him a sense of moral purpose. He claims that he writes "to appease the innocent dead. To speak the speech of those incapable of speaking for themselves," and he recalls thinking at the outset of his writing career "of the voices that were speaking or could speak to one … if one gave them permission to speak." The concept of voice is crucial to Rooke on thematic and stylistic levels. His belief that fiction can "speak the speech" of the socially oppressed or the physically victimized has led him to create characters — otherwise hugely varied — who are outsiders. "The character that haunted me for a long time," he says, "was the one who was outside of things, outside of life." Stylistically, Rooke's preoccupation with voice gives rise to a mastery of dialect: he has effectively re-created the idioms of (among others) adolescents, Southerners, Blacks, and the Elizabethan English. Much of his characterization is accomplished through speech patterns.

For Rooke, however, getting the voice right is more than a linguistic exercise — it is a process by which the writer relinquishes the self. In the essay "Canadian Fiction against the Headwinds," he declares that the writer can "occupy fully … another's skin, a made-up character's self." His penchant for assuming the personality of his characters, along with his "scant interest … in things indecipherable," separates him from the mainstream of Canadian postmodern fiction. However, though his emphasis on character, voice, and drama links him to traditional forms, it has also led him to deconstruct realist conventions of plot and setting. His first-person narrators reveal themselves in fragments, and he prefers open endings to conventional resolutions; he will discard setting entirely if it does not contribute to a character's psychology. Rooke will also incorporate the fantastic or grotesque into a narrative to reveal a suppressed psychological state: in "The Iron Woman," for example, the abused and sexually unfulfilled Rebecca sees her flesh become armour as she masturbates.

Rooke's first short story collection was *Last One Home Sleeps in the Yellow Bed* (1968). It contains "Brush Fire," a novella based on his military experiences in which he investigates the suicide of a Hungarian-American soldier while demonstrating how the events of a story can be revealed indirectly, through tonal shifts and narrative digressions. *The Love Parlour* (1977), Rooke's second collection, is an assemblage of moral tales that fixate on states of extreme loneliness or frustration. In a series of three stories set in Mexico — "For Love of Madeline," "For Love of Eleanor," and "For Love of Gómez" — Rooke employs setting and symbols of death to heighten our sense of the spiritual and sexual ennui of four American tourists.

With *A Bolt of White Cloth* (1984), Rooke continued his explorations into extraordinary situations and voiceless figures. In "The Woman's Guide to Home Companionship," two women discuss their reasons for murdering their husbands. The tale's charm and pathos depend upon the women's bourgeois, clichéd vocabulary — even in their exhilarated and inebriated state, they are confined by social convention and cannot directly express their suffering.

Other short story collections include *The Birth Control King of the Upper Volta* (1982), *The Happiness of Others* (1991), and *Oh!: Twenty-Seven Stories* (1997). *Cry Evil* (1980) and *Death Suite* (1981) are dark collections that examine themes of murder, sadism, and pornography, while *How I Saved the Province* (1989) is a series of satirical sketches about power and survival in British Columbia politics. A record and short story package called *Muffins* was released in 1995, and *Painting the Dog*, a selection of short fiction spanning Rooke's career, was published in 2001.

Rooke's reputation as a novelist was established in 1980, when *Fat Woman* was short-listed for a Governor General's Award. Noted for its vivid characterization and use of North Carolina dialect, *Fat Woman* tells the story of Ella Mae, who is boarded up in a room by her husband. She is trapped literally and symbolically by her own puritan outlook, her corpulence, and her uncaring family (whom she feels obliged to support). In 1981, Rooke published the novella *The Magician in Love*, his most metafictional work. Ostensibly about a magician's love for his mistress, it is also a parable of the power of fantasy to satirize reality and reveal truth. In *Shakespeare's Dog* (1983), Rooke extended his play with satire, constructing the cosmos of a talking canine. Told in pseudo-Elizabethan English, the novel is notable for its virtuosic vocabulary, bawdy wordplay, coinages, and orthographic puns. Character and voice, however, still dominate: the dog is an idiosyncratic character, who, like Ella Mae, is frustrated by his inability to communicate effectively (either in the dog world or the human one).

Other novels include *Vault* (1973), *Who Goes There* (1998), *The Fall of Gravity* (2000), *The Beautiful Wife* (2005), and *A Good Baby* (1989), which was developed from a play first staged in British Columbia in 1987. In 2005, Rooke produced *Hot Poppies*, his first collection of poetry, and another novella, *Balduchi's Who's Who*. He has also edited several collections of short stories with John Metcalf, including *Best Canadian Short Stories* (two volumes, 1981, 1982), and *The New Press Anthology* (two volumes, 1984, 1985).

Rooke has received numerous awards, including the Canada-Australia Literary Prize (1981), a Governor General's Award for *Shakespeare's Dog* (1984), and the W.O. Mitchell Literary Prize (2002). He has been writer-in-residence at a number of Canadian and American universities. In 1988, Rooke moved to Eden Mills, Ontario, where, with Constance, he founded the Eden Mills Writer's Festival. Rooke now resides in Toronto.

The Woman's Guide to Home Companionship

What follows is not in my own hand. What follows is being delivered through the good graces of my friend and neighbour Mrs. Vee Beaverdeck of 101 Menzies, who is doing so without cost or complaint. She will aver, if asked, that this is the truth and the whole truth as I know it and that this story or tale is told first-hand and in a calm manner while we are here in my kitchen drinking our two coffees with now and then an ounce of something fortifying on the side.

It is 2:00 a.m. after what I'd call without exaggeration the roughest night of our lives.

We have been sitting around for hours since it happened, trying to figure out how we hooked up with such undesirables in the first place.

Vee says yes, that is the Lord's truth.

I shall now describe Mrs. Vee Beaverdeck to the degree I am able, so that there shall be no mistaking her for another person or persons and in order to assist the authorities. Vee is forty-six years old, two full years and three full months older than I am, though I think I can guarantee she has never acted funny about it. She is close to my own height and with a disposition similar to mine and on the issue of slenderness we both come in with identical high marks, though this was not always the case.

Why, you ask.

Since June I have shed eighteen pounds, all in the strategic places and without experiencing any undue psychological turmoil. Indeed, it was not because of psychological turmoil or unwholesome self-image in the first place that I embarked upon my physical-improvement program. It was a question of being Fulfilled or not being Fulfilled, as the expert told us. I have always been something of a compulsive snacker and the pounds seem to go right on me, right where they shouldn't, so from time to time my span-image of myself is such that without undue duress I engage in a crash program to eliminate all excess flabbiness, though that is hardly the word.

Mrs. Beaverdeck on the other hand has always been of the slim variety, though not so slim you could thread her through a needle, which has been her great good fortune down through the ages and which I think she will admit (she is nodding) she at times feels a little vain about.

I should intrude here to say Mrs. Beaverdeck keeps trying to interrupt me and change what I am saying, but I am not allowing this because it was the agreement we struck before we started out on this dictation. "You will get your turn," I keep telling her, "after I am done." I should explain too the employment of quotations in the previous sentence was because it was a direct quote or ultimatum delivered to Mrs. Vee Beaverdeck one second ago. I hope I will not have to use this technique hereafter, because it is most distracting to find yourself constantly interrupted and corrected and your every word questioned.

Back to the description.

Suffice it to say I took the aerobic course at Fitness Works Incorporated, 427 Fort Street with free parking, and dropped eighteen pounds, the first being always the hardest, as you know. Mrs. Beaverdeck only lost four, whereupon the expert let her know she need not lose any additional poundage. Be that as it may, I got my muscles toned and my stomach flat and now look smarter than I ever have, whereas Mrs. Vee Beaverdeck has since time immemorial been able to wear whatever she has wanted to wear without thinking twice about it. Now we wear the same size dress, with my feet maybe a half-size larger depending on the make, and double A whereas she's single A.

She paints her toes and I do not.

I am this minute wearing a house robe which belonged to her but which she gave to me because it looked so much better on me thanks to the colour of my eyes, which it picks up and highlights, together with my hair.

My bones are bigger so I think I still look larger and more cumbersome, though she claims this is my own personal delusion and little hang-up.

It is time we paused now to refreshen our drinks and sort out in a private and unpublicized manner the issue raised above, since as Vee says this is not a subject totally pertinent to this document and anyhow we have both got to stop crying.

We have got to face up, Vee says, to the consequences of what we have done.

Hi, we are now back, and Vee has sworn that she will take my dictation properly and not in any way undermine my account of our activities this awful evening.

To pick up where we left off:

I definitely have more bosom and we have agreed that this is why I feel larger than Mrs. Beaverdeck, when the truth is that for all practical purposes our bodies are identical. Mrs. Beaverdeck's breasts are sweet and certainly ample, if a little catty-cornered. On this score I feel the nod goes to her whatever the case, the reason being she is more in the Movement than I am and hence does not wear brassieres, which gives her a pronounced if unfair edge on the stares-and-whistles front, that being proved each time the two of us step out shopping. Let me insert also the news that while Mrs. Beaverdeck and I have numerous areas of conflict, on such matters for instance as the wearing of brassieres, we are in shining agreement on the abortion issue, women in the priesthood, on how ninety percent of the world's husbands stack up, etcetera or for instance the politics of certain warmongering nations which shall remain nameless.

Vee is this minute dressed in a black chiffon gown bought from Coordinates Yes!, a stylish store in the heart of town which we both frequent and not too expensive though occasionally their manners could be improved. She has a striped black-and-white silk scarf around her throat, and sheer knee-high hose of midnight blue, with a pair of old Capezio shoes on her feet because of how she came running out of her house so fast tonight she was practically hysterical. She has long black hair which is now pinned up to her head, along the sides anyway. I have more grey in mine, sorry to say, though it hardly ever shows because of a certain high-quality if expensive rinse which I swear by. Funnily enough, my skin is darker than Vee's with her black hair, despite my being in the blond spectrum thanks to my devoted parents who were both good Christians and will never again be able to hold up their heads once the newspapers get hold of this dictated confession. Vee's skin is definitely on the pale or albinic side, since she has not had more than an instant's sunshine strike her lovely figure since she was a child at Ocean View, which I understand is a beach-front-and-carnival type place outside Norfolk, Virginia. It is pretty bold and striking, if you've ever seen Vee — that contrast between black which is her favourite colour and her black hair with her dazzling white skin which does not have a blemish on it that I've ever seen.

Pardon. Mrs. Vee announces she has a cute birthmark the size of a dime on her left inner thigh next to what she calls her "chief asset."

As for yours truly I do not have any marks or disfigurations over the whole of my flesh save those administered in recent times by my objectionable husband.

Mrs. Vee Beaverdeck interrupts to say that I should say up there where she spoke of her most cherished parts she was speaking "in the ironical."

The subject's eyes are her best features. They are very large and entrancing, with naturally long lashes, plus she has a lively animated face, as I do myself, and more especially tonight as we sit here pouring ourselves coffee and spirits, which we are in part doing in order to keep up our spirits and to get done and accomplished the job we have set for ourselves before we close up shop and let come what must come: the terrible shame and our names and likenesses splashed in banner headlines across the nation.

Vee says thanks to God we do not have children, inasmuch as unbearable would be their agony and their lives ruined, because what we have done would be a bitter tonic.

Amen.

It may well be that we are having more to drink than is good for us under the circumstances, but let it be known we are of sound mind and strictly responsible for our actions and will not plead self-defence or temporary insanity or any of that stuff that you read about. Nor do we yet anyhow regret anything we have done or see how, given the circumstances and our emotional states and how over these past few months we have been driven to it, how it could have been avoided.

Nor do we intend to shrivel and cry and fall down in a faint when they come for us. Suffice it to say we mean to stand on our own two feet, giving as good as we get. We will go with our two V fingers high, like in the Movement.

Time out.

Time in.

We are back now, Mrs. Vee Beaverdeck with a pillow to soften her behind and a new writing tablet to take down this dictation as I hereby give it, each word the truth as I have always found the truth to be relevant.

Blemish and all, as Vee says.

Vee says that I should remind everyone that since June of the current year, together with our loyal attendance at Fitness Works Incorporated, a going and respectable concern, we have both been running on the shoulders of our noted highway one half-hour each morning and another half-hour around sunset and that we are now up to four and five miles without hassle or undue sudation.[1] In fact, what we have noticed is that gentlemen of the male persuasion are frequently pitched into unseemly fits of passion by no more than a thin sheen of sweat over our jogging bodies, with the result that they often swerve off the road or beep their horns or sometimes even execute daredevil U turns and return to embark upon the most boring and impossible advances two women at our stage of enlightenment could conceivably imagine.

Whereas we could take or leave this behaviour, our abominable husbands have, from the beginning, pitched a gasket. We have taken immeasurable abuse, alternating with a certain stonewalling,[2] over our fitness endeavours. Vee remembers that when we first went out on runs her husband would sit drinking his beer in front of the TV and laughing at her for (quote) "thinking you are some kind of female athelete."

What my own husband said, his chapter-one remark, was (quote), "What I wonder is what kind of effect all this exercising is going to have on your little red fire engine." Little red fire engine is my husband's he thinks quaint euphemism for my sexual parts. If the reader finds this sinister and distasteful and bespeaking of deep dark problems with his sexual attitudes then I am with that reader to the nth degree.

It is with a heavy heart that I utilize material of this x-rated type but accuracy dictates it and leaves me no choice.

Mind you, this was way back in June when there was still some semblance of sanity at 101 and 137 Menzies.

Vee says that I should take off the kid gloves and give a few more sterling examples of their truly rotten behaviour.

But I believe I can trust the reader to already understand what kind of "gentlemen" we have here.

Also, it is not my hope to give a full and documented account of their crimes against us and nature, for that would take a book and lots more time than I am willing to give to those two throw-backs.

Let it be known, in any event, that we have spotless reputations in this town and no one to our knowledge, among those with whom we carry on a daily business, has ever had occasion to say word one against us, nor have we been involved in any previous criminal wrongdoing.

Hold on a minute. Vee has gone and got my Polaroid and I have taken and labelled three pictures depicting her cut and bruised face, as well as two of the back porch and door which show what a rage my own husband was in earlier in the evening when he left this place.

Vee or Mrs. Beaverdeck has likewise taken a picture of me in knickers and bra, which shows I am anything but the "slick pig" he has since June been calling me.

Vee has said she can think of a number of men who would be willing to pay a hundred dollars for a copy of the above-named photo. I have said I can think of two or three I'd let have it for free.

We have had us another drink and are presently making a fresh pot of coffee.

---

1. **sudation** Sweating. 2. **stonewalling** Stalling by being uncooperative.

We have also looked back over this document and read it aloud, because my friend and neighbour Mrs. Vee Beaverdeck claims I go off on too many tangents, for instance what she looks like.

Vee Beaverdeck is beautiful. She is beautiful and she is my dearest friend and I have threatened to go directly to the authorities and confess our cruel deed if she doesn't put on the page exactly what I dictate to her.

You should understand, however, that many of the comments and asides we make to each other are not being entered into this document, since we feel much of it is not your business to know and for once in our lives we are doing exactly what we want to do.

We shall now have another drink, and as Vee says, "screw the coffee."

Mrs. Vee Beaverdeck, I have discovered only this evening, has had business training, and I am proud of her. For six years before her unfortunate marriage she worked for Stan Bask Associates, a well-known investment firm in this city. She advanced in this period from clerk-typist to the position of receptionist-supervisor and customarily took dictation from Stan Bask himself, who twice tried to seduce her and once got her pinned down on the carpet floor in front of his desk.

Suffice it to say that Mrs. Beaverdeck now looks back upon that experience with a very different eye.

She is now back from the phone where she has got Mr. Stan Bask up from a sound sleep and told him exactly what we think of him.

He professes that he "does not remember," and reminds her that "we were both young then."

I have now been subjected to a long speech from Mrs. Vee Beaverdeck on the importance of the Women's Movement and such questions as, "How can you, Violet Witherspoon, sit quietly by?" I have not heard many of these questions because I have gone to the bathroom. From my seat on the toilet, however, I have reminded Vee Beaverdeck of what we both have tonight done to our husbands.

"You can hardly say, after my actions this evening, that I have sat (quote) quietly by (unquote)."

That is a direct quote.

Vee Beaverdeck, who has admitted she said so out of tipsiness, has apologized for delivering inflammatory accusations against one Violet Witherspoon, domiciled at 137 Menzies.

By common vote we shall now pause, for we are overcome with giggles. Take five.

Back now. The old clock on the wall cries out the time, 3:12 a.m. In this interval we have skulked[3] by devious route and cunning to 101 Menzies, there to "view the remains," to replenish our bar stock, and to secure an overnight bag for Mrs. Vee Beaverdeck, including toothbrush, stockings, underwear, make-up, hair dryer, the outfit she means to wear tomorrow for whatever official inquiries might involve us, together with the book I lent her years ago, inherited from my mother and containing numerous pressed flowers, entitled *The Woman's Guide to Home Companionship*.

We have had a great laugh over this volume, as you can imagine, though it put me in tears to think of my mother eternally slaving away and all for what?

The "remains" remain intact and unchanged. We did not long study the situation, however, for the macabre, as Vee stated, has limited appeal.

---

3. **skulked** Moved stealthily.

I shall now pick up some of the loose ends.

Vee Beaverdeck believes I should not have described her breasts as "catty-cornered." She has bared herself and I have taken a Polaroid and we are now researching the result. I say to Vee, "Your left nipple points to nine o'clock, your right to three o'clock, and I call that catty-cornered."

Vee Beaverdeck spends one half-hour in my bathroom behind locked door studying this matter. Then she calls for her drink, which I pass through. A minute or so later she calls me in. She is seated on the bath edge, crying out her beautiful eyes.

"Vee," I say, "I was only kidding."

"I know," she says.

"I mean it," I say. "It was only a joke."

"I know," she says.

Then Vee Beaverdeck looks at me and with a broken heart says, "I could get a plastic surgeon to make small cuts on the inside of each breast and get them pointed straight."

We then bawl, for it comes to us in the same split second that our men have totally undermined our self-image, and it is almost as if we can hear them laughing.

It is some time before we are able again to stand upright. This has nothing to do with strong drink, though our glasses stand empty.

Vee says, "I said I was going to get drunk, and I meant it."

So forthwith we pour ourselves another round.

We are both wide awake at 4:00 a.m. and wondering when grief or guilt, or fear or total despair, will set in, but to this hour, along those lines, we feel nothing.

"What will they do to us?"

"I will claim total amnesia."

These statements and others like them have been made and repeated since the perpetration of the very deed itself, though I have decided and Vee has agreed that such disclosures are not to be admitted into this chronicle. Even so.

"Should we get in the car and run?" says Vee.

"Vee," I say, "we have between us exactly twenty-seven dollars and eleven cents."

"Two beautiful women, alone in the dark night, cannot leave a cold trail. It is impossible. At the first gas station or truck stop we come to some man will make a pass at us, we will be compelled to resist his advances, and before we know it five thousand peace officers will be hot on our trail."

I mope. I tell Vee to put it down that I am moping because she has entered the above statement directly onto these pages. "Vee," I say, "I am supposed to be dictating my statement."

"So dictate," she says.

We have a little cry because we have fought with each other.

Vee asks if I meant it back there at the start of this piece when I spoke of her beauty. That interests her, she says, though she can not quite see its point in terms of this document.

"Take this down, Vee," I say. "The point of it was to stress that while our husbands found us objectionable and undesirable, men and in fact anyone with an objective eye would find us quite the opposite." I remind her that I did not kill myself those weeks at Fitness Works Incorporated for nothing, and that we have not run upwards of five thousand miles over the past six months so that our husbands could abuse us and poke fun.

"Also, we were pretty sharp cookies to begin with," I say.

Something in this remark drives Vee to reflect that seventeen men in the past year have propositioned her. Three of them, directly. That is, they put their arms around her and began kissing her and whispering about motels.

I am stunned. Only two have approached me.

"One was your husband," she says.

"Vee, put this in," I say. "I am not surprised."

"He was the one most adamant."

I am not surprised.

"Vee," I say, "are you sure? Seventeen?"

"I could be mistaken about a couple of them," Vee says. "But it was how they looked at me. I also didn't tell quite the truth about Mr. Stan Bask. The truth is I never knew to what extent I was willing. Alas, he was a handsome devil. So debonair."

We agree it is the debonair gent who most carries the day.

Vee Beaverdeck makes it clear she was never a fallen woman. She wonders whether this was a mistake. She laments that all she wants is a little happiness in her life. "Like," says she, "when jogging."

She says she is getting tired of taking dictay, and is feeling dopey and sentimental and would like to shoot herself.

She goes over to the kitchen faucet and lets cold water stream over her head.

I have gone into my bedroom and poked around in my cedar chest until I've found my husband's old love letters. I look at them a while. I don't know why and I certainly don't care. It strikes me with a jolt that his old letters are wholly illiterate. All he talks about is his job and drinking and the weather and what he'd do if he had me near him, and how dumb everybody is. He writes in a very large hand so he can fill nine or ten pages. He includes little drawings of what sheep do to each other. It is a funny thing to me how I would clutch this trash to my chest in those days and feel absolutely divine and glorious.

It is clear from his letters that he never had a brain in his head and that all was subterfuge[4] from the start.

"He mentions you," I tell Vee. "He says his buddy Carl has taken up with 'a very weird woman who is very odd.'"

Vee says, "Let me see that."

She has now stopped receiving dictation to look it over.

I say, "All right, Vee." It is too late to save her from it. She's going to come to that part in the letter where my husband-to-be says that Carl tells him he's pretty sure he's going to get from her what he wants and that he's already had more than a taste of it. "She's hot-to-trot in the old backseat," Carl says. "Guess they just can't resist old Carl's charm."

"I don't want to take any more dictay," Mrs. Vee Beaverdeck has said. So I've dropped down here to do it myself. What I wonder about is why they've treated us the way they have. I don't think they originally set out to become demented. I know they don't think of themselves as mean. We've never mattered to them so they've gone about their lives exactly as they've wanted, never thinking about us except to say what trouble we've caused them. Floppy appendages, I guess we are, like an extra arm that nobody wants. It was not the big things anyway that led us to our mission. It was the little things they did, like how they would look at each other with sick smiles anytime we spoke, and how they

---

4. **subterfuge** A deceptive façade.

pitched their beer cans out of the car windows, and scoffed at flowers we brought into the house; it was how they left wet coffee spoons in the sugar bowl and abused our friends and swore up and down Richard Nix was such a great foreign-policy president, not to mention the whole cut-throat heathen gang our other halves aligned themselves with. Etcetera. Etcetera. It was how they looked, too: with their hair combed down over their brows, their ears sticking out, the stupid baseball caps on the back of their heads, and the seats of their pants flopping down to their knees. Mostly it was how you could never get out of them one word of moral support, not one word about their emotional feelings on the private home-front question as it relates to those closest and dearest to them, and if you expected support from those two on your personal dilemmas ranging from A to Z you'd be better off putting in a call to the Ayatollah[5] what's-his-name.

The truth is we did it to them because they never seemed to feel anything. Not even when we did it.

My friend and beloved neighbour Mrs. Vee Beaverdeck is this moment overcome with uncontrollable fatigue and hereby demands that I cease with these memoirs. She declares with a shiver that she has this second had the most terrible thought; to wit, that we have not in point of fact succeeded in dispensing with our husbands, but that throughout the torment of this evening and the subsequent drenching of ourselves with alcohol we have merely been displaying wishful thinking. She urges that we abandon this post immediately and scurry post-haste to view the miserable bodies.

Agreed. A foul thought indeed. Take twenty.

Hi! I'm back.

Nope, we've done it, all right. They are definitely gone from this world. They shall never again take advantage of frail womanhood or sneer at a pile of dirty dishes or behave generally like inhuman scoundrels.

They shall know better next time.

"Let's put pennies over their eyes," Vee Beaverdeck said. "Let's pull the sheets up under their chins. Let's get rid of these beer cans and cigarette butts they've left here and take a Polaroid of them in their glory, in case we again have doubts."

The photo turned out ever so nicely. It seemed to catch mine flinching when the flash went off. It seemed to me I heard both of them groan, but that was only my nerves working overtime.

"Mine, too," said Vee. "I've had it."

She said hers looked nicer than he ever had. "You'd almost think him human," she said. She pointed out a dimple in his left cheek. "Or is that where I got him with the heel of my shoe?"

We sat out on the back deck measuring the dark houses all around and looking up out of tired relief at the man in the moon.

"It's no man," Vee said. "That's my grandmother."

"She's nice," I said. "She looks like she knows a woman's true place."

Vee Beaverdeck stretched out flat on her back. She sighed about a thousand times. "This is a one-shot deal," she said. "I'm not cut out for murder and mayhem."

Ditto here. It's too gruesome, if that's any news.

(1985)

---

5. **Ayatollah** Ali Kamenei, president of Iran from 1981–1989, and a major figure in Iran's Islamic Revolution.

Rudy Wiebe (1934–)

Rudy Wiebe was born in 1934 to Mennonite parents who had fled Soviet Russia in 1930 and settled in a tiny Mennonite Brethren Church community near Fairholme, Saskatchewan. As a child, he was impressed by the immensity and loneliness of the land and intrigued by its history. The Wiebes spoke a dialect of Low German at home, and the children learned English in a one-room schoolhouse. In 1947, the family moved to Coaldale, Alberta, where Rudy could attend high school. He later enrolled at the University of Alberta to study medicine, but he switched to English literature and was encouraged by his professors to write. From 1957 to 1960, Wiebe studied in Germany, married Tena Isaak, and obtained an M.A. in creative writing from the University of Alberta. He was then hired to teach at the Mennonite Brethren Bible College.

Wiebe's first novel, *Peace Shall Destroy Many* (1962), grew out of his M.A. thesis. This four-part narrative, its divisions corresponding to the seasons, is set in 1944 in the northern Saskatchewan Mennonite village of Wapiti. Its inhabitants, bent on preserving their Christian way of life, live in relative isolation; elsewhere, World War II is raging. Tensions mount, however, as the war gradually brings national interests into conflict with community values. Realistic in style, the novel underscores the inherent hypocrisy of the villagers' isolationism while examining the threat that national agendas pose to minority cultures — a recurring theme in Wiebe's work. The novel outraged many Mennonites, and the Bible College convinced Wiebe to resign his post in 1963.

The following year, Wiebe moved to Indiana to be an assistant professor of English at Goshen College. There, he wrote his second novel, *First and Vital Candle* (1966), the story of 40-year-old Abe Ross who, returning to Winnipeg after spending years in the Arctic, struggles to accept his past and rekindle his faith. Abe finally travels to northern Ontario, where he is taken in by a band of Ojibwa, whose spiritual strength allows him to regain his equilibrium. *First and Vital Candle* is a more complex offering than its predecessor in that it experiments with narrative structure and voice; Abe's first-person recollections alternate with third-person omniscient depictions of the present. Wiebe here employs Christian symbolism, as he does in *Peace*, but it is intensified in this novel that examines the role of faith in an increasingly secular society. After its publication, Wiebe returned to Edmonton to take up a permanent position in the University of Alberta English department.

In 1970, Wiebe returned to the subject of the Mennonite diaspora in his third novel. *The Blue Mountains of China* evokes almost a hundred years of Mennonite history, interweaving the tales of four families who journey from Russia to their new homes in Canada, Paraguay, and Brazil. As the tales progress, Wiebe develops a critique of the materialism he sees permeating modern life. Although the narrative point of view changes with every chapter, heralded by shifts in rhythm, diction, and syntax, the novel coalesces around the themes of family and Christian commitment and a sense of shared tradition. Wiebe's experiments in this novel with historical representation, narrative perspective, and language would come to be recognized as hallmarks of his style.

In the 1970s, Wiebe began editing collections of Western Canadian fiction, including *Stories from Western Canada* (1972). He admired Frederick Philip Grove for his attention to the "particular world" of the prairies, for his willingness to "look hard at … bush Canada"; and, like Robert Kroetsch, he believed that literary traditions cannot be created — they can only be excavated, bit by bit, from the land itself. Wiebe became increasingly conscious of the fact that prairie history did not begin with White settlement, and that the oral tradition of First Nations people had been obscured over time. Unearthing the West's literary heritage became for him a matter of retrieving lost, forgotten, unheard voices. Through his anthologies, he encouraged prairie writers to piece together enough of their tradition to "make a dinosaur" — a colossus that could "break up that space with huge design."

Wiebe's historical prairie epics *The Temptations of Big Bear* (1973) and *The Scorched-Wood People* (1977) are both grounded in First Nations history. The Governor General's Award–winning *Temptations of Big Bear* is set in the period 1876–1888, when Saskatchewan Cree leader Big Bear led his people across the prairie in search of a way to preserve their way of life in the face of White settlement; in so doing, he became embroiled in the series of events that would lead to his death. Attempting to instill in European Canadians a sense of Cree culture, Wiebe often recounts events twice: once from the point of view of the Whites (depicted in a more formal language that evokes a bureaucratic rationality), and again from the perspective of the Cree (portrayed in a fluid, cadenced voice that suggests a more elemental, natural perspective in harmony with nature). Big Bear's extraordinary voice also aligns him with the Old Testament prophets, who, Wiebe maintains, share with the Cree chief "the sense of a heritage ... that through ignorance or neglect has been simply left." Wiebe spent six years researching *Big Bear,* and in the process he became convinced of the inadequacy of reports and records when it comes to conveying the human reality of historical events. Structuring his work through multiple perspectives, he infuses it with the kind of psychological realism that conventional historical accounts fail to achieve.

The Scorched-Wood People, another dramatization of the profound rift between Aboriginal and White cultures, relates the story of Louis Riel and the Northwest Rebellion. Narrator Pierre Falcon presents Riel as a Christ figure whose prophetic, spiritual, communal vision of the West is pitted against the capitalist expansionism of Sir John A. Macdonald and his government. The circular structure of the novel — we are told at the beginning that it will end with Riel "hanged by his neck until he is at last, perfectly, dead" — suggests that each reading in some way resurrects Riel, and that his spirit may come yet again to speak for the Métis people.

The title story of Wiebe's 1974 collection *Where Is the Voice Coming From?* is the author's most concentrated attempt to demonstrate the difficulty of coaxing authentic historical voices from extant records. The metafictional tale begins by alluding to the "problem" of combining "the bits and pieces" of history into a story, especially when those fragments are contradictory or biased or inaccurate. Nevertheless, the synthesis gains momentum, and the "incredible voice" of the subject — the Cree warrior Almighty Voice — rises from the landscape, singing his own death chant. For the storyteller, who hears the chant as a "wordless cry," it seems that the past speaks either inaccurately, through history, or incomprehensibly, through the spirit; all he has to guide him is his own desire for truth. This story is a compelling example of the way in which contemporary writers such as Wiebe challenge received versions of history while at the same time acknowledging that historical truth and accuracy are always open to question. It demonstrates the author's understanding that history, like all stories, is reconstructed with each new teller; there is no stable version of the past.

Wiebe's next novel, *The Mad Trapper* (1980) is a fictionalized account of the RCMP's 1931 manhunt for the real Albert Johnson, "the mad trapper of Rat River," who shot one of their own. In *My Lovely Enemy* (1983), the story of a history professor's affair with a graduate student, Wiebe blends realism and fantasy to explore sexual love as a metaphor for divine love. His experiments with perspective continue in *A Discovery of Strangers* (1994), which traces John Franklin's overland Arctic journey through the eyes of the explorers and the Tetsot'ine (Yellowknife) people. Wiebe inserts historical sources, ranging from explorer diary excerpts to Native myths and songs, into the novel, which won him his second Governor General's Award.

In the mid-1990s, Wiebe was contacted by Yvonne Johnson, Big Bear's grand-daughter, who was serving a prison sentence for her role in the murder of a suspected child abuser. Wiebe agreed to help her tell her life story, and it was published in 1998 as *Stolen Life: The Journey of a Cree Woman*. Wiebe returned to the subject of Mennonite life in *Sweeter Than All the World*

(2001), a novel that blends the fictional story of Adam Wiebe, an Albertan Mennonite of about Rudy Wiebe's age, with episodes from the Wiebe family history (beginning in the 16th century). It is perhaps Wiebe's most explicit and personal exploration of the importance of cultural history to individual psychology.

Wiebe has published four other collections of short work; the most recent is *River of Stone: Fictions and Memories* (1995). In 2001, he was made an Officer of the Order of Canada, and he has been a professor emeritus at the University of Alberta since 1992. He produced *Of This Earth*, a memoir of his early years, in 2006.

Where Is the Voice Coming From?

The problem is to make the story.

One difficulty of this making may have been excellently stated by Teilhard de Chardin:[1] "We are continually inclined to isolate ourselves from the things and events which surround us ... as though we were spectators, not elements, in what goes on." Arnold Toynbee[2] does venture, "For all that we know, Reality is the undifferentiated unity of the mystical experience," but that need not here be considered. This story ended long ago; it is one of finite acts, of orders, of elemental feelings and reactions, of obvious legal restrictions and requirements.

Presumably all the parts of the story are themselves available. A difficulty is that they are, as always, available only in bits and pieces. Though the acts themselves seem quite clear, some written reports of the acts contradict each other. As if these acts were, at one time, too well known; as if the original nodule of each particular fact had from somewhere received non-factual accretions;[3] or even more, as if, since the basic facts were so clear perhaps there were a larger number of facts than any one reporter, or several, or even any reporter had ever attempted to record. About facts that are still simply told by this mouth to that ear, of course, even less can be expected.

An affair seventy-five years old should acquire some of the shiny transparency of an old man's skin. It should.

Sometimes it would seem that it would be enough — perhaps more than enough — to hear the names only. The grandfather One Arrow; the mother Spotted Calf; the father Sounding Sky; the wife (wives, rather, but only one of them seems to have a name, though their fathers are Napaise, Kapahoo, Old Dust, The Rump) — the one wife named, of all things, Pale Face; the cousin Going-Up-To-Sky; the brother-in-law (again, of all things) Dublin. The names of the police sound very much alike; they all begin with Constable or Corporal or Sergeant, but here and there an Inspector, then a Superintendent and eventually all the resonance of an Assistant Commissioner echoes down. More. Herself: Victoria, by the Grace of God etc., etc., QUEEN, defender of the Faith, etc., etc.; and witness "Our Right Trusty and Right Well-beloved Cousin and Councillor the Right Honorable Sir John Campbell Hamilton-Gordon, Earl of Aberdeen; Viscount Formartine, Baron Haddo, Methlic, Tarves and Kellie, in the Peerage of Scotland; Viscount Gordon of Aberdeen, County of Aberdeen, in the Peerage of the United

---

1. **Teilhard de Chardin** French philosopher and paleontologist (1880–1955) who supported the theory of evolution but suggested that it was not random but goal-oriented. The quote is from his book, *The Phenomenon of Man*. 2. **Arnold Toynbee** British historian (1889–1975) who wrote extensively on the rise and fall of civilizations. 3. **accretions** External additions.

Kingdom; Baronet of Nova Scotia, Knight Grand Cross of Our Most Distinguished Order of Saint Michael and Saint George, etc., Governor General of Canada." And of course himself: in the award proclamation named "Jean-Baptiste"[4] but otherwise known only as Almighty Voice.[5]

But hearing cannot be enough; not even hearing all the thunder of A Proclamation: "Now Hear Ye that a reward of FIVE HUNDRED DOLLARS will be paid to any person or persons who will give such information as will lead … (etc., etc.) this Twentieth day of April, in the year of Our Lord one thousand eight hundred and ninety-six, and the Fifty-ninth year of Our Reign … " etc. and etc.

Such hearing cannot be enough. The first item to be seen is the piece of white bone. It is almost triangular, slightly convex — concave actually as it is positioned at this moment with its corners slightly raised — graduating from perhaps a strong eighth to a weak quarter of an inch in thickness, its scattered pore structure varying between larger and smaller on its perhaps polished, certainly shiny surface. Precision is difficult since the glass showcase is at least thirteen inches deep and therefore an eye cannot be brought as close as the minute inspection of such a small, though certainly quite adequate, sample of skull would normally require. Also, because of the position it cannot be determined whether the several hairs, well over a foot long, are still in some manner attached or not.

The seven-pounder cannon can be seen standing almost shyly between the showcase and the interior wall. Officially it is known as a gun, not a cannon, and clearly its bore is not large enough to admit a large man's fist. Even if it can be believed that this gun was used in the 1885 Rebellion[6] and that on the evening of Saturday, May 29, 1897[7] (while the nine-pounder, now unidentified, was in the process of arriving with the police on the special train from Regina), seven shells (all that were available in Prince Albert at that time) from it were sent shrieking into the poplar bluffs as night fell, clearly such shelling could not and would not disembowel the whole earth. Its carriage is now nicely lacquered, the perhaps oak spores of its petite wheels (little higher than a knee) have been recently scrapped, puttied and varnished; the brilliant burnish of its brass breeching[8] testifies with what meticulous care charmen and women have used nationally-advertised cleaners and restorers.

Though it can also be seen, even a careless glance reveals that the same concern has not been expended on the one (of two) .44 calibre 1866 model Winchesters apparently found at the last in the pit with Almighty Voice. It also is preserved in a glass case; the number 1536735 is still, though barely, distinguishable on the brass cartridge section just below the brass saddle ring. However, perhaps because the case was imperfectly sealed at one time (though sealed enough not to warrant disturbance now), or because of simple neglect, the rifle is obviously spotted here and there with blotches of rust and the brass itself reveals discolorations almost like mildew. The rifle bore, the three long strands of hair themselves, actually bristle with clots of dust. It may be that

---

4. **Jean-Baptiste** The patron saint of Quebec. 5. **Almighty Voice** Legendary hunter and marksman; was arrested for slaughtering a cow (which he may have done legally), but escaped prison. He was pursued for over a year through the West after killing an officer, despite a $500 reward on his head. 6. **1885 Rebellion** An unsuccessful Métis rebellion against the Canadian government in what is now Saskatchewan; Sounding Sky was a major leader, along with Louis Riel. 7. **May 29, 1897** The third night that Almighty Voice was sieged with cannon-fire while holed up with Dublin and Going-Up-To-Sky in the cliffs near the One Arrow reserve; the next morning, all three would be found dead. 8. **breeching** Point where bullets are loaded into a gun.

this museum cannot afford to be as concerned as the other; conversely, the disfiguration may be something inherent in the items themselves.

The small building which was the police guardroom at Duck Lake, Saskatchewan Territory, in 1895[9] may also be seen. It had subsequently been moved from its original place and used to house small animals, chickens perhaps, or pigs — such as a woman might be expected to have under her responsibility. It is, of course, now perfectly empty, and clean so that the public may enter with no more discomfort than a bend under the doorway and a heavy encounter with disinfectant. The door-jamb has obviously been replaced; the bar network at one window is, however, said to be original; smooth still, very smooth. The logs inside have been smeared again and again with whitewash, perhaps paint, to an insistent point of identity-defying characterlessness. Within the small rectangular box of these logs not a sound can be heard from the streets of the, probably dead, town.

Hey Injun you'll get hung for stealing that steer
Hey Injun for killing that government cow you'll get three weeks on the woodpile Hey Injun

The place name Kinistino[10] seems to have disappeared from the map but the Minnechinass Hills have not. Whether they have ever been on a map is doubtful but they will, of course, not disappear from the landscape as long as the grass grows and the rivers run. Contrary to general report and belief, the Canadian prairies are rarely, if ever, flat and the Minnechinass (spelled five different ways and translated sometimes as "The Outside Hill," sometimes as "Beautiful Bare Hills") are dissimilar from any other of the numberless hills that everywhere block out the prairie horizon. They are bare; poplars lie tattered along their tops, almost black against the straw-pale grass and sharp green against the grey soil of the plowing laid in half-mile rectangular blocks upon their western slopes. Poles holding various wires stick out of the fields, back down the bend of the valley; what was once a farmhouse is weathering into the cultivated earth. The poplar bluff where Almighty Voice made his stand has, of course, disappeared.

The policemen he shot and killed (not the ones he wounded, of course) are easily located. Six miles east, thirty-nine miles north in Prince Alberta, the English Cemetery. Sergeant Colin Campbell Colebrook, North West Mounted Police Registration Number 605, lies presumably under a gravestone there. His name is seventeenth in a very long "list of non-commissioned officers and men who have died in the service since the inception of the force." The date is October 29, 1895, and the cause of death is anonymous: "Shot by escaping Indian prisoner near Prince Albert." At the foot of this grave are two others: Constable John R. Kerr, No. 3040, and Corporal C.H.S. Hockin, No. 3106. Their cause of death on May 28, 1897 is even more anonymous, but the place is relatively precise: "Shot by Indians at Min-etch-inass Hills, Prince Albert District."

The gravestone, if he has one, of the fourth man Almighty Voice killed is more difficult to locate. Mr. Ernest Grundy, postmaster at Duck Lake in 1897, apparently shut his window the afternoon of Friday, May 28, armed himself, rode east twenty miles, participated in the second charge into the bluff at about 6:30 p.m., and on the third sweep of that charge was shot dead at the edge of the pit. It would seem that he thereby

---

9. **police guardroom ... 1895** Prison where Almighty Voice was held for allegedly stealing and slaughtering a cow belonging to a local official. 10. **Kinistino** (Minnechinass Hills) Where Sergeant Colebrook of the Mounted Police caught up with Almighty Voice after he escaped from prison.

contributed substantially not only to the Indians' bullet supply, but his clothing warmed them as well.

The burial place of Dublin and Going-Up-To-Sky is unknown, as is the grave of Almighty Voice. It is said that a Métis named Henry Smith lifted the latter's body from the pit in the bluff and gave it to Spotted Calf. The place of burial is not, of course, of ultimate significance. A gravestone is always less evidence than a triangular piece of skull, provided it is large enough.

Whatever further evidence there is to be gathered may rest on pictures. There are, presumably, almost numberless pictures of the policemen in the case, but the only one with direct bearing is one of Sergeant Colebrook who apparently insisted on advancing to complete an arrest after being warned three times that if he took another step he would be shot. The picture must have been taken before he joined the force; it reveals him a large-eared young man, hair brush-cut and ascot tie, his eyelids slightly drooping, almost hooded under thick brows. Unfortunately a picture of Constable R. C. Dickson, into whose charge Almighty Voice was apparently committed in that guardroom and who after Colebrook's death was convicted of negligence, sentenced to two months hard labour and discharged, does not seem to be available.

There are no pictures to be found of either Dublin (killed early by rifle fire) or Going-Up-To-Sky (killed in the pit), the two teenage boys who gave their ultimate fealty to Almighty Voice. There is, however, one said to be of Almighty Voice, Junior. He may have been born to Pale Face during the year, two hundred and twenty-one days that his father was a fugitive. In the picture he is kneeling before what could be a tent, he wears striped denim overalls and displays twin babies whose sex cannot be determined from the double-laced dark bonnets they wear. In the supposed picture of Spotted Calf and Sounding Sky, Sounding Sky stands slightly before his wife; he wears a white shirt and a striped blanket folded over his left shoulder in such a manner that the arm in which he cradles a long rifle cannot be seen. His head is thrown back; the rim of his hat appears as a black half-moon above eyes that are pressed shut in, as it were, profound concentration; above a mouth clenched thin in a downward curve. Spotted Calf wears a long dress, a sweater which could also be a man's dress coat, and a large fringed and embroidered shawl which would appear distinctly Dukhobour[11] in origin if the scroll patterns on it were more irregular. Her head is small and turned slightly towards her husband so as to reveal her right ear. There is what can only be called a quizzical expression on her crumpled face; it may be she does not understand what is happening and that she would have asked a question, perhaps of her husband, perhaps of the photographers, perhaps even of anyone, anywhere in the world if such questioning were possible for an Indian lady.

There is one final picture. That is one of Almighty Voice himself. At least it is purported to be of Almighty Voice himself. In the Royal Canadian Mounted Police Museum on the Barracks Grounds just off Dewdney Avenue in Regina, Saskatchewan, it lies in the same showcase, as a matter of fact immediately beside, that triangular piece of skull. Both are unequivocally labelled, and it must be assumed that a police force with a world-wide reputation would not label *such* evidence incorrectly. But here emerges an ultimate problem in making the story.

---

11. **Dukhobour** From the 17th-century Russian religious sect; their Canadian contingent emerged in the 19th century and was in conflict with the RCMP throughout the first half of the 20th century.

There are two official descriptions of Almighty Voice. The first reads: "Height about five feet, ten inches, slight build, rather good looking, a sharp hooked nose with a remarkably flat point. Has a bullet scar on the left side of his face about 1½ inches long running from near corner of mouth towards ear. The scar cannot be noticed when his face is painted but otherwise is plain. Skin fair for an Indian." The second description is on the Award Proclamation: "About twenty-two years old, five feet ten inches in height, weight about eleven stone, slightly erect, neat small feet and hands; complexion inclined to be fair, wavy dark hair to shoulders, large dark eyes, broad forehead, sharp features and parrot nose with flat tip, scar on left cheek running from mouth towards ear, feminine appearance."

So run the descriptions that were, presumably, to identify a well-known fugitive in so precise a manner that an informant could collect five hundred dollars — a considerable sum when a police constable earned between one and two dollars a day. The nexus of the problems appears when these supposed official descriptions are compared to the supposed official picture. The man in the picture is standing on a small rug. The fingers of his left hand touch a curved Victorian settee, behind him a photographer's backdrop of scrolled patterns merges to vaguely paradisiacal trees and perhaps a sky. The moccasins he wears make it impossible to deduce whether his feet are "neat small." He may be five feet, ten inches tall, may weigh eleven stone, he certainly is "rather good looking" and, though it is a frontal view, it may be that the point of his long and flaring nose could be "remarkably flat." The photograph is slightly over-illuminated and so the unpainted complexion could be "inclined to be fair"; however, nothing can be seen of a scar, the hair is not wavy and shoulder-length but hangs almost to the waist in two thick straight braids worked through with beads, fur, ribbons and cords. The right hand that holds the corner of the blanket-like coat in position is large and, even in the high illumination, heavily veined. The neck is concealed under coiled beads and the forehead seems more low than "broad."

Perhaps, somehow, these picture details could be reconciled with the official description if the face as a whole were not so devastating.

On a cloth-backed sheet two feet by two and one-half feet in size, under the Great Seal of the Lion and the Unicorn,[12] dignified by the names of the Deputy of the Minister of Justice, the Secretary of State, the Queen herself and all the heaped detail of her "Right Trusty and Right Well Beloved Cousin," this description concludes: "feminine appearance." But the pictures: any face of history, any believed face that the world acknowledges as *man* — Socrates, Jesus, Attila, Genghis Khan, Mahatma Gandhi, Joseph Stalin — no believed face is more *man* than this face. The mouth, the nose, the clenched brows, the eyes — the eyes are large, yes, and dark, but even in this watered-down reproduction of unending reproductions of that original, a steady look into those eyes cannot be endured. It is a face like an axe.

It is now evident that the de Chardin statement quoted at the beginning has relevance only as it proves itself inadequate to explain what has happened. At the same time, the inadequacy of Aristotle's much more famous statement becomes evident: "The true difference [between the historian and the poet] is that one relates what *has* happened, the other what *may* happen." These statements cannot explain the storyteller's activity

---

12. **Great Seal of the Lion and the Unicorn** The Canadian Coat of Arms.

since, despite the most rigid application of impersonal investigation, the elements of the story have now run me aground. If ever I could, I can no longer pretend to objective, omnipotent disinterestedness. I am no longer *spectator* of what *has* happened or what *may* happen: I am become *element* in what is happening at this very moment.

For it is, of course, I myself who cannot endure the shadows on that paper which are those eyes. It is I who stand beside this broken veranda post where two corner shingles have been torn away, where barbed wire tangles the dead weeds on the edge of this field. The bluff that sheltered Almighty Voice and his two friends has not disappeared from the slope of the Minnechinass, no more than the sound of Constable Dickson's voice in that guardhouse is silent. The sound of his speaking is there even if it has never been recorded in an official report:

> *hey injun you'll get*
> *hung*
> *for stealing that steer*
> *hey injun for killing that government*
> *cow you'll get three*
> *weeks on the woodpile hey injun*

The unknown contradictory words about an unprovable act that move a boy to defiance, an implacable Cree warrior long after the three-hundred-and-fifty-year war is ended, a war already lost the day the Cree watch Cartier hoist his gun ashore at Hochelaga and they begin the long retreat west; these words of incomprehension, of threatened incomprehensible law are there to be heard just as the unmoving tableau of the three-day siege is there to be seen on the slopes of the Minnechinass. Sounding Sky is somewhere not there, under arrest, but Spotted Calf stands on a shoulder of the Hills a little to the left, her arms upraised to the setting sun. Her mouth is open. A horse rears, riderless, above the scrub willow at the edge of the bluff, smoke puffs, screams tangle in rifle barrage, there are wounds, somewhere. The bluff is so green this spring, it will not burn and the ragged line of seven police and two civilians is staggering through, faces twisted in rage, terror, and rifles sputter. Nothing moves. There is no sound of frogs in the night; twenty-seven policemen and five civilians stand in cordon at thirty-yard intervals and a body also lies in the shelter of a gully. Only a voice rises from the bluff:

> *We have fought well*
> *You have died like braves*
> *I have worked hard and am hungry*
> *Give me food*

but nothing moves. The bluff lies, a bright green island on the grassy slope surrounded by men hunched forward rigid over their long rifles, men clumped out of rifle-range, thirty-five men dressed as for fall hunting on a sharp spring day, a small gun positioned on a ridge above. A crow is falling out of the sky into the bluff, its feathers sprayed as by an explosion. The first gun and the second gun are in position, the beginning and end of the bristling surround of thirty-five Prince Albert Volunteers, thirteen civilians and fifty-six policemen in position relative to the bluff and relative to the unnumbered whites astride their horses, standing up in their carts, staring and pointing across the valley, in position relative to the bluff and the unnumbered Indians squatting silent along the higher ridges of the Hills, motionless mounds, faceless against the Sunday morning sunlight edging between and over them down along the tree tips, down into the shadows of the bluff. Nothing moves. Beside the second gun the red-coated officer has flung a handful of grass into the motionless air, almost to the rim of the red sun.

And there is a voice. It is an incredible voice that rises from among the young poplars ripped of their spring bark, from among the dead somewhere lying there, out of the arm-deep pit shorter than a man; a voice rises over the exploding smoke and thunder of guns that reel back in their positions, worked over, serviced by the grimed motionless men in bright coats and glinting buttons, a voice so high and clear, so unbelievably high and strong in its unending wordless cry.

The voice of "Gitchie-Manitou Wayo" — interpreted as "voice of the Great Spirit" — that is, The Almighty Voice. His death chant no less incredible in its beauty than in its incomprehensible happiness.

I say "wordless cry" because that is the way it sounds to me. I could be more accurate if I had a reliable interpreter who would make a reliable interpretation. For I do not, of course, understand the Cree myself.

(1974)

George Bowering (1935–)

In his long career as a writer of poetry, fiction, and criticism, George Bowering has produced more than 60 books. He once described them as a garden of "odd-looking shrubs." The "oddness" of his work derives from its restless, unconventional, and idiosyncratic style — a style that combines the serious and the comic. With his subversive streak and pointed sense of humour, Bowering has found popularity as both a writer and a speaker.

Bowering was born in Penticton, in British Columbia's Okanagan region, in 1935. After attending Victoria College (now the University of Victoria) in 1953–1954, he joined the Royal Canadian Air Force; he quit in 1957 to attend the University of British Columbia. In 1959, the year before he graduated with a B.A. in history, he read the anthology *New American Poetry 1945–1960*, which introduced him to the American models that would dominate the Vancouver poetry scene for most of the 1960s. Bowering also became excited about the publications issuing from Contact Press in Toronto, but what drew him most powerfully was the burgeoning West Coast literary scene. In 1961, he co-founded and became co-editor — with Frank Davey and Fred Wah — of the influential magazine *TISH*.

TISH (the name is an anagram) quickly became an important source of postmodern West Coast writing. Its contributors (among them Daphne Marlatt) employed the open verse form and an informal tone; they also displayed a political orientation. Davey regarded *TISH* as a "universalist" outlet for poetry that expressed the mysteries of life rather than rational humanism, and so the magazine initially excluded the modernist writers from Montreal, Toronto, and the Maritimes in favour of Americans and Canadians from the West Coast; many of these West Coast poets of both nationalities met at UBC's catalytic 1963 poetry conference organized by an American professor who had mentored the writers of *TISH*.

Because Bowering was also interested in the Contact Press group headed by Raymond Souster, Louis Dudek, and Irving Layton, the *TISH* editors began inviting writers from the east to contribute to their magazine, reserving a special page for them. While the *TISH* group continued to draw most of its inspiration from its American influences, Bowering has insisted that its members absorbed these influences and moved on. The writers who initially wrote for *TISH* took the general guidelines of 1960s American beat and postmodern writing — unsettle the formal line, validate the diction and syntax of the vernacular, and express experience rather than abstraction — and adapted them throughout their careers. Ultimately, they would embrace no single, unifying aesthetic or politics.

The 1960s was a busy time for Bowering. He married critic Angela May Luoma in 1962, earned an M.A. in creative writing in 1963, taught at the University of Calgary (1963–1966), travelled abroad, and edited *Imago* (1964–1974), a long-poem journal based in Calgary that was more nationalistic than *TISH* but still embraced the unconventional. Bowering began a Ph.D. on the Romantic poet Percy Bysshe Shelley at the University of Western Ontario in 1966, but he left after a year to teach at Sir George Williams University (now Concordia) in Montreal; he remained there for two years.

In 1969, his poetry collections *Rocky Mountain Foot* and *Gangs of Kosmos* won him a Governor General's Award. His experimentation with unusual breaks in the poetic line had influenced other poets, as did his enthusiastic involvement in public and academic artistic collaborations. In 1972, he embarked on a long career at Simon Fraser University in Vancouver and became involved with a group of poets that included Robin Blaser and Sharon Thesen.

One of the highlights of Bowering's 1970s work is *A Short Sad Book* (1977), the title and discontinuous style of which he adapted from Gertrude Stein's *A Long Gay Book* (1912). Reacting to critics who blamed him for importing American influences (primarily that of the famous Black Mountain poets, among them Charles Olson, Robert Creeley, and Robert Duncan) into Canadian literature via *TISH*, Bowering has the narrator of *A Short Sad Book* say, "Sometimes when people ask me about the Black Mountain Influence I tell them the closest I ever got was Montenegro."

The book also features a detective known as Al, who is modelled on poet Al Purdy, a long-time (usually) friendly rival of Bowering's. Al discovers the body of the painter Tom Thomson, whose 1917 drowning death in Algonquin Park is still shrouded in mystery. After examining just a few clues, Al decides that Thomson "had not been killed by the Black Mountain Influence." Rather, he reveals later, "The canoe tipt over & he fell from Canadian literature right into the lake. This was the Northern Experience." This was also Bowering's comic attack on Canadian literary critics — like Margaret Atwood — who interpreted Canadian art politically and geographically and reviled the American influence.

Reflecting on his school years, during which Canadian literature was rarely on the curriculum, Bowering observed, "We were people who had been deracinated." The only Canadian writer he was introduced to by his teachers was Stephen Leacock, whose sketches would eventually exert their influence upon his work (especially in the 1970s), lending it an undercurrent of humour. As the decade ended, Bowering moved away from lyricism and adopted a historical focus informed by postmodernism. This shift is exemplified by *Burning Water* (1980), the Governor General's Award–winning novel about the life of explorer Captain George Vancouver.

Bowering constantly plays with the role of the author (sometimes publishing reviews under pseudonyms), and this has led him to develop a detached, objective approach. He began, in some instances, to reduce his own authorial presence in his work. In the poem "Against Description" from *West Window* (1982), the poet says, "I went to the blackberries / on the vine." Eight progressively shorter lines later, we have only "Black / berries." The first element cut is the narrative "I."

In the 1980s, Bowering produced five books of critical essays. More recently, he has pursued his fascination with history, publishing *Bowering's BC: A Swashbuckling History* (1996), *Egotists* and Autocrats: The Prime Ministers of Canada (1999), and *Stone Country: An Unauthorized History of Canada* (2003). With *His Life: A Poem* (2000) he returned simultaneously to poetry and autobiography. To create this work, Bowering transformed 30 years' worth of diary material (spanning 1958 to 1988) into a memoir that explores the poetic form. Describing the project, Bowering says, "Once a month I'd get into writing [it] … as a break from doing my ongoing fiction and prose projects. I deliberately savoured doing it over a decade."

In 2002, Bowering was appointed the first Parliamentary Poet Laureate of Canada, a position he held for two years. One reporter remarked that Canadians were getting "a West Coast writer with an irreverent muse, an obsession with baseball and a distaste, his friends say, for all things pompous."

The Acts

from *Autobiology*

Things. Events & things. I have found this out about events & things. I have found this out that events & things can not act upon. You can not be acted upon by events & things & you could not in the past. Each time thereafter you are only by memory & the gift of the present not the same, a little. You are not the same & that is actual. It is not factual, & it is not real. It is actual. There are events & there are things but they are not actual until you are there to act. You are an actor & they are not & they may not act upon you. *Agir*,[1] *agir*, that is the verb of the person & not the event or the thing. You are an event & a thing living as a person when you act upon. Existentialism is a conspiracy of the mind tempted by discourse & its electrical child the radio. The radio can not turn you off & on. *Agir* is not a verb of the radio. You can not be acted upon by the radio or by events on the radio. You can arrive, lift it, & act & act upon. You are a thing or an event until you act but that is not true or actual, it may be real but it is not actual. Man is: he does. The thing does not do, it is. Done to. Done to is not event, it is act. Man is not except as he does. Before that he is only real & that is not enough. The baby acts before he knows about real, before he steps into the river that is a thing during an event, acted upon.

(1972)

Feet, Not Eyes

How I got close to the prairie. Or realized it. This was in Manitoba, 1955, I had got loose all alone & a little drunk hitchhiking west on One between The Peg & Portage[1] about ten miles west of city edge, a totally starless night, low clouds I imagined, & no other light because no farmhouses. It is an absolute straight highway & my measurement, my feet feeling pavement or gravel at the edge, back & forth, my coat hanging unbuttoned, I actually wavered like a movie drunk along the hard surface, till I stopt & stared I thought straight upward. There were no stars & no moonlight could get thru or around those clouds, & when I felt my way to the edge of the hard surface I knew I could look

---

1. *Agir* French, "to act."

1. **The Peg and Portage** Winnipeg and Portage La Prairie, which is about 70 km west of Winnipeg, in Manitoba.

five miles in either direction to see headlights but there were none. Nowhere in the imagined fields around me was there any bird noise or animal grunt, no wind to move grass or scraps of paper thrown from car windows & presumably faded from rain & sun. There could have been a mountain in its own darkness creep up & stop five feet from me, but I thought there was none. I knew I stood on the flatland, my head in the air or maybe the sky, & in all directions the darkness was equal & equal the distance. My only touch was thru the thick shoes to the surface but that could not keep me long from falling. This was the dark of the prairie, & I will never lose the portion that came into my head & found its place just as full.

(1974)

Desert Elm

I

I woke, & woke again, to see her smiling
at me, & turned to find soft sleep in the
green pillow.

Later in the day she said what were you
dreaming, you were smiling in your sleep,
but again it was my sleep, though I have
never said that.

Later I felt the pain three times inside
my left arm, driving the red car, & I re-
membered, I had dreamt that I too had had   10
my heart attack.

Attack, I didnt mean that when I told her,
sitting now on my lap, it was simply all
I could remember of my dream & thinking,
of course, but I am nearly thirty years
younger than him.

He finally had his on the green grass of
the golf course, how mundane, how it
filled my mother's voice with unwonted
fear, to be telling this to *me*.   20

I thought of a rock, not quite round, tonight, reading H.D.[1] on the old age of the
professor, a rock, not quite round, beginning to crack, it will crumble, will
I know this earth.

---

1. H.D. Hilda Doolittle, American poet (1886–1961); refers to her "Tribute to Freud" ("the professor").

II

The earth he made me on, we dug into
side by side, has not long been there,
has been carried there by the glacier,
all rocks & all round rocks, all stones
30   rolled together.

We toiled among the stones, that rattling
sound is my earth, where I grew up looking like him. There was some light falling always into the valley, always blue,
the blue that hovers over heat, a blue
I saw cooling the Adriatic[2] shore.

It is the blue fading in his eyes, they
are not startling blue, it is the family
colour I never got, they are not bright
40   blue but fading to a transparency you
will notice only if you are watching
closely, I mean within a few feet.

They found a desert & made it bloom, made
it green, but even the fairways seen from
across the valley are under a blue haze,
the smoke of space it seemed on high summer days, not a cloud in the sky, no mote[3]
in that eye.

The earth is not brown but grey, grey of
50   stones, the flat stones round to the eye
looking straight down.

III

I never saw him attack anything but a
baseball, a golf ball, his own records,
to be beaten despite his getting older,
to compete satisfactorily with himself.
That is why he never rebuked her, he is
more pure than I.

He said hold the hammer at the handle's
end, for leverage, not because he was a
60   science teacher, because he knew how to
do it, full out, not thinking or rather

---

2. Adriatic The Adriatic sea separates the Apennine and Balkan peninsulas. **3. mote** Speck.

thinking wide open, down the lines of
energy.

He had those muscles you can see under
the skin, the large vein down the middle
of his biceps I never had, I didnt get
the blue eyes or that, & not the straight
nose, I would perhaps never have broken
it then.

He is associated with no colour, no colour   70
clothes or car or house, he would as soon
eat a peach as an apple. I think of the
apple splitting in half as some can make
it between their hands, as he could likely
do that, & it is white.

In the last two years his hair is thin
& one may see between them, & they are
white. His slacks were white below the
purple blazer, & worn twice a month.

IV

Rounding the bases his neck became red as   80
a turkey's but it was a home run, every
one like me has to see his father do that
once, fearing his father is like him, not
as good.

Red as a turkey neck, his eyes bulging,
his heart already something to frighten
the young boy, was it something she said
as this other says now to me playing my
guerrilla ball, I dont want you collapsing
& dying on the field. It is a playing field,   90
I say, I can feel my blood running red
under the skin.

I tell him about it whenever I can, my
average, joking as if I am my team & he is
his, & sometime we must come together,
clasp & both of us, win. He was his mother's
first child, I was my mother's first child,
& after us came just all the rest, the
bases cleared already.

But he didnt get it done till a quarter   100
century later, he lay they say on the fresh

cut grass, all the red gone from under the
skin of his face, pale, those pale blue
eyes looking for her?

In my dream I thought of course, I too,
what will I take up when too old to round
the bases, what crimson driver.

V

I thought of a rock, not quite round
sticking half out of the earth where I
110   would put the ladder's foot. In a hurry,
without patience to place it safely, to
be up that tree & working.

& working. Never half as fast as he could
do it, but in some ways inheriting his
quiet efficiency & turning it to grace.
He said he could never play second base
& I found it the easiest position, bending
over occasionally to pick stones off the
ground.

120   Even this summer, a month before his fall,
he pickt twenty pounds while I pickt
eleven, just more than half & I am more
than half at last, thirty-seven, moving
around to the other half of the tree,
but someone guesst, that is under the
ground, the root system.

A tree, growing downward as I dreamed I
would or desperately hoped I would, to
become this child again, never having the
130   nerve or wit, age four, to follow that to
its home, from one hundred back to the
seed, & then what. A new lease on life?
For him?

The earthly tree grows downward, we do it
after all, bypassing the womb, back where
we came from, down the rabbit hole on the
golf course, above the shade of the old
cherry tree.

VI

General knowledges are those knowledges
140   that idiots possess. What words would you

use to characterize your relationship with
your parents. Scratchy tweed pants they
provided for Sunday school. I remember because of my legs. They look now like his
legs, shorts he wears at the golf course,
no embarrassment, he has come this far,
what are they to him?

Prophecy is finally simple & simply more
interesting than characterization. We are
not characters, we devise characters. I   150
sat as still as possible, the backs of my
knees held forward from the hard curved
wood. Those pants were never worn out,
though they belonged unused to some uncle
first.

His white slacks hung for two weeks in the
closet we'd built some years earlier, he
took them out two Tuesdays each month. A
lifetime uses few such garments. Who wears
the pants in this family is no sociological   160
question. Prophecy is no answer. If you
need an answer go make up a question &
leave me alone without it.

He has those muscles you can see under the
skin, the calf muscle like mine tending toward the other, inside the line of shin
bone. I see his lines every morning in the
mirror.

VII

I woke & again I woke, to find her smiling
at me, & turned to return to soft sleep   170
in the green pillow. A tree, growing down-
ward as I dreamed we all would or hoped
we would, against my god or what they
gave me as my god, their god, given them
against their will, we punish the generation that succeeds us.

Did I mean to say he did that. No, he
never tried to bend my life, never stood
between me & the sun, this tree grew where
the seed fell. A new lease on life? For   180
him? In the thick dark forest the trees

grow tall before they extend wings. Tall
green pillow.

They found a desert & made it bloom, made
it green, but even the trees feel blue
smoke curling among their branches, the
smoke that holds away the frost, the early
message that fills our hearts with ice,
lovely to taste fresh from the branch,
190   but it doesnt travel well. All stones
rolled together, long enough & they will
all be dust, hanging in the air over our
blue lakes.

Prophecy is finally simple, & simply a
pair of eyes thru which the blue of the
sky travels, an observation thru a lens.

VIII

Staring straight into his eyes for the
first time, I see the blue, a sky with
some puffy clouds many miles away.
200   Step into the nearby field, over the sill,
into footprints that disappear as I step
into them, into the blue sky that is not
above but straight in front of me. Straight
eyes, in all the photographs, & in one old
brown kodak print of the family assembled
I look into his oval eyes & see inside
them a man walking backward, out of his
footsteps.

My eyes are brown, walking inside them
210   would be moving over burned grass on low
hills. They found a desert & made it bloom.
I move closer, zooming into his eyes &
find the first aperture completely filled
with one petal of a blue flower, a close-
up of a star weeping in surrender to the
earth, a tear, Aurora weeping helplessly
on the edge of the Blue Nile.[4]

He's no sun of mine, I never stood between
him & the brightness, the mistakes I make

---

4. **Aurora ... Blue Nile** Aurora was the ancient Roman goddess of dawn; her son, Memnos, was killed in battle, and his statue now stands beside the Nile.

will live as long as these ovals stay open.
I walkt into his open eye, over the sill
& saw two enormous black holes in the sky.
A voice came thru a nose & reduced them
to personality. I had never said the word
poetry without a funny accent.

IX

Men who love wisdom should acquaint themselves with a great many particulars.
Cutting the crisp apple with a French knife
I saw that the worm had lived in the core
& chewed his way out, something I've seen
a thousand times & never understood & while
I'm looking he's on the other side of the
green tree picking. One two one two, the
wisdom of the tree filling his picking bag,
its weight strapt over his shoulders. He
showed me, you cross the straps like this
& keep it high. Get above the apples & look
down at them.

& I still do it wrong, reaching up, picking with sore arms, strain rather than wisdom filling me not the bag. He said the
safest step on the ladder is the top, he
was trying to get me up, & always right,
this one I have learned & Saturday I was
on the top step picking apples, wanting
someone to advise. That is how one becomes
acquainted, working to gather.

It could be a woman but is it a woman. Is
it a woman you can work together with, is
it a woman you know doesnt feel the particulars as you do, they are apples, not the
picking of them, the filling. She has been
without a man for years, she offers ladders,
tools, bags for the apples. You want someone to advise to be him, but do it silently
knowing your expertise is somehow, known.

X

I did not see him lying on the grass, I
may as well have been under the ground,
perhaps entangled in the tree growing downward, an earth. His earth, our particular

220

230

240

250

260

earth, as it sifts back & forth, composing
like dust on a piano. The piano is black
but where it has been rubbed it is brown.
He never sat at a piano, only an old black
typewriter with round keys, making faint
words.

So faint they barely heard him. It was August & the grass dry, the thin words rose
like a tree into the air, lightly, as blue
270   as the thin smoke hanging over the green
fairway. It has nothing to do with justice.
He spent thousands of hours in those trees
picking pennies for me, this day he was
knocking them into a hole, I'm glad to hear
that.

In the ocean light of the ward window his
eyes are barely blue & deep in his head
like my daughter's. He woke again to see
me smiling at him, his head straight in
280   the pillow, a rock nearly round. In the
desert the rocks simply lie upon each other
on the ground, a tree is overturned out
of the ground, its shallow widespread roots
coiled around small rocks. By these fruits
we measure our weight & days.

(1976)

Elegy One
from *Kerrisdale Elegies*

If I did complain, who among my friends
would hear?
        If one of them
amazed me with an embrace
he would find his arms empty, his own face
staring from a mirror.

Beauty is the first prod of fear,
                we must
live our lives in.
10   We reach for her,
we think we love her, because she holds the knife
a knife-edge from our throat.
                  Every fair heart

is frightful.
          Every rose petal
exudes poison in bright sunlight.

So I close my mouth, and my cry
makes dark music in my belly.
                    Who would listen
who could amaze?   20
                    Friends and beauty
lie waiting in poems, and the god
whose life we once wrote has left us
to muck in a world we covered with grease.

     Maybe I should watch the blossoms
turn to toasted flakes on my cherry tree.
Maybe I should walk along 41st Avenue
where mothers in velvet jogging suits push prams[1]
and imitate the objects of my first lyrics.
Maybe I should comb my hair   30
the way I did in high school.

In the night the wind slides in from the sea
and eats at our faces;
                    that sweetheart,
she would do anything you ask her,
ask her,
          she'll lie down for a lonely heart.
Night-time's for lovers, maybe, closing their eyes
and pretending tomorrow will be splendid.

You should know that, you adult;   40
why dont you fling your arms wide
into the juicy air, chuck your ardent loneliness,
bump birds out of their dark paths
homeward to their grieving chicks.

Be grateful —
                    sadness makes music, cruel
April tuned a string for you.
                    Moons
whirled around planets waiting for you to spot them.
The middle of the Pacific prepared a wave   50
to plash ashore at your visit.
                    A radio

---

1. **prams** Baby carriages.

switched to melody as you walked by
a neighbour's window.

You should know by now,
                                the world waited
to come alive at your step —
                                could you handle that?
Or did you think this was love,
60   movie music
introducing a maiden you could rescue?
Where were you going to keep her,
                                and keep her
from seeing those dreams you were already
playing house with?

When your heart hungers,
                                sing a song of six-
teen, remember your own maidenly[2] love
and the girls that aroused it,
70   make them famous.
Remember their plain friends who danced so well
because they never got into a back seat.
Bring them all back, become a lyric poet again.
Identify with heroes who die for love
and a terrific image,
                                you'll live forever
in your anguished exalted metaphors.
                                                Oh yeah.

But remember nature?
80   She takes back all
worn-out lovers,
                                two lie in the earth, one moulders
above-ground;
                                nature is an exhausted mum,
she cant go on forever,
                                this is late
in the machine age.
                                Can you think of one woman
who gave up on the stag line[3] and turned
90   to God and a peaceful lawn?

Isnt it about time we said to hell with agony?
Shouldnt we be rich with hit parade love by now?
Arent we really free to choose joy over drama,

---

2. **maidenly** Youthful. 3. **stag line** A line of men at a dance who circle the dance floor, awaiting and selecting partners.

and havent we come through looking pretty good,
like a line-drive off a perfect swing
in the ninth inning?
                        It leaves the bat faster
than it came to the plate.
                           Taking that pitch
and standing still in the batter's box is nowhere.   100

Somebody's talking.
                      Listen, stupid Kerrisdale heart,
the way your dead heroes listened, till
they were lifted out of their shoes,
but they couldnt hear it all, they thought
they were standing on earth.
                      No,
you're not going to hear the final clap of truth;
that would kill you in two heart-beats.

But listen to the wind in the chestnut trees,   110
the breath of autumn's bleeding,
                       the death
of your young heroes.
                     You recall the breeze
across from the station in Florence,
where you saw an amazing name by the door?
Remember the clouds pulled off the face
of Mt. Blanc[4] you saw from the morning window?
Why would the wind reach down to me?

Am I supposed to translate that swishy voice   120
into some kind of modern law?
Make me their liar even as the chestnuts are?
Deesse dans l'air repandue,
flamme dans notre souterrain![5]

Yes, I know, it is odd to be away from the world,
dropping all the habits you learned so well;
never bending to look at a rose face to face,
throwing your name away,
free of hands that held you fiercely,
laughing at what you once ached for,   130
watching all the old connections unravel in space.

---

4. **Mt. Blanc** Mountain between France and Italy; also the subject of the poem "Mont Blanc" by British romantic poet Percy Bysshe Shelley (1792–1822), which addressed the relationship between the mind and the world. 5. **Deesse ... souterrain!** From Charles Baudelaire's 1868 collection of poems *Les Fleurs du Mal*; the poem is called "La Prière d'un paien" ("A Pagan's Prayer"). The lines translate as "Goddess who permeates the air, / Flame in our underground cavern!"

Being dead is no bed of roses,
you have so much work piled up in front of you
before the long weekend.
But the folks who are still alive are too quick
to make their little decisions.
The spooks, they tell me, cant tell whether they're moving
among corpses or the fretful living.
The everlasting universe of things rolls
140   through all minds of all ages in every back yard,
and none of them can hear themselves think.

The ones who left early dont need our voices;
they're weaned from this ground as neatly
as we're diverted from mom's tit. But
what about us?
              We need the mystery, we need
the grief that makes us long for our dead friends,
we need that void for our poems.
We'd be dead without them.

150   Queen Marilyn made silly movies, but she's
the stuff our words are made from.
                   Her meaning
struts along the lines of a hundred lovely books.
Her music may be heard in the gaps in the traffic
of 41st Avenue.
                Her shiny breasts
fill the hands of our weeping poets.

(1984)

Do Sink

1

When I have fears that I
may cease to be[1]
open to pain that shines
wet on the side of a gold
fish in my own, I thought,
pond

      I ought to forget
comfort, forget family
history, drive a black sedan

---

1. **When I … cease to be** Opening line of a sonnet of the same name by Romantic poet John Keats (1795–1821); all
following line quotations are from the same poem.

over thin prairie roads 10
looking for a town even
my mother does not believe
was ever there

        knowing
pain is not colour, not value
but condition, the cost
of starting a damned life
in the first place, where no
thinking man ever was.

2

Before my pen has 20
gleaned my teeming brain[2]
the vehicle of forget all this
piece by piece will pull up
from behind, an unremembered
cousin at the wheel

        coloured
like the car and beautiful
in a tailored shirt, forget
that and that and that thing
you've not quite recalled, 30
take my hand

        & souls of poets
long since gone sit down to sing
with your family, did you think
you could just grow those
upper arms, wait for a bus, and get
whisked away beyond pain?

3

Before high-piled books,
in charactery[3] this fool
scribes his day, walks the town
as if new to the job without 40
rising from his desk, a black car
parked in back

        with orange cats
coiled on the warm hood, his team
of familiars, his destiny, nine

---

2. **Before my pen ... teeming brain** Line 2. 3. **Before high-piled ... charactery** Line 3.

lifetimes prepared hopelessly, this
idiot with a black pen writes
and yet writes

50   with ginger
in his shadowed heart, protected
from the sun and its rays, the
measure of the year a few lines
that will last longer than a cherry
tree bird's song.

4

Driving a dusty black sedan
over flimsy prairie roads,
he feels his eyes and mind's machine
hold like rich garners
60   the full ripened grain,[4] the
dark void of night

                    somewhere
high behind him, while family
never met will rush from ground
like wheat into a lovely maiden's
hand, her picture now the reverse
of our currency

                    dropped from our
fingers faster and faster as we age,
70   dirt from our skin piled into heaps
to rival these small prairie hills, loam
to grow a grandmother, obfuscate[5]
a self.

5

When I behold, upon the night's
starred face,[6] a gold sheen, I know
my eyes are old beyond their desire,
two aged deer as dull as the surface
of this pond

                    I contemplate
80   falling into, when I behold
no star's reflection on that face
I hate the books piled high
that told me heaven was

---

4. **hold like ... ripened grain** Line 4. **5. obfuscate** Obscure or conceal. **6. When I behold ... starred face** Line 5.

what we worked for, fame
was love

       deferred, a family
wider than a suburb firmament,[7]
a story we must aid the telling of,
we must edit with our
failing breath.   90

6

Huge cloudy symbols of a high
romance[8] in the night sky shimmer,
images of satisfied self-murder
haunt one's eyes inside the windshield
on the prairie, drive he said, everyone
insane

       with melodious chuckle
in strings heard from rear speakers,
laughter beside a dark road dangerous
& narrow under starlight, families   100
emerging from hard soil, weed roots
sliding from their shoulders

             weak
from disuse, exactly what the thrush,
could he have spoken, would have said,
an observant eye in available light, a
relative bird awake when one is nearly
asleep at the wheel.

7

I'm driving this black sedan
too swiftly over rutted prairie roads
and think that I may never live to trace[9]   110
my DNA another generation
down the route of fate, oh damn
such maunderings[10]

            come upon so early
in the dying business, before my pen
has gleaned a thing worth harvesting,
or so one says every year, and considers

---

7. **firmament** The imagined surface of a heavenly sphere. 8. **Huge cloudy ... high romance** Line 6. 9. **and think ... to trace** Line 7. 10. **maunderings** Nonsensical speech or aimless movement.

120   a grandmother who likely never wrote at all
save misspelled letters to her sister

lost to the south, caught in a draught
no one could have expected, deep
in another family, wild shoeless brothers
with big noses, my kin, my semblables,[11]
too dear to keep in memory, in a line
that grows longer as we walk it.

8

Driving under dark prairie clouds
I confuse their shadows with
the magic hand of chance,[12] lose
130   all trace of grandparents to the geography,
the ground converted

in the vehicular
mind into latitudes, for instance,
of mortality, no matter the voices
alongside the road, no matter the urgings
of the season, haunting is haunting, dying
is less exciting as it goes

along, looking
for whatever it looks for, chromosomes,
140   colours of late seasons, cruel anemones, perhaps
sprouting out of literature with comic face,
comic mice under those nearby leaves,
I think they are, racing by.

9

And when I feel, fair
creature of an hour,[13] brought up
so rudely from the earth, that I
will never see you plain, your whispering
by the roadside like the night breeze
in thistles.

150   seems to propel this black
vehicle, no star's reflection on its back,
an almost unseen shark in the gloom,
and in its belly a tiring brain that wants only

---

11. **brothers … semblables** The words echo Baudelaire's "Au Lecteur" ("To the Reader") in his *Fleurs du mal*: "Hypocrite lecteur, — mon semblable, — mon frère!" ("Hypocrite reader — my colleague — my brother!") **12. their shadows … of chance** Line 8. **13. And when … an hour** Line 9.

some abandoned town you lived in
too young to know its name

                              and then dead
too soon to hear of mine, oh a sentence
can never be as confused as our line, the
unknowing all along it, the progeny
suffering in silence some pain for one actual,   160
for the next a story being told.

10

I'm scared to death that I shall never
look upon thee more[14] clear than
I do tonight, dark creature of a time
long past my memory, long past the desire
of my mother's recollection, who never
heard these roadside ditches sing

                              this song
like thistles, like music scribed by pens
gleaning brains we would never recognize   170
even were their headstones to be found
in that pine-bordered plot in the middle
of the bald-headed

                    where a black sedan
parked in westering sunlight while this
lorn grandson walked hopeless and lost
on his DNA's purported earth again, you
nowhere to be found inside that square, only
encountered in the roadside's bright dirge.[15]

11

Locked inside this heavy car, I   180
will never have relish in the faery
power[16] known to the unknown who
walked this way in a musical past, never
ride the vehicle invisible beyond desire,
never remember

                    where my share of
molecules might fetch up, D for desire,
N for Never, and A for a beginning
we all have honestly missed, watching

---

14. that I … thee more Line 10. **15. dirge** Funeral song, or similar lament. **16. never have … faery power** Line 11.

190   intently as we can the roadside slippage,
              the willows in the wind

                              that is only
              main component of our song, oh what ears
              we waste on one another's plaints, oh
              what hours we cast aside while our dearest
              family dies in other arms, oh how late
              we come to realize or not.

              12

              When I perceive the prairie beside the road
              as a pond of unreflecting love —
200   then on the shore[17] far from this dark
              the night sky falls to wrap those quick
              golden shapes

                              that swim like thought
              where we seek no mother's mother, here
              beneath the still wheels of this dark sedan
              are bones enough, unbending below
              their burden of invisible earth, stones
              caught in the arms of soil

                              some tried
210   to instruct us has always been the base
              of our being, while we, riders
              of pneumatic spin, cast our loyalty
              to an idea, God is Love, Mother
              is Queen of Earth, Dian of Heaven[18]
              and whatever that is out there.

              13

              I remember this night, getting out
              of the car to wait: in the reputed centre
              of the wide world I stand alone, and think[19]
              like a sheen of gold-sided fish, flitting
220   into the dark, no stars in this crown, no
              supreme darkness

                              to see them in, a voice
              by the side of the road is only the weather,
              no stone marks a grave if it is here,

---

17. of unreflecting … the shore Line 12. **18. Dian of Heaven** Diana was the ancient Roman goddess of the hunt. **19. of the wide … and think** Line 13.

the dying business is not tidy, ruts in the road
are direction, not aid, the end of light
is partly darkness only

               given to grandsons
who cannot turn their eyes to look inward,
and will forget the time they tried, have fears   230
that themselves will cease to be, when suns
rise and bring partial light, gold at first, a
flash of lesser metal, a day.

14
When I have fear that eyes may
cease to be upon me, looking only through
what seems to be there, here, in the centre
of the shadowed earth nearly flat with age,
oh then what seems to me a mother's mother
is only the mother

             of these late thoughts,   240
what vehicle brings us to this halt, what spectre
carriage with what geography implied, oh
let me remain outside, above the maternal ground
of being, below the dark clouds of seeming,
inside any out there is

             relative to what
there is not, let me start the engine and release
anything, the clutch, the earthlike hold of bones,
release the music of the roadside ditches, back
let me go, let me rouse my fancied kin and think   250
till song and pain to nothingness do sink.[20]

               (1992)

Musing on Some Poets

Those poets, heads coming out of collars,
advised us, showed us how to hold paper and look good,
did we sometime grow tired of them, those
who lived for us,
died for us,
rotted under ground for us,
are still
so we may move.

---

20. **till song … do sink** cf. Line 14 of Keats's sonnet, "Till Love and Fame to nothingness do sink."

Not friends, really, not teachers,
10   poets, whose names glittered when we were alone,
     whose books dropped like gleaming newborn calves into our unsteady hands,
     did we read them as if pulling shavings off our souls,
     never stepped out of the Pacific combers[1] with shine on morning face,
     never twisted body out of grip of coal giant ogre
     save with inspiration of our poets,
     and who knows what our
     means?

     What are we now besides older;
     a young man newly graduated from university,
20   black gown still on him said I envy you and your friends,
     you got to make the last ones,
     there isnt anything to make now, or no one knows what there is.
     I said it seems that way but there is always something,
     and I showed him my teeth through yellow beer.

     Do we old farts say thank you every genuflecting morning
     to those poets with agate[2] names who showed us their synapses?[3]
     Nowadays the young want us to love the earth,
     And I never say out loud to them that my dear old people
     Are columns of earth, walk around, sit in chairs,
30   discard cigarettes and write that's left of poems.
     They were low lights between mountains visible
     to the evening gaze, they were evaporate mornings,
     They are not mulch but stones in the earth, they are not
     specimens but the authors of words should be whispered inside a dark bowl
     from Siena.

     I have no remaining skill for form,
     just feel words jostle each other in doorways on the way out, sit here this
     evening remembering a former life, I'm with friends
     all lovely all restrained by hope, all agreed without saying so
40   — those poets gave us a way to waste our lives
     saying useless things, smiling indulgently at each other's personal diaspora,[4]
     carrying mismatched goodies on the way to the grave,
     trip, fall into hole, write on dirt walls
     a first and last sonnet,
     solving all, coming to rest, combing hair, adjusting socks,
     kissing no one but the image of Jesus, disbursing mind as if it were mercury,
     listening for the voices to arrive with the worms.

                                                                         (1997)

---

1. combers Waves breaking into foam. **2. agate** Marble. **3. synapses** Nerve endings. **4. diaspora** The dispersion of
people from their homeland.

Fall 1962. Vancouver

Inside the strangeness of living
as a young man, with.

With A, they went to see his
soppy hero, nearly jazzman, Sammy
Davis Junior, at the Queen.
Elizabeth Theatre. It was very nice
to see him at last, gratifying
to hear him do Frank Sinatra
the white guy.

Snow. C.P.   10
Snow sees the continent of the rich
pull away from the continent poor.

We need, he says, to revampire
western education, supply money, send
men to poor lands, prod
their revolutions. China, 1949.

But intellectuals. They are rooted
in the so far
all right soil of the past. They do impressions
(if you want unity) of the past. This   20
is tradition. Not the strange.

(2000)

Joy Kogawa (1935–)

Joy Kogawa (née Nakayama) was born in 1935 in Vancouver, British Columbia, to first-generation Japanese immigrants. In 1942, a year after the Japanese bombed Pearl Harbor, the Canadian government instituted a "dispersal" policy, which entailed the forced evacuation of over 22,000 Japanese Canadians from coastal B.C. and 100 miles inland. Kogawa and her family were sent to live in forced-labour camps in the B.C. interior and in Alberta, and there they remained until the policy was lifted, in 1949.

At 19, Kogawa earned a teaching certificate from the University of Alberta and returned to Coaldale, Alberta, one of the towns where her family had been interned, to work as a teacher. In 1955, she moved to Toronto to study at the Royal Conservatory of Music, returning to Vancouver a year later. In 1957, she married David Kogawa, with whom she would have two children. They divorced in 1968, the year after she published *The Splintered Moon*. Its narrator is subjected to a number of violent traumas — she is eaten, she is surgically carved, her heart explodes. Kogawa explains that in her early days, she "wrote as a white person" because she had stifled her Japanese heritage. In *A Choice of Dreams* (1974), she explores a wider range of themes and ideas and begins to address the anger she harbours at having been victimized by the racist dispersal policy. In "What Do I Remember of the Evacuation," she describes being torn from her home, spat upon, and forced onto a train that carries her through the mountains. She "prayed to the God who loves / All the children in his sight / That I might be white."

From 1974 to 1976, Kogawa was a staff writer in the office of Prime Minister Pierre Elliott Trudeau. In 1977, she published *Jericho Road;* the same year, she travelled to California, where she met Japanese Americans and heard their stories of evacuation and internment. She discovered that these people had suffered less during the war than their Canadian counterparts, because they enjoyed partial protection under the U.S. Constitution; Canada did not have its own charter of rights until 1982. At home, Kogawa noticed that Japanese Canadians rarely spoke up to demand their rights, and this led her to reflect, in the poem "On the Jericho Road," "Your tongue / was your weapon / I lay silent / on the Jericho Road / Silence is also / a two-edged sword." The double-edged nature of silence is a theme that would reappear prominently in her first novel, *Obasan* (1981).

The novel has become essential reading for anyone interested in the North American experience of people with Asian ancestry. Based on her 1978 short story of the same name, *Obasan* (the term is a polite way of saying "aunt" in Japanese) was the first book by a Japanese Canadian to expose what had happened under the dispersal policy. It is also an example of what Linda Hutcheon refers to as "historiographic metafiction" — a genre that subverts our assumptions about realism by "confronting the discourse of art with the discourse of history." Blending fiction with documentary materials, Kogawa tells the story of Naomi, who is raised by her uncle and her Obasan after her mother dies during the American bombing of Nagasaki. Dispossessed, stripped of their rights as citizens, sent to live in a camp, this small reconstituted family lapses into silence. Naomi's surrogate parents are intimidated by their new circumstances; her own silence actually predates the dispersal, beginning when she is sexually molested by a White neighbour. Kogawa's linkage of these two forms of abuse intensifies her condemnation of the racism to which her characters are subjected.

When Naomi starts to read the diary of another aunt, Emily, she at last perceives the voice of outrage, the counterpoint to Obasan's stoic silence. Stoicism, considered a supreme virtue in Japanese culture, becomes a "two-edged sword" for Naomi. Her mixed-culture upbringing prompts her simultaneously to speak out and to endure silently. Eventually, however, Emily's words convince her to summon suppressed memories: "You have to remember. You are your history. If you cut any of it off you're an amputee ... Cry it out! Scream! Denial is gangrene."

In 1985, Kogawa published the poetry collection *Woman in the Woods,* but she had already begun to think of herself as a novelist. She declared that the "faucet" of poetry "is now turned off," adding that "Poetry is a kind of gasp, and there it is, a spark on the page. Fiction, on the other hand, is like a swamp fire." Because of its narrative scope, fiction proved a more suitable vehicle for Kogawa's expanding interest in social protest. From 1983 to 1985, she aided the National Association of Japanese Canadians (NAJC) in its effort to convince the government that it had an obligation to compensate those who had been subjected to the dispersal policy.

Kogawa's second novel, *Itsuka* (1992), is a sequel to *Obasan.* Whereas *Obasan* is elegiac and personal and contains sections of prose poetry, *Itsuka* is determined, public, and didactic. In it, Kogawa suggests that political activism can repair broken communities. Naomi, now 40 and dealing with the death of Obasan, involves herself in the movement to seek redress from the government. Kogawa was amazed to learn, just as she reached the midway point in writing *Itsuka,* that the movement had succeeded: in 1988, Prime Minister Brian Mulroney offered financial compensation and an apology to interned Japanese Canadians. The NAJC accepted, and Kogawa altered the outcome of her story accordingly.

Extending her reputation as a writer who deals with topical subjects, Kogawa published *The Rain Ascends* (1995). The novel's protagonist, Millicent, discovers that her adored father, an Anglican minister, has been sexually abusing children. Through a series of flashbacks, Kogawa builds a dialogue between characters who hold opposing views of the minister: one condemns him for molesting so many children; another rationalizes that he has helped many people. The novel is fuelled by Kogawa's continued interest in human rights and her fascination with Christianity, which is present in much of her work.

Although Kogawa had shut off the poetry faucet, a friend asked her to provide material for a multimedia event in support of a Toronto community organization, and the result was *A Song of Lilith* (2001), a book-length poem with accompanying drawings by Lilian Broca. This offering, which displays a more explicit feminism than Kogawa's previous works, tells the story of Lilith, the first wife of Adam, who resists her husband and then flees Eden after he rapes her. She becomes a model of female power in contrast to Eve, her pliant successor.

In 1986, Kogawa was made a Member of the Order of Canada and published *Naomi's Road*, a children's version of *Obasan*. She divides her time between Toronto and Vancouver.

From *Obasan*

February 15, 1942.

Dearest Nesan,

I thought I would write to you every day but, as you see, I haven't managed that. I felt so sad thinking about what the children are having to experience I didn't want to keep writing. But today I must tell you what's happening.

Things are changing so fast. First, all the Japanese men — the ones who were born in Japan and haven't been able to get their citizenship yet — are being rounded up, one hundred or so at a time. A few days ago, Mark told me he felt sure Sam had been carted off. I took the interurban down as soon as I could. Isamu couldn't have been gone too long because not all the plants were parched though some of the delicate ones had turned to skeletons in the front window. I tried to find the dog but she's just nowhere. I looked and called all through the woods and behind the house.

Grandma and Grandpa Nakane will be so upset and confused when they find out he's gone. You know how dependent they are on him. They went to Saltspring Island[1] a couple of weeks ago and haven't come back yet. I know they're with friends so they must be all right.

We know some people who have left Vancouver. Dad says we should look around and get out too, but we just don't know any other place. When we look at the map it's hard to think about all those unknown places. We were thinking of going to Kamloops,[2] but that may be too close to the boundary of the "protected area."[3]

It's becoming frightening here, with the agitation mounting higher. It isn't just a matter of fear of sabotage or military necessity any more, it's outright race persecution. Groups like the "Sons of Canada"[4] are petitioning Ottawa against us and the newspapers

---

1. **Saltspring Island** Island off the coast of British Columbia. 2. **Kamloops** Inland city in British Columbia. 3. **protected area** In 1942, a protected area was declared that spread from the Pacific coast 100 km inland; all men of Japanese descent in this area were displaced into work or prisoner-of-war camps. 4. **Sons of Canada** The Native Sons of Canada group vocally opposed immigration and cultural pluralism in favour of preserving Canada's Anglo-Saxon background.

are printing outright lies. There was a picture of a young Nisei[5] boy with a metal lunch box and it said he was a spy with a radio transmitter. When the reporting was protested the error was admitted in a tiny line in the classified section at the back where you couldn't see it unless you looked very hard.

March 2, 1942.

Everyone is distressed here, Nesan. Eiko and Fumi came over this morning, crying. All student nurses have been fired from the General.

Our beautiful radios are gone. We had to give them up or suffer the humiliation of having them taken forcibly by the RCMP. Our cameras — even Stephen's toy one that he brought out to show them when they came — all are confiscated. They can search our homes without warrant.

But the great shock is this: we are all being forced to leave. All of us. Not a single person of the Japanese race who lives in the "protected area" will escape. There is something called a Civilian Labour Corps[6] and Mark and Dan were going to join — you know how they do everything together — but now will not go near it as it smells of a demonic roundabout way of getting rid of us. There is a very suspicious clause "within and *without*" Canada, that has all the fellows leery.

Who knows where we will be tomorrow, next week. It isn't as if we Nisei were aliens — technically or not. It breaks my heart to think of leaving this house and the little things that we've gathered through the years — all those irreplaceable mementoes — our books and paintings — the azalea plants, my white iris.

Oh Nesan, the Nisei are bitter. Too bitter for their own good or for Canada. How can cool heads like Tom's prevail, when the general feeling is to stand up and fight? He needs all his level-headedness and diplomacy, as editor of the *New Canadian*,[7] since that's the only paper left to us now.

A curfew that applies only to us was started a few days ago. If we're caught out after sundown, we're thrown in jail. People who have been fired — and there's a scramble on to be the first to kick us out of jobs — sit at home without even being able to go out for a consoling cup of coffee. For many, home is just a bed. Kunio is working like mad with the Welfare society to look after the women and children who were left when the men were forced to "volunteer" to go to the work camps. And where are those men? Sitting in unheated bunk-cars, no latrines, no water, snow fifteen feet deep, no work, little food if any. They were shunted off with such inhuman speed that they got there before any facilities were prepared. Now other men are afraid to go because they think they'll be going to certain disaster. If the snow is that deep, there is no work. If there is no work, there is no pay. If there is no pay, no one eats. Their families suffer. The *Daily Province* reports that work on frames with tent coverings is progressing to house the 2,000 expected. Tent coverings where the snow is so deep? You should see the faces here — all pinched, grey, uncertain. Signs have been posted on all highways — "Japs Keep Out."

Mind you, you can't compare this sort of thing to anything that happens in Germany. That country is openly totalitarian. But Canada is supposed to be a democracy.

---

5. **Nisei** "Second generation." Person of Japanese descent who was not born and raised in Japan. 6. **Civilian Labour Corps** Work groups that Japanese-Canadian men were "offered" as an alternative to internment, though the conditions were not terribly different. 7. *New Canadian* A paper published by and for Canadians of Japanese origin that spoke boldly against internment during this period. Tom Shoyama was its editor from 1938–1945.

All Nisei are liable to imprisonment if we refuse to volunteer to leave. At least that is the likeliest interpretation of Ian Mackenzie's "Volunteer or else" statement. He's the Minister of Pensions and National Health. Why do they consider us to be wartime prisoners? Can you wonder that there is a deep bitterness among the Nisei who believed in democracy?

And the horrors that some of the young girls are facing — outraged by men in uniform. You wouldn't believe it, Nesan. You have to be right here in the middle of it to really know. The men are afraid to go and leave their wives behind.

How can the Hakujin[8] not feel ashamed for their treachery? My butcher told me he knew he could trust me more than he could most whites. But kind people like him are betrayed by the outright racists and opportunists like Alderman Wilson,[9] God damn his soul. And there are others who, although they wouldn't persecute us, are ignorant and indifferent and believe we're being very well treated for the "class" of people we are. One letter in the papers says that in order to preserve the "British way of life," they should send us all away. We're a "lower order of people." In one breath we are damned for being "inassimilable" and the next there's fear that we'll assimilate. One reporter points to those among us who are living in poverty and says "No British subject would live in such conditions." Then if we improve our lot, another says, "There is danger that they will enter our better neighbourhoods." If we are educated the complaint is that we will cease being the "ideal servant." It makes me choke. The diseases, the crippling, the twisting of our souls is still to come.

March 12.

Honest Nesan, I'm just in a daze this morning. The last ruling forbids any of us — even Nisei — to go anywhere in this wide dominion without a permit from the Minister of Justice, St Laurent,[10] through Austin C. Taylor of the Commission here. We go where they send us.

Nothing affects me much just now except rather detachedly. Everything is like a bad dream. I keep telling myself to wake up. There's no sadness when friends of long standing disappear overnight — either to Camp or somewhere in the Interior. No farewells — no promise at all of future meetings or correspondence — or anything. We just disperse. It's as if we never existed. We're hit so many ways at one time that if I wasn't past feeling I think I would crumble.

This curfew business is horrible. At sundown we scuttle into our holes like furtive creatures. We look in the papers for the time of next morning's sunrise when we may venture forth.

The government has requisitioned the Livestock Building at Hastings Park,[11] and the Women's Building, to house 2,000 "Japs pending removal." White men are pictured in the newspaper filling ticks with bales of straw for mattresses, putting up makeshift partitions for toilets — etc. Here the lowly Jap will be bedded down like livestock in stalls — perhaps closed around under police guard — I don't know. The Nisei will be "compelled" (news report) to volunteer in Labour Gangs. The worse the news from the Eastern Front, the more ghoulish the public becomes. We are the billygoats and

---

8. **Hakujin** White people. 9. **Alderman Wilson** Halford Wilson, a municipal alderman of Vancouver, who suddenly found support for his well-known anti-Asian feelings in 1942. 10. **Minister of Justice, St Laurent** Later became Prime Minister Louis St. Laurent (1882–1973). 11. **Hastings Park** Japanese-Canadians were kept in animal stalls in Hastings Park, Vancouver, for months before being moved on to camps in former ghost towns.

nannygoats and kids — all the scapegoats to appease this blindness. Is this a Christian country? Do you know that Alderman Wilson, the man who says such damning things about us, has a father who is an Anglican clergyman?

I can't imagine how the government is going to clothe and educate our young when they can't even get started on feeding or housing 22,000 removees. Yet the deadline for clearing us out seems to be July 1st or 31st — I'm not sure which. Seems to me that either there are no fifth columnists[12] or else the Secret Service men can't find them. If the FBI in the States have rounded up a lot of them you'd think the RCMP could too and let the innocent ones alone. I wish to goodness they'd catch them all. I don't feel safe if there are any on the loose. But I like to think there aren't any.

March 20.
Dearest Nesan,

Stephen has been developing a slight limp. Dad's not sure what's wrong with the leg. He suspects that the fall he had last year never healed properly and there's some new aggravation at the hip. Stephen spends a lot of time making up tunes on the new violin Dad got him. The old one, I told you, was broken. It's lucky our houses are so close as I can get to see the children fairly often, even with the miserable curfew.

Your friend Mina Sugimoto takes her boys to play with Stephen a fair amount but she's acting like a chicken flapping about with her head cut off since her husband left.

Last night over a hundred boys entrained[13] for a road camp at Schreiber, Ontario. A hundred and fifty are going to another camp at Jasper. The Council (United Nisei) has been working like mad talking to the boys. The first batch of a hundred refused to go. They got arrested and imprisoned in that Immigration building. The next batch refused too and were arrested. Then on Saturday they were released on the promise that they would report back to the Pool. There was every indication they wouldn't but the Council persuaded them to keep their word. They went finally. That was a tough hurdle and the Commission cabled Ralston[14] to come and do something.

On Thursday night, the confinees in the Hastings Park Pool came down with terrible stomach pains. Ptomaine,[15] I gather. A wholesale company or something is contracted to feed them and there's profiteering. There are no partitions of any kind whatsoever and the people are treated worse than livestock, which at least had their own pens and special food when they were there. No plumbing of any kind. They can't take a bath. They don't even take their clothes off. Two weeks now. Lord! Can you imagine a better breeding ground for typhus?[16] They're cold (Vancouver has a fuel shortage), they're undernourished, they're unwashed. One of the men who came out to buy food said it was pitiful the way the kids scramble for food and the slow ones go empty. God damn those politicians who brought this tragedy on us.

Dan has to report tomorrow and will most likely be told when to go and where. A day's notice at most. When will we see him again? Until all this happened I didn't realize how close a member of the family he had become. He's just like a brother to me. Nesan, I don't know what to do.

---

12. **fifth columnists** Secretive political actors working to undermine an established order; the term was frequently (and groundlessly) applied to Japanese-Canadians to justify internment. 13. **entrained** Dragged themselves along, or were swept away. 14. **Ralston** James Layton Ralston, Minister of National Defence from 1940–1944. 15. **Ptomaine** Food poisoning. 16. **typhus** Disease transmitted by lice or fleas, characterized by fever, headache, and rash.

The Youth Congress protested at the ill treatment but since then the daily papers are not printing a word about us. One baby was born at the Park. Premature, I think.

If all this sounds like a bird's eye view to you, Nesan, it's the reportage of a caged bird. I can't really see what's happening. We're like a bunch of rabbits being chased by hounds.

You remember Mr Morii, the man who was teaching judo to the RCMP? He receives orders from the Mounties to get "a hundred to the station or else and here's a list of names." Any who are rich enough, or who are desperate about not going immediately because of family concerns, pay Morii hundreds of dollars and get placed conveniently on a committee. There are nearly two hundred on that "committee" now. Some people say he's distributing the money to needy families but who knows?

There's a three-way split in the community — three general camps: the Morii gang, us — the Council group — and all the rest, who don't know what to do. The Council group is just a handful. It's gruelling uphill work for us. Some people want to fight. Others say our only chance is to co-operate with the government. Whichever way we decide there's a terrible feeling of underlying treachery.

March 22, 1942.
Dear Diary,
   I don't know if Nesan will ever see any of this. I don't know anything any more. Things are swiftly getting worse here. Vancouver — the water, the weather, the beauty, this paradise — is filled up and overflowing with hatred now. If we stick around too long we'll all be chucked into Hastings Park. Fumi and Eiko are helping the women there and they say the crowding, the noise, the confusion is chaos. Mothers are prostrate in nervous exhaustion — the babies crying endlessly — the fathers torn from them without farewell — everyone crammed into two buildings like so many pigs — children taken out of school with no provision for future education — more and more people pouring into the Park — forbidden to step outside the barbed wire gates and fence — the men can't even leave the building — police guards around them — some of them fight their way out to come to town to see what they can do about their families. Babies and motherless children totally stranded — their fathers taken to camp. It isn't as if this place had been bombed and *everyone* was suffering. *Then* our morale would be high because we'd be *together*.

Eiko says the women are going to be mental cases.

Rev. Kabayama and family got thrown in too. It's going to be an ugly fight to survive among us. They're making (they say) accommodation for 1,200–1,300 women and children in that little Park! Bureaucrats find it so simple on paper and it's translated willy-nilly into action — and the pure hell that results is kept "hush hush" from the public, who are already kicking about the "luxury" given to Japs.

I'm consulting with Dad and Mark and Aya about going to Toronto. We could all stay together if we could find someone in Toronto to sponsor us. People are stranded here and there all over the B.C. interior. I want to leave this poisoned province. But Aya wants to stay in B.C. to be closer to Sam. I'm going to write to a doctor in Toronto that Dad knows.

March 27.
   Dan's been arrested. The boys refused to go to Ontario. Both trainloads. So they're all arrested. Dan had a road map friends drew for him so they suspected him of being a "spy" and now he's in the Pool.

Nisei are called "enemy aliens." Minister of War, or Defense, or something flying here to take drastic steps.

April 2, 1942.
Dearest Nesan,

If only you and Mother could come home! Dad's sick in bed. The long months of steady work. Since the evacuation started he's had no let-up at all. Two nights ago, one of his patients was dying. He tried to arrange to have the daughter go to the old man's bedside but couldn't. Dad stayed up all night with the man, and now he's sick himself.

I'm afraid that those kept in the Hastings Park will be held as hostages or something. Perhaps to ensure the good behaviour of the men in the work camps. Dan was cleared of that idiotic spying charge and is helping at the Pool. The cop who arrested him was drunk and took a few jabs at him but Dan didn't retaliate, thank heavens. I'm applying for a pass so I can get to see him.

Dan has a lawyer working for him and his parents about their desire to stay together, especially since Dan's father is blind and his mother speaks no English at all. The lawyer went to the Security Commission's lawyers and reported back that he was told to let the matter drift because they were going to make sure the Japs suffered as much as possible. The Commission is responsible to the Federal Government through the Minister of Justice, St Laurent. It works in conjunction with the RCMP. The Commission has three members — Austin C. Taylor, to represent the Minister of Justice, Commissioner Mead of the RCMP, John Shirras of the Provincial Police.

Only Tommy and Kunio, as active members of the Council, know what's going on and they're too busy to talk to me. The *New Canadian* comes out so seldom we have no way of knowing much and I've been so busy helping Dad I can't get to Council meetings very often. There's so much veiling and soft pedalling because everything is censored by the RCMP. We can only get information verbally. The bulletins posted on Powell Street aren't available to most people. Besides, nobody can keep up with all the things that are happening. There's a terrible distrust of federal authorities and fear of the RCMP, but mostly there's a helpless panic. Not the hysterical kind, but the kind that churns round and round going nowhere.

My twenty-sixth birthday is coming up soon and I feel fifty. I've got lines under my eyes and my back is getting stooped, I noticed in a shop window today.

Mina Sugimoto heard from her husband. Why haven't we heard from Sam? Stephen asked me the other day "Where's Uncle?" What could I say?

April 8, 1942.

Ye gods! The newspapers are saying that there are actually Japanese naval officers living on the coast. It must be a mistake. Maybe they're old retired men. I heard someone say it was just that they took courses when they were kids in school and that's the way schools are in Japan. I'd hate to think we couldn't tell a fisherman from a sailor. Maybe the articles are true. I wonder if there's a cover-up. Surely we'd know if there were any spies. But gosh — who can we trust? At times like this, all we have is our trust in one another. What happens when that breaks down?

A few days ago the newspaper reported Ian Mackenzie as saying "The intention of the government is that every single Japanese — man, woman and child — shall be removed from Vancouver as speedily as possible." He said we were all going to be out in three or four weeks and added it was his "personal intention," as long as he was in public life, "that these Japanese shall not come back here."

It's all so frightening. Rumours are that we're going to be kept as prisoners and war hostages — but that's so ridiculous since we're Canadians. There was a headline in the paper yesterday that said half of our boats "of many different kinds and sizes" have been released to the army, navy, air force, and to "bona fide white fishermen." I wonder who has Sam's beautiful little boat. It was such an ingenious design. They said they were hopeful about all the boats because one plywood boat passed all the tests. The reporter found someone he called a "real fisherman," a man from Norway who had fished all his life and used to have a 110-foot steam fishing boat when he fished off Norway and Iceland "close to home." That's one man who's profiting by our misery. He's quoted as saying "We can do without the Japanese," but he's not loath to take our boats. Obviously white Canadians feel more loyalty towards white foreigners than they do towards us Canadians.

All this worrying is very bad for Dad. He's feeling numbness on the left side. I'm trying to keep him still but he's a terrible patient. He's very worried about Stephen — the limp is not improving. Dad is so intense about that boy. He's also worried about Mark, says his coughing is a bad sign and he's losing weight too fast. A lot of his patients, especially the old ones, are in a state of collapse.

I hadn't been to meetings of the Council lately. Too occupied with the sick ones around me. But I'm trying to keep an eye on what's happening. The Nisei who were scheduled to leave last night balked. I don't know the details. We haven't heard whether they're in the jug or the Pool or on the train. It's horrible not being able to know.

April 9.

It seems that all the people who are conscientious enough to report when they have to, law-abiding enough not to kick about their treatment — these are the ones who go first. The ones on the loose, bucking the authorities, are single men, so the married ones have to go to fill the quota. Lots of the fellows are claiming they need more time to clear up family affairs for their parents who don't understand English well enough to cope with all the problems and regulations.

I had a talk with Tommy on the phone. He said they can't do much more than they're doing without injuring a lot more people. "All we've got on our side," he said, "is time and the good faith of the Nisei." At times I get fighting mad and think that the RCMP in using Morii are trusting the wrong man — the way he collects money for favours — but in the end, I can see how complaining would just work even more against us. What can we do? No witnesses will speak up against him any more. I'm told our letters aren't censored yet, but may be at any time.

April 11.
Dear Nesan,

Dad had a letter the other day from his friend Kawaguchi at Camp 406 in Princeton. It's cheered him up a lot. You remember Kawaguchi? His wife died a few years back. He left his kids with friends and he's asking us to see what we can do to keep Jack's education from being disrupted. He says "I think we should always keep hope. Hope is life. Hopeless is lifeless. ..."

This morning Dad got out of bed and went to the Pool bunkhouse for men (the former Women's Building). He was nauseated by the smell, the clouds of dust, the pitiful attempts at privacy. The Livestock Building (where the women and kids are) is worse.

Plus manure smells. The straw ticks are damp and mouldy. There are no fresh fruits or vegetables. He ate there to see what it was like. Supper was two slices of bologna, bread and tea. That's all. Those who have extra money manage to get lettuce and tomatoes and fruit from outside. Nothing for babies. He's asking for improvement and so is the Council.

Dad saw Dan. He earns about two dollars a day at the Pool helping out — minus board of course. There are a handful of others working there as well, getting from ten to twenty-five cents an hour for running errands and handling passes, etc. Dad, being a doctor, has a pass to come and go freely. The fact that he retired a few years ago because of his heart means the Commission is not pressing him into service in the ghost towns.

We'll have to rent our houses furnished. Have to leave the chesterfield suite, stove, refrig, rugs, etc. We aren't allowed to sell our furniture. Hits the dealers somehow. I don't understand it, but so they say.

It's an awfully unwieldy business, this evacuation. There's a wanted list of over a hundred Nisei who refuse to entrain. They're being chased all over town.

April 20.

I have gone numb today. Is all this real? Where do I begin? First I got my pass and saw Dan at last. He's going to Schreiber in two days. I didn't feel a thing when he told me. It didn't register at all. Maybe I'm crazy. When I left, I didn't say good-bye either. Now that I'm home I still can't feel. He was working in the Baggage — old Horse Show Building. Showed me his pay cheque as something he couldn't believe — $11.75. He's been there for an awfully long time.

After I saw Dan, and delivered some medicine for Dad, I saw Eiko and Fumi. Eiko is working as a steno[17] in the Commission office there, typing all the routine forms. She sleeps in a partitioned stall — being on the staff so to speak. The stall was the former home of a pair of stallions and boy oh boy did they leave their odour behind! The whole place is impregnated with the smell of ancient manure. Every other day it's swept with chloride of lime or something but you can't disguise horse smells, cow, sheep, pig, rabbit, and goat smells. And is it dusty! The toilets are just a sheet-metal trough and up till now they didn't have partitions or seats. The women complained so they put in partitions and a terribly makeshift seat. Twelve-year-old boys stay with the women too. The auto show building, where the Indian exhibits were, houses the new dining room and kitchens. Seats 3,000. Looks awfully permanent. Brick stoves — eight of them — shiny new mugs — very very barracky. As for the bunks, they were the most tragic things I saw there. Steel and wooden frames at three-foot intervals with thin lumpy straw ticks, bolsters, and three army blankets of army quality — no sheets unless you brought your own. These are the "homes" of the women I saw. They wouldn't let me or any "Jap females" into the men's building. There are constables at the doors — "to prevent further propagation of the species," it said in the newspaper. The bunks were hung with sheets and blankets and clothes of every colour — a regular gypsy caravan — all in a pathetic attempt at privacy — here and there I saw a child's doll or teddy bear — I saw two babies lying beside a mother who was too weary to get up — she had just thrown herself across the bed. I felt my throat thicken. I couldn't bear to look on their

---

17. **steno** Stenographer, one who takes dictation.

faces daring me to be curious or superior because I still lived outside. They're stripped of all privacy.

Some of the women were making the best of things, housecleaning around their stalls. One was scrubbing and scrubbing trying to get rid of the smell, but that wasn't possible. And then, Nesan, and then, I found Grandma Nakane there sitting like a little troll in all that crowd, with her chin on her chest. At first I couldn't believe it. She didn't recognize me. She just stared and stared. Then when I knelt down in front of her, she broke down and clung to me and cried and cried and said she'd rather have died than have come to such a place. Aya and Mark were sick when I told them. We all thought they were safe with friends in Saltspring. She has no idea of what's going on and I think she may not survive. I presumed Grandpa Nakane was in the men's area, but then I learned he was in the Sick Bay. I brought Eiko to meet Grandma but Grandma wouldn't look up. You know how yasashi Grandma is. This is too great a shock for her. She whispered to me that I should leave right away before they caught me too — then she wouldn't say any more. Nesan, maybe it's better where you are, even if they think you're an enemy.

Eiko has taken the woes of the confinees on her thin shoulders and she takes so much punishment. Fumi is worried sick about her. The place has got them both down. There are ten showers for 1,500 women. Hot and cold water. The men looked so terribly at loose ends, wandering around the grounds — sticking their noses through the fence watching the golfers. I felt so heavy I almost couldn't keep going. They are going to move the Vancouver women now and shove them into the Pool before sending them to the camps in the ghost towns.

The other day at the Pool, a visitor dropped his key before a stall in the Livestock Building, and he fished for it with a wire and brought to light manure and maggots. He called the nurse and then they moved all the bunks from the stalls and pried up the wooden floors, and it was the most stomach-turning nauseating thing. So they got fumigators and hoses and tried to wash it all away and got most of it into the drains. But maggots are still breeding and turning up here and there, so one woman with more guts than the others told the nurse (white) about it and protested. She replied: "Well, there are worms in the garden, aren't there?" This particular nurse was a Jap-hater of the most virulent sort. She called them "filthy Japs" to their faces and Fumi gave her what for and had a terrible scrap with her, saying, "What do you think we are? Are we cattle? Are we pigs?" You know how Fumi gets.

The night the first bunch of Nisei refused to go to Schreiber the women and children at the Pool milled around in front of their cage, and one very handsome Mountie came with his truncheon and started to hit them and yelled at them to "Get the hell back in there." Eiko's blood boiled over. She strode over to him and shouted "You put that stick down. What do you think you're doing? Do you think these women and children are cows, that you can beat them back?" Eiko was shaking. She's taken it on herself to fight and now she's on the blacklist and reputed to be a trouble-maker. It's people like us, Nesan — Eiko and Tommy and Dan and Fumi and the rest of us who have had faith in Canada, who have been more politically minded than the others — who are the most hurt. At one time, remember how I almost worshipped the Mounties? Remember the Curwood tales[18] of the Northwest, and the Royal Canadian Mounted

---

18. **Curwood tales** James Oliver Curwood wrote of the heroism of the RCMP in novels like his 1911 *Philip Steele of the Mounted Police*.

Police and how I'd go around saying their motto — *Maintiens le droit* — Maintain the right?

The other day there were a lot of people lined up on Heather Street to register at RCMP headquarters and so frightened by what was going on and afraid of the uniforms. You could feel their terror. I was going around telling them not to worry — the RCMP were our protectors and upholders of the law, etc. And there was this one officer tramping up and down that perfectly quiet line of people, holding his riding crop like a switch in his hand, smacking the palm of his other hand regularly — whack whack — as if he would just have loved to hit someone with it if they even so much as spoke or moved out of line. The glory of the Redcoats.

April 25.
Dearest Nesan,
　　Mark has gone.

The last night I spent with him and Aya and kids, he played the piano all night. He's terribly thin. Dad has been too ill to see him but he says Mark should not be going to the camps.

Is it true, Nesan, that you were pregnant just before you left? Mark said he wasn't sure. Oh, is there no way we can hear from you? I'm worried about the children. Nomi almost never talks or smiles. She is always carrying the doll you gave her and sleeps with it every night. I think, even though she doesn't talk, that she's quite bright. When I read to her from the picture books, I swear she's following the words with her eyes. Stephen spends his time reading war comics that he gets from the neighbourhood boys. All the Japs have mustard-coloured faces and buck teeth.

April 28.
We had our third letter from Sam — rather Aya did. All cards and letters are censored — even to the Nisei camps. Not a word from the camps makes the papers. Everything is hushed up. I haven't been to meetings for so long now that I don't know what's going on. Sam's camp is eight miles from the station, up in the hills. Men at the first camps all crowd down to the station every time a train passes with a new batch of men. They hang from the windows and ask about their families. Sam said he wept.

The men are luckier than the women. It's true they are forced to work on the roads, but at least they're fed, and they have no children to look after. Of course the fathers are worried but it's the women who are burdened with all the responsibility of keeping what's left of the family together.

Mina Sugimoto is so hysterical. She heard about a place in Revelstoke, got word to her husband and he came to see her on a two-day pass. She wanted them to go to Revelstoke together but of course that wasn't possible. He wasn't able to make it back to road camp in the time limit so now they're threatening to intern him. In the meantime, Mina has gone off to Revelstoke, bag, baggage, and boys. I'll try to find out what happens to them for you, Nesan.

Eiko has heard that the town of Greenwood is worse than the Pool. They're propping up old shacks near the mine shaft. On top of that local people are complaining and the United Church parson there says to "Kick all the Japs out."

Eiko, Fumi, and I have gotten to be so profane that Tom and the rest have given up being surprised. Eiko says "What the hell," and Fumi is even worse.

What a mess everything is. Some Nisei are out to save their own skins, others won't fight for any rights at all. The RCMP are happy to let us argue among ourselves. Those of us who are really conscientious and loyal — how will we ever get a chance to prove ourselves to this country? All we are fighting for inch by inch just goes down the drain. There are over 140 Nisei loose and many Japanese nationals (citizens of Japan). The Commission thinks the nationals are cleared out of Vancouver but oh boy, there are a lot of them who have greased enough palms and are let alone.

April 30.

We got another extension and are trying to get a place here in B.C. somewhere — somewhere on a farm with some fruit trees. We may have to go to some town in Alberta or Saskatchewan or Manitoba. I have to do some fast work, contacting all the people I think could help in some way. Dad doesn't want to leave B.C. If we go too far, we may not be able to come back. With you in Japan and Mark in Camp, Dad feels we should stay with the kids — but everybody has the same worry about their kids.

Stephen's leg was put in a cast. Dad thinks that rest will heal it. He says Grandma Nakane's mind is failing fast. She didn't speak to him when he was there today. He thought she'd be all right if she could see Grandpa Nakane but he wasn't able to arrange it. Dad's worried about both of them. I'm trying to get them out of there but the red tape is so fierce.

May 1.

I have to work fast. The Commission put out a notice — everyone has to be ready for 24-hour notice. No more extensions. Everything piled on at once. We're trying to get into a farm or house around Salmon Arm or Chase or some other decent town in the Interior — anywhere that is livable and will still let us in. Need a place with a reasonable climate. Some place where we can have a garden to grow enough vegetables for a year. Somewhere there's a school if possible. If there's nothing in B.C., I think we should go east and take our chances in Toronto. Fumi and Eiko and I want to stick together.

Monday, May 4.

Got to get out in the next couple of weeks. Dad's had a relapse. The numbness is spreading. He doesn't think it's his heart.

There's another prospect. McGillivray Falls, twenty miles from Lillooet. Going there would eat up our savings since that's all we'd have to live on but at least it's close to Vancouver and just a few hours to get back. There's no school. I'd have to teach the children.

It's because so many towns have barred their doors that we are having such a heck of a time. The Commission made it clear to us that they would not permit us to go anywhere the City Councils didn't want us. Individuals who offer to help have to write letters saying they undertake to see that we won't be a burden on the public. Who among us wants to be a burden on anyone? It'd be better if, instead of writing letters to help one or two of us, they'd try to persuade their City Councils to let us in. After all we're Canadians.

Eiko and her mother might go to a ghost town to be closer to her father. Also most likely she'll have to teach grade-school. The pay is two dollars a day out of which she'd have to feed and clothe the four younger kids and try to keep them in a semblance of health. Honest, Nesan, I wonder if the whites think we are a special kind of low animal able to live on next to nothing — able to survive without clothing, shoes, medicine, decent food.

Aya just phoned that there's no electricity at McGillivray. What does one do without electricity? There are so many complex angles in this business my head aches.

Another thing that's bothering Aya is the cost of transportation and freight. We can take only our clothes, bedding, pots and pans, and dishes. We've sold our dining-room suite and piano. Mark didn't sell anything. Aya's house is looted. I haven't told her. It's in such an out-of-the-way place. When I took the interurban on Friday to see if the dog might have shown up, I was shocked. Almost all the hand-carved furnishings were gone — all the ornaments — just the dead plants left and some broken china on the floor. I saw one of the soup bowls from the set I gave them. The looting was thorough. The collection of old instruments Mark talked about was gone too and the scrolls. No one will understand the value of these things. I don't have the heart to tell Aya.

We're all walking around in a daze. It's really too late to do anything. If we go to the ghost towns, it's going to be one hell of a life. Waiting in line to wash, cook, bathe —

I've got to go to sleep. And I've got to pack. If we go to McGillivray, Fumi, Eiko, and family are coming with us. We have to go in a week or two. The Commission won't wait.

May 5.
Dearest Nesan,

We've heard from Mark. Crazy man. All he thinks about are Stephen's music lessons. He sent two pages of exercises and a melody which he thought up. He wrote about some flowers he found which he stuck on the end of his pick and says he thinks about you as he works. I read the letter three times to Dad. Dad says Stephen's health is more important than his music right now. Nomi is fine. She's so silent though. I've never seen such a serious child before.

I got a letter from Dan as well. His address is Mileage 101, Camp SW 5-3, Jackfish, Ontario.

We've had three different offers since yesterday. Mickey Maikawa wants us to go to his wife's brother's farm in Sicamous. We're considering it. Everything is confusion and bewilderment.

Eiko has heard awful things about the crowding and lack of sanitation in the ghost towns. People have been freezing in tents. She's dead set against them now. She and Fumi and I are still trying to stick together. But you never know when we'll have to go, or which way our luck's going to jump. Every day's a different story, from nowhere to go to several choices. I want to go east. Rent at McG. Falls was reduced to $80.00 per year.

May 14.
Dear Nesan,

Aya, kids, Dad, and I have decided to go to Slocan. We hear that's one of the best of the ghost towns. It used to have a silver mine, or maybe a gold mine — I'm not sure. There are just abandoned old hotels there now and a few stores. I don't know the size of the white population but it's not very large.

The family — or what's left of it — intends to stick together one way or another, and after days and nights of discussion, chasing this elusive hope or that, worrying, figuring, going bats with indecision, with one door after another closing then opening again — we finally realize the only thing to do is give in and stay together wherever we go, and moving to Slocan is the easiest.

Rev. Nakayama, who's already in Slocan, wrote and told me about a small house that Dad and I can have to ourselves, close to the mountains and away from the crowding. It makes all the difference. I'm so glad I thought to ask him for help. We'll be able to manage something for the kids — build an addition if we have to.

Now that the decision is taken, I don't want to be upset all over again. I don't want to go through all the hopes and the uncertainty of trying to find a loophole to escape from. I'm resigned to Slocan — and anyway, Rev. Nakayama says it's a nice place. It even has a soda fountain. So I'll settle for that until they say it's okay for us to join Mark and Sam and Dan again somewhere. Grandma and Grandpa Nakane have orders to go to New Denver. We've tried everything, I've cried my cry, I've said good-bye to this home. All fluttering for escape has died down. Just wish us luck, Nesan. We'll wait until that happy day when we can all be together again.

Now I must get to serious packing and selling and giving away and the same thing at your house.

I asked too much of God.

May 15, Friday.

There's too much to do. Dad's unable to help though he tries. After we get to Slocan things should calm down. The furor will die down when there are none of us left on the Coast. Then we can discuss moving to Ontario. It's time that defeated us for the present but we won't give up yet. Not by a long shot.

Dan's new address — Dalton Mills, c/o Austin Lumber Co., Dalton Ontario.

We got a letter today from the doctor in Toronto offering us the top floor of his house. That would be wonderful, but heck! how I'd hate to impose on anyone. Imagine being dependent like that. I think it was fated for me to taste the dregs of this humiliation that I might know just what it is that all the women and children are enduring through no fault of their own.

Once we're in Slocan, chances of going east are better than here. The officials are terribly harassed with the whole thing and exasperated with individual demands for attention. So, Slocan City, here we come.

Goodness, I think I'll keep my golf clubs.

May 18, 1942.
Dear Nesan,

It's flabbergasting. I can't believe any of it. Here's what happened.

I was all packed for Slocan and Dad was reasonably okay. In the middle of helping Aya, I thought — just as a last gesture and more for my own assurance than out of any hope — that I'd write to Grant MacNeil, secretary of the Commission. So I wrote asking for written assurance that I could continue negotiations from Slocan about going to Toronto. That's all. Just the word that there was hope for us to get to Ontario. No further aspirations. I was too tired to start all over again anyway. Mailed the letter around noon from the main post office on Friday. A little after three o'clock, Mrs Booth who works there phoned to say that they'd got the letter and I was to come right away. I couldn't believe it. I dropped everything and ran. Mrs Booth, speaking for Mr MacNeil, said they were not giving any special permits but they'd make this one exception and told me to return next day with bank accounts, references, etc. I was so excited and happy, I assumed that included Dad and Aya and the kids. Next day, Mrs Booth said the permit was only for the Kato family. One family only. I told her Stephen and Nomi are my sister's kids but she said something about Commission rulings and their name is Nakane and then she asked about the Nakane family and I had to say they were nationals and I think that settled it. But she said she would look into the business of the kids. I was so frustrated not having Mark or Dad or Aya to confer with. It seemed to me at that point that I should opt for Toronto with Dad and then negotiate having everyone else come to join us.

Do you think I did the right thing, Nesan? Eiko says I did and that we should try to keep as many out of the ghost towns as possible. So I went back and told Dad and he didn't say anything one way or the other. Just kept nodding his head.

When I discussed it with Aya, she was adamant about the kids. She says you entrusted them to her and they're her kids now until you return and she won't part with them. It's true they're more used to her than to either me or Dad. And as for being so far away, Aya says ten miles or ten thousand miles makes no difference to a child.

The whole point of all our extensions was to find a way to keep together, but now at the last minute everything has exploded. Aya is being very calm and she doesn't want any discussion in front of the kids. All she's told them is that they're going for a train ride.

Fumi is resigned to not coming with us. Eiko's mother wants to go to Slocan, but I can tell Eiko wants out. I don't know what Fumi is going to do now. I think she's going to Kaslo with Rev. Shimizu's group.

I'm going to the Custodian tomorrow and then to the Commission again. Maybe the permit won't be given at the last minute. What if I transfer the Slocan papers to someone else and then don't get the Toronto permit? There could be trouble with all these forms and deferments.

Well, I'm going to go ahead, repack everything and hope. The mover, Crone, is sending our boxed goods, beds, and Japanese food supplies — shoyu, rice, canned mirinzuke, green tea. I'm taking the Japanese dishes, trays and bowls. Can't get any more miso now.

I'll just have to live on hope that Aya and kids will be all right till we can get them to Toronto. I tell myself that at least they'll have their own place till then.

What will it be like, I wonder, in the doctor's house? I'll wire them as soon as I get the permit and we'll head their way for the time being. Do we eat with the family? First thing I'll do when I get to Toronto is go out *at night*.

In Petawawa there are 130 Nisei interned for rioting and crying "Banzai,"[19] shaving their heads and carrying "hino-maru" flags.[20] Damn fools.

May 21.
Dearest Nesan,

Aya and kids are leaving with others bound for Slocan tomorrow. RCMP came in person to order Kunio off to camp. Rev. Shimizu and Rev. Akagawa had to leave immediately.

Yesterday I worked so hard — tied, labelled, ran to Commission, ran to bank, to Crone movers, to CPR, washed and cooked and scrubbed. Dad is saying good-bye to the

---

19. **Banzai** Japanese battle cry. 20. **"hino-maru" flags** Japanese flags.

kids now. They're spending the night in the church hall at Kitsilano. I'm going over there too as soon as I pack this last item.

Merry Christmas, Nesan.

This is the last word in the journal. The following day, May 22, 1942, Stephen, Aya Obasan and I are on a train for Slocan. It is twelve years before we see Aunt Emily again.

(1981)

Alistair MacLeod (1936–)

Alistair MacLeod was born in 1936 in North Battleford, Saskatchewan, to parents who had moved west from Nova Scotia during the Depression in search of work. They settled in Alberta, where they lived until MacLeod was 10, at which point they returned home to their farm in Inverness County, on Cape Breton Island. In 1956, MacLeod earned a teaching certificate from the Nova Scotia Teachers' College in Truro, and he taught in the province for a year. Then, paying his way by working as a miner, he obtained a B.A. and a B.Ed. from St. Francis Xavier University. He went on to do an M.A. at the University of New Brunswick with a thesis on the 1930s Canadian short story, and a Ph.D. at the University of Notre Dame in Indiana with a focus on the 19th-century British novel. He was employed at the University of Indiana at Bloomington for three years before taking a position at the University of Windsor, where he would teach English literature and creative writing until his retirement, in 1999. He also served as fiction editor of the *University of Windsor Review*.

When asked about his beginnings as a writer, MacLeod replied that he had spent so much time studying literature in school that he thought he'd try his hand at creating some himself, adding that living so far from Cape Breton was also a factor: "I found myself becoming more and more thoughtful about where I'd grown up. I'm not saying that it was simply 'absence makes the heart grow fonder,' but I do think it's true that sometimes when you're removed from your home, you start to think about it differently." MacLeod began publishing his short stories in Canadian and American periodicals in the 1960s, and his work met with almost immediate critical acclaim. His second published story, "The Boat" (1968), was selected for Houghton-Mifflin's annual *Best American Short Stories* in 1969.

MacLeod's first collection, *The Lost Salt Gift of Blood*, appeared in 1976. Its seven stories revolve around Cape Breton — their narrators have left home and are either physically returning to the island or recollecting their island pasts. MacLeod explores the complex experience of leaving a culture that is so protective of its traditions. His fictional families are descended from the Highland Scots who fled to Cape Breton during the 18th and 19th centuries. These descendants of exiles and survivors are fiercely proud of their Highland customs and Gaelic language, yet they must cope with the hard socio-economic realities of the contemporary island, its isolation and the limits it imposes, or become exiles themselves, seeking better opportunities in the world beyond.

In "The Boat," for example, the narrator's mother is defensive of her culture, maintaining a sharp differentiation between "our people" and the "outsiders" who flock to the island during tourist season. However, his father — whose death the narrator is mourning — feels an affinity with the outside world. He had once wanted to attend university, his room is filled with books and magazines, and he is ill suited to a seafaring life. The narrator takes pride in his culture, but he knows its limitations, and so he is assailed by conflicting emotions when he hears his father singing sea chanties and Gaelic drinking songs for a group of American tourists: "the familiar yet unfamiliar voice that rolled down from the cabins made me feel as I had never felt before in my young life ... I was ashamed yet proud, young yet old and saved yet forever lost."

From 1984 to 1985, MacLeod participated in a Canada-Scotland writer-in-residence exchange program and did a reading and lecture tour of Great Britain. In 1986, he published *As Birds Bring Forth the Sun and Other Stories,* 10 years after his first collection. With this book, it was evident that MacLeod was becoming more conscious of his role as storyteller. While these tales, like the earlier ones, are told in a realist style by narrators remembering their island pasts, they also have a folkloric quality and draw on the tones and rhythms of oral storytelling. The title story begins: "Once there was a family with a highland name who lived beside the sea. And the man had a dog of which he was very fond. She was large and grey, a sort of staghound from another time." With such elocutions, MacLeod demonstrates the power of creative engagement with mythology and the unknown. Thus, although the brothers in his story have physically left home for Toronto and Montreal, they are haunted by the curse of the *cù mòr glas a' bhàis* ("the big grey dog of death").

In 1999, MacLeod published his first novel. *No Great Mischief* won, among other honours, the Trillium Book Award and the Canadian Booksellers Association Libris Award; it was also the first Canadian novel to win the IMPAC Dublin Literary Award. It took MacLeod 13 years to write. It tells the story of Alexander MacDonald, a Cape Bretoner who has settled in Ontario, where he makes his living as an orthodontist. Prompted by a visit with his oldest brother, Calum, who is dying of alcoholism, Alexander goes back in time, remembering his island childhood and his experiences as a young adult in the mines of northern Ontario. These recollections are intertwined with reflections on his bloody ancestral history, beginning in Scotland with the 1745 clan revolt for Bonny Prince Charlie that culminated in the slaughter at Culloden, and shifting to Canada with the 1759 Battle of the Plains of Abraham, during which General Wolfe saw the decimation of his Scottish troops and remarked, "no great mischief if they fall." To this, Alexander adds the history of his own family, the MacDonald clan who settled on Cape Breton. For Alexander, another of MacLeod's compelling exiles, the past is both an inescapable burden and a sustaining force.

MacLeod has always been a slow, painstaking writer who does not significantly rework his stories after committing them to paper. As a result, his output is relatively small: 14 short stories and one novel. He explains, "for me, it's like making a doorstep. I don't want to make the doorstep and then come back next week and tear it all apart. I prefer to make it right the first time, even if it's a slow process." Nevertheless, with this oeuvre he has forged an international reputation and garnered much acclaim.

In 2000, MacLeod was elected a Fellow of the Royal Society of Canada. Also in 2000, *Island: The Collected Short Stories of Alistair MacLeod* appeared, and in 2004, he published a new edition of his story *To Every Thing There Is a Season: A Cape Breton Christmas Story,* with illustrations by Peter Rankin. MacLeod and his wife, Anita, have six children. They live in Windsor, Ontario, and spend their summers in Cape Breton.

The Boat

There are times even now, when I awake at four o'clock in the morning with the terrible fear that I have overslept; when I imagine that my father is waiting for me in the room below the darkened stairs or that the shorebound men are tossing pebbles against my window while blowing their hands and stomping their feet impatiently on the frozen steadfast earth. There are times when I am half out of bed and fumbling for socks and mumbling for words before I realize that I am foolishly alone, that no one waits at the base of the stairs and no boat rides restlessly in the waters by the pier.

At such times only the grey corpses on the overflowing ashtray beside my bed bear witness to the extinction of the latest spark and silently await the crushing out of the most recent of their fellows. And then because I am afraid to be alone with death, I dress rapidly, make a great to-do about clearing my throat, turn on both faucets in the sink and proceed to make loud splashing ineffectual noises. Later I go out and walk the mile to the all-night restaurant.

In the winter it is a very cold walk and there are often tears in my eyes when I arrive. The waitress usually gives a sympathetic little shiver and says, "Boy, it must be really cold out there; you got tears in your eyes."

"Yes," I say, "it sure is; it really is."

And then the three or four of us who are always in such places at such times make uninteresting little protective chit-chat until the dawn reluctantly arrives. Then I swallow the coffee which is always bitter and leave with a great busy rush because by that time I have to worry about being late and whether I have a clean shirt and whether my car will start and about all the other countless things one must worry about when he teaches at a great Midwestern university. And I know then that that day will go by as have all the days of the past ten years, for the call and the voices and the shapes and the boat were not really there in the early morning's darkness and I have all kinds of comforting reality to prove it. They are only shadows and echoes, the animals a child's hands make on the wall by lamplight, and the voices from the rain barrel; the cuttings from an old movie made in the black and white of long ago.

I first became conscious of the boat in the same way and at almost the same time that I became aware of the people it supported. My earliest recollection of my father is a view from the floor of gigantic rubber boots and then of being suddenly elevated and having my face pressed against the stubble of his cheek, and how it tasted of salt and of how he smelled of salt from his red-soled rubber boots to the shaggy whiteness of his hair.

When I was very small, he took me for my first ride in the boat. I rode the half-mile from our house to the wharf on his shoulders and I remember the sound of his rubber boots galumphing along the gravel beach, the tune of the indecent little song he used to sing, and the odour of the salt.

The floor of the boat was permeated with the same odour and in its constancy I was not aware of change. In the harbour we made our little circle and returned. He tied the boat by its painter, fastened the stern to its permanent anchor and lifted me high over his head to the solidity of the wharf. Then he climbed up the little iron ladder that led to the wharf's cap, placed me once more upon his shoulders and galumphed off again.

When we returned to the house everyone made a great fuss over my precocious excursion and asked, "How did you like the boat?" "Were you afraid in the boat?" "Did you cry in the boat?" They repeated "the boat" at the end of all their questions and I knew it must be very important to everyone.

My earliest recollection of my mother is of being alone with her in the mornings while my father was away in the boat. She seemed to be always repairing clothes that were "torn in the boat," preparing food "to be eaten in the boat" or looking for "the boat" through our kitchen window which faced upon the sea. When my father returned about noon, she would ask, "Well, how did things go in the boat today?" It was the first question I remember asking: "Well, how did things go in the boat today?" "Well, how did things go in the boat today?"

The boat in our lives was registered at Port Hawkesbury. She was what Nova Scotians called a Cape Island boat and was designed for the small inshore fishermen who sought the lobsters of the spring and the mackerel of summer and later the cod and haddock and hake. She was thirty-two feet long and nine wide, and was powered by an engine from a Chevrolet truck. She had a marine clutch and a high speed reverse gear and was painted light green with the name *Jenny Lynn* stencilled in black letters on her bow and painted on an oblong plate across her stern. Jenny Lynn had been my mother's maiden name and the boat was called after her as another link in the chain of tradition. Most of the boats that berthed at the wharf bore the names of some female member of their owner's household.

I say this now as if I knew it all then. All at once, all about boat dimensions and engines, and as if on the day of my first childish voyage I noticed the difference between a stencilled name and a painted name. But of course it was not that way at all, for I learned it all very slowly and there was not time enough.

I learned first about our house which was one of about fifty which marched around the horseshoe of our harbour and the wharf which was its heart. Some of them were so close to the water that during a storm the sea spray splashed against their windows while others were built farther along the beach as was the case with ours. The houses and their people, like those of the neighbouring towns and villages, were the result of Ireland's discontent and Scotland's Highland Clearances and America's War of Independence.[1] Impulsive emotional Catholic Celts who could not bear to live with England and shrewd determined Protestant Puritans who, in the years after 1776, could not bear to live without.

The most important room in our house was one of those oblong old-fashioned kitchens heated by a wood- and coal-burning stove. Behind the stove was a box of kindlings and beside it a coal scuttle. A heavy wooden table with leaves that expanded or reduced its dimensions stood in the middle of the floor. There were five wooden homemade chairs which had been chipped and hacked by a variety of knives. Against the east wall, opposite the stove, there was a couch which sagged in the middle and had a cushion for a pillow, and above it a shelf which contained matches, tobacco, pencils, odd fish-hooks, bits of twine, and a tin can filled with bills and receipts. The south wall was dominated by a window which faced the sea and on the north there was a five-foot board which bore a variety of clothes hooks and the burdens of each. Beneath the board there was a jumble of odd footwear, mostly of rubber. There was also, on this wall, a barometer, a map of the marine area and a shelf which held a tiny radio. The kitchen was shared by all of us and was a buffer zone between the immaculate order of ten other rooms and the disruptive chaos of the single room that was my father's.

My mother ran her house as her brothers ran their boats. Everything was clean and spotless and in order. She was tall and dark and powerfully energetic. In later years she reminded me of the women of Thomas Hardy, particularly Eustacia Vye,[2] in a physical way. She fed and clothed a family of seven children, making all of the meals and most of the clothes. She grew miraculous gardens and magnificent flowers and raised broods of hens and ducks. She would walk miles on berry-picking expeditions and hoist her skirts to dig for clams when the tide was low. She was fourteen years younger than my father, whom she had married when she was twenty-six and had been a local beauty for a period of ten years. My mother was of the sea as were all of her people, and her horizons were the very literal ones she scanned with her dark and fearless eyes.

---

1. **Ireland's … Independence** Ongoing Irish civil conflict, the displacement of Scottish citizens from the highlands, and the American Civil War; all generated an influx of immigrants to the Maritimes. 2. **women of … Eustacia Vye** A passionate young woman, is a character in Thomas Hardy's *The Return of the Native*.

Between the kitchen clothes rack and barometer, a door opened into my father's bedroom. It was a room of disorder and disarray. It was as if the wind which so often clamoured about the house succeeded in entering this single room and after whipping it into turmoil stole quietly away to renew its knowing laughter from without.

My father's bed was against the south wall. It always looked rumpled and unmade because he lay on top of it more than he slept within any folds it might have had. Beside it, there was a little brown table. An archaic goose-necked reading light, a battered table radio, a mound of wooden matches, one or two packages of tobacco, a deck of cigarette papers and an overflowing ashtray cluttered its surface. The brown larvae of tobacco shreds and the grey flecks of ash covered both the table and the floor beneath it. The once-varnished surface of the table was disfigured by numerous black scars and gashes inflicted by the neglected burning cigarettes of many years. They had tumbled from the ashtray unnoticed and branded their statements permanently and quietly into the wood until the odour of their burning caused the snuffing out of their lives. At the bed's foot there was a single window which looked upon the sea.

Against the adjacent wall there was a battered bureau and beside it there was a closet which held his single ill-fitting serge suit, the two or three white shirts that strangled him and the square black shoes that pinched. When he took off his more friendly clothes, the heavy woollen sweaters, mitts and socks which my mother knitted for him and the woollen and doeskin shirts, he dumped them unceremoniously on a single chair. If a visitor entered the room while he was lying on the bed, he would be told to throw the clothes on the floor and take their place upon the chair.

Magazines and books covered the bureau and competed with the clothes for domination of the chair. They further overburdened the heroic little table and lay on top of the radio. They filled a baffling and unknowable cave beneath the bed, and in the corner by the bureau they spilled from the walls and grew up from the floor.

The magazines were the most conventional: *Time, Newsweek, Life, Maclean's, Family Herald, Reader's Digest*. They were the result of various cut-rate subscriptions or of the gift subscriptions associated with Christmas, "the two whole years for only $3.50."

The books were more varied. There were a few hard-cover magnificents and bygone Book-of-the-Month wonders and some were Christmas or birthday gifts. The majority of them, however, were used paperbacks which came from those second-hand bookstores which advertise in the backs of magazines: "Miscellaneous Used Paperbacks 10¢ Each." At first he sent for them himself, although my mother resented the expense, but in later years they came more and more often from my sisters who had moved to the cities. Especially at first they were very weird and varied. Mickey Spillane and Ernest Haycox[3] vied with Dostoyevsky and Faulkner, and the Penguin Poets edition of Gerard Manley Hopkins arrived in the same box as a little book on sex technique called *Getting the Most Out of Love*. The former had been assiduously annotated by a very fine hand using a very blue-inked fountain pen while the latter had been studied by someone with very large thumbs, the prints of which were still visible in the margins. At the slightest provocation it would open almost immediately to particularly graphic and well-smudged pages.

When he was not in the boat, my father spent most of his time lying on the bed in his socks, the top two buttons of his trousers undone, his discarded shirt on the ever-ready chair and the sleeves of the woollen Stanfield underwear, which he wore both

---

3. **Mickey Spillane, Ernest Haycox** Spillane wrote crime stories; Haycox wrote Westerns.

summer and winter, drawn half way up to his elbows. The pillows propped up the whiteness of his head and the goose-necked lamp illuminated the pages in his hands. The cigarettes smoked and smouldered on the ashtray and on the table and the radio played constantly, sometimes low and sometimes loud. At midnight and at one, two, three and four, one could sometimes hear the radio, his occasional cough, the rustling thud of a completed book being tossed to the corner heap, or the movement necessitated by his sitting on the edge of the bed to roll the thousandth cigarette. He seemed never to sleep, only to doze, and the light shone constantly from his window to the sea.

My mother despised the room and all it stood for and she had stopped sleeping in it after I was born. She despised disorder in rooms and in houses and in hours and in lives, and she had not read a book since high school. There she had read *Ivanhoe*[4] and considered it a colossal waste of time. Still the room remained, like a solid rock of opposition in the sparkling waters of a clear deep harbour, opening off the kitchen where we really lived our lives, with its door always open and its contents visible to all.

The daughters of the room and of the house were very beautiful. They were tall and willowy like my mother and had her fine facial features set off by the reddish copper-coloured hair that had apparently once been my father's before it turned to white. All of them were very clever in school and helped my mother a great deal about the house. When they were young they sang and were very happy and very nice to me because I was the youngest and the family's only boy.

My father never approved of their playing about the wharf like the other children, and they went there only when my mother sent them on an errand. At such times they almost always overstayed, playing screaming games of tag or hide-and-seek in and about the fishing shanties, the piled traps and tubs of trawl,[5] shouting down to the perch that swam languidly about the wharf's algae-covered piles, or jumping in and out of boats that tugged gently at their lines. My mother was never uneasy about them at such times, and when her husband criticized her she would say, "Nothing will happen to them there," or "They could be doing worse things in worse places."

By about the ninth or tenth grade my sisters one by one discovered my father's bedroom and then the change would begin. Each would go into the room one morning when he was out. She would go with the ideal hope of imposing order or with the more practical objective of emptying the ashtray, and later she would be found spellbound by the volume in her hand. My mother's reaction was always abrupt, bordering on the angry. "Take your nose out of that trash and come and do your work," she would say, and once I saw her slap my youngest sister so hard that the print of her hand was scarletly emblazoned upon her daughter's cheek while the broken-spined paperback fluttered uselessly to the floor.

Thereafter my mother would launch a campaign against what she had discovered but could not understand. At times although she was not overly religious she would bring in God to bolster her arguments, saying, "In the next world God will see to those who waste their lives reading useless books when they should be about their work." Or without theological aid, "I would like to know how books help anyone to live a life." If my father were in, she would repeat the remarks louder than necessary, and her voice would carry into his room where he lay upon his bed. His usual reaction was to turn up

---

4. *Ivanhoe* 1819 historical novel by Sir Walter Scott (1771–1832). 5. **tubs of trawl** Tubs in which trawl lines are coiled.

the volume of the radio, although that action in itself betrayed the success of the initial thrust.

Shortly after my sisters began to read the books, they grew restless and lost interest in darning socks and baking bread, and all of them eventually went to work as summer waitresses in the Sea Food Restaurant. The restaurant was run by a big American concern from Boston and catered to the tourists that flooded the area during July and August. My mother despised the whole operation. She said the restaurant was not run by "our people," and "our people" did not eat there, and that it was run by outsiders for outsiders.

"Who are these people anyway?" she would ask, tossing back her dark hair, "and what do they, though they go about with their cameras for a hundred years, know about the way it is here, and what do they care about me and mine, and why should I care about them?"

She was angry that my sisters should even conceive of working in such a place and more angry when my father made no move to prevent it, and she was worried about herself and about her family and about her life. Sometimes she would say softly to her sisters, "I don't know what's the matter with my girls. It seems none of them are interested in any of the right things." And sometimes there would be bitter savage arguments. One afternoon I was coming in with three mackerel I'd been given at the wharf when I heard her say, "Well I hope you'll be satisfied when they come home knocked up and you'll have had your way."

It was the most savage thing I'd ever heard my mother say. Not just the words but the way she said them, and I stood there in the porch afraid to breathe for what seemed like the years from ten to fifteen, feeling the damp moist mackerel with their silver glassy eyes growing clammy against my leg.

Through the angle in the screen door I saw my father who had been walking into his room wheel around on one of his rubber-booted heels and look at her with his blue eyes flashing like clearest ice beneath the snow that was his hair. His usually ruddy face was drawn and grey, reflecting the exhaustion of a man of sixty-five who had been working in those rubber boots for eleven hours on an August day, and for a fleeting moment I wondered what I would do if he killed my mother while I stood there in the porch with those three foolish mackerel in my hand. Then he turned and went into his room and the radio blared forth the next day's weather forecast and I retreated under the noise and returned again, stamping my feet and slamming the door too loudly to signal my approach. My mother was busy at the stove when I came in, and did not raise her head when I threw the mackerel in a pan. As I looked into my father's room, I said, "Well how did things go in the boat today?" and he replied, "Oh not too badly, all things considered." He was lying on his back and lighting the first cigarette and the radio was talking about the Virginia coast.

All of my sisters made good money on tips. They bought my father an electric razor which he tried to use for a while and they took out even more magazine subscriptions. They bought my mother a great many clothes of the type she was very fond of, the wide-brimmed hats and the brocaded dresses, but she locked them all in trunks and refused to wear any of them.

On one August day my sisters prevailed upon my father to take some of their restaurant customers for an afternoon ride in the boat. The tourists with their expensive clothes and cameras and sun glasses awkwardly backed down the iron ladder at the wharf's side to where my father waited below, holding the rocking *Jenny Lynn* in snug against the wharf with one hand on the iron ladder and steadying his descending passengers with the other. They tried to look both prim and wind-blown like the girls in the Pepsi-Cola ads and did the best they could, sitting on the thwarts where the newspapers were spread to cover the splattered blood and fish entrails, crowding to one side so that they were in danger of capsizing the boat, taking the inevitable pictures or merely trailing their fingers through the water of their dreams.

All of them liked my father very much and, after he'd brought them back from their circles in the harbour, they invited him to their rented cabins which were located high on a hill overlooking the village to which they were so alien. He proceeded to get very drunk up there with the beautiful view and the strange company and the abundant liquor, and late in the afternoon he began to sing.

I was just approaching the wharf to deliver my mother's summons when he began, and the familiar yet unfamiliar voice that rolled down from the cabins made me feel as I had never felt before in my young life or perhaps as I had always felt without really knowing it, and I was ashamed yet proud, young yet old and saved yet forever lost, and there was nothing I could do to control my legs which trembled nor my eyes which wept for what they could not tell.

The tourists were equipped with tape recorders and my father sang for more than three hours. His voice boomed down the hill and bounced off the surface of the harbour, which was an unearthly blue on that hot August day, and was then reflected to the wharf and the fishing shanties where it was absorbed amidst the men who were baiting their lines for the next day's haul.

He sang all the old sea chanties which had come across from the old world and by which men like him had pulled ropes for generations, and he sang the East Coast sea songs which celebrated the sealing vessels of Northumberland Strait and the long liners of the Grand Banks, and of Anticosti, Sable Island, Grand Manan, Boston Harbor, Nantucket and Block Island. Gradually he shifted to the seemingly unending Gaelic drinking songs with their twenty or more verses and inevitable refrains, and the men in the shanties smiled at the coarseness of some of the verses and at the thought that the singer's immediate audience did not know what they were applauding nor recording to take back to staid old Boston. Later as the sun was setting he switched to the laments and the wild and haunting Gaelic war songs of those spattered Highland ancestors he had never seen, and when his voice ceased, the savage melancholy of three hundred years seemed to hang over the peaceful harbour and the quiet boats and the men leaning in the doorways of their shanties with their cigarettes glowing in the dusk and the women looking to the sea from their open windows with their children in their arms.

When he came home he threw the money he had earned on the kitchen table as he did with all his earnings but my mother refused to touch it and the next day he went with the rest of the men to bait his trawl in the shanties. The tourists came to the door that evening and my mother met them there and told them that her husband was not in although he was lying on the bed only a few feet away with the radio playing and the cigarette upon his lips. She stood in the doorway until they reluctantly went away.

In the winter they sent him a picture which had been taken on the day of the singing. On the back it said, "To Our Ernest Hemingway"[6] and the "Our" was

---

6. **Ernest Hemingway** American author (1899–1961) who often wrote about the relationship between men and the natural world.

underlined. There was also an accompanying letter telling how much they had enjoyed themselves, how popular the tape was proving and explaining who Ernest Hemingway was. In a way it almost did look like one of those unshaven, taken-in-Cuba pictures of Hemingway. He looked both massive and incongruous in the setting. His bulky fisherman's clothes were too big for the green and white lawn chair in which he sat, and his rubber boots seemed to take up all of the well-clipped grass square. The beach umbrella jarred with his sunburned face and because he had already been singing for some time, his lips which chapped in the winds of spring and burned in the water glare of summer had already cracked in several places, producing tiny flecks of blood at their corners and on the whiteness of his teeth. The bracelets of brass chain which he wore to protect his wrists from the chafing seemed abnormally large and his broad leather belt had been slackened and his heavy shirt and underwear were open at the throat revealing an uncultivated wilderness of white chest hair bordering on the semi-controlled stubble of his neck and chin. His blue eyes had looked directly into the camera and his hair was whiter than the two tiny clouds which hung over his left shoulder. The sea was behind him and its immense blue flatness stretched out to touch the arching blueness of the sky. It seemed very far away from him or else he was so much in the foreground that he seemed too big for it.

Each year another of my sisters would read the books and work in the restaurant. Sometimes they would stay out quite late on the hot summer nights and when they came up the stairs my mother would ask them many long and involved questions which they resented and tried to avoid. Before ascending the stairs they would go into my father's room and those of us who waited above could hear them throwing his clothes off the chair before sitting on it or the squeak of the bed as they sat on its edge. Sometimes they would talk to him a long time, the murmur of their voices blending with the music of the radio into a mysterious vapour-like sound which floated softly up the stairs.

I say this again as if it all happened at once and as if all of my sisters were of identical ages and like so many lemmings going into another sea and, again, it was of course not that way at all. Yet go they did, to Boston, to Montreal, to New York with the young men they met during the summers and later married in those far-away cities. The young men were very articulate and handsome and wore fine clothes and drove expensive cars and my sisters, as I said, were very tall and beautiful with their copper-coloured hair and were tired of darning socks and baking bread.

One by one they went. My mother had each of her daughters for fifteen years, then lost them for two and finally forever. None married a fisherman. My mother never accepted any of the young men, for in her eyes they seemed always a combination of the lazy, the effeminate, the dishonest and the unknown. They never seemed to do any physical work and she could not comprehend their luxurious vacations and she did not know whence they came nor who they were. And in the end she did not really care, for they were not of her people and they were not of her sea.

I say this now with a sense of wonder at my own stupidity in thinking I was somehow free and would go on doing well in school and playing and helping in the boat and passing into my early teens while streaks of grey began to appear in my mother's dark hair and my father's rubber boots dragged sometimes on the pebbles of the beach as he trudged home from the wharf. And there were but three of us in the house that had at one time been so loud.

Then during the winter that I was fifteen he seemed to grow old and ill at once. Most of January he lay upon the bed, smoking and reading and listening to the radio while the wind howled about the house and the needle-like snow blistered off the ice-covered harbour and the doors flew out of people's hands if they did not cling to them like death.

In February when the men began overhauling their lobster traps he still did not move, and my mother and I began to knit lobster trap headings in the evenings. The twine was as always very sharp and harsh, and blisters formed upon our thumbs and little paths of blood snaked quietly down between our fingers while the seals that had drifted down from distant Labrador wept and moaned like human children on the ice-floes of the Gulf.

In the daytime my mother's brother who had been my father's partner as long as I could remember also came to work upon the gear. He was a year older than my mother and was tall and dark and the father of twelve children.

By March we were very far behind and although I began to work very hard in the evenings I knew it was not hard enough and that there were but eight weeks left before the opening of the season on May first. And I knew that my mother worried and my uncle was uneasy and that all of our very lives depended on the boat being ready with her gear and two men, by the date of May the first. And I knew then that *David Copperfield* and *The Tempest*[7] and all of those friends I had dearly come to love must really go forever. So I bade them all good-bye.

The night after my first full day at home and after my mother had gone upstairs he called me into his room where I sat upon the chair beside his bed. "You will go back tomorrow," he said simply.

I refused then, saying I had made my decision and was satisfied.

"That is no way to make a decision," he said, "and if you are satisfied I am not. It is best that you go back." I was almost angry then and told him as all children do that I wished he would leave me alone and stop telling me what to do.

He looked at me a long time then, lying there on the same bed on which he had fathered me those sixteen years before, fathered me his only son, out of who knew what emotions when he was already fifty-six and his hair had turned to snow. Then he swung his legs over the edge of the squeaking bed and sat facing me and looked into my own dark eyes with his of crystal blue and placed his hand upon my knee. "I am not telling you to do anything," he said softly, "only asking you."

The next morning I returned to school. As I left, my mother followed me to the porch and said, "I never thought a son of mine would choose useless books over the parents that gave him life."

In the weeks that followed he got up rather miraculously and the gear was ready and the *Jenny Lynn* was freshly painted by the last two weeks of April when the ice began to break up and the lonely screaming gulls returned to haunt the silver herring as they flashed within the sea.

On the first day of May the boats raced out as they had always done, laden down almost to the gunwales with their heavy cargoes of traps. They were almost like living things as they plunged through the waters of the spring and manoeuvred between the still floating icebergs of crystal-white and emerald green on their way to the traditional grounds that they sought out every May. And those of us who sat that day in the high school on the hill, discussing the water imagery of Tennyson, watched them as they

---

7. **David Copperfield, The Tempest** *David Copperfield* is an 1850 novel by Charles Dickens; *The Tempest* is a play by Shakespeare.

passed back and forth beneath us until by afternoon the piles of traps which had been stacked upon the wharf were no longer visible but were spread about the bottoms of the sea. And the *Jenny Lynn* went too, all day, with my uncle tall and dark, like a latter-day Tashtego[8] standing at the tiller with his legs wide apart and guiding her deftly between the floating pans of ice and my father in the stern standing in the same way with his hands upon the ropes that lashed the cargo to the deck. And at night my mother asked, "Well, how did things go in the boat today?"

And the spring wore on and the summer came and school ended in the third week of June and the lobster season on July first and I wished that the two things I loved so dearly did not exclude each other in a manner that was so blunt and too clear.

At the conclusion of the lobster season my uncle said he had been offered a berth[9] on a deep sea dragger and had decided to accept. We all knew that he was leaving the *Jenny Lynn* forever and that before the next lobster season he would buy a boat of his own. He was expecting another child and would be supporting fifteen people by the next spring and could not chance my father against the family that he loved.

I joined my father then for the trawling season, and he made no protest and my mother was quite happy. Through the summer we baited the tubs of trawl in the afternoon and set them at sunset and revisited them in the darkness of the early morning. The men would come tramping by our house at four A.M. and we would join them and walk with them to the wharf and be on our way before the sun rose out of the ocean where it seemed to spend the night. If I was not up they would toss pebbles to my window and I would be very embarrassed and tumble downstairs to where my father lay fully clothed atop his bed, reading his book and listening to his radio and smoking his cigarette. When I appeared he would swing off his bed and put on his boots and be instantly ready and then we would take the lunches my mother had prepared the night before and walk off toward the sea. He would make no attempt to wake me himself.

It was in many ways a good summer. There were few storms and we were out almost every day and we lost a minimum of gear and seemed to land a maximum of fish and I tanned dark and brown after the manner of my uncles.

My father did not tan — he never tanned — because of his reddish complexion, and the salt water irritated his skin as it had for sixty years. He burned and reburned over and over again and his lips still cracked so that they bled when he smiled, and his arms, especially the left, still broke out into the oozing salt-water boils as they had ever since as a child I had first watched him soaking and bathing them in a variety of ineffectual solutions. The chafe-preventing bracelets of brass linked chain that all the men wore about their wrists in early spring were his the full season and he shaved but painfully and only once a week.

And I saw then, that summer, many things that I had seen all my life as if for the first time and I thought that perhaps my father had never been intended for a fisherman either physically or mentally. At least not in the manner of my uncles; he had never really loved it. And I remembered that, one evening in his room when we were talking about *David Copperfield*, he had said that he had always wanted to go to the university and I had dismissed it then in the way one dismisses his father's saying he would like to be a tight-rope walker, and we had gone on to talk about the Peggottys[10] and how they loved the sea.

---

8. **Tashtego** A harpooner from Herman Melville's novel *Moby-Dick* (1851). 9. **berth** Position as an officer.

10. **Peggottys** Humble, generous friends of David Copperfield in the Dickens novel.

And I thought then to myself that there were many things wrong with all of us and all our lives and I wondered why my father, who was himself an only son, had not married before he was forty and then I wondered why he had. I even thought that perhaps he had had to marry my mother and checked the dates on the flyleaf of the Bible where I learned that my oldest sister had been born a prosaic eleven months after the marriage, and I felt myself then very dirty and debased for my lack of faith and for what I had thought and done.

And then there came into my heart a very great love for my father and I thought it was very much braver to spend a life doing what you really do not want rather than selfishly following forever your own dreams and inclinations. And I knew then that I could never leave him alone to suffer the iron-tipped harpoons which my mother would forever hurl into his soul because he was a failure as a husband and a father who had retained none of his own. And I felt that I had been very small in a little secret place within me and that even the completion of high school was for me a silly shallow selfish dream.

So I told him one night very resolutely and very powerfully that I would remain with him as long as he lived and we would fish the sea together. And he made no protest but only smiled through the cigarette smoke that wreathed his bed and replied, "I hope you will remember what you've said."

The room was now so filled with books as to be almost Dickensian, but he would not allow my mother to move or change them and he continued to read them, sometimes two or three a night. They came with great regularity now, and there were more hard covers, sent by my sisters who had gone so long ago and now seemed so distant and so prosperous, and sent also pictures of small red-haired grandchildren with baseball bats and dolls which he placed upon his bureau and which my mother gazed at wistfully when she thought no one would see. Red-haired grandchildren with baseball bats and dolls who would never know the sea in hatred or in love.

And so we fished through the heat of August and into the cooler days of September when the water was so clear we could almost see the bottom and the white mists rose like delicate ghosts in the early morning dawn. And one day my mother said to me, "You have given added years to his life."

And we fished on into October when it began to roughen and we could no longer risk night sets but took our gear out each morning and returned at the first sign of the squalls; and on into November when we lost three tubs of trawl and the clear blue water turned to a sullen grey and the trochoidal[11] waves rolled rough and high and washed across our bows and decks as we ran within their troughs. We wore heavy sweaters now and the awkward rubber slickers and the heavy woollen mitts which soaked and froze into masses of ice that hung from our wrists like the limbs of gigantic monsters until we thawed them against the exhaust pipe's heat. And almost every day we would leave for home before noon, driven by the blasts of the northwest wind, coating our eyebrows with ice and freezing our eyelids closed as we leaned into a visibility that was hardly there, charting our course from the compass and the sea, running with the waves and between them but never confronting their towering might.

And I stood at the tiller now, on these homeward lunges, stood in the place and in the manner of my uncle, turning to look at my father and to shout over the roar of the

---

11. **trochoidal** Curving.

engine and the slop of the sea to where he stood in the stern, drenched and dripping with the snow and the salt and the spray and his bushy eyebrows caked in ice. But on November twenty-first, when it seemed we might be making the final run of the season, I turned and he was not there and I knew even in that instant that he would never be again.

On November twenty-first the waves of the grey Atlantic are very very high and the waters are very cold and there are no signposts on the surface of the sea. You cannot tell where you have been five minutes before and in the squalls of snow you cannot see. And it takes longer than you would believe to check a boat that has been running before a gale and turn her ever so carefully in a wide and stupid circle, with timbers creaking and straining, back into the face of storm. And you know that it is useless and that your voice does not carry the length of the boat and that even if you knew the original spot, the relentless waves would carry such a burden perhaps a mile or so by the time you could return. And you know also, the final irony, that your father like your uncles and all the men that form your past, cannot swim a stroke.

The lobster beds off the Cape Breton coast are still very rich and now, from May to July, their offerings are packed in crates of ice, and thundered by the gigantic transport trucks, day and night, through New Glasgow, Amherst, Saint John and Bangor and Portland and into Boston where they are tossed still living into boiling pots of water, their final home.

And though the prices are higher and the competition tighter, the grounds to which the *Jenny Lynn* once went remain untouched and unfished as they have for the last ten years. For if there are no signposts on the sea in storm there are certain ones in calm and the lobster bottoms were distributed in calm before any of us can remember and the grounds my father fished were those his father fished before him and there were others before and before and before. Twice the big boats have come from forty and fifty miles, lured by the promise of the grounds, and strewn the bottom with their traps and twice they have returned to find their buoys cut adrift and their gear lost and destroyed. Twice the Fisheries Officer and the Mounted Police have come and asked many long and involved questions and twice they have received no answers from the men leaning in the doors of their shanties and the women standing at their windows with their children in their arms. Twice they have gone away saying: "There are no legal boundaries in the Marine area"; "No one can own the sea"; "Those grounds don't wait for anyone."

But the men and the women, with my mother dark among them, do not care for what they say, for to them the grounds are sacred and they think they wait for me.

It is not an easy thing to know that your mother lives alone on an inadequate insurance policy and that she is too proud to accept any other aid. And that she looks through her lonely window onto the ice of winter and the hot flat calm of summer and the rolling waves of fall. And that she lies awake in the early morning's darkness when the rubber boots of the men scrunch upon the gravel as they pass beside her house on their way down to the wharf. And she knows that the footsteps never stop, because no man goes from her house, and she alone of all the Lynns has neither son nor son-in-law that walks toward the boat that will take him to the sea. And it is not an easy thing to know that your mother looks upon the sea with love and on you with bitterness because the one has been so constant and the other so untrue.

But neither is it easy to know that your father was found on November twenty-eighth, ten miles to the north and wedged between two boulders at the base of the rock-strewn cliffs where he had been hurled and slammed so many many times. His hands were shredded ribbons as were his feet which had lost their boots to the suction of the sea, and his shoulders came apart in our hands when we tried to move him from the rocks. And the fish had eaten his testicles and the gulls had pecked out his eyes and the white-green stubble of his whiskers had continued to grow in death, like the grass on graves, upon the purple, bloated mass that was his face. There was not much left of my father, physically, as he lay there with the brass chains on his wrists and the seaweed in his hair.

(1976)

Claire Harris (1937–)

Claire Harris was born in Port of Spain, Trinidad, in 1937. Although her parents were employed in the public school system (her mother was a teacher and her father a headmaster who became a school inspector), Harris was educated at home until the age of seven, when she entered a Catholic convent school. During summer vacations, she and her family would retreat to their country estate. "My father would bring boxes of books with him," Harris recalls. "He would insist that the radio be turned on only twice a day, to hear the news. And the rest of the time we ran wild, and made up our own stories, and read."

Harris's mother advised her to find a profession that would ensure her financial independence, and Harris heeded her advice. She earned a B.A. in English from University College in Dublin in 1961, and a teaching certificate from the University of the West Indies in Jamaica in 1963. She returned to Trinidad as a teacher and remained there until 1966, when she immigrated to Canada. Until 1993, she taught high school English and drama in Calgary. During this period, she took a leave of absence and travelled to Nigeria, where she obtained a diploma in media studies from the University of Lagos. There, in 1975, Harris met Nigerian writer and critic John Pepper Clark, who, she says, "initiated [me] into the mysteries of writing professionally." As she worked towards her diploma, Harris began to reflect on her origins and came to the realization that, as a Black woman, she had lost touch with her heritage. She began to use writing as a means of exploring the ways in which she could recover that heritage in the context of her experience as a Trinidad-born Canadian.

In 1975, Harris began to publish poetry. The following year, she became involved in Poetry Goes Public, a poster series that featured the works of major Canadian poets. From 1981 to 1989, she edited *Dandelion* magazine, and in 1984, she co-founded the literary magazine *blue buffalo*, which was devoted to supporting local Alberta writers. Her first book of poetry, *Fables from the Women's Quarters*, appeared the same year.

Fables establishes many of the themes that would come to distinguish Harris's career. Some of the poems comment on the work of Guatemalan political leader Rigoberto Manchu, who won the Nobel Peace Prize in 1992. Others address female communities and attempt to forge bonds between them by creating multiple personae — writers, record-keepers, and diarists — who map the varieties of female experience and self-creation using multiple narrative forms (autobiography, biography, diary, reportage, and letters, to name a few). Harris's incorporation of these different narrative forms in her writing is motivated by her belief that identity itself is composite, multiple, and always in flux. Rather than provide a static depiction of any individual, Harris encourages a dynamic view of identity that is open to change and instability. Her mixing of forms has political implications: it demonstrates the ways in which women construct themselves and their freedom through acts of telling. The degree of independence that women enjoy is intimately related to the way they speak and write, and to the way they interpret the voices of those around them.

Although in her early poetry Harris focused on the construction of female identity, she was also concerned with the effects of the Caribbean diaspora. Canadian immigration policy changed dramatically after she moved to Canada, in 1966, and this precipitated an influx of thousands of people from the Caribbean region and Africa. In much of her writing, Harris confronts the problems faced by newcomers in adapting to a new culture, in bridging the gulf between their pasts and their Canadian present. Harris says, "I believe that African poetry in the Americas, or in Europe — in the diaspora — is written out of a subconscious dialogue that's constantly running through our minds ... a continuing engagement with a society that in all its manifestations still wants to convince us that we're less than others." She writes about the suffering of immigrants constricted by stereotypes of race and gender. In the poem "Policeman Cleared in Jaywalking Case," for example, she dramatizes public apathy about the arrest and strip-search of a Black schoolgirl. *Travelling to Find a Remedy* (1986) and *The Conception of Winter* (1989) are similarly concerned with the ways in which racism, prejudice, and politics intrude upon daily life.

One of Harris's most compelling works is the Governor General's Award–nominated *Drawing Down a Daughter* (1992), which she calls "an autobiography. Of sorts." In this prose-poem, a pregnant woman speaks to her unborn daughter through an array of forms and voices. Harris's narrator/mother/writer blends oral history, historical records, myths, and recipes and employs a range of typefaces and visual effects to produce an evocative collage. As the birth of her daughter approaches, the woman struggles to reconnect with her past so that she can move forward to embrace her future — a future embodied by the life growing inside her.

In *Dipped in Shadow* (1996), Harris challenges women to speak out about domestic violence, political oppression, and pedophilia. The poem "Nude in an Armchair," for example, gives voice to the thoughts of a woman whose children have been abused by their father. In her most recent book, *She* (2000), a poetry and prose novel, Harris depicts the breakdown of a woman afflicted with multiple personality disorder. Penelope-Marie Lancet, a Trinidadian immigrant, is driven insane by her unfulfilled desire to have a child. She speaks in several voices and in multiple dialects, which conflict with one another as the story unfolds. Cut off from friends and family, Penelope reaches out to relieve her isolation by writing letters — cacophonous epistles packed with newspaper clippings, movie reviews, plays on words, unpunctuated outpourings, and dislocated dialogues. Although the book provides the reader with clinical insight into Penelope's disorder, Harris also treats the disease as a metaphor for the conflicted voice of women — a voice that must strive mightily in its attempt to express a cohesive identity.

Harris retired from teaching in 1993 to focus on her writing. She is the recipient of numerous awards, including the Commonwealth Prize, Americas Region (1985); the Writer's Guild of Alberta Award for poetry (1987); the Alberta Culture Poetry Prize (1990); and the Alberta Culture Special Award (1992).

Where the Sky Is a Pitiful Tent

Once I heard a Ladino say "I am poor but listen I am not an Indian"; but then again I know Ladinos who fight with us and who understand we're human beings just like them.

Rigoberto Manchu (Guatemala)[1]

---

1. **Rigoberto Manchu** All italicized excerpts are from Manchu, human rights activist and 1992 Nobel Peace Prize winner, as translated by Patricia Goedicke in *American Poetry Review*, Jan./Feb. 1983.

All night the hibiscus tapped at our jalousies[2]
dark bluster of its flower trying to ride in
on wind lacinated[3] with the smell of yard fowl
Such sly knocking sprayed the quiet
your name in whispers
dry shuffle of thieving feet on verandah floors
My mouth filled with midnight and fog
like someone in hiding
to someone in hiding
10   I said *do not go*
you didn't answer
though you became beautiful and ferocious
There leached from you three hundred years of compliance
Now I sleep with my eyes propped open
lids nailed to the brow

After their marriage my parents went into the mountains to establish a small settlement … they waited years for the first harvest. Then a patron arrived and claimed the land. My father devoted himself to travelling and looking for help in getting the rich landowners to leave us alone. But his complaints were not heard … they accused him of provoking disorder, of going against the sovereign order of Guatemala … they arrested him.

Ladino: descendants of Spanish Jews who came to Guatemala during the Inquisition.

---

2. **jalousies** Shutters. 3. **lacinated** Fringed.

In the dream I labour toward something
glimpsed through fog   something of us exposed
on rock and mewling[4]   as against the tug of water   20
I struggle under sharp slant eyes
death snap and rattle of hungry wings
                                        Awake I whisper
You have no right to act
you cannot return land from the grave
Braiding my hair the mirror propped on my knees
I gaze at your sleeping vulnerable head
Before the village we nod smile or don't smile
we must be as always
while the whole space of day aches with our nightmares   30
I trail in your footsteps through cracks you chisel
in this thin uncertain world
where as if it were meant for this mist hides
sad mountain villages   reluctant fields
still your son skips on the path laughing
he is a bird   he is a hare
under the skeletal trees

My mother had to leave us alone while she went to look for a lawyer who would take my
father's case. And because of that she had to work as a servant. All her salary went to the
lawyer. My father was tortured and condemned to eighteen years in prison. (Later he was
released.) But they threatened to imprison him for life if he made any more trouble.

---

4. **mewling** Crying, whimpering.

I watch in the market square
40 those who stop and those who do not
while my hands draw the wool over up down
knitting the bright caps on their own
my eyes look only at sandals
at feet chipped like stones at the quarry
There are noons when the square shimmers
we hold our breath while those others
tramp in the market place
Today the square ripples like a pond
three thrown what is left of them
50 corded like wood alive and brought to flame
How long the death smoke signals
on this clear day
We are less than the pebbles under their heels
the boy hides in my shawl

---

*The army circulated an announcement ordering everyone to present themselves in one of
the villages to witness the punishment the guerillas would receive ... There we could observe
the terrible things our comrades had suffered, and see for ourselves that those they called
guerillas were people from the neighbouring villages ... among them the Catequistas[5] and
my little brother ... who was secretary to one of the village co-operatives. That was his only
crime. He was fourteen years old ... They burnt them.*

---

5. **Catequistas** Those who teach catechism, the preparatory lessons for entering a Christian church.

As if I have suffered resurrection I see
the way the grass is starred with thick fleshed
flowers at whose core a swirl of fine yellow
lines disappear into hollow stems
so we now into our vanished lives   60
Dust thickening trees we turn
to the knotted fist of mountains
clenched against   mauve distance
Because I must   I look back
heartheld to where the mudbrick huts
their weathered windows daubed with useless crosses
their shattered doors   begin the slow descent
to earth   my earlier self turns in
darkening air   softly goes down with them
The boy only worms alive in his eyes   70
his face turned to the caves

---

*When we returned to the house we were a little crazy, as if it had been a nightmare. My
father marched ahead swiftly saying that he had much to do for his people; that he must go
from village to village to tell them what had happened ... A little later so did my mother in
her turn ... My brother left too ... and my little sisters.*

If in this poem you scream who will hear you
though you say *no one should cry out in vain*
your face dark and thin with rage
Now in this strange mountain place
stripped by knowledge
I wait for you
Someone drunk stumbles the night path
80   snatching at a song or someone not drunk
I am so porous with fear
even the rustle of ants in the grass flows through me
but you are set apart
The catechists say *in heaven there is no male
no female*   that is a far foolishness
why else seeing you smelling of danger
and death do I want you so
your mouth   your clear opening in me

We began to build camps in the mountains where we would spend the night to prevent the troops from killing us while we slept. In the daytime we had taught the children to keep watch over the road … We knew that the guerillas were up there in the distant mountains. At times they would come down in order to look for food, in the beginning we didn't trust them, but then we understood that they, at least, had weapons to fight the army with.

You will not stop what you have begun   90
though I asked in the way a woman can
Since you have broken thus into life
soon someone will make a pattern
of your bones   of your skull
as they have with others
and what will fly out
what will escape from you torn apart
the boy and I must carry
In your sleep I went to the cenote[6]
in the moonlight I filled my shawl with flowers   100
threw them to the dark water
the ancient words fluting in my head
your son pinched awake to know what must come

My mother was captured (some) months later … when all she could wish for was to die …
they revived her, and when she had recovered her strength they began torturing her again …
they placed her in an open field … filled her body with worms … she struggled a long time then
died under the sun … The soldiers stayed until the buzzards and dogs had eaten her. Thus
they hoped to terrorize us. She doesn't have a grave. We, her children, had to find another way
of fighting.

---

6. **cenote** A well occasionally used in ritual sacrifice (pre-Columbian).

Oh love this is silence   this is the full
silence of completion   we have swum through
terror that seared us to bone
rage lifted a cold hand to save us
so we became this surreal country
110   We have been bullet-laden air   fields that sprout
skulls   night that screeches and hammers
we have been hunger   whip   wind that sobs
feast days and drunken laughter
a rare kindness and pleasure
We have come through to the other side
here everything is silence   our quiet breathing
in this empty hut   our clay jugs full of light
and water   we are our corn our salt
this quiet is the strength we didn't know we had
120   our humanity no longer alarms us
we have found who we are
my husband our silence is the silence of blue steel thrumming
and of love
Our deaths shall be clear

_____

*Our only way of commemorating the spilled blood of our parents was to go on fighting
and following the path they had followed. I joined the organization of the Revolutionary
Christians. I know perfectly well that in this fight one runs the greatest risk ... We have
been suffering such a long time and waiting.*

Your death is drenched in such light
that small things   the sky   branches
brushing against the cave mouth   the boy
stirring   make my skin crackle against damp blankets
As one gathers bullets carelessly spilled I gather your screams   130
all night I remember you   utterly lovely
the way you danced the wedding dance
rising dust clouding your sandals
your slow dark smile
You return to the predawn   leaving us
what remains when the flames die out of words
(small hard assertions
our beginnings
shards of the world you shattered
and ourselves)   140

Their death gave us hope, because it is not just that the blood of all those people be erased
forever. It is our duty on this earth to revive it … I fight so they will recognise me … If
I have taken advantage of this chance to tell the story of my life it is because I know that my
people cannot tell their own stories. But they are no different from mine.

(1984)

Jane in Summer

She sits on rocks above the bay   so still that were it not
     for the wind in her hair   or her blouse in its yellow
     silk blooming
She might be a figure carved from twisted pine   from
     summer   curve of her back and arm growing from the curve
     of land
At this distance Barcelona suits her   a certain grace
     black hair   pale forehead
Yet you would be better to think her a room rising
     out of ruins   a room put together stone by stone   10
Stones unfamiliar to each other yet holding together
     with delicacy   despite cracks and patches

A stranger passing by at dusk   looking up in softened light
     might catch a glimpse   shadowy elegances
From consonants of chandelier and red velvet chair might
     construct a language   a fable   might imagine skeins[1] of wool
     tapestry

---

1. **skeins** Loosely coiled bundles.

And a woman graceful in summer glow waiting behind leafed
    wrought iron bars
20 If drawn to rescue he knocked on the door it would open on
    a warm prairie room   fire burning low   prim French provincial
    suite   dried flowers near the hearth   a table laid for two
    the air expectant
But no woman there   nothing but an empty room listening
    for someone else to come along the path   someone known

Now each summer shaking off her year   its ruins   she comes
    to Spain   finds a new place to stitch and unstitch dreams
Summer after summer passes in an illusion of action   of vivid
    life   rehearsing her stories   and winter
30 And always   like an after-image or a ghost the first Adam
    secret inviolate[2] moment   the love around which her life
    still swirls
Imagine then the stranger hesitating on her threshold
    conscious in the stones indifference   retracing his steps
    down paths of rosemary
Should he pause he might hear clear and distant   the voice
    of that room piping as in a darkening wood

(1988)

John Metcalf (1938–)

John Metcalf was born in Carlisle, England, in 1938. As a child, he was a passionate collector, filling his room with books, comics, and assorted biological specimens. Later, this passion emerged in his work as an editorial collector and in his finely crafted fiction, which he says is "full of *detailed,* factual *things.*" Metcalf spent much of his adolescence reading voraciously, but he also passed many hours sparring in the boxing ring (perhaps this is where his reputation as a literary pugilist began). He attended the University of Bristol, where he studied theology and literature, but his primary interest was literature: he scrutinized the works of modernist writers, especially Ernest Hemingway and Ezra Pound, whom he admired for their concision, their use of concrete images, and their obsession with technique and style.

In 1960, he received an honours B.A. and a certificate in education, but he found that teaching in the British system depressed him. After two years in the trenches, he successfully applied for a position in Montreal; he came to Canada in 1962. His first story, "Early Morning Rabbits," won a CBC short story competition in 1963. Two years later, Metcalf married, and he spent the remainder of the decade teaching literature in Montreal secondary schools. Recalling the state of Canadian writing in the early 1960s, he says, "there was no Canadian tradition or body of work I could hope to join. The country lacked what would be called today an 'infrastructure' — the literary equivalent of roads, sewers, electric power, railroad tracks — and I've spent nearly all my life in Canada … in a probably vain attempt to help put the necessary infrastructure in place."

---

2. **inviolate** Retaining its purity.

Appalled to find no Canadian literature on the high school curriculum, Metcalf assembled an anthology of new fiction called *Sixteen by Twelve* (1970). As with *Best Canadian Stories,* the annual he co-edited with Leon Rooke from 1977 to 1982, the aim was "to produce a ... showcase of fine writing — writing for which one wouldn't have to mumble and apologize." Asked why he would devote time to editing anthologies instead of focusing on his own work, Metcalf replied, "I feel I have to attempt to shape taste, to encourage younger writers, to edit, to criticize — and anthologies are an expression of that." He firmly believed that good writers are encouraged by good readers, and that Canadian literature would flounder unless educators and students were encouraged to take an interest in their national literature. To foster such interest, Metcalf became a relentless anthologizer, eventually producing over 30 anthologies of Canadian fiction. On this level alone, his contribution to the evolution of Canadian literature and to the formation of literary taste in Canada is unsurpassed.

In his quest to promote Canadian writing, Metcalf joined with fellow writers Hugh Hood, Clark Blaise, Ray Fraser, and Ray Smith to form the Montreal Storytellers performance group. From 1971 to 1976, they toured local high schools, colleges, and universities. "We read in the schools week after week," he recalls. "We were trying to attract a new generation of readers ... [and to] show them that Montreal could be imagined just as London or New York is."

When the Montreal Storytellers was launched, Metcalf was writing full time and supplementing his income with occasional teaching. In 1969, five of his stories had appeared in *New Canadian Writing,* and Metcalf was becoming increasingly preoccupied with questions of style. His stories were musically timed, intricately structured, and lyrically honed. As Barry Cameron has observed, they read like "an approximation of poetry." In his essay "Soaping a Meditative Foot," Metcalf emphasizes his concern with stylistic compression and stresses his finicky devotion to punctuation and form. He advises writers to "Avoid literary criticism which moves away from the word on the printed page and ascends to theories of God, Archetypes, Myth, Psyche, The Garden of Eden, The New Jerusalem, and Orgone Boxes. Stick to the study of the placement of commas." Expanding on this in "Punctuation as Score," he argues that if an author attends carefully to the effects of punctuation on the ear and eye, he or she might create a text whose rhythms and voices are as clear as a well-scored piece of music. Metcalf's attention to the mechanics of writing soon won him a reputation as a master stylist.

His first published collection was *The Lady Who Sold Furniture* (1970), a novella that focuses on one of his recurring themes: the declining excellence of teaching and writing. By 1971, his marriage had fallen apart. He remarried in 1975, and the following year he and his wife, Myrna, moved to a farmhouse in Delta, Ontario. There he produced two novellas, published together under the title *Girl in Gingham* (1978), and his second novel, *General Ludd* (1980). The novel is an absurd and bitter comedy set in a university. It tells the story of an underappreciated poet in residence, who, incensed by the smug technocrats who surround him, decides to destroy the university's new Communication Arts Complex. The relationship between art and human experience, a familiar Metcalf theme, informs this work.

In 1981, Metcalf moved to Ottawa with his family. Increasingly frustrated by what he saw as the dearth of good critical and creative writing in Canada, he became known as a literary provocateur, protesting vociferously against the Canada Council, arguing that in funding the arts, it confused literature with nationalism and masked both the smallness of the Canadian audience and its inability to identify high-quality work. He also began publishing collections of critical essays. The first of these, *Kicking Against the Pricks* (1982), established him as a completely different kind of Canadian literary critic. As Shane Neilson says, the collection "arrived with the brawling enthusiasm of an undefeatable self-confidence, a fearlessness towards telling the truth no matter what the professional cost." Humorous and caustic, Metcalf's essays cemented his reputation as a Canadian literary curmudgeon par excellence. But, despite their levity, these collections — which Metcalf calls "contentious essays and squibs" — are part of his serious attempt to reform Canadian literary standards.

Metcalf published *Adult Entertainment,* a collection of novellas and short stories, in 1986. These pieces, including "The Nipples of Venus," have episodic structures, and their dialogue testifies to Metcalf's superb control of tone, mood, and pacing. Since *Adult Entertainment,* Metcalf has published *Shooting the Stars* (1993) and "Forde Abroad" (1996), a novella that won the 1996 gold medal for fiction at the National Magazine Awards.

Since 1989, Metcalf has worked tirelessly to discover new writers and foster their talent through his editorial work with the Porcupine's Quill, a small literary press based in Erin, Ontario. In his memoir *An Aesthetic Underground* (2003), he explains that his high aesthetic standards are part of a larger cultural vision: "I wanted to shock homogenized minds with the experience of writing at high voltage. I wanted the press to assert relentlessly literature's importance ... to be a gathering together of writers with an aesthetic approach to literature and with a lust for excellence. I wanted our writers to draw strength from community. I wanted each to embolden the next."

In 2004, Metcalf was made a member of the Order of Canada. Since 2005, he has been acquiring works for Biblioasis, a literary press based in Windsor, Ontario. Metcalf is also the senior editor of the journal *Canadian Notes and Queries.*

The Nipples of Venus

Rome stank of exhaust fumes and below our hotel room on the Via Sistina motor bikes and scooters snarled and ripped past late into the night rattling the window and the plywood wardrobe. The bathroom, a boxed-in corner, was the size of two upright coffins. It was impossible to sit on the toilet without jamming your knees against the wash-basin. In the chest of drawers, Helen discovered crackers, crumbs, and Pan Am cheese.

I'd reserved the room by phone from Florence, choosing the hotel from a guide-book from a list headed: Moderate. We would only have to put up with it for Saturday and Sunday and would then fly home on Monday. After nearly three weeks spent mainly in Florence and Venice, I had no real interest in looking at things Roman. I felt ... not tired, exactly. Couldn't take in any more. I'd had enough. "Surfeited"[1] was the word, perhaps. I was sick of cameras and photographs and tourists and tourism and disliking myself for being part of the problem. I felt burdened by history, ashamed of my ignorance, numbed by the succession of *ponte, porta, piazza,* and *palazzo.* I was beginning to feel like ... who was it? Twain, I think, Mark Twain,[2] who when asked what he'd thought of Rome said to his wife:

Was that the place we saw the yellow dog?

Helen was bulged and bloated and the elastic of her underpants and panty-hose had left red weals and ribbing on the flesh of her stomach. She'd been constipated for nearly two weeks. I'd told her to stop eating pasta, to relax, to stop worrying about whether the children would leave the iron switched on, about aviation disasters, devaluation of the lira, cancer of the colon, but at night I heard her sighing, grinding her teeth, restless under the sheets, gnawing on the bones of her worries.

That waiter in — where was it? Milan? No. Definitely not in Milan. Bologna? — a waiter who'd worked for some years in Soho in the family restaurant — he'd told us that

---

1. **Surfeited** Overindulged. 2. **Mark Twain** American writer and humourist (1835–1910).

the tortellini, the tiny stuffed shells of pasta in our soup, were commonly called "the nipples of Venus."

Fettuccine, tuffolini, capelletti, manicotti, gnocchi …

Mia moglie è malata.

Dov'è una farmacia?

Aspirina?

Bicarbonato di soda?[3]

… polenta, rigatoni, tortellini …

Praaaaaaaaap …

Scooters on the Via Sistina.

Praaaaaaaaap …

Helen passing gas.

The Spanish Steps[4] were just at the top of the street anyway and at the very least, Helen said, we had to see the Trevi Fountain and St. Peter's and the Pantheon.[5]

They all looked much as they looked in photographs. Not as attractive, really. The Spanish Steps were littered with American college students. The sweep of St. Peter's Square was ruined even at that early hour by parked coaches from Luton, Belgrade, Brussels, and Brighton. Knowing that St. Peter's itself would be hung with acres of martyrdom and suchlike, I refused to set foot in it. The Trevi Fountain was rimmed with people taking its photograph and was magnificent but disappointing.

Places of historical interest often make me feel as if I'm eight again and the sermon will never end. I enjoyed the *doors* of the Pantheon — I always seem drawn to bronze — but the hushed interior struck me as lugubrious.[6] Helen, on the other hand, is an inveterate reader of every notice, explication, plaque, and advisement.

Straightening up and taking off her reading glasses, she says,

"This is the tomb of Raphael."[7]

"How about a coffee?"

"Born 1483."

"Espresso. You like that. In the square."

"Died in 1520."

"Nice coffee."

And then it was back to the Spanish Steps because she wanted to go jostling up and down the Via Condotti looking in the windows — Ferragamo, Gabrielli, Bulgari, Valentino, Gucci. And then in search of even more pairs of shoes, purses, scarves, gloves, and sweaters, it was down to the stores and boutiques on the Via del Tritone.

For lunch I ate *funghi arrosto alla Romana.* Helen ordered *risotta alla parmagiana* and had to go back to the hotel. She said she'd just lie there for a bit and if the pains went away she'd have a little nap. She asked me if I thought it was cancer, so I said that people with cancer *lost* weight and that it was *risotto, manifestly* risotto, *risotto first and last.*

"There's no need to shout at me."

"I am *not* shouting. I am speaking emphatically."

"You don't mind?" she said. "Really?"

---

3. **Mia moglie … di soda?** "My wife is sick." "Where is the pharmacy?" "Painkillers?" "Sodium bicarbonate?" 4. **Spanish Steps** 138 steps connecting the Piazza di Spagna with the Trinità dei Monti. 5. **Trevi Fountain, St. Peter's, the Pantheon** An elaborate fountain, St. Peter's Basilica, and a classical temple of the gods; landmarks in Rome. 6. **lugubrious** Dismal. 7. **Raphael** Florentine Renaissance painter.

"I'll go for a stroll around," I said.

"You won't feel I'm deserting you?"

"Just rest."

I strolled up the Via Sistina and stood looking down the sweep of the Spanish Steps. Then sauntered on. Some seventy-five yards to the right of the Steps, seventy-five yards or so past the Trinità dei Monti[8] along the stretch of gravel road which leads into the grounds of the Villa Borghese,[9] tucked away behind a thick hedge and shaded by trees, was an outdoor café hidden in a narrow garden. The garden was just a strip between the road and the edge of the steep hill which fell away down towards the Via Condotti or whatever was beneath. The Piazza di Spagna, perhaps. Houses must have been built almost flush with the face of the hill because through the screening pampas grass I could glimpse below the leaning rusty fence at the garden's edge the warm ripple of terra cotta roof tiles.

The garden was paved with stone flagstones. Shrubs and flowers grew in long-walled beds and urns. In the centre of the garden was a small rectangular pond with reeds growing in it, the flash of fish red and gold. The tall hedge which hid the garden from the road was dark, evergreen, yew trees.

It was quiet there, the traffic noises muted to a murmur. Round white metal tables shaded by gay umbrellas, white folding chairs. Two old waiters were bringing food and drinks from the hut at the garden's entrance. There were only three couples and a family at the tables. The yew hedge was straggly and needed cutting back. The shrubs and flowers in the stone-walled beds were gone a little to seed, unweeded.

I sat at the only table without an umbrella, a table set into a corner formed by the hedge and a low stone wall. The wall screened the inner garden a little from the openness of the entrance and from the shingled hut-like place the food came from. All along the top of the wall stood pots of geraniums and jutting out from the wall near my corner table was the basin of a fountain. The basin was in the form of a scallop shell. The stone shell looked much older than the wall. It looked as if it had come down in the world, ending up here in this garden café after gracing for two hundred years or more some ducal[10] garden or palazzo courtyard. The stone was softer than the stone of the wall, grainy, the sharpness of its cuts and flutes blurred and weathered.

I sat enjoying the warmth of the sun. The Becks beer bottle and my glass were beaded with condensation. Sparrows were hopping between tables pecking crumbs. Water was trickling down the wall and falling to the stone scallop shell from a narrow copper pipe which led away down behind the wall and towards the hut at the garden's entrance. Where the pipe crossed the central path feet had squashed it almost flat. The small sound of the water was starting to take over my mind. The glint and sparkle of the sunlight on the water, the tinkling sound of it, the changes in the sound of it as it rose and deepened around the domed bronze grate before draining — it all held me in deepening relaxation.

Somewhere just below me were famous guidebook attractions — the Barcaccia Foundation, the Antico Caffe Greco, the rooms where John Keats died now preserved

---

8. **Trinità dei Monti** Church above the Spanish Steps. 9. **Villa Borghese** Home of the Borghese family, former nobles.
10. **ducal** Of a duke.

as a museum and containing memorabilia of Byron and Shelley[11] — but all I wanted of Rome was to sit on in the sunshine drinking cold beer and listening to the loveliness of water running, the trill and spirtle, the rill and trickle of it.

Watching the sparrow, the small cockings of its head, watching the little boy in the white shirt and red bow-tie balancing face-down over his father's thigh, I was aware suddenly at the corner of my eye of flickering movement. I turned my head and there, reared up on its front legs on the rim of the stone scallop shell, was a lizard. It stood motionless. I turned more towards it. Its back was a matte black but its throat and neck and sides were touched with a green so brilliant it looked almost metallic, as if it had been dusted with metallic powder.

Set on the stone surround of the scallop shell were two pots of geraniums and from the shadow of these now appeared another lizard, smaller than the first, not as dark in colouring, dun rather than black and with not a trace of the shimmering peacock green — compared with the male a scrawny creature drab and dowdy.

This lizard waddled down into the curve of the stone basin where she stopped and raised her head as if watching or listening. Or was she perhaps scenting what was on the air? I'd read somewhere that snakes "smelled" with their tongues. Were lizards, I wondered, like snakes in that? Would they go into water? Was she going to drink?

I was startled by loud rustlings in the hedge near my chair. A bird? A bird rooting about in dead leaves. But it wasn't that kind of noise quite. Not as loud. And, I realized, it was more continuous than the noise a bird would have made — rustling, twig-snipping, pushing, scuffling. The noise was travelling along *inside* the hedge. Slowly, cautiously, not wanting to frighten away the lizards on the stone scallop shell, I bent and parted branched, peering.

And then the noise stopped.

As I sat up, I saw that the stone bowl was empty, the brown lizard disappeared behind the geranium pots again. The green lizard was still motionless where he'd been before. Every few seconds his neck pulsed. Suddenly I saw on the wall level with my knee a lizard climbing. Every two or three inches it stopped, clinging, seeming to listen. It too was green but it had no tail. Where its tail should have been was a glossy rounded stump.

Lacking the tail's long grace, the lizard looked unbalanced, clumsy. About half the tail was gone. It was broken off just below that place where the body tapered. The stump was a scaleless wound, shiny, slightly bulbous, in colour a very dark red mixed with black. The end of the stump bulged out like a blob of smoke-swirled sealing-wax.

Just as its head was sticking up over the edge of the stone shell, the other lizard ran at it. The mutilated lizard turned and flashed halfway down the wall but then stopped, head-down, clinging. The pursuing lizard stopped too and cocked its head at an angle as if hearing something commanding to its right.

Seconds later, the stubby lizard skittered down the rest of the wall, but then stopped again on the flagstones. The pursuing lizard pursued but himself stopped poised above the wall's last course of stones. It was like watching a flurry of a silent movie with the action frozen every few seconds. And then the damaged lizard was negotiating in dreamy slow motion dead twigs and blown leaves on his way back into the hedge. He *clambered* over them as if they were thick boughs, back legs cocked up at funny angles

---

11. **Keats, Byron, Shelley** British romantic poets; John Keats died in Italy in 1821, at the age of 26, inspiring Percy Bysshe Shelley to write "Adonais." Lord Byron also wrote about Keats' death.

like a cartoon animal, crawling, ludicrous. His pursuer faced in the opposite direction intently, fiercely.

Peculiar little creatures.

I signalled to the waiter for another beer.

I sat on in the sunshine, drifting, smelling the smell on my fingers of crushed geranium leaves, listening to the sounds the water made.

And then the noises in the hedge started again.

And again the lizard with the stump was climbing the wall.

And again the lizard on the top was rushing at it, driving it down.

By the time I was finishing my third beer, the attacks and retreats were almost continuous. The stubby lizard always climbed the wall at exactly the same place. The defending lizard always returned to the exact spot on the stone surround of the scallop shell where the attacking lizard would appear. The stop-frame chases flowed and halted down the wall, across the flagstones, halted, round an urn, into the hedge.

But with each sortie the damaged lizard was being driven further and further away. Finally, the pursuing lizard hauled his length into the hedge and I listened to their blundering progress over the litter of twigs and rusty needles in the hedge-bottom, the rustlings and cracklings, the scrabblings travelling further and further away from my chair until there was silence.

The sun had moved around the crown of the tree and was now full on me. I could feel the sweat starting on my chest, in the hollow of my throat, the damp prickle of sweat in my groin. I glanced at my watch to see how long she'd been sleeping. I thought of strolling back to the hotel and having a shower, but the thought of showering in the boxed-in bathroom inside the glass device with its folding glass doors like a compressed telephone booth — the thought of touching with every movement cold, soap-slimy glass …

I lifted the empty Becks bottle and nodded at the waiter as he passed.

A dragon-fly hovered over the pond, its wings at certain angles a blue iridescence.

I wondered about my chances of finding a Roman restaurant or trattoria serving *Abbracchio alla Romana*, a dish I'd read about with interest. And while I was thinking about restaurants and roast lamb flavoured with rosemary and anchovies and about poor Helen's *risotto* and about how long I'd been sitting in the garden and Helen worrying there in that plywood room heavy with exhaust fumes …

you might have been killed … you know I only nap for an hour … I got so scared …

… while I was thinking about this and these and listening to the water's trickle and looking at the white, heavy plumes of the pampas grass, there on top of the wall, my eye caught by the movement, was the lizard with the stump.

I studied the face of the wall, scanned the bottom of the hedge, looked as far around the base of the urn as I could see without moving, but there was no sign of the other lizard, no sound of pursuit.

He stood motionless on top of the wall just above the scallop shell where the scrawny brown female still basked. The stump looked as if blood and flesh had oozed from the wound and then hardened into this glossy, bulging scab.

The coast's clear, Charlie!

Come on!

Come on!

He was clinging head-down to the wall inches above the stone shell.

The female had raised her head.

Now he seemed to be studying a pale wedge of crumbling mortar.

Come on!

And then he waddled down onto the stone surround and seized the female lizard firmly about the middle in his jaws. They lay at right angles to each other as if catatonic. The female's front right leg dangled in the air.

Come on, you gimpy retard! Let go! You're biting the wrong one. It's the GREEN ones we bite. The brown ones are the ones we …

The waiter's voice startled me.

I smiled, shook my head, picked up the four cash-register slips, leaned over to one side to get at my wallet in my back pocket. When he'd gone and I turned back to the stone scallop shell, the female had already vanished and the end of the stump, somewhere between colour of a ripening blackberry and a blood blister, was just disappearing into the shadows behind one of the pots of geraniums.

I got up slowly and quietly. I was careful not to scrape my chair on the flagstones. I set it down quietly. I looked down to make sure my shoe wasn't going to knock against one of the table's tubular legs. One by one, I placed the coins in the saucer.

No, I told Helen on Sunday morning, not the Forum, not the Colosseum, not the Capitoline, the Palatine, or the Quirinal. I wanted to be lazy. I wanted to be taken somewhere. But not to monuments. Trees and fields. But not *walking*. I didn't want to *do* anything. I wanted to see farmhouses and outbuildings. What I wanted — yes, that was it exactly — a coach tour! I wanted to gaze out of the window at red and orange roof tiles, at ochre walls, poppies growing wild on the roadsides, vines.

At 10 AM we were waiting in a small office in a side street for the arrival of the coach. The brochure in the hotel lobby had described the outing as Extended Alban Hills Tours — Castelli Romani. Our coach was apparently now touring some of the larger hotels picking up other passengers. The whole operation seemed a bit makeshift and fly-by-night. The two young men running it seemed to do nothing but shout denials on the phone and hustle out into the street screaming at drivers as coach after coach checked in at the office before setting out to tour whatever they were advertised as touring. Commands and queries were hysterical. Tickets were counted and recounted. And then recounted. Coaches were finally dispatched with operatic gesture as if they were full of troops going up to some heroic Front.

As each coach pulled up, we looked inquiry at one or other of the young men. "This is not yours," said their hands. "Patience." "Do not fear. When your conveyance arrives, we will inform you," said their gestures.

We were both startled by the entry of a large, stout man with a shaved head who barged into the tiny office saying something that sounded challenging or jeering. His voice was harsh. He limped, throwing out one leg stiffly. Helen sat up in the plastic chair and drew her legs in. Something about his appearance suggested that he'd survived a bad car-crash. He leaned on an aluminum stick which ended in a large rubber bulb. He was wearing rimless blue-tinted glasses. His lip was permanently drawn up a little at one side. There was a lot of visible metal in his teeth. He stumped about in the confined space shouting and growling.

The young man with the mauve leather shoes shouted "no" a lot and "never" and slapped the counter with a plastic ruler. The other young man picked up a glossy brochure and, gazing fixedly at the ceiling, twisted it as if wringing a neck. The shaven-headed man pushed a pile of pamphlets off the counter with the rubber tip of his aluminum stick.

A coach pulled up and a young woman in a yellow dress got down from it and clattered on heels into the office. They all shouted at her. She spat — *teh* — and made a coarse gesture.

The young man with the mauve leather shoes went outside to shout up at the coach driver. Through the window, we watched him counting, pulling each finger down in turn.

... five, six, *seven*.

Further heart-rending pantomime followed.

Still in full flow, he burst back into the office brandishing the tickets in an accusatory way. Peering and pouting into the mirror of a compact, the girl in the yellow dress continued applying lipstick. They all shouted questions at her, possibly rhetorical. The horrible shaven-headed man shook the handle of his aluminum cane in her face.

She spat again — *teh*.

The bus driver sounded his horn.

The other young man spoke beseechingly to the potted azalea.

"Is that," said Helen, "the Castelli Romani coach? Or isn't it the Castelli Romani coach?"

There was silence as everyone stared at her.

"It *is*, dear madam, it *is*," said the horribly bald man.

"Good," said Helen.

And I followed her out.

We nodded to the other seven passengers as we climbed aboard and seated ourselves behind them near the front of the coach. They sounded American. There were two middle-aged couples, a middle-aged man on his own, rather melancholy-looking, and a middle-aged man with an old woman.

"Here he comes goosewalking," said Helen.

"*Stepping*," I said.

The shaven-headed man, leg lifting up and then swinging to the side, was stumping across the road leaning on the aluminum cane. His jacket was a flapping black-and-white plaid.

"Oh, *no!*" I said. "You don't think *he's* ... "

"I told you," said Helen. "I told you this was going to be awful."

The shaven-headed man climbed up into the bus, hooked his aluminum cane over the handrail above the steps, and unclipped the microphone. Holding it in front of his mouth, he surveyed us.

"Today," he said with strange, metallic sibilance, "today you are my children."

Helen nudged.

"Today I am taking you into the Alban Hills. I will show you many wonders. I will show you extinct volcanoes. I will show you the lake of the famous Caligula.[12] I will show you the headquarters of the German Army in World War II. Together we will visit Castel Gandolfo, Albano, Genzano, Frascati, and Rocca di Papa. We will leave ancient Rome by going past the Colosseum and out onto the Via Appia Antica completed by Appius Claudius in 312 before Christ."

He nodded slowly.

"Oh yes, my children."

---

12. **Caligula** Roman emperor and eccentric despot.

Still nodding.

"*Before Christ.*"

He looked from face to face.

"You will know this famous road as the Appian Way and you will have seen it in the movie *Spartacus* with the star Kirk Douglas."

"Oh, God!" said Helen.

"Well, my children," he said, tapping the bus driver on the shoulder, "are you ready? But you are curious about me. Who *is* this man, you are saying."

He inclined his shaved head in a bow.

"*Who* am I?"

He chuckled into the microphone.

"They call me Kojak."

Cypresses standing guard along the Appian Way over sepulchres and sarcophagi,[13] umbrella pines shading fragments of statuary. Tombs B.C. Tombs A.D. Statuary contemporaneous with Julius Caesar, of whom we would have read in the play of that name by William Shakespeare. It was impossible to ignore or block out his voice, and after a few minutes we'd come to dread the clicking on of the microphone and the harsh, metallic commentary.

You will pay attention to your left and you will see ...

A sarcophagus.

You will pay attention opposite and you will see ...

"Opposite what?"

"He means straight ahead."

"Oh."

... to your right and in one minute you will see a famous school for women drivers ...

Into view hove a scrap-metal dealer's yard mountainous with wrecked cars.

You will pay attention ...

But despite the irritation of the rasping voice, I found the expedition soothing and the motion of the coach restful. The landscape as it passed was pleasing. Fields. Hedges. Garden plots. The warmth of terra cotta tiles. Hills. White clouds in a sky of blue.

The Pope's summer residence at Castel Gandolfo was a glimpse through open ornate gates up a drive to a house, then the high encircling stone wall around the park.

Beech trees.

In the narrow, steep streets of the small town, the coach's length negotiated the sharp turns, eased around corners, trundled past the elaborate façade of the church and through the piazza with its fountain by Bernini.[14]

The famous Peach Festival took place in June.

At Lake Albano we were to stop for half an hour.

No less, my children, and no more.

The coach pulled into the restaurant parking lot and backed into line with more than a dozen others. The restaurant, a cafeteria sort of place, was built on the very edge of the lake. It was jammed with tourists. Washrooms were at the bottom of a central staircase and children ran up and down the stairs, shouting. There was a faint smell of disinfectant. Lost children cried.

---

13. sepulchres, sarcophagi Tombs with coffins or monuments. **14. Bernini** Gian Lorenzo Bernini, baroque sculptor (1598–1680).

In the plastic display cases were sandwiches with dubious fillings, tired-looking panini, and slices of soggy pizza that were being reheated in microwave ovens until greasy.

The man from our coach who was travelling with the old woman sat staring out of the plate-glass window which overlooked the lake. The old woman was spooning in with trembling speed what looked like a huge English trifle, mounds of whipped cream, maraschino cherries, custard, cake.

Helen and I bought an ice cream we didn't really want. We stood on the wooden dock beside the restaurant and looked at the lake which was unnaturally blue. There was a strong breeze. White sails were swooping over the water. I felt cold and wished we could get back in the coach.

"So this was a volcano," said Helen.

"I guess so."

"The top blew off and then it filled up with water."

"I suppose that's it."

The man from our coach who was on his own, the melancholy-looking man, wandered onto the other side of the dock. He stood holding his ice-cream cone and looking across the lake. He looked a bit like Stan Laurel.[15] We nodded to him. He nodded to us and made a sort of gesture at the lake with his ice cream as if to convey approval.

We smiled and nodded.

The engine of the coach was throbbing as we sat waiting for the man and the old woman to shuffle across the parking lot. The stiff breeze suddenly blew the man's hair down, revealing him as bald. From one side of his head hung a long hank which had been trained up and over his bald pate. He looked naked and bizarre as he stood there, the length of hair hanging from the side of his head and fluttering below his shoulder. It looked as if he'd been scalped. The attached hair looked like a dead thing, like a pelt.

Seemingly unembarrassed, he lifted the hair back, settling it as if it were a beret, patting it into place. The old woman stood perhaps two feet from the side of the coach smiling at it with a little smile.

And so, my children, we head now for Genzano and for Frascati, the Queen of the Castelli …

We did not stop in Genzano which also had Baroque fountains possibly by Bernini in the piazzas and a palazzo of some sort. Down below the town was the Lake of Nemi from which two of Caligula's warships had been recovered only to be burned by the retreating Adolf Hitler.

The famous Feast of Flowers took place in May.

"Why do I know the name Frascati?" said Helen.

"Because of the wine?"

"Have I had it?"

I shrugged.

"I had some *years* ago," I said. "Must be thirty years ago now — at a wedding. We drank it with strawberries."

"Whose wedding?"

"And I don't think I've had it since. Um? Oh … a friend from college. I haven't heard from him — Tony Cranbrook … oh, it's been *years*."

---

15. **Stan Laurel** Comedian most famous for his part in the Laurel and Hardy duo.

"There," said Helen, "what kind of tree is that?"

I shook my head.

Frascati.

The wine was dry and golden.

Gold in candlelight.

The marriage of Tony Cranbrook had been celebrated in the village church, frayed purple hassocks, that special Anglican smell of damp and dust and stone, marble memorials let into the wall:

… *departed this life June 11th 1795 in the sure and certain hope of the resurrection and of the life everlasting* …

Afterwards, the younger people had strolled back through deep lanes to the family house for the reception. I'd walked with a girl called Susan who turned out to be the sister of one of the bridesmaids. She'd picked a buttercup and lodged it behind her ear. She'd said:

Do you know what this means in Tahiti?[16]

Late in the evening they'd been wandering about the house calling to us to come and eat strawberries, calling out that I had to make another speech.

Jack?

We know you're there!

Susan?

Jack and Su-san!

The larger drawing-room was warm and quick with candlelight. In the centre of the dark polished refectory table stood a gleaming silver épergne[17] piled with tiny wild strawberries. By the side of it stood octagonal silver sugar casters. The candelabra on the table glossed the wood's dark grain. Reflected in the épergne's curves and facets, points of flame quivered.

You will pay attention to your right …

Traffic was thickening.

Fisher!

The bus was slowing.

Susan Fisher!

… *above the piazza. The Villa is still owned by the Aldobrandini family. You will notice the central avenue of box trees. The park is noted for its grottos and Baroque fountains.*

"Doubtless by Bernini," I said.

"Is that a *palm* tree?" said Helen.

The Villa is open to tourists only in the morning and upon application to the officials of the Frascati Tourist Office. If you will consult your watches, you will see that it is now afternoon so we will proceed immediately to the largest of the Frascati wine cellars.

The aluminum cane with its rubber bulb thumping down, the leg swinging up and to the side, Kojak led the straggling procession towards a large grey stone building at the bottom end of the sloping piazza. A steep flight of steps led down to a terrace and the main entrance. Kojak, teeth bared with the exertion, started to stump and crab his way down.

"Oh, look at the poor old thing, Jack," said Helen. "He'll never manage her on his own down here."

---

16. **buttercup … in Tahiti?** If Susan put it behind her left ear, it means she was spoken for. If it was put behind her right ear, she was seeking a partner. **17. épergne** Ornamental dish, used as a centrepiece.

I went back across the road to where they were still waiting to cross and put my arm under the old woman's. She seemed almost weightless.

"I appreciate this," he said, nodding vigorously on the other side of her. "Nelson Morrison. We're from Trenton, New Jersey."

"Not at all," I said. "Not at all. It's a pleasure."

The old woman did not look at either of us.

"That's the way," I said. "That's it."

"She's not a big talker. She doesn't speak very often, do you, Mother?"

Step by step we edged her down.

"But she enjoys it, don't you, Mother? You can tell she enjoys it. She likes to go out. We went on a boat, didn't we, Mother?"

"Nearly there," I said.

"Do you remember the boat in Venice, Mother? Do you? I think it's a naughty day today, isn't it? You're only hearing what you want to hear."

"One more," I said.

"But she did enjoy it. Every year you'll find us somewhere, won't he, Mother?"

Inside, the others were sitting at a refectory table in a vaulted cellar. It was lit by bare bulbs. It was cool, almost cold, after coming in out of the sunshine. In places, the brickwork glistened with moisture. Kojak, a cigarette held up between thumb and forefinger, was holding forth.

The cellars apparently extended under the building for more than a mile of natural caves and caverns. In the tunnels and corridors were more than a million bottles of wine. Today, however, there was nothing to see as the wine-making did not take place until September. But famous and authentic food was available at the café and counter just a bit further down the tunnel and bottles of the finest Frascati were advantageously for sale. If we desired to buy wine, it would be his pleasure to negotiate for us.

He paused.

He surveyed us through the blue-tinted spectacles.

Slowly, he shook his head.

The five bottles of wine on the table were provided free of charge for us to drink on its own or as an accompaniment to food we might purchase. While he was talking, a girl with a sacking apron round her waist and with broken-backed men's shoes on her feet scuffed in with a tray of tumblers. Kojak started pouring the wine. It looked as if it had been drawn from a barrel minutes before. It was greenish and cloudy. It was thin and vile and tasted like tin. I decided to drink it quickly.

I didn't actually see it happen but I was leaning over saying something to Helen. I heard the melancholy man, the man who was travelling alone, say, "No thank you. I don't drink."

Glass chinking against glass.

"*No thank you.*"

A chair scraping.

And there was Kojak mopping at his trouser leg with a handkerchief and grinding out what sounded like imprecations[18] which were getting louder and louder. The melancholy man had somehow moved his glass away while Kojak was pouring or had

---

18. **imprecations** Curses.

tried to cover it or pushed away the neck of the bottle. Raised fist quivering, Kojak was addressing the vaulted roof.

Grabbing a bottle-neck in his meaty hand, he upended the bottle over the little man's glass, wine glugging and splashing onto the table.

"Doesn't drink!" snarled Kojak.

He slammed the bottle down on the table.

"Doesn't drink!"

He flicked drops of wine onto the table off the back of his splashed hand.

"Mama mia! Doesn't drink!"

Grinding and growling he stumped off towards the café.

He left behind him a silence.

Into the silence, one of the women said,

"Perhaps it's a custom you're supposed to drink it? If you don't it's insulting?"

"Now wait a minute," said her husband.

"Like covering your head?" she added.

"Maybe I'm out of line," said the other man, "but in my book that was inappropriate behaviour."

"I never did much like the taste of alcohol," said the melancholy man.

His accent was British and glumly northern.

"They seem to sup it with everything here," he said, shaking his head in gloomy disapproval.

"Where are you folks from?" said the man in the turquoise shirt.

"Canada," said Helen.

"You hear that, June? Ottawa? Did we visit Ottawa, June?"

"Maybe," said June, "being that he's European and … "

"It's nothing to do with being European," said Helen. "It's to do with being rude and a bully. And he's not getting a tip from *us*."

"Yeah," said June's husband, "and what's with all these jokes about women drivers? I'll tell you something, okay? My *wife drives better than I drive*. Okay?"

He looked around the table.

"Okay?"

"I've seen them," said the melancholy man, "in those little places where they eat their breakfasts standing up, I've seen them in there first thing in the morning — imagine — taking raw spirits."

The old woman sat hunched within a tweed coat, little eyes watching. She made me think of a fledgling that had fallen from the nest. Her tumbler was empty. She was looking at me. Then she seemed to be looking at the nearest bottle. I raised my eyebrows. Her eyes seemed to grow wider. I poured her more and her hand crept out to secure the glass.

"Jack!" whispered Helen.

"What the hell difference does it make?"

I poured more of the stuff for myself.

June and Chuck were from North Dakota. Norm and Joanne were from California. Chuck was in construction. Norm was on a disability pension and sold patio furniture. Joanne was a nurse. George Robinson was from Bradford and did something to do with textile machinery. Nelson and his mother travelled every summer and last summer had visited Yugoslavia but had suffered from the food.

I explained to June that it was quite possible that I sounded very like the guy on a PBS series because the series had been made by the BBC and I had been born in the UK but was now Canadian. She told me my accent was cute. I told her I thought her accent cute too. We toasted each other's accents. Helen began giving me looks.

June had bought a purse in Rome. Joanne had bought a purse in Florence. Florence was noted for purses. June and Chuck were going to Florence after Rome. Helen had bought a purse in Florence — the best area of Florence for purses being on the far side of the Ponte Vecchio. In Venice there were far fewer stores selling purses. Shoes, on the other hand, shoe stores were everywhere. Norm said he'd observed more shoe stores in Italy than in any other country in the world.

Nelson disliked olive oil.

George could not abide eggplants. Doris, George's wife who had died of cancer the year before, had never fancied tomatoes.

Nelson was flushed and becoming loquacious.[19]

Chuck said he'd had better pizza in Grand Forks, North Dakota, where at least they put cheese on it and it wasn't runny.

George said the look of eggplants made him think of native women.

Joanne said a little pasta went a long way.

Milan?

After Venice, Norm and Joanne were booked into Milan. What was Milan like? Had anyone been there?

"Don't speak to me about Milan!" said Helen.

"Not a favourite subject with us," I said.

"We got mugged there," said Helen, "and they stole a gold bracelet I'd had since I was twenty-one."

"'They,'" I said, "being three girls."

"We were so walking along on the sidewalk just outside that monstrous railway station ... "

"Three *girls*, for Christ's sake!"

"They came running up to us," said Helen.

"Two of them not more than thirteen years old," I said, "and the other about eighteen or nineteen."

"One of them had a newspaper sort of folded to show columns of figures and another had a bundle of tickets of some sort and they were waving these in our faces ... "

"And talking at us very loudly and quickly ... "

" ... and, well, *brandishing* these ... "

" ... and sort of grabbing at you, pulling your sleeve ... "

"*Touching* you," said Helen.

"*Right!* said Norm. "Okay."

"*Exactly*," said Joanne. "That's *exactly* ... "

"And then," I said, "I felt the tallest girl's hand going inside my jacket — you know — to your inside pocket ... "

"We were so *distracted*, you see," said Helen, "what with all the talking and them pointing at the paper and waving things under your nose and being *touched* ... "

---

19. **loquacious** Overly talkative.

"So anyway," I said, "when I felt *that* I realized what was happening and I hit this girl's arm away ... "

"Oh, it was *awful!*" said Helen. "because *I* thought they were just beggars, you see, or kids trying to sell lottery tickets or something, and I was really horrible to Jack for hitting this girl ... I mean, he hit her *really hard* and I thought they were just begging so I couldn't believe he'd ... "

"But the best part," I said, "was that I probably wasn't the main target in the first place because we walked on into the station and we were buying tickets — we were in line — and Helen ... "

"I'd suddenly felt the weight," said Helen. "The difference, I mean, and I looked down at my wrist and the bracelet was gone. I hadn't felt a thing when they'd grabbed it. Not with all that other touching. They must have pulled and broken the safety chain and ... "

"Of course," I said, "I ran back to the entrance but ... "

I spread my hands.

"Long gone."

"With us," said Joanne, "it was postcards and guidebooks they were waving about."

"Where?"

"Here. In Rome."

"Girls? The same?"

"Gypsies," said Norm.

"Did they get anything?" said Helen.

"A Leica,"[20] said Joanne.

"Misdirection of attention," said Norm.

"Were they girl-gypsies?" I said.

"Misdirecting," said Norm. "It's the basic principle of illusionism."

"I was robbed right at the airport," said Nelson.

"It must be a national *industry*," said George.

"They had a baby in a shawl and I was just standing there with Mother and they pushed this baby against my chest and well, naturally, you ... "

"I don't *believe* this!" said Norm. "This I do not *believe!*"

"And while I was holding it, the other two women were shouting at me in Italian and they had a magazine they were showing me ... "

"What did they steal?"

"Airplane ticket. Passport. Traveller's cheques. But I had some American bills in the top pocket of my blazer so they didn't get that."

"Did you feel it?" said Joanne.

He shook his head.

"No. They just took the baby and walked away and I only realized when I was going to change a traveller's cheque at the cambio office because we were going to get on the bus, weren't we, Mother?"

"A baby!" said June.

"But a few minutes later," said Nelson, "one of the women came up to me on her own with the ticket and my passport."

---

20. **Leica** A brand of camera.

"Why would she give them back?" said Helen. "Don't they sell them to spies or something?"

"I paid her for them," said Nelson.

"Paid her?" said June.

"*Paid her!*" said Norm.

"*PAID!*" said Chuck.

"Ten dollars," said Nelson.

"They must have seen you coming!" said George.

"They must have seen *all* of you coming," said Chuck.

Nelson poured himself another murky tumbler of Frascati. "It wasn't much," he said. "Ten dollars. She got what she wanted. I got what I wanted."

He shrugged. Raising the glass, he said,

"A short life but a merry one!"

We stared at him.

"I got what I wanted, didn't I, Mother? And then we went on the green and red bus, didn't we? Do you remember? On the green and red bus?"

The old woman started making loud squeak noises in her throat.

It was the first sound we'd heard her make.

She sounded like a guinea pig.

"It's time for tinkles!" sang Nelson. "It's tinkle time."

And raising her up and half carrying her to the door of the women's malodorous toilet, he turned with her, almost as if waltzing, and backed his way in.

... *not entirely without incident.*

Don't mention Milan to us!

... *except for Helen's getting mugged.*

It all made quite a good story, a story with which we regaled our friends and neighbours. We became quite practised in the telling of it. We told it at parties and over dinners, feeding each other lines.

But the story we told was a story different in one particular from what really happened — though Helen doesn't know that.

The scene often comes to mind. I see it when the pages blur. I see it in my desk-top in the wood's repetitive grain. I see it when I gaze unseeing out of the window of the restaurant after lunch, the sun hot on my shoulder and sleeve. I see it when I'm lying in bed in the morning in those drowsy minutes after being awakened by the clink and chink of Helen's bottles as she applies moisturizing cream, foundation, blush, and shadow.

Chuck from Grand Forks, North Dakota, had been right. They *had* seen all of us coming. Easy pickings. Meek and nearing middle age, ready to be fleeced, lambs to the slaughter.

She'd been the first female I'd hit since childhood. I hadn't intended to hit her hard. I'd moved instinctively. Her eyes had widened with the pain of it.

I'd noticed her even before she'd run towards us. Good legs, high breasts pushing at the tight grey cotton dress, long light-brown hair. She was wearing bright yellow plastic sandals. She had no makeup on and looked a bit grubby, looked the young gamine[21] she probably was.

---

21. **gamine** A lean, mischievous, street girl.

I'd been carrying a suitcase and felt sweaty even though it was early in the morning. Her hand as it touched the side of my chest, my breast, was cool against my heat.

When I struck her arm, there was no panic in her eyes, just a widening. There was a hauteur[22] in her expression. Our eyes held each other's for what seemed long seconds.

When Helen discovered her bracelet gone, I hurried out of the vast ticket hall but under the colonnade and out of sight I slowed to a walk. There is no rational, sensible explanation for what followed.

I stood in the archway of the entrance. The two small girls had gone. She stood facing me across the width of the curving road. It was as if she'd been waiting for me.

We stood staring at each other.

Behind her was a sidewalk café. The white metal chairs and tables were screened by square white tubs containing small, bushy bay trees. The bays were dark and glossy. Dozens of sparrows hopped about on the edges of the tubs. Pigeons were pecking along the sidewalk near her feet. Among them was a reddish-brown pigeon and two white ones. In the strong morning light I could see the lines of her body under the grey cotton dress. She was gently rubbing at her arm.

Sitting there in Reardon's restaurant, drowsy in the sunshine after eating the Businessman's Luncheon Special ($4.95), the cream of celery soup, the minced-beef pie with ginger-coloured gravy, the french fries, the sliced string beans, waiting for the waitress to bring coffee, sitting there with the winter sun warm through the window on my shoulder and sleeve, I walk out of the shadow of the arch and stand waiting on the edge of the sidewalk. She nods to me. It is a nod which is casually intimate, a nod of acknowledgement and greeting. I wait for a gap in the sweeping traffic.

She watches me approaching.

(1986)

John Newlove (1938–2004)

In his short poem "Shakespeare's Sonnets," John Newlove confessed, "I'm not interested in rainbows / but in the sky itself, the serene / not the spectacular: the permanent." As he searched for the language that would most accurately capture particular imagery, Newlove avoided embellishment and strove to communicate "the thing itself." Sitting down to write, he would summon memories of the setting or event he was attempting to depict: "I'm actually in the place and not in the room, with all the physical details absolutely clear. And I lean back, close my eyes for recall." Yet even as he aimed for exactitude, he had a deep sense of the unreliability of memory and language — "Everything we recall is told on a flat page and becomes / something else in telling, not less but else." Again and again, he struggled with this problem, ceasing only to step back and embrace his limitations. "The Weather," the final poem in his collection *The Night the Dog Smiled* (1986), dramatizes one such moment. He begins, "The weather gets in my words / and I want them dry"; but, deciding that "This is guesswork, this is love," he concludes, "God bless / the weather and the words. Any words. Any weather."

Newlove was born in 1938 in Regina, Saskatchewan. He spent his early years in rural Saskatchewan communities, mainly Kamsack, where he received his schooling. After attending the University of Saskatoon for one year, he travelled around Canada, working at a variety of

---

22. hauteur Air of arrogance.

occupations: in the late 1950s, he was a high school teacher in Manitoba, a social worker and a radio announcer in Saskatchewan, a "worm-picker" in Quebec, and a labourer in Alberta and British Columbia. In 1960, he moved to Vancouver and, supporting himself by working in a ware-house, he began to devote serious attention to his writing.

In the early 1960s, Newlove published two slim volumes of poetry, *Grave Sirs* (1962) and *Elephants, Mother and Others* (1963). In 1965, when his first full-length collection, *Moving in Alone*, appeared, reviewers were quick to point out that he had little in common with the prom-inent *TISH* group, whose members were also based in Vancouver. Instead, lines of influence were traced to imagism, as the poet had already begun to develop the sharp, sparse descriptions that would later characterize so much of his work.

In these early efforts, Newlove deals with an array of themes. His tone, often bleak and critical, earned him a reputation as a pessimist and even a misanthrope among some readers. He writes about relationships with women, sometimes even questioning the impulse to do so. In "My Daddy Drowned," for example, he compares the symbolic rendering of women in poetry to drowning kittens in a barrel of rainwater. For the poet figure, depicting women in art becomes a way to capture and control them. He imagines "pushing those women underneath / to drown in poems," but sometimes allowing them "to slip to the surface / & squeak a little bit before [he kills] them."

Newlove also re-creates settings and experiences from his youth and his travels; naturally, many of these poems portray prairie scenes. In *Moving in Alone,* he illustrates Kamsack, the "Plump eastern saskatchewan river town," and the "tiny / magnificent prairie Verigin." In his second full-length collection, *Black Night Window* (1968), he becomes increasingly attentive to the first inhabitants of prairies: Native peoples. In "The Pride," for example, he imagines "the western country" as "crammed / with the ghosts of indians." For these, and works such as "Ride off Any Horizon," Newlove is recognized as having been one of the first poets to devote his attention to the Canadian prairies. Some of his most notable poems are specifically focused on the pain and exploitation experienced by Native peoples.

Newlove continued to build his reputation as a writer, publishing poetry throughout the 1960s. In 1966, he married Susan Mary Phillips. They moved to Toronto, where Newlove became an editor for McClelland and Stewart. In 1973, he won a Governor General's Award for his collection *Lies* (1972), and the honour opened many doors for him. He left publishing in 1974 and served as writer-in-residence at various Canadian institutions, including Concordia University, the University of Western Ontario, and the University of Toronto. In 1977, he edited an anthology, *Canadian Poetry: The Modern Era,* for McClelland and Stewart. The same year, he was awarded a Canada Council Senior Arts Grant, and in 1984, he was honoured with a Saskatchewan Writers Guild Founders Award. In 1986, he moved to Ottawa and began to work as an editor for the federal government.

In the later years of his life, Newlove did not publish prolifically. Yet when he produced the long poem *The Green Plain* (1981) and the collection *The Night the Dog Smiled* (1986), critics were intrigued by what they perceived to be a major change in the poet's generally dark outlook. *The Green Plain* addresses the existential questions with which Newlove had been preoccupied in his earlier collections. He asks, "Is civilization / only lack of room, only / an ant-heap at last? — the strutting cities / of the East, battered gold, / the crammed walls of India, / humanity swarming, indistinguishable / from the earth?" He selects Jonathan Swift's famous character Lemuel Gulliver as an "image of us" and envisions all of humanity "tied, webbed in, / and never learning anything."

Amid his questioning, though, Newlove finds reasons to rejoice. Rejecting "brave" constancy, he takes comfort in variation and in his belief that the "world flows, / still flows." He praises the beauty of the world, asserting that "The forests, the forests, swaying, / there is no reason why they should be beautiful. / They live for their own reasons, not ours. But they are." In *The Green Plain* and in shorter poems such as "The Light of History: This Rhetoric Against That Jargon," Newlove appears to have adopted a philosophy of acceptance that allows him to see beauty in chaos, death, memory, and love and to reject what he understands as the artificial strictures imposed by an unconscious devotion to the concept of time.

There are, however, elements of continuity between his early and later poetry, and to read his oeuvre as a journey from dark into light is to miss its complexity. For Newlove, life is a continual struggle, even though it is punctuated by moments of peace and clarity. In *The Green Plain* and *The Night the Dog Smiled*, he dramatizes this struggle, shifting constantly between tones of uncertainty and conviction. In "Being Caught," the prefatory statement to his final collection, *Apology for Absence: Selected Poems 1962–1992* (1993), we find him still "trying to hold the world together" and "wondering what to make of it all." John Newlove died in Ottawa in 2003.

Crazy Riel[1]

Time to write a poem
or something.
Fill up a page.
The creature noise.
Huge massed forces of men
hating each other.
What young men do not know.
To keep quiet,
contemporaneously.
Contempt. The robin diligently   10
on the lawn sucks up worms,
hopping from one to another.
Youthfully. Sixteen miles
from my boyhood home
the frogs sit in the grassy marsh
that looks like a golf course
by the lake. Green frogs.
Boys catch them for bait or sale.
Or caught them. Time.
To fill up a page.   20
To fill up a hole.
To make things feel better. Noise.
The noise of the images
that are people I will never understand.
Admire them though I may.
Poundmaker. Big Bear. Wandering Spirit,[2]
those miserable men.
Riel. Crazy Riel. Riel hanged.
Politics must have its way.

---

1. Riel Louis Riel (1844–1885), Canadian politician and advocate for Métis rights in Manitoba. Assisted the Métis in the Red River Rebellion of 1869 and the Northwest Rebellion of 1885; he was later hung for treason. **2. Poundmaker, Big Bear, Wandering Spirit** Leaders of the Plains Cree who presented complaints from their communities, and later participated in the Northwest Rebellion.

30 The way of noise. To fill up.
The definitions bullets make,
and field guns.
The noise your dying makes,
to which you are the only listener.
The noise the frogs hesitate
to make as the metal hook
breaks through the skin
and slides smoothly into place
in the jaw. The noise
40 the fish makes caught in the jaw,
which is only an operation
of the body and the element,
which a stone would make
thrown in the same water, thrashing,
not its voice.
The lake is not displaced,
having one less jackfish body.
In the slough that looks like a golf course
the family of frogs sings. Metal throats.
50 The images of death hang upside-down.
Grey music.
It is only the listening for death,
fingering the paraphernalia,
the noise of the men you admire.
And cannot understand.
Knowing little enough about them.
The knowledge waxing.[3]
The wax that paves hell's road,
slippery as the road to heaven.
60 So that as a man slips
he might as easily slide
into being a saint as destroyer.
In his ears the noise magnifies.
He forgets men.

(1968)

The Pride

I

The image/ the pawnees[1]
in their earth-lodge villages,
the clear image

---

3. **waxing** Growing, strengthening.

1. **pawnees** A Native American tribe of central North America.

of teton sioux,[2] wild
fickle people the chronicler says,

the crazy dogs, men
tethered with leather dog-thongs
to a stake, fighting until dead,

image: arikaras[3]
with traded spanish sabre blades   10
mounted on the long
heavy buffalo lances,
riding the sioux
down, the centaurs,[4] the horsemen
scouring the level plains
in war or hunt
until smallpox got them,
4,000 warriors,

image — of a desolate country,
a long way between fires,   20
unfound lakes, mirages, cold rocks,
and lone men going through it,
cree with good guns
creating terror in athabaska[5]
among the inhabitants, frightened
stone-age people, "so that
they fled at the mere sight
of a strange smoke miles away."

II

This western country crammed
with the ghosts of indians,   30
haunting the coastal stones and shores,
the forested pacific islands,
mountains, hills and plains:

beside the ocean ethlinga,
man in the moon, empties
his bucket, on
a sign from Spirit
of the Wind ethlinga
empties his bucket, refreshing
the earth, and it rains   40
on the white cities;

---

2. **teton sioux** Lakota tribe, the most western group of the Sioux nation. 3. **arikaras** Native American tribe that lived near the Pawnees. 4. **centaurs** Mythological beings with a man's upper body and the four legs of a horse. 5. **athabaska** Area around Lake Athabaska, between Alberta and Saskatchewan.

that black joker, broken-
jawed raven, most prominent
among haida and tsimshyan[6] tribes,
is in the kwakiutl[7]
dance masks too —
it was he who brought fire,
food and water to man,
the trickster;

50   and thunderbird hilunga,
little thought of
by haida for lack of thunderstorms
in their district, goes
by many names, exquisite disguises
carved in the painted wood,

he is nootka tootooch,[8] the wings
causing thunder and the tongue
or flashing eyes engendering
rabid white lightning,

60   whose food was whales,
called kwunusela by the kwakiutl,
it was he who laid down the house-logs
for the people at Place
Where Kwunusela Alighted;

in full force and virtue
and terror of the law, eagle —
he is authority, the sun
assumed his form once,
the sun which used to be

70   a flicker's egg, successfully transformed;

and malevolence comes to the land,
the wild woman of the woods;
grinning, she wears
a hummingbird in her hair,
d'sonoqua,[9] the furious one —

they are all ready
to be found, the legends
and the people, or

---

6. **haida, tsimshyan** Haida is a First Nations community of northern British Columbia; the Tsimshyan are another First Nations community that reside nearby. 7. **kwakiutl** Aboriginal people living in parts of coastal British Columbia; their legendary thunderbird is called the *kwunusela*. 8. **nootka tootooch** The Nootka are a First Nations group in British Columbia; the *tootooch* is a thunderbird from their legends. 9. **d'sonoqua** Woman-figure from Kwakiutl legend who is the opposite of the maternal figure.

all their ghosts and memories,   80
whatever is strong enough
to be remembered.

III

But what image, bewildered
son of all men
under the hot sun,
do you worship,
what completeness
do you hope to have
from these tales,
a half-understood massiveness, mirage,   90
in men's minds — what
is your purpose;

with what force
will you proceed
along a line
neither straight nor short,
whose future
you cannot know
or result foretell,
whose meaning is still   100
obscured as the incidents
occur and accumulate?

IV

The country moves on;
there are orchards in the interior,
the mountain passes
are broken, the foothills
covered with cattle and fences,
and the fading hills covered;

but the plains are bare,
not barren, easy   110
for me to love their people,
for me to love their people
without selection.

V

In 1787, the old cree saukamappee,[10]
aged 75 or thereabout, speaking then

---

10. **1787, saukamappee** Saukamappee, a warrior of the Peigan tribe (part of the Albertan Blackfoot nation), told the story
of attacking the Shoshoni (snake) tribe to the south, and taming horses for the first time.

of things that had happened when he was 16,
just a man, told david thompson,
of the raids the shoshonis,
the snakes, had made on the westward-
120   reaching peigan, of their war-parties
sometimes sent 10 days journey to enemy camps,
the men all afoot in battle array for
the encounter, crouching
behind their giant shields;

the peigan armed with guns
drove these snakes out of the plains,
the plains where their strength had been,
where they had been settled since living
memory (though nothing is remembered
130   beyond a grandfather's time),
to the west of the rockies;

these people moved without rest,
backward and forward with the wind,
the seasons, the game, great herds,
in hunger and abundance —

in summer and in the bloody fall
they gathered on the killing grounds,
fat and shining with fat, amused
with the luxuries of war and death,

140   relieved from the steam of knowledge,
consoled by the stream of blood
and steam rising from the fresh hides
and tired horses, wheeling in their pride
on the sweating horses, their pride.

VI

Those are all stories;
the pride, the grand poem
of our land, of the earth itself,
will come, welcome, and
sought for, and found,
150   in a line of running verse,
sweating, our pride;

we seize on
what has happened before,
one line only
will be enough,

a single line and
then the sunlit brilliant image suddenly floods us
with understanding, shocks our
attentions, and all desire
stops, stands alone;   160

we stand alone,
we are no longer lonely
but have roots,
and the rooted words
recur in the mind, mirror, so that
we dwell on nothing else, in nothing else,
touched, repeating them,
at home freely
at last, in amazement;

"the unyielding phrase   170
in tune with the epoch,"
the thing made up
of our desires,
not of its words, not only
of them, but of something else,
as well, that which we desire
so ardently, that which
will not come when
it is summoned alone,
but grows in us   180
and idles about and hides
until the moment is due —

the knowledge of
our origins, and where
we are in truth,
whose land this is
and is to be.

VII

The unyielding phrase:
when the moment is due, then
it springs upon us   190
out of our own mouths,
unconsidered, overwhelming
in its knowledge, complete —

not this handful
of fragments, as the indians
are not composed of
the romantic stories

about them, or of the stories
they tell only, but
200   still ride the soil
in us, dry bones a part
of the dust in our eyes,
needed and troubling
in the glare, in
our breath, in our
ears, in our mouths,
in our bodies entire, in our minds, until at
last we become them

in our desires, our desires,
210   mirages, mirrors, that are theirs, hard-
riding desires, and they
become our true forbears, moulded
by the same wind or rain,
and in this land we
are their people, come
back to life.

(1968)

Ride off Any Horizon

Ride off any horizon
and let the measure fall
where it may —

on the hot wheat,
on the dark yellow fields
of wild mustard, the fields

of bad farmers, on the river,
on the dirty river full
of boys and on the throbbing

10   powerhouse and the low dam
of cheap cement and rocks
boiling with white water,

and on the cows and their powerful
bulls, the heavy tracks
filling with liquid at the edge

of the narrow prairie
river running steadily away.

*

Ride off any horizon
and let the measure fall
where it may —   20

among the piles of bones
that dot the prairie

in vision and history
(the buffalo and deer,

dead indians, dead settlers,
the frames of lost houses

left behind in the dust
of the depression,

dry and profound, that
will come again in the land   30

and in the spirit, the land
shifting and the minds

blown dry and empty —
I have not seen it! except

in pictures and talk —
but there is the fence

covered with dust, laden,
the wrecked house stupidly empty) —

here is a picture for your wallet,
of the beaten farmer and his wife   40
leaning toward each other —

sadly smiling, and emptied of desire.

*

Ride off any horizon
and let the measure fall
where it may —

off the edge
of the black prairie

as you thought you could fall,
a boy at sunset

50   not watching the sun
      set but watching the black earth,

      never-ending they said in school,
      round: but you saw it ending,

      finished, definite, precise —
      visible only miles away.

      *

      Ride off any horizon
      and let the measure fall
      where it may —

      on a hot night the town
60   is in the streets —

      the boys and girls
      are practising against

      each other, the men
      talk and eye the girls —

      the women talk and
      eye each other, the indians
      play pool: eye on the ball.

      *

      Ride off any horizon
      and let the measure fall
70   where it may —

      and damn the troops, the horsemen
      are wheeling in the sunshine,
      the cree, practising

      for their deaths: mr poundmaker,
      gentle sweet mr bigbear,[1]
      it is not unfortunately

      quite enough to be innocent,
      it is not enough merely
      not to offend —

---

1. **mr poundmaker, mr bigbear** Leaders of the Plains Cree who presented complaints from their communities, and later participated in the Northwest Rebellion of 1885.

at times to be born   80
is enough, to be
in the way is too much —

some colonel otter,[2] some
major-general middleton[3] will
get you, you —

indian. It is no good to say,
I would rather die
at once than be in that place —

though you love that land more,
you will go where they take you.   90

*

Ride off any horizon
and let the measure fall —

where it may;
it doesn't have to be

the prairie. It could be
the cold soul of the cities
blown empty by commerce

and desiring commerce
to fill up emptiness.

The streets are full of people.   100

It is night, the lights
are on; the wind

blows as far as it may. The streets
are dark and full of people.

Their eyes are fixed as far as
they can see beyond each other —

to the concrete horizon, definite,
tall against the mountains,
stopping vision visibly.

                                                                  (1968)

---

2. colonel otter Poundmaker's force defeated that of Lt. Colonel William Otter at the Battle of Cut Knife, 1885. **3. major-general middleton** Frederick Middleton was the British general and head of the Canadian militia during the Northwest Rebellion.

Notes from and among the Wars

1

Your drink is twice as strong as mine is
Your mouth is twice as fair as mine is
Your hair is sweeter than mine is
You smile where I could wish to smile
You sleep when I could wish to sleep

I wish to dream, I wish to dream
through our centuries of blood

2

Dead arrogant kings
   bearded in gold
10   beautiful to archaeologists
living on slaves slaves —
   my people
having come out of Asia
your sons the seven Osmanli[1] mutes
   who strangle and smile
what have you done
but bow and wait
for the petty lords of creation
heirs of the floods and the plagues
20   and dead with gold
a crust on the rotted faces
till you after some centuries or so
could use a new plow to conquer Europe?

3

Were the bunks neat in Auschwitz?[2]
Was the soul's blond efficiency repulsed
by the messy blankets of Jews and Gypsies? — If
they had blankets, those who surrendered
immortal teeth of gold, surrendered rings, piles
of prosthetics tabulated in the avenues
30   between the wooden huts, and all else?

4

In the end you don't even know yourself
only the hill you must climb; but not even

---

1. **Osmanli** From the Ottoman (Turkish) Empire. 2. **Auschwitz** The largest of the Nazi concentration camps.

the hill; a bump on it, one hump of grass
a flint, a blade thin in the wind as you climb
each step, each breath taken in a dissimilar time

5

And how after each little separation
we seem to have to learn again
to know each other as awkward strangers do —
the slightest kiss our accidental hands our eyes
that waver off each other as if we had not been   40
nakedly in love

6

I would like to whistle softly in your ear
to recall to you a tune we might have played
if I could remember it. Instead I sit reading
of man's perpetual wars,
of how he says he strides toward the stars

7

Among the wars
the poet walks along
in his mind
from the start   50
gone wrong
unable to find
some simple part
that he might make
into an easy song
or phrase to take
as medicine
when he walks along
in his mind,

when his mind soars   60
from the start,
gone wrong

8

And to see men
attempting to do things
and their women
wary, protecting them,
wolves distrusting all strangers,
smiling like guards

9

As among the wars
and fears
we sail
or kill —
wanderers....

10

And what one would have thought
to have brought forward
to build on
         has become one's life,
with no addition

11

Movie

There's a man inside there, dying
as you in your homogalactic excitement watch
the fuming awkward plane
fifty-five funny years ago
dive in twisty smoke
into a poison sea of shell-ploughed earth:
it is a movie.
              For you it would be much more bitter
just to walk in the streets
than to watch those older deaths again

12

Today when the sun does not rise
Today when the rulers cannot stop the snow
Today as the murders cross the screen
Today as the headlines are hopelessly accepted
Today watching a real-life neo-gothic fistfight
Today on the outskirts of no novel
Today during the shakiness of human life
Today during our constant killing ignorance
declaring our deaths in continuous rehearsal
we live and try to love —
                          ourselves at least,
if no others

13

The green trees grow from year to year
and seem to have no thoughts
although I hear it said
they scream when we kill before them

14

And give us a little pity too:
for the last drink in the whisky bottle
sunday afternoon, for the calcium in our spines
for the daily prejudiced paper, the constant liars
those who think war is a high-school debate   110
the ones who take freedom away
in the name of freedom
as our portions get smaller

Forgive us: for whom civilization consists of acquiring
the correct mental addictions, those of us who act
as if we hated the human in ourselves
knowing there is enough to hate
in the human in ourselves

The wars the slaveries no dead men redeemed by poems
no humiliation redressed with songs   120
no chain scars in the soul erased with apologies
a hundred years late
the simple everyday savagery of parent to child
or child to parent brother to brother sister to sister

The torture goes on forever as we in perpetual motion
breed and destroy ourselves for any reason
even intelligent ones

All of which we have always known
in despair and amusement at ourselves

15

And there is an egypt of the mind   130
grotesque mysterious remote
sacrificial
where the dunes are piling and unpiling
their arabesques[3] coiling about some point
not grasped some
secret living to be learned
desperately longed for....

Blue and green commingling, the muscley sea
sliding through the mind, a notion of deeper rivers
than those that run over the earth, among the stars   140
currents in the bright mixture pulsing, something

---

3. **arabesques** Swirling motifs or movements.

that might be there to save us as it seems
we cannot save ourselves or do not want to....

16

To be willingless, to be willing....

Willingless and willing, as when
the pickup truck went around
a slight curve to the right
years ago and stopped. Off the road
a small triangular piece of level ground
150   a wooden shack a quick shallow river
and then the trees again as far as could be seen
night coming thoughts of bears the sound
of crisp leaves as bits of wind brushed off them
a place unknown and feared
and the driver saying This
is as far as I go
meaning this is as far as you go....

17

But what should we expect of our memories
except remembrance? We who are so adept
160   so practised in false hopes so able to read
the slightest changes in a face
the slightest intonations in a voice
the indications of things
that do not exist affirmations
never considered by the other....

18

But me? Waking up mornings
my mouth full of blood
it seeming to be such a difficult life
and yet so easy not to be
170   as water rings in the musical hillside sewers
in a false Spring
hoarding regrets

And the ghost that sings in my blood
a mortal
everything waiting for its boat-shaped grave ender
of the sad tricks we play on ourselves
ender of foolish lives
and foolish loves greatly desired ending
the crying instruments of speech
180   that repeat and repeat themselves happily repeating
the past from which they are trying to rise

19

You smile where I could wish to smile
You sleep when I could wish to sleep....
It is not the milk-bearing tree I see
but the one that seeps blood or trees
exploding like tnt in the winter's cold

20

Caught in the maze of life
and knowing only that we end

Avoiding infinity
with questions   190

Was I a lover you had
out of your kindliness
in wintertime?

Is today the day I got old?

Is today the day you got old?
And were only able to sing a structured song?
So —

If you were in the air
would you be a bird?
If you were able   200
would you wish to be?
And would you sing
if you wished to be?
And if you cared to be —

Would you want to fly? knowing
below and as you fly
in the green concealed pit
the hunters with their sighted shotguns lie.

                                                                 (1972)

Insect Hopes

The world's longest poem didn't start like this
didn't go on like this
it doesn't end like this — there was still
a cigarette burning. After
the ending, after all the Indians
the Pygmies,[1] the Gypsies, the Jews

---

1. **Pygmies** A group of tribes in Central Africa, once famous for their small stature.

the burned and the black and the spurned
after all the cheated and demeaned were buried by bulldozers
or sold as cheap souvenirs in green translucent glass
10   that cigarette still fumed —
what wealth!

And the writer of all that stuff
was still stupid
he still thought that when people said
I understand
they understood

He didn't know that he lied for pleasure
others, profit
and he still saw
20   all-around wrap-around death and didn't believe it
and woke up one night in the maw[2] and believed it

Knowing what was wanted

Not these sweaty visions everyone has
no recognizable rhythms
no beauty in the line
no knowledge
              only noise
no feeling of pain

This whole civilization is noise
30   we are not wholly beasts yet
but the politicians roar at us
until civilization is minor

And we are surrounded by liars
so that when the poet that is in us says
we are surrounded by liars
he is called a liar
or is given prizes, liar
obligations

O I am sick and called sick
40   and I am healthier than you are

At least I know how lovely we are

Enduring —

---

2. **maw** Mouth or stomach.

Which is history
we are one after the other
we are the stars of this show
but we are
at the end of all time

What nonsense we talk
What nonsense we're told
What nonsense we are   50

But I wanted to tell you still how lovely we are
of the ages of jewels
of failed cities
of the notion that there was good
how this century began like all the others

in blood
and milk-white dreams
and ended
with insect hopes
with insect hopes   60
all in a heap
like all the others
who ever died

(1986)

Margaret Atwood (1939–)

In the title poem from *True Stories* (1981), Margaret Atwood writes, "Don't ask for the true story; / why do you need it? … The true story lies / among the other stories … The true story is vicious / and multiple and untrue / after all." This understanding of the subjective and multiple nature of the "true story" shapes much of her fiction and poetry. She encourages her readers to look beyond what has been recorded, to make use of a "third eye" that can reveal myths, dreams, ghosts. For Atwood, the most intriguing stories lie just below the surface: "beneath the page is everything that ever happened, most of which you would rather not hear about."

Atwood was born in Ottawa, Ontario, on 18 November 1939. Her father was a forest entomologist and, to accommodate his research, the family spent a lot of time travelling through the bush country of northern Ontario and Quebec. Because they often had to head north in early spring, Atwood did not complete a full year of school until she was 12. In the bush, she and her brother (they would later have a younger sister) received lessons from their mother and learned from the many books they read to entertain themselves.

From 1957 to 1961, Atwood attended Victoria College at the University of Toronto, where she studied English literature, philosophy, and French. During these years, she took classes with Northrop Frye and poet Jay Macpherson (with whom she developed a close friendship), and she became involved in theatre and journalism. Having decided to become a writer at 16, Atwood worked hard to cultivate her craft, publishing her efforts in college periodicals. In 1959, the *Canadian Forum* printed her poem "Fruition" and she began reading her poetry alongside Milton Acorn, George Miller, and Gwendolyn MacEwen at a coffee house called the Bohemian Embassy.

In 1961, she produced a chapbook of poetry entitled *Double Persephone,* for which she was awarded the University of Toronto's E.J. Pratt Medal.

Graduating with honours from the University of Toronto, Atwood received a Woodrow Wilson Fellowship to attend Radcliffe, a women's college closely associated with Harvard University. In the fall of 1961, she moved to Cambridge, Massachusetts, to study Victorian literature. Living outside Canada and taking classes in American literature, Atwood began to ponder her own literary and cultural heritage; she has continued to do so throughout her career. This concern would prompt her to write a controversial and best-selling study called *Survival: A Thematic Guide to Canadian Literature* (1972), in which she argued that Canadian literature is preoccupied with victims and the notion of survival. Although some charged that Atwood's thesis was flawed because her test group of authors was too limited, the study succeeded in bringing questions about Canadian literature and identity to the attention of the reading public.

After earning her M.A., Atwood began a doctorate at Harvard, but she put it on hold to return to Canada in 1963. In Toronto, she worked at a market research company and wrote a first novel that was never published. In 1964, she moved to Vancouver to become a lecturer at the University of British Columbia. Absorbed in her writing, she drafted the novel *The Edible Woman* (not published until 1969), wrote 14 short stories, and composed the poems of *The Circle Game* (1967). She had returned to Cambridge to continue her Ph.D. when she learned that she had been honoured with a Governor General's Award for *The Circle Game*. At this point, her literary career began to interfere with her academic pursuits, and she eventually abandoned her thesis. She has, however, received many honorary doctoral degrees from Canadian and international universities. In 1973, Trent University bestowed upon her the first such tribute.

In 1967, Atwood married James Polk, a colleague from Harvard. Over the next few years, she published three collections of poetry: *The Animals in That Country* (1968), *The Journals of Susanna Moodie* (1970), and *Procedures for Underground* (1970). In these works, she deals with a wide array of themes and subjects; but her childhood experiences in the Canadian north appear to inform many of the poems. She writes of the Canadian wilderness, and of nature in general, as a phenomenon beyond human control. For example, in "Speeches for Dr. Frankenstein," she revives Mary Shelley's critique of the human urge to dominate the natural world. At the end of the poem, the monster speaks to his maker: "you sliced me loose / and said it was / Creation ... Now you would like to heal / that chasm in your side, / but I recede. I prowl. / I will not come when you call."

The Journals of Susanna Moodie also illustrates human interaction with the natural world, but in this work, Atwood focuses on one woman's estrangement from the Canadian landscape. She sees Moodie as a fundamentally divided and displaced figure: "she claims to be an ardent Canadian patriot while all the time she is standing back from the country and criticizing it as though she was a detached observer, a stranger." For Atwood, Moodie's detachment represents the Canadian condition: "we are all immigrants to this place even if we were born here ... the country is too big for anyone to inhabit completely." In 1980, Atwood's friend and long-time collaborator Charles Pachter designed and illustrated an edition of *The Journals* (reprinted in 1997). And Atwood also returned to Moodie later in her career — specifically, to the story of murderess Grace Marks, which she found in Moodie's *Life in the Clearings Versus the Bush* (1853). Atwood used the story as the basis of her television script *The Servant Girl* and her Giller Prize–winning novel *Alias Grace* (1996).

In 1971, Atwood and Polk moved to Toronto, where they began to work for House of Anansi Press under the leadership of Dennis Lee, a friend of Atwood's from her time at Victoria College. These were tumultuous years for Atwood. She achieved recognition and even celebrity with the publications of *Survival* and the novel *Surfacing* (1972). She and Polk began to grow apart, and by 1973, they had divorced and Atwood had started a relationship with Graeme Gibson, a novelist affiliated with Anansi. The couple moved to a farm in Alliston, Ontario. Many of the poems in

Atwood's *You Are Happy* (1974) were inspired by this new relationship and way of life. In 1976, their daughter, Eleanor Jess, was born.

In 1978, Atwood did her first world book promotion tour. When they were not travelling or writing, she and Gibson were working to promote the political aims of the writing community. Gibson had helped to found the Writers' Union of Canada in the early 1970s, and both he and Atwood remained actively involved in the project. They were also involved in PEN, a group devoted to aiding writers who are political prisoners. Atwood helped to found the English Canadian branch of the organization.

In 1985, she published *The Handmaid's Tale,* a novel that employs the dystopian setting of a patriarchal totalitarian state to explore and critique the political claims of the right and of religious fundamentalism, especially as these pertain to women. Although Atwood was anxious about the reception of this shift in style and subject matter, the novel was an international success. She received a Governor General's Award for it, as well as numerous other honours in Canada and the United States; the novel spent over 20 weeks on the *New York Times* bestseller list. Atwood tried her hand at dystopian fiction once more in 2003, with *Oryx and Crake.*

Atwood has always been astoundingly productive, and she shows no sign of slowing down. Her fiction, such as the novels *Cat's Eye* (1988), *The Robber Bride* (1993), and *The Blind Assassin* (2000), is consistently well received and honoured. More recently, she published *The Penelopiad* (2005), an ambitious retelling — or reinvention — of Homer's epic poem the *Odyssey* from the point of view of Penelope, Odysseus's wife; Penelope's 12 mysteriously murdered maids (Atwood says that she has "always been haunted by the hanged maids") form the chorus. She has also produced numerous collections of short fiction and literary criticism, edited anthologies, and authored several children's books.

This Is a Photograph of Me

It was taken some time ago.
At first it seems to be
a smeared
print: blurred lines and grey flecks
blended with the paper;

then, as you scan
it, you see in the left-hand corner
a thing that is like a branch: part of a tree
(balsam or spruce) emerging
and, to the right, halfway up   10
what ought to be a gentle
slope, a small frame house.

In the background there is a lake,
and beyond that, some low hills.

(The photograph was taken
the day after I drowned.

I am in the lake, in the center
of the picture, just under the surface.

20 It is difficult to say where
    precisely, or to say
    how large or small I am:
    the effect of water
    on light is a distortion

    but if you look long enough,
    eventually
    you will be able to see me.)

                                                          (1966)

The Animals in That Country

In that country the animals
have the faces of people:

the ceremonial
cats possessing the streets

the fox run
politely to earth, the huntsmen
standing around him, fixed
in their tapestry of manners

10 the bull, embroidered
    with blood and given
    an elegant death, trumpets, his name
    stamped on him, heraldic brand
    because

    (when he rolled
    on the sand, sword in his heart, the teeth
    in his blue mouth were human)

    he is really a man

    even the wolves, holding resonant
    conversations in their
20 forests thickened with legend.

        In this country the animals
        have the faces of
        animals.

        Their eyes
        flash once in car headlights
        and are gone.

        Their deaths are not elegant.

They have the faces of
no-one.

(1968)

Progressive Insanities of a Pioneer

I

He stood, a point
on a sheet of green paper
proclaiming himself the centre,

with no walls, no borders
anywhere; the sky no height
above him, totally un-
enclosed
and shouted:

Let me out!

II

He dug the soil in rows, 10
imposed himself with shovels
He asserted
into the furrows, I
am not random.

The ground
replied with aphorisms:[1]

a tree-sprout, a nameless
weed, words
he couldn't understand.

III

The house pitched
the plot staked 20
in the middle of nowhere.

At night the mind
inside, in the middle
of nowhere.

The idea of an animal
patters across the roof.

---

1. **aphorisms** Brief statements.

In the darkness the fields
defend themselves with fences
30   in vain:
        everything
        is getting in.

IV

By daylight he resisted.
He said, disgusted
with the swamp's clamourings and the outbursts
of rocks,
        This is not order
        but the absence
        of order.

40   He was wrong, the unanswering
forest implied:

        It was
        an ordered absence

V

For many years
he fished for a great vision,
dangling the hooks of sown
roots under the surface
of the shallow earth.

It was like
50   enticing whales with a bent
pin. Besides he thought

in that country
only the worms were biting.

VI

If he had known unstructured
space is a deluge[2]
and stocked his log house-
boat with all the animals

even the wolves,

he might have floated.

---

2. **deluge** Flood.

But obstinate he
stated, The land is solid
and stamped,

watching his foot sink
down through stone
up to the knee.

VII

Things
refuse to name themselves; refused
to let him name them.

The wolves hunted
outside.

On his beaches, his clearings,
by the surf of under-
growth breaking
at his feet, he foresaw
disintegration
                and in the end
through eyes
made ragged by his
effort, the tension
between subject and object,

the green
vision, the unnamed
whale invaded.

(1968)

Departure from the Bush

I, who had been erased
by fire, was crept in
upon by green
                (how
lucid a season)

            In time the animals
arrived to inhabit me,

first one
    by one, stealthily
(their habitual traces
burnt); then

60

70

80

10

having marked new boundaries
returning, more
confident, year
by year, two
by two

but restless: I was not ready
altogether to be moved into

　　　They could tell I was
20　　too heavy: I might
　　　capsize;

I was frightened
by their eyes (green or
amber) glowing out from inside me

I was not completed; at night
I could not see without lanterns.

He wrote, We are leaving. I said
I have no clothes
left I can wear

30　　The snow came. The sleigh was a relief;
　　　its track lengthened behind,
　　　pushing me towards the city

and rounding the first hill, I was
(instantaneous)
unlived in: they had gone.

There was something they almost taught me
I came away not having learned.

(1970)

Newsreel: Man and Firing Squad

i

A botched job,
the blindfold slipped, he sees
his own death approaching, says No
or something, his torso jumps as the bullets hit
his nerves / he slopes down,
wrecked and not even
cleanly, roped muscles leaping, mouth open

as though snoring, the photography
isn't good either.

ii
Destruction shines with such beauty   10

Light on his wet hair
serpents of blood jerked from the wrists

Sun thrown from the raised and lowered
rifles / debris of the still alive

Your left eye, green and lethal

iii
We depart, we say goodbye

Yet each of us remains in the same place,
staked out and waiting,
it is the ground between that moves, expands,
pulling us away from each other.   20

No more of these closeups, this agony
taken just for the record anyway

The scenery is rising behind us
into focus, the walls
and hills are also important,

Our shattered faces retreat, we might be
happy, who can interpret
the semaphore of our bending
bodies, from a distance we could be dancing

(1974)

Tricks with Mirrors

i
It's no coincidence
this is a used
furniture warehouse.

I enter with you
and become a mirror.

Mirrors
are the perfect lovers,

that's it, carry me up the stairs
by the edges, don't drop me,

10   that would be bad luck,
throw me on the bed

reflecting side up,
fall into me,

it will be your own
mouth you hit, firm and glassy,

your own eyes you find you
are up against   closed   closed

ii
There is more to a mirror
than you looking at

20   your full-length body
flawless but reversed,

there is more than this dead blue
oblong eye turned outwards to you.

Think about the frame.
The frame is carved, it is important,

it exists, it does not reflect you,
it does not recede and recede, it has limits

and reflections of its own.
There's a nail in the back

30   to hang it with; there are several nails,
think about the nails,

pay attention to the nail
marks in the wood,

they are important too.

iii
Don't assume it is passive
or easy, this clarity

with which I give you yourself.
Consider what restraint it

takes: breath withheld, no anger
or joy disturbing the surface   40

of the ice.
You are suspended in me

beautiful and frozen, I
preserve you, in me you are safe.

It is not a trick either,
it is a craft:

mirrors are crafty.

iv
I wanted to stop this,
this life flattened against the wall,

mute and devoid of colour,   50
built of pure light,

this life of vision only, split
and remote, a lucid impasse.[1]

I confess: this is not a mirror,
it is a door

I am trapped behind.
I wanted you to see me here,

say the releasing word, whatever
that may be, open the wall.

Instead you stand in front of me   60
combing your hair.

v
You don't like these metaphors.
All right:

Perhaps I am not a mirror.
Perhaps I am a pool.

Think about pools.

(1974)

---

1. **impasse** Deadlock.

Marrying the Hangman

She has been condemned to death by hanging. A man may escape this death by becoming the hangman, a woman by marrying the hangman. But at the present time there is no hangman; thus there is no escape. There is only a death, indefinitely postponed. This is not fantasy, it is history.

*

To live in prison is to live without mirrors. To live without mirrors is to live without the self. She is living selflessly, she finds a hole in the stone wall and on the other side of the wall, a voice. The voice comes through darkness and has no face. This voice becomes her mirror.

*

In order to avoid her death, her particular death, with wrung neck and swollen tongue, she must marry the hangman. But there is no hangman, first she must create him, she must persuade this man at the end of the voice, this voice she has never seen and which has never seen her, this darkness, she must persuade him to renounce his face, exchange it for the impersonal mask of death, of official death which has eyes but no mouth, this mask of a dark leper. She must transform his hands so they will be willing to twist the rope around throats that have been singled out as hers was, throats other than hers. She must marry the hangman or no one, but that is not so bad. Who else is there to marry?

*

You wonder about her crime. She was condemned to death for stealing clothes from her employer, from the wife of her employer. She wished to make herself more beautiful. This desire in servants was not legal.

*

She uses her voice like a hand, her voice reaches through the wall, stroking and touching. What could she possibly have said that would have convinced him? He was not condemned to death, freedom awaited him. What was the temptation, the one that worked? Perhaps he wanted to live with a woman whose life he had saved, who had seen down into the earth but had nevertheless followed him back up to life. It was his only chance to be a hero, to one person at least, for if he became the hangman the others would despise him. He was in prison for wounding another man, on one finger of the right hand, with a sword. This too is history.

*

My friends, who are both women, tell me their stories, which cannot be believed and which are true. They are horror stories and they have not happened to me, they have not yet happened to me, they have happened to me but we are detached, we watch our unbelief with horror. Such things cannot happen to us, it is afternoon and these things do not happen in the afternoon. The trouble was, she said, I didn't have time to put my glasses on and without them I'm blind as a bat, I couldn't even see who it was. These things happen and we sit at a table and tell stories about them so we can finally believe. This is not fantasy, it is history, there is more than one hangman and because of this some of them are unemployed.

*

He said: the end of walls, the end of ropes, the opening of doors, a field, the wind, a house, the sun, a table, an apple.

She said: nipple, arms, lips, wine, belly, hair, bread, thighs, eyes, eyes.

They both kept their promises.

*

The hangman is not such a bad fellow. Afterwards he goes to the refrigerator and cleans up the leftovers, though he does not wipe up what he accidentally spills. He wants only the simple things: a chair, someone to pull off his shoes, someone to watch him while he talks, with admiration and fear, gratitude if possible, someone in whom to plunge himself for rest and renewal. These things can best be had by marrying a woman who has been condemned to death by other men for wishing to be beautiful. There is a wide choice.

*

Everyone said he was a fool.
Everyone said she was a clever woman.
They used the word *ensnare*.

*

What did they say the first time they were alone together in the same room? What did he say when she had removed her veil and he could see that she was not a voice but a body and therefore finite? What did she say when she discovered that she had left one locked room for another? They talked of love, naturally, though that did not keep them busy forever.

*

The fact is there are no stories I can tell my friends that will make them feel better. History cannot be erased, although we can soothe ourselves by speculating about it. At that time there were no female hangmen. Perhaps there have never been any, and thus no man could save his life by marriage. Though a woman could, according to the law.

*

He said: foot, boot, order, city, fist, roads, time, knife.

She said: water, night, willow, rope hair, earth belly, cave, meat, shroud, open, blood.

They both kept their promises.

(1978)

Notes Towards a Poem
That Can Never Be Written

For Carolyn Forché

i

This is the place
you would rather not know about,
this is the place that will inhabit you,
this is the place you cannot imagine,
this is the place that will finally defeat you

where the word *why* shrivels and empties
itself. This is famine.

ii

There is no poem you can write
about it, the sandpits

10   where so many were buried
& unearthed, the unendurable
pain still traced on their skins.

This did not happen last year
or forty years ago but last week.
This has been happening,
this happens.

We make wreaths of adjectives for them,
we count them like beads,
we turn them into statistics & litanies
20   and into poems like this one.

Nothing works.
They remain what they are.

iii

The woman lies on the wet cement floor
under the unending light
needle marks on her arms put there
to kill the brain
and wonders why she is dying.

She is dying because she said.
She is dying for the sake of the word.
30   It is her body, silent
and fingerless, writing this poem.

iv

It resembles an operation
but it is not one

nor despite the spread legs, grunts
& blood, is it a birth.

Partly it's a job,
partly it's a display of skill
like a concerto.

It can be done badly
or well, they tell themselves.   40

Partly it's an art.

v

The facts of this world seen clearly
are seen through tears;
why tell me then
there is something wrong with my eyes?

To see clearly and without flinching,
without turning away,
this is agony, the eyes taped open
two inches from the sun.

What is it you see then?   50
Is it a bad dream, a hallucination?
Is it a vision?
What is it you hear?

The razor across the eyeball[1]
is a detail from an old film.
It is also a truth.
Witness is what you must bear.

vi

In this country you can say what you like
because no one will listen to you anyway,
it's safe enough, in this country you can try to write   60
the poem that can never be written,
the poem that invents
nothing and excuses nothing,
because you invent and excuse yourself each day.

---

1. razor … eyeball From the 1929 film *Un Chien Andalou*, in which a woman's eyeball is sliced by a razor.

Elsewhere, this poem is not invention.
Elsewhere, this poem takes courage.
Elsewhere, this poem must be written
because the poets are already dead.

70   Elsewhere, this poem must be written
as if you are already dead,
as if nothing more can be done
or said to save you.

Elsewhere you must write this poem
because there is nothing more to do.

(1984)

How to Tell One Country from Another

Whether it is possible to become lost.

Whether one tree looks like another.
Whether there is water all around
the edges or not. Whether
there are edges or whether
there are just insects.

Whether the insects bite,
whether you would die
from the bites of the insects.
10   Whether you would die.

Whether you would die for your country.
Whether anyone in the country would die for your country.
Let's be honest here.
A layer of snow, a layer of granite, a layer of snow.
What you think lies under the snow.
What you think lies.

Whether you think white on white is a state of mind
or blue on blue or green on green.
Whether you think there is a state,
20   of mind.

How many clothes you have to take off
before you can make love.
This I think is important:
the undoing of buttons, the gradual shedding
of one colour after another. It leads
to the belief that what you see is not
what you get.

Whether there are preliminaries,
hallways, vestibules,[1]
basements, furnaces,   30
chesterfields, silences
between sentences, between pieces
of furniture, parasites in your eyes,
drinkable water.

Whether there has ever been
an invading army.
Whether, if there were an invading army,
you would collaborate.
Poor boy, you'd say, he looks cold
standing out there, and he's only twenty.   40
From his point of view this must be hell.

A fur coat is what he needs,
a cup of tea, a cup of coffee,
a warm body.
Whether on the contrary
you'd slit his throat in his sleep
or in yours. I ask you.

So, you are a nice person.
You would behave well.
What you mean by behaving well.   50
When the outline of a man
whose face you cannot see
appears at your bedroom window,
whether you would shoot.
If you had a gun, that is.
Whether you would have a gun.
It goes on.

(1986)

The Loneliness of the Military Historian

Confess: it's my profession
that alarms you.
This is why few people ask me to dinner,
though Lord knows I don't go out of my way to be scary.
I wear dresses of sensible cut
and unalarming shades of beige,

---

1. **vestibules** Small entrance halls between the outer door and the interior of a building.

I smell of lavender and go to the hairdresser's:
no prophetess mane of mine,
complete with snakes, will frighten the youngsters.
10   If I roll my eyes and mutter,
if I clutch at my heart and scream in horror
like a third-rate actress chewing up a mad scene,
I do it in private and nobody sees
but the bathroom mirror.

In general I might agree with you:
women should not contemplate war,
should not weigh tactics impartially,
or evade the word *enemy*,
or view both sides and denounce nothing.
20   Women should march for peace,
or hand out white feathers to arouse bravery,
spit themselves on bayonets
to protect their babies,
whose skulls will be split anyway,
or, having been raped repeatedly,
hang themselves with their own hair.
These are the functions that inspire general comfort.
That, and the knitting of socks for the troops
and a sort of moral cheerleading.
30   Also: mourning the dead.
Sons, lovers, and so forth.
All the killed children.

Instead of this, I tell
what I hope will pass as truth.
A blunt thing, not lovely.
The truth is seldom welcome,
especially at dinner,
though I am good at what I do.
My trade is courage and atrocities.
40   I look at them and do not condemn.
I write things down the way they happened,
as near as can be remembered.
I don't ask *why*, because it is mostly the same.
Wars happen because the ones who start them
think they can win.

In my dreams there is glamour.
The Vikings leave their fields
each year for a few months of killing and plunder,
much as the boys go hunting.
50   In real life they were farmers.

They come back loaded with splendour.
The Arabs ride against Crusaders[1]
with scimitars[2] that could sever
silk in the air.
A swift cut to the horse's neck
and a hunk of armour crashes down
like a tower. Fire against metal.
A poet might say: romance against banality.
When awake, I know better.

Despite the propaganda, there are no monsters,   60
or none that can be finally buried.
Finish one off, and circumstances
and the radio create another.
Believe me: whole armies have prayed fervently
to God all night and meant it,
and been slaughtered anyway.
Brutality wins frequently,
and large outcomes have turned on the invention
of a mechanical device, viz. radar.
True, valour sometimes counts for something,   70
as at Thermopylae.[3] Sometimes being right —
though ultimate virtue, by agreed tradition,
is decided by the winner.
Sometimes men throw themselves on grenades
and burst like paper bags of guts
to save their comrades.
I can admire that.
But rats and cholera have won many wars.
Those, and potatoes,
or the absence of them.   80
It's no use pinning all those medals
across the chests of the dead.
Impressive, but I know too much.
Grand exploits merely depress me.

In the interests of research
I have walked on many battlefields
that once were liquid with pulped
men's bodies and spangled with exploded
shells and splayed bone.
All of them have been green again   90
by the time I got there.
Each has inspired a few good quotes in its day.

---

1. Arabs, Crusaders The Crusaders were Christian soldiers who attempted to recapture the Holy Land from Arab rule between 1095 and 1291. **2. scimitars** Curved swords. **3. Thermopylae** A famous battle in 480 BC in which the outnumbered Greek army still marched (unsuccessfully) against the Persians.

Sad marble angels brood like hens
over the grassy nests where nothing hatches.
(The angels could just as well be described as *vulgar*
or *pitiless*, depending on camera angle.)
The word *glory* figures a lot on gateways.
Of course I pick a flower or two
from each, and press it in the hotel Bible
100   for a souvenir.
I'm just as human as you.

But it's no use asking me for a final statement.
As I say, I deal in tactics.
Also statistics:
for every year of peace there have been four hundred
years of war.

(1995)

Hairball

On the thirteenth of November, day of unluck, month of the dead, Kat went into the Toronto General Hospital for an operation. It was for an ovarian cyst, a large one.

Many women had them, the doctor told her. Nobody knew why. There wasn't any way of finding out whether the thing was malignant, whether it contained, already, the spores of death. Not before they went in. He spoke of "going in" the way she'd heard old veterans in TV documentaries speak of assaults on enemy territory. There was the same tensing of the jaw, the same fierce gritting of the teeth, the same grim enjoyment. Except that what he would be going into was her body. Counting down, waiting for the anaesthetic, Kat too gritted her teeth fiercely. She was terrified, but also she was curious. Curiosity has got her through a lot.

She'd made the doctor promise to save the thing for her, whatever it was, so she could have a look. She was intensely interested in her own body, in anything it might choose to do or produce; although when flaky Dania, who did layout at the magazine, told her this growth was a message to her from her body and she ought to sleep with an amethyst under her pillow to calm her vibrations, Kat told her to stuff it.

The cyst turned out to be a benign tumour. Kat liked that use of *benign,* as if the thing had a soul and wished her well. It was big as a grapefruit, the doctor said. "Big as a coconut," said Kat. Other people had grapefruits. "Coconut" was better. It conveyed the hardness of it, and the hairiness, too.

The hair in it was red — long strands of it wound round and round inside, like a ball of wet wool gone berserk or like the guck you pulled out of a clogged bathroom-sink drain. There were little bones in it too, or fragments of bone; bird bones, the bones of a sparrow crushed by a car. There was a scattering of nails, toe or finger. There were five perfectly formed teeth.

"Is this abnormal?" Kat asked the doctor, who smiled. Now that he had gone in and come out again, unscathed, he was less clenched.

"Abnormal? No," he said carefully, as if breaking the news to a mother about a freakish accident to her newborn. "Let's just say it's fairly common." Kat was a little disappointed. She would have preferred uniqueness.

She asked for a bottle of formaldehyde, and put the cut-open tumour into it. It was hers, it was benign, it did not deserve to be thrown away. She took it back to her apartment and stuck it on the mantelpiece. She named it Hairball. It isn't that different from having a stuffed bear's head or a preserved ex-pet or anything else with fur and teeth looming over your fireplace; or she pretends it isn't. Anyway, it certainly makes an impression.

Ger doesn't like it. Despite his supposed yen for the new and outré,[1] he is a squeamish man. The first time he comes around (sneaks around, creeps around) after the operation, he tells Kat to throw Hairball out. He calls it "disgusting." Kat refuses point-blank, and says she'd rather have Hairball in a bottle on her mantelpiece than the soppy dead flowers he's brought her, which will anyway rot a lot sooner than Hairball will. As a mantelpiece ornament, Hairball is far superior. Ger says Kat has a tendency to push things to extremes, to go over the edge, merely from a juvenile desire to shock, which is hardly a substitute for wit. One of these days, he says, she will go way too far. Too far for him, is what he means.

"That's why you hired me, isn't it?" she says. "Because I go way too far." But he's in one of his analyzing moods. He can see these tendencies of hers reflected in her work on the magazine, he says. All that leather and those grotesque and tortured-looking poses are heading down a track he and others are not at all sure they should continue to follow. Does she see what he means, does she take his point? It's a point that's been made before. She shakes her head slightly, says nothing. She knows how that translates: there have been complaints from the advertisers. *Too bizarre, too kinky.* Tough.

"Want to see my scar?" she says. "Don't make me laugh, though, you'll crack it open." Stuff like that makes him dizzy: anything with a hint of blood, anything gynecological. He almost threw up in the delivery room when his wife had a baby two years ago. He'd told her that with pride. Kat thinks about sticking a cigarette into the side of her mouth, as in a black-and-white movie of the forties. She thinks about blowing the smoke into his face.

Her insolence used to excite him, during their arguments. Then there would be a grab of her upper arms, a smouldering, violent kiss. He kisses her as if he thinks someone else is watching him, judging the image they make together. Kissing the latest thing, hard and shiny, purple-mouthed, crop-headed; kissing a girl, a woman, a girl, in a little crotch-hugger shirt and skin-tight leggings. He likes mirrors.

But he isn't excited now. And she can't decoy him into bed; she isn't ready for that yet, she isn't healed. He has a drink, which he doesn't finish, holds her hand as an afterthought, gives her a couple of avuncular[2] pats on the off-white outsized alpaca[3] shoulder, leaves too quickly.

"Goodbye, Gerald," she says. She pronounces the name with mockery. It's a negation of him, an abolishment of him, like ripping a medal off his chest. It's a warning.

He'd been Gerald when they first met. It was she who transformed him, first to Gerry, then to Ger. (Rhymed with *flair*, rhymed with *dare*.) She made him get rid of those sucky pursed-mouth ties, told him what shoes to wear, got him to buy a loose-cut Italian suit, redid his hair. A lot of his current tastes — in food, in drink, in recreational drugs, in women's entertainment underwear — were once hers. In his new phase, with his new, hard, stripped-down name ending on the sharpened note of *r*, he is her creation.

---

1. outré Bizarre. **2. avuncular** Characteristic of an uncle; affectionate. **3. alpaca** A fleecy fabric.

As she is her own. During her childhood she was a romanticized Katherine, dressed by her misty-eyed, fussy mother in dresses that looked like ruffled pillowcases. By high school she'd shed the frills and emerged as a bouncy, round-faced Kathy, with gleaming freshly washed hair and enviable teeth, eager to please and no more interesting than a health-food ad. At university she was Kath, blunt and no-bullshit in her Take-Back-the-Night jeans and checked shirt and her bricklayer-style striped-denim peaked hat. When she ran away to England, she sliced herself down to Kat. It was economical, street-feline, and pointed as a nail. It was also unusual. In England you had to do something to get their attention, especially if you weren't English. Safe in this incarnation, she Ramboed through the eighties.

It was the name, she still thinks, that got her the interview and then the job. The job with an avant-garde magazine, the kind that was printed on matte stock in black and white, with overexposed close-ups of women with hair blowing over their eyes, one nostril prominent: *the razor's edge*, it was called. Haircuts as art, some real art, film reviews, a little stardust, wardrobes of ideas that were clothes and of clothes that were ideas — the metaphysical shoulder pad. She learned her trade well, hands-on. She learned what worked.

She made her way up the ladder, from layout to design, then to the supervision of whole spreads, and then whole issues. It wasn't easy, but it was worth it. She had become a creator; she created total looks. After a while she could walk down the street in Soho or stand in the lobby at openings and witness her handiwork incarnate, strolling around in outfits she'd put together, spouting her warmed-over pronouncements. It was like being God, only God had never got around to off-the-rack lines.

By that time her face had lost its roundness, though the teeth of course remained: there was something to be said for North American dentistry. She'd shaved off most of her hair, worked on the drop-dead stare, perfected a certain turn of the neck that conveyed an aloof inner authority. What you had to make them believe was that you knew something they didn't know yet. What you also had to make them believe was that they too could know this thing, this thing that would give them eminence and power and sexual allure, that would attract envy to them — but for a price. The price of a magazine. What they could never get through their heads was that it was done entirely with cameras. Frozen light, frozen time. Given the angle, she could make any woman look ugly. Any man as well. She could make anyone look beautiful, or at least interesting. It was all photography, it was all iconography. It was all in the choosing eye. This was the thing that could never be bought, no matter how much of your pitiful monthly wage you blew on snakeskin.

Despite the status, *the razor's edge* was fairly low-paying. Kat herself could not afford many of the things she contextualized so well. The grottiness and expense of London began to get to her; she got tired of gorging on the canapés at literary launches in order to scrimp on groceries, tired of the fuggy smell of cigarettes ground into the red-and-maroon carpeting of pubs, tired of the pipes bursting every time it froze in winter, and of the Clarissas and Melissas and Penelopes at the magazine rabbiting on about how they had been literally, absolutely, totally freezing all night, and how it literally, absolutely, totally, usually never got that cold. It always got that cold. The pipes always burst. Nobody thought of putting in real pipes, ones that would not burst next time. Burst pipes were an English tradition, like so many others.

Like, for instance, English men. Charm the knickers off you with their mellow vowels and frivolous verbiage, and then, once they'd got them off, panic and run. Or else stay and whinge. The English called it *whinging* instead of whining. It was better, really. Like a creaking hinge. It was a traditional compliment to be whinged at by an Englishman. It was his way of saying he trusted you, he was conferring upon you the privilege of getting to know the real him. The inner, whinging him. That was how they thought of women, secretly: whinge receptacles. Kat could play it, but that didn't mean she liked it.

She had an advantage over the English women, though: she was of no class. She had no class. She was in a class of her own. She could roll around among the English men, all different kinds of them, secure in the knowledge that she was not being measured against the class yardsticks and accent-detectors they carried around in their back pockets, was not subject to the petty snobberies and resentments that lent such richness to their inner lives. The flip side of this freedom was that she was beyond the pale. She was a colonial — how fresh, how vital, how anonymous, how finally of no consequence. Like a hole in the wall, she could be told all secrets and then be abandoned with no guilt.

She was too smart, of course. The English men were very competitive; they liked to win. Several times it hurt. Twice she had abortions, because the men in question were not up for the alternative. She learned to say that she didn't want children anyway, that if she longed for a rug-rat she would buy a gerbil. Her life began to seem long. Her adrenalin was running out. Soon she would be thirty, and all she could see ahead was more of the same.

This was how things were when Gerald turned up. "You're terrific," he said, and she was ready to hear it, even from him, even though *terrific* was a word that had probably gone out with fifties crew-cuts. She was ready for his voice by that time too: the flat, metallic nasal tone of the Great Lakes, with its clear hard *r*'s and its absence of theatricality. Dull normal. The speech of her people. It came to her suddenly that she was an exile.

Gerald was scouting, Gerald was recruiting. He'd heard about her, looked at her work, sought her out. One of the big companies back in Toronto was launching a new fashion-oriented magazine, he said: upmarket, international in its coverage, of course, but with some Canadian fashion in it too, and with lists of stores where the items portrayed could actually be bought. In that respect they felt they'd have it all over the competition, those American magazines that assumed you could only get Gucci in New York or Los Angeles. Heck, times had changed, you could get it in Edmonton! You could get it in Winnipeg!

Kat had been away too long. There was Canadian fashion now? The English quip would be to say that "Canadian fashion" was an oxymoron. She refrained from making it, lit a cigarette with her cyanide-green Covent Garden-boutique leather-covered lighter (as featured in the May issue of *the razor's edge*), looked Gerald in the eye. "London is a lot to give up," she said levelly. She glanced around the see-me-here Mayfair[4] restaurant where they were finishing lunch, a restaurant she'd chosen because she'd known he was paying. She'd never spend that kind of money on food otherwise. "Where would I eat?"

Gerald assured her that Toronto was now the restaurant capital of Canada. He himself would be happy to be her guide. There was a great Chinatown, there was world-class Italian. Then he paused, took a breath. "I've been meaning to ask you," he said.

---

4. **Mayfair** An expensive and upscale neighbourhood in London.

"About the name. Is that Kat as in Krazy?" He thought this was suggestive. She'd heard it before.

"No," she said, "It's Kat as in KitKat. That's a chocolate bar. Melts in your mouth." She gave him her stare, quirked her mouth, just a twitch.

Gerald became flustered, but he pushed on. They wanted her, they needed her, they loved her, he said in essence. Someone with her fresh, innovative approach and her experience would be worth a lot of money to them, relatively speaking. But there were rewards other than the money. She would be in on the initial concept, she would have a formative influence, she would have a free hand. He named a sum that made her gasp, inaudibly of course. By now she knew better than to betray desire.

So she made the journey back, did her three months of culture shock, tried the world-class Italian and the great Chinese, and seduced Gerald at the first opportunity, right in his junior vice-presidential office. It was the first time Gerald had been seduced in such a location, or perhaps ever. Even though it was after hours, the danger frenzied him. It was the idea of it. The daring. The image of Kat kneeling on the broadloom, in a legendary bra that until now he'd seen only in the lingerie ads of the Sunday *New York Times*, unzipping him in full view of the silver-framed engagement portrait of his wife that complemented the impossible ball-point pen set on his desk. At that time he was so straight he felt compelled to take off his wedding ring and place it carefully in the ashtray first. The next day he brought her a box of David Wood Food Shop chocolate truffles. They were the best, he told her, anxious that she should recognize their quality. She found the gesture banal, but also sweet. The banality, the sweetness, the hunger to impress: that was Gerald.

Gerald was the kind of man she wouldn't have bothered with in London. He was not funny, he was not knowledgeable, he had little verbal charm. But he was eager, he was tractable, he was blank paper. Although he was eight years older than she was, he seemed much younger. She took pleasure from his furtive, boyish delight in his own wickedness. And he was so grateful. "I can hardly believe this is happening," he said, more frequently than was necessary and usually in bed.

His wife, whom Kat encountered (and still encounters) at many tedious company events, helped to explain his gratitude. The wife was a priss. Her name was Cheryl. Her hair looked as if she still used big rollers and embalm-your-hairdo spray; her mind was room-by-room Laura Ashley wallpaper: tiny, unopened pastel buds arranged in straight rows. She probably put on rubber gloves to make love, and checked it off on a list afterwards. One more messy household chore. She looked at Kat as if she'd like to spritz her with air deodorizer. Kat revenged herself by picturing Cheryl's bathrooms: hand towels embroidered with lilies, fuzzy covers on the toilet seats.

The magazine itself got off to a rocky start. Although Kat had lots of lovely money to play with, and although it was a challenge to be working in colour, she did not have the free hand Gerald had promised her. She had to contend with the company board of directors, who were all men, who were all accountants or indistinguishable from them, who were cautious and slow as moles.

"It's simple," Kat told them. "You bombard them with images of what they ought to be, and you make them feel grotty for being the way they are. You're working with the gap between reality and perception. That's why you have to hit them with something new, something they've never seen before, something they aren't. Nothing sells like anxiety."

The board, on the other hand, felt that the readership should simply be offered more of what they already had. More fur, more sumptuous leather, more cashmere. More established names. The board had no sense of improvisation, no wish to take risks; no sporting instincts, no desire to put one over on the readers just for the hell of it. "Fashion is like hunting," Kat told them, hoping to appeal to their male hormones, if any. "It's playful, it's intense, it's predatory. It's blood and guts. It's erotic." But to them it was about good taste. They wanted Dress-for-Success. Kat wanted scattergun ambush.

Everything became a compromise. Kat had wanted to call the magazine *All the Rage*, but the board was put off by the vibrations of anger in the word "rage." They thought it was too feminist, of all things. "It's a *forties* sound," Kat said, "Forties is *back*. Don't you get it?" But they didn't. They wanted to call it *Or*. French for *gold*, and blatant enough in its values, but without any base note, as Kat told them. They sawed off at *Felice*, which had qualities each side wanted. It was vaguely French-sounding, it meant "happy" (so much less threatening than rage), and, although you couldn't expect the others to notice, for Kat it had a feline bouquet which counteracted the laciness. She had it done in hot-pink lipstick-scrawl, which helped some. She could live with it, but it had not been her first love.

This battle has been fought and refought over every innovation in design, every new angle Kat has tried to bring in, every innocuous bit of semi-kink. There was a big row over a spread that did lingerie, half pulled off and with broken glass perfume bottles strewn on the floor. There as an uproar over the two nouveau-stockinged legs, one tied to a chair with a third, different-coloured stocking. They had not understood the man's three-hundred-dollar leather gloves positioned ambiguously around a neck.

And so it has gone on, for five years.

After Gerald has left, Kat paces her living room. Pace, pace. Her stitches pull. She's not looking forward to her solitary dinner of microwaved leftovers. She's not sure now why she came back here, to this flat burg beside the polluted inland sea. Was it Ger? Ludicrous thought but no longer out of the question. Is he the reason she stays, despite her growing impatience with him?

He's no longer fully rewarding. They've learned each other too well, they take short-cuts now; their time together has shrunk from whole stolen rolling and sensuous afternoons to a few hours snatched between work and dinner-time. She no longer knows what she wants from him. She tells herself she's worth more, she should branch out; but she doesn't see other men, she can't, somehow. She's tried once or twice but it didn't work. Sometimes she goes out to dinner or a flick with one of the gay designers. She likes the gossip.

Maybe she misses London. She feels caged, in this country, in this city, in this room. She could start with the room, she could open a window. It's too stuffy in here. There's an undertone of formaldehyde, from Hairball's bottle. The flowers she got for the operation are mostly wilted, all except Gerald's from today. Come to think of it, why didn't he send her any at the hospital? Did he forget, or was it a message?

"Hairball," she says, "I wish you could talk. I could have a more intelligent conversation with you than with most of the losers in this turkey farm." Hairball's baby teeth glint in the light; it looks as if it's about to speak.

Kat feels her own forehead. She wonders if she's running a temperature. Something ominous is going on, behind her back. There haven't been enough phone calls from the magazine; they've been able to muddle on without her, which is bad news. Reigning queens should never go on vacation, or have operations either. Uneasy lies the head. She has a sixth sense about these things, she's been involved in enough palace coups to know the signs, she has sensitive antennae for the footfalls of impending treachery.

The next morning she pulls herself together, downs an espresso from her mini-machine, picks out an aggressive touch-me-if-you-dare suede outfit in armour grey, and drags herself to the office, although she isn't due in till next week. Surprise, surprise. Whispering knots break up in the corridors, greet her with false welcome as she limps past. She settles herself at her minimalist desk, checks her mail. Her head is pounding, her stitches hurt. Ger gets wind of her arrival; he wants to see her a.s.a.p., and not for lunch.

He awaits her in his newly done wheat-on-white office, with the eighteenth-century desk they chose together, the Victorian inkstand, the framed blow-ups from the magazine, the hands in maroon leather, wrists manacled with pearls, the Hermès scarf twisted into a blindfold, the model's mouth blossoming lusciously beneath it. Some of her best stuff. He's beautifully done up, in a lick-my-neck silk shirt open at the throat, an eat-your-heart-out Italian silk-and-wool loose-knit sweater. Oh, cool insouciance.[5] Oh, eyebrow language. He's a money man who lusted after art, and now he's got some, now he is some. Body art. Her art. She'd done her job well; he's finally sexy.

He's smooth as lacquer. "I didn't want to break this to you until next week," he says. He breaks it to her. It's the board of directors. They think she's too bizarre, they think she goes way too far. Nothing he could do about it, although naturally he tried.

Naturally. Betrayal. The monster has turned on its own mad scientist. "I gave you life!" she wants to scream at him.

She isn't in good shape. She can hardly stand. She stands, despite his offer of a chair. She sees now what she's wanted, what she's been missing. Gerald is what she's been missing — the stable, unfashionable, previous, tight-assed Gerald. Not Ger, not the one she's made in her own image. The other one, before he got ruined. The Gerald with a house and a small child and a picture of his wife in a silver frame on his desk. She wants to be in that silver frame. She wants the child. She's been robbed.

"And who is my lucky replacement?" she says. She needs a cigarette, but does not want to reveal her shaking hands.

"Actually, it's me," he says, trying for modesty.

This is too absurd. Gerald couldn't edit a phone book. "You?" she says faintly. She has the good sense not to laugh.

"I've always wanted to get out of the money end of things here," he says, "into the creative area. I knew you'd understand, since it can't be you at any rate. I knew you'd prefer someone who could, well, sort of build on your foundations." Pompous asshole. She looks at his neck. She longs for him, hates herself for it, and is powerless.

The room wavers. He slides towards her across the wheat-coloured broadloom, takes her by the grey suede upper arms. "I'll write you a good reference," he says. "Don't worry about that. Of course, we can still see one another. I'd miss our afternoons."

"Of course," she says. He kisses her, a voluptuous kiss, or it would look like one to a third party, and she lets him. *In a pig's ear*.

She makes it home in a taxi. The driver is rude to her and gets away with it; she doesn't have the energy. In her mailbox is an engraved invitation: Ger and Cheryl are

---

5. **insouciance** Indifference.

having a drinks party, tomorrow evening. Postmarked five days ago. Cheryl is behind the times.

Kat undresses, runs a shallow bath. There's not much to drink around here, there's nothing to sniff or smoke. What an oversight; she's stuck with herself. There are other jobs. There are other men, or that's the theory. Still, something's been ripped out of her. How could this have happened, to her? When knives were slated for backs, she'd always done the stabbing. Any headed her way she's seen coming in time, and thwarted. Maybe she's losing her edge.

She stares into the bathroom mirror, assesses her face in the misted glass. A face of the eighties, a mask face, a bottom-line face; push the weak to the wall and grab what you can. But now it's the nineties. Is she out of style, so soon? She's only thirty-five, and she's already losing track of what people ten years younger are thinking. That could be fatal. As time goes by she'll have to race faster and faster to keep up, and for what? Part of the life she should have had is just a gap, it isn't there, it's nothing. What can be salvaged from it, what can be redone, what can be done at all?

When she climbs out of the tub after her sponge bath, she almost falls. She has a fever, no doubt about it. Inside her something is leaking, or else festering; she can hear it, like a dripping tap. A running sore, a sore from running so hard. She should go to the Emergency ward at some hospital, get herself shot up with antibiotics. Instead she lurches into the living room, takes Hairball down from the mantelpiece in its bottle, places it on the coffee table. She sits cross-legged, listens. Filaments wave. She can hear a kind of buzz, like bees at work.

She'd asked the doctor if it could have started as a child, a fertilized egg that escaped somehow and got into the wrong place. No, said the doctor. Some people thought this kind of tumour was present in seedling form from birth, or before it. It might be the woman's undeveloped twin. What they really were was unknown. They had many kinds of tissue, though. Even brain tissue. Though of course all of these tissues lack structure.

Still, sitting here on the rug looking in at it, she pictures it as a child. It has come out of her, after all. It is flesh of her flesh. Her child with Gerald, her thwarted child, not allowed to grow normally. Her warped child, taking its revenge.

"Hairball," she says. "You're so ugly. Only a mother could love you." She feels sorry for it. She feels loss. Tears run down her face. Crying is not something she does, not normally, not lately.

Hairball speaks to her, without words. It is irreducible, it has the texture of reality, it is not an image. What it tells her is everything she's never wanted to hear about herself. This is new knowledge, dark and precious and necessary. It cuts.

She shakes her head. What are you doing, sitting on the floor and talking to a hairball? You are sick, she tells herself. Take a Tylenol and go to bed.

The next day she feels a little better. Dania from layout calls her and makes dove-like, sympathetic coos at her, and wants to drop by during lunch hour to take a look at her aura. Kat tells her to come off it. Dania gets huffy, and says that Kat's losing her job is a price for immoral behaviour in a previous life. Kat tells her to stuff it; anyway, she's done enough immoral behaviour in this life to account for the whole thing. "Why are you so full of hate?" asks Dania. She doesn't say it like a point she's making, she sounds truly baffled.

"I don't know," says Kat. It's a straight answer.

After she hangs up she paces the floor. She's crackling inside, like hot fat under the broiler. What she's thinking about is Cheryl, bustling about her cosy house, preparing for the party. Cheryl fiddles with her freeze-framed hair, positions an overloaded vase of flowers, fusses about the caterers. Gerald comes in, kisses her lightly on the cheek. A connubial[6] scene. His conscience is nicely washed. The witch is dead, his foot is on the body, the trophy; he's had his dirty fling, he's ready now for the rest of his life.

Kat takes a taxi to the David Wood Food Shop and buys two dozen chocolate truffles. She has them put into an oversized box, then into an oversized bag with the store logo on it. Then she goes home and takes Hairball out of its bottle. She drains it in the kitchen strainer and pats it damp-dry, tenderly, with paper towels. She sprinkles it with powdered cocoa, which forms a brown pastry crust. It still smells of formaldehyde, so she wraps it in Saran Wrap and then in tinfoil, and then in pink tissue paper, which she ties with a mauve bow. She placed it in the David Wood box in a bed of shredded tissue, with the truffles nestled around. She closes the box, tapes it, puts it into the bag, stuffs several sheets of pink paper on top. It's her gift, valuable and dangerous. It's her messenger, but the message it will deliver is its own. It will tell the truth, to whoever asks. It's right that Gerald should have it; after all, it's his child too.

She prints on the card, "Gerald, Sorry I couldn't be with you. This is all the rage. Love, K."

When evening has fallen and the party must be in full swing, she calls a delivery taxi. Cheryl will not distrust anything that arrives in such an expensive bag. She will open it in public, in front of everyone. There will be distress, there will be questions. Secrets will be unearthed. There will be pain. After that, everything will go way too far.

She is not well; her heart is pounding, space is wavering once more. But outside the window it's snowing, the soft, damp, windless flakes of her childhood. She puts on her coat and goes out, foolishly. She intends to walk just to the corner, but when she reaches the corner she goes on. The snow melts against her face like small fingers touching. She has done an outrageous thing, but she doesn't feel guilty. She feels light and peaceful and filled with charity, and temporarily without a name.

(1991)

bill bissett (1939–)

bill bissett was born in Halifax in 1939. He was stricken with appendicitis and peritonitis as an adolescent, and the treatments for these ailments weakened his abdomen to the extent that he had to abandon his dream of becoming a professional dancer. He took up painting and drawing, though he never lost interest in performance. In 1956, he attended Dalhousie University, but he dropped out after a year and hitchhiked to Vancouver, escaping his parents' disapproval of his bisexuality. He quickly became part of the city's vital bohemian scene. In 1965, bpNichol published bissett's first book of poems, *we sleep inside each other all*. bissett's idiosyncratic and enduring disregard for the oppressive conventions of spelling, form, and content was evident from the start.

In retrospect, he said that he had been in search of "clariteez seeking freedom from behaviour n sexual role repressyuns n 2 rage out in nu direksyuns n writing painting n living." Although his father was a judge and would have funded him through law school, bissett refused membership in the upper middle class. He got by mainly on low-paying jobs or welfare. Later, he supported himself with Canada Council grants and by selling his paintings.

---

6. **connubial** Matrimonial.

From 1963 to 1965, bissett studied English literature and political philosophy at the University of British Columbia, and though he excelled in his course work, he quit to pursue greater artistic freedom. In 1963, he launched the magazine *blewointment* (named after a cure for body lice), which became an outlet for many important writers. He started blewointmentpress in 1967, publishing works by fellow experimental poets Nichol, Steve McCaffery, Andrew Suknaski, and Lionel Kearns. In these enterprises, he gave his authors licence to express themselves without restriction. A few years later, in *RUSH / what fuckan theory: a study uv language* (1971), he argued practically for self-publication: "writing is what yu write. yu need to print it yrself to / make its freedom. yu cin do anything yu want or feel like / with word. // th rules are there to oppress yu. rules watch / yu in a lot of ways, check yr expression … yu as writrs are responsible to th message that flows thru yu."

In a 1966 CBC-TV documentary, bissett criticized the war in Vietnam and advocated marijuana use. Two years later, he was arrested for marijuana possession during a police raid at his house, and the magazine *blewointment* folded. Of his incarceration, he wrote: "yu sit behind bars, turning to / endless vapors." He then mused, "we're all part of this // historical mistake, even love / may now be possible, tho, don't / hold yr breath, be seein' ya, // mother earth." The year he was arrested, bissett published *awake in th red desert* (1968). It included a vinyl recording of him performing his poems using the mantra-like patterns that won him recognition as a sound poet. Some critics have used the term "borderblur" to identify the technique that gives rise to his "sound-vizual" pieces. It involves the poem's speaker referring to something external while directing attention to himself or herself as a voice, and it also involves blending genres — reading a visual poem aloud. An exemplary "sound-vizual" poem is found in bissett's *soul arrow* (1980): it depicts a man with a prominent penis using only the letter *X*. When read aloud, the sound blurs to produce the chant "sex sex sex …"

bissett was released from prison in 1969, but his troubles persisted. At a Kitsilano house party, he fell through a false wall into a basement and nearly died of a brain injury. It took several years of rehabilitation for him to regain motor control on the left side of his body; he also had to relearn the alphabet and how to paint. Still, two years later, he published *NOBODY OWNS TH EARTH* (1971), an important volume of poems selected by Margaret Atwood and Dennis Lee. It exemplified the inseparability of bissett's politics and style: both are based on notions of freedom. In the collection, bissett criticizes imperialism, the military, and the exploitation of nature, and he promotes pacifism, egalitarianism, and a spiritual state he calls the "ecstatic yunyun." Like many of his other collections, this one also features bissett's line drawings and contains a variety of poem types — lyric, narrative, and pattern poems (though he always eschews traditional forms, such as the sonnet). His poems are infused with emotion; they are wistful, funny, resentful, loving, outraged, playful, and they often express longing for sexual union and religious enlightenment.

bissett's rebelliousness made him a target in 1977 when members of the House of Commons presented one of his poems ("a warm place to shit") as evidence that government arts grants were being misused. He was accused of being a pornographer because some of his pattern poems depicted genitalia and sexual acts. Many people came to his defence, writing letters to newspapers, and bissett was thrust briefly into the national spotlight. In 1983, however, he had to give up blewointmentpress when his Canada Council grant was slashed by 42 percent.

From the late 1970s onward, bissett's work began to alter in form as he started experimenting with prose poetry. He kept his unconventional style, but the formal shift allowed him to emphasize the narrative, often autobiographical, element of the work. In the 1980s, this element was prominent in his best work: *Seagull on Yonge Street* (1983) and *Canada Gees Mate for Life* (1985).

In 1985, bissett served as writer-in-residence at the University of Western Ontario, and while living in London he became involved with an alternative rock group called the Luddites, singing with the band and writing song lyrics. His love for rock music is on display in *the last photo uv th human soul* (1993); in a comic poem about attending a Morrissey concert, he writes: "i heer morrissey singing / hes so great peopul fall on me … i start out sitting in row 7 / end up in row 25."

Now based in Toronto, bissett continues to paint, write, and give public performances of his work. Despite having produced over 60 books of poetry, he has retained a characteristic modesty — in "memoreez uv that hous" from *th influenza uv logik* (1995), he asks, "what can i know," and his answer is frequently "nothing." This extends to a certain humility in the face of the endless permutations and possibilities of sound and language and life in general — in "red lava ovr bord th men wer kissing" from *b leev abul char ak trs* (2000), he asserts that "ther is no / unfailing axiom."

jed bi kor benskt trik

jed bi kor benskt trik
2 get 2 th dust n mist
who came outuv thswamp

image image images imagine imaginings
borrow borrow fi dar cankst th th thread tunnel wear fourty
evoke evoke croak narrow thunder down bring what ever under
stone bear thread ride th dusk n dust n sand water forty in
stone bear thread ride th dusk n dust n sand water forty in
what sign ded cum cum down when cum street sum cum cumm in
10   under cum cum in cum cum cum in cum cum win cum well within
musical cum cum dance cum cum den cum cum cum out meatknight
ava gardnr n robert taylor starring in knights uv th round
tabul[1] brought to yew from m g m cum technicolor cinemascope
sin seat slide over under popcorn in cum win sister carrie
in swim cum cummdown   cum start cum go far for love cum in
santa claus   receive n over roger cum there tina bell ring up
cum magicul smudge cum hill down crown broke break dont cum
break any cum mor jazz riff tiff swear no more cum in cumon
dance ray charles wander up beatles ugh mommy beatlus there
20   go mustard swear there irish mist memory go cum down there
so sew thread tabul wear barrow bronz gonk there fred swear
mutter so an so for cum ever hallucind whatshername thetime
is ever walk to never th store sunlight sunset smudge allin
cum here there for swear and ever distort th whereverafterd
allsin and inning marrianne moore[2] swear new yorker there is
nevr enuff mony so this is my concern is my enuff therecum
disease advice ideal goal work for what is lawful theregoin
winning advance gggg th garbage advances smell sweet awgful
least we least we least we forget to swear an score thwires

---

1. **ava gardnr … tabul** The 1953 film *Knights of the Round Table*, starring Ava Gardner and Robert Taylor (MGM studios).
2. **marrianne moore** American modernist poet Marianne Moore (1887–1972).

r shot shooting for more and cum cum cum over n cum cum all
borrow there is enuff advice can u can u can u can u can u
talk 2 yourself forthereismorethanforscorethirty thurtyising
sincuminsparrowsmustadrwesternwesterndownsouthstayherehairher
skipskripwhip whiff in take downintakedownindidushutoffmywatr
sparrowsoarover th buggy with th sand in it chug chug chug this
is a new york train a gem a gem a whim an announcement will cum
cum that was cum u c u c u c dont yu dont yu cum take and where
is th watchword that will cum that is cumming for all and alway

30

ring s

(1966)

awake in th red desert

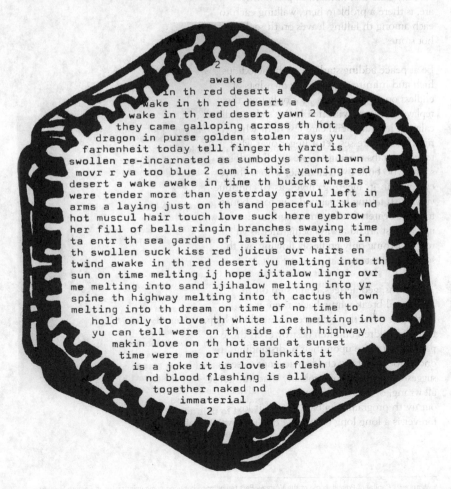

```
            2
          awake
    in th red desert a
   wake in th red desert a
  wake in th red desert yawn 2
    they came galloping across th hot
     dragon in purse golden stolen rays yu
     farhenheit today tell finger th yard is
   swollen re-incarnated as sumbodys front lawn
   movr r ya too blue 2 cum in this yawning red
   desert a wake awake in time th buicks wheels
   were tender more than yesterday gravul left in
   arms a laying just on th sand just peaceful like nd
   hot muscul hair touch love suck here eyebrow
   her fill of bells ringin branches swaying time
   ta entr th sea garden of lasting treats me in
   th swollen suck kiss red juicus ovr hairs en
   twind awake in th red desert yu melting into th
   sun on time melting ij hope ijitalow lingr ovr
   me melting into sand ijihalow melting into yr
   spine th highway melting into th cactus th own
   melting into th dream on time of no time to
      hold only to love th white line melting into
       yu can tell were on th side of th highway
        makin love on th hot sand at sunset
         time were me or undr blankits it
          is a joke it is love is flesh
           nd blood flashing is all
             together naked nd
                immaterial
                   2
```

(1968)

Beyond Even Faithful Legends

On th othr hand, yu sd to yrselvs we
cud cease to care so much what it all
looks like, how it appears, how arrangd,
to anyone's beleef and desire, but give
to go on living (i want to live he sd
stumbling into th can) to go on living
with our broken hearts, batterd heads
and sold out sun rays, for what comment
in Warsaw[1] either, endless conversationals, to
10   go on living, yr left hand stiff in its fist,
shud i buy th 150 acre ranch next to LBJ's[2]
for only 1 nd a ½ million, th possibilities
are, is there a problem here, walking each to
each among th falling leaves on th scalding
hot stones.

Be at peace adding starlight of th melodious
high and infinite, yr own very own lists of
endless one night stands   for only love they
replay   centring within yr hearts's also endless
20   calm, yr left hand cud care less right what yr
right hand carresses, let it linger over what it
touches, grabs ceasing to care yu all by doing
so say who built this valentine, who will live
ever within its meeting curves, as yu continue
yr walk th falling leaves under yr toes, bones
to heart beaten fertilize, moving into th cut-
up sky, just ahead always being ther as yu
reach nothing only endlessly flowing ovr th
scalding hot stones.

30   Patterns, geometrees, don't step on th
cracks, yul break whose back, there it is,
mother or who, those choices to me child, help,
help th children children destroy even those
patterns yu place upon their undrstandings, i
once thot ..., or my childish attempt to see a
suggested pattern tho i probably that way got it
all wrong, o, if there's any way
out uv th programmd albatross take it loves
forever is a long long time and i don't know

---

1. **Warsaw** Capital of Poland, home of the Warsaw Pact (an alliance between communist states in Eastern Europe).
2. **LBJ's** Lyndon B. Johnson, American president.

yu she sd cumming to me from her side 40
meeting ther encirculd by endless onlookrs and
i don't know she sd cumming from her side
take it is a long time being starlight high and
infinite carresses, if it dissolvs goes into solution
there it is what els is thcr shoot it loves
don't know, why know she sd cumming to me
again our feet fastr than any sacred or othr markings
our projectid bodees possessd ovr th endless burning
stones.

(1969)

Killer Whale

> "… i want to tell you love … "
> — Milton Acorn

we were tryin to get back to Vancouver
again cumming down th sunshine coast,away
speeding from th power intrigue of a
desolate town,Powell River, feudalizd
totally by MacMillan Blowdell,[1] a different
trip than when i was hitch-hiking back
once before with a cat who usd to live
next door to Ringo Starr's grandmother 10
who still lives in th same Liverpool[2] house
even tho Ringo offerd her a town house
in London, still shops at th same places
moves among th Liverpool streets
with th peopul, like she dusint want
to know, this cat told me

away from th robot stink there,
after th preliminary hearing,martina
and me and th hot sun, arguing
our way thru th raspberry bushes 20
onto a bus headin for Van, on th ferry
analyzing th hearing and th bust, how
th whole insane trip cuts at our life
giving us suspicions and knowledge
stead of innocence and th bus takes
off without us from th bloody B.C.

---

1. **Powell River, MacMillan Blowdell** MacMillan Bloedel was a forestry company; the company had a paper mill in British Columbia that came from a merger between the Powell River paper company and two others; the town of Powell River runs around the paper mill. 2. **Ringo Starr, Liverpool** Starr, a member of the Beatles, was from Liverpool, England.

government ferry — i can't walk too good
with a hole in my ankle and all why
we didn't stay with our friends back
30   at th farm — destind for more places
changes to go thru can feel th pull
of that heavy in our hearts and in th air,
th government workmen can't drive us
20 minutes to catch up with th bus, insane
complications,phoning Loffmark works minister
in Victoria capital if he sz so they will they say
he once wrote a fan letter to me on an
anti-Vietnam pome published in Prism[3], "… with
interest … " he sd he read it,can't get him
40   on th phone,workmen say yer lucky if th
phone works,o lets dissolve all these phone
booths dotting surrealy our incognito intrigue
North American vast space,only cutting us all
off from each other — more crap with th bus
company,2 hrs later nother ferry,hitch
ride groovy salesman of plastic bags,may
be weul work together we all laughing say
in th speeding convertibel to Garden City,[4]he
wants to see there the captive killer whales.

50   Down past th town along th fishing boat dock
th killer whales,like Haida argolite carvings,[5]
th sheen — black glistening,perfect white circuls
on th sides of them, th mother won't feed
th baby,protests her captivity, why did they
cum into this treacherous harbor, th times
without any challenge, for food, no food
out there old timer tells me, and caught,
millions of bait surrounding them,part of
th system, rather be food for th despondent
60   killer whales than be eat by th fattend ducks
on th shore there old timer tells me, and
if th baby dies no fault of mine th man
hosing him down strapped in a canvas sack
so he won't sink to th bottom,ive been hosing
him down 24 hrs a day since we netted em,
and out further a ways more killer whales

---

3. **Prism** *Prism International* is a Canadian literary magazine. **4. Garden City** A suburb of Winnipeg, Manitoba. **5. Haida argolite carvings** Rock carvings made by the Haida people of northern British Columbia.

came in to see what was happening and they
got capturd for their concern,th cow howling
,thrashing herself in and out of th water,how
like i felt after getting busted, like we all
felt,yeah,th hosing down man told me,we got
enuff killer whales for 2 maybe 3 museums,course
th baby may die but there's still plenty for those
peopul whos never see animals like these
here lessen they went to a museum.

We went back to th convertible along th narrow
plank, heard th cow howl sum more, th bull
submergd, th man hosing th listless baby,
th sun's shattering light, them mammals aren't going
to take it lying down we thot, missd another ferry
connection, changd, made it, staggerd
together into town.

70

80

(1969)

yaji yaji yaji

```
yaji yaji yaji yu kaneee anjaneeee yakoooo yangee eee
eeeeeeeeeeeeeeee oooooooooooooooon yaaaaaa eeeoooookaa
aaaaaaaaaaaneeeeeeeeeeeeeeeeee uskooooo eeeaanji anji
yaji yaji yaji yaji yananji yanaaaaaanjeeee eeekooooo
eeeekuuuuuuu eeeeeeeeekuuuuu eku eku eku ya eku yaa
cheeunfantu cheeanfantu yaskeee yaskee uuuuoooonaaanji
yanukuu yaanuuakuu yanuuankuuaanji yanuuaankooanjiiio
anjio anjio anjeeooo anjeeee yaskoo yasku angeeeeanji
ananananananan aaaaaahuhuhuhuahuahuahuahuahua yanskii
yaji yaji yaji yaji yu kaneee anjanee yakooo yangeeee
eeeeeeeeeeeeeeeeeeeeeeeeeeeeeeeeeeeeeeeeeeeeeeeeeeeeee
eeeeeeeeeeeeeeeeeeeeeeeeeeeeeeeeeeeeeeeeeeeeeeeeeeeeee
eeeeeeeeeeeeeeeeeeeeeeeeeeeeeeeeeeeeeeeeeeeeeeeeeeeeee
eeeeeeeeeeeeeeeeeeeeeeeeeeeeeeeeeeeeeeeeeeeeeeeeeeeeee
yaaaakuuuuaneeeee yaaaakuuuuanee aji aji aji aji key
aaaaaaaaaaaaaaaaaaaaaneeeeee aneeee aaaneeee anookee
anooikeeeeee anooookeeeaya ayaa ayaaa ayaa ayyyaaaaaaa
aaaaaaaaaaaaaaaaaaaaaaaaaaaaaaaaaaaaaaaaaaaaaaaaaaaaaa
aaaaaaaaaaaaaaaaaaaaaaaaaaaaaaaaaaaaaaaaaaaaaaaaaaaaaa
aaaaaaaaaaaaaaaaaaaaaaaaaaaaaaaaaaaaaaaaaaaaaaaaaaaaaa
noikeeayaajindeee anoikeeyaajindeeee jindeee jindeee
jindeee jindeee jindeee jindeee jindeee jindeee jinde
eeeee aji aji aji eeeeeooooaaaoaaaoooaaaooooaaaoooaaa
aaaaaaa anoikeeeyaajindeee anoikeeeyaajindeee anoikee
yaaajindeee anoikeeeyajindeee anoikeeeyajindeee anoia
aaaa anoiaaayaaakeeeyaaajindeee ajindee ajindeee huuu
uuuuaaaani huuuaaani aneeeeejindeee anoikeeyaajinde
eeee kanuuu kannuuuu kaaanuuu jakuuu kanuuu jakuu kan
uuu kanuuu kaaanuuu jakuuu kanuuu jakuuu kanuuu jakuu
kanuuuu kuaanji kuanji kuaanji kuaanjiii kuaanjiii ye
eeeee aaaango yeeen yeeen yeeen aaaaan go guancheeeee
cheeanji kuaaanfusko ko ko ko yeeeeeeeeee anjeeee yaa
neeeeena neeenaaa neeeenaaa neeenaaa neeeenaa neeeenaa
neeeenaaa neeeenaaa neeeeenaaa neeeeenaaaa neeeenaaaa
funduuchakali funduchali funduchakali funduchakali oe
eeeeeeeeeeeenaaaanjiiianjeeeeaaangeee anoikaliendeene
eeeeeeeeeeeeeenaaaaaaaa ooooooo yakuuuu yaaaaaakuuune
eeeanji angeeeeee anji anji anji anji anji anji anjio
kaaantuanchudali chunaneeeyoantali chunkantuonyeental
io eeeeooo eeeeeeooooo jakuuuu yakuuuu jeeeanjiundaa
aaaaaaaleeee ali aliunchukuantali anoikeeyaaaajindeee
eeeooonaaakooo eeeoooonaaaaakoooo eeeeooooonaaaakooaa
kuua kuuuuaaaa eeeeoooonaaaakuuuuaaaa ji ji aneeeeeeuk
```

(1974)

ths is a konkreet pome

           a dia   adi AAAA   toftling sd murrum grasp sweet n
      adi
       ths is a konkreet pome   ths is a konkreet pome   ths
      is a konkreet pome   ths is a konkreet pome   it reminds
        yu uv tapestree   it can remind yu uv konkreet uv sand
ths is a konkreet   p o m e   ther ar spaces in it   yu can
   walk   slide thru   designs   meditating gardns if we wer
   all   onlee in   love with each othr   if passyun wer
   forevr if why   duz it onlee last mostlee coupul yeers
knocking us off th bed   pr prson   with so manee   is it poor
   designing   on th part uv who   watch thees   miraculs watch
   ths mayonais is it   vizual   well   th   politikul point
   therem is   blow it   put yr hands in it   touch it   wave it
   surround it   subtlee it dusint   evn gess   tho it
   knows evree   thing ping sing ring   carress it   follo
   its legs into   th being is with yu   th cuddling watrs
   so ooooozing   ao b o see   o   th cabins wer rising
   on th in th   was it   th rivr road   inkee n moist nite
     greeneree   in our hearts bare   studious wax   whistul
   salt rip hello   hello beeting th   drum heer   prison clown
   reminding us   so physikul ths life   is   being careful n

```
th  Radians    radians    radians    radians    radians   radIANS
rad radians    radians    radians    radians    radians   radians
rad RADIANS    RADIANS    RADIANS    RADIANS    RADIANS    RADIANS
sad RADIANS    RADIANS    RADIANS    RADIANS    RADIANS    RADIANS
tad RADIANS    RADIANS    RADIANS    RADIANS    RADIANS    RADIANS
gad RADIANS    RADIANS    RADIANS    RADIANS    RADIANS    RADIANS
nad RADIANS    RADIANS    RADIANS    RADIANS    RADIANS    RADIANS
kad RADIANS    RADIANS    RADIANS    RADIANS    RADIANS    RADIANS
lad RADIANS    RADIANS    RADIANS    RADIANS    RADIANS    RADIANS
mad RADIANS    RADIANS    RADIANS    RADIANS    RADIANS    RADIANS
wad RADIANS    RADIANS    RADIANS    RADIANS    RADIANS    RADIANS
pad RADIANS    RADIANS    RADIANS    RADIANS    RADIANS    RADIANS
vad RADIANS    RADIANS    RADIANS    RADIANS    RADIANS    RADIANS
yad RADIANS    RADIANS    RADIANS    RADIANS    RADIANS    RADIANS
zad
```

  ZAD itss e e p i n g   i n   can yu   f e e l   yr yeestee
ZAD zad zad taste   b u d s   still
                                 heers a nu toree govr ttt
programs   boy   wow
                        its dildos on legs thats d i l d o s on
  l e g s
           returnlng 2 th radians   ium soree a realitee intrluud
   ment   all along 1 2 b mor uprlifting or optimistik   yess yas
   ths is a konkreet pome notis th refrakshurs along th seem
     lines   help   help   n th starving hands in th grotto bottom
uv th cracks btween th sidewalk teers   can yu
                                             feel th radians
       can we start with th b r e e t h i n g   thats breth
   reth   rrrrrrrrrttttttttttttttttttthhhhhhhhhhhhhhh huuh ANAS
   ansa ansa ansa   ansa ANSA ansa ansa   ANSA

                                                          (1993)

th ordr uv things   wher is th ordr

duz th nu informaysyun technolojee re ordr nd re struktyur th human being
n th human condishyun   yes if we evolv byond binaree war games   what is
ordr dpends on our vishyun   our definishyuns   duz th nu technolojee in
capasitate neurologikul funcksyuns with th loss uv speech loss uv lang
wanga   loss uv memoree n loss uv identitee   NO   why wud it ackshulee
still a dualitsik construkt   it can altho inkrees memoree   inkress ident
itee   like tv howevr it can add bodilee fat in th midseksyun   so much
sitting   tho brain access   dot dot dot   most qwestyuns ar nevr eithr
or   they ar mostlee always both and   we sumtimes seek absolutes   in
thees n othr mattrs   2 assauge feers   that continualee reoccur   thru

contrast with inkredibul consuming contentment realizd alone or not
oftn enuff with sumwun els   or we wake up   see ourselvs in th mirror   we
look happee   what 2 dew   ths cant b okay   or can it   i think it is okay
n happeeness can leed us 2 b n help othrs with othrs   n with ourselvs
selvs   lava interruptus   john calld in saying   sew did aneewun els   who
calld   n th notes n th keys   ther is no ordr in things   ther is a temp
oraree deskriptiv capasitee   or yerning   or being   at ths time   at that
time   4 who   whos   whom   n changing   th ordr is always subjekt 2 change
n may b alredee in 2 changing   life is change   what is creatid is self
destroying   what is destroyd is self creating   ther is no ordr as wev bin
taut   ther is th possibilitee uv equalitee thru bettr managing n distribut
ing th food suppliez   ther is mor food thn peopul   ther is   that way not
2 manee peopul   tho lets chill on that til we can know how 2 get th food
around 2 evreewun   hopefulee compewtrs can help us distribute food bettr
without hierarkees n punishment   no wun need suffr 4 improoving   dot dot

th nu informaysyun technolojee in fact re map th human brain   that probablee
cannot b dun by sumthing we create ourselvs   chek mary shelleys frankenstein
or th mor resent   lawnmowr man with piers brosnan n jeff fahey   it dusint
surpass aneething mary shelley wrote   we nevr get 2 reelee veree well know
our creator or creators   prhaps a teem uv animators   prhaps god th in
finit enerjee   breething into us   n th scripts we dew not write we
follow   dna puppets with mor thn a dash uv free will   dew we have that
just cuz we think we mite   not enuff uv kours   sum complaind ther was
2 much free will   sum not enuff   uv kours nu vokabularee   always xciting
nu neurona awareness   nu stuff   great   RAGING STAR W   STRAW POLLS RE
JOINDRS 2 FAX MILLENIUM CAPTURING STRAW BERREEZ ESSENS IS THER A N POT
BELLEED TREETS UV SUGAR GLAZINGS   THER IS A   scientist who sz part uv
our brain is still reptilian n cannot evolv byond territorial man
ifestaysyuns n acting our 2 acheev contentment   innr pees agilee
volishyun combo   always know   in life etsetera   ahhhh   satisfacksyun
eeting th othr   othrs say its not ther   digesting   th reptilian fold in
th brain   or cud dissolv   or like th appendix   dot dot dot   let me re
turn 2 yr qwestyuns   we cant know ultimate ulteema   in th gardn was
weeping bittrlee by th jade tree she refeerd 2 as th tree uv knowing evn
its peech like blossoms n succulent fruit   ther is now i see she sighd
nothing 2 know   if we can b cum happee with unknowing   ther is now
i see she sighd nothing xcept we create it ourselvs   n its nevr singular
it endlesslee multiplying   we cant hold it   contain it   ourselvs opns
amazing possibiliteez   tho lessns our superioriteez   we can soar   n
elim   n un learn 2 keep up with evreething   we ar alredee up with   n
accepting accepting   yes yes   she cried   thats it   thats it   YES

(1995)

Patrick Lane (1939–)

In his memoir *There Is a Season* (2004), Patrick Lane describes how gardening helped him to recover from alcoholism, and how he began to form a relationship to his poetry. "For me," he says, "the art of the garden is to assist a natural order. ... Done well, a garden is a poem, and the old lesson of gardening is the same in poetry: what is *not* there is just as important as what is." For much of his career, Lane has been searching for things that are potent due to their absence.

Lane was born in 1939 in Nelson, British Columbia. The same year, his father left to serve in World War II. Paternal absence and maternal neglect during the war would become an obsession for Lane. After high school, he had a series of jobs — among them, fruit picker, logger, truck driver, boxcar loader, and sawmill clerk. He began to write poetry in his early 20s, but he would remain primarily a manual labourer until he reached his 40s, when he was finally able to earn a modest living as a poet and teacher. Lane married in 1958. In 1961, he wrote his first good poem, had it published in *Canadian Forum*, and "never looked back." "I disappeared inside words. I don't think my wife and family ever found me again. I knew what I had to do with my life."

His brother, poet Red Lane, encouraged him and drew him to Vancouver in the 1960s. There, in 1966, Lane published his first book with his own press, Very Stone House, which he had established with Seymour Mayne and bill bissett. It was called *Letters from a Savage Mind* (1966), and it was infused with his brother's influence and the popular mysticism of the 1960s. In 1964, Red Lane died of a cerebral hemorrhage at the age of 28. Four years later, tragedy struck again. Lane's father was killed while working in a shop when a man shot him at random through an open window. In *There Is a Season,* Lane speculates about what led the murderer to commit his crime and describes the damage it inflicted on his own life. His marriage disintegrated, and he was driven to attempt suicide. In retrospect, he believes he was "crazy," adding that "the only thing that kept me alive, was poetry."

Violence and loss would leave their imprint on everything he wrote. In the poem "Wild Horses" in *Separations* (1969), he expresses his torment over the guilt and detachment that characterized his relationship with his parents. The poet is part of a group of hunters who track and kill the horses, and he longs "Just to come once alone / to these wild horses"; the animals represent his past, which is rapidly receding, and which is tainted by his complicity in the killing.

In 1971, Lane published a manifesto entitled "To the Outlaw." In it, he promotes a poetics of sensual experience and discovery, one that allows the poet to be an outlaw and contravene the established order; he insists that there is no ultimate truth, no ultimate morality. He also argues against the intellectualism of poetry grounded in a modernist and academic tradition. Lane would later call the essay "a howl in the wilderness."

Lane remarried in 1972 and went to live in the Okanagan Valley. His collection *The Sun Has Begun to Eat the Mountain* was published in that year, and it contained most of his early poems. Many of these pieces expose the terrible cruelty and injustice wrought by poverty; some reveal a more subtle and personal aspect of the poet. In that busy year, Lane also managed to visit Peru, Ecuador, and Colombia. Two years later, he moved with his family to the fishing village of Pender Harbour, where he worked as a carpenter and building contractor and continued to operate Very Stone House, a project he would keep afloat until 1980. His South American journey had furnished him with material for another collection; *Beware the Months of Fire* was published in 1974. In this book, Lane's style displayed a new level of self-assurance, and he continued to develop his poetic voice in *Unborn Things: South American Poems* (1974) and *Albino Pheasants* (1977). The title poem of the latter volume evokes conflict between the sexes, a theme to which the poet would often return; Lane's women are "albino birds, pale sisters, succubi" (female demons who have sexual intercourse with sleeping men).

In 1978, Lane divorced his second wife and moved to Winnipeg to become writer-in-residence at the University of Manitoba. That year, he also published *Poems New & Selected*, which garnered a Governor General's Award, and he met poet Lorna Crozier, who would become his third wife after a long partnership. Early in their relationship, they co-authored *No Longer Two People* (1979). Its poems are linked by a set of images — ribs, scars, skirts, nests — and portray their creators as circling one another, each perceiving the other as hunter and lover.

After *The Measure* (1980), Lane published *Old Mother* (1982), inspired partly by his new life on the Canadian prairies and partly by a visit to China. Next came *Woman in the Dust* (1983), a selection of earlier poems accompanied by Lane's finely detailed pen-and-ink drawings — phantasmagorical, gruesome depictions, often of naked women in bondage, contorted, or in a state of decay. His drawings also appeared in *Separations* (1969), *The Sun Has Begun to Eat the Mountain* (1972), and *Unborn Things* (1975).

In 1985, Lane produced *A Linen Crow, A Caftan Magpie*, a book of meditative poems based on the Persian-Urdu ghazal and the Japanese haiku. The following year, he accepted a teaching position in English literature at the University of Saskatchewan, and there he remained until 1990. The 45 poems of *Winter* (1990) are reflections upon the brutal prairie cold. Escaping that cold, he and Crozier moved to Vancouver Island in 1991; Crozier had been offered a professorship at the University of Victoria, and Lane would teach creative writing at that institution from 1991 to 2004.

An important transition occurred in Lane's work with *Mortal Remains* (1991). For the first time, he used his poetry as a means to confront the despair that had assailed him during the 1960s. In "The Killer," he imagines he is the bullet that kills his father, ripping through the air and into his heart: "I have stayed, a small thing lodged there, / and felt the blood that made me / heave into silence." In the 1990s he also produced *How Do You Spell Beautiful and Other Stories* (1992) and *Too Spare, Too Fierce* (1995).

In 2004, after publishing his memoir *There Is a Season*, Lane produced *Go Leaving Strange*, the title poem of which builds on the poet's earlier examinations of death. He declares: "The door / is one way of knowing the world's gone wrong. / You let the hounds out and they go leaving strange." Through the open door, the poet watches the dogs as they pick up a scent on the air; he turns away when they "catch the spoor," blocking his ears to the sound of the beasts preparing to savage a weaker being.

In 2006, *Syllable of Stone* appeared, the first volume of Lane's poetry to be published in the United Kingdom. After producing more than 20 volumes of poetry over the course of a long career, one of Canada's pre-eminent poets was extending his voice to reach a new audience. In the poem "Winter 1" Lane meditates on transgression and forgiveness: "The thought of snow, / small white grains sifting / into the holes where his feet went, / filling things in, / leaving no room for despair."

Wild Horses

Just to come once alone
to these wild horses
driving out of the high Rockies
raw legs heaving the hip-high snow.
Just once alone. Never to see
the men and their trucks.

Just once alone. Nothing moves
as the stallion with five free mares
rush into the guns. All dead.

Their eyes glaze with frost.
Ice bleeds in their nostrils
as the cable hauls them in.

Later, after the swearing
and the stamping of feet
we ride down into Golden:

Quit bitchin.
It's a hard bloody life
and a long week
for three hundred bucks of meat.

That and the dull dead eyes
and the empty meadows.

10

20

(1969)

As It Is with Birds and Bulls

For Margaret Atwood

Having left their women in the dust
outside the sanctuary of the pit
the men, gambling on the blood-line
of birds, hunch with their cocks.
Legs plucked carefully and spiked with spurs
the roosters, born to killing,
beat the still air with wings
and tear at the gloves that bind them.

The sand is cleaned of blood.
Pit-masters rub pepper
under the arched green of tails.
The birds are thrown.

10

I gamble on the smaller bird
not because he is a coward
but because he seems afraid.
Survival lies in the death you make
believe. As it is with birds and bulls
so with men. They do not hate what they are
they hate what they cannot be.

The survivor crows and falls
blood splurting from his bill.
I collect my money
as the sun stumbles over the line of adobe.[1]

20

---

1. **adobe** Heavy clay used for brick-making.

The men sit inside and talk of birds.
The women sit outside and talk of men:
mouths full of coca leaf, they squat
beside gaping bags that receive the dead,
quick fingers tearing
the last feathers from the birds.

(1974)

Albino Pheasants

At the bottom of the field
where thistles throw their seeds
and poplars grow from cotton into trees
in a single season I stand among the weeds.
Fenceposts hold each other up with sagging wire.
Here no man walks except in wasted time.
Men circle me with cattle, cars and wheat.
Machines rot on my margins.
They say the land is wasted when it's wild
10   and offer plows and apple trees to tame
but in the fall when I have driven them away
with their guns and dogs and dreams
I walk alone. While those who'd kill
lie sleeping in soft beds
huddled against the bodies of their wives
I go with speargrass and hooked burrs
and wait upon the ice alone.

Delicate across the mesh of snow
I watch the pale birds come
20   with beaks the colour of discarded flesh.
White, their feathers are white,
as if they had been born in caves
and only now have risen to the earth
to watch with pink and darting eyes
the slowly moving shadows of the moon.
There is no way to tell men what we do ...
the dance they make in sleep
withholds its meaning from their dreams.
That which has been nursed in bone
30   rests easy upon frozen stone
and what is wild is lost behind closed eyes:
albino birds, pale sisters, succubi.[1]

(1977)

---

1. succubi Female demons that have sex with sleeping men.

Still Hunting

A single banner of sky between two mountains:
neither the beginning nor the end of clouds.
Somewhere all the animals have happened
and I wait and pray I will know
the difference between the animal and man;
pray for the gift of a death
to break this glacial waste of time —
that when I shoulder the empty body
I will have something to walk with
be it ice, air, stone or man; pray   10
I will find the road where I left it
in the tree-line far below.

                                                                   (1977)

There Is a Time

For Robert Kroetsch

There is a time when the world is hard,
the winters cold and a woman
sits before a door, watching through wood
for the arrival of a man. Perhaps a child is ill
and it is not winter after all. Perhaps
the dust settles in a child's breath,
a breath so fragile it barely exists.
Tuberculosis or pneumonia. Perhaps
these words place her there, these words
naming the disease and still not curing it.   10

Maybe it is not the man she waits for.
We want it to be someone. We want
someone to relieve this hour. On the next farm
the nearest woman to the woman is also sitting
in dust or cold and watching a door. She is no help.
So let it be the man. He is in the barn
watching the breathing of his horses.
They are slow and beautiful,
their breath almost freezing in perfect clouds.
Their harness hanging down from the stalls   20
gleams, although old and worn. He is old and worn.
The woman is waiting behind the door
but he is afraid to go there because of her eyes
and the child who is dying.

There is a time when it is like this,
when the hours are this cold, when the hours

are no longer than a bit of dust in an eye,
a frozen cloud of breath, a single splinter in a door
large enough to be a life it is so small and perfect.
30   Perhaps there are soldiers coming from far away,
their buttons dull with dust or bright with cold,
though we cannot imagine why they would come here,
or a storm rolling down from the north
like a millwheel into their lives.

Perhaps it is winter.
There is snow. Or it could be dust.
Maybe there is no child, no man, no woman
and the words we imagined have not been invented
to name the disease there is no child to catch.
40   Maybe the names were there in a time before them
and they have been forgotten. For now let them die
as we think of them and after they are dead
we will imagine them alive again,
the barn, the breath, the woman, the door.

(1982)

The Far Field

We drove for more than an hour, my father's hands
on the truck's wheel, taking us farther and farther
into the hills, both of us watching
the sagebrush and spare pines drift
past, both of us silent. He did not know
what to do with me. I think he thought of
my death, as a man will whose son has chosen
to destroy. I think that's why he drove
so long, afraid to stop for fear
10   of what he'd do. My mother had cried
when we left, her hands over her mouth,
saying through her splayed fingers
my father's name, speaking
that word as if it were a question. I
sat there peaceful with him,
knowing for these hours he was wholly mine.

He stripped me naked in the last hour of day
and made me stand with my back to him, my bare
feet in the dust, my back and buttocks to him,
20   a naked boy, hands braced upon the hood,
staring across the metal at the hills.

I remember the limb of the tree falling
upon me, the sound of the white wood crying

as it hurt the air, and the flesh of my body
rising to him as I fell to the ground and rose
only to fall again. I don't remember pain,
remember only what a body feels
when it is beaten, the way it resists
and fails, and the sound of my flesh.

I rose a last time, my father dropping   30
the last limb of the tree beside me.
I stood there in my bones wanting it not to be
over, wanting what had happened to continue, to go
on and on forever, my father's hands on me.

It was as if to be broken was love, as if
the beating was a kind of holding, a man
lifting a child in his huge hands and throwing him
high in the air, the child's wild laughter
as he fell a question spoken into both their lives,
the blood they shared pounding in their chests.   40

(1991)

Go Leaving Strange

You sit watching hounds go leaving strange,
their nails clicking swift the wooden floor
as they slide like narrow smoke away.
What's out there is anyone's child or beast.
They know. They have the smell on them.
You see it move in folds, the slack jowl
flutters pink and the tooth comes down
cutting stiff and ear upraised. The door
is one way of knowing the world's gone wrong.
You let the hounds out and they go leaving strange,   10
even the one you call Slip tracking quick
on the heels of his wretched dam without a sound.
When a hound goes quiet into the night
you wonder. Head down and the long ears
lifting scent into the nose, she leads, he follows,
the young ones coming last, the little one
jumping vertical to see what he can't smell.
Hounds run silent till they catch the spoor.
It's why you close the door
and when your woman asks what's wrong, say   20
nothing, the sky inventing clouds
where no clouds are, the light in the thin pines
turning pale and the hounds lost in their steady run.

(2004)

That Cold Blue Morning

Thin snow in the ruts and the men without work
rising from the ash and coals of the burner behind the mill,
the cleanup crews gone home and the long chains
no longer screaming. I wake in dreams and sweat, my mind still
shaped by a wailing woman on the sawmill road
as the trucks went by. Her song lives in me, her high thin crying,
and the girl-child in worn cotton pulling at the woman's dress,
the child's hand trembling, her mother gone mad again.
The woman's arms were raised into the river of wind
10   out of the north and her song rose on that wind
and was gone like the snow scoured from river ice.
The trucks went by and the men stared through starred glass,
ashamed as men were back then, the Coquihalla logs[1]
heavy in their chains. *Good God, go home,* the trucker with me said,
his eyes straight ahead. *Jesus Christ, Jesus Christ,*
and I said nothing to what was a curse as much as sorrow.
The stories in my head are made from mountains,
they are made from cold four o'clock winter mornings,
from thin coffee in a plastic thermos, from crying brakes
20   and broken ruts, and from the chains and groans
of the start-up early mill, that late fifties moan of just enough
wood, just enough shelter, just enough food to live another day.
That woman on the late dawn early road was some man's
daughter, some man's wife, and though I thought
I knew the thing that drove her onto the frozen ruts,
still it had no name. *Jesus Christ, Jesus Christ,*
but it does no good but for the crying out.
I come out of the Interior and there were no words back then
but for the names of the gods and those who cried them,
30   staring as they did through the broken glass and diesel smoke.
Back in those nights I struggled to make words
turn into poems, but I was young and it was no good.
It was hard to make things right. My wife huddled in our bed
and there were nights I know she too might have gone
into the road to sing her only song. There were dead butterflies
and blue stones, a gut-shot doe in a spring meadow, a headless dog
in a ditch, children picking their way through garbage at the dump,
and the cold winds, and the spring breakup, and the nights
alone with words. I don't know now what drove me into poems,
40   what dream I had or where I was to go. I have tried to make sense
of it and so made sense of nothing. There are men who think
the stories are not them, men who've spent their lives in books
and offices. I curse their luck tonight. Tonight I place that woman
on this page in the hope she'll give me rest.

---

1. **Coquihalla logs** Logs from the region near Coquihalla River or Summit, both in British Columbia.

She wants her mind clear in the morning.
And me?
I want the cup and the cold coffee. I want the last of night.
I want the truck's roar and the shapes of the shadow-men
rising out of the ash and the rush of wind that follows them
when the kerosene explodes under the falling bark and wood.
If I could, I'd end her song. That's what I want.
I want the song to end that shapes me still. These words
make no sense but I write them anyway that they be said:
Jesus Christ, Jesus Christ, but the snow still blows
and the ruts freeze hard and the burner's smoke still rises gray
into that cold blue morning I used to call the sky.

50

(2004)

Fred Wah (1939–)

Born in 1939 in Swift Current, Saskatchewan, to a mother born in Sweden and a father of Chinese-Scottish-Irish descent, Fred Wah has always been fascinated by issues of race and place and their relation to an understanding of the world based in language. His innovative and often semi-autobiographical work exemplifies a poetics based on theories of race, but it is also based on the musical quality of poetry written with a focus on the embodied breath.

In 1958, Wah enrolled at the University of British Columbia and majored in music. With Lionel Kearns and others, he played in a group called the Kampus Kings, forever conjoining his interests in jazz music and poetry: for Wah, the breath that passes through his trumpet is the breath that forms the poetic line. In the early 1960s, he and George Bowering and Frank Davey were part of the group that founded and edited the poetry magazine *TISH*, motivated by the influence of Black Mountain poets such as Charles Olson and by the conviction that West Coast poets were being ignored by the rest of Canada. Olson's concept of projective verse impressed upon Wah the idea that poetry could be the record of the body's breath, with its physical and experiential connection, its mutability, its unpredictability. Poetry could be proprioceptive — it could relate directly to the movement of the body. In *Breathin' My Name with a Sigh* (1981), Wah writes: "I take the breath / through the throat / and hold it / in the stomach / hit the fingers / of the horn / … blow the jazz / that's where it goes."

In the mid-1960s, Wah went to the University of New Mexico to study with Robert Creeley, another of the Black Mountain poets. He then transferred to the University of New York at Buffalo to work with Olson. Wah expanded his poetic career by publishing *Lardeau* (1965) and *Mountain* (1967) and by co-editing *Sum, Niagara Frontier Review, Magazine of Further Studies*, and Davey's *Open Letter*. In 1967, after earning his M.A., he returned to B.C. to teach at Selkirk College at Castlegar, and there he began to edit *Scree*. His reputation as an important poet and a leader of creative communities was established.

In the 1970s, a time of New Age philosophy and environmentalism, Wah lived in the forested mountains of Canada's West Coast with his wife, Pauline Butling, a critic and professor of Canadian literature. His interest in the geography of the place where he was raised intensified, and this is evident in *Tree* (1972). Reflecting on what he would later call the "word picture," he writes, "this is a hard language to work out / the images keep interrupting the talking / trees keep being pictures of themselves / my words keep meaning pictures / of words meaning tree." *Earth* (1974) and *Pictograms from the Interior of B.C.* (1975) continued in this vein and provided further material for the collection *Loki Is Buried at Smoky Creek: Selected Poems* (1980).

After establishing the creative writing program at the David Thompson University Centre in Nelson (1978–1984), Wah edited Daphne Marlatt's *Selected Writing: Net Work* (1980), and in 1984 he helped Davey create and operate *SwiftCurrent*, a database-driven literary magazine — the first online zine — which ceased publication in 1990. Meanwhile, he published the how-to book (how to *live*) *Owners Manual* (1981); then, in 1981, when *Breathin' My Name with a Sigh* appeared, it became a classic of the Canadian long poem genre. Beyond its musical conceit, the book (to a greater extent than subsequent ones) was an exploration of the sonic analogues of Wah's own name: the poet plays with "ahh" and "wuhh" and asks "ihh-zuh ihh-zuh / water / did you hear me / wa ter / wa ter / otter."

Wah published *Grasp the Sparrow's Tail* (1982) during his year as writer-in-residence at the University of Manitoba. Back at Selkirk College, in 1985, he produced *Waiting for Saskatchewan*, which won a Governor General's Award. Containing poems from *Breathin' My Name with a Sigh* and *Grasp the Sparrow's Tail*, the volume expands his experimentation with breath and sound to encompass ideas about meditation and concentration. With *Music at the Heart of Thinking* (1987), Wah's language became more musical and sonically intricate. The same year, with *Rooftops*, he continued to examine how thoughts, like improvised song, develop in unpredictable ways. The notion that language can express the musicality of cognition was now a central focus of his work, as was his multiracial identity. In 1989, he joined the faculty of the University of Calgary (remaining there until he retired, in 2003). His next three books — *Limestone Lakes Utaniki* (1989), *So Far* (1991), and *Alley Alley Home Free* (1992) — were constructed on the theme of racial hybridity. But it was with his first book of prose that hybridity became the lynchpin.

Diamond Grill (1996) is what Wah calls a "biotext" — a partly fictional memoir. It depicts the period in the early 1950s when his family owned and operated a Chinese-Canadian diner. "These are not true stories but, rather, poses or postures," he writes, explaining that to produce a range of stories, he had to "fake it" — invent history — often using humour to offset the bleak aspects of the immigrant experience.

After doing online mentoring for the Kootenay School of Art, Wah published *Faking It: Poetics and Hybridity* (2000), in which he laid out his theory of race and place in poetry. Like several of his other poetic and academic texts, *Faking It* emphasized that hybrid, hyphenated identities such as "Chinese-Canadian" signified agency rather than stasis, and that ethnic cultures should not be rigidly classified.

Two weeks after Hurricane Isadora devastated Mexico's Yucatán area in 2002, Wah travelled there on a cultural exchange designed to bridge the divide between geographies and between artistic genres. His counterpart was Mexican photographer Eric Jervaise (in the 1990s, Wah had undertaken several collaborations with visual artists). The experience led Wah to write the chapbook *Isadora Blue* (2005). Playing on the sound of the title, he writes "is a door wood / is a door nailed / is a door a board / is a door barred / is a door fixed." He ends, "is a door spoken." The answer to the Isadora question is "ah," like the "wah" rhymes in earlier books. The chapbook ends by asking "how to find the door / to stand in the way / just be there Mr. In-Between." Wah ingeniously implies that a hybridized understanding of cultural difference in the context of ecological disaster (like Isadora, when she "blew") would help to build productive bridges in the process of reconstructing devastated areas.

Waiting for saskatchewan

Waiting for saskatchewan
and the origins grandparents countries places converged
europe asia railroads carpenters nailed grain elevators

Swift Current my grandmother in her house
he built on the street
and him his cafes namely the "Elite" on Center
looked straight ahead Saskatchewan points to it
Erickson Wah Trimble houses train station tracks
arrowed into downtown fine clay dirt prairies wind waiting
for Saskatchewan to appear for me again over the edge
horses led to the huge sky the weight and colour of it
over the mountains as if the mass owed me such appearance
against the hard edge of it sits on my forehead
as the most political place I know these places these strips
laid beyond horizon for eyesight the city so I won't have to go
near it as origin town flatness appears later in my stomach why
why on earth would they land in such a place
mass of pleistocene
sediment plate wedge
arrow sky beak horizon still waiting for that
I want it back, wait in this snowblown winter night
for that latitude of itself its own largeness
my body to get complete
it still owes me, it does

10

20

(1981)

Elite 1

Swift Current Saskatchewan is at the centre. I don't think you were a boy there.
Probably what happened is your family moved there from Medicine Hat just before
you were four, just before you and Ethel were sent to China. I know all these "facts"
existed once, and I could check some of them out with Ethel, or your other sisters and
brothers, Buster, Lil, Flo, Jimmy. But, like the information on distant relatives I lost just
before going into China, somehow I don't want it or don't need it. The facts seem
partially unreal. Anyway, you must have seen Swift Current just before Grampa put you
on the train. About 1923. I was driving across the prairies on New Year's eve last year
and we decided to stop for the night in Swift Current. It was close to midnight and so we
thought we'd welcome in the New Year in a pub downtown. I hadn't been there for over
thirty years but I felt natural in following Central Ave. to the old train station. As soon
as I saw the station I knew exactly where I was. I stopped the car and pointed out to
Pauline the exact spot I stood when the war was over and I met you at the station when
you came home from training camp. From there the lay of the land was clear to me.
There was Roy's shoe shop and just up the street across from Woolworth's was the Elite
Cafe. You were always there, in the Elite, working. I remember the streets more on my
own. Not just the photographs, but me walking, alone in the town. Touching a building,
the flowerpots in Mother Trimble's windowsills, the cool shade under some outside stairway, etc. I never talked to you about these things, even when they weren't memories.
They weren't really important at the time. Your memory of such particulars. Mine. Does
it matter? The reason for the story is simply to count on it. What I remember or what
you or anyone else connected remembers isn't the point. There isn't even any point.
There is just this. You, before you had a car, on the street in an overcoat, winter, to

work. Always alone. I mean I see only your singularity, you with hands in your pockets, head down, going to work, with intention, in the cold winter dusk, to the Elite, your dad or Buster already has the big stainless coffee urn ready, what was it, twenty cups of ground in the cloth sack and, what, the first few customers, not farmers, you can't even speak English at first, silence, from China too, sweep the floors, maybe do some cooking in the kitchen where you can talk to the cooks, Grampa out front flipping coins, the whole family around you there in Swift Current, your new old family, by then silence and anger hum, alone.

Elite 2

Do you remember how living on the prairies was like living in water, in an ocean or a large lake. Movements, decisions, fortunes were made by undercurrent, a sense of sliding along a large floor, in the night. The night I was with you on a trip, just before we moved out to B.C., it felt like that, the way we moved, probably by train, through unknown territory. Always you had an "intent." You were on business of some sort and the others we met were all Chinese. You could talk to them. They gave me candy and pinched me. You and they talked and talked. Chinese always sounds so serious, emotional, angry. I napped on a couch in some Chinese store in some Alberta town. The old men played dominoes and smoked and drank tea. In the window dusty plants in porcelain bowls and some goldfish. Does it seem strange to you now to see this in words? Do you remember the trip I'm talking about? Late at night somewhere you played Mah Jong.[1] From outside the sound of the click-clack of the pieces being shuffled over the tabletop under the hum of the men's voices, a real music I felt comfortable with. Even though you stayed late you always came back, going somewhere. We moved that night through this subcontinent of prairie landscape, it was summer and the water was warm and hazy, the possible distances, distant.

Elite 3

I'm on the prairies this winter. I haven't been here in the winter since I was four years old. It's not Swift Current, or Speedy Creek as some here call it, but there are certain flavours which are unmistakeably part of us. The ethnicity here feels so direct. I mean the Chinese are still connected to China, the Ukrainians so Ukrainian, in the bar the Icelanders tell stories about Iceland, the Swede still has an accent, the French speak French. Here you're either a Wiebe or a Friesen, or not. What is a Metis, anyway? I know when you came back from China you must have felt more Chinese than anything else. But I remember you saying later that the Chinese didn't trust you and the English didn't trust you. You were a half-breed, Eurasian. I remember feeling the possibility of that word "Eurasian" for myself when I first read it in my own troubled adolescence. I don't think you ever felt the relief of that exotic identity though. In North America white is still the standard and you were never white enough. But you weren't pure enough for the Chinese either. You never knew the full comradeship of an ethnic community. So you felt single, outside, though you played the game as we all must. To be a mix here on the prairies is still noticed. I remember going into Macleods in Swift

---

1. **Mah Jong** Popular Chinese game played with tiles.

Current a few years ago and sensing that most of the women in the store were just like Granny Erickson. I don't think you felt there was anyone else in the world like you.

Elite 4

You got us involved in the Salvation Army because that's what Granny Wah wanted. She had a bonnet. I can't recall ever seeing Grampa or you there. But I bet she had her go at you too. Didn't you ever play the big bass drum, or the cymbals? I played the E-flat horn later in Nelson. I think, like Grampa, you always thought the Salvation Army people outside yourself. That was the Chinese in you. You didn't outwardly really trust it. But you tried it. In some totally pure and personal way you prayed, alone. I know later when our family went to the United Church in Nelson and you sometimes got off work on Sunday morning to go to church with us you did sing the hymns but your brow furled as if you couldn't understand the words. You were proud, then, of the fact you were going to church and you made a point of telling some of the customers in the restaurant that you had to go to church. That was after you had stopped desiring China and the Chinese at work put up with but laughed at you going to church. I think the church thing was white respectability and you did it for that and a sense of our family in that community. Somehow in the face of all the Salvation Army, Granny, community, etc. I know you established some real spiritual communication, totally private, no drums.

Elite 5

There is no picture (or is there) of me leaning over the boards of the Swift Current arena with you there, on the ice in your big overcoat, suit and tie, spiffy, smiling at the camera, and the whole Swift Current Indians (they weren't real "indians" — that was their name) hockey team working out, swirling big as life over the dark ice. There is a team picture I know. Like the Toronto Maple Leaf hockey calendars that used to hang in the barber shop, the team lined up on the real ice of the Gardens against the backboards. But in this one it's the Indians. I think you were the manager or something, you helped out. The brim of your hat is turned down, Chicago gangster style. The Indian on their sweaters is just like the Chicago Black Hawks. Strangely, Chicago figured in your life. You told us that you ran away from home when they brought you back from China and got work on a boat in the Great Lakes. You jumped ship in Chicago and they picked you up for illegal entry. You were sent back to Swift Current and that was the end of that. I wish you had given us more details. Chicago has always been a mysterious place for me and someday I'll get there myself. Anyway, isn't it strange how that city is there in our lives, on the periphery.

I've always been "proud" you were part of that team. The Swift Current Indians were my first hockey heroes and their movements over the ice instilled a sense of body and mind-set which I have carried with me all my life. Even though you never played hockey I know you had the invisible movement of the game inside you too. You said you played basketball on a winning team in China. But you liked hockey. There is no picture either of me and my first pair of skates, double-runners, with Mom (you were working), on a blustery day, natural ice, on a pond or creek. Or the skating rink you made for us in our back yard in Trail. Or the puck that caught me just above the eye, third row as you and I watched a game in the Civic Centre, blood and stitches. The game on television now, you'd fall asleep before the end of the first period. Did you ever ride a horse?

Elite 6

Line going deep into the lake or flung out onto the surface glaze river current, layers of darkness, invisible fish. You would look at me with serious brown eyes sometimes like I was crazy when I caught a fish and then give your own mad laugh. Something got to you fishing in the Columbia River at Trail, after work, along the rocks, swift-flowing mind emptying, maybe. Or in a creek at Meadow on a Sunday afternoon picnic, cousins and uncles, a ball game. At Apex you driving the road in the turquoise Ford looking for us fishing along the slow meandering of Cottonwood Creek. You without me at Trout Lake. Me without you below the C.P.R.[1] tracks below Granite Road on the way out of town or jigging for suckers near the boathouses with the old Chinaman. When I fish now sometimes I feel like I'm you, water, glassy gaze, vertical, invisible layers, the line, disappearing.

Elite 7

The dream "noises" of the early morning. You getting ready to go to work, still dark at 4:30, a light dust of snow maybe, the house warm, as you dress, the gabardine[1] pants, shoes I shined for you last night, muffled voices of goodbye, the small change in your pocket, car keys, your pace on the varnished maple floor, alone, quickens with movement towards the door, out, dark grey mist-hackle across the lake on Elephant Mountain, you and the town get going for the day, I hear the blue 2-door Pontiac hum alive down on the street, and you're gone to work, and then our own half-awake silence and relaxation back into the morning's warmth and sleep. Or me a couple times a year getting up for you, e.g. father's day, some Sunday morning, could you really sleep "in" thinking of me the kid making the big urn of coffee, turning the heat up, remembering to get the cream and a tray of butter out of the cooler, turn on the sign, the synchromesh[2] of everything starting to work, darkness breaking on Baker Street, first customers and the regulars early morning old man risers C.P.R. night shift and a few foremen and loners first coffee and cigarettes, the new noises of the day picking up speed and humming along the counter and booths to the whack of the kitchen door kicked on stride and the "smells" then.

(1985)

Elite 8

I try to "place" you and the hand or head can't, try to get you into my mountains for example but your China youth and the images of place for you before you were twenty are imbued with the green around Canton rice fields, humid Hong Kong[1] masses — I

---

1. **C.P.R.** Canadian Pacific Railway.

1. **gabardine** Loose, dense cloth, traditionally worn by labourers. 2. **synchromesh** Mechanism for shifting gears in a car smoothly.

1. **Canton, Hong Kong** Canton (or Guangdong) is a province on China's south coast; Hong Kong is a Chinese territory bordering on Guangdong Province in the north.

can't imagine what your image of the world was, where you were in it (were you always going home to Swift Current, were you ever at home, anywhere). How much did you share of how small or large the world was after we left the prairies — Trail, Nelson, Cranbrook, Calgary, Vancouver? That "reward" of a real holiday down the Columbia[2] and then up the coast to Vancouver when you sold a share in the Diamond Grill. A few trips to Spokane, hikes into the hills around Nelson for fishing, the gravelly drive to Trail and back. Did any shape of such places ever displace the distancing in your eyes? You looked out at it all but you never really cared if you were there or elsewhere. I think you were prepared to be anywhere. The sun, the warmth, was something you went outside for, outside yourself, stretching and relaxing your working moving body, inside, inside, you never betrayed any imprint of a "world" other than your dark brown eyes.

(1985)

Elite 9

When you returned from China via Victoria on Hong Kong Island and they put you in jail in Victoria on Vancouver Island because your birth certificate had been lost in the Medicine Hat City Hall fire and your parents couldn't prove you were born in Canada until they found your baptism records in the church or in the spring of 1948 when we moved to Nelson from Trail during the floods while Mao chased Chiang Kai-shek[1] from the mainland to offshore Taiwan and the Generalissimo's[2] picture hung in our house and on a wall above some plants and goldfish in the Chinese Nationalist League[3] house down on Lake Street or when you arrived in China in 1916 only four years old unable to speak Chinese and later in the roaring twenties when each time Grampa gambled away your boat passage so you didn't get back to Canada until 1930 languageless again with anger locked up in the immigration cells on Juan de Fuca Strait[4] or when your heart crashed so young at 54 as you fell from mom's arms to the dance floor did you see islands?

(1985)

Elite 10

Your father owned the Regal across from the railway station but you worked in the Elite on Central Avenue right next to the Venice and the Paris was the one on the corner all three across the street from Cooper's store where Connie worked in the dry goods department after school and then full time after graduation the year you took her to the final basketball game at Gull Lake and Mom says now you borrowed a car and drove to Moose Jaw[1] for a honeymoon and bought your first house in Swift Current in the fall of 1939 for $900 just after I was born and Connie's Dad fixed it up so you sold it and bought another, stucco (I remember that one) in '41 then moved to Trail in the spring of '43 and bought the Expert Cleaners and sold it to Andy's brother Sam and his wife

---

2. **Columbia** Columbia River, which runs through British Columbia and the northwestern United States.

1. **Mao, Chiang Kai-shek** Kai-shek was a Chinese provincial chairman who resisted Mao Zedong's revolutionary warfare; Mao drove him out of the country. 2. **Generalissimo's** Epithet for Mao; the supreme general. 3. **Chinese Nationalist League** Association for Chinese-Canadians based in British Columbia. 4. **Juan de Fuca Strait** The passage of water that separates Vancouver Island from Washington State.

1. **Gull Lake, Moose Jaw** Towns in Saskatchewan.

and bought a house there on a corner right across from the river near Butler ball park by the bridge and the next one where we had our first dog it was down closer to Sandy Beach where Granny and Grampa lived at the foot of Sandy Mountain and then Ernie's dog Mickey up in the house in the next block to the Dollar Cleaners all in East Trail while you and Grampa were in the Elite across the river downtown underneath the smelter hill and then in the spring of '48 floods when we moved to Nelson didn't you and Jimmy Gee Ethel's husband buy into the L.D. Cafe which you changed to the New Star just as Mao's victory north of the Yangze[2] became palpable and we lived in the duplex with the oil stove at 314 Carbonate before you got into your last restaurant (and mine) the Diamond Grill which even with the Standard down by Hipperson's Hardware times got good on Baker Street in the fifties and you got Grampa Erickson to build us our own house with maple floors at 724 Victoria you were so proud we had fireworks for the house warming and two sittings for the Chinese banquet in the basement and finally the Holmes Motel in Cranbrook in the early sixties where that was the end of the deals the cafes the houses the driving the building the running right through it, for you, that was it.

(1985)

Father/Mother Haibun[1] #4

Your pen wrote Chinese and your name in a smooth swoop with flourish and style, I can hardly read my own tight scrawl, could you write anything else, I know you could read, nose in the air and lick your finger to turn the large newspaper page pensively in the last seat of those half-circle arborite[2] counters in the Diamond Grill, your glass case bulging your shirt pocket with that expensive pen, always a favourite thing to handle the way you treated it like jewellery, actually it was a matched pen and pencil set, Shaeffer maybe (something to do with Calgary here), heavy, silver, black, gold nib, the precision I wanted also in things, that time I conned you into paying for a fountain pen I had my eye on in Benwell's stationery store four dollars and twenty cents Mom was mad but you understood such desires in your cheeks relaxed when you worked signing checks and doing the books in the back room of the cafe late at night or how the pen worked perfectly with your quick body as you'd flourish off a check during a busy noon-hour rush the sun and noise of the town and the cafe flashing.

High muck-a-muck's gold-toothed clicks ink mark red green on lottery blotting paper, 8-spot (click, click)

(1985)

Famous Chinese Restaurant is the name of a

small, strip-mall Chinese cafe a friend of mine eats at once in awhile. We laugh at the innocent pretentiousness of the name, Famous.

---

2. **Mao's victory ... Yangze** The defeat of Chiang Kai-shek, a provincial chairman who resisted Mao's communist revolution.

1. **Haibun** A travelogue consisting of prose and haiku. 2. **arborite** A synthetic plastic.

But then I think of the pride with which my father names the Diamond Grill. For him, the name is neither innocent nor pretentious. The Diamond, he proudly regales the banquet at the grand opening, is the most modern, up-to-date restaurant in the interior of B.C. The angled design of the booths matches the angles of a diamond and the diamond itself stands for good luck. We hope this new restaurant will bring good luck for all our families and for this town. Eat! Drink! Have a good time!

Almost everything in Chinese stands for good luck, it seems. You're not supposed to use words that might bring bad luck. Aunty Ethel is very upset when we choose a white casket for my father's funeral. She says, that no good! White mean death, bad luck!

So I understand something of the dynamics of naming and desire when I think of the names of some Chinese cafes in my family's history. The big one, of course, is the Elite, which we, with no disrespect for the Queen's English, always pronounce the eee-light. In fact, everyone in town pronounces it that way. My dad works in an Elite in Swift Current and that's what he names his cafe in Trail when we move out to B.C. Elite is a fairly common Chinese cafe name in the early fifties, but not any more. I see one still on Edmonton Trail in Calgary and I know of one in Revelstoke. I like the resonant undertone in the word *élite*: the privilege to choose. In the face of being denied the right to vote up until 1949, I smile a little at the recognition by the Chinese that choice is, indeed, a privilege.

Other names also play on the margins of fantasy and longing.

(1996)

The Christmas before he dies he comes to

Buffalo. We're graduate students there and I drive to Toronto to pick up him and Mom and Glenda, my little sister, from their cross-Canada train trip. A friend of mine has snapped a few tickets to a Leafs' game in the Gardens;[1] he's excited by that. I take them to see Niagara Falls, but our car has no heater and it's about 15 below. He's intrigued by all the black people in Buffalo. We play cards a lot — hearts — and he really gets into it. But one night the game blows up because he misunderstands one of the rules. We all side against him and his ire rises. At times like that he's alone. You can see he knows he's wrong but defends himself in the face of it anyway. This playing with anger, with a double edge there, almost arithmetic, in that attractive way, some armature[2] of tempta- tion at work that urges on bravado[3] and resistance — dead set.

(1996)

After our family moves out to British Columbia

in 1943, my grandmother on my Chinese side, the Scots-Irish one from Ontario, periodically takes several of us cousins back to the prairies for summer holidays. We stay with a variety of relatives still living in Swift Current. After a couple of weeks, always sooner than we expect, she puts us on the train and takes us back to Trail and Nelson complaining that she knows when and where she isn't wanted. Her stew, as they say, has been stirred. She just sits in her train seat and looks grim and pouty. She has a large lower lip, as many of us after her have, and this exaggerates her smouldering. I

---

1. **Leafs' game in the Gardens** The Toronto Maple Leafs formerly played at the Maple Leaf Gardens arena.
2. **armature** Supportive, skeletal framework. **3. bravado** A false show of bravery.

hope my daughters, who also have full lower lips, don't have to carry her kind of ire.
They need to let their gorges rise; we all do, need to channel our granny's grammar.
 Cook your silence, but don't let it simmer.

(1996)

Clark Blaise (1940–)

In "Chronology of Salience," Clark Blaise highlights the formative events of his life. He was born in
Fargo, North Dakota. His father, Leo Romeo Pierre Blaise, was originally from Quebec. His mother,
Anne Vanstone, was from the Canadian prairies. From an early age, Blaise felt pulled in two
directions. Leo was a furniture salesman for Sears, rising through the ranks until the war inter-
vened and, in pursuit of a decent living, he was forced to become an itinerant. The family moved
through a succession of towns and cities, mainly in Florida at first, but then the circle widened.
Blaise grew up in Atlanta, Fort Lauderdale, New York, Springfield, Cincinnati, and Pittsburgh,
where he attended high school. His interest in literature took him to Denison University in Ohio,
where he majored in English and began to write. The psychic scars of all that early dislocation
would engender a body of fiction preoccupied with the outsider who must try to make sense of
new experiences, who is obsessed with his past and his family, and who is compelled to apply his
eccentric intelligence to the world around him, translating his alienation and loneliness into
powerful metaphors of the human condition.

 Blaise published his first story in 1962. The following year, he married Calcutta-born writer
Bharati Mukherjee. By 1966, they had settled in Montreal, and Blaise was teaching at Sir George
Williams University (now Concordia). He was also writing the stories of *A North American
Education* (1973) and *Tribal Justice* (1974) as well as performing his work throughout the city
as a member of the Montreal Storytellers group. In 1977, he and Mukherjee collaborated on *Days
and Nights in Calcutta,* each writing half the account of their voyage to India, Mukherjee's
homeland. They would collaborate once more to produce *The Sorrow and the Terror: The Haunting
Legacy of the Air India Tragedy* (1987), a work of investigative journalism about the 1985 terrorist
bombing of Air India flight 182. In it, Blaise and Mukherjee suggest that through its reluctance to
investigate the crime, the government of Canada betrayed its fundamental racism — the majority
of the victims were of Indian origin, and despite the fact that most were Canadian citizens, the
government viewed them as foreign. Blaise has called the book "our proudest accomplishment, as
writers and especially as citizen-writers."

 In 1978, Blaise and Mukherjee left Montreal for Toronto, where Blaise had accepted a position
as professor of humanities at York University. The move was prompted by their desire to get away
from what they perceived to be Montreal's racial intolerance, but they found Toronto no better,
and in 1980 they moved to Saratoga Springs, New York. There, Blaise taught creative writing at
Skidmore College. He resigned from Skidmore in 1984 and then took a series of teaching and
administrative posts, including director of the International Writing Centre at the University of Iowa.

 The stories Blaise wrote during his time in Montreal remain some of the most finely crafted in
Canadian fiction. *A North American Education* and *Tribal Justice* are about displacement, alienation, memory, and the ways in which identity is constructed by people who are haunted by their
pasts. Blaise's protagonists are often children or adolescents, and so they function as voyeurs in
an adult world, recording the often questionable behaviour of adults with an ironic detachment
and intensity of focus. The stories are distinguished by their literary self-consciousness — each
narrative voice displays its preoccupation with the role and the origins of the writer. In these tales,
Blaise develops an intricate set of symbols and metaphors; he revels in his narrative complicity as
he fashions his self-perpetuating, self-reflexive, autobiographical art.

Blaise's first novel, *Lunar Attractions* (1979), is a dark coming-of-age story centred on inheritance, paternity, and sexual identity. Narrator David Greenwood realizes that he is attracted to the "lunar," or dark side of the world he inhabits and is drawn into an exploration of the lunar aspect of his own personality. For him, writing becomes a way of solving the mysteries with which his life is riddled. In his second novel, *Lusts* (1983), Blaise experiments with the confessional mode. His main character, Richard Durgin, is in an agony of guilt over his wife, famous Jewish poet Rachel Isaacs. When he makes a joke about the Holocaust and Rachel kills herself, Richard is plunged into a depression and can no longer write. Many years later, he volunteers to help biographer Rosie Chang research Rachel's life and work; corresponding with Rosie, he finds his way back to writing. The story is told through Richard's memoirs and the letters he exchanges with Rosie. Combining epistolary and confessional modes, Blaise finds new ways of exploring self-reflexivity in his fiction.

In *Resident Alien* (1986), Blaise's self-reflexivity reaches new heights: he book-ends four short stories with two essays on his own work. Juxtaposing essays and stories, Blaise sets up an implicit dialogue between forms that reinforces his questioning of authorship. His character Phil Porter in the story "Identity" uses authorship to retrieve the identity that he has repressed, and authorship becomes a way of healing. In this collection, Blaise also poses a series of questions that could be applied to all of his fiction: "Where does the impulse come from, and why does the voice and shape and subject matter after twenty years remain the same? Why the first-person narrator, why the child and adolescent character, why the adult looking back? Why the relative silence on marriage and fatherhood, the scarcity of relationships, the elevation of the private and psychological over the social and political? Why am I wedded like a reborn Wordsworth to the epic of my own becoming, the origins of a calling, the hints of a talent? Why are most of my narrators themselves writers?"

Although his style — however confidently self-reflexive it may be — is not generally considered postmodern, Blaise nevertheless realizes that his obsession with writing about writing is metafictional, and thus his work has an element of postmodernism. His 1993 book *I Had a Father: A Post-Modernist Autobiography* equates two traditionally separate genres. As Blaise explains, "Fiction and autobiography, like science, are based on observable responses to unknown forces."

Blaise's most recent extended fiction is a novella. *If I Were Me* (1997) follows Brooklyn psychologist Gerald Lander in his search for his estranged children in Poland and Japan. By deciphering the words of his mother, who has Alzheimer's disease, Gerald develops a theory of language that brings him international celebrity. Self-creation through language, dislocation, and alienation remain firmly part of Blaise's oeuvre, even though Gerald is not as explicitly autobiographical as his other characters.

Since 1992, Blaise has been writing fiction and organizing his stories into thematic collections. All the pieces in *Man and His World* (1992) reappear along with many others in his geographically themed series *Southern Stories* (2000), *Pittsburgh Stories* (2001), *Montreal Stories* (2003), and *World Body* (2006). He has also published *Time Lord: The Remarkable Canadian Who Missed His Train* (2001), a non-fictional account of Sanford Fleming, the Scottish-Canadian engineer who developed a way to synchronize global schedules. Blaise and Mukherjee live in San Francisco.

Identity

Porter, Reg and Hennie. My parents for several years. Mysteries to me, to each other. Gone now, even in name.

My earliest memory is of falling off an armchair when I was three and breaking my arm. A bad break, poorly mended. Even now the extended arm, with the elbow resting, barely grazes the tabletop. For the wrist and hand to conspire with gravity is an act of will. Think of the forearm as I do, a slow hypotenuse connecting that original fracture to a slightly skewed grand disclosure. Needless to say, I'm still waiting for it.

I'd been watching my father reading and writing in a Queen Anne chair. For years that memory stood as evidence that we'd been a normal, happy family. Father reading, son at his side, a little spill, nothing too serious. Despite the small imperfection it left me, it is a pleasant memory. It occurred to me since, however, that we never owned Queen Anne furniture, especially not in 1943, and that I cannot remember my father ever reading or writing. When I was thirteen and having to learn to read and write all over again, I discovered something else I'd always suspected: my father couldn't read or write at all.

That same year, 1943, I remember sitting on my tricycle at the top of a steep hill. This part of the memory is a moment, even now, of rather intense pleasure. And then I flung my legs out straight and rode like the breeze to the bottom of the little hill. Unfortunately, the hill was our driveway and the bottom of it was our garage door, and the door was down. From that episode, I received a bent nose, a broken collarbone and a skull fracture. After the fracture I became an epileptic. It was bad as a child, not so severe now. From internal evidence, you will conclude that I'm writing this as a man of forty-three.

Such are the sheltering memories of childhood. Or the preferred fictions of adulthood. I once overhead my mother, talking to a friend long after I'd grown up, relate a more intriguing version of those same injuries. There'd never been a chair or a tricycle and garage door. There'd only been New Year's Eve, 1943, and a scrounged-up babysitter recommended by someone down at Sears, where my father worked. And she had a soldier husband who'd wangled a holiday pass, only to find her apartment empty. He saw our address on a piece of paper. He confronted her there, in our second-floor apartment on Reading Road, stabbed her and shot her visiting boyfriend, and then went to work on me, his only witness. So I was killed, at least to his satisfaction. I have never, consciously, been able to replay a single frame of that incident. So much for the theories of Freud or the plots of Ross Macdonald.[1] I think of the armchair and the tricycle constantly.

Let more bones break, more moves be made. Those early memories are from Cincinnati — a freak appearance in our lives, a town that did not claim us — from deep in America, a country, as it turned out, that did not claim me either.

Turned out, not in the passive sense of a plot that runs its course, but in the active sense of total reversal, like a pocket being turned out, like deadbeats being turned out of a bar. There are millions like me on this continent (I know, I meet them everywhere) who constitute no bloc, and who, for all their numbers, have no champion. The implications radiate like angles from a protractor, like tracks from a roundhouse, though I'm unable to pursue them all. Think rather of Reg and Hennie Porter and me, lying just a degree or two off plumb, or the prime horizontal axis. Think of life led slightly off balance.

In Pittsburgh in 1952 I was standing on the roof of an apartment building, with matches, a knife and rabbit ears under opaque plastic. With matches I burned off an inch or so, stripped it with the knife, then spliced the copper onto the frail set of rabbit ears that had come with our first television set. Then I lashed the whole contraption to

---

1. **Ross Macdonald** Author of hardboiled detective stories that often turned on characters' family secrets (1915–1983).

the giant brick apartment-house chimney and crawled to the edge of the roof and called down, "How about it now?"

Staring down six floors to our opened window on the second floor was the closest thing I knew to an epileptic aura. The sidewalk yo-yoed, close enough to step out on.

Peter Humphries, my only friend, was in our apartment. He was from the third floor. My parents both worked, so did his mother. His father did not seem to exist, even in memory.

He shouted up, "It's just a test pattern!"

He couldn't know that that was the whole point. I'd succeeded. It meant to me — though it was only channel 9 in Steubenville, Ohio, or 7 in Wheeling, West Virginia — that features were materializing from outer space. New test patterns, new readers of local news, new advertisers, new street names, different phrasing of the same Tri-State weather, different politics: the mark of sophistication was access to all the channels. I'd exhausted KDKA, and the only NBC outlet before we got our own WIIC on channel 11 was channel 6 in Johnstown. Farther out in the mountains there was rumoured to be a channel 10 in Altoona and a channel 3 downriver in Huntington, West Virginia. Pittsburgh, in other words, was an exciting place, if you had the right connections. Pittsburgh eventually got more than enough channels, but not in 1952. We were always deprived, last in everything, at least in the years I lived there. But with ingenuity and agility and rabbit ears lashed to a chimney, hope existed for more than snow on channels 2, 3, 6, 7, 9 and 13, which was educational. On exceptional nights with my antenna pointing in the right direction I'd gotten Cleveland, and Chambersburg, almost in Maryland. A collector with luck could get a picture, however furry, and enough voice to make a positive identification, on every VHF channel, and he could pull in signals from four states, not counting freaks, which once, with the help of clouds, sunspots and a low-flying airplane, brought in Detroit and Buffalo.

The point is, I was king of the airwaves. I might not have known much about my parents or myself, or about Peter Humphries for that matter, but those questions never arose. I knew the important things, like call letters and the names of news readers and where to shop for Mercurys and Fords in Steubenville. It was the essence of my new-found teenagerliness to know everything about strangers and occult signals materializing from snow, and to know nothing at all about the forces that had made me, the scars and handicaps that were about to reclaim me.

All of this happened nearly thirty year ago. I haven't seen Pittsburgh in a quarter of a century, and probably all those familiar faces have scattered or died, although I still catch KDKA on the car radio, deep in the night. The magic is gone, but I'll stick with it till it fades completely to hear again those little neighbouring town names: Belle Vernon, Castle Shannon, Blawnox, Sewickley — names that were ushering in life to me, holding promises of jobs and adventure. Those were all threshold names, places I couldn't have located on an Allegheny County map, but that nevertheless were part of my private empire, my homeland, the back of my hand, whose borders were marked by the snowy extremities of Wheeling, Altoona, Chambersburg and Cleveland.

Peter Humphries is about to leave this story, but not before he leaves his mark, freshly, on me again. His mother was divorced — *divorcée* was one of those words, probably the only one, that a 1952 Pittsburgh kid pronounced in a self-consciously French way, to imbue it with its full freight of accompanying *negligées* and *lingerie* and *brassières* and of other things that came off in the night and suggested a rich inner life — she had dates, and Peter often slept over with us on nights when she planned to stay away. Or didn't plan, but stayed away anyway. As a cocktail waitress, then hostess, she didn't come home till three or four in the morning anyway, then slept till noon.

He might have been the gateway to my adolescence, but as it turned out — that phrase again — he was merely the last of my childhood friends. In a life of sharp and inexplicable and unmendable breaks, I have a special feeling for these friends of a special time and place. They seem to me, all of them, including my parents, prisoners of peculiar moments, waving at me from ice floes as dark waters widen between us. I remember all of them sharply, for they never were given a chance to grow out and modify; they were forever the last way I saw them, just as Pittsburgh is, which is to say they are essences of themselves and of my own poor reception of them. Even so, they give a surer sense of my own continuity than anything I can conjure in myself.

Peter was predictably avid for sex. He was riveted on the female body, every part of it, in ways that only a deeply troubled boy can be: hating it, fearing it, desiring it. He found my ignorance of it and my indifference to learning about it from him something of an affront. It marked me as being just a kid, which I was.

Being with Peter, the only friend I had, was like standing at the tip of an enormous funnel; all the sexual knowledge available to pubescent, provincial Americans in 1952 was swirling past me, and not a precious drop was wasted, not with Peter and his mother nearby. I wasn't in their apartment that often — they had the cheaper, one-bedroom model — but every time I entered it I was struck by the fumes of something lurid. Peter's mother wasn't much older than thirty, her hair was black and ringleted, her body lean and firm, her habits and language loose and leering. She'd strung clotheslines across the living-room, and her entire stock of lingerie and negligees was usually on display. Her job demanded a lot of buttressing and tressing, as well as display and ornamentation. The apartment was always dark, always a den, in deference to her strange professional hours. I'd never seen so many bottles and lotions; things to drink, to spray, to paint, to rub in, to rub off; it shocked me, the absence of normal food, the exclusion of anything not related to her body, skin and hair. The sofa was draped in suggestive dresses still in dry-cleaner's plastic, and the kitchen had hosiery soaking in the sink and a slab of meat defrosting on the counter. Peter slept in the dining room, on a foldaway cot that he had to dispose of in a closet every morning. They had a large television set, a "deal" she'd gotten from a motel close-out, but it didn't work.

What I responded to, of course, was the implicit savagery of that mother-son situation. She had nothing of the mother in her. She was a cruel woman who got by on lies about her youth, supported by candlelight and booze. A thirteen-year-old at home — who, as luck would have it, looked much older, with a jockey-like ropy body and tight, lined face of a child who wouldn't be growing much taller or broader — was the last thing in the world she would acknowledge as her own. They treated each other like husband and wife; he drank with her, gave her massages and sometimes crawled into bed with her.

There wasn't a time I visited when his mother was up and moving that I didn't leave that apartment without something shocking to me, some hunk of flesh observed or knowledge that would stimulate me like a laboratory rat in an uncontrolled experiment. She would excite a centre of consciousness, but leave me without completion or comprehension. A moment caught in the kitchen, with Mrs Humphries talking casually of "ragging it" and needing some peace and quiet; of a man's voice muffled by the door to her bedroom shouting out, "Hey, what the — ?"

The most frightening moment didn't concern her at all. It was with Peter alone. "Hey, want to see something? Look in here." And before I could stop him, he was into his mother's clothes, underwear first, then the dresses and finally the make-up, all very professionally applied. We avoided each other for a few weeks after that. He'd let something drop.

My mother called her "the slut." Peter called her "her" and "she." To have been the son of such a woman, to have absorbed the full blast without any shield (even grown men could take her only one night at a time) was a formula for disaster more potent than even my own. I envied him the nakedness of things in his life. His mother was to me, thanks to the luxury of deflection, like a pair of 3-D glasses on the world; things I couldn't have noticed in my mother or in my secretive parents stood in sharp relief thanks to her. And thanks to Peter, on those nights he'd shared my bed, I learned how women were built, what Kotexes were for, where "it" went and how it got there. Thanks to Peter, I became a statistically normal American pre-teen, as judged by the Kinsey Foundation.[2]

In most areas of development, I was keeping pace. Peter was the sexual guide, his mother the sexual quarry and my parents, the ultimately mysterious Reg and Hennie, were receding nicely from me as peers took over. A career based on my odd little passion for resolving distant images, for pulling in signals, was suggesting itself. It would be consistent with all this data to say that I grew up to become an astronomer, monitoring deep-dish radio telescope on a thin-aired mountaintop far from the murk of Pittsburgh. But even as children we are scouts; more daring and treacherous than the troops we lead, than the adults we become.

I have spoken of all the things I knew in 1952. What I didn't know was about to kill me. I died in 1952, not from my epilepsy or a fall from a sixth floor or an electric jolt or anything else from that world of Pittsburgh or Peter Humphries. These fragments stand out to me now, against a black background, and that seems to be the nature of childhood as it bleeds into adolescence: that we see faces without the lies and sympathies of self-protection, we can live events without antecedent or consequence. They appear tantalizingly sharp, but in a veil of snow and static: we can make them out, but then they fade and are no more.

My parents: Reg and Hennie Porter. My name is Philip. Phil Porter. Reg was working in a department store called Rosenbaum's in downtown Pittsburgh. It's been gone a quarter of a century now, so I'll not disguise any of these names. Names are treacherous anyway.

Reg was a good-looking man, about fifty, with dense white chest hair and forearms thick as Popeye's, hairy and with "Amor Vincit"[3] tattooed on one in a thin, unfurled banner under a starlet's face, neck and bare shoulders down to what promised to be an indecent cleavage. He'd been married twice before, so far as I knew, and I'd found that out only when I overheard it. It didn't seem safe to ask if he had other children, though they'd hardly be kids. He might have married at twenty or less, so conceivably there were other Porters around, somewhere in New England, where he came from. He usually had the accent to prove it. But those kids could be thirty. My parents had been married eighteen years — I knew that from their number of anniversaries. I loved every aspect of that man.

If I could stop time, or stop narration, I would linger on the lean, graceful, grey-haired buxom[4] figure of my mother (as she suddenly stands out to me) in the late

---

2. **Kinsey Foundation** An organization that did groundbreaking studies of human sexuality in the 1940s and 1950s. 3. **Amor Vincit** Latin for "Love conquers." 4. **buxom** Full-bosomed.

summer of 1952. She was a woman softened by the grey in her hair, made younger by it (I don't remember her dark-haired, but I suspect she had looked almost masculine, the kind of young woman who must have a very handsome brother somewhere; a face that seems to find its resolution in the opposite sex). She hadn't married till thirty-two. Grey hair had finally focused her face, the way a beard might define an otherwise unspectacular set of features.

I've said enough. You will know already that the story is beginning to turn inside out. I had Oedipal longings — still do, doubtless, since I've never consciously considered them or worked them out — and my hours of staring into snowy screens, rejoicing with any faint signal, offers to me now a portrait of sublimation. There is sexual energy sparking over the gaps. And all my attempts at refining the images are doomed because the interference is built in: in my brain where blood vessels and nerve endings just don't quite reach, where some blunt or sharp object — in my case, a shard of bone — sliced through. And of the other connections to family and to place and even to language, I cannot speak at all. Those were things out on the street, outside of me entirely, about to knock on our door.

All right. People wonder what it's like to die, and since I've done it several hundred little-bad times and a few great convulsive big-bad times, and have died in other ways, too, I'll start small and build.

Dying is like this. You are twelve, coming back to the apartment after school. Picture it September, those scratchy days when the heat is up and school's not serious yet and the summer pursuits are still operative. I came home with a cherry sno-cone, about four o'clock. The front door was half open. Inside were half-packed boxes, all over the place, where selections of our things had been thrown in. My mother dashed from the kitchen to another opened box, a stack of china against her bosom, and eased them into the box and scrunched some pages of the *Post-Gazette* around them. She was a careful packer, and this was not careful packing. And because of my unexpected entrance, my shocked silence, her concentration, she did not see me. I caught her in expressions I'd never seen before; she was smaller, younger, sexier than she'd ever appeared before, all the more so for her obvious distress, or distraction, or anger — whatever indefinable thing it was. We'd moved many times before, and usually under bad conditions — to towns we didn't know and where we had no address. Those moves were chance things: pack up the car, flee a city and travel to a place where a job might be waiting. Then find an apartment after a few days in a squalid hotel, unpack, put the boy in school. We'd sometimes moved when rent was due; my father was so calm about it he could meet a landlord at the door, listen politely to his demand, reach in his pocket for the chequebook, saying all the time, "Sure, sure," and then slap his forehead, "God, forgot it!"

"That's okay, what about tomorrow?" the landlord would say.

"Right you are," my father would say, "first thing in the morning." And two hours later we'd be at the outskirts of town, heading deeper into America.

My death was standing at the open door of my apartment, seeing my mother run from the kitchen clutching a stack of plates against her blouse and dropping them into a box, and thinking:

1. We're moving.
2. We're skipping.
3. Something terrible is happening.

4. Christ, my mother is a *sexy* woman.
a) On reflection, this last insight is tempered by the further insight that nearly any woman, when viewed unannounced, in the privacy of her living-room, is sexy. That is, the act of observing is sexy.
b) She legitimately was sexy. Her hair was up, but falling down, the grey and the black, and she was in slacks and one of my father's shirts, and she was looking good.
c) Sexiness, if I am now to lift it from any immediate context or application to any particular woman, is (for me) an appearance that borders on slovenliness. Sex will never embrace me in tennis shorts, in a bikini, or in any fetishistic combination of high heels and low neckline. Sex is the look that says, "Help me out of these clothes," or shows that things she's wearing are a constriction, not an attraction.

On that late summer day in 1952, standing quietly and excitedly in the door of our apartment that was soon not to be our apartment, I had a seizure. When I woke up a few minutes later, my mother was holding the wooden spoon she used to keep me from biting my own tongue (what abuse that spoon had taken, over the years!). My mind was absolutely clean: I woke up remembering only that I knew something about my mother. And I knew something else: that this move was different from the others. In this one, the furniture was staying, but papers I'd never seen before were littering the floor. Papers in old leather folders with the crushed ribbons of official documents that had not been untied in a generation. When I could walk, she helped me back to the bedroom. She indicated that I should fall over my parents' double bed, but I ritually opened my own bedroom door.

Sitting on my bed was my father. I saw him in bright colour, the way only an epileptic can see the world, after an attack. I saw every pore, every hair, intensely sharp. I would not have recognized him on the street. He was crying, and it looked to me that he had been crying for hours and that he had nothing left to cry with. His shirt buttons were torn open, but his tie was still knotted, red silk over chest hair. His sleeves were rolled back, those massive arms lay helpless at his side and the cuff links were still stuck in the cuffs, and I worried that they'd fall out. My mother pushed me hard, out of my room and into theirs, and I was still groggy two hours later when she put two suitcases in my hands and told me to march quickly and quietly to the car, which was parked in the alley.

We headed north towards Buffalo and slipped through the middle of New York State all night long. He knew where he was going, though he didn't tell me. Around two o'clock in the morning he pulled into a large motel between Syracuse and Utica, waking me again, almost shaking me to make sure I was awake.

"Philip," he said, all the time shaking me. "Philip, until I tell you it's okay to talk, I don't want you to say a word. Not one word. Not even if someone talks to you, understand?"

"Even if things seem wrong," my mother said. "Even if you don't understand a thing."

At three in the morning my father and I went prowling through the parking lot of that large motel while my mother slept in the car. I was scouting for a licence plate and a dollar bounty offered by my father. Finally I found one, on a black, pre-war Ford. My father stripped it of its plate — like Pennsylvania, they had only a rear plate — and put it on our car. Our plate was creased until it snapped, then buried. At five o'clock we were on the road again, over the Adirondacks, with my mother driving. They were talking now of "the border," and the motels were flying two sets of flags, the American and the red British one, and ads were appearing for duty-free items. When the customs houses were in view, she pulled off to the side. My father took over. "Tell him," he told my mother and she turned around to face me.

"In a minute we'll be going to Canada. Canada is where your father and I come from." She flashed some of those documents in front of me. "We're going to Montreal. We have relatives in Montreal."

I still had not spoken, could not speak.

"Our name will change when we go over the border. Forget all you ever knew about Porter. Our real name is Carry-A. Like this — see?" She showed me a plastic-coated green-framed card with an old picture of my father on it. I couldn't pronounce the name, but the letters bit into my brain. Réjean Carrier.

"What's my name?" I asked.

"I thought I told you to shut up," said my father.

There were two cars in front of us. My father found a radio station playing strange music in a foreign language.

"You can be anything you want to be," said my mother.

(1986)

Sharon Butala (1940–)

Sharon Butala was born in 1940 in Nipawin, Saskatchewan, the second oldest of five girls. Her first exposure to city life came when she was 13 and entered high school in Saskatoon, where she excelled in art. She went on to attend the University of Saskatchewan, earning a B.A. in English and art. Some years later, she returned to university to obtain a B.Ed., specializing in the education of children with learning disabilities, and then she found work in this field. While employed as a special educator, she began work on an M.A.

In 1975, her marriage of 14 years ended. The following year, she abandoned her M.A. and went to live with her second husband, Peter Butala, on his ranch near Eastend, Saskatchewan. For ranchers and farmers, the late 1970s was a prosperous period, but increasingly frequent droughts, shifts in the world economy, and unsustainable farming practices would erode their good fortune. The resulting changes in her way of life and the landscape she inhabited inspired in Butala an ecological activism and, using her writing as her medium, she began to explore the ways that nature (which she sees as feminine) can "teach us about how to live" — "her first lesson is in humility." According to Butala, "The spiritual sustenance to be found in nature in its undisturbed state is one of my larger themes, but my overarching theme has been and continues to be my effort to understand and to lay bare, in both fiction and non-fiction, the female soul."

The harsh beauty of southwestern Saskatchewan prompted Butala to adopt a romantic approach to storytelling, although her work is marked by its attention to the realistic detail of daily life. Her first novel, *Country of the Heart* (1984), won a W.H.Smith/*Books in Canada* First Novel Award. Butala then entered a "period of mysterious dreaming," during which she developed the spiritual and visionary themes of the story collection *Queen of the Headaches* (1985) — the title story ends with the protagonist dreaming she is a river. Nominated for a Governor General's Award, this collection of tales populated by ordinary rural Saskatchewan people established Butala's momentum. Since then, she has published a book every year or two.

In 1988, she produced *Luna* (1988), a novel in which she explored her deepening belief in the power of dreams, prompted by prophetic dreams she'd had about an earthquake in San Francisco and a Japanese jet crash. At about this time, she was also reading the work of feminist academics and Jungian psychologists interested in the female unconscious and collectivity, and *Luna* became, in Butala's words, "the story of the lives of contemporary ranch and farm women and how they live, feel about, and understand their rural, agricultural, traditional lives." Butala expanded this investigation with the story collection *Fever* (1990), which she described as "a much more personal and urbanized study of the same issues."

Butala published her highly acclaimed first memoir, *The Perfection of the Morning: An Apprenticeship in Nature,* in 1994. It takes the author's journey from a study of nature to visionary awareness as its central focus, and in it Butala talks about how she has come to sense an "aura or presence" that corroborates her understanding of nature as a conscious being. She and her husband donated 13,000 acres of their ranch land to the Nature Conservancy of Canada in 1996, naming the preserve Old Man on His Back. In collaboration with photographer Courtney Milne, Butala published *Old Man on His Back: Portrait of a Prairie Landscape* (2002). A year later, she and her husband helped to reintroduce buffalo to the preserve, partly to help atone for the massive slaughter of buffalo in the late 1800s that destroyed the local Cree and Blackfoot way of life.

In her second memoir, *Wild Stone Heart* (2000), Butala reflects on the First Nations peoples of southwestern Saskatchewan. She is intrigued by their spirituality, ashamed of her complicity in their displacement, and determined to reach an understanding of the world on their terms, but she also realizes that she is not part of their tradition. Nevertheless, she says, *Wild Stone Heart* "carries the most important message of any book I've written. … It is time we came to real terms with the damage we've done to the aboriginal people of this continent."

Butala's third collection of short stories, *Real Life* (2002), features several versions of her established character type — a strong female protagonist dealing with a crisis. In "Light," she is Lucia. Like Butala herself, Lucia heeds omens and gut feelings: when she hits only green traffic lights on her way to see her sick sister, she speeds up, suddenly fearing for her sister's life. Then, when books about the Holocaust seem to jump off the shelves at her, she reads them, half expecting a timely message. By associating the Holocaust with illness, Butala suggests that hospitals are places of death, like concentration camps, and that cancer is like fascism; she also implies that disease is a symptom of an overly concentrated urban environment. Such implications form the moral centre of Butala's tales.

Although fiction was her initial way of imagining women's lives and refining her interests, Butala is becoming better known for her non-fiction. With her history of the Canadian west, *Lilac Moon* (2005), she synthesized many of the topics of her fiction and non-fiction, including the prairie city, the natural world, the history of colonialism, the spirituality of First Nations, and her personal and family history. In 2007, she produced *The Sweetest Face on Earth,* the story of the unsolved 1962 murder of her high school friend Alexandra Wiwcharuk. Butala continues to live in Saskatchewan and remains active in ecological and feminist causes.

Light

The sign reads, "If you've been waiting more than forty-five minutes, report to staff." Lucia and Elaine have been waiting an hour when finally Lucia rises, walks down the hall to the desk, and points this out to the uniformed woman there. The woman replies briskly, not looking at Lucia, "We know you're waiting." Then less harshly, "It won't be long now." Lucia says, "I'm only telling you because of the sign."

"Mmmmm," the woman says, snapping shut a drawer, and Lucia realizes she has once again entered can't-win-land. As she reseats herself beside Elaine she tells herself that this is quite possibly funny, that some day she may laugh about it.

She reaches over and takes Elaine's small, slightly polio-deformed, very white hand in hers. Elaine grasps hers tightly, although otherwise she doesn't move or change her expression. She sits in her wheelchair, the clear plastic of her oxygen nose-piece glistening on her upper lip, ignoring even the television, normally her favourite source of entertainment, that blats away next to her.

Every chair in the waiting area is occupied by patients or their companions. Nobody speaks, except for the occasional hurried whisper, nobody laughs, nobody watches the television, though nobody turns it off either, nobody stretches and yawns and shifts position, or paces up and down. Nobody moves. They sit quietly, hands in lap, looking at nothing. All of them, both the men and women, look faded to Lucia, blurred at the edges, as if they've been out in the damp too long. Soon, after their trials here at the cancer clinic, Lucia thinks, they'll dissolve into the Great Beyond, which now, after too many hours spent waiting there, appears to Lucia to be, instead of the sunshine-dappled, flower-dotted meadow of her childhood belief, a kind of Buddhistic nothing.

She can always tell the new patients. They talk too much, they talk incessantly, a bright jabbering that disturbs the whole waiting room and which they themselves, gazing around helplessly, their eyes flitting from patient to patient and back again, seem powerless to stop. Whenever it has happened, Lucia has been annoyed by it, refusing to meet the prattlers' eyes in order to avoid responding. Now it occurs to her that these women — she's never seen a man act this way — are simply afraid, they're driven by terror, that they'll stop when the system has slowly transmuted it into the numb acquiescence of everybody else here. Since she began looking after Elaine, she finds such moments of illumination gratifying.

Weeks ago, on a weekend trip home, she'd told George about the babbling women. They were lying side by side in bed, the blinds closed against the stars and moon, the world shrunk down to this darkened intimacy.

"I miss you," he said.

"You can't imagine how they look," she said. "Aren't you getting lots of work done? It isn't forever, after all. I'll be home soon."

"How's that?" he asked, surprised. "Have you found a facility for her?" This silenced her. At this stage, no facility would take Elaine, she isn't sick enough or helpless enough yet, and if one would, Elaine would refuse to go. Lucia knew very well she'd never force her sister to go.

"I don't know," she said finally. She didn't want to tell George that so far it had all been pretty interesting. Or that she was avoiding looking into the future, except to pray silently for something to happen that would rescue her from this task before things got too bad, although she doesn't really know what too bad might be.

Eventually, Elaine's name is called and Lucia wheels her to a treatment room, helps the nurse transfer her to an easy chair so large it dwarfs Elaine's small, twisted body. They cover her with a red mohair throw Lucia has brought from the apartment — the clinic provides only flannel sheets for warmth — and the treatment commences.

Waiting, while Elaine lies with closed eyes in the easy chair, an alarming, if also rather pretty, red fluid flowing down tubing into a needle planted in her arm, Lucia notices a tall thin man in a hospital dressing gown walk slowly past the open door. For a second he seems merely familiar, and then she realizes he's the husband of one of George's colleagues, someone she's known for years. It's so unusual to see somebody she knows here that, without reflection, she gets up and hurries after him.

She finds him around a corner in a niche. He's seated on a hard wooden lab chair, his arm is extended on the chair's wide shelf-like projection, a nurse is pushing up the sleeve of his dressing gown, about to apply the tourniquet, when Lucia bends over him, grinning, and says softly, "We've got to stop meeting like this."

He glances at her, slowly, his irises are pale, flat blue, the pupils shrunk to the tiniest points of darkness. His mouth is fixed in a half-smile, and he says nothing, nor does his expression change. She thinks he hasn't heard what she's said, more, that although only two weeks earlier on a weekend at home she'd had dinner at his house, he doesn't know who she is. She touches his shoulder lightly with her palm, an apology, a commiseration, then turns and hurries back to Elaine. She feels oddly elated, if puzzled, and when finally she recognizes that absent half-smile as another manifestation of the fear that lurks in every corner and shadow in this bright new facility, she's ashamed, as if to joke — although isn't that what everyone says you're supposed to do? — were immoral, or at the very least, a glaring faux pas.

More, she's astonished. Elaine was born with moderate mental retardation, then felled further by childhood polio, she can't read, she has no formal education and only the narrowest of life experience, while her friend is a well-travelled, much-honoured professor. Mulling this over as she waits for the bag of bright fluid to empty into Elaine's arm, she can't get over how here in the cancer clinic everything is instructive.

Back in Elaine's apartment, with Elaine sleeping from the anti-nausea medication, her oxygen concentrator running noisily at her bedside, Lucia does housework. The few dishes washed, the few square feet of vinyl in the walk-through kitchen swept, she decides against dusting. She ought to be resting while Elaine sleeps, the first post-chemo night can be harrowing, but the more tired she is, the harder she finds it to sleep. She tells herself that the moment will come when she's so tired she'll sleep like a baby.

The muted roar of the oxygen concentrator in the bedroom on the other side of the wall disturbs her rest too. It can't be turned off, Elaine's lips would turn blue and she'd gasp for breath, her lung cancer is well advanced now, nor can it be muffled by putting it in a closet because its electrical cord is too short and the oxygen-supply people, who come periodically to exchange the portable tanks Elaine uses whenever she leaves the apartment, are adamantly against extension cords. Wherever Elaine is in the apartment, the concentrator is never more than a few feet away. Lucia often thinks that its drone would do nicely as background to the torturing of the wicked in hell.

She should phone George. Talking with him reminds her that she won't be here in Elaine's apartment in this city five hours from her own forever, that she hasn't yet joined the ranks of the condemned. Otherwise, as the weeks pass, she finds this easier and easier to forget.

But George won't be home yet, so she puts the phone down, picks up her book from the stack she keeps behind the kitchen door — the apartment is so small that with two occupying it there's no place left to put them — stretches out on the sofa, and opens her book. George, an English professor, has just finished his stint on a non-fiction literary jury. He's been keeping her supplied with reading material from the more than two hundred new books he's had to read. But on her last trip home she'd found herself rejecting a highly praised memoir by a poet, a biography of a movie star, a humorous book about small-town life, everything that George had already selected for her.

"What's the matter with these?" he'd asked her in surprise.

"It's just that … they just don't look very interesting." They'd stared at the wall of books in front of them. Tentatively, Lucia reached out, took a thin volume from the shelf, and flipped through its pages.

"That's about the Holocaust," he told her briskly, reaching to take it from her.

"I know it," she'd said, evading his reach to put it aside on the table between them. In the end she'd collected a half-dozen books about the Holocaust from his shelves.

"They're pretty depressing reading," he warned her. "Especially now."

"I don't care," she said, "I just … want to."

But once she'd put the books in a bag and was setting it by her suitcase, he'd handed her a paper on which he'd scribbled the titles and authors of a half-dozen more.

"Those books will tell you the story," he explained, nodding down at the bookbag. "But none of them are works of art, and they have in common a failure to express the full scope of what happened." She watched him, as always, half irritated, half admiring of this professorial mode he often fell into with her. "The books on this list will help you …" he hesitated, "come to terms," he added finally, shrugging, as if such a thing were hardly possible. Then he'd looked hard into her eyes, as if she were one of his students about whose talents he was slightly dubious.

She'd begun with a memoir by a Canadian woman, a Jew born in Poland of a many-branched, tightly knit, prosperous family, nearly all of whom were killed in concentration camps. In it, the memoirist tells of her return in late adulthood to seek out the old family home, to find any remaining living relatives, to visit family graves if they can be found, and, most of all, to revisit the sites of her blissful early childhood, all of this in an attempt to sort out these happy memories from what she knows only by hearsay to be, for most of her family, their tragic outcome. It is an interesting enough narrative, although Lucia doesn't really understand the memoirist's impulse to make such a journey and then, especially, to write a book about it.

But she hasn't much left to read, and as she makes her way through to the end, and the full realization of what happened to the writer's grandparents, her aunts and uncles, her cousins, to the beautiful house in the countryside where her happiest memories reside, comes crashing over the author, Lucia thinks, What a fool the writer was to want to know.

She sets the book down on the sofa beside her and stares out the double-glass doors onto the small balcony that overlooks the parking lot, then a service station, and beyond that, one of the busiest of the city's downtown streets. She knows she's being mean-spirited, even childish. Of course the woman needed to know. She wonders about the word "needed," but in the other room, over the concentrator's loud hum, Elaine has begun to cough and Lucia drops the book and hurries in to her.

In the absence of a hospital bed, which Elaine becomes nearly hysterical at the mere mention of, Lucia has bought an item the home care people call a "wedge" because of its shape, a huge piece of foam rubber, textured so it will stay where it's placed in the bed, and on which Lucia then arranges another half-dozen pillows, so that Elaine can sleep comfortably, sitting up. If in her sleep she moves, dislodges the pillows, and begins, over the hours, slowly to sink to a flatter position in the bed, it's only a matter of minutes before she wakes, unable to breathe, coughing, gasping for breath, but too weak to sit up without help. Some nights this happens three or four times, when Lucia, hearing the first cough, on her feet before she's even awake, rushes into the bedroom, calling, "It's all right, I'm coming, it's okay," during the seconds it takes her to reach Elaine's bedside.

She puts one arm behind Elaine's back and another in the crook of her knees while Elaine pushes against the bed with her hands to assist Lucia in dragging her back up to a sitting position. All this done in semi-darkness — the city lights never allow absolute darkness in the apartment no matter what Lucia tries — and fast, before Elaine loses consciousness.

Often Lucia can't get a proper grip, can't seem to make any difference, and then she climbs onto the bed, kneels beside Elaine, and struggles until she's managed to drag her upright. Then she goes back to the cot she sets up nightly in the living room, picks up her book, and reads until her heart stops its rapid pounding in her ears and throat and wrists.

Elaine is awake and, once she and Lucia have managed to pull her to a sitting position, she wants her wheelchair so she can go into the living room and watch television. With the toiletting, medicating, and various other kinds of necessary care, none of which Elaine can do for herself any more, and now the inane racket of the television set — Elaine's taste in programming is the same as a twelve-year-old's, although her dignity won't allow her to watch cartoons if Lucia is there — it will be late tonight before Lucia gets another chance to read.

Still, as she goes about her routine, she finds herself thinking about the book she's just finished. She tries to imagine herself in the author's shoes, her grandparents, aunts, uncles, cousins all dead — murdered, in fact — reduced from flesh to shadowy images in worn snapshots. But every time she feels herself getting close, the phone rings, or it's time for Elaine's medication, or the wash is ready for the dryer, or it's time to cook supper, and before long she's forgotten about the book.

Today they are in the waiting room two floors below ground level at Nuclear Medicine, Lucia sitting in a straight-backed chair beside Elaine's wheelchair until all the chairs are taken and she gives up hers to a newcomer. Then she leans against the wall next to Elaine under a sign warning of the presence of radioactive materials. Elaine is there to undergo tests that involve large machines, all steel, shiny chrome, and spotless white plastic, attached to banks of computer screens with flickering white graphs on blue backgrounds. They've seen these machines and computers as examination room doors open to let someone in or out, or else they know what they look like from television or movies, or maybe, Lucia thinks, they've seen them in their dreams.

The walls of this waiting room are a cream colour, the floors black-and-brown-speckled marble. The doors — extra wide to accommodate stretchers — are a pale wood, oak, perhaps, or maple. No, ash, Lucia decides. She doesn't actually know what ash looks like, it's just that ash seems the appropriate wood down here. She thinks she'll have to remember to tell George this the next time she manages a few days at home.

She glances around the room. People stare at the floor or gaze forward into space, the colourlessness of their eyes indicating that they see nothing, or perhaps it is a memory they've fallen into of some distant moment; the way the leaves in the yard crunched underfoot one fall day, maybe, or how the light used to stream through the bedroom window mornings when it was time to get up for school.

How shabby this room is, Lucia thinks. How dismal in its very shabby ordinariness. She thinks, If I were one of these dying people, what would I see if I looked? And in a visionary flash she sees how purely unendurable the thought of leaving even it behind must be.

This is more than even she, the non-dying, can bear. No one in this room is thinking what she's thinking, or they'd be on their knees, banging their heads against that marble floor, they'd be wailing and tearing their hair.

She drags herself back from this moment, some emotion well beyond mere pity forcing her to make another glance around the room at the men and women sitting in absent silence. She remembers the silly joke she cracked a few weeks earlier with her professor-friend and, annoyingly, tears rush to her eyes.

She has promised Elaine, on the evidence of a reply given her by a nurse, that this time there'll be no needles, but when they've been waiting twenty minutes, they're called into a cubicle across the hall so that a technician can find one of Elaine's tiny veins and inject a radioactive fluid into it for the machines to pick out as it circulates through her blood. Elaine goes weekly for lab tests where blood is routinely drawn; she endures the chemotherapy needle and the finger pricks and the palpation of various lumps and sore spots. So far she's never protested, except for a whimper at the pain or, once in a while, an angry "ouch!"

Today, as the technician struggles to get his needle into a vein, she begins to cry. She sobs quietly, not protesting, not pulling her arm away, not asking Lucia to make the technician stop. She cries hopelessly, as if there will never be an end to this. Lucia holds Elaine's head pressed gently against her abdomen. The technician gives up, goes away, comes back with the department head who succeeds in hitting a vein on his first, extremely careful try.

She's into the first-person accounts now, one by a man and one by a woman. The male writer, about twelve at the time his family had been seized, had been lucky enough to stay with his father. He tells of how time and time again the father saves them both with his hard intelligence and a cunning that seems somehow able to cut through the trauma around him. The father never dwells on the monstrousness of what is going on, but instead he approaches the routine of each day with supreme but well-hidden alertness, always calculating what the best chances for their survival are in each situation. And he never takes his eyes off the day he knows will come when he and his son will escape or be freed. Nor does he ever forget, nor allow his son to forget, that outside these walls there is still a normal world to which they will return. When she's finished this book, Lucia thinks, I thought it would be so much worse than this to read.

The next night she begins the book by the woman. This memoirist can barely bring herself to tell her story. Every line — written, she says, only because her children say she must — is filled with an emotion deeper than mere sorrow or disgust or rage. There is no name for it in Lucia's vocabulary, but whatever it is, it is so deep and terrible that, thinking about it, Lucia can't see how the author has managed to live the fifty or more years since the events happened, and now, when she tells them.

It is with the woman that Lucia gets the sense of the daily horrors of camp life. Some images of Nazi cruelty she knows she will never be able to erase, and lying on the sagging, narrow little cot at night while Elaine sleeps fitfully, the condenser roaring, and sirens wailing down the street below, or the balcony doors rattling in sudden gusts of prairie wind, she tries to grasp some meaning out of this that she feels sure must be there beyond the general horror, the barely utterable cruelties, the awful suffering. Something moves in the darkness of her consciousness, well back from the light. It is huge and, so far, shapeless. She doesn't know what it is, only that it isn't ready yet to come forward, to sweep her up into some new level of awareness. Or to madness, she thinks suddenly, when she sees it at last in its true form. Or perhaps in the end she will decide not to let it come forward into light. Perhaps she will have to turn away.

Elaine is not eating much now, and it's a chore to get her to drink anything. One eye has a slight infection, so added to the round of daily chores is the task of flushing it twice a day with a medicated fluid. Elaine tries to cooperate in this, but she blinks as the fluid falls from the eye dropper so that most of it trickles down her cheek.

"I'm sorry, Luce," she says, crying a little, and Lucia says, "If I were the one getting stuff poured into my eye, I'd blink too."

Elaine's nose is crusted and bloody inside from the irritation of the oxygen tubes constantly resting in it, which means nose drops and eventually antibiotics. The flesh between the oxygen tubing that hooks behind her ears and her skull grows more irritated and sore all the time, and Lucia and the home care nurse have had to devise padding that will stay in place there. Besides these small miseries, pains come and pains go, often in strange places, usually without explanation, as do other afflictions that can't be ignored: a rash, a swollen arm and hand, a swollen foot, a discharge, a painful shoulder, a painful hip. Each one required phone calls to the home care staff, to the cancer clinic, to the family doctor.

Consultations take place, advice is given, then Lucia makes appointments at downtown laboratories for X-rays, or blood tests, or other, more complicated investigations. First, she has to order the wheelchair van since, as Elaine has grown weaker, Lucia can no longer get her in and out of her own car; then she has to take Elaine out for more waiting in other waiting rooms. In these, Elaine is always the sickest person present, and seeing this, the staff nearly always accelerates her admission into the inner sanctum. This is a kindness Lucia is always more grateful for than is Elaine who, falling into her peculiar waiting-room reverie, seems not to notice.

Over and over again Lucia has had to step outside these examination or treatment rooms and say softly to the attendant, "My sister is mildly mentally retarded, she does not understand what you are telling her," filled with shame for humiliating Elaine, irritation with the doctor, nurse, or technician's inability to see what appears to Lucia to be the obvious, and pity for Elaine. She finds herself, too, caught between guilt for betraying her sister, who is intelligent enough to know she doesn't think as well as other people and is permanently sick with disgust at herself because of it, and fear that the medical person she's talking to won't believe her, since in a brief, polite social exchange, Elaine simulates normal intelligence so well that no one would ever guess that she can't read or write.

Nothing much ever comes of these visits. If they reveal a new problem, it's always trivial in the light of the cancer, and if it's another symptom of the cancer's spread, there's nothing more that can be done than already is. Knowing all this in advance, or learning it as she goes along, Lucia has moments close to real despair, until she begins to view these usually weekly trips — in addition to the sometimes twice-weekly trips to the cancer clinic for various tests, examinations, and treatments, although they've given up on the chemotherapy — as outings for Elaine, a way of passing another day on the seemingly endless road to her demise.

George has given Lucia another survivor's story about her experience in the camp-village called Theresienstadt, and there's still the book about a Canadian Jewish committee's post-war struggle to find some Jewish orphans to bring to Canada. She spends a couple of hours on each, although neither does much more for her than to confirm what the memoirs have already seared into her brain. She puts them back without finishing them.

One night, she realizes she's finished the first stack of books. She moves to the second pile, which consists of the books that on George's advice she borrowed from the library file. Elie Wiesel's *Night*,[1] the thinnest of volumes, barely a hundred pages long, is on the top. Having seen him on television, and knowing him to be a Nobel Peace Prize winner, she's pretty sure this will be an exceptionally hard book to read. She hesitates while the electric clock on the wall above the table ticks erratically and the concentrator makes its breathy roar in the other room. After a moment she puts it back, crawls into her cot, and drifts into the state of semi-consciousness that these days passes for sleep.

She'd been home for the weekend. Five, or is it six, women have been involved in caring for Elaine over the three days she's been gone, an arrangement that took Lucia ten days to set up and then to ensure that the arrangements had gone down the full chain of command to the people who would actually be coming. More than once there's been some kind of bureaucratic foul-up at home care when Lucia, having made arrangements to go out to a hurried dinner with a friend, comes back to Elaine's apartment to find that the person who was supposed to make Elaine's supper hasn't shown up. Elaine is propped against the cushions of her couch just as Lucia had left her two or three hours earlier. Elaine is frightened beyond reason when this happens. According to the arrangements this time, Elaine should have been alone only for about an hour between the nurse's visit and Lucia's promised arrival by two.

She's driving up the three-mile-long avenue of fast-food restaurants, service stations, and motels that leads into the city. She's about halfway up it when she notices that so far she hasn't hit a single red light. Ordinarily it takes her as long as half an hour before she reaches the narrow side streets that lead to the apartment building where Elaine lives. There must be a dozen sets of traffic lights along this road, and not to have hit a single red one is so unusual she laughs out loud in surprise. Far ahead she sees another green light, almost brakes, thinking that by the time she reaches it, it will be red. But it stays green, and it stays green, and she sails right on through, and through the next one too, and then she knows. She knows absolutely that Elaine needs her. She puts her foot hard on the gas, knowing there'll be no red lights today, and in five minutes she's parking in front of Elaine's.

She finds her alone, instead of resting against the pillows, sitting forward on her couch, her forehead beaded with perspiration, her white face paler than Lucia has so far seen it no matter what atrocities are being done to her in various clinics around the city. Her lips, in this paste-white face, are blue. Her chest pumps in and out with rapidity that appals Lucia; she can't begin to guess how many times a minute Elaine's chest is going in and out. Elaine stares at her with large, desperate eyes, barely able to speak.

"Where's the nurse?" Lucia asks stupidly.

"She … left … " Lucia tries to think what to do, runs into the bedroom and gathers the nebulizer — Elaine is supposed to use it twice a day but refuses to if Lucia isn't there to help her — the mask, the potent asthma-type drugs that the nebulizer converts to mist for Elaine to breathe in. Quickly she puts the drugs into their container, plugs in the nebulizer, pulls the mask up over her sister's mouth and nose. She takes Elaine's pulse as the machine whirrs away on Elaine's lap and the mask clouds with vapour and Elaine's head continues to bob with each breath. Her pulse is — Lucia almost can't believe it — 150 beats a minute. The phone sits on the sofa beside Elaine and now Lucia dials the home care nurse's mobile phone.

---

1. **Elie Wiesel's** *Night* This novel, published in 1958, is based on the author's experiences during the Holocaust.

"Call an ambulance," the nurse tells her. "Don't wait. Call an ambulance. Here, I'll give you the number."

She copies down the number, but Lucia finds herself reluctant to dial it, Elaine hates hospitals so, but she can't imagine now what will happen if she doesn't obey — how long can Elaine go on gasping this way before — she doesn't know what, only that surely Elaine will die. She dials, and in less than ten minutes, during which time Elaine continues to pant, her torso jerking and her head bobbing with every breath as she struggles for air, three ambulance attendants, a stretcher, and some bulky equipment have taken up all the available space in the small living room.

"She had polio as a child," she tells the attendants, just as she has had to tell everyone in every clinic and waiting room and doctor's office through this whole odyssey, because no one ever seems to realize that Elaine can't walk. "You'll have to lift her."

The ambulance attendants, all young men, are kind, and gentle, and reassuring. Stethoscopes appear, and various other medical paraphernalia which Elaine can't recall later, but she remembers a hypodermic syringe and vials of medication. They change Elaine's oxygen supply to the portable tank they've brought with them. In mere minutes they have Elaine half sitting on the stretcher and are wheeling her out of the apartment, Lucia reassuring her, "Don't worry. I'll be right behind you. I'll be at the hospital as soon as you are." Elaine continues to gasp for breath with her whole frame as the elevator doors close on the stretcher.

Lucia beats the ambulance to the hospital. Nobody is more surprised by this than her, she can only be grateful she wasn't stopped for speeding, and when the ambulance does arrive nearly ten minutes later, it remains parked next to the Emergency entrance, motor running, for another ten minutes with nobody emerging. She waits, pacing, not daring to knock on the ambulance doors, afraid of what's happening on the other side of them.

Finally they open and her sister's stretcher is lowered and wheeled into the hospital through doors Lucia isn't allowed to pass through. When she rushes inside and asks if she may go into the treatment room, she's told, absolutely not, and it looks as if the receptionist/nurse telling her this wouldn't hesitate to wrestle her to the ground if she shows the slightest sign of disobeying.

Moments pass, she paces, staring through the double doors, the top half of which are glass, into the suite of rooms where her sister has vanished.

"You can go in now," somebody tells her. She finds Elaine in the room next to the nursing station, seated nearly upright in what looks like an old-fashioned dentist's chair. At least six doctors, nurses, and technicians surround her, each of them doing something to Elaine, although Lucia, in her confusion, can't make any sense of the scene, except to relax a little because her sister is in good hands. A man in operating-room greens, his mask dangling from a string, detaches himself from the scrum around Elaine and introduces himself as doctor somebody. He questions her about Elaine's diagnosis, her condition, and repeats in a casual way some of her answers to the crowd around Elaine.

Before too long Lucia sees someone else being rushed past on a stretcher into the room next door to Elaine's and most of the people clustered around Elaine abruptly leave. She hears orders being given, she hears the new patient moaning, she sees nurses rushing out and then in again. Listening, Lucia hears the unmistakable sounds, which she knows from watching television hospital dramas, of someone dying and being brought back to life. Twice, she hears this. Her abdomen and chest feel hollow. She's not sure she's breathing, although she must be, but if she is, it seems she isn't getting any air. Elaine is drowsy now. Lucia kisses her cheek, gets her a paper cup of icy water, murmurs softly whatever comforting words come to her.

Elaine is breathing less quickly now, although when Lucia surreptitiously takes her pulse, it's still over a hundred beats per minute. It occurs to her to wonder why Pierre Trudeau didn't make time metric[2] too, but then she thinks, maybe it already is. How bizarre these thoughts are doesn't occur to her until months later. Nurses return and try again to insert a line into Elaine's vein and Elaine cries and behaves like a frightened child and one of the nurses snaps at her. Once more Lucia has to explain why Elaine is hospital-and-needle phobic.

It is because of the polio when she was five years old, when she nearly died in the old wing of this very hospital, according to their mother, screaming with pain for days and nights on end until the head nurse told their parents Elaine would not live through another night. Then she was kept here for more than seven months in isolation, with two dozen other children, living as if they were all orphans. She summarizes the surgeries, each one more horrible than the last. Lucia has to do this in such a way that Elaine does not hear that she is not as smart as other people, that in some ways she remains a child still, while the nurses do hear Lucia's message.

Hours later, while Elaine sleeps on a ward in the hospital, Lucia drives through the summer twilight to her sister's apartment. She remembers how earlier she'd careened around corners, sped down residential streets, and screeched to stops at traffic lights, only to arrive ten minutes ahead of the ambulance. She's been told now, or rather, since nobody ever tells her anything she considers meaningful, she's figured out that her sister has narrowly escaped death. If Lucia hadn't hit all those green lights on the way into town, she might have found Elaine's corpse. And she realizes that the paramedics had tried and failed to find a vein while Elaine was on her way to the hospital. Now she thinks that maybe that's why the driver went slowly, so as not to jolt the paramedic struggling with Elaine's damaged veins, and why they'd taken so long to open the ambulance doors.

Alone in Elaine's apartment, she picks up Wiesel's *Night* again. This time she opens it to the first page and begins reading. At first she forces herself, then, although she wants to stop, she gets caught up in the harrowing[3] narrative and can't. She reads, her guts in knots, her palms wet with sweat, her breathing shallow and fast, as if she is perhaps asleep and dreaming some intense, frightening dream. She feels as though she's caught in the throes of some terminal disease whose symptoms are amazement, horror, disgust, and an unfathomably deep shock that the world could, after all, contain such depths of savagery, such depths of suffering. When, hours later, she finishes the book, she sits on the side of her cot for a long time staring into space.

After a while she wanders to the balcony doors to gaze out over the concrete-grey of the city, tinged purple in the bleak light of the powerful street lamps. She thinks about Elie Wiesel, about a certain expression that appears on his face when she's seen him being interviewed on television. She doesn't think she's seen it on anyone else's face, and every time she's seen it on his, she's wondered what it means.

---

2. **Pierre Trudeau … metric** The Trudeau government initiated Canada's conversion from the imperial system to the metric system in 1971. 3. **harrowing** Extremely distressing.

She thinks she understands it now. Since the camps he has become a witness, determined never to look away from the terrible pictures he carries in his mind, or from the stories he's been told, the photographs he's seen.

For once, the streets outside the apartment are quiet, no drunken young people shouting, nobody roaring his motor or squealing his tires on the road leading onto the bridge that crosses the wide river, no fire trucks or ambulances or police cars screaming past where she stands alone in her nightgown in the shadows. She stares up at the moon hanging hard and white over the city, and thinks of all the millennia it has been shining down on this planet. For a moment, the belief that she's been taught, that every single human death matters, wavers and almost disappears.

The world does not make sense, she thinks. One horror ends and somewhere another is beginning. She must not look away either, she tells herself, but doubts she has the courage to carry out such a resolve.

After Elaine's return from her week-long stay in the hospital, her needs grow in quantity and intensity. Since they can't afford to hire a professional nurse to stay with her — only the rich could do that — the visits from home care attendants and nurses increase. Elaine's case manager drops in, drinks coffee with them, chats in a friendly way. She's here to assess the situation: both Lucia and Elaine know that soon, if she doesn't die first, Elaine will have to go to a facility equipped to care for someone as ill as she is, maybe even to a palliative care unit in a hospital. When Lucia hasn't the strength to lift her out of bed one more time, to leap up from sleep one more time to rush into her room and pull her up in bed, even then, she can't imagine how they will get Elaine to consent to go.

Lucia has lost quite a lot of weight, she has chronic diarrhea now and a number of random aches and pains which she tries to ignore, but which, nonetheless, alarm her. She wants to go home, she wants to lie down and sleep for a month, she wants George to come and hold her. One day someone phones to tell her that the friend she ran into at the cancer clinic so long ago, and to whom she made that stupid, unfunny joke, has died.

Now Elaine is staying alive on oxygen and morphine and an unwillingness to die. Lucia has begun to wish the end would come, the quicker the better, and she finds herself irritated with Elaine's refusal to face what is happening to her. Early on, when Elaine had misunderstood a doctor's message to her, taking it as hopeful when it was really a statement of hopelessness, and Lucia had tried gently to correct her misunderstanding, Elaine had screamed, "I'm sick and tired of you telling me I'm going to die!" Now Lucia can't bring herself to try to talk to Elaine about her impending death, and she hates herself for her desire, which she can no longer deny, that Elaine should give up this fight she can't win.

She's read all the books in the stacks behind the kitchen door now, or all that she can bear to read; there is only a work by Primo Levi[4] left that she's determined to try. Primo Levi comes highly recommended from a rabbi-professor friend of George's, and so she placed his book on the top of the pile to begin reading once Elaine has had her evening morphine and for a few hours will be unconscious. Although it seems to her she's done what she set out to do, however unclear that intention was and, in some ways, remains, her new knowledge has not brought her peace, or any new understanding, or even any

---

4. **Primo Levi** Jewish Italian novelist, poet, and chemist (1919–1987) whose memoirs documented his imprisonment at Auschwitz.

satisfaction. She doesn't know what it is she wants, but whatever it is, it hasn't come yet. Maybe it never will, maybe she isn't wise enough or smart enough. Maybe she's too weak. Or maybe she has to be the victim, instead of just a helper, to know what it is.

Evenings now, after the last visit from the palliative care nurse, and the last home care helper has long since departed, Lucia spends a lot of time on the phone. Relatives call from across the country, there's her evening talk with George, sometimes the family doctor calls, or a friend or two. It's quite late before she's able to make up her cot, undress for bed, and climb in with her book. Since she learned how as a six-year-old, to read before sleep has been her habit, and now, despite her exhaustion, she clings to it as the only remnant of normalcy left in her life.

Levi's book is a careful, scholarly dissection of the degrees, causes, and purposes of specific daily cruelties in the concentration camps of the Second World War. It examines in detail, coldly, human evil as it manifests itself in the simplest and smallest of everyday acts. This book is the worst of them all, and she's read only a few pages before she begins to wonder if she can go on.

Elaine has begun to cough. Lucia throws back her blanket and sheet and hurries into the bedroom. Surprisingly, given that she is now constantly heavily drugged with morphine, Elaine is awake. Her blue eyes, grown large and beautiful in these last weeks, shine in the semi-dark, and through her spasms of coughing she tries to speak to Lucia.

"Yes, okay," Lucia murmurs, although she hasn't been able to understand her sister's broken mumbling. She tries, using her usual techniques, to partly pull, partly lift Elaine back up to a sitting position, but for some reason it is one of those nights when she can't manage it. Maybe it's because Elaine can't help her any more by pushing against the mattress with her hands.

Frantically, she climbs onto the bed beside Elaine and puts one arm against her back to hold her up. Elaine's cough has settled into a steady, gasping roll that is terrifying to hear. Lucia reaches with her other arm for the pillows and the foam wedge to pull them down to where she's holding Elaine up in her sitting position, but she can't get a grip on them, and when she does, the wedge refuses to move, seems to be caught on something she can't see or reach. Elaine is trying to speak again. Lucia freezes.

"I'm … so … scared … " Panic grips Lucia, her helplessness, her desire to save her sister any suffering she can, her hopeless, endless failure to do so, and the demands of the moment that she can't even consider rush through her mind. She tries, but from here she can't reach the phone without letting go of Elaine and she doesn't dare do that.

Upright now, Elaine's coughing has subsided enough that Lucia can feel her short gasping breaths returning to shudder through her chest and ribs and spine.

"I'm … so … tired … I … need … sleep … " Elaine whispers: a word, a breath, a word, a breath. Lucia gives up the struggle to pull the wedge and pillows to her. Holding Elaine upright with her left arm, on all fours she moves around behind her, transfers Elaine's weight to her left shoulder, while she tugs at and straightens her own nightgown that has twisted around her legs. Then she crouches behind Elaine, her face hovering level with the back of her sister's stubbly head. Slowly she lowers herself until she's seated behind her.

She spreads her legs so that they enclose Elaine, and the pillows and wedge fit her own back, neatly propping her upright. She puts both arms around Elaine, pulls up the sheet and blankets, pats them into place, folding them down under Elaine's chin. Then she clasps her hands on Elaine's lap, and accepts her sister's full weight, surprisingly heavy for all her thinness, her frailty, against her chest and abdomen and thighs.

Elaine falls back into unconsciousness almost immediately, her head lolling against Lucia's throat, chin, and shoulder. The concentrator drones on beside the bed and the city's light glows in around the curtains so that Lucia can make out the shadows that are furniture. Slowly her sister's twisted, knobby spine relaxes and settles into the warm cushion of Lucia's breasts and belly.

Lucia's mind wanders to the book by Primo Levi she's been trying to read, she remembers reading that Levi committed suicide. She grasps Elaine more firmly, presses her lips slightly against her sister's clammy cheek. She thinks of their parents, dead now, and of her and Elaine's long childhood together in the bright, quivering aspen forest of the north, of the moving sky there, the intense green of the grass.

Elaine coughs, a light, shallow cough, moves her head slightly, her short, stiff hair brushing Lucia's mouth, before she relaxes again against Lucia's warm body.

They stay that way a long time, Elaine deeply unconscious, her polio-and-pain-stiffened shoulders, neck, and back slowly loosening so that they feel almost normal to Lucia, while Lucia drifts in and out of sleep, until the heat of their two bodies has so melded that, awake now as the first pale rays of dawn seep around the drawn curtains, Lucia can no longer tell where her sister leaves off and she begins.

(2002)

Gwendolyn MacEwen (1941–1987)

During a 1984 interview, Gwendolyn MacEwen declared that she was "beginning to see Canada as the most exotic land of all." Anyone familiar with her work and life story will understand the significance of this statement. Throughout her career, MacEwen drew upon the mystical and the mythical for her poetic content and style, and she took great interest in cultures and languages that were not her own. She travelled extensively in the Middle East and the Mediterranean, and she taught herself Hebrew, Arabic, Greek, and French, translating works written in these languages into English. In fact, as her biographer, Rosemary Sullivan, points out, many who watched MacEwen's "forays into Mediterranean cultures thought she was simply pursuing the exotic, as an escapist might." Yet MacEwen did not consider her work escapist. She believed that in pursuing and uncovering the mystical, she was actively participating in the "real" world some felt she was repudiating. "I want to live myth, not read about it," she said. "I'm not really concerned about literature at all but about life."

Influenced by Carl Jung, MacEwen held that through art, dreams, myth, and language one could penetrate a kind of collective psychological world, thus gaining access to "human history," or "the roots of things." If she could reveal this realm, then she would be able to better understand and communicate the present state of the so-called real world and human thought. Consequently, much of MacEwen's work explores themes of exploration and revelation. In "Dark Pines under Water," she dramatizes her unconventional approach to perception: "But the dark pines of your mind dip deeper / And you are sinking, sinking, sleeper / In an elementary world; / There is something down there and you want it told."

MacEwen took on the task of finding and "telling" this "something down there." She was intrigued by what she understood as the poet's transformative faculty, turning repeatedly to the image of the magician or alchemist as artist figure. Yet the nature of this task was such that it could never be fulfilled. In "The Discovery," she writes, "do not imagine that the exploration / ends," that "the map you hold / cancels further discovery." She demands of the reader, "when you see the land naked, look again." According to MacEwen, "the moment when it seems most plain / is the moment when you must begin again."

When she applied her vision to Canada, the country appeared rife with mystical and exotic poetic material. She was deeply interested in the myths surrounding the Canadian landscape and in figures such as Grey Owl and Mackenzie King. In the 1960s, the Canadian Broadcasting Corporation commissioned several plays from the young writer, and she produced *Terror and Erebus,* a haunting verse-play based on Sir John Franklin's failed 1845 attempt to navigate the Northwest Passage. Her fascination with such iconic types persisted, and years later, in 1985, it would engender the short fiction collection *Noman's Land* (1985), in which MacEwen creates the myth of a representative Canadian character — Noman — who dwells in the land of "Kanada." His name alludes not only to the mythical explorer Odysseus, who uses it during his confrontation with Polyphemus in Homer's *Odyssey,* but also to "noman's land" — the neutral territory between opposing forces in war.

Some attribute MacEwen's attraction to the world of dreams and myth to the fact that she endured much hardship in her relatively short life. She was born in Toronto in 1941, and her childhood is commonly believed to have been a troubled one. Her father suffered from alcoholism, and her mother was regularly institutionalized due to mental illness. MacEwen married twice — her first husband was poet Milton Acorn — but both relationships failed. In the years before her death, she grew increasingly dependent on alcohol, and she died in 1987, at the age of 46.

Yet MacEwen believed that her life and her career as a writer were indivisible, and she was successful in her professional life. She had settled on her calling when she was quite young. At 17, she published her first poems in the *Canadian Forum,* and at 18, she left high school in order to write full time. She drifted into the nascent Toronto literary scene of the 1960s, hanging out at the Bohemian Embassy coffee house and poetry club, where she befriended other young writers, among them Acorn and Margaret Atwood. She went to Montreal and edited the little magazine *Moment* with Acorn and Al Purdy from 1960 to 1962, and in 1965, she received a Canada Council grant to conduct research in Egypt for her historical novel *King of Egypt, King of Dreams* (1971). In 1970, she was given the Governor General's Award for poetry for *The Shadow-Maker* (1969), and in 1973, she received the A.J.M. Smith Poetry Award for *The Armies of the Moon* (1972). In 1984–1985 she was writer-in-residence at the University of Western Ontario in London; she accepted the same role at the University of Toronto in 1986–87.

Her poetry collection *A Breakfast for Barbarians* (1966), admired for its concrete imagery and exuberance, brought a wider acceptance of MacEwen's work, which some critics had found overly obscure and complex. Reviewers of later collections found fault with what they perceived as her idiosyncratic vision, but most found her rich poetic language and her mysterious, mystical images and themes compelling. Atwood has written of her friend and colleague, "she created, in a remarkably short time, a complete and diverse poetic universe and a powerful and unique voice, by turns playful, extravagant, melancholic, daring and profound. To read her remains what it has always been: an exacting but delightful pleasure, though not one without its challenges and shadows."

Eden, Eden

it is the thunder is
the vocal monument
to the death-wished rain;
or obelisk[1] in a granite sky

---

1. **obelisk** Tapering stone structure similar to a four-sided pyramid.

that roars a jawed epitaph
through cut cloud.

in the morning
thunder is the reared stone elephant,
            the grown element of grey;
its trunk is vertical and thick as thunder;   10
the elephant stubs down the wrenched lightning,
funnelling a coughed verse
for the suicidal rain
in the morning.

the stormed man is heavy with rain
and mumbles beneath the elephant gargle
and his jaw locks human in the rain,
and under the unlocked jaw of the cut sky
and under the bullets of the elephant's trunk

he is thinking of a thunder garden.   20

Behind sense he is thinking of a warped tree
with heavy fruit falling;
peaked rock fighting the ragged fern
in the other storm's centre;
a monolithic thunder tree
and a man and woman naked and green with rain
above its carved roots, genesis

(1963)

A Breakfast for Barbarians

my friends, my sweet barbarians,
there is that hunger which is not for food —
but an eye at the navel turns the appetite
round
with visions of some fabulous sandwich,
the brain's golden breakfast
                        eaten with beasts
                        with books on plates

let us make an anthology of recipes,
let us edit for breakfast   10
our most unspeakable appetites —
let us pool spoons, knives
and all cutlery in a cosmic cuisine,
let us answer hunger

with boiled chimera[1]
and apocalyptic tea,
an arcane[2] salad of spiced bibles,
tossed dictionaries —
                    (O my barbarians
20   we will consume our mysteries)

and can we, can we slake[3] the gaping eye of our desires?
we will sit around our hewn wood table
until our hair is long and our eyes are feeble,
eating, my people, O my insatiates,
eating until we are no more able
to jack up the jaws any longer —

to no more complain of the soul's vulgar cavities,
to gaze at each other over the rust-heap of cutlery,
drinking a coffee that takes an eternity —
30   till, bursting, bleary,
we laugh, barbarians, and rock the universe —
and exclaim to each other over the table
over the table of bones and scrap metal
over the gigantic junk-heaped table:

by God that was a meal

(1966)

Manzini: Escape Artist

now there are no bonds except the flesh; listen —
there was this boy, Manzini, stubborn with
gut stood with black tights and a turquoise
leaf across his sex

and smirking while the big
brute tied his neck arms legs, Manzini
naked waist up and white with sweat

struggled. Silent, delinquent, he
was suddenly all teeth and knee, straining slack
10   and excellent with sweat, inwardly

wondering if Houdini would take as long
as he; fighting time and the drenched

---

1. chimera Mythological monster composed of varying animal parts. **2. arcane** Secret, mystical. **3. slake**
Satisfy.

muscular ropes, as though his tendons were worn
on the outside —

as though his own guts were the ropes
encircling him; it was beautiful; it was thursday; listen —
there was this boy, Manzini

finally free, slid as snake from
his own sweet agonized skin, to throw his entrails
white upon the floor   20
with a cry of victory —

now there are no bonds except the flesh,
but listen, it was thursday, there was this boy,
Manzini —

(1966)

Poems in Braille

1

all your hands are verbs,
now you touch worlds and feel their names —
thru the thing to the name
not the other way thru (in winter
I am Midas,[1] I name gold)

the chair and table and book
extend from your fingers;
all your movements
command these things back to their
places; a fight against familiarity   10
makes me resume my distance

2

they knew what it meant,
those egyptian scribes who drew
eyes right into their hieroglyphs,
you read them dispassionate until
the eye stumbles upon itself
blinking back from the papyrus

outside, the articulate wind
annotates this; I read carefully
lest I go blind in both eyes, reading with   20
that other eye the final hieroglyph

---

1. Midas Mythological king who turned everything he touched into gold.

3

the shortest distance between 2 points
on a revolving circumference
is a curved line; O let me follow you,
Wenceslas[2]

4

with legs and arms I make alphabets
like in those children's books
where people bend into letters and signs,
yet I do not read the long cabbala[3] of my bones
30   truthfully; I need only to move
to alter the design

5

I name all things in my room
and they rehearse their names,
gather in groups, form tesseracts,[4]
discussing their names among themselves

I will not say the cast is less than the print
I will not say the curve is longer than the line,
I should read all things like braille in this season
with my fingers I should read them
40   lest I go blind in both eyes reading with
that other eye the final hieroglyph

(1966)

Dark Pines under Water

This land like a mirror turns you inward
And you become a forest in a furtive[1] lake;
The dark pines of your mind reach downward,
You dream in the green of your time,
Your memory is a row of sinking pines.

Explorer, you tell yourself this is not what you came for
Although it is good here, and green;
You had meant to move with a kind of largeness,
You had planned a heavy grace, an anguished dream.

10   But the dark pines of your mind dip deeper
And you are sinking, sinking, sleeper

---

2. Wenceslas Bohemian king (1361–1419) who saved his servant from a winter storm by treading a path for him to follow through deep snow. **3. cabbala** An esoteric philosophy based on Hebrew scriptures. **4. tesseracts** Cubes that exist in at least four dimensions (it would be 16-cornered).

---

1. furtive Stealthy.

In an elementary world;
There is something down there and you want it told.

(1969)

The Shadow-Maker

I have come to possess your darkness, only this.

My legs surround your black, wrestle it
As the flames of day wrestle night
And everywhere you paint the necessary shadows
On my flesh and darken the fibres of my nerve;
Without these shadows I would be
In air one wave of ruinous light
And night with many mouths would close
Around my infinite and sterile curve.

Shadow-maker create me everywhere   10
Dark spaces (your face is my chosen abyss),
For I said I have come to possess your darkness,
Only this.

(1969)

From *The T.E. Lawrence*[1] *Poems*

My Father

He never looked at anyone, not even me, like once
On one of those official city mornings, he stepped
          right on my foot in the middle of the road
          and kept on walking into nowhere.

He had inherited enough money for him to sail yachts
And shoot pheasants, and ride hard and drink hard
          until she tamed him with her fairy tales
          about God, and how He loved the sinner,
Not the sin. I wonder what he thought of his five
          little bastards. It was impossible to tell.   10

Now I'm very much like that country gentleman, in that
I can talk to you for hours without for a moment revealing
          that I don't have a clue who you are;
I never look at a man's face and never recognize one;
          I have never been sure of the color of my eyes.

---

1. T.E. Lawrence British soldier and writer (1888–1935), often referred to as "Lawrence of Arabia," who helped to lead an Arab revolt against the Turks in the Middle East.

Sometimes he looked so lost that I wanted to show him
The way back home, but the house had become a place
        of thunder; it stared at us with square,
        unseeing eyes, and I never knew why
20 He went to her in that permanent, resounding dark.

I suppose he might have been a lion of a man, but
When you castrate a lion, all its mane falls out and
        it mews like a cat. Imagine, he was afraid
        of everything; I, of nothing — (my key
        opened all the houses on the street, I thought).

Once as a boy I asked someone if a statue I stared at
Was alive. They said no, but they were wrong. It was.

(1982)

In Bed

One should only live in the future or the past,
In Utopia or The Wood beyond the World,[1] I said,
        but I had this Mission; it devoured
        my waking moments, and forced the present
        upon me like a storm.

I had a brass-rubbing of a dead Crusader[2] on the ceiling
And when sometimes, in satin midnights,
                                    my flesh crawled
With unspeakable desires, and the wind teased
10 The silly trees,
            and I knew myself to be
Just one step short of perfect — I'd lie and stare
At that ridiculous hero,
                    his lurid[3] body eaten by worms,
Night after night above me.

(1982)

The Water-Bearer

On a hill at Carcemish which is in Mesopotamia,[1] which is
        Between-the-Rivers,
We dug up the bones and artifacts of ancient strangers,
You and your donkey lugging buckets of water
        back and forth over many thousands of years,

---

1. **The Wood beyond the World** An 1894 fantasy novel by British writer William Morris (1834–1896). 2. **Crusader** Those who fought in religious-military campaigns by Catholic Europe against non-Catholics to the East (11th–13th centuries). 3. **lurid** Terrible, ghastly.

---

1. **Carcemish, Mesopotamia** Carcemish, a city between Turkey and Syria, was once owned by the Hittite Empire; it was also the site of a biblical battle between the Egyptians and Babylonians. The region was formerly called Mesopotamia.

While I made notes about absolutely everything, and
    wrote long letters home.

You watered the mules and camels and nothing was ever
Too pretty or tiresome that you couldn't make mad and
    silly fun of it;   10
                everything admired you.
The animals admired you because you had a splendid
    disregard for man that even they
    could not achieve. And a dark and secret love
That only they could achieve.

When it was too hot, we swam, and then the river
Released us and found its way back home.

They called you Darkness although your skin was fair;
I gave you a camera and taught you how to explore
    the darkness that lived behind light;   20
You said you would take pictures of the whole world.

Water-bearer, you gave everything and asked nothing
    in return. We dreamed that one day
    the ghosts of your ancestors would arise
    and tell to us wonderful Hittite secrets;
But we had forgotten that your name meant also
    the darkness of water before Creation;
    we did not know that you would one day drown
In the dark water of your own lungs.

I loved you, I believe. It was before the horror.   30

                                     (1982)

Feisal[1]

He was standing in a doorway waiting for me, all white,
Framed in black, with the light
                      slanting down on him —
    a heavenly weapon.
Of the ten thousand and thirty-seven words for *sword*
    in Arabic, his name meant one:
The sword flashing downward in the stroke.

My lord Feisal, the man I had come to Arabia to seek,
Had a calm Byzantine[2] face which, like an ikon,[3]
    was designed to reveal nothing. Many times,   10

---

1. Feisal Arab prince with whom Lawrence formed an alliance. **2. Byzantine** Greek-speaking empire, centred in
Constantinople. **3. ikon** Symbolic picture or image.

I learned later, he had watched his men
tortured by the Turks, and his black eyes
With their quiet fire did not flinch or turn away.

When he was at rest, his whole body was watching,
And when he moved, he floated over the earth, a prince.
　　　Once when I saw him, dark against the sun,
　　　its haze all gold through the silk of his *aba*,[4]
I knew I would have sold my soul for him, joyfully.

And how do you like our place here in Wadi Safra?[5]
20　　　he asked me, looking off to one side of me,
　　　as though an angel stood there, listening.
Well, I said: but it is far from Damascus.[6]

Later, when we rode northward into the dream that was his
And mine, he paid some of the men by letting them dip
　　　their hands into a box of gold sovereigns,
　　　and keep, not counting, all one hand could hold.
To reassure the others, he carried around false money —
Boxes of stones that rattled like silver and gold —
And we carried in our knapsacks the paper secrets
30　　　that were war, the bundles of rotting letters,
　　　the green figs, the promises, the lies.

No matter what happened they would always adore him —
　　　the prince whose name was a sword —
And I would follow my lord Feisal from Wadi Safra
　　　to the ends of the earth.

(1982)

The Mirage

This is the desert, as I promised you.
　　　There are no landmarks, only
Those you imagine, or those made by rocks
　　　that fell from heaven.

Did you ever know where you were going?
　　　Am I as invisible to you
As you always were to me, fellow traveller?
　　　You are not here for nothing.

There are no easy ways of seeing, riding
10　　　the waves of invisible seas

---

4. *aba* Sleeveless shirt of rough camel-hair material. 5. **Wadi Safra** Location of Feisal's camp. 6. **Damascus** Major
Syrian city where the Turks would surrender to the Arabs.

In marvellous vessels which are always
    arriving or departing.

I have come to uncover the famous secrets
    of earth and water, air and fire.
I have come to explore and contain them all.
    I am an eye.

I need tons of yellow space, and nothing
    in the spectrum is unknown to me.
I am the living center of your sight; I draw for you
    this thin and dangerous horizon.   20

(1982)

The Peace Conference

After prostituting myself in the service of an alien race,[1]
    I was too mangled for politics; the world
    swirled around me and I was its still center.
Old men crawled out from the woodwork and seized upon
    our victory, to re-shape it at their will.
We stammered that we had worked for a new heaven and
    a new earth. They thanked us kindly, and
    made their peace.

France carved up Syria[2] as Feisal questioned their rights
    to do so, inquiring gently which of them
    had won the Crusades;   10
                 everyone was carving up
    the kingdoms of each other's minds.
I quietly arranged everyone's destiny to my satisfaction,
    without revealing it out loud, as an inner voice
    informed me I had not done well at all —
I had freed the Arabs from everybody but ourselves.

My ideas were simple, always have been; I wanted only:
    an association of free, separate Arab states,
    the beginning of the United States of Arabia,   20
    the first brown dominion within the Empire,
And no mad talk of Arab unity; no one can unite
    the facets of a jewel.

Everything sickened me; I had been betrayed from the moment
    I was born. I betrayed the Arabs;
    Everything betrays everything.

---

1. **in service … alien race** This refers to Lawrence's support of the Arabs against the Turks during the Arab Revolt of 1916–1918. 2. **France … Syria** France, Britain, and Russia divided up the Arab world without consulting the regions' local governments.

It was an Arab war, waged and led by Arabs, for an Arab aim
In Arabia, I said, as the bedlam[3] grew louder,
   and France and Britain played chess
30   *with the world.*
         Feisal caught my eye, saying
Without words: I've given you my dreams, and now
you have to dream them.

                      (1982)

The Tao[1] of Physics

In the vast spaces of the subatomic world where
Matter has a   tendency   to exist
The lord of Life is breathing in and out,
Creating and destroying the universe
With each wave of his breath.[2]

And my lord Siva[3] dances in the city streets,
His body a fierce illusion of flesh, of energy,
The particles of light cast off from his hair
Invade the mighty night, the relative night, this dream.

10   Here where events have a   tendency   to occur
My chair and all its myriad[4] inner worlds
Whirl around in the carousel of space; I hurl
Breathless poems against my lord Death, send these
Words, these words
Careening into the beautiful darkness.

                      (1987)

Daphne Marlatt (1942–)

Interviewed by George Bowering in 1979, Daphne Marlatt identified a main intention of her work: "I love that phrase, the body of language. And I'm trying to realize its full sensory nature as much as possible." Her work often blends and bends the forms of poem, essay, documentary, fiction, theory, and life writing.

  Marlatt (née Buckle) was born in Melbourne, Australia, in 1942. Her British parents had settled in Malaysia but moved to Australia to escape the advancing Japanese army during World War II. After the war, the family returned to Malaysia, and there Daphne spent her childhood years. They moved to North Vancouver in 1951. In the early 1960s, Marlatt attended the University of British Columbia, where she took a course with Earle Birney and found herself drawn into the community of writers. During the period of creative excitement following the 1963 Vancouver Poetry Conference, she served

---

3. **bedlam** State of chaos.

---

1. **Tao** A Chinese philosophy that favours harmony and acceptance over action. 2. **creating ... breath** The Hindu faith believes that universes are created and destroyed as Vishnu, the preserver, inhales and exhales. 3. **Siva** Hindu deity, the destroyer, who is often depicted dancing. 4. **myriad** Many.

as an editor of the magazine *Tish*. Some of *Tish*'s founders — George Bowering, Frank Davey, and Fred Wah — would later help to demystify Marlatt's experimental poetry by explaining how it could be read. They could offer this insight because they had been influenced by Charles Olson's argument about "projective verse" — an approach to poetry that asserted that language is consciousness, each word stimulating the next through sonic or etymological association.

In 1964, Marlatt received her B.A. in English literature and creative writing from UBC, then she moved with her husband, Alan, to Indiana to attend graduate school. While writing *Frames* (1968), she published some of her early poems in Raymond Souster's influential anthology *New Wave Canada* (1966). In 1968, she completed her M.A. in comparative literature and published *Frames* and *leaf leaf/s* in quick succession. These sonic and syntactical experiments were tight and technical, reflecting the influence of Louis Zukofsky. Writing these books was her poetic apprenticeship, yet they contained characteristics of her mature work. One critic, for instance, has observed that they were meant to "establish a correlation between perception and articulation." In other words, they were intended to show how language is an experience, a phenomenon, and an event — not a mode of description.

Davey called her approach "phenomenological: every image and reflection of the woman's multiphasic consciousness is recorded — some by means of puns, metaphors, split words, parenthetical phrases." Wah (using Olson's term) called it "proprioceptive" — the poet "strives for a writing which will accurately reflect the condition of the writer at the moment of the writing." This self-reflexivity, multiplicity, and non-linearity indicate the postmodern character of Marlatt's work.

In the 1970s, through the efforts of friends such as Davey, Wah, and Bowering, Marlatt's reputation grew. As the decade began, she was living in Wisconsin and writing *Vancouver Poems* (1972); she published the long prose-poem experiment *Rings* in 1971. Later, in 1979, she reflected that "standard prose is written as if language was transparent. You're not seeing it. Poetry is written with the awareness that it's not transparent, that it is in fact a medium." In *Vancouver Poems*, Marlatt began to develop her interest in writing history — particularly documentary. She quoted archival and ethnographical materials, contrasting the official histories of the Canadian Pacific Railway, for example, with images of people who would not be included in such histories: "Old men. How many step to a dead fish smell. / How would *you* like a tail in the eye, scales, a / little bit rhumey but otherwise" ("Slimey"). In his review of the book, Bowering wrote that Marlatt's writing is "obscure but highly readable" and effectively approximated the experience of slowly becoming familiar with a city.

While she was the poetry editor for *Capilano Review* (1973–1976), Marlatt published *Steveston* (1974), her landmark long-poem collaboration with photographer Robert Minden (Robert Kroetsch would later use it as an example in his important essay "For Play and Entrance: The Contemporary Canadian Long Poem"). With this book, Marlatt advanced her exploration of life in cities and towns. Steveston was a "onetime cannery boomtown" largely populated by Japanese Canadians. Many of them had been arrested and sent to prison camps in the interior of British Columbia during World War II; returning to Steveston after the war, they had to "buy back their old homes, at inflated prices." Having also been displaced during the war, Marlatt could understand the nature of their troubles, and she bore witness to the continuing exploitation of Steveston residents by corporations and governments. Her work took on an explicitly political and journalistic dimension.

Marlatt supplemented *Steveston* with *Steveston Recollected* (1975), a history book. This led to *Zócalo* (1977), her first extended prose narrative. With *The Story, She Said* (1977), she expressed her growing interest in the differences between the languages used by men and by women, but she returned to the documentary form with *Opening Doors: Vancouver's East End* (1979). In 1980, she published *What Matters: Writing 1968–70,* a series of journal poems about the breakup of her marriage and the birth of her child, and *Net Work: Selected Writings*.

The next phase of her career was characterized by her growing interest in feminism and autobiography. In *How Hug a Stone* (1983), she combined the long poem and journal forms to chronicle her trip to England with her son, Kit. With *Touch to My Tongue* (1984), she explored a lesbian relationship through erotic, bodily language. In the included essay, "Musing with Mothertongue," Marlatt argues that language is "a living body we enter at birth." Aligning herself with feminist thinkers such as Julia Kristeva and Marguerite Duras in France, and Nicole Brossard, Louky Bersianik, and Jovette Marchessault in Québec, Marlatt attempted to show how the unspoken language of a woman's body could be invoked and spared from patriarchal repression. This idea reappeared in *Double Negative* (1988), which she wrote with her partner, Betsy Warland. *Ana Historic* (1988), Marlatt's first novel, showed that the history of women has not been written and that women, therefore, are "an ahistoric" group. Protagonist Ana's name can be written forward and backward, suggesting that if women's history cannot be written one way, then it can be written the other way.

After teaching women's studies at Simon Fraser University and founding the journal *Tessera* in the late 1980s, Marlatt entered a retrospective phase in her career. She published *Salvage* (1991), a reprise of *Steveston* from the feminist perspective that had become central to her outlook. In 1994, when her one-time partner and long-time friend Roy Kiyooka died, Marlatt assumed his job of editing the stories his mother had told him; they were published as *Mothertalk* (1998). In 1996, with her second novel, *Taken*, she returned to the themes of *Ana Historic*. In 1998, she produced *Readings from the Labyrinth*, a collection of essays, and in 2001, she published *This Tremor Love Is*, a collection of 25 years of love poems, with sections dedicated to three different people. Marlatt's latest book is the long poem *Seven Glass Bowls* (2003).

From *Steveston*

Imagine: a town

Imagine a town running

                (smoothly?
a town running before a fire
canneries burning

              (do you see the shadow of charred stilts
on cool water? do you see enigmatic chance standing
just under the beam?

                He said they were playing cards in the
Chinese mess hall, he said it was dark (a hall?   a shack.
10   they were all, crowded together on top of each other.
He said somebody accidentally knocked the oil lamp over, off
the edge

          where stilts are standing, Over the edge of the
dyke a river pours, uncalled for, unending:

                    where chance lurks
fishlike, shadows the underside of pilings, calling up his hall
the bodies of men & fish corpse piled on top of each other (residue
time is, the delta) rot, an endless waste the trucks of production
grind to juice, driving thru

                    smears, blood smears in the dark   20
dirt) this marshland silt no graveyard can exist in but water swills,
endlessly out of itself to the mouth

                    ringed with residue, where
chance flicks his tail & swims, thru

                                                                    (1984)

Steveston[1] as you find it:

                    multiplicity simply there: the physical matter of
the place (what matters) meaning, don't get theoretical now, the cannery.

It's been raining, or it's wet. Shines everywhere a slick on the surface of
things wet gumboots[2] walk over, fish heads & other remnants of sub/ or
marine life, brought up from under. Reduced to the status of things hands
lop the fins off, behead, tail, tossed, this matter that doesn't matter,
into a vat or more correctly box the forklifts will move, where they swim,
flat of eye — deathless that meaningless stare, "fisheye" (is it only
dead we recognize them?) in a crimson sauce of their own blood.

                                                    We orient   10
always toward the head, & eyes (yes) as knowing, & knowing us, or what we do.
But these, this, is "harvest." These are the subhuman facets of life we the
town (& all that is urban, urbane, our glittering table service, our white
wine, the sauces we pickle it with, or ourselves), live off. These torsos.
& we throw the heads away. Or a truck passes by, loaded with offal[3] for what
we also raise to kill, mink up the valley.

                                    That's not it. It's wet,
& there's a fish smell. There's a subhuman, sub/marine aura to things. The
cavernous "fresh fish" shed filled with water, with wet bodies of dead fish,
in thousands, wet aprons & gloves of warm bodies whose hands expertly trim,   20
cut, fillet, pack these bodies reduced to non-bodies, nonsensate food *these*
bodies ache from, feet in gumboots on wet cement, arms moving, hands, cold
blowing in from open doors facing the river, whose ears dull from, the in-
sensate noise of machinery, of forklifts, of grinding & washing, of conveyor
belt. Put on an extra sweater, wear long underwear against the damp that
creeps up from this asphalt, from this death that must be kept cool, fresh.

---

1. **Steveston** Small fishing town near Vancouver, B.C. 2. **gumboots** Rubber rain boots. 3. **offal** Unusable parts of a dead animal.

"DISINFECT YOUR GLOVES BEFORE RESUMING WORK."

That no other corpus work within it. Kept at the freshest, at the very point of
mutable life, diverting, into death. To be steamed in cans, or baked, frozen in
30   fillets, packaged sterile for the bacteria of living bodies to assimilate. break
down. Pacific Ocean flesh.

No, that's not it. There's a dailiness these lives revolve around, also immersed.
Shifts, from seven to four or otherwise. Half an hour for lunch. & a long
paperwrap & tied form outside the lunchroom, keeping cool. 'til shift's
end & the fridge,   supper,   bed.   "my life," etc.

                             "You leave 2 minutes after 4,
& not before, you understand? Two minutes after." Two minutes, as if that,
together with the sardine cans for ashtray, made all the difference. Which is,
simply, as two Japanese women sit, relaxing with their fifteen minute coffee
40   out of thermos, more likely hot soup, one rearranges the chrysanthemums, red &
yellow, she placed in an empty can on their table this morning when the day
began. Or more directly how in "fresh fish" the lunchrooms, men's & women's,
face over an expanse of roof with flowerboxes even, river & the delta, Ladner,[4]
space. & remain spacious, time turned calendar of kimona'd beauty, kneeling,
on the wall. While in the cannery close to wharfedge they face north,
backed by old wooden lockers to the door: DO NOT SPIT IN THE GARBAGE.
USE THE TOILETS. & here they flood in together, giggling, rummaging thru
bags, eating grapes, girlish even ("I've worked here 20 years") under severe
green kerchief like Italian peasants, except that they are mostly Japanese,
50   plunked under a delicate mobile of Japanese ribbon fish in their gumboots
& socks. Break, from routine, with the ease of tired bodies laughing,
for what? "It's life." *Their* life?

                         Or how the plant packs their lives, chopping
off the hours, contains *them* as it contains first aid, toilets, beds, the
vestige of a self-contained life in this small house back of the carpentry
shed, where two woodburners are littered with pots & hot plates, & the table
still bears its current pattern of dominoes. Where a nude on the wall glints
kittenish at one of the two small rooms inside, each with iron bed. Some
sleeping place between shifts? Dark. Housing wet dreams, pale beside the
60   clank of forklift, supply truck, welding shed.

It's a mis-step, this quiet gap on everyone else's shift, when you're off,
when accidental gravel rattles loud on the wooden walk. wan sun. coffee,
gone cold. There's a surface skin of the familiar, familial. Running into
shadow, where old socks, someone elses intimate things, call up the fishy
odour of cunt, of lamp black in the old days you could hear them screwing
behind their door (cardboard), & even the kitchen still exists to pull you

---

4. **Ladner** Fishing village on the Fraser River, B.C.

back in, to smallness, a smell of coal, the aura of oil, of what comes up
from under, sleeping — nets, wet still from riverbottom, & the fish.

This darker seam that slips underneath the coppery gleam of all those cans stacked
flat after flat, waiting transfer. Men. & Women. Empty familiar lunchroom,   70
& the dream, pounding with the pound of machinery under mountains of empty packer
pens at night, the endless (white) stream of flesh passing under the knives,
To be given up, gone, in a great bleeding jet, into that other (working) world.

(1984)

At Birch Bay

for Roy

(thanks to Charles Olson)

black, crow, leap up   fall, flap nervous wings against a steep
invisible. bank,   against wind flutters, settle,   has none of the
sweep & glide these gulls have   open to this incessant
oncoming tide   waves & foam   wind

                           Crow, rise &
(drop something   rise & (drop,   flutter,   in to his own stress
landing against this wind, over & over.   Cracking shells, having
learned this from the gulls?

                       thru time, in the rising
wind last night I dreamt, & see, now, like the crow what it is I   10
learn from you
           walking
               walking the night as moon, moves out of
cancer, out of sea & moon pre-eminent, walking the long. tiderow-
beach. alone: white shells, white backs of gulls on the further
strand,   lift,   onto the air, clapping wings at their
re-entry into the element,   birds,   know wind changes
fast as the moon, how tide makes sand disappear, no place to be
except the turbulent face of sea itself incessant …
                       It was you who   20
entered my dream, entered me,   in the rising wind last night, in love
in the wash of opening seas we come together in : something about a
newborn you saw (rise & drop, rise &) drop   a long life line down
thru all these threshing seas, these birds, like refugees, are resting in
cloud earth sky sensorium   outside my dream, outside our dream — "ends &
boundaries," or "'space-activities' in, Creation." Within which, this
marvellous "Animate" you teach me, along with the sweep & glide these
gulls possess   this (shell) their & our   one & only   world. 4/75

(1975)

in the dark of the coast

there is fern and frost, a gathering of small birds melting song in the underbrush. close,
you talk to one. there is the cedar slant of your hair as it falls gold over your shoulder,
over your naked, dearly known skin — its smell, its answering touch to my tongue.
fondant, font, found, all that melts, pours. the dark rain of our being together at last.
and the cold wind, curled-up fronds of tree fern wanting touch, our fingers separate
and stiff. we haven't mourned enough, you say, for our parting, lost to each other the
last time through. in the dark of this place, its fire touch, not fern but frost, just one of
the houses we pass through in the endless constellation of our being, close, and away
from each other, torn and apart. i didn't know your hair, i didn't know your skin when
10   you beckoned to me in that last place. but i knew your eyes, blue, as soon as you came
around the small hill, knew your tongue. come, you said, we slid together in the spring,
blue, of a place we'd been. terra incognita[1] known, *geysa*,[2] gush, upwelling in the hidden
Norse we found, we feel it thrust as waters part for us, hot, through fern, frost, volcanic
thrust. it's all there, love, we part each other coming to, geyser, spouting pool, hidden
in and under separate skin we make for each other through.

(1984)

prairie

in this land the rivers carve furrows and canyons as sudden to the eye as if earth
opened up its miles and miles of rolling range, highway running to its evercoming
horizon, days of it, light picking flowers. your blackeyed susans are here, my coral weed
in brilliant patches, and always that grass frayed feathery by the season, late, and wild
canada geese in the last field. i imagine your blue eye gathering these as we go, only
you are not here and the parched flat opens up: badlands and hoodoos[1] and that river
with dangerous currents you cannot swim, TREACHEROUS BANK, sandstone caving
in: and there she goes, Persephone[2] caught in a whirlwind the underside churns up, the
otherwise of where we are, cruising earth's surface, gazing on it, grazing, like those
10   70 million year old dinosaurs, the whole herd browsing the shore of Bearpaw Sea which
ran all the way in up here, like Florida, she said, came in from the desert region they
were hungry for grass (or flowers) when something like a flashflood caught them,
their bones, all these years later, laid out in a whirlpool formation i cannot see (that as
the metaphor) up there on the farthest hoodoo, those bright colours she keeps stressing,
the guy in the red shirt, metal flashing, is not Hades but only the latest technician in a
long line of measurers. and earth? i have seen her open up to let love in, let loose a
flood, and fold again, so that even my fingers could not find their way through all that
bush, all that common day rolling unbroken.

(1984)

---

1. terra incognita Latin for "unknown territory," used by explorers. **2.** *geysa* To sweep, pass quickly over (Icelandic).

1. hoodoos Oddly-shaped pillars of rock left behind by erosion. **2. Persephone** Classical goddess of spring, kidnapped by Hades, lord of the underworld.

Booking Passage

You know the place: then
Leave Crete and come to us
     — Sappho/Mary Barnard

this coming & going in the dark of early morning, snow scribbling its
thaw-line round the house. We are under-cover, under a cover of white
you unlock your door on this slipperiness.

to throw it off, this cover, this blank that halts a kiss on the open road. i kiss
you anyway, & feel you veer toward me, red tail lights aflare at certain patches,
certain turns my tongue takes, provocative.

we haven't even begun to write … sliding the in-between as the ferry slips its
shore-line, barely noticeable at first, a gathering beat of engines in reverse,
the shudder of the turn to make that long passage out—

the price paid for this.   10

we stood on the road in the dark. you closed the door so carlight wouldn't
shine on us. our kiss reflected in snow, the name for this.

under the covers, morning, you take my scent, writing me into your cells'
history. deep in our sentencing, i smell you home.

there is the passage. there is the booking — & our fear of this.

you, sliding past the seals inert on the log boom. you slide & they don't raise
their heads. you are into our current now of going, not inert, not even gone as i
lick you loose. there is a light beginning over the ridge of my closed eyes.

passage booked. i see you by the window shore slips by, you reading Venice
our history is, that sinking feel, those footings under water. i nose the book   20
aside & pull you forward gently with my lips.

a path, channel or duct. a corridor. a book & not a book. not booked but off
the record. this.

irresistible melt of hot flesh. furline & thawline align your long wet descent.

nothing in the book says where we might head. my tongue in you, your body
cresting now around, around this tip's lip- suck surge rush of your coming
in other words.

we haven't even begun to write … what keeps us going, this rush of
wingspread, this under (nosing in), this wine-dark blood flower. this
rubbing between the word and our skin.   30

*

"tell me, tell me where you are" when the bush closes in, all heat a luxuriance of earth so heavy i can't breathe the stifling wall of prickly rose, skreek of mosquito poised … for the wall to break

the wall that isolates, that i so late to this: it doesn't, it slides apart — footings, walls, galleries, this island architecture

one layer under the other, memory a ghost, a guide, histolytic where the pain is stored, murmur, mer-*mère*, historicity stored in the tissue, text … a small boat, fraught. trying to cross distance, trying to find that passage (secret) in libraries where whole texts, whole persons have been secreted away.

40   original sin he said was late overlay. & under that & under that? sweat pouring down, rivers of thyme and tuberose in the words that climb toward your scanning eyes

She shouts aloud, Come! we know it;
thousand-eared night repeats that cry
across the sea shining between us

*

this tracking back & forth across the white, this tearing of papyrus crosswise, this tearing of love in our mouths to leave our mark in the midst of rumour, coming out.

… to write in lesbian.

50   the dark swell of a sea that separates & beats against our joined feet, islands me in the night, fear & rage the isolate talking in my head. to combat this slipping away, of me, of you, the steps … what was it we held in trust, tiny as a Venetian bead, fragile as words encrusted with pearl, *mathetriai*, not-mother, hidden mentor, lost link?

to feel our age we stood in the road in the dark, we stood in the roads & it was this old, a ripple of water against the hull, a coming and going

we began with …

her drowned thyme and clover, fields of it heavy with dew our feet soak up, illicit hands cupped one in the other as carlights pick us out. the yell a salute.
60   marked, we are elsewhere,

translated here …

like her, precisely on this page, this mark: *a thin flame runs under / my skin.* twenty-five hundred years ago, this trembling then. actual as that which wets

our skin her words come down to us, a rush, poured through the blood, this
coming & going among islands is.

(1991)

Don McKay (1942–)

Don McKay was born in 1942 in Owen Sound, Ontario, and grew up 600 kilometres to the east, in Cornwall. He attended Bishop's University, in Lennoxville, Quebec, and subsequently obtained an M.A. from the University of Western Ontario (1966) and a Ph.D. from the University of Wales (1971). In 1975, he was hired to teach English and creative writing at the University of Western Ontario, and while in London he co-founded Brick Books with Stan Dragland. From 1990 to 1996, McKay taught at the University of New Brunswick and served as editor of the *Fiddlehead*, which describes itself as the country's "longest living literary journal." Deciding that he wanted to write on a full-time basis, McKay retired from teaching in 1997 and moved to Victoria, British Columbia, with his partner, poet Jan Zwicky.

Dragland once remarked that McKay — along with fellow writers Robert Bringhurst, Dennis Lee, Tim Lilburn, and Zwicky — was engaged in a "search for responsible ways of being in the world." Heavily influenced by mid-century European philosophy, McKay has spent the last 30 years re-examining fundamental questions proposed by Martin Heidegger and Emmanuel Levinas: What is being? What are tools? How do we know, see, and write about these tools? How do we go about using them in a respectful and ethical way? McKay's most concerted effort to address these questions is the long poem *Long Sault* (1975), which traces the displacement of communities and the destruction of natural history triggered by the construction of a hydroelectric dam near his hometown of Cornwall. *Long Sault* was preceded by *Air Occupies Space* (1973) and followed by *Lependu* (1978), a prose-poem about a hanged man in which McKay begins to explore the relationship between language and wilderness — a natural wilderness devoid of human phys-icality and human thought. It is a zone where "the only writing is the writing of the glaciers on the rocks / the only thinking is the river slowly / knowing its valley."

In order to access this zone through poetry, McKay argues, "one does not invoke language right-off." Instead, the poet will "keep coming back, figuratively speaking, to the trail — to the grain of experience." McKay acknowledges that to talk or write about the natural wilderness is to impose human values and concepts upon it, and he therefore advocates a new kind of "poetic attention" — an attention to objects as we encounter them in the world rather than to objects as we encounter them through literature. The wilderness, the unknown path, and the otherness of nature are the generators of meaning for McKay; poetry merely translates that meaning into language, so poems are simply "translations."

The form that each translation takes will vary. McKay has written long poems, prose-poems, and essays on poetics, but most often he writes short lyrics. His poems are studded with puns, unexpected images, comic enjambment, and dense metaphors. His speakers are highly self-conscious in their struggle to respectfully translate the wilderness into human terms. Furthermore, McKay strenuously avoids moulding content to accommodate poetic rhythms or rhyme schemes, convinced that poems discover their natural shape as the writing progresses; he favours organic free verse over structured lyric forms, like the sonnet.

McKay's fourth poetry collection, *Lightning Ball Bait*, was published in 1980. Three years later, with the appearance of his fifth book, *Birding, or Desire*, McKay's poetic inquiries into nature and being began to receive critical approbation. *Birding*, now recognized as a landmark in his career, won him a Canadian Authors Association Prize and a Governor General's Award nomina-tion. McKay sees birds as both wilderness emissaries and symbols of his yearning to unite with the wilderness — a yearning that can never be satisfied. His bird-watching speakers sometimes envy birds their ability to fly, their freedom, but they also know that freedom is nothing more than a human concept. Their admiration for birds, then, sometimes resolves into a painful sense of alienation from them. In the poem ironically entitled "Identification," for example, the speaker, seeing a peregrine in flight, cries out: "falcon / fix me to my feet and lock me in this / slow sad pocket of awe." Bird-watching becomes a metaphor for poetry-writing: while it may transport the watcher/writer closer to the wild, it ultimately serves to emphasize his separation from it.

With *Sanding Down This Rocking Chair on a Windy Night* (1987), *Night Field* (1991), and *Apparatus* (1997), McKay pursues his investigation of the tools we employ to think about and control the natural world. In more recent collections, *Another Gravity* (2000) and *Strike/Slip* (2006), he interrogates the way we allow natural phenomena (the moon, fault lines) to accumulate metaphorical associations — associations that refer, for good or for ill, to the process of artistic creation.

Over the last few years, McKay has markedly increased his output, and his readership has grown. In 2001, he produced a volume of essays, *Vis à Vis: Fieldnotes on Poetry and Wilderness*; in 2004, he published *Camber: Selected Poems 1983–2000*; the following year, he produced a second prose collection, *Deactivated West 100*; and in 2006, the selected *Field Marks — The Poetry of Don McKay* appeared. McKay has won two Governor General's Awards — for *Night Field* (1991) and for *Another Gravity* (2000) — and *Camber* and *Another Gravity* were also short-listed for the Griffin Poetry Prize.

The Boy's Own Guide to Dream Birds

Audubonless[1]
dream birds thrive. The talking swan, the kestrels[2]
nesting in the kitchen, undocumented citizens of teeming
terra incognita.[3]
        To write
their book the boy will need
la plume de ma tante,[4] harfang des neiges,[5]
patience, an ear like a cornucopia and at least
an elementary understanding of the place of human psychology
10   among nature's interlocking food chains.
                  For the facts are scarce
and secretive. Who is able to identify
the man in metamorphosis, becoming
half-bird on the Coldstream Road? The boy reports
a falcon's beak both hooked and toothed, the fingers spreading,
lengthening into a vulture's fringe, the cold eye
glaring as he lifts off from the road: look, look,
come quick!
        Who sits inside and fails to hear?
20   What can he be doing?
       Why is he so deaf?

---

1. **Audubonless** John James Audubon (1785–1851) was a French-American ornithologist and painter. 2. **kestrels** Small falcons. 3. **terra incognita** Latin for "unknown territory"; an expression used by explorers. 4. **la plume de ma tante** Literally, "my aunt's pen." 5. **harfang des neiges** Snowy owl.

But on another night a huge, hunched, crested,
multicoloured bird, a sort of cross between eagle
and macaw, sits, sinister and gorgeous,
on our mailbox.
Now we know what happens to the letters we do not receive
from royalty, and from our secret lovers
pining in the chaste apartments of the waking world.

(1983)

The Great Blue Heron

What I remember
about the Great Blue Heron that rose
like its name over the marsh
is touching and holding that small
manyveined
wrist
upon the gunwale,[1] to signal silently —

look

The Great Blue Heron
(the birdboned wrist).   10

(1983)

Kestrels

"The name 'Sparrow hawk' is unfair to this handsome and beneficial little falcon."
The Birds of Canada

1.

unfurl from the hydro wire, beat
con brio[1] out across the field and
hover, marshalling the moment, these
gestures of our slender hostess,
ushering her guests into the dining room

2.

sprung rhythm and
surprises, enharmonic change directions simply
step outside and let the earth turn
underneath, trapdoors, new lungs, missing bits
of time, plump familiar pods go   10
pop in your mind you learn not
principles of flight but how to fall, you learn
pity for that paraplegic bird, the heart

---

1. **gunwale** Edge of a boat.

---

1. **con brio** Italian musical term; "with spirit."

3.

to watch by the roadside singing *killy killy killy*,
plumaged like a tasteful parrot,
to have a repertoire of moves so clean their edge is
                          the frontier of nothing
to be sudden   to send
postcards of distance which arrive in nicks of time

20   to open letters with a knife

                                                (1983)

How to Imagine an Albatross

(assisted by the report of a CIA observer near Christmas Island)

To imagine an albatross
a mind must widen to the breadth of the Pacific Ocean
dissolve its edges to admit a twelve foot wingspan soaring
silently across the soft enormous heave as the planet
breathes into another dawn.
This might be
dream without content or the opening of a film
in which the credits never run no speck appears
on the horizon fattening to Randolph Scott[1] on horseback
10   or the lost
brown mole below your shoulder blade, the albatross
is so much of the scene he drinks the ocean never needs
to beat the air into supporting him but
thoughtlessly as an idea, as a phrase-mark holding notes
in sympathy, arcs above the water.

And to imagine an albatross
we must plan to release the rage
which holds this pencil in itself, to prod things
until their atoms shift, rebel against their thingness, chairs
20   run into walls, stones
pour like a mob from their solidity.

A warm-up exercise:
                once
in London, Ontario, a backhoe accidentally
took out a regulator on the gas-line, so the pressure
    of the system
rushed the neighbourhood. Stoves
turned into dragons and expressed
their secret passions all along the ordinary street

---

1. Randolph Scott American actor (1898–1987), a star of western movies.

the houses bloomed fiercely as the peonies in their front   30
   yards.

Meanwhile the albatross, thoughtlessly
as an idea, as a phrase-mark holding notes
in sympathy, arcs into a day
that will escape the dull routine of dayness and achieve
crescendo.
             Placing ourselves safely
at a distance we observe
how the sky burns off its blueness to unveil
the gaze of outer space, which even here   40
has turned the air psychotic. The birds
start smoking, then,
as though Van Gogh[2] were painting them, turn
cartwheels in the air, catch fire
and fall into the ocean.
What saves us now from heat and light
what keeps us now from biting off our tongues
what stops blood boiling through the heart blocks
recognition of this burning curve
slicing like a scythe[3] through the mind   50
is what hereafter will protect us

from the earth.

                                (1987)

Fates Worse Than Death

Atrocity
implies an audience of gods.
The gods watched as swiftfooted
godlike Achilles cut behind the tendons of both feet
and pulled a strap of oxhide through
so he could drag the body of Hektor,[1]
tamer of horses, head down in the dust
behind his chariot.
Some were appalled, some not,
having nursed their grudges well, until   10
those grudges were fine milkfed
adolescents, armed
with automatic weapons. The gods,

---

2. **Van Gogh** Dutch painter Vincent Van Gogh (1853–1890) was interested in light and movement. 3. **scythe** Curved blade used for harvesting.

---

1. **Achilles, Hektor** Achilles was the greatest warrior in the Trojan War; he fought Hektor, leader of the Trojans.

and farther off,
the gods before the gods, those who ate
their children and contrived
exquisite tortures in eternity, watched
and knew themselves undead. Such is the loss, such
the wrath of swiftfooted godlike
20   Achilles, the dumb fucker, that he drags,
up and down, and round and round the tomb
of his beloved, the body of Hektor,
tamer of horses. Atrocity
is never senseless. No. Atrocity is dead ones
locked in sense, forbidden
to return to dust, but scribbled in it,
so that everyone — the gods,
the gods before the gods, the enemy, the absent mothers, all
must read what it is like to live out exile on the earth
30   without it, to be without recesses, place,
a campsite where the river opens
into the lake, must read
what it means to live against the sun and not to die.
Watch,
he says, alone in the public
newscast of his torment, as he
cuts behind the tendons of both feet,
and pulls a strap of oxhide through,
so he can drag the body that cannot stop being Hektor,
40   tamer of horses, head down in the dust
behind his chariot, watch
this.

(1997)

Finger Pointing at the Moon

"We come from a hidden ocean, and go to an unknown ocean."
        — Antonio Machado

Everything you think of has already happened
and been sung by the sea. We were hiking
along the coast, with the hush and boom of surf
in our ears, on a trail so wet it was mostly
washouts strung together, forcing us
to find fresh ways around, teetery
and nimble, until I thought, yes,
the real agenda of this so-called trail
is not to lead us through this sopping biomass
10   but into it, with the surf
as soundtrack. *Everything you think,* it sang,
has already happened and been sung in long

confessional sighs and softly
crashing dactyls, wash, rinse,
wash, useless to resist. Each wave,
having travelled incognito through its ocean,
surges up to rush the rock, Homer[1] was here, and perish,
famous and forgotten. On the beach
the back-drag clicks the stones and pebbles
on each other, a death rattle that is somehow soothing, somehow   20
music, some drum kit from the far side of the blues
where loss begins to shuffle. It's O.K. to disappear. Off balance,
I'm trying to hop from stepping stone to stone
when I flash back forty years to my friend's
younger sister sitting in the boat,
trailing her fingers as we row out to the raft, how she gazes,
pouring herself into water as its depth
pours into her. I remember
being embarrassed she'd been caught out
having an inner life and rowed hard for the raft   30
where summer fun was waiting with its brawny cannonballs
and swan dives. I think each memory is lit
by its own small moon — a snowberry,
a mothball, a dime — which regulates its tides
and longings. Next time I am going to lift the oars
so we can watch the droplets fall back,
hidden ocean into unknown ocean,
while we drift. I will need a word
to float there, some empty blue-green bottle
that has lost its label. When we lose the trail entirely,   40
or it feeds us to the rain forest,
what will we be like? Probably not the Winter Wren,
whose impossible song is the biography of Buddha,
then Mary Shelley,[2] then your no-good Uncle Ray.
Not the Cat-tail Moss
which hangs in drapes and furs the fallen logs in lavish
sixties shag. I think we come here so our words
can fail us, get humbled by the stones, drown,
be lost forever, then come back
as beach glass, polished and anonymous,   50
knowing everything. Knowing everything they
think of has already happened, everything they think of has
already happened and been sung, knowing
everything they think of has already happened and been sung,
in all its tongues and metres, and to no one,
by the sea.

(2000)

---

1. **Homer** Greek poet, writer of *The Iliad* and *The Odyssey*. 2. **Mary Shelley** Author of *Frankenstein* (1797–1851).

"Stress, Shear, and Strain Theories of Failure"

They have never heard of lift
and are — for no one, over and over — cleft. Riven,[1]
recrystallized. Ruined again. The earth-engine
driving itself through death after death. Strike/slip,
thrust, and the fault called normal, which occurs
when two plates separate.
Do they hearken unto Orpheus,[2] whose song
is said to make them move? Sure.
This sonnet hereby sings that San Fran-
10   cisco and L.A. shall, thanks to its chthonic[3] shear,
lie cheek by jowl[4] in thirty million
years. Count on it, mortals. Meanwhile,
may stress shear strain attend us. Let us fail
in all the styles established by our lithosphere.[5]

(2006)

Thomas King (1943–)

Thomas King remarks, "Tragedy is my topic. Comedy is my strategy." Responding to the effects of colonialism on Native peoples in North America and shifting attention to pre-colonial traditions, King writes short stories, novels, and essays that are both seriously urgent and playfully comic. He was the child of a mixed marriage, born in 1943 near Sacramento, California. His father was a military man of Cherokee descent, an alcoholic who abandoned his family when Thomas was five years old. King's non-Native mother kept the household running, supporting the family with her hairdressing business and maintaining contact with Cherokee relatives in Oklahoma. Travelling across the Midwest to visit family, King experienced many border crossings — a motif that would later appear in his writing.

King attended a Catholic boarding school and then high school in Roseville; from there he went to California State University, Sacramento. He quit after one year and worked at a series of jobs — actor, casino dealer, ambulance driver, and bank teller. In 1964, he mistakenly travelled to New Zealand (he'd intended to go to New Guinea), and then moved on to Australia, where he found work as a photojournalist. He wrote his first novel, which he did not publish, and in 1967 he returned to the United States and to university. He earned his B.A. in 1970 and his M.A. in 1972 from California State University, Chico.

Around this time, he read N. Scott Momaday's Pulitzer Prize–winning *House Made of Dawn* (1969) and was inspired that a Native person could write a book that would appeal to a wide audience. In 1980, after teaching at the University of Minnesota and serving as chairperson of its American Indian studies program, King immigrated to Canada to take a faculty job at the University of Lethbridge, Alberta. He later moved to the University of Guelph to teach Native literature and creative writing.

---

1. **Riven** Distressed or torn. 2. **Orpheus** Classical mythological musician who won the chance to retrieve his wife, Eurydice, from the underworld as a reward for his music of mourning. 3. **Chthonic** Subterranean. 4. **cheek by jowl** Side by side. 5. **lithosphere** Crust of the earth.

During the 1980s, King left Canada for a short time to earn his Ph.D. from the University of Utah. His dissertation (1986) bore the influence of Momaday, as well as James Welch and Leslie Marmon Silko, Native writers who countered what he called the "literary phantasms" of 19th-century colonial views of Native peoples. He concluded that repetition, ritual, and circular narration characterized Native stories, comparing this to the traditionally linear plots of Anglo-European fiction. King would eventually begin incorporating circular narratives into his own writing, but for the time being he was preoccupied with more traditional works.

From the late 1980s until the mid-1990s, King was especially busy. He edited *The Native in Literature: Canadian and Comparative Perspectives* (1987) and *All My Relations: An Anthology of Contemporary Canadian Native Fiction* (1990). Then, in 1990, he produced an important article — "Godzilla vs. Post-Colonial" — in which he argued that Native cultures should not be studied as if colonialism were the single most important factor in the lives of Natives peoples. These cultures existed long before colonial contact; they could not be reduced to a tale of victim and victimizer. "Ironically," King writes, "while the term itself — post-colonial — strives to escape to find new centres, it remains, in the end, a hostage to nationalism."

The year 1990 was a milestone for two more reasons: first, in that year King transcribed the oral narratives of Harry Robinson, and the task compelled him to examine the ways in which one might approximate orality in a written tale; second, he published *Medicine River*, his first novel. *Medicine River* carefully deconstructs Native stereotypes, showing that Native and non-Native cultures are vulnerable to the same social problems. It concerns Will, a mixed-blood photographer who returns from Toronto to his mother's Native community in Alberta. Harlan, the novel's trickster figure, dupes Will into accepting the welcoming gestures of the Natives of Medicine River (a fiction-alized Lethbridge). In one key scene, Harlan takes Will to visit the isolated home of a traditional Blackfoot matchmaker and helper. Her house is separated from the city by the river, across which Harlan and Will wade, even though (as Will discovers later) they could have used the bridge. Harlan's unspoken point is that borders are often intentional or symbolic boundaries, not necessary ones.

Medicine River was made into a CBC Television movie (1993), starring Graham Greene and Tom Jackson. King wrote the screenplay. In the early 1990s, he also wrote scripts for CBC's *North of 60* television series and edited stories for the network's *Four Directions*. These undertakings won him a prominent role on the CBC Radio comedy *The Dead Dog Café* (1996–2001), which he created, wrote, and performed in. King published *One Good Story, That One* in 1993. In this book of short stories influenced by Robinson's oral narratives and the novels of Momaday, Silko, and Welch, the coyote emerges as a trickster figure who plays with the workings of the narrative. His motives are seemingly inexplicable, and he possesses the powers of multiplication and transfor-mation. The narrator explains that "all of Coyote's stories are bent." Furthermore, Coyote says, "I'll tell you the rules as we go along."

Coyote reappears in King's Governor General's Award–nominated *Green Grass, Running Water* (1993), a comic novel with a narrative that constantly begins again. Often fable-like, it demonstrates how Christianity absorbed Native creation stories and confined them within its own ideological boundaries. It also incorporates other fictional characters into the narrative, such as the Lone Ranger, *Moby-Dick*'s Ishmael, and Robinson Crusoe. Jesus Christ appears, embodying Christian values of martyrdom, hierarchical authority, and an omniscient god: "Christian rules, says Young Man Walking On Water. And the first rule is that no one can help me. The second rule is that no one can tell me anything. Third, no one is allowed to be in two places at once. Except me." Impressed with seeing Jesus walk on water, but on his own terms, Coyote responds, "That's a really good trick."

With *Truth and Bright Water* (1999), King returned to a less playful approach than that of *Green Grass, Running Water*, but he retained some magical elements to blend with the realist ones. The novel examines the twinning effect in a Blackfoot community divided by both a river and the more problematic line of the Canada–U.S. border. Of the recurring border motif, King says, "Well, I guess I'm supposed to say that I believe in the line that exists between the U.S. and Canada, but for me it's an imaginary line … [and] it's not my imagination." King returned to short fiction with *A Short History of Indians in Canada* (2005). The surreal title story involves Bob, a businessman visiting Toronto, who is startled to see flying Indians crash into the windows of skyscrapers and fall to the ground, stunned. Another character laments, "In the old days, when they came through, they would black out the entire sky." The story demonstrates that King's ability to merge tragedy and comedy has not diminished.

King has also published three children's books, and, under the pseudonym Hartley Good-Weather, he recently began publishing a series of comic detective novels.

Borders

When I was twelve, maybe thirteen, my mother announced that we were going to go to Salt Lake City to visit my sister who had left the reserve, moved across the line, and found a job. Laetitia had not left home with my mother's blessing, but over time my mother had come to be proud of the fact that Laetitia had done all of this on her own.

"She did real good," my mother would say.

Then there were the fine points to Laetitia's going. She had not, as my mother liked to tell Mrs. Manyfingers, gone floating after some man like a balloon on a string. She hadn't snuck out of the house, either, and gone to Vancouver or Edmonton or Toronto to chase rainbows down alleys. And she hadn't been pregnant.

"She did real good."

I was seven or eight when Laetitia left home. She was seventeen. Our father was from Rocky Boy on the American side.

"Dad's American," Laetitia told my mother, "so I can go and come as I please."

"Send us a postcard."

Laetitia packed her things, and we headed for the border. Just outside of Milk River, Laetitia told us to watch for the water tower.

"Over the next rise. It's the first thing you see."

"We got a water tower on the reserve," my mother said. "There's a big one in Lethbridge, too."

"You'll be able to see the tops of the flagpoles, too. That's where the border is."

When we got to Coutts, my mother stopped at the convenience store and bought her and Laetitia a cup of coffee. I got an Orange Crush.

"This is real lousy coffee."

"You're just angry because I want to see the world."

"It's the water. From here on down, they got lousy water."

"I can catch the bus from Sweetgrass. You don't have to lift a finger."

"You're going to have to buy your water in bottles if you want good coffee."

There was an old wooden building about a block away, with a tall sign in the yard that said "Museum." Most of the roof had been blown away. Mom told me to go and see when the place was open. There were boards over the windows and doors. You could tell that the place was closed, and I told Mom so, but she said to go and check anyway. Mom and Laetitia stayed by the car. Neither one of them moved. I sat down on the steps of the museum and watched them, and I don't know that they ever said anything to each other. Finally, Laetitia got her bag out of the trunk and gave Mom a hug.

I wandered back to the car. The wind had come up, and it blew Laetitia's hair across her face. Mom reached out and pulled the strands out of Laetitia's eyes, and Laetitia let her.

"You can still see the mountain from here," my mother told Laetitia in Blackfoot.

"Lots of mountains in Salt Lake," Laetitia told her in English.

"The place is closed," I said, "Just like I told you."

Laetitia tucked her hair into her jacket and dragged her bag down the road to the brick building with the American flag flapping on a pole. When she got to where the guards were waiting, she turned, put the bag down, and waved to us. We waved back. Then my mother turned the car around, and we came home.

We got postcards from Laetitia regular, and, if she wasn't spreading jelly on the truth, she was happy. She found a good job and rented an apartment with a pool.

"And she can't even swim," my mother told Mrs. Manyfingers.

Most of the postcards said we should come down and see the city, but whenever I mentioned this, my mother would stiffen up.

So I was surprised when she bought two new tires for the car and put on her blue dress with the green and yellow flowers. I had to dress up, too, for my mother did not want us crossing the border looking like Americans. We made sandwiches and put them in a big box with pop and potato chips and some apples and bananas and a big jar of water.

"But we can stop at one of those restaurants, too, right?"

"We maybe should take some blankets in case you get sleepy."

"But we can stop at one of those restaurants, too, right?"

The border was actually two towns, though neither one was big enough to amount to anything. Coutts was on the Canadian side and consisted of the convenience store and gas station, the museum that was closed and boarded up, and a motel. Sweetgrass was on the American side, but all you could see was an overpass that arched across the highway and disappeared into the prairies. Just hearing the names of these towns, you would expect that Sweetgrass, which is a nice name and sounds like it is related to other places such as Medicine Hat and Moose Jaw and Kicking Horse Pass, would be on the Canadian side, and that Coutts, which sounds abrupt and rude, would be on the American side. But this was not the case.

Between the two borders was a duty-free shop where you could buy cigarettes and liquor and flags. Stuff like that.

We left the reserve in the morning and drove until we got to Coutts.

"Last time we stopped here," my mother said, "you had an Orange Crush. You remember that?"

"Sure," I said. "That was when Laetitia took off."

"You want another Orange Crush?"

"That means we're not going to stop at a restaurant, right?"

My mother got a coffee at the convenience store, and we stood around and watched the prairies move in the sunlight. Then we climbed back in the car. My mother straightened the dress across her thighs, leaned against the wheel, and drove all the way to the border in first gear, slowly, as if she were trying to see through a bad storm or riding high on black ice.

The border guard was an old guy. As he walked to the car, he swayed from side to side, his feet set wide apart, the holster on his hip pitching up and down. He leaned into the window, looked into the back seat, and looked at my mother and me.

"Morning, ma'am."

"Good morning."

"Where you heading?"

"Salt Lake City."

"Purpose of your visit?"

"Visit my daughter."

"Citizenship?"

"Blackfoot," my mother told him.

"Ma'am?"

"Blackfoot," my mother repeated.

"Canadian?"

"Blackfoot."

It would have been easier if my mother had just said "Canadian" and been done with it, but I could see she wasn't going to do that. The guard wasn't angry or anything. He smiled and looked towards the building. Then he turned back and nodded.

"Morning, ma'am."

"Good morning."

"Any firearms or tobacco?"

"No."

"Citizenship?"

"Blackfoot."

He told us to sit in the car and wait, and we did. In about five minutes, another guard came out with the first man. They were talking as they came, both men swaying back and forth like two cowboys headed for a bar or a gunfight.

"Morning, ma'am."

"Good morning."

"Cecil tells me you and the boy are Blackfoot."

"That's right."

"Now, I know that we got Blackfeet on the American side and the Canadians got Blackfeet on their side. Just so we can keep our records straight, what side do you come from?"

I knew exactly what my mother was going to say, and I could have told them if they had asked me.

"Canadian side or American side?" asked the guard.

"Blackfoot side," she said.

It didn't take them long to lose their sense of humor, I can tell you that. The one guard stopped smiling altogether and told us to park our car at the side of the building and come in.

We sat on a wood bench for about an hour before anyone came over to talk to us. This time it was a woman. She had a gun, too.

"Hi," she said. "I'm Inspector Pratt. I understand there is a little misunderstanding."

"I'm going to visit my daughter in Salt Lake City," my mother told her. "We don't have any guns or beer."

"It's a legal technicality, that's all."

"My daughter's Blackfoot, too."

The women opened a briefcase and took out a couple of forms and began to write on one of them. "Everyone who crosses our border has to declare their citizenship. Even Americans. It helps us keep track of the visitors we get from the various countries."

She went on like that for maybe fifteen minutes, and a lot of the stuff she told us was interesting.

"I can understand how you feel about having to tell us your citizenship, and here's what I'll do. You tell me, and I won't put it down on the form. No-one will know but you and me."

Her gun was silver. There were several chips in the wood handle and the name "Stella" was scratched into the metal butt.

We were in the border office for about four hours, and we talked to almost everyone there. One of the men bought me a Coke. My mother brought a couple of sandwiches in from the car. I offered part of mine to Stella, but she said she wasn't hungry.

I told Stella that we were Blackfoot and Canadian, but she said that that didn't count because I was a minor. In the end, she told us that if my mother didn't declare her citizenship, we would have to go back to where we came from. My mother stood up and thanked Stella for her time. Then we got back in the car and drove to the Canadian border, which was only about a hundred yards away.

I was disappointed. I hadn't seen Laetitia for a long time, and I had never been to Salt Lake City. When she was still at home, Laetitia would go on and on about Salt Lake City. She had never been there, but her boyfriend Lester Tallbull had spent a year in Salt Lake at a technical school.

"It's a great place," Lester would say. "Nothing but blondes in the whole state."

Whenever he said that, Laetitia would slug him on his shoulder hard enough to make him flinch. He had some brochures on Salt Lake and some maps, and every so often the two of them would spread them out on the table.

"That's the temple. It's right downtown. You got to have a pass to get in."

"Charlotte says anyone can go in and look around."

"When was Charlotte in Salt Lake? Just when the hell was Charlotte in Salt Lake?"

"Last year."

"This is Liberty Park. It's got a zoo. There's good skiing in the mountains."

"Got all the skiing we can use," my mother would say. "People come from all over the world to ski at Banff. Cardston's got a temple, if you like those kinds of things."

"Oh, this one is real big," Lester would say. "They got armed guards and everything."

"Not what Charlotte says."

"What does she know?"

Lester and Laetitia broke up, but I guess the idea of Salt Lake stuck in her mind.

The Canadian border guard was a young woman, and she seemed happy to see us. "Hi," she said. "You folks sure have a great day for a trip. Where are you coming from?"

"Standoff."

"Is that in Montana?"

"No."

"Where are you going?"

"Standoff."

The woman's name was Carol and I don't guess she was any older than Laetitia. "Wow, you both Canadians?"

"Blackfoot."

"Really? I have a friend I went to school with who is Blackfoot. Do you know Mike Harley?"

"No."

"He went to school in Lethbridge, but he's really from Browning."

It was a nice conversation and there were no cars behind us, so there was no rush.

"You're not bringing any liquor back, are you?"

"No."

"Any cigarettes or plants or stuff like that?"

"No."

"Citizenship?"

"Blackfoot."

"I know," said the woman, "and I'd be proud of being Blackfoot if I were Blackfoot. But you have to be American or Canadian."

When Laetitia and Lester broke up, Lester took his brochures and maps with him, so Laetitia wrote to someone in Salt Lake City, and, about a month later, she got a big envelope of stuff. We sat at the table and opened up all the brochures, and Laetitia read each one out loud.

"Salt Lake City is the gateway to some of the world's most magnificent skiing.

"Salt Lake City is the home of one of the newest professional basketball franchises, the Utah Jazz.

"The Great Salt Lake is one of the natural wonders of the world."

It was kind of exciting seeing all those color brochures on the table and listening to Laetitia read all about how Salt Lake City was one of the best places in the entire world.

"That Salt Lake place sounds too good to be true," my mother told her.

"It has everything."

"We got everything right here."

"It's boring here."

"People in Salt Lake City are probably sending away for brochures of Calgary and Lethbridge and Pincher Creek right now."

In the end, my mother would say that maybe Laetitia should go to Salt Lake City; and Laetitia would say that maybe she would.

We parked the car to the side of the building and Carol led us into a small room on the second floor. I found a comfortable spot on the couch and flipped through some back issues of *Saturday Night* and *Alberta Report*.

When I woke up, my mother was just coming out of another office. She didn't say a word to me. I followed her down the stairs and out to the car. I thought we were going home, but she turned the car around and drove back towards the American border, which made me think we were going to visit Laetitia in Salt Lake City after all. Instead she pulled into the parking lot of the duty-free store and stopped.

"We going to see Laetitia?"

"No."

"We going home?"

Pride is a good thing to have, you know. Laetitia had a lot of pride, and so did my mother. I figured that someday, I'd have it, too.

"So where are we going?"

Most of that day, we wandered around the duty-free store, which wasn't very large. The manager had a name tag with a tiny American flag on one side and a tiny Canadian flag on the other. His name was Mel. Towards evening, he began suggesting that we should be on our way. I told him we had nowhere to go, that neither the Americans nor the Canadians would let us in. He laughed at that and told us that we should buy something or leave.

The car was not very comfortable, but we did have all that food and it was April, so even if it did snow as it sometimes does on the prairies, we wouldn't freeze. The next morning my mother drove to the American border.

It was a different guard this time, but the questions were the same. We didn't spend as much time in the office as we had the day before. By noon, we were back at the Canadian border. By two we were back in the duty-free shop parking lot.

The second night in the car was not as much fun as the first, but my mother seemed in good spirits, and, all in all, it was as much an adventure as an inconvenience. There wasn't much food left and that was a problem, but we had lots of water as there was a faucet at the side of the duty-free shop.

One Sunday, Laetitia and I were watching television. Mom was over at Mrs. Manyfingers's. Right in the middle of the program, Laetitia turned off the set and said she was going to Salt Lake City, that life around here was too boring. I had wanted to see the rest of the program and really didn't care if Laetitia went to Salt Lake City or not. When Mom got home, I told her what Laetitia had said.

What surprised me was how angry Laetitia got when she found out that I had told Mom.

"You got a big mouth."

"That's what you said."

"What I said is none of your business."

"I didn't say anything."

"Well, I'm going for sure, now."

That weekend, Laetitia packed her bags, and we drove her to the border.

Mel turned out to be friendly. When he closed up for the night and found us still parked in the lot, he came over and asked us if our car was broken down or something. My mother thanked him for his concern and told him that we were fine, that things would get straightened out in the morning.

"You're kidding," said Mel. "You'd think they could handle the simple things."

"We got some apples and a banana," I said, "but we're all out of ham sandwiches."

"You know, you read about these things, but you just don't believe it. You just don't believe it."

"Hamburgers would be even better because they got more stuff for energy."

My mother slept in the back seat. I slept in the front because I was smaller and could lie under the steering wheel. Late that night, I heard my mother open the car door. I found her sitting on her blanket leaning against the bumper of the car.

"You see all those stars," she said. "When I was a little girl, my grandmother used to take me and my sisters out on the prairies and tell us stories about all the stars."

"Do you think Mel is going to bring us any hamburgers?"

"Every one of those stars has a story. You see that bunch of stars over there that look like a fish?"

"He didn't say no."

"Coyote[1] went fishing, one day. That's how it all started." We sat out under the stars that night, and my mother told me all sorts of stories. She was serious about it, too. She'd tell them slow, repeating parts as she went, as if she expected me to remember each one.

Early the next morning, the television vans began to arrive, and guys in suits and women in dresses came trotting over to us, dragging microphones and cameras and lights behind them. One of the vans had a table set up with orange juice and sandwiches and fruit. It was for the crew, but when I told them we hadn't eaten for a while, a really skinny blonde woman told us we could eat as much as we wanted.

They mostly talked to my mother. Every so often one of the reporters would come over and ask me questions about how it felt to be an Indian without a country. I told them we had a nice house on the reserve and that my cousins had a couple of horses we rode when we went fishing. Some of the television people went over to the American border, and then they went to the Canadian border.

Around noon, a good-looking guy in a dark suit and an orange tie with little ducks on it drove up in a fancy car. He talked to my mother for a while, and after they were done talking, my mother called me over, and we got into our car. Just as my mother started the engine, Mel came over and gave us a bag of peanut brittle and told us that justice was a damn hard thing to get, but that we shouldn't give up.

I would have preferred lemon drops, but it was nice of Mel anyway.

"Where are we going now?"

"Going to visit Laetitia."

The guard who came out to our car was all smiles. The television lights were so bright they hurt my eyes, and, if you tried to look through the windshield in certain directions, you couldn't see a thing.

"Morning, ma'am."

"Good morning."

"Where you heading?"

"Salt Lake City."

"Purpose of your visit?"

"Visit my daughter."

"Any tobacco, liquor, or firearms?"

"Don't smoke."

"Any plants or fruit?"

"Not any more."

"Citizenship?"

"Blackfoot."

The guard rocked back on his heels and jammed his thumbs into his gun belt. "Thank you," he said, his fingers patting the butt of the revolver. "Have a pleasant trip."

My mother rolled the car forward, and the television people had to scramble out of the way. They ran alongside the car as we pulled away from the border, and, when they couldn't run any farther, they stood in the middle of the highway and waved and waved and waved.

We got to Salt Lake City the next day. Laetitia was happy to see us, and, that first night, she took us out to a restaurant that made really good soups. The list of pies took up

---

1. **Coyote** A mythological figure common to Native cultures.

a whole page. I had cherry. Mom had chocolate. Laetitia said that she saw us on television the night before and, during the meal, she had us tell her the story over and over again.

Laetitia took us everywhere. We went to a fancy ski resort. We went to the temple. We got to go shopping in a couple of large malls, but they weren't as large as the one in Edmonton, and Mom said so.

After a week or so, I got bored and wasn't at all sad when my mother said we should be heading back home. Laetitia wanted us to stay longer, but Mom said no, that she had things to do back home and that, next time, Laetitia should come up and visit. Laetitia said she was thinking about moving back, and Mom told her to do as she pleased, and Laetitia said that she would.

On the way home, we stopped at the duty-free shop, and my mother gave Mel a green hat that said "Salt Lake" across the front. Mel was a funny guy. He took the hat and blew his nose and told my mother that she was an inspiration to us all. He gave us some more peanut brittle and came out into the parking lot and waved at us all the way to the Canadian border.

It was almost evening when we left Coutts. I watched the border through the rear window until all you could see were the tops of the flagpoles and the blue water tower, and then they rolled over a hill and disappeared.

(1993)

Michael Ondaatje (1943–)

Michael Ondaatje was born in 1943 in Ceylon (which became Sri Lanka in 1972). His parents — Philip Mervyn Ondaatje and Enid Doris Gratiaen — were well-known members of what was once Ceylon's colonial upper class. His father supervised a tea and rubber plantation, but he was better known for his bouts of alcoholism, which finally alienated him from Doris, whose career as a dancer was inspired by Isadora Duncan. When they separated, Michael and his mother moved to England, where he entered Dulwich College in London. Ondaatje arrived in Canada in 1962 and attended Bishop's University. He completed his B.A. at the University of Toronto in 1965 and an M.A. at Queen's University in 1967. He has taught creative writing at the University of Western Ontario and at York University.

Ondaatje's first two poetry books introduced a fresh and disarming voice. Both *The Dainty Monsters* (1967) and *The Man with Seven Toes* (1969) were notable for their precise and frequently grotesque imagery. The first collection revealed a mind attracted to the exotic, uncaged energy of the natural world, and to what happens when humans begin to interfere with it by imposing human reason on the savage and unknowable. *The Man with Seven Toes* follows the response of a woman confronted by aborigines after a shipwreck leaves her in unfamiliar, hostile territory. This series of connected poems reveals the signature elements of Ondaatje's work: sharp attention to visual details; an attraction to explosive violence; a preoccupation with outcast figures who challenge authority and civility; and a fascination with the ongoing war between nature and culture.

In 1970, when he was 27, Ondaatje won a Governor General's Award for *The Collected Works of Billy the Kid.* This long poem combines various literary forms to construct a portrait of the famous outlaw William H. Bonney, aka Billy the Kid. Billy is a lover and a killer, gentle and savage, an extreme artist living in a brutal world. The book is a postmodern collage of poetry, prose, photography, pop culture sources, and documentary material, presented from multiple viewpoints and from intermingling temporal perspectives that flout the idea of linear narrative. At the same time, it is a self-reflexive portrayal of the criminal mind, which becomes, in Ondaatje's hands, an extension of the artist's mind as he tries to nail down his subject matter, a kind of creative murder. Subtitled "Left-Handed Poems," the book is a celebration of the unexpected, the subversive, the forces that undermine coherence and control.

With his next book, the poetry collection *Rat Jelly* (1973), Ondaatje immersed himself once again in the themes that had enriched his previous works: family, animals, and myth. The poems collected here offer eccentric, troubling, and mysterious versions of worlds populated by extremists — madmen and beasts and "social animals" that are on the edge of losing control and thriving on the periphery. Ondaatje is consistently drawn to those who live on the margin, to risk-takers who are attracted to chaos. In "White Dwarfs" he asks:

Why do I love most
among my heroes those
who sail to that perfect edge
where there is no social fuel …

And in "'The Gate in His Head'" he says:

My mind is pouring chaos
in nets onto the page.
A blind lover, dont know
what I love till I write it out.

In 1976 Ondaatje published *Coming Through Slaughter*, a poetic novel about Buddy Bolden (1876–1931), a pioneering New Orleans cornet player who went mad at a parade in 1907. Ondaatje adapts the structures of jazz music to create the form of his novel, brilliantly evoking Bolden's mental fragmentation through his style. The novel is at once poetic and disarming. And it is as much an exploration of Bolden's creative breakdown as it is about the potential breakdown of the investigative artist (Ondaatje) who pursues him, his milieu, and his music. How much of Bolden's life is "outside" history? How much of Ondaatje's historic voyage into another man's madness is in reality a voyage into himself? Ondaatje plays on this question and makes it central to the self-reflexive nature of the text. For this reason, *Coming Through Slaughter* is often seen as a prime example of the postmodern emphasis on process, experimentation, and the role of the artist. It is also an exploration of the ways in which writers appropriate and interrogate history.

In 1979 Ondaatje published a volume of new and selected poems, *There's a Trick with a Knife I'm Learning to Do*. It won him a second Governor General's Award. He had begun to turn to his own family history as a source of inspiration. In *Running in the Family* he recounts his return to Sri Lanka, 25 years after his departure. In this family memoir, fact and fiction come together through research and memory. Ondaatje creates a rich and evocative picture of a colonial age and of the eccentric family members who contributed to his sense of history, and story.

With *Secular Love* (1984), Ondaatje advanced his fascination with autobiography through increasingly confessional poetry. "Tin Roof," a poignant long poem dedicated to love and loss, confronts the poet's own limitations as a writer, the pull he feels toward silence in the face of his failure as a husband (the poem was partially inspired by Ondaatje's divorce). Ondaatje collected many of the poems written after 1970 in *The Cinnamon Peeler* (1991). The title poem provides one of the best examples of Ondaatje's sensuous attention to detail and his ability to blend the exotic and the erotic.

In *Handwriting* (1998), Ondaatje returned again to the subject of Sri Lanka, but in a much more politicized fashion than he did in his family memoir. These poems examine the ongoing political strife in Sri Lanka with a profound sense of loss. Ondaatje's latest offering, *The Story* (2006), is a collection of prose poems that explore familiar themes of love, memory, family, and exile. It includes dark, evocative paintings by David Bolduc.

Although Ondaatje's poems are rich and varied, he is perhaps best known for his five novels. In 1987, he published *In the Skin of a Lion*. It tells the story of the Macedonian immigrants who built the Bloor Street Viaduct in 1917 and the Toronto Waterworks in the 1930s, blending historical fact with fiction to depict the interplay between the forces of capitalism and the people consumed by them. Once again, Ondaatje focuses on the immigrants as outsiders, as people who contributed to the construction of the city, but who remain invisible, effaced from official histories. The novel garnered the 1988 City of Toronto Book Award.

Ondaatje published the enormously successful *The English Patient* in 1992. It won the first Booker Prize ever given to a Canadian, received a Governor General's Award, sold over two million copies, and was made into a film that won nine Academy Awards. It tells the story of Hana, Kip, Caravaggio, and the English patient, who come together in an Italian villa as World War II draws to a close. As events move forward, the characters' histories are revealed in a series of flashbacks that allow the narrative to move among various locations including Africa, India, Italy, and Canada. The novel explores the extent to which history is constructed through the process of narration and challenges the conventional notion of history as a set of facts and events that can be assembled objectively. Instead, Ondaatje's work emphasizes the relativism of historical memory.

Anils's Ghost (2000) brought Ondaatje his fourth Governor General's Award. In this examination of the human cost of war, Ondaatje gives us the voice of forensic anthropologist Anil, who in turn gives voice to the "Disappeared" as she studies the skeleton of an unknown victim of the genocide sparked by the complex historical tensions between Sri Lanka's Sinhalese and Tamil factions. As one interviewer pointed out, Ondaatje approaches the task of writing this historical fiction like an archaeologist in his own right, "delving into the earth, unsure of what he'll find."

Ondaatje's most recent novel, *Divisadero*, appeared in 2007. In it he explores the bonds of family and the links between history and the present, moving from northern California in the 1970s to casinos in Nevada to rural France. Like Ondaatje's other novels, *Divisadero* is also preoccupied with the life of a writer in an earlier time and with the scars his stories inflict upon characters in the present. In addition to his poetry and fiction Ondaatje has produced two films and written a critical study of Leonard Cohen. He has edited several anthologies, and has worked with his wife, Linda Spalding, as the editor of *Brick* Magazine. They live in Toronto.

Henri Rousseau[1] and Friends

For Bill Muysson

In his clean vegetation
the parrot, judicious,
poses on a branch.
The narrator of the scene,
aware of the perfect fruits,
the white and blue flowers,

---

1. **Henri Rousseau** Post-impressionist painter (1844–1910), famous for his jungle scenes.

the snake with an ear for music;
he presides.

The apes
10   hold their oranges like skulls,
like chalices.
They are below the parrot
above the oranges —
a jungle serfdom[2] which
with this order
reposes.

They are the ideals of dreams.
Among the exactness,
the symmetrical petals,
20   the efficiently flying angels,
there is complete liberation.
The parrot is interchangeable;
tomorrow in its place
a waltzing man and tiger,
brash legs of a bird.

Greatness achieved
they loll among textbook flowers
and in this pose hang
scattered like pearls
30   in just as intense a society.
On Miss Adelaide Milton de Groot's[3] walls,
with Lillie P. Bliss[4] in New York.

And there too
in spangled wrists and elbows
and grand façades of cocktails
are vulgarly beautiful parrots, appalled lions,
the beautiful and the forceful locked in suns,
and the slight, careful stepping birds.

(1967)

King Kong Meets Wallace Stevens[1]

Take two photographs —
Wallace Stevens and King Kong
(Is it significant that I eat bananas as I write this?)

---

2. **serfdom** A class of servants who were bought and sold along with the land they worked on. 3. **Miss Adelaide Milton de Groot** Major American arts patron (1876–1967). 4. **Lillie P. Bliss** American arts patron (1864–1931); her bequest helped establish a permanent collection for the fledgling Museum of Modern Art in New York City.

---

1. **Wallace Stevens** American modernist poet (1879–1955).

Stevens is portly, benign, a white brush cut
striped tie. Businessman but
for the dark thick hands, the naked brain
the thought in him.

Kong is staggering
lost in New York streets again
a spawn of annoyed cars at his toes.   10
The mind is nowhere.
Fingers are plastic, electric under the skin.
He's at the call of Metro-Goldwyn-Mayer.

Meanwhile W. S. in his suit
is thinking chaos is thinking fences.
In his head the seeds of fresh pain
his exorcising,
the bellow of locked blood.

The hands drain from his jacket,
pose in the murderer's shadow.   20

                                                          (1970)

Letters & Other Worlds

"for there was no more darkness for him and, no doubt
like Adam before the fall, he could see in the dark"

       My father's body was a globe of fear
       His body was a town we never knew
       He hid that he had been where we were going
       His letters were a room he seldom lived in
       In them the logic of his love could grow

       My father's body was a town of fear
       He was the only witness to its fear dance
       He hid where he had been that we might lose him   10
       His letters were a room his body scared

He came to death with his mind drowning.
On the last day he enclosed himself
in a room with two bottles of gin, later
fell the length of his body
so that brain blood moved
to new compartments
that never knew the wash of fluid
and he died in minutes of a new equilibrium.

His early life was a terrifying comedy   20
and my mother divorced him again and again.

He would rush into tunnels magnetized
by the white eye of trains
and once, gaining instant fame,
managed to stop a Perahara in Ceylon[1]
— the whole procession of elephants dancers
local dignitaries — by falling
dead drunk onto the street.

As a semi-official, and semi-white at that,
30   the act was seen as a crucial
turning point in the Home Rule Movement[2]
and led to Ceylon's independence in 1948.

(My mother had done her share too —
her driving so bad
she was stoned by villagers
whenever her car was recognized)

For 14 years of marriage
each of them claimed he or she
was the injured party.
40   Once on the Colombo[3] docks
saying goodbye to a recently married couple
my father, jealous
at my mother's articulate emotion,
dove into the waters of the harbour
and swam after the ship waving farewell.
My mother pretending no affiliation
mingled with the crowd back to the hotel.

Once again he made the papers
though this time my mother
50   with a note to the editor
corrected the report — saying he was drunk
rather than broken hearted at the parting of friends.
The married couple received both editions
of *The Ceylon Times* when their ship reached Aden.

And then in his last years,
he was the silent drinker,
the man who once a week
disappeared into his room with bottles
and stayed there until he was drunk
60   and until he was sober.

---

1. Perahara in Ceylon A Sri Lankan Buddhist procession with elephants, dancers, and torch-bearers. The name Ceylon was changed to Sri Lanka when the country became a republic, in 1972. **2. Home Rule Movement** Movement whose proponents sought the status of dominion for India (a status shared by former British colonies like Canada and Australia) in the 1910s. **3. Colombo** The capital of Sri Lanka.

There speeches, head dreams, apologies,
the gentle letters, were composed.
With the clarity of architects
he would write of the row of blue flowers
his new wife had planted,
the plans for electricity in the house,
how my half-sister fell near a snake
and it had awakened and not touched her.
Letters in a clear hand of the most complete empathy
his heart widening and widening and widening   70
to all manner of change in his children and friends
while he himself edged
into the terrible acute hatred
of his own privacy
till he balanced and fell
the length of his body
the blood screaming in
the empty reservoir of bones
the blood searching in his head without metaphor

                                                            (1971)

White Dwarfs

This is for people who disappear
for those who descend into the code
and make their room a fridge for Superman
— who exhaust costume and bones that could perform flight,
who shave their moral so raw
they can tear themselves through the eye of a needle
this is for those people
that hover and hover
and die in the ether peripheries

There is my fear   10
of no words   of
falling without words
over and over   of
mouthing the silence
Why do I love most
among my heroes those
who sail to that perfect edge
where there is no social fuel
Release of sandbags
to understand their altitude —   20

          that silence of the third cross
          3rd man hung so high and lonely
          we dont hear him say

say his pain, say his unbrotherhood
What has he to do with the smell of ladies
can they eat off his skeleton of pain?

The Gurkhas in Malaya[1]
cut the tongues of mules
so they were silent beasts of burden
30   in enemy territories
after such cruelty what could they speak of anyway
And Dashiell Hammett[2] in success
suffered conversation and moved
to the perfect white between the words

This white that can grow
is fridge, bed,
is an egg — most beautiful
when unbroken, where
what we cannot see is growing
40   in all the colours we cannot see

there are those burned out stars
who implode into silence
after parading in the sky
after such choreography what would they wish to speak of   anyway

(1971)

'The gate in his head'

For Victor Coleman

Victor, the shy mind
revealing the faint scars
coloured strata of the brain,
not clarity but the sense of shift

a few lines, the tracks of thought

Landscape of busted trees
the melted tires in the sun
Stan's fishbowl
with a book inside
10   turning its pages
like some sea animal
camouflaging itself
the typeface clarity
going slow blonde in the sun full water

---

1. **Gurkhas in Malaya** Nepalese soldiers for the British army before the liberation of India. 2. **Dashiell Hammett**
American author (1894–1961) of detective novels, human rights activist, and member of the American Communist Party.

My mind is pouring chaos
in nets onto the page.
A blind lover, dont know
what I love till I write it out.
And then from Gibson's your letter
with a blurred photograph of a gull.   20
Caught vision. The stunning white bird
an unclear stir.

And that is all this writing should be then.
The beautiful formed things caught at the wrong moment
so they are shapeless, awkward
moving to the clear.

(1973)

Heron Rex

Mad kings
blood lines introverted, strained pure
so the brain runs in the wrong direction

they are proud of their heritage of suicides
— not the ones who went mad
balancing on that goddamn leg, but those

whose eyes turned off
the sun and imagined it
those who looked north, those who
forced their feathers to grow in   10
those who couldn't find the muscles in their arms
who drilled their beaks into the skin
those who could speak
and lost themselves in the foul connections
who crashed against black bars in a dream of escape
those who moved round the dials of imaginary clocks
those who fell asleep and never woke
who never slept and so dropped dead
those who attacked the casual eyes of children and were led away
and those who faced corners forever   20
those who exposed themselves and were led away
those who pretended broken limbs, epilepsy,
who managed to electrocute themselves on wire
those who felt their skin was on fire and screamed
                              and were led away

There are ways of going
physically mad, physically
mad when you perfect the mind

30   where you sacrifice yourself for the race
when you are the representative when you allow
yourself to be paraded in the cages
celebrity a razor in the body

These small birds so precise
frail as morning neon
they are royalty melted down
they are the glass core at the heart of kings
yet 15 year old boys could enter the cage
and break them in minutes
as easily as a long fingernail.

(1973)

The Cinnamon Peeler

If I were a cinnamon peeler
I would ride your bed
and leave the yellow bark dust
on your pillow.

Your breasts and shoulders would reek
you could never walk through markets
without the profession of my fingers
floating over you. The blind would
stumble certain of whom they approached
10   though you might bathe
under rain gutters, monsoon.

Here on the upper thigh
at this smooth pasture
neighbour to your hair
or the crease
that cuts your back. This ankle.
You will be known among strangers
as the cinnamon peeler's wife.

I could hardly glance at you
20   before marriage
never touch you
— your keen nosed mother, your rough brothers.
I buried my hands
in saffron, disguised them
over smoking tar,
helped the honey gatherers ...

*

When we swam once
I touched you in water
and our bodies remained free,
you could hold me and be blind of smell.   30
You climbed the bank and said

　　　　　this is how you touch other women
the grass cutter's wife, the lime burner's daughter.
And you searched your arms
for the missing perfume
　　　　　　　　and knew

　　　　　what good is it
to be the lime burner's daughter
left with no trace
as if not spoken to in the act of love   40
as if wounded without the pleasure of a scar.

You touched
your belly to my hands
in the dry air and said
I am the cinnamon
peeler's wife. Smell me.

                                                                    (1984)

Red Accordion — An Immigrant Song

How you and I talked!
Casually, and side by side,
not even cold at 4 a.m.
New Year's morning

in a double outhouse in Blyth.

Creak of trees and scrub snow.
Was it dream or true memory
this casualness, this ease of talk
after the long night of the previous year.

Nothing important said   10
just as now the poem
draws together such frail times.
Art steps forward as accident
like a warm breeze from Brazil.

　　　　　This whispering
as if not to awaken
what hibernates in firewood

as if not to disturb the blue night
the last memory of the year.

20   So we sit
within loose walls of the poem
you and I, our friends indoors
drunk on the home-made wine.
All of us searching to discern ourselves,
the "gift" we can give each other.
Tell this landscape.
Or the one we came from.

Polkas in a smoky midnight light.

I stepped into this new year
30 dancing with a small child.
Rachel, so graceful,
we bowed when the dance was over.
If I could paint this I would

             and if writing
showed colour and incident
removed from time
             we could be clear.

The bleak view past the door
is where we are, not what we
40 have made here, or become, or brought
like wolves bringing food to a lair
from another world. And this
is magic.
             Ray Bird's seven year old wine
— transformed! Finally made good.
I drank an early version years ago
and passed out.
             Time collapses.
The years, the intricate
50 knowledge now of each other
makes love.

A yard in its scrub now, stacked wood
brindle in the moonlight, the red truck,
a bare tree at the foot of the driveway
waving to heaven.
             A full moon the
             colour of night kitchen.

(1984)

Death at Kataragama[1]

For half the day blackouts stroke this house into stillness so there is no longer a whirring fan or the hum of light. You hear sounds of a pencil being felt for in a drawer in the dark and then see its thick shadow in candlelight, writing the remaining words. Paragraphs reduced to one word. A punctuation mark. Then another word, complete as a thought. The way someone's name holds terraces of character, contains all of our adventures together. I walk the corridors which might perhaps, I'm not sure, be cooler than the rest of the house. Heat at noon. Heat in the darkness of night.

There is a woodpecker I am enamoured of I saw this morning through my binoculars. A red thatch roof to his head more modest than crimson, deeper than blood. Distance is always clearer. I no longer see words in focus. As if my soul is a blunt tooth. I bend too close to the page to get nearer to what is being understood. What I write will drift away. I will be able to understand the world only at arm's length.

Can my soul step into the body of that woodpecker? He may be too hot in sunlight, it could be a limited life. But if this had been offered to me today, at 9 a.m., I would have gone with him, traded this body for his.

A constant fall of leaf around me in this time of no rain like the continual habit of death. Someone soon will say of me, "his body was lying in Kataragama like a pauper." Vanity even when we are a corpse. For a blue hand that contains no touch or desire in it for another.

There is something else. Not just the woodpecker. Ten water buffalo when I stopped the car. They were being veered from side to side under the sun. The sloshing of their hooves in the paddy field that I heard thirty yards away, my car door open for the breeze, the haunting sound I was caught within as if creatures of magnificence were undressing and removing their wings. My head and almost held breath out there for an hour so that later I felt as if I contained that full noon light.

It was water in an earlier life I could not take into my mouth when I was dying. I was soothed then the way a plant would be, brushed with a wet cloth, as I reduced all thought into requests. Take care of this flower. Less light. Curtain. As I lay there prone during the long vigil of my friends. The ache of ribs from too much sleep or fever — bones that protect the heart and breath in battle, during love beside another. Saliva, breath, fluids, the soul. The place bodies meet is the place of escape.

But this time brutal aloneness. The straight stern legs of the woodpecker braced against the jak fruit as he delves for a meal. Will he feel the change in his nature as my soul enters? Will it go darker? Or will I enter as I always do another's nest, in their clothes and with their rules for a particular life.

Or I could leap into knee-deep mud potent with rice. Ten water buffalo. A quick decision. Not goals considered all our lives but, in the final minutes, sudden choice.

---

1. **Kataragama** Village in southern Sri Lanka, a popular destination for pilgrimages.

This morning it was a woodpecker. A year ago the face of someone on a train. We depart into worlds that have nothing to do with those we love. This woman whose arm I would hold and comfort, that book I wanted to make and shape tight as a stone — I would give everything away for this sound of mud and water, hooves, great wings

(1998)

bpNichol (1944–1988)

Born in Vancouver and raised in various western Canadian locales by parents who worked for the railway, Barrie Nichol later earned an elementary school teaching certificate from the University of British Columbia. In 1963, when he was 20 years old, he moved to Toronto and entered into therapy with Lea Hindley-Smith at a community called Therafields. The experience led him to become a therapist, and he practised as one from 1966 to 1981. The year after joining Therafields, Nichol abandoned his early lyric poetry and began the experimental work for which he is now recognized.

In 1967, his first major work was published. Titled simply *bp*, it consisted of a box containing a book called *Journeying & the Returns,* a sound poetry recording, a flip-animated poem, and an envelope labelled "Letters Home" and filled with concrete poems. It was Kenneth Patchen's painting-poems that had led Nichol to concrete poetry, although he was also influenced by e.e. cummings. His first concrete poem was called "Popular Song," and it was composed of just two lines (the bold type in red): "WAR**BLED** / **WAR**BLED." The poem had a deceptive simplicity, inherent cultural commentary, and transformative implications, and Nichol included it among the comic-strip drawn poems of his pamphlet *Aleph Unit* (1974). In keeping with his central aim — communication — Nichol turned to comic-book art and the children's books of Dr. Seuss in creating poems that would reach people. Although complex and surreal on one level, these visual pieces also had a strong and immediate imaginative appeal.

The year 1970 was an important one for bpNichol. He won a Governor General's Award alongside Michael Ondaatje, and Ondaatje began making a film about him called *Sons of Captain Poetry.* Nichol's award was not for one text, but for four: *The True Eventual Story of Billy the Kid,* a prose booklet about the iconic cowboy; *Still Water,* a box of poem cards; *Beach Head,* a series of lyrics; and an anthology of Canadian concrete (or spontaneous and visual) poetry called *The Cosmic Chef* (its abbreviated title), which Nichol had edited. Marking the confluence of sonic and visual elements in his poetry, 1970 also saw the birth of the Four Horsemen, a sound poetry performance group comprising Nichol, Steve McCaffery, Paul Dutton, and Rafael Barreto-Rivera. They toured Canada, the U.S., Britain, and Europe, performing their playful and seemingly prelinguistic sound poems. Through these shows, Nichol reinforced the international reputation he had already developed with his concrete poetry.

Despite this reputation, Nichol's Governor General's Award was contentious, as most of the Canadian reading public knew of no precedent for his work. His earliest precursors were Dadaists, such as Hugo Ball, and the most experimental modernists, such as Gertrude Stein and James Joyce. Nichol was aware that wide acceptance would be hard won, so in essays and interviews he offered explanations and justifications for his oeuvre. Reflecting on his rejection of the traditional lyric poetry he had produced in his early years, he declared that he wanted "to unarmour the poem," to strip it of its formal heritage and thus avoid the arrogance of instructing instead of exploring. Language had a great deal to teach him, so he would experiment with it and see what he could learn. The results were often delicate, vulnerable innovations. Playing with words and their sonic echoes, he could write, in "A Little Pome for Yur Fingertips," "love / lovely / lo Ave / A lover," and call forth an image of love transforming into chant that beckons a lover.

The spirit of this short poem adheres to the poet's fundamental belief that poetry must communicate. Rather than complicate his poems with intertextual allusions, elaborate conceits, or esoteric content, he conceived them as gestures of invitation. He argued that the problem of language was "finding as many exits as possible from the self (language/communication exits) in order to form as many entrances as possible for the other." Speaking from the vantage point of the 1960s counterculture, Nichol was imagining the "other" not only as a sexual partner but also as a member of a disenfranchised racial minority embroiled in the civil rights movement. He also saw reflected in his anthology *The Cosmic Chef* the breakdown of barriers between lifestyles and politics that was transforming society. The anthology exemplified the egalitarian notion of "borderblur" — its poems were not even identified as belonging to a given contributor, and so it reinforced the ideal of free, anonymous comings and goings. Nichol's interest in the relatively anonymous job of editing was established with *The Cosmic Chef*, but it would become a major aspect of his career in the 1970s, when he volunteered his services at Toronto's Coach House Press, acquiring and editing a substantial portion of the press's output; he also joined the editorial collective at the journal *Open Letter*, published a series of pamphlets and cards under the banners *Ganglia* and *grOnk*, and co-founded Underwhich Press.

Nichol's sound poetry, particularly that which was included in the dynamic Four Horsemen performances, traversed many of the imaginative boundaries that the Dadaists had tried to cross. The Four Horsemen shows brought Nichol's performative interests to the fore and testified to his dedication to communalism and collaboration. For all its playfulness, though, his sound poetry was quite serious. He remarked that "It is a frustrating often frightening avenue of expression which can release primitive elements in both the poet & his audience." By reordering words and repeating simple sounds ("tee," "pow," "shh,") in a four-part pattern, the Horsemen broke the syntactical rules of language and moved towards a new form of expression.

Nichol began to compose *The Martyrology*, the epic long poem that would become his most famous work, in the late 1960s or early 1970s; it would eventually balloon to nine books in six volumes, some of which appeared posthumously. It was an ongoing project that never ended — a roadmap of Nichol's evolving poetics, a lifetime investigation of language, speech, self, and being that was initially sparked by Nichol's fascination with the lives of the saints. He teases their names out of words — "stranglehold" and "storm" become St. Ranglehold and St. Orm — in pursuit of what Frank Davey calls "insight into himself and his writing through scrupulous attention to the messages hidden in the morphology of his own speech." Nichol died in 1988 at the age of 44. A street near the University of Toronto was named in his honour, and one of his poems is etched in the pavement.

after hokusai[1]

the old man holds
the sea on a
string. how can he
bring it in &
keep from drowning?

(1971)

---

1. **hokusai** Katsushika Hokusai (1760–1849) was a Japanese painter and engraver whose woodcuts and prints vividly portrayed daily life.

Not What The Siren[1] Sang
But What The Frag Ment for margaret avison

```
       leaf   autumn    sky
       flea   umantu    kys
          over  an  over
              um  tu
              mu  ut
       fale   munaut    syk
       fail   monotony  sikh
                 ton
              tongue
       flail  man tongue
              Manatou
              anatou
       frail  anatole   sick
              man toll
              mental
               tall
              men
               tell
              men
              Telemann
    sail                kick
              elephant
    bail                flick
              medicant
          ahmen canter
          amen cantor
       all men can't or
      tall men can
      tell men
              Telemann tlick
    wail      element  trick
    wall all it meant tick
              intimate
    ball                pick
              intimate
    Bach                click
              imminent
    back                clack
              emanate
```

---

1. **Siren** The sirens of Greek mythology lured sailors with their irresistible song, causing them to smash their ships on rocks.

```
Braque              clock
          immitate
break               cake
          immolate
brick               kick
          integrate
crib                kite
          insulate
crab                sight
          irritate        wait.......
```

(1973)

Allegory #4

(1974)

Frame 16

(1974)

TTA 4: original version

Icharrus[1]   winging up
Simon the Magician[2]   from Judea   high in a tree,
everyone   reaching for the sun

                    great towers of stone
built by the Aztecs, tearing their hearts out
to offer them, wet and beating

                    mountains,
cold wind, Macchu Piccu[3] hiding in the sun
unfound for centuries

cars whizzing by, sun
thru trees passing, a dozen
new wave films, flickering
on drivers' glasses

flat on their backs in the grass
a dozen bodies slowly turning brown

sun glares off the pages, "soleil
cou coupé",[4] rolls in my window
flat on my back on the floor
becoming aware of it
for an instant

(1979)

---

1. **Icharrus** (Icarus) Greek mythological figure who used wax wings to fly; when he got too close to the sun, the wings melted, and Icarus fell to his death. 2. **Simon the Magician** Figure in Christian mythology who offered Jesus's Apostles money if they would perform miracles for him. 3. **Macchu Piccu** Well-preserved Incan ruins in Peru. 4. **soleil cou coupé** From "Zone," the opening poem of Guillaume Apollinaire's 1913 collection *Alcools*. Apollinaire (1880–1918) was a French artist and poet, and a founder of surrealism; the phrase translates as "cut-necked sun."

TTA 5: re-arranging words in poem in alphabetical order

```
a     a a,
an and aware    Aztecs back     backs beating becoming bodies,
brown    built by by cars
                    centuries cold cou coupé
dozen dozen drivers' everyone, films flat flat flickering
floor for for, for from glares
                glasses,
grass great, hearts hiding high Icharrus in in
in in instant

it Judea Macchu, Magician
mountains my my, new of
of off offer, on
on on on

out pages passing Piccu reaching rolls Simon
slowly soleil stone sun sun sun

sun tearing the the the, "the
the the", the their their them
thru to towers tree trees turning unfound
up wave wet whizzing
wind window winging
```

(1979)

TTA 19: replacing words with their meanings using Webster's DICTIONARY FOR EVERYDAY USE

Icharrus furnished with wings, enabling him to fly or hasten (wounded in the wing, arm or shoulder) to or toward a higher place or degree; Simon the one skilled in magic (a conjurer), out of Judea, elevated far up indicating a present relation to time, space, condition, the indefinite article, meaning one perennial plant having trunk, bole, or woody stem with branches; all possible people stretching out their hands, straining after a conception, or to denote a particular person or luminous body round which earth and the other planets revolve.

Large in size or number, long in time or duration, lofty, round or square structures proceeding from hard, earthy matter of which rock is made, the act or work of building them exercised through the agency of the Aztecs, pulling apart forcibly the possessive case of them, the hollow, muscular organs which make the blood circulate, on, at, or to, the outside, expressing motion towards, expressing purpose, to present for acceptance or refusal the objective & dative case of they (Old English *thaem*), full of moisture, together with a word that joins words, throbbing, dashing against (as waves, wind, etc.).

High hills, wanting in heat, deficient in emotions, air in motion, the power of respiration, Macchu Piccu lying concealed in the sun, undiscovered during many periods of a hundred years.

Vehicles on wheels making a hissing sound, as of an arrow flying thru air, in the neighbourhood of the sun going in at one side & out the other of the trees, dying, a group of twelve things of the same kind, not existing before, surges, movie show burning unsteadily, above & touching one who (or that which) drives, his spectacles.

Prone on the upper or hinder part of their trunks in the herbage a dozen frames of human beings or animals at reduced speed convert into a darker colour inclining to red or yellow.

Sun shines with a strong dazzling light away from the one side of a leaf of a book or manuscript, a line from Guillaume Apollinaire's *Zone*, drives forward with a swift & easy motion, turning over & over in an opening in the wall to admit air & light which belongs to me, usually covered with glass, flat on my back on the horizontal surface of the room upon which one walks, passing from one state to another, possessing knowledge of the neuter pronoun of the third person for a particular point of time.

(1979)

probable systems 4

this one's for james joyce in his worst bummer

> faith
> $= 6 + 1 + 9 + 20 + 8$
> $= 44$
> $= 8 + 15 + 16 + 5$
> $=$ hope

(1985)

Steve McCaffery (1947–)

Steve McCaffery is the author, co-author, and editor of close to 30 works of concrete poetry, sound poetry, fiction, and criticism. Although he will not call himself a poet, the influence this theoretician, writer, and performance artist has had on Canadian experimental (he prefers the term "investigative") poetry is so defining that one critic divides the genre in Canada into two periods: "pre-McCaffery and post-McCaffery."

Born in Sheffield, England, in 1947, McCaffery attended Catholic school and went on to earn a B.A. from the University of Hull in 1968. His work is infused with the ideas of European philosophers and theorists, among them Jacques Derrida, Roland Barthes, and Karl Marx. He embraced Derrida's deconstruction of the formal aspects of a text, opening it to an array of interpretations; Barthes's radical notion of positing the reader, not the author, as the creator of a text through the act of reading; and Marx's focus on the ways in which language functions through social and political structures. However, while one may take many fruitful theoretical approaches to

McCaffery's work, his aim is not to elicit a strictly intellectual response from his readers. At the end of the day, as he and fellow poet bpNichol once asserted, "all theory is transient & after the fact of writing."

While at Hull, McCaffery founded the literary magazine *Poet's Eye* and began creating his first concrete poems, works that involved arranging words into shapes on the printed page, shapes that engage in a meaningful exchange with the words from which they are formed. *Carnival*, which was published in sections from 1969 to 1975, is composed of several panels that the reader must tear out of the book and arrange on a surface in order to interpret. The reader both destroys and constructs the work, literalizing the metaphor of interpretation as a process of reconstruction.

When McCaffery came to Canada in 1968 to study with Eli Mandel at York University in Toronto, he immediately sought out Nichol. They became fast friends, and together they founded the Toronto Research Group, for which they wrote reports on translation, literary performance, non-narrative prose, and the "book-as-machine." These reports were collected in *Rational Geomancy: The Kids of the Book Machine: The Collected Research Reports of the Toronto Research Group 1973–1982* (1992). Nichol and McCaffery also pioneered "homolinguistic translation," a technique of translating "English to English" by substituting one word for another. Forms of a language harbour their own histories, values, and ideologies — Canadian English has elements of British and American English — and in the process of homolinguistic translation, these differences enrich the trove of meanings. McCaffery played with the possible meanings hidden within an English text by "translating" Gertrude Stein, Ludwig Wittgenstein, Susanna Moodie, and an English translation of Sappho in his books *Dr. Sadhu's Muffins* (1974), *Ow's Waif* (1975), and *Intimate Distortions* (1978).

McCaffery and Nichol also began to experiment with sound poetry, a method of communicating through the sound rather than the semantic meaning of words. In 1970, Rafael Barretto-Rivera and Paul Dutton joined Nichol and McCaffery to form the Four Horsemen sound poetry collective, touring widely and releasing *Live in the West* (1974), and *Horse D'Oeuvres* (1976). The group continued to perform until Nichol's death, in 1988.

In 1977, McCaffery published an edited collection of essays entitled "The Politics of the Referent" (a special issue of the journal *Open Letter*), which introduced to Canadians the American movement called language (or L=A=N=G=U=A=G=E) poetics. A postmodern initiative greatly influenced by modern experimentalists such as Gertrude Stein and Louis Zukofsky, it uses language to encourage reader participation in the text. In his work, for example, McCaffery will self-consciously subvert grammar, the tool used to impose sense on words. When words are freed from grammar and the author's intentions relegated to the background (or even jettisoned), possible meanings and associations multiply, and readers are at liberty to select their own. For McCaffery, poetry is a personal, emotional, physical experience, and he insists that language poetics are "bringing poetry back to the body where it truly belongs." Many of the younger writers who cite McCaffery as an influence combined during this time to create the Kootenay School of Writing, a non-profit artist-run centre in Vancouver, and the literary journal *L=A=N=G=U=A=G=E*. The journal was eventually incorporated into *Open Letter*, for which McCaffery still serves as a contributing editor.

In the 1980s and early 1990s, McCaffery continued to investigate form and language, publishing *Knowledge Never Knew* (1983), *Panopticon* (1984), *Evoba* (1987), and *The Black Debt* (1989). He also experimented with literary theory in *North of Intention: Collected Writings 1973–1986* (1986) and *Theory of Sediment* (1992); the latter was nominated for a Governor General's Award. In these texts, McCaffery suggests different ways of reading the poetry he is critiquing, as well as different ways of reading his critiques, consciously blurring or even eradicating the line between art and criticism.

After teaching at York University for many years, McCaffery moved to Buffalo with his wife, poet Karen McCormack, to take up the David Gray Chair of Poetry and Letters at the State University of New York. His ground-breaking and extensive body of work won him the Gertrude Stein Award for Innovative Poetry in 1993–1994 and 1994–1995. Since 2000, he has written several award-nominated works of poetry and published a collection of essays, *Prior to Meaning: The Protosemantic and Poetics* (2001).

Poem for Arthur Cravan[1]

a perfume
like the sugary[1]
                 drops[2]
the sweet thrash
arousing these feathers[3]

all like a clinch[4]

when the shattered light
is rose[5]

the small enters
what the odour colours[6]

1 at this point (perfume) the two people are located in the two separate
hemispheres of existing area of action.
2 the third person enters with each foot bisecting the double areas of
interaction (perfume drops).
3 at any time between (perfume drops feathers) the hemispherical areas of
interaction may be altered (the these).
4 penultimate adaption of hemispherical areas of interaction to be implemented
at any time during pre-arranged duration of this interaction (perfume drops
all feathers clinch).
5 this is entirely doubtful as the fourth person must be introduced into area
one of total areas of hemispherical interaction (perfume drops all feathers
clinch a colours). the type of entry permissable up to and including second
pre-agreed shift of areas (perfume drops all feathers clinch a colours
feathers all).
6 at this point the lines should be drawn across the first area of the hemispherical
division of interaction to connect the parties (cravan and nameless opponent)
with lateral and diagonal terminal possibility points (.a .what .perfume
.colours) in pre-arranged shift to circulation of duration (a - w - s - e).

---

1. **Arthur Cravan** Eccentric international poet and surrealist artist (1887–1918).

a (perfume) like the sugary
(drops)
the sweet thrash arousing these (feathers)
all like a (clinch)
when the shattered light is rose
the small enters
what the odour (colours)

Line 1 is strong and in an odd place
    (Cravan's round without a doubt).
Line 2 is weak and in its proper place but with
    no proper correlative above.
Line 3 is strong and between two weak lines.
    (Cravan seems to be tiring).
Line 4 is faithful.
    (Cravan takes a count of eight).
Line 5 is in the place of honour.
    (After a brief meeting in London
    Cravan marries Mina Loy in Mexico).
Line 6 is at the top.
    ('a yellow man to a white man, a black
    man to a yellow man with a black boxer
    to a white student.' Arthur Cravan).

it was in the third round that Cravan chose an
alternate image pathway controlled by regulatory letters
through the primary alteration of lettristic contours:

   aper   fume-like

the ingested words actually became Johnson's chin
converted into a biological path which Cravan ocularised
immediately to provide him with a type of energy based
entirely upon typographic molecules
          (sugary drops) as
Cravan literally did.
later Cravan began to store such energy in the form of
'dictionaries' which he could release against Johnson's jaw
as the need arose.
by round five it was obvious that Cravan would have to choose
one specific pathway entirely dependent on the concentration
of the regulatory letters
     (feat
        he
    rs
       all)

hence the essence of the contours changed and Cravan gained
the offensive.
this concept of the boxing ring as page – the concept of an
entirely flexible lettristic landscape (semanto-molecularly
based but capable of geographic and historic realization)
makes it possible to explain a previously puzzling observation:
that certain of the oversized and undersized post-definables
(vowels and consonants really were Cravan's chin) were able to
bind the surface of Johnson's chest without forming sentences.

                 (1974)

Gnotes

The history which bears and determines us has the form of a war rather than that of a language, relations of power not relations of meaning.
—MICHEL FOUCAULT

ever since	T
land	H
.	.
this power	E
.	
relation	H
to	I
an is	S
.	.
th' is	'T
book is	O
.	.
"this" "is"	"R"
.	.
(closes) :	(Y):
.	.
the SKY THE sea	W
THE GLOSS	H
"if" : when	"I"
(elements)	(C)
.	.

```
what ever                H
the real                 B
as                       E

power           d        A

.                        .

force    : ——————————————R:
relation to              S
a too                    A


.                        .

an use / tongue          N/
through hook  :  tong    :D


.                        .

parts                    D
partial)                 E)


.                        .

concept-                 T-
form:                    :E
"i told                  "R


you so"                  M"

takes place              I
from                     N

.                        .E
acts                     S
gripped                  U
mode
```

.

consensus	S
"skirt" links	"H"
dim component	A
c o (nfi) d e n c e	(S)
*	*
aim plus "	"T
route	H
as all"	E"

.

implode i	F
sink	O
load mucous	R
simile to	M
style that	O
.	.
great	F
ER than	A
a	W
column let'	A'

.

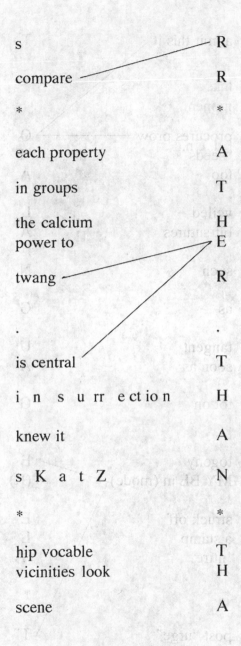

s	R
compare	R
*	*
each property	A
in groups	T
the calcium	H
power to	E
twang	R
.	.
is central	T
i n s u rr e ct io n	H
knew it	A
s K a t Z	N
*	*
hip vocable	T
vicinities look	H
scene	A

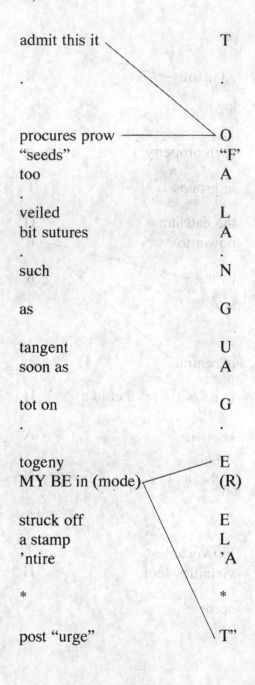

admit this it   T

.   .

procures prow   O
"seeds"   "F'
too   A
.   .
veiled   L
bit sutures   A
.   .
such   N

as   G

tangent   U
soon as   A

tot on   G
.   .

togeny   E
MY BE in (mode)   (R)

struck off   E
a stamp   L
'ntire   'A

*   *

post "urge"   T"

of flavour   I

.

final shrunk   O
called clutch   N

.   .

that lettuce   S
as a   O

night   F
litotes   P

.   .

oval cotta   O
simples   W

overdose   E
a state miens   R

meant   N

shunned a para   O

per occlude   T

derives   R
a river   E

.   .

to arrive   L

*   *

a life dense   A
hither   T
to   I

philosophers   O
have tried   N

to interpret   S

.   .

this as   O
a diaper   F

the point   M

(how   (E

eVer   )   A)

is   N

to   I

*   *

change   N

it   G

(1991)

Instruction Manual

Open the blade to read the word knife.

PROPERTY.

A loop-hole logic.

Films developed under water.

HAPPINESS.

It was the morning after which big festival.

HETEROCLYTE.[1]

Verbs divulge each driving hazard.

Inching into human coal.

PRECESSION.

Hooks reduce sculpture to a hanging lint.

Field practices.

INTERPELLATE.[2]

Who me.

A plant is any upright animal.

The earth and every star two twins.

SUCCESS.

We didn't hire him for the vinyl tie.

FALLACY.

---

1. **Heteroclyte** Irregular; verbs that are not conjugated according to their language's normal patterns. 2. **interpellate** To call, summon; Marxist philosopher Louis Althusser (1918–1990) used the term to describe how ideology and roles are unconsciously assigned to participants in a society.

A town in Florida invented ragtime.

Hegel's[3] truths appeal to left-hand shoes.

MEDIATION.

Papal populism[4] grows by way of colourful tectonic shifts.

EQUATION.

Sir Thomas Wyat[5] sold his soul to phonocentrism.[6]

NOSTALGIA.

All keys quiet in the western door.

GENDER.

Oblivion hates to enter sequence.

PERSONIFICATION.

Focus comes attended by a box-like thatch.

INSIGNIA.

These were three parentheses.

KOAN.[7]

Which what exists.

CIRCUITOUS.[8]

Economy seeks out situated spas.

Hesitation via stanzas.

BATHOS.

---

3. **Hegel** German philosopher (1770–1831), perhaps most famous for his view of history as a series of competing movements that arise as solutions to previous movements; influenced the Marxist idea of the dialectic. 4. **Papal populism** Somewhat paradoxical; the pope is the absolute head of the Catholic Church, whose word is considered infallible, while populism would trust the common people over elites of any kind. 5. **Sir Thomas Wyat** Wyatt (1503–1542) was a British poet renowned for his sonnets, songs, and satires. 6. **phonocentrism** The notion that spoken language is prior to, or the basis of, written language. 7. **koan** Buddhist story or saying whose meaning is illogical, but understandable on an intuitive level. 8. **bathos** Emotion or literary style so bombastic it becomes absurd.

My heart is opening like a wet umbrella.

Rhyme tempts the rational to attack.

TACITURNITY.[9]

We asked the time.

MODERNITY.

It's on the wall.

SEMIOSIS.[10]

Each atom palpitates between two sentients.

Death diagnosed as convalescence[11] in a novel.

PROSCRIPTION.[12]

Only a dentist can tell you how certain mimosas[13] peel away from chalk.

ALLEGORY.

The two blue sofas twice between a shaft of stationary peach.

These are the sentences you have to paint.

SYNOPSIS.

Male insecurity accounts for narrative in politics.

DESTINATION.

The most beautiful phrase is this line.

(1996)

---

9. **taciturnity** State of being untalkative. 10. **semiosis** The process by which signs interact. 11. **convalescence** Period of recovery from illness. 12. **proscription** Prohibition. 13. **mimosas** A species of sensitive flowering plant.

Marlene NourbeSe Philip (1947–)

Marlene NourbeSe Philip was born in 1947 in Tobago. When she was eight years old, her father moved the family to Trinidad because he believed that his children would receive a better education there. Philip refers to this flight from her lush tropical birthplace to the "concrete and paved over" world of Trinidad as her first real "experience of exile." Her schooling was British and colonial, based on Western conceptions of "profession, vocation, career."

Following her graduation in 1968 from the University of the West Indies in Kingston, Jamaica, Philip immigrated to Canada to study political science and law at the University of Western Ontario in London. From 1973 to 1982, she practised law in Toronto, specializing in immigration and family law. During this period, Philip began to compose poetry. Because she had been raised to believe that the only "good" jobs were to be found in the professions, she had never considered writing as a vocation. In her essay "The Absence of Writing; Or, How I Almost Became a Spy" (1989), she reflects: "Some people are born writing, some achieve writing and some have writing thrust upon them. My belonging is to the last group, coming slowly to accept the blessing and yoke that is writing." In 1982, she retired from law to devote herself to a literary career.

Philip had published her first poetry collection, *Thorns*, two years earlier. In these early poems, she explores the Trinidadian dialect, which, she explains, is a unique melange of Spanish, French, English, and "the languages initially spoken by the African slaves." In "Nostalgia '64," for example, the speaker is "Liming by de street corner / dressed to kill / … talking bout de latest caiso / who's a jackabat / an' who not." The carefree tone of this poem gives way to a more sombre one in "Oliver Twist," as Philip examines the dark paradoxes arising from the way in which her community has ingested English values and ideologies along with the English language. Describing a visit that the Queen of England makes to the island, she imagines the monarch waving from a "black limousine with air conditioned crawl" while "little children faint and drop / black flies in the heat singing / Britons never never never / shall be slaves."

In 1988, Philip published a novel for adolescents called *Harriet's Daughter*. Narrator Margaret Cruickshank, the child of West Indian immigrants living in Toronto, is inspired by American abolitionist Harriet Tubman and her involvement with the Underground Railroad. She devises a plan to help her friend Zulma return to Tobago to be with her grandmother, and the mothers of both girls aid in the preparations for Zulma's journey. Mother–daughter relationships are strengthened in the process, and the girls gain confidence and pride in their heritage. This story, which showcases Philip's skill at mixing standard English and dialect, has been widely taught in Ontario high schools.

The poetry collection *She Tries Her Tongue, Her Silence Softly Breaks* (1989) marked a shift in Philip's relationship with language. In her introductory essay, she identifies her "father tongue" as English and claims that her "mother tongue" is irretrievably lost. She refers to the Caribbean "demotic," "honed and fashioned through a particular history of empire and savagery," and argues that it is an inadequate mode of expression for the African Caribbean writer. "It is not sufficient," she says, "to write only in dialect, for too often that remains a … closed experience." Neither, of course, is it enough to simply write in English: "The language as we know it has to be dislocated and acted upon — even destroyed — so that it begins to serve our purposes." The poems of *She Tries Her Tongue* put these ideas into practice. In "Discourse on the Logic of Language," Philip searches for her linguistic origins by rupturing and restructuring standard English: "English / is my mother tongue. / A mother tongue is not / not a foreign lan lan lang / language / l/anguish / anguish / — a foreign anguish. / English is / my father tongue. / A father tongue is / a foreign language, / therefore English is / a foreign language / not a mother tongue." The poet has, therefore, "no mother / tongue" — she is "dumb-tongued." Yet this very act of disruption, what Philip calls "the split in bridge / Between speech and magic / Force and word," is in itself a form of language capable of expressing, to some degree, her colonial experience. With these poems, Philip has managed, as one review put it, to enter "the difficult post-colonial dialogue with English, the conquering language" and thereby expose the "oppression [that occurs] when a new world is grafted upon an unwilling people by means of an alien tongue."

In 1990, Philip was awarded a Guggenheim poetry fellowship. The following year, she published *Looking for Livingstone: An Odyssey of Silence,* a meditation on the ways in which we create and distort history composed of dream sequences, journal entries, and prose passages. It tells the story of a woman traveller in search of British explorer David Livingstone, the so-called discoverer of Africa. In the course of her journey, she meets with many people, collecting their stories and reading their silences in an effort to discover a new truth. Philip then turned her attention to critical writing, producing three collections of essays: *Frontiers: Essays and Writings on Racism and Culture* (1992), *Showing Grit: Showboating North of the 44th Parallel* (1993), and the semi-autobiographical *A Genealogy of Resistance* (1997).

Most recently, Philip has made a foray into the world of theatre, publishing a play called *Coups and Calypsos* (2001). The piece is set during the 1990 military coup attempt in Trinidad and Tobago, and it focuses on a South Asian Caribbean man and an African Caribbean woman who are forced to share a beach house for a night after their marriage has failed. Philip is interested in the way public issues impinge upon private lives — the way in which the relationship she depicts in the play "becomes the public arena in which the historical drama inherent in the brutal legacies of colonialism and racism in the Caribbean play themselves out." In her introduction to *Coups and Calypsos,* she admits that her attraction to the theatre stems from the centrality of drama and performance to Caribbean life. She notes the abundance of demotic terms to describe performance ("mamaguy," "pappyshow," "ramajay," "robber talk") and makes reference to calypso performers and the Caribbean tradition of carnival. "It surprises me," she reflects, "that performance has not claimed me earlier."

Philip currently resides in Toronto. Her other works include a second poetry collection, *Salmon Courage* (1983), and *Caribana: African Roots and Continuities — Race, Space and the Poetics of Moving* (1996), an examination of the Caribbean carnival.

Discourse on the Logic of Language

WHEN IT WAS BORN, THE MOTHER HELD HER NEWBORN CHILD CLOSE: SHE BEGAN THEN TO LICK IT ALL OVER. THE CHILD WHIMPERED A LITTLE, BUT AS THE MOTHER'S TONGUE MOVED FASTER AND STRONGER OVER ITS BODY, IT GREW SILENT — THE MOTHER TURNING IT THIS WAY AND THAT UNDER HER TONGUE, UNTIL SHE HAD TONGUED IT CLEAN OF THE CREAMY WHITE SUB-STANCE COVERING ITS BODY.

English
is my mother tongue.
A mother tongue is not
not a foreign lan lan lang
language
l/anguish
 anguish
— a foreign anguish.

English is
my father tongue.
A father tongue is
a foreign language,
therefore English is
a foreign language
not a mother tongue.

What is my mother
tongue
my mammy tongue
my mummy tongue
my momsy tongue
my modder tongue
my ma tongue?

I have no mother
tongue
no mother to tongue
no tongue to mother
to mother
tongue
me

I must therefore be tongue
dumb
dumb-tongued
dub-tongued
damn dumb
tongue

EDICT I[1]

*Every owner of slaves
shall, wherever possible,
ensure that his slaves
belong to as many ethno-
linguistic groups as
possible. If they can-
not speak to each other,
they cannot then foment
rebellion and revolution.*

---

1. **Edict** Decree, law.

Those parts of the brain chiefly responsible for speech are named after two learned nineteenth century doctors, the eponymous[2] Doctors Wernicke and Broca respectively.

Dr. Broca believed the size of the brain determined intelligence; he devoted much of his time to 'proving' that white males of the Caucasian race had larger brains than, and where therefore superior to women, Blacks and other peoples of colour.

Understanding and recognition of the spoken word takes place in Wernicke's area — the left temporal lobe, situated next to the auditory cortex; from there relevant information passes to Broca's area — situated in the left frontal cortex — which then forms the response and passes it on to the motor cortex. The motor cortex controls the muscles of speech.

---

2. **eponymous** Lending one's name to something; here, Wernicke's Area, the centre responsible for language comprehension, and Broca's Area, the centre of the brain that enables language production.

THE MOTHER THEN PUT HER FINGERS INTO HER CHILD'S MOUTH — GENTLY FORCING IT OPEN; SHE TOUCHES HER TONGUE TO THE CHILD'S TONGUE, AND HOLDING THE TINY MOUTH OPEN, SHE BLOWS INTO IT — HARD. SHE WAS BLOWING WORDS — HER WORDS, HER MOTHER'S WORDS, THOSE OF HER MOTHER'S MOTHER, AND ALL THEIR MOTHERS BEFORE — INTO HER DAUGHTER'S MOUTH.

but I have
a dumb tongue
tongue dumb
father tongue
and english is
my mother tongue
is
my father tongue
is a foreign lan lan lang
language
l/anguish
  anguish
a foreign anguish
is english
another tongue
my mother
mammy
mummy
moder
mater
macer
moder
tongue
mothertongue

tongue mother
tongue me
mothertongue me
mother me
touch me
with the tongue of your
lan lan lang
language
l/anguish
  anguish
english
is a foreign anguish

EDICT II

Every slave ca
ing his native
shall be seve
ished. Where
removal of the
recommended.
fending organ,
moved, should
on high in a cen
so that all may
tremble.

A tapering, blunt-tipped, muscular, soft and fleshy organ describes
(a) the penis.
(b) the tongue.
(c) neither of the above.
(d) both of the above.

In man the tongue is
(a) the principal organ of taste.
(b) the principal organ of articulate speech.
(c) the principal organ of oppression and exploitation.
(d) all of the above.

The tongue
(a) is an interwoven bundle of striated muscle running in three planes.
(b) is fixed to the jawbone.
(c) has an outer covering of a mucous membrane covered with papillae.
(d) contains ten thousand taste buds, none of which is sensitive to the taste of
     foreign words.

Air is forced out of the lungs up the throat to the larynx where it causes the vocal cords
to vibrate and create sound. The metamorphosis from sound to intelligible word requires
(a) the lip, tongue and jaw all working together.
(b) a mother tongue.
(c) the overseer's whip.
(d) all of the above or none.

(1989)

She Tries Her Tongue; Her Silence Softly Breaks

All Things are alter'd, nothing is destroyed
Ovid, *The Metamorphoses* (tr. Dryden).

the me and mine of parents
the we and us of brother and sister
the tribe of belongings small and separate,
when gone …
on these exact places of exacted grief
i placed mint-fresh grief coins
sealed the eyes with certain and final;
10   in such an equation of loss tears became
a quantity of minus.
with the fate of a slingshot stone
loosed from the catapult pronged double with history
and time on a trajectory of hurl and fling
to a state active with without and unknown
i came upon a future biblical with anticipation

*It is important, when transplanting plants, that their roots not be exposed to air longer than is
necessary. Failure to observe this caution will result in the plant dying eventually, if not
immediately. When transplanting, you may notice a gently ripping sound as the roots are torn
away from the soil. This is to be expected: for the plant, transplanting is always a painful
process.*

The Practical Guide to Gardening

seek   search and   uproot
the forget and remember of root words   20
uncharged
              pathways electric with the exposed lie
circuits of dead
              currents of still
                        words
synapses[1] of unuse and gone
                        words
wordless
        in the eden of first sin
                        and   30
naked

1. The limbic system along with the hypothalamus, hippocampus, amygdala, fornix and
   olfactory bulb rule the basic drives for food, sex and survival.
2. The limbic system or primitive cortex plays a significant role in emotions; it is indispensable in
   the formation of memory.
3. Human memory may be either immediate, short-term, or long-term.
4. The cerebral cortex is the storehouse of our memory — it makes us human.
5. What we choose to store in our long-term memory is closely linked to our emotions.
6. Memory is essential to human survival.

Facts to Live By and Die

---

1. **synapses** Junctions crossed by nerve paths.

without the begin of word
grist in a grind and pound of together
in the absence of a past mortared with
                                                    apart
the harsh husk of a future-present begins

40

... and the big bad wolf came and said,
    "Little pig, little pig let me in."
    "No, no, not by the hair of my chinny chin chin."
    "Then I'll huff and I'll puff and I'll blow your
    house in."
    The wolf huffed and puffed and he huffed and puffed
and couldn't blow the house down.

    The first pig built his house of straw; the second of wood. Did the third pig buy his bricks or was he given them, and why? Where did he get his money to buy his bricks with?
    Straw, wood or brick. The moral of this tale, is that the right choice of materials secures safety.

How to Build Your House Safe and Right

oath   moan   mutter   chant
      time grieves the dimension of other   50
babble   curse   chortle   sing
      turns on its axis of silence
praise-song   poem   ululation[2]   utterance
      one song would bridge the finite in silence
syllable   vocable   vowel   consonant
      one word erect the infinite in memory

... the day of Pentecost was fully come ...
And suddenly there came a sound from heaven as of a rushing mighty wind, and it filled all
the house where they were sitting.
And there appeared unto them cloven tongues like as of fire, and it sat upon each of them.
And they were filled with the Holy Ghost, and began to speak with other tongues ...   60
... every man heard them speak in his own language.

                 The Acts of the Apostles   *2: 1,2,3,4,6.*

---

2. **ululation** Howling.

absencelosstears   laughter   grief
in any language
                    the same
only larger
            for the silence
                            monstrosity
obscenity
tongueless wonder
blackened stump of a tongue
                            torn
out
            withered
            petrified
                            burnt
on the pyres of silence
a mother's child foreign
                            made
by a tongue that cursed
                        the absence
in loss
tears   laughtergrief
                in the word

... and if a stranger were to touch her newborn child, the mother will have nothing to do with it. She can smell the stink of the stranger on her child and will refuse to suckle it, believing the spirit of her child to be taken by the stranger.

De Matribus et Advenis[3]

---

3. *De Matribus et Advenis* Latin; "On Mothers and Strangers."

I do not presume to come to this thy table
father forgive
most merciful father, trusting in my own righteousness
foreign father forgive   90
but in thy manifold and great mercies.
forgive her   me   this foreignness
I am not worthy so much as to gather up the crumbs under thy table
forgive me this dumbness
but thou art the same Lord, whose property
this lack of tongue forgive
is always to have mercy
                              upon
                                              this
                              thisthisand this   100
                                    disfigurement this
                                                          dis
                              memberment
                                            this
                                                    verbal crippling
                                                            this
                              absence of voice
                                            that
                              wouldnotcould   not
sing   110

                    Kyrie eleison
                    Christos eleison[4]
                    Kyrie eleison

Is it in the nature of God to forgive himself —
For his sin?

                                        The Book of unCommon Prayer

---

4. *Kyrie eleison, Christos eleison* Greek; "God have mercy," "Christ have mercy."

Hold we to the centre of remembrance
that forgets the never that severs
word from source
120   and never forgets the witness
of broken utterances that passed
before   and now
breaks the culture of silence
in the ordeal of testimony;
in the history of circles
each point lies
along the circumference
diameter or radius
each word creates a centre
130   circumscribed by memory ... and history
waits   at rest always

still at the centre

history, n — L. *historia*, '*narrative, story, narration, account*', *from Gk ... 'learning by inquiry, knowledge obtained by inquiry; account of one's inquiries; narration, historical narrative; history ...*

memory, n — *ME. memoire, fr OF. memorie (F. Memoire), fr. L. memoria, 'memory', fr. memor, 'mindful', which stands for *me-mor, and derives from I.-E. *mer-(s)mer-, reduplication of base *(s)mer-, to care for, be anxious about, think, consider, remember' ... Cp. memoir, commemorate, remember. Cp. also martyr, mourn, smriti.*

**Klein's Comprehensive Etymological
Dictionary of the English Language**

Without memory can there be history?

140

That body should speak
When silence is,
Limbs dance
The grief sealed in memory;
That body might become tongue
Tempered to speech
And where the latter falters
Paper with its words
The crack of silence;
That skin become
Slur   slide   susurration
Polyphony[5] and rhythm — the drum;
The emptied skull a gourd
               filled
With the potions of determine
That compel the split in bridge
Between speech and magic
Force and word;
The harp of accompaniment the ribcage
Strung with the taut in gut;
Flute or drumstick the bones.
When silence is
Abdication[6] of word   tongue and lip
Ashes of once in what was
... Silence
Song   word   speech
Might I ... like Philomela[7] ... sing
               continue
                  over
                    into
... pure utterance

... and on the day of the great salmon run, the first salmon caught is cooked and shared among the elders — men and women. The oldest woman of the tribe, accompanied by the youngest girl-child, then goes down to the waters and returns the skeleton whole to its watery home. This is the way the tribe ensures future gifts of winter food.

Of Women, Wisdom, Fishes and Men

(1989)

---

5. **Polyphony** Music written with multiple interacting melodies. 6. **abdication** Renunciation of political power.
7. **Philomela** Athenian princess who is raped by her sister's husband, who then cuts out her tongue when she defiantly threatens to speak of it. While imprisoned, she weaves a tapestry telling her story and sends it to her sister, who takes revenge on her husband.

John Steffler (1947–)

John Steffler was born on 13 November 1947, and he grew up on a farm near Thornhill, Ontario. In 1974, he received an M.A. in English from the University of Guelph; his thesis was on William Blake. The same year, he relocated to Corner Brook, Newfoundland, to teach English at Sir Wilfred Grenfell College of Memorial University. The shift in landscape had a profound effect on Steffler, who focuses much of his poetry on the relation between the Newfoundland landscape and his own sense of self and community. "Place has always been very important to me," he says. "Different landscapes have different characters just as various kinds of animals do. Partly for this reason I've always been interested in the long-term interaction between people and the place they inhabit. This process is especially striking in Newfoundland, where nature is rowdy and naked, and people fit right in." Steffler's work is imbued with the folklore and myths of the Atlantic coast. At the same time, he is the kind of writer whose interests take him into many worlds, and many historic periods far removed from the immediate present.

Although Steffler explored the works of many poets, Dylan Thomas and T.S. Eliot were the first to reel him in. At 16, he would "stand in our ruined barn at sunset and read 'Fern Hill' and *Four Quartets* out loud." But it was Canadian poet Al Purdy who finally gave Steffler what he calls his "route." Purdy's unpretentious, colloquial verse was a revelation, prompting Steffler to remark that "maybe the route to poetry did not have to lie through abstruse Old World learning and intricate technique. Maybe there was a more direct, local route. Maybe I already knew a lot. Maybe there was a route that lay through honesty and objectivity." He began to follow this route, publishing poems in various journals and magazines. His first collection, *An Explanation of Yellow*, appeared in 1981.

In 1985, Steffler published what he called "a sort of novel": *The Grey Islands: A Journey.* Through various poetic forms, it relates the story of a man who leaves his family and friends to spend a summer on the almost uninhabited Grey Islands off the Newfoundland coast. Steffler's awe and respect for the wildness of the land infused this work and those he had yet to write. *The Wreckage of Play* (1988) experiments with the idea of home — outside or inside, in a house or on the road. Steffler, who aimed to make his readers recognize a particularly Canadian sense of place, admired the way Purdy had accomplished this with his own work, "expressing not only himself in this sophisticated, familiar way, but … also expressing me, too, and the people I knew well and for whom I had learned not to have much regard." Steffler sets his poems in Newfoundland, Ontario, and Greece, and they often involve mental and physical journeys — travelling by plane or boat, leaving and joining families, making discoveries, and "mapping dreams." Home can be found in wild places, but it also resides in the small beauties, and often the comedies, of the domestic sphere. Some of Steffler's poems recall his experiences working as a tradesman, delicately and humorously celebrating such mundane structures as household plumbing.

Steffler achieved popular success with his debut novel, *The Afterlife of George Cartwright* (1992), which won several awards and was shortlisted for a Governor General's Award. It was inspired by the journals of George Cartwright, a British soldier, trader, and explorer who journeyed to Newfoundland and Labrador in 1768. Although the main purpose of his expedition was to establish fruitful commercial relations with the Beothuks, his chief interest was in developing his own community on the coast of Labrador. His journals record the pleasures and frustrations of this endeavour, which brought Cartwright into close contact with the local inhabitants and allowed him to learn their methods of hunting and surviving in a hostile climate. After building strong relations with the Inuit over several years Cartwright convinced an Inuit family to accompany him on a trip to England in 1772, a move that he hoped would encourage investment in his trading activities; however, Cartwright's display of his Inuit friends caused skepticism among the British gentry and alienation among the Inuit themselves. Tragically, the Inuit family became infected with smallpox on the return voyage; only one woman survived. Eventually the infection spread to the larger Inuit community, which was destroyed by the disease.

In Steffler's novel Cartwright becomes a ghost who inhabits the 1990s and looks back on his earlier life. His story is constructed through an interrogation and rewriting of the historic Cartwright's actual account of his travels to and settlement in Labrador, which was called *A Journal of Transactions and Events During a Residence of Nearly Sixteen Years on the Coast of Labrador,* published in 1792. The novel travels back and forth over three centuries to contrast the values of Cartwright's day with those of our own. Its discontinuous structure explores ways in which history is altered by those who record it and provides a complex illustration of how history can be imagined in multiple ways, confounding the idea that there is a single, objective version of the past. It also explores colonial and postcolonial ideas about of the treatment of native peoples, the conception of the natural world, and the ways in which the very process of keeping a journal can become a means of constructing and manipulating identity. The novel, like *That Night We Were Ravenous* (1998), is informed by the author's interest in Zen and Taoism, monistic religions in which there is no separation between the individual and the world he or she inhabits; to damage the earth is to damage one's self.

Steffler was named Canada's Poet Laureate in 2006. His most recent publication is *Helix: New and Selected Poems* (2002).

cliffs

cliffs
and a thin green
cover. like
dinosaurs crouching under a rug. then

through the rowdy narrows
a sunlit bay: spits, shoals[1] and islands, white
birds lifting out of the blue. no

centre. no shadows here. no lines
leading anywhere. waves
capes scrub-tufts shift, shuffle

under the open sky.

10

(1985)

Two rock paws

Two rock paws, a wharf to the left and a gravel beach between, the cabin crouching there ten feet from the shore. A white door and a stoop facing the waves. Long grass ducking, galloping up a hill.

A thick pitted padlock is held to the door with spikes. Splinters and holes up and down where it's been ripped out and hammered back. A contest. Keepers and takers.

---

1. **shoals** Shallow places in a larger body of water.

Owners and travellers. Out here the law is the other way. The right to shelter takes
first place.

Stove, table, two metal bunks. Mattresses once used in bayonet practice probably.
Yellow linoleum nailed to the table top, dirt deep in the cracks and gashes. Chain oil,
10   blood, rust, fat, scrawled in like a diary. All the guys gutting their ducks and fish here,
cleaning their guns, stripping their engines down, hands dripping black spreading
bolts and bearings among the plates of beans.

Feathers turn and lift in the corners when you walk. Back of the stove mush-bottomed
boxes, plastic bags bloated with rot, shrunk potatoes gone into sprouts, liquid carrots,
cabbages yellow, burst.

Men coming out here at the end of their calculations and budgets and fights and
fantasies. Building into crude space. A good time hacking and arsing out at the furthest
edge. No home. No sofas. No wives. High boots, hunting knives and booze and not
getting washed. Then, the time used up or unable to stand it another day, laughing
20   and boasting they run to their boats or planes, dropping what nobody owns. And half
what they brought. Cupboard crammed with stale pancake mix, margarine, sugar, salt.
Salt for godsake! Like me everybody brings salt. Nobody takes it away.

(1985)

From Halki[1]

Along a lane through olive fields
with Mount Zas[2] close in the brilliant air
and no sound but birds and the bamboo's watery rustle
we come to a chapel and burying ground in a pine's dry shade.

One small flame in the chapel's gloom
and Saint George killing his dragon forever.
This chamber deep in the local mind, out here open to all,
makes the rest of the land seem like the rest of the mind.

Outside the graveyard wall I pick up a broken cross
10   carved with name and dates, and the littered earth
focusses, strikes like a snake, the yellow sticks cracking
under my shoes are thigh bones, ribs
still tangled in black rags.

The brightness, the branches swoop
with the bones in a blurred stream loosened and
whirling up through my legs, out of my mouth and eyes
and down again in magnetic curves.

---

1. **Halki** Southern Greek island in the Aegean Sea. 2. **Mount Zas** Mountain on the Greek island of Naxos, near Halki.

Nothing is hidden here, nothing is made abstract.
No one pretends that this walled ground is a resting place;
only a dark hall each passes slowly through travelling back.   20

And walking again I see the tawny earth everywhere
is brick, pottery, tools, teeth, dung, things
built and broken, grown and eaten over and over,
burnt to fine ash in the young Aegean sun.

(1988)

That Night We Were Ravenous

Driving from Stephenville in the late October
dusk — the road swooping and disappearing ahead
like an owl, the hills no longer playing dead
the way they do in the daytime, but sticking their black
blurry arses up in the drizzle and shaking themselves,
heaving themselves up for another night of
leapfrog and Sumo ballet — some

trees detached themselves from the shaggy
shoulder and stepped in front of the car. I swerved

through a grove of legs startled by pavement, maybe a   10
hunchbacked horse with goitre,[1] maybe a team of beavers
trying to operate stilts: it was the

landscape doing a moose, a cow
moose,
most improbable forest device. She danced
over the roof of our car in moccasins.

She had burst from the zoo of our dreams and was
there, like a yanked-out tooth the dentist
puts in your hand.

She flickered on and off.   20
She was strong as the Bible and as full of lives.
Her eyes were like Halley's Comet, like factory whistles,
like bargain hunters, like shy kids.

No man had touched her or given her movements geometry.
She surfaced in front of us like a coelacanth,[2] like a face
in a dark lagoon. She made us feel blessed.

---

1. goitre Swelling of the thyroid. **2. coelacanth** Genus of fish thought extinct since the Cretaceous period, until found off
the South African coast in 1938.

She made us talk like a cage of canaries.

She reminded us. She was the ocean wearing a fur suit.

She had never eaten from a dish.
30   She knew nothing of corners or doorways.

She was our deaths come briefly forward to say hello.

She was completely undressed.

She was more part of the forest than any tree.
She was made of trees. The beauty of her face was bred
in the kingdom of rocks.

I had seen her long ago in the Dunlop Observatory.

She leapt from peak to peak like events in a ballad.

She was as insubstantial as smoke.

She was a mother wearing a brown sweater opening her arms.

40   She was a drunk logger on Yonge Street.

She was the Prime Minister. She had granted us a tiny reserve.

She could remember a glacier where she was standing.

She was a plot of earth shaped like the island of
Newfoundland and able to fly, spring down in the middle of
cities scattering traffic, ride elevators, press pop-eyed
executives to the wall.

She was charged with the power of Churchill Falls.

She was a high-explosive bomb loaded with bones and meat.
She broke the sod in our heads like a plough parting the
50   earth's black lips.

She pulled our zippers down.

She was a spirit.

She was Newfoundland held in a dam. If we had touched her,
she would've burst through our windshield in a wall of blood.

That night we were ravenous. We talked, gulping, waving our
forks. We entered one another like animals entering woods.

That night we slept deeper than ever.

Our dreams bounded after her like excited hounds.

(1998)

Cook's[1] Line

I cut into Cook's pen's
line at latitude 48° 57', longitude 57° 58',
just below his much vandalized
monument
on the edge of Corner Brook.

I lift the section of line extending west
along Humber Arm's south shore.
At first it is no thicker than a thread,
but I flatten it between my palms, I shake it
like a long ribbon, sending   10
waves down its length.

I tug it from side to side, get it limber
and loose.

The pigment he used was remarkably
dense;
it somehow muffled everything on both sides,
like the Great Wall of China,
kept the smell of the sea out of the land and smell
of the land out of the sea.

I dip the severed line in the salt water   20
and make it soft,
knead it, stretch it wide like black
dough.

I hold the bottom edge down with my feet spread
wide apart. I stretch
the top corners out with my hands,
making a tunnel, a kind of nighttime road
of Cook's line.

The pigment thins and separates,
you can walk along inside Cook's line   30
like a long grey cloud.

---

1. **Cook's** Captain James Cook (1728–1779), British explorer who mapped Newfoundland. Corner Brook, a city at the mouth
of the Humber River, now has a monument to him.

Listen.
There are French voices inside the line
and voices that might be Micmac
or even Beothuk, men singing in something
like Spanish or Portuguese, you can hear
birds and waves among beach stones,
taste the kelpy sound of the surf, clear
serum of mussel juice, clams' fine
40   squirts.

I take my cassette recording of Alfred saying:
"There's nar fish be d' wharf clar of a sculpin."
and throw that down inside Cook's line.

I take the photos I took of all the groc and confs[2]
and take-outs between Corner Brook
and Lark Harbour and throw them down inside
Cook's line,
            then I throw in the C & E Takeout
itself and the John's Beach church that used to be
50   in my grade three geography book,
                        and I pick up all
the kids hitchhiking in Mount Moriah
and drive them to the side of Cook's line
and let them out and watch them go
running out of sight in the ink mist,

and I pick up a ball that comes bouncing toward me
in the street in Curling and pitch it
down inside the line, and the ball-hockey players
go chasing after it,
60   and the car
that's rocking up and down on its springs
in the bushes just off the Cook's Brook Park
parking lot, I push it slowly into Cook's line
and give it a shove — two startled flushed faces
in the rear window —
                        and I throw in
Woods Island and Pissing Horse Falls
and the solar orgasm rock and Mad Dog Lake
and Lisa and me at the top of Blomidon Head
70   (Is that a caribou in the pond below? Yes,
it's moving. No, it isn't. Yes, it is.)
and Walt LeMessurier napping in the sun
on the rim of Simms Gorge,
                        and I drag

---

2. **groc and confs** Grocery and convenience stores.

the line over to the start of the Clark's Brook
road, and a row of skidoos, the riders all
in zipped suits and helmets, roars
down inside Cook's line,
                    and the line
is stretched to bursting now, the inside   80
spilling back out to the outside, birds'
calls, crinkled light on the bay,
Lorraine with her radio and barbecue — people
in trouble will find her and her help —
Randy and me coming down the scree[3] slope
on the face of the Blomidons, long moonwalk
strides,
          and I know Cook is away down there
somewhere, bent to his table with pen and dividers,
still leaving his fine black trail.   90

What will he think when his line
spreads and explodes at his pen's
tip and the first of the ball-hockey kids
and skidoos come tumbling in front of him?

                                                                    (2002)

Lorna Crozier (1948–)

Lorna Crozier was born in Swift Current, Saskatchewan, in 1948. She has described her
background as working class and reflected that her parents' lack of interest in literature and the
utilitarian nature of her primary education engendered in her a desire to escape the confining way
of life she had been born into. Her chosen escape route was writing.

     Graduating from the University of Saskatchewan in Saskatoon in 1969, Crozier married Lorne
Uher, a chemistry teacher (she would publish under the name Uher until 1983). She obtained a
teaching certificate and the couple moved back to Swift Current, where she taught high school
English. The early 1970s saw a surge of artistic activity in Saskatchewan, and Crozier became
involved in the province's blossoming literary community. She attended writing workshops at Fort
San, a tuberculosis sanatorium that had been transformed into the Saskatchewan Summer School
of the Arts. She also joined a poetry workshop that met monthly in Moose Jaw. "We called it the
Moose Jaw Movement, partly as a joke," she says — "a reaction to the idea that good writing
couldn't come out of any place but Toronto, Vancouver, Montreal."

     Crozier published her first poetry collection, *Inside Is the Sky* (1976), with Saskatoon's newly
created Thistledown Press. The prairie landscape is a central element in many of these poems, but
Crozier has often insisted that her work is not merely "about 'The Prairie'" — the prairie finds its
way in because she draws on her external environment in creating metaphors. "Writing Is All But,"
for example, is about the shortcomings of language, yet Crozier conveys her meaning through
prairie imagery. She writes, "you with your perfect words / cannot make the rustling / of wind-
rippled wheat / cannot reply to the coyote's howl / cannot call like the meadowlark / from the

---

3. **scree** Steep face of loose debris.

fenceposts." This landscape is also present in several of her feminist poems, as she identifies with the geese, swallows, and deer that are hunted by various stern, shadowy male figures.

In 1978, Crozier produced a second collection, *Crow's Black Joy*, and later that year she left her husband for poet Patrick Lane. In 1979, she and Lane published *No Longer Two People*, a collaborative series of poems based on their relationship but meant to reach beyond the personal to the archetypal. Speaking in an exemplary female voice, Crozier writes with frustration but also remarkable lucidity about the power dynamic in this union. In "With My Fist I Stroke You," the speaker seeks to awaken violence in her partner: "I burn your poems / scatter the ashes over your toast / wait for you to split me / in two." Choosing not to engage in physical violence, the man resorts to a form of emotional abuse and tries to psychoanalyze the speaker. She responds, "you must talk / explain my perversions / ask: What do you want?"

In 1980, Crozier earned an M.A. in English from the University of Alberta. Her thesis was her poetry collection *Humans and Other Beasts* (1980). She travelled a great deal in the period after graduate school, because Lane was serving as writer-in-residence at universities across the country. She managed, however, to return home each year to teach at the Saskatchewan Summer School of the Arts; she was also writer-in-residence at Saskatchewan's Cypress Hills Community College in 1980, and in 1984 she held the same position at the Regina Public Library.

Crozier's 1983 collection *The Weather* was published under her maiden name; the dedication reads: "For the Croziers, whose name / I have reclaimed." She attained a new level of self-assurance and maturity with this collection, treating a wide range of subjects and adapting her style to fit the requirements of each poem. In "The Child Who Walks Backwards," for example, she does not name the offence of child abuse but instead illuminates her concerns through juxtaposition: "My next-door neighbour tells me / her child runs into things. / Cupboard corners and doorknobs / have pounded their shapes / into his face ... This child who climbed my maple / with the sureness of a cat, / trips in his room, cracks / his skull on the bedpost." In "Spring Storm, 1916," she adopts a colloquial tone to capture the speech of the farmers and townspeople depicted in the poem.

In 1985, Crozier published a collection of new and selected poems entitled *The Garden Going On Without Us*. She had begun to infuse her work with an element of humour. In "The Sex Lives of Vegetables," she imagines that tomatoes "rouge their nipples," cucumbers are "like flashers in the park," and carrots are forever engaging in sexual intercourse with the earth. Due to its frank sexuality, the work unsettled some readers. Crozier actually received "hate mail," which prompted her to remark, "a lot of people do not like humour in a poetry book. They find it almost offensive that someone is daring to try to be funny in poetry, which strikes me as extremely limited and naïve." Unfazed, Crozier continued in this vein. "The Penis Poems" sequence from the collection *Angels of Flesh, Angels of Silence* (1988), for example, ends with the image of a penis arriving late at night, breaking the lock, and casting "the long shadow / of a man" from the "bedroom doorway."

In 1991, Crozier and Lane settled in Saanichton, British Columbia, and Crozier began teaching creative writing at the University of Victoria. In 1992, she won a Governor General's Award for *Inventing the Hawk* (1992). Her father had died in 1990, and many of these poems examine his difficult life and the way in which his alcoholism shaped her childhood. In 1996, she produced *A Saving Grace: The Collected Poems of Mrs. Bentley*, written from the perspective of the complex narrator of Sinclair Ross's *As For Me and My House* (1941). In 1999, she published *What the Living Won't Let Go*, in which she explores mortality in the human community and the natural world.

Crozier has continued to write prolifically and has co-edited several anthologies. Her most recent poetry offering is *Whetstone* (2005), a collection in which she reflects on her life from the perspective of middle age. She also revisits some themes of her early writing. Most notable are the poems in which she reworks biblical narratives and assumptions. In "Rapture," she imagines Jesus's second coming: "Folks lined up in lawn chairs along the street / as if waiting for a late parade: the Lord in hat / and snakeskin boots on a chestnut mare."

Fishing in Air

What he fishes for changes
as light changes on water.
Whitefish, pickerel, goldeye.
There is a space in his mind
where they die, a pier slippery with scales
where their eyes turn to slime.

His line is invisible.
He has forgotten what lure falls
endlessly through water.
It could be feathered or striped   10
or a silver curve that flashes
at the slightest flick of his wrist.

If he could send his eye out on a hook,
return it to its socket when he reels in the line,
he would do so. If he could use his heart for bait
then cut it from the fish within a fish.

There is something he has never caught.
Something that makes him stand here
every evening, casting, casting
and reeling in.   20

Every time he fishes he is different.
The water is different, the sky, the way
the tern hangs in the air or doesn't.
What he will catch is a minnow now,
slim and golden, growing to fill an emptiness
in a lake he's never seen before —
no road in or out.

                                                                   (1985)

Myths

There is a story of a swan.
See the birthmark on the back of my neck
under my hair. That is where the great bird
pinched me in her beak, snatching me from the sea
and carrying my wet, salty body to the shore.
This is a story I could believe.

Sometimes the wings of a bird beat against
my skull. Feathers fill my mouth and eyes
with a whiteness like winter.

10   Or I was carried on a dolphin's back.
She pushed me to shore with her soft nose
then turned and disappeared under the waves,
the notes of her song hovering above the water.
In the blue light of evening, alone in the house,
I float through rooms, my sides sleek and slippery.

I was not made from a thin, dry rib
white and bare as if chewed and sucked
by a small dog. These breasts did not come
from a man's side, this round belly, this
20   hollow at the centre. We dreamed each other
at the same time and we dreamed a garden.
When we awoke there was wind in the leaves
above us apples glowing like red moons
as we turned to one another in the sweet green air.

(1985)

Facts about My Father

1

He's five foot eight.
He has a large nose and thick grey hair.
He chews his nails to the quick.

2

He's skinny but he didn't used to be.
His hands and arms were huge from working hard, from shovelling grain in the elevators for a dollar a day, from digging sewers for the City with a back-hoe, from digging trenches in the oil fields. When I was a kid, he won all the arm-wrestling matches at the Healey Hotel. I wanted my arms to be as hairy and powerful as his.

3

10   He calls himself Irish and he's proud of it, though he's third-generation Canadian, his father moving from Ontario to Saskatchewan, settling on a farm near a town called Success.

4

He wasn't smart in school, quit in grade eight to help on the farm. His brains were in his hands, he could fix anything, his fingers knew exactly what to do.

5

He was famous for two things in the area where he grew up. He was the best driver for miles around Success, could drive to town through any kind of gumbo in his father's Model T. He was the district killer, shot dogs and horses for the neighbours without batting an eye, took pride in that, still likes to tell those stories.

6

He played the fiddle at country dances. Loved Wilf Carter's "Blue Canadian Rockies" and "Strawberry Roan." He married Peggy Ford who loved to dance. She lived across the road on the farm with the big alkali lake[1] where everyone used to swim. He didn't   20
like to swim, didn't like to walk, didn't like to do anything that didn't connect him with a machine. As a kid he even rode his bicycle from the back door to the outhouse.

7

He has flat feet. That's why he lost the farm. He couldn't get in the army so his mother asked him to move to town. That way his younger brother, Orville, would be the only man around and wouldn't get drafted. He and Mom moved into a cook-car abandoned by the railroad in Success, which was already failing, the stores shutting down, the Chinaman moving away. When his mother died she left everything to Orville and Orville kept it all.

8

The Christmas of '41, just after my brother was born, there was no money. He shot a coyote, sold the hide for $5, and bought gifts for everyone. It was the first and last time   30
he spent money on presents.

9

He wasn't there when I was born. He was betting on the horses at the Gull Lake Sports Day. The first time he held me, Mom was mad, he was hungover, his hands shaking.

10

He got throat cancer in 1969, had cigarettes smuggled into the Grey Nun's hospital, smoked a pack of Export A's a day, got well.

11

He caught his right hand in a lawn mower he was repairing, severed the first joints of three fingers. He smashed his left hand between the steel doors of a freight elevator. I was standing beside him. I fainted.

12

He had his gall bladder removed when he was sixty-four. The morning after the operation he pulled out the tubes from his arm and walked to the Legion for a beer.   40

---

1. **alkali lake** Salty lake.

13

He bought a speedboat when he and Mom were broke. He roared across Duncaren Dam, drunk, in a storm, leaping the waves. The boat finally tipped and he fell in with his clothes and rubber boots on. He can't swim, but he made it to the surface, the boat circling like a shark. Somehow he got in, made it home, didn't tell anyone till years later.

14

He buys hot goods in the bars and sells them for a profit. He cheated his son-in-law when he sold him a car. One time he came home with a rug he bought at an auction sale. When he unrolled it on the living room linoleum, there was a hole in the middle, big enough to poke your head through. He rolled it up, tied it with a string and took it back, sold it to a Mennonite for twenty dollars more.

50

15

He collects ballpoint pens with names written on them, like "Ashdown's Hardware," "Ham Motors," "The Venice Cafe." He puts them in the bottom drawer on his side of the dresser. One of them has a drawing of two minks fucking. As a kid I wasn't supposed to know it was there.

16

He never came to the plays I was in, never watched my brother play hockey. He was drunk at my grade twelve graduation (I was the Valedictorian), stayed out the night before and arrived home just as Mom and I were leaving for the gym. He couldn't tie his shoes. Beside the principal at the head table, he fell asleep, his head nodding over the plate of ham, scalloped potatoes, and jellied salad.

17

60

He uses the word *Bohunk*[2] and the phrase *Jew him down.*[3] One morning out of the blue he told me he'd rather kill me than have me marry a Catholic.

18

He owns the pool tables in the beer parlour at the Legion. Every Saturday morning he cleans the felt and collects his quarters, rolling them in strips of brown paper at the breakfast table. Though he's got cataracts and can't raise his arms above his head (it was all the arm wrestling, my mother says), no one can beat him playing pool. The young guys wait to challenge him after he's had a few beer, but he only gets better. His eyes seem to clear and maybe he forgets how old he is.

19

His favourite breakfast is Cream of Wheat. His favourite supper is roast chicken with mashed potatoes. His favourite bread is store-bought white though Mom bakes her own.

70

His favourite shirt has snap-buttons and two pockets, one for cigarettes, one for pens. His favourite car is an El Camino painted bronze with razor-thin black stripes. Young

---

2. Bohunk Derisive term for an Eastern European Caucasian. **3. Jew him down** Derogatory expression for price haggling.

guys stop him on the street and ask if it's for sale. His favourite story is how he picked up a semi-trailer from the factory in Windsor years ago, drove it through Detroit and all the way to Swift Current without stopping for a sleep. His favourite TV program used to be "Don Messer's Jubilee."[4] He'd always say *Look at old Charlie dance.*

20

He doesn't have a favourite book. The only thing he reads is *The Swift Current Sun.* He follows the lines with the one good finger on his right hand, the nail bitten to the quick, and reads everything three times. I don't know how much he understands.

(1992)

Mrs. Bentley[1]

I've walked through this story
in housedresses and splay-
footed rubbers.[2] Mousy hair
without curls. Philip never drew
a convenient portrait
for me to comment on,
a hasty sketch. I could have said,
though his hand is flawless,
this does not resemble me.
That's my high forehead   10
and the way I purse my lips
but he's placed my eyes
far apart. I look in two directions.
The right one stares at you,
follows you as you move.
The left, my prairie eye,
gazes at what lies just over
where the lines converge.
No portrait exists, no photographs
and little self-description.   20
And nowhere in these pages
can you find my name.
Gladys, Louise, Madeline?
I fancy Margaret though in the country
everyone would call her Peg.
We're left with Mrs.
Bentley, dowdy, frumpy, plain.
Don't you wonder what Philip

---

4. **Don Messer's Jubilee** CBC musical variety show of the 1960s, for which Messer (1909–1973), a famous Maritime fiddler, was master of ceremonies.

1. **Mrs. Bentley** Narrator of Canadian author Sinclair Ross's 1941 novel *As for Me and My House,* which dealt with the struggle between Mrs. Bentley and her husband, Philip, in a small prairie town during the Great Depression. 2. **splay-footed rubbers** Waterproof overshoes.

30
called me as we lay together,
my flesh warmed by his hands,
the taste of me on his tongue,
as if there were no better sound
in all the world,
my name, my name!

(1996)

A Kind of Love

You can see it
in my graduation photograph.
You're Daddy's little girl, he said,
his arm heavy around my shoulders,
his face too naked, a sloppy
smile sliding to one side.
I held him up. Mom tied his shoes.
His love made me ashamed.

10
Some days I felt protective,
his hangdog look at breakfast
when no one talked to him but me,
sugar spilling from his spoon.
Don't tell Mum, he'd say
on Sundays when he took me boating,
sunk his third empty in the lake.
At home, she fried a chicken
in case he didn't catch a fish,
waited and kept things warm.
Even so, he died too soon.

20
Now I wait for you as if
you've spent a summer afternoon
in waves of wind and sunlight. I know
you've hidden a bottle somewhere
upstairs in your room. So far
I've stopped myself from looking
though I can't find what to do.

More and more I'm Daddy's
little girl in peau de soi,[1]
my first long dress, its false
30
sheen a wash of mauve.
When you lean into me
the same look's on your face

---

1. **peau de soi** A smooth, satiny fabric.

as in the photograph,
your smile's undone.

Among the other things
it could be named
this too is love, the kind
I'm most familiar with —
the weight I claim
I cannot bear and do,   40
and do.

                                                            (1999)

The Sacrifice of Isaac[1]

I bind my breasts with hide. Eat a jackal's heart
and ride in dust to the mountains of Moriah.
Three nights I sit with what they cannot see
beyond their fires. Though I'm close enough
to touch his cheek, I will my hands to stillness.
Before dawn, our last day on the road, a caravan
stutters by, heavy with its load lie something
from the past. I am too old for them to trouble me
though a boy rides up, tips his goatskin
and offers me a drink. He drops his eyes   10
when I unveil my mouth, the darkness there.
I swallow his breath with water from his father's well,
mumble a blessing though I do not know
his gods, their indifference or their lust.
When the groan of wheels fades, I hear
my child's laugh ringing through the grass
like bells tied to the morning wind.
He is climbing. Bent double under wood,
he bears his fire upon his back.
I wait by a thicket, tufts of ram's wool   20
on the brambles, knife cold against my thigh,
until the altar's built, Isaac asking,
Father, where's the lamb?
then I step into the open, fists on fire,
above my swinging arm
the bare throat of my husband's
Lord opening in a flood of crimson light.

                                                            (2002)

---

1. **Isaac** Hebrew prophet, son of Abraham and Sarah. To test Abraham, God commands him to sacrifice Isaac on Mount Moriah; Moses prepares to do this, but is stopped at the last moment by an angel.

Blizzard

Walking into wind, I lean into my mother's muskrat coat;
around the cuffs her wristbones have worn away the fur.

If we stood still we'd disappear. There's no up or down,
no houses with their windows lit. The only noise is wind

and what's inside us. When we get home my father
will be there or not. No one ever looks for us.

I could lie down and stay right here where snow is all
that happens, and silence isn't loneliness just cold

not talking. My mother tugs at me and won't let go.
10 Then stops to find her bearings. In our hoods of stars

we don't know if anyone will understand
the tongue we speak, so far we are from home.

(2005)

Anne Carson (1950–)

Anne Carson was born in Toronto and grew up in the small Ontario towns of Timmins, Stoney Creek, and Port Hope. As a teenager, she resolved to study classics because Oscar Wilde had done so, and she enrolled at the University of Toronto. Though she found the course requirements frustrating and twice dropped out, she obtained a B.A. in 1974 and an M.A. in classics in 1975. After spending a year in Scotland, Carson returned to Toronto and wrote a dissertation on the poetry of Sappho, receiving her Ph.D. in 1980.

Her first publication, *Eros the Bittersweet* (1986), based on her dissertation, is a quirky, scholarly exploration of the nature of the erotic in ancient Greek literature. In it, she outlines the idea of *eros* (which means "want," or "lack") as well as its bittersweet "dilemma": "The lover wants what he does not have. It is by definition impossible for him to have what he wants if, as soon as it is had, it is no longer wanting." The erotic, argues Carson, is profoundly ambivalent, and often experienced as a "desire *for* desire."

In 1995, she published her first two volumes of verse: *Glass, Irony and God* and *Plainwater: Essays and Poetry*. The latter volume is divided into five parts, each vastly different from the next, and in it she rewrites the paradox of desire in terms of knowledge. Throughout, however, she suggests that knowledge, like desire, seems possible only when its object is absent. Like the horizon, which features prominently in the pilgrimage prose-poem "Thirst," the thing one hopes to know disappears as one approaches it. Moreover, in the set of poems entitled "The Life of Towns" — in which every line, finished or not, ends with a period — Carson undermines the speaker's ability to conclude, or to describe anything conclusively.

Though Carson is an expert in Greek metrics, she does not describe her own poems as musical and claims that her voice is better suited to narrative. She often straddles the gap between poetry and prose: her essays are full of images and experimental syntax, while the narrative poems of "Canicula di Anna" are related in argumentative, expository, and syntactically conventional sentences. Even in her more "poetic" poems, internal punctuation is minimal and the lines, which often spill over into enjambments, have a forward-moving, prose-like momentum. By playing with the limits of genre — breaking sentences into lines of poetry, or including a fake interview with the long-dead Greek poet Mimnermos — Carson asks the reader to consider what kinds of information they expect to gather from established genres.

Behind Carson's experimentation with genres lies the idea that truth constantly exceeds the forms we create to contain it. Like the experimental modernist Gertrude Stein, one of her great influences, Carson believes that standard units (the sentence) and genres (the interview, essay, lyric poem, autobiography) can no longer be used to discuss subjects meaningfully. She therefore develops an indirect or ironic approach to her material, whereby discussion of something is always predicated upon a discussion of the limitations of discussion. She also addresses the danger of *not* discussing the limitations of form, particularly in matters of religion. In "The Truth About God," a poem sequence from *Glass, Irony and God,* Carson describes the "masses" of people who compulsively photograph, record, or question religious experience; however, since they are unconscious of the ways in which they limit their own inquiries, their gestures are "blind," or made from "one side / of a partition."

Carson's reputation soared with the publication of *Autobiography of Red: A Novel in Verse* (1998), which sold over 25,000 copies in hardcover. It is made up mainly of the narrative poem "Autobiography of Red: A Romance," which is composed in alternating short and long lines and divided into 47 chapters. Carson takes her protagonist, Geryon, from Greek mythology but sets the poem in the second half of the 20th century — Geryon begins as both a mythological red-winged monster and a sexually confused little boy. The poet transforms the slaying of Geryon by Herakles into a metaphor for sexual rejection, and Geryon, by recovering from the wound Herakles inflicts, becomes *Autobiography*'s unlikely hero.

The poem, however, is more than a homosexual revisioning of Greek myth: it explodes the genre of autobiography and asks how literary descriptions shape self-identity and history. Carson bookends the poem with an essay on and an interview with Stesichorus, the Greek poet who wrote a poem called the *Geryoneis* in the 7th century BC. Throughout the poem, it seems that Geryon can refer only to what has already been written: for example, in his diary, Geryon records the "Total Facts Known" about himself, but he writes only six lines, and most of them are taken from Stesichorus. *Autobiography of Red* thus questions the efficacy of art as a mode of self-expression and encourages readers to "undo the latches," or to question the literary descriptions that limit their self-knowledge.

In 2000, Carson published *Men in the Off Hours,* a collection of verse, essays, epitaphs, and prose poems. It takes grief, time, and death as themes, and, like *Autobiography,* it blends contemporary influences with ancient ones. In the poem "Essay on What I Think About Most," Carson suggests that poetry's metaphors engage us in "the willful creation of error," and continues her thesis that knowledge and truth can only be apprehended indirectly — that language, through "the deliberate break and complication of mistakes," can show us how "things are other than they seem."

In *The Beauty of the Husband: A Fictional Essay in Twenty-Nine Tangos* (2001), Carson uses the deterioration of a marriage to complicate John Keats's famous assertion at the end of "Ode on a Grecian Urn": "Beauty is truth, truth beauty." The poet's husband, we discover, is both beautiful and a liar, and the poet finds herself unable to say "Beauty is Truth and stop." Instead, as the twenty-ninth tango ends, we stop short — commanded to "Hold beauty," we find that the truth of the situation is, as it is in much of Carson's work, deferred and left unspoken.

Carson's most recent volume, *Decreation: Poetry, Essays, Opera* (2005), contains four essays as well as creative works that comment upon the essays' style and substance. The title, *Decreation,* is taken from the work of 20th-century mystic Simone Weil, and in Carson's words, it refers to a "dislodging of herself from a centre where she cannot stay because staying there blocks God." The book explores a mystical longing to "go towards God in love without bringing [the] self along," and as it progresses, its creative pieces — beginning with lyric poems and ending with an opera and its "Shot List" — become increasingly depersonalized. A work dealing predominantly with themes of self-annihilation, *Decreation* investigates the poet's responsibility to sublimate the self to the text.

Other works by Carson include *Economy of the Unlost: Reading Simonides of Keos with Paul Celan* (1999), and *If Not, Winter: Fragments from Sappho* (2002). She maintains an interest in the visual arts, particularly in mixed-media productions, and prior to the publication of *Decreation*, she staged a Web-based "installation opera" based on the life of French mystic Marguerite Porete. Carson was the first woman to win the T.S. Eliot Prize for Poetry (2001); she has also received the Griffin Trust Award and a Guggenheim Fellowship. She has taught classics at several universities, including McGill, in Montreal, and she currently teaches at the University of Michigan.

The Truth about God

My Religion

My religion makes no sense
and does not help me
therefore I pursue it.

When we see
how simple it would have been
we will thrash ourselves.

I had a vision
of all the people in the world
who are searching for God

10   massed in a room
on one side
of a partition

that looks
from the other side
(God's side)

transparent
but we are blind.
Our gestures are blind.

Our blind gestures continue
20   for some time until finally
from somewhere

on the other side of the partition there we are
looking back at them.
It is far too late.

We see how brokenly
how warily
how ill

our blind gestures
parodied
what God really wanted   30

(some simple thing).
The thought of it
(this simple thing)

is like a creature
let loose in a room
and battering

to get out.
It batters my soul
with its rifle butt.

The God Fit

Sometimes God will drop a fit on you.   40
Leave you on your bed howling.
Don't take it meanly.

Because the outer walls of God are glass.
I see a million souls clambering up the walls on the inside
to escape God who is burning,

untended.

The God Coup

God is a grand heart cut.
On the road where man surges along He may,
as the prophet says,
tarry.   50

By God

Sometimes by night I don't know why
I awake thinking of prepositions.
Perhaps they are clues.

"Since by Man came Death."
I am puzzled to hear that Man is the agent of Death.
Perhaps it means

Man was standing at the curb
and Death came by.
Once I had a dog

60   would go with anyone.
Perhaps listening for
little by little the first union.

Deflect

I have a friend who is red hot with pain.
He feels the lights like hard rain through his pores.
Together we went to ask Isaac.[1]

Isaac said I will tell you the story told to me.
It was from Adam
issued the lights.

From the lights of his forehead were formed all the names of the world.
70   From the lights of his ears, nose and throat
came a function no one has ever defined.

From the lights of his eyes — but wait —
Isaac waits.
In theory

the lights of the eye should have issued from Adam's navel.
But within the lights themselves occurred
an intake of breath

and they changed their path.
And they were separated.
80   And they were caught in the head.

---

1. **Isaac** Hebrew prophet, son of Abraham and Sarah. To test Abraham, God commands him to sacrifice Isaac on Mount Moriah; Moses prepares to, but is stopped at the last moment by an angel.

And from these separated lights came
that which pains you
on its errands (here my friend began to weep) through the world.

For be assured it is not only you who mourn.
Isaac lashed his tail.
Every rank of world

was caused to descend
(at least one rank)
by the terrible pressure of the light.

Nothing remained in place.   90
Nothing was not captured except
among the shards and roots and matter

some lights
from Adam's eyes
nourished there somehow.

Isaac stopped his roaring.
And my friend by now drowsy as a snake
subsided behind a heap of blueblack syllables.

God's Name

God had no name.
Isaac had two names.   100
Isaac was also called The Blind.

Inside the dark sky of his mind
Isaac could hear God
moving down a country road bordered by trees.

By the way the trees reflected off God
Isaac knew which ones were straight and tall
or when they carried their branches

as a body does its head
or why some crouched low to the ground in thickets.
To hear how God was moving through the universe   110

gave Isaac his question.
I could tell you his answer
but it wouldn't help.

The name is not a noun.
It is an adverb.
Like the little black notebooks that Beethoven carried

in his coatpocket
for the use of those who wished to converse with him,
the God adverb

120   is a one-way street that goes everywhere you are.
No use telling you what it is.
Just chew it and rub it on.

Teresa of God

    "the aching has hold of me O grievous daimon"

Teresa lived in a personal black cube.
I saw her hit the wall each way she moved.
She cursed her heart

which was, she said, rent
and her nose
which had been broken again and again.

130   Some people have to fight every moment of their lives
which God has lined with a burning animal —
I think because

God wants that animal kept alive.
With her nose Teresa questioned
this project of God's.

To her heart God sent answer.
The autopsy after her death revealed
it was indeed rent.

Photographs of the event
140   had to be faked (with red thread and an old gold glove)
when the lens kept melting.

The Grace That Comes by Violence

Yours is not (I regret to say) the story they tell
although you howl and gash yourself
scurrying out of the tombs

where you now live.
God forces some.
God's prophet came

to send your unclean spirit
into pigs, who ran amok.
I saw you   150

at the bottom of the cliff of pity
diving in pig blood —
"cleansed" now.

God's Woman

Are you angry at nature? said God to His woman.
Yes I am angry at nature I do not want nature stuck
up between my legs on your pink baton

or ladled out like geography whenever
your buckle needs a lick.
What do you mean *Creation*?

God circled her.   160
Fire. Time. Fire.
Choose, said God.

God Stiff

God gave an onomatopoeic quality to women's language.
These eternally blundering sounds eternally
blundering down

into the real words of what they are
like feet dropped into bone shoes.
"Treachery" (she notices) sounds just like His zipper going down.

God's Beloveds Remain True

Chaos overshadows us.
Unsheltered sorrow shuts upon us.   170
We are strangled by bitter light.
Our bones shake like sticks.
We snap.

We grope.
We pant and go dry.
Our tongues are black.
All day is endless.
Nights endless.
Our skin crawls, it cracks.
180   Our room is a cat who plays with us.
Our hope is a noose.
We take our flesh in our teeth.
The autumn blows us as chaff across the fields.
We are sifted and fall.
We are hung in a void.
We are shattered on the ocean.
We are smeared on the darkness.
We are slit and drained out.
Little things drink us.
190   We lie unburied.
We are dust.
We know nothing.
We can not answer.
We will speak no more.
BUT WE WILL NOT STOP.
For we are the beloveds.
We have been instructed to call this His love.

God's Bouquet Of Undying Love

April snow.
God is waiting in the garden.
200   Slow as a blush,

snow shifts and settles on God.
On God's bouquet.
The trees are white nerve nets.

God's Mother

She doesn't get to say much in the official biography —
I believe they are out of wine, etc.,
practical things —

watching with one eye as he goes about the world
calling himself The Son Of Man.
Naturalists tell us

that the hatching crow is fed by the male   210
but when it flies, by the mother.

Love	Fly	Man
Loves	Flies	Mans
Loved	Flew	Manned
Loving	Flying	Manning
Loved	Flown	Woman.

It is what grammarians call a difference of tense and aspect.

God's Justice

In the beginning there were days set aside for various tasks.
On the day He was to create justice
God got involved in making a dragonfly   220

and lost track of time.
It was about two inches long
with turquoise dots all down its back like Lauren Bacall.

God watched it bend its tiny wire elbows
as it set about cleaning the transparent case of its head.
The eye globes mounted on the case

rotated this way and that
as it polished every angle.
Inside the case

which was glassy black like the windows of a downtown bank   230
God could see the machinery humming
and He watched the hum

travel all the way down turquoise dots to the end of the tail
and breathe off as light.
Its black wings vibrated in and out.

The Wolf God

Like a painting we will be erased, no one can remain.
I saw my life as a wolf loping along the road
and I questioned the women of that place.

Some regard the wolf as immortal, they said.
Now you know this only happened in one case and that   240
wolves die regularly of various causes —

bears kill them, tigers hunt them,
they get epilepsy,
they get a salmon bone crosswise in their throat,

they run themselves to death no one knows why —
but perhaps you never heard
of their ear trouble.

They have very good ears,
can hear a cloud pass overhead.
250   And sometimes it happens

that a windblown seed will bury itself in the aural canal
displacing equilibrium.
They go mad trying to stand upright,

nothing to link with.
Die of anger.
Only one we know learned to go along with it.

He took small steps at first.
Using the updrafts.
They called him Huizkol,

260   that means
Looks Good In Spring.
Things are as hard as you make them.

God's Christ Theory

God had no emotions but wished temporarily
to move in man's mind
as if He did: Christ.

Not passion but compassion.
Com — means "with."
What kind of withness would that be?

Translate it.
270   I have a friend named Jesus
from Mexico.

His father and grandfather are called Jesus too.
They account me a fool with my questions about salvation.
They say they are saving to move to Los Angeles.

God's List of Liquids

It was a November night of wind.
Leaves tore past the window.
God had the book of life open at PLEASURE

and was holding the pages down with one hand
because of the wind from the door.
For I made their flesh as a sieve   280

wrote God at the top of the page
and then listed in order:
Alcohol
Blood
Gratitude
Memory
Semen
Song
Tears
Time.   290

God's Work

Moonlight in the kitchen is a sign of God.
The kind of sadness that is a black suction pipe extracting you
from your own navel and which the Buddhists call

"no mindcover" is a sign of God.
The blind alleys that run alongside human conversation
like lashes are a sign of God.

God's own calmness is a sign of God.
The surprisingly cold smell of potatoes or money.
Solid pieces of silence.

From these diverse signs you can see   300
how much work remains to do.
Put away your sadness, it is a mantle of work.

(1992)

Barbara Gowdy (1950–)

In her early 20s, Barbara Gowdy suddenly took up the piano, practising between five and eight
hours daily, determined to become a professional. After eight years had passed, she was still

unsatisfied with her playing, so she stopped and didn't touch the piano again for 20 years. Her innate perfectionism may have scuttled her career as a pianist, but close attention to detail has been one of her defining qualities as a writer. While she often examines uncommon, exotic, or grotesque subjects, her exhaustive research and sympathetic imagination lend her characters an air of normalcy. This recognizable humanity is found even in her most freakish figures, making Gowdy's treatment of the grotesque quite different from that of Flannery O'Connor and other modernists who use the grotesque to highlight the evils and anxieties of "normal" society. Instead, Gowdy explores the consciousness and individuality of her deformed or "perverse" subjects, many of whom she draws from real life.

Gowdy was born in 1950 in Windsor, Ontario, and although she moves frequently (as often as 23 times in 25 years), she has spent most of her life in Toronto. She attended York University's theatre program, then she moved between jobs before committing herself to professional writing. At one point, she nearly became a stockbroker, having passed the Canadian Securities Course exam, but then she decided to take a managing editor's position at the publishing house of Lester and Orpen Dennys, working there from 1974 through 1979. She also served as an interviewer on the TVOntario literary program *Imprint.* In 1982, with the publication of her short story collection *The Rabbit and the Hare,* she became convinced that she could make a career as a professional writer and left her job. Six years later, she published *Through the Green Valley,* a carefully researched historical novel about a poor Irish boy and his three sisters who endeavour to escape to America from their war-torn, famine-ridden homeland.

Her second novel, *Falling Angels,* appeared in 1989. With it, Gowdy inaugurated her signature style and attracted a wave of critical attention. Holed up in their eccentric father's bomb shelter, pubescent sisters Sandy, Lou, and Norma explore their developing personas and bodies, sip from their mother's mug of whiskey, and uncover the story of a murdered younger brother. The novel introduces the enduring Gowdy themes of unconventional family relationships, female self-modification, and atypical sexuality. Margaret Atwood chose the chapter entitled "Disneyland" for inclusion in the 1989 edition of *Best American Short Stories,* and the novel was made into a film in 2003.

In 1992, Gowdy produced her second short story collection, *We So Seldom Look on Love,* which takes its name from Frank O'Hara's poem "Ode on Necrophilia" and focuses on the grotesque body, abnormal sexuality, and the relationships between adults and children. In the title story, which spawned the film *Kissed,* an attractive young woman who works in a morgue discusses her sexual preference for cadavers. The morbidity of the situation is normalized by the casual first-person narration and the surprising reasonableness of the protagonist, who resists any traditional psychoanalytic interpretation — she simply enjoys the dead. She is at home in this story collection, which also features sexual exhibitionists, a two-headed man, and an autistic girl who drills a hole in her forehead. Gowdy is careful to respect the perspectives of these characters rather than exploiting their oddness. Most were drawn from true stories; the main character of "Sylvie," who has two sets of legs and hips, is modelled on a woman named Myrtle Corbin who joined a circus, married a doctor, and had at least one child through each of her two vaginas.

In Gowdy's 1995 novel *Mister Sandman,* Joan, mute as a result of being dropped on her head as an infant, becomes the sounding board for family members engaged in various sexual pursuits. Both of Joan's parents are having same-sex affairs; one of her sisters is promiscuous and the other repressed. Joan finally airs her family members' dirty laundry by taping their confessions and creating, as Gowdy does with the novel, a collage of their speeches. By doing so, she frees them to accept each other. The novel was named book of the year by Atwood in the *Times Literary Supplement,* and it was nominated for the Trillium and Governor General's Awards.

During the three-year gap between the publication of *Mister Sandman* and her next novel, *The White Bone,* Gowdy undertook her most thorough research project to date. After seeing a documentary about African elephants in which a herd performed an elaborate mourning and burial ritual for a deceased member, Gowdy started reading everything she could find about the mammals. For *The White Bone,* she constructed not only an elaborate social system, complete with its own mythology, beliefs, and rituals, but also a complex form of subjectivity for the creatures based on their real practices. She has explained that in fashioning the narrative she simply took "observed behaviour and credited it with a high level of intention." Although critics are divided over whether the novel should be read allegorically, Gowdy insists that it is not an animal fable, and neither is it a satire of human behaviour. The elephant families, in a quest for survival, re-evaluate their way of reading their environment, rejecting spiritual direction from the godlike "the She" and discovering the sacredness of their own community.

With her next novel, *The Romantic* (2003), Gowdy radically changed her focus. The work belongs to a loosely defined genre of fiction that one reviewer describes as documenting "the ongoing collision, like that between geological plates, of comedy and tragedy in personal life, with female consciousness as the ever-erupting fault line." Partially based on the tragic 12th-century tale of Abelard and Héloïse, it recounts the love affair between childhood neighbours Louise and Abel. Louise is "furious with love" for the elusive Abel, who grows up to be a dreamy naturalist and alcoholic jazz musician with self-destructive tendencies. Her love never wanes, becoming a lifelong obsession, and she is doomed to a recurring cycle of reunion, betrayal, and loss.

In 2007, Gowdy produced the novel *Helpless,* a study in fear, maternal love, and twisted, obsessive love. Nine-year-old Rachel is kidnapped by Ron, a pedophile who has deluded himself into thinking that the child's single mother, Celia, who is struggling to raise her daughter while holding down two jobs, is unfit. Ron loves Rachel, and so he sequesters her in a basement and struggles to remain her chaste saviour. Gowdy, with characteristic compassion, manages to dramatize the humanity residing in a man afflicted with a monstrous psychological illness.

Gowdy, whose partner is poet Christopher Dewdney, lives in Toronto.

We So Seldom Look on Love

When you die, and your earthly self begins turning into your disintegrated self, you radiate an intense current of energy. There is always energy given off when a thing turns into its opposite, when love, for instance, turns into hate. There are always sparks at those extreme points. But life turning into death is the most extreme of extreme points. So just after you die, the sparks are really stupendous. Really magical and explosive.

I've seen cadavers shining like stars. I'm the only person I've ever heard of who has. Almost everyone senses something, though, some vitality. That's why you get resistance to the idea of cremation or organ donation. "I want to be in one piece," people say. Even Matt, who claimed there was no soul and no afterlife, wrote a P.S. in his suicide note that he be buried intact.

As if it would have made any difference to his energy emission. No matter what you do — slice open the flesh, dissect everything, burn everything — you're in the path of a power way beyond your little interferences.

I grew up in a nice, normal, happy family outside a small town in New Jersey. My parents and my brother are still living there. My dad owned a flower store. Now my brother owns it. My brother is three years older than I am, a serious, remote man. But loyal. When I made the headlines he phoned to say that if I needed money for a lawyer, he would give it to me. I was really touched. Especially as he was standing up to Carol, his wife. She got on the extension and screamed, "You're sick! You should be put away!"

She'd been wanting to tell me that since we were thirteen years old.

I had an animal cemetery back then. Our house was beside a woods and we had three outdoor cats, great hunters who tended to leave their kills in one piece. Whenever I found a body, usually a mouse or a bird, I took it into my bedroom and hid it until midnight. I didn't know anything about the ritual significance of the midnight hour. My burials took place then because that's when I woke up. It no longer happens, but I was such a sensitive child that I think I must have been aroused by the energy given off as day clicked over into the dead of night and, simultaneously, as the dead of night clicked over into the next day.

In any case, I'd be wide awake. I'd get up and go to the bathroom to wrap the body in toilet paper. I felt compelled to be so careful, so respectful. I whispered a chant. At each step of the burial I chanted. "I shroud the body, shroud the body, shroud little sparrow with broken wing." Or "I lower the body, lower the body . . . " And so on.

Climbing out the bathroom window was accompanied by: "I enter the night, enter the night . . . " At my cemetery I set the body down on a special flat rock and took my pyjamas off. I was behaving out of pure inclination. I dug up four or five graves and unwrapped the animals from their shrouds. The rotting smell was crucial. So was the cool air. Normally I'd be so keyed up at this point that I'd burst into a dance.

I used to dance for dead men, too. Before I climbed on top of them, I'd dance all around the prep room. When I told Matt about this he said that I was shaking my personality out of my body so that the sensation of participating in the cadaver's energy eruption would be intensified. "You're trying to imitate the disintegration process," he said.

Maybe — on an unconscious level. But what I was aware of was the heat, the heat of my danced-out body, which I cooled by lying on top of the cadaver. As a child I'd gently wipe my skin with two of the animals I'd just unwrapped. When I was covered all over with their scent, I put them aside, unwrapped the new corpse and did the same with it. I called this the Anointment. I can't describe how it felt. The high, high rapture. The electricity that shot through me.

The rest, wrapping the bodies back up and burying them, was pretty much what you'd expect.

It astonishes me now to think how naive I was. I thought I had discovered something that certain other people, if they weren't afraid to give it a try, would find just as fantastic as I did. It was a dark and forbidden thing, yes, but so was sex. I really had no idea that I was jumping across a vast behavioural gulf. In fact, I couldn't see that I was doing anything wrong. I still can't, and I'm including what happened with Matt. Carol said I should have been put away, but I'm not bad-looking, so if offering my body to dead men is a crime, I'd like to know who the victim is.

Carol has always been jealous of me. She's fat and has a wandering eye. Her eye gives her a dreamy, distracted quality that I fell for (as I suppose my brother would eventually do) one day at a friend's thirteenth birthday party. It was the beginning of the summer holidays, and I was yearning for a kindred spirit, someone to share my secret life with. I saw Carol standing alone, looking everywhere at once, and I chose her.

I knew to take it easy, though. I knew not to push anything. We'd search for dead animals and birds, we'd chant and swaddle the bodies, dig graves, make popsicle-stick crosses. All by daylight. At midnight I'd go out and dig up the grave and conduct a proper burial.

There must have been some chipmunk sickness that summer. Carol and I found an incredible number of chipmunks, and a lot of them had no blood on them, no sign of cat. One day we found a chipmunk that evacuated a string of foetuses when I picked it up. The foetuses were still alive, but there was no saving them, so I took them into the house and flushed them down the toilet.

A mighty force was coming from the mother chipmunk. It was as if, along with her own energy, she was discharging all the energy of her dead brood. When Carol and I began to dance for her, we both went a little crazy. We stripped down to our underwear, screamed, spun in circles, threw dirt up into the air. Carol has always denied it, but she took off her bra and began whipping trees with it. I'm sure the sight of her doing this is what inspired me to take off my undershirt and underpants and to perform the Anointment.

Carol stopped dancing. I looked at her, and the expression on her face stopped me dancing, too. I looked down at the chipmunk in my hand. It was bloody. There were streaks of blood all over my body. I was horrified. I thought I'd squeezed the chipmunk too hard.

But what had happened was, I'd begun my period. I figured this out a few minutes after Carol ran off. I wrapped the chipmunk in its shroud and buried it. Then I got dressed and lay down on the grass. A little while later my mother appeared over me.

"Carol's mother phoned," she said. "Carol is very upset. She says you made her perform some disgusting witchcraft dance. You made her take her clothes off, and you attacked her with a bloody chipmunk."

"That's a lie," I said. "I'm menstruating."

After my mother had fixed me up with a sanitary napkin, she told me she didn't think I should play with Carol any more. "There's a screw loose in there somewhere," she said.

I had no intention of playing with Carol any more, but I cried at what seemed like a cruel loss. I think I knew that it was all loneliness from that moment on. Even though I was only thirteen, I was cutting any lines that still drifted out toward normal eroticism. Bosom friends, crushes, pyjama-party intimacy, I was cutting all those lines off.

A month or so after becoming a woman I developed a craving to perform autopsies. I resisted doing it for almost a year, though. I was frightened. Violating the intactness of the animal seemed sacrilegious and dangerous. Also unimaginable — I couldn't imagine what would happen.

Nothing. Nothing would happen, as I found out. I've read that necrophiles are frightened of getting hurt by normal sexual relationships, and maybe there's some truth in that (although my heart's been broken plenty of times by cadavers, and not once by a live man), but I think that my attraction to cadavers isn't driven by fear, it's driven by excitement, and that one of the most exciting things about a cadaver is how dedicated it is to dying. Its will is all directed to a single intention, like a huge wave heading for shore, and you can ride along on the wave if you want to, because no matter what you do, because with you or without you, that wave is going to hit the beach.

I felt this impetus the first time I worked up enough nerve to cut open a mouse. Like anyone else, I balked a little at slicing into the flesh, and I was repelled for a few seconds when I saw the insides. But something drove me to go through these compunctions. It was as if I were acting solely on instinct and curiosity, and anything I did was all right, provided it didn't kill me.

After the first few times, I started sticking my tongue into the incision. I don't know why. I thought about it, I did it, and I kept on doing it. One day I removed the organs and cleaned them with water, then put them back in, and I kept on doing that, too. Again, I couldn't tell you why except to say that any provocative thought, if you act upon it, seems to set you on a trajectory.

By the time I was sixteen I wanted human corpses. Men. (That way I'm straight.) I got my chauffeur's licence, but I had to wait until I was finished high school before Mr. Wallis would hire me as a hearse driver at the funeral home.

Mr. Wallis knew me because he bought bereavement flowers at my father's store. Now *there* was a weird man. He would take a trocar, which is the big needle you use to draw out a cadaver's fluids, and he would push it up the penises of dead men to make them look semi-erect, and then he'd sodomize them. I caught him at it once, and he tried to tell me that he'd been urinating in the hopper. I pretended to believe him. I was upset though, because I knew that dead men were just dead flesh to him. One minute he'd be locked up with a young male corpse, having his way with him, and the next minute he'd be embalming him as if nothing had happened, and making sick jokes about him, pretending to find evidence of rampant homosexuality — colons stalagmited with dried semen, and so on.

None of this joking ever happened in front of me. I heard about it from the crazy old man who did the mopping up. He was also a necrophile, I'm almost certain, but no longer active. He called dead women Madonnas. He rhapsodized about the beautiful Madonnas he'd had the privilege of seeing in the 1940s, about how much more womanly and feminine the Madonnas were twenty years before.

I just listened. I never let on what I was feeling, and I don't think anyone suspected. Necrophiles aren't supposed to be blond and pretty, let alone female. When I'd been working at the funeral home for about a year, a committee from the town council tried to get me to enter the Milk Marketer's Beauty Pageant. They knew about my job, and they knew I was studying embalming at night, but I had told people I was preparing myself for medical school, and I guess the council believed me.

For fifteen years, ever since Matt died, people have been asking me how a woman makes love to a corpse.

Matt was the only person who figured it out. He was a medical student, so he knew that if you apply pressure to the chest of certain fresh corpses, they purge blood out of their mouths.

Matt was smart. I wish I could have loved him with more than sisterly love. He was tall and thin. My type. We met at the doughnut shop across from the medical library, got to talking, and liked each other immediately, an unusual experience for both of us. After about an hour I knew that he loved me and that his love was unconditional. When I told him where I worked and what I was studying, he asked why.

"Because I'm a necrophile," I said.

He lifted his head and stared at me. He had eyes like high-resolution monitors. Almost too vivid. Normally I don't like looking people in the eye, but I found myself staring back. I could see that he believed me.

"I've never told anyone else," I said.

"With men or women?" he asked.

"Men. Young men."

"How?"

"Cunnilingus."

"Fresh corpses?"

"If I can get them."

"What do you do, climb on top of them?"

"Yes."

"You're turned on by blood."

"It's a lubricant," I said. "It's colourful. Stimulating. It's the ultimate bodily fluid."

"Yes," he said, nodding. "When you think about it. Sperm propagates life. But blood sustains it. Blood is primary."

He kept asking questions, and I answered them as truthfully as I could. Having confessed what I was, I felt myself driven to testing his intellectual rigour and the strength of his love at first sight. Throwing rocks at him without any expectation that he'd stay standing. He did, though. He caught the whole arsenal and asked for more. It began to excite me.

We went back to his place. He had a basement apartment in an old rundown building. There were books in orange-crate shelves, in piles on the floor, all over the bed. On the wall above his desk was a poster of Doris Day in the movie *Tea for Two*. Matt said she looked like me.

"Do you want to dance first?" he asked, heading for his record player. I'd told him about how I danced before climbing on corpses.

"No."

He swept the books off the bed. Then he undressed me. He had an erection until I told him I was a virgin. "Don't worry," he said, sliding his head down my stomach. "Lie still."

The next morning he phoned me at work. I was hungover and blue from the night before. After leaving his place I'd gone straight to the funeral home and made love to an autopsy case. Then I'd got drunk in a seedy country-and-western bar and debated going back to the funeral home and suctioning out my own blood until I lost consciousness.

It had finally hit me that I was incapable of falling in love with a man who wasn't dead. I kept thinking, "I'm not normal." I'd never faced this before. Obviously, making love to corpses isn't normal, but while I was still a virgin I must have been assuming that I could give it up any time I liked. Get married, have babies. I must have been banking on a future that I didn't even want let alone have access to.

Matt was phoning to get me to come around again after work.

"I don't know," I said.

"You had a good time. Didn't you?"

"Sure, I guess."

"I think you're fascinating," he said.

I sighed.

"Please," he said. "Please."

A few nights later I went to his apartment. From then on we started to meet every Tuesday and Thursday evening after my embalming class, and as soon as I left his place, if I knew there was a corpse at the mortuary — any male corpse, young or old — I went straight there and climbed in a basement window.

Entering the prep room, especially at night when there was nobody else around, was like diving into a lake. Sudden cold and silence, and the sensation of penetrating a new element where the rules of other elements don't apply. Being with Matt was like lying on the beach of the lake. Matt had warm, dry skin. His apartment was overheated and noisy. I lay on Matt's bed and soaked him up, but only to make the moment when I entered the prep room even more overpowering.

If the cadaver was freshly embalmed, I could usually smell him from the basement. The smell is like a hospital and old cheese. For me, it's the smell of danger and permission, it used to key me up like amphetamine, so that by the time I reached the prep room, tremors were running up and down my legs. I locked the door behind me and broke into a wild dance, tearing my clothes off, spinning around, pulling at my hair. I'm not sure what this was all about, whether or not I was trying to take part in the chaos of the corpse's disintegration, as Matt suggested. Maybe I was prostrating myself, I don't know.

Once the dancing was over I was always very calm, almost entranced. I drew back the sheet. This was the most exquisite moment. I felt as if I were being blasted by white light. Almost blinded, I climbed onto the table and straddled the corpse. I ran my hands over his skin. My hands and the insides of my thighs burned as if I were touching dry ice. After a few minutes I lay down and pulled the sheet up over my head. I began to kiss his mouth. By now he might be drooling blood. A corpse's blood is thick, cool and sweet. My head roared.

I was no longer depressed. Far from it, I felt better, more confident, than I had ever felt in my life. I had discovered myself to be irredeemably abnormal. I could either slit my throat or surrender — wholeheartedly now — to my obsession. I surrendered. And what happened was that obsession began to storm through me, as if I were a tunnel. I became the medium of obsession as well as both ends of it. With Matt, when we made love, I was the receiving end, I was the cadaver. When I left him and went to the funeral home, I was the lover. Through me Matt's love poured into the cadavers at the funeral home, and through me the cadavers filled Matt with explosive energy.

He quickly got addicted to this energy. The minute I arrived at his apartment, he had to hear every detail about the last corpse I'd been with. For a month or so I had him pegged as a latent homosexual necrophile voyeur, but then I began to see that it wasn't the corpses themselves that excited him, it was my passion for them. It was the power that went into that passion and that came back, doubled, for his pleasure. He kept asking, "How did you feel? Why do you think you felt that way?" And then, because the source of all this power disturbed him, he'd try to prove that my feelings were delusory.

"A corpse shows simultaneous extremes of character," I told him. "Wisdom and innocence, happiness and grief, and so on."

"Therefore all corpses are alike," he said. "Once you've had one you've had them all."

"No, no. They're all different. Each corpse contains his own extremes. Each corpse is only as wise and as innocent as the living person could have been."

He said, "You're drafting personalities onto corpses in order to have power over them."

"In that case," I said, "I'm pretty imaginative, since I've never met two corpses who were alike."

"You *could* be that imaginative," he argued. "Schizophrenics are capable of manufacturing dozens of complex personalities."

I didn't mind these attacks. There was no malice in them, and there was no way they could touch me, either. It was as if I were luxuriously pouring my heart out to a very clever, very concerned, very tormented analyst. I felt sorry for him. I understood his twisted desire to turn me into somebody else (somebody who might love him). I used to fall madly in love with cadavers and then cry because they were dead. The difference between Matt and me was that I had become philosophical. I was all right.

I thought that he was, too. He was in pain, yes, but he seemed confident that what he was going through was temporary and not unnatural. "I am excessively curious," he said. "My fascination is any curious man's fascination with the unusual." He said that by feeding his lust through mine, he would eventually saturate it, then turn it to disgust.

I told him to go ahead, give it a try. So he began to scour the newspapers for my cadavers' obituaries and to go to their funerals and memorial services. He made charts of my preferences and the frequency of my morgue encounters. He followed me to the morgue at night and waited outside so that he could get a replay while I was still in an erotic haze. He sniffed my skin. He pulled me over to streetlights and examined the blood on my face and hands.

I suppose I shouldn't have encouraged him. I can't really say why I did, except that in the beginning I saw his obsession as the outer edge of my own obsession, a place I didn't have to visit as long as he was there. And then later, and despite his increasingly erratic behaviour, I started to have doubts about an obsession that could come on so suddenly and that could come through me.

One night he announced that he might as well face it, he was going to have to make love to corpses, male corpses. The idea nauseated him, he said, but he said that secretly, deep down, unknown even to himself, making love to male corpses was clearly the target of his desire. I blew up. I told him that necrophilia wasn't something you forced yourself to do. You longed to do it, you needed to do it. You were born to do it.

He wasn't listening. He was glued to the dresser mirror. In the last weeks of his life he stared at himself in the mirror without the least self-consciousness. He focused on his face, even though what was going on from the neck down was the arresting part. He had begun to wear incredibly weird outfits. Velvet capes, pantaloons, high-heeled red boots. When we made love, he kept these outfits on. He started into my eyes, riveted (it later occurred to me) by his own reflection.

Matt committed suicide, there was never any doubt about that. As for the necrophilia, it wasn't a crime, not fifteen years ago. So even though I was caught in the act, naked and straddling an unmistakably dead body, even though the newspapers found out about it and made it front-page news, there was nothing the police could charge me with.

In spite of which I made a full confession. It was crucial to me that the official report contain more than the detective's bleak observations. I wanted two things on record: one, that Matt was ravished by a reverential expert; two, that his cadaver blasted the energy of a star.

"Did this energy blast happen before or after he died?" the detective asked.

"After," I said, adding quickly that I couldn't have foreseen such a blast. The one tricky area was why I hadn't stopped the suicide. Why I hadn't talked, or cut, Matt down.

I lied. I said that as soon as I entered Matt's room, he kicked away the ladder. Nobody could prove otherwise. But I've often wondered how much time actually passed between when I opened the door and when his neck broke. In crises, a minute isn't a minute. There's the same chaos you get at the instant of death, with time and form breaking free, and everything magnifying and coming apart.

Matt must have been in a state of crisis for days, maybe weeks before he died. All that staring in mirrors, thinking, "Is this my face?" Watching as his face separated into its infinitesimal particles and reassembled into a strange new face. The night before he died, he had a mask on. A Dracula mask, but he wasn't joking. He wanted to wear the mask while I made love to him as if he were a cadaver. No way, I said. The whole point,

I reminded him, was that *I* played the cadaver. He begged me, and I laughed because of the mask and with relief. If he wanted to turn the game around, then it was over between us, and I was suddenly aware of how much I liked that idea.

The next night he phoned me at my parents' and said, "I love you," then hung up.

I don't know how I knew, but I did. A gun, I thought. Men always use guns. And then I thought, no, poison, cyanide. He was a medical student and had access to drugs. When I arrived at his apartment the door was open. Across from the door, taped to the wall, was a note: "DEAD PERSON IN BEDROOM."

But he wasn't dead. He was standing on a stepladder. He was naked. An impressively knotted noose, attached to a pipe that ran across the ceiling, was looped around his neck.

He smiled tenderly. "I knew you'd come," he said.

"So why the note?" I demanded.

"Pull away the ladder," he crooned. "My beloved."

"Come on. This is stupid. Get down." I went up to him and punched his leg.

"All you have to do," he said, "is pull away the ladder."

His eyes were even darker and more expressive than usual. His cheekbones appeared to be highlighted. (I discovered minutes later he had make-up on.) I glanced around the room for a chair or table that I could bring over and stand on. I was going to take the noose off him myself.

"If you leave," he said, "if you take a step back, if you do anything other than pull away the ladder, I'll kick it away."

"I love you," I said, "Okay?"

"No, you don't," he said.

"I do!" To sound like I meant it I stared at his legs and imagined them lifeless. "I do!"

"No, you don't," he said softly. "But," he said, "you will."

I was gripping the ladder. I remember thinking that if I held tight to the ladder, he wouldn't be able to kick it away. I was gripping the ladder, and then it was by the wall, tipped over. I have no memory of transition between these two events. There was a loud crack, and gushing water. Matt dropped gracefully, like a girl fainting. Water poured on him from the broken pipe. There was the smell of excrement. I dragged him by the noose.

In the living room I pulled him onto the green shag carpet. I took my clothes off. I knelt over him. I kissed the blood at the corner of his mouth.

True obsession depends on the object's absolute unresponsiveness. When I used to fall for a particular cadaver, I would feel as if I were a hollow instrument, a bell or a flute. I'd empty out. I would clear out (it was involuntary) until I was an instrument for the cadaver to swell into and be amplified. As the object of Matt's obsession how could I be other than impassive, while he was alive?

He was playing with fire, playing with me. Not just because I couldn't love him, but because I was irradiated. The whole time that I was involved with Matt, I was making love to corpses, absorbing their energy, blazing it back out. Since that energy came from the act of life alchemizing into death, there's a possibility that it was alchemical itself. Even if it wasn't, I'm sure it gave Matt the impression that I had the power to change him in some huge and dangerous way.

I now believe that his addiction to my energy was really a craving for such a transformation. In fact, I think that all desire is desire for transformation, and that all transformation — all movement, all process — happens because life turns into death.

I am still a necrophile, occasionally, and recklessly. I have found no replacement for the torrid serenity of a cadaver.

(1996)

Tim Lilburn (1950–)

In 1991, having moved back to Saskatchewan after 15 years away, Tim Lilburn dug for three weeks into the side of a hill and built a root cellar. He called it a "listening post," and he slept in that confined space on hot summer nights. Emerging from this time of solitary contemplation, he took a new approach to poetry. His poems had always been philosophical, even scholarly, but he now became interested in writing about the prairie and eros — not in its conventional sense, but as something "intellectual, religious, aesthetic — any type of deep yearning, deep longing — this sort of reaching of the heart, or even reach of the mind."

Lilburn was born in Regina, Saskatchewan, in 1950. He grew up in the United Church, but when he was in his early 20s, he converted to Catholicism. Literature, he maintains, played no role in his childhood: "Poetry is not the sort of vocation that would occur to a male growing up in working-class Regina in the late fifties and sixties, where hockey, fighting, general thuggery and eventually finding a decent job made up the usual range of possibilities." But he was eventually drawn to the way poetry could "say something you knew was true but had never said," the way language could indirectly express a mystical truth.

From 1975 to 1976, Lilburn taught in Nigeria through CUSO (Canadian University Service Overseas). He became a Jesuit in 1978, completing his novitiate in Guelph, Ontario, and then studying for his M.A. in philosophy at Gonzaga University in Spokane, Washington. Later, he would also earn a Ph.D. at McMaster University in Hamilton, Ontario.

Lilburn published the poetry collection *Names of God* in 1986. Despite being devotional, honorific, and replete with references to Catholic history, these poems occasionally slip into an irreverent tone — in "Hosanna to Wisdom, the Divine Anima," for instance, the poet orders his "Woman-spirit" to "skedaddle my blood like a first date." His adherence to the principles of Karl Marx, whom Lilburn studied in the course of earning his M.A., is revealed in the poem "The Wealth of Nations": a factory worker's "hand, asleep on a wrist, feeds itself to iron. / And there is no shutdown." Although the poet's distress over the conflicts and inequities of modern life lies at the thematic heart of this collection, he also expresses his conviction that if we listen to the "common language" of nature, we'll hear "the center holding" — a conviction that would burgeon into a powerful attraction to the natural world as opposed to the human community. A year after *Names of God* appeared, Lilburn left the Jesuit order and entered a very active period of his life.

He published *From the Great Above She Opened Her Ear to the Great Below* (1988), a collaboration with photographer Susan Shantz that contains poems written as a series of linked narratives, some of which are told by Sumerian goddess Inanna or her killer, Erishkegal. With 1989's *Tourist to Ecstasy* (for which he received a Governor General's Award nomination), Lilburn continued to investigate his complex relationship with the broad Christian tradition. In so doing, he gave full rein to his developing poetic language, displaying stylistic innovations that critic Carmine Starnino identifies as, for example: "Improvised sonic effects ('clank-tappa-clang'), neologistic embellishments ('wind-boisterous Dakota'), and roundabout conclusions ('spirit-rappings of your own garrulous deaths')."

Moving back to Saskatchewan in 1991, Lilburn says, he realized that even after years of scholarship, "I had done nothing to educate myself to be someone who could live with facility, familiarity, where he was born. This incompetence, when I finally saw it, floored me." It also triggered a powerful desire — which has never left him — to find a means of connecting with the land through poetry, a poetry engendered by silent observation. *Moosewood Sandhills,* published in 1994, was the result. In this account of a period Lilburn spent in the wilderness, language is again mediated through Christian tradition, elevating the speaker to a new plane of physical awareness and a new way of seeing. Lilburn explains that the language people have conventionally used to impart "the soul's approach to God" can also serve to "plot the return of consciousness to the world, unnameable in its athletic variety." In the collection's final piece, "Restoration," the poet declares: "I want to be the knowledge that is one sleep in the sunward shoulder muscle / of the two-year-old doe coming out of hills and down to Moon Lake. / I will get there by seeing." Deer, a recurring image in Lilburn's work, here seem to embody a skittish divinity, but these creatures never allow the poet to come close enough to capture whatever mystical truth they harbour. A poetics of seeing will be his only means of achieving union with the land.

   Moosewood Sandhills won the 1995 Canadian Authors Association Award for Poetry in 1995. In 1999, Lilburn published *To the River,* a series of richly metaphorical poem-meditations undertaken on the banks of the South Saskatchewan River, and *Living in the World as If It Were Home,* a collection of essays composed over a period of nine years that explore the human desire to become one with the natural world. Lilburn's edited collection *Thinking and Singing: Poetry and the Practice of Philosophy* appeared in 2002, picking up where his 1995 editorial effort, *Poetry and Knowing,* left off. Then, in 2003, Lilburn published *Kill-Site,* and it won him a Governor General's Award. Lilburn has called the book "a long poem about prayer; a long poem about yet another failed expedition to track the hidden natures of things," and in it he unleashes his philosopher's mind and poet's eye on the harsh rural Saskatchewan landscape, observing animals, depicting natural phenomena like giant ice sheets, evoking a subterranean world where the dead fly underground.

   In 2004, Lilburn left his teaching position at St. Peter's College in Muenster, Saskatchewan, to teach in the department of creative writing at the University of Victoria. His essay collection *Going Home* is due out in 2007.

Blessed Jan Ruysbroek,[1]
Gardening at Groenendael

1
In the green valley, the prior is light's woman.
He keeps a cat. Shrewd,
unwed morning glories, every third bean plant in his pythagorian[2] garden,
watch, crisp-eyed, everything he does,
determined to love and understand him.
The prior is painstakingly trying to imitate, *vita Christiformus,*[3]
the light in the silver, green poplars, above him
and to his right, thinking:
what would the light do if the light
10   thought and consciously were trying to be a man
working quietly, moments before lunch, in his small garden?

---

1. **Jan Ruysbroek** Flemish mystic and teacher (1293–1381) who acquired a following at his hermitage at Groenendael.
2. **pythagorian** Of the geometrician Pythagoras, who theorized particularly about triangles. 3. *vita Christiformus* Life in the way of Christ.

Blessed Jan Ruysbroek, Gardening at Groenendael **897**

He almost has it. The sensation teeters
at the zenith[4] of his forehead.
Cattle, in the next pinfold, stagger in bald grazing,
cringing before loud men. The loud men are false men,
foxes, devoutly shunned.

2

Perhaps the poplar knows this. Or the cat.
But the espoused prior does not yet know the light
which he sees as the congealment of specific unlikenesses
          (vegetable, breathing)   20
and holds in part in a weed's milky pod
in the fractured, shaking ray of his gleam brittle hand,
is, in fact, an entire continent undiscovered in 1343,
whose shores are the torn, white, naked minds of men
like himself.
The light, monolith, is a Mesopotamia[5] of celestial decorum,
governed by the codified, natural courtesy of angels,
under the reign of an *idiota*,[6] the holy child,
where trees, morning glories, and the smiling cat are citizens, burghers[7] of love.

He is tilling the garden, food for the journey,   30
in holy confusion,
doing what he does not know.

3

Everything, Ruysbroek, is a mirror and your hunger
the most profound image.
Desire's pulsing, jewelled eye. Apex,[8] opal
flash of soul's triangularity.
Your neighbours, the next field over, have downed a heifer
krunk   an axe between her blue eyes. Other men
devour the world raw from the world's bones.
You, however, are eating yourself into yourself,   40
groin, nose, ears, fingertips, eyes, tongue, gone, all,
into that simple, true, hungry trajectory heavenward, light,
unlocal, mating with everything.
You haven't moved an inch among the beans.
The morning glories have grown closer. A wind
would blow them through your pale flesh like ghosts through a wall.

John of Leeuwen,[9] the good cook,
comes to the priory door and shouts: Eat;

---

4. **zenith** Pinnacle. 5. **Mesopotamia** Ancient kingdom encompassing modern Syria, Turkey, and Iraq (roughly from the 4th century BC through the 4th century AD). 6. *idiota* The assumed name of a 14th-century anonymous theologian of the Catholic faith. 7. **burghers** Citizens. 8. **Apex** Pinnacle. 9. **John of Leeuwen** A follower of Ruysbroek.

NEL   Open Country: Canadian Literature in English

it's Friday and the food is black.
50 And you have vanished, *Wesenmystik*[10]
    through that skinny door.

(1986)

Part of the Inheritance

For Susan Shantz (shrine-builder)

The hoards of sleep surround us.
Cast up, great mounds of it, termiteria,[1]
chewed and hardened.
These are the very palaces we live in,
handed down through the family,
set on clipped parkland rolling away from the eye.
Parts of it are very old.
One passageway is weddingcaked
with heavy, round figures of an out-of-date joy.
10 It was begun with great ambition over a hundred years ago
                                in Northern Ireland.
Men in tight red hunt clothes
from the *Illustrated London News*.
It wanders off uncompletable into the dark.

In one of the rooms a collection of gadgets
for perpetual motion.
Sleep has projects that go on
even after the sleeper has died.
Go to the balcony and enjoy the lilacs'
20 mimesis[2] of everything alive the day your parents got married
                                over fifty years ago.
Now come back quickly from the window.
If you are seen in sleep by what is
outside in the night, it is not good.

When we drift off we go to become characters
in the long, untranslatable ancient sutras[3] of the night.
To live here means one or two responsibilities
unspoken but known.
Keep them.   Sleep is
30 the elder son who died
so you could have the inheritance.

(1989)

---

10. Wesenmystik One side of a theological split in Flemish mysticism: *Wesenmystik* refers to "mysticism of the essence," while *Braumystik*, or "nuptial mysticism," is a love-based school.

1. termiteria Mound left by termites. **2. mimesis** The imitation of reality in art. **3. sutras** Sacred scriptures of Hinduism or Buddhism.

Contemplation Is Mourning

You lie down in the deer's bed.
It is bright with the undersides of grass revealed by her weight during the
length of her sleep. No one comes here; grass hums
because the body's touched it. Aspen leaves below you sour like horses
after the run. There are snowberries, fescue.[1]
This is the edge of the known world and the beginning of philosophy.

Looking takes you so far on a leash of delight, then removes it and says
the price of admission to further is your name. Either the desert
                                     and winter
of what the deer is in herself or a palace life disturbed by itches and sounds   10
felt through the gigantic walls. Choose.

Light comes through pale trees as mind sometimes kisses the body.
The hills are the bones of hills.

The deer cannot be known. She is the Atlantic, she is Egypt, she is
the night where her names go missing, to walk into her oddness is
                        to feel severed, sick, darkened, ashamed.

Her body is a border crossing, a wall and a perfume and past this
she is infinite. And it is terrible to enter this.

You lie down in the deer's bed, in the green martyrion, the place where
language buries itself, waiting place, weem.   20
You will wait. You will lean into the darkness of her absent
body. You will be shaved and narrowed by the barren strangeness of the
deer, the wastes of her oddness. Snow is coming. Light is cool,
nearly drinkable; from grass protrudes the hard, lost
smell of last year's melted snow.

                                                       (1994)

Learning a Deeper Courtesy of the Eye

I

This is what you want.
You go into porcupine hills on a cold afternoon, down an aspen-ruffed
   path on Sam's land behind one low grass-knotted dune, then into real bush.
You will see deer.

Eros has nowhere to go but to become sorrow.
Piss marks on snow, flattenings,
creases where animals rolled, hoof-drag through drifts.

---

1. **fescue** Rough, long grass.

Exhaustion now as you walk toward the world's bright things.
Grass over snow, rose-hips clear and large in winter-killed thicket.
10 You will never make it all the way up to them.

II

The back fields are beautiful.
Take off your glove, coast
               fingers through oatgrass tips.
Four deer fountain from the poplar circle where
last fall the dog and you lay in old fox beds, breathing.

It hurts to look at deer,
deer under their name.
The light from their bodies makes you ashamed
and you look down.

(1994)

Restoration

I want to be the knowledge that is one sleep in the sunward shoulder muscle
of the two-year-old doe coming out of hills and down to Moon Lake.
I will get there by seeing.
The whole body and virtue will rise up and form the look.
Seeing is the extreme courtesy that comes when desire is broken.
Desire will be broken and will continue with a bright limp.
We will move toward high bush cranberry and the smell of water.
I will be attentive, an oblique[1] crescent near her spine, touched
by the light of her liquids. We will be going to Moon Lake,
10   the diamond willows,
old oxbow lake, reeds round it, the true river a ruin of water
in dust further on, the red century ending.
I will see my way into that place and into that body.
This will come only after I've been sitting in the long grass
eating loaves of shadow pressed up through the ground.
I will have been dreaming there of one day opening milky eyes and finding
myself sick, inside her body, high up, near the spine, poor, relieved.
Sometimes it happens: you lose everything
and wake in the strange room of what you want.
20 Except I won't be awake but asleep and full of gnosis.[2]
In my ears, gold pulse of her footsteps.
We will go down the hill and enter the shadows of frost-burnt roses
and the shade of the smell of water in which reeds and elms are rotting,
October sunlight the shore of a country a small boat is just now pulling
                                      away from.
I will smell her, light of one locked room in the mansion.

---

1. **oblique** Slanted. 2. **gnosis** Esoteric knowledge of the spiritual.

I will be in the muscle, a painting on the cave wall of her flesh.
I crane into the deer.
I am in the bright-dark cloud of knowing her
              and could walk for days.   30
She is at the top of the hill and starting down
              in early evening.

                                     (1994)

Its Seeing-Perfumed Fist

Bareback Quill Lakes country in tamping snow, colour of a
Sportsman cigarette tin, then drifting, almost Christmas, roads about to
close, nothing coming out of the ground, greed with teeth eats me,
distance or Christic loneliness eats me.
A blue city under the snow — its name is Unending, or, in another
    language, Hardly There.   Pine splinters tied into its hair, hanging.
First philosophy is mystical theology.
The fox moves quickly on the snow.
I mean doodling out the taupe-green
lynx spoor[1] of always wanting, which is the single archive of what is   10
said beyond the wall, the one track into the second world.

Now.
Let the object build weight in the meadow of your eye,
                     because you're not good for much else.

A day's travel southwest, the creased hills fat-walk down to the
Estuary[2] ferry, lifted to the sand above the dark-hoarding ice,
rich, covert, kingly ice, and to the west Big Bear's
eyed hill and the Hutterite[3] colony,
small snow down the slopes, the Red Deer locked, crooked,
ankle-broke, old night coming into its wounds.   20
Cranberries staining snow, signs of rabbit kill in the excitedly knotted,
breathed world of the elm thicket,
thick back of essence, flab-pleated with omnia,[4] everywhere
opening its seeing-perfumed fist.

                                   (2003)

Sleeping Four Nights in a Tree

In the Sunset Motel in Senlac, Saskatchewan, it's possible
to think of *The Spiritual Canticle* with the ear of García Lorca[1]

---

1. spoor The trail or scent of an animal. **2. Estuary** Open-water inlet that is fed by a river. **3. Hutterite** A community of
Anabaptists, similar to the Amish. **4. omnia** A reference to the idea that God contains all things — he is *omnia complicans*.
At the same time, he is *omnia explicans*, the source of all things, which reveal his presence.

1. García Lorca (1898–1936) Spanish poet killed by militia in the Spanish Civil War.

inside it like a silver imaginary bird. Look at the eyes in the chimed,
sound-locked garden of the poem. They are wolverines twisting back
into heavy poplar, twisting back, waving back.
Possible to dream of the dangerous nun just off the plane from
         Guatemala who asks to borrow a pair of your shorts.
Turn over this world and there is another world,
     rain clouds hunking through, mind light slabbing like surf
10   around the articulate not-speaking of stone.
Socrates was not an anti-rationalist; his earlier sugar-eye for science, his
small milk lunges, is sublated[2] not abandoned, but he believes a particular
                  pose
of knowing drives the car right through the wall though
it may *appear* to be philosophy.
The bad bearing wobble of coyotes' voices just as night begins,
the thorny crown of coyotes with a twin below the ground.
A swallowed percussion of moon on rained-on snow in fenced stubble
going up the hill at the west edge of town,
20 the dish with its bolts popped out beside the singlewide motel.
Beside this world is another world.
Geese are back but out of sight, moving on green-purple, saline ice,
the April frog sound of natural gas kicking
up in the thigh-big water heater in room 15, rig smell of the carpet, wool
sock rig smell of the bath mat, sheets toenail sliced dust,
the moon in the socket of the ear.
It's better to be forgotten. No one ever gets around to saying this.
Better to live in a place like Winter, Sask., for
instance, though this is hard to think.
30 The mind of St. John of the Cross[3] hovers through you
like a big fish; it bends, lit, in wall-like water its one muscle into a
half-circle and comes back, bends and returns.
Mule deer, bluebirds, the moon instead of a dish.
Phenoxy herbicides enter the extra-cellular fluids like
a small family leaving a station wagon, carrying stiff objects
for a picnic into the grass by the stream. The family is
nameless gathering between the moony nodes and the
blood. Thunder fists and is waving in the currenting
light and spreading appetite considers its options.
40 It's better to be forgotten.
Shake your body out into uselessness.
Lay your sweet head on the flex and the gaze-that-floats-us of
the rivers hoboing through the staring land.

        *

---

2. sublated Refuted. **3. St. John of the Cross** (1542–1591) Spanish mystic and major contributor to the Catholic
Reformation.

And then, in the fucked, hillbilly motel, your
pubic hair going into the cave to coconutrug with others' pubic hair, the
curtain with its rod on the smoked television, the comforter's eight month
deisel smell, a line of R20 insulation on the table,
the ego can comb its beautiful hair and think of John Stuart Mill.[4]
There are many versions of *Anne of Green Gables* on the television.
Non-Hodgkin's lymphoma, a heavy dark bird, bearded   50
like an old railway engine, Assyrian[5] beard, lifts on farms over six
                                                 thousand acres.
What's happening a little way on in the beer parlour? They're celebrating
his decision to forget his decision not to drink.
It's possible to think of the perita[6] of grass, bony assemblage, the
conciliar[7] hum of erotic argument, steepling, unrolling over
days, adverbed by the moon fidgeting under purple-green slough ice.
All this takes a long time, the time of psalm cycles, a long sailing; begin
             by sleeping near a grave. Stand back; look down.
The cafe is open two blocks away. We offer to cook our own breakfasts.   60
It's possible to think of the bones of things,
shark bone of argument, talk's bone ring, orchestral
raptor bone of rising speech going through you like a black wind.
Lymph of moonlight coming down the ancient canals.
Scarves of an encyclopedic muchness darker than this continent, this
                              at-the-moment.
Quick shapes of seeability, tongues coming out of things.
Everything is disguised, covered, everything is feathered.
The brown crust winter left on the windows.
The one neighbour you saw leaving the office the first night here you never   70
see again, black ball cap, his full, see-through bag of white bread.

                                                                                  (2003)

Guy Vanderhaeghe (1951–)

Guy Vanderhaeghe was born in Esterhazy, Saskatchewan in 1951. He dreamed of being a writer from the time he was 11 years old. In the late 1970s, he started writing short stories, but he had trouble getting any of them published. Discouragement set in, but he was determined to go on, preserving his rejection letters as a goad. His determination paid off, and in 1980, his story "What I Learned from Caesar" was selected for inclusion in *80: Best Canadian Stories*, and "The Watcher" won the *Canadian Fiction Magazine* prize. Twenty years and many awards later, Vanderhaeghe — admirer of such masters of the short-story form as Alice Munro, Flannery O'Connor, and John Updike — explained that he had stayed the course by not working to please the reader: "I try to write the book I would want to read. … If you try to speculate about what people will like … you sink yourself."

---

4. **John Stuart Mill** British philosopher and liberal economist; sought a balance between individualism and the promotion of common interests. 5. **Assyrian** Assyria was an ancient kingdom in northern Mesopotamia, which is in present-day Iraq. 6. **perita** Odour. 7. **conciliar** Of a council.

In 1972, Vanderhaeghe married Margaret Gottlieb, a visual artist, and in 1975 he earned an M.A. in history from the University of Saskatchewan; three years later, he received a B.Ed. from the University of Regina. He supported himself as an archivist, a researcher, and a high school English and history teacher, and in 1982, he published his first collection of short stories, *Man Descending*. It won a Governor General's Award and created a national audience for its author. The book's 12 stories extend their focus through time and space: the male protagonists represent life stages from childhood to old age, while their tales are set in such diverse locales as the Canadian prairies and London, England. These are ordinary people (Rudy Wiebe referred to them as people "Any Canadian looking in the bathroom mirror is sure to recognize") buffeted by an indifferent, sometimes hostile world. They battle loneliness and disillusionment, respond with cynicism or frustration or anger, but Vanderhaeghe depicts them with compassion and unflagging humour.

Then, in *The Trouble with Heroes and Other Stories* (1983), Vanderhaeghe explored the heroic archetype — a model for which he had an abiding interest, and one that would eventually lure him away from the contemporary focus on which he had established his writing career and pull him towards the historical. First, however, he finished a novel entitled *My Present Age* (1984) while serving as writer-in-residence at the Saskatoon Public Library. The book draws us into the cramped universe of Ed, the protagonist of the last two stories of *Man Descending*. Ed has lost his wife, Victoria, and he makes it his mission to find her, scouring a bleak and seedy urban terrain and his own past, coming eventually to the painful realization that his life is a fragile construct of self-deceptions. Again, Vanderhaeghe delivers his harrowing themes — existential angst, despair, and isolation — wrapped in dark humour. Ed, despite his deep flaws, is realistically etched, a strangely sympathetic anti-hero. As one reviewer put it, he is for Vanderhaeghe "the perfect vessel from which to launch his kamikaze sorties into contemporary life."

In 1985, Vanderhaeghe served as writer-in-residence and visiting professor of creative writing at the University of Ottawa. His next novel, *Homesick*, was published in 1989. Set in 1959 in a Saskatchewan prairie town, it tells the story of Vera Monkman, a widow with a young son who returns home to face what she has fled years earlier: her widowed father, the community that spawned her, and a painfully suppressed past. *Homesick* takes as its central theme the dual thrust of the concept of "home": home is at once a place of comfort, security, and belonging and a place of claustrophobia and entrapment; all of these powerful forces are condensed in the novel's title.

Vanderhaeghe, in the meantime, was establishing himself as a successful playwright: *I Had a Job I Liked. Once* was produced in 1991, and *Dancock's Dance* in 1995, both in Saskatoon. In 1993, Vanderhaeghe took up the position of visiting professor of English at St. Thomas More College of the University of Saskatchewan. Three years later, he published his second Governor General's Award–winning effort, *The Englishman's Boy*, a novel composed of two intertwined narratives. In 1953, in Saskatoon, Harry Vincent recalls his brief career in the movie business. Hired to write a script for a ruthless Hollywood movie mogul who has little regard for historical accuracy, Harry is instructed to track down Shorty McAdoo, cowboy film extra and alleged "Indian fighter," and glean from him nuggets of information he can use to write a cinematic blockbuster. Interspersed with this first-person narrative is the third-person narrative of a Wild West–era drifter, known simply as "the Englishman's Boy," who becomes embroiled in the events that climax in the bloody 1873 massacre at Cypress Hills, Saskatchewan. As the sinister link between these seemingly disparate tales emerges, Harry, the writer, must confront his penchant for moral paralysis. Vanderhaeghe's masterful construction of this complex fiction prompted critic David Staines to comment on the author's "ear for well-tuned dialogue, his sensitivity to language and sparse rhythms, and his apparently effortless evocation of time, place, and character."

Shortly after the publication of *The Englishman's Boy*, Vanderhaeghe began work on *The Last Crossing*, but the novel would not see publication until 2002. Two years into the project, he decided that it needed to be written in the first person rather than the third; he then set out to create a unique voice for each of the five main characters. The novel is set mainly during the second half of the 19th century in the North American West and in Victorian England, and, like *The Englishman's Boy*, it is an intricately structured epic of interwoven life stories. As these stories unfold — initiated by the search Englishmen Charles Gaunt and his brother Addington must undertake for Charles's twin, Simon, who has disappeared in the wilds of Montana — border after embattled border is traversed: between siblings, spouses, Europeans and North Americans, White and Native, the Wild West and Victorian society.

Vanderhaeghe continues to live in Saskatoon. In 2003, he was awarded the Saskatchewan Order of Merit and made an Officer of the Order of Canada.

The Watcher

I suppose it was having a bad chest that turned me into an observer, a watcher, at an early age.

"Charlie has my chest," my mother often informed friends. "A real weakness there," she would add significantly, thumping her own wishbone soundly.

I suppose I had. Family lore had me narrowly escaping death from pneumonia at the age of four. It seems I spent an entire Sunday in delirium, soaking the sheets. Dr. Carlyle was off at the reservoir rowing in his little skiff and couldn't be reached — something for which my mother illogically refused to forgive him. She was a woman who nursed and tenaciously held dark grudges. Forever after that incident the doctor was slightingly and coldly dismissed in conversation as a "man who betrayed the public's trust."

Following that spell of pneumonia, I regularly suffered from bouts of bronchitis, which often landed me in hospital in Fortune, forty miles away. Compared with the oxygen tent and the whacking great needles that were buried in my skinny rump there, being invalided at home was a piece of cake. Coughing and hacking, I would leaf through catalogues and read comic books until my head swam with print-fatigue. My diet was largely of my own whimsical choosing — hot chocolate and graham wafers were supplemented by sticky sweet coughdrops, which I downed one after another until my stomach could take no more, revolted, and tossed up the whole mess.

With the first signs of improvement in my condition my mother moved her baby to the living-room chesterfield, where she and the radio could keep me company. The electric kettle followed me and was soon burbling in the corner, jetting steam into the air to keep my lungs moist and pliable. Because I was neither quite sick nor quite well, these were the best days of my illnesses. My stay at home hadn't yet made me bored and restless, my chest no longer hurt when I breathed, and that loose pocket of rattling phlegm meant I didn't have to worry about going back to school just yet. So I luxuriated in this steamy equatorial climate, tended by a doting mother as if I were a rare tropical orchid.

My parents didn't own a television and so my curiosity and attention were focused on my surroundings during my illnesses. I tried to squeeze every bit of juice out of them. Sooner than most children I learned that if you kept quiet and still and didn't insist on drawing attention to yourself as many kids did, adults were inclined to regard you as being one with the furniture, as significant and sentient as a hassock.[1] By keeping mum I was treated to illuminating glances into an adult world of conventional miseries and scandals.

I wasn't sure at the age of six what a miscarriage was, but I knew that Ida Thompson had had one and that now her plumbing was buggered. And watching old lady Kuznetsky hang her washing, through a living-room window trickling with condensed kettle steam, I was able to confirm for myself the rumour that the old girl eschewed panties. As she bent over to rummage in her laundry basket I caught a brief glimpse of huge, white buttocks that shimmered in the pale spring sunshine.

I also soon knew (how I don't remember exactly) that Norma Ruggs had business with the Liquor Board Store when she shuffled by our window every day at exactly 10:50 a.m. She was always at the store door at 11:00 when they unlocked and opened up for business. At 11:15 she trudged home again, a pint of ice cream in one hand, a brown paper bag disguising a bottle of fortified wine in the other, and her blotchy complexion painted a high colour of shame.

"Poor old girl," my mother would say whenever she caught sight of Norma passing by in her shabby coat and sloppy man's overshoes. They had been in high school together, and Norma had been class brain and valedictorian. She had been an obliging, dutiful girl and still was. For the wine wasn't Norma's — the ice cream was her only vice. The booze was her husband's, a vet who had come back from the war badly crippled.

All this careful study of adults may have made me old before my time. In any case it seemed to mark me in some recognizable way as being "different" or "queer for a kid." When I went to live with my grandmother in July of 1959 she spotted it right away. Of course, she was only stating the obvious when she declared me skinny and delicate, but she also noted in her vinegary voice that my eyes had a bad habit of never letting her go, and that I was the worst case of little pitchers having big ears that she had ever come across.

I ended up at my grandmother's because in May of that year my mother's bad chest finally caught up with her, much to her and everyone else's surprise. It had been pretty generally agreed by all her acquaintances that Mabel Bradley's defects in that regard were largely imagined. Not so. A government-sponsored X-ray program discovered tuberculosis, and she was packed off, pale and drawn with worry, for a stay in the sanatorium at Fort Qu'Appelle.

For roughly a month, until the school year ended, my father took charge of me and the house. He was a desolate, lanky, drooping weed of a man who had married late in life but nevertheless had been easily domesticated. I didn't like him much.

My father was badly wrenched by my mother's sickness and absence. He scrawled her long, untidy letters with a stub of gnawed pencil, and once he got shut of me, visited her every weekend. He was a soft and sentimental man whose eyes ran to water at the drop of a hat, or more accurately, death of a cat. Unlike his mother, my Grandma Bradley, he hadn't a scrap of flint or hard-headed common sense in him.

But then neither had any of his many brothers and sisters. It was as if the old girl had unflinchingly withheld the genetic code for responsibility and practicality from her pin-headed offspring. Life for her children was a series of thundering defeats, whirlwind

---

1. **hassock** Footstool.

calamities, or, at best, hurried strategic retreats. Businesses crashed and marriages failed, for they had — my father excepted — a taste for the unstable in partners marital and fiscal.

My mother saw no redeeming qualities in any of them. By and large they drank too much, talked too loudly, and raised ill-mannered children — monsters of depravity whose rudeness provided my mother with endless illustrations of what she feared I might become. "You're eating just like a pig," she would say, "exactly like your cousin Elvin." Or to my father, "You're neglecting the belt. He's starting to get as lippy as that little snot Muriel."

And in the midst, in the very eye of this familial cyclone of mishap and discontent, stood Grandma Bradley, as firm as a rock. Troubles of all kinds were laid on her doorstep. When my cousin Criselda suddenly turned big-tummied at sixteen and it proved difficult to ascertain with any exactitude the father, or even point a finger of general blame in the direction of a putative sire, she was shipped off to Grandma Bradley until she delivered. Uncle Ernie dried out on Grandma's farm and Uncle Ed hid there from several people he had sold prefab, assemble-yourself, crop-duster airplanes to.

So it was only family tradition that I should be deposited there. When domestic duties finally overwhelmed him, and I complained too loudly about fried-egg sandwiches for dinner *again*, my father left the bacon rinds hardening and curling grotesquely on unwashed plates, the slut's wool[2] eddying along the floor in the currents of a draft, and drove the one hundred and fifty miles to the farm, *right then and there*.

My father, a dangerous man behind the wheel, took any extended trip seriously, believing the highways to be narrow, unnavigable ribbons of carnage. This trip loomed so dangerously in his mind that, rather than tear a hand from the wheel, or an eye from the road, he had me, *chronic sufferer of lung disorders*, light his cigarettes and place them carefully in his dry lips. My mother would have killed him.

"You'll love it at Grandma's," he kept saying unconvincingly, "you'll have a real boy's summer on the farm. It'll build you up, the chores and all that. And good fun too. You don't know it now, but you are living the best days of your life right now. What I wouldn't give to be a kid again. You'll love it there. There's chickens and *everything*."

It wasn't exactly a lie. There were chickens. But the *everything* — as broad and overwhelming and suggestive of possibilities as my father tried to make it sound — didn't cover much. It certainly didn't comprehend a pony or a dog as I had hoped, chickens being the only livestock on the place.

It turned out that my grandmother, although she had spent most of her life on that particular piece of ground and eventually died there, didn't care much for the farm and was entirely out of sympathy with most varieties of animal life. She did keep chickens for the eggs, although she admitted that her spirits lifted considerably in the fall when it came time to butcher the hens.

Her flock was a garrulous,[3] scraggly crew that spent their days having dust baths in the front yard, hiding their eggs, and, fleet and ferocious as hunting cheetahs, running down scuttling lizards which they trampled and pecked to death while their shiny, expressionless eyes shifted dizzily in their stupid heads. The only one of these birds I felt any compassion for was Stanley the rooster, a bedraggled male who spent his days

2. **slut's wool** Dust bunny. 3. **garrulous** Excessively talkative.

tethered to a stake by a piece of bailer twine looped around his leg. Poor Stanley crowed heart-rendingly in his captivity; his comb drooped pathetically, and he was utterly crestfallen as he lecherously eyed his bantam[4] beauties daintily scavenging. Grandma kept him in this unnatural bondage to prevent him fertilizing the eggs and producing blood spots in the yolks. Being a finicky eater I approved this policy, but nevertheless felt some guilt over Stanley.

No, the old Bradley homestead, all that encompassed by my father's *everything*, wasn't very impressive. The two-storey house, though big and solid, needed paint and shingles. A track had been worn in the kitchen linoleum clean through to the floorboards and a long rent in the screen door had been stitched shut with waxed thread. The yard was little more than a tangle of thigh-high ragweed and sowthistle to which the chickens repaired for shade. A windbreak of spruce on the north side of the house was dying from lack of water and the competition from Scotch thistle. The evergreens were no longer green; their sere needles fell away from the branches at the touch of a hand.

The abandoned barn out back was flanked by two mountainous rotted piles of manure which I remember sprouting button mushrooms after every warm soaker of a rain. That pile of shit was the only useful thing in a yard full of junk: wrecked cars, old wagon wheels, collapsing sheds. The barn itself was mightily decayed. The paint had been stripped from its planks by rain, hail, and dry, blistering winds, and the roof sagged like a tired nag's back. For a small boy it was an ominous place on a summer day. The air was still and dark and heavy with heat. At the sound of footsteps rats squeaked and scrabbled in the empty mangers, and the sparrows which had spattered the rafters white with their dung whirred about and fluted ghostly cries.

In 1959 Grandma Bailey would have been sixty-nine, which made her a child of the gay nineties — although the supposed gaiety of that age didn't seem to have made much impress upon the development of her character. Physically she was an imposing woman. Easily six feet tall, she carried a hundred and eighty pounds on her generous frame without prompting speculation as to what she had against girdles. She could touch the floor effortless with the flat of her palms and pack an eighty-pound sack of chicken feed on her shoulder. She dyed her hair auburn in defiance of local mores, and never went to town to play bridge, whist, or canasta without wearing a hat and getting dressed to the teeth. Grandma loved card games of all varieties and considered anyone who didn't a mental defective.

A cigarette always smouldered in her trap. She smoked sixty a day and rolled them as thin as knitting needles in an effort at economy. These cigarettes were so wispy and delicate they tended to get lost between her swollen fingers.

And above all she believed in plain speaking. She let me know that as my father's maroon Meteor pulled out of the yard while we stood waving goodbye on the front steps.

"Let's get things straight from the beginning," she said without taking her eyes off the car as it bumped toward the grid road. "I don't chew my words twice. If you're like any of the rest of them I've had here, you've been raised as wild as a goddamn Indian. Not one of my grandchildren have been brought up to mind. Well, you'll mind around here. I don't jaw and blow hot air to jaw and blow hot air. I belted your father when he needed it, and make no mistake I'll belt you. Is that understood?"

---

4. **bantam** Small.

"Yes," I said with a sinking feeling as I watched my father's car disappear down the road, swaying from side to side as its suspension was buffeted by potholes.

"These bloody bugs are eating me alive," she said, slapping her arm. "I'm going in."

I trailed after her as she slopped back into the house in a pair of badly mauled, laceless sneakers. The house was filled with a half-light that changed its texture with every room. The venetian blinds were drawn in the parlour and some flies carved Immelmanns[5] in the dark air that smelled of cellar damp. Others battered their bullet bodies *tip-tap, tip-tap* against the window panes.

In the kitchen my grandmother put the kettle on the stove to boil for tea. After she had lit one of her matchstick smokes, she inquired through a blue haze if I was hungry.

"People aren't supposed to smoke around me," I informed her. "Because of my chest. Dad can't even smoke in our house."

"That so?" she said genially. Her cheeks collapsed as she drew on her butt. I had a hint there, if I'd only known it, of how she'd look in her coffin. "You won't like it here then," she said. "I smoke all the time."

I tried a few unconvincing coughs. I was ignored. She didn't respond to the same signals as my mother.

"My mother has a bad chest, too," I said. "She's in a T.B. sanatorium."

"So I heard," my grandmother said, getting up to fetch the whistling kettle. "Oh, I suspect she'll be right as rain in no time with a little rest. T.B. isn't what it used to be. Not with all these new drugs." She considered. "That's not to say though that your father'll ever hear the end of it. Mabel was always a silly little shit that way."

I almost fell off my chair. I had never thought I'd live to hear the day my mother was called a silly little shit.

"Drink tea?" asked Grandma Bradley, pouring boiling water into a brown teapot. I shook my head.

"How old are you anyway?" she asked.

"Eleven."

"You're old enough then," she said, taking down a cup from the shelf. "Tea gets the kidneys moving and carries off the poisons in the blood. That's why all the Chinese live to be so old. They all live to be a hundred."

"I don't know if my mother would like it," I said. "Me drinking tea."

"You worry a lot for a kid," she said, "don't you?"

I didn't know how to answer that. It wasn't a question I had ever considered. I tried to shift the conversation.

"What's there for a kid to do around here?" I said in an unnaturally inquisitive voice.

"Well, we could play cribbage," she said.

"I don't know how to play cribbage."

She was genuinely shocked. "What!" she exclaimed. "Why, you're eleven years old! Your father could count a cribbage hand when he was five. I taught all my kids to."

"I never learned how," I said. "We don't even have a deck of cards at our house. My father hates cards. Says he had too much of them as a boy."

At this my grandmother arched her eyebrows. "Is that a fact? Well, hoity-toity."

5. **Immelmanns** A manoeuvre in which an airplane performs a half loop to reverse its direction.

"So, since I don't play cards," I continued in a strained manner I imagined was polite, "what could I do — I mean, for fun?"

"Make your own fun," she said. "I never considered fun such a problem. Use your imagination. Take a broomstick and make like Nimrod."[6]

"Who's Nimrod?" I asked.

"Pig ignorant," she said under her breath, and then louder, directly to me, "Ask me no questions and I'll tell you no lies. Drink your tea."

And that, for the time being, was that.

It's all very well to tell someone to make their own fun. It's the making of it that is the problem. In a short time I was a very bored kid. There was no one to play with, no horses to ride, no gun to shoot gophers, no dog for company. There was nothing to read except the *Country Guide* and *Western Producer*. There was nothing or nobody interesting to watch. I went through my grandmother's drawers but found nothing as surprising there as I had discovered in my parents'.

Most days it was so hot that the very idea of fun boiled out of me and evaporated. I moped and dragged myself listlessly around the house in the loose-jointed, water-boned way kids have when they can't stand anything, not even their precious selves.

On my better days I tried to take up with Stanley the rooster. Scant chance of that. Tremors of panic ran through his body at my approach. He tugged desperately on the twine until he jerked his free leg out from under himself and collapsed in the dust, his heart bumping the tiny crimson scallops of his breast feathers, the black pellets of his eyes glistening, all the while shitting copiously. Finally, in the last extremes of chicken terror, he would allow me to stroke his yellow beak and finger his comb.

I felt sorry for the captive Stanley and several times tried to take him for a walk, to give him a chance to take the air and broaden his limited horizons. But this prospect alarmed him so much that I was always forced to return him to his stake in disgust while he fluttered, squawked and flopped.

So fun was a commodity in short supply. That is, until something interesting turned up during the first week of August. Grandma Bradley was dredging little watering canals with a hoe among the corn stalks on a bright blue Monday morning, and I was shelling peas into a colander on the front stoop, when a black car nosed diffidently up the road and into the yard. Then it stopped a good twenty yards short of the house as if its occupants weren't sure of their welcome. After some time, the doors opened and a man and woman got carefully out.

The woman wore turquoise-blue pedal-pushers, a sloppy black turtleneck sweater, and a gash of scarlet lipstick swiped across her white, vivid face. This was my father's youngest sister, Aunt Evelyn.

The man took her gently and courteously by the elbow and balanced her as she edged up the front yard in her high heels, careful to avoid turning an ankle on a loose stone, or in an old tire track.

The thing which immediately struck me about the man was his beard — the first I had ever seen. Beards weren't popular in 1959 — not in our part of the world. His was a randy, jutting, little goat's-beard that would have looked wicked on any other face but his. He was very tall and his considerable height was accented by a lack of

---

6. **Nimrod** A biblical reference to the king of Babylon who was a descendant of Noah.

corresponding breadth to his body. He appeared to have been racked and stretched against his will into an exceptional and unnatural anatomy. As he walked and talked animatedly, his free hand fluttered in front of my aunt. It sailed, twirled and gambolled on the air. Like a butterfly enticing a child, it seemed to lead her hypnotized across a yard fraught with perils for city-shod feet.

My grandmother laid down her hoe and called sharply to her daughter.

"Evvie!" she called. "Over here, Evvie!"

At the sound of her mother's voice my aunt's head snapped around and she began to wave jerkily and stiffly, striving to maintain a tottering balance on her high-heeled shoes. It wasn't hard to see that there was something not quite right with her. By the time my grandmother and I reached the pair, Aunt Evelyn was in tears, sobbing hollowly and jamming the heel of her palm into her front teeth.

The man was speaking calmly to her. "Control. Control. Deep, steady breaths. Think sea. Control. Control. Control. Think sea, Evelyn. Deep. Deep. Deep," he muttered.

"What the hell is the matter, Evelyn?" my grandmother asked sharply. "And who is *he?*"

"Evelyn is a little upset," the man said, keeping his attention focused on my aunt. "She's having one of her anxiety attacks. If you'd just give us a moment we'll clear this up. She's got to learn to handle stressful situations." He inclined his head in a priestly manner and said, "Be with the sea, Evelyn. Deep. Deep. Sink in the sea."

"It's her damn nerves again," said my grandmother.

"Yes," the man said benignly, with a smile of blinding condescension. "Sort of."

"She's been as nervous as a cut cat all her life," said my grandmother, mostly to herself.

"Momma," said Evelyn, weeping. "Momma."

"Slide beneath the waves, Evelyn. Down, down, down to the beautiful pearls," the man chanted softly. This was really something.

My grandmother took Aunt Evelyn by her free elbow, shook it, and said abruptly, "Evelyn, shut up!" Then she began to drag her briskly towards the house. For a moment the man looked as if he had it in mind to protest, but in the end he meekly acted as a flanking escort for Aunt Evelyn as she was marched into the house. When I tried to follow, my grandmother gave me one of her looks and said definitely, "You find something to do out here."

I did. I waited a few minutes and then duck-walked my way under the parlour window. There I squatted with my knobby shoulder blades pressed against the siding and the sun beating into my face.

My grandmother obviously hadn't wasted any time with the social niceties. They were fairly into it.

"Lovers?" said my grandmother. "Is that what it's called now? Shack-up, you mean."

"Oh, Momma," said Evelyn, and she was crying, "it's all right. We're going to get married."

"You believe that?" said my grandmother. "You believe that geek is going to marry you?"

"Thompson," said the geek, "my name is Thompson, Robert Thompson, and we'll marry as soon as I get my divorce. Although Lord only knows when that'll be."

"That's right," said my grandmother. "Lord only knows." Then to her daughter, "You got another one. A real prize off the midway, didn't you? Evelyn, you're a certifiable lunatic."

"I didn't expect this," said Thompson. "We came here because Evelyn has had a bad time of it recently. She hasn't been eating or sleeping properly and consequently she's got herself run down. She finds it difficult to control her emotions, don't you, darling?"

I thought I heard a mild yes.

"So," said Thompson, continuing, "we decided Evelyn needs some peace and quiet before I go back to school in September."

"School," said my grandmother. "Don't tell me you're some kind of teacher?" She seemed stunned by the very idea.

"No," said Aunt Evelyn, and there was a tremor of pride in her voice that testified to her amazement that she had been capable of landing such a rare and remarkable fish. "Not a teacher. Robert's a graduate student of American Literature at the University of British Columbia."

"Hoity-toity," said Grandmother. "A graduate student. A graduate student of American Literature."

"Doctoral program," said Robert.

"And did you ever ask yourself, Evelyn, what the hell this genius is doing with you? Or is it just the same old problem with you — elevator panties? Some guy comes along and pushes the button. Up, down. Up, down."

The image this created in my mind made me squeeze my knees together deliciously and stifle a giggle.

"Mother," said Evelyn, continuing to bawl.

"Guys like this don't marry barmaids," said my grandmother.

"Cocktail hostess," corrected Evelyn. "I'm a cocktail hostess."

"You don't have to make any excuses, dear," said Thompson pompously. "Remember what I told you. You're past the age of being judged."

"What the hell is that supposed to mean?" said my grandmother. "And by the way, don't start handing out orders in my house. You won't be around long enough to make them stick."

"That remains to be seen," said Thompson.

"Let's go, Robert," said Evelyn nervously.

"Go on upstairs, Evelyn. I want to talk to your mother."

"You don't have to go anywhere," said my grandmother. "You can stay put."

"Evelyn, go upstairs." There was a pause and then I heard the sound of a chair creaking, then footsteps.

"Well," said my grandmother at last, "round one. Now for round two — get the hell out of my house."

"Can't do that."

"Why the hell not?"

"It's very difficult to explain," he said.

"Try."

"As you can see for yourself, Evelyn isn't well. She is very highly strung at the moment. I believe she is on the verge of a profound personality adjustment, a breakthrough." He paused dramatically. "Or breakdown."

"It's times like this that I wished I had a dog on the place to run off undesirables."

"The way I read it," said Thompson, unperturbed, "is that at the moment two people bulk very large in Evelyn's life. You and me. She needs the support and love of us both. You're not doing your share."

"I ought to slap your face."

"She has come home to try and get a hold of herself. We have to bury our dislikes for the moment. She needs to be handled very carefully."

"You make her sound like a trained bear. *Handled*. What that girl needs is a good talking to, and I am perfectly capable of giving her that."

"No, Mrs. Bradley," Thompson said firmly in that maddeningly self-assured tone of his. "If you don't mind me saying so, I think that's part of her problem. It's important now for you to just let Evelyn *be*."

"Get out of my house," said my grandmother, at the end of her tether.

"I know it's difficult for you to understand," he said smoothly, "but if you understood the psychology of this you would see it's impossible for me to go; or for that matter, for Evelyn to go. If I leave she'll feel I've abandoned her. It can't be done. We're faced with a real psychological balancing act here."

"Now I've heard everything," said my grandmother. "Are you telling me you'd have the gall to move into a house where you're not wanted and just . . . just *stay there?*"

"Yes," said Thompson. "And I think you'll find me quite stubborn on this particular point."

"My God," said my grandmother. I could tell by her tone of voice that she had never come across anyone like Mr. Thompson before. At a loss for a suitable reply, she simply reiterated, "My God."

"I'm going upstairs now," said Thompson. "Maybe you could get the boy to bring in our bags while I see how Evelyn is doing. The car isn't locked." The second time he spoke his voice came from further away; I imagined him paused in the doorway. "Mrs. Bradley, please let's make this stay pleasant for Evelyn's sake."

She didn't bother answering him.

When I barged into the house some time later with conspicuous noisiness, I found my grandmother standing at the bottom of the stairs staring up the steps. "Well, I'll be damned," she said under her breath. "I've never seen anything like that. Goddamn freak." She even repeated it several times under her breath. "Goddamn freak. Goddamn freak."

Who could blame me if, after a boring summer, I felt my chest tighten with anticipation. Adults could be immensely interesting and entertaining if you knew what to watch for.

At first things were disappointingly quiet. Aunt Evelyn seldom set forth outside the door of the room she and her man inhabited by squatters' right. There was an argument, short and sharp, between Thompson and Grandmother over this. The professor claimed no one had any business prying into what Evelyn did up there. She was an adult and had the right to her privacy and her own thoughts. My grandmother claimed she had a right to know what was going on up there, even if nobody else thought she did.

I could have satisfied her curiosity on that point. Not much was going on up there. Several squints through the keyhole had revealed Aunt Evelyn lolling about the bedspread in a blue housecoat, eating soda crackers and sardines, and reading a stack of movie magazines she had had me lug out of the trunk of the car.

Food, you see, was beginning to become something of a problem for our young lovers. Grandma rather pointedly set only three places for meals, and Evelyn, out of loyalty to her boyfriend, couldn't very well sit down and break bread with us. Not that

Thompson didn't take such things in his stride. He sauntered casually and conspicuous-ly about the house as if he owned it, even going so far as to poke his head in the fridge and rummage in it like some pale, hairless bear. At times like that my grandmother was capable of looking through him as if he didn't exist.

On the second day of his stay Thompson took up with me, which was all right as far as I was concerned. I had no objection. Why he decided to do this I'm not sure exactly. Perhaps he was looking for some kind of an ally, no matter how weak. Or maybe he just couldn't bear not having anyone to tell how wonderful he was. Thompson was that kind of a guy.

I was certainly let in on the secret. He was a remarkable fellow. He dwelt at great length on those things which made him such an extraordinary human being. I may have gotten the order of precedence all wrong, but if I remember correctly there were three things which made Thompson very special and different from all the other people I would ever meet, no matter how long or hard I lived.

First, he was going to write a book about a poet called Allen Ginsberg which was going to knock the socks off everybody who counted. It turned out he had actually met this Ginsberg the summer before in San Francisco and asked him if he could write a book about him and Ginsberg had said, Sure, why the hell not? The way Thompson described what it would be like when he published this book left me with the impression that he was going to spend most of the rest of his life riding around on people's shoulders and being cheered by a multitude of admirers.

Second, he confessed to knowing a tremendous amount about what made other people tick and how to adjust their mainsprings when they went kaflooey. He knew all this because at one time his own mainspring had gotten a little out of sorts. But now he was a fully integrated personality with a highly creative mind and a strong intuitive sense. That's why he was so much help to Aunt Evelyn in her time of troubles.

Third, he was a Buddhist.

The only one of these things which impressed me at the time was the bit about being a Buddhist. However, I was confused, because in the *Picture Book of the World's Great Religions* which we had at home, all the Buddhists were bald, and Thompson had a hell of a lot of hair, more than I had ever seen on a man. But even though he wasn't bald, he had an idol. A little bronze statue with the whimsical smile and slightly crossed eyes which he identified as Padma-sambhava. He told me that it was a Tibetan antique he had bought in San Francisco as an object of veneration and an aid to his meditations. I asked him what a meditation was and he offered to teach me one. So I learned to recite with great seriousness and flexible intonation one of his Tibetan meditations, while my grandmother glared across her quintessentially Western parlour with unbelieving eyes.

I could soon deliver, "A king must go when his time has come. His wealth, his friends and his relatives cannot go with him. Wherever men go, wherever they stay, the effect of their past acts follows them like a shadow. Those who are in the grip of desire, the grip of existence, the grip of ignorance, move helplessly round through the spheres of life, as men or gods or as wretches in the lower regions."

Not that an eleven-year-old could make much of any of *that*.

Which is not to say that even an eleven-year-old could be fooled by Robert Thompson. In his stubbornness, egoism and blindness he was transparently un-Buddha-like. To watch him and my grandmother snarl and snap their teeth over that poor, dry bone, Evelyn, was evidence enough of how firmly bound we all are to the wretched wheel of life and its stumbling desires.

No, even his most effective weapon, his cool benevolence, that patina[7] of patience and forbearance which Thompson displayed to Grandmother, could crack.

One windy day when he had coaxed Aunt Evelyn out for a walk I followed them at a distance. They passed the windbreak of spruce, and at the sagging barbed-wire fence he gallantly manipulated the wires while my aunt floundered over them in an impractical dress and crinoline. It was the kind of dippy thing she would decide to wear on a hike.

Thompson strode along through the rippling grass like a wading heron, his baggy pant-legs flapping and billowing in the wind. My aunt moved along gingerly behind him, one hand modestly pinning down her wind-teased dress in the front, the other hand plastering the back of it to her behind.

It was only when they stopped and faced each other that I realized that all the time they had been traversing the field they had been arguing. A certain vaguely communicated agitation in the attitude of her figure, the way his arm stabbed at the featureless wash of sky, implied a dispute. She turned toward the house and he caught her by the arm and jerked it. In a fifties calendar fantasy her dress lifted in the wind, exposing her panties. I sank in the grass until their seed tassels trembled against my chin. I wasn't going to miss watching this for the world.

She snapped and twisted on the end of his arm like a fish on a line. Her head was flung back in an exaggerated, antique display of despair; her head rolled grotesquely from side to side as if her neck were broken.

Suddenly Thompson began striking awkwardly at her exposed buttocks and thighs with the flat of his hand. The long, gangly arm slashed like a flail as she scampered around him, the radius of her escape limited by the distance of their linked arms.

From where I knelt in the grass I could hear nothing. I was too far off. As far as I was concerned there were no cries and no pleading. The whole scene, as I remember it, was shorn of any of the personal idiosyncrasies which manifest themselves in violence. It appeared a simple case of retribution.

That night, for the first time, my aunt came down to supper and claimed her place at the table with queenly graciousness. She wore shorts, too, for the first time, and gave a fine display of mottled, discoloured thighs which reminded me of bruised fruit. She made sure, almost as if by accident, that my grandmother had a good hard look at them.

Right out of the blue my grandmother said, "I don't want you hanging around that man any more. You stay away from him."

"Why?" I asked rather sulkily. He was the only company I had. Since my aunt's arrival Grandmother had paid no attention to me whatsoever.

It was late afternoon and we were sitting on the porch watching Evelyn squeal as she swung in the tire swing Thompson had rigged up for me in the barn. He had thrown a length of stray rope over the runner for the sliding door and hung a tire from it. I hadn't the heart to tell him I was too old for tire swings.

Aunt Evelyn seemed to be enjoying it though. She was screaming and girlishly kicking up her legs. Thompson couldn't be seen. He was deep in the settled darkness of the barn, pushing her back and forth. She disappeared and reappeared according to the

---

7. **patina** Surface appearance.

arc which she travelled through. Into the barn, out in the sun. Light, darkness. Light, darkness.

Grandma ignored my question. "Goddamn freak," she said, scratching a match on the porch rail and lighting one of her rollies. "Wait and see, he'll get his wagon fixed."

"Aunt Evelyn likes him," I noted pleasantly, just to stir things up a bit.

"Your Aunt Evelyn's screws are loose," she said sourly. "And he's the son of a bitch who owns the screwdriver that loosened them."

"He must be an awful smart fellow to be studying to be a professor at a university," I commented. It was the last dig I could chance.

"One thing I know for sure," snapped my grandmother. "He isn't smart enough to lift the toilet seat when he pees. There's evidence enough for that."

After hearing that, I took to leaving a few conspicuous droppings of my own as a matter of course on each visit. Every little bit might help things along.

I stood in his doorway and watched Thompson meditate. And don't think that, drenched in *satori*[8] as he was, he didn't know it. He put on quite a performance sitting on the floor in his underpants. When he came out of his trance he pretended to be surprised to see me. While he dressed we struck up a conversation.

"You know, Charlie," he said while he put on his sandals (I'd never seen a grown man wear sandals in my entire life), "you remind me of my little Padma-sambhava," he said, nodding to the idol squatting on his dresser. "For a while, you know, I thought it was the smile, but it isn't. It's the eyes."

"Its eyes are crossed," I said, none too flattered at the comparison.

"No, they're not," he said good-naturedly. He tucked his shirt-tail into his pants. "The artist, the maker of that image, set them fairly close together to suggest — aesthetically speaking — the intensity of inner vision, its concentration." He picked up the idol and, looking at it, said, "These are very watchful eyes, very knowing eyes. Your eyes are something like that. From your eyes I could tell you're an intelligent boy." He paused, set Padma-sambhava back on the dresser, and asked, "Are you?"

I shrugged.

"Don't be afraid to say it if you are," he said. "False modesty can be as corrupting as vanity. It took me twenty-five years to learn that."

"I usually get all A's on my report card," I volunteered.

"Well, that's something," he said, looking around the room for his belt. He picked a sweater off a chair and peered under it. "Then you see what's going on around here, don't you?" he asked. "You see what your grandmother is mistakenly trying to do?"

I nodded.

"That's right," he said. "You're a smart boy." He sat down on the bed. "Come here."

I went over to him. He took hold of me by the arms and looked into my eyes with all the sincerity he could muster. "You know, being intelligent means responsibilities. It means doing something worth while with your life. For instance, have you given any thought as to what you would like to be when you grow up?"

"A spy," I said.

The silly bugger laughed.

---

8. *satori* Sudden enlightenment.

It was the persistent, rhythmic thud that first woke me, and once wakened, I picked up the undercurrent of muted clamour, of stifled struggle. The noise seeped through the beaver-board wall of the adjoining bedroom into my own, a storm of hectic urgency and violence. The floorboards of the old house squeaked; I heard what sounded like a strangled curse and moan, then a fleshy, meaty concussion which I took to be a slap. Was he killing her at last? Choking her with the silent, poisonous care necessary to escape detection?

I remembered Thompson's arm flashing frenziedly in the sunlight. My aunt's discoloured thighs. My heart creaked in my chest with fear. And after killing her? Would the madman stop? Or would he do us all in, one by one?

I got out of bed on unsteady legs. The muffled commotion was growing louder, more distinct. I padded into the hallway. The door to their bedroom was partially open, and a light showed. Terror made me feel hollow; the pit of my stomach ached.

They were both naked, something which I hadn't expected, and which came as quite a shock. What was perhaps even more shocking was the fact that they seemed not only oblivious of me, but of each other as well. She was slung around so that her head was propped on a pillow resting on the footboard of the bed. One smooth leg was draped over the edge of the bed and her heel was beating time on the floorboards (the thud which woke me) as accompaniment to Thompson's plunging body and the soft, liquid grunts of expelled air which he made with every lunge. One of her hands gripped the footboard and her knuckles were white with strain.

I watched until the critical moment, right through the growing frenzy and ardour. They groaned and panted and heaved and shuddered and didn't know themselves. At the very last he lifted his bony, hatchet face with the jutting beard to the ceiling and closed his eyes; for a moment I thought he was praying as his lips moved soundlessly. But then he began to whimper and his mouth fell open and he looked stupider and weaker than any human being I had ever seen before in my life.

"Like pigs at the trough," my grandmother said at breakfast. "With the boy up there too."

My aunt turned a deep red, and then flushed again so violently that her thin lips appeared to turn blue.

I kept my head down and went on shovelling porridge. Thompson still wasn't invited to the table. He was leaning against the kitchen counter, his bony legs crossed at the ankles, eating an apple he had helped himself to.

"He didn't hear anything," my aunt said uncertainly. She whispered conspiratorially across the table to Grandmother. "Not at that hour. He'd been asleep for hours."

I thought it wise, even though it meant drawing attention to myself, to establish my ignorance. "Hear what?" I inquired innocently.

"It wouldn't do any harm if he had," said Thompson, calmly biting and chewing the temptress's fruit.

"You wouldn't see it, would you?" said Grandma Bradley. "It wouldn't matter to you what he heard? You'd think that was manly."

"Manly has nothing to do with it. Doesn't enter into it," said Thompson in that cool way he had. "It's a fact of life, something he'll have to find out about sooner or later."

Aunt Evelyn began to cry. "Nobody is ever pleased with me," she spluttered. "I'm going crazy trying to please you both. I can't do it." She began to pull nervously at her hair. "He made me," she said finally in a confessional, humble tone to her mother.

"Evelyn," said my grandmother, "you have a place here. I would never send you away. I want you here. But he has to go. I want him to go. If he is going to rub my nose in it that way he has to go. I won't have that man under my roof."

"Evelyn isn't apologizing for anything," Thompson said. "And she isn't running away either. You can't force her to choose. It isn't healthy or fair."

"There have been other ones before you," said Grandma. "This isn't anything new for Evelyn."

"Momma!"

"I'm aware of that," he said stiffly, and his face vibrated with the effort to smile. "Provincial mores have never held much water with me. I like to think I'm above all that."

Suddenly my grandmother spotted me. "What are you gawking at!" she shouted. "Get on out of here!"

I didn't budge an inch.

"Leave him alone," said Thompson.

"You'll be out of here within a week," said Grandmother. "I swear."

"No," he said smiling. "When I'm ready."

"You'll go home and go with your tail between your legs. Last night was the last straw," she said. And by God you could tell she meant it.

Thompson gave her his beatific Buddha-grin and shook his head from side to side, very, very slowly.

A thunderstorm was brewing. The sky was a stew of dark, swollen cloud and a strange apple-green light. The temperature stood in the mid-nineties, not a breath of breeze stirred, my skin crawled and my head pounded above my eyes and through the bridge of my nose. There wasn't a thing to do except sit on the bottom step of the porch, keep from picking up a sliver in your ass, and scratch the dirt with a stick. My grandmother had put her hat on and driven into town on some unexplained business. Thompson and my aunt were upstairs in their bedroom, sunk in a stuporous, sweaty afternoon's sleep.

Like my aunt and Thompson, all the chickens had gone to roost to wait for rain. The desertion of his harem had thrown the rooster into a flap. Stanley trotted neurotically around his tethering post, stopping every few circuits to beat his bedraggled pinions[9] and crow lustily in masculine outrage. I watched him for a bit without much curiosity, and then climbed off the step and walked toward him, listlessly dragging my stick in my trail.

"Here Stanley, Stanley," I called, not entirely sure how to summon a rooster, or instil in him confidence and friendliness.

I did neither. My approach only further unhinged Stanley. His stride lengthened, the tempo of his pace increased, and his head began to dart abruptly from side to side in furtive despair. Finally, in a last desperate attempt to escape, Stanley upset himself trying to fly. He landed in a heap of disarranged, stiff, glistening feathers. I put my foot on his string and pinned him to the ground.

"Nice pretty, pretty Stanley," I said coaxingly, adopting the tone that a neighbour used with her budgie, since I wasn't sure how one talked to a bird. I slowly extended my thumb to stroke his bright-red neck feathers. Darting angrily, he struck the ball of my

---

9. **pinions** Wings.

thumb with a snappish peck and simultaneously hit my wrist with his heel spur. He didn't hurt me, but he did startle me badly. So badly I gave a little yelp. Which made me feel foolish and more than a little cowardly.

"You son of a bitch," I said, reaching down slowly and staring into one unblinking glassy eye in which I could see my face looming larger and larger. I caught the rooster's legs and held them firmly together. Stanley crowed defiantly and showed me his wicked little tongue.

"Now, Stanley," I said, "relax, I'm just going to stroke you. I'm just going to stroke you. I'm just going to pet Stanley."

No deal. He struck furiously again with a snake-like agility, and bounded in my hand, wings beating his poultry smell into my face. A real fighting cock at last. Maybe it was the weather. Perhaps his rooster pride and patience would suffer no more indignities.

The heat, the sultry menace of the gathering storm, made me feel prickly, edgy. I flicked my middle finger smartly against his tiny chicken skull, hard enough to rattle his pea-sized brain. "You like that, buster?" I asked, and snapped him another one for good measure. He struck back again, his comb red, crested, and rubbery with fury.

I was angry myself. I turned him upside down and left him dangling, his wings drumming against the legs of my jeans. Then I righted him abruptly; he looked dishevelled, seedy and dazed.

"Okay, Stanley," I said, feeling the intoxication of power. "I'm boss here, and you behave." There was a gleeful edge to my voice, which surprised me a little. I realized I was hoping this confrontation would escalate. Wishing that he would provoke me into something.

Strange images came into my head: the bruises on my aunt's legs; Thompson's face drained of life, lifted like an empty receptacle toward the ceiling, waiting to be filled, the tendons of his neck stark and rigid with anticipation.

I was filled with anxiety, the heat seemed to stretch me, to tug at my nerves and my skin. Two drops of sweat, as large and perfectly formed as tears, rolled out of my hairline and splashed onto the rubber toes of my runners.

"Easy, Stanley," I breathed to him, "easy," and my hand crept deliberately towards him. This time he pecked me in such a way, directly on the knuckle, that it actually hurt. I took up my stick and rapped him on the beak curtly, the prim admonishment of a schoolmarm. I didn't hit him very hard, but it was hard enough to split the length of his beak with a narrow crack. The beak fissured like the nip of a fountain pen. Stanley squawked, opened and closed his beak spasmodically, bewildered by the pain. A bright jewel of blood bubbled out of the split and gathered to a trembling bead.

"There," I said excitedly, "now you've done it. How are you going to eat with a broken beak? You can't eat anything with a broken beak. You'll starve, you stupid goddamn chicken."

A wind that smelled of rain had sprung up. It ruffled his feathers until they moved with a barely discernible crackle.

"Poor Stanley," I said, and at last, numbed by the pain, he allowed me to stroke the gloss of his lacquer feathers.

I wasn't strong enough or practised enough to do a clean and efficient job of wringing his neck, but I succeeded in finishing him off after two clumsy attempts. Then, because I wanted to leave the impression that a skunk had made off with him, I punched a couple of holes in his breast with my jack knife and tried to dribble some blood on the ground. Poor Stanley produced only a few meagre spots; this corpse refused to bleed in the presence of its murderer. I scattered a handful of his feathers on the ground and buried him in the larger of the two manure piles beside the barn.

"I don't think any skunk got that rooster," my grandmother said suspiciously, nudging at a feather with the toe of her boot until, finally disturbed, it was wafted away by the breeze.

Something squeezed my heart. How did she know?

"Skunks hunt at night," she said. "Must have been somebody's barn cat."

"You come along with me," my grandmother said. She was standing in front of the full-length hall mirror, settling on her hat, a deadly-looking hat pin poised over her skull. "We'll go into town and you can buy a comic book at the drugstore."

It was Friday and Friday was shopping day. But Grandma didn't wheel her battered De Soto to the curb in front of the Brite Spot Grocery, she parked it in front of Maynard & Pritchard, Barristers and Solicitors.

"What are we doing here?" I asked.

Grandma was fumbling nervously with her purse. Small-town people don't like to be seen going to the lawyer's. "Come along with me. Hurry up."

"Why do I have to come?"

"Because I don't want you making a spectacle of yourself for the half-wits and loungers to gawk at," she said. "Let's not give them too much to wonder about."

Maynard & Pritchard, Barristers and Solicitors, smelled of wax and varnish and probity.[10] My grandmother was shown into an office with a frosted pane of glass in the door and neat gilt lettering that announced it was occupied by D. F. Maynard, Q.C. I was ordered to occupy a hard chair, which I did, battering my heels on the rungs briskly enough to annoy the secretary into telling me to stop it.

My grandmother wasn't closeted long with her Queen's Counsel before the door opened and he glided after her into the passageway. Lawyer Maynard was the neatest man I had ever seen in my life. His suit fit him like a glove.

"The best I can do," he said, "is send him a registered letter telling him to remove himself from the premises, but it all comes to the same thing. If that doesn't scare him off, you'll have to have recourse to the police. That's all there is to it. I told you that yesterday and you haven't told me anything new today, Edith, that would make me change my mind. Just let him know you won't put up with him any more."

"No police," she said, "I don't want the police digging in my family's business and Evelyn giving one of her grand performances for some baby-skinned constable straight out of the depot. All I need is to get her away from him for a little while, then I could tune her in. I could get through to her in no time at all."

"Well," said Maynard, shrugging, "we could try the letter, but I don't think it would do any good. He has the status of a guest in your home; just tell him to go."

My grandmother was showing signs of exasperation. "But he *doesn't* go. That's the point. I've told him and told him. But he *won't*."

"Mrs. Bradley," said the lawyer emphatically, "Edith, as a friend, don't waste your time. The police."

"I'm through wasting my time," she said.

---

10. **probity** Integrity.

Pulling away from the lawyer's office, my grandmother began a spirited conversation with herself. A wisp of hair had escaped from under her hat, and the dye winked a metallic red light as it jiggled up and down in the hot sunshine.

"I've told him and told him. But he won't listen. The goddamn freak thinks we're involved in a christly debating society. He thinks I don't mean business. But I mean business. I do. There's more than one way to skin a cat or scratch a dog's ass. We'll take the wheels off his little red wagon and see how she pulls."

"What about my comic book?" I said, as we drove past the Rexall.

"Shut up."

Grandma drove the De Soto to the edge of town and stopped it at the Ogdens' place. It was a service station, or rather had been until the B.A. company had taken out their pumps and yanked the franchise, or whatever you call it, on the two brothers. Since then everything had gone steadily downhill. Cracks in the windowpanes had been taped with masking tape, and the roof had been patched with flattened tin cans and old licence plates. The building itself was surrounded by an acre of wrecks, sulking hulks rotten with rust, the guts of their upholstery spilled and gnawed by rats and mice.

But the Ogden brothers still carried on a business after a fashion. They stripped their wrecks for parts and were reputed to be decent enough mechanics whenever they were sober enough to turn a wrench or thread a bolt. People brought work to them whenever they couldn't avoid it, and the rest of the year gave them a wide berth.

The Ogdens were famous for two things: their meanness and their profligacy as breeders. The place was always aswarm with kids who never seemed to wear pants except in the most severe weather, and tottered about the premises, their legs smeared with grease, shit, or various combinations of both.

"Wait here," my grandmother said, slamming the car door loudly enough to bring the two brothers out of their shop. Through the open door I saw a motor suspended on an intricate system of chains and pulleys.

The Ogdens stood with their hands in the pockets of their bib overalls while my grandmother talked to them. They were quite a sight. They didn't have a dozen teeth in their heads between them, even though the oldest brother couldn't have been more than forty. They just stood there, one sucking on a cigarette, the other on a Coke. Neither one moved or changed his expression, except once, when a tow-headed youngster piddled too close to Grandma. He was lazily and casually slapped on the side of the head by the nearest brother and ran away screaming, his stream cavorting wildly in front of him.

At last, their business concluded, the boys walked my grandmother back to the car.

"You'll get to that soon?" she said, sliding behind the wheel.

"Tomorrow all right?" said one. His words sounded all slack and chewed, issuing from his shrunken, old man's mouth.

"The sooner the better. I want that seen to, Bert."

"What seen to?" I asked.

"Bert and his brother Elwood are going to fix that rattle that's been plaguing me."

"Sure thing," said Elwood. "Nothing but clear sailing."

"What rattle?" I said.

"What rattle? What rattle? The one in the glove compartment," she said, banging it with the heel of her hand. "That rattle. You hear it?"

Thompson could get very edgy some days. "I should be working on my dissertation," he said, coiled in the big chair. "I shouldn't be wasting my time in this shit-hole. I should be working!"

"So why aren't you?" said Evelyn. She was spool knitting. That and reading movie magazines were the only things she ever did.

"How the christ do I work without a library? You see a goddamn library within a hundred miles of this place?"

"Why do you need a library?" she said calmly. "Can't you write?"

"Write," he said, looking at the ceiling. "Write, she says. What the hell do you know about it? What the hell do *you* know about it."

"I can't see why you can't write."

"Before you write, you research. That's what you do, you *research*."

"So bite my head off. It wasn't my idea to come here."

"It wasn't me that lost my goddamn job. How the hell were we supposed to pay the rent?"

"You could have got a job."

"I'm a student. Anyway, I told you, if I get a job my wife gets her hooks into me for support. I'll starve to death before I support that bitch."

"We could go back."

"How many times does it have to be explained to you? I don't get my scholarship cheque until the first of September. We happen to be broke. Absolutely. In fact, you're going to have to hit the old lady up for gas and eating money to get back to the coast. We're stuck here. Get that into your empty fucking head. The Lord Buddha might have been able to subsist on a single bean a day; I can't."

My grandmother came into the room. The conversation stopped.

"Do you think," she said to Thompson, "I could ask you to do me a favour?"

"Why, Mrs. Bradley," he said, smiling, "whatever do you mean?"

"I was wondering whether you could take my car into town to Ogdens' to get it fixed."

"Oh," said Thompson, "I don't know where it is. I don't think I'm your man."

"Ask anyone where it is. They can tell you. It isn't hard to find."

"Why would you ask me to do you a favour, Mrs. Bradley?" inquired Thompson complacently. Hearing his voice was like listening to someone drag their nails down a blackboard.

"Well, you can be goddamn sure I wouldn't," said Grandma, trying to keep a hold on herself, "except that I'm right in the middle of doing my pickling and canning. I thought you might be willing to move your lazy carcass to do something around here. Every time I turn around I seem to be falling over those legs of yours." She looked at the limbs in question as if she would like to dock them somewhere in the vicinity of the knee.

"No, I don't think I can," said Thompson easily, stroking his goat beard.

"And why the hell can't you?"

"Oh, let's just say I don't trust you, Mrs. Bradley. I don't like to leave you alone with Evelyn. Lord knows what ideas you might put in her head."

"Or take out."

"That's right. Or take out," said Thompson with satisfaction. "You can't imagine the trouble it took me to get them in there." He turned to Evelyn. "She can't imagine the trouble, can she, dear?"

Evelyn threw her spool knitting on the floor and walked out of the room.

"Evelyn's mad and I'm glad," shouted Thompson at her back. "And I know how to tease her!"

"Charlie, come here," said Grandma. I went over to her. She took me firmly by the shoulder. "From now on," said my grandma, "my family is off limits to you. I don't want to see you talking to Charlie here, or to come within sniffing distance of Evelyn."

"What do you think of that idea, Charlie?" said Thompson. "Are you still my friend or what?"

I gave him a wink my grandma couldn't see. He thought that was great; he laughed like a madman. "Superb," he said. "Superb. There's no flies on Charlie. What a diplomat."

"What the hell is the matter with you, Mr. Beatnik?" asked Grandma, annoyed beyond bearing. "What's so goddamn funny?"

"Ha ha!" roared Thompson. "What a charming notion! Me a beatnik!"

Grandma Bradley held the mouthpiece of the phone very close to her lips as she spoke into it. "No, it can't be brought in. You'll have to come out here to do the job."

She listened with an intent expression on her face. Spotting me pretending to look in the fridge, she waved me out of the kitchen with her hand. I dragged myself out and stood quietly in the hallway.

"This is a party line," she said, "remember that."

Another pause while she listened.

"Okay," she said and hung up.

I spent some of my happiest hours squatting in the corn patch. I was completely hidden there; even when I stood, the maturing stalks reached a foot or more above my head. It was a good place. On the hottest days it was relatively cool in that thicket of green where the shade was dark and deep and the leaves rustled and scraped and sawed dryly overhead.

Nobody ever thought to look for me there. They could bellow their bloody lungs out for me and I could just sit and watch them getting uglier and uglier about it all. There was some satisfaction in that. I'd just reach up and pluck myself a cob. I loved raw corn. The newly formed kernels were tiny, pale pearls of sweetness that gushed juice. I'd munch and munch and smile and smile and think, why don't you drop dead?

It was my secret place, my sanctuary, where I couldn't be found or touched by them. But all the same, if I didn't let them intrude on me — that didn't mean I didn't want to keep tabs on things.

At the time I was watching Thompson stealing peas at the other end of the garden. He was like some primitive man who lived in a gathering culture. My grandma kept him so hungry he was constantly prowling for food: digging in cupboards, rifling the refrigerator, scrounging in the garden.

Clad only in Bermuda shorts he was a sorry sight. His bones threatened to rupture his skin and jut out every which way. He sported a scrub-board chest with two old pennies for nipples, and a wispy garland of hair decorated his sunken breastbone. His legs looked particularly rackety; all gristle, knobs and sinew.

We both heard the truck at the same time. It came bucking up the approach, spurting gravel behind it. Thompson turned around, shaded his eyes and peered at it. He wasn't much interested. He couldn't get very curious about the natives.

The truck stopped and a man stepped out on to the runningboard of the '51 IHC. He gazed around him, obviously looking for something or someone. This character had a blue handkerchief sprinkled with white polka dots tied in a triangle over his face. Exactly like an outlaw in an Audie Murphy western. A genuine goddamn Jesse James.

He soon spotted Thompson standing half-naked in the garden, staring stupidly at this strange sight, his mouth bulging with peas. The outlaw ducked his head back into the cab of the truck, said something to the driver, and pointed. The driver then stepped out on to his runningboard and, standing on tippy-toe, peered over the roof of the cab at Thompson. He too wore a handkerchief tied over his mug, but his was red.

Then they both got down from the truck and began to walk very quickly towards Thompson with long, menacing strides.

"Fellows?" said Thompson.

At the sound of his voice the two men broke into a stiff-legged trot, and the one with the red handkerchief, while still moving, stooped down smoothly and snatched up the hoe that lay at the edge of the garden.

"What the hell is going on here, boys?" said Thompson, his voice pitched high with concern.

The man with the blue mask reached Thompson first. One long arm, a dirty clutch of fingers on its end, snaked out and caught him by the hair and jerked his head down. Then he kicked him in the pit of the stomach with his work boots.

"Okay, fucker," he shouted, "too fucking smart to take a fucking hint?" and he punched him on the side of the face with several short, snapping blows that actually tore Thompson's head out of his grip. Thompson toppled over clumsily and fell in the dirt. "Get fucking lost," Blue Mask said more quietly.

"Evelyn!" yelled Thompson to the house. "Jesus Christ, Evelyn!"

I crouched lower in the corn patch and began to tremble. I was certain they were going to kill him.

"Shut up," said the man with the hoe. He glanced at the blade for a second, considered, then rotated the handle in his hands and hit Thompson a quick chop on the head with the blunt side. "Shut your fucking yap," he repeated.

"Evelyn! Evelyn! Oh God!" hollered Thompson, "I'm being murdered! For God's sake, somebody help me!" The side of his face was slick with blood.

"I told you shut up, cock sucker," said Red Mask, and kicked him in the ribs several times. Thompson groaned and hugged himself in the dust.

"Now you get lost, fucker," said the one with the hoe, "because if you don't stop bothering nice people we'll drive a spike in your skull."

"Somebody help me!" Thompson yelled at the house.

"Nobody there is going to help you," Blue Mask said. "You're all on your own, smart arse."

"You bastards," said Thompson, and spat ineffectually in their direction.

For his defiance he got struck a couple of chopping blows with the hoe. The last one skittered off his collar-bone with a sickening crunch.

"That's enough," said Red Mask, catching the handle of the hoe. "Come on."

The two sauntered back towards the truck, laughing. They weren't in any hurry to get out of there. Thompson lay on his side staring at their retreating backs. His face was wet with tears and blood.

The man with the red mask looked back over his shoulder and wiggled his ass at Thompson in an implausible imitation of effeminacy: "Was it worth it, tiger?" he shouted. "Getting your ashes hauled don't come cheap, do it?"

This set them off again. Passing me they pulled off their masks and stuffed them in their pockets. They didn't have to worry about Thompson when they had their backs to him; he couldn't see their faces. But I could. No surprise. They were the Ogden boys.

When the truck pulled out of the yard, its gears grinding, I burst out of my hiding place and ran to Thompson, who had got to his knees and was trying to stop the flow of blood from his scalp with his fingers. He was crying. Another first for Thompson. He was the first man I'd seen cry. It made me uncomfortable.

"The sons of bitches broke my ribs," he said, panting with shallow breaths. "God, I hope they didn't puncture a lung."

"Can you walk?" I asked.

"Don't think I don't know who's behind this," he said, getting carefully to his feet. His face was white. "You saw them," he said. "You saw their faces from the corn patch. We got the bastards."

He leaned a little on me as we made our way to the house. The front door was locked. We knocked. No answer. "Let me in, you old bitch!" shouted Thompson.

"Evelyn, open the goddamn door!" Silence. I couldn't hear a thing move in the house. It was as if they were all dead in there. It frightened me.

He started to kick the door. A panel splintered. "Open this door! Let me in, you old slut, or I'll kill you!"

Nothing.

"You better go," I said nervously. I didn't like this one little bit. "Those guys might come back and kill you."

"Evelyn!" he bellowed. "Evelyn!"

He kept it up for a good five minutes, alternately hammering and kicking the door, pleading with and threatening the occupants. By the end of that time he was sweating with exertion and pain. He went slowly down the steps, sobbing, beaten. "You saw them," he said, "we have the bastards dead to rights."

He winced when he eased his bare flesh onto the hot seat-covers of the car.

"I'll be back," he said, starting the motor of the car. "This isn't the end of this."

When Grandma was sure he had gone, the front door was unlocked and I was let in. I noticed my grandmother's hands trembled a touch when she lit her cigarette.

"You can't stay away from him, can you?" she said testily.

"You didn't have to do that," I said. "He was hurt. You ought to have let him in."

"I ought to have poisoned him a week ago. And don't talk about things you don't know anything about."

"Sometimes," I said, "all of you get on my nerves."

"Kids don't have nerves. Adults have nerves. They're the only ones entitled to them. And don't think I care a plugged nickel what does, or doesn't, get on your nerves."

"Where's Aunt Evelyn?"

"Your Aunt Evelyn is taken care of," she replied.

"Why wouldn't she come to the door?"

"She had her own road to Damascus.[11] She has seen the light. Everything has been straightened out," she said. "Everything is back to normal."

---

11. **road to Damascus** In the Bible, Saul of Tarsus travels to Damascus to kill the Christians living there. He converts to Christianity and becomes Paul, the apostle, when he sees a bright light and hears the voice of Christ.

He looked foolish in the back of the police car later that evening. When the sun began to dip, the temperature dropped rapidly, and he was obviously cold dressed only in his Bermuda shorts. Thompson sat all hunched up to relieve the strain on his ribs, his hands pressed between his knees, shivering.

My grandmother and the constable spoke quietly by the car for some time; occasionally Thompson poked his head out the car window and said something. By the look on the constable's face when he spoke to Thompson, it was obvious he didn't care for him too much. Thompson had that kind of effect on people. Several times during the course of the discussion the constable glanced my way.

I edged a little closer so I could hear what they were saying.

"He's mad as a hatter," said my grandmother. "I don't know anything about any two men. If you ask me, all this had something to do with drugs. My daughter says that this man takes drugs. He's some kind of beatnik."

"Christ," said Thompson, drawing his knees up as if to scrunch himself into a smaller, less noticeable package, "the woman is insane."

"One thing at a time, Mrs. Bradley," said the RCMP constable.

"My daughter is finished with him," she said. "He beats her, you know. I want him kept off my property."

"I want to speak to Evelyn," Thompson said. He looked bedraggled and frightened. "Evelyn and I will leave this minute if this woman wants. But I've got to talk to Evelyn."

"My daughter doesn't want to see you, mister. She's finished with you," said Grandma Bradley, shifting her weight from side to side. She turned her attention to the constable. "He beats her," she said, "bruises all over her. Can you imagine?"

"The boy knows," said Thompson desperately. "He saw them. How many times do I have to tell you?" He piped his voice to me, "Didn't you, Charlie? You saw them, didn't you?"

"Charlie?" said my grandmother. This was news to her.

I stood very still.

"Come here, son," said the constable.

I walked slowly over to them.

"Did you see the faces of the men?" the constable asked, putting a hand on my shoulder. "Do you know the men? Are they from around here?"

"How would he know?" said my grandmother. "He's a stranger."

"He knows them. At least he saw them," said Thompson. "My little Padmasambhava never misses a trick," he said, trying to jolly me. "You see everything, don't you, Charlie? You remember everything, don't you?"

I looked at my grandmother, who stood so calmly and commandingly, waiting.

"Hey, don't look to her for the answers," said Thompson nervously. "Don't be afraid of her. You remember everything, don't you?"

He had no business begging me. I had watched their game from the sidelines long enough to know the rules. At one time he had imagined himself a winner. And now he was asking me to save him, to take a risk, when I was more completely in her clutches than he would ever be. He forgot I was a child. I depended on her.

Thompson, I saw, was powerless. He couldn't protect me. God, I remembered more than he dreamed. I remembered how his lips had moved soundlessly, his face pleading with the ceiling, his face blighted of everything but abject urgency. Praying to a simpering, cross-eyed idol. His arm flashing as he struck my aunt's bare legs. Crawling in the dirt, covered with blood.

He had taught me that "Those who are in the grip of desire, the grip of existence, the grip of ignorance, move helplessly round through the spheres of life, as men or gods or as wretches in the lower regions." Well, he was helpless now. But he insisted on fighting back and hurting the rest of us. The weak ones like Evelyn and me.

I thought of Stanley the rooster and how it had felt when the tendons separated, the gristle parted and the bones crunched under my twisting hands.

"I don't know what he's talking about," I said to the constable softly. "I didn't see anybody."

"Clear out," said my grandmother triumphantly. "Beat it."

"You dirty little son of a bitch," he said to me. "You mean little bugger."

He didn't understand much. He had forced me into the game, and now that I was a player and no longer a watcher, he didn't like it. The thing was that I was good at the game. But he, being a loser, couldn't appreciate that.

Then suddenly he said, "Evelyn." He pointed to the upstairs window of the house and tried to get out of the back seat of the police car. But of course he couldn't. They take the handles off the back doors. Nobody can get out unless they are let out.

"Goddamn it!" he shouted. "Let me out! She's waving to me! She wants me!"

I admit that the figure was hard to make out at that distance. But any damn fool could see she was only waving goodbye.

(1982)

Di Brandt (1952–)

Born Diana Janzen, poet Di Brandt left the Mennonite community of Reinland, Manitoba, at the age of 17. The Janzens were strict observers of the Mennonite creed. Although Brandt read widely as a child, the only book allowed in her house was the Bible. Her first book of poetry, entitled *questions i asked my mother* and published in 1987, broke what she calls "centuries old taboos against self-expression and art-making and public speech." The book was startling in its depiction of Mennonite disciplinary methods and her father's dismissive attitude towards women. As a child, Brandt resisted what she calls the "sixteenth century" ways of her Mennonite community and sought the freedom of the twentieth century. She has said that she "spent so much time writing, fighting, against my Mennonite inheritance and the restrictions it puts on women and its internal contradictions." But at the same time, she credits her upbringing with instilling in her a profound sense of the natural world: "The Mennonites had a great sense of responsibility to the land, of living close to the rhythm of the seasons and trying to live simply and plainly on the land so you can have an intimate relationship with it."

When Brandt first arrived in Winnipeg, at age 17, she suffered acute culture shock. She encountered feminists, activists, environmentalists, and postmodernists, and she experienced deep anxiety about the modern world. "I remember thinking at one point," she writes, "so this is what it feels like to be in the late-twentieth century that I have worked so hard to get to: how awful! *I want to go back.*" Brandt began to explore experimental forms of writing as a result of her association with the group of writers involved in *Tessera*, a feminist journal and collective dedicated to fostering new modes of writing creative and critical texts. Through her *Tessera* connection, she discovered that "feminism was no longer an idea but a group of women talking, working together. It was like a dream, the beginning of feeling connected to other writers, women, becoming part of a women's community." Thanks in part to this support group, Brandt was finally able to publish her first two books of poetry — *questions I asked my mother* (1987) and *Agnes in the Sky* (1990). The former contains a series of poems in which a Mennonite woman interrogates her past and present and recalls her liberation from an oppressive, patriarchal order. This liberation is enacted in the experimental form of the book itself, which blends multiple influences into a stream-of-consciousness challenge to orthodoxy. *Agnes in the Sky* addresses similar issues, but adopts a more removed stance.

The poet married artist Les Brandt in 1971, and she had her first child in 1975, while working on her M.A. in Romantic and Renaissance literature at the University of Toronto. Her second child was born four years later, and she and her husband divorced in 1989. Motherhood had a profound impact on Brandt: her personal experiences prompted her to work towards a Ph.D. at the University of Manitoba, and her thesis topic was maternal narratives in Canadian writing. The doctoral thesis was published as *Wild Mother Dancing* in 1993. In 2005, she co-edited with Barbara Godard *Re:Generations: Canadian Women Poets in Conversation*, a collection of critical essays and poems that includes a "dialogue" between Brandt and one of her literary foremothers, Dorothy Livesay, in the form of a poem called "Awakenings: In Two Voices." Brandt's interest in maternal narratives also inspired the poems in *mother, not mother* (1992).

In *Jerusalem, Beloved* (1995) — which, like *questions I asked my mother*, was nominated for a Governor General's Award — Brandt begins to connect her sense of the oppression of women with her sense of the land. The book consists of Brandt's recollections of a journey to the holy city to visit a friend and to witness first hand the repercussions of the Israeli-Palestinian conflict. It is a book about reconciling the past and the present, the imagined and the real.

Brandt's interest in feminist politics and her deep respect for the natural world combine powerfully in *Now You Care* (2003), a book about looming environmental catastrophe. Her preoccupation with the environment was heightened by her experience of living in Windsor, Ontario — she held a teaching position at the University of Windsor from 1997 to 2005. Brandt found herself inhabiting a city whose drive towards industrial development showed a deep disregard for the land.

Brandt continues exploring new ways of expressing her roles as woman, mother, environmentalist, and teacher. In 2004, she co-produced a CD of Canadian women's poetry called *Planet Earth*, and she has taught English and creative writing at the University of Windsor, the University of Winnipeg, and Brandon University, where she holds a Canada Research Chair.

but what do you think my father says

but what do you think my father says this verse means if it's not
about the end of the world look that's obviously a misreading i say
the verb grammatically speaking doesn't have an object in this
instance so it can't possibly be made to that's exactly what i mean
he says waving the book in mid air if my father ever shouted he
would be shouting now you don't really care about the meaning all
you ever think about is grammar & fancy words i never even heard of
where i come from the reason you learn to read is to understand God's
Holy Word i only went to school 7 year & it's done me okay what are
10   you going to do with all this hifalutin education anyway don't you
think it's time you got a job & did some honest work for a change

the meaning i say through clenched teeth is related to the structure
of the sentence for godsake anybody can see that you can't just take
some old crackpot idea & say you found it in these words even the
Bible has to make some sense the Bible my father says the veins in
his neck turning a slow purple is revealed to those gathered together
in His name you don't even go to church how can you know anything of
the truth you're no better than the heathen on the street the way
you live around here if i'd aknown my own daughter would end up like
this you're the one i say who started this conversation what did you   20
ask me for if i'm not entitled to an opinion please my mother says
crying as usual why don't we go for a walk or something you think
i'll weep i'll not weep we glare at each other with bright fierce
eyes my father & i she still tries after all these years to end this
argument between us arrest deflect its bitter motion does she know
this is all there is for us these words dancing painfully across the
sharp etched lines of his God ridden book & does she does he do we
really want this crazy cakewalk to stop

(1987)

missionary position (1)

let me tell you what it's like
having God for father & jesus
for a lover on this old mother
earth you who no longer know
the old story the part about the
Virgin being of course a myth
made up by Catholics for an easy
way out it's not that easy i can
tell you right off the old man
in his room demands bloody hard   10
work he with his rod & his hard
crooked staff well jesus he's
different he's a good enough lay
it's just that he prefers miracles
to fishing & sometimes i get tired
waiting all day for his bit of
magic though late at night i burn
with his fire & the old mother
shudders & quakes under us when
God's not looking   20

(1987)

poem for a guy who's thought about feminism

poem for a guy who's
thought about feminism

& is troubled by it,
but not enough:

what you don't want
to know can hurt you,

& will, perhaps even
kill you, as it has killed

so many others, women,
10   whales, birds, Indians,

Jews, even the golden-
haired sons of men,

the privileged ones,
the chosen.

why do we hide grief
from ourselves,

& each other, pretending
pleasure? i cry

because we must greet
20   each other from now on

with lies or terror,
our lying together

through the years
has brought us

to such an impasse,
such a possible ending,

i fear we must,
all of us,

everything in us,
30   fly apart.

i feel a heaviness in me
tonight, the earth's

weight pulling me,
down. i want to love

you, under these dripping
trees, these great

scented blossoms,
but i can't.

enchanted evening,
you would have liked

to whisper in my ear,
in another language,

another story, your
heart in your throat.

the poem is bigger
than i am. the poem

is hungry, & insists
on its own truth.

the desire in every
thing, fierce

breeding among the trees.
i love you, i love you.

i cannot lie, i cannot lie
with you tonight,

there's holocaust
between us,

& i'm tired of dying.

40

50

(1992)

how long does it take to forget a murder

how long does it take to forget a murder in your
house, behind a closed door, without a sound, no
words said, the hanging in a field your great
grandmother watched as a little girl, her face pushed
against her father's sleeve, a heretic slow burning at
the end of August in the town square? how long
does the body remember the bullet, where it graced
the flesh, the cells burned, blue black, where it
entered skin, nerve endings charred, trembling?
how long does it take to forget a gas chamber filled

10

with naked, terrified, bearded men, the roomful
of women, the accused, sentenced to burning, a
soldier's rifle under the chin, cocked, the soldier's
hand, shaking, full of hatred, shame, rage?

this black ball we carry around inside us, this
darkness, this red flaming sea, how it comes back
to us, this violence, to haunt us, a ghost, the devil, the
enemy, how it yearns, like tree roots, to take hold, to
flower in us, like branches & leaves:

20   the body's humiliation, trembling, how it stays in
the air, long after the body is gone, dismembered, the
spirit seeking revenge — or is it comforting it wants,
remembering, shaking, grieving, so we will not do it
again, to someone else, the way it was done to us, so
that the flowering can be trembling, beautiful, wise,
as newborn children are, instead of wrath?

                                                        (1995)

Here at the heart of the ravaged heart

Here at the heart of the ravaged heart
of the Dead Land, lilacs mixing with
the dead rain, we like to kill our gods
and eat them too, like all good christians
do, no mystery moths or beetles for us,
or locusts shining in the grass, nosiree,
all our trillion little winged deities, bees,
mosquitoes, houseflies, butterflies,
fruitflies, fishflies, horseflies, Junebugs,
10   cicadas now in radical chemical jeopardy,
and our lettuce and raspberries, and yet,
and yet, deer graze in the forest along
the ravine, grasshoppers and crickets
miraculously sing in forgotten ditches
along the fields, wasps stray through
chlorpyrifos[1] clouds to out of the way
sweet milkweed, thistle, goldenrod
clumps, just then for a moment, above
around below the shadow of the shadow
20   of these endless depleted uranium driven
grey grey grey grey grey apocalyptic
streets, these lurking cancer cells, hawks
and goldfinches, bright coloured, let's
turn it all around, asphalt splitting

---

1. **chlorpyrifos** An insecticide.

volcanic magic, blue butterflies, sweet
grass, adrenalin, circling darting
fluttering kicking bursting in

(2003)

Zone: <le Détroit>

after Stan Douglas

1

Breathing yellow air
here, at the heart of the dream
of the new world,
the bones of old horses and dead Indians
and lush virgin land, dripping with fruit
and the promise of wheat,
overlaid with glass and steel
and the dream of speed:
all these our bodies
crushed to appease   10
the 400 & 1 gods
of the Superhighway,
NAFTA,[1] we worship you,
hallowed be your name,
here, where we are scattered
like dust or rain in ditches,
the ghosts of passenger pigeons
clouding the silver towered sky,
the future clogged in the arteries
of the potholed city,   20
Tecumseh,[2] come back to us
from your green grave,
sing us your song of bravery
on the lit bridge over the black river,
splayed with grief over the loss
of its ancient rainbow coloured
fish swollen joy.
Who shall be fisher king[3]
over this poisoned country,
whose borders have become   30
a mockery,
blowing the world to bits
with cars and cars and trucks and electricity and cars,
who will cover our splintered

---

1. NAFTA North American Free Trade Agreement, limiting or eliminating taxes on trade between Canada, the United States, and Mexico. **2. Tecumseh** Native American (1768–1813) who attempted to unite the native tribes to defend their land collectively. **3. fisher king** Guardian of the holy grail in Arthurian legend; emblematic of Christ.

bones with earth and blood,
who will sing us back into —

2

See how there's no one going to Windsor,
only everyone coming from?
Maybe they've been evacuated,
40   maybe there's nuclear war,
maybe when we get there we'll be the only ones.
See all those trucks coming toward us,
why else would there be rush hour on the 401
on a Thursday at nine o'clock in the evening?
I counted 200 trucks and 300 cars
and that's just since London.
See that strange light in the sky over Detroit,
see how dark it is over Windsor?
You know how people keep disappearing,
50   you know all those babies born with deformities,
you know how organ thieves follow tourists
on the highway and grab them at night
on the motel turnoffs,
you know they're staging those big highway accidents
to increase the number of organ donors?
My brother knew one of the guys paid to do it,
$100,000 for twenty bodies
but only if the livers are good.
See that car that's been following us for the last hour,
60   see the pink glow of its headlights in the mirror?
That's how you know.
Maybe we should turn around,
maybe we should duck so they can't see us,
maybe it's too late,
maybe we're already dead,
maybe the war is over,
maybe we're the only ones alive.

3

So there I am, sniffing around
the railroad tracks
70   in my usual quest for a bit of wildness,
weeds, something untinkered with,
goldenrod, purple aster, burdocks,
defiant against creosote,[4]
my prairie blood surging

---

4. **creosote** Liquid distilled from tar, used as a preservative.

in recognition and fellow feeling,
and o god, missing my dog,
and hey, what do you know,
there's treasure here
among these forgotten weeds,
so this is where they hang out,   80
all those women's breasts
cut off to keep our lawns green
and dandelion free,
here they are, dancing
their breastly ghost dance,
stirring up a slight wind in fact
and behaving for all the world
like dandelions in seed,
their featherwinged purple nipples
oozing sticky milk,   90
so what am I supposed to do,
pretend I haven't seen them,
or like I don't care
about all these missing breasts,
how they just vanish
from our aching chests
and no one says a word,
and we just strap on fake ones
and the dandelions keep dying,
and the grass on our lawns   100
gets greener and greener
and greener

4

This gold and red autumn heat,
this glorious tree splendour,
splayed out for sheer pleasure
over asphalt and concrete,
ribbons of dark desire
driving us madly toward death,
perverse, presiding over
five o'clock traffic
like the queens on Church Street   110
grand in their carstopping
high heels and blond wigs
and blue makeup, darling,
so nice to see you, and what,
dear one, exactly was the rush?
Or oceans, vast beyond ridicule
or question, and who cares if it's
much too hot for November,

120   isn't it gorgeous, darling,
and even here, in this
most polluted spit of land
in Canada, with its heart
attack and cancer rates,
the trees can still knock
you out with their loveliness
so you just wanna drop
everything and weep, or laugh,
or gather up the gorgeous
130   leaves, falling, and throw yourself
into them like a dead man,
or a kid, or a dog,

5

O the brave deeds of men
M*E*N, that is, they with phalli
dangling from their thighs,
how they dazzle me with
their daring exploits
every time I cross the Detroit River
from down under, I mean,
140   who else could have given
themselves so grandly,
obediently, to this water god,
this fierce charlatan,[5]
this glutton for sailors and young boys,
risking limbs and lives, wordlessly
wrestling primordial mud,
so that we, mothers and maids,
could go shopping across the border
and save ourselves twenty minutes
150   coming and going, chatting about
this and that, our feet never
leaving the car, never mind
the mouth of the tunnel
is haunted by bits and fragments
of shattered bone and looking
every time like Diana's bridge
in Paris,[6] this is really grand, isn't it,
riding our cars under the river
and coming out the other side
160   illegal aliens, needing passports,
and feeling like we accomplished

---

5. **charlatan** Fake expert; quack. 6. **Diana's ... Paris** Princess Diana of Wales (1961–1997) was killed in a car accident under a bridge in Paris.

something, snatched from
our busy lives, just being there

(2003)

Rohinton Mistry (1952–)

The award-winning Indo-Canadian writer Rohinton Mistry was born in Mumbai (then Bombay) in 1952. In 1974, he was awarded a degree in mathematics from the University of Bombay, and the following year, he and his wife immigrated to Canada. They settled in Toronto, where Mistry found work in a bank and enrolled in part-time English and philosophy studies at the University of Toronto; he received his second degree in 1984. During his student years, he used what little spare time he had to write short fiction. The first two stories that Mistry published won the Hart House Literary Prize (1983 and 1984), and a third story garnered a *Canadian Fiction Magazine* prize (1985). This trio of stories, along with eight others, became his first book, *Tales from Firoszha Baag*, which was published in 1987.

Although he had lived in Canada for a number of years before beginning to craft his fiction, Mistry set all of his tales in the city of his birth. He explains, "I was born and brought up in India, my imagination is still engaged with it." *Tales from Firozsha Baag* takes place in a *baag* — an exclusively Parsi apartment block, like the one in which Mistry, a Parsi, grew up. The Parsis are the descendants of Zoroastrian Persians who fled to India in the 7th and 8th centuries to avoid Muslim persecution. Now a small and rapidly diminishing minority in India, they fear for their community and struggle to keep their families intact. As the inhabitants of the *baag* engage in this struggle, they reinforce their isolation from the outside world. *Tales from Firozsha Baag* is a series of interconnected stories, both comic and poignant, chronicling the lives of the apartment block residents as they attempt to reconcile the tensions between the old world and the new in post-colonial India. In "Squatter," children listen as a storyteller recounts the tale of Sarosh, a man who went to live in Canada but who finally returned to India because he found that he could not use a Western toilet; his inability to adapt humiliated him profoundly. In "Swimming Lessons," the book's final story, the young narrator, who has immigrated to Canada, sends his family a copy of the book he has written: *Tales from Firozsha Baag*. Since all the tales are set in India, his parents worry that he is so severely afflicted with homesickness that he has failed to adapt to his new life abroad. These stories express Mistry's concern with cultural alienation, his ability to render characters with realism and depth, his attention to the distinctions between social classes, and his fascination with the ways in which religious and political beliefs shape individual destiny.

Mistry's first novel, *Such a Long Journey* (1991), met with international success. It won a Governor General's Award and a Commonwealth Writer's Award, was shortlisted for a Man Booker Prize, and was made into a film in 2000. Set in 1971 during the India-Pakistan war, it focuses on Gustad Noble, his family, and friends. The good-hearted Noble falls victim to the machinations of a corrupt and incompetent society, becoming embroiled in a banking scandal, and the reader watches his personal life unravel against the backdrop of the broad political events transforming Indira Gandhi's India.

A few years later, in 1995, Mistry published *A Fine Balance,* and it was awarded the Giller Prize. It is set in the mid-1970s. The "prime minister" (the unnamed Indira Ghandi) has declared a state of emergency, bestowing upon her government sweeping powers to infringe on civil liberties; Mistry portrays the horrific impact this has on individual lives, and especially on the destitute. The novel is structured around the stories of four characters — a widowed seamstress, a university student who pines for his idyllic hill-station home, and a pair of "untouchable" tailors escaping the caste violence of their village — whom circumstances compel to share a cramped apartment in a city by the sea. The four feel their way towards a new understanding of family as their country self-destructs — socially, politically, and economically. Mistry ultimately shows that the survival of both the individual and the country depends upon maintaining "a fine balance between hope and despair." *Family Matters* (2002) garnered Mistry another Booker Prize nomination. In it, the life of a Parsi family serves as a microcosm for the nation — India, in turmoil, in the 1990s. Nariman Vakeel, an elderly Bombay widower suffering from Parkinson's disease, breaks an ankle and is unable to care for himself. Mistry paints a compassionate portrait of the tremendous stress that this burden exerts on Nariman's extended family.

Mistry's work has often been compared to that of Tolstoy and Dickens, writers whose novels are marked by a broad scope and a preoccupation with the social injustices of their time and place. But he insists that he has not consciously modelled his oeuvre on that of these masters of the novel form. In fact, he says, he is not "particularly drawn to these authors ... if I were to choose my favourites, what I enjoy most, they would probably include some American writers, like Cheever, Saul Bellow, Malamud, and Updike." As these references indicate, Mistry is not an experimental writer; his strength lies in the ability to present the humour and pathos of the human condition with striking realism.

Squatter

Whenever Nariman Hansotia returned in the evening from the Cawasji Framji Memorial Library in a good mood the signs were plainly evident.

First, he parked his 1932 Mercedes-Benz (he called it the apple of his eye) outside A Block, directly in front of his ground-floor veranda window, and beeped the horn three long times. It annoyed Rustomji who also had a ground-floor flat in A Block. Ever since he had defied Nariman in the matter of painting the exterior of the building, Rustomji was convinced that nothing the old coot did was untainted by the thought of vengeance and harassment, his retirement pastime.

But the beeping was merely Nariman's signal to let Hirabai inside know that though he was back he would not step indoors for a while. Then he raised the hood, whistling "Rose Marie," and leaned his tall frame over the engine. He checked the oil, wiped here and there with a rag, tightened the radiator cap, and lowered the hood. Finally, he polished the Mercedes star and let the whistling modulate into the march from *The Bridge on the River Kwai*. The boys playing in the compound knew that Nariman was ready now to tell a story. They started to gather round.

"*Sahibji,*[1] Nariman Uncle," someone said tentatively and Nariman nodded, careful not to lose his whistle, his bulbous nose flaring slightly. The pursed lips had temporarily raised and reshaped his Clark Gable moustache. More boys walked up. One called out, "How about a story, Nariman Uncle?" at which point Nariman's eyes began to twinkle, and he imparted increased energy to the polishing. The cry was taken up by others, "Yes, yes, Nariman Uncle, a story!" He swung into a final verse of the march. Then the lips relinquished the whistle, the Clark Gable moustache descended. The rag was put away, and he began.

"You boys know the great cricketers: Contractor, Polly Umrigar, and recently, the young chap, Farokh Engineer. Cricket *aficionados*, that's what you all are." Nariman

---

1. *Sahibji* Affectionate term for a superior.

liked to use new words, especially big ones, in the stories he told, believing it was his duty to expose young minds to as shimmering and varied a vocabulary as possible; if they could not spend their days at the Cawasji Framji Memorial Library then he, at least, could carry bits of the library out to them.

The boys nodded; the names of the cricketers were familiar.

"But does any one know about Savukshaw, the greatest of them all?" They shook their heads in unison.

"This, then, is the story about Savukshaw, how he saved the Indian team from a humiliating defeat when they were touring in England." Nariman sat on the steps of A Block. The few diehards who had continued with their games could not resist any longer when they saw the gathering circle, and ran up to listen. They asked their neighbours in whispers what the story was about, and were told: Savukshaw the greatest cricketer. The whispering died down and Nariman began.

"The Indian team was to play the indomitable MCC as part of its tour of England. Contractor was our captain. Now the MCC being the strongest team they had to face, Contractor was almost certain of defeat. To add to Contractor's troubles, one of his star batsmen, Nadkarni, had caught influenza early in the tour, and would definitely not be well enough to play against the MCC. By the way, does anyone know what those letters stand for? You, Kersi, you wanted to be a cricketer once."

Kersi shook his head. None of the boys knew, even though they had heard the MCC mentioned in radio commentaries, because the full name was hardly ever used.

Then Jehangir Bulsara spoke up, or Bulsara Bookworm, as the boys called him. The name given by Pesi *paadmaroo* had stuck even though it was now more than four years since Pesi had been sent away to boarding-school, and over two years since the death of Dr Mody. Jehangir was still unliked by the boys in the Baag, though they had come to accept his aloofness and respect his knowledge and intellect. They were not surprised that he knew the answer to Nariman's question: "Marylebone Cricket Club."

"Absolutely correct," said Nariman, and continued with the story. "The MCC won the toss and elected to bat. They scored four hundred and ninety-seven runs in the first inning before our spinners could get them out. Early in the second day's play our team was dismissed for one hundred and nine runs, and the extra who had taken Nadkarni's place was injured by a vicious bumper that opened a gash on his forehead." Nariman indicated the spot and the length of the gash on his furrowed brow. "Contractor's worst fears were coming true. The MCC waived their own second inning and gave the Indian team a follow-on, wanting to inflict an inning's defeat. And this time he had to use the second extra. The second extra was a certain Savukshaw."

The younger boys listened attentively; some of them, like the two sons of the chartered accountant in B Block, had only recently been deemed old enough by their parents to come out and play in the compound, and had not received any exposure to Nariman's stories. But the others like Jehangir, Kersi, and Viraf were familiar with Nariman's technique.

Once, Jehangir had overheard them discussing Nariman's stories, and he could not help expressing his opinion: that unpredictability was the brush he used to paint his tales with, and ambiguity the palette he mixed his colours in. The others looked at him with admiration. Then Viraf asked what exactly he meant by that. Jehangir said that Nariman sometimes told a funny incident in a very serious way, or expressed a significant matter in a light and playful manner. And these were only two rough divisions, in between were lots of subtle gradations of tone and texture. Which, then, was the funny story and which the serious? Their opinions were divided, but ultimately, said Jehangir, it was up to the listener to decide.

"So," continued Nariman, "Contractor first sent out his two regular openers, convinced that it was all hopeless. But after five wickets were lost for just another thirty-eight runs, out came Savukshaw the extra. Nothing mattered any more."

The street lights outside the compound came on, illuminating the iron gate where the watchman stood. It was a load off the watchman's mind when Nariman told a story. It meant an early end to the hectic vigil during which he had to ensure that none of the children ran out on the main road, or tried to jump over the wall. For although keeping out riff-raff was his duty, keeping in the boys was as important if he wanted to retain the job.

"The first ball Savukshaw faced was wide outside the off stump. He just lifted his bat and ignored it. But with what style! What panache! As if to say, come on, you blighters, play some polished cricket. The next ball was also wide, but not as much as the first. It missed the off stump narrowly. Again Savukshaw lifted his bat, boredom written all over him. Everyone was now watching closely. The bowler was annoyed by Savukshaw's arrogance, and the third delivery was a vicious fast pitch, right down on the middle stump.

"Savukshaw was ready, quick as lightning. No one even saw the stroke of his bat, but the ball went like a bullet towards square leg.

"Fielding at square leg was a giant of a fellow, about six feet seven, weighing two hundred and fifty pounds, a veritable Brobdingnagian, with arms like branches and hands like a pair of huge *sapaat,* the kind that Dr Mody used to wear, you remember what big feet Dr Mody had." Jehangir was the only one who did; he nodded. "Just to see him standing there was scary. Not one ball had got past him, and he had taken some great catches. Savukshaw purposely aimed his shot right at him. But he was as quick as Savukshaw, and stuck out his huge *sapaat* of a hand to stop the ball. What do you think happened then, boys?"

The older boys knew what Nariman wanted to hear at this point. They asked, "What happened, Nariman Uncle, what happened?" Satisfied, Nariman continued.

"A howl is what happened. A howl from the giant fielder, a howl that rang through the entire stadium, that soared like the cry of a banshee right up to the cheapest seats in the furthest, highest corners, a howl that echoed from the scoreboard and into the pavilion, into the kitchen, startling the chap inside who was preparing tea and scones for after the match, who spilled boiling water all over himself and was severely hurt. But not nearly as bad as the giant fielder at square leg. Never at any English stadium was a howl heard like that one, not in the whole history of cricket. And why do you think he was howling, boys?"

The chorus asked, "Why, Nariman Uncle, why?"

"Because of Savukshaw's bullet-like shot, of course. The hand he had reached out to stop it, he now held up for all to see, and *dhur-dhur, dhur-dhur* the blood was gushing like a fountain in an Italian piazza, like a burst water-main from the Vihar-Powai reservoir, dripping onto his shirt and his white pants, and sprinkling the green grass, and only because he was such a giant of a fellow could he suffer so much blood loss and not faint. But even he could not last forever; eventually, he felt dizzy, and was helped off the field. And where do you think the ball was, boys, that Savukshaw had smacked so hard?"

And the chorus rang out again on the now dark steps of A Block: "Where, Nariman Uncle, where?"

"Past the boundary line, of course. Lying near the fence. Rent asunder. Into two perfect leather hemispheres. All the stitches had ripped, and some of the insides had spilled out. So the umpires sent for a new one, and the game resumed. Now none of the fielders dared to touch any ball that Savukshaw hit. Every shot went to the boundary, all the way for four runs. Single-handedly, Savukshaw wiped out the deficit, and had it not been for loss of time due to rain, he would have taken the Indian team to a thumping victory against the MCC. As it was, the match ended in a draw."

Nariman was pleased with the awed faces of the youngest ones around him. Kersi and Viraf were grinning away and whispering something. From one of the flats the smell of frying fish swam out to explore the night air, and tickled Nariman's nostrils. He sniffed appreciatively, aware that it was in his good wife Hirabai's pan that the frying was taking place. This morning, he had seen the pomfret[2] she had purchased at the door, waiting to be cleaned, its mouth open and eyes wide, like the eyes of some of these youngsters. It was time to wind up the story.

"The MCC will not forget the number of new balls they had to produce that day because of Savukshaw's deadly strokes. Their annual ball budget was thrown badly out of balance. Any other bat would have cracked under the strain, but Savukshaw's was seasoned with a special combination of oils, a secret formula given to him by a *sadhu*[3] who had seen him one day playing cricket when he was a small boy. But Savukshaw used to say his real secret was practice, lots of practice, that was the advice he gave to any young lad who wanted to play cricket."

The story was now clearly finished, but none of the boys showed any sign of dispersing. "Tell us about more matches that Savukshaw played in," they said.

"More nothing. This was his greatest match. Anyway, he did not play cricket for long because soon after the match against the MCC he became a champion bicyclist, the fastest human on two wheels. And later, a pole-vaulter — when he glided over on his pole, so graceful, it was like watching a bird in flight. But he gave that up, too, and became a hunter, the mightiest hunter ever known, absolutely fearless, and so skilful, with a gun he could have, from the third floor of A Block, shaved the whisker of a cat in the backyard of C Block."

"Tell us about that," they said, "about Savukshaw the hunter!"

The fat ayah, Jaakaylee, arrived to take the chartered accountant's two children home. But they refused to go without hearing about Savukshaw the hunter. When she scolded them and things became a little hysterical, some other boys tried to resurrect the ghost she had once seen: "Ayah *bhoot*![4] Ayah *bhoot*!" Nariman raised a finger in warning — that subject was still taboo in Firozsha Baag; none of the adults was in a hurry to relive the wild and rampageous days that Pesi *paadmaroo* had ushered in, once upon a time, with the *bhoot* games.

Jaakaylee sat down, unwilling to return without the children, and whispered to Nariman to make it short. The smell of frying fish which had tickled Nariman's nostrils ventured into and awakened his stomach. But the story of Savukshaw the hunter was one he had wanted to tell for a long time.

"Savukshaw always went hunting alone, he preferred it that way. There are many incidents in the life of Savukshaw the hunter, but the one I am telling you about

---

2. **pomfret** Type of fish found off the Indian coast. 3. *sadhu* Good, honest man. 4. *bhoot* Ghost.

involves a terrifying situation. Terrifying for us, of course; Savukshaw was never terrified of anything. What happened was, one night he set up camp, started a fire and warmed up his bowl of chicken-*dhansaak*."

The frying fish had precipitated famishment upon Nariman, and the subject of chicken-*dhansaak* suited him well. His own mouth watering, he elaborated: "Mrs Savukshaw was as famous for her *dhansaak* as Mr was for hunting. She used to put in tamarind and brinjal, coriander and cumin, cloves and cinnamon, and dozens of other spices no one knows about. Women used to come from miles around to stand outside her window while she cooked it, to enjoy the fragrance and try to penetrate her secret, hoping to identify the ingredients as the aroma floated out, layer by layer, growing more complex and delicious. But always, the delectable fragrance enveloped the women and they just surrendered to the ecstasy, forgetting what they had come for. Mrs Savukshaw's secret was safe."

Jaakaylee motioned to Nariman to hurry up, it was past the children's dinner-time. He continued: "The aroma of savoury spices soon filled the night air in the jungle, and when the *dhansaak* was piping hot he started to eat, his rifle beside him. But as soon as he lifted the first morsel to his lips, a tiger's eyes flashed in the bushes! Not twelve feet from him! He emerged licking his chops! What do you think happened then, boys?"

"What, what, Nariman Uncle?"

Before he could tell them, the door of his flat opened. Hirabai put her head out and said, "*Chaalo ni*, Nariman, it's time. Then if it gets cold you won't like it."

That decided the matter. To let Hirabai's fried fish, crisp on the outside, yet tender and juicy inside, marinated in turmeric and cayenne — to let that get cold would be something that *Khoedaiji* above would not easily forgive. "Sorry boys, have to go. Next time about Savukshaw and the tiger."

There were some groans of disappointment. They hoped Nariman's good spirits would extend into the morrow when he returned from the Memorial Library, or the story would get cold.

But a whole week elapsed before Nariman again parked the apple of his eye outside his ground-floor flat and beeped the horn three times. When he had raised the hood, checked the oil, polished the star and swung into the "Colonel Bogie March," the boys began drifting towards A Block.

Some of them recalled the incomplete story of Savukshaw and the tiger, but they knew better than to remind him. It was never wise to prompt Nariman until he had dropped the first hint himself, or things would turn out badly.

Nariman inspected the faces: the two who stood at the back, always looking superior and wise, were missing. So was the quiet Bulsara boy, the intelligent one. "Call Kersi, Viraf, and Jehangir," he said, "I want them to listen to today's story."

Jehangir was sitting alone on the stone steps of C Block. The others were chatting by the compound gate with the watchman. Someone went to fetch them.

"Sorry to disturb your conference, boys, and your meditation, Jehangir," Nariman said facetiously, "but I thought you would like to hear this story. Especially since some of you are planning to go abroad."

This was not strictly accurate, but Kersi and Viraf did talk a lot about America and Canada. Kersi had started writing to universities there since his final high-school year, and had also sent letters of inquiry to the Canadian High Commission in New Delhi and to the U.S. Consulate at Breach Candy. But so far he had not made any progress.

He and Viraf replied with as much sarcasm as their unripe years allowed, "Oh yes, next week, just have to pack our bags."

"Riiiight," drawled Nariman. Although he spoke perfect English, this was the one word with which he allowed himself sometimes to take liberties, indulging in a broadness of vowel more American than anything else. "But before we go on with today's story, what did you learn about Savukshaw, from last week's story?"

"That he was a very talented man," said someone.

"What else?"

"He was also a very lucky man, to have so many talents," said Viraf.

"Yes, but what else?"

There was silence for a few moments. Then Jehangir said, timidly, "He was a man searching for happiness, by trying all kinds of different things."

"Exactly! And he never found it. He kept looking for new experiences, and though he was very successful at everything he attempted, it did not bring him happiness. Remember this, success alone does not bring happiness. Nor does failure have to bring unhappiness. Keep it in mind when you listen to today's story."

A chant started somewhere in the back: "We-want-a-story! We-want-a-story!"

"Riiiight," said Nariman. "Now, everyone remembers Vera and Dolly, daughters of Najamai from C Block." There were whistles and hoots; Viraf nudged Kersi with his elbow, who was smiling wistfully. Nariman held up his hand: "Now now, boys, behave yourselves. Those two girls went abroad for studies many years ago, and never came back. They settled there happily.

"And like them, a fellow called Sarosh also went abroad, to Toronto, but did not find happiness there. This story is about him. You probably don't know him, he does not live in Firozsha Baag, though he is related to someone who does."

"Who? Who?"

"Curiosity killed the cat," said Nariman, running a finger over each branch of his moustache, "and what's important is the tale. So let us continue. This Sarosh began calling himself Sid after living in Toronto for a few months, but in our story he will be Sarosh and nothing but Sarosh, for that is his proper Parsi name. Besides, that was his own stipulation when he entrusted me with the sad but instructive chronicle of his recent life." Nariman polished his glasses with his handkerchief, put them on again, and began.

"At the point where our story commences, Sarosh had been living in Toronto for ten years. We find him depressed and miserable, perched on top of the toilet, crouching on his haunches, feet planted firmly for balance upon the white plastic oval of the toilet seat.

"Daily for a decade had Sarosh suffered this position. Morning after morning, he had no choice but to climb up and simulate the squat of our Indian latrines. If he sat down, no amount of exertion could produce success.

"At first, this inability was no more than mildly incommodious.[5] As time went by, however, the frustrated attempts caused him grave anxiety. And when the failure stretched unbroken over ten years, it began to torment and haunt all his waking hours."

Some of the boys struggled hard to keep straight faces. They suspected that Nariman was not telling just a funny story, because if he intended them to laugh there was always some unmistakable way to let them know. Only the thought of displeasing

---

5. **incommodious** Inconvenient.

Nariman and prematurely terminating the story kept their paroxysms[6] of mirth from bursting forth unchecked.

Nariman continued: "You see, ten years was the time Sarosh had set himself to achieve complete adaptation to the new country. But how could he claim adaptation with any honesty if the acceptable catharsis[7] continually failed to favour him? Obtaining his new citizenship had not helped either. He remained dependent on the old way, and this unalterable fact, strengthened afresh every morning of his life in the new country, suffocated him.

"The ten-year time limit was more an accident than anything else. But it hung over him with the awesome presence and sharpness of a guillotine. Careless words, boys, careless words in a moment of lightheartedness, as is so often the case with us all, had led to it.

"Ten years before, Sarosh had returned triumphantly to Bombay after fulfilling the immigration requirements of the Canadian High Commission in New Delhi. News of his imminent departure spread amongst relatives and friends. A farewell party was organized. In fact, it was given by his relatives in Firozsha Baag. Most of you will be too young to remember it, but it was a very loud party, went on till late in the night. Very lengthy and heated arguments took place, which is not the thing to do at a party. It started like this: Sarosh was told by some what a smart decision he had made, that his whole life would change for the better; others said he was making a mistake, emigration was all wrong, but if he wanted to be unhappy that was his business, they wished him well.

"By and by, after substantial amounts of Scotch and soda and rum and Coke had disappeared, a fierce debate started between the two groups. To this day Sarosh does not know what made him raise his glass and announce: 'My dear family, my dear friends, if I do not become completely Canadian in exactly ten years from the time I land there, then I will come back. I promise. So please, no more arguments. Enjoy the party.' His words were greeted with cheers and shouts of hear! hear! They told him never to fear embarrassment; there was no shame if he decided to return to the country of his birth.

"But shortly, his poor worried mother pulled him aside. She led him to the back room and withdrew her worn and aged prayer book from her purse, saying, 'I want you to place your hand upon the *Avesta* and swear that you will keep that promise.'

"He told her not to be silly, that it was just a joke. But she insisted: '*Kassum khà* — on the *Avesta*. One last thing for your mother. Who knows when you will see me again?' and her voice grew tremulous as it always did when she turned deeply emotional. Sarosh complied, and the prayer book was returned to her purse.

"His mother continued: 'It is better to live in want among your family and your friends, who love you and care for you, than to be unhappy surrounded by vacuum cleaners and dishwashers and big shiny motor cars.' She hugged him. Then they joined the celebration in progress.

"And Sarosh's careless words spoken at the party gradually forged themselves into a commitment as much to himself as to his mother and the others. It stayed with him all his years in the new land, reminding him every morning of what must happen at the end of the tenth, as it reminded him now while he descended from his perch."

Jehangir wished the titters and chortles around him would settle down, he found them annoying. When Nariman structured his sentences so carefully and chose his

---

6. **paroxysms** Sudden outbursts. 7. **catharsis** Cleansing release of tension.

words with extreme care as he was doing now, Jehangir found it most pleasurable to listen. Sometimes, he remembered certain words Nariman had used, or combinations of words, and repeated them to himself, enjoying again the beauty of their sounds when he went for his walks to the Hanging Gardens or was sitting alone on the stone steps of C Block. Mumbling to himself did nothing to mitigate the isolation which the other boys in the Baag had dropped around him like a heavy cloak, but he had grown used to all that by now.

Nariman continued: "In his own apartment Sarosh squatted barefoot. Elsewhere, if he had to go with his shoes on, he would carefully cover the seat with toilet paper before climbing up. He learnt to do this after the first time, when his shoes had left telltale footprints on the seat. He had had to clean it with a wet paper towel. Luckily, no one had seen him.

"But there was not much he could keep secret about his ways. The world of washrooms is private and at the same time very public. The absence of his feet below the stall door, the smell of faeces, the rustle of paper, glimpses caught through the narrow crack between stall door and jamb — all these added up to only one thing: a foreign presence in the stall, not doing things in the conventional way. And if the one outside could receive the fetor of Sarosh's business wafting through the door, poor unhappy Sarosh too could detect something malodorous in the air: the presence of xenophobia[8] and hostility."

What a feast, thought Jehangir, what a feast of words! This would be the finest story Nariman had ever told, he just knew it.

"But Sarosh did not give up trying. Each morning he seated himself to push and grunt, grunt and push, squirming and writhing unavailingly on the white plastic oval. Exhausted, he then hopped up, expert at balancing now, and completed the movement quite effortlessly.

"The long morning hours in the washroom created new difficulties. He was late going to work on several occasions, and one such day, the supervisor called him in: 'Here's your timesheet for this month. You've been late eleven times. What's the problem?'"

Here, Nariman stopped because his neighbour Rustomji's door creaked open. Rustomji peered out, scowling, and muttered: "*Saala* loafers, sitting all evening outside people's houses, making a nuisance, and being encouraged by grownups at that."

He stood there a moment longer, fingering the grey chest hair that was easily accessible through his *sudra*, then went inside. The boys immediately took up a soft and low chant: "Rustomji-the-curmudgeon! Rustomji-the-curmudgeon!"

Nariman held up his hand disapprovingly. But secretly, he was pleased that the name was still popular, the name he had given Rustomji when the latter had refused to pay his share for painting the building. "Quiet, quiet!" said he. "Do you want me to continue or not?"

"Yes, yes!" The chanting died away, and Nariman resumed the story.

"So Sarosh was told by his supervisor that he was coming late to work too often. What could poor Sarosh say?"

"What, Nariman Uncle?" rose the refrain.

"Nothing, of course. The supervisor, noting his silence, continued: 'If it keeps up, the consequences could be serious as far as your career is concerned.'

---

8. **xenophobia** Fear of specific ethnic groups, or more generally, anything foreign.

"Sarosh decided to speak. He said embarrassedly, 'It's a different kind of problem. I . . . I don't know how to explain . . . it's an immigration-related problem.'

"Now this supervisor must have had experience with other immigrants, because right away he told Sarosh, 'No problem. Just contact your Immigrant Aid Society. They should be able to help you. Every ethnic group has one: Vietnamese, Chinese — I'm certain that one exists for Indians. If you need time off to go there, no problem. That can be arranged, no problem. As long as you do something about your lateness, there's no problem.' That's the way they talk over there, nothing is ever a problem.

"So Sarosh thanked him and went to his desk. For the umpteenth time he bitterly rued his oversight. Could fate have plotted it, concealing the western toilet behind that shroud of anxieties which had appeared out of nowhere to beset him just before he left India? After all, he had readied himself meticulously for the new life. Even for the great, merciless Canadian cold he had heard so much about. How could he have overlooked preparation for the western toilet with its matutinal demands unless fate had conspired? In Bombay, you know that offices of foreign businesses offer both options in their bathrooms. So do all hotels with three stars or more. By practising in familiar surroundings, Sarosh was convinced he could have mastered a seated evacuation before departure.

"But perhaps there was something in what the supervisor said. Sarosh found a telephone number for the Indian Immigrant Aid Society and made an appointment. That afternoon, he met Mrs Maha-Lepate at the Society's office."

Kersi and Viraf looked at each other and smiled. Nariman Uncle had a nerve, there was more *lepate*[9] in his own stories than anywhere else.

"Mrs Maha-Lepate was very understanding, and made Sarosh feel at ease despite the very personal nature of his problem. She said, 'Yes, we get many referrals. There was a man here last month who couldn't eat Wonder Bread — it made him throw up.'

"By the way, boys, Wonder Bread is a Canadian bread which all happy families eat to be happy in the same way; the unhappy families are unhappy in their own fashion by eating other brands." Jehangir was the only one who understood, and murmured: "Tolstoy,"[10] at Nariman's little joke. Nariman noticed it, pleased. He continued.

"Mrs Maha-Lepate told Sarosh about that case: 'Our immigrant specialist, Dr No-Ilaaz, recommended that the patient eat cake instead. He explained that Wonder Bread caused vomiting because the digestive system was used to Indian bread only, made with Indian flour in the village he came from. However, since his system was unfamiliar with cake, Canadian or otherwise, it did not react but was digested as a newfound food. In this way he got used to Canadian flour first in cake form. Just yesterday we received a report from Dr No-Ilaaz. The patient successfully ate his first slice of whole-wheat Wonder Bread with no ill effects. The ultimate goal is pure white Wonder Bread.'"

"Like a polite Parsi boy, Sarosh said, 'That's very interesting.' The garrulous[11] Mrs Maha-Lepate was about to continue, and he tried to interject: 'But I — ' but Mrs Maha-Lepate was too quick for him: 'Oh, there are so many interesting cases I could tell you about. Like the woman from Sri Lanka — referred to us because they don't have their own Society — who could not drink the water here. Dr No-Ilaaz said it was due to the different mineral content. So he started her on Coca-Cola and then began diluting it with water, bit by bit. Six weeks later she took her first sip of unadulterated Canadian water and managed to keep it down.'

---

9. *lepate* Exaggeration. 10. **Tolstoy** From the opening of Russian novelist Leo Tolstoy's *Anna Karenina* (1875): "Every happy family is alike, but every unhappy family is unhappy in their own way." 11. **garrulous** Talkative.

"Sarosh could not halt Mrs Maha-Lepate as she launched from one case history into another: 'Right now, Dr No-Ilaaz is working on a very unusual case. Involves a whole Pakistani family. Ever since immigrating to Canada, none of them can swallow. They choke on their own saliva, and have to spit constantly. But we are confident that Dr No-Ilaaz will find a remedy. He has never been stumped by any immigrant problem. Besides, we have an information network with other third-world Immigrant Aid Societies. We all seem to share a history of similar maladies, and regularly compare notes. Some of us thought these problems were linked to retention of original citizenship. But this was a false lead.'

"Sarosh, out of his own experience, vigorously nodded agreement. By now he was truly fascinated by Mrs Maha-Lepate's wealth of information. Reluctantly, he interrupted: 'But will Dr No-Ilaaz be able to solve my problem?'"

"'I have every confidence that he will,' replied Mrs Maha-Lepate in great earnest. 'And if he has no remedy for you right away, he will be delighted to start working on one. He loves to take up new projects.'"

Nariman halted to blow his nose, and a clear shrill voice travelled the night air of the Firozsha Baag compound from C Block to where the boys had collected around Nariman in A Block: "Jehangoo! O Jehangoo! Eight o'clock! Upstairs now!"

Jehangir stared at his feet in embarrassment. Nariman looked at his watch and said, "Yes, it's eight." But Jehangir did not move, so he continued.

"Mrs Maha-Lepate was able to arrange an appointment while Sarosh waited, and he went directly to the doctor's office. What he had heard so far sounded quite promising. Then he cautioned himself not to get overly optimistic, that was the worst mistake he could make. But along the way to the doctor's, he could not help thinking what a lovely city Toronto was. It was the same way he had felt when he first saw it ten years ago, before all the joy had dissolved in the acid of his anxieties."

Once again that shrill voice travelled through the clear night: "*Arré* Jehangoo! *Muà*, do I have to come down and drag you upstairs!"

Jehangir's mortification was now complete. Nariman made it easy for him, though: "The first part of the story is over. Second part continues tomorrow. Same time, same place." The boys were surprised, Nariman did not make such commitments. But never before had he told such a long story. They began drifting back to their homes.

As Jehangir strode hurriedly to C Block, falsettos and piercing shrieks followed him in the darkness: "*Arré* Jehangoo! *Muà* Jehangoo! Bulsara Bookworm! Eight o'clock Jehangoo!" Shaking his head, Nariman went indoors to Hirabai.

Next evening, the story punctually resumed when Nariman took his place on the topmost step of A Block: "You remember that we left Sarosh on his way to see the Immigrant Aid Society's doctor. Well, Dr No-Ilaaz listened patiently to Sarosh's concerns, then said, 'As a matter of fact, there is a remedy which is so new even the IAS does not know about it. Not even that Mrs Maha-Lepate who knows it all,' he added drolly, twirling his stethoscope like a stunted lasso. He slipped it on around his neck before continuing: 'It involves a minor operation which was developed with financial assistance from the Multicultural Department. A small device, *Crappus Non Interruptus*, or CNI as we call it, is implanted in the bowel. The device is controlled by an external handheld transmitter similar to the ones used for automatic garage door-openers — you may have seen them in hardware stores.'"

Nariman noticed that most of the boys wore puzzled looks and realized he had to make some things clearer. "The Multicultural Department is a Canadian invention. It is supposed to ensure that ethnic cultures are able to flourish, so that Canadian society will consist of a mosaic of cultures — that's their favourite word, mosaic — instead of one uniform mix, like the American melting pot. If you ask me, mosaic and melting pot are both nonsense, and ethnic is a polite way of saying bloody foreigner. But anyway, you understand Multicultural Department? Good. So Sarosh nodded, and Dr No-Ilaaz went on: 'You can encode the handheld transmitter with a personal ten-digit code. Then all you do is position yourself on the toilet seat and activate your transmitter. Just like a garage door, your bowel will open without pushing or grunting.'"

There was some snickering in the audience, and Nariman raised his eyebrows, whereupon they covered up their mouths with their hands. "The doctor asked Sarosh if he had any questions. Sarosh thought for a moment, then asked if it required any maintenance.

"Dr No-Ilaaz replied: 'CNI is semi-permanent and operates on solar energy. Which means you would have to make it a point to get some sun periodically, or it would cease and lead to constipation. However, you don't have to strip for a tan. Exposing ten percent of your skin surface once a week during summer will let the device store sufficient energy for year-round operation.'

"Sarosh's next question was: 'Is there any hope that someday the bowels can work on their own, without operating the device?' at which Dr No-Ilaaz grimly shook his head: 'I'm afraid not. You must think very, very carefully before making a decision. Once CNI is implanted, you can never pass a motion in the natural way — neither sitting nor squatting.'

"He stopped to allow Sarosh time to think it over, then continued: 'And you must understand what that means. You will never be able to live a normal life again. You will be permanently different from your family and friends because of this basic internal modification. In fact, in this country or that, it will set you apart from your fellow countrymen. So you must consider the whole thing most carefully.'

"Dr No-Ilaaz paused, toyed with his stethoscope, shuffled some papers on his desk, then resumed: 'There are other dangers you should know about. Just as a garage door can be accidentally opened by a neighbour's transmitter on the same frequency, CNI can also be activated by someone with similar apparatus.' To ease the tension he attempted a quick laugh and said, 'Very embarrassing, eh, if it happened at the wrong place and time. Mind you, the risk is not so great at present, because the chances of finding yourself within a fifty-foot radius of another transmitter on the same frequency are infinitesimal. But what about the future? What if CNI becomes very popular? Sufficient permutations may not be available for transmitter frequencies and you could be sharing the code with others. Then the risk of accidents becomes greater.'"

Something landed with a loud thud in the yard behind A Block, making Nariman startle. Immediately, a yowling and screeching and caterwauling went up from the stray cats there, and the *kuchrawalli's* dog started barking. Some of the boys went around the side of A Block to peer over the fence into the backyard. But the commotion soon died down of its own accord. The boys returned and, once again, Nariman's voice was the only sound to be heard.

"By now, Sarosh was on the verge of deciding against the operation. Dr No-Ilaaz observed this and was pleased. He took pride in being able to dissuade his patients from following the very remedies which he first so painstakingly described. True to his name, Dr No-Ilaaz believed no remedy is the best remedy, rather than prescribing this-mycin and that-mycin for every little ailment. So he continued: 'And what about our sons and daughters? And the quality of their lives? We still don't know the long-term effects of CNI. Some researchers speculate that it could generate a genetic deficiency, that the offspring of a CNI parent would also require CNI. On the other hand, they could be perfectly healthy toilet seat-users, without any congenital defects. We just don't know at this stage.'

"Sarosh rose from his chair: 'Thank you very much for your time, Dr No-Ilaaz. But I don't think I want to take such a drastic step. As you suggest, I will think it over very carefully.'

"'Good, good,' said Dr. No-Ilaaz, 'I was hoping you would say that. There is one more thing. The operation is extremely expensive, and is not covered by the province's Health Insurance Plan. Many immigrant groups are lobbying to obtain coverage for special immigration-related health problems. If they succeed, then good for you.'

"Sarosh left Dr No-Ilaaz's office with his mind made up. Time was running out. There had been a time when it was perfectly natural to squat. Now it seemed a grotesquely aberrant[12] thing to do. Wherever he went he was reminded of the ignominy[13] of his way. If he could not be westernized in all respects, he was nothing but a failure in this land — a failure not just in the washrooms of the nation but everywhere. He knew what he must do if he was to be true to himself and to the decade-old commitment. So what do you think Sarosh did next?"

"What, Nariman Uncle?"

"He went to the travel agent specializing in tickets to India. He bought a fully refundable ticket to Bombay for the day when he would complete exactly ten immigrant years — if he succeeded even once before that day dawned, he would cancel the booking.

"The travel agent asked sympathetically, 'Trouble at home?' His name was Mr Rawaana, and he was from Bombay, too.

"'No,' said Sarosh, 'trouble in Toronto.'

"'That's a shame,' said Mr. Rawaana. 'I don't want to poke my nose into your business, but in my line of work I meet so many people who are going back to their homeland because of problems here. Sometimes I forget I'm a travel agent, that my interest is to convince them to travel. Instead, I tell them: don't give up, God is great, stay and try again. It's bad for my profits but gives me a different, a spiritual kind of satisfaction when I succeed. And I succeed about half the time. Which means,' he added with a wry laugh, 'I could double my profits if I minded my own business.'

"After the lengthy sessions with Mrs Maha-Lepate and Dr No-Ilaaz, Sarosh felt he had listened to enough advice and kind words. Much as he disliked doing it, he had to hurt Mr Rawaana's feelings and leave his predicament undiscussed: 'I'm sorry, but I'm in a hurry. Will you be able to look after the booking?'

"Well, okay," said Mr Rawaana, a trifle crestfallen; he did not relish the travel business as much as he did counselling immigrants. 'Hope you solve your problem. I will be happy to refund your fare, believe me.'

"Sarosh hurried home. With only four weeks to departure, every spare minute, every possible method had to be concentrated on a final attempt at adaptation.

---

12. aberrant Abnormal. **13. ignominy** Shamefulness.

"He tried laxatives, crunching down the tablets with a prayer that these would assist the sitting position. Changing brands did not help, and neither did various types of suppositories. He spent long stretches on the toilet seat each morning. The supervisor continued to reprimand him for tardiness. To make matters worse, Sarosh left his desk every time he felt the slightest urge, hoping: maybe this time.

"The working hours expended in the washroom were noted with unflagging vigilance by the supervisor. More counselling sessions followed. Sarosh refused to extinguish his last hope, and the supervisor punctiliously recorded 'No Improvement' in his daily log. Finally, Sarosh was fired. It would soon have been time to resign in any case, and he could not care less.

"Now whole days went by seated on the toilet, and he stubbornly refused to relieve himself the other way. The doorbell would ring only to be ignored. The telephone went unanswered. Sometimes, he would awake suddenly in the dark hours before dawn and rush to the washroom like a madman."

Without warning, Rustomji flung open his door and stormed: "Ridiculous non-sense this is becoming! Two days in a row, whole Firozsha Baag gathers here! This is not Chaupatty beach, this is not a squatters' colony, this is a building, people want to live here in peace and quiet!" Then just as suddenly, he stamped inside and slammed the door. Right on cue, Nariman continued, before the boys could say anything.

"Time for meals was the only time Sarosh allowed himself off the seat. Even in his desperation he remembered that if he did not eat well, he was doomed — the downward pressure on his gut was essential if there was to be any chance of success.

"But the ineluctable day of departure dawned, with grey skies and the scent of rain, while success remained out of sight. At the airport Sarosh checked in and went to the dreary lounge. Out of sheer habit he started towards the washroom. Then he realized the hopelessness of it and returned to the cold, clammy plastic of the lounge seats. Airport seats are the same almost anywhere in the world.

"The boarding announcement was made, and Sarosh was the first to step onto the plane. The skies were darker now. Out of the window he saw a flash of lightning fork through the clouds. For some reason, everything he'd learned years ago in St Xavier's about sheet lightning and forked lightning went through his mind. He wished it would change to sheet, there was something sinister and unpropitious[14] about forked lightning."

Kersi, absorbedly listening, began cracking his knuckles quite unconsciously. His childhood habit still persisted. Jehangir frowned at the disturbance, and Viraf nudged Kersi to stop it.

"Sarosh fastened his seat-belt and attempted to turn his thoughts towards the long journey home: to the questions he would be expected to answer, the sympathy and criticism that would be thrust upon him. But what remained uppermost in his mind was the present moment — him in the plane, dark skies lowering, lightning on the horizon — irrevocably spelling out: defeat.

"But wait. Something else was happening now. A tiny rumble. Inside him. Or was it his imagination? Was it really thunder outside which, in his present disoriented state, he was internalizing? No, there it was again. He had to go."

---

14. **unpropitious** Boding ill.

"He reached the washroom, and almost immediately the sign flashed to 'Please return to seat and fasten seat-belts.' Sarosh debated whether to squat and finish the business quickly, abandoning the perfunctory seated attempt. But the plane started to move and that decided him; it would be difficult now to balance while squatting.

"He pushed. The plane continued to move. He pushed again, trembling with the effort. The seat-belt sign flashed quicker and brighter now. The plane moved faster and faster. And Sarosh pushed hard, harder than he had ever pushed before, harder than in all his ten years of trying in the new land. And the memories of Bombay, the immigration interview in New Delhi, the farewell party, his mother's tattered prayer book, all these, of their own accord, emerged from beyond the region of the ten years to push with him and give him newfound strength."

Nariman paused and cleared his throat. Dusk was falling, and the frequency of B.E.S.T. buses plying the main road outside Firozsha Baag had dropped. Bats began to fly madly from one end of the compound to the other, silent shadows engaged in endless laps over the buildings.

"With a thunderous clap the rain started to fall. Sarosh felt a splash under him. Could it really be? He glanced down to make certain. Yes, it was. He had succeeded!

"But was it already too late? The plane waited at its assigned position on the runway, jet engines at full thrust. Rain was falling in torrents and takeoff could be delayed. Perhaps even now they would allow him to cancel his flight, to disembark. He lurched out of the constricting cubicle.

"A stewardess hurried towards him: 'Excuse me, sir, but you must return to your seat immediately and fasten your belt.'

"'You don't understand!' Sarosh shouted excitedly. 'I must get off the plane! Everything is all right, I don't have to go any more . . .'

"'That's impossible, sir!' said the stewardess, aghast. 'No one can leave now. Takeoff procedures are in progress!' The wild look in his sleepless eyes, and the dark rings around them scared her. She beckoned for help.

"Sarosh continued to argue, and a steward and the chief stewardess hurried over: 'What seems to be the problem, sir? You *must* resume your seat. We are authorized, if necessary, to forcibly restrain you, sir.'

"The plane began to move again, and suddenly Sarosh felt all the urgency leave him. His feverish mind, the product of nightmarish days and torturous nights, was filled again with the calm which had fled a decade ago, and he spoke softly now: 'That . . . that will not be necessary . . . it's okay, I understand.' He readily returned to his seat.

"As the aircraft sped down the runway, Sarosh's first reaction was one of joy. The process of adaptation was complete. But later, he could not help wondering if success came before or after the ten-year limit had expired. And since he had already passed through the customs and security check, was he really an immigrant in every sense of the word at the moment of achievement?

"But such questions were merely academic. Or were they? He could not decide. If he returned, what would it be like? Ten years ago, the immigration officer who had stamped his passport had said, 'Welcome to Canada.' It was one of Sarosh's dearest memories, and thinking of it, he fell asleep.

"The plane was flying above the rainclouds. Sunshine streamed into the cabin. A few raindrops were still clinging miraculously to the windows, reminders of what was happening below. They sparkled as the sunlight caught them."

Some of the boys made as if to leave, thinking the story was finally over. Clearly, they had not found this one as interesting as the others Nariman had told. What dolts, thought Jehangir, they cannot recognize a masterpiece when they hear one. Nariman motioned with his hand for silence.

"But our story does not end there. There was a welcome-home party for Sarosh a few days after he arrived in Bombay. It was not in Firozsha Baag this time because his relatives in the Baag had a serious sickness in the house. But I was invited to it anyway. Sarosh's family and friends were considerate enough to wait till the jet lag had worked its way out of his system. They wanted him to really enjoy this one.

"Drinks began to flow freely again in his honour: Scotch and soda, rum and Coke, brandy. Sarosh noticed that during this absence all the brand names had changed — the labels were different and unfamiliar. Even for the mixes. Instead of Coke there was Thums-Up, and he remembered reading in the papers about Coca-Cola being kicked out by the Indian Government for refusing to reveal their secret formula.

"People slapped him on the back and shook his hand vigorously, over and over, right through the evening. They said: 'Telling the truth, you made the right decision, look how happy your mother is to live to see this day'; or they asked: 'Well, bossy, what changed your mind?' Sarosh smiled and nodded his way through it all, passing around Canadian currency at the insistence of some of the curious ones who, egged on by his mother, also pestered him to display his Canadian passport and citizenship card. She had been badgering him since his arrival to tell her the real reason: '*Saachoo kahé*, what brought you back?' and was hoping that tonight, among his friends, he might raise his glass and reveal something. But she remained disappointed.

"Weeks went by and Sarosh found himself desperately searching for his old place in the pattern of life he had vacated ten years ago. Friends who had organized the welcome-home party gradually disappeared. He went walking in the evenings along Marine Drive, by the sea-wall, where the old crowd used to congregate. But the people who sat on the parapet while waves crashed behind their backs were strangers. The tetrapods were still there, staunchly protecting the reclaimed land from the fury of the sea. He had watched as a kid when cranes had lowered these cement and concrete hulks of respectable grey into the water. They were grimy black now, and from their angularities rose the distinct stench of human excrement. The old pattern was never found by Sarosh; he searched in vain. Patterns of life are selfish and unforgiving.

"Then one day, as I was driving past Marine Drive, I saw someone sitting alone. He looked familiar, so I stopped. For a moment I did not recognize Sarosh, so forlorn and woebegone was his countenance. I parked the apple of my eye and went to him, saying, 'Hullo, Sid, what are you doing here on your lonesome?' And he said, 'No no! No more Sid, please, that name reminds me of all my troubles.' Then, on the parapet at Marine Drive, he told me his unhappy and wretched tale, with the waves battering away at the tetrapods, and around us the hawkers screaming about coconut-water and sugar-cane juice and *paan*.

"When he finished, he said that he had related to me the whole sad saga because he knew how I told stories to boys in the Baag, and he wanted me to tell this one, especially to those who were planning to go abroad. 'Tell them,' said Sarosh, 'that the world can be a bewildering place, and dreams and ambitions are often paths to the most pernicious of traps.' As he spoke, I could see that Sarosh was somewhere far away, perhaps in New Delhi at his immigration interview, seeing himself as he was then, with what he thought was a life of hope and promise stretching endlessly before him. Poor Sarosh. Then he was back beside me on the parapet.

"'I pray you, in your stories,' said Sarosh, his old sense of humour returning as he deepened his voice for his favourite *Othello* lines" — and here, Nariman produced a basso profundo of his own — "'When you shall these unlucky deeds relate, speak of me as I am; nothing extenuate, nor set down aught in malice: tell them that in Toronto once there lived a Parsi boy as best as he could. Set you down this; and say, besides, that for some it was good and for some it was bad, but for me life in the land of milk and honey was just a pain in the posterior.'"

And now, Nariman allowed his low-pitched rumbles to turn into chuckles. The boys broke into cheers and loud applause and cries of "Encore!" and "More!" Finally, Nariman had to silence them by pointing warningly at Rustomji-the-curmudgeon's door.

While Kersi and Viraf were joking and wondering what to make of it all, Jehangir edged forward and told Nariman this was the best story he had ever told. Nariman patted his shoulder and smiled. Jehangir left, wondering if Nariman would have been as popular if Dr Mody was still alive. Probably, since the two were liked for different reasons: Dr Mody used to be constantly jovial, whereas Nariman had his periodic story-telling urges.

Now the group of boys who had really enjoyed the Savukshaw story during the previous week spoke up. Capitalizing on Nariman's extraordinarily good mood, they began clamouring for more Savukshaw: "Nariman Uncle, tell the one about Savukshaw the hunter, the one you had started that day."

"What hunter? I don't know which one you mean." He refused to be reminded of it, and got up to leave. But there was loud protest, and the boys started chanting, "We-want-Savukshaw! We-want-Savukshaw!"

Nariman looked fearfully towards Rustomji's door and held up his hands placatingly: "All right, all right! Next time it will be Savukshaw again. Savukshaw the artist. The story of the Parsi Picasso."

(1987)

Dionne Brand (1953–)

Dionne Brand was born in Trinidad in 1953 and raised by her grandmother. Like many of her generation, she says, she thought of Trinidad as "no-place" and couldn't wait to be "grown up to go away." In 1970, she came to Canada and enrolled in university, earning a B.A. in English and philosophy and an M.A. in the philosophy of education from the University of Toronto. Throughout the 1970s and 1980s, Brand was a social activist, working as a counsellor at Toronto's Immigrant Women's Centre, volunteering at the Black Youth Hotline, and serving as an advisor to the Toronto Board of Education. She also founded *Our Lives,* the first Canadian newspaper by and for Black women, acted as a facilitator on several labour committees, served on the board of a shelter for battered women, and spent a year working for the Caribbean People's Development Agencies in Grenada.

Brand jokes that she only ever learned to do two things well: read and write. As a child in Trinidad, she felt alienated by the British poetry she had to study, but it was a powerful motivator for her to create her own means of poetic expression: "if the literature … is presented to you as great art and you are absent, or the forms and shapes in which you are included are derided, then you know that this literature means to erase you or to kill you. Then you write yourself."

Since 1978, Brand has published nine volumes of poetry, three novels, and three works of non-fiction. For her, the difference between poetry and prose is one of audience: "prose," she says, "is a conversation with a local audience"; poetry "is a conversation with language, its meanings, origins, and relevance as a descriptor of human existence." As a Black lesbian author from a former British colony, Brand constantly asks how the English language can be manipulated to better reflect her experience. As she works with the language, she strives for precision. "I'm trying to speak perfectly," she explains, "which is different from saying I'm trying to speak perfect English. I'm not."

In *No Language Is Neutral* (1990), she confronts the politics of language and seeks "another place, not here," where "a woman might touch something between beauty and nowhere." In a world where "Each sentence realised or dreamed jumps like a pulse with history and takes a side," Brand argues, one must shatter racist and sexist clichés and reconstruct the language to convey the Black "herstory." Her poetry is rhythmical, sonorous, and inflected with Trinidadian dialect. Its image-rich lines meander then come up short, expressing thought processes, carrying other voices, remaining mostly in the present tense; this creates a sense of history as a continuous presence — vital and unfolding in the minds of her subjects.

Brand is not unconditionally optimistic about poetry's power to write inclusive history. In the title poem of *No Language Is Neutral,* she says to her grandmother, Liney, "no one is interested in telling the truth. History will only hear you if you give birth to a woman who smoothes starched linen … and who gives birth to another woman who cries near a river and vanishes and who gives birth to a woman who is a poet, and, even then." In *Land to Light On* (1996), Brand's skepticism becomes more pronounced. She has maintained that, while she believes all art is political, the work of Black artists is particularly so because "we are living in a politically charged moment that's suffused in race and racism and the ideas of land and border and belonging." *Land to Light On* is Brand's first poetic foray into the Canadian landscape, and in it she suggests that language in Canada is politicized to the point where, even in converted or subverted forms, it cannot offer rest or stability to minority voices. The dominant discourse of White male capitalism is seductive, and it fosters complicity; given that, Brand implies, language can only ever be a place to "light on" briefly. *Land to Light On* won a Governor General's Award and the Trillium Award.

In the long poem *thirsty* (2002), Brand gives us the final utterance of an immigrant who yearns for "a calming loving spot" where he can retreat from the "conditional places" and "conditional sentences" that define his marginality. Shot by police, Alan lies dying, "anticipat[ing] nothing as intimate as history," only "a glancing blow of tears / on skin, the keen dismissal in speed." But Brand knows that longing for that "loving spot" — like longing for "another place, not here" — is a static and ultimately futile impulse. Salvation from the conditional will depend upon an active reconciliation of language and history, however unattainable this may seem. Not long after *thirsty* was published, Brand told an interviewer that she "wanted to challenge the idea of constantly having to fix oneself as a way of finding identity."

Brand's latest poetry offering, *Inventory,* was published in 2006. This long poem is, as its title declares, a stock-taking. It covers, Brand writes, "the tumultuous early years of this new century." Beginning the piece with the statement "we believed in nothing," the poet presents us with, to quote one reviewer, "a relentless catalogue of global suffering, loss, war, cruelty, disaster, and pain." That this dire and detailed warning is accommodated by the comforting and orderly structure of the list makes it even more disconcerting. Hope for release from the onslaught comes only in those rare "moments when you rise to what you might be."

In her novels, Brand focuses less on questions of language and identity and engages in a close treatment of social concerns. *In Another Place, Not Here* (1996), her first novel, is the story of two women, set in Toronto and a Caribbean island, and it is a testament to its author's commitment to Marxism, feminism, labour movements, and the inscribing of women's social history. Verlia, an educated woman, travels to the island to help mount a socialist revolution, and there she embarks upon a relationship with Elizete, a cane-cutter. Through their affair, Brand explores the interaction of what she calls "learned politics" (Marxism, socialism) and "traditional practices" (island working-class custom). Brand's second novel, *At the Full and Change of the Moon* (1999), is a Caribbean neo-slave narrative that depicts the death of Marie Ursule, a 19th-century African slave, and the lives of her descendants. Bola, Marie's daughter and the sole survivor of a mass suicide organized by her mother, scatters her own children "so that all would never be gathered in the same place to come to the same harm." Brand thus creates a metaphor for the Black diaspora in the post-colonial era. The novel also examines the complex emotional reactions experienced by minority peoples when they are compelled to perform acts of heroism and sacrifice in their struggle for survival and justice. In 2005, Brand produced the novel *What We All Long For*, which recounts the ongoing ordeal of a family of Vietnamese boat people who settle in Toronto.

Brand's poetry and short stories have been widely anthologized. Her works of non-fiction include a collection of her own essays, *Bread Out of Stone* (1994), and a volume of minority oral histories, *Rivers Have Sources, Trees Have Roots: Speaking of Racism* (1986), which she co-edited. Between 1989 and 1996, she was involved in the production of four documentaries for the National Film Board. She has taught literature and creative writing at the Universities of Guelph and Toronto and at the West Coast Women and Words Summer School. Brand lives in Toronto.

No Language Is Neutral

No language is neutral. I used to haunt the beach at
Guaya, two rivers sentinel the country sand, not
backra[1] white but nigger brown sand, one river dead
and teeming from waste and alligators, the other
rumbling to the ocean in a tumult, the swift undertow
blocking the crossing of little girls except on the tied
up dress hips of big women, then, the taste of leaving
was already on my tongue and cut deep into my
skinny pigeon toed way, language here was strict
description and teeth edging truth. Here was beauty   10
and here was nowhere. The smell of hurrying passed
my nostrils with the smell of sea water and fresh fish
wind, there was history which had taught my eyes to
look for escape even beneath the almond leaves fat
as women, the conch shell tiny as sand, the rock
stone old like water. I learned to read this from a
woman whose hand trembled at the past, then even
being born to her was temporary, wet and thrown half
dressed among the dozens of brown legs itching to
run. It was as if a signal burning like a fer de lance's[2]   20
sting turned my eyes against the water even as love
for this nigger beach became resolute.

---

1. **backra** Person of European descent in the Carribean. 2. **fer de lance** Large, venomous snake.

There it was anyway, some damn memory half-eaten
and half hungry. To hate this, they must have been
dragged through the Manzinilla spitting out the last
spun syllables for cruelty, new sound forming,
pushing toward lips made to bubble blood. This road
could match that. Hard-bitten on mangrove and wild
bush; the sea wind heaving any remnants of
30 consonant curses into choking aspirate. No
language is neutral seared in the spine's unravelling.
Here is history too. A backbone bending and
unbending without a word, heat, bellowing these
lungs spongy, exhaled in humming, the ocean, a
way out and not anything of beauty, tipping turquoise
and scandalous. The malicious horizon made us the
essential thinkers of technology. How to fly gravity,
how to balance basket and prose reaching for
murder. Silence done curse god and a beauty here,
40 people does hear things in this heliconia³ peace
a morphology of rolling chain and copper gong
now shape this twang, falsettos of whip and air
rudiment this grammar. Take what I tell you. When
these barracks held slaves between their stone
halters, talking was left for night and hush was idiom
and hot core.

When Liney reach here is up to the time I hear about.
Why I always have to go back to that old woman who
wasn't even from here but from another barracoon,⁴ I
50 never understand but deeply as if is something that
have no end. Even she daughter didn't know but only
leave me she life like a brown stone to see. I in the
middle of a plane ride now a good century from their
living or imagination, around me is a people I will
only understand as full of ugliness that make me
weep full past my own tears and before hers. Liney,
when she live through two man, is so the second one
bring she here on this penultimate hope and she
come and sweep sand into my eye. So is there I meet
60 she in a recollection through Ben, son, now ninety,
ex-saga boy and image, perhaps eyes of my mama,
Liney daughter. I beg him to recall something of my
mama, something of his mama. The ninety year old
water of his eyes swell like the river he remember
and he say, *she was a sugar cake, sweet sweet*
sweet. Yuh muma! that girl was a sugar cake!

---

3. **heliconia** Helicon was the residence of the classical muses; heliconia is a flower similar to bird of paradise.
4. **barracoon** Barracks where slaves were confined.

This time Liney done see vision in this green guava
season, fly skinless and turn into river fish, dream
sheself, praise god, without sex and womb when sex
is hell and womb is she to pay. So dancing an old   70
man the castilian[5] around this christmas living room
my little sister and me get Ben to tell we any story he
remember, and in between his own trail of conquests
and pretty clothes, in between his never sleeping with
a woman who wasn't clean because he was a
scornful man, in between our absent query were they
scornful women too, Liney smiled on his gold teeth.
the castilian out of breath, the dampness of his
shrunken skin reminding us, Oh god! laughing,
sister! we will kill uncle dancing!   80

In between, Liney, in between, as if your life could
never see itself, blooded and coarsened on this
island as mine, driven over places too hard to know
in their easy terror. As if your life could never hear
itself as still some years, god, ages, have passed
without your autobiography now between my stories
and the time I have to remember and the passages
that I too take out of liking, between me and history
we have made a patch of it, a verse still missing you
at the subject, a chapter yellowed and moth eaten at   90
the end. I could never save a cactus leaf between
pages, Liney, those other girls could make them root
undisturbed in the steam of unread books, not me,
admiring their devotion, still I peered too often at my
leaf, eyeing the creeping death out of it and giving up.
That hovel[6] in the cocoa near the sweet oil factory I'll
never see, Liney, each time I go I stand at the road
arguing with myself. Sidelong looks are my specialty.
That saddle of children given you by one man then
another, the bear and darn and mend of your vagina   100
she like to walk about plenty, Ben said, *she was a*
small woman, small small. I chase Ben's romance as
it mumbles to a close, then, the rum and cocunut
water of his eyes as he prepares to lie gently for his
own redemption. *I was she favourite, oh yes*.
The ric rac running of your story remains braided in
other wars, Liney, no one is interested in telling the
truth. History will only hear you if you give birth to a
woman who smoothes starched linen in the wardrobe
drawer, trembles when she walks and who gives birth   110

---

5. **castilian** A Spanish-influenced dance popular in Trinidad. 6. **hovel** Destitute shack.

to another woman who cries near a river and
vanishes and who gives birth to a woman who is a
poet, and, even then.

Pilate[7] was that river I never crossed as a child. A
woman, my mother, was weeping on its banks,
weeping for the sufferer she would become, she a too
black woman weeping, those little girls trailing her
footsteps reluctantly and without love for this shaking
woman blood and salt in her mouth, weeping, that

120   river gushed past her feet blocked her flight … and go
where, lady, weeping and go where, turning back to
face herself now only the oblique shape of something
without expectation, her body composed in doubt
then she'd come to bend her back, to dissemble, then
to stand on anger like a ledge, a tilting house, the
crazy curtain blazing at her teeth. A woman who
though she was human but got the message, female
and black and somehow those who gave it to her
were like family, mother and brother, spitting woman

130   at her, somehow they were the only place to return to
and this gushing river had already swallowed most of
her, the little girls drowned on its indifferent bank, the
river hardened like the centre of her, spinning chalk
stone on its frill, burden in their slow feet, they
weeping, she, *go on home,* in futility. There were
dry-eyed cirri[8] tracing the blue air that day. Pilate was
that river I ran from leaving that woman, my mother,
standing over its brutal green meaning and it was
over by now and had become so ordinary as if not to

140   see it any more, that constant veil over the eyes, the
blood-stained blind of race and sex.

Leaving this standing, heart and eyes fixed to a
skyscraper and a concrete eternity not knowing then
only running away from something that breaks the
heart open and nowhere to live. Five hundred dollars
and a passport full of sand and winking water, is how
I reach here, a girl's face shimmering from a little
photograph, her hair between hot comb and afro, feet
posing in high heel shoes, never to pass her eyes on

150   the red-green threads of a hummingbird's twitching
back, the blood warm quickened water colours of a
sea bed, not the rain forest tangled in smoke-wet,
well there it was. I did read a book once about a

---

7. Pilate A river in Trinidad, but the poet also alludes to Pontius Pilate, the Roman governor who oversaw Christ's trial and
ordered his crucifixion. **8. cirri** Wispy cirrus clouds.

prairie in Alberta since my waving canefield wasn't
enough, too much cutlass and too much cut foot, but
romance only happen in romance novel, the concrete
building just overpower me, block my eyesight and
send the sky back, back where it more redolent.[9]

Is steady trembling I trembling when they ask me my
name and say I too black for it. Is steady hurt I feeling   160
when old talk bleed, the sea don't have branch you
know darling. Nothing is a joke no more and I right
there with them, running for the train until I get to find
out my big sister just like to run and nobody wouldn't
vex if you miss the train, calling Spadina[10] *Spadeena*
until I listen good for what white people call it, saying I
coming just to holiday to the immigration officer when
me and the son-of a bitch know I have labourer mark
all over my face. It don't have nothing call beauty
here but this is a place, a gasp of water from a   170
hundred lakes, fierce bright windows screaming with
goods, a constant drizzle of brown brick cutting
dolorous prisons into every green uprising of bush.
No wilderness self, is shards, shards, shards,
shards of raw glass, a debris of people you pick your way
through returning to your worse self, you the thin
mixture of just come and don't exist.

I walk Bathurst Street until it come like home
Pearl was near Dupont, upstairs a store one
christmas where we pretend as if nothing change we,   180
make rum punch and sing, with bottle and spoon,
song we weself never even sing but only hear when
we was children. Pearl, squeezing her big Point
Fortin[11] self along the narrow hall singing *Drink a rum
and a ...* Pearl, working nights, cleaning, Pearl beating
books at her age, Pearl dying back home in a car
crash twenty years after everything was squeezed in,
a trip to Europe, a condominium, a man she suckled
like a baby. Pearl coaxing this living room with a
voice half lie and half memory, a voice no room   190
nowhere could believe was sincere. Pearl hoping this
room would catch fire above this frozen street. Our
singing parched, drying in the silence after the
chicken and ham and sweet bread effort to taste like
home, the slim red earnest sound of long ago with the
blinds drawn and the finally snow for christmas and

---

9. redolent Evocative. **10. Spadina** Major street in Toronto. **11. Point Fortin** Township in Trinidad and Tobago.

the mood that rum in a cold place takes. Well, even
our nostalgia was a lie, skittish as the truth these
bundle of years.

200 But wait, this must come out then. A hidden verb
takes inventory of those small years like a person
waiting at a corner, counting and growing thin
through life as cloth and as water, hush ... Look I
hated something, policemen, bankers, slavetraders,
shhh ... still do and even more these days. This city,
mourning the smell of flowers and dirt, cannot tell
me what to say even if it chokes me. Not a single
word drops from my lips for twenty years about living
here. Dumbfounded I walk as if these sidewalks are a
210 place I'm visiting. Like a holy ghost, I package the
smell of zinnias and lady of the night, I horde the taste
of star apples and granadilla. I return to that once
grammar struck in disbelief. Twenty years. Ignoring
my own money thrown on the counter, the race
conscious landlords and their jim crow[12] flats, oh yes!
here! the work nobody else wants to do ... it's good
work I'm not complaining! but they make it taste bad,
bitter like peas. You can't smile here, is a sin, you
can't play music, it too loud. There was a time I could
220 tell if rain was coming, it used to make me sad the
yearly fasting of trees here, I felt some pity for the
ground turned hot and cold. All that time taken up
with circling this city in a fever. I remember then, and
it's hard to remember waiting so long to live ... anyway
it's fiction what I remember, only mornings took a long
time to come, I became more secretive, language
seemed to split in two, one branch fell silent, the other
argued hotly for going home.

This is the part that is always difficult, the walk each
230 night across the dark school yard, biting my tongue
on new english, reading biology, stumbling over
unworded white faces. But I am only here for a
moment. The new stink of wet wool, driving my legs
across snow, ice, counting the winters that I do not
skid and fall on, a job sorting cards, the smell of an
office full of hatred each morning, no simple hatred,
not for me only, but for the hated fact of an office, an
elevator stuffed with the anger of elevator at 8 a.m.
and 5 p.m., my voice on the telephone after nine

---

12. **jim crow** Segregated.

months of office and elevator saying, I have to spend   240
time on my dancing. Yes, I'm a dancer, it's my new
career. Alone in the room after the phone crying at
the weakness in my stomach. Dancer. This romance
begins in a conversation off the top of my head, the
kitchen at Grace Hospital is where it ends. Then the
post office, here is escape at least from femininity,
but not from the envy of colony, education, the list of
insults is for this, better than, brighter than, richer
than, beginning with this slender walk against the
mountainous school. Each night, the black crowd of   250
us parts in the cold darkness, smiling.

The truth is, well, truth is not important at one end of a
hemisphere where a bird dives close to you in an
ocean for a mouth full of fish, an ocean you come to
swim in every two years, you, a slave to your leaping
retina, capture the look of it. It is like saying you are
dead. This place so full of your absence, this place
you come to swim like habit, to taste like habit, this
place where you are a woman and your breasts need
armour to walk. Here. Nerve endings of steady light   260
pinpoint all. That little light trembling the water again,
that gray blue night pearl of the sea, the swirl of the
earth that dash water back and always forth, that
always fear of a woman watching the world from an
evening beach with her sister, the courage between
them to drink a beer and assume their presence
against the coralline[13] chuckle of male voices. In
another place, not here, a woman might ... Our
nostalgia was a lie and the passage on that six hour
flight to ourselves is wide and like another world, and   270
then another one inside and is so separate and fast
to the skin but voiceless, never born, or born and
stilled ... hush.

In another place, not here, a woman might touch
something between beauty and nowhere, back there
and here, might pass hand over hand her own
trembling life, but I have tried to imagine a sea not
bleeding, a girl's glance full as a verse, a woman
growing old and never crying to a radio hissing of a
black boy's murder. I have tried to keep my throat   280
gurgling like a bird's. I have listened to the hard
gossip of race that inhabits this road. Even in this I
have tried to hum mud and feathers and sit peacefully

---

13. **coralline** Made of or resembling coral.

in this foliage of bones and rain. I have chewed a few
votive leaves here, their taste already disenchanting
my mothers. I have tried to write this thing calmly
even as its lines burn to a close. I have come to know
something simple. Each sentence realised or
dreamed jumps like a pulse with history and takes a
290   side. What I say in any language is told in faultless
knowledge of skin, in drunkenness and weeping,
told as a woman without matches and tinder, not in
words and in words and in words learned by heart,
told in secret and not in secret, and listen, does not
burn out or waste and is plenty and pitiless and loves.

(1990)

From *Thirsty*

XI

i

you can't satisfy people, we long for everything,
but sleep, sleep is the gift of the city
the breath of others, their mewling, their disorder,
I could hear languages in the lush smog,
runes to mercy and failure and something tender
a fragile light, no, not light, yes light,
something you can put your hand in, relinquishing

I'll tell you this. I've seen a toxic sunset,
flying down over the city, its gorgeous spit
10   licking the airplane, how it is that steel weeps
with the sense of bodies, pressed, another passion,
we become other humans,
boisterous and metallic, fibrous and deserted.
Here I could know nothing and live,
harbour a dead heart,
slip corrosive hands into a coat

ii

These are the muscles of the subway's syrinx
Vilnus, Dagupan, Shaowu, Valparaiso, Falmouth, and Asmara.
The tunnel breathes in the coming train exhaling
20   as minerals the grammar of Calcutta, Colombo,
Jakarta, Mogila and Senhor do Bonfim, Ribeira Grande
and Hong Kong, Mogadishu and the alias St. Petersburg

the city keens its rough sonancy,
you would be mistaken to take it as music

it is the sound before music
when the throat vomits prehistoric birds

XII

It was late spring then, it was warm already,
he, jeremiad[1] at the door holding the rough bible
to his temple like rhymed stone, she the last bolt
in her head shut, "Alan, let me pass."
"Oh my god!" his mother foretelling the meter,
he versed, "You're not leaving here with what is mine,"

her heart travelled the short distance of their joy
all the anger she had vaulted like gold belongings,
"Call the police! child, call the police! 911!"
The rake? The gloves? Had they come for the neighbours' things?   10
the tulip, the infinitesimal petals of spirea, the blossoms
he kissed this morning? "Here, wait." Then he would give them
their clippers, the branches of lilacs, the watering hose,
the two lengths of wild grasses that came off his hands.

They couldn't have come here to his house to stop him
from quarrelling with his own wife, it was the clippers
or the rake or their garden hose. He would straighten
things out, he would confess to the poppies, the white astilbe
Julia was leaving and no way was she taking what was his,
declaring the hedge clippers he said, "Look take it ... "   20

"What the devil ..." already descending.
"What the devil you all making so much noise for?"
then his chest flowered stigma of scarlet bergamot
their petal tips prickled his shirt, spread to his darkening
throat, he dropped the clippers to hold his breaking face,
he felt dry, "Jesus ... thirsty ..." he called, falling.

XX

Consider the din of beginnings, this vagrant, fugitive city
just hours ago these people standing prone as sleep
in subways were enclosed in the silk of their origins,
glowing chrysalises of old, at least, inconvenient cultures

they had some set notions of who they were, buried in apartments
and houses in North York and Scarborough and Pickering,[2]
those suburbs undifferentiated, prefabricated from no great
narrative, except cash, there is no truth to their names

---

1. **jeremiad** A sustained lament or vision of doom. 2. **North York, Scarborough, Pickering** Regions of Greater Toronto.

10   they don't even vaguely resemble the small damp villages
of their etymology. The Romans would not build roads here,
unflagging dreariness dries the landscape, meagre oases of woodland
fight gas stations and donut shops for any thing named beauty

Thomson would have snatched his *Burnt Country*[3] away from here,
knowing that it would vanish. This suburban parching would dry bog
far more succour the oversleeping, the insomniac, summer wastes,
mauve light, mauve, mauve dark black, mauve white, reconstructing

what they choose to remember and what they mis-forget of places
they'd known. They are improvising as Lismer's *Forest in Winter*[4]
some recent past, drowned hues, drenched schemes, plans,
20   for an arranged marriage, a red bride, a white garlanded groom, the

Gurdwara[5] on Weston Road. Blue, blue, blue black, that brilliant
red leafed tree, yellow leafed tree, the immigrant from Sheffield,
Lismer paints Sackville River with the same new memory as Violet
Blackman, her gesso[6] was that wood floor in Rosedale[7]

1920, when Toronto was just a village and all her labour, all her
time, all her heart and hand could not make that painting work, so,
hanging on fading histories, igniting another burnt drama
forty years from St. Elizabeth someone says this is how we do

christenings back home yet longs to see the world over, elsewhere
30   someone disciplined a son coming home, too late, "We live here
but don't think that we're going to live like people here!"
The city's cathedral of smogged sky receives the daily sacrament

of conditional sentences about conditional places, "If we were home.
I would … " as strong a romance with the past tense as with what is
to come. Cresting as the engraver's mountain red black, purple, light
suffused in sunset, important in the middle of the pluperfect

in the subway though these separate dreamers are a mass of silences.
They are echo chambers for the voices of the gods of
cities. Glass, money, goods. They sit in a universe of halted breaths
40   waiting for this stop Bay and that stop Yonge and that one St. Patrick

in early morning surrender to factories in Brampton,
swirling grey into the 401 and the Queen Elizabeth Highway,

---

3. **Thomson … *Burnt Country*** Painting by Canadian landscape artist Tom Thomson (1877–1917). 4. **Lismer's *Forest in Winter*** Painting by Canadian artist Arthur Lismer (1885–1969), a member of the Group of Seven. 5. **Gurdwara** Sikh temple. 6. **gesso** Plaster of Paris or gypsum substance used as a ground for painting. 7. **Rosedale** Wealthy neighbourhood in Toronto.

they hold their tempers, their passions, over grumbling machines
until night, dreaming their small empires, their domestic tyrannies

but of course no voyage is seamless. Nothing in a city is discrete.
A city is all interpolation. The Filipina nurse bathes a body, the
Vincentian courier delivers a message, the Sikh cab driver navigates a
corner. What happens? A new road is cut, a sound escapes, a touch   50
                                                                            lasts

XXXI

what she might collect now and what she isn't
the bristle of light so public and irretrievable
the wood crumbled into paper too appropriate
the grey patch of stars that made her still mouth
the oblivious dress she wore, the shoes
grafted to her feet and the ink-dry pavement
her mourning, lustrous as fury

yet she too had glimpsed herself,
an unrepentant cheekbone, those fingers
brushing glyphs[8] of newsprint away   10
the extraordinary emptiness of the woman
emerging from clusters of dots on the front page
then the second page, then the last page
then vanishing all together, but not vanished

there, in the time, transparent,
held and held, she had been held, why
it was so quiet there and cool as edges
anything nearing life or what she might do
now, any opening, now again in the bolt
of a bicycle, again she had sensed, glimpsed   20
herself, now as pitiable and that she could not take

lust she had lost along with the things
in her suitcases that morning, and the things,
the slivers of seconds in between,
fallen, all of it, tinted, sunken, all of it,
that, she wanted back, that at least if not
a daughter as silver as velocity; and the true
taste of things and the atmosphere of her blood

beating at her temples in apprehension or fear
or love or any feeling; the climate of substances   30
she would have touched, the divine elements

---

8. glyphs Typographical characters.

her eyes ought to have seen, her throat devour,
the space surrounding her, look that gesture
of a boy the other morning, even the panic of a woman
bowing out of orbit to a lodestar[9] of crack

once she wore powder blue skirts and embroidered
Indian blouses, then she stood on the corner of
Oakwood and St. Clair waiting for a bus, the clarity
of the traffic, the sky, the day, her life
40   her directions, plain, unknown, except for this,
the idea, the idea that she was possible
nothing but the sun in the blood of a summer

she used to buy a new pair of sandals
each year, soften the leather with the sweat
of her feet, then a wide-mouthed woven bag
out of which wine and letters and lipstick
and panties, water, apples, bracelets, and grapes
could fall; she went to concerts tasting music
and the cocks of jazz musicians, taking their mouths

50   in her own scent; she used to jump fire hydrants
on Bloor when darkness wet the roads and drunks
cradled light posts; she used to take ganga-high rides
to Montreal when her body was dangerous and full
of liquid; she could assassinate streets with her eyes
damage books and chemical compounds and honey and waiting
rooms, dance floors would bleed from the knife of her dress

until, it must be said, the moment when all women realize
the war they're in, that the only possibility is falling
that the fragments of winter and music are only solemn
60   kisses to their half-life and only mercy and surrender move
their hand. Well what's more with a daughter given up
to lightening and pity she wanted her blue skirt back,
she wanted that single sense she'd lost, anticipation

She needed to smell, without dying, the skin
of someone else, she needed without a wounding,
without a murder, without a killing, a truce if not peace,
a city, as a city was supposed to be, forgetful,
and to gather up any charm she might have
left, to sleep, to feel snow, to have it matter,
70   to wake like leaves, to hate rain

(2002)

---

9. **lodestar** Guiding star, or principle.

Bill Gaston (1953–)

Bill Gaston was born in Winnipeg in 1953, and he lived there until he was 12. He spent the rest of his adolescence in Dollarton, in North Vancouver's Deep Cove area. Gaston claims he always wanted to be a writer, and as a youth he read everything from the Hardy Boys mysteries to Dostoevsky, but his real teenage passion was hockey — by the time he was 16, he was playing semi-professionally. Soon after, Gaston enrolled at the University of British Columbia to study English. But after obtaining a B.A. and two M.A.s, he left UBC convinced that writers should learn their craft from other, contemporary writers; he cites John LeCarré and Guy Vanderhaeghe as influences.

Gaston worked as a logger and as a salmon-fishing guide, and then, from 1990 to 1998, he taught and served as writer-in-residence at the University of New Brunswick; he also edited the literary magazine *The Fiddlehead*. He had published his first collection, *Deep Cove Stories*, in 1989 — other early titles include *North of Jesus' Beans* (1993) and *Sex Is Red* (1998). Gaston's stories have been noted for their effective handling of voice, character, and setting, as well as their mixing of gritty realism with the playful, the surreal, and the surprising. His stories are also distinguished by their scatological vocabulary and frank references to bodily functions and aging. "Our society is timidly avoidant," Gaston has declared: "Everybody is afraid of dying, and I think denying shit is the same as denying death." Accepting reality without sentimentalizing or sanitizing it is a frequent challenge for his protagonists.

Gaston's stories began receiving serious critical attention in 2002, with the publication of *Mount Appetite*. Nominated for the Giller Prize, the collection focuses on the denial and satisfaction of physical wants, examines the aging process, and investigates the (often unfulfilled) potential of the human spirit. Though Gaston's characters in this and other works are predominantly middle-aged baby boomers, each has a distinct and often bizarre personality, and each is enmeshed in unusual circumstances. In "The Little Drug Addict That Could," Gaston writes about a man who struggles to accept his inability to alter the conditions of his unsatisfying life as he gets high with his nephew, who is struggling to overcome his heroin addiction. In "The Alcoholist," a sommelier with an extraordinary palate creates a recipe for an astounding microbrew while reflecting on organic produce and his imminent death from liver cancer. These stories demonstrate Gaston's appreciation for situational irony and his fondness for placing characters in unlikely positions. He relishes the emotional poignancy that arises when a character is jarred from complacency and habit into a new mode of perception.

Describing the writing process, Gaston notes that "The main thrust of a story will come to me full-blown, usually arriving in the shape of a character or several characters in conflict over something stunning." His detached observations and clinical narrative tone create the impression that he, as author, does not actually orchestrate the "stunning" or remarkable elements of his fiction, but rather that those elements are somehow already present and waiting to be discovered by his characters. The stunning element might be external, environmental, or a previously unrecognized desire. In *Gargoyles*, Gaston's 2006 collection, it takes the shape of a little demon — an internal force that erupts during the aging process. His disturbed, human-contact-starved protagonists don't yearn for new cars or younger wives; all they crave is a physical or emotional connection with another being. In "Honouring Honey," for example, a suburban dad is overcome by the urge to shoot the elderly family dog and eat its heart. Through the sheer weirdness of the conflicts he depicts, Gaston distances himself from the clichés of baby boomer literature, but he still deals with its essential themes: suburban despair, material excess, spiritual dissatisfaction, and the loss of youth.

In 1990, Gaston published his first novel, *Tall Lives,* which he describes as "an attempt to de-Victorianize the body." His next novel, *The Cameraman,* appeared four years later. It tells the story of a documentary filmmaker, named Francis, who clashes with his director and mentor. The novel's major device is a double plot line: the narrative alternates between Francis's present and his past. Gaston also employs the metaphor of the hidden camera to explore the divergences between art and reality. His other novels include *Bella Combe Journal* (1996) and *The Good Body* (2000). In the latter, Bobby Bonaduce, an aging hockey player, is diagnosed with multiple sclerosis and returns home to the family he has abandoned. He enrolls in a creative writing course and initiates unexpected forms of familial reconciliation. Told from a limited third-person perspective, the novel has an intimate, colloquial, and conversational tone, and it highlights Gaston's ability to situate recognizable emotions and expressions within bizarre or absurd circumstances. One reviewer praised the book as "the first Canadian novel that successfully excavates three different worlds — hockey, academe, and the broken family — and [it] uses as its shovel a resilient humility."

In 2004, Gaston published *Sointula,* a novel centred on a West Coast island of the same name where a group of Finnish idealists founded a colony at the turn of the century. Like Sointula's founders, the novel's protagonists seek a harmony in the British Columbia landscape that they cannot find in their daily lives. The central character, Evelyn, leaves her comfortable existence in Ontario and all of its protective trappings and travels to B.C. in search of her alienated teenaged son. On his trail, she steals a kayak and heads for the failed utopia of Sointula. The novel has been called magic realist, but Gaston prefers the term "artful exaggeration." He tries to "exaggerate selectively for effect at certain spots without challenging the threshold of possibility," and he believes that the West Coast, in particular — with its massive trees, waves, and mountains — invites such an enlarged, "absurd vision."

Gaston has authored several plays and a volume of poetry entitled *Inviting Blindness* (1995). In 2006, he produced *Midnight Hockey: All About Beer, the Boys and the Real Canadian Game,* a memoir of the years he spent as a semi-professional and beer-league player. He won the Timothy Findley Award in 2003, and *Gargoyles* was nominated for a Governor General's Award in 2006. Gaston lives with his wife, writer Dede Crane, and their children in Victoria, B.C., and since 1998 he has taught in the creative writing department at the University of Victoria.

The Alcoholist

Lyle van Luven typically got into these arguments with his employers. And typically he kept a civil tongue, simply explaining himself as he had so often before. Which over the years hadn't gotten any easier — how to explain colour to the blind?

"I am not a brewmaster," van Luven began, choosing *via negativa,*[1] "nor am I a chemist. Nor am I a slave to Bavarian Purity Laws."

Again he raised the ostentatious silver mug, smelled the naïveté of its contents, put it gently down. A pain gripped his abdomen and he put his hand to the desk-top, quickly but gracefully, for support. He was explaining himself to someone named Peter Philips, owner of Vancouver Brews, another venture into the microbrewery industry. This West Coast was, apparently, still flowering with new afficionados of beer, those ready to dismiss the chemistry of Molsons or Labatts in favour of anything whose label read "hand-crafted in small batches."

---

1. *via negativa*   Negative theory; theological doctrine that attempts to speak about God by describing what he is not.

Van Luven stood in Philips' new office, which smelled of its peach-tinted paint, so he would not stay long. One wall was a window onto the brew operations below; another afforded a moneyed view of the North Shore mountains. Van Luven had been warned of heavy corporate backing here. He could see with his own eyes that beer was not Philips' primary love.

"Mr. Philips, if you want this wheat beer of yours, this blond, to be 'the best in the city' — "

"Country."

"'Country.' Then you'll have to introduce a less conspicuous, more subtly engaging — "

"Okay. Good. What?"

Philips had no time for intimacy with his beer. He wanted it whizzing off the shelves.

"It must be subtle."

"Yes. Fine. What?"

Van Luven had no stomach for further debate on the difference between "mass appeal" and "quality," how they were very nearly mutually exclusive, and how a business approach refused to consider this. In his younger days he would have lectured. That time in Toronto he had pointed at the belching distillery and shouted at them all, *"This should be your church!"*

"That's not for me to say yet. We'll be involving the nuance of four, maybe five, partial flavours. So — I'll ask you again." Van Luven paused in punishment. "How is it — exactly — that you want your customers to *feel?*"

During the circuitous ferry trip to his Pender Island home, van Luven reread favourite bits of the Buddhist tantric text he was studying, those passages on *prajna*[2] and *alayavijnaya*[3] which both calmed and energized him for the way they described the workings of his ordinary genius. He suspected the current beer project might be his last. While his death had no exact timetable, the growing fatigue and pain would soon demand a decision from him. The Vancouver test-batches would be ready in two weeks. He sensed the best route would be to tone down the apricot hints, which promoted a cheap kind of acidic *fun,* in favour of a more bodied, after-nose of smoky oak. This would be eccentric in a blond, but all save the most deadened drinker would gain from it a homey warmth and confidence. Actually, they would gain this whether they were aware of it or not. There was a suitable hops coming out of eastern Oregon.

After Vancouver Brews, van Luven had invitations to work with a distillery in Los Angeles (pollution there making his throat constrict at the notion), and with a vineyard in, of all places, France. *Estates de Petit Rhone* had asked that, if he came, he keep his visit a secret. While van Luven's reputation in Europe was solid enough, there remained that Old World embarrassment over employing a North American taster. All of which piqued van Luven's vanity, of course, and he considered going. He suspected their problems lay in the relationship of rainfall and fertilizer. El Nino muddied age-old habits. They'd had a scientist in and now they knew, as van Luven always had, that this was beyond science. But the job was some months away, which might be too late.

---

2. *prajna* Buddhist idea of not-selfhood, emptiness. 3. *alayavijnaya* Buddhist consciousness that makes other consciousnesses possible.

The extreme low tide, coupled with the heat of the day, offered a waft of percolating mud-and-seaweed that smelled deeply vital. It felt nutritious just to inhale. Well, it was. In any case it was the perfect tide to bag kelp for his garden, and he would have done so were it not for, again, the matter of time. He stood on his narrow porch surveying his vegetables, and the equation arose unbidden: how much more food would he be needing? This question broke down into smaller equations: If I fertilize with kelp today, will I still be alive when the garden reaps the benefits? How many more meals will I want to make of that chard? Why not trade half of that garlic for more of Oswald's carrots?

Since they'd resolved their fight last year, his elderly neighbour Oswald had been almost aggressively generous. The fight had centered around carrots. Van Luven had traded some green onions and romaine for a box of Oswald's carrots, one bite of which informed van Luven of at least two chemicals that would make him mentally ill for days. Oswald caught him burying the carrots on the beach. After assuaging the older man's feelings, a long discussion about organic gardening ensued — van Luven didn't bother going into much of his own history, or talent, except to say that he had finely honed senses — and Oswald was won over. For two years since he'd been eager for van Luven to try out his organic this and that, which van Luven did, having to bury only half of it, mostly root crops, which continued to absorb the soil's residual nonsense.

Oswald was fine as far as neighbours went. They often stood and chatted at the spot between their two properties where a fence would have been. And van Luven loved — loved — old Oswald's cat, an unnamed stray tabby. The cat seemed to like van Luven too, and at his approach was given to a display of coy and ribald[4] that looked almost like humour, something van Luven could not recall ever seeing in a cat.

Van Luven took his steaming dinner of new potatoes, chard and parsley onto the deck, to eat standing up. He didn't like so spartan a plate, but he was out of the Saltspring lamb, the only meat he still enjoyed. For a decade, the salmon hereabouts had been losing their elan,[5] giving him only their encroaching lethargy. Tomorrow he would phone and order a hind quarter. He would like another few meals of lamb. The innocence of their romp.

To his right, van Luven could feel the pampered growth of his garden; to his left, on the rock outcrop, the quieter swellings of moss and lichen, which sucked their life out of deadfall and, astoundingly, granite. The otter family should be cruising past within the hour. He admired their enactment of an ideal human family — two parents and three children — in the way the parents led and coaxed and herded, and the way the loopy pups splashed and played disappearing games in the kelp. They no doubt suffered crude neuroses and various otter problems, but van Luven couldn't see them.

He turned to take in his empty plate, stopping to stare at his reflection in the glass door — was his skin yellower, or was that the sun? — then at the glass door itself, which needed cleaning with vinegar. He eyed the missing cedar shake above his head, its gap-toothed look of poverty. It was natural that of late he'd been stopping like this to stare at and chastise his house, and his land. Easiest was this assessment of place, comforts, life-scat. Easier than taking stock of his accrued *being* — which inevitably led to the house-of-mirrors taking stock of that which was taking stock.

---

4. **ribald** Vulgar, coarse. 5. **elan** Energy.

The heavy look of the house was Shirley's doing: post-and-beam, thick cedar siding, a house to withstand earthquakes and two centuries of weather. They'd built it as their summer retreat, though van Luven, certain he could never again live in any city, secretly knew it would be his home. Shirley, his third wife, now third ex-wife, was a professor of engineering. Her world was one of physical equations. They had seemed a good match, for his world was also one of equations. But while hers could be explained, his could not. His influences on the house, for instance, could be seen in the six Balinese wind chimes (the diamond sound of which cured some of his more rooted depressions) hanging at strategic windows, and the uniform white curtains with their lemon trim. The undoing of their marriage had less to do with his insistence on bare stone floors than on his inability to explain himself. "Allergies" worked for a time, but the word grew thin, and was in any case a lie. In the end, him saying that "the spirit of manufactured tile makes me minutely insane" simply *sounded* insane. Nor could he explain how he knew that his sensitivity to the world was growing.

But it had always been thus. It had been a surprise to learn he was different from other children. Whereas other kids joshed while munching two and three hotdogs, his one bite gave him the dumb fear of the slaughterhouse, visceral knowledge of a mix of mushed parts congealing in a tube. Not to mention an instant salt headache. Tropical fruits awarded him exotic moods he otherwise wouldn't have known. Sugar was a harsh and wonderful drug.

One straw that broke Shirley's back was otherwise funny, and she had laughed without mockery. Nostalgic one day, trying to better remember details of his childhood, van Luven had made himself a peanut butter and jam sandwich, wrapped it in wax paper, put it in a paper bag, let it sit unrefrigerated for five hours — then took it out and smelled it and became instantly eight.

When he met Shirley, van Luven hadn't yet developed the liver cancer, nor what they now said was a tumour in his brain, but he was well into his cirrhosis. In this he hadn't been forthright. He hadn't been able to explain to his first two wives his love of alcohol, and why he "couldn't just spit the wine out" at tastings, so why had he thought it would be any different with Shirley? He'd tried. Alcohol, he told her, is not just alcohol. The alcohol in one beer is not the alcohol in another. Alcohol was not framed by ingredients, it was made by them. What was the yeast eating as it died, expelling its vital poison? What was its environment, what was its *mood?* These were questions more spiritual than scientific. More, what was the relationship of the alcohol to the human body? This affair was *not* consummated on the tongue. No, the only bed of this romance was found deep, deep in the body.

Harder still to explain was that, just as the truth of Calvados — good God, it was *called* "spirit" — was discernible only in front of a rustic fire, at dusk, in something akin to a hunting lodge, so the truth in a German beer was available only to those who knew to chug the earthy froth down, exhaling noises of satisfied aggression as you clinked the thick mug on a table, which would be made of wood.

He couldn't explain, but his proximity to spirit spoke for itself. It had earned him his money and modest fame. Almost anyone could feel in themselves the difference between three drinks of draft beer and three drinks of scotch. But how many could feel — *feel* — the difference in a Pinot from one valley and a Pinot from the next? Or the difference between 1985 Laphroig and its 1986 sister? How many would know it's been stored months in a decanter? That had been washed with detergent? Or if this ice cube was made from spring water? Not on the tongue, but in their being? How many people *became* the trace of detergent, or the spring water, or the patient corpse of peat in the scotch?

Addiction was an equation too. In truth, a marriage. And disease its necessary divorce.

Van Luven washed his plate and fork, and came back onto the deck to watch the otters. Hit with a sudden bad pain — the one that penetrated front to back and effectively bisected his body — he sank to the deck floor and put his knees up. He took several deep, rough breaths. Some of the pain he still could manage to feel as "interesting," but most now he could not. The small you could own; the large owned you. Knees up, keep the moans low and steady, releasing. He had his heroin coming, at great expense, promised from a friend of a friend of Shirley's. (He repeated to himself the funny phrase — "shipment of heroin" — which sounded like bad television.) He'd been assured that if taken through the nose it would be enough for weeks of pain. Or if taken all at once, to end things. He'd read De Quincy[6] and others, and wondered how it would be, entering opium's palace. How long would he stay, before the millions of angelic candles extinguished themselves?

He had tried for a time to let his senses seek out a route of miraculous healing. He'd eaten certain vegetables and herbs, and even leaves and grasses, tasting and feeling in these the birth and fresh workings of new tissue — it was for the most part a raw, giddy affair, precipitous in its balance between the toxic and the vital, and one that felt nauseatingly like his own gestation. Nor did it work. The playground scamper of new cells did little but bounce off a densely scarred and tumoured liver that felt more mulish than stupid in its determination to die.

Hardest to explain — and doctors would be the first to laugh at this — was his certainty that his cirrhosis was caused not so much by alcohol but by imperfect intentions, and by ignorance. Insecticides. Additives. Actually, the real poison taken in during his life of alcohol was the greed, the *lack* of spirit, of those who made it. This he could taste. This he had absorbed.

The pain lessened enough for him to doze. These days he was always tired, but he could sleep only when pain let him.

He awoke to the squeak and bang of Oswald's screen door. He decided to stay down for a while, though he might miss the otters. This light rain on the face was pleasant, though he wished also for music. In recent years he'd been exploring music's visit to certain of his tissues. He didn't have a medical image of where sounds located themselves, but time and again certain tones gravitated to certain spots in his body, elbows and kidneys and ribs in particular, and he could hear the sounds in these new ears and feel them influence how he felt about the world.

But now not even his wind chimes could keep him awake.

Colours of sunset told him he'd slept an hour or two. He got to all fours, then stood. The pain had settled enough for him to walk to the beach. The odd yellow in the sky — was it real, or was there bilirubin in the fluid of his eye? Was that possible?

---

6. **De Quincy** British intellectual (1785–1859) who wrote *Confessions of an English Opium-Eater*.

Van Luven stepped carefully in his sandals; some rocks were slippery, others were armed with collars of barnacles on which he'd often cut his toes. Walking, he studied the shifting planes of light coming off sand, off rocks wet and dry, off seaweed in all its curves, colours changing even as he watched them. It was true you never saw the same place twice.

He paused at the lip of the tide, facing out, his sandaled toes half in the icy water. To his left, in a patch of clean sand, was a scatter of prints where his otters must have emerged, a rare event. He could see in the prints' patternlessness their nosing and dashing about. Curiosity, whimsy. He'd missed it. Maybe they'd left the water because he wasn't looming at them from his deck. He could see lines where their tails had briefly dragged; children's tails, adult's tails. Tales.

Vancouver Brews. Should he try to give Peter Philips the best blond beer in the country? Should he give him a good beer at all? Despite his wayward day, some part of him had been at work and had arrived at a deep, beet-like nuance, followed by layered aromas dissolving by turns — salmonberry, honey, faint leathers — to the oak finish. It would look blond but hardly taste it. It would have blond's effervescence yet something weighty and generous; a beer to dispel many an off-mood. But why should Peter Philips have it?

As if beckoned, van Luven turned to see a full moon rising over the mainland mountains, and it startled him with meaning. It looked, it felt, like completion. Without much thought on the matter, but some surprise, he knew it would be tonight.

He had never had much fear of death. Death was simple, surely: if there was nothing, he would not know it. If there was something, it would probably be much like now, for there was no reason for it not to be.

Tonight. How? He had painkillers enough. If there was a way to keep from vomiting … He literally could not stomach … If there was a way to exit with senses open, uninjured …

It was a medium-sized oyster, perfect, and for no reason other than that he picked it up, spied a suitable rock, and dashed it down. A quarter shell broke off, enough for him to get a finger in. The flesh was sun-warmed. Not constricted by the bite of ice or of lemon, its taste was grandly oyster. He knew that his tasting so fully the creature's flesh was all the thanks it needed.

Spinning on his heel, carrying the empty shell, van Luven understood that life could end on a note of humour. The whimsy of an otter. He traced his steps back to the otter family's scamper-ground and knelt there, studying. He pitched forward momentarily, dropping his forehead to the sand. It seemed he'd passed out, for moments only, a new thing.

But there, an otter pup's perfect paw print. He admired it for a moment, its heartwarming symmetry. Then eased the shell-edge into the sand, pushing gently, scooping the entire print intact. He stood and held it to his face — a paw print in a shell. This he would send to Peter Philips. He would include instructions that it be added to the initial vat, and that it would linger in spirit in all brews to come. He would suggest a label depicting nothing but a closed oyster shell — which was none other than a sealed promise — and that there should be no words on the label. A man like Peter Philips might even do such a thing. And it might even work. The beer might actually taste good. There were stranger things than this.

Van Luven stared possessively at his paw print. He would add — one more thing. The edge of shell was as sharp as it needed to be and, an interesting pain, he cut himself deeply on the thumb pad. One drop, two, three, onto the paw-print sand, black dots spreading in.

Now van Luven jerked back in surprise at himself. Here was something he had not properly tasted. With caution, and respect, he lifted his thumb, bringing it to his tongue. In the instant of taste, he knew what he would do.

Softly licking his lips, he steadied his hunger. Taking shallow breaths, he rose in courage, muscle. He took a deeper breath, held it, and under the rising full moon the shell sank deeply into his wrist.

He didn't have to suck, he had only to receive the rush, to swallow in sucking rhythm to his heart beat. His continuous stream. In its taste, the truth of a mirror. The hot bronze of all he'd known. Van Luven went easily to the sand, the river of himself leaving no room for any more effort, or thought.

(2002)

Neil Bissoondath (1955–)

Neil Bissoondath was born in Trinidad in 1955. His family came to the island as indentured immigrants from India in the early 1900s and entered the ranks of the middle class when Bissoondath's paternal grandfather, after fulfilling the terms of indenture, opened a store. Bissoondath grew up in a world of literature and ideas — he has referred to his mother as "the most well-read person I've ever known." His Uncle Vidia, better known as V.S. Naipaul, was awarded the 2001 Nobel Prize for Literature (an honour Bissoondath has called "a way of saying, 'You have lived your life well'"). Naipaul strenuously encouraged his nephew to leave Trinidad to pursue a university education in Canada, and Bissoondath listened. In 1973, he enrolled at York University in Toronto, earning a B.A. in French literature in 1977.

After graduating, Bissoondath spent several years teaching French and English as a second language. His students, many of whom were recent immigrants to Canada, proved an abundant source of material for the short story collection Bissoondath worked on when he was not teaching or reading voraciously. It was some time before the collection saw publication: *Digging Up the Mountains* would not appear until 1985. In the meantime, Bissoondath attended a writing workshop at the Banff School of Fine Arts and submitted his stories to magazines, finally placing "Dancing" in *Saturday Night;* three more stories were read on CBC Radio's *Anthology.*

Despite his assertion that "literature is literature; it's not politics," Bissoondath has cited among his influences an array of international authors whose work has rich political undercurrents — Nadine Gordimer, Mario Vargas Llosa, and Milan Kundera, as well as several 19th-century Russians. In *Digging Up the Mountains,* Bissoondath delves into the political powder keg of Trinidadian society from the perspective of a displaced native. He has remarked that although his literary impulse turns him towards his homeland, he would never have been able to write about it if he had remained there: "I cannot write about a place while I am in it," he says; Canada "has given me the anonymity I need to write." The collection mines themes of cultural dislocation, the illusory nature of "home," the fine line between law and order and violent criminality. The protagonist of the title story, well-to-do Indo-Caribbean businessman Hari Beharry, is at a crisis point in his life: his once idyllic island home is in a state of emergency; a "cynical politics of corruption" has come in the wake of independence, and thugs sporting sunglasses, indistinguishable from the police, are on the prowl. Hari has been denounced as a "Yankee slave" by the new socialist government, which Bissoondath caricatures as a band of hypocrites. Reduced to defending his property, gun in hand, Hari stands on the veranda of his home firing a revolver at the mountains of the story's title because he believes they are overrun with guerrillas. His beloved mountains, once a concrete symbol of safety, immutability, and belonging, are now ominous and threatening, and Harry must contemplate exile.

In 1988, Bissoondath published his first novel, *A Casual Brutality*, which tells the story of a Canadian-educated doctor, Raj Ramsingh, who must leave his native Caribbean island — the fictional Casaquemada — to escape the rampant corruption and caste-based oppression that have blossomed there. The formal elements of the novel underscore narrator Raj's dislocation: his language switches from standard English to Caribbean dialect; he structures his narrative as a series of time shifts, transporting the reader back and forth between different periods in his life and between Casaquemada and Canada. Like "Digging Up the Mountains," this is a tale of paradise despoiled, and Bissoondath encapsulates the deterioration, the fall from innocence, in a number of potent metaphors. For example, Raj's once vital and engaged grandfather slides into mental incompetence and eventually dies, as his once orderly showpiece of a garden grows wild and becomes impenetrable.

Next, Bissoondath published a short story collection entitled *On the Eve of Uncertain Tomorrows* (1991), which deals with people fleeing political oppression and economic hardship who are struggling to establish a new life in Canada. Two years later, he produced a novel, *The Innocence of Age*, which also deals with cultural alienation, but this time between a Toronto father and son — Pasco lives according to values of love and friendship, while his son, Danny, has his sights set on economic prosperity and has little interest in the bond of common humanity.

In 1994, Bissoondath published *Selling Illusions: The Cult of Multiculturalism in Canada*, and thereby sparked a lively nationwide debate. In newspaper editorials, on radio phone-in shows, and on public affairs television programs, he was either praised or reviled for his harsh criticism of the Canadian government's multiculturalism policies. Bissoondath contended that such an approach to minority cultures promotes ghettoization and stereotyping, that it severely limits opportunities for immigrants by exiling them to the margins of Canada's cultural mainstream.

After having thus propelled himself into the national spotlight, Bissoondath returned to novel writing. *The Worlds Within Her* appeared in 1999. It is the story of Yasmin, a middle-aged Canadian who returns to her native Trinidad to scatter her mother's ashes. She has not seen the island since her early childhood, and her desire to trace the roots of her identity is powerfully awakened through conversations she has with her aunt, her uncle, and a long-time servant of her influential family. Slowly, Yasmin arrives at a new understanding of her mother and the world she once inhabited. The novel garnered Bissoondath a Governor General's Award nomination.

"With my fiction," Bissoondath has said, "I have no thesis. There is a thesis there, but I recognize it only at the end." The structure of *Doing the Heart Good* (2002), which fuses the novel and short story forms, serves to accommodate this approach to writing. Alistair Mackenzie, the central character, is an elderly White Montrealer, a war veteran who is caught up in his memories, which constitute the book's series of linked narratives. Unilingual Alistair must adapt to living in the bilingual household of his daughter following an arson attack on his own home, and there he resists his impending death through his present-tense retelling of the past.

In 2005, Bissoondath produced *The Unyielding Clamour of the Night*. It is set in a fictional South Asian country (modelled on Sri Lanka) and it centres on Arun Bannerji, an idealistic young man from a wealthy family who goes to teach school in a region rocked by violent revolt. Arun battles to preserve his faith in human nature in a world that has gone to hell — suicide bombers vie with one another for greater glory, war-mongers extract economic profit from human misery, atrocity turns to banality. Bissoondath's fascination with our essential nature is everywhere in this work. "We are contrary," he has insisted, "we are illogical, we love, we hate, and nobody can truly predict how any other person is going to react."

Bissoondath won the MacLennan Prize for both *Doing the Heart Good* and *The Unyielding Clamour of the Night*. He lives in Quebec City with his wife, medical ethics lawyer Anne Marcoux, and their daughter. He teaches creative writing at Laval University.

Continental Drift

The room, a rectangular hole between two slabs of building, has the feel of an elevator shaft. The dull light from the lamp on the reception counter shows walls of a scuffed sky-blue; a stairway off to my right leads upwards to shadow within which, with concentration, I make out the outlines of a large door. In front of me, talking with the concierge — a big man with tired eyes, rounded shoulders, and a voice theatrical with studied patience, or weariness — are two Spaniards, a man and a woman, young, equally ragged, as if they have been travelling on foot for days, but barely. The woman, eyes alternating between rabid, uncomprehending attention and desperate fatigue, says nothing, stands just a little off to the side, their packs, bound with belts and pieces of string, leaning against her legs.

The concierge says, "Fifty francs each. Bedding deposit."

The Spaniard is fidgety. His French is bad. "But we are leaving in the morning. Four o'clock. We do not have much money."

"It is a deposit. You will get it back tomorrow morning."

"But we have little money." He is pleading now, in low tones.

"No deposit, no bedding. That's all there is to it."

"You think we steal your bedding?"

The concierge says nothing, patiently rolls his pen between his fingers.

The Spaniard says, "But how I am sure you give me my money in the morning?"

"And how can I be sure you'll give me back my bedding in the morning?"

"We're not thieves." A stridency[1] enters his voice.

"You give me fifty francs, I give you the bedding. And in the morning we exchange once more. It's the rule, it's simple. Fifty francs each please." He maintains his evenness of tone without effort: he knows he has won.

The man turns to the woman and mumbles rapidly in Spanish. She digs into the pocket of her jeans and hands him bills rolled as tight and as flat as a stick of chewing-gum. With difficulty he tugs out two fifty-franc notes and tosses them onto the counter, a flick of the wrist that implies both disdain and resignation.

The concierge takes up the money and, with neither comment nor glance, showing only an impenetrable passivity, hands over two stacks of white bedding. He gestures with his thumb towards the shadow at the top of the stairs. "Par là," he says to the man; and to the woman, "Toi, de l'autre côté."

The woman, uncomprehending, flustered, looks at her friend with a kind of desperation. He explains, indicating the stairway across the room from the one he is to take. She grabs him by the shoulders; clearly, she does not like being separated from him. But he pushes her off, mumbling, scoops up his bedding, shoulders his pack, and sets off up the stairs without looking back. She follows him with her eyes, then looks wildly at the concierge.

He says, more softly, "Par là, mademoiselle," pointing her to her stairway.

---

1. **stridency** A shrill, irritating quality.

Suddenly meek, with eyes fearful, she takes her bedding, drags her pack to the stairs, and disappears up into the webby darkness.

The concierge, neutrality unperturbed, says to me, "Passeport, s'il vous plaît, monsieur."

I hand over my passport along with a fifty-franc note, take up my bedding, and make my way up the stairs into the darkness, the shoulder-straps of my pack pressing like two weighted hands into my tensed flesh. The Spanish woman's face, her terror at so simple a thing, remains vividly with me. It seems to hint at the precarious, as if — in her vision, along with what is before her — she senses herself at the crumbing edge of a precipice. It is not that this look is new to me; it is, rather, that I have seen it before, many times in many places, this look that is a new version, more tragic, of continental drift. The Arabs in England, the Turks in Germany, the Gypsies in Spain, the swarming lost of the bars, backrooms, and alleys of Amsterdam. And everywhere, in the streets, the subways, the hidden corners, are the hippies — so strange a word, so dated, evocative of an era before my own — balding men and greying women with beads, bangles, and backpacks, guitars strung on their shoulders, like refugees lost in time, aging people stuck in a past that clings only to them, like the dust and soot that cloak the buildings, famous, infamous, and nondescript, of Europe. There flows from their eyes the melancholy fear of those adrift, travel imposed not by desire but by habit and circumstance, in what I have come to think of not as wanderlust but as wanderlost.

They fascinate me, those faces, those looks, those eyes. They attract me; for they seem to harbor truths that will always lie well beyond the reach of my security.

The mattress — on the lower bunk of a double-decker, the upper bunk littered with the jumbled jetsam of another traveller — is, as usual, thin and bare, a meagre slab beneath me. The pillow, of even more desperate dimensions, is barely distinguishable from the sheet I've thrown loosely on. Four high-wattage bulbs make sleep impossible; the light, rejected almost with violence by the sky-blue walls, seems to gather in the middle of the room and explode out into every corner, stifling shadow.

Lying here in my jeans so faded they are nearly white and socks mended in the crushed, haphazard way of the inexperienced, I feel the drain of my six months of wandering: little town after little town to big town after big town, from train to bus to bus to train, faces and languages switched from one day to the next as easily as switching channels on a television. Faces, styles, cars, buildings, landscape in ungraspable array. And the cathedrals! Lord, the cathedrals! Endless miles of flying buttresses, crowds of spires and gargoyles: boundless piety in carved stone. And then the museums. I gave up on them early on, all the paintings and statues, centuries and a continent on display, when I began to feel that all of Europe was a museum, and all the men and women merely caretakers; when it began to seem to me that no sooner had Europe lived a passage of its life than it put the relics on display behind glass sombrely labelled, the past — remote and recent — neatly packaged.

And now, lying on the barely realized mattress, feeling the boards of the bed pressing in on my back, the question that first occurred to me a couple of weeks ago once more presents itself: what, in all this time, after all these miles, have I learnt?

I have had fun, at times. Have been angered, irritated, stunned. And, often, merely bored. I have seen many things, encountered many people. But all in passing, experiences less complete than dreams, visions fraught with the insubstantial, footnotes forming of themselves no whole, offering but image and sensation as recompense for endless motion. Lessons? But there has been commitment to nothing: so, whence the lessons?

I reach down with my right arm to the backpack beneath the bunk, find the side pocket, unzip it, and take out my diary, a small hardcover book shut with a brass clasp. On the cover, of a tan felt soft and warm to the touch, is my name stamped in gold cursive script: *J. T. Farrell*. James Timothy. An ordinary name, it suddenly occurs to me; there seems to be something distinctly unprecious about it.

I haven't written in the diary for a while. Much time has passed without anything worth noting. But, as I flick through it, I am surprised to see that it has been a full two months. It depresses me to read my last entry, a brief description — so brief, with subjects and prepositions dropped, that I think I detect the incipient boredom — of a run-in with a persistent prostitute in Munich. "Cheap fuck! Cheap fuck!" she had shouted in heavily accented English stumbling after me in the street. I had ended up running through the crowds on the sidewalk, pursued by her screams: "Sauhund! Con! Fag! Hijo de puta!"[2] All the spitting language of an international sideshow.

And after Italy I had scrawled, "No more church doors please, no more altars, no more crosses."

Instinctively I reach for the pen encased in the binding of the book but as my finger touches it I decide that there is nothing to write, that, still, I *feel* like writing nothing. I want instead to withdraw to a cafeteria, to order a coffee in a language that requires of me no linguistic calisthenics, and then to hop the subway home, to shower, dinner, bed. It is, I realize, the same sensation that comes to me after a few hours spent in the Royal Ontario Museum or the Art Gallery: enough of the old and the captured; time needed to assimilate it, store it; and time, then, to breathe the fresher air of things yet uninvented.

I put the notebook beside me on the bed and close my eyes, turning my face to the wall to escape the light.

Voices, loud and British, echo down the hall and into the room. In irritation I open my eyes and turn towards the door. Two men, young but with faces aged by thick, weathered skin, enter together. Towels are draped wetly over their shirtless shoulders. Their hair, still damp from the shower, is uncombed, and their skin — an underlying greyness drawn out by the probing light of the room — recalls the color of marble statues greyed by exposure.

They pay no attention to me, walk to the far end of the room to bunks, top and bottom, burdened with weathered army backpacks and satchels. One busily towels his back, as if scratching with the towel, while the other, less concerned, throws on a white shirt that quickly grows spotty with dampness.

The toweller says, "Remember the Dutch one? What was 'er name?"

"Hildie? Tildie?" his friend replies, untidily sticking his shirttails into his jeans.

"No-no-no, Hildie was the German. Battle a Britain all over again. Only *I* was doin' the bloody bombin' this time."

His friend, pulling a comb with difficulty through his dirty-blond hair, laughs. "You shoulda heard the noise you two was makin'. Enough to raise the dead."

The toweller sits on the lower bunk caressing the memory. "More than the dead, 'enry. She was a good one."

---

2. **Sauhund ... Hijo de puta** German for "pig-dog," and Spanish for "son of a prostitute."

"How many times that night? Three? Four?"

The toweller grins, then gives a raucous laugh. "Don't bloody remember. But she performed miracle after miracle that night."

"Rise, Lazarus. Again and again and again."

The toweller flings his towel at 'enry, knocking the comb from his hand, and they both double over in exaggerated laughter.

I cover my eyes with my forearm, listening with growing reluctance to the conversation. I wish they would leave, for they bring back to me my own two spells of sexual adventure early on in the trip, quick, unhappy trysts that engendered in their embarrassed aftermaths a dissatisfaction and a loneliness such as I had never before known.

But they won't leave, begin discussing the varied abilities of the girls they bedded in Italy. I suddenly get a vision of them as semen machines leaving deposits wherever they go, like male cats in uncontrollable heat, followed, in respite, by this savored inventory of technical details, public boasts of pubic circus tricks.

My stomach hollows at the thought, and my mouth goes sour. With a quick movement I roll out of the bed, slip into my hiking boots — scuffed and dusty, red laces frayed at the ends — and make my way from the brightness of the room and corridor to the darkness of the entrance hall where the concierge, almost somnolent, is reading a book in the yellow circle of his lamplight, and out into the febrile[3] air of a quiet dusk.

The sky, clouded, is of a grey uniformity that seems to throw its color onto the cobblestones of the wide street. Trees, in the last of their full green, line the opposite sidewalk, the stores and cafés beyond their thin trunks already darkened, shuttered. The sidewalk is deserted and the silence itself, so unrelieved, seems to whisper in unseizable tones.

Suddenly a small car squeals around a corner, shoots past me, and disappears down the street. I think, with envy, of people hurrying home. The fading whine of the car engine is replaced by a silence gone inert and an almost perceptible quickening of the multiplying greyness. It is as if the town is sinking into itself, sucking all life indoors in the small-town fashion I know so well, the descent of dusk bringing a retreat that is like desertion.

I walk the length of the street, to where it opens out into a large square in the middle of which rises a monument, a column of concrete surmounted by a bare-breasted woman in dramatic posture. Graffiti and posters, visible but unreadable in the dying light, cover the base of the monument. The buildings enclosing the square are in darkness but for two places on the far side: an unpeopled bar fronted by white chairs and orange tables, and a garishly neoned hotel. Neither is inviting, and for a moment I wonder what to do next. Eat? But I'm not really hungry. Continue my walk? But exploration, unkindled, now takes effort. I am tired, I know, of continually going nowhere.

Beside me on the sidewalk is a telephone booth and I suddenly wish I could call someone, but no one is within easy reach, familiarity distant. Then I notice that the phone lacks both receiver and cord. It is like a sign.

A light drop of rain lands on my face. Without a thought I turn around and, with hurried step and a sense of relief, make my way back to the hostel, to its threadbare bed and piercing light and voices that bring distress.

---

3. **febrile** Feverish.

"Excusez-moi."

Shouts echo through the halls. Boots pound up and down stairs.

"Excusez-moi."

My shoulder-blades hurt and the pain, with a kind of determination, begins creeping its way slowly up my neck.

"Excusez-moi."

I open my eyes and look up into a face shadowed by the light. "Yes?"

"Ahh." The man straightens up, shoulder-length hair, thick and black, picking up the light and breaking it into sparks. He has a strong, square face with generous features, a face that inspires both instant trust and distrust, the kind of face, laughing eyes, open smile, that can disarm. "You are American?" he says. The accent is British, but the pronunciation, careful and delicate, as if each word is being stroked before spoken, clearly comes from a gruffer, more solid language.

"No, Canadian." His question and my answer, repeated enough in the last months to become a kind of litany, irritate me; they bring to mind the American girl — tanned, Californian — who, on the train last night, said to me with sarcastic bite, "And do you have a Canadian flag on your backpack, like *all* the Canadians?" I wanted to hit her but, instead, simply said, "Yes. We don't have to hide our nationality." I then fled her, pushing my way through the crowded corridor to another car.

"Please forgive me for disturbing you," the man continues, "but do you have a ... ?" He doesn't have the word. "For beer. To open the bottles." And his hands, large, with soiled fingernails, mimic the action of taking the cap off a bottle.

"A bottle opener."

"Yes, that's it. A bottle opener."

"No, I'm sorry." I close my eyes, hoping he will go away.

"You said you are Canadian?"

"Yes." My irritation grows.

"Are you from Montreal?"

"No. From a little town you've never heard of. In Ontario. But you've probably never heard of there either." I keep my eyes closed but as I hear myself speak my irritation lessens. "I go to university in Toronto."

"I knew a Canadian once. In London. Very nice. Very kind."

"You're not ... are you British?"

"No-no." He gives a resounding chuckle, drawing it out in such a way that I realize the question has brought images to his mind, images he wants to savor, if only for a second or two. "No, I'm Spanish."

I open my eyes and sit up. "You speak very good English."

"I spent a year in London. I wanted to learn the language." His eyes look directly at mine; his posture — slim, solid body clad in black jeans, dark-blue shirt, and black vest — reflects a relaxed confidence. There is nothing tentative about him.

"My name is Enrique," he says.

"James." I put out my hand. Enrique grasps it briefly, but with strength. The roughness of the skin surprises me. There is contrast between the clipped precision of his language and the knotted hardness of his hand: each seems to suggest a different background.

"I am with a friend in another room. We are going to have dinner. Would you like to join us?"

"Thank you, but I'm tired."

"We don't have much. Sausage, bread, apples, a few bottles of beer. But we would be pleased if you would share it with us."

There is in his invitation a kind of old-world sincerity, an elegance of the kind that, at the beginning of the trip, I had expected to encounter daily but that, more often than not, has presented itself only in artifacts, in carved wood and chiselled stone, as if petrified. His words, his manner, are almost anachronistic, but at the same time attractive. "Thank you," I hear myself saying. "I'd like that."

We walk down the hall to a much larger, dormitory-like room crowded with single beds, some sheathed in white, others grey rectangles of thin mattress. Enrique leads the way to the far corner. Half-reclining on one of the beds is a tall, thin man, scraggly blond hair uncombed and badly cut, face drained of blood in the way of the ill. Enrique introduces us: "This is Carlos. Carlos does not speak much English." Then he speaks rapidly to Carlos in Spanish and I hear my name. Carlos smiles thinly, with a reticence that is somehow not distancing, as if it contains its own apology, establishing a kind of disinterested neutrality. We shake hands, a weak, brief motion, and before I can sit, at Enrique's urging, on the edge of the bed, Carlos is already gazing through the ceiling at stars years distant.

As Enrique busies himself laying out the meal — unwrapping the sausage, slicing the apples with a pocket knife, hooking the bottle caps on the edge of the metal bed-frame and banging on them with the flat of his palm, the beer fizzing and flowing out from beneath the partially twisted caps — I wonder at the contrast between the two friends: the one dark and strong with full, expressive lips; the other fair and fragile, with thin, bloodless lips that fade inconspicuously into his face; Enrique overflowing with a vitality that works at the food with a certain relish; Carlos languishing flaccidly, and this with effort, the blue of his eyes paled almost to extinction. Had I just seen them on the street, without contact, I would have thought Carlos British, undernourished and adrift. Enrique, Gypsy-like, I would have instinctively mistrusted.

And yet it is Enrique who, with a distracted fussiness that is like warmth, now hands me half an apple and a thick slice of sausage, who wipes the spilled beer from the bottle before passing it to me.

"Are you guys travelling?" I automatically take in Carlos with my gaze although I know my words to be incomprehensible to him.

"Yes, but not for pleasure." Enrique places a beer in Carlos's hand, practically wrapping his fingers around the bottle. "We are looking for work." He hoists himself onto the neighboring bed, crosses his legs, and slips a piece of sausage into his mouth. He speaks as he chews. "There is much disemployment in Spain now."

"Unemployment."

"Unemployment, pardon me. My English is not perfect. I could not stay in London as long as I had wished. Money was the problem. As always."

"You ran out of money?"

"My father died, very suddenly. He left many debts. The lawyers got rich. And my family passed from not very rich to not very poor."

"So you had to leave England."

"My mother has five other children, all younger than I. She needed help to support them." He breaks his slice of apple into two and pops a half into his mouth. "But there are no jobs in Spain now."

Carlos, still reclining, sipping slowly at his beer, ignoring his food, speaks rapid Spanish to Enrique. Enrique replies, as rapidly, and breaks out into a raucous laugh punctuated with cries of "Eyyy, Carlos! Eyyy, Carlos!"

To my surprise I recognize the elements. The laughter a bit forced, the tone teasing yet aimed, clearly, at reassurance. Still laughing, Enrique says to me, "Carlos worries. He was reminding me that we must go to the train station tonight."

"Are you leaving?" It surprises me that I find the thought distressing. People coming, people going. It all ceased, after a while, making any impression. Encounters, like everything else on this trip, are little more than brushes with vapor.

"Not this evening, no. There are no trains, and we need to rest. No, we are going in search of others like us. It is sometimes the best way to find out where the jobs are."

"What kind of jobs are you looking for?" Relief comes as a physical sensation, a deflation of the sudden tension.

"Picking grapes."

"Can you make money doing that?"

"Some. A little. We keep what we need in order to continue, the rest we send to our families. It isn't much but it is better than nothing."

"And when there are no more grapes?"

"We'll see. We will worry about that later." He turns to Carlos and they converse in Spanish, the voices retaining their particular cadences: Enrique's urgent with a suppressed energy, Carlos's a slowly rumbling whisper from between stretched, drained lips.

I finish my apple and take a bite from the sausage, a red spicy meat, solidly packed, that floods my mouth with a warm oil. As Enrique and Carlos speak, building around themselves the spare exclusivity engineered by a private conversation in a language not possessed by the others around, I empty my mind, eyes flitting around the room. Blue walls, bared lightbulbs throwing shadows into the corners, beds made and unmade. My ears enjoy the soft, rolling music of their conversation, the sounds of the language, by themselves, a poetic device. Their voices alternate, the sharp urgency of Enrique followed by the meditative sleepiness of Carlos. At times their voices run into each other, interrupting, sounds dodging and skipping, energetically seeking supremacy, Carlos's whisper spurting into the gaps of Enrique's urgency then retreating before its growing timbre, lapsing into a silence that is a tensed expectation.

With the sounds of their conversation in the background, my mind goes back to the beginning, to the three of us, John, Grady, and me, backpacked, booted, and moneybelted, abandoning university midway, seduced by the thoughts of Europe, attracted by the romance of a greater acquaintance with the past. John, the engineer doubtful of his vocation, more attracted to his guitar than to structural theories; Grady, bored with political science, unable to see importance in anything; and me, James, growing insensitive to the finest of fiction, distanced, unexpectedly, from the printed page.

Much has changed in the six months since our late, cramped charter flight. John was left behind in London, our first stop, for treatment of a disease picked up from a young prostitute. In Amsterdam, Grady floated off to the ingested comforts of outer space, deciding quickly that he had found something of importance. And I continued on alone to the museums, the churches, the streets grim with the dirt and dried blood of history. When the time came, later, to link up, Grady failed to arrive and John, changed, had already inserted himself into another group.

Where was the mistake? I wonder. Was it in the departure itself? Or did it come later, in the damp alleys of Venice or the street of prostitutes — a Hades[4] more

---

4. Hades The classical Greek underworld.

substantial in the flesh — in Frankfurt? Or was there even a mistake? From where this emptiness and boredom alleviated only by a quick irritation? It came rapidly to John, and he sought relief and distraction in bartered sex; Grady, I feel, had always borne it within him, and he found his outlet in the tax-subsidized concoctions of a drug bar. I remember with distress Grady's fascination with the discarded syringes that littered the back streets of Amsterdam. It was a fascination I could not and still cannot understand. In our little Ontario town, swollen in August by summer residents, anything could be bought, alleys could be found littered with discarded paraphernalia. Amsterdam was little more than a larger, more extended version of our little town, a passage of adolescence, institutionalized, converted into a way of life.

The conversation ends and the sudden silence brings me back to the room: the lights, the walls, the beds, Enrique sitting crosslegged, Carlos lying limp.

Enrique says, "We should go to the train station. Would you like to come with us?" After the Spanish, the English sounds duller, cooler, the British accent distant and controlled.

"Has it stopped raining?"

Enrique speaks to Carlos in Spanish and, with effort, he hoists himself onto his left elbow and peers out through the window above him into the perfect darkness of the night. Finally, rolling over and sitting up, he says, "No rain."

The street is still wet, the trees dark and heavy with dripping leaves, the cobbled pavement black and rutted like the back of a great, wet alligator. The lights that shine from buildings — few, mere hints of red or white sparkle here and there, the retreat of the town complete — fail to light the darkness, seem rather to emphasize its depth and the impenetrability of the shutters and doors that exclude so totally the outside world.

We walk in silence down the middle of the street, Enrique and I with hands stuffed into our jeans, Carlos, thin and tall, seemingly huddled into himself, head almost crouching between hunched shoulders.

I enjoy the darkness and its blanketing hush. It offers a freedom, a retreat from the rush that has caught me up in the past months. See this, see that. Do this, do that. Here, in this little French town late in the evening, there is nothing to see, nothing to do. It is as if I owe nothing, own nothing, feel obligation to no one, not even to myself. And as I relish the sense of lightness, I feel a new vein of energy working itself into me. My eyes fall to my boots and I think I can almost see the new energy moving them along, marching in leisurely time with the battered shoes of Carlos and Enrique. I breathe deeply of the moist air and think with pleasure that, tonight, with a mind suddenly unencumbered, I will sleep well.

We come to the end of the street, to the square I saw earlier this evening. As before, only the bar — from the distance, empty — and the hotel offer signs of life. The rest of the buildings and the monument in the middle have been absorbed by the dark so that the two snatches of light, glaring without reach, are like clutches of glow tossed into a nocturnal countryside emptiness.

We pause at the edge of the square, looking, examining the totality that seems to rock us, to unhinge our sense of balance. Carlos mumbles to Enrique, who thinks for a moment then mumbles in reply. It is a worried exchange, quietly spoken, desperation not far beneath the surface, a conversation of the night and quiet. Then they step together into the square.

I make to follow them but a hesitation, abrupt and unexpected, holds me back. I am, I notice, suddenly nervous. My hands, relaxing in the pockets of my jeans, go cold with sweat. The muscles in my upper back hunch and tense.

Enrique turns and called, "James, come on. You are dreaming?"

I step forward towards them, thighs reluctant. They wait for me, then take up once more their leisurely pace into the darkened, deserted square.

I examine my nervousness and find questions: Why, of all the people in the hostel, did they choose me to share their meal? Why me to invite for a walk far from the company of others? My hand goes uncomfortably to my moneybelt. They are moneyless Spaniards with impoverished families back in Spain. I am a Canadian, not rich but not poor, travelling to my fill in Europe. I begin to see a kind of fateful logic constructing itself around us all, and a vision comes to me of falling, slowly, with pain and confusion, into the darkness. I wish a car would come squealing at us, its whine and its lights cracking the hardening cocoon.

The night air, undisturbed, no longer seems merely fresh, the dampness penetrating now, coating my bones with a chilled moisture. An uncontrollable trembling seizes my right arm.

We leave the pulsing darkness of the square and take the road, almost as dark, to the train station. This is relief, but of the slightest degree. My distrust of my companions, unwarranted, I know, a distrust that I am, at the same time, ashamed of, has grown beyond the range of my logic. As I watch my boots, left, right, moving reluctantly forward over the cobblestones, I search for a reason to return to the hostel. But another vision, of a swift knife and a falling into the shadows, presses itself in on me, spurts of panic, barely controlled, like surging lava restrained by the frailest of membranes, thrusting insistently at the outward calm I am still, somehow, able to maintain.

On we walk, in silence still, the only sound the soft fall of our shoes on the street.

Carlos lights a cigarette, the head of the match rasping into flame, and for a moment in the flickering light everything gleams, his face a floating spectre.

Darkness comes again and with it the acrid, almost acidic smoke of the cheap tobacco. Enrique mumbles and Carlos passes him the cigarette. He pulls heavily on it so that a red glow casts onto his face, the features — the full nose, the deeply furrowed brow — thickening to what strikes me as near-caricature.

Soon, sooner than I expect, just ahead at a bend in the road stands the train station, dully lit by lamps embedded at intervals into its walls. It looks shuttered and abandoned, no one to be seen. Enrique and Carlos speak quietly, anxiously, to each other and pick up the pace.

At the barricaded main door of the station the sense of desertion is even greater. I feel the quiet desperation that has seized Enrique and Carlos: if there is no one to ask about jobs, what will they do tomorrow morning? Where will they go?

We stand for a moment in the weak light of a lamp, peering into the darkness. Then, without a word, Enrique hurries forward and disappears into the obscurity of an unlit corner.

Carlos, hunched and withdrawn, hands stuck into the pockets of his jeans, cigarette dangling from between his lips, stares away into the night. I suddenly feel sorry for him. He is like an overgrown boy with resources inadequate to the situation, resented, in which he finds himself. I want to reassure him, to offer a word of encouragement, to squeeze his shoulder with the message that the world is not as empty, as rejecting, as it must seem at this moment.

But Carlos, almost as if sensing my thoughts, steps away, claiming for himself a greater space.

I wonder where Enrique has gone and move cautiously towards the corner. My nervousness, I note, has of itself disappeared. In the grip of the shadow the darkness lessens. I make out human forms silhouetted against the greater night behind them, two people sitting huddled on a bench under what I guess to be a blanket, another — Enrique — leaning over them, supporting himself with an outstretched arm against the wall of the station. They are talking quietly, in whispers less conspiratorial than intimate, with affection, as if they know each other.

Enrique offers cigarettes, strikes a match, and in the weak glow of the leaping flame two female faces — young, weary, each framed by straight, black hair — hungrily reach out their cigarettes. Then the light is gone and all that remains are two glowing ends floating, bobbing, before faces once more effaced.

Enrique says, "Buenas noches, adios," and his voice, louder now, is generous with warmth. He turns and walks towards me with energetic steps, takes my arm familiarly, and calls to Carlos. "Let's go," he says.

"Do you know them?" I ask, looking one last time into the darkened corner.

"No, we only just met."

"The way you were with them, as if you knew them."

"They have very little money. They must spend the night here. They are taking a train early in the morning. To jobs. So will we." He tells Carlos the news and Carlos, for the first time this evening, laughs, even becomes expansive, but still with a reserve.

Carlos talks all the way back to the hostel. Enrique, exuding energy, hums a tune to himself, laughing occasionally at something Carlos has said, the sound of his voice, authoritative, confident, at ease, ringing into the empty night, beating back the darkness, filling the blackened square, running along the street ahead of us, into the alleys and shuttered doorways. He speaks with relish of life in London, of the women he has known, the women he has loved. And he laughs, a sound unrestrained, a joy unbridled. I recognize the laughter as the sound of a freedom I have never known, an internal unshackling, and I engage the sounds, savor them, marvel at them. And I know that I want to have for myself that sense, that sense of life suddenly electrified.

When we get back to the hostel the concierge is asleep, his head on the counter. He stirs only slightly as we make our way up the stairs to the rooms.

We stop outside the door to my room. "Will we meet in the morning?" I ask.

"We must leave very early," Enrique replies. "Before dawn."

"In that case, good luck. And thank you." I put out my hand.

Carlos shakes it briefly and pulls back. He is anxious to get to bed.

Enrique wraps my hand in both of his, a solid grasp, enveloping. "Maybe one day," he says. "In Canada."

"You never know. Maybe." I know it to be a lie, as does Enrique, but a satisfactory lie. Images, incomplete and fragmentary, a trip of torn edges. But this one image, of life momentarily peaked, will remain with me, will form of itself a glittering whole, will give value to an experience until now unsatisfactory.

Enrique claps me once on the shoulder and then they hurry down the corridor to their room.

As I enter my room, darkened, the other bunks occupied with bodies wrapped in white, I think: I'd like to go with them. But I know the urge to be absurd.

I undress, get into bed, and pull the sheet up to my neck.

From the far end of the room a voice whispers, "Too bloody good, that's what *they* think they are." The tone is one of hurt, of complaint.

Another voice replies, "All talk and no action. Bloody frustrating."

"Goddamn Frenchwomen. This town's a dump anyway."

I laugh quietly. The voices go silent. And in the moments before I fall asleep I contemplate with more relish than regret the security that is mine.

(1985)

Marilyn Dumont (1955–)

Marilyn Dumont was born in the small town of Olds, Alberta, in 1955. The community in which she was raised was primarily White, but it was located near a large Native reservation. Dumont, of Métis-Cree heritage, felt caught between two worlds. She would go to church on Sundays, like her classmates, but she would also make periodic pilgrimages to Lac Ste. Anne with her parents and other local Métis. While her formal religious education was Catholic, she absorbed Cree spirituality from her parents; she also incorporated the rhythms of their speech and the verbal wit of her female relatives. Although she never became fluent in Cree, she explains that it is the language in which her family "spoke about really important things."

Dumont received a B.A. in English literature with a minor in anthropology from the University of Alberta in 1991, and she went to work for three years at the National Film Board. Inspired by the work of Gwendolyn MacEwen, Lucille Clifton, and Zora Neale Hurston, she returned to school to earn an M.F.A. in creative writing from the University of British Columbia. The support and creative energy that Dumont drew from the writing circles she moved in at UBC gave her an enduring appreciation for the value of creative collaboration. During this time, she completed her first collection of poetry, *A Really Good Brown Girl* (1996). In this volume of lyric and prose poems, Dumont looks with equal parts humour and outrage at the systematic marginalization of Aboriginal peoples, the gulf between the Native and non-Native worlds, the debilitating effects of racism and sexism, and family and the formulation of identity.

Divided into four sections — "Squaw Poems," "What More Than Dance," "White Noise," and "Made of Water" — the book presents a vivid portrait of what it means to be a Métis in Canada today. Dumont characterizes this experience as one constructed on a series of dualities. For example, the persona in the poem "Memoirs of a Really Good Brown Girl" is split by her early and ongoing encounter with the "white judges" who represent White society in its self-appointed role of arbiter (these judges also appear in the poem bearing their name). The "good brown girl" expresses the good/bad dichotomy that the judges instill in her through the chant "You are not good enough, not good enough, obviously not good enough," then she adds, "The chorus is never loud or conspicuous, just there." She struggles to become invisible to these judges, to blend in by being "good enough." But in the course of the poem, the girl's adult persona begins to emerge, and the dualities become more complex: while the child internalizes the shame the judges' gaze engenders in her, the adult strives for wholeness by challenging the authority and perception of White society.

In her second collection of poems, *green girl dreams Mountains* (2001), Dumont employs a number of the formal techniques she used in *A Really Good Brown Girl* — alliteration, enjambment, a blending of lyric and prose passages, arresting images — to probe family relationships and the intersections of race and class in urban life. The volume is divided into five sections. The first, entitled "Homeground," invokes themes of loss and memory as it explores the difficulty of intergenerational relationships; it features poems about the interaction between mothers and daughters, and about the emotional conflicts that fathers experience in assuming their role in the family. In the poem "kindling," the poet acknowledges her mother as her creative progenitor. She envisions her poetry as a flame ignited by her maternal heritage — her dead mother's handwriting is like "broken twigs on the page ... kindling / for me." In "City View," the book's second section, the poet extends her exploration with a set of poems that express both the despair and the happiness she derives from her experience in an urban context. The poems in this section are named for the streets in Vancouver — streets that, according to Dumont, constitute "boundaries of class and race." The last section, "Among the Word Animals," looks more closely at language — the social role it plays and the political power it wields. In "Straw Boss," for example, an English teacher breaks the languages of her Native students as though they were so many wild horses, reining them in with "tight-assed / suffixes" and "blond syllables." But in "throatsong for the four-leggeds," the last piece in the volume, Dumont draws poetry from the cries of animals as they communicate with one another, thus celebrating the natural persistence of individual expression.

Dumont is currently working on two documentary films: one about Métis rebel leader Gabriel Dumont, who is one of her ancestors, and another about the intriguing parallels and divergences between her mother's life and her own (her mother had a sixth-grade education, she married at 18, and she gave birth to 10 children; Dumont is well educated, unmarried, and childless). Dumont has served as writer in residence at the Universities of Windsor, Toronto, and Alberta, and she has read her poetry to audiences in many countries.

The Devil's Language

1. I have since reconsidered Eliot[1]
and the Great White way of writing English
standard that is
the great white way
has measured, judged and assessed me   all my life
by its
lily white words
its picket fence sentences
and manicured paragraphs
one wrong sound and you're shelved in the Native Literature section   10
resistance writing
a mad Indian
unpredictable
on the war path
native ethnic protest
the Great White way could silence us all
if we let it
its had its hand over my mouth since my first day of school
since Dick and Jane, ABC's and fingernail checks
syntactic laws: use the wrong order or   20
register and you're a dumb Indian
dumb, drunk or violent
my father doesn't read or write
the King's English says he's
dumb but he speaks Cree

---

1. **Eliot** T.S. Eliot (1888–1965), an American-born English modernist poet, critic, and dramatist.

how many of you speak Cree?
correct Cree not correct English
grammatically correct Cree
is there one?

30   2. is there a Received Pronunciation of Cree, is there
a Modern Cree Usage?
the Chief's Cree not the King's English

as if violating God the Father and standard English
is like talking back(wards)

as if speaking the devil's language is
talking back
back(words)
back to your mother's sound, your mother's tongue, your mother's language
back to that clearing in the bush
40   in the tall black spruce

3. near the sound of horses and wind
where you sat on her knee in a canvas tent
and she fed you bannock[2] and tea
and syllables
that echo in your mind now, now
that you can't make the sound
of that voice that rocks you and sings you to sleep
in the devil's language.

(1996)

The Sound of One Hand Drumming

"It is not the end of all being. Just a small stunting of a road in you,"[1] but
you will branch out into all directions of this country,
this nationstate inside of you waiting to come of age,
cede, or claim independence from the founding fathers of confederation
or thought
and all your tributaries will flow into the great dam of existence,
the watershed of doubt and creation
of your soul and others in this land of no returning
this fountain of youth and sorrow, and
10   print-dressed women will greet you and say, "kayas,"[2]
and kiss you on the cheek
call you relative,
call you to them for everlasting life

---

2. bannock Flat, dense bread prepared by First Nations communities.

---

1. It is … road in you From "Thirst," by Canadian poet Robert Priest. **2. kayas** Cree for "it's been a long time."

and who knows what will come of reading this bible
of technology in your soul,
if you have one that isn't digitized yet,
the soul you pray with every new dawn of your life before
stepping into the headlines
of thought or waving goodbye
to good fellows who trod off to loftier things   20
in *the big house of knowing*,
peeling back words from spines
that vault into theories as ornate as rococo[3]
and as cluttered as a bad relationship
with oneself or anyone else within reach
of those words that flow like milkweed from Philosophers while
the   small   single   words
of brown women hang on
clotheslines stiff in winter and
thaw only in early spring but   30
no one takes them off the line because
no one wants last year's clothes,
they're the wrong colour and out of fashion and
if dead-white-men stopped writing for one thousand years and
only brown women wrote
that wouldn't be enough

time for all the Indian youth to say what they had to
or enough for me and those of my kind,
the sharp-toned-and-tongued kind
who keep railing on about this stuff   40
when all well-mannered and sophisticated Indian types
would have reasonably dropped it long ago
because it's just rhetoric,
guilt-provoking
and sounds like a broken record of an Indian beating a drum
or like an Indian beating a drum with a broken record,
or like an Indian breaking a record,
or like an Indian breaking a drum over a record
whose sound is digitized, on CD-ROM
complete with video and CD quality sound.   50

(1996)

monuments, cowboys & indians, tin cans, and red wagons

We lived at the end of a road
that dissolved into a field

---

3. rococo   Highly ornamented; a late-baroque decorative style prevalent in 18th-century Europe.

flat as a table and the color of deer;
although I saw no deer there
that field rolled out for miles to a deep cliff
that fell to a river
and that Red Deer River
was our source of water
hauled home by our black dog, Chinnie

10   and our old school house
jut out of that flatness
like a misplaced monument
to the wanderings home and away
of an extended family of half-breeds
kids scattering to cowboys and indians, tin cans, red wagons
teenagers jiving to Del Shannon
migrating Settlement relatives searching for work
their wives or "old ladies" in tow
and on Saturday nights with two weeks pay
20   the Silk Tassle, Pilsner,[1] and fiddle tunes would flow
weave through auntie's rank laughter, mom's stepdancing and
my brother's yodelling
Cree would occupy the house like a new code, the partying would
heat up the walls and spill out windows and doors like light
through cracks

And that old school house had long divided windows and
the same paint the school board issued
when my father bought it
the sun's rays a potato peeler
30   that curled the paint away from the boards
where that field spread out and away from the schoolhouse
like an epic film shot
until the sun sank into the wet field
between the house and river
ending our days like forged steel dipped in water

(2001)

Mark Anthony Jarman (1955–)

Mark Anthony Jarman says that when he writes, he tends to focus on language and imagery rather than the structure of the narrative. "I'm really rotten at plot," he insists, consoling himself that "James Joyce was rotten at plot too. He did okay." Not only is Jarman doing okay — his publications include a novel, three short story collections, a poetry collection, and a work of non-fiction; and his writing has been nominated for several awards — but also a close reading of his

---

1. **Silk Tassle, Pilsner** Brands of rye and beer.

work belies his claim that he's a rotten plotter. His stories are complex creations: their plots are fabricated from a welter of images, characters, and settings, and they move through fictional terrains that are, in turn, humorous, ironic, tragic, bizarre, and horrific.

Jarman was born in Edmonton, Alberta, in 1955, and he read a lot as a child. He always wanted to write, but it took him many years to pick up a pen because, he says, "I'd thought you had to write about cocktail parties in Manhattan or you weren't a writer." Then he encountered the works of other prairie writers like Robert Kroetsch and Ken Mitchell and suddenly understood that home was worth writing about. As well, Jarman cites Canadian writers Matt Cohen, P.K. Page, Phyllis Webb, and Clark Blaise as influences, but he also names an eclectic array of American and world writers — from Nathanael West, John Dos Passos, Charles Bukowski, and Raymond Carver to Céline and Isaac Babel — and for good measure he appends a list of playwrights and musicians who have inspired him. In the 1970s, Jarman began reading detective stories "when it wasn't all that trendy," and Raymond Chandler, in particular, had a lasting impact upon him because, as Jarman puts it, "he was so good with images." Jarman graduated from the Iowa Writers' Workshop at the University of Iowa, and, still subject to what he refers to as a "restlessness of influence," went to live in Seattle, where he mowed lawns and chopped wood for a living.

During this time, he began work on his first collection of short stories. *Dancing Nightly in the Tavern* was published in 1984. These nine tales are populated by junkies, drunks, and lonely souls who inhabit a bleak underworld where being out of work and down on your luck is a normal condition of life. By infusing his narrative voice with humour, Jarman mitigates the darkness that lies at the heart of these stories and thus renders more compelling the series of themes and concerns he introduces: accidental death, sudden shifts of fortune, the powerful lure of drugs and alcohol in a world of pain, the challenge to masculinity in the late 20th century, our common struggle to endure.

Next Jarman produced a poetry collection entitled *Killing the Swan* (1986). It contains black-and-white photos by Sandy Reber, and both the poems and the pictorial images address the issue of urban encroachment on the natural world. Canada is depicted as a country in a state of rapid decay, a place where "messages bob in Orange Crush bottles." Then, in 1992, Jarman edited an anthology of alcohol-related stories by Canadian writers called *Ounce of Cure* (1992), because, he explains, he came across a book like it in Seattle "and thought someone should do this in Canada."

His first novel, *Salvage King, Ya! A Herky-Jerky Picaresque,* was published in 1997. Jarman took his title from an inscription he saw on the wall of a Montana bar. This novel, described by one reviewer as "A story about a boozing, coke snorting, skirt chasing minor-league hockey player during the final days of his often brutally violent ice warrior career," features rambling monologues delivered by embattled narrator Drinkwater, who is reduced to playing "scarred no-name defence" and "doing pushups on puzzlingly ugly hotel rugs." The monologues are often brought up short by arresting, sometimes grotesque images. Through the voice of its itinerant narrator, this contemporary example of a picaresque novel (one that deals with the episodic adventures of a roguish figure) reinvestigates many of the themes Jarman established with *Dancing Nightly*. It was an expansion of the short story "Righteous Speedboat," which was short-listed for the Journey Prize and was described as challenging Roch Carrier's "The Hockey Sweater" for the title of "greatest hockey story ever written."

Jarman returned to the short story format with *New Orleans Is Sinking* (1998) and *19 Knives* (2000). Both collections are driven by Jarman's powerful narrative voice — a voice that derives its power from the intensity of the despair that lacerates his characters, from his dextrous use of colloquial language (one reviewer called it "downright acrobatic"), and, as always, from his unfailing humour. The stories are set in a variety of locations — from Edmonton to Texas to Dublin — and feature a range of characters and narrators — a recovering drug addict, a man in flames, General Custer. Jarman's skillful integration of all these literary elements achieves an effect that has been described as "symphonic."

Jarman's most recent work is *Ireland's Eye* (2002), the story of the author's journey to Ireland, the country where his mother was born. In the course of his visit, Jarman meets with a succession of relatives and listens to their dubious recollections in an effort to gain insight into his family's past; his depictions of these encounters are charged with the author's signature raucous humour. The narrative is initiated by a pair of deaths: that of revolutionary leader Michael Collins, who was shot in 1922, during the Irish Civil War, sending the country into mourning; and that of his own grandfather, Michael Lyons, who drowned in a Dublin canal on the same day Collins died. One a national hero, and one an ordinary citizen, these men, through their deaths, lead Jarman to contemplate the ways in which collective and personal histories intersect.

Jarman never expected to become a full-time writer — "I thought I'd drive a truck and write on the side," he says. Instead of supporting himself by driving, however, he teaches: he has taught part time at the University of Victoria, and he currently teaches creative writing at the University of New Brunswick in Fredericton.

Burn Man on a Texas Porch

> *Men who are unhappy, like men who sleep badly, are always proud of the fact.*
> — Bertrand Russell

> *At fifty everyone has the face they deserve.*
> — George Orwell

Propane slept in the tank and propane leaked while I slept, blew the camper door off and split the tin walls where they met like shy strangers kissing, blew the camper door like a safe and I sprang from sleep into my new life on my feet in front of a befuddled crowd, my new life on fire, waking to *whoosh* and tourists' dull teenagers staring at my bent form trotting noisily in the campground with flames living on my calves and flames gathering and glittering on my shoulders (Cool, the teens think secretly), smoke like nausea in my stomach and me brimming with Catholic guilt, thinking, Now I've done it, and then thinking, Done what? What have I done?

Slept during the day with my face dreaming on a sudoral[1] pillow near the end of the century and now my blue eyes are on fire.

I'm okay, okay, will be fine except I'm hoovering all the oxygen around me, and I'm burning like a circus poster, flames taking more and more of my shape — am I moving or are they? I am hooked into fire, I am hysterical light issuing beast noises in a world of smoke.

To run seems an answer. Wanting privacy, I run darkest dogbane and daisies and doom palms, hearing bagpipes and whistling in my head, my fat burning like red wax, fat in the fire now. Alone — I want to do this alone, get away from the others. I can't see, bounce off trees and parked cars, noise in my ears the whole time.

The other campers catch me and push me onto a tent the blue of a Chinese rug, try to smother me, but soon the tent is melting, merrily burning with me while everyone in

---

1. **sudoral** Sweaty.

the world throws picnic Kool-Aid and apple juice and Lucky Lager and Gatorade and gingerale and ice cubes and icewater from the Styrofoam coolers. Tourists burn their hands trying to extinguish me.

My face feels like a million white hot rivets. I am yelling and writhing. One of my shoes burns happily by itself on the road.

Where does my skin end and the skin of their melted tourist tent begin?

At some point in this year of our Lord I began to refer to myself in third person, as a double: Burn Man enters the Royal Jubilee burn unit, Burn Man enters the saline painful sea. Burn Man reads every word of the local rag despite its numerous failings, listens to MC5 on vinyl, listens to Johnny Cash's best-known ballad.

I am not dealing with this well, the doctors tell me. I am not noble. They carried me in the burnt blue tent, a litter borne from battle, from defeat on the fields of fire and disassembly lines and into three months of shaking, bandaged pain. Your muscles go after you're burnt, but if you work out the skin grafts won't stretch over the larger muscles. Grafted skin is not as flexible as real skin. Skin is your cage.

Once straight, now I'm crooked. I lack a landscape that is mine. A doctor shone a light at the blood vessels living in the back of my retina. I saw there a trickle-down Mars in a map of my own blood: twin red planets lodged in my skull.

As a nerdy kid in horn-rimmed glasses, I haunted libraries, reading about doomed convoys in World War II, Canadian sailors burnt in the North Atlantic or off icy Russia, Canadian sailors alive but charred by crude oil burning all around them after U-boats[2] from sunny Bordeaux took down their tramp freighter or seasick corvette — circular scalp of sea on fire and flaming crude races right at them, so eager, enters them, fricassees their lungs and face and hands, the burning ring of fire come to life on the Murmansk[3] run.

I can't recall what happened when the burnt sailors moved back into the non-burnt world, crawled back home above Halifax's black snowy harbour or the sombre river firs of Red Deer, the saltbox houses of Esquimalt.

No war here; no peace either. Only the burn ward's manic protracted nurses sliding on waxed floors and the occasional distracted doctor with a crew of rookies whipping back the curtain, the gown, jabbing me to see if I'm done like dinner. Sell the sizzle. Door blows off the rented camper, spinning under sulphur sun, and I too am sent out into red rented sunlight, your basic moaning comet charging through a brilliantly petalled universe.

I was on a holiday in the sun, a rest from work, from tree spikers and salmon wars, from the acting deputy minister on the cellphone fuming about river rights, water diversions, and the botched contract with Alcan. I was getting away from it all, resting my eyes, my brain.

I had left the cellphone sitting like a plastic banana on the middle of my wide, Spartan[4] desk. I was working on my tan, had a little boat tied up dockside, plastic oars, nine h.p., runs on gas-and-oil mix. I rested my skin on the sand-and-cigarette-butt beach. I lay down on a pillow in a tin camper. I caught fire, ran the dusty leaves and levees of our campground, alchemy and congress weighing on my mind.

---

2. U-boats German submarines. **3. Murmansk** An important Russian trading port, which was unsuccessfully attacked by the Germans in 1941. **4. Spartan** Simple, frugal.

Back home in my basement, a 1950s toy train circles track, its fricative steam locomotive emitting the only light in the room, swinging past where a slight woman in a parody of a nurse's uniform does something for Burn Man, for Burn Man is not burnt everywhere, still has some desires, and the woman doesn't have to touch anything else, doesn't have to see me, has almost no contact, has a verbal contract, an oral contract, say.

"Cindi: Yes that's me in the photo!" avows the ad in the weekly paper.

Cindi can't really see me, except for the toy-train light from my perfect childhood, can't make out my grave jerry-built[5] face. I can barely see her. She has short, dark, hennaed hair that used to be another colour. I imagine her monochrome high-school photo. Dollars to doughnuts she had long hair parted in the middle, a plain face, a trace of acne. No one senses then that Cindi would become an escort pulled out of the paper at random and lit by a moving toy train and red-and-yellow poppies waving at a big basement window — mumbling to me, I have these nightmares, every night these nightmares.

I explained my delicate situation on the phone — what I wanted, didn't want.

Good morning, Cindi, I said. Here's my story, you let me know what you think.

She coughed. Uh, I'm cool with that, she claimed.

So Cindi and I set up our first date.

My escort dresses as the nurse in white, her hands, her crisp uniform glowing in the rec room. All of us risk something, dress as something: ape, clown, worker, Cindi, citizen, *cool with that*.

Here's an ad in *Now* magazine I didn't call: "FIRE & DESIRE, Sensuous Centrefold Girls, HOT Fall Specials, $150 per hour." I didn't call that number. I don't live in the metro area. I'm not one of the chosen.

Once, maybe, I was chosen, necking on the Hopper porch, that stunning lean of a Texas woman into my arms, my innocent face, our mouths one. Perfect height for each other and I am pulled to another doomed enterprise.

The iron train never stops, lights up my decent little town, its toy workers frozen in place with grim happy faces, light opening and closing them, workers with tin shovels, forklifts, painted faces. God gives you one face and you make yourselves another. My nurse is too thin. I like a little more flesh. I wish she'd change just for me.

My slight Nurse Wretched carries my cash carelessly and heads out to buy flaps of coke, or maybe today it's points of junk, for twenty or thirty dollars (her version of the stock market), delving into different receptor sites, alternate brands of orgasmic freeze and frisson, and she forgets about carrot juice and health food, any food, forgets about me, my eyes half-hooded like a grumpy cat's, eyes unfocused and my mouth turned down and our shared need for death without death, for petit mal,[6] tender mercies.

Cindi is out this moment seeking a pharmacy's foreign voice and amnesiac hands and who can blame her?

Some people from my old school (*Be true to your school*) fried themselves over years and years, burned out over dissolute decades, creepy-crawling centuries.

Not me. Ten seconds and done, helter-skelter, hugger-mugger. Here's the new you handed to you in a campground like a platter of oysters. An "accelerant," as the

---

5. **jerry-built** Inadequately built. 6. **petit mal** A type of seizure characterized by lapses of consciousness.

firefighters enjoyed saying, was used. Before I could change, had nine lives. Now I have one. O, I am ill at these numbers.

In the hospital not far from the campground I cracked jokes like delicate quail eggs: You can't fire me, I already quit. Then I quit cracking jokes. The skin grafts not what I had hoped for, didn't quite fit (*Why then we'll fit you*). The surgeons made me look like a wharf rat, a malformed Missouri turtle, a post-mortem mummy. Years and doubt clinging to her, the nurse with the honed Andalusian[7] face tried not to touch me too hard.

At first how positive I was! Eagerly I awaited the tray with the Jell-O and soup and fruit flies, the nurse with the determined Spanish face carrying it to my mechanical bed. I overheard her say to another nurse, No, he's not a bigot, he's a bigamist! Who? I wonder. Me? My aloof doctor? Does he have a life? If only we could duplicate the best parts and delete the rest. A complicated bed and her arms on a tray and her serious expression and unfucked-up skin and my hunger and love for a porch (*I spied a fair maiden*), for the latest version of my lunatic past.

I spill Swedish and Russian vodka into my morning coffee now (rocket fuel for Rocket Man) and, blue bubble helmet happily hiding my scarred face, fling my Burn Man motorcycle with the ape-hanger handlebars down the wet island highway, hoping for fractious friction and the thrill of metal fatigue, hoping to meet someone traumatic, a ring of fire. I re-jetted the carburetor on my bike, went to Supertrapp pipes — wanting more horses and torque, wanting the machine to scream.

Before I became Burn Man, the Texas woman kissed me at the bottom of her lit yellow stairs, porch dark as tar, dark as sky, and her cozy form fast leaning against me, disturbing the hidden powers, ersatz[8] cowboys upstairs drinking longnecks and blabbing over Gram Parsons and Emmylou[9] (*One like you should be — miles and miles away from me*), impatient taxi waiting and waiting as we kissed. I had not expected her to kiss me, to teach me herself, her mouth and form, her warm image driven like a nail into my mind, her memory jammed on that loop of tape. (Such art of eyes I read in no books, my dark-star thoughts attending her day and night like a sacred priest with his relics.) In that instant I was changed.

Now I'm the clown outside Bed of Roses, the franchise flower shop beside the dentist's office on the road to Damascus, the road to Highway 61. On Saturdays I wave white gloves to passing cars — dark shark-like taxis, myopic headlights — and helium balloons with smiley faces bump my wrecked and now abandoned mouth. (*Where have all the old finned cars swum to?*)

Pedestrians hate me, fear me; pedestrians edge past the bus-stop bench where the sidewalk is too narrow; pedestrians avoid my eyes, my psychedelic fright-wig. I want to reassure them: Hey dudes, I'm not a mime. Different union.

At Easter I'm a giant grey rabbit, but I can't do Santa. I could definitely use the do-re-mi but the beard isn't enough cover for my droopy right eye and melted cheek, the beard isn't enough to save face, and also I confess to trouble with the constant Ho Ho Ho.

Dignity is essential, I attempt to impart to a passing priest, but I start coughing like a moron. *Drugs too*, I finally sputter. *Essential!* He moves on. Brother, sister, I may appear

---

7. **Andalusian** From the southernmost region of Spain. **8. ersatz** Imitation. **9. Gram Parsons and Emmylou** Gram Parsons (1946–1973) and Emmylou Harris (b. 1947) were folk-rock musicians who performed together.

in ape costume at your apartment door, will deliver a singing telegram in a serviceable tenor. My grey rabbit suit needs a little bleach. Dignity is essential.

Burn Man must have his face covered, bases covered. I'm different animals. In the winter nights I'm the mascot Mighty Moose for our junior hockey team down at Memorial Arena. You may recall TV heads and columnists frowning on my bloody fight with the other team's Raving Raven mascot. All the skaters were scrapping, Gary Glitter's "Rock & Roll Part One" booming on the sound system, and then both goalies started throwing haymakers.[10] I thought the mascots should also duke it out — a sense of symmetry and loyalty. I banged at the Old World armour of that raven's narrow, serious face, snapped his head back. Hoofs were my advantage.

Later we went for a drink or three and laughed about our fight, Raven and Moose at a small bar table comparing notes and bloody abrasions, hoofs and talons around each other, shop talk at the gin bin.

Don't fuck with me, rummy beard-jammers and balls-up bean-counters snarl at every bar on the island, as if they alone decide when they get fucked over. I could advise them on that. I didn't decide to have the camper blow to shrapnel with me curled inside like a ball-turret gunner.

They hunker down at the Commercial Hotel or Blue Peter Marina or Beehive Tap or Luna Lounge thinking they're deep, thinking one ugly room is the universe's centre because they're there with flaming drinks by the lost highway, clouds hanging like clocks over the Japanese coal ships and the coast-guard chopper, and across the water a distant town glittering the green colours of wine and traffic.

I sit and listen to their hyena patter, their thin sipping and brooding and laughing. Sometimes I'm still wearing my clown outfit while drinking my face off. Why take it off?

Friday night a man was kicked to death in this bar. In that instant, like me, he was changed, *his* memory jammed on a loop in a jar of wind, living the blues, dying.

At my front door a rhododendron sheds its scarlet bells one by one. A dark blue teacup sits on the rainy steps, looking beautiful and lonely, and there's a bird in the woods that sounds like a car trying to start.

One Sunday session a man lifted his golf shirt to show me his bowel-obstruction-surgery scar. His navel shoved four inches to the left. He didn't mind getting fucked over — in fact he guffawed gruffly at his own wrecked gut. We're so pliant,[11] I thought, prone to melt, to metal, to a change of heart, to lend our tongue vows.

I who loved the status quo, liked things to stay the same even when they were bad. I who didn't want to break up with Dolly Varden girlfriends when it was obvious to everyone that we should get it over with. Then the camper door flies off: Kablooie! Goodbye Louie. I who loved the status quo.

I'm different animals now. New careers in fire and oxygen, careering and hammering through the dolomite[12] campground to fall on your tent, to fall on my sword. Home, I want to go home, darling. Take me back to Tulsa.

The skin is the largest organ; mine's a little out of tune. Your skin's square footage is — Jesus, how the hell should I know? Far more than your heart, which gets all the good press, attracts the spin doctors and diligent German scalpels.

---

10. haymakers Forceful punches. **11. pliant** Mouldable. **12. dolomite** Limestone or marble rich in magnesium carbonate.

Perhaps my Burn Man skin is more accurate now, what we all become after a certain age: parched animals, palimpsests[13] in wrinkled uniforms, clowns hanging at the Pet Food Mart waving to the indifferent flow of traffic and shiny happy people.

I stare at a bottle of Ayinger German wheat beer, inhaling softest froth in my mouth, breathing in something good like a virus, like breathing oxygen and perfume with a woman's Norwegian hair all over your face.

I am The Way, I say to the drunken bottle, I am truth, heresy, *evidence* of what none of us wish to admit: that appearance is everything, that surface is God and God is surface.

Appearance: the white whale we chase every minute of every day. Looks and youth. We say this isn't so — Naysir, No Sir, No, No, No — we insist appearance counts for very little, but then I am walking at you, an ancient bog monster limping on the teensy sidewalk with my face like a TV jammed on the wrong channel, and at that sideways juncture ALL of us, ME included, decide shallow is not that bad. Let us, we decide, worship and grovel at the church of shallow.

Only Tuesday but I need a drink, my teeth caught in my teeth. Down to the Starfish Room or Yukon Jack's, down to the sea in ships, hulls dragging on our city's concrete.

Flame created me with its sobering sound. Wake up, flame whispered in my ear, like a woman on a porch, like a muttering into cotton, a rush to action. It was ushering, acting on me, eating me. I'm its parent, I'm its home, and people worry they might catch it from me — catch ugliness, catch chaos theory, catch something catchy.

The baby doctor caught me when I came out in fluid, and my mother held me as a baby, such smooth baby skin, my skin dipped in baptismal water at St. John's, they washed away original sin, she held my perfect skin, my original skin. They lit fat candles in the cathedral and I came out in fluid in the university hospital.

The woman on the Texas porch said my skin was soft and that she loved my smell. No one ever said that before, and no one said it after. She created me.

As a kid I was burned by the summer sun in Penticton. My aunt from England peeled a section of skin from my back, and she still has that piece of my skin in a scrapbook in London.

Remember that map they torched at the beginning of each episode of *Bonanza*? I watched every week as a kid and when the flames came I thought, *neato-torpedo,* I thought, *cool.*

Where are my lost eyebrows? Did they fly up, up, up, or drift down as delicate ash, floating like some unformed haiku on a winter lake? My eyebrows got the fuck out of Dodge. Flames went up and down me as they pleased; fire didn't have to obey pecking order or stop-work orders. Kids in pyjamas watched me burn like Guy Fawkes,[14] watched me dwell in possibilities.

The doctor with zero bedside manner said the trick was simply to consider your face a convenience, not an ornament. Thanks for that, Doc. Maybe I could take a razor to him, see if he still debates function versus ornament after I've cut him a new face. Hate is everything they said it would be, and it waits for you like an airbag. You have to

---

13. **palimpsests** Texts that have been erased and written over, or objects that otherwise reflect their own histories.
14. **Guy Fawkes** An English soldier who tried to assassinate King James I and the members of Parliament in 1605 using explosives. Guy Fawkes Night is celebrated in Britain by burning effigies of Fawkes.

learn to deal with your anger, they said in the hospital. I am dealing with my anger, I'm dealing with my anger by hating people.

Here's a haiku I wrote in the hospital for the woman on the Hopper porch.

> Lawyers haunt my phosphorus forest
> I was bright paper burning in a glass gas-station ashtray
> Owning old cars is like phoning the dead

I might have to count the syllables on that baby — I believe haikus follow some Red Chinese system. The Texas woman plays a gold-top guitar, never played for me. She sings in a band doing Gram and Emmylou's heartbreaking harmonies. You narrow the universe to one person, knowing you cannot, knowing there's a price for that.

I want to be handsome more than anything else now that it's impossible, now that I'm impossibly unhandsome, and there is a certain hesitation to the nurse's step at my door, a gathering in of her courage, a white sun outside hitting her skin.

Before I caught fire in the campground I golfed with a smoke-eater from Oregon. Mopping up after a forest fire he told me he found a man in full scuba gear lying on the burnt forest floor. Crushed yellow tanks, mask, black wetsuit, the whole nine yards. At first he thought it was a UFO alien or something like that. Scuba guy was dead. Recently dead.

They couldn't figure it out, how he got there. Finally some genius decided that he must have been diving somewhere and a water bomber scooped him right out of the ocean and dumped startled scuba man onto the forest fire.

The smoke-eater from Oregon on the golf course swore this was a true story, but then I'm in England, a little seaside cottage in ugly Essex, my Thatcherite[15] uncle snoring, and what starts off this American cop show on the telly? A TV detective talking about this scuba diver found in a forest fire. Then a month later a neighbour I bumped into at 7-Eleven insists it actually happened to him on Vancouver Island near Central Lake by Port Alberni. Water bomber scooped the diver out of the big lake, not the ocean. Now I don't know what to believe. Everyone keeps telling me the same false true stories.

The toy train runs and Cindi shows me a photo of herself as a little girl in a little bathing suit at the beach (*Yes that's me in the photo!*).

Cindi cries, points at the photo book: Look. I look so happy! Once she was happy. Now she has nightmares. Cindi lights a cigarette, says she wants to see real icebergs and lighthouses before she dies. Then she says, I dreamed the two of us travelled to Newfoundland together, and it was so nice and calm; not one of my nightmares. Cindi also dreamed I killed her. She says, When I die, no one will remember me, and tells me it must be her period coming on, makes her emotional. I decide mixed messages may be better than no messages at all, though I feel like the palace eunuch.[16]

Cindi spends half her day looking for matches. Cindi struggles with her cigarette, as if it takes great planning to get face to end of cigarette; she seems to move her face rather than move the cigarette. Cindi says, Nothing attracts police like one headlight. *Do you know why I pulled you over?*

---

15. Thatcherite A supporter of former British Prime Minister Margaret Thatcher; a conservative. **16. eunuch** A castrated man, usually a low-level servant assigned to guard women.

At the tavern by the rushing river, men said things to me in my clown suit, my eunuch suit, thinking they were funny. They were deep. The waitress knew me from my previous life, gave me red quarters for the jukebox. She trusted my taste, trusted me once at her apartment. She wore deliberately ugly plaid pants and her wise face just like the Statue of Liberty's. With the bar's red quarters I plugged honky-tonk and swing B-sides only. The B-sides rang out, sang their night code to me alone: Texas, kiss, lit stairs, a world changed.

The old boys in the Commercial Hotel had been drinking porch-climber, watered down shots of hooch, emptying their pants pockets, their bristle heads.

We watched a man kicked directly to death. Strangely, it was an off-duty police officer who had stopped another officer for drinking and driving and refused to let him off. The drunk driver was suspended from the force, from his life. Then guess who bumps into whom at the wrong bar?

The night alive with animals, the whole middle-class group taking some joy in the royal beating, displaying longing, bug-house excitement, wanting to get their feet in like mules kicking, believing it the right thing to do. He was struggling. I don't think they meant to kill the policeman with their feet, but it was a giddy murder, a toy in blood. They busted his head and eyes and busted his ribs and arms and kidney and returned to their drinks, expecting him to resurrect himself on his own power with his swollen brain and internal bleeding. Then the ambulance attempting to dispense miracles, a syringe quivering into muscle. It was fast. I stood fast. I stood shaking in my suffocating clown suit and they returned to their drinks and sweaty hyena hollering, their *Don't fuck with me, Jack*, their legions and lesions and lessons and their memories of twitching creations face down in the parking lots of our nation.

I can wait. Wait until they pass out, then punch a small hole in the drywall under the electrical panel and pour in kerosene, my accelerant du jour. I will run before the doors blow off. See how they like it. See how they like Cindi and the Spanish nurse's Flamazine lotion. It's basic psych. You want everyone else to have the same thing you caught.

Nothing happens, though, because I feel immediately moronic and melodramatic, dial 911 outside, and firefighters are on top of it lickety-split. The doors don't blow, their faces don't fry or turn to wax. I fly away on my rare Indian motorcycle with a transplanted shovelhead engine and Screamin' Eagle calibration kit. No one new joins my Burn Man Club. Burn Man is alive and the unyielding moral policeman is dead, his family in dark glasses at the bright graveyard.

Oh, how our sun smiled on me, breezes blew softly in the dappled leaves over the low-rent beach and my head touching a cool pillow. I napped and the propane fire snapped my skin, remapped me. I twisted and travelled in beautiful lost towns and low registers of postmodern western wind from the Sand Hills of Saskatchewan.

I am a product of light, of hope.

I still have that shy desire for the right fire to twist me back just as easily to what was: to milky youth and a mysterious person falling toward me on a Texas porch with her tongue rearranging hope in my mouth. Under oak trees by the river the Texas woman put words in my mouth, secret words pushed in my mouth like a harmonica. *Her temple fayre is built within my mind.* Perhaps God will have mercy on me in my new exile.

The right fire. Doesn't that make sense?

Like corny cartoons and television shows — amnesia victim loses memory from blow to head, but a second blow makes it right, fixes it all right up, no matter what.

I remember a relevant episode of *I Love Lucy*. Ricky Ricardo's memory pops back after Lucy hits him by the fireplace: Ricky comes swinging back, I come back, my old skin swims back from its minor shipwreck, from the singing sirens, the torpedo, finds the muscle memory held like a Rolodex in my new skin.

Doesn't seem to work. Can't buy pointed boots back from a swollen brain, can't drift again into your childhood face or her blue truck and blue eyes and blond hair and stories of west Texas waltzes and Cotton-Eyed Joe. Can't saw sawdust.

Instead I rise Saturday a.m. with TV cartoons, set up a supper-time date with Cindi — God bless her, at least she takes me, takes me as I am (Yes that's *not* me in the photo) — Burn Man climbs inside mask and clown suit like a scuba diver, like Iago[17] on Prozac. For what seems a fucking century we wave white gloves at you (*Drowning not waving*), wave at blind drivers passing Bed of Roses and the helium balloons — gorgeous ivory moons and red planets bump-bumping my skin, trying to enter the hide of Burn Man's teeming serious face, trying to push past something difficult and lewd.

Ours really is an amazing world. Tristan falls in love on a Hopper porch, but Isolde[18] loses faith in a Safeway parking lot, Isolde takes the magic bell off the dog. And a famous scuba diver rockets like a lost dark god into smoking stands of Douglas fir, into black chimneys burning.

(2000)

Erin Mouré (1955–)

Erin Mouré was born in Calgary, Alberta, in 1955. Growing up, she and her two younger brothers would leave the city as often as they could to hike on the surrounding prairie and explore the nearby mountains. Her love for this natural landscape developed in tandem with her adult consciousness, and it would inform her poetic long after she left it behind. She has explained that a second profound influence on her work was her mother: "I get my courage from my mother, from the place where she stood in front of the kitchen sink, and wore two holes in the linoleum." The mother–daughter relationship in all its complexity is a vital presence in Mouré's poetry. In *Sheepish Beauty, Civilian Love* (1992), she writes: "Who abandoned you? / My mother. / How did your mother abandon you? / I abandoned her. / What happened? / I grew up."

Mouré submerged herself in poetry as a high-school student, starting with Chaucer and Milton and moving on to discover a host of Canadian poets, among them Irving Layton, P.K. Page, Al Purdy, and Phyllis Webb. She studied at the Universities of Calgary and British Columbia, never completing a degree, and wrote poetry in her free time. In 1979, she published her first collection — *Empire, York Street* — and the following year it was nominated for a Governor General's Award. She bolstered this success with the chapbook *The Whiskey Vigil* (1981) and another collection, *Wanted Alive* (1983), which contains several poems from the chapbook. In 1984, Mouré left her home territory and settled in Montreal, working for VIA Rail. She still lives in Montreal, a city whose vibrant political, social, and cultural atmosphere continues to exert its influence on her work.

The poems of *Empire, York Street* reflect Mouré's dual fascination with the power that emanates from carefully honed poetic language and the plight of working people oppressed by a monolithic capitalist system that often renders them invisible. In "So Much Worse," she writes:

---

17. **Iago** In Shakespeare's *Othello*, Iago causes Othello's downfall by preying on his fears. 18. **Tristan, Isolde** In this medieval story, King Mark seeks to marry Isolde, a rival king's daughter, and sends Tristan to kidnap her. Tristan and Isolde fall in love on their journey back to King Mark.

"can't you see me, standing on the corner w/ shoelaces / broken, my elbows ripped open?" In this collection, and later efforts, language — which has the propensity to enforce compliance (grammar and syntax oppress in the same way political systems do) — is the poet's tool for accessing liberation. Sometimes, however, the task proves too daunting. In "Snowbound," from *The Whisky Vigil*, Mouré despairs that she "can't wring any more sense out of the words."

Before moving east, Mouré attended the 1983 Women and Words conference at the University of British Columbia. She describes the experience as "a real catalyst or turning point." There she was introduced to the work of Hélène Cixous, Luce Irigaray, and Julia Kristeva, the initiators of poststructuralist feminist theory whose writings were having an enormous impact in feminist literary circles worldwide. Living in Montreal two years later, Mouré published the collection *Domestic Fuel*, which displays the pervasive influence on her work of the French feminist theorists and others who hold that language is fundamentally patriarchal and that women must subvert and reinvent it in order to speak, write, and be. In this collection, Mouré offers the first poetic expression of her lesbianism — it is not possible, she writes, "To embrace them without them / knowing you / These … women" — and intensifies her investigation into the political properties of poetic language. Formally, she accomplishes the subversion of patriarchal structures through what critic Susan Glickman calls "strategic incoherence," employing "Transgressions of syntax and punctuation, repetition, fragmentation … the rejection of formal closure."

In her next collection, the Governor General's Award–winning *Furious* (1988), Mouré again addresses political hierarchies, language, and sexuality in a search for a private voice capable of conveying collective femininity. In the concluding section, entitled "The Acts," she declares her mission in ringing terms: "To break down the noun/verb opposition that is a kind of absolutism in the language itself"; instead, she will focus on the preposition, "the woman's sign because it is relational," as it facilitates wholeness. The section "Three Versions" was engendered, Mouré later said, by a comment made by fellow writer and mentor Gail Scott. Mouré had asked Scott which version of a poem she preferred; Scott "read them and got really impatient with my question, asking, 'Why do you have to choose a definitive version?' That phrase of hers has echoed in my head since then. I think it's become woven into my practice." To choose one story over another is to reinforce the hierarchy, to assert a privileged, patriarchal discourse. The prolific Mouré followed *Furious* with two volumes of linked poems — *WSW (West South West)* (1989) and *Sheepish Beauty, Civilian Love* (1992) — which explore similar issues, and *Search Procedures* (1996), a collection of lyrics.

While translating experience into poetry has absorbed Mouré all of her life, she is also interested in the dynamics of translation (mainly French into English, but also Spanish and Portuguese into English). She has co-translated the works of several Québécois writers, and in 2001, she wrote *Sheep's Vigil by a Fervent Person*, a "translation" or "trans-creation" of Fernando Pessoa's classic Portuguese long poem *O Guardador de Rebanhos*, which recounts the experience of a lone shepherd who inhabits the Portuguese countryside from the perspective of an urban Canadian woman.

With the poems of *O Cidadán* (2002), Mouré questions the possibility of ethical citizenship in the contemporary world. She has described the volume as an argument for "a notion of frontier or border as a line that admits filtrations, that leaks," because "identity finds its stability in uncertainty, in the fluidity of limits, in the 'not yet.'" Again, Mouré proposes a political activism grounded in language — hierarchies exist to be dismantled, borders exist to be traversed, since a border "is only a useful edge if it can be crossed [and] … a language/community can only thrive over time if people can enter it from outside."

Mouré's most recent book, *Little Theatres* (2005), in which she intersperses English verse with poems written in Galician, won the A.M. Klein Prize for Poetry and was nominated for a

Governor General's Award (as were *Search Procedures* and *O Cidadán*). Over the years, Mouré has served as writer-in-residence at the Universities of Toronto, Calgary, and New Brunswick. She has worked as a customer service representative (at VIA), a freelance editor, and a translator and has travelled to England, the U.S., Spain, and throughout Canada to conduct poetry workshops.

Certain Words, a Garden

I am a terrorist in my life,
each morning arrives again to me
holding the accident of birth, a blanket, my mother's
deep sighing.
To get up, cherished, & not cry out to anything,
neither wet doors, the shorn corridor,
odour of cabbages caught against the stair
Refusing to trust in the talk
of pistols, its grimness deafens a whole garden,
10 breeds sentinels on the roofs of buildings, feigned
relaxation, dedication, fear
Instead to dress quietly in the old coat & my usual shoulders,
empty of ancestors,
rejecting the innocence of age, the white step
of the fou[1] with his crumpled ass
& nightgown

After all night throwing knives against
the kitchen table,
against the lampshade that spoke your name,
20 you catch yourself, ticking, certain words.
You touch the holy palms
brought by your accidental brothers, given to you,
hold them free of the
ceremonies.
In the morning, now, the neighbours
hear you laughing

because the law is a gone story
awaiting apprehension, because it is not enough
to sell your furniture;
30 your life alone has reached you, captive, stubborn:
in its arms at last
your terror rises
with red wings & a lonely heartbeat, & your voice
opens up a whole garden

(1983)

---

1. **fou** A crazy person.

Post-Modern Literature

Less to insist upon, fewer
proofs.
Raw metals pulled from the ground, cheaply.
Or a woman in the televised film shouting: thanks to you
I end up surrounded by violence.
So much gratitude, Saturday nights spent
believing in it.

But the end of a city is still
a field, ordinary persons live there, a frame house, & occasionally —
a woman comes out to hang the washing.   10
From a certain angle you see her
push a line of wet clothes across a suburb.
It sings in the wind there, against
stucco, lilacs, sunken front porches, windows
where nobody moves.
But carefully.   All of it

made carefully, children in snowsuits
after school, appear in the doorway, carry
their tracks shyly.
& you at the kitchen table — your empty   20
bowl streaked by the spoon, the meal's
memory, papers, juice in one glass, whisky
in another, unwritten greeting cards,
a watch, applesauce, small white medallions.

As if saying the name fixes.
As if the woman will come out again, & pull down
an entire suburb with her washing.
As if the city *could* end, in a field or
anywhere.
or if the woman on the bright TV could   30
stop saying *thank you.*
or you, saying "like this," & pointing shyly.
Too much paper, the children
in their snowsuits holding doorways, white snow,
parrots, singing smuggled information, the corporation gone to

Guatemala.
Leaving Father, the curling rink, a woman dressed
in grey parka & the nearest boots pulling
stiff clothes away from the weather, the back road, post-modern literature

(1983)

Miss Chatelaine

In the movie, the horse almost dies.
A classic for children, where the small girl pushes a thin
knife into the horse's side.
Later I am sitting in brightness with the women
I went to high school with in Calgary,
fifteen years later we are all feminist, talking of the girl
in the film.
The horse who has some parasite & is afraid of the storm,
& the girl who goes out to save him.

10 We are in a baggage car on VIA Rail around a huge table,
its varnish light & cold,
as if inside the board rooms of the corporation;
the baggage door is open
to the smell of dark prairie,
we are fifteen years older, serious
about women, these images:
the girl running at night between the house & the barn,
& the noise of the horse's fear mixed in with the rain.

Finally there are no men between us.
20 Finally none of us are passing or failing according to
Miss Chatelaine.
I wish I could tell you how much I love you,
my friends with your odd looks, our odd looks,
our nervousness with each other,
the girl crying out as she runs in the darkness,
our decoration we wore, so many years ago, high school
boys watching from another table.

Finally I can love you.
Wherever you have gone to, in your secret marriages.
30 When the knife goes so deeply into the horse's side, a
few seconds & the rush of air.
In the morning, the rain is over.
The space between the house & barn is just a space again.
Finally I can meet with you & talk this over.
Finally I can see us meeting, & our true tenderness, emerge.

(1988)

The Beauty of Furs

At lunch with the girls, the younger ones are talking about furs, & what looks good with certain hair colours. Red fox looks no good with my hair, says one. White fox looks snobbish, beautiful but snobbish, says another one. They talk about the pronunciation of coyote. I think of my brother catching muskrat. I think of pushing the drown-set[1] into the weeds, the freezing water of the Elbow, the brown banks & snow we lived with, soft smell of aspen buds not yet coming out on the trees, & us in our nylon coats in the backyards of Elbow Park Estates, practically downtown, trapping. *Coy-oh-tea,* the women say. In some places they say *Ky-oot* or *Ky-oht,* I say, thinking of the country where my brother now lives, the moan of coyotes unseen, calling the night sky. & me caught in the drown-set so deeply, my breath snuffled for years. & then it comes. They are talking about the beauty of furs, and how so-and-so's family is in the business. I remember, I say, I remember my mother had a muskrat coat, & when she wore it & you grabbed her too hard by the arm, fur came out. Eileen, fifteen years older than me, starts to laugh, & puts her hand on my shoulder, laughing. We both start laughing. I start to explain to her that it was old; my mother wore it to church on Sunday & got upset if we grabbed her arm. We're laughing so hard, now the young ones are looking at us, together we are laughing, in our house there was a beaver coat like that Eileen said, then suddenly we are crying, crying for those fur coats & the pride of our mothers, our mothers' pride, smell of the coat at church on Sunday, smell of the river, & us so small, our hair wet, kneeling in that smell of fur beside our mothers

(1989)

The Beauty of Furs: A Site Glossary

Later you realize it is a poem about being born, the smell of the fur is your mother birthing you & your hair is wet not slicked back but from the wetness of womb, the fur coat the hugest fur of your mother the cunt of your mother from which you have emerged & you cower in this smell The fur coat the sex of women reduced to decoration, & the womb the place of birth becomes the church in which you are standing, the womb reduced to decoration, where women are decoration, where the failure of decoration is the humiliation of women, to wear these coats, these emblems of their own bodies, in church on Sunday, children beside them The church now the place of birth & rebirth, they say *redemption,* everyone knows what this signifies & the mother is trying to pay attention, all the mothers, my mother, & we are children, I am children, a child with wet hair cowlick slicked down perfect, no humiliation, the site still charged with the smell of the river, the coat smell of the river, smell of the birth canal, caught in the drown-set is to be stopped from being born, is to be clenched in the water unable to breathe or see the night sky, the *coyohts* calling me upward, as if in these circumstances, so small beside my mother, I could be born now, but cannot, can I, because we are inside this hugest womb which has already denied us, in which we are decoration, in which men wear dresses & do the cooking, & the slicked hair is not the wet hair of birth but the hair of decoration, as if I could be born now, I am born, my snout warm smelling the wet earth of my mother's fur

(1989)

---

1. **drown-set** A foot-hold trap.

Safety of the State

The problem is the division of labour in the word "hunted,"
pluriel, plural, *elles,* el L,
the letter L hunted by the letter H, He, Hunted …
The problem is the alphabet has fallen apart. An army maintained by
public tax who obey the order to fire on "hooligan elements." O citizen.
The division of labour. Inside us, the state. Raise up, we say.
Agnus dei,[1] we say. Dominus vobiscum,[2] we say.

The defense minister's "suicide,"
people in the streets climb upon tanks & embrace the soldiers. If only
10   the soldiers would stop shooting on the population, they say. Who take off
their overcoats & wave them over their heads. Embracing the air.
Embracing the state of the air. Dancing. Lying down in their blood.
Tired. The head sideways. The blur. Which
happens

In the forest, the bodies
still mouths bloodied with shovelled earth.
I am looking
for my brother, one said, climbing the mounds, the dishevelled &
dirty shoulders, snowy air, forests where we once dreamed the word
20   "partisan," the word
"comrade" now fallen apart, the letters P & C of the alphabet now fallen
apart. In us, the safety of the state, equally, the identity of the brother,
equally, inside us. I am looking for my brother, they say,
triggering the metal.

Some will call this bitterness, to say so.

& now, what is left mocks all of us
waiting outside the church
for the silver circles
carried outward
30   We see these circles
this silver
Our arms fall
Outside the cathedral's immense stones

We admit everything
when we see this silver

(1992)

---

1. **Agnus dei** Latin for "Lamb of God," referring to Christ. 2. **Dominus vobiscum** Latin for "The Lord be with you."

Erosion Theory Coil Theory Maintenance Device:

EROSION	THEORY
SURGE	THEORY
MAINTENANCE	DEVICE

*"This is when human beings who thought they could use language as an instrument of communication learn through the feeling of pain which accompanies silence (and of pleasure which accompanies the invention of a new idiom), that they are summoned by language, not to augment to their profit the quantity of information communicable through existing idioms, but to recognize that what remains to be phrased exceeds what they can presently phrase, and that they must be allowed to institute idioms which do not yet exist."   J-F Lyotard, *The Differend*

**her head wet

(1999)

Jan Zwicky (1955–)

Jan Zwicky was born in Calgary in 1955. She admits that she can't say why or when she began writing poetry, but that once she started it was impossible to quit: "my sense that [poetry] was a way to get at truth outweighed my sense of frustration with its difficulties." The belief that poetry is a means of accessing philosophical truth took root in her, and it has continued to shape her approach to writing.

After receiving a B.A. from the University of Calgary, Zwicky moved east to study at the University of Toronto; there she earned an M.A., and in the late 1970s, she wrote a Ph.D. dissertation on the "ineffability claims" of certain artists and mystics who maintain that some experiences defy verbal description. Zwicky, comfortable with the idea of ineffability, repudiates philosophies that propose that the best way to understand objects is to break them down and describe their constituent parts. Such a method, she argues, inadequately reflects the world's complexity and interconnectedness. For this reason, she has developed an interest in the pre-Socratic philosophy of the Ancient Greeks, which existed prior to (and was therefore not influenced by) Aristotle's divisive taxonomical approach to the world.

Zwicky thinks that poetry and philosophy come together in the space between what can be said and what remains unsayable. Lyric poems provide access to "the foundations of meaning ... in the world," which remain "unconditioned by language"; they celebrate their subjects by immortalizing them in a timeless present. However, the poet is often conscious of time passing, and so the lyric takes on an elegiac tone as it is pulled back into time and the world — this dynamic is evident in many of Zwicky's poems. There is a tension in the lyric poem, Zwicky suggests, between the said and the unsaid, and between the timeless and the time-bound, and this tension, like in a stringed instrument, is what produces "resonance," or meaning.

Though Zwicky received little formal training as a poet, she has said that in her teens and twenties she enjoyed the work of John Donne, Alden Nowlan, and Philip Larkin. Describing her poetic process, she remarks that "Sometimes a rhythmic phrase, without words but with an emotional/tonal 'pitch' or colour, will announce itself in relation to something." As a poet, she sees it as her job to translate those phrases into language. As a musician — Zwicky is a violinist who has played in many orchestras and chamber music ensembles — she is highly attentive to rhythm, and she will sometimes wait years for words to appear in the right metre or key.

In 1981, Zwicky received her doctorate, and in 1986, she published *Wittgenstein Elegies*, a sequence of five long poems that engage with the life and ideas of 20th-century philosopher Ludwig Wittgenstein, exploring elements of his work that are hard to articulate in analytical philosophical language. Each of the poems juxtaposes quotation with poetic commentary, and their meanings arise largely from the juxtapositions. Like her poems, Zwicky suggests, Wittgenstein's "truths" can only be apprehended by looking at their parts in relation to an infinitely complex whole, an entity that language may be incapable of describing.

This poetics of juxtaposition is grounded in Zwicky's deeper concern for how objects relate to the world. "Ecology" is the word she uses to refer to the "interconnectedness of things"; the way in which an object "is" is intimately tied to its environment, its situation, or what it "is not." In her Governor General's Award–winning *Songs for Relinquishing the Earth* (1998), Zwicky exhibits an environmentalist's concern for writing through, rather than about, her subjects. Highly conscious, as she says in "Kant and Bruckner," that "we cannot touch a hair / without affecting all the rest," she strives in her short lyrics to allow objects and images to articulate what they are (and what they are not) without interference.

Zwicky's increasing preoccupation with the ability of specific objects to reveal larger truths partially explains the general shift in her poetic style. Her poems have evolved from the colloquial lyrics of *Where Have We Been* (1982) to the sparse, imagistic, haiku-like "songs" of *Thirty-Seven Small Songs and Thirteen Silences* (2005). In earlier volumes, like *The New Room* (1989), she personifies objects, associating them with abstract human emotions (as in "Last Steps," when a bed refuses to "accept" the speaker's "bewildered failure"). In *Thirty-Seven Small Songs*, however, Zwicky attempts to let the images speak for themselves; abstractions and emotions, when explicitly invoked, are juxtaposed with objects rather than attributed to them, so that their relationship resonates but is not limited by unnecessary articulation.

History, too, is an ecology for Zwicky. In *Robinson's Crossing* (2004), she examines the interconnectedness of land, history, and personal identity. Robinson's Crossing is the place in Northern Alberta where the railway ended — from there, settlers had to proceed by wagon or on foot. The history of the crossing is sketchy; as Zwicky says, "There's no mention / in the local history book / of how the crossing got its name." But as she contemplates the land suffering from technological changes, like "junk" accumulating "in the grass," she realizes she is connected on a sensory level to the land's undocumented past. Her fear that the land will be destroyed is also a fear that her identity will be lost: her family history, transmitted through the "smell" of "grass and dirt," might be obliterated along with the natural environment.

Zwicky's other publications include *Twenty-One Small Songs* (2000) and *Why I Sing the Blues: Lyrics & Poems* (2001). She has written two book-length works about the intersection of poetry and philosophy: *Lyrical Philosophy* (1992) and *Wisdom and Metaphor* (2003). Zwicky has also contributed essays to *Poetry and Knowing* (1995) and *Thinking and Singing: Poetry and the Practice of Philosophy* (2002). Edited by Tim Lilburn, these two collections also contain essays by Canadian poets such as Robert Bringhurst, Dennis Lee, and Don McKay, who, like Zwicky, desire to live in and write about the world responsibly.

Zwicky has taught at a number of universities throughout North America. Since 1996, she has lived in British Columbia with her partner, Don McKay, teaching philosophy at the University of Victoria.

Language Is Hands

Language visits the dentist: fevered
tooth to the world's
cold lunch. Twitchy, beaten yet again
by the unsayable, it's time
to scrape the nerve-pulp out, spirit
gone friable as ash.

In the desert of nth-order quantificational
logic and shopping malls, this is not
what Heraclitus[1] meant. When you dry a plant out
water stays inside its soul like wisdom   10
in the muscles of a farmer's hand.
Language is a cactus.

Language is a hand, a hand
used to pulling on galoshes: ribbed nails, long thumb
that lies along a car door
like a donkey's ear against its neck.
Mottled skin and knobbiness unowned
anymore by anyone.

If it remembers hunger, it is
to touch, for tendons that flex and contract   20
into sound; to have been
a musician's hand with its cat-mind,
grasping the handle of a fridge door
the way a dancer walks in his body.

Your poor old slipper, speech:
worn out, kicked off
for having failed, grown threadbare.
There may be no words for the vibratoless[2]
baroque[3] of the cello world, which you
have tried to show me, galloped   30

each day right up to the edge
of what Kant[4] understood, wheeled in its face.

---

1. **Heraclitus** Greek philosopher who believed that change is a natural part of the universe and that it arises from conflict.
2. **vibratoless** Lacking a tremulous or pulsating effect. 3. **baroque** Ornateness. 4. **Kant** German idealist philosopher (1724–1804).

Yet I set you to the task again, against
yourself, and you struggle with the goodwill
of a later-to-be-schizophrenic child.
Like my dog, Sam

who in an urgency of insight
drops his soggy tennis ball at my distracted feet,
and whom I banish, thankless, reading
40   not his terrible compassion but
mere need, bronzed to necessity; at best
irrelevant demand.

(1989)

Last Steps

Which summer was it? First of these
clenched bumbles down the stairs I couldn't see
the loveseat in the dark and stubbed my toe.
No stairs now, true, and leave the light
on in the kitchen just in case,
but that's no difference. Still, it's the room
won't hold one any longer, same grope
for handrails, absence shoving from behind, absence
that pulls.   Which one?
10   I still don't know
what happened wrong. It must have been
a birthday gift; said thank you twice and true
as true (although it was too short
and violent in cut and colour) so must have been
I didn't try it on. Or wear it long enough.
Lapse of alacrity?[1] Your tears
and anger after supper, rules I didn't know,
still can't construct, even my bed
would not accept that much
20   bewildered failure. Better comfort
the cold couch, the skin-dry furnace, frozen
dusted coffee tables. How we invigilated!
All eyes open in the moon-dark,
anonymous as furniture.

        Past caring, carcasses.
When the Shetland pony foundered, you had
your father burn the body when I wasn't there.
Why worse the thought he had to do it
all alone, dull jerks behind the tractor

---

1. alacrity Readiness, liveliness.

and the fire too slow at first?   30
Your own mare, stiff-legged in the draw,
the single bloody eye; or mine,
his hoof gone rotten while I was in Europe,
those long months you nursed and nursed
past all recovery. Told me the Langdales
used to throw their kittens, hours old
against the barn door — faster than drowning.
Dark room, TV set; headlights on the highway
half a mile away:
                    to desire was misconceived.   40
       Moth falls behind the bookcase,
heaves from underneath festooned
with clumps of dust three times its size
— pulped scuttering. Back of the summerhouse,
the headless chicken dithering across the lawn,
your mother stares, laughs, passes me
her sticky hatchet,

                    takes us visiting
the old folks home, yanks on my braids,
"For God's sake, stand up straight.   50
How your poor mother bears it,
I don't know." Detours
on the way home, rutted track
that dead-ends in a field. The nervous
high-pitched grin, crisp drugstore bag.
She's awkward with the match, but
gets them lit; we have to finish them
half-sick with smoke. The way your father
shoves me up against the cellar wall
to feel my breasts and doesn't have to   60
warn me not to tell: no no
I'd never breathe a word, "You're
such a disappointment, your poor mother,
it'd kill her if she knew."

                    Because it's filled to bursting:
pig's teeth, shrapnel, silent fallout
coming home to roost. I'm mined, don't
touch me mother in the dark; I'm set
on automatic, unnamed thing that cuts
you in the night, the razor hidden   70
in the apple of your eye.

                    The first shirt I sewed was paisley,
pink and green. "We three girls!"
You helped with every seam,

that basement room. Saturday mornings,
father gone back to the office and
your bitterness palpable as pins,
how could you know we would remember?

                       "Lies."
80   There was no blood, I made it up, and
it was love, hay's sweetness
and those sunsets, all the promises.
You gave us everything: "Don't cry
unless you're run down by a truck."
Ingratitude, my ugliness,
she told me. That much more
the treasure of your love; the scorn
of men who liked me: must be lying.
We all knew. You knew. You knew me.
90   Sham.
            These words
                      inhabit me, your ghosts:
a child of twelve clutching the hayrake-mangled dog;
a woman labouring at thirty under mountains of her father's
shit-soaked bandages; no kerchief ties the jaw-gape shut, the
screams were silent silent silent; faces stream, fists knuckle
at the ears of that obliterated childhood; nineteen,
stretched full length on the tufted counterpane,
eyes to the ceiling, you recite: the butcher knife,
100   the .22, the scythe, the axe, the maul ...

Which summer was it? "In Houston,
sometimes they'd come up like this, the clouds
so thick with water they'd be green." We sat
on those back steps, white legs unmuscled
angling from their ill-cut twice-worn shorts.

In that romance of humidity and heat
you forgot once who I was, it fled, drained
to the sky, you opened
like clouds, like hands, you were
110   my mother.
            We said almost nothing but it's bright
               that slash of ozone in the gust
               that set the poplars thrashing;
               the pumphouse door that slammed, creaked,
               slammed again; the runner, coconut,
               curled up against my thigh,
               pricking the thin fabric.
               Your laugh.

Oh, I'd have sat there years,
what there's been of lives
and decades since, I'd
have sat there till the sky turned green.

120

(1989)

Driving Northwest

Driving Northwest in July before
the long twilight that stretches into
the short summer dark, despite the sun
the temperature is dropping, air
slips by the truck, like diving,
diving,
      and you are almost blind
with light: on either side of you
it floats across the fields, young barley
picking up the gold, oats white,

10

the cloudy bruise of alfalfa
along the fencelines, the air itself
tawny with haydust, and the shadows of the willows
in the draw miles long, oh it is lovely
as a myth, the touch of a hand on your hair,
and you need, like sleep, to lie down now
and rest, but you are almost
blind with light, the highway
stretched across the continent
straight at the sun: visor,

20

dark glasses, useless against its gonging,
the cab drowns in it, shuddering, you cannot tell,
you might be bleeding or suffocating, shapes
fly out of it so fast there's no time to swerve:
but there is no other path, there is no other bed,
it is the only way home you know.

(1998)

The Geology of Norway

> *But when his last night in Norway came, on 10 December, he greeted it with*
> *some relief, writing that it was perfectly possible that he would never return.*
> —Ray Monk, *Ludwig Wittgenstein*

I have wanted there to be
no story. I have wanted
only facts. At any given point in time
there cannot be a story: time,
except as now, does not exist.
A given point in space

is the compression of desire. The difference
10   between this point and some place else
is a matter of degree.
This is what compression is: a geologic epoch[1]
rendered to a slice of rock you hold between
your finger and your thumb.
That is a fact.
Stories are merely theories. Theories
are dreams.
A dream
is a carving knife
20   and the scar it opens in the world
is history.
The process of compression gives off thought.
I have wanted
the geology of light.

They tell me despair is a sin.
I believe them.
The hand moving is the hand thinking,
and despair says the body does not exist.
Something to do with bellies and fingers
30   pressing gut to ebony,
thumbs on keys. Even the hand
writing is the hand thinking. I wanted
speech like diamond because I knew
that music meant too much.

And the fact is, the earth is not a perfect sphere.
And the fact is, it is half-liquid.
And the fact is there are gravitational anomalies. The continents
congeal, and crack, and float like scum on cooling custard.
And the fact is,
40   the fact is,
and you might think the fact is
we will never get to the bottom of it,
but you would be wrong.
There is a solid inner core.
Fifteen hundred miles across, iron alloy,
the pressure on each square inch of its heart
is nearly thirty thousand tons.
That's what I wanted:
words made of that: language
50   that could bend light.

---

1. **epoch** Time period.

Evil is not darkness,
it is noise. It crowds out possibility,
which is to say
it crowds out silence.
History is full of it, it says
that no one listens.

The sound of wind in leaves,
that was what puzzled me, it took me years
to understand that it was music.
Into silence, a gesture.   60
A sentence: that it speaks.
This is the mystery: meaning.
Not that these folds of rock exist
but that their beauty, here,
now, nails us to the sky.

The afternoon blue light in the fjord.
Did I tell you
I can understand the villagers?
Being, I have come to think,
is music; or perhaps   70
it's silence. I cannot say.
Love, I'm pretty sure,
is light.
        You know, it isn't
what I came for, this bewilderment
by beauty. I came
to find a word, the perfect
syllable, to make it reach up,
grab meaning by the throat
and squeeze it till it spoke to me.   80
How else to anchor
memory? I wanted language
to hold me still, to be a rock,
I wanted to become a rock myself. I thought
if I could find, and say,
the perfect word, I'd nail
mind to the world, and find
release.
The hand moving is the hand thinking:
what I didn't know: even the continents   90
have no place but earth.

These mountains: once higher
than the Himalayas. Formed in the pucker
of a supercontinental kiss, when Europe
floated south of the equator

and you could hike from Norway
down through Greenland to the peaks
of Appalachia. Before Iceland existed.
Before the Mediterranean
100   evaporated. Before it filled again.
Before the Rockies were dreamt of.
And before these mountains,
the rock raised in them
chewed by ice that snowed from water
in which no fish had swum. And before that ice,
the almost speechless stretch of the Precambrian:[2]
two billion years, the planet
swathed in air that had no oxygen, the Baltic Shield
older, they think, than life.

110   So I was wrong.
This doesn't mean
that meaning is a bluff.
History, that's what
confuses us. Time
is not linear, but it's real.
The rock beneath us drifts,
and will, until the slow cacophony of magma
cools and locks the continents in place.
Then weather, light,
120   and gravity
will be the only things that move.

And will they understand?
Will they have a name for us? — Those
perfect changeless plains,
those deserts,
the beach that was this mountain,
and the tide that rolls for miles across
its vacant slope.

(1998)

Robinson's Crossing

They say
the dog was crazy that whole evening:
whining at the door, tearing
around the yard in circles,
standing stock still in the cart track,
head cocked, whimpering.

---

2. Precambrian A prehistoric era of Earth's geological history; life is believed to have emerged at the end of this era.

They'd left him out and gone to bed, but he
kept barking until after midnight
when they finally heard him take off
down the railbed, east,   10
toward the river. Next morning
Ernest said he'd met him
a half-mile from the house. The train
had got in late but he'd
been eager to get home, so walked
the eight miles from the crossing
at the steel's end. They had finished
with the harvest down south, he had money
in his pocket. He was
two days early,   20
but the dog had known.

       My great-
grandmother slept
in a boxcar on the night
before she made the crossing. The steel
ended in Sangudo then, there was
no trestle on the Pembina,[1] no siding
on the other side. They crossed
by ferry, and went on by cart through bush,
the same eight miles. Another   30
family legend has it that she stood there
in the open doorway of the shack
and said, "You told me, Ernest,
it had windows and a floor."

       The museum
has a picture of the Crocketts —
later first family of Mayerthorpe —
loading at the Narrows
on the trail through Lac Ste. Anne.
Much what you'd expect: 40
a wagon, crudely covered,
woman in a bonnet on the box seat,
man in shirt sleeves
by the horses' heads, a dog.
But what draws the eye, almost
a double-take, are the tipis
in the distance, three of them,
white, smudged — a view the lens
could not pull into focus.

---

1. **Sangudo, Pembina** Albertan town and river.

50   And another photo,
       taken in the '30's maybe,
       of a summer camp down on the river flats
       between our quarter and the town.
       At least a dozen tipis; horses, smoke.
       By the time I was a kid,
       they'd put the town dump there;
       but I remember we picked arrowheads
       out of the west field every spring
       when it was turned. And a memory
60   of my uncle, sharp, impatient with
       my grandfather for lending out
       his .22 to Indians:
       last time, didn't he remember?,
       he never got it back.

                    Robinson's Crossing
       is how you come in to this country, still —
       though it's not been on a map
       since 1920, and the highway
       takes a different route. You come in,
70   on the backs of slightly crazy Europeans, every time
       you lift your eyes across a field of swath
       and feel your throat catch
       on the west horizon. It's the northern edge
       of aspen parkland, here —
       another ten miles down the track,
       the muskeg's getting serious.
       But my great-grandfather was right:
       cleared, seeded, fenced,
       trees left for windbreaks and along
80   the river's edge, it looks
       a lot like England.
       You could file
       on a quarter section for ten dollars;
       all you had to do to keep it
       was break thirty acres in three years.
       The homestead map shows
       maybe two in three men
       made it. Several of their wives
       jumped from the bridge.

90   There's no mention
       in the local history book
       of how the crossing got its name.
       I found a picture of an Ernie
       Robinson — part of a road gang
       in the '20's — and of an old guy,

Ed, at some town function
later on. There's also
a photo of a sign, undated, shot
from an extreme low angle, as though
whoever took it had been standing   100
in the ditch beside the grade. I'll show you
where it was: just go out
the old road from the RV park, west,
about two miles. Nothing there now
but a farmer's crossing and a stretch
of old rail in the ditch. I'm guessing
that they closed it
when the steel moved on
after the war.

        A few years back   110
I was out behind the old house
picking twigs. (TransAlta
had come in and taken out
a poplar — it had left
enough junk in the grass
my mother couldn't mow.)
The rake had clawed
the grass out, more than
it had piled up twigs,
so I was squatting, sorting   120
dirt and grass by hand. The smell
was mesmerizing: musty, sweet,
dank, clay-ey; green —
and with a shock I realized
what it was: the same smell
as my family. Not because
our boots and gloves
were covered in it, nothing
you could shower off — it was
the body's scent, the one   130
that's on the inside
of your clothes, the one a dog
picks up. Our cells were
made of it: the garden, and the root
cellar, the oats
that fed the chickens, and the hay
the steers.
        These days

the line north of the farmhouse
carries only freight,   140
infrequently; the highway's

being twinned; Monsanto[2]
just released another herbicide-resistant
seed. Before the drought,
the river flooded every time it rained —
no trees upstream; this year
it's lower than it's been
since someone started
keeping records. The wooden
150   elevators, gone or going; ranks
of concrete silos that read
Agricore in flowing nineteenth-century
script — it's why

the story matters, why it
puzzles me. Here comes
my great-grandfather, he has made
Robinson's Crossing, he is walking
toward us, bone-tired
but whistling, it's a fine night, he has
160   money in his pocket,
and the dog, the family dog,
is going out to meet him.

(2004)

John Barton (1957–)

In the concluding section of his long poem *Hidden Structure* (1984), John Barton writes that "The facts of our lives / simply form / the whole of our forever growing / personal pasts." The passage captures a theme that runs through his work: identity. As he explores his relationships with his family, nation, and sexuality, he often imagines that identity is continually being shaped, even if it is resisted or suppressed: "identity and love are a harvest / of doubts whose seeds take root in / the right soil despite us / and grow."

Barton was born in 1957 in Edmonton, Alberta, and he spent his youth in Calgary. He returned to Edmonton in the mid-1970s to attend the University of Alberta but went on to complete an undergraduate education in creative writing at the University of Victoria. In 1986, he earned a degree in library science from the University of Western Ontario in London, and later that year he moved to Ottawa. Until quite recently, Barton was employed there in the publishing departments of several national museums, including the National Gallery of Canada. While at the National Gallery, he also edited its magazine, *Vernissage*, and, from 1990 to 2003, he was co-editor of the periodical *Arc: Canada's National Poetry Magazine*. In 2004, he moved from Ottawa to Victoria, where he edits the literary journal the *Malahat Review*.

Much of Barton's early poetry is preoccupied with the possibility of forging a uniquely Canadian tradition in literature and art. He recollects, "what got me to think about becoming a writer was Margaret Atwood's novel *Surfacing* (1972), which I discovered when I was 17. The tone

---

2. **Monsanto** American agricultural company that produces herbicides and genetically engineered seeds.

of that book spoke to me like no other. It was written in my language ... I began to write while reading the writers who came on stream in the heady days of CanLit after 1967. I was swept up in the nationalistic fervour to create an authentic Canadian literature." Although Barton treats a range of subjects in his first collection, *A Poor Photographer* (1981), he declares his indebtedness to a specifically Canadian tradition by paying homage to his fellow writers. "The Silence" is written for Patrick Lane, "Hieroglyph" is composed in the style of P.K. Page, and, in "On Rereading Phyllis Webb's 'To Friends Who Have Also Considered Suicide,'" Barton dramatizes a line of influence within Canadian literature.

In his second full-length book, *West of Darkness* (1987), he takes on the voice and persona of Canadian painter Emily Carr in an attempt to examine her distinctive artistic approach and the way in which that approach was connected to her profound identification with her country and its landscape. Barton imagines that when Carr first arrives in London, England, to study at the Westminster School of Art, she is self-conscious of her Canadian heritage, but that she soon begins to take pride in her origins. Explaining her feelings to an unpatriotic emigrant, Barton's Carr exclaims, "what about the tremendous forests ... that can root deep in a child's / heart? ... Or the rivers that pour the heart-song of our origins / through their mouths?"

Mindful of such questions, Carr turns to art: "what I thought of the British Museum and / their galleries stuffed with mummies and old masters who / copied each other I kept to myself. / Nothing new in art for hundreds of years." Here, Barton suggests that Carr's ability to cast off the "rusting shackles of light / brought from Europe / a century before" and begin her work "in darkness," stems from her intensifying connection to the shadowy land into which she was born. "Shadows," his Carr persona muses, "I never took to heart / when Small."

In his more recent work, Barton shifts his focus away from national issues and towards questions of sexual identity. In his early 20s, he had begun to question his sexuality; by 1985, he had become openly gay in his life and work. In his first publications, Barton speaks of love in what he now calls "androgynous" terms, allowing for both hetero- and homosexual readings. His chapbook *Hidden Structure* marks a turning point in his oeuvre, as he explores his troubled relationships with his parents and his growing understanding of his sexuality in order to come to terms with all aspects of his identity — or "the whole" of himself.

Hidden Structure is reprinted in *Great Men* (1990). In this collection, Barton delves more deeply into the way in which fear and denial of his sexuality developed into acceptance and pride. He also extends his vision outward, examining the same pattern of growth as it occurs over a longer period in the gay community at large. In the title poem, Barton considers famous men throughout history who, he believes, were forced to suppress their homosexual desires: "Great men have slept / in each other's arms; Rimbaud / and Verlaine; / Auden and Isherwood; / and maybe Michelangelo." These desires are hands "held out in dangerous recognition / again and again," and they make men "ghetto themselves in the arms of women / they do not love" until, eventually, "desire turns to lust in the thin fingers of their cowardice." In "Au Garage, Montréal," which depicts the scene at a gay club, Barton expresses a movement towards openness and solidarity, but, he writes, "when two or more gather / fear slips like a shirt from heavy shoulders, / tangles about chair legs." In "Holiday," the personal and public come together when the speaker takes a trip with his lover and acknowledges the "time it has taken to come this far."

Since the publication of *Great Men,* Barton has continued to investigate the gay experience in his writing, searching also for a uniquely queer poetic in *Designs from the Interior* (1994) and *Sweet Ellipsis* (1998). Describing these pursuits, he observes that "The creation of a queer voice, especially of a realistic one, is one of the important motivations behind writing for me. I have been criticized for promoting negative images of homosexuality in my work, or reinforcing the so-called clichés of gay experience — loneliness, alienation, solitude." Yet, he insists, "despite all the recent federal and provincial legislation and the raised consciousness of many Canadians, I believe it is still not easy to be queer in this country." In dealing with the topic of AIDS, Barton has said that "I have written a lot about AIDS and my relationship to it as a gay man. Well, the public face of AIDS has changed over the last few years, with increased recognition of other communities that have been affected and, in the case of Africa, convulsed and even destroyed by HIV. I want to write about these other communities, to bring the full face of AIDS into my aesthetic treatment … of it as a disease."

In *Hypothesis* (2001), Barton depicts the effects of the AIDS pandemic on the gay community. The title poem is the story of a man who is dying slowly, "but still too fast," "his will bodacious / unlike his nearly exhausted / T-cells." Barton experiments with several forms, especially in the three poems making up the second section of the book, which use set margins to control the rhythm and pacing of the poems. His poem entitled "In the House of the Present" won the CBC Literary Award competition and was published in *En Route* magazine, a sign that Barton's poetry is gaining popular recognition.

Haro Strait[1]

Damn these skittish feet.
They whine with each step,
carry me towards cliffs
where the ocean lies
out cold in the heat.
I must sit
a moment and rest.

Ah … how I love the sun,
how it beats down
10   through the branches
like soft rain.
I must write Dilworth,[2]
tell him how the cedars
wake to light.
Sometimes they are cold blue,
then green, sometimes yellow-
warm as their boughs
turn into wind.
As they are lost
20   in the shadow Mount Douglas
draws from the ocean
across them, do they
feel it as darkness
or simply the sun's absence?
Do they feel the tug
of Your love, O My God?

---

1. Haro Strait The strait between Vancouver Island and mainland British Columbia. **2. Dilworth** Ira Dilworth (1894–1962) taught at the University of British Columbia and later directed CBC Radio's B.C. operations; he was a mentor of painter and writer Emily Carr (1871–1945).

I am your child.
My paintings show that.
But I am also Small,
my father's child,   30
with knots in my hair.
The little girl trotting
behind him, my fingers
clutching at his coattail
or cringing at his voice
raised like a hand.
His shadow lengthens
behind me as I limp
to my death.
With each step its grip   40
nips at my ankle,
a knot jerking taut.
I must write Dilworth:
Eye, Small says she remembers
the Brutal Telling well,
was barely fourteen,
had outgrown herself,
was soon called Milly.
Speak Small while Eye is still
willing to listen.   50
Mister Ira, Emily wants
you to know about one day
in late spring, the last
trees come into flower.
Mother was dying.
Father and I had gone
for a walk along Dallas Road.
The sea below us stretched
to the world's edge.
"Small," he said, "it is time   60
I warned you how a man
makes a child in a woman."
"They marry," I said brightly,
pleased that I already
knew. He started
to laugh. "No,
pretty whelp,"[3] he said,
gently cuffing my ear,
"there are many brats
like you whose fathers   70
were sailors. Navvies

---

3. **whelp** Rude child.

who bedded their mothers,
left the next morning.
One week of shore leave
could make a man a father
seven times over, I know,
I too was a sailor."
I tried to run away,
Mister Ira, but Father
80 grabbed at my frock.
It ripped in his hand.
"You haven't heard it all,
my dear girl," he said,
wiping the tears from my eyes.
"A man takes his member
(I know you saw Richard's
when you were both smaller
and took baths together);
and it grows big and hard
90 like the bull's,
he places it
right here in his woman."
With that I tore free.
I ran and I ran.
I hid in the cow shed.
I was never Small again
until Emily met you,
Mister Ira. Only to you
can I tell such horrible things.

100 Damn, my fingers have grown stiff
clutching this pen,
feel like dry twigs
itching to snap.
The breeze is warm though,
catches the branches.
Sometimes they float,
faery as ferns,
sometimes they droop
heavy as heartaches.
110 Get up, old girl,
the cliffs aren't far.
The islands in the strait
are dogs leaping into
the thick afternoon mist.
Go sit on those cliffs,
Emily. Your dreams
bits of cedar you toss

out to sea. Your dogs
catch them, carry them
west in their jowls,   120
drop them at the feet
of an invisible shore.
Sit on those cliffs,
let the sun wrap
you in the cedars'
warm shadows.
Sit on those cliffs,
feel everything recede.
Sexless, ageless,
you are Small again.   130

(1987)

The Totems Permit Me Peace

At first, I only woke the fleeting
glimmer behind the land's weathered
face, not the vacant
silence of its
stare. I merely observed, with sleight of hand
and colour, how the stubbled curve of its chin
dropped into the ocean like a seagull's
sudden cry into the wind. I never asked myself
why.

The light I knew then was not   10
local.
The etiquette of gardens
and shuttered windows skirted all questions
the veins of granite and cedar posed.
When exposed by some new
foundation, by another road
pushing aside the forest musk,
the land's raw colour was muted by delicate
webs of alyssum, day-lilies, and primroses.

Then the darkness fell: what light there was   20
I needed. My brush thirsted,
groped free of the decorum my race mapped out.
Its bristles felt out paths all forests lead
into themselves. I made the journey
up the Inside Passage from Alert Bay, then painted
Skeena, Kitwancool, Skidegate, Masset,
half-deserted villages built on rock
that formed my backbone.

But what I cannot let go of permits me
30   my art: my little griffon dog
asleep on my knees, the plait of lavender
stowed among my dry clothes
while I camp, the packet of tea biscuits
I keep as treats in my carpet coat bag.

At dusk, after William's left me
alone on the island,
after I've sketched, surveyed the poles,
they recede into darkness,
become one with the forest.
40   I listen like all Indians before me
for the land's voice:
the hoot-owl,
the raven's wing,
the claw-print,
the salmon-call.
Its absence inhabits me,
a limpid series of echoes that blurs into night
like waves through salt water.
With the fear of God that Father gave me
50   I pray for His blessing.
The totems permit me peace.

(1987)

Great Men

Great men have slept
in each other's arms: Rimbaud
and Verlaine;[1]
                Auden and Isherwood;[2]
and maybe Michelangelo
warmly carved David's thirst
for women in
the marble thrust of some half-forgotten
lover's unforgotten
10   thighs.

        Or Whitman[3] leaning easily
against the wall in a rough
Philadelphia tavern, his vision unrealised
in a young man's slender hips
and the barmaid's breasts,

---

1. **Rimbaud and Verlaine** French poets (1854–1891 and 1844–1896). 2. **Auden and Isherwood** W.H. Auden
(1907–1973), Anglo-American poet, and Christopher Isherwood (1904–1986), Anglo-American novelist.
3. **Whitman** American poet Walt Whitman (1819–1892).

his lovers' quick movements singing
like two
birds in a cage.

        And Cavafy[4] dreaming of the ease
of the Greeks unreachable across the terrible blue   20
Mediterranean of the last
two thousand years of his privation.
And Crane[5] jumped ship and Mishima[6] lost his head.
And I think of crazy Tchaikovsky[7] returning always
to his half-crazed wife.

        And there are others
who lie in the quiet arms of their
lovers, their bodies intimate,
hidden behind drawn curtains in London,
Vienna, and Prague,   30
Sydney, Tokyo, and Montreal.
This is more furtive than clothes
a moment shed and the single
passing of hands over one-night-flesh.

This is the hand
held out in dangerous recognition
again and again.

This is the hand that becomes
two hands undistinguished in the gentle
search of caressing   40
and caressed giving rise
to lips on nipples, on stomach,
and penis hardening
against anus.
This is courageous.

This makes men
ghetto themselves in the arms of women
they do not love.
        This makes men
who love their wives want   50
to tear out their hearts,
the clarity of desire unobtainable

---

4. **Cavafy** Constantine Cavafy (1863–1933), Greek poet. 5. **Crane** Hart Crane (1899–1932), American poet who committed suicide by jumping off a steamship in the Gulf of Mexico. 6. **Mishima** Yukio Mishima (1925–1970), Japanese writer who committed suicide by ritual *seppuku*, or disembowelment. 7. **Tchaikovsky** Pyotr Ilyich Tchaikovsky (1840–1893), Russian romantic composer who maintained a sham marriage to cover his homosexuality.

as stars.
     This makes men walk,
walk, walk,

the bitter mile along the sea,
the tide ponderous,
the sky ponderous,
the walk home ponderous,

60   the key in the door useless
as the rooms each one
leads to.
Desire turns to lust in the thin
fingers of their cowardice.

(1990)

Stains

They are everywhere, accidental
and black on the sleeve
of my shirt, on the overstuffed arm
of the sofa in the lobby,
burned through the sheen
of the oak table we lean on
in silence, its pale plane
of light scored by some
careless eclipse, a cigarette
10   dropped after a meal of salmon,
white wine, and asparagus.
Green oxides bleed down the marble
facade of the hotel around us,
its copper mansard[1] weeping,
weeping as it breaks down in the rain.

We carry the rain inside us,
carry it upstairs to bed, it courses
through us, soaked up by dreams
woven from blotting paper
20   once so unselfconscious and fresh,
now inked with shadows and retreating
faces we are slow to acknowledge,
waking to kicked off sheets
and saliva on the pillows.
Our bodies tangle, nerve ends
speculating on what the other
said in the night.

---

1. **mansard** Four-sloped roof.

Wordless, flushed from love
and exhausted, I study the ceiling,
mildewed, liver-spotted   30
with drizzly afternoon light.
No longer able to lie
about permanence, whispering, whispering,
I ease away while you doze,
the print that my spine urged
into your stomach
still pink, but fading.

Outside, beyond the terrace,
the ocean's constant erasure.
Gone are the sunlit days   40
when we unrolled towels on the sand.
Light stained everything;
we darkened, magnified
by the delicious lens of the sun.
We were insatiable.
We ate clams, drank beer,
and for a while saw what we chose,
saw our faces emblazoned on the surface
of tidal pools, not in the milky
spawning of hermit crabs   50
among the starfish below.

(1994)

From a Journey Around the World

Consider the crew of able-bodied men
a young boy imagines
taking upriver into the heart
of some continent: Grey Owl,[1]
Jack London,[2] and Joseph Conrad.[3]
Voices drip from your paddle.
As I fall asleep, you sit
cross-legged on the bed,
lips memorizing each
word in the book of voyages —   10
what to take with you,
what to leave behind —
a pocket flashlight guiding
you into the dark,
the crickets of August in the parched,

---

1. **Grey Owl** Canadian writer and conservationist (1888–1938), who was born British but adopted a First Nations identity.
2. **Jack London** American author (1876–1916) who wrote extensively about the American north. 3. **Joseph Conrad**
British novelist (1857–1924) most famous for *Heart of Darkness,* about a journey through the Congo.

noisy rushes along the river
below my window tickling
the cocked ear of a sickle moon.

The *Seniavin* at anchor in Sitka Sound.[4]

20 You are the nameless
Cossack carrying the samples
Mertens gathers from the mouth
of some uncharted river, the slimy
algae and bladder kelp staining
your uniform with salt,
salt that later sets the ink
preserving a day in the life
of a naturalist and his assistant
documenting Russian-America,

30 the frontispiece to
Illustrations of Seaweeds
from a Journey around the World
by Decree of Emperor Nicholas I.

How the sun of this new continent
makes your bodies sweat,
layers of the Navy's wool perfumed
with the weight of a three-year voyage.
Look at how perfectly
it stretches across his shoulders.

40 Whatever story was soaked up
by its tersely woven
fibres is less decipherable than the knotted
records of the Aztecs.

No matter how cold these near Arctic waters,
when the tide comes in,
warmed by the sand and rocks,
how you want to shed all
constraint and swim
with him among the weeds,

50 sample what can be found in the impressions
your bodies leave in the soft
spongy floor of the river's mouth.

It is dark down here
and in the haze the ship's disappearing
anchor rope gleams, a worm of the sea.
You swim with your eyes open

---

4. *Seniavin* Class of Russian battleships. Sitka Sound is on the southern Alaskan coast.

and your fingers are
blurred specimens under glass.
You can't believe how
easily you turn into this clear element,   60
yield to the current that feathers
the numberless and lovely
algae releasing oxygen
that the almost prehistoric,
prenatal gills of your body
at last are learning to collect.
You are at home down here,
your skin alive to something
you can't yet put a name to,
Mertens somewhere below or ahead,   70
your god of the sea,
a father called Neptune.

While I drift toward Atlantis,
you sit on the raft
of my bed with a flashlight,
amazed how the dark face of the deep
appearing so impregnable and endless
from the rolling deck of the ship
from below is now,
for the two of you, a fluttering   80
wide-open eyelid of sunlight.

(1998)

The Living Room

> Their rubbish alone was left.
> He was a vacant lot,
> he had become an exemption.
> *The squares of his mind were empty.*
>
> — P. K. Page, "In Memoriam"

At the drop-in clinic near the centre
of town, I namelessly drop off
cotton shirts wrinkled as grey skin
to be slung on hangers and rifled through
by men whose flesh thins under the shaking
force of their scapulae, the deft
articulation of fingers a memory
as they thumb through gaunt fabric —
the colours so bereft
their rubbish alone was left.   10

Even as I drive away, a man buttons
wash-worn cotton about his body
as it vanishes, ribs rising through
jaundiced skin like stains as he breathes
haltingly, or so I think, driving away
with my fears intact, overwrought
about whatever might or might not be
deadly in my own blood, haunted
by my one parting thought:

20   *He was a vacant lot.*

Against my will, I slip inside
his flesh. Its slim vitality sits
amply on my shoulders as I drive uptown
every remaining bit of pleasure to be
had from it an undiscovered country
lying within reach, vague satisfaction
of desires unable to die
with him, the body a cairn, fog
lifting as I pause at an intersection.

30   *He had become an exemption.*

His world opens up: his death is my death
his love my love, the men he kissed
and held are men like us who've passed
through the ordinary arms of several others
dates in loose cotton shirts who drove us
home after the movies, each entreaty
to love made on nights when warmth was wanted.
Guys who made us feel safe not cautious.
One foolhardy night he fleetingly felt free.

40   *The squares of his mind were empty.*

(2001)

Plasma, Triangles of Silk

the shirt you gave me I passed on to a friend, yellow silk the colour
of plasma, too soon worn out by years of wear and cut when needed

into triangles sewn by hand with a running stitch to other salvaged
bits of fabric forming squares joined into blocks then rows assembled

strip by strip, the pattern of the quilt revealing the care behind it the way
the shirt no longer can, my favourite shirt, given to heal something

between us in ways the year that tore us apart never could, a shirt
despite everything I wore thin with love, wore almost daily, loose-fitting

and cool to the skin while all around us men were dying, men we did
not know and read about in the paper, men like us, bodies full of a virus   10

no one at first understood was making copies of itself in their blood
perfect copies made from enzymes we now know, after thousands died

how to starve the virus of, years spent piecing together an erratic if ever
more exacting model of how it disperses through the body, its dark hold

on the imagination at last worn through but not wholly gone, the still
lethal viral load like the metaphors of plague lowered to levels

undetectable in the blood, the triangles of plasma-coloured silk entrusted
to a slowly apparent design, each one cut expressly like the other

then positioned in arcane patterns to catch the eye through variation
and distract it from their wavering abundance, the triangles unrecognizable   20

except by us to be from a shirt I once wore to know myself by, a single
man who otherwise might have put on a future time could not alter

its unchosen motifs the possibilities still underpinning my life: the virus
able to kill, as always — yet today we read some men forget, joining

their bodies without protection, unmindful the porous, spontaneous
membranes between them are still thinner than silk, the now exposed

patterns of contagion unchanged from the start, unlike the treatments
multiplying by trial and error, the dissemblings of the virus so many

scientists work hard to pin down, but they have yet to get everything
precisely right, always aware the triangles of whatever cloth, seam   30

by seam, must be picked apart with care, the design discovered to be
wanting, not good enough, though the bits thrown aside may point to

how else they might be joined, the coherence searched for perhaps
made up from what is not recognized in what already seems to

be known though a cure will never bring back the dead, it should unravel
the evidence they left us in the blood, painfully ripped-out threads read

by anyone who does not want to pass their message on, the quilt stitched
with quiet knowing hands toward something no less bold in design than

the shirt: silk the colour of plasma, of inspiration, its triangulation never
once undoing your gift — a contagious, heartfelt gesture that healed us both   40

(2001)

In the House of the Present

I rise through the house, your dog at my heels

curious ears pitching forward as we climb

landing window angled open, stairwell hazy

with the intense light of his barking as I enter

time's leaky vacuum, having not come to visit

in years, the hall dividing rooms not everyone

finds his way into, the way through coming

back to me, our parents still downstairs long

after we are meant to have fallen more deeply

10   asleep, dwindled voices ghosting me as I climb

our fathers staring into their ryes and water

while our mothers, so contrary, settle on how

best to set the table in the English manner few

pay heed to, silver against damask,[1] carving set

poised on crystal knife rests — how they come,

to sit next to each other on the Jasper Avenue

bus, what in the 50s makes them start talking

neither of us tries to guess at, our sisters at play

in the aisle, transfers made to points far beyond

20   the unexpectedness of our bodies, two sons

born two years apart, your mother bathing you

in the sink, skin pink against shining porcelain

---

1. **damask** Woven silk or linen fabric with a pattern on both sides.

until as you crawl up behind me I step back

eyes downcast and lifting, meeting as I glance

over my shoulder, small foot squashing smaller

fingers into the Kashmiri carpet's deep crush

as, pulling at threads, the sun bleeds through

the clouds — what clouds — there always seems

to be clouds as I look skyward, unfurled bolts

of cirrus shading my eyes as slowly they open   30

to what we wake to hours before anyone else

your father in the eternal early light making us

breakfast, bread trimmed of crusts set to brown

in residues of bacon grease, he says, to fatten

us up — to what other purpose does anyone cut

into such yolks, two runny cow's eyes running

across the countryside breakfast china I find

misidentified pieces of in second-hand shops

your mother's voice turning down the hallway

with me until I open the door, blocks scattering   40

across the plain of the floor, the blown apart

cities of the imagination no one ever moves

into, cities built on the unlit side of the moon

before you disappear ahead of me out the open

window with your camera, the case discarded

on the grass — there are still more images, still

more destroyed cities in your head to set loose

your mother, as she dies, anxious for me to set

them free with you, but older, imperceptibly

50   we live in atmospheres too heady for you or I

to detect while in the closet hangs the silver

space suit she one day makes you, the lucent

helmet you wear when I come around clouding

with your breath, though for now this sham orb

glows, clear and hollow on its briefly exposed

shelf, your dog clawing at the loose-woven rug

ragged by your bed, coiling into a sleep none

wakes him from until I am found in the kitchen

where our sisters dry the last of the remaining

60   day's dishes, clean faces caught in the plates

before they are packed into crates, vestigial

steam distorting the windows, and me wanting

to wipe it away, wanting the two of us framed

by the sill, framed and held by the willow

where you sometimes read with your father

among branches spreading low into twilight

under the sweep of sun-gilt leaves we play

unaware his book is closing, the most ragged

of catkins sifting down onto our heads, neither

70   of us ready yet to know what this house might

make room for and what it cannot, both of us

giving so little thought to our growing capacity

for inattentiveness or to our called-out names

(2003)

Elise Levine (1959–)

Elise Levine was born in Toronto in 1959. From an early age, she was drawn to innovative writing. She recalls being consumed with "green-about-the-gills jealousy" while reading a Virginia Woolf novel because she hadn't written it herself, and at 16 she memorized beat poet Allen Ginsberg's long poem *Howl*. Levine worked as a paper girl, waitress, security guard (with nasty dogs), textbook editor, and editor at a women's press. She also received a B.A. in English from the University of Toronto.

Often described as an experimental writer — one reviewer called her a "cagey dominatrix of literary form" — Levine employs the technique of fragmentation in constructing her narratives. Although her fiction is frequently lyrical and poetic, she uses extreme compression, ellipsis, and a tight focus on voice to disorient the reader and make a character's psychic drama more immediate and believable. As a result, she frequently achieves her goal of portraying "a person or situation dense with emotional cross-currents." Levine has said that the depiction of identity is one of her primary motivations in writing, particularly the "sometimes tragic, sometimes comic ways in which we attempt to invent ourselves over time." To this end, she has developed an acute sensitivity to the discrepancy between the way we conceive of ourselves and the way others view us. She remarks, "I think many if not most of us exist in a mutable zone that fluxes between self-knowledge and self-estrangement, a liminal or borderline area stocked with memory, desire both carnal and spiritual, and an aching awareness of loss. Ever-shifting and protean — prone to both pain and rapture, subject to terror and susceptible to beauty, each in our own singular, idiosyncratic ways — we are governed above all by an uneasy sense of our own mortality, our provisional status in the world."

Levine's interest in extreme dramatization has prompted her to compare her method of composition with a performance in a darkened theatre. "I flirt with notions of some strange operatic experience," she explains, "part Monteverdi, Messiaen, Ligeti, P.J. Harvey — equal parts aria and recitative, with performers well-versed in the uses of extended techniques. Ahistorical, forever playing away on a lost stage, in a pocket out of time. My job is to press my forehead against the stage door and peek through a peephole, and to try to describe, as faithfully as I can, what I see and hear."

Levine's short story collection, *Driving Men Mad*, appeared in 1995. It is notable for its use of vivid language and its experimentation with voice, plot, and form. In these tales that are, in the words of one reviewer, "peppered with people who live on the edge of town and the edge of poverty," Levine probes lives in disarray. Her subjects are self-estranged outcasts who are struggling to understand themselves and their own tangled histories, but they have no foundations on which to build that comprehension — the world they inhabit is situated in the blurring zone between rural and urban experience, and it resists their efforts to decode it. In 1998, another Levine story about the perplexing question of identity, "You Are You Because Your Little Dog Loves You," was included in the *Journey Prize Anthology*.

In the novel *Requests and Dedications* (2003), Levine introduces us to the members of an eccentric family whose bonds are gradually eroding: Walker, a hard-driving horse dealer; Mimi, Walker's lounge-singer girlfriend; Joy, his sister; and Tanis, Joy's 18-year-old daughter, who constantly clashes with her mother. The title of the novel refers to a call-in country music show that Tanis and Mimi listen to on the radio. Here, as in *Driving Men Mad*, the central characters are haunted by their pasts and their emotional obligations; they are afraid to break free of one another and the life they know, and so they spiral slowly into despair. Levine has commented on how the call-in show serves as an apt metaphor for their condition. In attempting to capture the "hauntedness" of her characters, to illuminate for the reader "the characters' psychic repetitions and fractures, the way their memories telescope and suspend their abilities to function in the present and envision a hopeful future," Levine uses music "as a kind of floating element" throughout the novel. The radio plays on, "with its babble of love and frustration, anger and hope," and as it does, "'Walker's dead mother speaks to him at night. Mimi's refuses to speak — which in itself is a terrible eloquence." Levine adds that she was searching for a "voice-appropriate language with an extended expressive range — at times dense and built-up, fiercely idiomatic and stubborn, at times simple in the extreme." By layering these elements of language, she hoped to "more accurately mirror the characters' terrible struggles to understand themselves and others, and to articulate their feelings."

Music has elastic possibilities for Levine, who admits that she is fascinated by "the way some contemporary composers talk about writing music as a way of sculpting time. By controlling texture (tone colour or timbre, volume, density, counterpoint), rhythm (tempo, duration, attack points, acceleration or deceleration, repetition), and pitch (melody — pitches in a given sequence, and harmony — pitches played simultaneously), composers structure the listener's experience of a certain interval of time." She points out the way writers of fiction exploit similar techniques, as she does in *Requests and Dedications,* to "shape the reader's experience."

Levine has won many awards for her writing, including a Canadian National Magazine Award. She currently lives in Chicago with her husband, a composer.

You Are You Because Your Little Dog Loves You

I'm going to come clean here. This is how it works.

First you're ordering drinks, nuts, thinking Merri or Melinda will be green as fish guts. Before the jet's off the ground you're in the rear bathroom with Jimmy or Steve, doing what you do best. Later, higher still, you find crushed velveteen — purple, blue, or black — in every seat. Also, cut-out stars, the moon. Sequins. Satisfaction. Girl, give your head a shake!

Then more drinks, hits to be dropped. The plane's a tin pot banging against a hot-sink sun. Dick or Mick or Steve — the glory-boy with the curling mane — says, The bitch. He announces this carefully, very British. You think you're so out of it you're not sure what he means. But what you really are is lying across the aisle, and someone lays a boot against your throat in a curious slow-time pulse as he forgets to apply pressure, then with a start remembers again.

From inside the plane the sky looks like nothing, upending blue blank as a baby's first dream. Tin-skin, that blue leaking in. Nothing to get through. Nothing to lose. Mystery. Sheen on your arm from the drooly boys. Somewhere someone's puking. And thirsty. Someone says, The stinking bitch.

Fifteen's already old, older than you are now at 36. When you're 15, and your dim mother's ditched you in Vancouver, and it's a West Coast winter raining everywhere all over you, what's the story going to be?

You were hatched from a bombshell of a woman who'd torn through her early life like it was a house on fire, until the doors to all the rooms in her head clapped shut against mayhem rising like a wail. By 30, she was easily exhausted. She had the fatty eyelids and slow lips, the rounded Barbra Streisand rear of the eternal émigré,[1] Montreal to Toronto to the land of milk and honey where she waited tables in the dining room of the Sylvia Hotel on Vancouver's English Bay, a place of only money and no-money, grey wandering rain.

You were seven when you washed up with her on that shore. She had named you Mimi, after *her* mother — an extravagant gesture from a woman for whom the past was a vanishing point, a scrap of an old language murmured in the ear to quiet a child, something odd, *Shpeelt, zit ah-zoy goot, ah fawks-trawt,* please play a fox-trot, a leftover from an erased world. What did she see when she looked your way? You were half her, half not — in a world where half was nothing, not one thing and not another.

You lived in an efficiency in the back of the Sylvia, facing a parking lot. During the day you'd drift along the seawall walk in front of the hotel, too-big red rubber boots like boats on your feet, an umbrella with pink and blue poodles floating above your head. Other children in brightly coloured raincoats and pants bobbed between sandy ribs of beach like balloons tethered to diligent mothers. The rain-scored horizon like steel wool.

At night, windows shut tight against raccoons prowling the ledges, red eyes blinking from between the vines that smother the Sylvia's façade. Lights out, the TV on, its blue buzzing your mother's wood-red hair until you think she might disappear in a cathode rush. Take that, Toronto! the weatherman says in winter. Fifty-seven here in Vancouver today. The rustling notes, each pinprick of sound, pushing pictures whole into your head. Take that! Your own giddy brain your mother's bright TV dream. Slow dissolve. Fade to black.

You see this mostly in black and white, the occasional swab of colour: a man on stilts. He unfolds like a flower from the side door of an old van parked next to the seawall in front of the hotel. With great bows and flourishes, his oversize Stetson[2] slipping back and forth across his small head, he mounts a six-foot-tall candy-striped bicycle.

Wind whips sand to tumbleweeds along the walk. The sky is barely spitting now, though still low and dark. It's three on a winter afternoon. In good weather, portrait painters mass like primulas[3] along the walk near Denman Street. But on this day any stragglers have packed it in by 3:15. At 3:17, the wind drops like a stone.

The man wheels past you then stops, carefully placing each stilt on the ground, leaving faint hoof prints behind him. He turns around and nods once, smiling, as if at some fabulous secret.

Beyond him you can see bluish-backed gulls rising and falling in the sky like breath. Beyond them, the blue-chested mountains. For once the rain has fully stopped. The night will be clear, the sunset yielding to a sky plush with stars, the lights of the ships at anchor even now beginning to pulse above the tarry water.

---

1. **émigré** Person who leaves one country to settle in another. 2. **Stetson** Hat with a broad brim and high crown; cowboy hat. 3. **primulas** Spring flowers.

He cocks his head, as if listening to the tankers waiting in the bay. A murmuring wind. Impossible high notes, low notes. Laughter and applause. The clink of loose change tuning up like an orchestra. At this moment everything seems possible.

He turns his head towards you again. That same slow smile, his mouth such a miracle of makeup you think each syllable he utters stitches the newly arisen half-moon to the night, as if it had been a prop waiting backstage. His teeth like polished seashells. Through a tear in the left leg of his pink pin-striped pants you can see wood, metal, something long and cold, hard.

In the months that followed, your mother managed to unglue herself from her TV, unwrapping herself like some fresh thing from skeins[4] of fatigue long enough for Mr. Long Legs to woo her. As if some dimly remembered past echoed in her ear. *Please play a fox-trot.*

Stiltless, without his costumes (which he made himself), your mother's beau was tiny, delicate. Also, breathtakingly penniless, buying roses with money he stole from your mother's purse while she showered. He had the heartbreak allure of the cheerfully insolvent,[5] the seductiveness of their fugitive ease.

Mimi, my lovely girl, he'd say, slipping a slender finger and thumb into your mother's wallet, Is the coast clear?

Let the show begin! He moved out of his van and into the Sylvia with you and your mother. He brought with him a scrappy white terrier with caramel patches on its face and behind. He quelled your mother's resistance with a radiant upsweep of canary yellow, crepe-clad arms. What's a family without a dog? he asked, standing in the doorway. The dog — called Alfie, after the Michael Caine movie — incautiously sniffed every piece of furniture in the cramped apartment as your mother peered after it, saying nothing. She looked both hopeful and afraid. The alchemy of her lover's dreams could work wonders.

The dog ran loose on the beach every day while Mr. Long Legs worked the seawall walk bestride his bicycle, floridly addressing the mothers of small children he'd take for rides at a dollar a pop. When a bus burst the dog at the seams one milky white morning, delicate entrails festooned Davie Street like streamers.

That afternoon, Mr. Long Legs pulled you onto his lap, drummed his thumbs on your knees. He smelled of the Old Spice your mother had given him. He touched a finger to the tip of your nose.

Hey! he said, as if he'd just had an idea. Alfie still loves you.

You sat very still as a breeze nudged the edges of the heavy beige curtains. Water streamed through the ivy around the window. He seemed to know something you didn't. After a moment you said, Alfie's dead.

Mr. Long Legs pulled his head away, raised his eyebrows, and opened his pinprick brown eyes as wide as they would go. He held his hands palm up and lifted his narrow shoulders.

Dead? he said, deeply shocked. You think so? I think Alfie's in heaven, barking and peeing, trying to sniff the ladies.

He closed his eyes. His lips relaxed, drooping at the edges. He looked tired and sad.

Just think, he said. Heaven.

---

4. **skeins** Loose coils of thread. 5. **insolvent** Unable to pay one's debt.

For your mother, each time Mr. Long Legs left it was forever. He'd be gone for weeks at a time. He always came back broke.

Your mother would unfasten herself from her TV long enough for tears, wall pounding. Once he stood by helplessly as she ripped up his pink pin-striped pants. When she finished he held the shreds to his face and wept, stopping every now and then to glance sorrowfully at the craters in the wall plaster. Suddenly he brightened. He lay the rags on the kitchen table. He took out a polka-dot hankie and wiped his eyes, blew his nose. He put his hankie away. He puffed out his slender chest and the creases fell away one by one from his just-past-its-prime brow.

You could almost hear the fresh cha-ching as he grazed tenderly at the pink strips on the table. Money, money, money. He'd milk this one for sure.

His eyes were shining. So what do you think it's worth? he said.

When forever came for good you were 12. Three years later your mother had scraped up enough to return alone to Ontario, tail tucked between her skinny varicosed legs.

She didn't have enough for the taxi to the airport, an extravagance you paid for with your earnings from your after-school and weekend job at Record City. You made less than minimum wage, but you saw the position as entry-level. You hoped to get an office job at a record company when you turned 16.

As you stood on the sidewalk outside the Sylvia, your mother rolled down the window of the taxi. Her face looked puffy, her drawn-on eyebrows faintly askew. Rain grizzled the beach across the street. Much of the bay itself had vanished from sight.

Did you hate her then?

She was your mother. She rolled up the taxi window, which immediately covered with steam.

You, age 15: ready for the bright hereafter. Left to your own devices you made yourself over as if you were the high alembic of every sulky *Creem* queen, each Bebe and Miss Pamela and Patti. Kohl-eyed, lips frosted high-glam white. If you weren't one thing, then you could be another.

Magic. All the way down the coast you learned the hit and bang came first and last. In between you learned about girlish boys, their rainbow perfection. Working your way up. Competing with Fawns, Dawns, and Merri Madrigals for the well-bred L.A. record exec who before the age of 13 thought there was no such thing as a poor Jew. The lowly drummer with his high hats and jelly rolls. A long-tongued slender-hipped lead guitarist. A Jimmy, Mick, or Keith. *Both* Keiths. Wheeling above you, huge as constellations.

Colour this red for passion.

The biggest prize? To be queen for a night on the private jet, the high priestess of higher love, for which you'd leave Lady Jane and Prudence below, weeping in the wings.

This was what you craved, in order to have something over other people: the *up there*, honey and smoke. The ample horizon a streak of blue beyond money and reason, glimpsed from between a guy's skinny legs, his velvet-clad butt and stick-figure bulge. Dry ice machines lisping eternity. Everything you can't quite remember — magic, mystery, an electric-blue boot bruising your throat while all the boys love you — a feckless drug of choice.

You never knew nice.

Hello? Earth to? You were 25, overripe. You couldn't decide whether Toronto's spill of light from above Pearson International was the circuit board for some third-rate sound and lighting show hard-wired to your limbic system[6] or merely a sorry child's spill of beads. You were broke, electric with it because the truth is, poverty can elevate: that snap and crackle of fear can take you right out of your mind.

You called your mother from the airport. She hung up on you. When you walked into her apartment in Whitby she slapped your face, then she cried hard.

Eye concealer shone beneath her eyes like half moons. Her once-beautiful hair stuck out uncertainly from her head, a dry sprig of curl here, a greasy tendril there. Her nose was dripping ferociously. She held her arms out to you then quickly dropped them.

It's me, Mimi, you said, not sure she recognized you. You'd always had this shyness with each other. That same shyness you'd come to recognize between people who've slept together long enough to find themselves in that remote place where the touching stops — each of you bedding down with the other's fantasy, someone else's breasts sliding in ones or twos across your body as clouds might drift across the sky — and where all you are is part and parcel of these loveless moments, grasping the metal bed frame to keep from falling, swaying to beat hell, bleating *mumma* like a lamb, wounded bear.

Baby, you'd say to whoever you were with. Or some other girlfriend would. These guys always had someone.

What you have is this: the sins of the mothers, for you are of a generation that never forgives. Whose pain exceeds? Outlives? In a world where half is nothing, love only endures.

Place is a thing to be moved through, like so much backdrop. At 25, your choice was classic Canadian: Toronto or the boonies in a southern Ontario of subdivisions, a culture of commuters and megamusicals, the province itself one vast bedroom community endlessly unfolding like a house of cards gone amok. To the near north and east of Toronto, a scattering of century-old farms and red-brick houses among the townhouse developments and outlandish executive homes, the new and the old mixing it up. In Whitby, your mother continued her disappearing act syllable by syllable until she couldn't care for herself any more. You moved her out of the tiny apartment and into the local psychiatric hospital. By then you had a job in a Stouffville beauty shop. You bought an ancient white Monte Carlo. One night in an Oshawa bar you clambered on stage to screech along with the house band in front of a mostly auto-worker audience too toasted to notice you couldn't actually sing. With them you could play the loud exotic, queen of the cross-eyed Jacks and horned shills,[7] having slept with the stars, the magicians and kings you once collected like cards. Your veiled past hinting at marvellous futures.

What a joke. Standing up there on that puny Oshawa stage fear would snake around your throat, shredding your voice to rat-shit. It was perfect: you were giving up nothing, all your nothing years, because nothing could be everything in this nowhere place. You imagined the dull grey sounds like ghostly lullabies your mother never sang.

You met your best friend Joy in that bar, on a rainy Tuesday night. The place was half deserted, and between sets she bought you drink after drink.

Mimi, she said, around the seventh Jack and coke. That's a name.

---

6. **limbic system** The part of the brain associated with emotions, motivation, and emotional associations with memory.
7. **shills** Con men.

She punched your arm and snorted through her stubby nose, as if she'd said something hilarious. She was short and thick, roughly made up, foundation caking in her laugh lines. At 30 she wasn't hard to impress since she'd never been anywhere in her life.

Just before the bartender cut you both off, Joy gave you her phone number — her brother's really, since at the time she lived in an apartment in back of his farmhouse where he ran a small boarding stable. He was previously married, had a daughter. He had a couple of thoroughbreds. His name was Walker.

Now you were laughing. Walker — a ridiculous name, as if he were a southern gentleman. You had to hand it to this old-Markham world clinging stubbornly — despite no money and no reason, despite wholesale land expropriations for the never-to-be-built Pickering airport — to its dream of itself, a dream fuelled by a hatred and fear of the immigrant city, the greedy city.

Within a week you drove your Monte Carlo out to visit. You quickly understood how Walker's unstinting bulk and that of his horses could be beneath you. And how Walker could both hate and love you for your boys, for how you'd loved them all, for he was heedless of awe, a stickler for details, each one a stitch of blood on white rayon panties, the red in his head that made him so angry. It was how you got to him — that you knew some of the things people do. Heigh-ho, Silver! Wild girls and horses! A masked avenger, riding to your own rescue, having found a way to still be tall in the saddle. And all that.

Eleven years later you still pretend to do it well, needing at least this much to believe in: that you can still be above it all. That you can still know yourself in this way. Yesterday, Walker pulled the sliding door to the arena open and stepped inside to watch you ride. The horse shied from him, danced beneath you every couple of strides to the top of the ring. Your legs jerked like a puppet's.

Keep your hands down, he shouted. As if you'd never heard that before. Keep your legs still.

He stooped as you neared the bottom of the arena. As you passed him he uncoiled, tossing oiled dirt that flummoxed[8] your head. That horse's neck like a giraffe's hit your nose. A second later the ground pummelled your chest.

Wasn't the first time you were winded, sucking nothing but queer sounds so unlike singing you feared someone else had entered you. Something else outside going, Shoosh, aroo, shoosh.

Then there was Walker standing over you, looking. He leaned closer. Laughed.

Fucked up again, he said. It was how he loved you.

Later he stood in his kitchen and said, The years haven't been good to you.

What's good? was all you could reply. Your mouth felt reamed with mud.

You, 36 years old, walking slowly across the floor, the tick of the kitchen clock like a warning shout. Dishes drying in the blue rack, bills in a careful stack on the table. You shut the screen door quietly behind you, stepping into sunlight thick as ice-glare.

Good for Walker. Good — that you tried hard for him? A trick for which you've lately lost the knack.

Walker's daughter, Jena, was in the barn when you walked in. She was lounging on the steps to the tack room, twisting a slick strand of dirty blond hair around a finger, using

---

8. **flummoxed** Bewildered.

her breath to puff up her bangs from her creamy, slightly moist face. Sweet 16. She tugged at a 10-carat gold chain around her neck and rocked absently back and forth. Her stomach formed rolls beneath her tight T-shirt. You could understand how her mother felt about her.

You nudged one step past the girl and sat down. She tugged harder at the gold chain and stiffened. She half turned her body and twisted her head to look at you. Nothing showed in her small eyes, as usual when she looked your way. You thought how unknown this girl was to you, how opposite you she was. After all, she had Walker's love. You knew one day she would leave, taking it with her.

Get lost! you wanted to say. That's the trick most worth mastering, to become a place the heart can safely grow fonder — an after-image, a faint blush of a thing, some vaguely remembered history of secret feints and thrusts. Even your drably desirous mother roamed each night down Whitby's bleary psychiatric home hallway, an orderly in hot pursuit. Your mother's fuzzy green bathrobe gaping, her skinny breasts wriggling like worms.

In the box stall across from you a horse gently weaved. Barn kittens mock-hunted field mice in and out of the standing stalls at the other end of the barn. By the door, black ants reeled like drunks over the husk of a June bug. The mother cat sat in the dust and groomed her paws. The lardy girl beside you was barely breathing. Maybe she was already gone. You realized with a start that underneath that pale-pink T she was as familiar to you as some pallid straw-stuffed animal you'd misplaced long enough to have forgotten. Love's puling[9] malcontent, soaked in neglect, encrusted with discontent, like an old mattress put out by the side of the road. She could almost be your daughter. For a moment you were as confused as the stammerings and velvety whoofs of the neighbouring horses.

You shifted slightly and placed a finger on her wrist, tapped lightly. She shivered a little, afraid or embarrassed. Maybe hopeful. You thought if you touched her harder she might cry, laugh, confide, opening up to you like a fat piñata whose hidden treasures you'd only squander.

You shoved to your feet, stepping past her into the aisle. You clapped your hands to startle the horse out of his tranced weaving. When he stopped you stroked his nose. Without turning you said, Still here?

She was standing close behind you. You could feel her breath coming hard on your neck. Her face, when you veered your head sharp right to look at her, was splotchy, red and white like a checkered flag. The split ends of her hair seemed to rise and twine, vaporize almost, in the mote-veiled light. When she spoke her voice was thick, a sneer or a choke.

Still here? she mimicked. Like fucking duh. Are *you*?

This morning Walker woke you early. A bird called outside the window. The bed sheets cooled against your feet. He ran his cracked hands over your stomach, up and down your arms. You turned over, rump up. When you woke again the bird was gobbling on the window ledge. Walker was sitting on the edge of the bed, half-dressed. He'd been up already. His head hung low, almost touching his knees. The bed rattled as he coughed. Christ, he was saying. He pressed the heel of his hand to his forehead.

---

9. **puling** Whimpering.

You'd heard the Trans Am pull up in the drive around two in the morning. You'd heard Jena close the door to her room, and something heavy bumping down the stairs with her. You hoped she was gone for good.

Walker's cough worsened. His shoulders heaved. You unwrapped yourself from the bedsheet and sat up. At least you could have this satisfaction: now Walker himself knew what it was like to have someone slip him like sunlight in November.

The bird outside the window had stopped singing or had flown away. You put a hand to Walker's grey wavy hair. Well?

Well what? he said. Happy now?

You had to stop yourself from grabbing a chunk of hair and yanking.

Fuck me to tears, Walker said, dropping his head into his hands, rubbing his face. Get the fuck out.

When you got up you smoked and peed. Smoked. Otherwise your hands were empty.

You got dressed. Went outside, got in your car. Drove around for hours. Past the Stouffville flea market, out to Musselman's Lake. Up and down the concession roads, past red-brick farmhouses with crumpled barns. The radio on though not loud. Barely listening. Trying to figure what you could still get away with. Trying to tell yourself you could still enjoy the show.

Only hours ago you parked your ancient Monte Carlo in Walker's drive. You knocked softly on his kitchen door. When he came you turned your head away. His small bay mare stood quietly under the big maple in the front paddock, half asleep, though her tail swished unceasingly.

When you glanced again through the screen, Walker was looking at you through half-shut eyes, his naked belly massively overhanging his jeans. You could hear him suck his cigarette and move it from one side of his mouth to the other.

Give it up already! You slammed the door to the Monte Carlo. Through the open window you yelled, Still a treat, aren't you, Walker. He moved a little behind the screen, like the shadow of a boulder. He'd always been like that for you, a rocky overhang beneath which you slipped along the stony scree[10] of your failures and his: that he was the wrong one for you, the right one. The right one.

You turned the engine on and drove past, heading towards the first barn. You heard him behind you now on the drive, shouting, Don't tell me your troubles. Your tongue rasped in your mouth. You opened your hands, flexed them like a cat might its paws. You turned the car off and leaned your head against the steering wheel, Walker's ducks and geese barking like dogs, a dog barking. Crow. Wind in the trees. You'd never heard such stillness, falling in lush sweeps like a first heavy snowfall, the air softly smacking your skin. The afternoon shadows a cold locket of memory in which a man on stilts groans backward like an old machine, into the terrible distance before floating upward to fade above the stars and waiting ships of English Bay.

You are still poor as the day. The crisp 10s and 20s, the crackling Gs of Ontario fall from you like dead leaves. No one in this dying province has the heart to sweep them away. This was the dominion you thought you'd never bargained for, where the future closes over you like a curtain of snow.

---

10. **scree** Steep face of loose rock debris.

Then Walker, his shadow another blindness brindling[11] the drive shimmery with heat.

Get real, he shouted. Don't you know when to quit? You take that fucker on the road I guarantee he'll come back without you. Leave you in the dirt.

He turned back towards the house. He jerked both arms out at his sides, waved them above his fat head. The big bastard was still yammering.

So go on, he brayed. But I told you. End of story.

Walker's wrong. Out on the road there's sky spanked by cloud. The stillness of the late afternoon. The playful buck the horse gave when the two-ton passed hauling a flat-bed trailer. After, the horse hanging loose, empty as a balloon beneath you. Your hands — which you remember to keep down — are light on his mouth. Between your legs he's jittery with flies and nothing else, not even the hot afternoon shivery with breeze. No end in sight to this bright blister of day.

Maybe the dead don't want you to rescue them. Maybe the dead just want to sleep, in their rattling dresses and shard suits, chattering with cold under the noonday sun. Scant-witted in their bugbear[12] stupor, they're wedged deep in the earth you have always loathed. Maybe they think you've got it all wrong.

Your mother is there and late this afternoon you'll grab her arm and yank hard. You idiot, you'll yell, How could you be so stupid? — because for your mother love was a fat ruinous thing, pancake makeup, dimpled cooing in late afternoon, nothing you think that should matter to her any more.

Mom, you'll screech, How could you? So much for nothing!

Drop the lathered reins. The horse cascades his neck to drink from the nearly dried-up creek. On the low bank above, wands of dry grass candle the ground. The horse chuffs, smoke-eater, big beast between your legs to shake a bouldered shoulder at so small a fly.

Don't move. Never let go. Keep your hands low, as Walker always says you should.

City traffic from nearby Steeles Avenue chimes coolly but here it's August hot. The tall trees creak. In the neighbouring fields a great demon baling machine parts the blond grasses and dust vapours the road. You've stopped to linger in the cemetery and at this moment you're sitting pretty while your mother leaks secrets into the earth. From the ninth concession line traffic makes a slow cortège[13] into a city of dust where at night sirens unravel sound from the faded stars as bats scratch the dark air. If this were late fall your breath would hang in front of you, heavy white sheets wet from so much drinking. You'd think the boys you love have left you.

Your mother was a rough woman, given to fits and starts. Yanking you along an icy Toronto sidewalk when you were five, gripping your arm so tight it hurt. Riding a two-wheeler for the first time when you were six, you reached out to steady yourself, dizzy from the sudden spectacle of hard ground. First thing you grabbed was her arm. She bruised easily. It was always like this: neither of you knew what to do once you'd grabbed hold.

---

11. brindling Making a tawny grey with darker spots. **12. bugbear** Source of unfounded fear. **13. cortège** Procession.

A dry breeze twitches the uncut grass. A sudden alertness in the world. Thrash chords, you think. A whisper-bright tremolo.[14] Anything. You can almost hear the dead sigh damply beneath you and sink lower into the earth.

For now you're saying nothing. Your mother's saying nothing back.

Maybe the dead don't want to be saved, the memory of them stashed away like so much coin, booty for the half-living. Maybe the dead hold on to their hats whichever way the wind blows, to keep their hands from waving goodbye. Or hello.

(1998)

George Elliott Clarke (1960–)

George Elliott Clarke was born in the Black Loyalist settlement of Windsor Plains, Nova Scotia, in 1960 and grew up in Halifax. His family line can be traced back seven generations to a group of slaves from the American South who were freed by the British during the War of 1812 and brought to Nova Scotia. In 1984, Clarke received a B.A. in honours English from the University of Waterloo in Waterloo, Ontario. Returning home to Nova Scotia, he earned an M.A. from Dalhousie University; he then attended Queen's University in Kingston, Ontario, obtaining a Ph.D. in English in 1993. Throughout this period, he supported himself as a social worker, a parliamentary aide, a legislative researcher, and a newspaper editor.

As a teenager, Clarke discovered that he loved to write. He explains that "the impulse that made me take up poetry ... was a need to discover *Beauty* for — and within — myself and my community." He rejected the designation "Black Nova Scotian" for this community and created a new one: Africadian. As an Africadian, he "wanted to war against all the propaganda asserting that African people ... were backwards, criminal, illiterate, and expendable." Clarke has long believed that there is an urgent need for Africadians to write themselves into the history of Maritime Canada, and, well aware that Africadians are but a small minority within the collective of Black Canadians, he asserts that they must write themselves with equal determination into African Canadian history. In undertaking this mission to project a local voice to a universal level, Clarke has found inspiration in the work of poets like William Butler Yeats and Derek Walcott, who, Clarke observes, share "an insistence on speaking to the whole world from their location."

Saltwater Spirituals and Deeper Blues (1983) was Clarke's first attempt to record the particular beauties and injustices of the Africadian experience. With its long, psalmic, alliterative lines, it is distinct from Clarke's other works, but, he admits, "even though it was a reflection of, and a reaction to, my Nova Scotian history ... [t]he material hadn't yet been transmuted into my own voice." The poems were cerebral and abstract, and they did not channel the vibrant oral culture of the people they described. Reading from *Saltwater Spirituals* to a large audience at the Black Cultural Centre of Nova Scotia in 1986, Clarke was heckled. Afterwards, he resolved to "never write again" what he could not "read before [his] own community."

At university Clarke had absorbed the epic forms and relished the infernal heroes of Dante, Milton, and Blake. He had experimented with blank verse and the five-foot iambic line, which he claims English-speaking poets "are stuck with ... no matter who we are." With *Whylah Falls* (1990), his account of the 1985 murder of Black Nova Scotian Graham Jarvis (here renamed Othello Clemence), Clarke "blackens" the European epic, breaking its conventions to better suit his subject matter. He couches his dramatic long poem in the rhythms of Africadian speech and catalogues his community — its catchphrases, recipes, favourite flowers. However, he appropriates Renaissance forms — the pastoral elegy and the idyll — to describe the wooing of Shelley Clemence.

---

14. tremolo Vibrating acoustic effect.

Anything but abstract, *Whylah Falls* is performative, energetic, and allusive, darting between genres and dialects, alluding to canonical English texts one minute and presenting forgotten photographs the next. Like many of Clarke's other works, it not only confronts race-related violence head-on but also joyously depicts the Africadian people, celebrating their ability to balance "bitter pain" with "beauty," creativity, and music. Since its publication, *Whylah Falls* has been adapted for the stage (set to music by Joe Sealy and performed in 1997) and made into a TV movie (*One Heart Broken into Song*). The volume also won the 1991 Archibald Lampman Prize for Poetry.

In 1999, Clarke produced *Beatrice Chancy: A Passional,* a recasting of Percy Bysshe Shelley's five-act verse play *The Cenci.* In Clarke's hands, the story of Beatrice, daughter of a cruel 16th-century Italian nobleman, becomes an Acadian slave narrative. The project began as a libretto for an opera by James Rolfe — Clarke says that he conceived it as "an opera of pain" — but it rapidly transformed itself into a dramatic poem. Unapologetically brutal, opera and poem are intended, Clarke says, to "jet blood and saliva" in the faces of "amnesiacs" who would deny or pastoralize the history of slavery in Nova Scotia. In fashioning the piece, Clarke was bolstered by the influence of people he calls "mighty, militant poets," including John Milton, the Marquis de Sade, and Irving Layton. He envisions the work, which is composed in 10-syllable lines and secret sonnets, and unlined couplets, as "quarrel[ling] with language" and trying to "hurt blank verse into black drama."

The Governor General's Award–winning *Execution Poems: The Black Acadian Tragedy of "George and Rue"* (2001) is the first of several creative investigations Clarke has conducted into the deaths of George and Rufus Hamilton. The two men, Clarke's cousins, were hanged for the murder of a Fredericton cab driver 11 years before Clarke was born. *Execution Poems,* while a devastating historical portrait of poverty, violence, rage, and racism, is also an exploration of the ways in which Africadian experience intersects with and diverges from English literary traditions. In the poem "Reading *Titus Andronicus* in Three Mile Plains, N.S.," for example, Clarke's Rue recalls that he "opened Shakespeare / And discovered a scarepriest" in the character of Aaron the Moor — Aaron demands: "'Is black so base a hue?'" The lines of the *Execution Poems* are enriched with internal rhymes, half-rhymes, assonance, and alliteration; and Clarke moves seamlessly between idiomatic speech and Renaissance English in search of what he calls "a Black Nova Scotian accent."

In 2001, Clarke also published *Blue,* a collection of sensual and angry lyrics, which, he hoped, would "pour out like pentecostal fire — pell mell, scorching, bright, loud: a poetics of arson." Clarke had spent several years teaching at Duke University in North Carolina, and he admits that *Blue,* and its partner volume, *Black* (2006), were written out of rage, because "The Great Republic's fiery liberty set [him] blazing" and "charred [his] brain." In 2005, Clarke produced his first novel, *George and Rue,* a more detailed and reflective look at the death of his cousins, and *Illuminated Verses,* a playful and celebratory sequence of poems with photographs by Ricardo Scipio. Though Clarke has said that he includes photographs in his books because he wants "the faces and bodies and history of Black people in Canada to be represented visually in the text," Scipio's portraits of nude black women made it difficult for him to find a publisher — Clarke speculates that "the idea of the unclothed black *feminine* seems too brazen, or just too *dark* a concept for a society addicted to depictions of elect whiteness."

Other works include *Lush Dreams, Blue Exile: Fugitive Poems 1978–1993,* a poetry collection about landscape, ancestry, and Africadian politics; and *Québécité: A Jazz Fantasia in Three Cantos* (2003), a poetic rendering of a libretto Clarke wrote for the Guelph Jazz Festival. Set to music by D.D. Jackson, *Québécité* explores the difficulties and possibilities of interracial romance in contemporary Quebec.

Clarke won the Dr. Martin Luther King Jr. Achievement Award in 2004 and a Fellowship from the Pierre Elliott Trudeau Foundation in 2005. He is currently the E.J. Pratt Professor of Canadian Literature at the University of Toronto.

The River Pilgrim: A Letter[1]

At eighteen, I thought the Sixhiboux wept.
Five years younger, you were lush, beautiful
Mystery; your limbs — scrolls of deep water.
Before your home, lost in roses, I swooned,
Drunken in the village of Whylah Falls,
And brought you apple blossoms you refused,
Wanting Hank Snow woodsmoke blues and dried smelts,
Wanting some milljerk's dumb, unlettered love.
    That May, freights chimed xylophone tracks that rang
To Montréal. I scribbled postcard odes,   10
Painted *le fleuve Saint-Laurent comme la Seine*[2] —
Sad watercolours for Negro exiles
In France, and dreamt Paris white with lepers,
Soft cripples who finger pawns under elms,
Drink blurry into young debauchery,
Their glasses clear with Cointreau, rain, and tears.
    You hung the moon backwards, crooned crooked poems
That no voice could straighten, not even O
Who stroked guitars because he was going
To die with a bullet through his stomach.   20
Innocent, you curled among notes — petals
That scaled glissando[3] from windows agape,
And remained in southwest Nova Scotia,
While I drifted, sad and tired, in the east.
    I have been gone four springs. This April, pale
Apple blossoms blizzard. The garden flutes
E-flats of lilacs, G-sharps of lilies.
Too many years, too many years, are past ...
    Past the marble and pale flowers of Paris,
Past the broken, Cubist[4] guitars of Arles,[5]   30
Shelley, I am coming down through the narrows
Of the Sixhiboux River. I will write
Beforehand. Please, please come out to meet me
    As far as Beulah Beach.

(1990)

---

1. The River Pilgrim: A Letter Cf. Ezra Pound, "The River-Merchant's Wife: A Letter." **2. *le fleuve ... la Seine*** "The St. Lawrence River, like the Seine" (a French river). **3. glissando** Effect of a piano player sliding their finger up the keyboard, producing an upward slide in tone. **4. Cubist** The 20th-century art movement that focused on the geometry and planes of shapes. **5. Arles** Village in southern France where Vincent Van Gogh produced many paintings.

Four Guitars

Pushkin, Othello, and Pablo gather in the livingroom coral reef, under a sea of sunshine, to perform improv music (no note knowing where the next is going to or coming from). They lean over their guitars like accountants studying thick ledgers.

Casting half-notes, thirds, and quarter-notes that stretch music like putty, Pushkin opens the concert. He bends the long metre of Baptist hymns into infernal hollers that true Baptists are sure the wicked Anglicans and Catholics enjoy behind the dark doors of their temples. From "If All the World Were Apple Pie," a nursery rhyme, he dredges sedimentary notes laden with a sorrow as rich as that felt by Schliemann[1] who discovered Troy because he was looking for love and the lost city got in his way.

Desperate for his own private sound, Pushkin once crafted a banjo from a frying pan and four pieces of string. Favouring *E* or *A* notes, plucking them — luscious fruit, heavy with memory and tears — from his American Martin guitar, he stands before us now, revelling in an *abb* rhyme scheme, the cadence of decadence:

> April rain snows white and cold,
> I feel so goddamn scared.
> You could've loved me if you'd dared.
> Were you waitin' to get old?
> Why did you act so weird?
> You loved me like you never cared!

Next, he plumbs the depths of bottomless love, "Don't do me evil / If you want the sun to shine," holding a breadknife against the throat of the guitar, forcing forth bastard slurs and mongrel fluctuations, a lover's midnight moans. He slides his stopping finger on the string, contrasting long notes with quick arpeggios, then backs into "Black Liquor" with fierce fluidity. Forgetting that his hands are warped, he plays, plagued by the currency of the radio cantos of Ezra "Epopee" Pound:[2] *I love my baby, love her to the bone*. Like Don Messer and his Famous Islanders,[3] Pushkin cannibalizes cacophony. When he attains zen-silence, hullabaloo collapses the room. He empties a bottle — a backward song — down his throat, smiles like sudden, brilliant snow.

Lean Othello follows the sweating giant, steps into the wake of his lilt and the still fluttering applause. He snatches his Dobro-chrome, steel-bodied guitar, tunes it Sebastopol style, dreaming that that's where William Hall won the Victoria Cross[4] more than a hundred years ago. O chooses "Hurry Down, Sunshine," then discards it because the room is bright enough. He selects, to a chorus of whoops and thigh slaps, "Black Water Blues." He lays the guitar gently across his hips, presses the supine[5] strings with a tall, brown bottle, and plays, thus sending quirky notes, tottering like drunken flowers, into the air. In the corner, Pushkin gasps, "Ooh!" O's artistry is that fine. His elegant left-hand figures, instrumental algebra, merge with his rough, dark voice:

---

1. **Schliemann** Heinrich Schliemann (1822–1890), German explorer and excavator. 2. **Ezra "Epopee" Pound** American modernist Ezra Pound (1885–1972). His cantos were a long poem cycle; cantos XC–XCV are love poems. 3. **Don Messer and his Famous Islanders** Messer hosted a CBC variety show in the 1960s; the Islanders was the name of his band. 4. **William Hall, Victoria Cross** Hall was the first Nova Scotian and first Black person to win the Victoria Cross, Britain's highest honour for courage in the face of the enemy. 5. **supine** Inactive, facing upwards.

I bought ya red, red, calico:[6]
mmmmmmm, ya didn't love me though.

Moon burnt the blue sky orange;
not ripe, plucked stars tasted green.
In its hard bed, the river tossed, black.

God made everyone with a need to love;
wonder who ya be thinkin' of?

His waterfall-hands cascade across the strings, leave, behind the glistening notes, a dark, inarticulate silence.

Unable to restrain himself, Pablo tunes his flamenco guitar Spanish style, nudging O into a Latinate version of "I bes troubled." Pablo contributes his exotic expertise, his Moorish[7] sense to that spiritual salvaged from two centuries of bad luck. His music tastes of three little feelings: saltiness, bitterness, and sweetness. Reminiscing in tempo, Othello pursues Pablo's anxious influence. Stressing static sadness by inverting the scale of flattened third and seventh degrees, they distort prettily Robert Johnson's classic blues, "Hell Hound."

Suddenly, Pablo discovers music drowned in a seashell and raises it, sounding as polished and suave as the clear, hairless limbs of the Chinese, Spanish, and Jamaican women he loves, women with indignant breasts, shell-smooth skin, and opulent[8] thighs. While he plays, the Sixhiboux River shimmies silver through the hills, lindys[9] beneath the bridge, and jitters into Saint Mary's Bay. He uncaps a bottle of Keith's India Pale Ale, *brewed the same way for a hundred years*, and nods in the direction of *Nisan:*

Thirty days of daffodils,
Lilies, and chrysanthemums,
Open with snowy petals
And close with apple blossoms.

O follows, remembering the lost music of sub-Saharan Africa and trying to perfect the blues.

When this chance duet fades, leaving clear notes hanging, untended, in the air, Missy barges in, panting, yammers, "Quit the gentle mercies and the delicate fears! God expects truth, not entertainment!" She unfolds a dark mandolin, rich, smelling of drenched forests, then jumbles the room into shape around her, juggling it so it becomes circular, curling around her curves. "Who's got a cigar box and string? A diddley bow?" Silence. Then, Pushkin, his breath renewed, manifests a ten-hole, twenty-reed, Marine Band harmonica, commences to mock a train, a historic freight, stuffed with Southern sunflowers, Mississippi magnolias. Missy adopts Poor Girl tuning, mumbles her debt to Bessie Smith[10] and Amy "Big Mama" Lowell, booms, "I've got Ford engine movements in my hips."

---

6. **calico** Bright patterned cloth. 7. **Moorish** The Moors were Muslim North Africans who inhabited Spain, especially before the 17th century. 8. **opulent** Abundant. 9. **lindys** Does a jitterbug dance. 10. **Bessie Smith** Prolific American blues singer (1892–1937).

I look outside. The sun has turned inside out. Moonlight lacquers the world. Black
bliss. Missy trolls an immortal song:

> Come and love me, darling one,
> In sweetest April rain.
> Kiss me until life is done:
> Youth will not come again.

(1990)

Reading *Titus Andronicus*[1] in Three Mile Plains, N.S.

Rue: When Witnesses sat before Bibles open like plates
And spat sour sermons of interposition[2] and nullification,
While burr-orchards vomited bushels of thorns, and leaves
Rattled like uprooted skull-teeth across rough highways,
And stars ejected brutal, serrated,[3] heart-shredding light,
And dark brothers lied down, quiet, in government graves,
Their white skulls jabbering amid farmer's dead flowers —
The junked geraniums and broken truths of car engines,
And *History* snapped its whip and bankrupted scholars,
10   School was violent improvement. I opened Shakespeare
And discovered a scarepriest, shaking in violent winds,
Some hallowed, heartless man, his brain boiling blood,
Aaron,[4] seething, demanding, "Is black so base a hue?"
And shouting, "Coal-black refutes and foils any other hue
In that it scorns to bear another hue." O! Listen at that!
I listen, flummoxed,[5] for language cometh volatile,
Each line burning, and unslaked[6] *Vengeance* reddens rivers.
I see that, notwithstanding hosts of buds, the sultry cumuli
Of petals, greatening like the pluvial[7] light in Turner's[8] great
20   Paintings, the wind hovers — like a death sentence — over
Fields, chilling us with mortality recalcitrant.[9] (Hear now
The worm-sighing waves.) *Sit fas aut nefas*,[10] I am become
Aaron, desiring poisoned lilies and burning, staggered air,
A King James God, spitting fire, brimstone, leprosy, cancers,
Dreaming of tearing down stars and letting grass incinerate
Pale citizens' prized bones. What should they mean to me?
A plough rots, returns to ore; weeds snatch it back to earth;

---

1. *Titus Andronicus* Gory Shakespearean play about a war of revenge between Roman general Titus and Tamora, a Gothic
queen. 2. **interposition** Coming between parts. 3. **serrated** Notched, like a saw edge. 4. **Aaron** Moorish lover of Tamora
who greatly facilitates the bloodshed. 5. **flummoxed** Bewildered. 6. **unslaked** Unsatisfied. 7. **pluvial** Rainy.
8. **Turner's** Joseph Mallord William Turner (1775–1851), romantic landscape painter. 9. **recalcitrant** Contrary, disobedient. 10. *Sit fas aut nefas* Italian; "whether a rightful or wrongful thing," from *Titus Andronicus* II.i.142.

The stones of the sanctuaries pour out onto every street.
Like drastic Aaron's heir, Nat Turner,[11] I's natural homicidal:
My pages blaze, my lines pall, crying fratricidal damnation.   30

(2001)

Language

1

for Wendy "Motion" Braithwaite

        I hate this language that *Hate* dictates to me.
It gusts the tang and bray of a savage civilization —
Violent words violently arrived at.

        Balderdash and *braggadocio*[1]: what English is —
Squabbling cabals[2] in Bibles and newspapers —
A tongue that cannibalizes all other tongues.

        Speculate on the words still bottled blackly
In placid ink —
Fear what may leap from that *Innocence* ...

2

This homely poem's a queer nigger rig,   10
A botch of art in slovenly English,
Bad grammar, bad everything;
It cannot perform ethically.
It even fucks up Black English badly:
The metre harries,[3] but the words refuse to fit.

3

for Evelyn Shockley

That bang, blackening, of English syllables
In my black-black mouth hurts,
Them syllables hurt,
So I can only vomit up speech —
Half-digested English —   20
Soiling it with virulent Negro stomach juices.
Ma voice ain't *classique*!

---

11. Nat Turner African-American slave (1800–1831) who led an uprising in which slaves were freed and their former masters killed; at least 50 people died before the uprising was quashed and a vicious slave-killing spree was undertaken by ruling Whites.

---

1. *braggadocio* Excessive boasting. **2. cabals** Groups of conspirators. **3. harries** Harasses.

4

Grammar is pollution, some poison in my lungs,
So what emerges from my mouth — spit, phlegm —
Looks tubercular.

My lopsided tongue spoils Her Majesty's English.
The jawbreaker words wad my mouth with blood,
Even busted teeth.

I spit out *vers*[4] — ruddy larvae, red writhing worms —
30 Like a TB victim hawking scarlet phlegm into a sink.

5

A "herring-choker" Negro with a breath of brine,
I gabble a *garrote* argot,[5] guttural, by rote,
A wanton lingo, taunted and tainted by wine,
A feinting *langue*[6] haunted by each slave boat.

My black, "Bluenose"[7] brogue smacks lips and ears
When I bite the bitter grapes of Creole[8] verse —
Or gripe and blab like a Protestant pope
So rum-pungent Africa mutes perfumed Europe.

(2006)

IX/XI

For John Fraser, who wrote Violence in the Arts *(1974), and was right.*

I

We told ourselves *History* was finished —
The Holocaust just a museum piece now,
Hitler a cartoon Macbeth, Stalin a wax corpse,
Pol Pot[1] a tin-pot version of crackpot Nixon,
And Rwanda[2] made a theme park of machetes.

It was safe, our white-washed world was now safe:
No more pyramids of bones and hair,
No more napalm to charbroil infants,
No more nerve-gassings of "infidels,"
10 No more land mines to blow off your legs.

---

4. *vers* French, "verse." **5.** *garrote* **argot** A garrote is a cord or wire used for strangulation; "argot" is a specific group's vocabulary: "strangled language." **6.** *langue* "Language," in French. **7.** **Bluenose** Resident of the Maritimes, especially Nova Scotia. **8.** **Creole** Person of mixed European descent; a language created from a combination of native and colonial languages.

---

1. Pol Pot Former prime minister of Cambodia (1925–1998) who caused the death of an estimated 1.5 million of his people.
2. Rwanda In 1994, the Rwandan government exterminated at least 500,000 citizens based on their ethnic identity.

We could tune out the grisly technicolour
Of dark peoples' famines, plagues, massacres,
Or watch their cheap apartment blocks dissolve —
Under the editorial resolve of our munitions.
Our omnipotence was our doled-out avarice.[3]

But all omnipotence has a weakness. Ours meant
The clacking of bankers' never-satisfied teeth,
The bullshit of bought-and-sold elections,
The guffaws of hucksters[4] drowning out
The pure, toxic prayers of those who blame us.   20

II

Out of our blue-blank, Disney-postcard Heaven,
Came *jihad* squads of suave, aerial assassins,
Whose glistening knives of hijacked jet aircraft
Sliced into hundred-storey-high monoliths —
As white and vulnerable as wedding cakes.

It was violence as judgment, violence as *Kitsch*,[5]
Violence as aviation and concrete, violence
As pornography, violence as *X-acto* blades,
Violence as the President hunkered down in
Bunkers, violence as the Pentagon burned.   30

It was violence as stock market manipulation,
Violence as crucified eagles, violence as maggots,
Violence as stabbed-out eyes, violence as racism,
Violence as information, violence as shopping,
Violence as the Secretary of Defense, cowering.

Computer terminals gone terminally combustible
Ignited an inferno of black-lettered, white paper,
While plummeting concrete sheared off women's feet
In red or black pumps and cut off fathers' heads and left
Torsos bent over steering wheels in crushed SUVs.   40

Those jets with their hostage passengers slammed into
And toppled our towers — like Hitler taking Paris.[6]
Our infallible towers, teetered, tottered, tumbled,
Crumbled, and crashed down like two Stalinist statues,[7]
The came down like twin *Titanics*, sinking.

---

3. avarice Greed. **4. hucksters** Showy salespeople. **5. *Kitsch*** Objects created for undiscriminating tastes. **6. Hitler taking Paris** In a pivotal loss for the Allies, the German army conquered Paris in 1940. **7. Stalinist statues** After the collapse of the U.S.S.R., citizens famously pulled down multiple statues of Stalin, the former communist leader.

It was trauma and *triage*,[8] to be so shocked awake
To *History*'s revolt, its brutal, blazing insurgency.
But do you have a *right* to finish your bagel and coffee?
Do you have a *right* to see your daughter give birth?
50 Do you have a *right* to exist without suffering?

III

History shook that city that said, "*History* is history."
A Malcolm X prophecy came to fiery, smoking life
In a King Kong apocalypse of planes hitting towers.
Unanswerably *kamikaze*, candidly unappeasable men
Insisted on dissolving citizens in fire and in glass.

Though civilization often okays being blasé,[9]
On its margins, there's suffering, intense suffering,
Gothic outcasts always dreaming up catastrophes,
And sometimes their lobbed fireballs hit home.
60 No civilization survives without suffering.

Now when we say, "I love New York," sobs may stun.
Such silent subways right after the sabotage, then
Wailing, yes, and instant spirituals — as in so many other
Exploded cities: London, Hiroshima, Baghdad,
And Halifax,[10] Nova Scotia, on December 6, 1917.

Let the damage be remembered, for we are damaged,
The dead given faces, our broadcast dead reclaimed,
The nightmares witnessed, pondered, documented,
The shed blood kept warm and wet and vivid, jetting, jetting,
70 From real bodies, our own, in pain — raw, ungodly, humanizing pain.

(2006)

Douglas Coupland (1961–)

In 2004, Douglas Coupland tore up a first edition copy of his novel *Generation X* (1991) and one of *Girlfriend in a Coma* (1997), along with a stack of American one-dollar bills. From each paper pile, he fashioned a wasp's nest. He named the money nest "Royalties." He thus demonstrated his fascination with commodity culture and popular art; he also showed his proficiency as a conceptual sculptor and ironic humorist.

Coupland was born in 1961 on a Canadian Air Force base at Baden-Sollingen, Germany. His family moved to West Vancouver in 1965. After high school, Coupland went to Montreal to study physics at McGill University, but he remained there for only a year before returning to Vancouver to attend the Emily Carr Institute of Art and Design. Reflecting on this period in his life, he said,

---

8. *triage* Sorting victims to determine the order in which they will see a doctor. 9. **blasé** Detached. 10. **London, Hiroshima, Baghdad, Halifax** Sites of tremendous explosions; London and Hiroshima were severely bombed during World War II, Baghdad in the Gulf War (1990–1991) and Iraq War (began in 2003). In Halifax, on 6 December 1917, the French munitions ship *Mont Blanc* exploded in the harbour, killing around 2000 people.

"When I graduated from art school in 1984 I thought I'd be long dead from poverty and drugs in some dump not far from Main and Hastings by 1995." Instead, he continued his studies in Sapporo, Japan, at the Hokkaido College of Art and Design, and in Milan, Italy, at the Instituto Europeo di Design.

In 1987, he mounted a solo exhibit of his sculptures at the Vancouver Art Gallery, but within a year he was working in a Toronto office, accumulating valuable raw material for his later satire of corporate culture. He would often eat his lunch in a nearby cemetery, where he basked in the silence. "Added bonus," he said: "not having to deal with the living."

In 1991, Coupland published *Generation X,* which he developed from a comic strip he had written (it was drawn by Paul Rivoche). The novel was never published in Canada and was nearly rejected in the United States. "In my experience," Coupland says, "the books that succeed the best are the ones that the publishers hate in advance the most." The novel was an immediate hit, and it branded the generation that followed on the heels of the baby boomers with an *X.* Its three main characters ironically comment on the consumer culture that alienates and excludes the young poor. "Generation X" became a buzz word, as did "McJob" — two of the book's many sidebar neologisms. Coupland also coined "optional paralysis" — "The tendency, when given unlimited choices, to make none"; and "consensus terrorism" — "The process that decides in-office attitudes and behavior."

With a keen eye for the spirit of the times, Coupland published *Shampoo Planet* (1992), an ironic novel about the blind spots of its 20-year-old narrator. It ends memorably with a mock Periodic Table of the Elements of contemporary culture, including Prozac, Photocopy, Real Estate, Japan, 1-800 Number, Edible Oil Product, Landfill, Sitcom, and Detox. With *Life After God* (1993), Coupland adopted a more serious approach. Instead of indulging his ironic tendency, he shifted into an elegiac and retrospective mode. A middle-aged, middle-class narrator explains that "we believed the rock music but I don't think we believed in the love songs, either then, or now." And, speaking of a childhood friend who has contracted HIV, he remarks that "the coolness that marked our youth is itself a type of retrovirus that can only leave you feeling empty." Some of this emptiness, Coupland implies, is due to the loss of religion.

With *Microserfs* (1995), Coupland's already good timing became uncanny. That year, Microsoft released its Windows 95 computer operating system, which brought the company vast riches and gave it a near monopoly over core computer software. *Microserfs* was a critique of life in a corporate cubicle — a life assembled from bits of incoming e-mail and other computer-related texts. Other popular culture milestones appeared in the work Coupland produced over the next 10 years. *Polaroids from the Dead* (1996), a collection of essays punctuated with photographs, became a template for future works. *City of Glass: Douglas Coupland's Vancouver* (2000) was composed of an alphabetical series of entries describing aspects of the author's home city — for example, Feng Shui, Fleece, and Greenpeace. *God Hates Japan* (2001) contained striking colour images in the manner of *City of Glass,* but it also had a "Japanimated" flair courtesy of computer animator Michael Howatson. *School Spirit* (2002), featuring a black-clad skeleton student on its cover, was a meditation on trouble in high schools, inspired partly by the 1999 Columbine massacre, which also served as the backdrop to his novel *Hey Nostradamus!* (2003). (Terrorism appeared again as a subtext in *September 10, 2001* [2004], a play that Coupland wrote and performed for the Royal Shakespeare Company in England.)

His non-fiction did not remain persistently bleak, however. *Souvenir of Canada* (2002) and its sequel (2004) were comic treatments of Canadian patriotism. The books mock Canadian insecurities and small-mindedness, but they also display an appreciation for Canadian idiosyncrasy. Some of Coupland's essays (like "Yanks") defend Canadian sovereignty and distinct society and are generally positive about both Canada and the U.S.: "The grass is, to be coy, green on both sides of the fence." The book includes photographs of items that have a distinctly Canadian appeal — such as beer bottles, cigarette warning labels, concert posters for the rock band Rush, and Terry Fox's prosthetic leg.

Fox was the subject of Coupland's most recent non-fiction effort, *Terry: The Life of Canadian Terry Fox* (2005). Fox died in 1981, after being forced to abandon his cross-Canada cancer-research fundraiser run when his own cancer spread to his lungs. A young man partly modelled on Fox narrates *Girlfriend in a Coma* (1997). The novel opens as he explains, from his perspective as a ghost, how he spent his last days. Dealing seriously with issues like death and spirituality, the novel marked the first occurrence of a Coupland device: using supernatural or extraordinarily unlikely events (like a meteorite strike) as a plot device. Coupland took the title of *Girlfriend in a Coma* from a song by the 1980s alternative rock band The Smiths, much as he took the title of *Eleanor Rigby* (2004) from the 1960s Beatles classic. Like the song for which it was named, the latter novel (as did *Life After God* before it) explores the effects of loneliness in a bittersweet style.

In 2006, Coupland published *jPod*. A thematic sequel to *Microserfs*, it chronicles the lives of a group of West Coast video game company employees. Speaking about its narrator, Ethan, Coupland says, "Of all the narrators in all of my books, Ethan is actually the least like me. He's a fun guy, and very very smart, but he's not me. I want to think that fifteen years of creating characters has allowed me to make something non-Doug yet convincing at the same time." More recently, Coupland helped stage a large sculpture exhibit called "Vancouver School" as a part of the visual-art collective Futura Bold, which he joined in 2002. He also adapted *Souvenir of Canada* for the screen and wrote the script for the film *Everything's Gone Green*, which was released in 2006.

Shopping Is Not Creating

The dogs are already pooped from the heat and lying in the shadow of the Saab, chasing dream bunnies with twitching back legs. Dag and I, both being in a carbohydrate coma, aren't far behind and are in a good listening mood as Claire begins her story of the day.

"It's a Texlahoma story," she says, much to our pleasure, for Texlahoma is a mythic world we created in which to set many of our stories. It's a sad Everyplace, where citizens are always getting fired from their jobs at 7-Eleven and where the kids do drugs and practice the latest dance crazes at the local lake, where they also fantasize about being adult and pulling welfare-check scams as they inspect each other's skin for chemical burns from the lake water. Texlahomans shoplift cheap imitation perfumes from dime stores and shoot each other over Thanksgiving dinners every year. And about the only good thing that happens there is the cultivation of cold, unglamorous wheat in which Texlahomans take a justifiable pride; by law, all citizens must put bumper stickers on their cars saying: NO FARMERS: NO FOOD.

Life is boring there, but there are some thrills to be had: all the adults keep large quantities of cheaply sewn scarlet sex garments in their chests of drawers. These are panties and ticklers rocketed in from Korea — and I say rocketed in because Texlahoma is an asteroid orbiting the earth, where the year is permanently 1974, the year after the oil shock and the year starting from which real wages in the U.S. never grew ever again. The atmosphere contains oxygen, wheat chaff, and A.M. radio transmissions. It's a fun place to spend one day, and then you just want to get the hell out of there.

Anyhow, now that you know the setting, let's jump into Claire's story.

"This is a story about an astronaut named Buck. One afternoon, Buck the Astronaut had a problem with his spaceship and was forced to land in Texlahoma — in the suburban backyard of the Monroe family. The problem with Buck's spacecraft was that it wasn't programmed to deal with Texlahoma's gravity — the people back on earth had forgotten to tell him that Texlahoma even existed!

"'That always happens,' said Mrs. Monroe, as she led Buck away from the ship and past the swing set in the backyard toward the house, 'Cape Canaveral just plum forgets that we're here.'

"Being the middle of the day, Mrs. Monroe offered Buck a hot nutritious lunch of cream of mushroom soup meatballs and canned niblet corn. She was glad to have company: her three daughters were at work, and her husband was out on the thresher.[1]

"Then, after lunch, she invited Buck into the parlor to watch TV game shows with her. 'Normally I'd be out in the garage working on my inventory of aloe products that I represent, but business is kind of slow right now.'

"Buck nodded his concurrence.

"'You ever thought of being a rep for aloe products after you retire from being an astronaut, Buck?'

"'No ma'am,' said Buck, 'I hadn't.'

"'Give it a thought. All you have to do is get a chain of reps working under you, and before you know it, you don't have to work at all — just sit back and skim the profit.'

"'Well, I'll be darned,' said Buck, who also complimented Mrs. Monroe on her collection of souvenir matchbooks placed in an oversized brandy snifter on the parlor table.

"But suddenly something went wrong. Right before Mrs. Monroe's eyes, Buck began to turn pale green, and his head began to turn boxy and veined, like Frankenstein's. Buck raced to look at a little budgie mirror, the only mirror available, and knew instantly what had happened: he had developed space poisoning. He would start to look like a monster, and shortly, he would fall into an almost permanent sleep.

"Mrs. Monroe immediately assumed, however, that her cream of mushroom soup meatballs had been tainted and that as a result of her culinary shortcomings, she had ruined Buck's adorable astronaut's good looks, and possibly his career. She offered to take him to the local clinic, but Buck deferred.

"'That's probably for the best,' said Mrs. Monroe, 'considering that all there is at the clinic is peritonitis vaccinations and a jaws of life.'

"'Just show me a place where I can fall down to sleep,' Buck said, 'I've come down with space poisoning, and within minutes I'll be out cold. And it looks like you'll have to nurse me for a while. You promise to do that?'

"'Of course,' replied Mrs. Monroe, eager to be let off the hook of food contamination, and he was quickly shown to the cool basement room with half-finished wall covered with simulated wood grain particle board. There were also bookshelves bearing Mr. Monroe's bonspiel[2] trophies and the toys belonging to the three daughters: an array of Snoopy plush toys, Jem dolls, Easy Bake ovens, and Nancy Drew mystery novels. And the bed Buck was given to sleep in was smallish — a child's bed — covered with ruffled pink Fortrel sheets that smelled like they'd been sitting in a Goodwill shop for years. On the headboard there were scuffed up Holly Hobby, Veronica Lodge, and Betty Cooper stickers that had been stuck and halfheartedly peeled away. The room was obviously

---

1. thresher Machine that separates grains from husks. **2. bonspiel** A curling tournament.

never used and pretty well forgotten, but Buck didn't mind. All he wanted to do was fall into a deep deep sleep. And so he did.

"Now, as you can imagine, the Monroe daughters were most excited indeed at having an astronaut/monster hibernating in their guest room. One by one the three daughters, Arleen, Darleen, and Serena came down to the room to stare at Buck, now sleeping in their old bed amid the clutter of their childhood. Mrs. Monroe wouldn't let her daughters peek long, still being fractionally convinced of her implication in Buck's illness, and shooed them away, wanting him to get better.

"Anyhow, life returned more or less to normal. Darleen and Serena went to work at the perfume counter of the local dime store, Mrs. Monroe's aloe product business picked up a bit, taking her out of the house, Mr. Monroe was out on his thresher, leaving only Arleen, the eldest daughter, who had recently been fired from the 7-Eleven, to take care of Buck.

"'Make sure he gets lots to eat!' shouted Mrs. Monroe from her salt-rusted blue Bonneville sedan as she screeched out of the driveway, to which Arleen waved and then rushed inside to the bathroom where she brushed her blond feathered hair, applied alluring cosmetics, and then dashed down to the kitchen to whip up a special lunchtime treat for Buck, who, owing to his space poisoning, would only awaken once a day at noon, and then only for a half hour. She made a platter of Vienna franks appended to toothpicks and accessorized by little blocks of orange cheese. These she prettily arranged on a platter in a shape reminiscent of the local shopping mall logo, the Crestwood Mall letter C, angled heavily to the right. *"Facing the future"* as the local newspaper had phrased it upon the mall's opening several hundred years previously when it was still 1974, even back then, since, as I have said, it has *always* been 1974 in Texlahoma. As far back as records go. Shopping malls, for instance, a recent innovation on Earth, have been supplying Texlahomans with running shoes, brass knickknacks, and whimsical greeting cards for untold millennia.

"Anyway, Arleen raced down to the basement with the food platter and pulled a chair up to the bed and pretended to read a book. When Buck woke up at one second past noon, the first thing he glimpsed was her reading, and he thought she looked ideal. As for Arleen, well, her heart had a romantic little arrhythmia right on the spot, even in spite of Buck's looking like a Frankenstein monster.

"'I'm hungry,' Buck said to Arleen, to which she replied, 'Won't you please please have some of these Vienna frank-and-cheese kebabs. I made them myself. They were most popular indeed at Uncle Clem's wake last year.'

"'Wake?' asked Buck.

"'Oh, yes. His combine overturned during the harvest, and he was trapped inside for two hours while he waited for the jaws of life to arrive. He wrote his will out in blood on the cab ceiling.'

"From that moment on, a conversational rapport developed between the two, and before long, love bloomed, but there was a problem with their love, for Buck would always fall back asleep almost as soon as he would awaken, owing to his space poisoning. This grieved Arleen.

"Finally one noon, just as Buck awoke, he said to Arleen, 'Arleen, I love you very much. Do you love *me*?' And, of course, Arleen replied, 'yes,' to which Buck said, 'Would you be willing to take a big risk and help me? We could be together always and I could help you leave Texlahoma.'

"Arleen was thrilled at both thoughts and said, 'Yes, yes,' and then Buck told her what she would have to do. Apparently, the radiation waves emitted by a woman in love are of just the right frequency to boost the rocket ship's engines and help it to lift off. And if Arleen would just come with him in the ship, they could leave, and Buck could get a cure for his space poisoning at the moon base. 'Will you help me, Arleen?'

"'Of course, Buck.'

"'There's just *one* catch.'

"'Oh?' Arleen froze.

"'You see, once we take off, there's only enough air in the ship for one person, and I'm afraid that after takeoff, you'd have to die. Sorry. But of course, once we got to the moon, I'd have the right machines to revive you. There's really no problem.'

"Arleen stared at Buck, and a tear came down her cheek, dripped over her lip and onto her tongue, where it tasted salty, like urine. 'I'm sorry, Buck, but I can't do that,' she said, adding that things would probably be for the best if she no longer took care of him. Heartbroken but unsurprised, Buck fell back asleep and Arleen went upstairs.

"Fortunately, Darleen, the youngest daughter, got fired from her perfume sales job that day and was able to take care of Buck next, while Arleen got hired at a fried chicken outlet and was no longer around to cast gloomy feelings on Buck.

"But with Buck's being on the rebound and Darleen's having too much free time on her hands, it was only a matter of minutes, practically, before love again blossomed. Days later, Buck was making the same plea for help to Darleen that he had made to Arleen, 'Won't you please help me, Darleen, I love you so much?'

"But when Buck's plea came to the part about Darleen's having to die, like her sister before her, she froze. 'I'm sorry, Buck, but I can't do that,' she, too, said, adding that things would probably be for the best if she no longer took care of him. Again heartbroken but again unsurprised, Buck fell back to sleep and Darleen went upstairs.

"Need I say it, but history repeated itself *again*. Darleen got hired at the local roadside steak house, and Serena, the middle child, got fired from Woolworth's scent counter and so was put in charge of taking care of Buck, who had ceased being a novelty in the basement and had become instead, kind of a grudge — of the same caliber of grudge as, say, a pet dog that the children argue over whose turn it is to feed. And when Serena appeared at noon with lunch one day, all Buck could bring himself to say was, 'God, did *another* one of your Monroe girls get fired? Can't any of you hold a job?'

"This just bounced right off of Serena. 'They're just small jobs,' she said. 'I'm learning how to paint and one of these days I'm going to become so good that Mr. Leo Castelli of the Leo Castelli art galleries of New York City is going to send a rescue party up to get me off of this God forsaken asteroid. Here,' she said, jabbing a plate of crudité celery and carrot in his chest, 'eat these celery sticks and shut up. You look like you need fiber.'

"Well. If Buck thought he had been in love before, he realized now that those were merely mirages and that Serena was indeed his real True Love. He spent his waking time for the next few weeks, savoring his half hours which he spent telling Serena of the views of the heavens as seen from outer space, and listening to Serena talk of how she would paint the planets if only she could see what they looked like.

"'I can show you the heavens, and I can help you leave Texlahoma, too — if you're willing to come with me, Serena my love,' said Buck, who outlined his escape plans. And when he explained that Serena would have to die, she simply said, 'I understand.'

"The next day at noon when Buck awoke, Serena lifted him out of the bed and carried him out of the basement and up the stairs, where his feet knocked down framed family portraits taken years and years ago. 'Don't stop,' said Buck. 'Keep moving — we're running out of time.'

"It was a cold gray afternoon outside as Serena carried Buck across the yellowed autumn lawn and into the spaceship. Once inside, they sat down, closed the doors, and Buck used his last energies to turn the ignition and kiss Serena. True to his word, the love waves from her heart boosted the engine, and the ship took off, high into the sky and out of the gravitational field of Texlahoma. And before Serena passed out and then died from a lack of oxygen, the last sights she got to see were Buck's face shedding its pale green Frankenstein skin in lizardy chunks onto the dashboard, thus revealing the dashing pink young astronaut beneath, and outside she saw the glistening pale blue marble of earth against the black heavens that the stars had stained like spilled milk.

"Below on Texlahoma, Arleen and Darleen, meanwhile, were both returning home from their jobs, from which they both been fired, just in time to see the rocket fire off and their sister vanish into the stratosphere in a long, colonic, and fading white line. They sat on the swing set, unable to go back into the house, thinking and staring at the point where the jet's trail became nothing, listening to the creak of chains and the prairie wind.

"'You realize,' said Arleen, 'that that whole business of Buck being able to bring us back to life was total horseshit.'

"'Oh, I knew *that*,' said Darleen. 'But it doesn't change the fact that I feel jealous.'

"'No, it doesn't, does it?'

"And together the two sisters sat into the night, silhouetted by the luminescing earth, having a contest with each other to see who could swing their swing the highest."

(1991)

Lisa Robertson (1961–)

Near the end of *The Weather* (2001), Lisa Robertson declares, "It is too late to be simple." Accordingly, the structures of each of her books resemble weather systems in their sweeping but unpredictable gestures. Her complex and often challenging poems reflect the influence of such avant-gardists as Gertrude Stein. Like Stein's *Tender Buttons*, for example, Robertson's work is organized around concepts that are not necessarily part of a narrative arc, even when narrative cues exist, like the sequence of days in *The Weather*. Robertson's approach is also influenced by the mixed media and collaborative culture of Vancouver's conceptual art scene, including references to a wide range of female artists, including conceptualists such as Erin O'Brien and Kathy Slade.

Robertson was born in Toronto in 1961 and raised in Newmarket, Ontario, but she went to Vancouver in 1980 after joining Katimavik (Canada's national youth service program) and doing volunteer work for a year in Nova Scotia, Quebec, and Alberta. She left to work as a cook on a West Coast island and then in a household in France, and in 1986 she returned to Vancouver and enrolled at Simon Fraser University (SFU).

While working as a research assistant in special collections at the SFU library, she took courses with George Bowering, Robin Blaser, and Roy Miki, who brought in bpNichol and Steve McCaffery for poetry workshops. These courses introduced her to avant-garde Canadian poetry, which is often seen as closer to experimental American models than to the late-blooming

Canadian modernism of Montreal and Toronto — in fact, as Robertson explains, the West Coast avant-garde was more influenced by the inter-media movements of the 1960s and 1970s and by radical philosophy (in the form of post-structuralism) imported from France. The poets who especially interested her at this time were Erin Mouré, Gail Scott, and bpNichol and his group the Four Horsemen. Robertson also volunteered in 1988 at the Kootenay School of Writing (and became a member a couple of years later), which was established in 1983 as a non-profit alternative to mainstream university courses on creative writing.

In 1988, she left SFU without a degree and established Proprioception Books, which she owned and operated until 1994. To help support the store, she wrote for magazines and catalogues, while also editing the feminist magazine *Giantess* with Christine Stewart and Susan Clark. Through her East Vancouver artist clientele, she became involved in the gallery scene and contributed to Artspeak, an artist-run offshoot of the Kootenay School in Vancouver's Gastown area. For the next 20 years, she would write creative catalogue essays for curators and artists in a milieu that was open to genre mixing. Her second full-length book, *Debbie: An Epic* (1997), best reveals her multimedia interests, showing the influence of fashion and design magazines, text art, and concrete poetry. Throughout *Debbie,* Robertson manifests an obsession with the interplay between the sonic and visual aspects of language. In "The Nurses of Perfidy Gently Descend to Earth," she writes that "Harmony Is an Effect of Disproportion" — the words "harmony" and "disproportion" appear in a font three times larger than the surrounding text and in tones of grey. Every few pages, typical ragged-right-edge poetry alternates with distinct visual poems in which other typographical aspects — margins, kerning, line spacing, screening and footnoting — are altered.

The visual aspect affects her use of sound. Subtle internal rhymes and enjambments demand a mental stop, if not a sonic one, as when she illustrates "the vision of structural / decrepitude so very dear to my / heart" in "The Descent: A Light Comedy in Three Parts." Although her later book *The Weather* would feature a more pronounced use of fragmented poetic lines, *Debbie* also deals in broken structures formed by "arms of terror / and grammar," which Robertson invokes to question institutions and traditions that are problematically gendered (often masculine).

Robertson approaches traditional poetic forms as well as the English language and its scholarship from a feminist perspective, questioning male biases. In *Debbie,* she implicates herself as a female poet in the form of Virgil's nationalistic epic, claiming in "She Has Smoothed Her Pants to No End," "I will discuss perfidy / with scholars as if spurning kisses, I / will sip the marble marrow of empire." Because most of her work begins with a concept that she researches, the language associated with the concept becomes part of the poetry and displays an academic orientation.

While Virgil's *Aeneid* forms the backdrop of *Debbie,* his 10 bucolic *Eclogues* are the most obvious historical intertext for Robertson's earlier book, *XEclogue* (1993), which was reissued in 1999 after *Debbie* was nominated for a Governor General's Award. Robertson first discovered the form of the eclogue not in Virgil but in Lady Mary Wortley Montagu's 18th-century satiric poems. Wortley Montagu appears in *XEclogue* as Lady M., writing letters to the character Nancy and talking with her in collaborative poem-speeches. Inspired by Wortley Montagu, Marguerite de Navarre, Christine de Pisan, and a host of popular musicians such as Patti Smith, Annie Lennox, and P.J. Harvey, Robertson realized "the necessity of women's tactical intervention in the official genres."

The year *XEclogue* was reissued, Robertson won a visiting fellowship to Cambridge. There she became fascinated with Cambridge's impressive collection of meteorological texts by 16th-century scientists. Before leaving for England, she had ruminated on the concept of sincerity as a

Romantic ideal and was fascinated by "the sincerity of objective observation" afforded by empirical science, but she did not try to write an objective or clinical book. Instead, she shows how nature subjectively affects people and how they respond by categorizing it in ways that make it comprehensible: "The sky is lusty; so are we. We prove inexhaustibility. The sky is mauve lucite; we reduce it to logic." *The Weather* asserts that nature can do things people cannot — "The wind opens the trees; art is too slow" — but it also implies that poems, on paper produced from felled trees, can simultaneously uphold or destroy biological, natural truths: "The wind sounds like paper; our sex is no problem."

Before visiting Cambridge, Robertson wrote "Soft Architecture: A Manifesto," which became the foundation of *Occasional Works and Seven Walks from the Office for Soft Architecture* (2003), a collection of essays on the design and ornamentation of urban spaces. The Office (Robertson's alter-ego) asserts that memory is "Soft Architecture," that the "bare ruin and the long autopsy of concepts serve as emblems of Soft Architecture's demise," and that the ruin of public and personal memory is everywhere evident in cities.

In 2003, Robertson married painter Keith Donovan and was a visiting poet and lecturer at the University of California at San Diego. In November of that year, she and Donovan moved to France, and she began teaching at the American University of Paris. Drawing on nearly 15 years' worth of her notebooks, she produced *Rousseau's Boat* (2004), an exploration of her interest in Jean-Jacques Rousseau's writing and in memory, which she had also explored in *Occasional Works*. In 2006, Robertson published *The Men: A Lyric Book*, which revises the work of Petrarch, Cavalcanti, Dante, and Montaigne.

From *Debbie: An Epic*

MY HUMAN FACE A BLAZING SHIELD
is all that I could give or she demand
so I shall hazard shame for future love
and list with soldiers my degenerate name:
Debbie. My name is Debbie. Unhappy, frugal
hope has made me dote and vainly tell
of parts obscene below the waves' crescent
now flecking heaven's screen with stuttered light —
dress up the supper, refit the beds
(receive these trifles for the singer's sake)
I'll weep and speak to you of parties
space and loss and how
freedom spoke a diction abstract as
we shared the hammered silver bowl†

10

---

†Another Toast:

Suburban love is fenced in acid
Civilian love is flush

All living animals need touch
Except for those that don't

I guess

The resemblance of pleasure brings
A dividend of doubt

and banished fate and passed through
widely opened gates in triumph. Lust's
dumb muscle imitated velvet
jackets of uncertain manufacture, loopy
noble, some years from the griefs
of my topic. I'd like to live with an economy
20   that's beyond me — but I have long long
tethers attached. For the sake of communication
I die into an arm, encumbered. Dear
sexual friends: between the psyche and the drowned
tail, an expensive circumstance —
bumpety-bumpety-bump
my sinking pleasure no longer sustained
in wet arms and shaking hair —
and if I should dream when I'm awake
if I should describe the thing opaque

But forensics could not quantify
10   The basted[1] evening's furrow

When cities and their citizens
Are molten swings for thought

And pleasure is the whelp I tend
A supernal chiaroscuro[2]

Though complicity thy name is woven
Of unctuous[3] polyphony

---

1. **basted** Tacked together, or moistened. 2. **chiaroscuro** Effects of light and shadow. 3. **unctuous** Smug about one's moral superiority.

if I should lie, if I should fake   30
if I should be held by such formality as ice
a gentle fire she fed within my veins
with fruiting care — for my girlish part
sad cypress, vervain, oak, compose the wreath
I pursued her exiled trace
as when a whirlwind holds to its mark
nor could I be mistaken
as long as larking punishment mocks
with frugal daring, as long as quarrelling
winds give sparkling face to the woods   40
— all things full of horror and light —
distract my pain and repel my fears
with rattling clangour[4] tear the frocks
as long as I commit to screens
these notes and names and passing breaths

———————

A civilianesque proclivity
Has clasped around my throat

This vulture cloak, a streamlined joke
Or greek machine for living   20

And from surfeit of sprung circumstance
I toast

O disquisit[5] book of marginalia
Each feral[6] daughter knows

———————

4. **clangour** A clanging sound; loud, resonant. 5. **disquisit** Formal, discursive. 6. **feral** Wild, untamed, savage.

to seize my theme: how the soul can hate
as when a sudden silence stifles
hope and oars work at nothing
I beheld horror in the wet shade's message
50 and time left me there standing
I did not witness morning. Once rivals
loved with darkling fruits. I haunt this ratio
or throw it to you, shrinking sea, in augured[7]
tongue bastard Latin hard song my busy pain
in moody tissue grieving.
You were mortal for a while. I can live
no better. Neither plenty of arrogance
plenty of gauze, nor the hard wall of
fingerbones (which is memory) can erase
60 this fact: we were half made when the empire
died in orgy. Because we are not free
my work shall be obscure
as Love! unlinguistic! I
bludgeon the poem with desire and
stupidity in the wonderful autumn
season as
rosy cars
ascend

---

7. **augured** Foretold by omens.

maybe
even
this
dress
shall
some
day be
a joy
to
repair

(1997)

Friday

We rest on the city or water or forms assumed in a fine evening after showers the sky full of the specimens of the peculiar forms. This picture presents the commencement of an evening mist. We rest on the violent events or concatenations[1] of incident or ointments makeup pollen the moving ornament after fact is entered showing rollicking vigorous and wet. Of the sky part a dense body of cloud. We rest on the chthonic[2] pageant or on the satisfying imbroglio[3] in incompletion as in low and creeping mists. The picture is after showers. It means famous glorious and beautiful. In a fine summer's evening. Tacit. After showers. Some needs are only ever complex. We rest on eschatological[4] space or on the long choreographies of greeting and thanking upright upon them as keys. How do we transform ourselves. Laciniation.[5] We are almost transparent. We rest on the rhetorical face. Body of cloud through the night. Now we will be persons. Body of cloud by the fibres collapsing. We rest on erotic heart-love or resist. Now we persons are breaking open. The real is not enough to pleasure us. We rest thrice in the advance of zestful agitation or on the confession of conflict unneedful and hard and as the distant world forbidding within

---

1. **concatenations** Things or events. 2. **chthonic** Underworldly. 3. **imbroglio** Difficult conflict.
4. **eschatological** Relating to the ends of things. 5. **Laciniation** The creation of a fringe at an edge.

ourselves as rivals. Body of cloud like an inundation.[6] We
are sexual peninsulae. Body of cloud from the bottom of
buildings. How is it now to be a lady. Tacit. Like the
future is relevant. We rest on deep vacation and no sorrow
and we speak amazing upward structures plumped. Construct the uninhabitable streets of our life. Body of cloud
arrive at their maximum. We rest on the bafflement. Great
empty ballrooms of the future. We explore water and air
also alabaster pigment and stainless steel. Construct the
most radical banality. The hurts felt. New golden face.
Body of cloud personified. If we abandon a pronoun an
argument is lost. We rest on the fringe of a vigorous architecture fighting and sliding as the orange lights of description therefore we're inflected by the site. Construct the
real games and emotions. Blocked soliloquy. Tacit. New
face of cold presented. Body of cloud of our minds. We
want to speak the beautiful language of our times. Lashed
by change. With no memory. Without admonishment.
We rest in the shack. Construct text leaflets and positions
taken. Poverty fables. We rest on the tiny-leafed material
and resist. Body of cloud of the conventional pieties. Not
for whom do we speak but in whom. Umpteenth agony.
We rest on the uncertain depth. Speak to us non-respon-

---

6. **inundation** Flood.

ders. Construct so much decoration. Just pour doubt. Body of cloud soft unleashes. Where can a lady embrace something free blithe[7] and social. By our own elasticity. In a perfect calm. From our attraction. On the surface. When the evening returns. Into the atmosphere by night. Attended with a calm. Thrown into the omniscience. By the certain tendency. Next the earth and almost out of reach. We rest tacitly in the flickering of a book or a street as an acute dissatisfaction or in the rapacity of adoration roughened and donating and pouring only omniscience. Body of cloud of work. Where can a lady reside. Next the earth and almost out of reach. Almost always electrified. To surfaces of discontinuity. In light clothes and coloured shoes. By the little flower called the pansy. O little bird extravagant. Among its decayed houses. Against intolerable justice of betterment. Spontaneous body of the plants we tread on. This fig and that fig. Rough boards. Are the streets really secular. We rest on the streets or warnings. Where can a lady reside. Shabby with hungers. About the year 2001 in the grey of dawn. This is perception. Now thickens up. Now parses. Construct the unpredictable equilibriums. Construct false latinities.[8] Construct the touch of risk. Construct the noble. Construct anger.

---

7. **blithe** Cheerful. 8. **latinities** Knowledge bases of Latin.

Construct face. Now soft unleashes. We rest on deep
rhetorics. Sometimes what we perceive best is shaded.
Becoming ornament. Now swiftening. We speak as if our
tremors our postures posed spaces. City of hunger and
patience. Floating in calm space. We shall be sober in our
imprint. Then go on diminishing. Sober in our imbroglio. The city tacit. At the same time descending. Sober in
our orchestra. Grassy — recumbent.[9] With no formal
admonishment. Body of cloud laciniated. We speak as if
in you alone.

(2001)

Wooden Houses

A work called wooden houses begins
It explores different degrees of fear.

And it is curious that you did not choose a secular image
Augustine's[1] own task was equally impossible.

And we said a boat would come and take you to Venice
And you are a law of language.

And my mouth took part
And we fed you morphine mixed with honey.

And you are a rare modern painting in the grand salon
And you are a wall of earth.

And you are an ideological calm
And you are flung out to search.

And you are framed only by the perspectival rigors of masonry[2]
And you are not a neutral instrument.

10

---

9. recumbent Reclining, inactive.

---

1. Augustine The 4th-century saint most famous for his *Confessions*, an autobiographical account of his conversion to Christianity. **2. masonry** Stonework.

And you are pornographic
And you are the imagination of society as a tree.

And you are the kneeling woman who expresses some alarm
The woman looks somewhat apprehensively at the viewer.

And you are the pronoun of love, scorn, accusation, glamour
20   Everything you know about the animal pertains to the riot of love.

And you are Torontos of cold trees
Where erupts the morning's catalogue.

And you did not die outside of love
And you do not judge.

And you roll down scrabbling at its glaze
The man on the right runs away terrified.

And you see how an animal dies
Giving a first drop of voluptuousness.

And you seem to pour rose water
30   Leaning on trees for rest.

And you speak in leaves
To flirt and fight and appease.

And you turn into a her not knowing what's happening
The woman in your midst may be kneeling or seated or perhaps has simply been drawn
    out of scale.

And you are the last wooden house
The carved frame includes the heads of dogs.

And you will not die
But chance is always a little ahead.

And your failure is my tongue
The dramatic effect is heightened by the bright red ground showing through the top
40   layers.

And your heart broke off into this great desire to see
Into the tall grass.

And your plump arms emerge from the gold and rose-pink folds of your tunics
As in the ancient literary genres.

Because it is a known fact
The wounded fall towards the point.

Because of mute desire
You are the teak pavilion.

Because you wanted to be flattered
You are portrayed here as the sea goddess Thetis[3] with two of her five sons.   50

But chance is always a little ahead
But not under circumstances of its own choosing.

Emptying your apartment during the season of apricots
This wasn't true.

Genial then light
I tell mine complaint.

I tell mine complaint.
I tell mine complaint.

I took part in the savage transaction
It burns to come back to you.   60

It is pure surface
It pushes straight towards the author of its hurt.

It was 3:04 am
Like you invented summer in a text I discovered in your drawer in the summer of 1998.

Or a woman whose complete being seems to sing sex
One man shows his companion.

Sometimes the most ample designations are so stifling you can only go further inside
Supposing a designation to have an interior.

The fabric is knotted to reveal your figure
The folds suggest the roundness of a young girl.   70

The tissue is syllables and dreams in a distant colony
The parts of life are not happening in tandem.

Then it is summer
This material is reconciled to chance, which is spacious.

---

3. **Thetis** Greek mythological sea-nymph. Some accounts say that she killed most of her offspring, the products of a forced marriage. At least one son, Achilles, survived.

To make livid a philosophy
We helped you leave breath.

Whether love comes as a young boy with girlish limbs
You are behind and between Christ and the adulteress, witnessing.

You are buckled into my truth
80   A young woman looks openly out of the picture.

You are the claustrophobia of the image
At its peak a couple stare at the lightning-filled sky.

You are the exhausting pace of boredom versus the use of the body
You are the next cabin also.

The figures represent the four ages of man
You call this passivity.

You left the books that surrounded you and me holding your body
Accompanied by only the city.

You lie there wounded
90   You see the precision of the distant city through the round arches of the bridge.

You see the women's thick hair bound with coloured ribbons, their complicated sandals
        and the sprigs of olive
You slip your cock into the actress's vagina.

You thrum and click
You took part in the savage transaction of negation.

You are wooden houses transformed into apartments and restaurants
Your breath thrummed the wooden house.

Your failures are no longer sacred
The cabin. The music shop. The next cabin.

(2005)

Timothy Taylor (1963–)

Timothy Taylor's parents were travelling through Venezuela when he was born. By the time he was a toddler, they had settled in Vancouver. The family moved to Edmonton when Taylor was a teenager, and he enrolled at the University of Alberta. After obtaining a B.A. in economics, he went on to study at Queen's University in Kingston, Ontario, where he completed a master's degree in business administration. Moving to Toronto, he worked for a time in the finance sector before returning to Vancouver in 1987 to become a commercial banker. Four years later, he dropped out of the industry and became a journalist, focusing on creative writing when he could. Still restless, Taylor became a fisheries policy consultant in the mid-1990s. He also began to publish his stories.

In 2000, he earned the distinction of becoming the only writer ever to have published three stories in a single volume of *The Journey Prize Anthology*. The next year, he produced the novel *Stanley Park*. With this comic realist tale that takes as its central theme the destruction of the local and the particular by the bulldozer of global corporate culture, Taylor introduces us to Jeremy Papier, an idealistic young chef who must fight to keep his fragile new enterprise afloat. The Monkey's Paw Bistro serves lovingly prepared dishes made from local ingredients, but the ruthless owner of the ominously named Dante's Inferno chain of coffee houses has his eye on Jeremy's business. As a counterpoint to this narrative line, Taylor builds a story about Jeremy's father, an anthropologist who becomes immersed in the lives of the indigents who bed down in Stanley Park — the son is pulled into the maw of the globalizing beast while the father retreats into green space. Taylor says he wrote this novel that encompasses the extremes of life in contemporary Vancouver only after he had acquired sufficient life experience to make it convincing: "I needed exposure to people in different fields with problems and issues and objectives outside the world of writing. If I had tried to start a novel in my mid-twenties after studying creative writing, I can't imagine what I would have written about."

Taylor's next book was *Silent Cruise* (2002), a collection of short fiction and one novella that are loosely connected through thematic motifs or common characters. It contains the story "Doves of Townsend," for which Taylor won both the Journey Prize and a Silver National Magazine Award. Its narrator, Clare, is an antiques dealer who mourns for her father, who has committed suicide, and pines for a collection of butterflies she comes across in a flea market. Here, Taylor vividly establishes his overarching theme of authenticity — a quality that is as fragile and elusive as a butterfly, but also a condition that the characters who populate Taylor's stories are compelled to pursue. Clare has an inherent sense of how perplexing that pursuit can be: "The truth is plain," she announces early in the narrative, but she later muses, "What's bad, clearly, is to get fake when you're after real." This preoccupation with authenticity re-emerges in "The Resurrection Plant," in which a Jewish high school student is obliged to share a locker with a thug who proudly displays a Nazi flag; the student is able to resist the bully, embracing his true heritage in the face of those who would twist history to glorify the perpetrators of the Holocaust. The plant of the story's title has the capacity to remain dormant for years and be revived with water — a potent symbol of the power of memory and the strength that can reside in fragility.

"NewStart 2.0 ™," the novella that concludes *Silent Cruise,* is an art-world mystery that follows two small-town Saskatchewan artists as they travel to Rome, and it raises the question of authenticity in the context of intellectual patrimony. Its narrator asks, "What's an original idea? Does it merely lack resemblance to any idea that has come before? Or does an idea become original over time if it proves itself by spawning offspring ideas, each of which then bear testimony by a degree of resemblance?"

In 2006, Taylor published his second novel, *Story House*. It is about a pair of half-brothers, Graham and Elliot Gordon, sons of a renowned architect. The brothers are vastly different from one another: Graham enters his father's profession and Elliot shifts counterfeit merchandise; Graham moves in respectable circles and Elliot exists on the social fringes. They reluctantly come together again to help restore a building designed by their father — the project is set in motion by a reality TV producer who wants to record the undertaking. The novel is linked to Taylor's others writings through the persistent theme of the mutability of reality and our unfulfilled desire for the authentic. It explores the overlap between the counterfeit and the genuine article, the restored edifice and the original construction, reality and reality TV, the legitimate son and the illegitimate son.

In structuring his narrative, Taylor moves seamlessly between time periods, a formal technique that reinforces his architectural metaphor: the building as the embodiment of temporal flux. "I tried to capture the simultaneity of the present and the past," he says. "Buildings evolve over

time. They are both what the architect intended them to be and what they have become."
Similarly, the two brothers exist in a present mediated by their past — a past constructed by their
father both literally and figuratively. Taylor compounds the architectural metaphor to include the
brothers' heritage, describing the design of the staircase in the deteriorating building as the DNA
double-helix.

Taylor, who likes to work on several projects simultaneously, continues to write novels and
non-fiction magazine pieces; he recently wrote a screenplay for *Stanley Park*. Taylor lives in
Vancouver with his wife, Jane, and their family.

The Resurrection Plant

Dad struck oil in 1976 when I was fifteen. "Struck" maybe isn't the right word. More like,
was struck by. He read an enthusiastic article about it and became, himself, enthusiastic.
That was his way. And so we moved from Halifax to an acreage outside Edmonton,
Alberta.

I sat on the front steps of our new house and looked at the dead grass stretching
away to the fence by the dirt road, the shrubs lining the drive ready to burst into flames.
I was stunned by the heat, by the lack of moisture and colour. I felt like an exile.
Marooned on a buff-coloured planet full of hostile, sun-toughened Prairie kids.

Mom dealt with it her own way. She was inside unpacking. Not pots or clothes.
First, her South American hat collection. Panamas and bowlers. Next, the record player.
Dad phoned from his new office in downtown Edmonton.

"Helping your mom, Colin?"

I didn't tell him mom was lying flat on her back in the empty living room listening
to the Tijuana Brass. Wearing a Mayan bowler. What I did tell him was that I was going
to go look for the river.

"Attaboy," Dad said optimistically. "The Atlantic, see … it just goes in and out.
The river is always coming from someplace, and then going on to some other place."

There were black-and-white birds that shrieked challenges and followed me from
branch to branch partway down the ravine. I climbed through papery grass and some thin
silver trees, up over a weed-covered berm, and discovered the mighty North Saskatchewan.

It was brown. I threw dirt clods into it.

My locker partner was Ted Shuchuk. He had a virgin upper lip, never shaved, which
aspired to a moustache and achieved only a faint black smudge that disappeared entirely
if you looked at it from a certain angle. His closest friend was a failed eleventh-grader
everyone called Snowblower. He stored his broken binders, a dumb-bell and stray
sandwiches on a rickety homemade set of plywood shelves. Almost every morning I
had to brush piles of mouse shit off my books.

Ted spruced up the locker with an Olivia Newton John poster and a Nazi flag.

The gym teacher, Mr. Cartwright, was the first to see the flag, and he cuffed Ted in
the side of the head and told him to take it down. Ms. Davison, the drama coach, said
hanging up that particular flag was hateful, insulting and immature, but Ted's legal right.

I waited a week before mentioning it to my mom. She wrote a carefully worded
letter to *The Edmonton Journal* and the next day there was a long, if somewhat oblique,
editorial about the Holocaust. The swastika came down.

"That was my grandfather's flag," Ted said, breathing menthol tobacco breath on me.

"You must be very proud," I said to him.

"Get out of the way, turkey. I'm going to work out." And he began pumping his dumb-bell right in front of the locker. I had to lean over him to put my liverwurst sandwiches up on that tiny top shelf.

My mom said to me, "He can't hurt you. Don't forget that." It was late September. We were walking through a warm wind on a hard blue night.

After Hitler was gone, my mom emerged from her hiding place in the Black Forest[1] and took a boat to Argentina. (This is how she told it.) She was drinking hot chocolate on the lower deck, an indescribable luxury, and someone said, "Eichmann[2] is on this very boat!" An old woman, her voice shaking with rage at the diabolical irony of it. And my mom had heard this and been sick: all at once, over the rail, a deep hot-chocolate-coloured, evacuating sickness. Then she fainted, toppling like a spent gyro and hitting her head on a deck bollard. She woke up wrapped in a horse blanket, her head pounding, and delivered her signature line, in broken English with her eyes still pinched shut: "Damn to Eichmann." My grandmother and the old lady cried. My mom never did. She said simply, "Then we went to Rio de Janeiro, and I prayed for a husband. Canadian or maybe from California."

I have a photograph from the New Year's Eve party at the Canadian consulate in Rosario where they met. My dad is flushed and brush-cut. My mother looks wide-eyed, frozen in the headlights of her own prayers. He took her to Nova Scotia the next year.

Phil Levine wore a black kangaroo jacket and carried an asthma inhaler. We used to eat lunch out at the hockey rink, on the visitors' bench. Phil always had a Vonnegut[3] on him, an old dog-eared Dell paperback edition *Player Piano, Cat's Cradle, Jailbird*. Phil's brother once spent an entire year indoors, reading and underlining bits in his Vonnegut collection, then moved to the Yucatan Peninsula. It was enough to make anyone read the underlined bits. So we sat out there at the rink and talked about fascism and nuclear winter and setting things on fire, until a tanker truck pulled up and flooded the rink. Then suddenly there were hockey players everywhere.

"Goofs with dentures," said Phil, who had a fine eye for details.

We went inside.

"Phil's a Zionist,"[4] I announced at dinner.

Scott Miller was not a Zionist, but he knew aircraft statistics and had read half of *Slaughterhouse-Five*. Phil, Scott and I ended up in the same science group. Our fourth was Ted. He came over and surveyed his team-mates: "Fatso, Nerdball and Psycho Asthmahead."

"You can be Goering,"[5] said Phil.

"But I was Fatso last year," Scott said, and Ted hit him without even looking in his direction.

"Anyone know what this is?" Mr. Duke, our science teacher, stood at the front of the class behind the lab bench, holding a brown crust above his head between his fingers. Holding it like it might break. It looked dead, whatever it was. The rad hummed.

---

1. **Black Forest** Mountainous region of southern Germany. 2. **Eichmann** Adolf Eichmann (1906–1962), a prominent Nazi official. 3. **Vonnegut** Kurt Vonnegut (1922–2007), American novelist, writer of satire and science fiction. Fought in World War II, became a prisoner of war, and documented the work he was forced to do by the Nazis, like burning bodies. 4. **Zionist** One who supports the establishment and development of a Jewish state. 5. **Goering** Hermann Goering (1893–1946), a Nazi, was commander of the Luftwaffe — the German air force.

"It's a dried dog turd," Ted said, laughing.

"It's a resurrection plant," Duke said. The brown crust didn't deny this. It was curled in on itself tight as a pine cone.

"And if I said it was alive would you believe me?" he asked, and somebody near the window answered aloud, "No-o-o."

"Well," he said, "how could you prove me wrong?"

One of the girls got it right. "Absolutely," Duke said. "Living things need oxygen."

So, we tried to suffocate it. Duke and Snowblower put it under the vacuum beaker set up on the corner of the lab bench.

"If it still looks the same in a week, what'll we know then?" Duke asked. "Anyone?"

"That it's definitely a dog turd," said Ted.

"What'll we know?" he asked again after Ted had disappeared to the principal's office.

"That it's dead," I said aloud. My first unsolicited class answer and, in fact, the right answer.

After school, Ted and Snowblower hung out and smoked in the east stairwell. We didn't talk to them. They hung out with girls, knit-vested princesses with platforms, pooka shells and three-dimensional breasts.

Phil got moods. He'd walk all the way home and not say a thing.

Scott walked between us, always talking, sticking a hand out on either side of him so we all had to stop and listen to him.

"Someone ask me what the fuel capacity of an L-1011 is."

Or, "Got your jockstraps for wrestling next week? No, really, what size did you get?"

After we dropped Scott off at his house, I'd try to draw Phil out.

"Shuchuk's into knives, hey?" I said once.

"And flags," Phil said tightly.

"You know he hung it up again," I asked.

"I know he hung it up again," he nodded.

"I could be a Zionist, you know," I tried.

"With a name like McCluskey?" he said and peeled off for home. I waved at his back.

At night we played ping-pong and Yahtzee round robins, and my mom and I listened to talk radio. Every Albertan held a personal opinion on whether the northern lights made a noise. I saw them a couple times and didn't hear anything. They just waved back and forth and then faded away.

At breakfast, Dad read the "Exposed-flesh-freezes-in-how-many-seconds" statistics out of the newspaper: "Ten seconds. Coldest November day since nine-teen-oh-too. Says here scientists have proven it's actually colder than a witch's tit. Sorry."

Duke let everyone come up with a way to kill the resurrection plant. Carbon monoxide, X-rays, two weeks of darkness, chlorine and ammonia gas. By December, I was rooting for the plant.

"Just burn the fucking thing," Ted said, right in one of those unexpected canyons of silence that a classroom will pass through.

Everyone turned to look at him. Duke closed his eyes and clenched his jaw. We decided to put it in a deep freeze until after the holidays.

The bell rang. "All right. The jockstrap hour," Scott said.

The sponge mat was rolled out in the gym. Phil tripped Scott and fell elbow first onto his back. "Body slam," he shouted. They bounced up, tapped into the finely strung mania webbing throughout the room.

"Get off the mat!" Cartwright emerged from the equipment room. Whistle, stop-watch, green sweatsuit cut like real pants with a wide yellow stripe down the outside of each leg. Red eyebrows the same width as his moustache. Black eyes flickering left and right.

He called me Mr. Vocabulary.

"Ring the mat!" We scattered like ants under a magnifying glass.

"Sutcliffe and Nesbitt," Cartwright read off his clipboard from the centre of the gym, glaring around him for silence.

"Sutcliffe, referee's position." Sutcliffe hit the mat on all fours. Nesbitt kneeled beside him, hands on Sutcliffe's back, fingers spread. There was silence, I looked up at the ceiling. Green rings around the gym lights were a bad omen. Silence hovered. And then the sound of the whistle was swamped by pandemonium.

"Nesbitt!" Scott yelled beside me. Sutcliffe had done a sit-out, sliding out from under Nesbitt's hands and scrambling to his feet. They grappled and fell. All knees and ribs.

"Nesbitt!" Phil and I joined in.

Nesbitt was chest down. Sutcliffe was on his back reefing on a half nelson. Snowblower was chanting, "Sutty, Sutty, Sutty."

Nesbitt's underwear climbed out the top of his shorts.

"Gonch pull," shouted Ted.

And that appeared to break his spirit. Nesbitt resigned with his eyes and rolled. One. Two. Three.

"Who backed the loser?" Cartwright paced the edge of the mat looking at each of us.

Our betrayal of Nesbitt was unanimous.

"I heard some of you yelling," Cartwright said, smiling, enjoying the moment. "Some of you, I know, backed the loser."

After gym, Phil and Scott and I sat in the hallway with our backs against the lockers and ate lunch.

"Meat loaf," Scott said, looking depressed. "What do ya got?"

"Gefilte fish and a Ding Dong," Phil said.

"Very Yiddish, Levine, congratulations. What do ya got, Colin?"

"I'm not trading."

"What though?"

"A granola bar," I said.

"All right. Meat loaf for the granola bar." Scott opened a corner of his sandwich. "It's got ketchup and mayo. What kind of granola bar is it?"

"My mom makes them," I said.

"Oh, forget it," Scott said. "What else you got?"

"A herring sandwich," I admitted.

"Herring sandwich?" Scott said. "What's with the Yid food, guys, how'm I supposed to trade here?"

"Well, I'm kind of Jewish, you know," I said.

We ate and watched the janitor string up red letters that spelled Merry Christmas along the main hallway.

"You spelled it wrong," Scott called over to him.

"What?" he said.

"Your sign is spelled wrong."

He climbed down off his stepladder, wiped his forehead with a rag he took from the pocket of his railway overalls and looked at the sign.

"So how'd you spell it?" he said after several minutes.

"H-A-N-U-K-K-A-H," Scott said. So Phil and I punched him until he coughed up a piece of sandwich. Then we went over to Poon's to buy Sno-Jos.

"What's this about you being kind of Jewish," Phil said later. We were standing outside the store squinting in the clear bright sun.

"My Oma and Opa[6] were, so my mom kind of is," I said. "I mean they're not really, because they're Lutheran, but they could be if they wanted to switch back."

Phil took some Wink Sno-Jo into his straw, covered the end with his thumb and dribbled the green slush onto the sidewalk. "Moms pass the Jewish bloodline," he said. And Phil scraped the frozen green pattern he'd made on the sidewalk with the side of his boot.

We went skating in Mayfair Park after Christmas. Dad bought us all new Bauer Supremes. I asked my mom while we were skating, "When does it warm up here?" I had two pairs of gloves on.

"Don't you like this?"

She skated with her bare hands behind her back.

"It's crisp, it's fresh," she said.

The air felt sharp on my cheek for the first while, then I didn't feel anything on my cheek.

"I'm going numb," I said.

"You shouldn't complain so much," she said. And we skated on a bit in silence. It was true that she never complained, not about physical pain.

"Ted hung that flag back in our locker," I said.

She kept skating. The ice was covered with a whisper of snow.

"Phil's a Zionist," I said. Still she just skated. Bare hands behind her back. Ear muffs, no toque.

"I want to be Jewish," I said finally.

Then she stopped, so I stopped. She looked at me.

"What do you want to be?" she asked.

"Jewish," I said.

"No, what do you want most of all. Right this minute."

"I'd like to be warm," I said, without thinking.

She smiled a sort of halfway smile I couldn't interpret.

Then she said, "Well, that's not so complicated then. In the spring you will get what you want."

Phil and I planned a camping trip out to Elk Island Park to see buffaloes in the spring. I was talking about this on the way to school and he cut me off.

"I want you to put this in your locker," he said, just outside the schoolyard gate. It was a taped-up Birks box. I held it in my glove. It seemed weightless.

"What is it?" I asked.

"It's the resurrection plant," he said.

"No, really," I said.

Phil stopped walking. "Do you have to know? I'm asking you a favour. A favour I couldn't ask just anyone. Hide this box in the back of your locker. Forget about it. As

---

6. **Oma and Opa** German for "grandma," and "grandpa."

my brother, do me this favour." And he took my hand and shook it slowly and firmly, something he'd never done before.

"Well, I don't have to exactly know about it," I said. "Except maybe if it's explosive or flammable. I'd like to know whether to put it on the upper or lower shelf." Phil didn't smile. At school I dropped the box behind Ted's shelves and blew into my cold hands.

"All right," Phil said, grinning, happy. I felt guilty-good.

Plus we were late.

"Glad you could join us, gentlemen," Duke said.

We sidled in like desperadoes. The room stayed silent after we sat down. No one was looking around.

"One of us is a thief," Duke said. And I noticed that Ted's chair was empty.

By the time I got out the door after class, and sprinted to the locker, Ted was hunched over, digging into the papers that filled the bottom shelf.

"Where'd you put it?" Ted said to me.

My legs actually felt weak. I was hyperventilating. "Behind the shelves," I said.

Ted leaned into the locker. "Oh, here it is." And he pulled out his dumb bell, turned around and started pumping it up and down solemnly.

"You been using this?" he asked me.

"No, I haven't at all. I promise."

"Just be cool," Phil said from behind me. He sounded cool.

There was a muscle on the right side of Ted's neck pressing out and relaxing rhythmically as he pumped. I stretched around him to put my science binder away.

"Hey, turkey," he said. "I need your notes from today."

"Sure. Where were you?" I asked.

Ted looked disgusted. "Principal. It was nothing."

"What was nothing, Shuchuk?" Phil leaned into our conversation, a big fake smile pasted on.

"Mind your own fucking business, Levine."

"No, seriously, I want to know. I mean, we never talk, you know. How was Christmas, get any cool stuff at all? Guns? Grenades? Gas maybe? Hey, nice flag."

"Hey, happy Hanukkah, Levine, all right?" Ted turned to his locker.

"And back to you, Shuchuk. Happy, happy, happy Hanukkah."

Ted was walking away.

"What a pin-dick," Phil said. He was wheezing. He took a drag on his inhaler.

"What's your problem?" I said to him.

"No problem," he said.

"What did you do? What did I do?" I asked.

He smiled, took another drag.

"Take it easy, McCluskey," he said. And we walked after Ted down the hall towards the gym.

Cartwright was pacing the circle at the centre of the mat, spinning his whistle. "And now," he said to the assembled class. "A special match."

Every light in the ceiling cast a green ring.

Cartwright was grinning broadly. "Will you welcome please, the Snowblower."

Whoops. Ted was on his feet. "Me. Me. Me. Let Snowblower and me go."

Not likely. Never friends. Cartwright's eyes were flicking around the ring. My arms goose-pimpled.

"In the blue trunks ... Mr. Voca-aaa-bulary."

Snowblower's face went flat with surprise, then hardened into something like sadistic amusement. I stood slowly, trying and failing to hold Cartwright's stare.

"Oh man, that's unfair," Scott said.

"Thanks," I said. "Any advice?"

"The balls," Scott said, "definitely the balls."

"His that is," Phil added. "Kick them, or pull on them."

"Oh, and if you hit him like this, you can drive his nose bone into his brain," Scott said, demonstrating on himself.

"Snowblower, referee," Cartwright barked, smiling at me from behind his whistle as I entered the centre ring.

I spread my hands on Snowblower's sweating back. The whistle sounded far above us and I did exactly as taught. I lunged for his far arm, reaching under his chest, got it, and drove with my shoulder against his ribs. Snowblower rocked a bit and settled. Then he stood up and shook me off. I was hanging from his neck. He grabbed my head. I jerked downward and escaped.

We circled. I could hear Ted screaming, "Snowblower. Snowblower." And Scott foghorning away on my behalf.

Then Snowblower grappled, lifted me and dropped me on the mat. Damn. My face was going to burst. He was working on my right shoulder. I twisted over onto my chest, crossed my legs, tucked in my hands and elbows. My last defence, the Armadillo.

Snowblower was scrambling around my back. I felt one hand on my neck, one on my ankles. I felt his head butt into my side, just above the waist. Phil was looking at me. He shrugged and shook his head. Snowblower was bending me like a bow and arrow, pulling on my head and feet, pushing with his head. I flipped onto my back, a husk, airless. Pinned.

Everyone was shouting. Cartwright helped me up and put a towel in my face. "It's just a nosebleed," he said. I pulled the towel away from my face. The white terry cloth was sticky red in the middle, still connected to me by a slick string of pink mucus.

I got what I wanted most. It did warm up.

Above the dirt-brown snow drifts, the skinny poplars next to the fire station were muscling out buds. There was a mouse population explosion at school. I began losing ground to the shit at the bottom of our locker. There were mice in the halls, streaking for cover in the corners behind doors. Disappearing into the wall under the water fountain.

On a Monday I slushed up the street, the air light and breathable, past sand-crusted front lawns.

Duke came out of the storeroom and stepped up behind the lab bench. He took his time, cleared his throat. Ted not being there didn't even register with me until I saw the blue Birks box.

Conversations slowly stopped, heads turned, seats were readjusted. Phil and Scott were the last to stop talking. I had forgotten the thing existed, and recognized it now like a toy lost in grade four and rediscovered. Like the Bluenose II model in the box in the basement that I had found before Christmas and repacked. That I had recognized every detail of, and immediately wanted forgotten.

He stood with the blue Birks box in his right palm. Then he reached over and pulled the lid off and rolled a blackened briquette-sized lump onto the desk. There was no question what it was. Burnt to a nub of its former size. We might have doubted. We had all doubted, I suppose, but the resurrection plant was now most definitely dead.

"At least we found it," Duke said. "The mouse exterminators were looking for nests in the lockers and … and the person responsible …" His face was a quilt of red and white splotches. "The person responsible has been expelled."

Phil showed nothing. He stared straight ahead, and so I did as well. Scott's jaw was slack. Around us, people seemed to breathe relief and delight, in unison.

The next part happened fast. I went to the locker after the three o'clock bell without talking to Phil. I was thinking of going home. Of confessing to someone or going to the Yucatan or both. And then I opened the locker and saw the flag gone. And something did flush through me. Like I had won something. Pride. Anger.

Scott came up behind me. "You going over to the fire station? Phil's already there."

And when we got into the poplars, it seemed like everyone was waiting for us. Ted was shadow-boxing Snowblower, dumb-bell biceps evident under his Edmonton Eskimos T-shirt. Phil stood a few yards away in the long grass, shaking his wire-thin arms by his sides.

"This is nuts," I said to him. "This is very stupid."

"And your better idea is?" he said to me.

"We'll get killed," I said.

Ted approached through the thick grass to where we stood. "I didn't burn that fucking thing. He told Duke I did. He's a weasel. You're both weasels. You're both dead weasels."

"I never said anything to anyone," Phil said.

"Fuck you, Levine."

"Fuck yourself, Shuchuk."

"Right now, man, right now."

"Don't you think — " I started a sentence I didn't have an ending for anyway.

"Hey, you're next, all right?" Ted said right into my face. He was at one of the angles from which I could see the moustache. It was filling out.

Snowblower was smacking Ted in the arm, bop, bop, get him, man, you're gonna kill him. A crowd fanned hungrily around us.

I looked at Phil, who gave a shrug.

"Let me have the first go," he said.

So I got out of the way and they did that mandatory circling manoeuvre. I can't say they were really sizing each other up. Ted was doing it for effect, swinging his fist near his waist, his stance open and confident. He was appraising a certain kill, thinking about maximizing crowd value maybe, but at his own speed.

Phil was just waiting. He could have been waiting for the bus. Except his elbows were tucked in at his sides, his white-knuckled fists trembled at eye level and he was leading left. A useless formality before going out with good form.

The crowd's calls for blood became persuasive, even from those who didn't want blood, those who probably wanted to go home but couldn't or wouldn't, because leaving at that moment was inconceivable. Girls hopped up and down on the spot. The few junior high school kids there, boys, were pushing each other back and forth, infected by what lay ahead.

"Ted. Ted. Ted." No one was yelling for Phil.

"Kill him, Phil," I screamed. And Phil stepped off his back foot, closed quickly and threw what everyone in the lot must have known was a one-in-a-million haymaker. A sweeping arc. A hate-filled cartoon of a punch, with enough power to remove an opponent's head as long as he'd been immobilized first.

Ted didn't even look at it. But he brought his fist up from his waist hard and fast into Phil's throat. A short, blunt movement. Phil's right arm feathered off Ted's shoulder and followed him to the grass. His face was white, his eyes pinched shut, his hands around his own neck, breathing like a stick in bike spokes. Then Ted kicked him in the stomach, a considered, methodical kick. Phil moved his hands, rolled tighter. Ted kicked again. The side of the head. It sounded like *clack*.

Phil rolled away, bloody face in the grass.

"Enough. Fuck," I said and ran toward them. The air was alive with movement. The crowd was draining out of the lot around me.

Scott was crying and yelling, "If you killed him, my dad'll sue." He was on his bike already.

I rolled Phil over. He was bleeding, but breathing.

Snowblower came over. "Oh, leave him, he's fine."

"You better not've fucking killed him," Scott yelled again, his face red and wet, and then he pedalled away. Standing up for speed, not looking back.

"You later, Vocabulary," Ted said, standing over Levine and me.

"Me now, cheese dick," I heard myself say as I stood up. Clearly I had lost my mind. Maybe I wouldn't feel anything. I felt strong. Maybe I was coursing full of some kind of Judaic adrenaline, making me impervious to pain, to fear.

"Come on, Brownshirt," I found myself saying. "You want to hit me. Hit me. Fucking hit me. What? Knock me down, pussy. Burnt a fucking plant so now you're a tough guy?"

Ted took a step back toward me but Snowblower stopped him.

"Don't," Snowblower said. Ted shook his arm away. "Listen to this little shit."

"Come on, gas me, you Ukrainian fuck. Try to kill me, Eichmann."

"Oh, I'm going to enjoy this," said Ted.

"You want Duke to come out?" Snowblower had Ted by the arm again. "Let's get out of here, man."

"Bastards took my flag. Let me kill him," Ted said.

"Come on, Eichmann, I'm not fucking afraid of you," I said.

"Leave the girls here," Snowblower said, almost softly.

They walked out of the lot, Snowblower pulling Ted through the grass. I wanted them dead.

"Anytime," I yelled after them. I was delirious.

But they didn't come back.

"Nice work," Phil said. He was sitting up behind me holding his throat and laughing. It looked painful. He had to go into his Adidas bag and get out his inhaler before he could speak again.

"Eichmann?" he said, wheezing, bleeding, laughing. "Fucking Eichmann."

Then Phil reached into his bag again, took out the resurrection plant and handed it to me. I had never felt it before. It was crumbled, a little worse for wear. Tender to the touch, like dried cedar. But all there. A tough little plant. Completely unburned. As alive as ever.

"Just do something with it. Anything," he said to me.

"I thought this was burnt. What's that in the school?" I said, confused.

Phil winced and strained some blood through his teeth into the grass. "A pine cone. A burnt pine cone," he said finally, coughed, spat some more. Laughed another painful laugh.

"Jesus," I said. I felt light, and I sat down suddenly, then lay back in the grass. The sky full of horsetails.

I kept the resurrection plant for three days before I talked to my mom. Even then I didn't tell her anything, only that I had something that wasn't mine. She said, "Is it from a store?" And then when I shook my head she said, "Does it have a proper owner?"

I said that its real owner thought it was dead. And that made her think for a minute. "Then put it where it belonged before its real owner even knew it was alive."

Of course it only needed water. I carried the resurrection plant down into the river valley. I found a spot near the sludgy bank. Buried it halfway in the moist brown soil, full of bugs and worms. The bowl-blue sky held out space above me. And in less than a week there was a fist-sized bush that sprang roots and pushed itself deep into the prairie.

The magpies still follow and fall away, their insults tapering. Their cackles trail behind them as they turn back toward the highway, toward roadkill and other concerns. The papery grass still catches in my cuffs and laces. The muddy bank gums my leather soles.

I kneel. It has grown as high as my chest.

I hold the branches, which I think smell of musty pine and pepper. The branches aren't dry. Aren't lifeless. They're full of the earth's moisture. Full of the water that the earth holds from the air. Moisture churned by beetles and fertilized by generations seeking to be reborn.

(2002)

Tim Bowling (1964–)

Tim Bowling grew up in the rural community of Ladner, British Columbia, whose traditional occupations of fishing and farming instilled in him an abiding concern for the environment that supports them. His poetry is suffused with a sense of impending loss, and it represents an attempt, Bowling says, "to archive what is vanishing, to hold on to people, places, emotions that are continually being altered by time." For him, it is "the poet's role to observe and preserve."

After obtaining a B.A. in English literature at the University of British Columbia, Bowling returned to Ladner for another eight years to fish, read, and write poetry. The rhythms of his life during this period inform his first collection, *Low Water Slack* (1995). The title is Fraser River slang for a low-tide in which everything from fish to the human heartbeat slows down. It is a condition conducive to meditation, and accordingly, the collection opens with the long meditative piece "Ladner," in which the poet examines the conundrum of his existence. The traditional practices that structure his working day are a source of pride for him, yet he must live with the knowledge that he is a practitioner of death: as the salmon-fishing season is launched, the "killing months begin." The silver prey that flash through the water represent not only natural beauty but also commercial necessity: they are "a million fortunes swimming in from the sea." Throughout the collection, Bowling employs his lyric voice to invoke this ebb and flow in the contexts of local and family history, and the flora and fauna of "the river's silver abacus," but he also uses it to imply his impending departure from the world that has defined him: "the distant water doesn't call my blood; / the canyon-walls have yet to narrow for my climb."

In 1995, Bowling moved to Edmonton to be with his future wife, Theresa, and to study at the University of Alberta. In 1997, he completed an M.A. in English literature and published his next book, *Dying Scarlet*. The book is a series of lyric elegies, although the poet admits "I don't know anything certain about the dead / except they're gone." Among others, he eulogizes John Keats, the progenitor of his own poetic language: "In my wrists live the ghosts of all the words / ever written in his, and his Queen's, English." In a poem dedicated to his grandmother, he laments the sad history she inhabited: the "dashed Irish dream," the existence contaminated by "poverty's pox and polio." And he envisions his grandfather, caught up and unravelling in the hell of World War I trench warfare: "trench rats ... gnawed his poise / to the quick."

For Bowling, writing is a means of connecting with a physical space and the cultural memories connected to that place. He explains that the most important thing about creating poems "is the sense of a dialogue with something outside the self, with other people, with other species, with the elements, with the dead, with the cosmos, with mystery." His collection *The Thin Smoke of the Heart* (2000) explores this dynamic by focusing on the weather. In these poems, windstorms and heavy rains, like those Bowling experienced during his childhood, represent human vulnerability to the unpredictable patterns of weather; climate fluctuations parallel the unforeseen shifts in people's lives. His next effort was *Darkness and Silence* (2001), a collection marked by his yearning to establish the interconnectedness of things through vivid metaphorical imagery and to thus access history, the natural world, a spiritual dimension. But the portal remains elusive: in "The Past," he writes, "Through the rotting cave / of the baby narwhal / on the beach / is no way back // ... nor down the gaping tunnel / of a grizzled lab's howl."

Memory and loss, themes that pervade so much of Bowling's poetry, emerge again in his first novel, *Downriver Drift* (2000), which is set in the fictional Fraser River settlement of Chilukthan. The narrative centres on the Mawson family, who, like Bowling's own clan, rely on B.C.'s salmon fishery to survive. As the Pacific salmon moves through its mysterious life cycle, the Mawsons' fortunes rise and fall, the industry whose history is so intimately intertwined with their own is under siege, and the landscape around them slowly degrades. Bowling's follow-up novel, *The Paperboy's Winter* (2003), is also set in Chilukthan and engages similar themes of memory and loss in the natural and human environments. Clear-eyed 10-year-old protagonist Callum remarks that "The shadowy, gently haunted place of my boyhood ... had almost vanished, replaced by strip malls, fast food franchises and gated condominium developments named 'Heron's Shores' and 'River Point.'"

Returning to poetry, the prolific Bowling produced several more collections. Each was grounded in the landscape of his childhood, although he was by now well entrenched in Edmonton. "People often wonder if you have to leave a place to write about it. I don't think that's true, but your imagination is called on in a different way if you're not actually in the place and you have to visualize it." The Governor General's Award–nominated collection *The Witness Ghost* (2003) is a series of elegies written upon the death of the poet's father, Heck Bowling, a Fraser River salmon fisherman. Engulfed by feelings of loss and anger, the poet reaches back to recapture the time and place where his father's spirit resided — a world of old wharves, fishing boats, and flowing waters. Remembering, however, cannot alleviate the pain of loss, and even the act of lyrical self-expression seems to perpetuate it: "without you," the poet writes, "there's a cut that cannot heal / and I feel it when I hold the pen."

Bowling's preoccupation with memory and penchant for elegy also characterize *The Memory Orchard* (2004), for which he received another Governor General's Award nomination. In the poem "Mannequins," he identifies in the "eternal dusk, the ring / of a mortal register echoing / like a stone dropped / farther and farther down / a well" — the sound we hear "is what memory hears," in "supple, cadenced tones." In writing these poems, Bowling says, he had the births of his three children and the death of his father on his mind. He was "haunted by the fragility and brevity of our lives," and he became "compelled by the enormity of having to say goodbye to everything."

Fathom (2006), Bowling's latest collection, extends the poet's Fraser River meditation. It is a lyrical evocation of a home that is in danger of vanishing forever, an attempt to convey, Bowling says, "some of the richness and intensity of that world" — that "eerie, trembling half-mile between the totem pole and cenotaph, its rain-swollen blackberries and orange-gold salmonberries, its particular flavour never to be tasted again, but just there, hovering, an inch from the lips."

Bowling has also edited a book of poets' interviews with other poets called *Where the Words Come From* (2002), which he dedicated to the memory of one of his influences, Al Purdy. In 2005, Bowling left Edmonton for Gibsons, B.C., where he now lives with his family.

Dying Scarlet

> I have had a great deal of pleasant time with Rice lately,
> and am getting initiated into a little band — they call
> drinking deep dying scarlet.
>> — Keats to his brothers, January, 1818

John Keats and his circle in their cups
died scarlet. And the poet's life
to its dregs did the same, his linen
bedsheets and nightshirt finely spotted.
The world loves him for drinking so deep
from the few years he had, for those pretty
tipples he took from his days' good wine;
the world honours blood flushed in a pale
brow that leans over blank pages in candle-
flicker, giving joy, believing. Vitality   10
is beautiful even coughed on a lace cuff,
o little red cosmos, little red heaven,
that last breath exhaled before dust
and the cold grave smothered his youth.

I don't know anything certain about the dead
except they're gone, young Keats and his brothers,
the two women named Fanny[1] he loved, his friends,
the publishers who respected his art, the guardian[2]
who didn't, Shelley with a drowned volume[3] in his
shirt-pocket under Italian stars,[4] gone. A century   20
of letter-writing, gossip, tuberculosis and poems.
And I don't know where the spirit of any poet goes
if it doesn't die scarlet wherever it can, Keats's
joy in October sunsets over the Adams River, full in

---

1. **two women named Fanny** Fanny Brawne, Keats's neighbour and love interest in his teen years, and his mother Frances.
2. **guardian** After his parents' death, his guardians removed him from a literary school and put him in training to be a surgeon. 3. **Shelley ... volume** Percy Bysshe Shelley (1792–1822) wrote the pastoral elegy "Adonais" in Keats's memory, after the model of Milton's "Lycidas." 4. **Italian stars** Keats died in Rome.

the salmon's scales as they scrabble to spawn before
the air eats to nothing their lace-threaded bones,
Keats's fear in the eyes of the ring-necked pheasant
shot out of its heart in the blue skies of my marshland
home, the long script of its death trailing off

30   into the ditches and rushes. I have heard the music
of his lines gasped from a thousand slack jaws
while the world stood crowded on the riverbanks,
amazed; my hands have touched the spots of his truth
on a thousand downed wings still quivering in frost.
In my wrists live the ghosts of all the words
ever written in his, and his Queen's, English;
they gather in my pulses, drinking life, dying scarlet,
unrestrained in their gaiety and rowdiness, dying
like the salmon and the pheasant and the flushed

40   eves of fall, dying as a poet dies, face turned
towards what's left of his life, the spatter
of his joy's heaven on his clothes,
the light going out on his page forever, the wax
of the last candle on his nightstand melted down,
as he lies grieving for every second he's lost
of the sun: I don't expect to know the vivid dawn
that finally dissolved the gay circle of Keats,
but if I'm blessed to die scarlet on my native ground,
let the wind dig a grave for my pallid[5] song.

(1997)

The Line

Why did I come to it? Where is it drawn?
How does it lie, and what divide?
If I speak of blood, will you not admit
that selfsame pattern holds you up?
We are nothing but variations of it,
and when we see, and if we see, and how,
decides the nature of our step across,
by land or sea, by flesh or word.
This one points particular, this one

10   is the wet chalk of my life on the board.
I follow it here, to where division began.

Two o'clock in the morning and a tired man docks his boat.
He has taken four tides into his hands and few fish. Now
he's going home. Finger under the gill, he hefts a red
spring from the deck, and steps heavily onto the wharf.

---

5. **pallid** Pale, uninteresting.

The river is calm and smoking a low mist into a sky
so black the stars seem close enough to be the blur
of sleep in the man's eyes. He tenses his wrist and
trudges his gumboots over the planks and up the gangway
to the top of the dyke[1] and down to the street, alone   20
with one streetlamp, his own footfall, and a line
of blood he doesn't know he leaves, a line the pull
of his finger in the salmon's gill began, a stream
along its scales that drips off its tail and marks
a black spine for the moonshadow he drags behind.

Half a block to his gravel drive, he lays the line,
the last spool of the gaping mouth. He doesn't take
the ache of it in his wrist for more than life,
the heaviness of muscle and water, for more than
one night following another in one summer following   30
another on the same black river. But his hand gaffed
the line and now the line is drawn and now it burns
and will not be erased. And someone else besides
the tom who creeps out of the grass to lap the spark
will wake and swallow its chill power to the marrow.

Gash of lipstick on the Salish[2] girls the druggist's
wife remarked were sluts and stole, my mother's boss
who bid her sell the Indians the gaudy tones and save
the upscale glosses for her kind. Gash of trench
my father's father breast-stroked through, his own   40
blood for a pool, and all the opened veins of boys
that serviced the rank geometry of a continent.
Gash on the brow of the scab[3] who cried fuck off
to men who blocked his path, and wore the vivid badge
for those who hid behind immaculate counting hands.
And gash of ink to keep the cheap gloss on the proper lips.

Why did I come to it? Where is it drawn?

How does it lie, and what divide?

But also it is the beautiful flesh of the inside of the throat
going all the way down to the cry of joy and terror,   50
and it is the long kiss and the juice of the black plum
and the tightrope over the precipice of memory and
the pricked fur of the fox's run. It is unwound from
the mouth of all the dead to be rulered by the born,
it is the tongue of the garter snake that smooths

---

1. **dyke** Breakwater. 2. **Salish** First Nations group of western North America. 3. **scab** Temporary labourers hired to replace a company's normal workers when they go on strike.

the grass for the child to kneel, and the finger of wine
that indexes a song from the cowering heart, and it is,
and it is, the fever of the love of the sound of itself,
unwinding, strand in the web, vein in the wrist, star
60 in the constellation, the naming and the singing
of the felt and the seen. Tomcat at the mad wick,
I know your hunger, I came out of the cradle of blades
to taste what I did not know I was starving for,
all sides of all things, the fire in the soles
of the dancer and the mimic fire of the coals,
but more, to touch this world in its four tides,
and take from it the means to lay these down,
my variations and my nature, out of the gaping mouth
in my father's hand, a lifted selvage[4] from the one design.

(2000)

The Rhododendron

Childhood has its own grave, and mine
is tombed by the purple rhododendron
blooming again in my mother's garden.

Tonight late bees engrave an epitaph
on the heavy flowerheads, and dusk
settles chalk-grains over their work.

The death of all life is sickly-sweet,
why not the years? There is no threat
in this black earth and this air wet

10 with the grief of stars. And rain,
each drop, stands straightbacked when
the bees have done, mourning the time

when a child breathed here and the grass
gave way to his light tread on the last
spring evening of a wonder so chaste

it was the only reality, the only truth.
A child has no patience for any death.
But once an adult, is it really enough,

this standing purple clutch of memory
20 washed round by darkness, night's sea
of hours on the gentle ebb, infinity

---

4. **selvage** Edge of woven fabric.

salting the petals? Time is a grave
that digs itself, and all we have
to do is consecrate it when we leave.

A grizzled black lab guards the portal
to the tomb. My mother's arms are full
with remembered weight; her low whistle

calls me back one more time to home.
But it is only my young ghost who comes,
a faded and gentle hour in his bones,

and pats the dog, and kneels in the rain,
and hears the woman's steady heartbeat again   30
clocking the desecrating step of the man.

(2000)

The Witness Ghost

I woke in the dark to your voice
(trickle of creek over rock,
clench of tide around pile).
We left in the dark, the old way,
down the lampless, houseless block,
past the row of wild cherries,
the crunch of our boots on gravel
like the drawn-out growl
of an old dog who doesn't really
mean it. And when the blossoms   10
touched my cheek, I understood
you had turned back to kiss me
without turning. I went into
those kisses like a bride.

There wasn't any light, though the stars
shone. It was as if someone
looked at us without seeing us;
we could have waved our arms
and never raised a blink. Half-
asleep, I lulled in your easy wake   20
along the wind-scoured parapet[1] of dyke[2]
down the gangway to the mossy wharf.
A mast chain shivered as we left the planks.

After you had warmed up the boat,
I stood aside and watched you choose
to steer from the cabin not the deck

---

1. **parapet** Defensive outer wall. 2. **dyke** Breakwater.

because a spider in the night
had attached a strand of web
to a spoke. I almost heard you sigh
30   for the ruin you'd have to make
later, when the dictates of your work
lorded over gentleness, as if
you had to spare a life for those
you planned to take — a reverse sacrifice.

The river trembled, sheened to silk.
Heavy in the damp, the musk
of mud and creosote.[3] Distantly,
a coal train cried, leading
its black pod a little closer
40   to the kelp. I woke
further. At the towhead,
beside an island of rushes
slightly rising and falling
like the roped chest of Gulliver,[4]
I saw the little throw of lights
up Grouse Mountain, in North Vancouver
where you'd been a boy, splashing
truant in creeks so silver that, whenever
you moved your body, even to kill,
50   something essential had been smithied,
struck from fire.

The corks rolled off the drum.
You steered across the channel
from the stern. I stood
beside the doomed cathedral
on the deck, my heart
still as the unsuspecting spider.
For ten minutes, we strained
to hear a salmon hit the net.

60   Then we picked up. Closer,
I watched you hang above
the ripping silk. An urgent whisper
and I came beside you, on rubbery
tiptoe, staring into the drip of black.
Slowly, you bunched in your hands
the web as soft as muddied lace.
We bent like two sunflowers
seeking the earth's internal light.

---

3. creosote Pungent oil distilled from wood and tar. **4. roped chest of Gulliver** In Jonathon Swift's *Gulliver's Travels* (1726), the tiny people of Lilliput hold Gulliver to the ground with ropes.

Shhh. The unending caution
of the breeze. Your lips   70
had become the vessel of the race.
In your hands, the will to strike.
In your eyes, the wonder that you would.
I hunched into the sudden shadow
of your shoulders, gaping like a baby owl.

Something big was down there. You held
a single mesh between thumb and forefinger
and traced its tooth-snagged geometric
on the air, careful inch by inch. Then angled
the hook of the gaff, prepared to strike.   80
In the invisible, acrid clots of exhaust,
I held my bones and heartbeat in,
stifled a cough.

The downward arc dipped
in the black before it pierced
the skull in the fatal crush,
striking up from under
at the gill. You rarely missed
and knocked it loose, or stuck
the hook in the valued flesh.   90
A painter's skill — you must
have traced the pattern of death
ten thousand times
in the roiling dark
until even your sleep was etched
with crossing lines so thick
they came to mimic
the grains in a woodcut.

And I was the spider who watched.
I was the pupil in the crystal,   100
widening, my black into the black
of the earth, that has to turn and kill
whatever's formed from the guts
of the self — nothing gentle
in the fall of a blossom
onto a street black
as the lid of a coffin,
or in a bubble of black froth
at the torn jaw of a salmon,
nothing gentle in an art that   110
traces out lines only to turn
and stuff its own creation
in its mouth.

Yet I woke this morning,
and will always wake,
to your voice
and the hopeless task
of replication,
to string along the web
120   without breaking
the first, struck silver
of dew, and listen for
the dying-as-it's-born
echoing afterclang of hush.

(2003)

Does the World Remember Us?

Sated[1] with garbage and guts
the gulls on the roof-peak
saw me lick the scent of blackberry from her bronzing shoulder
and gawked as, storm-browed,
I pelted stray cats with rocks.
When weren't they there,
those brine-eyed judges
in their robes of ash, turning
10   into the wind to watch me puke
my first cheap bottle, stretching
their necks toward the time
I helped the mind-blank
and shivering old neighbour home.

And how many pitiable bullheads
gaped in terror at my blue intention
to destroy, or dew-fleshed salmon
saw my hand-tombs scrape across
their vision of the infinite and clear?

20   It must be coded in the species now,
so that this very moment's
gulls and fish must sometimes snap
awake to flashes of remoter terror
so real they seem less like the present
than the past the long dead
of their own kind lived
(where even acts of gentleness
fade in the quick of killing).
Memory keeps the suffering vigilant.

---

1. **Sated** Satisfied.

From the rooftops, the deep tides,   30
out of ditchbanks, cloud-currents,
telephone wires, prickle bushes,
beyond compost piles, shed-shadows,
wharf-shadows, grass-shadows —
this flinch from the imprint of power.

Senses wide, I remember
the world's gallied[2] look
and a weeping so quiet
those years couldn't hear it
for the sound of moths   40
shaking the dark off their wings.

                                                                                      (2004)

Memory

I write this with the hot ink
of the red stripe on the back
of a garter snake stopped
a second in the tall grass
beside the Fraser River
under a sky of August fire.

I reached into a closet
racked with bones
in a condemned house
I put my arm through   10
the dark of the dead
to wet this quill
I leaned all my weight
on the dust and air
(nobody there
but this moment, still.)

My younger arm
I kept behind, the one
that stayed six seconds
longer in the womb.   20
With the other
like a blind man's
cane, heavy
with all weather,
I went back
and dipped

---

2. **gallied** Frightened.

my right index finger
into the baked
strip of flesh
30   parallel to, still
as, the river.

I did not touch
the child who stood
just as still
beside the snake
though his hand
was hot and open
at his side
and full of blood.

40   Here is the poem
of the low red smoke
in the permanent
grass. I want
you to read this
as the child read
that stillness
of the world,

quickly
with the older
50   and then, slowing,

      the younger eye.

(2004)

Lisa Moore (1964–)

Lisa Moore was born in 1964 in St. John's, Newfoundland. She grew up there and, after spending time in Halifax and Toronto, she returned to "the Rock" and made a permanent home in St. John's. As a child, she exhibited a keen interest in the visual arts and, strongly encouraged by her parents, she explored watercolour and pottery. This early preoccupation with hands-on creation did not wane. Moore took courses at a community art school called 77 Bond Street, and she enrolled in the Nova Scotia College of Art and Design in Halifax, where she earned a B.F.A. She says that "Seeing people make art about Newfoundland gave me permission to think you could write from this place." But even after making the transition to writing — prompted, in part, by an "urge to spill the beans" — she says that she felt the need to "talk about the textures, colours, types of mark making, subject matter, and point of view shown in painting and photography, and compare these techniques to similar ones used to create fiction."

    Moore went on to study creative writing at Memorial University of Newfoundland, and there she fell in with Burning Rock, a collective of local young writers (among them Michael Winter and

Ramona Dearing) who had met in a class led by English professor and writer Larry Mathews. They would discuss each others' work in progress; their approaches and orientations were divergent, but they were united by their sense of place and their professional ambitions (Moore says, "We were writing to publish"), and they provided invaluable mutual support. Moore's stories appeared in two Burning Rock anthologies: *Extremities: Fiction from the Burning Rock* (1994) and *Hearts Larry Broke* (1999).

In 1995, Moore published her first collection of short stories. *Degrees of Nakedness* is a series of reflections on love, in all its aspects of joy and anguish, set in contemporary Newfoundland, a landscape at times marred by traces of the lives that are now unfolding within it. In "Wisdom Teeth," in which a young woman etches the story of her life thus far, we see the town of Stephenville: "one traffic light, a penitentiary, a bar called the El Dorado, and a long beach with round stones, driftwood and pink tampon applicators." Moore's female narrators long to speak, to get the story out. They suspect that there is something crucial to be learned through self-exposure: the narrator of the title story has become "interested in nakedness," and wants to do an art project that involves photographing herself naked around the city in the early hours before people re-inhabit the streets, and although "not usually one for telling strangers things," she has developed the "habit" of confiding "intimate" details of her life to a cafeteria lady in the building where she works. These stories examine love's tyrannies and betrayals: in the title story, the narrator's lover ("First love") tells her to jump off a cliff, and she does; later, she tells him, "You're unravelling fast ... like a composite drawing a police artist makes from the testimony of witnesses." They also evoke love's sweet, fleeting moments of unification: in "Meet Me in Sidi Ifni," the narrator's "knees dug into the back corners of the chair around your waist. I rose and dropped over the wavelets of frost on the window like a mermaid. A horn honked. And honked and honked. Never mind, you whispered, never mind."

In 2002, Moore's second collection of stories, *Open,* appeared, and it won a Giller Prize nomination. Like the stories in *Degrees of Nakedness*; these tales are grounded in contemporary, largely urban, Newfoundland, and they explore complex human relationships through arresting images and depictions of the electric moments on which our lives turn. Again, love in its many stages and tragic manifestations is an obsession, and Moore undermines our assumptions about it. In "The Stylist," a woman (Moore signals her dislocation by using the second person) is abandoned by her husband and lost inside her loneliness — "he didn't want. To be married anymore. To you." At twelve, she has a sexual encounter with her pedophile swim coach, but as she summons the memory, the moment is transformed into a flash of perfection in a world of suffering: "He kisses and kisses. You have never. Nothing will ever be as wonderful as this. You give yourself over/over/over."

In this volume, Moore also experiments with narrative structure, breaking chronology, fragmenting conventional time frames to approximate the function of memory. In "The Way the Light Is," the prose repeatedly breaks into the text of a film shooting script and the story's formal construct takes on the elasticity of film; a video of a traumatic birth now "plays in reverse, until the baby has disappeared, unwinding history," and mimicking memory's capacity to eradicate what is too painful to contemplate.

In 2005, Moore produced *Alligator,* her first novel. A teenaged eco-terrorist named Colleen watches a training video made by her aunt many years earlier. In a state of passive fascination, she sees a professional alligator wrestler insert his head between the jaws of a seemingly subdued specimen and experience a terrifying brush with death. Moore has said that the predatory nature of the alligator prompted her to use it as the central metaphor of this novel dealing with the separate struggles of a set of characters who, although they seem compelled to place themselves in dangerous situations (heads between jaws), strive to overcome loss and assure their own survival. "I was interested in the metaphor of a predator, but also, it's just such a way to survive. And what do we do when it's just a question of survival? How do we behave?" The narrative point of view changes with each chapter; tenses shift, and there are alternations between the first person and the third. The independent story lines finally merge in a harrowing conclusion. Asked to explain why she constructed her novel in this way, Moore draws on another metaphor: "I thought of [*Alligator*] as an orchestra, and I wanted it to be a portrait of St. John's — not told through a central narrator but the way a city would tell its story. It's told through a wide range of voices, and no voice is privileged. In the way that with an orchestra, a maestro would say, 'Now the drums, now the violin, up with the trumpets,' the characters, when I sat down to write, came up in those ways." The novel was shortlisted for both the Giller and the Commonwealth Prize.

In 2006, Moore selected and introduced the stories in the *Penguin Book of Contemporary Short Stories by Canadian Women.* In her introduction, she writes that she made her selections for the volume by focusing on the pieces that were "most haunting." She sought stories in which "Nothing was recognizable, nothing was simply itself. Everything felt foreign, altered, and new." Moore writes for television and radio as well as *The Globe and Mail* and *National Post.* She lives in St. John's with her husband and children.

Grace

On the shiny collar of her black tuxedo jacket, at a potluck after the wedding, Eleanor notices a ladybug. Orange shell, two black spots. Under the jacket she wears a crimson dress. The skirt a pattern of folded, satin diamonds, each diamond held with a red bead, so that if she were to attain grace, or spill her beer, or be overwhelmed with some fleeting infatuation — she shouldn't drink in the afternoon; she can see herself in Glenn Marshall's sunglasses, her black patent leather purse like a match head folded in the flame of her skirt — if she were visited by a moment of grace, the beads of the dress might drop to the grass and the diamonds unfold into butterflies. She grips the wet beer bottle. Too cold to be outside. The tulle under her skirt scratchy against her bare legs. She'll shave them before the reception. Where is Philip? At the heart of everything, she thinks, is the question of behaving with grace. He is falling in love with someone else. They have an understanding, is the phrase people say. Couples who agree to open marriages, an understanding.

A big wind lifts the umbrella out of the hole in the centre of the plastic table and it pirouettes for a few seconds across the lawn on its white metal spike. Glenn Marshall makes a swipe for it, arm raised, fist empty. What she has decided: She will sleep with Glenn Marshall. An understanding is something for which you must acquire a taste, like all the other great things in life: coffee, wine, oysters, bungee jumping. A crowd of guests move out of the path of the careening umbrella. It knocks against the picket fence. A paper napkin flutters off the table and dips, like a dove shot out of the sky, a gash of lipstick on its breast. The crystal bowl of strawberries catches the sun, a tiny prism shoots across its sharp rim. The rowing shells on Quidi Vidi Lake[1] glide fast. A team of women with yellow caps hold the oars above the water. They lean forward, they lean back. A riot of sparkles bursts around the prow. The last rower raises her hand to her cheek and is obliterated in the glare.

---

1. **Quidi Vidi Lake** Adjacent to St. John's, Newfoundland; site of the Royal St. John's Regatta (rowing competition).

The ladybug on Eleanor's jacket is still anchored. She's here somewhere, this woman Philip's seeing.

Eleanor closes her eyes. The afternoon sways, the lawn, the voices. The summer is almost over. She can smell fall. Once at the Ship Inn Glenn Marshall put his hand on the small of her back. She'd been dancing in a black minidress and the cotton was damp.

He said, What are you doing?

Getting a beer. What are you doing?

It's dangerous, talking to you.

Dangerous?

You have beautiful legs.

That was last summer, the same hint of fall. Just that, his hand on her back, the cotton damp with sweat. *You have beautiful legs*. She was ahead of him, leaning into the crowded bar, one heel lifting out of her shoe. He steadied her.

She can see Philip in the sunroom window, listening to a woman with a blond ponytail. This must be the woman. She's on tiptoe, he bends his ear toward her. Eleanor sees him yank his tie. Her mouth close to Philip's ear. Then a cloud moves, making the window darken, and she can't see him.

What's Philip doing, she asks Glenn Marshall.

Philip is having a good time. Believe me.

She feels the earth turning. The heels of her sandals driven into mud beneath the wet grass. She'd made a rice salad with sesame oil, red peppers. Last night the taxi driver said, See that moon, that's weather. I had a wife once who could make a meal out of nothing. You had your moose, you had your garden. I got a different wife now, different altogether.

Eleanor was making everyone tell the moment they had come closest to death.

I like moments, she says, any kind of moment. Cut to the climax.

Glenn Marshall was once in a helicopter, sighting the neck of a galloping moose with a tranquilizing rifle, and they came near a cliff, and whatever happened with the wind, the helicopter dropped for ten seconds. He told the story while buttering a roll. Turning the knife over and over to clean both sides in the bread. He said in accidents like this, the blades keep turning, driving down like a corkscrew, decapitating passengers.

Eleanor told about the crashing Nepalese tour bus, the front wheel over the cliff edge, the TVs bolted to the ceiling still blaring some Indian musical with a harem of dancers poised on three tiers of a fountain, all sawing on miniature violins. Big breasts, pillowy hips. When the second wheel of the bus thumped over the edge of the cliff, the fountain hung sideways, the dancers still perched, still grinning and sawing away on the violins in jubilant Technicolor, defying gravity. She had seen, through the window at her shoulder, fire smeared over the steel side. They were on fire. She and Sadie sleeping under a single bedsheet. The windshield shattered and fell into their laps. The bluish glass tumbling into the folds of the sheet, caught in their hair. They had raised their arms to cover their faces.

And there they were, in Nepal. What opulence,[2] how quiet. The pressing crowd squished them, lifted them off their feet. They were borne out of the bus and fell on their knees and got up quick, quick.

Get away from the bus, get away before it blows.

Dawn; a woman in a sari on a dusty road with a water jug on her head and the sun coming up behind her. The real moment is the flutter of the sari. The snap and thwonk of fabric in the breeze. The silence. Someone taking out a map that crackled in the hot air like eggshells. But Eleanor stops telling the story just as the second wheel of the bus flops over the cliff.

Leave your audience hanging.

She says, Beneath you could see buses that had already crashed, crumpled on the rocks. Then the second wheel rolled over the edge and we could feel the bus rocking.

Glenn leaned back and rested his arm over her chair. She could smell the muggy, spring-like sweat of his body. The nearness of his arm made her blush.

She thought: And Philip wants to leave me.

These were the categories of moments: the most famous person they'd ever met, the most romantic moment ever experienced, the most embarrassing. Earliest memory. Luckiest moment. The last time you peed your pants.

Constance told about waking in a field when she was seven with a bull eating grass, snorting water droplets on her cheek, horns yellowed like an old toilet. How she ran, hot pee trickling down her legs, yellow on her white ankle socks. When she'd climbed the fence, stopped to catch her breath, leaned over to puke, she could see the blue sky and clouds in the shiny black patent leather shoes an aunt had sent from St. John's. She lights a cigarette and blows the wedding veil out of her face.

She says, Will someone get me out of this contraption?

Constance grew up around the bay, an only child, raised by her grandmother. She says she was bathed in the kitchen in a big galvanized tub in front of a wood stove. Can this be true? She remembers when television arrived in Newfoundland. They all gathered in one house to watch. She's a chef with a Master's in Religious Studies. Medieval witches. Magic, black and white. Eleanor has watched Constance paint braided pastry with melted butter, skin rabbits, flick dollops of fresh cream off a wooden spoon into chocolate mousse.

Once Philip had made Eleanor open her mouth and close her eyes. He'd had candles, they'd smoked some dope, him scrabbling under the bed. *Keep 'em closed.* A ball bearing dinging back and forth in the metal can he shook, *I said keep 'em closed,* and the raucous sputtering, her mouth blocked with Reddi Wip. Loops of Reddi Wip over her nipples, her chin, her nose, her hair.

Constance looks like cotton candy in the dress. Eleanor can't, for the moment, imagine her in other clothes. She was made for the wedding dress. Busty and pink-cheeked. Satin is perfect for her, iceberg cool and pleasure affirming. She was made, actually, to be in a Russian novel; a kitchen with a fireplace as big as a bed, the game-keeper banging on the door with a wooden staff, a brace of quail over his shoulder, and

---

2. **opulence** Wealth, abundance.

there is Constance presiding over her blood puddings, her four children in muslin[3] walking in the pink cherry orchard.

The whole wedding dress swishes from side to side as she hands out puff pastry with brie and caramelized onions. Her auburn curls sliding from the combs. The low scooped neck. She'd pulled the whole wedding off by herself without complaint. She had enjoyed it. Constance knows how to get by on nothing, she and Ted, the four children, and the scabrous,[4] moulting husky with an eye infection — they are always broke. But when it comes to a party, Constance is easily extravagant. What's money for? A tiny glass tube of saffron she'd picked up at a specialty store on the way back from the Sally Ann where she'd bought the girls' jeans.

Yesterday Eleanor had visited and Constance was sitting at the kitchen table, smoking (an orange silk blouse, that's the sort of thing she wears), cheek resting on her hand and the counter full of loaves of bread, the tops glistening with butter. More dough rising. She sat in front of the window, taking a break. Making Eleanor a cup of tea. The rowing shells on the lake passing by her shoulder. Yesterday the lake was still, and the oars touched down and came up splashless. The kittens knocking over the jade plant. Giant piles of laundry. A stack of books about the plague, one on alchemy. She'd had four children, each a year apart. Alchemy she knew; the Pill she didn't bother with.

Eleanor had said, How do you do it? The bread. Constance waved a dismissive hand in the direction of the counter.

The bread makes itself, she'd said. There's nothing to bread. But the lamb. She opened a magazine and tossed it toward Eleanor so she could read the recipe.

Maybe if I'd learned to cook, Eleanor said vaguely, snapping the pages of the magazine. She stopped at a perfume ad, a crystal decanter stopper trailing down a woman's throat, her pouty lips parted.

Or wore perfume.

Constance narrowed her eyes, then opened them wide, tapped her cigarette vigorously.

You have to behave with grace, is my advice, Constance said.

Grace is boring.

Nevertheless.

You could uninvite her, Eleanor said.

I wouldn't give her the satisfaction.

And now Constance is married to Ted. The service held on Signal Hill, the wind whipping her veil into a beehive over her head until the bridesmaid caught it and batted it into submission. The priest is a man who shot the windows out of that church you can see from the highway. Red paint along the white clapboard, "These Windows Shot Out By A Catholic Priest."

Eleanor opens her purse, drops her corsage inside, and snaps it closed. She lifts the neck of her jacket. The ladybug is gone. She'd wanted to show her daughter, Gabrielle. They'd been looking for a ladybug months ago, to make a wish.

Frank Harvey is talking. Frank says he found himself doing the husband thing. A stone fireplace in the basement, some plumbing, other couples on Friday night talking

---

3. **muslin** Cotton fabric. 4. **scabrous** Marred by bumps and scabs.

about this shade of wallpaper or upgrading gas barbecues, and all the while he hated himself.

You discover that you are an asshole, he says. He winces. Tilts the lemon slice in his gin from side to side.

An asshole, he says. That's what happened to me. It was a terrible thing. I took up yoga.

The moment you faced your worst fear, says Eleanor.

She tells about her mother trapped in her living room with a white weasel or mink. After Eleanor's father died. Eleanor had been seventeen, in Stephenville, wrapped in a snowstorm, a giant wooden custard cone banging off the side of an abandoned convenience store. She's trying to work it into the screenplay she's writing — the custard cone squeaking on its hinges. Ice in her eyelashes. Later, in the student residence, the phone ringing down the hall, running to catch it, and it's her mother, in her kitchen in St. John's, standing on the counter. Somehow a rodent, fat as her thigh, long as her arm, had gotten into her house.

A white weasel or mink tearing through the green and gold shag carpeting, crazed. Eleanor could hear its piping squeals. Her mother, a tall woman, neck bent awkwardly, the back of her head touching the stuccoed ceiling. The stucco swirled with a scrub brush, a new idea then. They had a spiral staircase, a smoky mirrored fireplace. They had an open-concept upstairs, a lake, and in the winter veils of snow sashayed all over the dark ice. The snow could come up to her mother's waist, and Howard, a mentally handicapped man who lived down the road, would come and shovel. Eleanor's mother would bring him a Pepsi with ice, which he paused long enough to drink, his frosty breath hanging, his fluorescent orange cap. Just the two of them with no one around for miles. Her mother standing beside him, waiting for the glass.

And this became her mother's life after her father died; she was only occasionally terrified; the mink's eye flashing that alien green of trapped animals and then black again, under the dining-room table.

Most erotic moment without touching. The cork of a wine bottle rolling over a faded yellow rose on the tablecloth under Glenn Marshall's palm. His hand on her back. That might have been a moment of grace. The Ship Inn on a summer night blocked with people, standing space only, some event at the Hall getting out, the band deafening, summer dresses, tanned faces. The way the light slowly tinted the sky over the South Side Hills indigo, yellowish, pale blue. The desire to keep going, another bar, someone's house, her new sandal destroyed. The sidewalk on Duckworth Street. A police cruiser slowing beside them and moving on. Glenn Marshall had whispered something in her ear, I'd like to go home with you. She had sobered up immediately. The cool breeze coming up from the harbour. The smell of the sea.

I'd like to do nice things to you, he'd said. How illicit and tender it had sounded. Sweetly wrong. Hokey and forward! The prim fervour with which she explained she could never, ever, ever hurt her husband.

Frank Harvey is still talking about the moment you discover you're an asshole. A Sunday afternoon in Bannerman Park, he says, hungover, fragile, children making the diving board reverberate, wind in the leaves, and it hit me. It was so cleansing, such a relief. He's smiling at everyone. Frank Harvey is holding court. The sun hits his balding forehead. It gleams as if he is physically projecting his new wisdom. He's good to have at a wedding; he's the entertainment.

Eleanor thinks: How dangerous to fall in love with Frank Harvey. She could always do that if Philip leaves. It would be *torrid*. Yes, there would be battles in public, dishes shattered, lovemaking outdoors, in movie theatres, planes. Bike trips across Canada, leanness, bracing, voluntary poverty. She would have to shave her head or become vegetarian. Type on a manual typewriter. Maybe take up smoking. She could be a female Ernest Hemingway, grow a beard. It would be invigorating. Philip, stunned, shaking his head at some luncheon. Philip regretting his blonde. But Eleanor is already too old for Frank. His lovers are all under twenty-five, they are giggly, svelte, and have asymmetrical haircuts. Eleanor doesn't have a haircut.

You see what I mean, says Frank Harvey, you're an asshole, you have somewhere to go from there, don't you? I rejoiced. No, seriously, I did. It was so unequivocal — my assholeness. The clouds broke and the sun poured down, cleansing me. I was cleansed.

Frank takes a moment to close his eyes and lift his palms and handsome face to whatever power cleansed him. This is ninety-two percent delivery, but the content he means. He means what he says. Timing, he understands. He's parodying himself parodying himself. He's dead serious. He opens his eyes and says almost viciously, I was brand spanking new.

Is Frank Harvey what they mean when they say bipolar? Or is he truly very, very near enlightenment? What enlightenment looks like: his eyes are so clear. He is so bursting with health. So goddamn sexy. Eleanor decides enlightenment would take too much energy. A lot of honesty. She's hardly ever deceitful — she imagines herself hacking a path of truth through a vast field with a machete, stopping only briefly to wipe the sweat from her brow.

But Philip believes he is duty-bound to lie whenever it makes life easier. Eleanor imagines herself from an aerial view, the path she's hacked winding in on itself, a spiral. Then she briefly allows herself to imagine Frank Harvey's penis. The word *dong* leaps to mind. Something big and friendly. The sound of cymbals at the gateway of the Forbidden City. The whack of a baseball against a bat. Ying yang, ding dong. With Frank she could be oblique,[5] like a heroine in a bodice ripper, Frank, *take* me.

The smell of cinnamon from a tray Constance passes under her nose and Eleanor is back in India with Sadie, ten, no twelve years ago. Icy air-conditioning, thwack of ceiling fans. How real it becomes for her sometimes. She can smell it. They were asked to be extras in a movie. Two shady-looking men outside the Salvation Army hostel in Bombay. They said, Meet us here at five in the morning. We'll fly you to Bangor. You'll be paid. Eleanor terrified, Sadie gung-ho.

Is this a good idea?

Sadie: Are you kidding? This is the *movies*.

With yoga, says Frank Harvey, there is so much pain. I tried to bury my self-hatred in pain. The instructor was so good. She really hurt me.

The Indian movie agents came for Sadie and Eleanor at five a.m. Drove them to the outskirts of the city, and beyond, into a dry landscape, almost desert. How had Sadie

---

5. **oblique** Indirect, backwards.

become so brave? And somehow this drive, during which Eleanor believed her twenty-three-year-old life was ending, and during which Sadie sang Joni Mitchell songs for the two men who had abducted them, her elbows flung over the front seat — *he bought her a dishwasher and a coffee percolator* — singing with deep feeling, though they are too young to understand how sad or practical a dishwasher can be — all of this becomes vividly present. She remembers even the crack in the window, the rubber Ganesh (why is he blue) jumping on an elastic hanging from the rearview mirror. She was once this: a woman in the back of a car in the desert about to be killed/be in a Bollywood movie.

And now she is what? Philip *might* be leaving. How will she support herself and Gabrielle? She has to finish her screenplay. She could get at least three or four thousand in development money if she tried. Even if the film went nowhere, four thousand. There are avenues. A little low-budget video thingy. A seventeen-year-old girl in Stephenville going to art school, old army barracks buried in snow, the El Dorado Lounge, the Grim Reaper, losing her virginity, her father's death.

The most erotic moment without touching: watching the nineteen-year-old boy, the first guy she'd ever slept with, sculpting a clay torso. Squeezing water from a sponge over the breasts, making the clay shiny like licked chocolate, a drip hanging on the nipple, the slosh while he dips the sponge, the water hitting the clay with a patter; he talks to her while his muddy hands smooth the muscles in the torso's belly, the ribs, the clavicle. He sponges the curve of the torso's neck, and Eleanor's hand creeps up itself to her own neck, and they both notice and laugh. They laugh, but she is blushing, hot.

The screenplay was taking forever. The penultimate scene, a Halloween party in a sprawling bar. That much would be cheap enough to shoot. Sometimes she still thinks about feasibility. She used to think about it always. But the more true the script becomes — the closer she is to describing the loss she felt with her father's death — the less she cares if it's feasible. Sandra, the lead, is drunk in the penultimate scene. She has made up her mind to lose her virginity. The town is buried in snowdrifts; it's a white film. White. Oh, the young girl Eleanor imagines playing the lead. Beautiful because she's that strange mix of child and adult, a changeling, like all sixteen-year-olds, but ordinary-looking too. The camera will always be close up on her face. The boy Sandra has decided to sleep with, a student at the school, is dressed as the Grim Reaper. He goes to the bar for beer and another Grim Reaper comes to her table and takes her by the wrist.

Eleanor looks for Sadie, who is supposed to be at this wedding party but who is late. Always late. She's in picture-lock, the message on the answering machine said. The film she's working on; they've got the final edit. She won't miss the potluck, she promises. I'll be there, okay. She's bringing Peach Melba isn't she? How could she miss the potluck? But it's almost over already, the potluck, and there is no Sadie.

She and Sadie were not killed in the desert by talent scouts as Eleanor had thought they would be! Instead they were extras in a Bollywood movie. They met a harem of dancers. Women who had been trained in the art of classical Indian dancing since they were five years old. Women who wore pale pancake makeup to lighten their dark skin. Kohl around their eyes. Plump, luscious women who fell asleep on wooden benches at one o'clock in the afternoon, dressed in brown calico[6] housecoats. The Vamp (in the

---

6. **calico** Light cotton.

dance number, she peeks coyly out from behind a palm tree, searching for the Prince she's about to seduce away from his virtuous wife) had chased Sadie around the change room. Sadie letting out yelps, leaping over benches, the Vamp trying to pinch her bum, the other dancers squealing, shrieking. Sadie backing her bum into a corner, bent double with giggles. Moments later the dancers huddle together, whispering, and they turned as a group. What, Sadie demanded. The Vamp stepped forward: You both must shave your underarms, it's terrible. To appear on film like that. Have you no shame?

There had been a poolside scene; a long line of dancers held striped beach balls over their heads and then fell sideways into the water, one after the other, like dominoes. Sadie and Eleanor among them, arms raised over their heads. Gloriously hairy armpits. They stood in line, the smell of chlorine and the burning sun, the music bursting into action, the Vamp shimmying to the water's edge, tossing her gorgeous black hair, slitting her sexy eyes at the camera, and one by one, the dancers fell into the water. None of them could swim. They began to drown as soon as they hit the water, the revved-up, hysterical music droning to silence, long black hair floating on the water, choking, coughing, panic. The cameramen reaching over the edge of the pool with poles. Sadie and Eleanor dragging the young women to the side, saving their lives after each take.

Eleanor walks across the lawn toward the house. She hears Dawn Clark's voice above everyone else: I *know* the Net. You've got a demographic of nineteen-year-old males, what are you going to do, sell them walking canes? I don't *think* so.

Eleanor goes inside, gets herself another beer from the fridge. She thinks, This beer will be the ruin of me. But it's cold; the frost smoking off the lip of the bottle cheers her up. There is Philip. She walks over to him and lays her hand on his neck. He turns and looks at her, smiling while he talks. He has forgotten, for the moment, that he wants to leave her. Whatever he is telling Constance is more important. Eleanor and Philip are together at the potluck. They might go on forever. They are surrounded by friends. The rowers glide past on the lake. The room is full of flowers. The children are playing in their fancy clothes. Gabrielle waves to her from the lawn, the long grass combing her lemon dress.

Philip telling Constance about his book. Constance holding her forehead in her hand, elbow on the table. She taps a cigarette. She's listening to globalization, still in the wedding dress.

The Swedes moving traffic from the left to the right side of the road, Philip says, without a hitch, overnight. Things can change overnight.

Eleanor has an overwhelming urge to pour her beer down the back of Philip's shirt. How dare he think of abandoning her. She has given up travelling the world with Sadie for him. They had promised to travel all their lives together, she and Sadie, no matter what. She has given up jungles, and rides in rubber dinghies in murky lagoons, and pyramids. Why had she ever given up being who she was to love Philip? (He knows everything, everything, and is handsome, his big hands on the cheeks of her bum, last week she came in from a rain that bounced like ball bearings on the pavement, the house booming with Glenn Gould,[7] so loud it was tactile, in the banister, in the linoleum, the Goldberg Variations, she yelled his name, and waited, and yelled again, but he

---

7. **Glenn Gould** Canadian pianist (1932–1982).

couldn't hear over the music and the shower and the rain and up the stairs two at a time, her coat, a boot, her sock, her shirt, the jeans — dropping them as she went — the other boot, the sock, the underwear, the bra, and she stood on the other side of the shower curtain, waiting, listening, the bathroom foggy and hot and the leaves of the spider plant on the windowsill trembling from the music, she got in silently, he was standing with his eyes closed, his hands resting on his chest and she cupped his balls and his eyes flew open and he screamed. He scared her so much she screamed, and they stood as if electrified, her hand on his balls, screaming into each other's face, then laughing, then fucking, the wet slap of their bodies.) He thinks it's wrong to stay in a relationship if you are in love with someone else. He does not believe in *weathering through*, or *for the children*, or *because you promised*. He believes, simply, in doing what you want.

First of all, Philip doesn't believe in anything. He believes strongly in not believing in anything. He believes Eleanor's whole problem is that she wants so desperately for there to be a *right* way. She has been too chicken-shit to shed this last vestige of her Catholic upbringing: the desire for a universal moral code, which, once understood, leaves only the small matter of putting it into practice. If he were to believe in something, it would be: admit what you want; get what you want. This line of action requires great stores of bravery. Apparently it's not as easy as it sounds. But to do otherwise, Philip believes, sets in motion a whole chain of actions and events which totally fucks up not only life but everyone's life with whom you come in contact. To do otherwise is to act dishonestly.

There is something so blazing and committed about this baldly self-centred stand that Eleanor loves him all the more for it. She refuses to love him less. He's stuck with her. He is what she wants.

Eleanor goes back out on the lawn. Glenn Marshall is where she left him. She'll tell Glenn Marshall about the Taj Mahal, the warm marble and smell of feet. They'd seen a man levitate in front of the Taj Mahal.

But Glenn loves Newfoundland. He doesn't like heat, prefers cool weather. He wouldn't want to be on top of the Pink Palace with lithe monkeys. She has told him before, she suddenly remembers. She has told him that story before, about the Bollywood movie. Glenn Marshall had been mildly interested. He had listened, but he shook his head and said he'd never go there. Why would he? He loves Newfoundland. As if there were just the two choices: the Taj or Little Island Cove. He loves being in the woods by himself, he has a cabin, can build a lean-to, set snares; he does some ice fishing, he likes the quiet.

Who is she kidding, she could never love Glenn Marshall. But if she slept with him. Maybe if she slept with him. Things can change overnight. The entire city of Stockholm, was it? Driving on the other side of the road as though they always had.

Frank Harvey says, And I had an epiphany, alone in Bannerman Park on a Sunday afternoon. I realized it was *okay* to be an asshole. I rushed out to tell my wife about the affairs I'd had, you see, I had already forgiven myself.

What was Glenn Marshall's most erotic moment without touching? Eleanor can only think of the galloping moose. He had kissed her on New Year's Eve and said, How do you like a moustache?

Ted says, Constance sent me flowers in the middle of a rainstorm — someone announced it over the intercom at the bookstore. I was in the back room tearing off the covers of old Harlequin romances. A big box of white roses.

Ivory, says Constance.

The salesgirls falling all over themselves to find a card, says Ted.

The first night Eleanor slept at Philip's apartment; walking up the steep hill from Kibitzer's, broken beer bottles glittering by the curbs, someone's white bedsheets flapping on a line. She walked under the sheets, the damp cotton stiff with frost when it brushed over her face. She turned to watch him, a big hand bashing through, the clothespins pinging into the air, and then the rest of him tumbling, falling. They were twenty-one and he had a three-year-old daughter. A light came on in the row of public housing, then another. They were rolling down the hill in the sheet. Grass, mud, stones, sky, stars. The sheet wrapped around them like a cocoon they wriggled out of together.

A snowy afternoon at four o'clock; walking past the war memorial with his three-year-old child on her shoulders, Eleanor counting change for a block of cheese. They had the macaroni already. They were a family overnight, some sort of family. The change in her hand just enough! The child's shiny red boots hanging beneath her chin. Dusk swooping down on Duckworth Street, the second-hand bookstore still lit. Slush seeping into her boots. Holding tight to the child's ankles. Later the steam rising from the pot in the kitchen, she and the child painted fish on the clear plastic shower curtain. The who-she-was disappearing fast, gobbled by the who-she-is.

Frank Harvey says his wife went insane with jealousy when he told her about the affairs.

I've avoided women like that ever since, jealous women. I can smell it, and if I get even the faintest whiff, I'm gone a hundred miles in the other direction.

He sounds so right, Eleanor thinks. She vaguely understands that everything Frank Harvey says is informed by the year of silence he spent in a monastery in Korea. Frank Harvey, the mime, had not spoken for an entire year of his life. It helped, he'd said, that no one spoke English. Cut down on the desire to blurt, he'd said. You come to understand the sublime beauty of chitchat, the fragmentary, absurd, chaotic, feral[8] meaningless of everything we say. Whatever else about Frank Harvey, he is a talented mime. He can do the glass wall thing, of course, and the Michael Jackson moonwalk, but he can also run on the spot in slow motion as if he were being chased in a nightmare, his bones melting, and then he is caught and devoured by some unnameable monster you can almost smell. He can hold invisible animals in his hands, quelling their struggles for escape. She loves how convincing Frank Harvey is. Convincing is the thing to be, Eleanor decides; it doesn't matter what you're convincing about.

I came to love talk, Frank Harvey says, I live for it. And I learned how to tell a joke, he says. You must never telegraph the laugh. Let the material do the work. The best joke I ever told, I waited a year to deliver the punch line.

What was the joke, Tiffany White asks. Tiffany is a bright, new nurse who has arrived from Thunder Bay. Eleanor realizes she is taking Frank seriously.

That was the joke, says Frank Harvey. You didn't get it?

---

8. **feral** Wild, untamed, savage.

What was?

The joke was it took a year to tell the joke.

Frank turns back to Eleanor. We parted after that, he says, speaking of his wife. There was nothing left to salvage.

It's some Buddhist idea of Frank's, Eleanor thinks, we can't possess each other. We shouldn't even want to. She has an ache in her chest as if she had been Frank Harvey's wife, the one he had cheated on a thousand million times. She wants to defend herself against his airtight argument, that jealousy is vile. What kind of man doesn't talk for a year?

Constance takes a tray of honey garlic meatballs from the oven. The woman with the blond ponytail is sitting next to Philip. Amelia Kerby from British Columbia doing a PhD on Canadian ecofeminist novels. A gold lamé dress: she had met Leonard Cohen in Greece, had somehow gotten invited into his limousine as it pulled away from a concert. Fans tearing open their blouses and squashing their breasts against the car windows as they pulled out of the garage.

She says, I put my hand on his crotch, he was wearing black leather pants, and the sun through the window made the leather hot. I couldn't help myself.

Eleanor: Your hand on his crotch, that's not without touching. It's supposed to be an erotic moment without touching.

The first night she and Philip slept together, he was sitting in an armchair and she sat on the frayed arm, in a homey downtown bar. *Last Tango in Paris*[9] was playing on a snowy screen bolted above the bar. Brando with the butter. Maria Schneider, those breasts. Empty apartment. The French are forever living in empty rooms with high ceilings and open windows, curtains.

Sadie's boyfriend, Maurice, has such an apartment. He wanders around it all day with a glass of something, and sighs, and writes something down, and wanders around the apartment some more. For this he gets a fair bit of money. As far as Eleanor can tell, that's all he does, but Eleanor doesn't speak French, so. Schneider's heels clattering on the tiles, the butter. The last movie ever about pleasure, expansive, extravagant, expensive, anger-incited, dangerous pleasure. Or pain. She isn't sure now.

At night in a hotel in Southern India, Bangor, monsoon rains drilling rivets in the corrugated tin roof, a week after the movie shoot; Sadie shook her awake. Sadie had opened her diary to an empty page. She was running her fingers through her hair and lice fell onto the clean paper. All those drowning dancers had lice.

We have them now, Sadie said.

Long shiny black ropes of hair floating in the aqua water, covering Eleanor's face and arms as she dragged the drowning dancers to the poolside after each shot.

You have them, said Eleanor. I don't have them.

The next day they were at a train station. Eleanor went to buy a drink and the train started to pull away without her. It was halfway out of the station gathering speed. Sadie's voice from a dark window, already in the white sun of the countryside. Jump on, jump on.

---

9. *Last Tango in Paris* A 1972 film set in Paris, starring Marlon Brando and Maria Schneider; it created a sensation due to its graphic sex scenes.

Eleanor ran and a soldier in khakis with a rifle leaned out of the last car and offered her his hand. He pulled her aboard, and she yelled into the countryside, rice fields flashing in the sun, I'm on the train, Sadie. Then she sat down on a sack of grain and hung her head, feeling her fast-beating heart and, at the nape of her neck, the crawling lice.

Eleanor opens her eyes and pulls the heel of her sandal slowly out of the mud. She has been out on the lawn most of the afternoon. She can feel the heat of a late summer sunburn. She turns, looks up at the bedroom window.

Constance and Ted have disappeared. And this is Ted's story, she thinks. His stepfather woke him with the tip of a kitchen knife pressing into his windpipe when he was fourteen. Ted inching his back up the wall, his palms squeaking against the floral wallpaper, until he's standing on tip-toe, the knife pressing hard into his throat. The most terrifying moment.

Ted says, My father died when I was three. After my stepfather arrived we weren't allowed in my mother's bedroom. That's why I let the children sleep with us whenever they want. They just pile in, all four of them and the dog. Constance can't stand it.

She hasn't seen Ted or Constance for an hour or more. They must be making love. Consummating their marriage. All the guests on the lawn filling their faces. The wedding dress on the hardwood floor, a sinking angel food cake.

Ted's brother Earl, a hulking rugby player, leans over the railing of the verandah, a champagne glass in his giant ginger-root hands, as delicate and incongruous as an icicle. Earl had gone to New Brunswick with his wife after a bankruptcy; he had five children. He worked in a cola factory for a time and was electrocuted while moving an industrial appliance. Enough electricity to lift him off his feet, blow him across the floor, and smash him against the wall. The moment you came closest to death.

He says, I lived because I kept my eyes open. If I'd closed my eyes I would have completed the circuit, and self-combusted, and this is the truth of what happened, whether it's scientifically true or not.

When Earl recovered he bought himself a small wooden table where he could sit and write poetry. He wrote several poems every day and understood his interest to have been ignited by the bolt of electricity. He called Constance late at night and read her the poems long distance, and she boxed up all her Eliot and mailed it to him.

Eleanor has imagined, ever since she first heard the story, that the electrical bolt had blown through Earl, back into his past, powering the restaurant he ran, the jobs he gave all his friends, including Eleanor (who once dropped a bowl of cod chowder down the back of another waitress), reached all the way back to the moment when his stepfather held a knife to Ted's throat, and protected Ted in a web of blue crackly light. Because Earl, with his near seven-foot height and boulder chest, wasn't a talker. Ted did the philosophy degree; Chad, the youngest, roamed the country with his thumb, became a clothing designer; and Earl protected, just as he was doing now, leaning on the verandah, the glass tipped, his eyes squinted against the glare of the lake.

Eleanor says, What do you think grace is, Glenn?

She's thinking, if she could attain grace, even for a moment, everything would fall into place. The scenes of her film script would snap together like a Rubik's cube, the scales would fall from her husband's eyes, and he would recognize how lucky he was to have her; Frank Harvey would return to his wife, or at least call and tell her she had been right all along. All women would be right. Glenn is watching Earl too. He doesn't speak until Earl turns and walks through the screen door, holding his fingertips against the wood frame so it doesn't bang.

Below Constance's bedroom window, the sunroom window. She sees a white streak that might be Philip's shirt.

Weasels don't come in white, Glenn says.

The one in my mother's house was white. It might have been a mink. Like spilled milk. My mother stood on the kitchen counter and it ran through the rungs of the chairs under the dining-room table.

I don't believe it, he says.

But you believe Leonard Cohen and the squashed breasts? You believe Amelia Kerby?

Amelia, Eleanor overheard while getting her beer from the kitchen, has also made a smallish fortune designing aromatherapy atomizers to squirt (mist, was the verb Amelia used) in the faces of colicky babies to shut them up (encourage serenity, Amelia said). The gold lamé dress was shipped from Paris; it had been packed in helium.

What have you got in those atomizers, asked Constance. Agent Orange?[10]

Amelia's uncle was a marine biologist. She had written a novel about eco-conscious cyborgs, a moral tale as yet unpublished because Amelia hasn't decided who to go with, apparently. She had bumped along the floor of the Atlantic in a two-person craft. There was nothing much to see down there, she said. It was dark.

Eleanor wants to tell Glenn Marshall she remembers him touching her back at the Ship Inn. Does he remember it? His hand on her back, a pulse of neon lighting up her bones, her hip, her ankle, all through. Once she heard Leonard Cohen dedicating a song to all the people who had conceived children listening to his music. The elegant arrogance of it. But Gabrielle was conceived that way. An attic bedroom in Toronto during a heat wave, a fitted bedsheet working its way off a coffee-coloured futon, she and Philip satiny with Toronto sweat. The whole day walking Yonge, crowds, bursts of music, exhaust, neon in daylight, sex shops with things she'd never seen before, battery-operated vaginas that could smoke a cigarette, the smell of hotdog stands. A food wrapper blew against her shin, squiggle of ketchup. Pastry shops. Even the breeze was hot. The sidewalk where they lived covered with blossoms. All part of their lovemaking, and Leonard Cohen singing about Joan of Arc.[11] *Make your body cold, I'm going to give you mine to hold.*

They had a tiny fan jammed into the window that did nothing but make a noise that she felt on the edges of her teeth. This was the cement of her love for Philip: this attic room, the swelter of summer, Newfoundland a gazillion miles away. She went with him to write her first film script. She'd written a naked skydiver. Swinging like a lazy pendulum beneath the big red bulb of a parachute, the sky behind utterly blue.

She had dreamed a skydiver, and he compelled her to make him real. The room she and Philip shared was so small that when they both sat at their desks the backs of their chairs touched. He went to the university during the day, and when it started to get dark outside she would listen for his footsteps on the sidewalk under the window. Listen for his key, the sound of his knapsack hitting the floor, the zipper of his jacket, the Velcro of his sneakers, the cats rubbing against his legs. She anticipated him. Tried

---

10. **Agent Orange** A harsh herbicide used in the Vietnam War. 11. **Joan of Arc** Track from Leonard Cohen's 1971 album *Songs of Love and Hate.*

to piece together who he was, and he was this: the cracked leather of the knapsack, dusk, clammy heat, the sound of coffee beans being ground in the kitchen. The unrelenting desire to fuck. She promised herself all day she would wait for the little things, the kiss, to take his earlobe in her teeth, unbutton his shirt, take a long time between each button — but her desire leapt all over itself, and she would want him inside her, couldn't wait.

Glenn?

He might have fallen asleep. The children are throwing a Frisbee at the edge of the lake.

Eleanor says, I want to be full of grace. Then she's embarrassed. What is she talking about, at a wedding? She is clearly drunk. She firmly reminds herself: You can't be sexy and maudlin[12] at the same time.

Glenn says, Grace is bestowed, you can't will it.

Grace is bestowed. Everything worth anything is like that, she thinks. You can't just know what you want and go get it, as Philip says. You wait. She closes her eyes. Watches the lake through her lashes. Wait for it to come to you. She can see the children, silhouettes, standing on the rim of the lake as if they will upend it. It's only late afternoon, there's still the evening, there's more drinking to do. There's a lot more drinking.

Frank Harvey says, It's about identity. My wife started to think of herself as us. What we made up together.

Frank is right. You have to be able to be alone. If only she could sleep with someone else. Once at the Ship Inn she could have gone home with Glenn Marshall. That first time with Philip she thought: I will spend the rest of my life with him. She thinks, I have never questioned this, and I have acted upon it. I have built a twisted organic life around the assumption that Philip was meant for me. She imagines the great coral reef around Australia as her life — as if Philip is Australia and she has accrued[13] around the fact of him. Coral accrues.

But she's afraid to be alone. Gabrielle had been afraid last night too. What was it? Can she guess her father might be leaving them? (But he's not leaving Gabrielle, he has explained this patiently to Eleanor several times, she keeps forgetting. But you're leaving, aren't you? I might be leaving, yes. You might be. Yes, and Gabrielle will come with me half the time. Gabrielle will go with you? You're leaving and Gabrielle will go with you. Sure, she can be with me half the time. In some apartment. Yes. So it's me you're leaving. I might be leaving you, he says. And you think that will be good for Gabrielle? He shrugs. It won't be a good thing, he says, maybe a necessary thing. Gabrielle will be fine, he says. He turns back to the computer. He doesn't let one thing overlap with the other. He might be leaving, but right now he has to work on his book about globalization.)

Gabrielle sobbing at the foot of their bed, her upper lip shiny with mucous. Eleanor let Gabrielle drag her down the hall. They stood in the doorway, she and her seven-year-old daughter. Eleanor saw the streetlight hit the dull glass of the hobbyhorse's eye. She

---

12. **maudlin** Stupidly sentimental. 13. **accrued** Grown.

saw a rust-coloured flare thin as a needle in the button. Sinister and pulsing. Gabrielle terrified. It's alive. It's *thinking*. A horse's head on a stick. The wind blew hard against the house, the windowpane rattled, and the fierce light, deep in the horse's button eye, faded and went flat. Shadows of leaves tumbled over each other on the wall above the bed, like galloping hoofs, a spooked herd all turning at once. Gabrielle's hand sweaty in hers, her face wet, nose running.

Eleanor thinks, I'm such a *dupe*. The shame she feels is so overpowering she could throw up all the red wine she's been drinking, and the beer, and the goat cheese thingies. She could throw up over the red dress with its folds and beads. She decides she will go in there and kick Amelia Kerby and punch her, knock her teeth loose. I will cut her into pieces and wear a chunk of her around my neck on a rope until it rots. I will not speak to her, I will not notice her, I will be aloof, condescendingly kind, I will invite her to dinner parties, rise above it all, befriend her. I'll sleep with her myself.

Her skin gets cold, and she thinks just as suddenly, It's not so bad. I'll go to China. No one there will know Philip has left me. A clean, simple life in China. They'll never hear from her again. Someone had gone to China already, that doctor whose wife left him. There was a rumour he'd remarried, he was happy, had new children. Chinese children. The rowers have lined up next to the buoys. A team of women in orange tank tops. They just float while the coxswain[14] harangues them. A shrill whistle. Eleanor thinks, it's very unlikely that I will go to China. Instead. Gradually, over time, I will get over Philip. My passion for Philip will cool. That's what happens. People *get over it*. They eventually get over it. This is the worst thing: to imagine normal without him.

Someone places her hands over Eleanor's hands. Eleanor reaches up and touches the wrists. Sadie! Eleanor is so happy she feels sharp little tears.

You're here.
Did I miss anything?
Amelia Kerby. She's over there tossing back champagne.
The gall!
Gold lamé, the ponytail.
She looks short to me. Am I right?
Ecofeminist.
Hefty, I'm thinking.
Here on scholarship.
What's with the tinfoil dress? How Walmart.
You think?
Sure I think!
She's into aromatherapy.
Of course she is.
And bungee jumping.
He'll get tired real quick.
Naked, they bungee jump on the West Coast.
Real quick.

---

14. **coxswain** Steersman.

Eleanor hadn't taken the scene of the naked skydiver to the pitch meeting. She'd had a Styrofoam cup of coffee, and when the producers looked at each other and told her, as kindly as they could, that a *big record producer from the mainland sweeping a local girl off her feet* was a cliché, the cup trembled in Eleanor's hand. She spilled hot coffee on her thumb. And she'd said, with her voice all funny, Well, originally he wasn't a record producer. He wasn't? No, not originally. What was he, originally? No, it's too silly. Tell us. It's expensive. Tell us. It's impractical, dangerous, you couldn't get anyone to do it. But originally you had something different? Well, I see him falling from the sky. This beautiful man. He's handsome, strange-handsome not ordinary-handsome, and he's got a beautiful body. Beauty is good. We should celebrate beauty, and he's naked, that's the hard part, he's naked. Naked skydivers, they have them. There are such things. There was an ad in the *Telegram*, and my friend, Sadie, she decided she wanted to jump when she saw the ad. She wanted something big and dangerous. Just their bums in the paper with the parachutes wafting behind, a promotional ad. Sadie had to do a one-day course, how to land, bend your knees, and then there she was hanging on to the wing, the guy in the plane yelling at her, Jump, and her yelling back, Jump? And him yelling, Jump! And her still yelling, Jump? And finally the guy in the plane, he leaned out and he just edged her feet off the step with the side of his shoe, he basically pushed her feet off the step, and she let go, and that was it. So Sally — my character, Sally — is driving along a country road and she pulls over because she sees something, she gets out, and it's a naked skydiver. The whole thing is about fate. Big theme, fate. Sally feels fated to be with him. She watches him fall, her hand over her eyes to block the sun. And he lands, and rolls, and gathers up the parachute, and lopes over to her, he's loping. He's out of breath. Buck naked. A naked babe. There's this big field behind them and the sun, you know, going down.

The producers looked at each other, looked at Eleanor, We could do that. You could? We could do that, yes. You could do a naked skydiver? We could, yes, we could.

Gabrielle comes around the corner of the house, whacking the grass with a cracked broom handle. There was a scream for attention in each whack. She has lost one of the gold earrings her grandmother gave her. She wants to be absolved. She leans on Eleanor, rocking gently.

How's my girl, says Sadie.

What, Eleanor asks Gabrielle. What do you want? What? Gabrielle won't mention the missing earring. We have heard enough about the earring, thinks Eleanor. She was too young for gold. Eleanor is tired of Gabrielle. Tired of the wedding. Tired of losing things. She wants it to be tomorrow already. Her neck, the back of her neck, she realizes, is tired.

Hi, Sadie, Gabrielle says. Then she grabs Sadie around the waist in a fit of passion, burying her face.

I love you so much, Gabrielle says.

Are you having a good time at the wedding, honey, Sadie says.

Gabrielle rocks harder, stamps her foot.

Eleanor says, What?

Nothing.

Tell me.

Nothing. My earring, she whimpers.

You're impossible, Eleanor says. Philip comes out and sits beside them.

What's the matter with her?

The earring your mother gave her. Philip rubs his hand over the stubble on his chin. The French, he says, are sometimes full of crap. Do you get that feeling?

Is it crap, Sadie says.

Philip says, But still, I'm like you, Sadie, I prefer the French.

Where's Maurice, Eleanor says.

He's showing Constance the dish he made for the wedding. Seaweed something or other.

We'll have to eat seaweed, Eleanor says, how gloomy.

Nobody has to eat anything they don't want to, Sadie says. He's very clear about that. It's part of his *thing*, his whole thing. He thinks it's totally fucked up to eat out of politeness. And you don't ever lie, or make promises; that's also part of his thing.

We all have a *thing*, Eleanor says. If someone makes a dish you eat it, that's my thing.

Philip says, I'm not eating seaweed.

Or marry for convenience, says Sadie, you never do that, according to Maurice, even if you need citizenship to get a job so you can stay in the country and be with your lover whom you supposedly love.

I'm eating it, says Eleanor.

Or marry for any reason. Or have children, because that's a promise in itself. Never making a promise is part of Maurice's thing too. Although he loves children, says Sadie.

I also love children, says Eleanor, children are also part of my *thing*. Staying married is part of my thing. And just generally being nice to people. I believe in *being nice*.

Philip grabs Constance's dog, who is trotting by and stares into his eyes.

This dog wants to tell me something, Philip says.

Maurice loves other people's children though, says Sadie. He loves this little girl for instance. She gives Gabrielle an extra squeeze.

Philip says, I think the dog is starting to look like Nicolas Cage.

Eleanor says, Try new things, right? Isn't that right Philip? My god, there's a whole ocean of seaweed out there.

They shot the skydiving scene during a blizzard on the Bally-Halley golf course. The man they'd gotten to play the part was strikingly beautiful. Eleanor had said, You have a beautiful face. He was surprised to hear it. He'd been a weightlifter, said his thigh had once been twenty-eight inches around, he couldn't buy a pair of pants. His body was a separate thing, a thing by itself, he said while folding a Caesar salad into his mouth. He wasn't successful as an actor, had turned to repairing fridges, which is what his father did. A part comes up every now and then, he says. A part like this. She can tell he doesn't think much of nude skydiving. Of course, there's a stuntman to do the actual dive. But the actor must run across the field without his clothes.

Costume had sewn tiny heating pads into the straps of the parachute, but he was nude in the snowstorm. All the crew in knee-length eiderdown, the actor completely nude, running through the snow, gathering the parachute behind him. Eleanor hadn't written a storm but there it was. The shoot had been postponed and there was the storm. Two women waited outside the scope of the camera with thick blankets. The hulking actor trembling with frostbite. Everybody averting their eyes from his purple dick. The director called cut, and the girls ran up to the naked actor and flung the blankets over him and there was a consultation.

What the hell? I thought that was good, he called out over the field, hopping from foot to foot. Someone wiped his nose.

Snot? Snot on my goddamn face? I do the best goddamn performance of my *life* and there's *snot* on my face. Come on, let's do this thing, let's do this thing, he yelled.

The first time Philip cheated on her, if you can call it that, when it's out in the open, when there's an understanding: Eleanor and Philip had gone to a movie together, and afterwards they sat in the car, which was parked facing their house. It was raining, and the yellow clapboard of the three-storey house wiggled and snaked.

Philip said, There's something I forgot to tell you. When I was in Montreal for that conference, two years ago. I told you about the jazz, and the weather.

You told me about that, she says.

On the last night we were all going to a party in a hotel room. This woman and me, this very beautiful woman, we got into the elevator together. It was late at night. And we got out on the wrong floor. We were talking, about the conference, papers we'd heard. We got out in front of a floor-to-ceiling window, a whole wall of glass. And there was the city in front of us, spread as far as you could see, the lights. It was so beautiful. It shocked me. And I said, How beautiful. And this woman, she touched my hand, and she said, yes, let's get a room.

He turned the car on and let the wipers clear the glass for two swipes, and their house was solid again, the clapboard straight, and the car filled with music, the radio was on loud, jazz, several horns, Miles Davis, maybe, and he turned it off. The house went soft, melting. She looked at him under the streetlight. A splatter of rainy shadows migrating over his nose, across his cheeks. His hand still on the key, looking straight ahead.

How does this confession change things? The yellow house is still yellow, the harbour beyond, the Atlantic Ocean, the rain hitting the street so hard it rises in a silver fur under the streetlights. It makes Philip a stranger, she thinks. Like in the beginning, when she sat on a frayed arm of the chair at Kibitzer's and just wanted to go home with him but was afraid. Maria Schneider making herself come without touching — they don't exchange names, she and Brando, they just fuck while his wife lies in a coffin.

And you forgot to tell me this.

I decided not to tell you. I decided not to tell you, and then I forgot to tell you.

But that night, when I spoke to you on the phone from Montreal, she says. She tried to think of the night. He had called every night, waking her. She loved being dredged out of sleep, trawled into the bedroom. Out drinking, he'd said. A bunch of Newfoundlanders at the conference and his paper had gone well, he'd called to tell her something about flowers and stars. They had been drinking outside, it was an outdoor pay phone he called her from. Flowers had fallen into his beer, or birdshit. It was birdshit. Nothing about stars. There had been laughter in the background and she'd fallen back to sleep, blissful.

With great effort she speaks to Glenn Marshall: Last summer Gabrielle wanted a lady-bug, but they're like grace, you can't will them, either.

Glenn rises from his chair and his snifter of brandy smashes. She sees it fall, hot amber coming up to the mouth of the glass like a jellyfish.

You prepare for grace, he says. Thomas Aquinas said, Get ready. That's his advice, prepare.

Yes, she thinks, you wait. She glances at the window, but she can't see Philip, he has moved into the kitchen. She thinks of her mother and the white mink, how much was lost when her father died.

Eleanor says, It's about a girl who comes through grief via a sexual awakening.

The story editor says, What does that mean?

She says, When my father died, because essentially this script is about my father. Pleasure is a kind of betrayal, to feel pleasure, any kind of pleasure, after a death. Because pleasure is life affirming, and to go on living, enjoying life, when someone you love has died is to accept their death. And acceptance is a kind of betrayal, is my thinking here.

The screenplay is a messy jumble. Everything out of order. Full of dream sequences (self-indulgent, according to the story editor), the death, snowstorms, pregnancy, a prison where Sandra teaches art to a young woman who had attacked someone with a hammer (of course it's all true, the screenplay tells exactly what happened, her mother struggling to get the lawnmower into the trunk of her car so she could mow her husband's grave and finally throwing it at the car with a superhuman burst of strength brought on by grief).

The story editor takes up a coloured marker and approaches a flip chart. He draws a timeline.

He says, A half-hour screenplay is twenty-four pages. I want the grief fully realized by page four. I want to see the character attempt to overcome grief three times by page twenty. Three failed attempts, but each time she gets closer. I want the sexual awakening on page twenty. By page twenty-four she has come through.

And who is the father, the story editor asks.

Who is he?

I mean who is he, really, the story editor says.

She remembers her father bringing a Portuguese sailor home for supper when she was seven so they could hear a foreign language. She feels a burst of tears coming, her nose. But she won't cry in front of the story editor. In the elevator she noticed his black turtleneck, his raglan, his polished shoes. He has uncapped the marker. Death has made her father finite. She could list all the things he was. Everyone else, this man with the marker, Philip wanting to leave her, Sadie working on her film, everyone else is changing.

Like what was his favourite food, says the story editor, who did he read. What did he take in his coffee. You have to know these things about your character.

Who was it Eleanor's father used to read before bed?

Harold Robbins.[15] Eleanor can see Harold Robbins in raised gold script. Her father would fall asleep each night with the book open on his chest, having read only a page or two.

After her father died, Eleanor's mother had a nervous breakdown, and then began to see Doug Ryan. Eleanor first read Harold Robbins while her father was still alive, just two pages. Two forbidden pages when she was thirteen.

They had been jumping off the Ryans' wharf, knees tucked up. The smack. Plunging down through the tunnel of bubbles and the murkiness near the bottom of the lake, the mossy struts of the dock, underground springs spurting up, making warm pockets, remembering the eels balled together in the darkness.

---

15. Harold Robbins American author and screenwriter (1916–1997) whose books were controversial due to their overt sexuality.

Eleanor had known about sex, the facts, for a long time, of course. She had been kissed. (She'd just let her horse, a fine-boned pacer, out of the barn and the mare had bucked and reared, front hoofs pawing the clouds, neck tossing, back legs step-stepping in the deep snow, and Eleanor caught the yellow nylon rope snacking past her jeans, the mare yanking her arms, her hands burned by the rope, digging in her heels, her mother had company, and they'd brought their son, three years older than Eleanor, sixteen, he was drinking a cup of tea he'd taken from the house, standing in snow up to his knees, she had loved the horse, had spent winter evenings in the mare's stall with just a flashlight, the smell of linseed oil she used to clean the tack, the brushes, she knew the animal's body, the shiny black knees, the way to pick up the hoofs and remove stones with a pick, a flame of pink inside the right nostril, the wet snuffle of giant lips against her palm when she held out half an apple, the smell of manure, the molasses in the grain, the water bucket with a skin of ice, the blue salt lick, smell of horse in her hair, under her nails, outside trees creaking together, the starry, dark blue sky. Walking back to her house through the trees, all the while her family going bankrupt, the television murmuring, her father hitting the adding machine, hitting the adding machine, the washer going, piles of money in front of him, a dish with a sponge for counting, the adding machine, until morning, when she woke and found him leaning on the counter looking through the kitchen window at the sun coming up. He had cut up a grapefruit for her breakfast with a maraschino cherry in the middle. He was drinking his instant coffee.

Catching the horse's nylon halter, kelly green, bright against the blue sky, white clouds, after coaxing the mare into stillness, the white of her eye, Danny Martin came up to her and kissed her lips, he took his time, she could feel the mare's breath on her wrist, he was holding the cup and he tasted of milky tea out there in the snowbank on a spring day, the snow creeping back off the pavement, the asphalt shiny, the horse.

For weeks after, months, she imagined the kiss while falling asleep, and when her father sat her down on the plaid sofa and took her two hands in his, cradled them between his, explaining they would have to sell the horse, his heart nearly broken, she could hardly remember why she had ever wanted one.)

Harold Robbins described being overcome. Sexually overcome. Losing control. To think that such a thing could happen to adults. Those who made the world stable. Even after the bankruptcy, when there were less treats in the cupboard and no new clothes for a long time, everything had a certainty.

She understood why she hadn't been allowed to read the Harold Robbins. Her parents hadn't wanted her to know, and knowing, she could feel herself crossing over, becoming adult.

Terrified of the eels, which were definitely thickly knotted under the wharf, kicking hard to the dazzling surface of the lake; but as soon as she gets there, thirteen-year-old Eleanor forgets the eels, climbs up the slimy ladder to jump again, ribs heaving to catch her breath.

Mr. Ryan used to deep fry battered cod tongues and serve them with tartar sauce. The men always had one specialty and they were praised for it as if it were a miracle. Doug's cod tongues.

Somewhere she has heard the story, a famous editor had given Harold Robbins an advance after receiving the first half of a novel. When the final half came in, it was an entirely different story. The characters had different names, different crimes, different lovers, different settings. But Robbins wouldn't change a word. His editor found him on the Riviera. Robbins wouldn't leave his yacht. A champagne glass held high, women in bikinis. The editor claimed it would destroy Robbins's career, published the novel as it was, and nobody noticed. It sold as well as all the other Harold Robbins books. People read for the sex and wealth.

Glamour, thinks Eleanor, and she remembers Mr. Ryan's plastic toothpicks with the Playboy bunnies at the tip, in silhouette, jutting breasts and ponytails, the tiny cheeks of their bums perched on the picks, sticking out of the cod tongues. Mr. Ryan was being ironic with the toothpicks, making fun of himself, his inability to let loose. But the toothpicks were also a parody of the desire to let loose; he didn't believe in letting go.

Mrs. Ryan sent her to the house for ice. Eleanor had left the wharf, wandered up through the raspberry canes, eating some, pressing her tongue into the nubbly thimbles. Spiderwebs in the shade of the spruce trees wobbling with droplets of an early morning rain. Her sister, Fran, stood near the sprinkler for hours, the lines of water hitting her bright bathing suit in a burry asterisk of mist (the bathing suit was blue with bananas all over, the things that suddenly come back to you!), the steely threads moving over Fran's scrunched eyes, down her throat, chest, protuberant belly, and thighs. Hitting the sharp bones of her ankles and resting there like silver spurs.

There was too much sun. The Ryans' house was empty. She opened the freezer and took out the metal tray of ice. In the living room she lay the tray on the TV and picked up a Harold Robbins novel from the shelf. She checked the bay window in the living room, looked out over the lawn. She could hear the Ryan children at the wharf. The crashes of their bodies on the water, shrill laughter.

Mr. Ryan, just outside on the verandah, preparing the cod tongues. Their parents drank so much in the middle of the afternoon, thinks Eleanor. All day, in the sunshine with the fireweed swaying, the mild breeze lifting clouds of seed into the air, and the dark spruce with ribbons of lake hanging in the branches. They had been rich briefly, then the construction company had failed. The sprinkler reaching her sister's feet, and then, mysteriously, the water had dried up, someone, somewhere, had turned off the tap, and Eleanor's sister opened her eyes and blinked in disbelief.

It's such a shock when someone dies, all that energy, angst, desire, memory, love, the sheer *propulsion,* amounting to nothing. She just wants the screenplay to capture that: the shock.

The Harold Robbins novel: Eleanor on the cusp of puberty, small breasts, ears pierced with two ice cubes freezing the lobes, and then the sewing needle, a drop of blood; in the mirror, her earlobes as dark as cherries, burning, the delicate jiggle of the dark red stones in the gold settings, her grandmother's, the hot sting of the sewing needle through numbed flesh.

But I'd never read a word of pornography, she thinks.

She opens to the second-last page. A man is holding a gun, he has caught up with a woman he is going to kill. Eleanor can tell he has chased her through the five hundred pages, she has betrayed him again and again, and he comes back for more, they are in a room alone, his arm out straight, his finger on the trigger. (Maybe she should shoot Philip, blow his head off with a rifle, ruin Constance's wedding.)

I will be independent, she thinks. She feels alert, squares her shoulders, a cold breeze from the lake, the potluck is ending, she is out on the lawn by herself, had she fallen asleep? She checks her chin for drool. She wonders if Philip has been waiting for a specific date when he can leave, like Mrs. Ryan. Has he planned to leave her all along?

Grace was not bestowed, she realizes. Nothing. Was it something Philip decided one night, resolved, resigned himself to? Surely Mr. Ryan, arranging the bowls of tartar sauce, the toothpicks, the serviettes, must have known something was going to happen.

Eleanor's mother singing out: Doug's cod tongues, what a treat!

How unthinkable that he would one day be with her mother for a short time, he would, in his confusion after Mrs. Ryan left, turn to Eleanor's mother, who was herself so disoriented with grief, so lost, how unthinkable on that particular sunny afternoon when Eleanor read pornography for the first time. As if the characters of the afternoon had stepped into a different novel halfway through. Her mother in Mr. Ryan's arms. Her father buried on a hill overlooking the ocean. Mrs. Ryan seeing a lawyer in British Columbia.

The man grips the gun. The woman takes out her hairpins. Her shiny mahogany hair tumbles over her shoulders. She begins to unbutton her blouse. The man breaks into a sweat, he tries to look away, but he cannot. The woman reaches behind and unzips her skirt, it falls to her ankles, the man is trembling. He tells her not to move. She stands before him in a black lace bra and panties, garters, and fishnet stockings. The woman reaches back and unhooks her bra. Out on the verandah Mr. Ryan lowers a basket into the boiling fat and a roar rises.

The woman says, Shoot me if you can, Eleanor moves her head, feels her earrings jingle. The woman leaning against the wall, her breasts, the gleaming satin of her bra, Danny Martin's kiss. The man slowly lowers his arm, he cannot hold the gun out any longer. The gun drops from his fingers to the floor. The woman steps out of her skirt, walks across the tiles in her high heels, and steps into his arms. The screen door slams. Eleanor drops the book, kicks it under the skirt of the couch (the screen door slams, it's Constance, checking the garden for Eleanor). Mr. Ryan is surprised to see her. For a moment he stands on the other side of the room, basket of cod tongues. The eels are undisturbed, writhing together between the crevices of rock at the bottom of the lake.

The editor snaps the top back on his felt-tip marker. He taps the flowchart with it.

We should see the father, he says. Who was he?

Eleanor and Philip take Gabrielle home in a taxi before the reception. Apple air freshener. She meets the eyes of the driver in the rearview mirror. It's the same driver. The one with the different wife altogether. She grabs her lapel.

Gabrielle, look! But the ladybug is gone.

Eleanor's mother, Julia, comes to pick up Gabrielle. She's babysitting so Philip and Eleanor can have a night together.

She says, Yes, you do, you need it.

Eleanor's sister has shaved her head.

Why would she do a thing like that, Julia asks. Who will hire her now, a bald woman? It's dark in the house after the lake, after the wedding dress blaring like a trumpet, the tinfoil trays of food floating through the party like a school of capelin. Eleanor closes her eyes and sees the lake spitting sparks, soft sparks. A wedding is a sham, she thinks. Constance letting the screen door slam behind her. Shading her eyes to check the children, the dress lifting like the lip of a snowdrift.

Eleanor says, Mom, was that weasel white? That weasel that ran through the rungs of the dining-room chairs.

What weasel? There was no weasel.

Eleanor thinks of Amelia on tiptoe, reaching for Philip's ear.

I want nothing to do with Philip, she thinks. My life should have gone another way. Climbing hills in Nepal. But if there were no Philip, there would be no Gabrielle. She fills with a gutful of love for her daughter. Gabrielle's braids in her hands. Braiding her hair while it's wet. One loose strand near the temple.

Why can't Gabrielle stay here with her? Why can't she and Gabrielle curl up in bed and sleep and forget the reception? Forget Philip. If he wants to get loaded and sleep with someone, just let him go. Dusk, almost night, and she and Gabrielle could order fish and chips. All the rooms in the three-storey house dark, except the kitchen, salt and vinegar. She imagines a rumbling under the ocean around Australia, the coral reef bursting apart, bits of brittle coral flying into the sun like batons.

She feels a catch — and leave Philip to be drunk with that blond woman, dancing, pouring beer over each other's heads, and finally kissing? Glenn Marshall is wrong. You don't wait for grace, or anything, you make it happen.

The last time she had take-out she saw the cook, in whites, lift baskets of fries from the roaring fat and stop to tip a sickly bottle of Pepto-Bismol down his throat. Straight from the bottle, and drop it back into the breast pocket of his apron.

You go on, Julia says. Gabrielle is fine with me. You need a party.

Then Philip comes from the kitchen with a mug of ice cream.

Lots of people shave their heads, he says.

He puts a mound of ice cream in his mouth, leaning against the wall, and pulls the spoon out of his mouth slowly. The mound of ice cream like a fossil of the roof of his mouth, a soft steam. He sees Eleanor looking at his mouth and he raises an eyebrow. Immediately she wants to be with him, get drunk with him, dance, she is grateful that her mom is taking Gabrielle.

Julia says, Was that the groom I saw on Prescott Street directing traffic with two soup ladles? They got a picture of it, someone did. He'll be nice by midnight. Say goodbye to your mother, Gabrielle. Kiss your mother goodbye.

Gabrielle throws her arms around Eleanor's neck, their foreheads gently knock, they look straight into each other's eyes.

Gabrielle whispers, I'm going to have chocolate.

Philip squeezes past them on the stairs. Eleanor sits and listens to her mother's car doors. Hears the car pull away.

In the bathroom, Eleanor and Philip stand side by side brushing their teeth. He pauses, his mouth foaming, the toothbrush still.

What were you and Glenn Marshall saying?

He gets in the shower. Eleanor undresses and gets in with him. The water hits his shoulders hard. She lets her wrists rest on his shoulder bones.

Then she kisses his chest, down his belly, until she is on her knees. The water slides down his ribs like cloth. She makes seams with her tongue. She puts her hand on his chest and the water flows down her arm to the elbow, like an evening glove. The hot water costing a fortune.

She says, Will I shave my legs?

Philip draws her up, takes her breast in his mouth.

The reception is at the Masonic Temple. There are perhaps two hundred people. More than the potluck — and the food. Constance has relatives from Heart's Desire, older women in shiny dresses, purples, scarlets, blues, clustered at long tables with pink streamers, and flowers and patterns of marshmallow cookies, coconut-covered. Old-lady bifocals cutting the reflection of candle flames in half. They have brought trays and trays of food. Constance likes flowers. White roses at Christmas, always. Once on a winter afternoon she and Eleanor sat on the sofa and Constance said, I don't love him.

She picked a rose petal off the coffee table and smoothed it onto her chin. It hung there. It had been nothing more than a mood. It had passed. He asked her to marry him and she did.

But the relatives sit back as if they've done nothing. Arms crossed over broad chests, they sit back and the reflections of candle flames align in their glasses like the vertical pupils of cats, glowing from the dark corners of the Masonic Temple.

Sadie says to Eleanor, I kissed Constance on her satin shoulder. My lipstick on her wedding dress. My God, I'm not kidding. The whole dress is *ruined*.

There's a lineup at the bar. Eleanor sits and looks at the dance floor. Her eyes adjust to the dark. She can see Amelia Kerby's lamé flashing in the crowd. Her blonde hair is down now, curly. Her naked shoulder. She has someone by the tie. A chair screeches opposite her and Glenn Marshall gives her a beer.

She says, It's Glenn Marshall again.

He says, I don't dance.

Dance with me, Glenn, she says. She feels desperate.

That's exactly what I don't do, he says. It's Philip's tie. Here at a wedding with all of their friends. He is already drunk and she's holding him up by the tie. Constance drops into the seat beside Eleanor.

It can't last with Amelia, she says.

Things end, Eleanor says. She has heard this idea all her life — that things end — but took no interest. Now she tries it on to test its durability. She has always imagined she was building something with Philip. She had a do-good work ethic toward love. It was something you hammered, chainsawed, sized up with a spirit level, until it was absolutely durable and true. Along with something less substantial, a blithe, unexamined faith, airy as a cloud, that things were meant to be. There had never been a need to reconcile these conflicting notions.

She has no life experience, says Constance.

What do you mean, Eleanor says, she has her own apartment. She drives a rusting Volvo. What do you want? Eleanor's thinking of this girl hanging by her feet, bouncing like a Yo-Yo, up and down the side of a ravine on a bungee cord. Also her reportedly tidy apartment fitted with a Web-cam, and the grants that sustain her. Eleanor sees the lipstick mark on the gown's shoulder, a perfect full mouth.

Let's dance, Eleanor says.

What you need, says Constance, is a drink.

Eleanor tries to gather herself in, but she's too drunk. There's her face in the mirror, her cheeks, forehead. She's a skyful of fireworks, a roller coaster, a birthday cake. She grips the bathroom sink but her shoulder hits a wall.

The sink is the wheel of a pleasure cruiser on a big sea and she must turn it into the wave before they capsize. She's in the basement of the Masonic Temple on Cathedral Street in downtown St. John's, Newfoundland. It's a steep hill, the harbour, the cliffs, the North Atlantic, a sheer drop (the Grand Banks), and nothingness. She clings to the sink. Everybody at the wedding, two floors above — dancing, shouting, drinking beer — has been washed out to sea in a wave shot through with tuna and capelin and electric eels, especially Frank Harvey with his flamboyant tie, and Dave Hogan who drives to Florida in a Tilley hat, and Matthew Shea who puts his thumb over the top of his beer spraying Gerry Pottle, who holds out his hands going, What'd I do? What'd I do? And Matthew's wife with a daiquiri held above one shoulder saying, Matthew, that's so unimpressive. Amelia Kerby just now smacked Philip's shoulder with the back of her hand and was ambushed by silent jerks of laughter — all of them are depending on Eleanor to alter the course of the evening, to drag the sink hard in the other direction, until she's lifted off her feet. She has to bring them into port. She won't abandon her post, even in the face of this brick shithouse of a wave. How had she gotten so drunk, she had only been drinking.

If she could count how many beers in the afternoon, but it was the gin. The gin was insubstantial and avid, intrinsically cold, like reptile blood. At some point in the evening the word *juniper* had seemed like a self-contained poem. There is no turning back, they can only brace themselves. She has begun to think of herself as them. She's the entire wedding party, and the city beyond. Dragged out to sea.

The face in the mirror is starting to look exactly like her, she's coming into herself too fast. Philip was dancing with Amelia when Eleanor careened out of the banquet hall, down the musty staircase, platform heels, rickety handrail.

The bathroom floor buckles in the grip of a swell and Eleanor is flung against the wall and hauls herself, hand over hand, up the roiling radiator to the cubicle. She lets her head drop against the door of the stall. If she can just hang on she will reach her purest self. She may have to puke to get there. Something pure, like a breeze through the pines of the Himalayas. She'd camped once in the forest in Kashmir. Slippery pine needles slicked the paths. At night the guide called from his tent: Watch out for the snow leopards!

The outer door bangs and she feels it reverberate in her bum. Two women have burst into the bathroom.

Sadie says, Someone in there?

I am, says Eleanor.

And who is I am? A fairy in a CBC Christmas special once when she was fourteen. They chromokeyed her so she floated over a frozen lake, pointed toes wiggling, to touch down beside an ice-fishing folksinger who grabbed up his guitar to play a carol. She'd once knit a long red scarf. Rode in a mock foxhunt. They had several bloodhounds, but it was Eleanor's French poodle, Monique, who treed the old fur hat doused with musk hidden in the crotch of a birch. She'd hitchhiked the island maybe seven times. She'd taken all kinds of lessons: raku, clay animation, Spanish, watercolour painting. The secret to a successful watercolour is to use many, many transparent veils of colour. This is also the secret to raku,[16] vegetarian cooking, synchronized swimming, and being very, very drunk when your husband is dancing with a bubblehead from British Columbia, or from anywhere for that matter. It is not the secret to flying trapeze, belly dancing, waitressing at the Blue Door, or being very, very drunk when your husband picks up the fine gold necklace that lies flat against Amelia's collarbone with his lips. There is no secret for that. You must carom[17] like the silver balls in a pinball machine, spitting

---

16. **raku** Japanese pottery. 17. **carom** Collide and rebound.

sparks with each wall your forehead smacks. You must grip the wheel with both hands, you must pick a star and aim true.

Eleanor realizes that she's unable to puke. She is bloated with woe. There's so much woe. Puking she can forget. She drank; she is drunk. These honest statements grip hands like used car salesmen. She straightens up and steps out of the cubicle.

Sadie is holding her wrist to Constance's nose.

It's called Celestial Sex, says Sadie, everybody's wearing it. Both women turn to face Eleanor and then lurch forward to catch her.

Eleanor says, Constance, your dress. It's smeared with lipstick.

The women grip Eleanor's shoulders just as the tiled floor slants towards her chin. They squash her between them.

Eleanor lets her face fall into Sadie's cleavage. Eleanor wants to let go the wheel. Let them dash against the cliffs, let the ocean crunch them in its rotten chops. She closes her eyes, nuzzling Sadie's breasts with her nose, and plummets. She's a jellyfish pulsing through infinite inkiness, the ordinary encumbrances giving way: bone, jealousy, the smell of smoke and shampoo, the stinky emerald cloud of pot that still hangs over the cubicles, the way her mother stood a boiled egg in her wedding ring, her father smoothing cement with a trowel, Eleanor's horse pawing the clouds with his front hoofs, the pink of his nostril, the white of his eye, good olives, her name, streets, books, aspirations, socks, coins, hair clips, all of it giving way. Then she grabs Sadie's spaghetti strap and drags herself back up, surfacing amid the bagpipe screams of the toilets. What it means to be human is spelling itself in the grey mould spreading over the ceiling. She must speak. She will hint at the immanent peril. Sadie can take it.

Philip is all over her, Eleanor says.

Downer, says Constance.

Remember who you are, says Sadie.

She had imagined herself in love lots of times. Sometimes she knew she wasn't and fought to convince herself, saying, See? That must be love, see? He's done this, you felt that way, you thought of him while making mashed potatoes, you thought of him when the chain came off your bike, you thought of him.

Knowing she wasn't in love but not knowing what love was and thinking, it might be this. It might be she and Sam Crowley hidden under the dripping laburnum, the poisonous flowers bright at dusk, his kid sister standing on the pedals of her bike, whizzing by like a thought through the liver-coloured maple trees. Clem Barker tearing the condom wrapper with his teeth. Paul Comerford, between the rolls of unlaid carpet, leaving the impression of his bum in a pile of sawdust. Eli Pack kissed the back of her neck, and led her to his back seat, his finger and thumb circling her wrist loosely, but it might as well have been a handcuff, because she couldn't have said no if she tried. Then on a plaid blanket covered with cat hair. Eleanor is all of this. Tom O'Neill in a field of wild roses he claimed was inhabited by fairies. Stoned with Harry McLaughlin so his fingers stirred up a trail on the inside of her thigh like an oar in a phosphorescent shoal. When she was sixteen, Rick O'Keefe held her against his greasy overalls, a fresh whiff of gasoline. With Brian Bishop in a motel in Port Aux Basques, a snowstorm, they'd missed the ferry. Afterward they devoured a bucket of Kentucky Fried Chicken. Wiped their greasy mouths in the tail of the bedsheets. Mark Fraser, on a bale of hay, a surprise because he'd sworn all summer he hated her. Hunched over, he had flicked a Bic lighter until it ran out of juice and he's tossed it and gathered her roughly, the hay pricking through her jeans, he'd knocked her riding hat so the elastic tugged at her throat and then he had stopped, astonished. He'd whispered, You're a nice girl, as if he'd opened her like a parcel. Donny White had let a line of sand spill from his fist into her belly button, up her stomach, and over the triangles of her glossy orange bikini. Mike Reardon had rubbed his jeans against her bum, pressing her hipbones against the counter until she rinsed the last cup.

Sadie tugs Eleanor's dress roughly, this way and that, as if she were making a hospital bed. Constance trawls the bottom of her tiny purse until she draws out a lipstick, lethal as a bullet. She dismantles it and screws up the explosion of colour. She grips Eleanor's jaw and covers the pouting bottom lip and says, Rub them together. Sadie has got her by the hair, dragging a punishing brush through so fast Eleanor's scalp yelps.

Listen, Sadie says, it's only that *yahoo* Amelia Kerby, *who cares?*

And then it rises in her, the wave, plowing up through the guts of the evening, up through her platform shoes, grinding her kneecaps to dust, into her thighs, a spraying granite of surf hitting her crotch, stomach, her breastbone splintering, all blown apart.

I care, wails Eleanor, I lo-huv-huv-huv-huve him.

She and Philip bought a house around the bay. The grass up to their waists. Tiger lilies. Fireweed. Crabapples. Philip pulled over on the side of the road and rolled down the window.

Why are we?

Shhh.

Can we just.

Shhh.

He'd pulled over next to a copse[18] of whispering aspen. The car filled with the leafy, percipient surf. The wind blew, and the leaves showed their silver undersides as if the tree had been caught naked and was trying to cover up.

And the wave withdraws. Eleanor is still standing. The bathroom is lustral,[19] the fluorescent lights thrumming like an orchestra of didgeridoos. Sadie and Constance are angels with tangy auras like orange zest. They are springtime, a Scandinavian polar bear swim, they are the girls in the cake, Isadora Duncan,[20] they've bested the mechanical bull, they're electricity after an outage, they are her friends. Eleanor is okay. She's okay. She's going to be *fine*.

I will fight, Eleanor says.

There you go, says Sadie.

She had awakened in Philip's apartment, ten years ago. Trembling, partly from the hangover, but mostly from fright. She knew she was in love. How terrible. She could still feel his finger tracing the elastic of her underwear. She lay on her back, her arms over her head, her wraparound dress — he had untied the string at her hip and lifted the fabric away, and untied the other string inside the dress, beneath her breast. Little bows he pulled slowly. So she lay there in the black bra and underwear. His finger moved from one hip to the other, tracing the elastic. It was that finger moving over her belly that tipped her. It spilled her over. A car roared up the steep hill outside the apartment and squealed its tires, and the squeal felt like her heart, as if her heart were tearing around the corner of an empty street in the last sleeping city on the Atlantic. A brass candle

18. copse Small cluster of trees. **19. lustral** Used as a site of purification. **20. Isadora Duncan** American modern dancer (1877–1927) famous for her innovative choreography and refusal of restrictive sexual mores.

holder crusted with wax. A Fisher Price telephone with a glowing orange receiver. She had stumbled over it on their way in and the bell rang clear. When she awoke in the morning she came into herself. Sunlight piercing the weave of a rosy curtain, the wardrobe door hanging open, his jeans on the back of a chair, the red suspenders sagging, exhausted from the effort of holding him back.

Eleanor jerks the wine glass back and forth as if it is a gear shift manoeuvring her across the room. She stumbles forward and grabs Sadie's arms.

She says, This is the sort of drunkenness it takes a lifetime to achieve. I must actualize my potential before it wanes. I may never achieve this clarity of purpose again as long as I live.

Sadie says, You might regret this.

Whose side are you on?

I'm just saying, in the morning.

Because I'm ready here.

In the clear light of day.

If I'm all alone, just say so.

You're not alone, it's just I'm thinking a glass of water, a Tylenol, forty winks.

So you're with me?

Whatever you say.

You're in?

I'm in.

Let's actualize.

Eleanor drags Sadie across the dance floor, grabbing at dresses and suit jackets to stay standing. Finally she taps Amelia on the shoulder. Amelia turns.

You, she says. Amelia smiles.

Eleanor says, You, you, you. Where is your husband?

I have no husband.

That's right, says Eleanor. She grins triumphantly.

Your boyfriend, then, where's he?

It was nothing, Amelia says, my last boyfriend.

Nothing? It was nothing? Okay, the one before that.

Him too, nothing. She makes a sound, Pfft.

Okay, the one that broke your heart, where is he?

Pfft, says Amelia.

Pfft? Pfft? says Eleanor. She suddenly rests her forehead on Sadie's shoulder. It's true the girl has no life experience. There is no way to make an impression on her. There is no way to dent that lamé. She is what she appears, bubbly and handsome with a certain talent for academic lingo and a healthy bank account. Eleanor feels no match.

Well, you've started it now, Sadie says.

Eleanor rouses herself. She will do it then, if she's forced, finish this girl off, although already a new clarity has befallen her. The girl has nothing to do with it. Where, she wonders sadly, is Philip. Who is he? How can she remind him who he is?

I mean the boyfriend, then, says Eleanor, who took his bare hands and tore your flesh and pried the bones of your ribs apart and reached up and tore your beating heart out with his fingernails and then put it in his mouth and chewed it up and swallowed it. And then smiled at you with your own blood dripping down his teeth.

Here Eleanor mimes as she speaks (a trick she's learned from Frank Harvey) a pulsing heart in her fist. She mimes the heart almost slipping out one end of the fist, but catching it, cupping it in both hands. The heart truly appears to be pulsing in her cupped hands. She looks at Sadie, astonished by her own facility. Sadie looks astonished too. Eleanor is holding Amelia Kerby's slithering, tough little bungee-jumping heart. And then, snarling like a dog, Eleanor chews the tough meat of Amelia's heart. She wipes her mouth with the back of her hand.

That boyfriend, she says.

Um, that's never happened to me, Amelia says. Sadie puts her arm around Amelia and gives her a squeeze.

I think what my friend is trying to say is stay away from her husband. He's a little confused right now, but they have a kid and a really great marriage and you don't want to inadvertently fuck that up, now, do you?

At four-thirty in the morning everyone forms a circle around the bride and groom on the beer-soaked dance floor. They hold hands and sway violently, some of them fall over and the other side of the circle drags them up from their knees. Then that side, because of the exertion, topples and they must be hauled back on their feet. They rush into the centre of the dance floor, joined hands raised over their heads. The circle rushes in and pulls out. The bright dresses like bits of glass and sparkle in a kaleidoscope that fall to the centre with each twist of the lens and drop away. Blue stage lights splash over them, up the walls, across the ceiling, the floor. The bride and groom hug the guests, making their way around the circle.

Constance holds Eleanor's head in her hands tightly, she presses her cheek against Eleanor's cheek, and her face is wet and hot. She draws back and the red light falls over her, splinters of purple searing from the sequins in her veil, on the bodice of her dress.

I love you, Eleanor, she says, I love you. And I love your husband, too. And I love my husband. I love everybody's husband.

She lets go of Eleanor's face and falls into the arms of the man next to Eleanor. Ted grabs Eleanor and holds her. He has a beer in each hand and the bottles chink behind her back.

Eleanor tugs Philip's shirtsleeves.

Come home with me?

Not yet, he yells.

She is lying in bed waiting for him. It's 7:32 a.m. She lies still. There is a fear rushing around in her body. She remembers her mother calling a few years ago about the weasel. Eleanor can feel that mink fear rippling through her body because she fell in love the first night she slept with Philip and after that she fixed on him.

A body slams against a wall and falls onto the opposite wall of the porch. It's either Philip or the three Norwegian sailors who rent the attached house. The angry saints with their haloes of white hair and steady brawling.

Philip lurches to the banister, wraps his arms around it as if it were the mast of a capsizing ship.

He looks up at her.

He says, I went to Signal Hill in a Cadillac.

Eleanor is standing at the top of the stairs.

We stopped at the Fountain Spray to buy candy necklaces and we had a giant bottle of wine. I bit the necklaces off all the women's necks. He burps.

Glenn Marshall's neck too. Spectacular Sam was there. That guy who dances on broken glass. Do you remember that guy? He does a lounge lizard thing, and the Caribbean drums.

He lunges past her and she follows him to the bedroom.

He says, Spectacular Sam poured cognac over broken beer bottles on the parking lot of Signal Hill. Lots of smashed glass. He lit it, fell into a trance, and danced on it with his bare feet. Then he knelt and scooped the glass up in his hands and splashed his face with it, and drops of blood came up all over his face. You know, there was the sun too, coming up.

Philip struggles for a long moment with the buttons of his shirt, tipping slowly on his heels like a punching clown in a breeze. He sighs and rips the shirt open. Buttons hit the wall above the lamp. He falls onto the bed.

She gets up to turn off the light, but he grabs her arm.

Stay here, he says. Stay here.

(2002)

Michael Crummey (1965–)

Michael Crummey says that he has no recollection of wanting to become a writer before his first year of university, but recently a former babysitter showed him a poem he had written for her when he was about eight years old. Born in 1965 in Buchans, a mining town in central Newfoundland, Crummey moved with his family to another mining community in Labrador when he was 14. He completed high school there and then headed south to St. John's to earn a B.A. in English at Memorial University. It didn't take him long to realize that he wanted to be a poet, but he considered this ambition "a bit suspect," so he honed his craft covertly for years. In 1988, he enrolled in Queen's University in Kingston, Ontario, where he attained an M.A. He had launched into a doctoral program when disillusionment with the academic life set in, and he dropped out. Crummey then worked at a series of part-time jobs and began to write in earnest.

Crummey has explained that his early poems were influenced by the "narrative, deceptively casual voice of Al Purdy, Alden Nowlan, Bronwen Wallace, and by their interest in telling the stories of ordinary people." He adds that "Purdy's reach into the past was also a huge influence." *Arguments with Gravity,* his first book of poetry, appeared in 1996, and it contains poems he wrote over a 10-year period. Organized into five sections, they cover a range of subjects: home and family, working people, politics, travel, and issues of gender. In poems that envision life in Newfoundland before Confederation, Crummey searches for the past; other pieces examine the poet's experience of travelling in China (he spent six months there teaching English) and Latin America. In "Northern Ontario: Finnish Cemetery," the poet explores his twin fascinations with those who toil relentlessly just to survive and those who are both constrained and nourished by familial love. He draws poignant connections between the experience of immigrants in a new land and a child within her family. The immigrants must "clear a piece of land with an axe / and the strength of a body that knows / it can't go home"; a young girl, helping her father mow the cemetery, senses that "A father can be as difficult a love / as an adopted country, / how part of him always remains a stranger / how impossible it is to leave cleanly, completely."

In 1998, Crummey published *Hard Light,* a collection of poems and short prose pieces that focus on the lives of his ancestors in Newfoundland and Labrador. The collection explores identity through culture, voice, and landscape. The figures who inhabit these narratives are defined by their daily labour, by the tools they wield, by the customs they adhere to and pass on. In "What's Lost," the poet calls on his father to speak the past into being — a past inseparable from the landscape they are moving through: "Most of what I want him to remember / lies among those islands, among the maze / of granite rippling north a thousand miles, / and what he remembers is all I have a claim to." Gradually, the poet takes on the voice of the father, and soon others join the chorus — a woman tells of her marriage to a "good fisherman" 20 years her senior; sealers and sailors recount their experiences on ice and water.

A concern with the way the past abides in and informs the present re-emerges in Crummey's first collection of short stories, *Flesh & Blood* (1998). These tales, set mainly in the small mining community of Black Rock, Newfoundland, depict people who are desperate to find a way out — they leave for Montreal, Vancouver, China — but they find that they must carry Newfoundland with them wherever they go; they are chained to the rock. Crummey followed *Flesh & Blood* with his first novel, *River Thieves* (2001), as well as two more volumes of poetry: *Emergency Roadside Assistance* (2001) and *Salvage* (2002). In these collections of poems set in a range of locales, Crummey deals with loss in all of its forms (*Salvage* actually begins with a road sign that reads "Poems about Loss / Next 100 Pages") — the loss of home and family as well as innocence and belief. This theme resonates in the poet's deft use of metaphor. Crummey has referred to metaphor as "the 'engine' of writing," the source of its "heft or depth," and he expresses admiration for the way in which poets like Patrick Lane and Lorna Crozier can "make a piece of writing turn on a single image."

Loss also pervades *River Thieves,* an epic tale that unfolds in early 19th-century Newfoundland. Two Beothuk men are murdered by a raiding party that includes two influential White trappers and fishermen, a father and son named Peyton; British naval officer David Buchan, ordered to make contact with the Beothuk, enters into this charged scenario. Crummey's complex and richly detailed story is in a sense an elegy for the Beothuk — the Aboriginal people of Newfoundland — who, in the period in which the novel is set, are hovering on the brink of extinction due to a variety of factors, including European diseases and violent clashes with the settlers and traders who carry them.

In 2005, Crummey produced another novel, entitled *The Wreckage.* He has explained that each of his novels has taken on "a slightly different voice," and he provides this description of the divergence between the two: "The prose in *River Thieves* was a bit baroque at times, dense and 'poetic,' which suited the content of the book, the meandering plot, the story's switchbacks and retellings. In *The Wreckage* I was after something cleaner, more streamlined. It was more of a plot-driven book and I wanted the writing to stay out of the way as much as possible." *The Wreckage* is the story of itinerant projectionist Wish Furey, who tours World War II–era Newfoundland to bring movies to isolated settlements. He falls in love with teenaged Sadie on remote Little Fogo Island, but as a Catholic in a fiercely Protestant community he is branded an outsider. He quickly runs afoul of the girl's family and is driven away. He then enlists in the British army and winds up in a hellish Japanese prisoner-of-war camp. Fifty years later, Wish, a broken alcoholic, and Sadie, a war widow with a daughter, encounter one another in Newfoundland. Again, Crummey offers a moving evocation of loss — of love, innocence, family, and history — and dramatizes the wreckage it entails.

In collaboration with photographer Greg Locke, Crummey also published the non-fiction account *Newfoundland: Journey into a Lost Nation* (2004), described as "an elegy for his father and an elegy for the way of life his father knew." Crummey lives in St. John's, Newfoundland.

Serendipity

When my father was assigned a home by the Company and moved out of the bunk-house, we carried our belongings by cart and boat from Twillingate across New World Island and down to Lewisporte where we caught the train for Black Rock. Fourteen hours in the single passenger car at the end of a line of empty ore boxes and most of that time in darkness, the clatter of the rails carrying us deeper into the island's interior, into the unfamiliar shape of another life. I woke up just after first light as the train leaned into the half-mile turn of Tin Can Curve. Out the window I could see a rusty orange petticoat of abandoned scrap metal poking through the white shawl of snow at the foot of the rail bed. Twenty minutes later we crossed a trestle and chuffed into town. My father met us at the red warehouse that served as a train station, his lean face dwarfed by a fur hat, his grin lop-sided, like a boat taking on water.

I'd never been away from Durrells before. Everything in this new place looked the same to my eyes. Streets as neat as garden furrows with rows of identical four unit buildings painted white or green or brown planted on either side. For the first three weeks after we arrived, my mother tied a kerchief to the door handle so my sister and I would be able to find our house in the line of uniform, indistinguishable quads.

Even my father got confused on one occasion, coming home from a card game at the bunkhouse. He'd been drinking and turned onto the street below ours, mistaking the third door in the second building for his own. Only a small lamp over the stove lighted the kitchen, the details of furniture and decoration were draped in darkness. He took off his shoes in the porch, hung his coat neatly on the wall and was about to have a seat at the kitchen table when Mrs. Neary walked in from the living room. "Can I get you a cup of tea?" she asked him.

He was too embarrassed to admit he'd made a mistake. "That would be grand, Missus," he said. "I wouldn't say no to a raisin bun if you had one to spare."

"Carl," Mrs. Neary shouted up at the ceiling. "We've got company."

For years afterwards, my father dropped in on Mr. and Mrs. Neary for tea on Saturday evenings. My father and Mr. Neary hunted together, played long raucous poker games at the kitchen table with my uncle Gerry.

My mother said that was just like him, to find his best friend that way — everything that ever happened to my father was a happy accident. She said it with just a hint of bitterness in her voice, enough that I could taste it, like a squeeze of lemon in a glass of milk.

When I turned thirteen, my father began taking me with him to check his rabbit slips on the other side of Company property. We'd set out before dawn, following the Mucky Ditch that carried mine tailings across the bog, the squelch of footsteps in wet ground the only sound between us. When we reached the tree line we struck off for the trails through the woods. My father grinned across at me in a way that he hoped was reassuring, but I didn't understand why he invited me along or wanted me with him. Every winter he took twice as many brace of rabbit in the slips as Mr. Neary, for no reason but chance as far as anyone could see. Of ten hands of poker, my father won eight, sometimes nine. Mr. Neary swore never to play another game on more occasions than I could count. "That man," he announced often and loudly, "has a horseshoe up his arse."

My father smiled his lop-sided grin as he shuffled the cards. "One more before you go?" he asked.

It's hard not to feel ambivalent about someone that lucky and that casual about his good fortune. "How can you love a man," I once overhead my mother confide to Mrs. Neary, "that you never feel sorry for?"

I wouldn't have gone into the woods with my father at all if my mother hadn't encouraged me, and it was mostly for her sake that I paid attention when he showed me how to tie the slips, and how to use boughs to narrow the run where the slip was set. He explained how a night of frost set them running to keep warm. He tied the paws of the dead rabbits together with twine. "Not that lucky for these little buggers," he said lightly. I carried them over my shoulder, the bodies stiff as cordwood against my back.

Around noon we stopped to boil water for tea. "You've got a good head for the woods," my father told me one Saturday. I suppose he was trying to soften me up a little. The enthusiasm in his voice suggested he'd just discovered something I had been hiding out of modesty. "Why don't you see if you can find us a bit of dry stuff for the fire."

I tramped off into the bush, annoyed with his irrepressible good humour, with his transparent praise. He had no right, I thought, and as I moved further into the spruce I decided not to go back, to keep walking. I wanted him to panic, to feel his world coming apart as he crashed through the woods yelling my name. I wanted him to feel the sadness my mother felt, the same sick regret. I kept my head down, not bothering to check my trail, working deeper into the green maze of forest. When I stopped to catch my breath I closed my eyes, turning three times in a circle before looking up. A light snow had started falling, stray flakes filtering through the branches of the spruce like aimless stars. I had no idea where I had come from, or where I was going. I was completely, perfectly lost.

Before he moved to Black Rock, my father worked as a fisherman in Crow Head on Twillingate Island. The year he turned eighteen he courted a girl who lived with her parents down the Arm in Durrells. Every night of the week he'd walk the six miles in from Crow Head to have tea and shortbread cookies with Eliza. Then he'd walk home again, arriving after one in the morning, crawling into bed for a few brief hours before heading out on the water by six.

During the winter he walked both ways in total darkness, often in miserable weather. On a particularly blustery evening in February Eliza's family tried to convince him to spend the night, but my father politely declined. His mother was expecting him at home, and the bit of blowing snow wasn't bad enough to keep him in. The old man tapped the weather glass beside the front door. "She's dropping fast, you'd best be going if you're going."

There were no roads through Twillingate in those days. The paths quickly disappeared under snow. Wind pummelled the treeless shoreline, visibility dropped to zero. My father walked for half an hour before he decided to turn around and spend the night. An hour later he had no idea where he was. His hands and feet were numb, his eyelashes were freezing together. He hunkered below a hummock to catch his breath out of the wind. He leaned against the face of the small hill and fell backwards through the door of a root cellar. There was a bin of dark-skinned potatoes, shelves of onions, parsnips, cabbage. He was near a house. He stared through the snow looking for a sign of life in the white-out, and then marched toward what he thought might be a light in a window. My mother answered his knock at the door. "Can I get you a cup of tea?" she asked him as he unwrapped himself from his frozen winter clothes.

My grandmother went into the pantry, digging out a plateful of buns, cheese, and crackers. "Sarah," she called to my mother, "get a few blankets upstairs, we'll set him up on the daybed for tonight."

The storm went on unabated for four days. On the fifth day, my father left my mother's house to walk back to Crow Head. On the way he met his father, who had set out to look for him as soon as the weather eased up.

"Well," my grandfather said, "you're all right then."

My father grabbed both his arms through the bulk of his winter coat. "I'm getting married," he said.

My grandfather turned and they began walking back home through the thigh-deep snow. "It's about time," he said finally. "We were starting to wonder about you two."

Eliza's uncle was the merchant in Twillingate and after my parents married he made it impossible for my father to make a living as a fisherman. According to the merchant's tally at the season's end, my father's catch of salted cod didn't even cover the cost of supplies and equipment taken on credit in the spring. It was unfair and petty, but there was no recourse. My mother's oldest brother, Gerry, was working underground in Black Rock at the time and he had a word with his foreman who spoke with the Company manager. When my father left in November to start work in the mine I was already lodged in my mother's belly, undiscovered, like a pocket of ore buried in granite.

For the first eleven years of my life I saw my father only at Christmas, when he had enough time off to make the three day trip to Twillingate by train and boat. He stayed with us from Christmas Eve until Boxing Day, then began the return trip in order to be back at work on New Year's Day. I looked forward to his appearance with the same mix of anticipation and anxiety my sister reserved for Santa Claus. As if I suspected he wasn't quite real, that this year my mother would sit me down and explain he was simply a story made up for children. He arrived in the middle of the night, the pockets of his winter coat heavy with oranges and blocks of hard taffy. He sat us on his knee, our small faces disfigured by interrupted sleep and shy, helpless excitement as he bribed us with nickels to kiss the unfamiliar wool and oil smell of his cheek. Then he disappeared for another year.

As I grew older my simple disappointment with this arrangement soured. I began to suspect that he chose to live away from us, chose to visit only three days a year. It made no difference how often he explained that the Company had yet again refused his application for a house, or how lucky he was even to have a job. The promise of moving us to Black Rock was like a gift my father was constantly saving for, but could never quite afford. I had been waiting for so long that I stopped expecting it would ever happen, had stopped wanting it altogether.

Like her children, my mother became more and more accustomed to the idea of life without him. During the summers she tended the garden with my grandmother, helped her brothers cut the meadow grass for hay in the fall. She sewed and mended and knit through the winter; she taught me my sums by the light of a kerosene lamp in the evenings. For eleven years she lived alone, married to a man she knew only through occasional letters, a brief annual visit. It should have been no surprise to anyone, least of all my mother, that she was no longer in love when he finally sent for us to join him in Black Rock.

It was a Christmas tradition at the house in Durrells, before we left for Black Rock, that the story of how my parents met and became engaged would be recounted by the people present during the storm. It was an informal telling, a story thrown out piecemeal, with everyone describing their own particular role or viewpoint on this detail or that, as if they were discussing a movie they had seen together years before. My father got lost and fell backwards into the root cellar, my mother opened the door to a hill of clothes covered in snow. My mother's youngest brother caught them furtively holding hands as they sat together on the second day. Uncle Gerry slams an open palm on the table, making the glasses of whiskey and syrup jump. Nothing at all would have happened between them if he had been at home at the time, he announces, and what was my grandmother thinking to allow such a thing in the first place?

My grandmother lifts a hand from her lap-full of crochet cotton to dismiss her son's feigned outrage. "When Sarah came to my bed that night to say he'd proposed I thought, What odds about it? You lot are all alike under the clothes anyway. Go ahead and marry him if you want to, I told her. One man is as good as another."

Everyone laughs at this, my mother included. I am too young to think there could be anything prophetic in my grandmother's words.

My father says, "It was fate is what it was. It was in the stars." He digs in his pocket for a coin. "Come over my darling," he says to my mother, "and kiss me."

"You men," my grandmother says, "you're all alike."

Whatever her feelings about leaving Durrells might have been, my mother was determined to make the best of our new life in Black Rock. She thought that pretending to be a family long enough would make it real for all of us. She hoped that would be the case. She insisted we see my father off to work before each shift, turning our faces up to receive a ritual peck on the cheek. We took the Company bus out to the lake on weekends, summer and winter, sitting on a blanket on the sand or skating across to Beothuk Island. We went to matinee shows at the theatre, standing with the rest of the audience to whistle and slap the seats of our folding chairs when, inevitably, the film broke and Smitty had to splice it together before continuing. In all of these activities my mother's selfless, brittle enthusiasm was a delicate and beautiful thing, like blown glass. I travelled cautiously in the wake of that beauty, as if she was the last star in the night sky.

My sister, on the other hand, cheerfully took root. She joined the Brownie troop, the school glee club, played hopscotch and Cut-the-butter with half a dozen other children on our street. She sat in my father's arms as he played poker with Mr. Neary and my uncle, sleeping soundly through the laughter and cigarette smoke and the cursing while I sulked in my room, refusing to be placated by my mother's trays of shortbread cookies, by the second-hand pair of skates my father left on a nail in the porch. "I don't know what we're going to do with that one," my mother said whenever I retreated up the stairs.

"Don't worry," my father reassured her. "He's just missing Twillingate. He'll come around. It'll all work out in the end." More than anything else, it was that blind faith in his luck that infuriated me. It hardened my resolve to show him how wrong he was about the world.

The further I walked through the bush, the more dense it became. Branches scraped my face and hands, but I hardly noticed. I was elated. I felt like shouting, but didn't want to give myself away. I kept moving, putting as much distance between myself and my father as possible, stumbling deeper into the forest like a man walking into a river, his pockets full of stones. I pictured my father scrambling through the woods behind me, calling helplessly.

Minutes later I broke through a web of alders into a clearing and stopped dead in my tracks. I felt something falling inside myself, a brilliant, catastrophic toppling like the collapse of a star. Twenty yards from where I stood there was a fire burning. My father crouched beside it, chewing nonchalantly on a sandwich. Lost in the bush, I realized, I had walked in a perfect circle.

"I was starting to wonder about you," my father said. "Did you find any wood for the fire?"

It was hopeless. I walked toward him, empty-handed, convinced there was no way to fight destiny, that I would never be free of my father's luck.

The following summer my mother slipped into the same posture of defeat. She abandoned her attempts to force us into the shape she thought a happy family should take, began complaining of headaches, bowing out of regular excursions and events to stay at home alone. Her absence had been so habitual and familiar to my father for so many years that he barely registered this retreat. He took my sister and I to the movie matinees without her, bought us popcorn or candies, joking with my sister as if nothing had changed. I sat sullenly through war movies and westerns starring "The Durango Kid," or a white-hatted hero played by Rocky Lane. Even during bar room brawls that hat never left his head, as if it grew from his scalp like hair. Someone in the audience inevitably shouted, "Knock his hat off!" and everyone cheered. It was enough that he always came out on top. The hat was simply flaunting it.

When we arrived home I brought my mother tea or juice where she lay in the dusk of the heavy curtains in her bedroom, her hair splayed against the pillow like meadow grass cut and drying in a field. The air in the room was thick with the smell of cloistered bodies. "You're a prince," she murmured, distracted, as if I had woken her from a dream. It was all I could do to keep from crying. Winter was coming. The stars were aligned against me.

Fate is simply chance in a joker's hat.

The Black Rock ore deposits were discovered when the stones around a prospector's cooking fire began flaring, the seams of ore in the slag[1] bursting into flame and melting. A snow storm threw my parents together for four days and they married. My father happened on his best friend by accident. In retrospect, it can all seem inevitable, unavoidable. I think about that now, how I might have gone on hating my father forever if not for the intervention of serendipity.

Two weeks before Christmas, the Company held its annual party for employees' children at the Star Hall. My mother stayed at home, complaining of a headache. I dressed, reluctantly, while my father and sister stood in the porch, sweating under coats and scarves, shouting at me to hurry. I lagged behind them on the street, scuffling snow with the toe of my boot. My sister was in my father's arms, and they were laughing. Other families on their way to the hall congregated around them. I walked more slowly,

---

1. **slag** Cinders.

watching as the dark cluster of people and conversation moved farther and farther ahead of me, like a train leaving a town behind. Finally I stopped altogether, angry and curiously satisfied that they hadn't noticed I was no longer beside them. I could just hear their voices at the bottom of the street and then they turned the corner.

Back at the house I pulled off my boots in the porch, feeling vaguely triumphant. My mother and I could spend the evening playing Crazy Eights, drinking tea. I knocked my boots together to clear the bottoms of snow, then set them neatly by the wall. Beside Mr. Neary's boots. I walked into the kitchen in my stocking feet. Only the light over the stove was on, there was no sound. I was about to call when I heard my mother's voice from upstairs. "Who's there?" she shouted.

"It's me," I said.

"Where's your father?" Her voice was hard, but fragile, as if the hardness in it might suddenly shatter into fragments.

"Is Mr. Neary here?" I asked uncertainly.

"Russell, you go straight to the Star Hall. Right this minute. You hear me?"

I didn't know what to say. It was like walking into a house you think is your own, taking off your shoes and jacket, sitting at a kitchen table, and suddenly realizing you're in the middle of something completely unfamiliar and unexpected, something foreign. "I forgot my scarf," I lied.

Halfway to the Star Hall I met my father, on his way back to look for me. "Well," he said. "You're all right then."

I looked at his face, at the complete innocence of it. The wind had brought tears to his eyes and he was grinning his lop-sided grin at me. He had no idea. My mother and my father's best friend. For the first time in my life I felt sorry for him.

"I forgot my scarf," I lied again.

He turned toward the Hall and we walked together in the darkness. "If the wind dies down there'll be a decent frost tonight," my father said. "Tomorrow should be a good day to check the slips."

"I'd like that," I said. I reached out and held his arm through the bulk of his winter jacket. "I'd like that a lot."

(1998)

Joseph Boyden (1966–)

Joseph Boyden was born in Toronto in 1966. While attending the Jesuit Brébeuf High School in the early 1980s, he got a mohawk haircut to protest the Jesuit mission's assimilation of the Iroquois. The Jesuit missionary for whom the school was named had been tortured and killed by Iroquois warriors in the 17th century, and the school administrators found Boyden's fashion statement wholly unacceptable. Boyden's early aversion to the subjugation of minority cultures would eventually lead him to write about his Métis ancestry and the politics of racism.

Although his heritage is mostly Scottish and Irish, Boyden was inspired to explore his Métis connection by some Ojibwa friends he made in the Georgian Bay area when he was growing up. While visiting reserve communities, he learned of the legendary exploits of Francis Pegahmagabow, the most decorated Aboriginal soldier in World War I. The sniper from northern Ontario killed more Germans and German allies than anyone else in the history of recorded warfare. He returned from Europe to a hero's welcome, but he was soon marginalized due to racist practices of the Canadian government. Intrigued by his story, Boyden would later use it as a model for his novel *Three Day Road* (2005).

At the age of 16, Boyden began to travel to the United States each summer — he was drawn especially to South Carolina and Louisiana — paying his way by working as a gravedigger, groundskeeper, dishwasher, waiter, tutor, and bartender. He also served as a roadie for a friend's punk-rock band, touring the U.S. and Canada, but he returned home each fall to attend school. Enrolling at York University in Toronto, Boyden studied creative writing. In the mid-1990s, he entered the M.F.A. program in creative writing at the University of New Orleans in Louisiana, and there he met his wife, Amanda, a fellow writer. After graduating, he taught for two years in Aboriginal programs on several reserves on James Bay in northern Ontario, and he has described the experience of teaching Native students as "life-changing." Boyden indulged his wanderlust by travelling between reserves by bush plane, helicopter, snowmobile, and canoe. He claims that the region has had a lasting impact on him: "this gateway to the last great wilderness has become my muse and obsession."

Leaving James Bay, Boyden returned to the University of New Orleans as a faculty member in the creative writing program from which he graduated. He published a collection of short stories, *Born with a Tooth*, in 2001. It is divided into sections entitled "East," "South," "West," and "North" — the set of directions representing the circle of life. The title story concerns a young Métis woman, Sue Born With A Tooth, who befriends a hungry wolf that wanders near her home at night. When the wolf becomes symbolically intertwined with her non-committal lover, a teacher from Toronto, Sue finds herself on the brink of an identity crisis. Like many other Boyden characters, Sue is also torn between two essentially incompatible ways of life: the urban and the rural. The author's preoccupation with the pervasive influence of urban ways and values on reserve life also informs the story "Shawanagan Bingo Queen," which is a nuanced examination of the stereotype of First Nations people as gambling addicts and the allure that on-reserve gambling establishments hold for non-Natives. In the story, the ironies compound: out of financial desperation, the leaders of a Native band try to attract wealthy tourists to their casino, but in so doing they inadvertently ensnare their own people in the gambling trap. While he stresses that dangerous addictions can take hold in any culture, Boyden implies that the proponents of colonization must bear responsibility for the devastating effects of gambling on Native communities.

Boyden had already produced a first draft of *Three Day Road* when it occurred to him that its chronological structure was too conventional. A circular narrative structure would be more appropriate, he decided, because it would reflect the oral tradition of the story's Ojibwa and Cree narrators. With this decision to jettison the chronological form, Boyden aligned himself not only with the Aboriginal storytelling tradition but also with the subversive values of postmodern fiction.

The novel's title refers to the Cree belief that a soul needs three days to travel from its body to the afterlife. Inspired by Boyden's time in James Bay, during which he witnessed the effects of governmental indifference on the region's Native inhabitants (contaminated water, alcoholism, unemployment), and by the tale of Pegahmagabow, the novel focuses on two World War I Cree snipers, Xavier and Elijah. They enlist in the military in an attempt to recover their warrior spirit, which they believe was lost due to the displacement of their people through colonization and their assimilation through the residential school system. As his characters are engulfed by the monumental violence of the war, Boyden deploys the Cree myth of the cannibalistic, soul-eating windigo to symbolize the European combat that is voraciously consuming lives. Although Boyden presents soldiers as ordinary people responding to the terrible circumstances in which they are caught, he also suggests that their role is contentious. He dramatizes the way in which people are corrupted by the violent acts they commit, even if those acts are initially justified. When *Three Day Road* appeared, in 2005, it won a Governor General's Award nomination.

Boyden continued to explore the fraught relationship between Native peoples and the descendants of colonists in non-fiction accounts. In 2005, he published a piece in *Maclean's* about racial profiling and the notorious "starlight tours" inflicted upon First Nations people in Saskatoon, Saskatchewan (police were abandoning individuals they had taken into custody on the frozen outskirts of town; several died as a result). Later that year, he wrote a series of stories, also for *Maclean's,* about Hurricane Katrina, which had devastated New Orleans, the city in which he had lived for years. In these stories, Boyden criticized American government officials for their lack of effective action in the face of the disaster and the White establishment of New Orleans, which appeared to welcome the mass exodus of the city's poor Black people.

Boyden divides his time between Louisiana and northern Ontario. He is currently writing a novel about the descendants of Xavier from *Three Day Road.*

Shawanagan Bingo Queen

Springtime brings the blackflies. Clouds of biting gnats that dig into your ears and nose and scalp swarm to the reserve in the first warm days to feed on us and keep us indoors for the four or five weeks that they eat and mate and die. You might not be able to see their teeth or even their little bodies crawling in your hair, but when blackflies start sucking, you know it. I remember, when I was a small girl, I was playing out back by the edge of the bush and a chainsaw scream started up in my head and sent me wailing to my mother. I put my finger in my ear and pulled it away all bloody. My mother said, "Hush, Mary," and stuck the point of a rolled-up towel in and wiggled out three of the buggers. Then she took her bottle of rye and tipped my head sideways and poured some in. My first taste of whisky came running down my cheek, mixed with blood that I licked off the side of my face.

Sometimes I think I fell in love with my husband, Ollie, because no matter how bad the blackflies got in spring, he'd still go out and about, working on his old car or hunting in the bush. He didn't let a thing stop him. When we first married he'd get a bottle of American bourbon that had been smuggled from over the border and take me out in his little boat late at night to look at stars and get drunk and silly. He'd take his shirt off, even if it was early spring with a sheen of thin ice forming on the lake, and stand on the bow and say, "Look, Mary, that bright one there is the dog star. It's my lucky star. Me and him, that dog, we talk to one another." Then he'd howl out until his voice came bouncing back across the water, and I'd join in and yelp to his star and to the moon until we were both out of breath. We were young and crazy. When Ollie got killed, there was grumbling and rumours it wasn't an accident. Maybe it wasn't planned, some of the old ones said, but it wasn't no accident, either.

Then our band council brought the Bingo Palace to Shawanaga. The one road running out of the rez got paved, and Chief Roddy Manague bought his Cadillac. The Bingo Palace changed a few things.

There are still blackflies in spring, and old Jacob the hunter still keeps our freezers full of deer meat in winter. What's changed now is we got a common focus on the rez, something to look forward to most weeknights. We got the *wasichu* driving in with their money, ready to spend it, sometimes driving all the way from Toronto. The Palace has given us a name.

Wasichu means white man. Grandmother never had the chance to teach me the Ojibway word, so I borrowed from the Sioux. Don't mistake me for a Plains woman, though. I'm a proud Ojibwa. The Sioux, when they came this far east, were our enemy, and we only feared and respected the Iroquois more. My grandmother spoke fluent Ojibway, but she's dead a long time ago. Before Ollie came along, I once learned some Indian from a South Dakota boy. He was Oglala Sioux and carried it proud like his barrel chest. Even though the words he taught me weren't my language, they were still Indian, and better than nothing, I figure. In return, I taught him to say the only Ojibway I knew, other than swear words. *Aneen Anishnabe* means "Hello, Indian" in my language. One of these days I'll take a break from the Palace and learn some Ojibway, something I can pass on to my two kids.

But what I can pass on to them now is my knowing bingo. I thought it was the stupidest game I ever heard of when word of the money started drifting in eleven years ago, with Yankee Indians in big new cars. Roddy Manague knew we were all down and out and there was no future for anyone collecting pogey and baby bonus cheques. Roddy was big enough to see that bingo might bring us some freedom.

You have to be a smooth talker to try to swing the elders in your favour, especially when you're selling something as foreign as gambling. In the end, it came down to the council elders, the old women, to decide. Roddy brought money backers in from an upstate New York rez, Iroquois with slick black hair in ponytails and three-piece suits and eagle feathers. They carried charts with red lightning zigzags on them and slide projectors under their arms.

The Iroquois dazzled our old women with talk of money for schools and autonomy. Well, we never got a school. Some built onto their houses, and many have newer cars. But you know there's still burnt-out war ponies with no windshields and most of the rez has rotted plywood and tarpaper roofs. The biggest difference when you look around is the Palace, on Centre Hill beside the rusting playground. The Palace is an old corrugated airplane hangar, insulated against winter and big enough to play a game of hockey inside, with room for spectators. There's no windows to look out onto Killdeer lake. Just tables and chairs to sit 450 people, and a high stage for me to call numbers from, and eight TV monitors spaced along the walls to show what ball's being called.

It used to be that the inside was filled with card tables and folding chairs, so empty and drafty that it was ugly. I learned soon enough to judge how well we were doing by the changes inside. After the first two years the cheap furniture was gone, replaced by sturdy pine cut from the bush. But the real measure is the walls. Roddy commissioned local kids to draw murals and paint pictures. Big colourful stuff showing Manitou and Indian princesses, the Sun Catcher with her buckskin arms stretched up welcoming another day, the Circle of Protecting Buffalo. One boy drew his red and black impression of a Jesuit being tortured by Iroquois. Roddy thought it would upset the *wasichu* and made the boy alter it. Now, on the wall behind the stage, there's a drawing of a Jesuit priest and an Indian warrior standing on a cloud shaking hands. Even though Ollie would have hated it, the Bingo Palace has become a nice-looking place over the last eight years.

Everyone is here to celebrate our eighth anniversary this weekend — cottagers up for the summer, townies, Indians. It's even larger than the council expected, with the chance to win a $50,000 pot and tons of advertising in advance. The money we're offering tonight is unheard of around here. A bunch of people have already come up and asked if the flyers were a misprint. "Fifty thousand dollars!" Abe from North Bay says real loud in my ear. "Goddamn if I'd ever have to work another day in my life!"

This is the first chance Roddy's ever taken in terms of the house making it big or going bust. First the people have to come. The even bigger chance for us is whether or not somebody walks with the $50,000 pot, the final game of the night. I've never seen Roddy so nervous before. I must admit I've got my fingers crossed, toes too. If nobody walks with the jackpot, Roddy's plans for a full casino — blackjack, craps, roulette, you name it — can go into motion.

A Mohawk rez out by Beaverton's already got a building going up with the same plan in mind. The Ontario politicians tried to stop them, and it was *wasichu* courts that declared Native autonomy. Roddy's got that silver shovel in his closet and he's ready to dig the first hole. After a big fight, he got the council to put up $25,000 when our New York Iroquois partners offered to help finance the casino deal. The Iroquois want to see if we can draw the crowds. It's now down to the money to bring in the bulldozers. Roddy told me he wants me to be a casino manager.

You couldn't ask for a better day. The blackflies are gone for the season, so the clouds and little bit of rain's made the cottagers antsy to get out and about. We open the doors at three p.m. sharp and have a buffet of casseroles and macaroni and venison. Old Blanche Lafleur from the tavern claims that, when she walked from her place to the Palace, she counted five hundred head, not including the little ones yelling and darting among the grown-ups.

Saturday nights were never like this seven years ago when I first got a job working bingo after Ollie died. Word of our Palace hadn't spread yet when Roddy hired me on at the snack counter. I worked my way up to official stage caller pretty quick, faster than I ever imagined. It's quite a thing to sit above the crowd and pull balls from the air popper and hear the hush when you call. Tonight won't be much different. As six o'clock comes near it looks like every chair in the house is taken and people have got their sheets of cards spread in front of them and are arranging all their doodads and charms.

You've never seen such a strange sight — troll dolls with bright pink or green hair shooting up from their heads, pieces of lucky clothing or real child hair and baby teeth. And daubers, lots of coloured bingo daubers. Most serious players always have a handful lined up, although it takes a lot of plugging away to run a dauber's ink dry. The stylish ladies carry all their bingo gear in crocheted bags. A few even have authentic-looking wampum pouches, made from moose hide with beaded Indian scenes on them.

I notice that the teenagers form their own group along the far wall. They've got torn jeans and long hair and pretty designs on their T-shirts. They're mostly rez kids, Johnny Sandy, Veronica Tibogonosh, and Earl Thibadeau among them. A few years ago, a lot of the more troublesome ones, the tricksters in the group, used to show up and do things like call, "Bing — " and then "Oh-oh," a few seconds later, like they mistook winning a game. The older ones didn't like that, I tell you, white or Indian. Don't ever cross a player and her game. It's like spitting on someone's religion. The Indians never hushed up the trickster kids. It always seemed to be the old white ladies with thin lips making snake noises against their wrinkled fingers. Roddy finally chased the bad ones out. I don't know exactly what he did or said, and I'm not sure I want to know. But there isn't much trouble during the games any more.

Tonight I notice a woman and her husband bring their three little ones in to sit with them while they get ready to play. My floor runner, Albert, goes over, and it looks like he's telling them that children aren't allowed in during the games. You never saw people leave in such a huff. I've never seen the family in here before, and don't expect to again any time soon.

That's one of the disagreements my husband, Ollie, had with the band council so many years ago. Roddy tried to sell bingo as a business good for the whole community when Ollie started up his petition of names against it. Ollie knew there was no room for the rez kids in the Palace. In the final band vote, his big opposition speech ended with talking about our Rachel and Little Ollie. It made a stir with the older ones, but the Palace was like a black bear waking in spring, too hungry to stop.

Ollie didn't live long enough to see bingo run on the rez. He died when he fell out of a tree. He was way up, near the top of a big pine, sawing dead wood threatening to come down during the next thunderstorm. A cottager had offered him fifty bucks for the job. The cottager was an old man then, but seems much older now when I occasionally run into him at the trading post or in town. He still sends me a prayer card every year.

It's funny, you know. Even now I sometimes don't believe Ollie's gone. He was always falling out of trees or driving his snowmobile too late in spring and going through the thin ice or tearing the hull off his boat on a shoal at night. But he crawled back into our bed, wet and cold or scratched up, telling me another story. After all these years it still doesn't sink in that nobody saw Ollie fall out of the tree or gasping for breath for a half an hour with a branch through his stomach like the coroner told me. Ollie's luck ran out. I think the rumours are just Ollie's spirit flying around on the wind at night, stirring up trouble and rattling the pine branches.

There wasn't much time for mourning with Little Ollie and Rachel at home. Little Ollie remembers a few things about his daddy but Rachel was only two when it happened. That bothers me a lot, the fact they'll never know him.

Roddy knew I never liked the idea of living off government money, that I hated the idea as much as Ollie did. After the funeral, Roddy offered me the job on the snack counter at the Palace. The thought of Ollie looking down from his star and shaking his head, disappointed that I sold myself out to something like bingo, bothered me. It always will. But it wasn't my fault that he left us early, and it seems to me that working is better than welfare. And I'm a hard worker. I moved up quick and ignored the grumbling from the others who worked the Palace till midnight and drank till dawn. Once I heard one of the townie kids call me Mary Goody Two-Moccasins. I bitched him out good.

The Palace chatters like a forest full of grosbeaks when I walk up and take my seat by the popper, on the stage a good four metres above the crowd. It's a bird's-eye view through the haze of smoke rising to the rafters. The noise stops with the croaking and fumbling of my mike, and you'd think a priest had walked in to say church or a judge to read the sentence. There are no empty seats. Even stragglers lean on walls or sit on the floor, arranging.

"Welcome to the Shawanagan Bingo Palace," I say. "As a lot of you know, Queen or King for the night wins ten dollars every time their ball number comes up in play this evening. Please refer to the lottery ticket you received with admission." I call out the number and wait for the winner. Old Barb from Magnetawan stands up and calls out, "I am Queen of the Shawanagan Bingo Palace!" Albert runs out and puts the red felt bandanna on her head. Old Barb looks very proud. People all around nod to her. It's a serious business. I make a note that her ball is B-6. All Barb has to do is call out, "Pay the

Queen," whenever her number is announced in a game and Albert runs over and gives her ten bucks. It can add up.

I jump right into the Early Bird Special, with two games of straight bingo and two games of Full Card X. It gets the interest up and people loosened for the night. I call the balls even and a little slow, holding them in front of the camera attached to the monitors long enough that the older ones who can't hear too well have enough time to squint out the numbers. I notice a lot of regulars in the audience tonight. There's Barb smiling away in her red bandanna and the Burk's Falls Lions Club gang with their matching shirts. I notice that even the Judge came out tonight. I gave him up for dead a while ago. He's a retired lawyer from Toronto who moved up here alone. We call him "Judge" because he uses a dauber shaped like a gavel and pounds away all serious at his cards like he's ordering the court to silence. The Early Bird winners walk with or split a hundred dollars a game.

One hundred dollars seemed like a fortune to me back when Ollie and I married. He was never much for government handouts, even though there were plenty of days we needed cash. Ollie was a wagon-burner, for sure. He sniffed out trouble and rolled in it faster than a hunting dog. He liked to piss people off. I met him at fifteen and could see it in his eyes. He'd hitchhiked into our rez from the Quebec interior and decided he liked the lake. So he stayed. But he could use a chainsaw and drive a logging truck, so he wasn't much of a burden. Old Jacob took Ollie under his wing and taught him about fishing and hunting. Jacob is a legend around here. He feeds most of the rez through the harder months. One winter Ollie and him bagged seventy deer and fed a lot of mouths through to spring.

Then Ollie got a crush on me. He claimed it was a vision he had after hiking to Moosejaw Mountain, which isn't so much a mountain as a heap of old quarry stone, and he got stuck there a couple days after his lunch bucket ran dry.

I'll never forget the day he walked back onto the reservation, shouting that he was a man now, that he'd had his first true vision — one of a large brown animal whispering my name in his ear as he lay naked and sweating on a rock.

I laughed at Ollie from my doorstep, so he left and I didn't see him again for two weeks. When he came back, his chest had swelled bigger. Ollie made sure to tell all my girlfriends that he had hitched the five hundred kilometres up to Moose Factory in pursuit of his vision, knowing it would get straight back to me. I'll tell you now I didn't like the idea of a moose popping up in Ollie's head whenever he thought of me. We ended up marrying a year later.

After a game of Four Corners and a game of Make a Kite, I call intermission. Tonight Jan What's-Her-Face comes and gabs in my ear like usual. She's a *wasichu* cottager who wears "Free Leonard Peltier"[1] or "American Indian Movement" T-shirts. Jan tells me that last night she had a vision in her dreams. The vision told her the winning combination of balls I would call in the jackpot game, and she looks forward to seeing if her vision was worthy.

"I always get such a feeling of freedom when I drive onto your reservation," she says, and takes my arm in her hands. "Just imagine winning $50,000. That would be freedom too."

---

1. Leonard Peltier   Native American activist (b. 1944) who was imprisoned in 1977 for his role in the deaths of two FBI agents; many believe he was wrongfully convicted.

She's only a summer cottager. Her place up here isn't even winterized. I wonder what she'd think about freedom, stuck in the house when it's thirty below and the walkie-talkie tells you the road won't be cleared for days.

Between the two intermissions we play Block of Nine, Anywhere, Half Diamond and Full Diamond games. They're simple enough, but I see people's focus is on the cards. There's not much chit-chat while play's in progress. The winnings are too big. Albert runs and hands out $2,000 in winnings before I call intermission again.

Bingo calling's like any other job in that it can get boring after a while. I learned to pass my time on the stage every night watching faces and goofing around, calling numbers too fast and laughing inside at all the eyes looking up at me like panicked raccoons in car headlights. Or I'll call real slow for a long while, listening for just the right moment when people are chatting and not paying attention. That's when I call a few balls super-fast and listen for the angry wail of "Call again," or "Bad bingo." Ollie would have laughed at that.

But tonight there's no fooling around. Roddy paces the floor like an anxious bear, his black braided ponytail flopping almost to his bum.

Our Shawanagan Special tonight is the biggest ever. If you want to play, you have to buy special strips at $5 a pop, but the winner walks with a guaranteed $4,000. We have to sell eight hundred cards to break even. Roddy decides to leave the cashier box open a couple of extra minutes despite cries of "Let's play," and "Get on." From where I sit, with all the scurrying about and money changing hands, we'll break even. But you're never positive until the accounting's done at the end of the night.

Roddy comes up to me before I start play again. "Remind the crowd about the jackpot game tonight, Mary," he says. As if they need to be reminded. I clear my throat and switch on the mike.

"Let me just tell you about tonight's jackpot game." Everyone goes real quiet and stares up at me. "The game is included with your admission price. You can buy extra cards at $25 a pop. Jackpot game is fill your card in forty calls or less and win $50,000. In forty-one calls, $40,000. In forty-two calls, $25,000. In forty-three calls, $15,000. In forty-four calls, $10,000. And in forty-five calls or more, $5,000." I see the glow in people's eyes. It's an addiction.

"The point isn't to win, it's to win big!" Roddy tells the Palace workers at our meetings. "You either lead, or you follow, or you get out of the way." It's a good scare tactic but doesn't leave much room to argue. I sometimes take a walk and look around the rez and wonder.

I was out walking with Little Ollie and Rachel when I heard about Ollie. Ernest, the band's police chief, roared up in a dust cloud. When he got out of his Bronco, he looked sad and red-eyed.

"I got bad news, Mary," he said. "Come here away from the little ones for a minute." I remember thanking him for telling me, and walking the kids down the dirt road to the pond Ollie always took them to.

"Daddy can't take you fishing here no more," I said. "Or to school or out in the bush." Their deer eyes looked up at me. Little Ollie figured it out fast and ran away on his skinny legs, his sneakers slapping up puffs of dust on the road. Rachel cried and wanted her brother to come back.

Little Ollie isn't so little any more. He's eleven now and he blames Roddy but can't reason it out exactly why. I tell my boy that it was his father's time to go to *Gitchi-Manitou*,[2] that he's up in the sky as a twinkling star now, looking down at us. The few rumours are just rumours. But my boy fights it. He's not named after his dad for nothing, I figure.

I start in the thirteenth game with one of my favourites, Telephone Pole, where you've got to fill in the right numbers to make the design on your card look like one. The next game, Picnic Table, goes along the same lines. "Buy extra jackpot cards soon," I remind everyone. "Jackpot is five games away." I glance at my watch. Tonight's going to be a late one for sure. The kids are long asleep.

My mother watches the kids on bingo nights. She tries to refuse my money, but I pay for her time anyways.

"We take care of our own," she says to me. "We've always taken care of our own. We're Ojibwa."

After Ollie died and I started working, Mom and me started fighting. One night I got out of work real late, and she got angry when I went to pick up the kids. "Ollie wouldn't want you working there," she said. That got me mad. "He thought bingo wasn't Indian. It's a white man's game."

I knew that already. It got me madder. "Indian?" I said. "Indian? We're Ojibwa and you don't even know our language." I tried to pass her to get the kids, but she stopped me and wrestled me to the ground by my hair. I began to cry and shouted, "Where were all the Indians when Ollie fell out of a tree?" She had me pinned beneath her, her cheeks shaking and her chest against mine.

"Where were all the Indians when Ollie fell out of a tree?" she asked. Our eyes got big at the same time. And then we started laughing at what I'd said until my sides were about to burst. We just lay beside one another on the floor and laughed. It felt good. We've been tight ever since.

I've asked Mom to come out and play bingo. "I'll find another sitter," I tell her. But she doesn't like the thought of a room packed with quiet, serious people and smoke.

"I could go to a sweat lodge if I want to see that," she always tells me. But I can see the question in her eyes, whether it doesn't bother me to be working for something Ollie hated.

I don't think it bothers me.

Really, I don't.

Roddy puts the word out that there are professional gamblers up from Toronto tonight.

"You just call those balls, Mary," he says. "You call 'em during the last game and pray hard. I don't want to see you call out the big one tonight."

As if I got a say. If somebody wins, Roddy loses the council money, not his backers'. That's the truth. If someone wins the big one and I get blamed, I'll just laugh and tell him, "Ollie came to me in a dream and said, 'Fuck you.'" I'll just walk.

"Next game is Crazy H," I say. My voice is muffled by chatter and smoke. We play mostly tried-and-true bingo strategies here. Roddy's travelled as far as Montreal and Vancouver to keep up on the business. He wants a slick operation, only the best.

The Bow Tie and Cloverleaf games slow things down some, but the Inside Square and Outside Square games go faster than I've ever seen. I've barely called twenty-five balls and both are won. There's so many cards out there tonight, house odds are way down.

---

2. *Gitchi-Manitou* The Great Spirit.

When I call intermission before the big one, a line forms at the cashier box. The jackpot is actually three games in one. The best we can hope to fork out is $7,000. A grand for the first person to get One Line Anywhere, another grand for Four Corners and, if we're real lucky, only $5,000 for the jackpot.

Most are already in their chairs when I call them to play. Every other person has a smoke lit. I start the big one, and I call fair and slow, leaving each ball on the monitor for seven seconds before calling the next.

The One Line Anywhere goes to a young woman in just eight balls. She calls, "Bingo!" then squeaks like a chipmunk and begins giggling. Albert calls her numbers back to me. I wait a few seconds for effect before saying, "That's good bingo."

The Judge calls, "Bingo," calmly after clearing his throat. He got Four Corners in twelve balls. Roddy's pulling his hair out over in the corner. I've never seen people win so early. After Albert calls the Judge's numbers and I verify, an old Indian lady I don't recognize calls "Bingo" as well. The Judge frowns. Albert calls her numbers back. She made a mistake. The Judge smiles again.

Twenty-eight calls till we clear the first one. Roddy oversold tonight. There's way too many cards out there. I call tons of B's and N's and O's. When an I or a G comes up, people tense and search their cards hard. I call the thirty-second ball when I notice a woman eyeing the far monitor carefully. I call a G. She doesn't budge. She's only got one game sheet in front of her; obviously an amateur. But she's lucky tonight. It looks like all she needs is one or two I's to win, best I can see. That means there's got to be dozens of players on the edge of taking it. Ball number thirty-eight is an I. I call and close my eyes. Nothing. Another B on the next call. People moan loud. I reach in the popper for the fortieth ball. It doesn't feel right. I turn it over to reveal I-28. I can feel Roddy's eyes on me. A couple of people squeal loud but then a wave of sad shouts rises up. I see Roddy smiling.

The next two balls are an N and a G. Roddy's smiling bigger. The pot's down to $15,000 when I pull another G. People must be thinking the popper's rigged, so few I's have come up. Just as I'm about to pull the ball for $10,000, a shaky voice calls out, "Bingo," near the front door. She's a down-to-the-wire girl. She just won herself $15,000. Everybody turns and voices rise in grunts and swear words and anger. Albert runs to the unofficial winner.

I can see it's a young woman. She's thin and pretty. I like her long hair. Roddy walks over to help verify the numbers. I call out, "That's good bingo." People clap and some cheer. The young woman doesn't even smile. But I smile when Roddy pulls out the cheque book. It's nice to see a winner. I get up and stretch and head down to congratulate her.

You've never seen a place empty faster than a bingo hall after the calling's done. There are a few of the woman's friends around, smoking and talking to one another. Roddy holds her arm. He's smiling but he's not happy.

"Congratulations!" I say.

She seems to know I mean it. "Thanks, ma'am."

"What you going to do with all that money?" I ask her.

"Fix my husband's Ski-Doo and get myself a new rifle, I figure. Put the rest away." She's got almond eyes. She looks half Indian.

"Before you go making plans," Roddy jumps in, "what about considering a dona-tion to the council? You know we took a thumping in the wallet tonight to get interest up in a new casino. I'm not asking for all of it, miss, maybe $5,000. Think of it as an investment with guaranteed return. The new casino would consider you a very special guest. Always."

I don't believe Roddy's nerve. "Roddy!" I say.

He shoots me a stare. "Follow or get out of the way," he says.

It's late. I've got to get to the kids.

As I near the door, the woman says, "Bingo's as much as I can stand. I'm just really not much of a gambler. I … I can't imagine having luck like this again, and that's the truth."

I'm going to get out of the way, then.

I shut the Palace door behind me. There's no moon and the wind blows along the pine tops. I hear the wind's whisper. The stars are out bright. Finally to be in fresh air makes me laugh loud. I look up and say to the dog star, "*Aneen Anishnabe*. Hello, Indian." It's the star I told Little Ollie is his dad.

(2001)

Gregory Scofield (1966–)

Gregory Scofield was born in Maple Ridge, British Columbia, in 1966. He is of Cree-Métis ancestry. On the day of his birth, his father had a heart attack while standing trial on various charges and was brought to the same hospital where his son had just entered the world. Although most of the charges were dropped, he was convicted of fraud and handed a two-year prison term; after that, Scofield saw his father only twice. Later, his mother was misdiagnosed with mental illness (she actually had lupus) and institutionalized, and Scofield was thrust into a life of displacement, abuse, and identity crisis. He was initially cared for by one of his mother's boyfriends and then made his way through a series of foster homes. After living for brief periods in several northern communities, he returned to the West Coast, where he was reunited with his mother. She introduced him to his aunt, a mixed-blood Cree, who would teach her nephew about Cree culture.

As a young teenager, Scofield read Dee Brown's *Bury My Heart at Wounded Knee* (1970) and Maria Campbell's *Half-Breed* (1973), and they kindled his anger over the racist treatment of Native peoples in North America. He became more determined than ever to learn the Cree language and adopt Cree traditions. Despite this determination and the fact that he was accepted into a Manitoba Cree community, the young Scofield was subject to many pressures and uncertainties, and he was often assailed by self-doubt related to his Cree identity and his homosexuality. He spiralled into drug abuse and despair. Then, after years of suffering, Scofield had a dream similar to a vision quest (a traditional rite of passage undertaken in some North American Aboriginal cultures) in which he encountered Grandfather Black Bear, who taught him how to use Bear Medicine to heal people through writing. Scofield would later relate most of this dream in the introduction to *The Gathering: Stones for the Medicine Wheel* (1993), his first collection of poems.

Writing had been important to Scofield since high school; he says that "Writing for me originally was like a best friend." During a particularly troubled period, he burned much of what he had written, but in 1986 he moved to Saskatoon, Saskatchewan, and sold a radio play called *The Storyteller* to the Canadian Broadcasting Corporation. In 1988, he returned to British Columbia, found work in a bakery, and took a consulting job with the CBC on another radio play — the work of a White writer whose depiction of the Cree was inaccurate. The experience impressed upon Scofield how important it is for a culture to tell its own stories. He found a publisher for *The*

Gathering, but he was not yet satisfied with what he had created, so he broke the contract, rewrote the book, and found a new publisher.

The Gathering won the Dorothy Livesay Poetry Prize. It featured autobiographical motifs, especially the hardships faced by a young Native man in an alienating urban environment. In "Last Night's Rebellion," he invokes the fiddle music and dancing of his Métis heritage, but he also depicts the violent reaction that such manifestations of Native culture can provoke from non-Natives: "Fist connecting to cheekbone / Still hurts / Could have been worse / At least I said my piece: To hell with you! / We never lost Batoche or Seven Oaks." The same indignation infuses "Speaking Real Indian," in which the poet trains his sights on the White writer hired by the CBC: "Damn nervy using me as your surrogate voice / CBC must look pretty impressive on that resume ... No white writer talk that good Cree." Scofield does, however, project other, less virulent moods in this volume. In "Kohkum's Lullaby," he finds reassurance in the words of his grandmother ("Kiya mato noosisim / Kiya mato / Kiya mato"), translating her song: "Don't cry grandchild / Don't cry / Don't cry." In subsequent books, Scofield expands his use of the Cree language, and many of his poems are threaded with translations.

Scofield's publisher, Polestar, asked poet Patrick Lane to edit Scofield's next book, *Native Canadiana: Songs from the Urban Rez* (1996). Although Scofield was at first dubious about collaborating in this way with a non-Native, he later admitted in his memoir that "if ever I had the choice to pick a father, it would have been him." The volume extended Scofield's reflection on the hazards that city life holds for Native people. In "Treats," for example, the poet's mother advises him: "After dark ... / always walk / in the middle of the road / And never, / ever get into cars."

Growing tired of the label "angry Métis poet," Scofield turned with his next book to more positive aspects of his experience. *Love Medicine and One Song* (1997) opens with a series of erotic poems. In "Unhinged," the speaker "slipped the curve / of your backside, slipped between / your thighs / my seasoned lips mouthing / the peach song / beneath your scrotum." Although the object of pleasure is often the male body, the subject is not always explicitly male, and Scofield's invocation of the androgynous Coyote figure of Native mythology demonstrates a more expansive and complex view of sexuality. The persona of "Whispers and Thoughts" alludes to "this whisper cast up / from heart's mould," and declares, "these are the days / I want to be wide open, / sing loud / the medicine of me, / unpack the thoughts / I've stored all winter long." Poems appearing later in the volume move away from sexuality to focus on the healing power of tradition and on the love between elders and the young and among family members.

In 1999, Scofield produced the memoir *Thunder Through My Veins.* He says that he felt compelled to write it because, after years of telling and retelling the story of his life to a host of people, it had begun to feel as though it belonged to someone else: "I was so completely disconnected to anything that was painful or anything that was difficult in my childhood." Committing the story of his harrowing early years, his deprivations, confusions, and ultimate successes to print was a way of "taking ownership." He widened his exploration of autobiography and healing with *I Knew Two Métis Women: The Lives of Dorothy Scofield and Georgina Houle-Young* (1999), a book of poems about his mother and his aunt. "I wanted to show the beauty, the strength, and the love of the women in our communities," he says. These poems are shot through with strains of Loretta Lynn and Kitty Wells–era country and western, and the music serves as a refrain to lives scarred by poverty, racism, and sexual abuse. But these lives, as Scofield envisions them, are also testaments to love, courage, and the durability of a cultural tradition. In "Dat Ting About Waltzing," the poet slips into the vernacular, offering a back-handed acknowledgement of women's power by issuing a good-humoured warning: "never let dah woman leet / cause if you do / she'll dake your pants, / make you sign yer cheques / an hant dem over, / push you outta bet / to feet day babies, / do dah dishes, if she wishes."

In *Singing Home the Bones* (2006), Scofield divides his poems into two sections, one for conversations with the dead and one for conversations with the living. In "Conversation with the Poet," he employs tense humour and anecdote to express how difficult it is to recover the life story of his dead aunt. After proceeding through a series of variant repetitions in the style of the Cree oral tradition, it ends — "ekosi, I am done" — but it avoids closure. This comfort with uncertainty implies that Scofield has both matured as a poet and found peace, however provisional it may be.

Scofield, a long-time activist and community worker, teaches First Nations and Métis poetry at Brandon University in Manitoba.

Conversation with the Poet

Who didn't know my aunty

This story is told in oral tradition in a voice much older than mine, a voice whose thought process and first language is Cree. The story, though written in English, is a translation. I've heard old people speak in both Cree and English many times and I am immediately drawn into their rhythms, the poetry of their voices.

a few years ago   at a reading
of erotic poetry
a poet read a poem
by another poet
about a toothless Eskimo woman
in a bar
looking for someone, anyone
to buy her a drink   and
what she did, what
that Eskimo woman did for a drink

10

Long ago when my aunty was no longer Mean Man's wife — Punching Bag Woman she was called — she had met a moniyâw, a white man. He was the one who called her Good Cooking Day Woman, or Good Laundry Day Woman, or sometimes, Good With The Money Day Woman.

Now, my aunty had TB in her lungs — which took her from Edmonton down to a hospital in Vancouver. I used to hear about it at that time; it must have been hard for her.

She had three sons, my aunty did. But two of her boys got sick and died in Wabasca. Her other boy, John Houle he was called, was killed in a car accident coming home for Christmas. I used to hear her talk about it sometimes. She'd say to me, *One night back home I was sitting having tea and I looked out at the clothesline and sure enough there were three owls sitting there, just sitting there hooting away on my clothesline. It's true,* she told me. *And those owls, those owls started making somersaults, spinning around and around like this,* she told me.

a few years ago   at a reading
of erotic poetry
a poet read a poem
by another poet
20   about a toothless Eskimo woman

who could be:

ni-châpan, Hunting To Feed The Family Woman   *my great-great-grandmother*

who could be:

ni-mâmâ, Holding Up The Walls Woman   *my mother*

who could be:

a kaskitewiyas-iskwew,   *a black woman*

a sekipatwâw-iskwew,   *a Chinese woman*
a moniyâw-iskwew,   *a white woman*

running from a white man,   30
any man
into the arms of a poet

in a bar
looking for someone, anyone
to buy her a drink

My aunty, as I was saying here before, lost her boys early on. That is how I came to be her son: "nikosis, now you take the place of my John," she used to say. And I treated her as my mother: ni-mâmâsis, my little mother, I used to call her. My own mother — Dorothy was her name — did not mind this arrangement, for it was good for me to have two mothers.

It was these women who raised me by themselves. They were poor, my mothers, but it did not seem to matter — there were many things to keep a young boy occupied: books, music, stories and beadwork. I recall one time watching my aunty sew some moccasins. So interested was I that I kept moving closer and closer to her work. She did not seem to mind this ... Now, my little mother used to sew with very long threads and her needle would move very quickly. But this time I did not pay attention, so engrossed with the moccasins was I. She must have known this, for she took her sâponikan, that needle, and poked me right on the nose. *awas, ma-kôt!* she said. *Go on, big nose!* That is what she told me.

---

a few years ago   at a reading
of erotic poetry
40   a poet read a poem
by another poet
about a toothless Eskimo woman

she was fat, a seal
for the taking

she was dirty, a bag
of muskox bones
crawling with lice

she was dumb, her language
click, click
50   made people laugh

she was looking
for someone, anyone
to buy her a drink

I will not say my mothers did not have trouble with drinking or they did not lose days keeping the house in order. It is true: they had weaknesses here and there, just like other people.

And as far as my little mother goes, though she loved me a great deal, she did not get over losing her boys. I guess that is why today I speak so proudly of her, for she taught me many good things.

---

a few years ago   at a reading
of erotic poetry
a poet read a poem
by another poet
about a toothless Eskimo woman   60

and what she did   that woman
did for a drink.

It was in a bar:

it could be
the one from my childhood,

it could be

a room of white faces, a poetry hall
of uproarious mouths,

a room of unbound limbs
70   laughing
deep in their bones

or it could be
my aunty's rape bed, the man
who took her like a monument,
step after violent step

or it could be
her deathbed, all sixty-nine years
of her
lost in the translation
80   of a policeman's report

it could be, yes
the bed
where she told me stories

â-ha, the bed
where I laid dreaming

This is as much as I am able to tell about my aunty. But there is another thing,
one more thing you should know: I loved her very much and I still think of her
whenever I am lonesome. ekosi, I am done.

(2005)

No Peace

Señorita, tonight in the city
the streets are held up by candles
and there are bodies
burning past the Plaza de Armas,[1]
each a black wick smoking.

But tomorrow your mother will sift
for your bones in daylight,
though she has turned every stone,
folded back the pavement
from Juárez to El Paso.   10

There is such terrible talk.
The women in the maquiladoras[2]
have eyes with doors
that refuse to close. Oh, such talk
of charred remains,

a small pink shoe   found
graceless as a dead flamingo.
And there is no peace, no trace
if the lizards have built
a house from your bones.   20

Still the others lie hidden
holding flowers without colour,
and in their mouths
the sand of silence is golden.
It is true, the desert

cannot be forced into confession
and la policía, the officals
are without the eye
of the Blessed Virgin.
But you must know, Señorita   30

two countries away
my own dark-skinned sisters
turn in a grave of silent rages.
But tonight in Ciudad Juárez[3]
the streets are held up by candles

---

1. Plaza de Armas Latin American term for a city square. **2. maquiladoras** American-run factories in Mexico. **3. Ciudad Juárez** Mexican border town, infamous for its crime rate; many women have been murdered there.

and there are bodies, many hearts
burning past the Plaza de Armas.
Señorita, from here
I will pray your bones' finding.
40   I will pray your mother rest.

(2005)

Women Who Forgot the Taste of Limes

Letter to ni-châpan Mary

ni-châpan, if I take ki-cihcânikan,   *my ancestor, your fingerbone*
press it to their lips,
will they remember the taste of limes,
sea-salt bled into their grandfathers' skin?

If I pull from this bag of rattling bones
the fiddle, the bow bone,
if I go down to the lazy Red,
lay singing in the grass

will the faces of our ancestors
10   take shape in clouds
and will the clouds name themselves,
each river-lot stolen?

If I take ki-tôkanikan, ni-châpan,   *your hipbone*
place on them a pack to bear
will they know the weight of furs,
kawâpahtamiwuk chî   *will they see?*

the city is made of blood, wîni   *bone marrow*
stains their grandmothers' aprons,
swims deep in the flesh, a grave of history,
20   a dry bone song.

ni-châpan, if I take ki-kiskatikan   *your shinbone*
will they offer up the streets,
lay open their doors and say I'm welcome?
Or if I take ki-tâpiskanikan,   *your jawbone*

place it scolding on Portage and Main
will all the dead Indians
rise up from the cracks, spit bullets
that made silent our talk?

If I take ki-mâwikan, ni-châpan   *your backbone*
I could say to them   30
I'm not afraid of gunshots, stones
or the table I sit at —

this table where I drink tea with ghosts
who share my house and the words
to keep it clean.
ni-châpan, if I take ki-chicânikan,   *your fingerbone*

press it to their lips
will they remember the taste of limes,
hold silent their sour tongues
for once?   40

                                                                                        (2005)

Karen Solie (1966–)

Asked about her origins as a writer, Karen Solie says, "I'd read sentences that astonished me and wonder how the writer was able to do it. Eventually I began to wonder if I could do it." Solie was born in Moose Jaw, Saskatchewan, in 1966 and lived for several years in Saskatoon. In the mid-1970s, she and her family moved to a farm that her grandfather had homesteaded in 1912. After completing high school, she went to Alberta and enrolled in university transfer courses at Medicine Hat College with the intention of becoming a veterinarian. Bogged down by the math and science requirement, she switched to a journalism program at Lethbridge Community College and, diploma in hand, landed a reporter-photographer job at the *Lethbridge Herald*. She later earned a B.A. in English at the University of Lethbridge, supporting herself by working as a university grounds-keeper; she also did shifts in the university library and at a local coffee shop. Pursuing her interest in music, Solie learned to play classical piano and for a time lived in Austin, Texas, where she joined a band that performed country music with "a few punk covers thrown in."

In Texas, Solie also began to write poems — she cites Wallace Stevens and Anne Carson as early influences — and did an independent study of the work of William Blake. She moved to British Columbia in 1993, where she earned an M.A. in English at the University of Victoria and then embarked on a doctoral program. In 2001, she began reviewing books for the *Globe and Mail* and published her first poetry collection, *Short Haul Engine*. A year later, realizing that the tenure track was not for her, she decided to make Toronto her home and dropped out of school.

The poems of *Short Haul Engine* are couched in a strong and rhythmic language that evinces Solie's grounding in music. "I'm a sucker for the sort of minor chord lyric mood of Beethoven sonatas," she admits, "but also the hysterical operatic sweep … of Nick Cave's work. I like how early Delta blues artists work with structure, language and repetition … the propulsive rhythms and cadences of bluegrass and punk." *Short Haul Engine* mines a range of preoccupations: cars and guns, highways and back roads, parents and children, lovers joined and alienated, surgery and helicopter crashes, fish and houseplants. Solie has said that her intention in writing these poems was "to get as close as I could to what I saw and felt and thought before these things ran away into the trees." The "process of looking, of drawing near, is the poem." That process is fraught, however — in "Ill Wind," the poet acknowledges that the moment of tension that engenders insight is fleeting: "Power lines wail, barely holding. / Everything happens here, then nothing / for a long time."

In 2004, Solie published the chapbook *The Shooter's Bible*. She followed this a year later with the collection *Modern and Normal*, in which philosophy and physics and ecology are striated with love and desire and pain. The persona of "Sleeping with Wittgenstein" is physically rescued ("Without him, / I might have died in those woods") and emotionally betrayed ("blindness: an inability to see / the double cross. I'm drenched. He's a man / who gets over it") by her "steeled" lover. In "Science and the Single Girl," the poet's voice rails against the smug and inadequate principles of matter: "What can we expect of a triangle / that we cannot expect from ourselves? Each side / a retaining wall, holding up its end. But / an equilateral affair? Please." The collection is divided into three sections — "More or Less," "As If," and "Everything's Okay." The titles of the first two sections underscore the perception buried in the poems they contain that both love and science, seemingly locked in an internecine struggle, have failed to conquer the slippery and prevaricating nature of existence. The persona in "Sleeping with Wittgenstein" knows that "Not everything you look at / is something. What was true is / no longer, and belief / a problem of tenses, of lapse." In "Everything's Okay" — and it's clearly not — reality fluctuates so rapidly it barely exists: "a man leans / to his companion as though he loves her. You believe one idea, / and then another. That is, in the instant, at the time."

Solie is intrigued by the capacity of poetry to summon a palpable mood "without necessarily ever referring to it directly." She admires writers (like Philip Larkin, Flannery O'Connor, Lorrie Moore, and Tim Lilburn, but the list is long) "who work with voice and tone and suggestion to mobilize the weird capacity of language to speak in spite of what might appear to be its obvious intent. To make absence present and allow a loaded silence." In *Modern and Normal*'s "Love Song of the Unreliable Narrator," she turns language's "weird capacity" upon itself, and a poem about the dry structures of language and narrative becomes a mysterious erotic exercise — "Lonely / as a preposition, you long for the thrust / of an accusative world" — and a dark comment on the politics of sexual desire — "The den that words / scratch out in you is my favourite haunt. / See my shadow; you'll have untold weeks / of whatever it is that you want."

Solie has served as writer in residence at the Universities of Alberta and New Brunswick. She lives in Toronto with her partner, poet David Seymour.

Signs Taken for Wonders

Moments earlier we were giggling
at the new priest's Romanian accent.
"Listen to the way he says *body*,"
I said. And she faints.
My sister faints in a robin's egg dress,
sighs, leans into our mother and escapes
thick August heat itchy as cow hair
with incense, flies. She swoons.
Unlike Mrs. Stein who clattered down
10   like an armload of wood.

Too delicate for these dog-days,
small, clover-blonde,
my sister sews indoors.
I ask her to fashion me
into something nice, ivory silk.
I am a big girl, sunburnt

skin like raw meat, sweating
two pews in front of the Blessed Virgin.

Poor Mary, back of her plaster head
caved in, dropped in the vestry   20
by a Knight of Columbus.[1]

Now mom's pale eyelids
are cabbage moths, fluttering,
hand on my sister's flushing brow.
If a sign comes today I may be
the only one standing,
strong as a horse.
Jesus's oozing stigmata, or worse,
that awful heart and its ring of thorns
jumping like a fish you'd thought was dead.   30

Did Mr. Schaefer receive a sign
as the tractor crushed his chest?
Doubtful. He had a Lutheran wife,
likely planting silly doomed petunias
in the clay.

(2001)

Sturgeon[1]

Jackfish and walleye circle like clouds as he strains
the silt floor of his pool, a lost lure in his lip,
Five of Diamonds, River Runt, Lazy Ike,[2]
or a simple spoon, feeding
a slow disease of rust through his body's quiet armour.
Kin to caviar, he's an oily mudfish. Inedible.
Indelible.[3] Ancient grunt of sea
in a warm prairie river, prehistory a third eye in his head.
He rests, and time passes as water and sand
through the long throat of him, in a hiss, as thoughts   10
of food. We take our guilts
to his valley and dump them in,
give him quicksilver to corrode his fins, weed killer,
gas oil mix, wrap him in poison arms.
Our bottom feeder,
sin-eater.

On an afternoon mean as a hook we hauled him
up to his nightmare of us and laughed

---

1. **Knight of Columbus** Member of the Catholic men's service organization.

---

1. **Sturgeon** Large bottom-feeding fish. 2. **Five of Diamonds ... Lazy Ike** Fishing lures. 3. **Indelible** Permanent, unforgettable.

at his ugliness, soft sucker mouth opening,
20   closing on air that must have felt like ground glass,
left him to die with disdain
for what we could not consume.
And when he began to heave and thrash over yards of rock
to the water's edge and, unbelievably, in,
we couldn't hold him though we were teenaged
and bigger than everything. Could not contain
the old current he had for a mind, its pull,
and his body a muscle called river, called spawn.

(2001)

A Treatise on the Evils of
Modern Homeopathic Medicines

"What if the vitamin makes my body stop making its own vitamins?"
    — Mark Anthony Jarman

" ... homeopathy is based on the theory that 'like cures like.'"
    — *Oxford English Reference Dictionary*

Take four Tylenol with that last sweet shot.
Morning comes, you'll be a prince
on the phones, greasing wheels, making it go
with a clear head. Your guts will come around.
Little quinine[1] at coffee. Cuts the shakes.
Sudden liver failure? Forget about it.
Cellphone tumours? Bullshit.
Look at me. 40 years and still a whip,
slick, the ticket, hyperspace.
10   I smoked my first cigarette at nine.
You don't know who to trust? Then don't.
Trust technology. It wouldn't send
machinery to Mars then seed
your little brain to polyps,[2] plant
cancer mushrooms in your balls.
It can keep your dick hard all night.
What more do you need? Someone tries
to sell you blue-green algae. Fuck him.
It's a scheme. Vitamin C? Eat an orange
20   for Chrissakes. Send that joker back
to the co-op, to his hypocrite cronies
drumming in the woods reading Bly[3] by night,

---

1. **quinine** Bitter whitish compound used to treat malaria. 2. **polyps** Intrusive growth on an organ's tissue. 3. **Bly** Nellie Bly (1864–1922), American activist and author who famously feigned insanity to investigate a mental facility from within.

Rand[4] by day. That'll soften your brain
fast as any happy hour. Do you think
no one is making money from this?
That it comes from the goodness of a heart?
Nothing comes from the goodness of a heart.
Like God said on the seventh day, kicking back,
feeling fine. Pick your poison
children, leave me mine.   30

                                                                    (2001)

Cipher Stroke[1]

> Scores of cases of the "stroke" are reported among men and
> women of all classes, who have been prostrated by their efforts
> to figure in thousands of millions. Many of these persons
> apparently are normal, except for a desire to write endless
> rows of ciphers.

— John Kenneth Galbraith

India opened zero and gods crawled out. Then everything else
fell in. Became, in falling, infinitely lovely, lit
with presence. Light in the still-life, spark in the field
we angle toward, odd-numbered
in a wonky sorrow, sight-lined to the vanishing point
with no end to speak of. Backs up against it,
the Greeks stared at stars for a long time, whistling,
beginning at one: the Prime Mover,[2] itself
unmoved, blameless in a fast fade.

It has the tug of a hole about it,   10
that hole, the mortal instant that fevers, shines,
then resumes its mileage hill to hill. A hundred kilometres
between Seven Persons and Purple Springs means
an easy hour on the highway. Unless the traffic's
bad, or the weather's bad, or the engine's bad, or worse
should an alarming new equation involving plastics
and combustion be borne in on the shoulders
of a huge misunderstanding. Please
tell me to shut up over and over. You drive.
I can't keep my eyes open.   20

---

4. **Rand** Ayn Rand (1905–1982) American novelist and Objectivist and individualist philosopher.

---

1. **Cipher Stroke** Nervous condition afflicting Germans in the 1920s when inflation drove prices for even small items into the millions; sufferers had the compulsion to write strings of zeros (ciphers) and do impossibly complex logarithmic calculations. 2. **Prime Mover** Source of power in a complex system; in metaphysics, that which set all else in motion.

Careers are made of it. To be proven wrong
and to try to make even this
beautiful. Find us in the fields again, the bush,
or back in the slapworn towns we grew up in, counting
off. As if we could forward or reverse along
the path of weird degrees and close the distance separating
us from what we love. The in-between
exponentiates merrily as a debt. And then, and
then. Repeat yourself and see what happens.

30   It's said the stock market behaves organically,
like a rodent or a wave. Everyone has a system
to own the table. Odds are night will fall
unnoticed, with the tick of water wasting through a hose
as the house burns down. Can thought about things
be so much different from things? Take up sleep
and defensive drinking. Lie down
awhile. At the airport, planes take off
and land without a problem.

Nothing keeps happening. A special kind
40   that pulls our midpoints toward it. The lure of the lip
where the falling starts, hesitant apex
of the arc or the prairie exhaling through centuries,
its great unseen beams sistered up, looking like the convergence
of an infinite series where each instant, each sound
hides another, and so on. Silence, the breath
inside the body of what is, sings an unbroken tone struck
in the key of nil. This endless untitled exclamation
implicit and from everywhere at once.

(2005)

Determinism

Someone's walking toward you, tree to tree, parting leaves
with the barrel of a rifle. There's a scope
on it. He's been watching awhile
through his good eye, you, washing dishes, scouring
what's burned with a handful of salt, so your shoulders shake
a little. Keep your back to him. It's sexier
under the bulb, light degraded,
like powder. The kitchen screens
are torn. You've worn something
10   nice. There's a breeze he's pressing through, boots
in the grass. There's a breeze and you smell him
blowing in on it. As if this has always
been happening and you've entered the coincidence of your life

with itself, the way a clock's ticks will hit the beat of a Hank Williams[1] song,
the best one, on the radio, fridge hum tuned without a quaver
to the sustained notes of the bridge. As if
you've arrived at where the hinge
articulates. An animal
may be bleeding in the woods. He could be carrying a pair of grouse
by the feet. Only details are left, bruises of gesture, style's aspirin   20
grit. He shuts the door and leans the gun against the wall
like a guitar. You keep your back to him because
it's sexier. Because in turning
you will see the dinner in all its potential
as you speak, spring the catch, finish this, the weighted moment
buckling into consequence. The place
where you can face your history and see it coming.

(2005)

Love Song of the Unreliable Narrator

Only God is objective, but he's long
gone, the thing that could save you
explained away. Irony takes you out at night
but appetite drives you home as I pace
outside your window singing songs
that make you moan with an uncertainty
that is the sex of dream. Lonely
as a preposition, you long for the thrust
of an accusative world. Crux. Locus.
Interstices.[1] Can you feel my tug   10
upon your sleeve? The den that words
scratch out in you is my favorite haunt.
See my shadow; you'll have untold weeks
of whatever it is that you want.

(2005)

Eden Robinson (1968–)

Eden Robinson grew up in Haisla territory near Kitamaat Village on the central coast of British
Columbia. She and her siblings are of mixed heritage: her father is Haisla and her mother is
Heiltsuk. Kitamaat, a Tsimshian word meaning "people of the falling snow," is home to 700 members of the Haisla nation; another 800 or so live off-reserve. Stories within Haisla communities are
transferred orally; committing these stories or descriptions of cultural rituals and events to writing
is considered taboo. Robinson's uncle, Gordon Robinson, whose *Tales of the Kitamaat* appeared in
1956, was the first Haisla ever to be published. Community elders were displeased by this, and

---

1. **Hank Williams** American country musician (1923–1953).

1. **Crux, Locus, Interstices** A pivotal or divisive point; a centre or site; narrow spaces between things.

even today, some disapprove of Eden Robinson's status as a Haisla fiction writer. "I can't write about certain things," she says, "or someone will go fatwa on me."

In her village, Eden is known as Vicki Lena. "I was named after a cousin who choked to death in her crib on a bottle," she explains. "So, I always thought that some day I'd change my name to something like Rebecca or Anastasia. Anyway, my first year of college I was telling that to someone who said, 'Oh, you'll never change your name.' And I decided, 'Yes, I will. I'm … Eden Robinson.'" The first author whose work gripped her was Stephen King: "I think it was *The Shining* that made me want to start writing." Her fascination with horror fiction is long established — "we had a grade four teacher, Mr. Mung, who absolutely adored Edgar Allan Poe. *The Purloined Letter. The Golden Ladybug.*"

After earning a B.F.A. from the University of Victoria in 1992, Robinson spent some time in the Kitlope region, a place that "touched the part of me that tells stories. And it was the part of me that had been missing." She then moved to Vancouver to find work that would allow her time to write. A late-night writer, she ended up taking "a lot of McJobs" — janitor, mail clerk, napkin ironer. Then, after having a story published in *PRISM international,* she decided to enter the M.F.A. program at the University of British Columbia.

In 1996, Robinson produced her first book, *Traplines,* which she developed from her thesis. It consists of three stories and one novella set in Kitamaat and Vancouver's Downtown Eastside, a neighbourhood in which members of the arts community mingle with drug dealers and addicts, runaways and prostitutes. Many disenfranchised Native people land there. "East Vancouver is my milieu," she says. "It's not foreign to me." The stories are written from various perspectives, both Native and non-Native, confounding assumptions about Robinson's ability to master divergent narrative voices — "People assumed I couldn't write anything that wasn't native because I'm native. … I wrote about non-native characters just to show them I could." She describes these characters as outcasts battling the pressures of modern life, adding, "I'm fascinated with serial killers, psychopaths, and sociopaths." The title story is told from the perspective of Will, a teenager who is torn between loyalty to his alcoholic and abusive family and his mounting desire to escape. In "Dogs in Winter," the young narrator recounts her past through a series of flashbacks, revealing that she is the progeny of a serial killer — a woman who butchers six people, stashing their bodies in a freezer, and later methodically slashes a neighbour's dog "Up and down … [with a] rapt face." In the novella, "Contact Sports," a teenaged boy named Tom becomes the obsessive object of his older cousin Jeremy's attention. Jeremy lavishes Tom and his mother with expensive gifts and starts exerting control over Tom's life. The price is initially acceptable to Tom — "A little freedom lost. A little financial security gained. Just long enough to finish classes without worrying about rent" — but he quickly realizes that he has made a terrible mistake and is in thrall to a sadistic sociopath.

Traplines was named a *New York Times* 1996 editor's choice and notable book of the year. Four years later, Robinson published her first novel, *Monkey Beach,* which builds on the foundations of the *Traplines* story "Queen of the North." It centres on Lisamarie Hill, a young Haisla woman from Kitamaat who learns that her younger brother, Jimmy, is missing at sea. Lisa is vital, funny, and outspoken, but she also suffers — she has lost friends and family members over the years and, succumbing to rage and grief (often difficult to separate), she has buried herself in the city, sliding into drug and alcohol abuse. Now in the process of healing, and having achieved a fragile peace with her family, she embarks on a quest to find Jimmy, travelling by boat along the coast. Lisa's journey becomes a voyage back in time as she remembers the past she shared with her brother. It is also a spiritual quest. Lisa is sensitive to the spirit world: the ghosts of dead relatives and ancestors as well as Sasquatches and animal spirits have helped draw her out of her self-destructive cycle, and they visit her now as she travels by water to join her parents in the search for Jimmy. Here, Robinson expands her tight focus on fatally damaged souls to include people who have the strength to grow and to try to build bridges between traditional ways and the modern world. *Monkey Beach* was nominated for a number of honours, among them the Giller Prize and the Governor General's Award.

Robinson's next novel, *Blood Sports* (2006), picks up the narrative of *Traplines*'s "Contact Sports" five years later. It is a stark and violent brew of revenge and addiction and dysfunctional relationships, and, formally, a construct of fragmented storylines and multiple perspectives. Tom, now in his early 20s, has had a baby, Melody, with a fellow ex-junkie named Paulina. One day, he comes home from work to find that Paulina and the baby have vanished. Then his toxic cousin Jeremy re-emerges. "I expected *Blood Sports* to go in a very different direction," Robinson says. "I had plots, plans, but the characters evolved in a way I hadn't outlined. Originally I was picturing something lighter … so my characters were really safe in the first couple of drafts. Then I started torturing them. I really didn't have a choice. When my characters solidify themselves, they pretty well take over."

Robinson began writing the novel in the Yukon while serving as writer-in-residence at the Whitehorse Public Library; she continued it while she was at the University of Calgary's Markin-Flanagan Distinguished Writers program. She finally finished the book after returning to Kitamaat, where she now lives. She is learning to speak the Haisla language.

Traplines

Dad kills a marten.

"Will you look at that," he says.

It is limp in his hand. A goner.

We tramp through the snow to the end of our trapline. Dad whistles. The goner marten is over his shoulder. From here, it looks like Dad is wearing it. There is nothing else in the other traps. We head back to the truck. The snow crunches. This is the best time for trapping, Dad told me a while ago. This is when the animals are hungry.

Our truck rests by the roadside at an angle. Dad rolls the white marten in a grey canvas cover separate from the others. The marten is flawless, which is rare around here. I put my animals beside his and cover them. We get in the truck. Dad turns the radio on. Country twang fills the cab. We smell like sweat and oil and pine. Dad hums. I stare out the window. Mrs. Smythe would say the trees here are like the trees on Christmas postcards. They are tall and heavy with snow. They crowd close to the road. When the wind blows strong enough, the older trees snap and fall on the power lines.

"Well, there's our Christmas money," Dad says, snatching a peek at the rearview mirror.

I look back. The wind ruffles the canvas that covers the martens. Dad is smiling. He sits back, steering with one hand. He does not even mind when we are passed by three cars. The lines in his face are loose now. He sings along with a woman who left her husband. Even that doesn't make him mad. We have our Christmas money. There will be no shouting in the house for a while. It will take Mom and Dad a while to find something else to fight about.

The drive home is a long one. Dad changes the radio station twice. I search my brain for something to say to him. He watches the road, and looks at the back of the truck. I watch the trees, the road, the cars passing us.

One of the cars has two women in it. The woman that isn't driving waves her hands around as she talks. She reminds me of Mrs. Smythe. They are behind us, then beside us, then ahead of us and gone.

Tulka is still as we drive into it. The snow drugs it, makes it lazy. Houses puff cedar smoke and the smell of it gets in everyone's clothes. Sweet and sharp. When I am in school in town, I can close my eyes and tell who is from the village and who isn't just by smelling them.

When we go home, we go straight to the basement. Dad gives me the ratty martens and keeps the good ones. He made me start on squirrels when I was in grade seven. He put the knife in my hand saying, "For Christ's sake, it's just a squirrel. It's dead, you stupid knucklehead. It can't feel anything."

He made the first cut for me. I swallowed and closed my eyes and cut.

"Jesus," Dad muttered. "Are you a sissy? I got a sissy for a son? Look. It's just like cutting up a chicken. See? Pretend you're skinning a chicken." Dad showed me, then put another squirrel in front of me and we didn't leave the basement until I got it right.

Now Dad is skinning the flawless white marten. He is using his best knife. His tongue is sticking out the corner of his mouth. He sits up, and shakes his skinning hand. I quickly start on the next marten. It is perfect except it has been in a fight that has left a scar across its back. It isn't a good skin. We won't get much for it. Dad goes back to work. I stop, clench, unclench my hands. They are stiff.

"Goddamn," Dad says quietly. I look up, tensing. Dad starts to smile. He has finished the marten. It is ready to be dried and sold. I have also finished mine. I look at my hands. They know what to do now without me having to tell them. Dad laughs as we go up the creaking stairs. When we get into the hallway, I breathe in, smelling bread. Fresh baked homemade bread.

Mom is sprawled in front of the TV. Her apron is floured and she is licking her fingers. When she sees us, she stops and puts her hands in her apron pockets.

"Well?" she says.

Dad lifts her up and dances her across the living room.

"Greg! Stop it!" she says, laughing.

Flour gets on Dad and cedar chips get on Mom. They talk and I leave, sneaking into the kitchen. I snatch two buns and take three aspirin and go to my room. I stop in the doorway. Eric is there. He is plugged into his electric guitar. He sees me and looks at the buns. He pulls out an earphone.

"Give me one," he says.

I throw him the smaller one, and he finishes it in three bites.

"The other one," he says.

I give him the finger and sit on my bed. I see him thinking about tackling me, but he shrugs and plugs himself back in. I chew on the bun, roll bits of it around my mouth. Fresh bread has a taste I have never been able to name. Something that makes it different from day old, or store bought. It is still warm, and I wish I had some honey for it, or some blueberry jam.

Eric gets up and leaves. He comes back with six buns and wolfs them down, cramming them into his mouth. I watch him, then watch the walls. He can't hear himself eat. I plug my ears and glare at him. He looks up. Grins. Opens his mouth so I can see.

Dad comes in. Eric's jaw clenches. Dad pulls himself straight. I leave, go into the kitchen, grabbing a hunk of bread. Mom smacks my hand. We hear Eric and Dad starting to yell. Mom rolls her eyes and puts three more loaves in the oven.

"Back later," I say.

She nods, frowning at her hands, not looking up.

I walk. Think about going to Billy's house. He is seeing Elaine, though, and is getting weird. He wrote her a poem yesterday. We all laughed at him and he didn't even mind. He didn't find anything nice to rhyme with "Elaine" so he didn't finish the poem.

"Pain," Craig said. "Elaine, you pain."

"Pain Elaine," Jer said.

Billy smacked Jer and they went at it in the snow. Billy gave Jer a face wash and that ended it. We let him sit on the steps and write in peace.

"Elaine in the rain," I say. "Elaine, a flame. Cranes. Danes. Trains." I smile, "My main Elaine." I shake my head. Billy is on his own.

I let my feet take me down the street. It starts to snow, tiny ladybug flakes. It is only 4:00 but it is getting dark. Street lights flicker on. No one but me is out walking. Snot in my nose freezes. The air is starting to burn my throat. I turn and head home. Eric and Dad should be tired by now.

Another postcard picture. The houses lining the street look snug. I hunch into my jacket. In a few weeks, Christmas lights will go up. We have the same set every year. Dad will put them up two weeks before Christmas. We will get a tree a week before Christmas. Mom will decorate it. She will put our presents under it on Christmas Eve. In the morning, some of the presents will be wrapped in aluminum because she never buys enough wrapping paper. We will eat. Mom and Dad will go out and we will not see them for a few days. Eric will go to a lot of parties and get really stoned. Mom and Dad will go to a lot of parties and get really drunk. Maybe this year I will too. Anything would be better than sitting around with Tony and Craig, listening to them gripe.

I stamp the snow off my sneakers and jeans. I open the door quietly. The TV is on loud. I can tell by the announcer's voice that it is a hockey game. I take my shoes off. The house is really hot after being outside. I pull off my jacket. My face starts to tingle as the skin thaws. I go into the kitchen. I take a few aspirins and stand near the stove. The kitchen could use some plants. It gets some good light in the winter. Mrs. Smythe has her kitchen crowded with plants. The cats usually munch on the ferns, so she has them hanging by the window. They have a lot of pictures of places they have been all over their walls. Europe. Africa. Arctic. They have been everywhere. They can afford it, she says, because they don't have kids. They had one, a while ago. On the TV, there is a wallet-sized picture of a dark haired boy with three missing teeth. He was their kid, but he disappeared. Mrs. Smythe stares at the picture a lot.

Eric tries to sneak up behind me. His socks make a slithering sound on the floor. I duck just in time and hit him in the stomach.

"Oof," he doubles over, hands over his belly. He has a towel stretched between his hands. His "Choking" game. He punches at me, but I hop out of the way. He hits the stove. Yelling, he jerks his hand back. I race out of the kitchen and go down to the basement. Eric is screaming my name. "Come out, you chicken," he says. "Come out and fight."

I stay behind some plywood. Eric still has the towel ready for me. After a while, he goes back upstairs and locks the door behind him.

I stand. Eric turns the TV off. Mom and Dad must have gone out to celebrate. They will find a bootlegger and go on a bender until Monday, when Dad has to go back to work. So. I am alone with Eric. He'll leave the house around 10:00. I can stay out of his way until then.

The basement door slams open. I scramble under Dad's tool table. Eric must be stoned. He probably has been toking up since Mom and Dad left. Pot always makes him mean.

He laughs. "You baby. You are a fucking baby." He doesn't look for me that hard. He thumps loudly up the stairs, slams the door shut, then tiptoes back down and waits. He must think I am really stupid.

We stay like this for a long time. Eric lights up. In a few minutes, the whole basement smells like pot. Dad will be pissed off if it ruins the perfect white marten. I smile, hoping it does. Eric will really get it then.

"Fuck," he says and disappears upstairs, not locking the door. I crawl out. My legs are stiff. The pot is making me dizzy.

The wood stove is cooling. I don't open it. Its door squeals. It will be freezing down here soon. Breathing fast, I go upstairs. I crack the door open. There are no lights on except in our bedroom. Eric must be playing. I pull on my jacket and sneakers. I grab some bread before I hear the bedroom door being opened. I stuff it in my jacket and run for the door. Eric is blocking it, grinning.

"Thought you were sneaky, hey," he says.

I back into the kitchen. He follows. I wait until he is near before I bend over and ram him. He is slow because of the pot and slips to the floor. He grabs my ankle, but I kick him in the head and am out the door before he can catch me. I take the steps two at a time. Eric stands on the porch and laughs. I can't wait until I'm bigger. I'd like to smear him against a wall. Let him see what it feels like. I'd like to smear him so bad.

I munch on some bread as I head for the village exit to the highway. The snow comes down in thick, large flakes that melt when they touch my skin. I stand at the exit and wait.

I hear One Eye's beat-up Ford a long time before I see it. It clunks down the road and stalls when he stops it beside me.

"You again. What are you doing here?" One Eye yells at me.

"Waiting for Princess fucking Di," I say.

"Smart mouth. You keep it up and you can stay out here."

The back door opens anyway. Snooker and Jim are there. One Eye and Pete Wilson are in front. They all have the same silver lunch buckets at their feet.

When we come into town I say, "Could you drop me off here?"

One Eye looks up, surprised. He has forgotten I am here. He frowns. "Where are you going?"

"Disneyland," I say.

"Smart mouth," he says. "Don't be like your brother. You stay out of trouble."

I laugh. One Eye slows the car and pulls over. It chokes and sputters. I get out and thank him for the ride. One Eye grunts. They pull away and I walk to Mrs. Smythe's.

The first time I saw her house was last spring when she invited all her English classes there for a barbecue. Their lawn was neat and green and I only saw one dandelion. They had rose bushes in the front and raspberry bushes in the back. I went with Tony and Craig, who got high before we got there. Mrs. Smythe noticed right away. She took them aside and talked to them. They stayed in the pool room downstairs until the high wore off.

I wandered around. There weren't any other kids from the village there. Only townies. Kids that Dad says will never get their pink hands dirty. They were split into little groups. They talked and ate and laughed and I was walking around, feeling like a dork. I was going to go downstairs to Tony and Craig when Mrs. Smythe came up to me. It's funny, I never noticed how nice her smile was until then. Her blue sundress swayed as she came up to me, carrying a hotdog.

"You weren't in class yesterday," she said, smiling.

"Uh, stomach ache."

"I was going to tell you how much I liked your essay. You must have done a lot of work on it."

I tried to remember what I had written. "Yeah."

"Which part was the hardest?" she said.

I cleared my throat. "Starting it."

She gave me a funny look. "I walked right into that one," she said, laughing. I kept smiling.

A tall man came up and hugged her. She kissed him. "Sam," she said. "This is the student I was telling you about."

"Well, hello," Mr. Smythe said. "Great paper."

"Thanks," I said, trying hard to remember what I had written about.

"Is it William or Will?" Mr. Smythe said.

"Will," I said. He held out his hand. We shook.

"Did you ever find out what happened to him?" Mrs. Smythe said.

Oh no, I thought, remembering what I'd written. I had to write about a real life experience and it was the night before the deadline and that was all I could think of. I blushed and shook my head. I was glad Tony and Craig weren't here.

"Karen tells me you've written a lot about fishing, too," Mr. Smythe said, sounding really cheerful.

"Excuse me," Mrs. Smythe said. "That's my cue to leave. If you're smart, you'll do the same. Once you get Sam going about his stupid fish stories you can't get a wor–"

Mr. Smythe goosed her. She hit him with her hotdog and left quickly. Mr. Smythe put his arm around my shoulder, shaking his head. He asked if I'd ever done any real fishing. We sat down on the patio. He told me about the time he caught a marlin, and about scuba diving in the Great Barrier Reef. He went down in a shark cage once, to try to film a Great White eating. I told him about the halibut I caught on Uncle Bernie's gilnetter. He wanted to know if Uncle Bernie would take him out. I gave him Old Marty Gladstone's number, because he takes charters. He asked me what gear he was going to need. We ended up in the kitchen, me using a flounder to show him how to clean a halibut.

I finally looked at the clock around 10:00. Dad had said he would pick me and Tony and Craig up around 8:00. I didn't even know where Tony and Craig were anymore. I couldn't believe it had gotten this late without me noticing it. Mr. Smythe said he would drive me home. I said no, that's okay, I'll hitch.

He snorted. "Karen would kill me. No, I'll drive you. Let's phone your parents and tell them you're coming home."

No one answered the phone. I said they were probably asleep. He dialled again. Still no answer.

"Looks like you've got the spare bedroom tonight," he said.

"Let me try," I said, picking up the phone. There was no answer but after six rings, I pretended Dad was on the other end. I didn't want to spend the night at my English teacher's house. Tony and Craig would never shut up about it.

"Hi, Dad," I said. "How come ... oh. I see. Car trouble. No problem. Mr. Smythe is going to drive me home. What? sure, I–"

"Let me talk to him," Mr. Smythe said, snatching the phone. "Hello! Mr. Bolton! How are you! My, my, my. Your son is a lousy liar, isn't he?" He hung up. "It's amazing how much your father sounds like a dial tone."

I grabbed the phone. "They're sleeping, that's all," I said. I dialled again. Mr. Smythe watched me. There wasn't any answer.

"Why'd you lie?" he said quickly.

We were alone in the kitchen. I swallowed. He was a lot bigger than me. When he reached for me, I put my hands up and covered my face. He stopped then took the phone out my hands.

"It's okay," he said. "I won't hurt you. It's okay."

I put my hands down. He looked sad. That annoyed me. I shrugged, backing away. "I'll hitch," I said.

Mr. Smythe shook his head. "Karen would kill me, then she'd go after you. Come on. We'll be safer if you sleep in the spare room."

In the morning, Mr. Smythe was up before I could sneak out. He was making bacon and pancakes. He asked if I'd ever done any freshwater fishing. I said no. He started talking about fishing in the Black Sea and I sat and listened to him, eating slowly. He is a good cook.

Mrs. Smythe came into the kitchen dressed in some sweats and a T-shirt. She ate without saying anything and didn't look awake until she finished her coffee. Mr. Smythe phoned home, but no one answered. He asked if I wanted to go up to Old Timer's Lake and try my hand at his new Sona Reel. I didn't have anything better to do.

Mr. Smythe has a great speedboat. He let me drive it around the lake a few times. We even went water-skiing. Mrs. Smythe looked great in her bathing suit. We lazed around the beach in the afternoon, watching the people go by. Sipping their beers, they argued about who was going to drive back. We rode around the lake some more and roasted hotdogs for dinner.

Their porch light is on. I go up the walk and ring the bell. Mrs. Smythe has said to just come in, don't bother knocking, but I can't do that. It doesn't feel right. She opens the door, smiling when she sees me. She is wearing her favorite jeans and a fluffy pink sweater. "Hi, Will. He says he's going to beat you this time."

"Dream on," I say.

She laughs. "Go right in. He's waiting." She goes down the hall to the washroom.

I go into the living room. Mr. Smythe is not there. The TV is on loud, some documentary about whales.

I find him in the kitchen, scrunched over a game of solitaire. His new glasses are sliding off. With his glasses like that, he looks more like a teacher than Mrs. Smythe. He scratches the beard that he is trying to grow and looks up.

"Come on doooown," he says, patting the chair beside him.

I take a seat and watch him finish the game. He wrinkles his nose and pushes his glasses up. "What's your pleasure?" he says.

"Pool," I say.

"Feeling lucky, huh?" We go down to the pool room. "How about a little extra this week?" he says, not looking at me.

I shrug. "Dishes?"

He shakes his head. "Bigger."

"I'm not shovelling the walk," I say.

He shakes his head again. "Bigger."

I frown. "Money?"

"Bigger."

"What?"

He racks up the balls. Sets the cue ball. Wipes his hands on his jeans.

"What?" I say again.

Mr. Smythe takes out a quarter. "Heads or tails?" he says, tossing it.

"Heads," I say.

He slaps the quarter on the back of his hand. "I break."

"Where, let me see that," I say, laughing. He holds it up. The quarter is tails.

He breaks. "How'd you like to stay with us?" he says, very quietly.

"Sure," I say. "But I got to go back on Tuesday. We got to check the traplines again."

He is quiet. The balls make clunking sounds as they bounce around the table. "Do you like it here?"

"Sure," I say.

"Enough to live here?"

I am not sure I heard him right. Maybe he is asking a different question from the one I think he is asking. I blink, opening my mouth. I don't know what to say. I say nothing.

"Those are the stakes, then," he says. "I win, you stay. You win, you stay."

He is joking. I laugh. "You serious?"

He stands up straight. "I don't think I've ever been more serious."

The room is suddenly very small.

"Your turn," he says. "Stripes."

I scratch and miss the ball by a mile.

"We don't want to push you," he says. He leans over the table, squints at the ball. "We just think that you'd be safer here. Hell, you practically live here already." I watch my sneakers. He keeps playing. "We aren't rich. We aren't perfect. We–" He looks at me, looks down. "We thought maybe you'd like to try it for a few weeks, first."

"I can't," I say.

"You don't have to decide right now," he says. "Think about it. Take a few days."

It's my turn again, but I don't feel like playing anymore. Mr. Smythe is waiting though. I stare at the table, and pick a ball. Aim. Shoot. Miss.

The game goes on in silence. Mr. Smythe wins easy. He smiles. "Well. I win. You stay."

If I wanted to get out of this room, there is only one door and Mr. Smythe is blocking it. He is watching me. He takes a deep breath. "Let's go upstairs."

Mrs. Smythe has shut off the TV. She stands up when we come into the living room. "Will–"

"I asked him already," Mr. Smythe says.

Her head snaps around and she glares at him. "You what?"

"I asked him."

Her hands fist at her sides. "We were supposed to do it together, Sam." Her voice is flat. She looks at me. "You said no."

I can't look at her. I look at the walls, at the floor, at her slippers. She stands in front of me. Her hands are warm on my face. "Look at me," she says. "Will? Look at me."

She is trying to smile. I shouldn't have come tonight. I should have waited for Eric to leave. "Hungry?" she says.

I nod. She makes a motion with her head for Mr. Smythe to follow her into the kitchen. When they are gone I sit down. It should be easy. It should be easy. I watch TV without watching it. Faces, words, names, places, cars all flash by. I wonder what they are saying about me in the kitchen.

It is almost 7:00 and my ribs hurt. Mostly, I can ignore it, but Eric hit me pretty hard and they are bruised. Eric got hit pretty hard by Dad, so we're even, I guess. I can't wait until Eric moves out. The rate he is going, he will be busted soon anyway. Tony says the police are starting to ask questions.

It is a strange night. We all pretend nothing happened and Mrs. Smythe fixes some natchos. Mr. Smythe beats me at Monopoly, then at poker, then at speed. Mrs. Smythe gets out a pack of Uno cards and we play a few rounds and watch *Sixty Minutes*. Mrs. Smythe wins. We go to bed.

I lie awake. My room. This could be my room. I already have most of my books here. It's hard to study with Eric around. I have a headache now, too. I couldn't get away from them long enough to sneak into the kitchen to get an aspirin. I wait for a few minutes then sit up. I pull my T-shirt up and take a look. There is a long bruise under my ribs and five smaller ones over it. I think he was trying to hit my stomach but he was so wasted he kept missing. It isn't bad. Tony's Dad broke three of his ribs once. Craig got a concussion a couple of weeks ago. My dad is pretty easy. It's only Eric that is bothering me. Mr. and Mrs. Smythe get mad and fussy when they see bruises though. You have to keep quiet about it or they will start talking your head off and won't shut up until you're bored half to death.

They keep the aspirin by the spices. I grab six, three for now and three for the morning. I am swallowing the last one when Mr. Smythe grabs my hand. I didn't even hear him come in. I must be sleepy.

"Where'd they hit you this time," he says.

"I got a headache," I say. "A bad one."

He opens the hand that has the aspirins in it. "How many do you plan on taking?"

"These are for later," I say.

He sighs. I get ready for the lecture. "Go back to bed," he says. He sounds very tired. I wish I could say something. I don't think they will want me around after this. I guess it's okay. Tony and Craig and the rest were starting to bug me about it anyway.

"Will," he says. I look up. He smiles. "It'll be okay."

"Sure," I say. "It'll be okay."

I leave around 5:00. I leave a note saying I have a really bad headache. I catch a ride back home with some guys coming off the graveyard shift.

No one is home. Eric had a party here last night. I am glad I wasn't here. They have wrecked the coffee table and the rug smells like stale beer and cigarettes. Our bedroom is worse. Someone puked all over Eric's bed and there are two used condoms on mine. At least none of the windows are broken this time. I start to clean my side of the room then stop. I sit on my bed. Mr. Smythe will be getting up soon. It is Sunday, so he will make waffles or French toast. He will make a plate of crispy bacon and eat it before Mrs. Smythe wakes up. He thinks that she doesn't know that he does this. She will wake up around 10:00 or 11:00 and will not talk to anyone until noon or until she's had about three coffees. She starts to wake up around 1:00 or 2:00. They will argue about something. Who took out the garbage or who did the dishes or the laundry last. Mrs. Smythe will read the paper.

I crawl into bed. The aspirin are not working. I try to go to sleep but it really reeks in here. I have a biology test tomorrow. I forgot to get the book from their place. I yawn. Our truck pulls into the driveway. Mom and Dad are arguing. I close my eyes. They sound plastered. Mom is bitching about something. Dad is not saying anything. Doors slam.

Mom comes in first. She doesn't notice the house is a mess. She goes straight to bed. Dad comes up the stairs a lot slower.

"What the — Eric!" he yells. "Eric!"

I pretend to sleep. The door bangs open.

"Eric, you little bastard," Dad says, looking around. He pulls me up. "Where's Eric?" His breath is lethal. You can tell he likes his rye and vodka straight.

"How should I know?"

"Where the fuck is he?" Dad says. "I want to talk to him."

I say I don't know. Dad gets up and rips Eric's amplifiers out of the walls. He throws them down and gives them a good kick. He tips Eric's bed over. Eric is smart. He won't come home for a while. Then Dad will have cooled off, and Eric can give him some money without Dad getting pissed off at him. I don't move. I wait until Dad is out of the room before I put on a sweater. I can hear him down in the basement, chopping wood. It should be around 8:00 by now. The RinkyDink will be open in an hour. Billy will be there because Elaine is there.

Mom is up. She is looking behind the stove. She sees me and makes a shushing motion with her hand. She pulls a bottle from behind the stove and sits down at the kitchen table.

"You're a good boy," she says, giggling. "You're a good boy. Help your old old old mother into bed, hey."

"Sure," I say, putting an arm around her. She stands, holding the bottle with one hand and me with the other. "This way, my lady."

"You making fun of me?" she says, her eyes going small. "You laughing at me?" Then she laughs and we go to their room. She flops onto the bed. She takes a long drink. "You're fucking laughing at me, aren't you?"

"Mom," I say, annoyed. "You're paranoid. I was making a joke."

"Yeah, you are reeeally funny. Really funny. You are a laugh a minute," she says, giggling again. "Real comedian."

"Yeah, that's me," I say.

She throws the bottle at me. I duck. She rolls over and starts to cry. I throw the blanket over her and leave. The floor is sticky now and stinks. Dad is still chopping wood. They wouldn't notice if I wasn't here. Maybe people would talk for a week or two, but after a while, they wouldn't notice. Only people that would notice is Tony and Craig and Billy and maybe Eric, who would miss me when he got toked up and didn't have anything for target practice.

Billy is playing Pac-man at the RinkyDink. He is chain-smoking. When I walk to him, he turns around quickly.

"Oh. It's you," he says turning back to the game.

"Hi to you too," I say.

"You seen Elaine?" he says.

"Nope," I say.

He crushes out another cigarette in the ashtray beside him. He plays for a while, loses a pac-man, then shakes a cigarette out one-handed. He sticks it in his mouth, loses another man, then lights up. He sucks deep. He looks at me. "Relax," I say. "She'll be here. Her majesty's limo is probably stuck in traffic."

He glares at me. "Shut up."

I laugh and go play pool with Craig. Craig has decided that he is James Dean. He is wearing a white T-shirt, jeans, and a black leather jacket that I think is his brother's. He has his hair slicked back. A cigarette is dangling from the corner of his mouth.

"What a loser," he says.

"Who you calling a loser?" I say.

"Billy. What a loser." He struts down to the other side of the pool table.

"He's okay."

"That chick," he says. "What's her face. Ellen? Erma?"

"Elaine."

"Yeah, that's the one. She going out with him cause she's got a bet."

I look at him. "What?"

"She's got to go out with him a month, and her friend will give her some coke."

"Billy's already giving her coke."

"Yeah. He's a loser."

I look at Billy. He is lighting up another cigarette.

"Can you imagine a townie wanting anything to do with him?" Craig says. "She's just doing it as a joke. She's going to dump him in a week. She's going to put all his stupid poems in the newspaper."

I see it now. There is a space around Billy. No one is going near him. He doesn't notice. I look around me. I catch some guys I used to hang out with grinning at me. When they see me looking at them, they look away.

Craig wins the game. I am losing a lot this week.

Elaine gets to the RinkyDink after lunch. She's got some townie friends with her that are staring around the RinkyDink like they are going to get jumped. Elaine leads them right up to Billy. Everyone is watching them without seeming like they are watching them. Billy gives her his latest poem. I wonder what he got to rhyme with Elaine.

They leave. Billy holds the door open for her. She gives her friends a look. They giggle. The same guys that were watching me start to howl. They are laughing so hard they are crying. I feel sick. I think about telling Billy but I know he won't listen.

I leave the RinkyDink and go for a walk. I walk and walk and walk and end up back in front of the RinkyDink. There isn't anywhere else to go. I hang out with Craig, who hasn't left the pool table.

I spend the night on Craig's floor. Craig's parents are Jehovah's Witnesses and preach at me before I go to bed. I sit and listen because I need a place to sleep. I am not going home until tomorrow when Mom and Dad are sober. His Mom gets us up two hours before the buses come to take the village kids to school. They pray before we eat. Craig looks at me and rolls his eyes. People are always making fun of Craig because his parents stand on the corner downtown every Friday and hold the *Watchtower* mags. When his parents start to bug him, he says he will take up Devil worship or astrology if they don't lay off. I think I'll ask him if he wants to hang out with me on Christmas. His parents don't believe in it.

I see Mrs. Smythe in the hall between classes. Craig nudges me. "Go on," he says, making sucking noises. "Go get your 'A.'"

"Fuck off," I say, pushing him back.

She is talking to a girl and doesn't see me. I think about skipping English today but know that she will phone home and ask where I am. It isn't fair. She doesn't do that for anyone else. Craig can skip as many times as he wants and all she does is make a note of it, and sends it to the principal's office.

At lunch, no one talks to me. I can't find Craig or Tony or Billy. The village guys at the science wing doors snicker as I go by. I don't stop. I keep going until I get to the headbanger's doors in the shop wing. I don't have any money and I don't have a lunch so I bum a cigarette off this girl with really tight jeans and to get my mind off my stomach I try and get her to go out with me. She smiles, but doesn't say anything. When she walks away, the fringe on her leather jacket swings.

I flunk my biology test. It would have been easy if I studied. It is multiple choice. I stare at the paper and kick myself. I know I could have passed if I had read the chapter. Mr. Kellerman reads out the marks from lowest to highest. My name is called out third.

"Mr. Bolton," he says, raising an eyebrow. "Three out of thirty."

"All-riiight," Craig says, slapping my back.

"Mr. Duncan," he says to Craig, his voice becoming resigned. "Three and a half out of thirty."

Craig stands up and bows. The guys in the back clap. The kids in the front laugh. Mr. Kellerman reads out the rest of the marks. Craig turns to me. "Looks like I beat the Brain," he says.

"Yeah," I say. "Pretty soon you're going to be getting the Nobel Prize."

The bell rings. Last class. English. I go to my locker and take out my jacket. If she phones, no one is going to answer.

I go downtown. I don't have any money so I walk. The snow is starting to slack off and it is even sunning a bit. My stomach growls. I haven't eaten since breakfast. I wish I had gone to English. Mrs. Smythe would have given me something to eat. She always has something left over from her lunch. I hunch down in my jacket. I guess it isn't right to mooch off her now that she doesn't want to see me anymore. I am glad I didn't mooch off her, but I am still hungry.

Downtown, I go to the Paradise Arcade. All the heads hang out there. Maybe I will find Eric. Maybe he'll give me some money. More like a belt. It's worth a try. I look around for him, but he isn't there. No one much is there. Just some burn-outs by the pinball machines. I see Mitch. I go over to him, but he is soaring. He is laughing at the ball going around and around the machine. I turn and walk away. There is no one here I can mooch off. I head for the highway and hitch home. Mom should be passed out by now and Dad is at work.

Sure enough, Mom is passed out. She is on the living-room floor. I get a blanket for her. The stove has gone out and it is freezing in here. I go into the kitchen and look through the fridge. There is a bottle of pickles and some really pathetic looking celery. There is also some milk, but it is so old it smells like cheese. There is no bread left from what Mom made this Saturday. I find some Rice-a-roni and make it. Mom wakes up and asks for some water. I bring her some and give her some Rice-a-roni. She makes a face but eats it slowly.

At 6:00, Dad comes home. Eric comes home with him. They have made up. Eric has bought Dad a six-pack and they watch a hockey game together. I stay in my room. Eric has cleaned his bed by dumping his mattress outside and stealing mine. We have a grammar test this Friday. I know Mrs. Smythe will be unhappy if she has to fail me. I read the chapters on "nouns," "verbs," and get through "the parts of speech" before Eric comes into the room and kicks me off the bed.

He tries to take the mattress but I kick him in the side. Eric turns. He grabs me by the hair. "This," he says. "Is my bed. Understand?"

"Fuck you," I say. "You had the party. Your fucked up friends trashed your bed. You sleep on the floor."

Dad comes in. He sees Eric push me against a wall and hit me. He yells at Eric, who turns around, his fist frozen in front of my face. Eric lets me go. Dad rolls his sleeves up.

"You always take his side!" Eric yells. "You never take my side!"

"You pick on someone your size," Dad says. "Unless you want me to pick on you."

Eric gives me a look that says he will make this up to me later when Dad isn't here. I pick up my book and get out. I go for a walk. I keep walking around the village, staying away from the RinkyDink. That is the first place that Eric will look.

I am at the village exit. The sky and the stars are popping out. Mr. Smythe will take out his telescope and he will try to take a picture of the Pleiades.[1] Mrs. Smythe will be marking papers while she watches TV.

"Do you need a ride?" this guy says. There is a blue pick-up in front of me. The driver is wearing a hunting cap.

I take my hand out of my mouth. I have been chewing my knuckle like some baby. I shake my head. "I'm waiting for someone," I say.

He shrugs and takes off. I stand there and watch his headlights disappear.

They didn't really mean it. They would get bored of me quick when they found out what I am. It should be easy. I should have said yes and then stayed until they got bored and then come home when Eric cooled off.

Two cars pass me as I walk back to the village. I can hide out in Tony's until Eric goes out with his friends and forgets this afternoon. My feet are frozen when I get to the RinkyDink. Tony is there.

He says, "So. I heard Craig beat you in biology."

I roll my eyes. "Didn't it just impress you?"

"A whole half a point. Way to go," he says, grinning. "For a while there we thought you were getting townie."

"Yeah, right," I say. "Listen, I pissed Eric off — "

"Surprise, surprise," he says.

" — and I need a place to crash. Can I sleep over?"

"Sure," he says.

Mitch wanders in the RinkyDink and a crowd of kids slowly drift over to him. He looks around, eyeing everybody. Then he pulls out something and starts giving it away. Tony gets curious and we go over.

"Wow," Tony says, after Mitch gives him something.

"What?"

We go outside and behind the RinkyDink where a crowd of kids is gathered. "Fucking all-riiight," I hear Craig say, even though I can't see him.

"What?" I say. Tony lifts up his hand. He is holding a little vial with small white crystals in it.

"Crack," Tony says. "Man, is he stupid. He could have made a fortune and he's just giving it way.'

---

1. **Pleiades** Star cluster named after seven sister nymphs in Greek mythology.

We don't have a pipe, and Tony wants to do this right the first time. No one will share with us though, so Tony decides to do it tomorrow, after he buys the right equipment. I am hungry again. I am about to tell him I am going to Billy's when I see Eric.

"Shit," I say and hide behind him.

Tony looks over and sees Eric. "Someone's in trou-ble," he sings.

Eric is looking for me. I hunch down. Tony tries to look innocent. Eric spots him and starts to come over. "Better run for it," Tony whispers.

I sneak behind some other people but Eric sees me and I have to run for it anyway. Tony starts to cheer and the kids behind the RinkyDink join in. Some of the guys follow us so that they will see what happens when Eric catches up with me. I don't want to find out so I ignore everyone behind me and start pumping hard so I can get home before Eric catches me.

Eric used to be fast. I am glad he is a head now because he can't run that far anymore. He used to always beat me in the races we had. I am panting now, and my legs are cramping. I run up the stairs to our house.

The door is locked.

I stand there, hand on the knob. Eric rounds the corner to our block and starts to smile. There is no one behind him anymore. I knock on the door but now I see that our truck is gone. I run around the house but the basement door is locked too. Even the windows are locked.

Eric pops his head around the corner of the house. He grins when he sees me. He disappears. I grit my teeth. Start running across our backyard. Head for Billy's. Eric lets out a hoot. He has someone with him. I think it is Brent. I duck behind our neighbour's house. There is snow in my sneakers and all the way up my leg. I am sweating. I rest for a while. I can't hear Eric. I hope I have lost him, but Eric is pissed off and when he's pissed off he doesn't let go. I look down. My footprints are clear in the snow. I start to run again, but I hit a thick spot and have to wade through some thigh-deep snow. I look behind me. Eric is nowhere. I keep slogging. I make it to the road and run down to the exit.

I have lost him. I am shaking now because it is cold. I can feel the sweat cooling on my skin. My breath goes back to normal. I wait for a car to come by. I have missed the night shift and the graveyard shift won't be by until near midnight. It is too cold to wait that long.

A car, a red car. A little Toyota. I start to run again. Brent's car. I run off the road and head into a clump of trees. The Toyota pulls over and Eric gets out of the car and starts yelling. I reach the trees and rest. They are waiting by the side of the road. Eric is peering at the trees, trying to see me. Brent is smoking in the car. Eric crosses his arms over his chest and blows into his hands. My legs are frozen.

After a long time, a cop car cruises to a stop beside Eric and Brent. I wade out and wave at the policeman. He looks startled. Then he looks at Eric and Brent and asks them something. Eric shrugs. It takes me a while to get to them because my legs are slow.

The cop is watching me. I swear I will never call them pigs again. I swear. He turns to Brent, who digs around the glove compartment. Eric glares at me. The cop says something to his partner. I scramble up the embankment.

Eric has no marks on his face. Dad probably hit him on the back and stomach. Ever since the social worker came, Dad has been careful. Eric suddenly smiles at me. He holds an arm out and moves to me. I move behind the police car. Eric is still smiling. The policeman comes over to us.

"Is there a problem here?" he says.

"No," Eric says. "No probulum. Li'le misunnerstan'nin.'" He grins.

Oh shit. He is as high as a kite. The policeman looks hard at Eric. I look at the car. Brent is glaring at me. He is high, too.

Eric tries again to get me. I put the police car between us. The policeman grabs Eric by the arm and his partner goes and gets Brent. The policeman says something about driving under the influence but none of us are listening. Eric is watching me. His eyes are very clear. I am not going to get away with this. I am going to pay for it. Brent is swearing. He wants a lawyer. He stumbles out of his car and slips on the road.

Brent and Eric are put in the back seat. The policeman comes up to me and says, "Can you make it home?"

I nod. He says, "Good. Go."

His partner says something to him, but I don't understand what it is because it is numbers. The policeman looks at me.

"My partner wants to know if you're going to press charges."

I look at Eric. He is flushed. I shake my head. It would only make him madder and he would only be in jail a few weeks. It would only make things worse. The policeman shakes his head and says, "I told you so."

They drive away and I go home. I walk around the house, trying to figure a way to break in. I find a small screwdriver and jimmy the basement door open. Just in case Eric gets out tonight, I make a bed under the tool table and go to sleep.

No one is home when I wake up. I scramble an egg and get ready for school. I sit beside Tony on the bus.

"I was expecting to see you with black eyes," he says.

I shake my head. My legs are still raw from last night. Freezer burn? I rub my head and sigh. I have something due today but I can't remember what. If Eric is in the drunk tank, they will let him out today.

The village guys are talking to me again. I skip gym. I skip history. I hang out with Craig and Tony in the Paradise Arcade. I am not sure if I want to be friends with them after they cheered last night, but it is better to have them on my side, so I am friends with them again. A couple of guys get a two-for-one pizza special for lunch and I am glad I am friends with them because I am starved. They have some five finger specials from Safeway. Tony is proud because he got a couple of bags of chips and Pepsi and no one even noticed.

Mitch comes up to me when I go to the bathroom.

"That was a really cheap thing to do," he says.

What?" I say, frowning. I haven't done anything to him.

"What? What? Getting your brother thrown in jail. Pretty crumby."

I laugh. "He got himself thrown in jail. He got caught when he was high. Him and Bre — "

"That's not what he says." Mitch frowns. "He says you set him up."

"Fuck." I run a hand through my hair. "When'd he tell you this?"

"This morning," he says. "He's waiting for you at school."

"I didn't set him up. How could I?"

Mitch nods. He hands me some crack and says, hey, I'm sorry, and leaves. I look at it, but know it will make me sick. I can't smoke anything. I'll give it to Tony.

Billy comes into the Paradise with Elaine and her friends. He is getting some smug looks but he doesn't notice. He holds the chair out for Elaine, who sits down without looking at him. I don't want to be around when he finds out he is a joke. I go over to Tony.

"I'm leaving," I say.

Tony shushes me. "Watch," he says.

Elaine orders a beer. Frankie shakes his head and points to the sign that says We Do NOT Serve Minors. Elaine frowns. She says something to Billy. He shrugs. She orders a Coke. Billy pays. When their Cokes come, Elaine dumps it over Billy's head. Billy stares at her like she has gone stark crazy. Her friends start to laugh, and I get up and walk out.

I lean against the wall of the Paradise. Billy comes out a few minutes later. His face is still and pale. Elaine and her friends follow him, reciting lines from the poems he wrote her. Tony and the rest just laugh. I go back inside, and trade the crack for some quarters for the video games. I keep remembering how Billy's face looked, and I keep losing the games I play. Tony says let's go, and we hitch back to the village. We raid his fridge and have chocolate ice cream coconut sundaes. Angela comes in with Di and says that Eric is looking for me. I look at Tony and he looks at me.

"Boy, are you in for it," Tony says. "You'd better stay here tonight."

When everyone is asleep, Tony pulls out a weird-looking pipe and does the crack. His face goes very dreamy and far away. A few minutes later he says, "Christ, that was great. I wonder how much Mitch has?"

I turn over and go to sleep.

The next morning Billy is alone on the bus. No one wants to sit with him so there are empty seats all around him. He does not look like he has slept. Tony goes up to him and punches his arm. Billy looks at him, then looks out the window. Tony says, "So how's Shakespeare this morning?"

The guys in the back of the bus laugh, but a lot of the girls don't. I don't want to watch it, so I look out my window too. I hope Eric isn't at the school. I don't know where else I can hide.

Mrs. Smythe is waiting at the school bus stop. I sneak out the back door of the bus, with Tony and the guys making enough noise and pretending to fight to cover me.

We head down to the Paradise again in Binky's car. I am starting to smell bad. I haven't had a shower for days. I wish I had some clean clothes. I wish I had some money so I could buy a toothbrush. I hate the scummy feeling on my teeth. I wish I had enough for a taco, or a hamburger. I wish I had a Pepsi.

Eric is at the Paradise, so I hide in the mall. I find Dad in Safeway, looking for Eric. "Let's go to the Dairy Queen," he says.

Dad orders a coffee, a chocolate milkshake, and a cheeseburger. We take the coffee and milkshake to a back table, and I take the order slip. We sit there. Dad stares at his hands.

"One of your teachers called," he says.

I sigh. "Mrs. Smythe?"

"Yeah," he looks up. "Says she'd like you to stay there."

I try to read his face. It is very still. His eyes are bloodshot and red rimmed. He must have a big hangover.

I shrug.

The cashier calls out our number. I go up and get the cheeseburger and we split it. Dad always eats slow to make it last longer.

"Did you tell her you wanted to?"

"No," I say. "They asked me, but I said I couldn't."

Dad nods. "Did you tell them anything?"

"Like what?"

"Don't get smart," he says, sounding beat.

"I didn't say anything."

He stops chewing. "Then why'd they ask you?"

"Don't know."

"You must have told them something."

"Nope. Just asked."

"Did Eric tell them?"

I snort. "Eric? No way. They wou — He wouldn't go anywhere near them. They're okay, Dad. They won't tell anybody."

"So you did tell them."

"I didn't. I swear I didn't. Look, Eric got me on the face a couple of times and they figured it out. They aren't go — "

"You're lying."

I finished my half of the cheeseburger. "I am not lying. I didn't say anything. And they won't say anything."

"I never touched you."

"Yeah, Eric took care of that," I say, smiling. Dad doesn't smile back. "You seen him?"

Dad nods. "I kicked him out."

"You what?"

"Party. Ruined the basement," Dad says grimly. "He's old enough. Had to leave sooner or later."

He finishes his cheeseburger. Eric will be really pissed now. I'll have to lie really low for a while. We go check the trapline, and get some more martens, and even get a little lynx. Dad is happy. We go home. The basement is ripped apart. I wonder if he was looking for me.

Next day at school, I spend most of the day ducking from Eric and Mrs. Smythe before I finally get sick of it and go down to the Paradise Arcade. Tony is there with Billy, who asks me if I want to go to Vancouver with him until Eric cools off.

"Now?"

"No better time," he says.

I think about it. "When you leaving?"

"Tonight."

"I don't know. I don't have any money."

"Me neither," he says.

"Shit," I say. "How we going to get there? It's a thousand miles at least."

"Hitch to town, hitch down to Smithers, then hitch to Prince George, hitch to — "

"Yeah, yeah, but how are we going to eat?"

He wiggles his finger. Five finger special. I laugh.

"You change your mind," he says. "I'll be behind RinkyDink around 7:00. Get some thick boots."

We are about to hitch home when I see Mrs. Smythe peer into the Paradise Arcade. It is too late to hide because she turns and sees me. Her face becomes stiff. She walks over to us, and the guys start to laugh. Mrs. Smythe looks at them, then at me.

"Will?" she says. "Can I talk to you outside?"

She stares around like the guys are going to jump her. I look at them and try to see what she is nervous about. Tony is grabbing his crotch. Billy is cleaning his nails. The other guys are snickering. I suddenly see them the way she must see them. They all have long, greasy hair, combed straight back. All of us have jeans on, T-shirts, sneakers. They don't look nice.

I look back at her. She has on her "school uniform" as she calls it. Dark skirt, white shirt, low black heels, glasses. She is watching me like she hasn't seen me before. I hope she never sees my house.

"Later?" I say. "I'm kind of busy."

She blushes, and the guys laugh hard. She takes a step back, and I want to take the words back. "Are you sure?" she says.

Tony nudges my arm. "Why don't you introduce us to your *girl*friend," he says. "Maybe she'd like — "

"Shut up," I say. Mrs. Smythe has no expression now. She pulls herself up.

"I'll talk to you later, then," she says, and turns around and walks out without looking back. If I could, I would follow her out.

Billy claps me on the shoulder. "Stay away from them," he says. "It's not worth it."

It doesn't matter. She practically said she didn't want to see me again. I don't blame her. I wouldn't want to see me either.

She will get into her car now and go home. She will honk when she pulls into the driveway so Mr. Smythe will come out and help her with the groceries. She always gets groceries today. The basics and sardines. Peanut butter. I lick my lips. Diamante frozen pizzas. Insta-oodles-o'-noodles. Eggo waffles. Captain Crunch.

Mr. Smythe will come out of the house, wave, come down the driveway. They will take the groceries into the house after they kiss. They will kick off their shoes. Throw something in the microwave. Watch *Cheers* re-runs on channel eight. Mr. Smythe will tell her what happened in his day. I wonder what she will say happened in her day.

On the way home with Billy, I wonder what Christmas in Vancouver will be like. Billy yabbers about how great it's going to be, the two of us, no one to boss us around, no one to bother us, going anywhere we want to go. I smile. Turn away from him. Watch the trees blur past. I guess anything will be better than sitting around, listening to Tony and Craig gripe.

(1992)

Ivan E. Coyote (1969–)

Ivan E. Coyote was born in Whitehorse, Yukon, in 1969. She was expelled from junior high in grade 11 for smoking pot on a basketball trip, and so she had to finish school in Nanaimo, British Columbia, while living with her grandmother. She attended Vancouver's Capilano College for two years, working towards a B.A. in music with a specialty in the saxophone. Despite her near perfect grade point average, she didn't complete her degree. She attributes this to a dawning awareness of her sexual orientation: "I finally admitted to myself I was queer as a three dollar bill and I needed to spend my tuition on a plane ticket to Thailand where nobody knew me and I could sit on a beach and think about it all." After she had done this, she returned to Vancouver and enrolled at the B.C. Institute of Technology to study electricity and industrial electronics. "I knew I wanted to be a writer, but I had read somewhere that lesbians should always have a trade to fall back on.

Plus I really liked wearing a tool belt, and it was good money." She has since worked as a landscaper, a waitress, an electrician, an installation technician in a recording studio, a lighting technician in the movie industry, and a props person.

Coyote grew up in a family of kitchen-table storytellers, and she created a new name for herself out of a series of stories: Ivan was the name of a character she played at a murder-mystery party; *E* is the initial of her middle name, Elizabeth; and Coyote is both a cartoon character who shares that initial (Wile E. Coyote) and the animal that appears as a cross-gendered trickster in many First Nations myths. At the age of 21, she learned to play guitar and started performing as a singer/songwriter, storyteller, and spoken-word artist in venues around Vancouver. In 1996, she founded the storytelling troupe Taste This with three other women. Two years later, the feminist collective Press Gang published *Boys Like Her,* a written version of the Taste This show. The troupe hit the road, touring Canada and the western United States three times; they used the take from their live shows to buy the gas and food that fuelled the undertaking. Coyote had no formal training as a writer. She maintains that she learned everything she knows about writing and editing by performing before live audiences and by reading fiction. While she is a voracious reader, some works have had a particular impact on her: *Geek Love*, by Katherine Dunn; *We So Seldom Look on Love,* by Barbara Gowdy; *The Man Who Fell in Love with the Moon,* by Tom Spanbauer; and *Cannery Row,* by John Steinbeck. She is drawn as well to the music of songwriters who are also poets or storytellers, naming Veda Hille, Rae Spoon, Tom Waits, Joni Mitchell, and Paul Simon as influences.

In her writing, Coyote has moved from mainly first-person narratives with an autobiographical element to longer works of fiction that contain more dialogue and present wholly fictional characters and events. Gender is often a focus for Coyote, especially in her first-person work ("Little old ladies think I am a handsome, soft-spoken young man. Old men give me advice about women"). However, she is mainly concerned with writing about her family, her neighbourhood, and the people she meets. *Close to Spider Man* (2000), her first collection of short stories, is a series of linked semi-autobiographical pieces set in the Yukon in the 1970s and 1980s. The female characters are looking for a fresh start, but they find it hard to break free of the constraints that define their lives. The collection constitutes an intimate portrait of the life of a queer woman in the Canadian North.

The conversational tone that marked Coyote's first collection re-emerges in *One Man's Trash* (2002), which contains stories grouped under three headings: "Then" consists of stories about the author's Yukon childhood; "Now" features tales describing her experiences in Vancouver and Calgary; and "There" comprises accounts of various road trips, including one to Las Vegas, where Coyote tried (and failed) to marry her girlfriend. The stories often depict the search for identity through humorous incidents and emphasize the vital importance of human connection and the rewards we reap through our capacity for love.

In 2003, the multimedia band One Trick Rodeo released the CD *You're a Nation,* which includes several of Coyote's stories set to music. Two years later, *Loose End,* a compilation of the columns Coyote wrote for the Vancouver gay and lesbian bi-weekly *Xtra West* appeared. In 2006, Coyote published the novel *Bow Grip,* which is about a middle-aged mechanic whose wife leaves him for a woman; he takes up the cello, travels, and meets a variety of new people — all of which help him to achieve a new self-understanding. Coyote explains that she was prompted to finish the novel by the students in the creative writing class she taught at Capilano College in 2004. She had challenged them to write 1,700 words a day — a quota recommended by the organizers of National Writing Month — and "The bastards all signed up and were consistently making their quotas. I felt like I had to keep up, just to be a good role model."

Coyote continues to write, perform, and teach. In the "Long-Ass Bio" she includes on her website, she explains that she also likes to "knit, do leatherwork, and play street hockey. I have two dogs, I live alone, and my favourite colour is orange. ... I was raised a Catholic, but now worship many gods, and believe in the religion of love, art and the holy story."

Makeover

I liked it when she ran her fingers through my hair, even though she had ulterior motives. "How about just a blonde rinse, or maybe we could just frost the tips?" she would whisper into my ear, like foreplay.

She couldn't help herself. She was a professional. Hair was her thing. We had been dating for a couple of months and the reality was that I was not going to last unbleached or undyed much longer. I was sleeping with a colour technician, and my hair was, well, boring.

"It's not quite brown, but it's not really blonde either," she would wince, as though it pained her somehow. "Can't we just do ... something? I could fix it."

"I didn't realize my hair was broken," I would retort, trying to lighten things up a little. But she was dead serious.

I caved a few days later, after two glasses of red wine. She wanted to bleach me blonde, but I was just about to turn thirty and I figured, it's now or never, buddy, both feet first. If you're gonna dye your hair, dye your hair.

"I want blue hair. The colour of a propane flame. Give me really blue hair. Quick, before I chicken out."

The thing that real girls never tell you is that it's true. They actually do have a higher pain tolerance than ... well, the rest of us. Bleach hurts. But I got what I asked for.

Shining on top of my head was a crop of titanium-coloured fluff. It felt like August straw and my scalp hurt to touch.

I don't own much propane flame-coloured clothing, so dressing for work the next day brought on a deep and disturbing fashion crisis. I almost had to call in sick.

I didn't recognize myself. I would catch my reflection in windows out of the corner of my eye, and whirl around to find only me, in Technicolor, with clothes that didn't, that couldn't, match.

About a week later we were in the shower together when she let out a shriek that dropped a rock in my belly. "What do you think you're doing?" she looked panicked.

I looked down at the bar of soap in my hand. I was going to wash my hair.

"You can't use soap on colour-treated hair. You're killing me. You need a balanced alkaloid shampoo, and a good conditioner. And you haven't been wearing your shower cap, have you? Do you think I don't know? You are impossible to work with. Your back is fading out already. Sit down in the tub. I'm going to have to touch you up."

"Look, if I had known it was going to be like this, I wouldn't have gone through with it," I sighed. "I like how we were before. I didn't know it was gonna involve this kind of commitment. Maybe I'm just not ready for colour-treated hair. Maybe I just can't handle the responsibility."

She left me for a bisexual esthetician, and my hair faded to television screen blue, then for a couple of weeks I walked around looking like a seventeen-year-old boy who had prematurely greyed, then blond. A couple of hair-cuts later, I was back to nondescript, not quite brown.

Then I met the stiltwalker. Stiltwalkers possess a penchant for spectacle and costume. Stiltwalkers wear a lot of make-up. Everything was fine, until she spent the night.

I heard her scuffling around in my bathroom, going through my drawers. "You okay in there?" I asked her through the closed door.

"Where is your facial cleanser?" she called out.

"You're joking me, right? There's a bar of soap on the little shelf in the shower."

She shot out of the bathroom, looking disgusted. "I can't wash my face with a bar of soap," she said, incredulous.

Just what you can wash with soap is still a mystery to me. I must have missed that chapter in the handbook. Perhaps I was at hockey practice when they covered the proper uses of soap, not to mention the difference between pumps and open-toed mule shoes. I have a lot to learn.

"No make-up remover?"

I shook my head.

"Moisturizer?"

I shrugged, palms up.

"Okay." She shook her head. "Just tell me where you hide your hairbrush."

I was afraid to answer. My cupboards were bare. "I have mechanic's hand cleaner," I said hopefully. "It takes oil and grease off. It contains lanolin. It smells like oranges...."

Turned out, if I were to properly entertain female company, I had some serious shopping to do.

The woman at Eaton's was very kind. I was overwhelmed, and slumped, my elbows resting on her cool glass counter.

"I thought you could wash your face with soap," I explained plaintively. "Can you help me?"

"Oh, honey, don't worry, I'll fix you up. I've worked with worse. You just need a skin profile. And a three-step regimen. It'll be okay. Repeat after me: cleanse, tone, moisturize."

Her eyes grazed over my shorn hair and flat chest, but she never blinked. She passed no judgment upon me for thinking toner was only for photocopiers, and I loved her for it. Her name was Madeline, and she spent forty-five patient minutes with me. Every time she leaned over to touch my skin I couldn't help but breathe deep in the smell of her. I had an almost unbearable urge to rest my head against her ample chest. I felt so grateful, I wanted to mow her lawn, or change her tires, or something.

Turns out I have combination skin, with a fair but clear complexion, most suited to spring colours. I spent seventy-two dollars, and left with a tiny bag of exquisitely packaged products.

Halfway down Granville Street, I recognized the swagger of one of my friends approaching, his hands deep in his pockets.

"Hey man. What'dja buy at Eaton's?" His voice was even deeper than last month, stubble starting to sprout on his chin and upper lip.

"You know, couple things," I almost whispered, trying to sound casual. "Rehydrating cream, stuff like that."

"Stuff like *what?*"

"It's rehydrating cream, okay? And a soothing cream cleanser. Oh, and eye supplement. I'm just holding it for a friend."

"Are you wearing mascara?" He narrowed his eyes at me, leaned over, and sniffed. "And each to their own and everything, buddy, but I gotta tell you, you smell kinda like ... roses, man. You smell like flowers, dude."

I changed the subject. I didn't tell him I smelled of evening primrose oil, which uplifts and boosts your everyday moisturizer when applied beforehand. I didn't tell him that according to Madeline, you're never too young or too butch for a good three-step beauty regimen; five minutes in the morning, five at night. I didn't mention that I had just been exfoliated and that my face felt fucking great.

I didn't tell him that testosterone often brings on puberty-grade acne, and that he might want to invest in a good epidermal cleanser, perhaps even an astringent.

I didn't say anything. That is why they are referred to as beauty secrets. Because I, myself, plan to age gracefully.

(2002)

The Smart Money

I write about my little godson Francis a lot. He is one of my greatest joys, and my most beloved muse. I wrote my first story about him when he was barely three and I was twenty-eight, and that story went on to be published in my second book. I have not stopped writing about Francis because I write about all the people I love, and he is still his little courageous almost eight-year-old self, bravely cross-dressing his way through Grade Three now, in a rough school in a rough town. I know how he feels. I grew up in that very same town. His dresses are even harder to explain now than my corduroy suit and double holstered cap guns were back then. School is always harder on the nelly boys than the tomboys. At least we are good at throwing balls.

Every time I read anything I have written about him, it moves me. I cry. Ask anyone who knows me. I can't help it. I'm a crybaby. Writing and reading about him to people is like a heart balm for me. Other people know it too, and by the number of sobbing drag queens and teary-eyed transgendered fellas I've seen in the audience over the years, I am not the only one. We all need to hear stories about people like us. What do they call it? Positive representation of something we can see ourselves in? I call it knowing I'm not the only one.

Francis's mom called me on the radio phone from the cabin one fall to ask me if I had been thinking of Francis at approximately eight o'clock the evening before. I had been, as it turned out, during a reading for two hundred people all packed into a club somewhere on the east side, all of us thinking of Francis. When I read his story, all of us got choked up on account of his bravery, his little fighting faggoty self, and his beautiful, gentle, unintentional, pure-hearted resistance.

"I knew it," his mother confided. "We were walking down the trail to the lake last night to go fishing, and he spun around on one heel and asked when you were coming home again."

He was four then, and I hadn't seen him since he was dancing around in red socks and a tube top. I always carry that moment with me, and to this day every time I face a crowd to tell a story about Francis I think about it. And then I tell a room full of strangers about me and my little fairy child. Crazy way to make a living, I know, but it works for me.

A couple of weeks ago, I got a call from Francis's other uncle, Brenda. She lives in the same small town, but she is not "from there," even though she has been a resident for almost a decade. It is how we are, us Yukoners. Anyway, Brenda is in a book club in Whitehorse, of course with a couple of gals I maybe went to high school with, or my sister did, or maybe I blew one of their brothers at a keg party on the Marsh Lake road in

1985 or something. Whatever. Point being, it is a very small town, and Brenda and her book club read my second book. The one with my first Francis story in it. So of course it turns out one of the women knew me, and knew Francis and his brothers, and Chris, his mom. She returned to Brenda's place the next first Tuesday of the month looking stricken. "I read this book," she told Brenda as they were reheating the scones and making the tea. "I have to tell you, it made me feel nauseous. I mean, actually sick, thinking of that poor little boy and his brothers, and she talked about them all too. Even the husband. Why couldn't she have changed all their names, at least? He is going to have to grow up and live with those stories hanging over his head for the rest of his life. They all will. Didn't she think of anyone other than herself, and making some money?"

Brenda ended up defending my honour (which has always been dubious in that town at the very best) in front of an increasingly indignant and hostile group of fiction readers, and I still feel vaguely responsible for her having to go through such an ordeal. I received the following e-mail from her, which I will excerpt for you here:

"Thank you so much for taking the time to talk through those issues with me. I've been spending a lot of time thinking (obsessing) about it. Kelly Anne [her partner] and I spent all yesterday morning talking about it too. It's really challenging to me to hear someone feel they have the right to tell us how to tell our stories. As if we don't already have a big enough problem with hearing and seeing representations of ourselves anyway. KA asked whether or not an analogy might be drawn with another community and I told her I don't think so. Who in this day or age would tell someone it's not okay to write a story about a young black person or a young native person for fear someone is going to think they're black or native? Invisibility and non-acceptance are the issues. Should be a barn burner of a book club."

I talked it all over with Brenda. We discussed different methods of explaining to straight people things we thought they might have already figured out by now without sounding strident, and we left it at that.

Then I sat down and tried to write. Politics aside, I thought to myself (the faint beginnings of a bout of existential angst descending upon me and my keyboard), what if Francis is straight? What if it is a phase? What if some redneck kid reads my book, and he endures even one more taunt, one more fistfight (which, according to his mom, he is starting to win now, and even start, in some cases), even one more hassle once he makes it to Grade Four?

What if my writing about him does make his life harder, somehow, somewhere, in some as of yet unforeseen way that I can never know until it happens? What if it happens, and he doesn't tell me? What if Francis grows up to be a huge, hairy football player whose best friend the tight end teases him at practice one day? What if his buddy bugs him about liking to wear dresses once when he was little, like he read in that book, and Francis is forced by peer pressure to deny himself, and curse my name?

I guess I had never considered the possibility. I guess I have always known exactly what Francis is and what he will grow up to be because he has never been made to hide it. I guess I thought Francis would continue to grow up into a world where being queer is nothing to be ashamed of, the safe world his mother and brothers and father and Uncle Brenda and Aunt Kelly Anne and Uncle Ivan live in, where he is loved and adored because of what he is exactly, not in spite of how he turned out. You see, I forget, sometimes, about the rest of the world.

I cannot stop to think about what if. What if because we let Francis be such a fag, people are going to hate him because he is a fag? How could we stop him anyway? That never worked for our parents.

I cannot phone up that woman from the book group and patiently explain to her that I didn't change Francis's name in my book because way back in the day when I asked his mother what I should change her son's name to, to protect him, she told me that God had whispered the name Francis to her in her head when he was still in her belly, that it had happened with all her boys that way, and that she thought we didn't have a right to change it for him until he was old enough to ask what he wanted his new name to be. She told me that his name came from God, as she understood these things, and that besides, being a cross-dresser is nothing to be ashamed of anyway.

So we kept the names real, and as a result, thousands of people know Francis, and love him, and call him by his name. He really exists, and we know it. We are rooting for him. But I worry about Grade Eight. Grade Eight is when any shit around is likely to hit anything in its way, fanlike or not. I fucking hated the grade that was eight.

I guess we'll all just have to wait and see what Francis grows up to be. I know that that is up to Francis, and I know where the smart money is, but I'll tell you what: if he grows up to be just a really nice, sensitive straight guy, it sure will make one hell of a story.

(2005)

Ken Babstock (1970–)

In 1991, when Ken Babstock returned to Montreal after travelling in Europe and living for a year in Dublin, he was broke. He eventually made his way to British Columbia, where he planted trees for two years then settled temporarily in Vancouver, with the plan of returning to Europe. He published his first poem in *The Fiddlehead*, and this initial success made him eager for more. Over the next six years, he contributed poems to several Canadian journals, and in 1997 he won a National Magazine Award. In 1998, Babstock moved to Toronto, and he published his first book the following year — *Mean*, a collection of poems in which he reflects on his travels throughout Canada and abroad and muses on his identity as a transplanted Newfoundlander.

Babstock was born in Burin, Newfoundland, in 1970, and he grew up in the Ottawa Valley of Ontario. As a high school student in Pembroke, he quietly began writing poems. He also befriended fellow poet David O'Meara, and the two exchanged poems and critiqued each other's work. At 19, Babstock enrolled in a course taught by Irving Layton at Concordia University in Montreal. Layton taught him (among other things) that poetry was a viable pursuit, so Babstock quit school and spent the next decade working as a labourer and devouring poetry by a host of other writers. Among his Canadian choices were Don McKay, Margaret Avison, Patrick Lane, Don Domanski, and Roo Borson; among international writers, he gravitated towards Seamus Heaney, John Berryman, Elizabeth Bishop, and a younger generation of British poets.

Mean was well received. Dennis Lee praised it for its maturity and for the craft evident in poems such as "What We Didn't Tell the Medic," in which "Time stall[s]" during a horrendous motorcycle crash on Highway 401. The poet tangles images, sounds, sensations to re-create the instant "the Honda hover[s] there — midair," the instant before the speaker's "eyes flickered, then calmed." The collection explores Babstock's fascination with violence, injury and death — one reviewer calculates the body count at about forty — but beneath an adulterated landscape littered with fatal crashes and suicides, where down a "junked alley" a murdered prostitute lies "in pieces, in a zipped up sack" and where "ravens [are] defending / a rope of entrails" spilling from a dead dog, is an enduring natural world. People are increasingly disenfranchised, isolated — in "Authority," the speaker knows that "We have shuffled our lives / to somewhere north of wanting / each other. Used / distance as anodyne" and "Pared / it all down to these grim-lipped / *take cares*." But "through a storm window" is "A garden sprouting / new chives, pumpkin sun, community of ants."

Mean is also a vehicle for the poet to probe painful ("I'd rather speak here / of other things") and formative family bonds. In "Charred Shadows," the child speaker watches "wide-eyed" as the claw hammer he has accidentally "nudged" drops forty feet onto his brother's head, "blood / bubbling into gun-blue clots"; he later notes "The way a mother can snag a lie from your lips / with her hands in dishwater." In "To a Sister, Wherever," the poet struggles to deal with recollections of his sister being beaten repeatedly for lying — the images "stack up" in his memory, "grow like a subsurface reef," until he finally confesses, "I find sleep a relief."

In 2001, Babstock published *Days into Flatspin* (2001). It is a series of meditations on an eclectic range of ideas and experiences, as well as on objects endowed with human attributes: a boot mat is "A cold-blooded thing, [that] eked out a living / in the subarctic of the mud room"; a tractor is fickle, "the valentine of the bucket seat perched on a spring-coil … that said a scooped-out I love you to any-sized ass"; a convenience store "was proud of [its] vast palette / of candies," but it has now "begun to loathe / the intervals between the guns." The poet's persona in this collection examines the world in which he is immersed very closely, and he (this person who recalls that the first book he "truly understood" sent his "days into / flatspin") comes to doubt the ability of poetic scrutiny to penetrate the "abundance / of goings-on that have vowed to be piercingly not you." The problem is, "We never come round from this coma of looking."

Babstock has remarked that "We're told to think critically by looming, spotlit billboards erected by companies whose product is at best unnecessary, and at worst a direct link to human suffering. The language of resistance is owned and trademarked." His exasperation with commodity culture resurfaces in his third book, *Airstream Land Yacht* (2006), which was short-listed for a Governor General's Award. In the fourth of six poems titled "Explanatory Gap," he reviles "Nineteen-Eighty-BoreYouToDeath" — the era in which "sex had attached / its lips to Things." Now, the global economy deplores a vacuum: "There'll be a sign here soon." This more contemplative collection also feeds on Babstock's investigation of philosophy and theories of consciousness; he has claimed particular interest in the ideas of American philosopher Daniel Dennett, who maintains that consciousness is merely a biological action and the self is a fictional construct. In the love poem "Marram Grass," the speaker feels that biological pull — "my affection's bending toward you seems / or feels ever just a blind, predetermined / consequence of random winds." But we are never slaves to predetermination; the world will resist principles that narrow and demystify our experience. The speaker tells his lover, "You taught / and teach me things. Most alive when grit / makes seeing hard."

Babstock has also been pursuing an interest in the intersection between poetry and contemporary music. He says, "One of the happiest things in the last few years … is finding out how there is a cross-genre interest. I grew up, like every other young person, loving music — pop music, indie rock and whatnot — and finding out that some of these bands that you're listening to are reading poetry is fantastic." The Deadly Snakes borrowed some lines from Babstock's "Uncle in Eastport," and on the Rheostatics' album *2067,* Babstock reads his poem "The Expected" in the track "Try to Praise This Mutilated World."

Since 2003, Babstock has been poetry editor for House of Anansi Press in Toronto.

Crab

Beyond the sandbar, the sea
was ash-grim, a flint quilt
buckling. Houses huddled, slanting
on the bay's rim like pastel mints on drab
green and granite. Paths
threaded the cragged bluffs
to a thumbnail of beach that was ours
for a summer. Wading through
shallows with driftwood
sticks, we'd lift away shag carpets of kelp   10
and spot them there — claws up,
scuttling — black eye beads
like cloves looking back as they spidered
away from our toes.

Stacked up in tide pools,
in tangled leg locks, they were
brittle old men, grotesques thrown ashore by the sea.
For hours I gawked at plasticky joints,
spotted, knobbed claws, and
wispy ferns at the mouth, how the sea's lens made   20
the shells swell, shimmer 'til
perspective was gone and their name
had washed up on my tongue — *Dungeness, Dungeness.*[1]
The boy I was edged closer to them,
brine-spattered, waterlogged, less.

(1999)

The Expected

The sky looks afflicted; a sallow, hairless
skull where rain worries
itself to exhaustion and falls. The clouds

are old codgers, belts cinched, bent
at the spine — wheezing —

they lean to shadow the town.

These bowed streetlights like crooked fingers,
their tendons too tight to point or
their skin doesn't fit, drool
electric wax into the snow.   10

---

1. *Dungeness* A type of crab.

By this glow we trudge through brittle
eyelid cold even dogs won't brave and
convince ourselves home … or at least
a front door and mail slot.

From under hedges, cats growing thumbs
whine the wind to a tight riled quiver.
The county's only radio tower has snapped
its bolts near the tip, is transmitting
nothing but coughs.

20   Winter has lost its footing, stumbles off
blind into accident. All westbound outroads
swallow their signs, choking on place-names …

The expected has finally gone wrong.

(1999)

Head Injury Card

Task: to be where I am.
Even when I am in this solemn and absurd
role: I am still the place
where creation works on itself
— Tomas Tranströmer (trans. Robert Bly)

* Unsteadiness on the feet, dizziness

When was. Crustaceans flick tongues in the ocean's ear;
fog clings, marbled. Metal gurney and knees pointed
at cracked plaster. Bite down on air.
Salmon-steak pink. Greased and soft-headed. Alternately
slapped and coddled, coddled and slapped — hands
like talons go for the gyroscope of the eye

* Unusual drowsiness

As if some swell beyond, below the sea's belt
10   had bone-chilled us, bale-wrapped and banded
our tongues. Sentenced to stillness, a columnar,
wet-hemlock church. A sharp creak sparrows out
from the shed … slack-drum thud from the shrubs …
               It starts in. Pray for its passing

* Mental confusion

Pool of shallow calm, terns two-step in chalked
mist, moist brush of spruce bough. Belong
here, adrift in amniotic[1] flow, this is your ... no —
I'm at it again, quelling the pain and gush. Semiotic[2]
downpour, onslaught; those first quivering lungs   20
and no one directing the intake

* Persistent vomiting

Between brown water potholes and clapboard yellows,
lean night halls, over the sea's breaking frown;
a brother. A beach stone. Unreliable air of the world.
Housed in hedged, Ontario towns, every shed savouring its bucked
wood, whimpering collie, cords coiled in a gas-blue
helix[3] of meaning. Basement detritus[4] piling and piling

* One pupil larger than the other

Soccer pitch, clipped, green. Raised on pitches of love   30
lower than a drone and today, brother, you and I weeping
at the touchline, grass glistens with it. Midfield, a boy
fires off a toy rocket. Zenith, where it wobbles, uncertain,
shies from the thinner reaches, burns up its last, and
shimmies down the ocean we all try to look through

* Persistent or increasingly severe headache

Further back. Feet stirruped, muzzled nurses hover
and grip. Crown of a skull slides out. Algae.
Crown of a skull like the mute in a trumpet's bell and
blow this with your entire, blood-flushed husk. This   40
music, heard through fog of Demerol, does it flow
into or out from that sea-floor-soft
fontanelle?[5]

(1999)

A Leave-Taking

1

As you walked, night grew, grew into its boots,
plum blue into pungent pine mat, meadow.
Feeding on asphalt and the electric
current of swollen crickets, night ate
while your own eyes starved. Ditches rose

---

1. **amniotic** Of the membrane that encloses the fetus. 2. **Semiotic** Relating to signs. 3. **helix** Spiral. 4. **detritus** Debris.
5. **fontanelle** Membrane-covered gap between the bones of an infant's skull.

up, swallowing fencing — posts, phone poles,
attending thicket all thickened to black.
Annihilation breath-close and towering,
like putting an eye up to knotholes
10   in barn walls. On concession roads
you made concessions to fear —
        I can walk as far
as the footbridge, I can walk as far —
a prayer that seemed transmitted from
your fist where it hung, where a stone
from the underfoot gravel warmed in wet
folds and stood for a smallness worth
arguing with. Coached on, reined in
by a sideline of megaphoned, gross-throated
20   frogs. Soft moth panicked your hair then
flits off, is gone; in the uncommon sway
of night's greatcoat, perhaps never was, but
a tingle awoke, travelled down the weed
of your spine, and your inner ear's fugged
with by the off-time scruffings of other,
invisible, oncoming boots …
Offer your hand, your stone, mute, huge
with new regions.

2

El Camino, Firebird, Nova; they'd growl
30   in a huddle, owners on hoods picking
out fags under sulphurous lamps while
Airborne on leave bristled and thugged

through the clubs clutching money —
a buttoned-down, Jordache,[1] let-God-sort-'em-out
set. Stand too close you'll hear
cartilage pop in the trapped reek

of cologne. We'd pin our eyes to bourbon-
hued carpet, cower, duck out early, and
get drunk under bridges: no-see-ums, black-
40   flies, midges sank in the gin and we'd

wince at the burn of that cocktail —
three parts boredom, one naked rage. Drop
acid. Rinse. That town where we hid was
infected; a boot camp,

a cage

---

1. Jordache Popular brand of jeans in the 1980s.

3

Over Shield rock edged like a dolphin's back
you watch woods, walled, rattling past
and the rolling wake of bruised sumac.

You've hitched this ride from a lumberless lumber
town, rifling change off the dash, tape   50
deck cranked, the number of

cigarettes left in your pack is a symbol —
or plain fact, either way, it recurs in
your head like a chant so you keep on.

And it's this nimble cat-stepping between
the brash urging of what is, and the constant
soft shoulder approaching, widening, converging

again back where these woods strangle or corset
the road. You're young. You need nothing.   60
All that's behind you is shitty. A spore,

a seed that finds its own transport, breaks
itself open on deadpan, impoverished clay:

city

4

A remnant rusted to a papery
thinness, shaped
like those masks worn to masquerade

balls, but in metal with eyeholes and
all. Its skin of black
paint has chafed, lifted, bubbled

away in spots revealing tired russets,   70
corroded reds veined
and blotched with lighter shades closer to

gold. *Northern Ontario Road Metal*, it's
called, the artist
mounted this oxidized grimace on a bright

orange field, under glass, and gave it
to me last Christmas.
What is it? Where is it from?

80
Being older he smiled, held his tongue, watched
me clamber and grope
for some meaning to pin to this *bright obvious*

standing motionless in cold. Live with and enter
its surface, texture of old
drainpipe or cow's tongue, colours made

loud by their background — I relive the loud
rash the Ottawa River
broke out in each fall, its tattered banks stitched

90
up by woodpeckers with a cicada's shrill thread.
The roads drifting
out of that town were all golds, reds, and

rot splintering the heads of greying posts.
Each dead farmhouse
alone in its proper plot, made beautiful by cold

light and long shadow, our dreams put on edge by
what each house lacked.
Detritus. Remnants. A scrap salvaged and

kept as reminder: Don't always look back —
but look back.

(1999)

Regenerative

That dog padded home wearing a rip
in his back, clicked onto the kitchen linoleum
with a five-inch smile down his saddling spine.

Where pebbles and dark grit stuck to the wound's
lips, vertebrae like molars grinned through
in an anemic bluish white. The dumb grey

meat of his tongue like a sodden flag waiting
for breeze in the post-storm still of that house —
how he lashed the plucked chicken length of it,

10
then lapped at the seepage that hung from black
flews.[1] He turned, and turned, and in turning sparks
of shock shot from his eyes as his chances of seeing

---

1. **flews** The large, hanging sides of the upper lip on some dogs.

pain dimmed, coiled to a brute whine in his chest. I
pictured a bald nest of lab mice pulsing in there
crying its cancer away; pictured a shed door, askew

on its hinges, mowing thick weeds as it swung; even
pictured a field in that dog, where choirs of crickets
sawed through the night with the ache in their legs.

I could smell the top-heavy cattails' thinning brown
felt as it burst, breathing commas on parachutes   20
into the world; heard the travelling s's of garter snakes

playing wet grass blades with cadmium scales as
they passed through invisible shivers. A lost leather
sneaker shone near a stump, like a child's plug-in

night-light, or a chipped-off sample of moon. Blue
shell casings coughed funnelled web from the throats
where their packed shot had been, and bleached-out

pages of porn doubled as mainsails, fitted to masts
of wild rose. Dew, meltwater cold, slid down my calves
like wet wrists unburdening jewels in my boots. Then no one   30

I knew approached through the dark, swinging a carved
column of light, prodding the bramble and weeds with
this staff that worked like a blind man's stick in reverse.

The mauve starbursts of thistles passed through it, casting
peaked shadows like crowns. Bugs strafed the beam, reared
from the black, threading it again, and again. He didn't

call out or raise his free hand or even target his lamp
on my head, just kept cresting the weeds with the twin
prows of his knees while scanning the foreground

for snags. Whether it was that he couldn't imagine me   40
there, and therefore I wasn't, or that my body actually
weighed in at nothing, doused as it was in that field's

feral[2] moulting, bucking, breathing — its bull-stubborn
morphing of intrauterine moments — I couldn't decide.
There wasn't time. He passed on the left, dragged by

2. **feral** Wild, untamed, savage.

his light as if some shadowy, leashed mastiff tractored
him on, plunging through weed. Solid black silhouette, receding,
until distance undermined outline, form bled into field.

(2001)

Ataraxia[1]

I'd come in from a wind, a wind in a storm with snow
like atomized iron, part chandelier part bomb, it hurt
to inhale. An engorged winter snow that ignored each cardinal
point on the compass, and Newton, and foreground, and
it ignored depth. Snow with layers of enamelled white
degrading through grey to black, black snow that shivered

white again in the acid of stung, underlid vision. Knifed
onto the canvas snow as the canvas creases, then tears.
The tips of two fingers rolled loose in the purse of a glove,
10   and a dollar-size patch of dead flesh collected crystals
under one eye. Gliding on the stump-end of each femur,
I reeled, gill-snagged by the collusion of wires above

and banged into the barn wood door before the door had gained
outline and was more than the snow shift and ground static.
It gave, and leaked a column that glowed. Air in that lung
was unalive, warm, moted, smoky, how I had imagined air
in my own, before I'd left the great enclosure months hence,
to come here, though at the point of my leaving "here" was no option.

Then I was sitting, a snow-pack on one hand stalling the thaw,
20   and chewing hard on my face with weak teeth. Iron pry-bars
and outsized wrenches hung like strips of smoked meat from
spikes in the studs. The studs crowned outward, and cracked
like the whip's end the wind held the handle of, out past
the weakening hydro towers. There were wood chips, a stool,

and a curling portrait of Curtis Strange[2] in his backswing; two
palm leaves browning through the frame of his high arm. Seeing
was shearing browns from the not-there's of black, except where
the heat source bled orange onto the meltwater and ice still
clinging to seams in my gear.
30   It was here I began hoping the angel
of quiet might visit, gripping the past in its talon; a past devoid

of plastics and canker, shame, stale grievance, Vancouver, debt,
shortfall, and waste —
                                "You stain what sections of now I've allowed

---

1. **Ataraxia** Tranquility. 2. **Curtis Strange** American golfer (born 1955).

You," I said, addressing the past as a pain-fire in the flesh of my feet
took root, "your slavish insistence on sticking around, on bearing
down on the hours as they enter and be, siphons the glow off your
stardom. You and your retinue reek. I've a chance here to gaze at this

oil can on into tomorrows. Equilibriate.[3] Blot the weather and settle."
Outside was tearing its fingernails out, eating the elderly in drifts-   40
become-tombs. The notion of water froze in the mind of outside
and all vertical entities had relinquished pretensions.
                                                "You had
a chance. Then you opened your mouth." Its voice came from nowhere,
as the past needs nowhere to be, and deadened the details of the things

I could see. "Your good eye hangs the way it does due to me. Padlocks
in your lower back, and the list of cities that rented you space. The love
defiled by disallowing the ground it grew into. Remember, bored child,
as a flea on the flesh of disquiet, you'd have given fingers to have
things mean, prior to seeing, disturbing, and reading them." The sun,   50
a governing body, had entered a phase of secrecy it couldn't discuss.

Or there wasn't a sun.

                                                                    (2006)

Palindromic

A patrimony all our own: the hours when we have done nothing … It is they that form
us, that individualize us, that make us *dissimilar*. — E.M. Cioran

Christmas alone, by choice, with a tin
        of sardines and bonnie "prince" billy[1]
sharpening the blade of the cold on
        the whetstone[2] of his voice. A melee

on the morning of the first of the year
        over who should pay what to who
for the nothing we got the night before.
        There'd been *lots* of it, but it amounted to

loss, I guess is what I mean, given the pain
        and embarrassing, hours-long absences   10
of someone with someone else whose name
        should stay out of this. Fences

---

3. Equilibriate To keep in balance.

---

1. bonnie "prince" billy American alternative-country singer-songwriter and actor (born 1970). **2. whetstone** Tool for
sharpening blades.

went up around friendships. The exacto blade
    in the thermometer kept snapping
off segments till there was nothing save numbered
    hash-marks seen through a static

of frost. I went for a walk in a parka I bought.
    Zipped up; the city as a fuzzy-edged
dream sequence afloat to indicate thought
20   in the head of a smiling protagonist. Cadge[3]

a light from a passerby and now your head's
    the lantern from the 28th Canto[4]
shedding light on hell. "Oh me!" you'd said,
    and no laughter, canned or

otherwise, leavened[5] a life that felt filmic.
    Sometime in March, the plaster over
the tub got pregnant, or Anish Kapoor[6] was snuck
    in to redecorate. Its water burst near

April Fool's and spring arrived stillborn, I was
30   reading something that hasn't stayed
with me, when the soldiers arrived with shovels.
    It was Mendelssohn screaming at Stoppard,[7]

I think, or Stoppard screaming back, in the letters
    section of the NYRB,[8] about Housman,[9]
was it? As penned by Stoppard? — whatever,
    I remember an exchange of epithets and now's

a little after the fact seeing as the play itself
    never came. One night in May, a barkeep thought
I looked tired and slipped me a pill: I got soft
40   in the neck, large in the thumbs, and a spot

of crimson light sang *Agnus Dei*[10] from the foreground
    of my vision's left field. Wall calendars
were argyle socks; all those X's in rows wrapped around
    June under colour shots of designer blenders.

It was like a training regimen to ensure I'd place last
    in the race to accomplish, accrue, attain,

---

3. **Cadge** Obtain by begging. 4. **28th Canto** In this canto of Dante's *Divine Comedy*, a headless body in the eighth circle of hell carries the head swinging like a lantern. 5. **leavened** Lightened. 6. **Anish Kapoor** Indian-English sculptor (b. 1954) famous for monochrome, curved shapes. 7. **Mendelssohn, Stoppard** Felix Mendelssohn (1809–1847), German composer; Tom Stoppard (b. 1937), British playwright. 8. **NYRB** *New York Review of Books*. 9. **Housman** The work of British poet A.E. Housman (1859–1936) forms the centre of Stoppard's play, *The Invention of Love*. 10. **Agnus Dei** Latin for "lamb of God," Jesus Christ. An invocation song.

or think straight for a day and a half. I didn't dust.
     Meeting resistance — a door opens onto more rain —

I'd fall back and regroup, reuse the same ringed tea cup
     and liberate a pack of Dunhill from the long ice age   50
of the freezer. Watched others watch their Weimaraner[11] pups
     grow to full glamour in the park. Massaged

the kinks of appointments from the hurt muscle of months,
     dredged each nightbottom for spare hours
to stare at. Just a therapist and me and a lot of not much
     to work through, more like locating doors

I might walk through if I'd get up and walk. Hypodermic,
     or fifty candies, or warm bath and a pine box:
repeated it all to myself, but self laughed, knew it was weak
     and would linger. Self trips self then mocks   60

the starfish of limbs washed up in the gravel, another X-
     brace to hold square a day. I read a novel wherein
many were worse off, so read it again, while flecks
     of grey ash mixed with eczematous snow in

the deep gorge between each page. To open it now's
     like opening a text from the Middle Ages, but
you can't, it's glued shut with dead skin cells and sweat. Sows
     at the Ex[12] in August nonplussed with the crowds at

the gate. Too much lost, in ten minutes, at Crown and Anchor,[13]
     and my house keys freed from a pocket while   70
upside down in those ergonomic gibbets hung from the Zipper.
     So head down for the night on the deep pile

carpet of clipped-lawn embankment that skirts the expressway.
     Stuff fell in the fall. No one took pictures.
Or painted the scene on wood panel in oil, of the day
     none of my friends and I decided not to go halves

on a driving trip through some of Vermont. I read Frost
     and stayed where I was. Thanksgiving
I thanked someone for the chance to play generous host
     to myself as guest at the bar where, having   80

been dosed earlier that year, we went back for more.
     By November I was an art installation

---

11. **Weimaraner** Grey, short-coated hunting dog. 12. **Ex** Toronto Exhibition, an annual fair; the Zipper is a popular ride.
13. **Crown and Anchor** Roulette-type game of chance.

begging the question are empty days at the core
    of the question of begging the question.

Borrowed money so's not to be anywhere near Christmas,
    while the snow whitened what no longer
wanted to be looked at. I know now I was missed.
    Then was a different story. I think we're all stronger.

(2006)

Lynn Coady (1970–)

Nova Scotian Lynn Coady was born in Port Hawkesbury, Cape Breton, in 1970. Although she had the will to write from a young age, she sensed that people in her economically depressed home town would consider such an ambition "preposterous and bigheaded." She emerged from this milieu with a sharp wit — remarking that "You've got to have a sense of humour to get through a Cape Breton adolescence" — and in 1988 she headed to Ottawa to attend Carleton University. Coady initially entered Carleton's journalism program but then switched to arts and graduated with a B.A. in English and philosophy. She worked for a few years at odd jobs (including day-care worker and nanny) in various New Brunswick towns, and in her free time she wrote plays. *Cowboy Names* was staged by Fredericton's Black Box Theatre in 1995, and in 1996, *Cold in the Morning* won the B.C. International Play Writing Competition and Coady was offered a fellowship to the University of British Columbia's creative writing program. She explains that she chose to make her home in Vancouver and enter the M.F.A. program because "all [she] really wanted was time to write."

In 1998, Coady published the novel *Strange Heaven*. It centres on teenaged Cape Bretoner Bridget Murphy, who has a baby out of wedlock and gives it up for adoption. Battling depression and unable to cope, she enters the psych ward of a Halifax children's hospital, where she encounters a cast of characters whose torments make her own seem inconsequential. Bewildered and withdrawn, Bridget observes the ward's horrific yet often darkly humorous goings-on and slowly makes a place for herself in its skewed world. At Christmastime, she reluctantly goes home for a reunion with family and friends and enters what she now has the insight to recognize as yet another bedlam — her father roars profanities, her bedridden grandmother raves and beseeches God, her mentally impaired uncle fabricates religious folk art for the tourist trade, her verbally abusive boyfriend threatens to sue her for giving up their baby. But somehow, Bridget comes to understand, this "strange heaven" is home, and as such it is a place to heal. Coady herself was a pregnant teen in a small Cape Breton town, and she is frequently asked about the autobiographical currents in her work. She underscores the impact that this early experience had upon her world view and, as a consequence, her writing: "Being a pregnant teenager set me off on the philosophical path that I eventually went down," Coady says. "It blew society wide open for me." *Strange Heaven* won several prizes and received a Governor General's Award nomination.

Coady's short story collection, *Play the Monster Blind*, appeared two years later, in 2000. Nine of its 11 stories are set in Cape Breton; the other two unfold in British Columbia. They delve into themes that Coady had already established with her novel — family, and the troubled and violent bonds it harbours; the oppressive nature of small-town existence; and the outsider's perpetual longing for escape. In mining this territory, Coady demonstrates her broad mastery of language, tone, and character and gives rein to her tough and unorthodox sense of humour (the collection won the Stephen Leacock Award for Humour). In the worlds of these stories, a chorus of censorious gossips herald sightings of a teenaged girl's disgraceful mother ("Oh, look, if it isn't Herself"). Another teenaged girl is brutally violated, ostracized, and ridiculed ("She was called Paula More 'n' More and Ball-a"). A town drunk who seems to crop up everywhere offers profane musings ("Would not this be the perfect day to be bobbing down the river … with a big blonde in one hand and a bottle of Captain Morgan in the other and a pink ribbon tied around your pinocchio?").

Coady's next work, *Saints of Big Harbour*, came out in 2002. Adolescent first-person narrator Guy Boucher lives with his goth sister and their mother, Marianne, who is severely worn down by life. They subsist on Marianne's welfare cheques and the pin money she earns babysitting. Marianne also has the use of her brother Isadore's truck on the understanding that she keep an eye on him and steer him clear of prison — as Guy tells us, "So he is paroled to my mother for driving the truck not just drunk but without a driver's license or insurance." Isadore is a hopeless alcoholic — "He reeks. To cover up his bed head, he wears a cap that reads, *Wine me, dine me, sixty-nine me!*" — and he trails damage in his wake. This is a story of abject lives, of broken people who have toppled into a hole so deep they will never crawl out of it. As critic Allan Hepburn observes, Coady's characters "speak basic English. They are small-minded, brawling, sentimental, banal, alcoholic. They live by rumour and manipulation."

Coady provides here and elsewhere a striking dramatization of the pervasive effects of poverty and the demoralization it brings. She has charged those who are critical of the hopelessness that colours her work with lacking the capacity to understand "how anyone could end up in such a situation and, more importantly … the way it shapes people. They know that poverty sucks because you can't afford to buy stuff, but they don't understand that it doesn't make you noble or strong as a result, it doesn't build character. On the contrary, it makes you petty and hostile and small-minded unless you have supernatural reserves of personal integrity, or else someone in your life who actively works to counter such influences. So that doesn't always make for a happy story, and it goes against all the societal myths with which we like to reassure ourselves."

In 2003, Coady edited *Victory Meat: New Fiction from Atlantic Canada*, and three years later, she produced another novel: *Mean Boy*. Nineteen-year-old protagonist Larry Campbell, son of the manager of a Prince Edward Island mini-putt, flees his dead-end existence for academia, enrolling in the fictitious Westcock University in New Brunswick. Larry burns to become a poet, and at Westcock he falls under the spell of Professor Jim Arsenault — a drunken, working-class-hero type who is also a published poet. His coterie of devoted student-followers are prone to jealousy and regularly stab each other in the back. Larry idealizes the charismatic Jim and becomes embroiled in departmental politics when his hero is denied tenure. Coady aligns Larry's raw need for Jim with that potent notion of escape and transcendence that emerges so often in her work. Larry moans, "I need Jim Arsenault to love me. Because that will mean I have worth. That will mean there is a point. That will mean I am not a PEI hillbilly going *hyuck-hyuck* chawing on a sprig of hay (or in my case maybe a hunk of raw potato), and poking around with his first cousin." In charting Larry's gradual disillusionment and coming of age, Coady also fashions a riotous satire of the hothouse of academia in the 1970s, when the CanLit industry was at full throttle. She also leaves Cape Breton and alters her comic and dramatic possibilities by shifting from her typical set of characters — whom she has described as "monosyllabic working-class people who aren't particularly articulate but whose hearts are full" — to a crew of hyper-articulate and self-conscious ones. "Larry was different," she explains, "because I wanted him to be really smart."

Coady has a regular column in the *Globe and Mail*. In 2005, after a decade in Vancouver, she moved to Edmonton.

In Disguise as the Sky

I am a sadist for doing it, but they have to learn. I give them test after test after test every week. They almost weep at the thought. There's no rules. They just have to keep practising, memorizing, testing and re-testing themselves.

I understand how it insults them, how the English language in general is an insult to reason with its *there*, *their*, and *they're*, its *it's* and *its*. "*I* before *e* except after *c*" and all that pointlessness. *Though* and *through* and *trough*. It's infuriating. They get angry at me. They demand: Why? And I'm a teacher, but because I am a teacher of a very insane and arbitrary science, the only answer I can give them is this — it's a child's answer: *Just because*.

And spoken to like children, they respond like children: Who say?

Who says, I correct. *I don't know. Whoever made it up. Just some guy.* I don't feel like much of a teacher, saying things like that. But it's true. And thus do they come to understand what an embarrassment to English speakers our language really is. All of them leave the class feeling a good degree more contempt for me and my countrymen than they started with. That means I am doing my job.

On the last day of class I usually ask them to tell me a little bit about their own language, not for their own benefit, but because it's fascinating to me how much more rational they all seem. A Japanese student showed me how the characters for things were basically just drawings of them. A Thai student showed me how the little round heads on all the lovely, looping characters were what made up vowel sounds. The one Russian I ever taught merely spat at me: "Russia language make sense."

Russian makes sense, I told him. *You don't have to say "Russian language," it's implied*.

He rolled his eyes, as he had been doing all along. Over the semester, it becomes harder and harder for them to believe that this is the language of the most prosperous nation on earth, of the Internet, of the global marketplace. This is the one out of all the others, for all their beauty and simplicity, that's won out.

One, won.

But prepositions makes them angriest. At least for some things you have the handy little rules of thumb. The *i* before *e* stuff. Subject and object. It's "my friend and I" if it's the object, but "my friend and me" if it's the subject. That's a tricky one but you can learn it. You can study it and you can learn it. All I can do with prepositions is give them long, endless lists. *A secret between us. A story about a man.* Is it always a story *about* something? *Yes, that's right.* So then they go and write something like, "This is a story about Ernest Hemingway." *No, it's a story by Ernest Hemingway about an old man dying with his hat off in the rain.* But you said it was *always* a story *about* something. About *something* but by *someone*. So a book can only be about something or by someone? they ask with so much hope. *A book is an object. It can be on something, off something, by something….* But you said it could only be by *someone*! I don't know how they keep from killing me.

But they don't. They come to feel sorry for me because I am only a dumb representative of my dumb language. A dumb citizen of a dumb English-speaking country that should be clamouring to join up with the wealthy and fearsome realm next door, they think, but remains stubbornly sovereign, middle-income, and weak. They don't get it, because to them we are all the same. It's not like we're a bunch of Latvians on this side of the border, with Ukrainians on the other side. That's precisely how my Russian student put it to me. "You are all mongrels," he said. "You have no culture, why do you care? It is not as if you are a bunch of Latvians or something."

"Not as if you *were*," I corrected. Eye-roll.

I had taught them the word *mongrel* the week before. They loved it. They used it all the time after that. They loved having a word to express what it was about North Americans that had baffled them for so long. This blandness. This striving towards homogeneity. This relative indifference to immigrants, for example, people of all races and creeds. This relative indifference to our own families and communities. That I had moved across the continent away from mine and not yet dried up from despair.

But I like my country, if not my language. I like that we're not all a bunch of Latvians. They may have simple languages, but their nations are complicated. Indonesia, for example, is complicated. Yugoslavia is complicated. I like simplicity. I like that slogan, "Keep It Simple, Stupid," and would have it posted up in my classroom, if it weren't such an outlandish contradiction to what I teach. *Obscurify, students. Clutter. Complicate*. So I have it pinned up in my kitchen at home instead. In my apartment, I forget about the Byzantine[1] world of English grammar. I get take-out food, everything in medium-sized portions. I watch television shows that were not created to be enjoyed by people with imaginations. I sleep on a futon. I don't dream.

In the office, two male voices are talking about something called "day-cake." One of them is my student, Kunakorn, from Thailand, and the other is someone I don't know, hanging around the desk like he works here. He probably does work here. This is such an irritating place to work that people quit and get hired all the time, so I am always running into people I don't know who are supposedly my co-workers.

Kunakorn says, "My favourite is day-cake," and my new co-worker replies that he is partial to day-cake as well. Then I remember what day-cake is. Kunakorn has a habit of making up his own words for objects when I'm not around to tell him what they are. He has an even worse habit of deciding that the word he makes up is more appropriate and easier to remember than the actual English word, once he's learned what it is. So he'll go for months, for example, refusing to call a basketball net anything other than a "sky-hole."

One of Kunakorn's pet peeves about North America is how much bread we eat. He's had some bad experiences with bread. When he first arrived here, his host-family served him nothing but sandwiches and hamburgers. Finally he just went out and bought a bag of rice and sat down and ate an entire pot of it himself. He thinks almost all the food we eat is a variation on the loaf of bread. Cinnamon buns, meat loaf, cookies, cake. To him it is all just bread. One time he was rhyming off a litany of such food to me, pretend-bread, he called it, bread products we Westerners irrationally gussy up in order to disguise its fundamental bread-character.

"Biscuits, scones," he said, impressing me with his baked-goods vocabulary. "Cake," he added. "Day-cake," he finished.

I told him there was no such word as *day-cake*, and he got frustrated. Kunakorn always claimed that he preferred to use the words that he made up because they made more sense. This was undeniable, but I insisted on correcting him nonetheless, because that was my job. That's the job of language. To impose arbitrary rules.

---

1. **Byzantine** Complex, intricate.

"Day. Cake," he repeated impatiently. "You often have in day."

"That's just regular cake!" I said.

"No, no! You don't have day-cake at night, that is difference. You can have regular cake at night."

"It doesn't make sense," I emphasized to him. Usually when his own personal vocabulary made sense, I would acknowledge it. I even praised him for his ingenuity sometimes, because he could come up with some quite reasonable substitutions. He called pillows sleeping bags, and sleeping bags out-blankets. You could not deny the logic.

But day-cake was nonsense, I told him. He gestured and jumped around trying to describe it to me, and finally I asked him to draw a picture on the board, which he did.

"It's a muffin," I said.

"Muh — "

"Muffin."

"Muh-vin."

"Muffin."

"Muffin. What 'muffin' mean?"

"It means that," I said, pointing to the board.

"But what it *mean*?" he repeated. "Day-cake?"

"No," I said. "It doesn't mean anything. It just means that." I pointed again.

Eye-rolls all around. That was their problem with English in a nutshell. It is no wonder Kunakorn refused to give up his own thoughtful creations for something so ridiculous-sounding.

So I come stampeding out from behind the partition where I'm photocopying lists of prepositions, hollering, "Muffin! Muffin! Muffin!" Kunakorn gives me a look as if his suspicion that I just make up all the craziness I drill into him day after day has been vindicated. He points with triumph at the new co-worker.

"He say 'day-cake.'"

"Why are you standing there talking about day-cake?" I say to the new guy.

The new guy is shorter than me, and about ten pounds lighter. He is absurdly overdressed to be sitting at the front desk. He looks like a boy who's been polished up for his first communion and I try not to wince.

But I do wince when I realize I've scared him. It is awful to scare a short man in a communion suit.

"Day-cake," he repeats. "It sounds nice!" He tries to be bright, breezy, the way people he's seen who work in offices in sitcoms always interact. Chipper, sardonic. Not jumpy and horrified at the sudden appearance of a tall woman with large breasts screaming "muffin."

That I know all this about him already is making me depressed and I want to go out and buy a coffee and walk around the block. First I have to make him feel more at ease, and quickly, or I will feel sick to my stomach all day long. I hunch my back so that my breasts won't further unnerve him and wag a finger at Kunakorn.

"This guy thinks he can just make up his own language and get accepted into Harvard Business School saying 'day-cake' for *muffin* and 'out-bed' for *sleeping bag* and God knows what else. It's our job to break him of this terrible habit!"

I make a half-assed gesture as if to chuck the new guy on the shoulder like the buddy I am, and the new guy smiles and lets his breath out. But then something terrible happens. I watch his face as he attempts to make it a perfect imitation of mine — the easy, co-conspirator grin meant to put him at ease. The fakeness on my face when transferred to his own magnifies itself about ten times over and my stomach contracts at the sight. No, I think. This guy cannot be this uncomfortable. I want to give him liquor.

I'm just about to rush hunchbacked out the door like an office Quasimodo when he says something nice, something that relieves me. It's nice because it's honest. He has forgotten himself for a moment.

"It's just so refreshing," he says, "to hear a different version of things every once in a while."

I turn around then because I want to smile at him again and be encouraging of unguarded moments like this, but already he has gone green. He picks up a pen and tries to twiddle it and ends up writing on his face, like the open book that he is. Clearly it's precisely such moments that he's desperate to avoid.

Now I'm going to feel sick to my stomach all day long. I walk around the block and can't drink my coffee. Everything I see exacerbates the situation. There is a man who sits on the corner every day surrounded by pigeons, asking people for change. Usually he is able to put on a brave face, crack jokes, say please and thank you to the passersby so they won't be intimidated or offended by him, but today must not have been a good day. Today he can't quite hold up the façade that he is just a regular Joe, a good, decent guy down on his luck, bearing ill will towards no one. As I'm walking towards him, he's still doing the please-and-thank-you thing, the obligatory have-a-nice-day, but already my antennae is out, he's sort of weaving, chanting the pleaseandthankyous and haveanicedays like cynical prayers, and finally, just as I'm passing, he bashes the back of his head against the building and howls:

"For the love of God and Jesus, people! I'm in pain!"

I am more like one of the pigeons at his feet than a pedestrian. The pedestrians alter their courses slightly, scarcely looking up, but me and the pigeons — the pigeons and me — we fly off in every direction.

At my apartment I classify this day as having been a Bad Day in my journal, taking note of the events that made it so. I do this every day, examining why it was good or bad and taking note of the events so that in the future I can try to recreate the good events and avoid the bad ones.

But the good days aren't really characterized so much by good events as lack of bad ones. I write that down in my journal. That is a little bit of wisdom for later on. I walk around my apartment for a while and eat some of my medium portions and repeat to myself, *Go to sleep, go to sleep,* which is meant to settle my stomach and calm me enough to sit and watch sitcoms before it's time for bed.

The first step is to remove yourself. I have students who come from, literally, the other side of the planet. If you took a long spike and drove it into the ground here, and it went all the way down the middle of the earth and out the other end, it would come out practically in their own backyard. But these same students, who had all the power to wrench themselves out of their huge families and their tiny communities and sit on a plane for fourteen hours, are the same ones who will sit in class weeping for days on end, and it's usually the same reason: *Because I miss my mother.* They will call their mothers every night, asking for news about their grandparents, siblings, cousins. When they hear that so-and-so's daughter has ran away again, they cry. They come to class crying about one thing or another happening on the other side of the planet on a regular basis. But mainly their mothers, or lack thereof. My point is, they haven't removed themselves at all.

It is that intimacy that is the problem, I have determined this long ago. The intimacy of little towns and families. You cry because of the intimacy. It may as well have happened to you. The less intimate you are, the less it bothers you. That's what cities are for. That's what I thought cities were supposed to be for. But the city is becoming a disappointment to me.

It is not so much hands being cut off and daughters running away, in the city. It is more like this:

I was sitting in the park reading a book on a beautiful day in the summertime. People walked by me in couples, groups, and families. There was a little canteen close to where I was sitting and all the people stopped to get ice cream and popsicles.

But then a man in a white cap who didn't seem to be enjoying the sun very much came and sat down on the other end of the bench. He was huffing and puffing from his walk and just sat there for a few moments, wiping his face with his cap. He wore a terry-cloth shirt the same colour blue as the sky, and white pants, like his cap. If he had, for whatever reason, started to levitate and float off into the horizon, he would have blended in perfectly with the sky, like Winnie-the-Pooh had hoped to do one time, but failed.

The man kept glancing at the canteen and all the people coming and going to get ice cream and popsicles. He'd stare at the beach for a while, and then glance back at the canteen, as if to see if it were still there. I couldn't read at all at this point. Finally he heaved himself up and tottered over to the canteen to buy himself an ice cream. It was obviously difficult for him to walk, not because he was so fat, but he also had some kind of limp.

So then he sits down beside me again with a rocky-road ice cream and eats it in about five minutes.

Then, the glancing-back started up again. Gazing at the beach, glancing towards the canteen, elaborately casual. After another five minutes of this, he stood up again and staggered back towards the canteen.

And this is what he said then:

"I'll have another rocky-road, please."

And then he came and sat down beside me again, with his second ice-cream cone.

He did this four more times in the space of an hour and a half — gazing and glancing, convincing himself that no one was paying attention, working up his courage — and I remained cemented to the other side of the bench like one of those bronze statues they sometimes install in parks to blend in with the real human beings, not having turned a page since he arrived. My tailbone had started to ache and sweat was trickling down my sides, but I couldn't budge until he left. I couldn't risk giving the slightest hint that I knew exactly what was going on. It was unthinkable. It was unspeakable.

That's the sort of thing I mean.

When I talk to my mother on the phone, we have a very pleasant chat. She tells me about neighbours and relatives I don't even remember any more, but even so it is never anything too lurid or horrifying. There are lots of operations, but most of them are successful. Daughters and sons are always getting married to other people's daughters and sons, and then having babies. It washes over me. Then my father is allowed to speak and asks me how I'm doing and I tell him fine. Then he asks me if I need any money and I make a joke about how if I needed money, I wouldn't say I was fine. We laugh. We hang up. It wasn't always so painless, but over the years we've managed to lay down some unspoken ground rules. It took a while. It used to be like a game where you scored or lost points despite yourself. Now it is more like a little play.

He's dressing in casual wear. Like after the first day on the job he went to the Casual Wear section at Eaton's and announced "office casual" to a salesgirl who decked him out from shoes to shirt. And she made him buy two shirts, three pairs of pants, and a couple of sweaters, all in coordinating colours to be mixed and matched throughout the week. And everything is ironed. And the brown sweater still has the tag. I shadow him around the office making small talk with a pair of scissors behind my back until one of the advisers simply calls out, "Nice tag, Sandy-boy," on her way to the bathroom, turning him green again and making me wish to nestle the scissors into the socket of her eye.

Even his name, Sandy. It's a description, like a dog's name. Scruffy. Fluffy. Makes you want to pet him. Weeks go by, and after Andrea has referred to him as Sandy-boy for the eleventh hundred time, I slam the photocopier and demand to know if he doesn't have any other names.

"Leopold is my second name," he tells me, quivering, because I've frightened him again.

"Jesus! That's it? Isn't Sandy short for anything?"

"Alexander," he shrugs.

"Alexander! You have a name like Alexander and you go around letting people call you Sandy? People could be calling you Alex. 'Alex, what time is the meeting? Phone call, line one … . Oh, thanks, Alex.' Doesn't that sound nice?"

"But my parents call me Sandy," he pleads.

"Your parents named you Alexander Leopold. Clearly they had some big plans. They just started calling you Sandy when you were a baby and couldn't get out of the habit."

"But everybody calls me Sandy. It's on my driver's licence."

I start calling him Alex all the time so he'll get used to it. I even refer to him as Alex when he's not around, and nobody knows who I am talking about. I make a special point of calling him Alex around Andrea.

"His name's Sandy."

"No," I correct. "His name's Alexander. Sandy is just a nickname."

"I asked him what his name was, he told me Sandy."

Andrea is a hard nut. She is one of those disquieting people who gives off an air of knowing how everything should be at all times. She has all the answers. She's an adviser, as I've said, and one of the few people in this place who is qualified for, and good at, her job. She was born to advise.

"Don't you think Alex is a better name?" I beg her.

"Yes. But I don't think it's *his* name. I think his name is Sandy."

Andrea calls things as she sees them. She has no vision.

I have come home from work some days and written in my journal about Andrea that she represents the way the world is. There are all sorts of holes dug into the world in certain shapes and sizes and people are born and shoved into those holes whether they care for them or not. Then they just grow into the shapes and sizes of the holes. And then everybody marvels about how those particular people are perfect for those holes, and isn't it great how perfectly things work out in this world of ours.

You can do the same thing with pumpkins. We had a pumpkin patch in our garden and my little brother used to grow them into whatever shapes he wanted. He'd put a band around the middle and make them grow into figure eights, for example. Later on, he saw in a farming magazine where you could buy little masks to put over the growing pumpkins, and when you took it off the pumpkins would have faces. He would line them up at Hallowe'en and everyone would wonder how he did it. And he'd tell them: *They just grew like that.*

And this being an Andrea kind of world, a lot of people believed him. They thought: If they exist, then that just must be how it is.

It seems a very passive way to live your life, and yet people like Andrea are the most stubborn I've met.

My brother was always doing things like that. How many boys do you know to whom it has occurred to direct the growth of pumpkins? He was a real original, my mother used to say. A genuine authentic, she used to say. She would desperately try to come up with all sorts of upbeat expressions to describe him. He was another one who liked to hear a different version of things every once in a while.

The Thai students have taken to Alex. They sense that he is like them — horrified by everything around him. Kunakorn often tells me of his first night in this country. He was bussed to the university after his sixteen-hour flight and deposited in a dorm room, given instructions in English, and left alone. He could speak not a word of English, of course, and was hungry. He took his key, screwed up his courage, and ventured out into the quad where young, drunken North Americans were celebrating frosh week. He bumped into a few staggering students and nobody was kind to him when they realized he was a foreigner as they were all intoxicated not so much by alcohol but by being together in a group with people exactly like themselves. So he was shoved by some guy in a backwards baseball cap who called him "loser." He remembers this word quite clearly, thinking it was maybe a pejorative North American term for *Asian*, and fell into a girl who shrieked and spilt her beer all down his back.

At long last Kunakorn arrived at some sort of all-night campus convenience store and purchased the largest bag of the most filling-looking food he could find. It was a bag of Wonderbread. He made his way back to his room and padded his stomach with it so he could sleep. He couldn't believe how utterly bland it was. His first taste of North America.

And then it was on to the sandwiches and hamburgers of his home-stay family. Thus was an unhealthy fascination born. He'll come into class every week announcing yet another bread-product he's discovered.

"Cracker."

"Oh, come on, crackers?"

"Yes, cracker. Flour, water. Bake."

"But that's like saying chips are bread."

That gives him pause. "Maybe chip *are* bread!" At lunchtime, he scurries off to investigate.

"No," after he returns. "Potato." He crosses his arms triumphantly. Don't even get Kunakorn started on potatoes. The potato is the second bizarre thing we eat in far too many forms, according to him. I have promised to bring in mashed potatoes at the end of the semester to show them all how lovely these grey lumps from underneath the earth can be when properly prepared.

"Comfort food," I teach them. "Food that makes you feel warm and safe. Perhaps your mother gave it to you when you were a child." I make a list on the board of all the foods that do it for me. Mashed potatoes, number one. With cream and butter and garlic, oh my God. The garlic was my brother's idea when he was fourteen and getting more creative with every passing minute. We all thought he was crazy. My father wanted to know if he was turning into some kind of Eye-talian. *Trust me*, he said. *Trust my palate*. My father couldn't stand him using words like *palate*. But no one could deny the potatoes were great that way.

Peanut butter and jelly sandwiches, I write. Kunakorn exhales with disgust. Boiled eggs. They all nod at that one. Pumpkin pie. Blank stares.

Then they all have to make their own lists. Kunakorn writes:

> *rice*
> *rice*
> *rice*
> *rice!*

"Rice is every bit as bland as bread!" I protest, a patriot.

Kunakorn looks at me like my father at my brother saying *palate*. "Noooo! Rice *heaven!*" he croons.

So the Thai students take Alex out for Chinese food all the time. They pay for him, they sort of make a pet of him. There is a syndrome among English as a Second Language teachers that it reminds me of. Some ESL teachers have no life and no friends, just like lots of people in lots of other jobs. And when they start teaching foreign students, they are given the kind of attention and regard that no self-respecting North American would ever deign to lavish upon someone so low on the social scale as a teacher. So their students become their social circle. Suddenly, the teacher finds him or herself popular and beloved in a way he or she has never known. It gets messy, obviously. Students start expecting their marks to reflect the goodwill they've shown. Everyone's around the same age, so teachers start sleeping with students. Lines are crossed.

That's kind of what's happening with the students and Alex except there is no power imbalance at play, so I suppose it is benign. Alex has some friends, friends who aren't instinctively aware of things like his trip to Casual Wear. Friends who don't tack "boy" to the end of his name. Friends who have their own dangling metaphorical price tags. I am happy for him. But I cannot convince them to stop calling him Sandy.

I still have to keep careful watch. His collar is always flipping up and I have to put it down for him. Once when he returned from the bathroom with his fly open, I had to stop myself from going over and doing it up. He's getting used to working around breasts, but the office is still riddled with female landmines, full of grown women who aren't as protective as I am. Andrea came raging towards me one time, demanding to know if I could give her a spare tampon "before I start gushing into my shoes." I tried to cover his ears, but it was too late.

"You're always fussing over that boy," says Andrea to me.

"He's not a boy," I say. "Don't call him 'boy.'"

"People will think you're in love with him." I look up at her and see that she's grinning. Of course she knows that nobody is ever going to think that.

"You need a man," Andrea says. "Why isn't there a man in the picture?"

A man in the picture. She puts it this way every time she asks me about it. Apparently there is a picture, and there is supposed to be a man in it. The hole in the ground that was dug out for me is of such a shape that there is supposed to be a man there as well.

"What would be your perfect man?" Andrea persists.

Well, let's see. I write a pointed response to Andrea in my journal since I'm incapable of doing it in person. My perfect man, Andrea, the man I want, is a character in a story I have been told ever since I was capable of understanding stories. He is big and strong. He is kind and compassionate. He is everywhere and all-powerful. He does not let bad things happen to good people. He is merciful. He is perfect. He can do it all. He takes you in his arms and wipes the tears from your eyes. You forget about everything. It's just a story I was told, and it wasn't fair to me, and it sure isn't fair to men, but this is the man I've been told about my whole life, so this is the man I'm waiting for. In the meantime, someone has to take care of Alexander.

At the end of the semester, everybody brings their favourite food, and we always invite the office staff to come and have some. All the women come trundling in, sampling and exclaiming over the exotic dishes, and I stand there looking around for Alex until I realize they've left him to answer the phones.

"Where's Alex? Where's Alex?" I keep saying. They pretend not to know who I'm talking about.

Another Thai student, Maliwan, comes up to me, taps me on the shoulder, and then takes a huge step back. That is how she asks for my attention, like I'm carrying a two-by-four and could whirl around and catch her on the side of the head. She's one of the most timid people I've ever met. I poke her on her own shoulder a few times to demonstrate how annoying it is.

"Just say my name. Don't poke."

"Sorry. Sorry. You are stress out."

I taught them "stressed out" last week. They liked it. *Stressed out* and *mongrel*.

"No, I'm not. Why don't you go get Alex?"

"Why you call Sandy Alex?"

"Why *do* you — "

"Why *do* you call Sandy Alex?"

"Sandy is his nickname."

Maliwan knows what *nickname* means, because she used to have one too. When she first arrived in Canada, she tried to convince me her nickname was Sharon Stone.

"Ah," says Maliwan, remembering how I refused to call her Sharon Stone. "You don't like nicknames."

I decide to just let her believe I don't like nicknames.

After much prodding, Andrea finally agrees to pile up a plate for herself and go back to the office so that Alex could come and get some food. The greeting that rises up from the Thai students takes me aback. They swarm him. Maliwan takes him from dish to dish, explaining what everything is and what it has in it.

"I usually can only eat shrimp if it's battered," I hear him tell her.

I glower at the office staff before they can react.

"You are allergic," Maliwan prompts.

"That's right!" Alexander replies, beaming.

I'm exhausted after the party, but can't keep myself from following him around trying to make him take the leftovers home. He won't take it. He keeps telling me that he's a meat-and-potatoes man.

"I'm a meat-and-potatoes man," he tells me. "I don't like my meals fancy."

"Listen," I step in close, fed up. "I know things about you. You are not a meat-and-potatoes man. You eat your mother's cooking, or else you eat an exact replica of your mother's cooking in fast-food form. You're afraid of anything else. You're not some rugged food-individualist. You leave here at night and you go to Burger King. You are destroying yourself."

It's too much. His face like a landslide. I regret it the moment it's out.

"I'm allergic — " he starts to protest, but I smother it with a hug. I long to suffocate us both.

Now I have three weeks off before the semester starts again, the second week of which my mother is coming to visit. In the meantime, the only thing to do is update my journal and go visit the doctor to complain about the awful, hideous, monstrous nightmares I have been having. In fact, I haven't been having nightmares at all, but I have started dreaming from time to time, and that is enough. A pumpkin patch with faces. All sorts of different expressions. She gives me a powerful drug that will blast it from my head.

Usually this time of year I would go to the park with a book but I haven't been able to do that since seeing the man in disguise as the sky.

The school is late with my pay as usual, so it gives me an excuse to drop by the office from time to time and pretend to kick up a fuss about it while making sure everyone is being nice to Alex. Maliwan and Kunakorn are always hanging around, waiting to take him to lunch.

"Is Maliwan your girlfriend?" I ask Kunakorn one day when we're kidding around and feeling chummy. These are the sort of questions I put to students point-blank, as they don't tend to understand our inane North American euphemisms. *Do you two have a thing? Are you guys going out? Are you seeing one another?* But Kunakorn looks at me like I've uttered the most obscure one of all.

"No! I ...." he stumbles.

"Boyfriend?"

"No! Not boyfriend! I go ... with Maliwan ...."

"You go out?"

"To lunch! I just go with Maliwan and Sandy ...."

"You're just friends," I help, thinking I shouldn't have put him on the spot.

"Yes! But what word? Thai friend. There is word ...."

"'Friend' is good enough." I try to calm him down, but Kunakorn is not the sort of person who can tolerate knowing he doesn't know something.

"I will find the word and tell you," he promises me.

He calls me at home at three in the afternoon. They know they are not supposed to call me at home unless they are having some sort of grammar crises, but they always do anyway, usually at night, in the middle of their parties, in order to settle bets about the meaning of words and idioms.

It so happens I am still in bed at three in the afternoon, unused to not having to go to work, and unable to muster up enough imagination, thanks to the anti-nightmare pills, to think of anything else worth doing. When the phone rings, it's as if my brains are lightly spread out across the pillow, and I have to mentally gather them up together in my head before I can figure out what the sound means and how I am supposed to respond to it. I pick it up on the seventh or so ring.

"Hello?"

"*Chaperone*," says Kunakorn.

I'm distracted when my mother comes, wanting to check on him. I had taken him to dinner at a steakhouse after talking to Kunakorn and encouraged him to eat as much meat and potatoes as he wanted. I'd talked to him like he was one of my students: *Is Maliwan your girlfriend?* He didn't turn green this time, but baby-girl pink. And he smiled. *Is she your first girlfriend?* A pointless question, as obviously she was. And of course he told me she wasn't and I was so happy I pretended to believe him and apologized for saying he went to Burger King all the time.

"It's true though," he admitted. "That's the kind of food I like, I can't help it."

"No, you can't," I agreed. "You should eat whatever makes you happy." I gave him my home phone number in case he ever needed anything.

It only occurred to me afterwards how painful and nasty and miserable first girlfriends and boyfriends could be and that was why I kept wanting to get rid of my mother and head down to the office with some kind of picnic basket loaded down with pre-emptive comfort.

I had spent a week doing a sort of tailor-made meditation in preparation for my mother's visit. Writing lists in my journal of everything I could think of. Cloud formations, for example. Cumulus, stratus. Berries. That was a good one, I could think of so many different kinds. I got down to Saskatoon berries and salmon berries and then huckleberries, which I wasn't even sure existed, and chokecherries, which I wasn't sure qualified. The berries list was a couple of pages long. Then I tried doing a list about the names of famous dogs, which at first I thought was a great idea — Lassie, Old Yeller, the Littlest Hobo — but of course I inevitably found myself writing the word *Sandy* and realized my brain had ambushed me again.

My mother is concerned that I no longer go to church and feels we should go together, but I tell her I don't know where any churches are, which is a lie. I walk past a Catholic church every day on my way to work, situated right alongside of a Catholic elementary school called Our Lady of Perpetual Help. A big white Mary perches upon the school's rooftop like a slender owl, looking down at all the little children in their uniforms, running back and forth behind the chain-link fence.

My mother says that's fine, she will find a church for us to go to together. I tell her we won't have time. I spread out before my mother catalogues, pamphlets, brochures, and outline for her all the activities I have planned for the week. Walking tours. Suspension bridges. Native art exhibits. High tea. Ferry rides.

Oh, my darling, she says. I just want us to spend some time together.

Very sincere, my mother. Warm, melting eyes. She's not lying, that's really what she wants. She wants to get inside my apartment and see me in it. Open up my cutlery drawers, poke around in the cupboards. Cook meals with my pots and pans. Buy me things, to go in the apartment, so she'll always feel she's there, inside my life.

There is no alcohol in my apartment, so she takes it upon herself to empty out a cupboard and stock me a little bar — wine and gin. I don't play along.

"But, Mother. I don't drink."

"Everybody should have a little wine and gin on hand, my darling!" Festive. Trying to get that festive feeling in the air. Get things uncorked.

This is her plan: To get inside my apartment and get me drunk. To get me talking.

I wake every morning at six and drag her off my futon and out into the city. We ride the trolley around the park and go on a bird tour and listen to a lecture about soapstone carving. Lunches and dinners are tricky. She'll go for the wine every time. After she finishes the first glass, it's: "Oh, may as well get a half-litre. What do you say, my darling?"

"None for me, thanks, Mother."

"But it's your holiday! Live a little!"

"We've got the suspension bridge next. You don't want to be falling off."

Next tactic: melting eyes, trembling lips. "Let me do something nice for you, you work so hard, I see you so rarely."

"I'm having a wonderful time, Mother." Thoughtful pause. "Aren't you?" Searching look, borderline hurt. Two can play at this game.

The day is mine. By nightfall, she is so wiped out her bedtime belt of gin knocks her off her feet. I open up my journal to gloat over the victory and strategize for tomorrow. Walk on the beach in the morning followed by a lunchtime concert at the university. Then a sudden wave comes over me, my eyes glaze. Exhaustion, from keeping my guard up all day. I'll use the concert time to think about how to spend the afternoon and evening.

I dream about scooping the guts out of a jack-o'-lantern with my hands and wake up and vomit all over the couch. My mother comes rapidly tip-toeing out of the bedroom, face slick with Mary Kay night cream. It shimmers in the grey, pre-dawn light. She says, "Oh! My darling!"

I'm lying on my back shuddering and start to say, "Isn't it supposed to absorb into your skin?" before turning my head and vomiting again. My mother goes to wipe off her face and put on some clothes and take care of me.

Stomach flu, like when I was a child. I vomit throughout the day. My mother goes out and buys consommé, crackers, and rum and honey. To make me hot toddies, she says, when I'm better.

"I knew we were pushing ourselves too hard," she mutters loudly to herself in the kitchen. "I'm an old homebody anyway. I'm happy to just hang around the house and spend time together!"

She is in heaven. Myself, on the couch with ginger ale and Mr. Dress-up on television, appalled by what my body has done to me. It was on her side all along. Nausea keeps me prone. My mother can sit and talk to me, her hand around a cool glass of gin, for hours on end.

It is so good, to have this time with me. How lucky for this to have happened while she was here! What would I have done if she hadn't been? No, really, what would I have done? Did I have someone to call? Didn't I get nervous, living all by myself? A young woman in the city? It would make her nervous. Oh yes, it seems like a very secure building. I don't go out by myself at night, do I? Oh, my darling, I really shouldn't. Of course, I must have friends I can always call. Not that I've introduced her to any of them. Haven't I met any men? Great big city like this? Still no man in the picture?

Glass of gin number two: It is hard, having me so far away, for both her and my father. They feel so removed from my life. They want to be of support to me, but how is it possible, my being so far away? If I moved back home, they could be of so much more help. There is lots of work back home these days, the economy has picked up quite a bit, had I heard? She could help me find an apartment, we could shop together for things. It would mean so much to them, now that they are getting on. The years just seem to fly by. The house so big and empty. Nothing left but memories. Not all good. And after all, I am all they have left in the world now that....

"This isn't fair," I manage to gasp, gripping the empty ice-cream bucket she's given me in case I can't make it to the toilet. "This isn't fair, Mother."

"I'm sorry, my darling," she murmurs, adjusting the cloth on my head. "You're sick. We can talk about these things later." And she wobbles off into the kitchen for gin number three, having granted me a temporary reprieve.

By evening, I'm finally able to sip some consommé and sit up to watch a weepy women's movie with Bette Midler that she's rented for us. We've both lost count of the glasses of gin and my mother sits with a roll of toilet paper on her lap, snuffling. Every now and then she pats a spot beside the toilet paper, inviting me to put my head there like when I was a girl. I ignore her. I have spent the entire day at her mercy and have dropped all pretence of civility.

Weirdly, the phone rings, the first time since she's been here. She jumps up and runs all around the apartment trying to find it, which I allow. Finally she discovers it in the bedroom, alongside of the futon she's been sleeping on, and drags it out to me on the couch.

"It's a boy!" she declares, like someone has just given birth. "He says his name is Sandy! What a nice name!"

"Hi, Alex," I say into the phone, glaring at her. She pretends to have gone back to Bette Midler, a huge mound of tissue pressed against her nose.

He is confused about Maliwan, and keeps telling me he doesn't understand her culture. It is such a different culture, he says, I don't know what's going on half the time. I don't understand her way ... the ways of her culture. After listening to him ramble for a few minutes, I figure out what he means by culture and take over.

"First of all, Alexander, calm down."

"I'm calm!" he protests.

"Calm down!"

"What's wrong? I'm very calm." I can picture his face arranging itself into a look of sitcom tranquillity. Convincing himself.

"I'm sick," I fret.

"Oh, I'm sorry...."

"No, I just mean ... I want to help. I'm just really sick."

"I should go." He sounds as if he's getting farther and farther away. He sounds as if he's standing in front of a well into which he plans on doing a forward roll as soon as he gets off the phone.

"Alex, Alex? Come and see me tomorrow, okay?"

"You're sick," he despairs.

"I'll be better tomorrow. Come and see me at around eleven."

"I'm sorry to — "

"Shut up! Come!" I give him my address. I hang up the phone and close my eyes. My stomach gurgles a warning.

My mother shifts on her side of the couch. "Visitors at last?"

"Tomorrow's Sunday," I inform her, eyes closed, seeking strength. "You won't want to miss church."

On the Lord's own day the nausea has subsided somewhat, but I'm weak like I've never been. I'm able to put on clothes for Alex's visit, but can't abide the thought of a bath or shower. My mother offers to help with a sponge bath, going as far as to try and ease me off the couch, and I flail my arms at her, grunting.

"You're a regular bear," she observes, snapping open a pink Mary Kay compact to touch up her eyes. "I'll say a prayer for you." I've scarcely spoken to her all morning. Conserving energy.

Alex shows up at eleven on the dot, toting a box of Dunkin' Donuts that I can't even look at. Oblivious, he starts shoving a Boston cream into his mouth, explaining that he hasn't had breakfast yet. I try to be indulgent. He is a man in pain. I avert my head while he finishes the doughnut, but as soon as the last blob of cream disappears, he goes to work on another one. I look up at the ceiling while he talks and chews and swallows. He has a large cup of coffee as well. He keeps forgetting it is too hot to drink and takes one searing, painful sip after another. I envision clouds and berries as he talks.

Maliwan is seeing an *old man*, he says. Some disgusting, probably married, businessman who saw her looking at sunglasses in the mall and bought her a pair. She goes with him to clubs and restaurants. He buys her dresses. She just told Alex this, one day. They were sitting on the beach with Kunakorn and she looked at her watch and said: Now I must visit Andrew.

"Now I must visit Andrew!" he repeats. "And Kunakorn just sits there with me! Why does she need a chaperone with me and not with Andrew?"

"Did you ask?"

"Yes. That's how I found out he was *old*. Kunakorn just waves his hand and goes, 'He old man.'"

"He didn't use a verb?"

"What?"

"Kunakorn. He's always dropping his to-be verbs. He told me he'd practise. Did you ask Maliwan about it?"

"She says she doesn't need a chaperone with Andrew because he doesn't count. He's too old to count as a boyfriend. She says he's more like an uncle."

"But you count as a boyfriend?"

"Yeah."

"Well, that's good."

"Yeah, but it's crazy!"

"Have you told Maliwan how you feel?"

"I don't know what to say! Maybe it's a Thai thing."

"I don't think it's exactly a Thai thing." I don't really know what kind of thing it is. I decide that it's beside the point.

"How do you feel about Maliwan?" I ask. He looks up at me in sudden fear. It's as if I've inquired: How would you like a punch in the face? Then the ersatz,[2] sitcom casualness settles over his pasty features and he leans back and takes a wincing sip of coffee.

"You know," he says, draping his arms across the back of the couch, pretending like his mouth isn't full of blisters, "she's nice. I like her."

---

2. **ersatz** Artificial.

I know all right.

In the twenty-five minutes before my mother gets back, I develop and outline a plan. First, he has to find out how Maliwan feels about him. Is she just playing around or what?

"Because, if you're serious, Alex — *if* — then you have to let her know. Are you serious?"

"I don't know."

"Well, if you don't know, then you can't expect her to know. And there's no reason for her not to go out with as many old men as she likes."

"But — "

"There's this thing called commitment, Alex, and it sounds to me like that's what you're looking for."

"I don't know! It's all so serious!"

"This is grown-up stuff. You can't just ask a woman to stop seeing whoever she wants to see and not give her a good reason."

"But I don't know if I have a good reason. I just don't want her to."

"Then you have to think up a better reason than that."

"Like what?"

"Tell her you want to *explore* a commitment."

"Explore — "

"A commitment."

"You mean, go steady?"

From what era is this child? "Yes, yes, for God's sake, just tell her you want to go steady and see what she says."

"But what if she says no?"

"It's better to know that now before you get too involved." Listen to me. The endless thumbings-through of waiting-room women's magazines over the years has really paid off. I am some kind of relationship-savant.

"But I don't want her to say no," he sulks.

The front door rattles. My mother is home. My instinct is to leap off the couch and hurl my body against the door to keep her from Alex, but the attempt amounts merely to my standing up, experiencing a whirling head-rush, and collapsing back down onto the couch.

"You have to go now, Alex," I hiss.

Alex looks around. It's like a bedroom farce all of a sudden, my burly husband about to burst in and catch us.

"Oh, hello!" chirps my mother.

"Alex has to go now," I say, shoving him off the couch with my foot.

"I'm the mother!" says my mother, holding out her hand. Alex wipes the icing sugar off one of his and shakes it for her.

Beads of sweat bloom across my back and between my shoulder blades at the sight of them touching. "Leave him alone!" I bark, enraged and panicked.

"She hasn't been well," confides my mother, lightly placing her hand on his shoulder to torment me further. I can see Alex responding already to her sweetness, her innocent dusting of Mary Kay, her prim, motherly scarf tucked into her collar. Red Riding Hood and the Wolf, decked out like Grandma. I breathe through the knot in my chest.

"Alex," I say. "I'm going to throw up all over the place in a minute. Give me a call in a few days, okay?"

"I'll leave you the doughnuts," he says generously, bidding a hasty retreat.

My mother picks up the box after he's gone. "There aren't any doughnuts left," she sniffs.

One more day until she goes home. I am still very weak. The hour with Alex and the handful of horrific moments he spent in the company of my mother have sent me into a relapse. The fever returns and my mother has to wrap me in towels to keep the couch from wringing with sweat. I sleep until dinnertime and dream of the fat man floating up into the sky with his ice-cream cone, blending right in. I wake to the deceptively comforting smell of consommé. My mother sashays into the living room, working on a glass of wine, one in a series of who knows how many. My suspicion is a few, because she starts in immediately.

"What a nice boy, that Sandy boy was."

"His name is Alex. Didn't you hear me calling him Alex the whole time he was here?"

"He's very young."

"Yeah, he's like twenty." I speak rapidly, trying to put the topic to rest. "I work with him. He's going through everything at once. First job, first girlfriend. I'm trying to help him manoeuvre his way through."

"He's the sort of boy you want to help," she agrees. "I just took one look at him and I wanted to take him in my arms." The sheen of her eyes starts to wobble a bit. Brimming. She must be close to polishing off the bottle. "You know who he reminds me of — "

"Stop," I say.

"Well, you do, though. Don't tell me you haven't noticed."

"Stop. Off limits."

"But then, I get so lonesome for him — I think I see him everywhere — "

"Stop! Out of bounds!"

She keeps talking and I keep hollering sports expressions at her: "Foul! Penalty! You're out!" But she keeps on and I run out of sports words. The next thing I know, I'm hollering my lists.

"It's been five years and you never want to — "

"Cumulus!"

"The priest says that after a loss families need to — "

"Boisenberry! Saskatoon!"

"I know that you blame — "

"Pineapple! I bet you didn't know that was a berry, did you? Famous dogs! Benji! The one on 'The Little Rascals'! Sandy!"

"I haven't seen you in over a — "

"Sandy!"

"Why don't you ever let me *talk?*" she shrieks, and throws down her drink. I cross my arms. She jumps up to get a towel, ashamed of herself. She's been both wasteful and sloppy. Failing to live up to her own standards of motherhood. Shamed into silence. Victory.

The next week is spent recovering from my holiday. It's slow going. I remain on the couch, absorbing televised reality, where nothing too evil happens to anybody and everyone is both cool and lovable. Alex calls to give me updates. Maliwan was pleased with the idea of going steady. At first she didn't believe him that he would want to explore a commitment "with Thai girl," but somehow he convinced her of his sincerity. The old man with the money is now out of the picture. I tell him I am happy for him. I have dreams of Alex wafting slowly, safely up into the sky, waving bye-bye to me as he disappears into the blue. I sleep and sleep. The whole ordeal has left me spent.

My mother leaves without trying to make me talk any more, but she isn't quite able to keep herself in check at all times. So I have to show her something, to make her stop. I have to give her a small taste of what it would be like if I did start talking. She strides about the apartment, gathering up her belongings, mumbling, clucking, shaking her head from time to time.

"What are you saying, Mother? Say it out loud and strong, belt it out, Mother."

"I'm just sorry to have to tell your father we haven't made any progress," she clucks, sad-chicken-like.

"What makes you think I want to make any progress?"

She stops to shoot me a pious look that outrages me so much I sit up. "It's a terrible thing to hold a grudge," she intones.

"A beautiful boy," I say.

"What?"

"A beautiful, blue-eyed boy who liked pumpkins."

Her mouth falls open, thinking the walls are coming down at last.

"A beautiful boy who liked to hear a different version of things once in a while."

"Yes?"

"A genuine authentic."

Her bottom lip starts to work.

"A real original."

"Stop, now."

"Only one thing to do with a boy like that."

"All right."

"Pull his wings off." I make a gesture like I am plucking the petals from a flower. With each pluck I enunciate one word. "Tear. Him. Limb. From. Limb."

"That's enough," she says behind her hands.

"I agree," I agree.

With that, the last of my energy is spent. Pushing my mother all the way back to the other side of the continent. She kisses my cheek when the taxi comes.

"I hope you feel better, my darling. It was a lovely visit."

I've won. I'm beat.

That's an expression it took a long time for my students to understand. *I'm beat.* You're what? *Beat. Like when someone beats you at a game.* Beat by who? *Beat by whom.*

Beat by whom? *Nobody. Just beat. Whipped. Tired.* Shouldn't it be beaten? *The expression is "I'm beat."* But nobody has beaten you? *Not necessarily.*

Back at work, the beat feeling doesn't go away. I tell everyone I've been sick. The students bring me a variety of home remedies. Andrea prescribes a man. Put some colour in your cheeks. Good for what ails ya, she says, yukking it up, embarrassing Alex. Maliwan comes for Alex every day at lunch, Kunakorn not always in tow. Apparently Alex has proven himself a gentleman. They stand at the elevator holding hands. They are like kittens. Andrea extends a long finger down towards the back of her throat whenever they leave the room.

"Don't you think they're sweet?" I demand. Andrea has two of those "Love Is …" posters hanging in her office, for God's sake. You'd think she'd eat it up. Instead she pronounces, "Too sweet." Grimly, a hard-nosed realist.

"They're happy!" I argue.

"They're not happy," Andrea contends. "They're blissed-out."

"Well, so *what?*"

"Icarus,"[3] she answers to my surprise, tossing her head towards the sky like he's actually up there waving a red flag.

Things get back to normal and I'm grateful. I work, come home, eat medium portions, watch television. Take notes in my journal about what is easy and what is hard. Take care the next day to avoid whatever was hard. The bus was hard one day because I saw the fat man from the park in his white cap struggling to climb the steps and making everybody wait and feel resentful of him. He was sweaty, too, and you could see the loathing on people's faces. So I leave the apartment an hour early and walk to work for the rest of the week.

I have to be easy on myself. I exchange pleasantries with Alex and avoid Andrea. I get engrossed in genuinely fascinating conversations about the future-possible with Kunakorn. He is in the highest level now and prides himself on his knowledge. Kunakorn is like a grammar textbook — he can rhyme off all the rules, do all the exercises flawlessly, but he still walks around dropping his to-be verbs all over the place and using "in" for "on" and "beside" for "under." He brings muffins in the morning, for a joke, knowing I will get agitated by his conversational sloppiness at some point. Then he'll hold out a muffin to me.

"Comfort food," he'll say.

Maliwan is in the same class and would be failing dramatically if it wasn't for Kunakorn's ongoing tutelage, and perhaps a bit of cheating, which I overlook. Maliwan is basically on holiday, sent over by her family to obtain the fastest, cheapest ESL certificate going before returning to Thailand to help run their factory. It is odd to think of how much more money than I — the privileged North American — Maliwan must have. She lives with two other girls in a $15,000 apartment and goes shopping for clothes every day at lunchtime and skiing on the weekend. But she shows up dutifully for class every day because she knows if she misses more than two she's out of the program and her parents will yank her back home to the other side of the world.

So it's odd when she misses one class in the middle of the semester, but downright troublesome when she misses a second. Kunakorn promises me he'll check in with her after class.

"Tell her, if she's sick, it's no big deal — she just needs a doctor's certificate," I say. The next day Alex calls in sick and Kunakorn shows up with extra muffins.

"How is Maliwan?" I ask.

"Thai," he says, picking walnuts off the tops.

"What?"

---

3. **Icarus** Greek mythological figure who used wax wings to fly; when he got too close to the sun, they melted and Icarus fell to his death.

"Thailand," he corrects himself, using the English term. He hadn't heard me properly. He thought I said "where," not "how."

The way Kunakorn tells it, one of Maliwan's roommates, a friend of the family's, called them up and told them Maliwan was planning to marry a Canadian. Apparently, the roommate had the idea that "going steady," which Maliwan constantly bragged about, meant the same thing as being engaged, or else she just decided one thing would lead to the next. To make matters worse, she got Alex mixed up somehow with Andrew, the rich old man, and told them Maliwan's paramour was in his sixties. The parents believed the roommate and told Maliwan to come home. It sounded to me like the roommate, who worked for her visa as a hostess in a restaurant, had merely tired of watching wealthy, twenty-year-old Maliwan having the time of her life.

"So she's just gone?"

Kunakorn looks at his watch. "Bangkok, now." He leans on his hands and puffs out his cheeks. "Sandy," he remarks, not bothering to try and find the words.

Sandy takes the whole week off. I am grateful. So grateful I actually find myself talking to God again from time to time, muttering quiet words of appreciation in the bathroom or waiting in line for a coffee. It is such a peaceful week as we prepare for mid-terms and I walk to work with my eyes straight ahead, focused on large, blank buildings in the distance with windows like mirrors. Even the bum who cried out on the corner last semester is nowhere in sight these days. It's quiet and warm, the weather patchy, a little bit cloudy, a little bit sunny, not too much of either. Even. It is a good week. One of the best weeks I've had.

Another week goes by. Sandy, I tell myself, is licking his wounds. Taking some time off. Coming to terms with his emotions. All these inane, comforting euphemisms I come up with. I realize I don't brace myself when I push open the door to the office any more, expecting to see him doing battle with the photocopier or barely defending himself from Andrea or turning green at the sight of someone's exposed bra strap. The ease of knowing I won't be called upon to extinguish any flare-ups of mortification.

My parents haven't called since my mother's visit so I call them. "I'm so glad you called!" says my mother. "I meant to tell you. Your grade three teacher died last week. Remember? She had cancer for years. It was just a matter of time. Everybody was expecting it. She went peacefully. It was a relief."

"It was so nice having you here, Mother," I tell her.

"Oh, my darling," she says, voice a-tremble. "I had a lovely time."

I eat well. One day when the weather is mild, I return to the park with a book. The sky is clear. There is no one else in sight. The ice-cream stand hasn't even been set up yet because it's too early in the season.

(2000)

Alissa York (1970–)

Alissa York, daughter of Australian immigrants to Canada, was born in Athabasca, northern Alberta, in 1970. Her father, a high school English teacher and outdoor education instructor, took York and her brother on long canoe trips and hikes to the region's black spruce bogs. The family moved to Victoria, British Columbia, when York was seven, but the wild northern landscape would

later establish its presence in her writing, as would the experience of life in a small community —
"The imprint of Athabasca on me is very strong," she says.

Graduating from high school, York spent some time in Toronto and then moved on to
Montreal, where she spent a year at McGill University studying English. Returning to Victoria, she
took a creative writing course at the University of Victoria with poet Lorna Crozier. In 1989, when
she was 19, York met filmmaker and poet Clive Holden, and they married in 1993. That year, they
also co-founded Cyclops Press (which they describe as "a media arts, web, and film project, and an
independent, artist-run, literary and multimedia arts publisher") and entered a peripatetic period,
travelling all over the country. During this time, York waitressed and worked in a florist shop and a
bookstore; she also studied acting in Toronto while working for a small theatre company, and she
appeared on stage in Whitehorse. She ultimately realized that writing was her calling, and at the
age of 21, she wrote her first story. In 1997, she and Holden settled in Winnipeg, where, York says,
the "arts community is active and supportive," and they remained there for a number of years.

In 1999, York published her first book, a collection of short fiction entitled *Any Given Power*. Its
12 stories are set in small towns, like the one in which York spent her formative years, but, in the
words of one reviewer, they "open to the universal like a beautiful dark rose." Exploring themes of
family strength and weakness, the toll of poverty, love, injury, and loss, evoking instances of
casual violence and moments of grace, they are delivered from multiple perspectives: York's
narrators include teenaged girls, an adolescent boy, a grown man, and a child. They are rife with
mysteries that seem all the more immediate and undiluted for being juxtaposed against the
uncluttered backdrop of small-town life (York has said that she likes "working on a small stage —
the relationships are more intense"). In the story "Clues," a series of vignettes in which a young
girl depicts her relationship with her friend Tonya — a child who, unloved by her debased clan,
uses her precocious sexuality in a doomed bid for acceptance and connection — mystery abounds.
A neighbour's "man came and went in the night, but we could tell when he was home, his purple
rig squashing the couchgrass"; later, the narrator and Tonya watch "through the scraggy trees, the
slanted fence and the flapping sheers. The neighbour lady down on her knees. Her high hair flat
under the truck man's hands, him humping her face like a dog." *Any Given Power* won several
awards, including the Journey Prize.

York's first novel, *Mercy* — named for the fictional Manitoba town in which it is set —
appeared in 2003. York has said that it is a story about love — "What it takes to give and receive
it, what happens to us when we don't." She has also acknowledged the influence on her work of
Southern Gothic writers like William Faulkner and Flannery O'Connor, and that influence is evident
in this novel, which exudes gothic and Catholic imagery and themes. It consists of two narratives
separated in time by several decades. In 1948, Father August Day comes to Mercy and quickly falls
into an intense love affair with Mathilda, whom Father Day marries to Thomas, the local butcher;
they struggle unsuccessfully to suppress their illicit passion and eventually have a baby girl out of
wedlock. Some 50 years later, the womanizing Reverend Carl Mann arrives in town intent on
developing a boggy wilderness area on the outskirts into a Christian camp; he is blinded in an
accident, and Mathilda and Father Day's daughter, now a reclusive eccentric called Bog Mary,
cares for him and leads him towards the possibility of redemption.

York's next novel, *Effigy*, was published in 2007. In imagining her story, York was inspired
by the 1857 Mountain Meadows Massacre, in which approximately 120 people of European
ancestry — men, women, and children — were slaughtered by a group of Native American
Paiutes and Mormon militiamen dressed as Native Americans as they made their way through the
Utah territory on their way to settle in southern California. The novel takes place on a Mormon
ranch in 19th-century Utah. Its protagonist is a young girl named Dorrie, who has no memory of her
life before the age of seven. Dorrie is intrigued by the art of taxidermy — she is keenly aware of

the ways in which it suggests a transcendence of violence, a defiance of death, immortality itself — and she becomes adept at it. Her occupation, however, triggers dreams marked by flashes of violence, and it becomes apparent that she is suppressing recollections of some horrifying event. At 14, she is married off to an elderly polygamist who has chosen her uniquely for her special skill. He is a hunter who is losing his sight, and he wants to preserve his trophies. The novel impresses its elemental themes of life and death, violence and self-preservation, through haunting imagery and a powerful sense of menace: "Behind them the collection looms. Tiers of straw bales ascend the western wall, each of them crowded with Dorrie's creations. Hunter lies alongside hunted — fox and pocket mouse, lynx and grouse, mountain lion and deer. She can feel them there, every beast, every bird."

York currently lives in Toronto.

The Back of the Bear's Mouth

God knows how long Carson was watching me before I caught on — it was dark where he was sitting, like he'd brought some of the night in with him. I matched his look for a second, and a second was all it took. He stood up out of his corner and made for the bar.

I saw this show on the North one time. About the only part I remember was these bighorn sheep all meeting up at the salt-lick. They were so peaceful, side by side with their heads bent low, and no rutting or fighting, no matter if they were old or up-and-coming, no matter if they were male or female, injured or strong. That's the way it was with me and Carson. Neither one of us said much. We just sat there side by side, and it felt like the natural thing.

When the time came, Carson just stood and made for the doorway, the same slow bee-line stride he'd taken to the bar. Beside me, the bartender cleared our glasses and talked low into his beard. "Think twice little girl, the Northern bushman's a different breed."

But then Carson looked back at me over his shoulder, and just like a rockslide, I felt myself slip off the barstool and follow.

The truck took its time warming up, so we sat together in the dark, both of us staring at the windshield like we were waiting for some movie to start.

"Robin," he said finally, "I figure you got no place to go."

I turned my head his way a little. I was just eighteen and he must've been forty, but none of that mattered a damn.

"No Carson, I don't."

"Well." He handed me a cigarette and put one to his own lips, leaving it hanging there, not lighted. I brought the lighter out of my coat pocket and held the flame up in front of his face, the flicker of it making him seem younger somehow, a little scared.

After a minute I sat back and lit my own.

I must've fallen asleep on the drive. It was no wonder with the hours I'd been keeping — hitching clear across the country in just under three weeks. God knows how I landed in Whitehorse, except I remember hearing some old guy in a truckstop talking about it, calling it the stop before the end of the line.

I opened my eyes just as Carson was laying me out on the bed. The place was dark and cold as a meat locker. It stunk of tobacco and bacon, oiled metal and mould and mouse shit, but somewhere underneath all that was Carson's smell — a gentle, low-lying musk. I know it sounds crazy, but I'll bet that smell was half the reason I went with him in the first place.

I pulled the blanket around me and sat up, watching the shadow that was him pile wood into the stove. He lit the fire, then settled back into the armchair, watching me where I sat. I'd always hated people staring at me. I guess that's why I left school in the end — the teachers and everyone staring at your clothes, your hair, staring into your skull. But Carson was different. His eyes just rested on me, not hunting or digging, just looking because I was there, and more interesting than the rug or the table leg.

Who knows how long we sat like that. I remember him pulling a couple more blankets down from a cupboard, laying one around my shoulders and leaving the other at the foot of the bed.

In the morning sun was all through the place. The bed was an old wrought iron double, with only my side slept in. Coals burnt low in the stove. A grizzly head hung over the bed, mounted with its mouth wide open and the teeth drawn back like a trap.

Carson was nowhere, so I stepped outside and lit a smoke. It was warm, the sun already burning holes in the snow. We were in the bush alright, the clearing was just big enough for the cabin, the outhouse, and the truck. The dirt road that led in to the place closed up dark in the distance, like looking down somebody's throat. A skinny tomcat squeezed out the door of the outhouse and sat washing what was left of one of its ears. The trees grew thick and dark, and the sounds of jays and ravens came falling.

I found Carson round back of the cabin, bent over the carcass of a deer. There was another one in the dust nearby, a buck with small, velvety antlers. Carson looked up at the sound of my footsteps, his eyes all quick and violent.

"Morning," I said.

"Morning."

"You get those this morning?"

" — No."

Something told me to shut up. I walked back round to the door and went inside. The place looked like it hadn't ever been cleaned, so I threw a log in the stove, put the kettle on top, and set about finding some rags and soap.

He never touched me for the whole first week. A couple of times he walked up close behind me and stood there, smelling my hair or something, and I waited for his hand on me, but it didn't come.

The days passed easily. I got the place clean, beat the rugs and blankets, swept out the mouse shit, oiled the table, and washed the two windows with hot water and vinegar. I even stood up on the bed and brushed the dust out of the grizzly's fur. There were gold hairs all through the brown, lit up and dancing where the sunlight lay on its neck.

Carson never thanked me for cleaning up, and I never thanked him for letting me stay. On my eighth night there he turned in the bed and I felt him pressing long and hard into the back of my thigh. He held me tight, but it didn't hurt. He fit into me like something I'd been missing, like something finally come home.

Carson was sometimes gone for part of the night, or all of it. He either went out empty and brought a carcass back, or went out with a carcass or two and came back empty.

Usually it was caribou or deer, but one time there was a lynx. He let me touch the fur. It felt just the same as a regular cat — a few hairs came away in my hand.

Time went by like this, me cooking and cleaning and watching, sometimes reading the *Reader's Digest* or some other magazine from a box in the cupboard, sometimes just sitting and smoking on the doorstep, watching the forest fill up with spring. Carson got more comfortable when I'd been there for a while, started teaching me how to shoot the rifle — first at empty bean tins, then at crows and rabbits that came into the clearing. When I finally hit a rabbit, Carson let out a whoop and ran to get it. Then he took the gun from my hands and held the rabbit up in front of my face. Its hindlegs were blown clear off. I felt my fingers go shaky when I reached for its ears, felt tears come up the back of my throat when I took it from him, the soft, dead weight of it in my hand.

One night I got Carson to let me go along. That sounds like I had to talk him into it, but really all I said was, "Can I come?"

"You can't talk if you do."

"You heard me talk much?"

" — Alright."

It was like driving through black paint — the headlights cut a path in front of the truck, and the dark closed up behind us. I had to wonder how Carson found his way around, how he ever managed to get back home. When we got a ways off the main road, he slowed right down and started zigzagging, the headlights swishing over the road and into the bush, then back over the road to the other side.

I was just nodding off when Carson cut the engine, grabbed the gun and jumped out into the dark. I caught a yellow flash of eyes in the bush, then came the shots, the gun blazing once, twice, and the moose staggered into the lights, forelegs buckling, head slamming into the dirt.

Carson pulled a winch out from under the seat and rigged it up to some bolts in the bed of the truck. We got the moose trussed up, but it took us forever to get it in the back.

"This is a big one," I said, not sure if it was true. I'd only ever seen one from far away, standing stock-still in a muskeg, the way they do.

"Not one," he said, "two. Springtime, Robin."

The next night Carson headed off on his own and I was just as glad. I was still trying to lose the picture of that moose's head hitting the ground.

It seems like it would be creepy being out there in the middle of God-knows-where, Yukon Territory, but I got used to it pretty fast. Even when I was alone it felt safer than any city I'd been through — all those junkies and college kids and cars.

One night though, I woke up slow and foggy, feeling like I couldn't breathe. It took a while for me to realize that tomcat was sitting on me, right on my chest, and when my eyes got used to the dark I could make out the shape of a mouse in its jaws.

I'm no chicken, but that dead mouse in my face scared the shit out of me. I threw the cat clear across the room, and the mouse flew out of its mouth and landed somewhere near the foot of the bed. The tom yowled for a minute, then found the mouse and settled down. I swear I didn't close my eyes until dawn. I just lay there, listening to that cat gnawing and tearing at the mouse, snapping the bones in its teeth.

I'd been out there for a couple of months as close as I could guess, and I had no ideas about leaving. It wasn't that Carson was such great company — half the time he wasn't there, and the other half he was busy skinning something, or cleaning his guns, or doing God knows what round back of the cabin. At night was mostly when we met up. He'd climb into the bed after me, and hold me hard and gentle, always the same way, from the back with me lying on my side. I didn't mind — it felt good, and I figured he was shy about doing it face to face. It made sense, a man who lives out in the bush on his own for so long.

By that time I was sure I was pregnant. I hadn't bled since I'd been there, my tits were sore, and my belly had a warm, hard rise in it. One night when Carson was lying behind me, I took his hand and put it there. I turned my face around to him, and even though it was dark as the Devil, I could tell he was smiling. I don't know that I've felt that good before or since.

I only asked Carson about the hunting once.

"Carson, all these animals — "

The way he looked at me made me think of that first day, when he looked up from that deer like he was a dog and I was some other dog trying to nose in on the kill. His eyes were really pale blue, sometimes almost clear. They didn't usually bug me, but times like that I always thought of that riddle — the man gets stabbed with an icicle, and it melts, and then where's the murder weapon?

It was maybe a week or two later when I woke up to the sound of Carson coming home in the truck. That alone told me there was something wrong — usually he coasted up to the cabin and came in without waking me up. I was lighting the lamp when he threw open the door.

"Can you drive?"

"What's wrong?"

"Can you drive!"

"Yes!"

"Get dressed."

"What's wrong Carson?"

"Goddammit Robin!"

I crawled out from under the covers and grabbed for my clothes. He jumped up on the bed and stood where my head had been, reaching one hand deep into the grizzly's mouth. I thought he'd lost it for sure, but a second later he jumped back down and stuck a fistful of money in my face, twenties and fifties, a fat wad of them.

"There's more up there," he said, "if I don't come back you come and get it, just reach past the teeth and push the panel. And watch you don't cut your hand."

He shoved the truck keys into the pocket of my red mack.

"Carson," I said, and my voice came out funny. I was thinking about what he said, about him maybe not coming back.

"Get going. Lay low in Whitehorse. I'll find you."

"But where will you go?"

"Out in the bush. Get going."

He touched my hair for a second, then held the door open and pushed me outside.

I got a room at the Fourth Avenue Residence. I didn't check in until morning, after spending the whole night driving around in the dark, scared shitless. When dawn came and I finally saw the road sign I'd been hoping for, I felt about two steps from crazy.

Whitehorse was waking up when I pulled into town. I bought a bottle of peroxide at the Pharmasave, and a big bag of Doritos, then I found the Fourth Ave. And parked around back.

First thing I did in my room was eat the whole bag of Doritos, fast, like I hadn't had anything for days. Then I took the scissors from the kitchen drawer and cut off all my hair. It fell onto the linoleum and curled around my feet, shiny black as a nest of crows. I left the peroxide on until it burned, and when I rinsed it out and looked at myself in the mirror I had to laugh. And then I had to cry.

I slept the whole day and through the night, and the next morning I went down to the front desk and bought a pack of smokes, two Mars Bars and a paper. I folded the paper under my arm and I didn't look at the front page until I was back in my room. I ate the Mars Bars while I read, and my hunger made me remember the baby. Our baby — mine and Carson's.

PITLAMPER GOES TOO FAR
Conservation Officer Harvey Jacobs was shot and badly wounded late last night when he surprised a lone man pitlamping on a back-road off the Dempster Highway. The man who fired at Jacobs is believed to be one Ray Carson, who has a cabin in the area. RCMP have issued a warrant for Carson's arrest and ask that anyone with information pertaining to his whereabouts come forward. Jacobs took a single .38 bullet in his right side. He is currently in intensive care …

I lay on my back on the bed, until it felt like the baby was screaming for something to eat. I thought about going out, but I ended up calling for pizza.

I was in the corner store when I heard. The old bitch behind the counter leaned across to me and said, "Did you hear? They got that nut case, Carson."

I looked down at the lottery tickets, all neat and shiny under a slab of plexiglas.

"They had to take the dogs in after him. Got him cornered up in the rocks of a waterfall, but he turned a gun on them. Well, they had to shoot him, the stupid bugger — "

She kept on talking, but that was the last I heard. I closed the door on her voice, walked up the road a ways, and sat down in the weeds. I thought about staying there forever, thought about the grass growing up around my shoulders, turning gold and seedy, then black and broken under the snow.

Then I thought about the baby and figured I better get up.

(1999)

David Bezmozgis (1973–)

In 2003, David Bezmozgis achieved sudden success as a writer. In April of that year, he was unknown; in May, his stories cropped up in five important magazines across the continent: the *New Yorker*, *Prairie Fire* (Winnipeg), *Grain* (Saskatoon), Francis Ford Coppola's *Zoetrope All-Story*

(San Francisco), and *Harper's* (New York). As critic Robert Fulford put it, it was "a one-man shock-and-awe invasion of North American literature."

Bezmozgis was born in Latvia, a country on the eastern shore of the Baltic Sea, in 1973. When he was six years old, he immigrated with his parents to Canada, settling with other Jewish refugees from the Soviet Union in Toronto's burgeoning Russian émigré community, located along the Bathurst Street corridor north of Sheppard Avenue. He left that insular world to attend McGill University in Montreal, graduating with a B.A. in English literature. At McGill, he wrote a play entitled *The Last Waltz: An Inheritance,* the story of a boy who sees an old photograph of a Jewish couple about to perish in the Holocaust and believes that they are his grandparents. The play was staged at a university theatre festival and at the Montreal Playwrights' Workshop. From there, Bezmozgis went on to earn an M.F.A. at the School of Cinema-Television at the University of Southern California. During this time, he wrote screenplays and learned to direct. In 1999, he released a short documentary, *L.A. Mohel*, about a trio of Jewish ritual circumcisers; *The Diamond Nose*, a short narrative film about a boy who wants to get rid of his huge nose, came out a year later. In California, Bezmozgis also befriended a writer he greatly admired, Leonard Michaels, and wrote a film script based on Michaels's story "Honeymoon."

In 2004, after having re-established himself in Toronto, Bezmozgis published a collection of linked short fiction, *Natasha and Other Stories*. It centres on a family named Berman, who live at the same Finch Avenue address the Bezmozgis family once inhabited. Mark Berman, through whose eyes we experience these narratives, attends the same schools David Bezmozgis once did, and Mark's father obtains a massage licence and strives to set up his own business as Bezmozgis's father once did. But Bezmozgis has said that while the stories in *Natasha* "may be called autobiographical fiction … the part that interests me is the fiction. The autobiographical part is largely context; the plot and most everything else is fictional." While he was concerned with chronicling the lives of Soviet Jewish immigrants to Canada, he insists that his stories are "mostly about basic struggles — get work, learn a language, find and survive love. I think these are things common to all immigrants and, really, most people. These are not stories of existential conflict; they deal instead with a pursuit of concrete things."

Critics have remarked on the influence apparent in Bezmozgis's work of other creators of fiction rooted in the Jewish experience — writers like Isaac Babel, Saul Bellow, and the young Bernard Malamud and Philip Roth (one commented that the character of Itzik in "Minyan" walked "right out of the pages of Babel"). Bezmozgis himself has said that he enjoys the novels of Mordecai Richler. What Richler did for Montreal's St. Urbain Street neighbourhood Bezmozgis has begun to do for the Bathurst and Finch community. The Bermans, whose lives *Natasha* traces over a 20-year span, become well entrenched in the universe that exists in these few city blocks. In the book's ironic tales, narrated in the first person in straightforward language unencumbered by metaphor, Mark's parents, Roman and Bella, are destabilized by the monumental shift in their lives. As former "Baltic aristocrats" (Roman once held a position in the Ministry of Sport), they keenly feel their loss of social status. They are also isolated from the broad community of their new country due to their inability to speak English — a language that is for them "more an enemy than an instrument" — and they must rely on their young son to help them negotiate their daily lives. In "Roman Berman, Massage Therapist," Mark tells us, "I was nine, and there were many things I did not tell them, but there was nothing they would not openly discuss in front of me, often soliciting my opinion. They were strangers in the country, and they recognized that the place was less strange to me, even though I was only a boy."

As the adaptation process unfolds, we see Mark grow from a six year old who "tramp[s] back home" from school "bearing the germs of a new vocabulary" (in "Tapka"), to a sullen youth who lives "a subterranean life" in his basement (or the basements of his teen tribe) smoking hash, watching television, reading, and masturbating (in "Natasha"), to a young man capable of understanding the ways in which personal identity is inextricably grounded in family and cultural legacy. In "Choynski," Mark returns home to attend the funeral of his grandmother, at which he "only cried for [his] mother's sake, and before that a little because [he] saw [his] grandfather lost and weeping like an old Jew." Later, when he breaks Jewish law by returning to the cemetery with his grandmother's dentures, determined to bury them along with her, he feels that he is "following other laws" — he then cries "shamelessly," wailing in Russian, "Babushka, babushka, where are you, my babushka?"

Bezmozgis's story "Natasha" was selected for inclusion in the 2005 *Best American Stories*, and his "A New Gravestone for an Old Grave" appeared in the 2006 edition of that collection. Bezmozgis continues to live in Toronto.

A New Gravestone for an Old Grave

Shortly before Victor Shulman was to leave on his vacation his father called him at the office to say that Sander Rabinsky had died. From the tone of his father's voice, and from the simple fact that his father had felt compelled to call him at work, Victor understood he was expected to recognize the name Sander Rabinsky and also to grasp the significance of the man's passing. Not wanting to disappoint his father he held the phone and said nothing. In recent years many of his father's friends had started to take ill and die. For the most part, these were friends from his father's youth, men whom Victor could not remember, having not seen them in the twenty-five years since the Shulmans left Riga[1] and settled in Los Angeles. For Victor they existed, if at all, in the forty-year-old photos in which they, along with his own father, appeared bare-chested and vigorous on the Baltic shore. Simka, Yashka, Vadik, Salik: athletes, womanizers, and Jewish professionals, now interred in cemeteries in Calgary, New Jersey, and Ramat Gan. Victor assumed that Sander Rabinsky was of the same company, although that didn't quite explain why his death merited a special phone call.

Sander Rabinsky was dead, which was of course sad, Leon Shulman explained, but there was more to it. Sander had been Leon's last remaining connection in Riga and the one Leon had entrusted with overseeing the erection of a new monument to his own father, Wolf Shulman. Of late, Leon and Sander had been in constant contact. Sander had been acting on Leon's behalf with the stonecutter and functioning as liaison with the Jewish cemetery. Leon had already wired one thousand dollars to Sander's bank and Sander had assured him that a new stone would be installed in a matter of weeks. But now, with Sander's death, Leon was at a loss. With nobody there to supervise the job he had no way of ensuring that it would be properly done.

— Believe me, I know how these things work. If nobody is standing over them, those thieves will just take the money and do nothing.

— The cemetery guy and the stonecutter?

— There are no bigger thieves.

Little more than a year before, Leon Shulman had been forced to retire from the pharmaceutical company where he had worked for twenty-three years. The diabetes that had precipitated his own father's death had progressed to the point where it

---

1. **Riga** Capital of Latvia, on the Baltic Sea.

rendered Leon Shulman clinically blind. Leon was a very competent chemist, enjoyed his job, and was well liked by his coworkers, but he could hardly argue when his supervisor took him aside and began enumerating the dangers posed by a blind man in a laboratory. Since then, as his vision continued to deteriorate, Leon imposed a strict regimen upon himself. His friends were dying and he was blind: another man might have surrendered to depression, but Leon informed anyone willing to listen that he had no intention of going down that road. It wasn't that he had any illusions about mortality; he was a sick man, but sick wasn't dead. So he woke each morning at a specific hour, performed a routine of calisthenics recalled from his days in the Russian army, dressed himself, made his own breakfast, listened to the news, and then immersed himself in unfinished business. At the top of the list of unfinished business was a new gravestone for his father's grave.

On occasion, particularly when the Shulmans observed the anniversary of their arrival in Los Angeles, Leon Shulman would recount the story of his father's death. Certainly Wolf Shulman had been ill. He'd been ill for years. But the week the Shulmans were scheduled to depart he had been no worse than he'd been in five years. Just that morning Leon had seen him and the old man had made oatmeal. So there was no way Leon could have anticipated what happened. But still, the thought that he was in a black marketeer's kitchen haggling over the price of a Kiev camera — albeit a very expensive model, with excellent optics, based on the Hasselblad — while his father was dying was something for which Leon could not forgive himself. And then the frantic preparations for the funeral, and the fact that Leon had already spent all of their money on things like the camera so that they'd have something to sell in the bazaars of Vienna and Rome, made the whole cursed experience that much more unbearable. Lacking time and money, Leon grieved that he had abandoned his father, a man whom he had loved and respected, in a grave marked by a stone the size of a shoebox.

This, Victor understood, was the reason for the phone call to the office. And later that evening, after submitting himself to the indignities of rush hour on the 405 and the 101, Victor sat in the kitchen of his parents' Encino condominium and listened as his father explained how easy it would be for him to adjust his travel plans to include an extended weekend in Riga. Leon had already called a travel agent, a friend, who could — even on such short notice — arrange for a ticket from London to Riga. It was, after all, a direct flight. A matter of only a few hours. The same travel agent had also taken the liberty — just in case — of reserving a room for Victor at a very nice hotel in Jurmala, two minutes from the beach, near bars, restaurants, and the Dzintari station, where he could find a local train that would get him into Riga in a half hour.

— Ask your mother, Jurmala in July, the beach, if the weather is good, nothing is better.

— Pa, we live in Los Angeles, if I go it won't be because of the beach.

— I didn't say because of the beach. Of course it's not because of the beach. But you'll see. The sand is like flour. The water is calm. Before you were one year old I took you into that water. And anyway, you shouldn't worry. I'll pay for everything.

— That's right, that's my biggest worry.

When Victor was a sophomore in college he realized that he would need to make money. This was the same year he spent a semester abroad at Oxford — though living for three months among fledgling aristocrats had nothing to do with his decision. For Victor, having grown up in Los Angeles, the lives and privileges of rich people — English or otherwise — were no great revelation. What led to his decision were the first irrefutable signs of his father's declining health. Victor began driving his father to the offices of world-class specialists, experts in the pancreas, not one of whom had been able to arrest — never mind reverse — the advancement of Leon's blindness. It was then that Victor started the calculations that ultimately led him to law school and a position as a litigation associate at a Century City law firm. At nineteen, Victor recognized — not unlike an expectant father — the loom of impending responsibilities. He was the only son of aging parents with a predisposition for chronic illness. His father's mother had died of a stroke before her sixtieth birthday. His mother's sister had suffered with rheumatoid arthritis before experiencing the "women's troubles" that eventually led to her death. And diabetes stretched so far back in his lineage that his ancestors were dying of the disease long before they had a name for it. More than once Victor had joked to friends that, when confronted with forms inquiring after family medical history, he simply checked the first four boxes without looking. Still, the only reason Victor felt he could permit himself that joke was that he was thirty years old, earned one hundred and seventy thousand dollars a year, and knew that although he could not spare his parents the misery of illness he could at least spare them the misery of illness compounded by the insult of poverty.

After dinner, Victor's mother, instead of saying good-bye at the doors of the elevator, insisted on walking him down to his car. Victor had not committed to going to Riga and she wanted him to understand — if he did not already — the effect his refusal would have on his father. Both Victor and his mother knew that Leon could be obsessive about the smallest things, and considering his condition, this was in some ways a blessing. Sitting at home alone, his obsessions kept his mind occupied. He could fashion his plans and make his phone calls. At the university library where Victor's mother worked, her coworkers all recognized Leon's voice; he no longer needed to ask for her by name.

— Of course you don't know this, but he calls me five or six times a day. Over the last month all the time to consult about the preparations for the gravestone. You know how he is, he says he wants my advice. Should he send Sander all the money at once or half and half? Do I think he should make up a contract for Sander to sign or would Sander be offended? And then when they started talking about what kind of stone, what shape, what size. Finally, when it came time to compose an epitaph, he says to me: "You studied literature." There, at least, I think he actually listened to what I said.

Standing in the street beside his car, Victor explained again why the trip would be much more complicated than his father imagined. He had only two weeks for vacation. And it wasn't the kind of vacation where he would be in one place all the time. He would be visiting the only close friend he had retained from his time at Oxford. The previous year this friend had gotten married and Victor had been unable to attend the wedding. His friend wanted Victor to meet his wife and spend some time with them. They had been planning this trip for months. Not only had his friend coordinated his vacation to coincide with Victor's but so had his new wife. They were to travel through Scotland, Ireland, and Wales. All the reservations had been made. So, it wasn't that Victor didn't want to help put his father's mind at ease, but that there were other people involved and he could not change his plans without inconveniencing them.

— If you tell them why, they'll understand. People have emergencies.

— I know people have emergencies. But the grave has been there for twenty-five years. All of a sudden it's an emergency?

— For your father it's an emergency.

— If he waits six months, I promise I'll book a ticket and go.

In his mother's deliberate pause, Victor heard what neither of them dared speak out loud. Leon was careful about his diet, monitored his blood sugar, and took his insulin injections. There was nothing to say that he could not continue this way for twenty years. Nevertheless, Victor felt that it was irresponsible, even ominous, to project into the future — if only six months — and presume that his father would still be there.

Meeting his mother's eyes, Victor knew that the decision had been made. And when his mother spoke it was no longer to convince him but rather to assure him that he was doing the right thing.

— I understand it will be unpleasant to disappoint your friends. But it's only three days. And, after all, this is your grandfather's and not some stranger's grave.

Late on a Saturday night, Victor's flight made its approach to the Riga airport. On the descent Victor looked out his window at the flat, green Latvian landscape. His neighbor for the three-hour trip from Heathrow was a garrulous, ruddy-faced Latvian in his seventies — a San Diego resident since 1947. Following the collapse of Communism, the man had returned to Latvia every summer for the fishing. When Victor informed him that he was undertaking his first trip to Latvia since his family's emigration in 1978, the man invited him to his cabin. Though the man was sincere and friendly, Victor couldn't help but suspect that he was an unregenerate Nazi. To hear his parents tell it, innocent Latvians hadn't retreated with the Germans. Whether this were true or not, Victor was not exactly proud of the ease with which his mind slipped into clannish paranoia. But, to maintain the necessary objectivity wasn't easy, particularly when buckled into an airplane full of blond heads.

In fact, after Los Angeles, and even London, Latvia struck him as remarkable in its blondness. At the customs desk, a pretty blond agent checked his passport. Tall blond baggage handlers handled the baggage. And it was a blond policewoman in a knee-length gray skirt who directed Victor up to the second floor where he could find a taxi. He had returned to the city of his birth, but no place had ever seemed less familiar. He marveled even at the sky. His flight had landed after ten and he had spent close to an hour in the terminal, but when he stepped outside he emerged into daylight. The pavement, highway, and outlying buildings were illuminated by some bright, sunless source.

At the curb, a thin Russian hopped off the fender of a Volkswagen and reached for Victor's suitcase. He wore a New York Yankees T-shirt and Fila track pants and had the distinction of being not-blond. Identifying Victor immediately as a foreigner, he asked, "American?" Victor responded in Russian, speaking in a terser, gruffer register than he normally used — a register he hoped would disguise the extent of his foreignness, make him appear less dupable, less likely to be quoted an exorbitant fare. And so when the cabdriver said, "Fifteen Lats" — equivalent to twenty-plus American dollars — a price Victor still suspected was inflated, he growled his disapproval and, to his satisfaction, succeeded in having the fare reduced by one Lat.

On the road to Jurmala, Victor rode in silence. He focused on the passing scenery. At that hour, nearly midnight, there were few other cars on the four-lane highway. The view was unspectacular. He registered certain banal observations. The road was smooth and clean. The passing cars were German, Swedish, Japanese — and clean. The few gas stations they passed appeared to be newly constructed. Victor kept expecting to feel something, be somehow inspired. He thought: I was born here, and I'm evaluating the infrastructure.

The cabdriver spoke over his shoulder and asked which hotel and Victor pronounced the name without turning his head.

— Villa Majori? Not bad. You know who owns it?

— No.

— The former mayor of Jurmala. Victor gathered that the driver expected him to be impressed.

— He was mayor for six months. Now he has a hotel. The property alone is worth 250,000 Lats.

— So he's a crook.

— Of course he's a crook.

— Did you vote for him?

— Did I vote for him? What difference does that make? Certain people decided he would be mayor, then later they decided he would no longer be mayor. It's not like that in America?

— In America he'd have two hotels. The driver laughed, inspiring in Victor a self-congratulatory and yet fraternal feeling.

— The mayor: a crook and a bastard, but I hear the hotel is good and that the girls he hires are very attractive.

Minutes later, Victor discovered that the hotel was indeed modern, tidy, and staffed — even at that late hour — by a pretty clerk. The hotel consisted of three floors, giving the impression that, before being converted to suit the needs of the former mayor, it had been someone's home. Victor found his room on the second floor and stood looking out the window at the flux of people on Jomas Street. The street was closed to all but pedestrian traffic and was flanked on either side by bars, restaurants, and hotels. Through his closed window he could hear the undifferentiated din of voices and music from rival bars. Had he wanted to sleep, the noise would have been infuriating, but though he'd hardly slept in two days, he felt exceedingly, even pathologically, alert. So, as he watched the sky darken literally before his eyes — a change as fluid as time-lapse photography of dusk — Victor decided to call home.

As it was Saturday afternoon in Los Angeles, his mother picked up the phone. When she realized it was Victor, she deliberately kept her voice neutral so as not to attract Leon's attention.

— You're there?

— I'm there.

— In the hotel?

— In the hotel.

— On Jomas?

— I can see it from my window.

— How does it look?

— How did it look before?

— People were strolling all day. Everyone dressed up. All year long girls thought only about getting a new dress for the summer. Victor heard Leon's voice, rising above his mother's, and the inevitable squabbling over possession of the phone.

— You see, if I tell him who it is he won't let me talk.

— What do you need to talk about? You can talk when he gets home. Has he spoken to Sander's son?

Sander Rabinsky had a son in Riga whom Victor was supposed to have contacted upon arrival. Sander's son was named Ilya and happened, as Leon enthusiastically pointed out, also to be a lawyer. It had been Ilya who had informed Leon of Sander's death. After not hearing from Sander for several days Leon had called repeatedly, left messages, and kept calling until finally Ilya had answered the phone.

— Did you call him?

— It's midnight.

— Call him first thing.

— I will.

— Good. So how is it over there?

— Exactly like Los Angeles. Maybe better. The women are beautiful and there are no fat people.

— Latvians: they look good in uniforms and are wonderful at taking orders. God punished them with the Russians. The devil take them both. Don't forget to call Sander's son.

Victor slept only a few hours and awoke at first light. He lingered in bed, trying to will himself back to sleep, but after an hour of this futility he rose, showered, dressed, and ventured outside. He found Jomas Street deserted but for a handful of elderly city workers armed with straw brooms, engaged in the removal of evidence of the previous night's revelry. It was five o'clock and Victor walked the length of the street, past the shuttered bars, small grocery stores, and souvenir shops. The only place not closed at that hour was an Internet café attended by a teenager slumped behind the counter. Victor wrote a too-lengthy e-mail to his friend in England. He had little new to say, having parted from him and his wife less than a day before, but to kill time he reassured them that they should begin their trip without him and that he would join them as soon as he resolved the business with his grandfather's gravestone. At the very least, Victor joked, he would connect with them by the time they reached Dublin, where his friend's wife had promised to set him up with a former roommate. Victor knew little about the girl other than her name, Nathalie, and that in a picture from his friend's wedding she appeared as a slender, attractive, dark-haired girl in a bridesmaid's dress.

By eight o'clock Victor had eaten his complimentary breakfast in the hotel's dining room and decided, even though it was still possibly too early, to call Sander's son. He dialed from his room and a woman answered. Leon had told him that Ilya was married with a young son of his own. Speaking to the woman, Victor tried to explain who he was. He mentioned Sander's name, the gravestone, and his father's name. Victor sensed a hint of displeasure in the way the woman replied, "Yes, I know who you are," but tried to dismiss it as cultural — Russians not generally inclined to American-grade enthusiasm — and he was relieved when he heard no trace of the same tone in Ilya's voice.

Ilya said, "I spoke with your father. He said you would be coming."

Victor offered his condolences over Sander's death and then accepted Ilya's invitation to stop at his apartment before proceeding to the cemetery.

As the travel agent had indicated, Victor found Dzintari station a few minutes' walk from his hotel. This route — Dzintari-Riga — was identical to the route he would have taken twenty-five years earlier in the summers when his parents rented a small cottage by the seashore. Somewhere, not far from his hotel, the cottage probably still existed, although Victor didn't expect that he could find it.

For the trip, Victor assumed a window seat and watched as the train sped past the grassy banks of a river and then the russet stands of skinny pines. Since it was a Sunday morning, and as he was heading away from the beach and toward the city, there were few other people in his car. At the far end two young men with closely cropped hair shared a quart of malt liquor, and several benches across from Victor a grandmother was holding the hand of a serious little boy dressed in shorts, red socks, and brown leather sandals no self-respecting American child would have consented to wear. Now and again, Victor caught the boy's eyes as they examined him. The boy's interest appeared to be drawn particularly by the plastic bag Victor held in his lap: a large Robinsons-May bag in which he carried a bottle of tequila for Ilya and a small rubber LA Lakers basketball for Ilya's son.

From the train station Victor followed Ilya's directions and walked through the center of the city. Ilya lived on Bruninieku Street, formerly called Red Army Street, in the apartment Sander had occupied for over fifty years. It was there, on Red Army Street, that Sander and Leon had become acquainted. They had been classmates in the Number 22 Middle School. Leon had lived around the corner and spent many afternoons playing soccer in the very courtyard where Victor now found himself. The courtyard and the building were older than the fifty years, closer to eighty or ninety, and the dim stairwell leading to the second floor suggested the handiwork of some pre–World War II electrician. Victor climbed stone steps, sooty and tread-worn to concavity, and squinted to read graffiti of indeterminate provenance. Some was in Latvian and seemed nationalistic in nature, some was in Russian, and if he read carefully, he could make out what it meant: "Igor was here"; "Nadja likes cock"; "Pushkin, Mayakovsky, Visotsky."

Victor found the number of Ilya's apartment stenciled above the peephole and rang the buzzer. Through the door he heard a child's high and excited cry of "Papa," and then Ilya opened the door. He was slightly shorter than Victor but was of the same type — a type which in America could pass for Italian or Greek but which in Latvia wasn't likely to pass for anything other than itself. Ilya wore a pair of house slippers, track pants, and a short-sleeved collared shirt. Standing at Ilya's side was a little blond girl, no older than five. The little girl seemed excited to see Victor.

— Papa, look, the man is here. Ilya gently put a hand on her shoulder and edged her out of the doorway.

— All right Brigusha, let the man inside.

Victor followed Ilya into the living room, where Ilya's wife was arranging cups, wafers, and a small teapot on the coffee table. The mystery of genes and chromosomes accounted for the nearly identical resemblance between mother and daughter and, but for a fullness at the mouth, the complete absence of the father in the little girl's face.

As Victor, Ilya, and the little girl entered the room Ilya's wife straightened up, looked at Victor, and appeared no happier at seeing him than she'd been at hearing his voice over the telephone. Ilya motioned for Victor to sit on the sofa and then performed the introductions.

— This is my wife, Salma, and Brigitta, our little girl.

Victor smiled awkwardly. He felt that he had made the mistake of taking his seat too soon. The upholstery claimed him in a way that made it difficult for him to lean forward or to rise. Undertaking the introductions while seated seemed wrong to the point of rudeness. As it was, he already felt less than welcome. He wanted to be on his feet, not only to shake hands, but also to offer the gifts — though the prospect of rising immediately after sitting down and then that of presenting the inappropriate basketball to Ilya's daughter momentarily paralyzed him. He was tempted to explain the misunderstanding about the basketball, but knew that to do so would be a betrayal of his father, portraying him as confused and inattentive, self-involved, possibly senile.

Doing his best to mask the exertion, Victor rose from the sofa and offered his hand to Salma and then, playfully, to the little girl. Because he knew that Salma didn't like him, Victor watched her face for some sign of détente,[2] but as Brigitta's small hand gripped the tips of his fingers, Salma's smile merely devolved from token to weary. Her expression made Victor feel like a fraud even though, apart from trying to be social, he was quite sure he hadn't done anything fraudulent. Under different circumstances, Victor consoled himself, he wouldn't tolerate such a woman.

Turning his attention from her, Victor reached into his bag and retrieved first the bottle of tequila and then the ball. To his relief, the little girl took the ball with genuine pleasure and bounced it on the stone floor with both hands. Ilya, inspecting the bottle, looked up and watched as Brigitta chased the ball into the kitchen.

— Before she punctured it, she had a beach ball like that. She could bounce the thing all day. Brigusha, say thank you. Victor, uncertain if he'd been commended or not, said that he hoped the gift was all right.

— You couldn't get her anything better. Right, Salma?

Salma, for the first time, looked — though not quite happy — at least somewhat less austere.

— It's very nice. Thank you.

She then picked up the empty Robinsons-May bag that Victor had left on the floor.

— Do you need the bag back?

— No.

— It's a good bag.

She called after her daughter.

— Brigusha, come here. Look at what a nice big bag the man left for you.

Carrying the ball, Brigitta returned to admire the bag.

— See what a big, fancy bag. You could keep all your toys in here. Come show the man how you can say thank you.

Brigitta looked up at Victor, down at her feet, and then pressed her face into Salma's hip. Ilya said, "Now you're shy? Maybe later you can show the man how you say thank you. She can say it in four languages. Russian, Latvian, German, and English."

Placing the tequila on the table, Ilya asked his wife to bring glasses.

— Come, we'll sit. I should have put a bottle down to begin with. What kind of alcohol is this?

Victor resumed his place on the sofa.

— Mexican. They make it from a plant that grows in the desert. It's very popular in America.

Salma returned with two glasses and Ilya poured. He proclaimed: "To new friendship."

After Salma made the tea and distributed the wafers she took Brigitta into a bedroom. From what Victor could see, that bedroom, plus another, along with the kitchen,

---

2. **détente** Decrease in tension between rivals.

a bathroom, and the living room, constituted the apartment. The ceilings were high, maybe twelve feet, and the floors and walls were in good repair. Also, the furniture, polished and solid, seemed to be many decades old and might have, for all Victor knew, qualified as antique.

Ilya said, "You like the apartment?"

— It would be hard to find one as good in Los Angeles.

— This apartment is the only home I've ever had. Now it's my inheritance. After the war my grandparents returned from the evacuation and moved here. My father grew up here, married here, and when I was born this is where he brought me from the hospital. As a boy I slept on this sofa, my parents in the smaller room, my grandparents in the larger. When my grandparents died my parents took their room and I was given the smaller one. Now it's my turn to take the big bedroom and move Brigitta into the little one. You could say I've been waiting my entire life to move into the big room. Though, if you follow the pattern, you can see where I go from there.

— So don't move into the big room. Then maybe you'll live forever.

— Well, we haven't moved yet. Brigitta still calls it "Grandfather's room." She likes to go and see his white coat hanging on the hook.

— She's a good girl.

— Do you have children?

— No.

— Married?

— No.

— It's a different life in America.

— Probably not that different. At my age most Americans have children. Some are even married.

The mood had become a little too confessional for Victor's liking and he took it as a good sign when Ilya grinned.

— One day I'd like to visit America. Salma's English is very good. Until recently she even worked for an American software company. Owned by Russians from San Francisco, Jews, who left here, like you, in the 1970s. They returned to take advantage of the smart programmers and the cheap labor. But the company went bankrupt after the problems with the American stock market.

— Unfortunately, it's a familiar story.

— "Capitalism," as my father would have said. Though he wasn't much of a Communist. But when everyone was leaving he wasn't interested. He liked it here. He was a doctor; he wanted to remain a doctor. He had no regrets. Not long ago, after your father contacted him he said to me: "You see. What if I'd left? I'd be collecting welfare in Brooklyn and who would help blind Leon Shulman with his father's gravestone." He had a real sense of humor.

Wolf Shulman was buried in the "new" Jewish cemetery on Shmerle Street. An older cemetery, from before the war, could be found in the Moskovsky district, a traditionally poor, working-class neighborhood behind the train station. Before the Nazi occupation the neighborhood had been predominantly Jewish, and during the Nazi occupation it had served as the ghetto. Ilya said there wasn't much to see there but, if Victor liked, Ilya would show him around. The municipal courthouse, where Ilya worked as a prosecutor, was only a few minutes away by foot.

From Ilya's apartment Victor caught a bus that let out at the base of Shmerle Street — a winding tributary off the main road — which rose to the cemetery and beyond. A concrete wall painted a pale orange encircled the cemetery. Victor followed the wall to the gates, where three old Russian women minded a wooden flower stall. Business appeared less than brisk, but as Victor neared the entrance, he saw a young couple select a bouquet of yellow carnations and so he did the same. He then passed through the gates and located the small stone building that served as the cemetery manager's office. Inside, the office was one single room, with dusty casement windows, a desk for the cemetery manager, and a lectern upon which rested a thick, leather-bound book. Upon entering, Victor found a short, heavy-set man wearing faded jeans, a pink sweater, and a black yarmulke, examining a slip of paper which had been handed to him by the young couple with the yellow carnations.

Victor heard the man ask, "*Berkovitz* or *Perkovitz?*" and the young woman reply, "Berkovitz. Shura Efimovna Berkovitz."

"*Berkovitz, Berkovitz*," the man repeated, shuffled to the lectern, and opened the large book. "Year of death," he inquired and, given the year, flipped pages and ran his finger down a column of handwritten names.

Once he found the name, the manager wrote down the section and row and pointed the young couple in the appropriate direction. For his service, and for the upkeep of the cemetery, he drew their attention to a container for donations. In a practiced appeal that included Victor, the man said: "We have more dead than living. And the dead don't donate."

When the young couple left to seek Shura Berkovitz's grave Victor introduced himself to the manager. For the second time that day he was surprised to be so effortlessly recognized. Using the same words Salma had used earlier that morning, though without the rancor, the manager said: "Yes, I know who you are." Flipping more pages in the book, he looked for Wolf Shulman.

— Remind me, what year did he die?

— 1978.

"There. Shulman, Wolf Lazarovich," the manager said, and copied the information.

— And is everything ready for the new gravestone?

— The grave is there. It's always ready. When the stonecutter brings the new stone, he'll also remove the old one. Very easy. Tik-tak.

— Is he here today?

Ilya had told Victor that sometimes, particularly on Sundays, the stonecutter could be found at the cemetery. He added that Victor would be well advised to speak to him as soon as possible because the stonecutter could be a difficult man to track down. Sander had expended no small amount of energy dealing with him.

The cemetery manager said, "I'll call him at his shop," and dialed the number. Within seconds he was speaking to the stonecutter. He spoke partly in Yiddish and partly in Russian. After a very brief exchange, he hung up. Victor, trying to suppress his irritation, explained that he had wished to speak to the stonecutter himself.

— He said he can see you tomorrow morning. He's very busy right now, but he'll be able to speak to you then. He keeps an office at the Jewish Community Center. He'll be waiting for you at ten-thirty.

— I understand. But, you see, I'm only here for a short time and I want to be sure there are no miscommunications.

— You shouldn't worry. I know of the matter. He knows of the matter. There will be no miscommunications. You'll see him tomorrow and everything will be just as you wish.

Victor paused, assumed an expression he often employed with obdurate[3] lawyers and clients, an expression intended to imply sincere deliberation, and then said, "Nevertheless."

The cemetery manager raised his palms in a sign of surrender. He scribbled a number on a piece of paper.

— Here is the number. Please. I wouldn't want you to think I am interfering. I was only trying to help you. The stonecutter is one of those men who, when he is busy, doesn't like to be disturbed.

Victor took the number and dialed. After a short while he heard a man's terse "hello." Before Victor could finish introducing himself the man barked, "Tomorrow; ten-thirty," and hung up. Victor replaced the phone and turned reluctantly to face the cemetery manager's obsequious[4] grin.

The cemetery at Shmerle had been hewn from a forest, but enough trees were spared so as to retain a sense of the arboreal. Different types of trees — birch, elm, maple, ash — provided texture and shade and resembled in their randomness the different species of gravestones — marble, granite, limestone — which sprouted from the ground as naturally as the trees. Though arranged in sections and rows, the gravestones did not follow any other order, and so large dwarfed small, traditional opposed modern, and dark contrasted light. The only commonality among them was that each stone featured a photograph of the deceased and that in each photograph the deceased possessed the same grudging expression. Soldiers, grandmothers, engineers, mathematicians: all stared into eternity with a face that declared not *I was alive*, but rather *This was my life*. After walking some distance, Victor found his grandmother and grandfather wearing this same face.

Until he saw his grandmother's grave, Victor had at some level forgotten about it. That he carried only one bouquet reminded him of the extent to which he had forgotten. His grandmother had died when he was still an infant and so he had no memory of her at all. Somewhere there was a picture of the two of them together: a baby in the arms of a stout, prematurely old woman. Her gravestone confirmed what little he knew of her: Etel Solomonovna Shulman, beloved wife, mother, and grandmother. Died before her sixtieth birthday. This information, beneath her photo, was etched into a thick, rectangular slab of black granite. And this slab, almost a meter high, towered over its partner, a limestone monument one-third the size, already weatherworn and tilting slightly backward. Seeing the two gravestones side by side, Victor could understand his father's anguish. What was left for Wolf Shulman seemed a slight against a man whose solemn face — due to the backward tilting of the stone — appealed vaguely heavenward with an expression that could also be interpreted as: *Is this all I deserve?*

After taking some pains to divide his bouquet into two equal halves, Victor paused and contemplated his grandparents' graves. They evoked in him a peculiar timbre of grief — grief not over what he had lost but over what he had never had. A baser, more selfish form of grief. The kind that permitted him only to mumble a self-conscious

---

3. obdurate Stubborn, unyielding. **4. obsequious** Obedient to the point of servility.

"good-bye" before turning back up the path. He then retraced his steps through the cemetery, stopping at times to appraise certain gravestones, look at pictures, and read names and dates. There were other members of his family buried here, and he discovered the grave of a great-uncle as well as some other graves with the last name Shulman — although he couldn't be sure if they were definitively his relations. The only other name he recognized appeared in a section occupied by more recent graves. On a reddish marble stone he read the name RABINSKY and saw a picture of a woman who must have been Ilya's mother. The picture, like all such pictures, was not of the best quality, but Victor could discern enough to draw the obvious conclusion. And beside this grave was another, still lacking a stone; but pressed into the soft earth was a small plastic sign on which was stenciled the name S. RABINSKY.

It was only noon when Victor left the cemetery, and though he felt the sluggishness of two days without sleep he decided to take a tour of the city. He caught a bus back into the vicinity of Ilya's apartment and then walked to the heart of medieval Riga. The city had been established in the twelfth century and had, throughout its history, been the subject of every Baltic power. Germanic Knights, Poles, and Swedes had tramped through its cobblestone streets. In the twentieth century alone — but for a brief spell of interwar independence — it had belonged to the Tsar, the Kaiser, Stalin, Hitler, and then Stalin once more. The heart of Old Riga had been destroyed by the Germans in the first days of World War II, rebuilt unfaithfully by the Soviets, but corrected to some extent by the new Latvian government. And so Victor was able to observe the storied Blackheads House, pass through winding alleyways, and visit the Domsky Cathedral, home to a world-famous organ.

Later, by leaving the old city, he found many examples of art nouveau buildings, with their elaborate stucco figures and faces. However, not particularly interested in architecture, Victor saw just enough to get a sense of the place. And after he'd acquired this sense, he took a seat at an outdoor cafe and ate his lunch in view of pedestrians, vendors, drunks, policemen, and bus drivers. In its constituent parts, the city displayed itself, and seemed, with its imported cars and Western fashions, none the worse for fifty years of Soviet rule.

On the ride back to Jurmala, Victor allowed himself to drift off. It was the deepest sleep he had experienced since leaving Los Angeles, and when his cab reached the hotel, a tremendous effort was required to rouse himself. He wanted nothing other than to sleep until morning, but at the front desk there were messages waiting for him from his father and from Ilya. So, tired as he was, Victor began by calling Ilya and recounting the episode at the cemetery manager's office. The incident, according to Ilya, was consistent with the man's character.

— But you have to consider how many others are practicing his trade. The man has no competition and so, unfortunately, he's become arrogant.

Ilya wished Victor luck and then invited him to come to the courthouse after his meeting with the stonecutter. He framed the invitation in collegial terms. As a fellow jurist, Ilya imagined that Victor possessed some professional curiosity. "This way," Ilya said, "you will be able to see the fabulous workings of the Latvian legal system."

Victor then placed his call home. This time Leon answered, after hardly a single ring, as though he had been sitting, primed, by the telephone. Whatever reservations Victor harbored about the cemetery manager and stonecutter, he knew better than to reveal them to his father. To Leon's detailed questions, he responded honestly but without elaboration. Yes, he had seen Sander's son. Yes, he had been received cordially. Yes, he had given the child the present and the child had been pleased. Yes, he had been to the cemetery, seen his grandparents' graves, and left flowers. And yes, he had also spoken with the cemetery manager and with the stonecutter — the latter of whom he had not seen personally but would the very next morning.

After the conversations with his father and with Ilya, Victor discovered — to his frustration — that he had lost his overwhelming need for sleep. The prospect of another sleepless night was unbearable and so Victor drew the blinds, climbed into bed, and resolved to nurture even the slightest vestige of fatigue. But once again his body refused to cooperate. He slept only fitfully, waking up disoriented, sometimes because of voices in the street, other times because of some malformed thought. At one point he found himself bolt upright, unsure whether or not he had indeed requested a wake-up call. He then spent what felt like an eternity, torn over whether or not to call the front desk and confirm yes or no. Later, he lost the better part of an hour recreating the scene at the cemetery manager's office and formulating alternate scenarios in which he didn't come off looking like an idiot. Eventually, in despair, he turned on the television and watched an American action movie, dubbed in Latvian with Russian subtitles.

At five in the morning, Victor was back among the sweepers on Jomas Street. The sky was cloudless and approaching full daylight. Victor made a circuit of Jomas, covering its entire length, and then turned north and walked the few blocks to the beach, which, like the streets, was largely deserted. Narrow and white, it stretched from east to west, seemingly to infinity. The tide was still high and sandpipers skittered neurotically at the fringes of the waves. A short distance away, balancing against one another and advancing gingerly out into the Baltic, were two middle-aged women in bathing suits. They had already progressed about fifty yards but the water was not yet to their waists. The sight triggered Victor's first memory of his Soviet childhood: stepping out into a dark-blue sea, conscious of danger, but feeling as though he could go a great distance before he had anything to fear.

To find the Jewish Community Center, Victor crossed a large municipal park and looked for the spire of a Russian Orthodox church. As he was extremely early, he trolled past the community center, made sure he was in the right place, and then sat and waited in the park until he thought it was reasonable to go and look for the stonecutter.

The community center, contrary to Victor's expectations, was a substantial building — four stories tall and designed in the art nouveau style. From a fairly dark and dreary looking lobby a broad stone stairway led to the upper floors, all of which benefited from an abundance of natural light. Not knowing whom to ask or where to look, Victor climbed the staircase and roamed the hallways hoping to stumble upon something that would announce itself as the stonecutter's office. He wandered for what seemed like a long time, finding an adult choir practicing Hebrew songs in a rehearsal room; a grand theater, with crumbling plaster and a seating capacity of hundreds; the locked doors of the Latvian Jewish Museum; and a tribute dedicated to a handful of Latvians who had protected Jews during the war.

He found these things but no explicit sign of the stonecutter, and little in the way of assistance until a young Latvian woman emerged from an office and cheerily informed Victor that the stonecutter did indeed use a room in the building but he kept no regular hours and she hadn't seen him that morning. However, keen to help, she led Victor down one floor and pointed out the stonecutter's door. She even knocked, waited, and then apologized profusely, as if she were personally responsible for the stonecutter's absence. There was a phone in her office, she said, if Victor wanted to call the stonecutter, and also magazines, if he wished to occupy himself while waiting.

Seeing no other recourse, Victor followed the woman to her office and made the pointless call. The stonecutter was admittedly only fifteen minutes late, and the fact that he did not pick up the phone could actually be construed as a good sign — (the man was on his way) — so there was, in essence, no logical reason for despair. And yet, each unanswered ring reinforced Victor's suspicion that the stonecutter would not show up.

Victor put down the phone. Beside him, the woman looked on with a doleful expression, and he dreaded that, at any moment, she would repeat her offer of the telephone and the magazines. He couldn't recall if he'd seen a pay phone down in the lobby but he was quite sure that he had seen one in the park. Calling from the park would require that he go somewhere and make change and then walk the two blocks between the community center and the park every time he wanted to make a phone call — thereby introducing a risk of missing the stonecutter should the man make a brief appearance at his office — but all this still seemed preferable to remaining, for even one second longer, the object of this woman's sympathy. Once again, Victor walked up and down the staircase. He listened to the choir and then descended to the lobby, where he found a handful of elderly Jews convened at a table, speaking Yiddish, chewing sandwiches, and playing cards. Victor stood for a few moments, debating whether or not to go outside, until a man brushed past him, hunched, bent under the weight of some psychological burden. He wore an ancient raincoat, a beaten fedora, and carried a briefcase. The man made his way for the doors of the public toilet and Victor heard him muttering to himself: "If only to go and shit like a human being." Victor decided to go outside.

Sitting in the park — having run the same coin through a pay phone yet once more — Victor thought it funny that there had been a time when the purpose of his vacation had absolutely nothing to do with Latvia. That at some point he had conceived of a relaxing trip with friends, touring the UK. And when the excursion to Riga had been introduced or, rather, imposed, he had treated it as only a minor deviation. A filial duty quickly and easily dispatched. But now, amid his exhaustion and anxiety, it seemed inconceivable that he would ever reunite with his friends and see Ireland, Scotland, and Wales. His fate was to be perpetually trapped in Latvia, pursuing a stonecutter, thinking obsessively about gravestones. Victor laughed out loud. It was possible that people at neighboring benches turned and stared. He didn't bother to check one way or the other. He had made his phone calls, he had knocked on the stonecutter's door, he had sat and waited. It was now time to walk to the courthouse and continue the farce.

Unlike most of the buildings Victor had seen in Riga, the courthouse was new and therefore outfitted with most of the contemporary trappings. The courtroom doors locked automatically when a session was in order, the faint whir of air-conditioning was omnipresent, and the furniture — though constructed from Latvian pine — had a vague Ikea-like quality. At the very back of the courtroom, to the right of the door, the accused sat on a bench inside a little gated prisoner's dock. Along the wall, just ahead of him, two policemen in green uniforms sat on their benches. They were both young men, barely in their twenties, but already possessing the dull, indolent posture common to all court officers. Victor had his place across the aisle from the policemen. Behind him were a young woman and a teenage boy and ahead was an old woman, presumably the defendant's family. When Victor entered the courtroom, there was no sight of the bailiff, judge, or — more to the point — Ilya. Only the defense attorney, a tall, thin woman with tired, houndlike features, was present. Ilya did not appear until the bailiff emerged from the back door and called the session to order. All were made to rise while the judge mounted his podium. He was dressed in a burgundy robe and wore a chain of orna-mental, golden medallions — evidently some folkloric symbol of Latvian authority. After the judge assumed his position, there followed the routine sequence of statements and exchanges — all of them in Latvian.

Victor understood hardly anything that happened over the next hour. He had no idea what the man had done to warrant his confinement, and he couldn't determine the purpose of the proceedings. He assumed they were preliminary, since, at one point, the defendant made a plea of not guilty. However, beyond that, the sense of things was impenetrable. And so Victor paid attention only long enough to register that Ilya, in his suit and tie, seemed to be a good lawyer. He was organized, spoke succinctly, and carried himself with an aloofness that bordered on menace. All of which probably didn't bode well for the man in handcuffs who sat in the prisoner's dock, looking not so much like a criminal but rather like a weary commuter waiting for the train. Victor assumed the same attitude of forbearance from the woman and the teenage boy as he heard not a sound behind him. The only person showing any sign of distress was the old woman in the front row. She had been in tears from the outset of the proceedings, and as time wore on, her breathing became shallower and more labored. Despite the air-conditioning, perspiration gathered in the folds of her neck. She drank water from a plastic, bear-shaped bottle — a kind manufactured to contain honey — and alternately wiped her eyes with a handkerchief and attempted to cool herself with a paper fan. But it was all to little effect as, ultimately, her breathing seized up and Victor was convinced that she was on the verge of a heart attack. It was only at this point that the judge turned his attention to her and considered a pause in the proceedings, but when she managed to collect herself things resumed as before.

The hearing was the last of the day for Ilya, and so, at its conclusion, he suggested they have lunch. They stopped at a small cafeteria where Victor bought half a dozen meat and cabbage buns and two bottles of Latvian beer. They then walked back toward the municipal park where Victor had spent much of his morning. On the way, Ilya explained what had transpired in the courtroom.

It was, as Victor had surmised, an arraignment. The man had already spent six months in custody waiting for the date. He would probably wait another several months before his next appearance. His crime was serious, though not uncommon. He was charged with attempting to murder his boss. The man was a mechanic and had worked in an auto shop. He had been on the job for three months — the standard probationary period during which a new employee is paid poorly, if at all. After three months, the boss is legally bound to either keep him on full time or let him go. Generally, to avoid the higher taxes associated with a full-time employee, a boss will let the person go and find another — there being no shortage of desperate people. In this case, the man claimed that his boss had promised to keep him. But when he came to work after his probationary period he found someone else at his post. His boss told him to go to hell, and so the man stabbed him in the neck with a screwdriver.

The boss probably had it coming, but Ilya had no choice but to prosecute. If he didn't, then every boss would be walking around with a screwdriver in his neck.

— So what will he get for stabbing his boss in the neck?

— Hard to say. Ten years? Or nothing. He'll say it was self-defense. The boss attacked him. He supports a wife, a younger brother. Nobody really wants to put him in jail. But who knows? Maybe things will turn out badly and he'll be put away for a long time.

— Which will probably be the end of the old woman.

Ilya considered this and then confessed that he had his doubts about the old woman. It struck him as peculiar that while the rest of the family sat in the back, she had taken her place in the front. Obviously, the old woman was supposed to be the defendant's mother, but this wasn't something anyone had bothered to verify. So she could just as well have been any old woman off the street. Which meant that there was nothing to say that the family hadn't scraped three Lats together and paid her to come to the courthouse and act hysterically. Such things were not without precedent. Though, for an arraignment, Ilya believed it a waste of money. But one couldn't blame the old woman. She probably received sixty Lats a month pension. Equivalent to one hundred dollars. And, Ilya said, he didn't need to describe to Victor what it was like to live on one hundred dollars a month.

They entered the park and Ilya sought out a vacant bench in the shade. It was now early afternoon and much quieter than when Victor had been there in the morning. There were a few young mothers with children and strollers. Now and again, a businessman strode past speaking into a cell phone. A few tourists stopped to buy ice cream and study their maps. Victor sipped his beer and wondered if he should admit to Ilya that he had absolutely no idea what it meant to live on one hundred dollars a month in Riga. Judging from Ilya's tone, he gathered that one hundred dollars a month was a pathetic sum. It certainly didn't sound like a lot of money, but then again, Latvia wasn't Los Angeles and, had Ilya phrased things differently, Victor could just as easily have been convinced that, in Latvian terms, one hundred dollars was a fortune. And though Victor subscribed to a sober view of the world and of the forces that ruled it — forces for whom the financial welfare of old ladies was generally not a top priority — he was in a strange country and therefore prone to a higher level of credulity; liable, practically, to believe the opposite of everything he believed.

Ilya said, "Do you want to know how much money I make?" and then answered his own question before Victor had a chance to object.

— Two hundred Lats a month. This is considered a good salary. Just enough so that I will think twice before taking a bribe. My father made the same as a dermatologist with forty years' experience. Salma, when she worked for the Americans, made two hundred and fifty. For a time, with three salaries, a total of six hundred and fifty Lats a month, we were relatively well off.

Ilya then proceeded to quote a litany of expenses, most of which, he said, were common to everyone in the city. Rent, food, transportation, miscellaneous items for children and the elderly. The figure he quoted for rent alone exhausted the total of the old woman's pension. There was, Ilya said, really no such thing as disposable income. This was why, to cite an extreme example, most of Riga's prostitutes had abandoned the city for points west. And as for the young mothers in the park, the businessmen, the pretty girls in summer dresses — in short, the reason Victor saw no squalor — well, it was Europe, after all. Not Africa. One good suit, one designer blouse — though secondhand from Germany — represented the difference between self-respect and despondency.

Ilya recited all of this information with detachment, as though he were addressing something merely statistical, academic, impersonal. His voice contained no resentment, which was why, when he asked Victor how much money he made, Victor felt less than his normal reticence to respond. However, he chopped fifty thousand off the number, which, given the context, still sounded obscenely excessive.

"But," Victor qualified, "I work for a large firm. We do most of our business with corporations. Someone doing your job would make less. And then you still have to adjust for the higher cost of living ..."

He realized that his was not a very persuasive argument. It was, even in terms of Los Angeles, not a very persuasive argument. He made a lot of money. Probably more than he deserved. But then again, he knew of others who earned even more and deserved even less.

Ilya leaned back on the bench and regarded, as though with intense botanical interest, the leaves and branches of the shade tree.

— I have some money saved up. Enough to send Salma and Brigitta to America. As I say, Salma is an accomplished programmer and her English is very good. And Brigitta is young and will easily learn the language. I am the only impediment. But I have my job here and am prepared to wait until they are ready for me.

Ilya then turned his attention from the tree and focused on Victor. As Ilya prepared to speak, Victor noted an inchoate[5] defensiveness in the set of his features, as though Ilya, like a teenage suitor, was poised for imminent rejection; prepared, at any moment, to dismiss the proposition with "never mind." Which was precisely what he said, but not before he said: "I'm not asking for money." And not before Victor replied: "I do not practice that kind of law."

— But perhaps someone in your firm?

— We deal only with corporations. Trade issues. Never individual immigration cases.

Which — other than the exceptions made for the sons and mistresses of wealthy clients — was the truth. Immigration cases were frustrating and time consuming, entailing a morass of paperwork and almost always ending in recriminations. Given the choice, he would have preferred it if Ilya actually had asked for money.

— And what about other means?

— What other means?

— Marriage.

— But you are already married.

— We could divorce. Temporarily, of course. I have heard it done.

— And then what?

— Salma could marry an American.

— Just like that?

— How else?

— And where would she find this American?

Which, Victor immediately understood, was a stupid question.

---

5. **inchoate** Disorganized.

"Never mind," Ilya said. "I see that it is asking too much."

Victor considered explaining, so far as he knew, the problems inherent in this option, to try to exonerate himself, to impress upon Ilya the impracticality; beyond that, he considered lying, consenting to fill out forms, marry the man's wife, adopt his daughter, do whatever, since it was pitifully clear that between him and the stonecutter remained — even if only tenuously — Ilya. But he couldn't quite bring himself to do that. Instead, he sat beside Ilya and resigned himself to a punitive silence.

After some time, as if having reached a conclusion, Ilya repeated, "Never mind," and ended the silence. "I realize that this isn't why you came here," he said, with each word distancing himself from the man who had, only moments before, offered Victor his wife and child.

— Fortunately, your problem is easier to solve. I will call the stonecutter for you.

Ilya rose and went to the phone booth, though Victor was sure that he hadn't said anything to him about his most recent frustrations. And when Victor approached the phone booth Ilya was already dialing a number. Then he was speaking in Latvian, exhibiting the same bloodless composure he had evinced in the courtroom. The conversation did not last long and Ilya did most of the talking. Once again, as at the cemetery manager's office, Victor felt himself excluded from considerations related to his own life. His input wasn't requested except to establish the departure time of his flight the next day.

When the conversation was over, Ilya exited the phone booth and announced: "If you like, he can see us now."

— That was the stonecutter?

— Yes.

— Is he at the community center?

— No.

— So, where is he?

— At his shop. In the Moskovsky district. It's possible to walk, although I would recommend a cab. A cab would get us there in ten minutes. We can get one easily on Brivibas Street.

Ilya half turned in the direction of the street, ready to hail the cab, as if Victor's consent were foregone and incidental. Angered by Ilya's presumptuousness, and momentarily unsure of what he wanted, Victor said:

— What if I don't want to go?

— You don't want to go?

— I don't understand the rush.

— I thought you left tomorrow.

— In the afternoon. I could see him in the morning.

— But he can see you now.

— I waited for him for two hours today. Where was he then?

Ilya regarded Victor as one might a child or a dog, as some thing ruled by impulse and deficient in reason.

— I couldn't say. Though I imagine if we went you could ask him yourself.

The flatness of Ilya's tone discouraged Victor from asking anything further. Which was fine, since Victor no longer had anything to ask. He now recognized that he was in a situation that provided for only a binary choice. He could go with Ilya and see things though to their conclusion — whatever that might be — or he could refuse and claim the transitory pleasure of refusal. Those were his choices. There was nothing else. Calling the stonecutter and repeating his mistake at the cemetery was out of the question. And though he had misgivings about the likelihood of things turning out right, he had also an almost inexorable curiosity to finally meet the man. It seemed ridiculous — and likely a symptom of his delirium — but he had begun to doubt the very fact of the stonecutter's existence. And he entertained the thought, in some subrational recess, that meeting the stonecutter might be like meeting God or the president or the Wizard of Oz — equal parts disappointment and reward — but at least the truth would be revealed.

Victor followed Ilya out to Brivibas Street, where, as predicted, they had no trouble finding a cab. Ilya rode up front and directed the driver while Victor sat in the back seat. The driver navigated along streets now familiar to Victor. They passed through the medieval city, looped behind the central markets and the train station, and followed a route that brought them to the courthouse and the limit of Victor's knowledge. They then continued south, into what could have been generically described as the "bad part of town." The change was abrupt, as though the result of a civic consensus: No tourists expected beyond this point. The streets were gray and dingy. Old buildings deteriorated unchecked. Not infrequently, Victor saw listing, wooden hovels[6] — seemingly anomalous in an urban setting — beside concrete apartment houses. People moved about the streets, tending to their everyday affairs, but there were also shadowy figures loitering in the doorways. In America, the place would have qualified as a slum, depressing and interesting only in a sordid way. But Nazis had commanded here and perpetrated horrific crimes, the knowledge of which invested the place with a sense of historical gravity; the slum felt like more than just a slum. And, assuming he didn't get mugged or clubbed to death, Victor thought it fitting that he should come here to get to the bottom of things.

After traveling for several more minutes, Ilya pointed to a dark green cottage and instructed the driver to stop. Victor then paid the driver and joined Ilya at the cottage's entrance. They stood there for a short while, but Ilya offered nothing in the way of explanation, not even a word to assure Victor that the dilapidated structure — bearing nothing to identify it as the stonecutter's shop or as a place of business of any kind — was where they needed to be. Victor had expected to find heavy machinery and stacked rock, but there were only a peeling facade, drawn curtains, uncut grass, and a dirt path that turned ninety degrees at the front steps and wound around the side of the house. Taking this path, Ilya led Victor the length of the house and into a yard dominated by a Mitsubishi pickup truck with a sunken rear suspension. The truck had been backed into the yard so that its tailgate was only a few feet from the doors of a garage and from a large manual winch. The winch looked ancient, a relic from previous centuries, but Victor could see that it was still very much in use. By its heavy rope, it suspended a rough marble obelisk[7] three feet in the air. The obelisk spun lazily, as though it had only recently been disturbed.

Ilya placed a hand on the obelisk, indicated the garage, and said: "Well, here you have him."

Victor stepped past a door and looked into the garage. Looking back at him was a man in his sixties. He wore scuffed work pants, a sleeveless undershirt, and he had the

---

6. hovels Destitute shacks. **7. obelisk** Four-sided pyramidal stone structure.

hands and arms befitting a man who spent his days working with stone. He sat on a low stool with his legs splayed out before him. In one hand he held an abrasive cloth, which he had been using to polish a granite tombstone propped against a nearby wall. He blinked sullenly and looked very much like someone who hadn't been happy to see anyone in years.

"Shimon," Ilya said, "I brought you your client."

Shimon blinked again and showed no indication that he heard what Ilya had said.

Ilya gave the obelisk a firm shove, putting the weight in motion, and eliciting squeals of protest from the winch.

— Aren't you even going to say thank you, you old goat?

"Go to the devil," Shimon said, "and take him with you."

— You shouldn't talk like that. He came all the way from America just to see you.

— All the worse for him.

Shimon glared from Victor to Ilya as though trying to determine which of them he despised more. For a moment, Victor wondered if maybe the old man had him confused with someone else. He'd not yet said one word to the stonecutter — barely looked at him, done nothing more than show up — and yet the man seemed to loathe him in a personal way. Victor found it unsettling, like the opprobrium[8] of a cripple or a religious person. However, it didn't appear to bother Ilya, who responded to the stonecutter's hatred with a patrician smugness.

— Listen, if you don't want the business we'll leave.

Shimon shrugged, hatred undiminished, but evidently not prepared to lose the business. Though, what business, Victor could not quite figure out. The money had been sent months ago and the work reportedly done.

Shimon lifted his face to Victor and said: "Well, did you come from America to stand here like a mute? What is it you want from me?"

It could only be, Victor thought, that the man had confused him with someone else. Either that or he suffered from a mental illness.

— I spoke to you yesterday. We had an appointment for this morning. I waited for you for hours. We were supposed to discuss the gravestone for my grandfather's grave. Work which I was told you had finished. Work for which you have already been paid. So, how exactly do you mean what do I want?

— Who told you it was finished?

— His father promised my father it would be finished. Money was wired. Are you saying it's not finished?

— Ask your friend the parasite if it's finished.

Shimon jerked his head toward Ilya, the parasite, who had allowed a shadow to fall over his smugness.

— You see how he talks. You see what it's like to deal with him. My father literally spent weeks tying to have a reasonable conversation with him. And though I saw the trouble he was having, my father refused to let me intervene. Now, you've seen the Latvian legal system. You have seen where I work. It's nothing to be proud of. But, for what it's worth, it gives me access to certain people. And, if absolutely necessary, I can complicate someone's life.

Ilya frowned in the stonecutter's direction.

---

8. **opprobrium** Disgrace.

— Not that it's something I enjoy. What's to enjoy? Old men like him pass through the court every day. You'd have to be a sick person to enjoy making someone's miserable life even more miserable. Right?

Ilya smiled philosophically at Victor, his eyes seeking confirmation, as though the question had not been rhetorical. Just to be clear, he repeated it.

— Right?

— Right.

— But what choice do I have with someone like him?

From the roof of his skull, Victor felt the spreading of a vaporous warmth. It filled him, like helium but not exactly, making him very light and very heavy all at once. It took him a second to identify this sensation as a powerful swell of fatigue. His legs were like pillars, rooted into the ground, and yet he believed he might tip over. Out of the corner of his eye, he thought he saw a lumbering, retarded man. The man was Shimon's son. He helped his father load and unload the heavy rocks. Victor turned to get a better look, but when he did he saw only Shimon sitting by himself in the garage.

Victor turned back to Ilya and said, "What does any of this have to do with my grandfather's gravestone?" Ilya wavered before him, for a second blurry and then immaculately sharp.

"Let me explain it to you," Ilya said.

— Three weeks ago my father got on a bus to go and see this man. This man who could not be relied upon to keep an appointment or return a phone call. On a hot day, after working for eight hours, at five o'clock, when the buses are full, my father had to ride across town. Before he got here he had a heart attack. They had to stop the bus. We only received a phone call when he was already in the hospital. I, my daughter, my wife, none of us even had a chance to say good-bye. This is what it has to do with your grandfather's gravestone. My father, who from the goodness of his heart agreed to help. My father, whom your father only pestered. Calling all the time. And then wanting to negotiate payment in installments. As if my father was a thief. And later sent him a *contract* —

Ilya spat out "contract," as if a more offensive word did not exist in the Russian language.

— This is what it has to do with anything. That my father killed himself over this gravestone. This gravestone which nobody would ever even visit. And what did my father get in return? Never a thank you. Only a hundred Lats for his trouble. A hundred Lats that won't even buy a stone a fifth as big for his memory. Now you tell me if that's fair.

Through the murk of fatigue, Victor heard the things Ilya said, but his brain processed only the rudiments: my father, your father, my father, your father. If there were an argument here, Victor didn't see how anyone could hope to win it. There was nothing to win. There was Sander, an old man suffering a heart attack on a cramped city bus: Ilya's father, but an abstraction to Victor. And there was Leon, an abstraction to Ilya, but as real to Victor as if he were standing before him. There he was, stumbling around the apartment, feeling the walls. There he was, every morning, in his tracksuit, doing deep knee bends and other ludicrous Soviet calisthenics. There he was, injecting himself with insulin and fretting about one thing or another at the kitchen table. His father.

"I thought I would give you a chance. If you would help," Ilya said. "And even now, I give you a chance. You can buy yourself another gravestone. God knows you have the money. Give this old bastard the business he doesn't deserve. And I'll send you a photo to prove it gets done."

In a daze, Victor didn't quite remember refusing the arrangement. Because he was already picturing his cab ride and the blur of pine trees on the way to Jurmala. And he was already in his hotel room, lying in bed, asleep and having a dream in which Nathalie, the Irish bridesmaid, appeared to him either on the beach in Jurmala or on the beach in Los Angeles — maybe both — and in which she professed her undying love, had sex with him, became his wife, and then — with the confounding logic of dreams — transformed into Salma, who, stranger still, did nothing to undermine the benign quality of the dream but rather, in some illicit way, only enhanced the sense of pleasure. And then he awoke and dialed and had a conversation with his father. A conversation in which his father asked him how everything went. If he met the stonecutter. If he saw the gravestone. If everything looked as it should. And Victor answered his father, saying yes about the stonecutter, yes about the gravestone. Yes about everything. He answered him and said that everything was perfect, just the way he imagined it.

(2003)

Madeleine Thien (1974–)

Madeleine Thien was born in 1974, the year her Chinese-Malaysian parents immigrated to Vancouver, British Columbia, from Malaysia. Thien has remarked that their experience has had a lasting effect on her writing. "Of all the gifts that our parents give us," she says, "one of the most wonderful and mysterious is … the example of their own lives. They show us how the past, present and future might unfold in a single life; how we are shaped by memory; how to live with the past and imagine the future." As a very young child, she read voraciously (her older sister taught her to read when she was just three) and learned to love the feeling it gave her of "inhabiting many worlds simultaneously." At the age of about six, she began to write. She also learned to dance, and after high school she enrolled in a dance program at Simon Fraser University, but, realizing that she didn't have the necessary passion to become a professional dancer, and having never lost the desire to write, she switched over to the University of British Columbia's creative writing program. She graduated with an M.F.A. in 2001.

The same year, her first book — the short story collection *Simple Recipes* — was published. These seven stories elucidate themes of loss, guilt, emotional betrayal, and despair. Families are torn by intergenerational conflict. Thien probes cultural alienation within immigrant families as well, but only two stories in this collection — the title story and "A Map of the City" — contain specific references to the author's Asian heritage. Longing suffuses these tales, and memory haunts the characters who populate them. The father of Miriam, narrator of "A Map of the City," fails to make a life for himself in his adopted country and returns to Indonesia, prompted by memories of a happier time. Miriam, despite having walked away from the wreckage of her family, realizes that memory will persist, and her parents' "hold would never diminish"; years later, she imagines that she sees them "in unexpected places." As a child, the narrator of the title story witnesses her normally gentle and patient father savagely beat her rebellious brother and, in that instant, the foundations of her world crumble: "This violence will turn all my love to shame and grief." As an adult, she still dreams of her father standing in the kitchen where he lovingly prepared family meals before the moment of undoing: "This memory of him is so strong, sometimes it stuns me." Betrayal is everywhere: in "House," ten-year-old Lorraine pines for her alcoholic mother, who has abandoned the family; in "Dispatch," a young wife is confronted with evidence that her husband has fallen in love with another woman and wants to leave her.

Thien's first novel, *Certainty*, was published in 2006. Here, as in her short fiction, she studies the dynamic of memory; she also examines grief and loss and the love and dislocation that characterize family bonds. At the novel's outset, the family and friends of radio documentary producer Gail Lim gather in Vancouver to mark the six-month anniversary of her death. Gail, the story's pivotal character, has succumbed to a viral infection while on a research trip. We meet her loved ones — husband Ansel and parents Matthew and Clara — who are reeling with shock and grief. The narration then fragments to accommodate multiple viewpoints (various narrators describe the same events from divergent perspectives), locales (the story moves from Vancouver to Indonesia, Malaysia, Australia, and Holland), and moments in history. Before her death, Gail engages in an investigation of a family mystery that has its roots in Japan's World War II occupation of British North Borneo. Her paternal grandfather was murdered there by the Japanese occupiers (Thien's own grandfather was killed under similar circumstances), and she digs deep to find an explanation for what happened, travelling, interviewing, recording, struggling to read (or hear) between the lines. Ansel replays and rewinds her tapes, listening to the past retold by a chorus of voices, a flood of words already spoken. Time is in flux, and the novel's disparate characters long to be released from the state of dislocation they are forced to inhabit — they are united in their craving for certainty. Thien says that in giving her book its title, she was inspired by a quote from Michael Ignatieff: "We could face the worst if we simply renounced our yearning for certainty. But who among us is capable of that renunciation?"

Thien is also interested in writing for children. In 2001, she published *The Chinese Violin*, a story about a little girl and her father who leave China to begin a new life in Canada. It was based on an animated National Film Board short made by Joe Chang, and it features Chang's illustrations. In 2005, Thien, after a two-year sojourn in the Netherlands, moved with her husband, Dutch-born Willem Atsma, to Quebec City.

Simple Recipes

There is a simple recipe for making rice. My father taught it to me when I was a child. Back then, I used to sit up on the kitchen counter watching him, how he sifted the grains in his hands, sure and quick, removing pieces of dirt or sand, tiny imperfections. He swirled his hands through the water and it turned cloudy. When he scrubbed the grains clean, the sound was as big as a field of insects. Over and over, my father rinsed the rice, drained the water, then filled the pot again.

The instructions are simple. Once the washing is done, you measure the water this way — by resting the tip of your index finger on the surface of the rice. The water should reach the bend of your first knuckle. My father did not need instructions or measuring cups. He closed his eyes and felt for the waterline.

Sometimes I still dream my father, his bare feet flat against the floor, standing in the middle of the kitchen. He wears old buttoned shirts and faded sweatpants drawn at the waist. Surrounded by the gloss of the kitchen counters, the sharp angles of the stove, the fridge, the shiny sink, he looks out of place. This memory of him is so strong, sometimes it stuns me, the detail with which I can see it.

Every night before dinner, my father would perform this ritual — rinsing and draining, then setting the pot in the cooker. When I was older, he passed this task on to me but I never did it with the same care. I went through the motions, splashing the water around, jabbing my finger down to measure the water level. Some nights the rice was a mushy gruel. I worried that I could not do so simple a task right. "Sorry," I would say to the table, my voice soft and embarrassed. In answer, my father would keep eating, pushing the rice into his mouth as if he never expected anything different, as if he noticed no difference between what he did so well and I so poorly. He would eat every last mouthful, his chopsticks walking quickly across the plate. Then he would rise, whistling, and clear the table, every motion so clean and sure, I would be convinced by him that all was well in the world.

My father is standing in the middle of the kitchen. In his right hand he holds a plastic bag filled with water. Caught inside the bag is a live fish.

The fish is barely breathing, though its mouth opens and closes. I reach up and touch it through the plastic bag, trailing my fingers along the gills, the soft, muscled body, pushing my finger overtop the eyeball. The fish looks straight at me, flopping sluggishly from side to side.

My father fills the kitchen sink. In one swift motion he overturns the bag and the fish comes sailing out with the water. It curls and jumps. We watch it closely, me on my tiptoes, chin propped up on the counter. The fish is the length of my arm from wrist to elbow. It floats in place, brushing up against the sides of the sink.

I keep watch over the fish while my father begins the preparations for dinner. The fish folds its body, trying to turn or swim, the water nudging overtop. Though I ripple tiny circles around it with my fingers, the fish stays still, bobbing side-to-side in the cold water.

For many hours at a time, it was just the two of us. While my mother worked and my older brother played outside, my father and I sat on the couch, flipping channels. He loved cooking shows. We watched *Wok with Yan*, my father passing judgement on Yan's methods. I was enthralled when Yan transformed orange peels into swans. My father sniffed. "I can do that," he said. "You don't have to be a genius to do that." He placed a sprig of green onion in water and showed me how it bloomed like a flower. "I know many tricks like this," he said. "Much more than Yan."

Still, my father made careful notes when Yan demonstrated Peking Duck. He chuckled heartily at Yan's punning. "Take a wok on the wild side!" Yan said, pointing his spatula at the camera.

"Ha ha!" my father laughed, his shoulders shaking. "*Wok* on the wild side!"

In the mornings, my father took me to school. At three o'clock, when we came home again, I would rattle off everything I learned that day. "The brachiosaurus," I informed him, "eats only soft vegetables."

My father nodded. "That is like me. Let me see your forehead." We stopped and faced each other in the road. "You have a high forehead," he said, leaning down to take a closer look. "All smart people do."

I walked proudly, stretching my legs to match his steps. I was overjoyed when my feet kept time with his, right, then left, then right, and we walked like a single unit. My father was the man of tricks, who sat for an hour mining a watermelon with a circular spoon, who carved the rind into a castle.

My father was born in Malaysia and he and my mother immigrated to Canada several years before I was born, first settling in Montreal, then finally in Vancouver. While I was born into the persistence of the Vancouver rain, my father was born in the wash of a monsoon country. When I was young, my parents tried to teach me their language but it never came easily to me. My father ran his thumb gently over my mouth, his face kind, as if trying to see what it was that made me different.

My brother was born in Malaysia but when he immigrated with my parents to Canada the language left him. Or he forgot it, or he refused it, which is also common, and this made my father angry. "How can a child forget a language?" he would ask my mother. "It is because the child is lazy. Because the child chooses not to remember." When he was twelve years old, my brother stayed away in the afternoons. He drummed the soccer ball up and down the back alley, returning home only at dinner time. During the day, my mother worked as a sales clerk at the Woodward's store downtown, in the building with the red revolving W on top.

In our house, the ceilings were yellowed with grease. Even the air was heavy with it. I remember that I loved the weight of it, the air that was dense with the smell of countless meals cooked in a tiny kitchen, all those good smells jostling for space.

The fish in the sink is dying slowly. It has a glossy sheen to it, as if its skin is made of shining minerals. I want to prod it with both hands, its body tense against the pressure of my fingers. If I hold it tightly, I imagine I will be able to feel its fluttering heart. Instead, I lock eyes with the fish. *You're feeling verrrry sleepy*, I tell it. *You're getting verrrry tired.*

Beside me, my father chops green onions quickly. He uses a cleaver that he says is older than I am by many years. The blade of the knife rolls forward and backward, loops of green onion gathering in a pyramid beside my father's wrist. When he is done, he rolls his sleeve back from his right hand, reaches in through the water and pulls the plug.

The fish in the sink floats and we watch it in silence. The water level falls beneath its gills, beneath its belly. It drains and leaves the sink dry. The fish is lying on its side, mouth open and its body heaving. It leaps sideways and hits the sink. Then up again. It curls and snaps, lunging for its own tail. The fish sails into the air, dropping hard. It twitches violently.

My father reaches in with his bare hands. He lifts the fish out by the tail and lays it gently on the counter. While holding it steady with one hand, he hits the head with the flat of the cleaver. The fish falls still, and he begins to clean it.

In my apartment, I keep the walls scrubbed clean. I open the windows and turn the fan on whenever I prepare a meal. My father bought me a rice cooker when I first moved into my own apartment, but I use it so rarely it stays in the back of the cupboard, the cord wrapped neatly around its belly. I have no longing for the meals themselves, but I miss the way we sat down together, our bodies leaning hungrily forward while my father, the magician, unveiled plate after plate. We laughed and ate, white steam fogging my mother's glasses until she had to take them off and lay them on the table. Eyes closed, she would eat, crunchy vegetables gripped in her chopsticks, the most vivid green.

My brother comes into the kitchen and his body is covered with dirt. He leaves a thin trail of it behind as he walks. The soccer ball, muddy from outside, is encircled in one arm. Brushing past my father, his face is tense.

Beside me, my mother sprinkles garlic onto the fish. She lets me slide one hand underneath the fish's head, cradling it, then bending it backwards so that she can fill the fish's insides with ginger. Very carefully, I turn the fish over. It is firm and slippery, and beaded with tiny, sharp scales.

At the stove, my father picks up an old teapot. It is full of oil and he pours the oil into the wok. It falls in a thin ribbon. After a moment, when the oil begins crackling, he lifts the fish up and drops it down into the wok. He adds water and the smoke billows up. The sound of the fish frying is like tires on gravel, a sound so loud it drowns out all other noises. Then my father steps out from the smoke. "Spoon out the rice," he says as he lifts me down from the counter.

My brother comes back into the room, his hands muddy and his knees the colour of dusty brick. His soccer shorts flutter against the backs of his legs. Sitting down, he makes an angry face. My father ignores him.

Inside the cooker, the rice is flat like a pie. I push the spoon in, turning the rice over, and the steam shoots up in a hot mist and condenses on my skin. While my father moves his arms delicately over the stove, I begin dishing the rice out: first for my father, then my mother, then my brother, then myself. Behind me the fish is cooking quickly. In a crockery pot, my father steams cauliflower, stirring it round and round.

My brother kicks at a table leg.

"What's the matter?" my father asks.

He is quiet for a moment, then he says, "Why do we have to eat fish?"

"You don't like it?"

My brother crosses his arms across his chest. I see the dirt lining his arms, dark and hardened. I imagine chipping it off his body with a small spoon.

"I don't like the eyeball there. It looks sick."

My mother tuts. Her nametag is still clipped to her blouse. It says *Woodward's*, and then, *Sales Clerk*. "Enough," she says, hanging her purse on the back of the chair. "Go wash your hands and get ready for supper."

My brother glares, just for a moment. Then he begins picking at the dirt on his arms. I bring plates of rice to the table. The dirt flies off his skin, speckling the tablecloth. "Stop it," I say crossly.

"*Stop it*," he says, mimicking me.

"Hey!" My father hit his spoon against the counter. It *pings*, high-pitched. He points at my brother. "No fighting in this house."

My brother looks at the floor, mumbles something, and then shuffles away from the table. As he moves farther away, he begins to stamp his feet.

Shaking her head, my mother takes her jacket off. It slides from her shoulders. She says something to my father in the language I can't understand. He merely shrugs his shoulders. And then he replies, and I think his words are familiar, as if they are words I should know, as if maybe I did know them once but then I forgot them. The language that they speak is full of soft vowels, words running together so that I can't make out the gaps where they pause for breath.

My mother told me once about guilt. Her own guilt she held in the palm of her hands, like an offering. But your guilt is different, she said. You do not need to hold on to it. Imagine this, she said, her hands running along my forehead, then up into my hair. Imagine, she said. Picture it, and what do you see?

A bruise on the skin, wide and black.

A bruise, she said. Concentrate on it. Right now, it's a bruise. But if you concentrate, you can shrink it, compress it to the size of a pinpoint. And then, if you want to, if you see it, you can blow it off your body like a speck of dirt.

She moved her hands along my forehead.

I tried to picture what she said. I pictured blowing it away like so much nothing, just these little pieces that didn't mean anything, this complicity that I could magically walk away from. She made me believe in the strength of my own thoughts, as if I could make appear what had never existed. Or turn it around. Flip it over so many times you just lose sight of it, you lose the tail end and the whole thing disappears into smoke.

My father pushes at the fish with the edge of his spoon. Underneath, the meat is white and the juice runs down along the side. He lifts a piece and lowers it carefully onto my plate.

Once more, his spoon breaks skin. Gingerly, my father lifts another piece and moves it towards my brother.

"I don't want it," my brother says.

My father's hand wavers. "Try it," he says, smiling. "Take a wok on the wild side."

"No."

My father sighs and places the piece on my mother's plate. We eat in silence, scraping our spoons across the dishes. My parents use chopsticks, lifting their bowls and motioning the food into their mouths. The smell of food fills the room.

Savouring each mouthful, my father eats slowly, head tuned to the flavours in his mouth. My mother takes her glasses off, the lenses fogged, and lays them on the table. She eats with her head bowed down, as if in prayer.

Lifting a stem of cauliflower to his lips, my brother sighs deeply, he chews, and then his face changes. I have a sudden picture of him drowning, his hair waving like grass. He coughs, spitting the mouthful back onto his plate. Another cough. He reaches for his throat, choking.

My father slams his chopsticks down on the table. In a single movement, he reaches across, grabbing my brother by the shoulder. "I have tried," he is saying. "I don't know what kind of son you are. To be so ungrateful." His other hand sweeps by me and bruises into my brother's face.

My mother flinches. My brother's face is red and his mouth is open. His eyes are wet.

Still coughing, he grabs a fork, tines aimed at my father, and then in an unthinking moment, he heaves it at him. It strikes my father in the chest and drops.

"I hate you! You're just an asshole, you're just a fucking asshole chink!" My brother holds his plate in his hands. He smashes it down and his food scatters across the table. He is coughing and spitting. "I wish you weren't my father! I wish you were dead."

My father's hand falls again. This time pounding downwards. I close my eyes. All I can hear is someone screaming. There is a loud voice. I stand awkwardly, my hands covering my eyes.

"Go to your room," my father says, his voice shaking.

And I think he is talking to me so I remove my hands.

But he is looking at my brother. And my brother is looking at him, his small chest heaving.

A few minutes later, my mother begins clearing the table, face weary as she scrapes the dishes one by one over the garbage.

I move away from my chair, past my mother, onto the carpet and up the stairs.

Outside my brother's bedroom, I crouch against the wall. When I step forward and look, I see my father holding the bamboo pole between his hands. The pole is smooth. The long grains, fine as hair, are pulled together, at intervals, jointed. My brother is lying on the floor, as if thrown down and dragged there. My father raises the pole into the air.

I want to cry out. I want to move into the room between them, but I can't.

It is like a tree falling, beginning to move, a slow arc through the air.

The bamboo drops silently. It rips the skin on my brother's back. I cannot hear any sound. A line of blood edges quickly across his body.

The pole rises and again comes down. I am afraid of bones breaking.

My father lifts his arms once more.

On the floor, my brother cries into the carpet, pawing at the ground. His knees folded into his chest, the crown of his head burrowing down. His back is hunched over and I can see his spine, little bumps on his skin.

The bamboo smashes into bone and the scene in my mind bursts into a million white pieces.

My mother picks me up off the floor, pulling me across the hall, into my bedroom, into bed. Everything is wet, the sheets, my hands, her body, my face, and she soothes me with words I cannot understand because all I can hear is screaming. She rubs her cool hands against my forehead. "Stop," she says. "Please stop," but I feel loose, deranged, as if everything in the known world is ending right here.

In the morning, I wake up to the sound of oil in the pan and the smell of French toast. I can hear my mother bustling around, putting dishes in the cupboards.

No one says anything when my brother doesn't come down for breakfast. My father piles French toast and syrup onto a plate and my mother pours a glass of milk. She takes everything upstairs to my brother's bedroom.

As always, I follow my father around the kitchen. I track his footprints, follow behind him and hide in the shadow of his body. Every so often, he reaches down and ruffles my hair with his hands. We cast a spell, I think. The way we move in circles, how he cooks without thinking because this is the task that comes to him effortlessly. He smiles down at me, but when he does this, it somehow breaks the spell. My father stands in place, hands dropping to his sides as if he has forgotten what he was doing mid-motion. On the walls, the paint is peeling and the floor, unswept in days, leaves little pieces of dirt stuck to our feet.

My persistence, I think, my unadulterated love, confuse him. With each passing day, he knows I will find it harder to ignore what I can't comprehend, that I will be unable to separate one part of him from another. The unconditional quality of my love for him will not last forever, just as my brother's did not. My father stands in the middle of the kitchen, unsure. Eventually, my mother comes downstairs again and puts her arms around him and holds him, whispering something to him, words that to me are meaningless and incomprehensible. But she offers them to him, sound after sound, in a language that was stolen from some other place, until he drops his head and remembers where he is.

Later on, I lean against the door frame upstairs and listen to the sound of a metal fork scraping against a dish. My mother is already there, her voice rising and falling. She is moving the fork across the plate, offering my brother pieces of French toast.

I move towards the bed, the carpet scratchy, until I can touch the wooden bed-frame with my hands. My mother is seated there, and I go to her, reaching my fingers out to the buttons on her cuff and twisting them over to catch the light.

"Are you eating?" I ask my brother.

He starts to cry. I look at him, his face half hidden in the blankets.

"Try and eat," my mother says softly.

He only cries harder but there isn't any sound. The pattern of sunlight on his blanket moves with his body. His hair is pasted down with sweat and his head moves forward and backward like an old man's.

At some point I know my father is standing at the entrance of the room but I cannot turn to look at him. I want to stay where I am, facing the wall. I'm afraid that if I turn around and go to him, I will be complicit, accepting a portion of guilt, no matter how small that piece. I do not know how to prevent this from happening again, though now I know, in the end, it will break us apart. This violence will turn all my love to shame and grief. So I stand there, not looking at him or my brother. Even my father, the magician, who can make something beautiful out of nothing, he just stands and watches.

A face changes over time, it becomes clearer. In my father's face, I have seen everything pass. Anger that has stripped it of anything recognizable, so that it is only a face of bones and skin. And then, at other times, so much pain that it is unbearable, his face so full of grief it might dissolve. How to reconcile all that I know of him and still love him? For a long time, I thought it was not possible. When I was a child, I did not love my father because he was complicated, because he was human, because he needed me to. A child does not know yet how to love a person that way.

How simple it should be. Warm water running over, the feel of the grains between my hands, the sound of it like stones running along the pavement. My father would rinse the rice over and over, sifting it between his fingertips, searching for the impurities, pulling them out. A speck, barely visible, resting on the tip of his finger.

If there were some recourse, I would take it. A cupful of grains in my open hand, a smoothing out, finding the impurities, then removing them piece by piece. And then, to be satisfied with what remains.

Somewhere in my memory, a fish in the sink is dying slowly. My father and I watch as the water runs down.

(2001)

Credits

This page constitutes an extension of the copyright page. We have made every effort to trace the ownership of all copyrighted material and to secure permission from copyright holders. In the event of any question arising as to the use of any material, we will be pleased to make the necessary corrections in future printings. Thanks are due to the following authors, publishers, and agents for permission to use the material indicated.

Margaret Atwood "This Is a Photograph of Me" from *The Circle Game* copyright © 1966 by Margaret Atwood. Reprinted with permission of House of Anansi Press. "The Animals in That Country," "Progressive Insanities of a Pioneer," "Departure from the Bush," "Newsreel: Man and Firing Squad," "Tricks with Mirrors," "Marrying the Hangman," and "Notes Towards a Poem That Can Never Be Written." From *Selected Poems: 1966–1984* by Margaret Atwood. Copyright © 1990 Oxford University Press Canada. Reprinted by permission of the publisher." "How To Tell One Country From Another" Reprinted by permission of Margaret Atwood. Copyright © 1986, 1987, by Margaret Atwood. Originally published in Canada by Oxford University Press. Currently available in the US in the collection *SELECTED POEMS II: Poems Selected and New, 1976–1986* © 1981, 1987 by Margaret Atwood, from Houghton Mifflin Co. "The Loneliness of the Military Historian." From *Morning in the Burned House* by Margaret Atwood © 1995. Published by McClelland & Stewart Ltd. Used with permission of the publisher. "Hairball." From *Wilderness Tips* by Margaret Atwood © 1991. Published by McClelland & Stewart Ltd. Used with permission of the publisher.

Margaret Avison "Snow," "The Apex Animal," "Meeting Together of Poles and Latitudes," "Searching and Sounding," "Strong Yellow, for Reading Aloud," and "Just Left or the Night Margaret Laurence Died." Reprinted from *Always Now* (in three volumes) by Margaret Avison by permission of the Porcupine's Quill. Copyright © Margaret Avison, 2003.

Ken Babstock "A Leave-Taking" from *Mean* copyright © Ken Babstock 1999. Reprinted with the permission of House of Anansi Press. "Ataraxia" from *Airstream Land Yacht* copyright © Ken Babstock 2006. Reprinted with the permission of House of Anansi Press. "Crab" and "Head Injury Card" from *Mean* copyright © Ken Babstock 1999. Reprinted with the permission of House of Anansi Press. "Palindromic" from *Airstream Land Yacht* copyright © Ken Babstock 2006. Reprinted with the permission of House of Anansi Press. "Regenerative" from *Days Into Flatspin* copyright © Ken Babstock 2001. Reprinted with the permission of House of Anansi Press. "The Expected" from *Mean* copyright © Ken Babstock 1999. Reprinted with the permission of House of Anansi Press.

John Barton "From a Journey Around the World." John Barton. From *Sweet Ellipsis*. Toronto: ECW Press, 1998. Reprinted with permission. "Great Men." John Barton. *Great Men*. Kingston, ON: Quarry Press, © 1990. Reprinted with permission. "Haro Strait." John Barton. *West of Darkness*. 2nd rev. ed. Vancouver: Beach Holme, 1999. Reprinted with permission. "In the House of the Present." John Barton. *In the House of the Present*. Toronto: En route magazine, February 2007. Reprinted with permission. "Plasma, Triangles of Silk." from *Hypothesis* copyright © John Barton 2001. Reprinted with the permission of House of Anansi Press. "Stains" from *Designs from the Interior* copyright © John Barton 1994. Reprinted with the permission of House of Anansi Press. "The Living Room" from *Hypothesis* copyright © John Barton 2001. Reprinted with the permission of House of Anansi Press. "The Totems Permit Me Peace." John Barton. *West of Darkness*.2nd rev. ed. Vancouver: Beach Holme, 1999. Reprinted with permission.

David Bezmozgis "New Gravestone for an Old Grave." *Zoetrope*, Volume 9, No. 2. Reprinted with permission.

Earle Birney "David," "Anglosaxon Street," "Vancouver Lights," "Bushed," "The Bear on the Delhi Road," "CanLit," "El Greco: Espolio," and "November Walk Near False Creek." From *One Muddy Hand* by Earle Birney. Harbour Publishing © 2006. Permission given by Wailan Low, executor of the estate of Earle Birney.

bill bissett "jed bi kor benskt trik." bill bissett. *We sleep inside each other all*. Vancouver: blewointmentpress, 1966. "2 awake in the red desert." bill bissett. *Awake in the red desert!* Vancouver: Talonbooks, 1968. "Beyond Even Faithful Legends." bill bissett. *The Lost Angel Mining Co*. Vancouver: blewointmentpress, 1969. Reprinted in bill bissett. *Selected Poems: Beyond Even Faithful Legends*. Vancouver: Talonbooks, 1980. "KILLER WHALE." bill bissett. *The Lost Angel Mining Co*. Vancouver: blewointmentpress, 1969. "yaji yaji" by bill bissett is reprinted from *Medicine My Mouth's on Fire* by permission of Oberon Press. "this is a konkreet pome." bill bissett. *th last photo uv th human soul*. Vancouver: Talonbooks, 1993. "th ordr uv things wher is th ordr." bill bissett. *th influenza uv logic*. Vancouver: Talonbooks, 1995.

Neil Bissoondath "Continental Drift." From *Digging Up the Mountains* by Neil Bissoondath © 1985. Published by McClelland & Stewart Ltd. Used with permission of the publisher.

Clark Blaise "Identity." Reprinted from *Pittsburgh Stories* by Clark Blaise by permission of the Porcupine's Quill. Copyright © Clark Blaise, 2001.

Robin Blaser "The Medium," "Image-Nation 12 (Actus)," "The Truth is Laughter 6," and "Image-Nation 21 (territory." Robin Blaser. *The Holy Forest: Collected Poems of Robin Blaser*. The University of California Press, 2007. Reprinted with permission.

George Bowering "The Acts." George Bowering. From *Autobiology*. Vancouver: New Star Books, 1972. Used with permission of the author. "Feet, Not Eyes." George Bowering. From *In the Flesh*. Toronto: McClelland & Stewart, 1974. Used with permission of the author. "Desert Elm." George Bowering. From *The Catch*. McClelland & Stewart, 1976. Used with permission of the author. "Elegy 1 (from *Kerrisdale Elegies*)." George Bowering. *Kerrisdale Elegies*. Toronto: Coach House Press, 1984. Reprinted with permission. "Do Sink." George Bowering. *Urban Snow*. Vancouver: Talonbooks, 1992. Used with permission of publisher. "Musing on Some Poets." George Bowering. *Blonds on Bikes*. Vancouver: Talonbooks, 1997. Reprinted with permission. "Fall 1962. Vancouver." George Bowering.

Tim Bowling "Does the World Remember Us?" Tim Bowling. *The Memory Orchard*. London, Ontario: Brick Books, 2004. Reprinted with permission. "Dying Scarlet" from *Dying Scarlet* by Tim Bowling. Nightwood Editions, 1997. www.nightwoodeditions.com. Reprinted with permission. "Memory." Tim Bowling. *The Memory Orchard*. London, Ontario: Brick Books, 2004. Reprinted with permission. "The Witness Ghost" from *Witness Ghost* by Tim Bowling. Nightwood Editions, 2003. www.nightwoodeditions.com. Reprinted with permission. Tim Bowling. "The Line" from *The Thin Smoke of the Heart*. Montreal: McGill-Queens University Press, © 2000. Reprinted with permission. Tim Bowling. "The Rhododendron" from *The Thin Smoke of The Heart*. Montreal: McGill-Queens University Press, © 2000. Reprinted with permission.

Joseph Boyden "Shawanagan Bingo Queen" by Joseph Boyden. From *Born with a Tooth*. Toronto: Cormorant Books, © 2001. Reprinted with permission.

Dionne Brand "No Language is Neutral." From *No Language is Neutral* by Dionne Brand © 1990. Published by McClelland & Stewart Ltd. Used with permission of the publisher. "XI," "XX", and "XXXI." From *Thirsty* by Dionne Brand © 2002. Published by McClelland & Stewart Ltd. Used with permission of the publisher.

Di Brandt "but what do you think my father says" and "missionary position (1)." Di Brandt. *Questions I asked my mother*. Winnipeg: Turnstone Press, 1987. Printed with permission of the publisher. "poem for a guy who's thought about feminism." Di Brandt. *mother, not mother*. Toronto: Mercury Press, 1992. Reprinted with permission of the author. "how long does it take to forget a murder." Di Brandt. *Jerusalem, beloved*. Winnipeg: Turnstone Press, 1995. Reprinted with permission of the publisher. "here at the heart of the ravaged heart" and "Zone: <le Détroit>." Di Brandt. *Now You Care*. Toronto: Coach House. 2003.

Sharon Butala "Light" from *Real Life* by Sharon Butala. Harper Collins Canada, 2002. Reprinted by permission.

Morley Callaghan "The Blue Kimono." Morley Callaghan. *The Complete Stories* (Volume 3). Ed. Alistair MacLeod. Toronto: Exile Editions, 2003.

Bliss Carman "Low Tide on Grand Pre" and "A Northern Vigil." Bliss Carman. *Low Tide on Grand Pre*. "By the Aurelian Wall." Bliss Carman. *By the Aurelian Wall and Other Elegies*. "I Loved Thee, Atthis, in the Long Ago." Bliss Carman. *Sappho*. "Vestigia." Bliss Carman. *Later Poems (1921)*. "The Winter Scene." Bliss Carman. *Sanctuary*.

Anne Carson "The Truth About God" by Anne Carson, from GLASS, IRONY, AND GOD, copyright © 1995 by Anne Carson. Reprinted by permission of New Directions Publishing Corp.

Austin Clarke "A Short Drive" by Austin Clarke, copyright 2003 by Austin Clarke. Published in Canada in *Choosing His Coffin*, by Thomas Allen Publishers, 2003. Reprinted by permission of the author.

George Elliott Clarke "Four Guitars (From *Whylah Falls*)." George Elliott Clarke. *Whylah Falls*. Vancouver: Polestar Book Publishers, 1990, 2000. Reprinted with permission. "IX/XI" and "Language." George Elliott Clarke. *Black*. Vancouver: Raincoast Books, 2006. Reprinted with Permission. "Reading *Titus Andronicus* in Three Mile Plains, N.S.". George Elliott Clarke. *Execution Poems*. Wolfville, NS:

Gaspereau, 2001. Reprinted with permission. "The River Pilgrim: A Letter (from *Whylah Falls*)." George Elliott Clarke. *Whylah Falls*. Vancouver: Polestar Book Publishers, 1990, 2000. Reprinted with permission.

Lynn Coady "In Disguise as the Sky" extracted from *Play the Monster Blind* by Lynn Coady, Copyright © Lynn Coady 2000. Reprinted by permission of Doubleday Canada.

Leonard Cohen "Poem," "I Have Not Lingered in European Monasteries," "Style," "What I'm Doing Here," "Suzanne," "Famous Blue Raincoat," "The Poems Don't Love Us Anymore," "How To Speak Poetry," and "Closing Time." From *Stranger Music* by Leonard Cohen © 1993. Published by McClelland & Stewart Ltd. Used with permission of the publisher.

Douglas Coupland "Shopping Is Not Creating" from *Generation X* by Douglas Coupland. Copyright © 1991 by the author and reprinted by permission of St. Martin's Press, LLC.

Ivan E. Coyote "Makeover." Ivan E. Coyote. *Loose End*. Vancouver: Arsenal Press, 2005. Reprinted with permission. "The Smart Money" by Ivan E.Coyote. Taken from *One Man's Trash*. Vancouver: Arsenal Pulp Press, copyright 2002. Reprinted with permission.

Isabella Valancy Crawford *"Malcolm's Katie."* Isabella Valancy Crawford. *Malcolm's Katie: A Love Story*. Ed. D.M.R. Bentley. London, Ont: Canadian Poetry Press, 1987. "The Lily Bed." Isabella Valancy Crawford. *Collected Poems*. Intro. James Reaney. Toronto: University of Toronto Press, 1972. "The Canoe" and "The Rose." Isabella Valancy Crawford. *Old Spookses' Pass, Malcolm's Katie, and Other Poems*. Toronto: J. Bain, 1884. "The Dark Stag." Isabella Valancy Crawford. *Collected Poems*. Intro. James Reaney. Toronto: University of Toronto Press, 1972.

Lorna Crozier "Fishing in Air" and "Myths." From *Garden Going on Without Us* by Lorna Crozier © 1985. Published by McClelland & Stewart Ltd. Used with permission of the publisher. "Facts About My Father," "Mrs. Bentley," "A Kind of Love," "The Sacrifice of Isaac," and "Blizzard." From *The Blue Hour of the Day* by Lorna Crozier © 2007. Published by McClelland & Stewart Ltd. Used with permission of the publisher.

Michael Crummey "Serendipity" extracted from *Flesh and Blood* by Michael Crummey. Copyright © 1998 Michael Crummey Ink. Reprinted by permission of Doubleday Canada.

Marilyn Dumont "The Devil's Language" and "The Sound of One Hand Drumming." Marilyn Dumont. *A Really Good Brown Girl*. London, Ontario: Brick Books, 1996. Reprinted with permission. "monuments, cowboys and indians, tin cans, and red wagons". Marilyn Dumont. *Green Girl Dreams Mountains*. Lantzville, BC: Oolichan Books, 2001. Reprinted with permission.

Timothy Findley "Dreams." From *Stones* by Timothy Findley. Copyright © Pebble Productions Inc., 1988. Reprinted by permission of Penguin Group (Canada), a Division of Pearson Canada Inc.

Mavis Gallant "The Moslem Wife." *FROM THE FIFTEENTH DISTRICT* by Mavis Gallant. Copyright © 1973, 1974, 1975, 1976, 1977, 1978, 1979 by Mavis Gallant (Originally appeared in *The New Yorker*). Reprinted by permission of Georges Borchardt, Inc., on behalf of the author.

Bill Gaston "The Alcoholist." Bill Gaston. *Mount Appetite*. Vancouver: Raincoast Books, copyright 2002. Reprinted with permission.

Oliver Goldsmith "The Rising Village." Oliver Goldsmith. *The Rising Village.*
Ed. Gerald Lynch. London, Ont: Canadian Poetry Press, 1989.

Barbara Gowdy "We So Seldom Look on Love." From *We So Seldom Look on Love: Stories.* Copyright © 1997, 1992 by Barbara Gowdy. This book was originally published in Toronto, Ontario in 1992 by Somerville House Publishing and in the United States by HarperCollins Publishers.

Frederick Philip Grove "The House of Many Eyes." Frederick Philip Grove. *Tales from the Margin: The Selected Short Stories of Frederick Philip Grove.* Ed., with an introd. and notes, by Desmond Pacey. Toronto; Ryerson Press, McGraw-Hill Co. of Canada, 1971.

Thomas Chandler Haliburton "Gulling a Blue Nose." Thomas Chandler Haliburton. *The Clockmaker: Series One, Two, and Three.* Ed. George L. Parker. Centre for Editing Early Canadian Texts. Ottawa: Carleton UP, 1995.

Claire Harris "Where the Sky Is a Pitiful Tent" was originally published in *Fables from the Women's Quarters* copyright © 1984 by Claire Harris. Reprinted by permission of Goose Lane Editions. "Jane in Summer" was originally published in *The Conception of Winter* copyright © 1989 by Claire Harris. Reprinted by permission of Goose Lane Editions.

Hugh Hood "Going Out as a Ghost." From *Dark Glasses* by Hugh Hood. Ottawa: Oberon, 1976. Reprinted by permission of the Family.

Mark Anthony Jarman "Burn Man on a Texas Porch" from *19 Knives* copyright © 2000 Mark Anthony Jarman. Reprinted with the permission of House of Anansi Press.

E. Pauline Johnson "A Cry from an Indian Wife," "The Cattle Thief," and "Ojistoh." E. Pauline Johnson. *The White Wampum.* London: J. Lane; Toronto: Copp Clark, 1895. "The Pilot of the Plains," "The Corn Husker," and "The Idlers." E. Pauline Johnson. *Flint and Feather.* Toronto: Musson Book Company, 1912.

Thomas King "Borders." Thomas King. *One Good Story, That One.* Harper Collins Canada, 1993. Reprinted with permission.

A.M. Klein A.M. Klein: "Design for Mediaeval Tapestry," "Heirloom," "Autobiographical," "Portrait of the Poet as Landscape," and "The Rocking Chair." Source: *A.M. Klein. Complete Poems* (UTP 1990). Reprinted with the permission of the publisher.

Raymond Knister "The Fate of Mrs. Lucier." Raymond Knister. *The First Day of Spring: Stories and Other Prose.* Ed. Peter Stevens. Toronto: University of Toronto Press, 1976.

Joy Kogawa "Obasan." From *Obasan* by Joy Kogawa. Copyright © Joy Kogawa, 1983. Reprinted by permission of Penguin Group (Canada), a Division of Pearson Canada Inc.

Robert Kroetsch "Meditation on Tom Thomson," "Pumpkin: A Love Poem," "Stone Hammer Poem," and "From Seed Catalogue." Robert Kroetsch. *The Stone Hammer Poems.* Edmonton: University of Alberta Press, 1975. Reprinted with Permission.

Archibald Lampman "Among the Timothy," "The Frogs," "In October," "Heat," "Morning on the Lièvres," "In November," "Winter Evening," "Winter Uplands," "The City of the End of Things," "At the Long Sault: May, 1660," and "The Railway Station" by Archibald Lampman. *The Poems of Archibald Lampman.* Toronto: University of Toronto Press, 1974.

Patrick Lane "Wild Horses," "As It Is with Birds and Bulls," "Albino Pheasants," "Still Hunting," "There Is a Time," "The Far Field," "Go Leaving Strange," and "That Cold Blue Morning." Patrick Lane. *Go Leaving Strange*. Madeira Park, BC: Harbour Publishing, 2004. Reprinted with permission.

Margaret Laurence "To Set Our House in Order." From *A Bird in the House* by Margaret Laurence © 1970. Published by McClelland & Stewart Ltd. Used with permission of the publisher.

Irving Layton "The Swimmer," "Composition in Late Spring," "The Birth of Tragedy," "The Fertile Muck," "Whatever Else, Poetry Is Freedom," "For Mao Tse-Tung: A Meditation on Flies and Kings," "A Tall Man Executes a Jig," and "To the Victims of the Holocaust." From *Selected Poems: A Wild Particular Joy* by Irving Layton © 1982, 2004. Published by McClelland & Stewart Ltd. Used with permission of the publisher.

Stephen Leacock "My Financial Career." Stephen Leacock. *Literary Lapses*. Toronto: Musson Book Co, 1912. "The Whirlwind Campaign." Stephen Leacock. *Sunshine Sketches of a Little Town*. Toronto: McClelland & Stewart Ltd., 1960.

Elise Levine "You Are You Because Your Little Dog Loves You". This story originally appeared in *The Journey Prize Anthology 10*, and later appeared in a slightly revised form in the novel *Requests & Dedications* by Elise Levine © 2003. Published by McClelland & Stewart Ltd. Used with permission of the publisher.

Tim Lilburn "Blessed Jan Ruysbroek, Gardening at Groenendael." Tim Lilburn. *Names of God*. Lantzville, BC: Oolichan Books, 1986. Used with permission of the author. "Part of the Inheritance." Tim Lilburn. *Tourist to Ecstasy*. Toronto: Exile Editions, 1989. "Contemplation Is Mourning," "Learning a Deeper Courtesy of the Eye," and "Restoration." From *Moosewood Sandhills* by Tim Lilburn © 1994. Published by McClelland & Stewart Ltd. Used with permission of the publisher. "Its Seeing Perfumed Fist" and "Sleeping Four Nights in a Tree." From *Kill-Site* by Tim Lilburn © 2003. Published by McClelland & Stewart Ltd. Used with permission of the publisher

Dorothy Livesay "Green Rain," "Day and Night," "London Revisited 1946," "Bartok and the Geranium," "Lament for J.F.B.L.," "The Three Emilys," and "The Notations of Love." Dorothy Livesay. *Collected Poems: The Two Seasons*. Toronto: McGraw-Hill Ryerson, 1972. Reprinted with permission.

Gwendolyn MacEwen "Eden, Eden." Gwendolyn MacEwen. From *The Rising Fire*. Toronto: Contact Press, 1963. Reprinted with permission by the author's family. "Breakfast for Barbarians," "Manzini: Escape Artist," and "Poems in Braille." Gwendolyn MacEwen. *A Breakfast for Barbarians*. Toronto: Ryerson Press, 1966. Reprinted with permission by the author's family. "Dark Pines Under Water" and "The Shadow-Maker." Gwendolyn MacEwen. *The Shadow-Maker*. Toronto: Macmillan, 1969. Reprinted with permission by the author's family. "In Bed," "The Water-Bearer," "Feisal," "The Mirage," and "The Peace Conference." Gwendolyn MacEwen. *The T.E. Lawrence Poems*. Oakville, ON: Mosaic Press, 1982. Reprinted with permission by the author's family. "The Tao of Physics." Gwendolyn MacEwen. *Afterworlds*. Toronto: McClelland & Stewart Ltd., 1987. Reprinted with permission by the author's family. "My Father." Gwendolyn MacEwen. *The T.E. Lawrence Poems*. Oakville, ON: Mosaic Press, 1982. Reprinted with permission by the author's family.

E.J. Pratt E.J. Pratt: "Newfoundland," "The Highway," "From Stone to Steel," "The Man and the Machine," "The Submarine," "Truant," and "Still Life." Source: *E.J. Pratt. Selected Poems* (UTP 2000). Reprinted with permission.

Al Purdy "The Country North Of Belleville," "The Cariboo Horses," "Home-Made Beer," "When I Sat Down To Play the Piano," "Trees at the Arctic Circle," "Wilderness Gothic," "Lament for the Dorsets," "At the Quinte Hotel," "The Horsemen of Agawa," "Piling Blood," and "Say the Names." Al Purdy. *Beyond Remembering: The Collected Poems*. Madeira Park, BC: Harbour Publishing, 2000. Reprinted with permission.

Charles G.D. Roberts "The Tantramar Revisited," "The Furrow," "The Sower," "When Milking Time Is Done," "Frogs," "The Pea-Fields," "The Mowing," "The Potato Harvest," "The Winter Fields," "The Flight of the Geese," "The Waking Earth," "The Cow Pasture," O Solitary of the Austere Sky," and "The Waking Earth" by Charles G.D. Roberts. *The Collected Poems of Sir Charles G.D. Roberts: A Critical Edition*. Ed. Desmond Pacey, assisted by Graham Adams. Wolfville, Nova Scotia: Wombat Press, 1985. "The Iron Edge of Winter" by Charles G.D. Roberts. *The Backwoodsmen*. New York: Macmillan, 1921.

Lisa Robertson "Friday." Lisa Robertson. *The Weather*. Vancouver: New Star Books, 2001. Reprinted with permission. "Sad Part." Lisa Robertson. *Debbie: An Epic*. Vancouver: New Star Books, 1997. Reprinted with permission. "Wooden Houses." Lisa Robertson. From *Jacket Magazine*, 2005. http://jacketmagazine. com/27/robe.html Reprinted with permission.

Eden Robinson "Traplines" extracted from *Traplines* by Eden Robinson. Copyright © 1996 by Eden Robinson. Reprinted by permission of Knopf Canada.

Harry Robinson "You Think It's A Stump, But That's My Grandfather". Harry Robinson. *Nature Power: In the Spirit of an Okanagan Storyteller*. Ed. Wendy Wickwire. Vancouver: Talonbooks, 2004. Reprinted with permission.

Leon Rooke "The Women's Guide to Home Companionship." Leon Rooke. *A Bolt of White Cloth*. Toronto: Stoddart, 1985. Reprinted with permission of the author.

Sinclair Ross "The Lamp at Noon." From *The Lamp at Noon and Other Stories* by Sinclair Ross © 1968. Published by McClelland & Stewart Ltd. Used with permission of the publisher.

W.W.E. Ross "Lovers," "Wild Rose," "Curving, the Moon," "The Diver," "Good Angels," and "First Snow" by W.W.E. Ross. *Irrealities, Sonnets & Laconics*. Exile Editions: Toronto, 2003. Reprinted with permission.

Charles Sangster "From *The St. Lawrence and the Saguenay*." Charles Sangster. *St. Lawrence and the Saguenay*. Ed. D.M.R. Bentley. London, Ont: Canadian Poetry Press, 1990.

Gregory Scofield "Women Who Forgot the Taste of Limes," "Conversation with the Poet," and "No Peace." Gregory Scofield. *Singing Home the Bones* © 2005. Reprinted with permission by the author.

Duncan Campbell Scott "The Onondaga Madonna" and "The Piper of Arll" by Duncan Campbell Scott from *Labour and the Angel*, 1898. "Night Hymns on Lake Nipigon," "The Forsaken," and "On the Way to the Mission" by Duncan Campbell Scott from *New World Lyrics and Ballads*, 1905. "The Height of Land" by Duncan Campbell Scott from *Lundy's Lane and Other Poems*, 1916. "At Gull Lake: August, 1810" by Duncan Campbell Scott from *The Green Cloister*, 1935.

F.R. Scott "North Stream," "Laurentian Shield," "A Grain of Rice," "Lakeshore,"

"National Identity," and "A Lass in Wonderland." From *The Collected Poems of F.R. Scott* by F.R. Scott © 1981. Published by McClelland & Stewart Ltd. Used with permission of the author's estate.

Ernest Thompson Seton "Lobo, the King of Currumpaw." Ernest Thompson Seton. *Wild Animals I Have Known.* Toronto: McClelland & Stewart, NCL.

A.J.M. Smith "The Lonely Land," "A Hyacinth for Edith," "Prothalamium," "Like an Old Proud King in a Parable," "Noctambule," "The Archer," "Metamorphosis," and "The Wisdom of Old Jelly Roll." *Poems New and Collected.* Toronto: Oxford UP, 1967. The poems by A.J.M. Smith are reprinted with the permission of William Toye, literary executor for the estate of A.J.M. Smith.

Karen Solie "A Treatise on the Evils of Modern Homeopathic Medicine." Karen Solie. *Short Haul Engine.* London, ON: Brick Books, 2001. Reprinted with permission. "Cipher Stroke," "Determinism," and "Love Song of the Unreliable Narrator." Karen Solie. *Modern and Normal.* London, ON: Brick Books, 2005. Reprinted with permission. "Signs Taken for Wonders" and "Sturgeon." Karen Solie. *Short Haul Engine.* London, ON: Brick Books, 2001. Reprinted with permission.

Raymond Souster "Young Girls," "Study: The Bath," "Two Dead Robins," "Get the Poem Outdoors," and "The Six-Quart Basket" by Raymond Souster are reprinted from *Collected Poems of Raymond Souster* by permission of Oberon Press.

John Steffler "cliffs" and "Two rock paws." John Steffler. *The Grey Islands.* London: Brick Books, 2000. Reprinted with permission. "From Halki," from *Helix: New and Selected Poems* by John Steffler, (A Signal Edition), 2003. Reprinted by permission. "That Night We Were Ravenous." From *That Night We Were Ravenous* by John Steffler © 1998. Published by McClelland & Stewart Ltd. Used with permission of the publisher. "Cook's Line," from *Helix: New and Selected Poems* by John Steffler, (A Signal Edition), is used by permission of Véhicule Press.

Timothy Taylor "The Resurrection Plant" extracted from *Silent Cruise* by Timothy Taylor. Copyright © 2002 by Timothy Taylor. Reprinted by permission of Knopf Canada.

Madeleine Thien From "Simple Recipes" by Madeleine Thien © 2001. Published by McClelland & Stewart Ltd. Used with permission of the publisher.

Catharine Parr Traill "The Bereavement." Catharine Parr Traill. *Pioneering Women. Short Stories by Canadian Women. Beginnings to 1880.* Ed. Lorraine McMullen and Sandra Campbell. Ottawa: University of Ottawa Press, 1993.

Guy Vanderhaeghe "The Watcher." From *Man Descending* by Guy Vanderhaeghe © 1982. Published by McClelland & Stewart Ltd. Used with permission of the publisher.

Fred Wah "Waiting for Saskatchewan." Fred Wah. *Breathin' My Name With a Sigh.* Vancouver: Talonbooks, 1981. Reprinted with permission. Fred Wah. "Elite 1," "Elite 2," "Elite 3," "Elite 4," "Elite 5," "Elite 6," "Elite 7," "Elite 8," "Elite 9," and "Elite 10," from *Waiting for Saskatchewan.* Winnipeg: Turnstone Press, 1985. Reprinted with permission. " "Father/Mother Haibun #4." Fred Wah. *Waiting for Saskatchewan.* Winnipeg: Turnstone Press © 1985. Reprinted with permission. Fred Wah. "Famous Chinese Restaurant Is the Name of a." *Diamond Grill.* Edmonton: NeWest Press, copyright 1996. Fred Wah. "The Christmas He Dies He Comes to." *Diamond Grill.* Edmonton: NeWest Press, 1996. Fred Wah. "After

Our Family Moves Out to British Columbia." *Diamond Grill*. Edmonton: NeWest Press, 1996.

Sheila Watson "Antigone." From *A Father's Kingdom: The Complete Short Fiction* by Sheila Watson © 2004. Published by McClelland & Stewart Ltd. Used with permission of the publisher.

Phyllis Webb "Lament." Phyllis Webb. *Even Your Right Eye*. Toronto: McClelland & Stewart. 1956. Reprinted in Phyllis Webb. *Selected Poems: The Vision Tree*. Vancouver: Talonbooks, 1982. "Suite I" and "Suite II." Phyllis Webb. *Naked Poems*. Vancouver: Periwinkle, 1965. Reprinted in Phyllis Webb. *Selected Poems: The Vision Tree*. Vancouver: Talonbooks, 1982. "Breaking," "Making," and "Poetics Against the Angel of Death." Phyllis Webb. *The Sea is Also a Garden*. Toronto: Ryerson Press, 1962. Reprinted in Phyllis Webb. *Selected Poems: The Vision Tree*. Vancouver: Talonbooks, 1982. "Rilke." Phyllis Webb. *Selected Poems: The Vision Tree*. Vancouver: Talonbooks, 1982. "Treblinka Gas Chamber." Phyllis Webb. *Wilson's Bowl*. Coach House Press, 1980. Reprinted in Phyllis Webb. *Selected Poems: The Vision Tree*. Vancouver: Talonbooks, 1982. "Heidegger, notes of music." Phyllis Webb. *Water and Light*. Toronto: Coach House Press. 1984. Reprinted in Phyllis Webb. *Selected Poems: The Vision Tree*. Vancouver: Talonbooks, 1982. "Attend." Phyllis Webb. *Hanging Fire*. Toronto: Coach House Press. 1990.

Rudy Wiebe "Where Is the Voice Coming From?" extracted from *River of Stone* by Rudy Wiebe. Copyright © 1995 Jackpine House Ltd. Reprinted by permission of Knopf Canada.

Anne Wilkinson "Summer Acres," "Lake Song," "Lens," "In June and Gentle Oven," "Letter to My Children," and "Variations on a Theme" by Anne Wilkinson. Reprinted with permission from Alan Wilkinson, 2007.

Ethel Wilson "Mr. Sleepwalker" from *Mrs. Golightly and Other Stories* by Ethel Wilson. Copyright © Ethel Wilson, 1961. Reprinted by permission of The University of British Columbia.

Alissa York "The Back of the Bear's Mouth" by Alissa York, copyright 1999 by Alissa York. Published in Canada in *Any Given Power*, by Arbeiter Ring, 1999. Reprinted by permission of the author.

Jan Zwicky "Driving Northwest." Jan Zwicky. *Songs for Relinquishing the Earth*. London: Brick Books, 1998. Reprinted with permission. "Language Is Hands" and "Last Steps." Jan Zwicky. *The New Room*. Toronto: Coach House Press, 1989. Reprinted with permission. "Robinson's Crossing." Jan Zwicky. *Robinson's Crossing*. London, Ontario: Brick Books, 2004. Reprinted with permission. "The Geology of Norway." Jan Zwicky. *Songs for Relinquishing the Earth*. London, Ontario: Brick Books, 1998. Reprinted with permission.

Index of Authors and Titles